D1571877

CASES AND MATERIALS

CHILDREN IN THE LEGAL SYSTEM

FOURTH EDITION

by

SAMUEL M. DAVIS
Dean and Jamie L. Whitten Professor of Law and Government
University of Mississippi School of Law

ELIZABETH S. SCOTT
Vice Dean and Harold R. Medina Professor of Law
Columbia University School of Law

WALTER WADLINGTON
James Madison Professor of Law Emeritus
University of Virginia School of Law

CHARLES H. WHITEBREAD
The Late George T. and Harriet E. Pfleger Professor of Law
University of Southern California Gould School of Law

FOUNDATION PRESS

2009

THOMSON
™
WEST

© 1983, 1997, 2004 FOUNDATION PRESS
© 2009 By THOMSON REUTERS/FOUNDATION PRESS

195 Broadway, 9th Floor
New York, NY 10007
Phone Toll Free 1–877–888–1330
Fax (212) 367–6799
foundation-press.com

Printed in the United States of America

ISBN 978–1–59941–433–1

 TEXT IS PRINTED ON 10% POST CONSUMER RECYCLED PAPER

In memory of
Charles H. Whitebread,
a mentor, a colleague and a dear friend

*

FOREWORD

The first edition of this casebook appeared twenty-five years ago. At the time, very few texts were available in this new and emerging field, and the first edition sought to fill a growing need and to augment the existing family law texts that were expanding in size because of the increasing number of cases and statutes in the area of children and the law.

As time has passed, a clearer conceptual framework has developed that helps define children and the law as a distinct area justifying separate treatment in depth. A major thread interwoven through the materials continues to be the tension between the authority of family, state and child. For these reasons the casebook's strengths are its breadth of coverage and its flexibility for use in courses with varying emphases and credit hours.

In this Fourth Edition we have maintained the basic organization of the previous edition while working to refine and update the materials, some of which have seen significant change. We have continued to select cases that will be particularly useful in setting a tone for stimulating classroom discussion. The courts have continued to oblige us by handing down many such opinions.

While the Fourth Edition was in press, our long-time friend and colleague Charlie Whitebread passed away following a brief illness. His participation in all of the editions of this book, including the present one, was invaluable. Charlie was a fabulous teacher and was an inspiration to all of us. He was larger than life, and we will miss him greatly. We dedicate the Fourth Edition to his memory. As always, Charlie would have dedicated this edition to his mother, Mrs. Helen M. Whitebread, and he would have wanted us to express his thanks to Katie Waitman and to his research assistants, Cristopher Briscoe and Karim Aoun.

Sam Davis acknowledges with appreciation the assistance of Connie Lamb and the research help of Jennifer Forman, Debra Giles and Kimberly Watson. Elizabeth Scott thanks her research assistant Sara Novick.

SAMUEL M. DAVIS
ELIZABETH S. SCOTT
WALTER WADLINGTON

*

NOTE ON EDITING

Some citations, footnotes, and text have been omitted in order to keep the materials at a manageable size. Footnotes that are retained bear the numbering from the original reporter or the publication from which the passage was excerpted. Citations to cases and secondary authorities (including some "string" citations with brief explanatory notes about specific cases in the string) have been deleted from some cases without notes or symbols to indicate their omission. Ellipses, or brackets containing summaries of omitted material, indicate other text has been deleted. Dates of statutory references (including dates of any supplements) have been omitted in this edition; the authors have endeavored to provide the most update versions of statutes as of the date of publication, but readers and other users are encouraged to check electronically for any more recent changes.

*

SUMMARY OF CONTENTS

*

TABLE OF CONTENTS

CHAPTER X   Delinquency: Differential Treatment of Juvenile and Adult Offenders

*

TABLE OF CASES

Principal cases are in bold type. Non-principal cases are in roman type. References are to Pages.

Brown v. Crosby, 249 F.Supp.2d 1285 (S.D.Fla.2003), 917, 1142

Brown v. Hot, Sexy and Safer Productions, 68 F.3d 525 (1st Cir.1995), **39**

Brown v. Johnson, 710 F.Supp. 183 (E.D.Ky. 1989), 344

Brown, In re, 33 Or.App. 423, 576 P.2d 830 (Or.App.1978), 981

Brown, In re, 183 N.W.2d 731 (Iowa 1971), 977

Brown, People v., 182 Ill.App.3d 1046, 131 Ill.Dec. 534, 538 N.E.2d 909 (Ill.App. 1 Dist.1989), 1131

Brown, State v., 879 So.2d 1276 (La.2004), 1146

Browning, People v., 45 Cal.App.3d 125, 119 Cal.Rptr. 420 (Cal.App. 2 Dist.1975), 980, 989

Brumfield v. Brumfield, 194 Va. 577, 74 S.E.2d 170 (Va.1953), 231

Brunelle v. Lynn Public Schools, 428 Mass. 512, 702 N.E.2d 1182 (Mass.1998), 34

Bullard, In re, 22 N.C.App. 245, 206 S.E.2d 305 (N.C.App.1974), 988

Bunker, People v., 22 Mich.App. 396, 177 N.W.2d 644 (Mich.App.1970), 1119

Burch v. Barker, 861 F.2d 1149 (9th Cir. 1988), 298

Burch v. Louisiana, 441 U.S. 130, 99 S.Ct. 1623, 60 L.Ed.2d 96 (1979), 898

Burge, United States v., 407 F.3d 1183 (11th Cir.2005), 1159

Burton, People v., 99 Cal.Rptr. 1, 491 P.2d 793 (Cal.1971), 1129

Bush v. State, 809 So.2d 107 (Fla.App. 4 Dist.2002), 552

Butler, State v., 294 Mont. 17, 977 P.2d 1000 (Mont.1999), 960

Cabalquinto, In re Marriage of, 100 Wash.2d 325, 669 P.2d 886 (Wash.1983), 397

Caban v. Mohammed, 441 U.S. 380, 99 S.Ct. 1760, 60 L.Ed.2d 297 (1979), 84

Cain, Commonwealth v., 361 Mass. 224, 279 N.E.2d 706 (Mass.1972), 1129

Cain, State v., 381 So.2d 1361 (Fla.1980), 960

California v. Green, 399 U.S. 149, 90 S.Ct. 1930, 26 L.Ed.2d 489 (1970), 612

California v. Hodari D., 499 U.S. 621, 111 S.Ct. 1547, 113 L.Ed.2d 690 (1991), 1089

California v. Patrick Steven W., 449 U.S. 1096, 101 S.Ct. 893, 66 L.Ed.2d 824 (1981), 1128

Calloway, United States v., 505 F.2d 311 (D.C.Cir.1974), 1073

Campbell v. Gahanna–Jefferson Bd. of Education, 129 Ohio App.3d 85, 717 N.E.2d 347 (Ohio App. 10 Dist.1998), 346

Canady v. Bossier Parish School Bd., 240 F.3d 437 (5th Cir.2001), 264

Care and Protection of Charles, 399 Mass. 324, 504 N.E.2d 592 (Mass.1987), 35

Carey v. Population Services Intern., 431 U.S. 678, 97 S.Ct. 2010, 52 L.Ed.2d 675 (1977), **222**

Carey, People ex rel. v. White, 65 Ill.2d 193, 2 Ill.Dec. 345, 357 N.E.2d 512 (Ill.1976), 895

Carr v. State, 545 So.2d 820 (Ala.Crim.App. 1989), 1129

Carrie W., In re, 89 Cal.App.3d 642, 152 Cal.Rptr. 690 (Cal.App. 5 Dist.1979), 945

Carroll v. Washington Tp. Zoning Commission, 63 Ohio St.2d 249, 408 N.E.2d 191 (Ohio 1980), 697

Carroll, In re, 260 Pa.Super. 23, 393 A.2d 993 (Pa.Super.1978), 1214

Carter v. Brodrick, 644 P.2d 850 (Alaska 1982), 438

Carter, Commonwealth v., 855 A.2d 885 (Pa.Super.2004), 1199

Carver, State v., 113 Wash.2d 591, 781 P.2d 1308 (Wash.1989), 482

Cason v. Cook, 810 F.2d 188 (8th Cir.1987), 1091

Cass, Commonwealth v., 551 Pa. 25, 709 A.2d 350 (Pa.1998), 373, 1103

Castle Rock, Colo., Town of v. Gonzales, 545 U.S. 748, 125 S.Ct. 2796, 162 L.Ed.2d 658 (2005), **569**

Castorina v. Madison County School Bd., 246 F.3d 536 (6th Cir.2001), 267

Castro v. State, 703 S.W.2d 804 (Tex.App.-El Paso 1986), 971

Causey, State ex rel., 363 So.2d 472 (La. 1978), **1167**

C.B., In re, 708 So.2d 391 (La.1998), 1146

C.C.M. v. State, 782 So.2d 537 (Fla.App. 1 Dist.2001), 1212

C.D.N., In re, 559 N.W.2d 431 (Minn.App. 1997), 1212

Chambers v. Mississippi, 410 U.S. 284, 93 S.Ct. 1038, 35 L.Ed.2d 297 (1973), 614

Chandler v. McMinnville School Dist., 978 F.2d 524 (9th Cir.1992), 261

Cheatham, State v., 80 Wash.App. 269, 908 P.2d 381 (Wash.App. Div. 1 1996), 1160

Child of Indian Heritage, Matter of Adoption of a, 111 N.J. 155, 543 A.2d 925 (N.J. 1988), 831

Christian, State v., 142 Wis.2d 742, 419 N.W.2d 319 (Wis.App.1987), 1159

City of (see name of city)

C.L., In re, 714 A.2d 1074 (Pa.Super.1998), 1132

C.L.A. v. State, 137 Ga.App. 511, 224 S.E.2d 491 (Ga.App.1976), 982

Clark v. Jeter, 486 U.S. 456, 108 S.Ct. 1910, 100 L.Ed.2d 465 (1988), 107

Clausen, In re, 442 Mich. 648, 502 N.W.2d 649 (Mich.1993), 98

Clay, In re, 246 N.W.2d 263 (Iowa 1976), 981

Cleveland v. State, 555 So.2d 302 (Ala.Crim. App.1989), 1137

Clutter, United States v., 914 F.2d 775 (6th Cir.1990), 1119

C.M. v. State, 676 So.2d 498 (Fla.App. 1 Dist.1996), 1214

Coats, State ex rel. v. Rakestraw, 610 P.2d 256 (Okla.Crim.App.1980), 1000

Coleman, State v., 271 Kan. 733, 26 P.3d 613 (Kan.2001), 980

Coley v. Morrow, 183 Or.App. 426, 52 P.3d 1090 (Or.App.2002), 917

Collin v. Smith, 578 F.2d 1197 (7th Cir.1978), 164

TABLE OF AUTHORS

CHILDREN IN THE LEGAL SYSTEM

*

CHAPTER I

ALLOCATING POWER OVER CHILDREN: PARENTAL RIGHTS AND STATE AUTHORITY

A. THE CONSTITUTIONAL PARAMETERS OF PARENTAL AUTHORITY

Legal policy affecting children is shaped by presumptions about particular attributes of childhood that set children apart from adults. Because children are immature, the law assumes that they are unable to care for themselves and incapable of making important decisions affecting their lives. As will become clear in Chapter III, this assumption has been subject to challenge in recent years. Nonetheless, a starting point in understanding the state's unique relationship to children is to recognize that adults, either parents or state agents, have legal authority to make decisions for children that adults are free to make for themselves. For example, parents decide where their child will live and what school she will attend, while the state decides that until she reaches a designated age, she must attend some school. Many of the interesting legal questions in this area therefore focus on whether, in a particular context, the child's parents or the state have authority to make decisions on behalf of the child.

To a considerable extent, this authority resides in parents. Under American law, the rearing of children generally takes place in families and is principally the responsibility of parents, who are given broad legal authority and discretion to make decisions involved in carrying out this role. The foundation of legal regulation of the family is the premise that parents are the "first best" caretakers of children and that parents have an interest in this role that warrants legal protection. The role of the state is a subsidiary one of support and supervision. State policies regulating parents thus are subject to constraint. Intervention is warranted only when an important interest of the state or of the child is implicated and that interest would be threatened by deference to parental authority. It is generally assumed that this basic arrangement is consistent with liberal political values and that it serves both the interests of children and of society. Of course, the childrearing roles of parents and the state could be quite different from that which is presumed "natural" in this country. For example, in *The Republic,* Plato proposed communal rearing of children by the state and in modern Israeli kibbutzim, parents have voluntarily participated in the communal rearing of their children. In some non-western societies, kinship groups have childrearing authority; in our country that authority resides with parents. Thus, the starting point in any analysis of

1

the state's relationship to the family is the acknowledgment of parents' primary role.

Until the latter part of the nineteenth century, parental authority was close to absolute and legal supervision was minimal. Parents decided about the extent of their children's education and they decided if and at what age their children would work to contribute economically to the family. Parents had broad authority to discipline their children and, before the establishment of juvenile courts and social service agencies in the early twentieth century, states did little to protect children if discipline was excessive and caused injury. Few issues arose regarding the parameters of parental and state authority over children.

State involvement in families and state authority over the lives of children grew in the early years of the twentieth century, partly in response to the influx of immigrants beginning in the late nineteenth century. With the creation of the Juvenile Court, the idea that the state has a responsibility for the welfare of children, and that society has an interest in how children are reared, emerged and became widely accepted. Policies designed to promote children's welfare need not restrict parental authority; for example, state provision of free public education and of health care services for poor children provide benefits that assist parents in caring for their children. However, state involvement in the family designed to benefit children often restricts and preempts parental authority. Analysis of policies regulating the family often takes the form of a rather inexact balancing of parents' interest in the authority to rear their children against the state's interest in children's welfare.

The allocation of authority over children between the parents and the state has shifted toward greater exercise of authority by the state. As the state expanded its role in family governance, questions arose both about whether particular policies involved an appropriate exercise of state authority in this realm and about the limits of state intervention in the family. As the cases in this Chapter reveal, the parameters of parental and state authority are defined not only by consideration of what policies serve the state's objective of protecting children; they are also subject to constitutional definition and constraint. The Supreme Court has clarified that parents' interest in rearing their children according to their own values is constitutionally protected under the Fourteenth Amendment.

Meyer v. Nebraska

Supreme Court of the United States, 1923.
262 U.S. 390, 43 S.Ct. 625, 67 L.Ed. 1042.

■ MR. JUSTICE MCREYNOLDS delivered the opinion of the Court:

[Plaintiff in error was convicted of violating the following Nebraska statute enacted in 1919:]

"Section 1. No person, individually or as a teacher, shall, in any private, denominational, parochial or public school, teach any subject to any person in any language other than the English language.

"Sec. 2. Languages, other than the English language, may be taught as languages only after a pupil shall have attained and successfully passed the eighth grade as evidenced by a certificate of graduation issued by the county superintendent of the county in which the child resides.

"Sec. 3. Any person who violates any of the provisions of this act shall be deemed guilty of a misdemeanor and upon conviction, shall be subject to a fine of not less than twenty-five ($25) dollars, nor more than one hundred ($100) dollars or be confined in the county jail for any period not exceeding thirty days for each offense.

"Sec. 4. Whereas, an emergency exists, this act shall be in force from and after its passage and approval." [Laws 1919, chap. 249.]

The supreme court of the state affirmed the judgment of conviction. It declared the offense charged and established was "the direct and intentional teaching of the German language as a distinct subject to a child who had not passed the eighth grade," in the parochial school maintained by Zion Evangelical Lutheran Congregation, a collection of Biblical stories being used therefor. . . .

. . .

The problem for our determination is whether the statute, as construed and applied, unreasonably infringes the liberty guaranteed to the plaintiff in error by the 14th Amendment. "No state . . . shall deprive any person of life, liberty, or property without due process of law."

While this court has not attempted to define with exactness the liberty thus guaranteed, the term has received much consideration, and some of the included things have been definitely stated. Without doubt, it denotes not merely freedom from bodily restraint, but also the right of the individual to contract, to engage in any of the common occupations of life, to acquire useful knowledge, to marry, establish a home and bring up children, to worship God according to the dictates of his own conscience, and, generally, to enjoy those privileges long recognized at common law as essential to the orderly pursuit of happiness by free men. The established doctrine is that this liberty may not be interfered with, under the guise of protecting the public interest, by legislative action which is arbitrary or without reasonable relation to some purpose within the competency of the state to effect. Determination by the legislature of what constitutes proper exercise of police power is not final or conclusive, but is subject to supervision by the courts.

The American people have always regarded education and acquisition of knowledge as matters of supreme importance, which should be diligently promoted. The Ordinance of 1787 declares: "Religion, morality and knowledge being necessary to good government and the happiness of mankind, schools and the means of education shall forever be encouraged." Corresponding to the right of control, it is the natural duty of the parent to give his children education suitable to their station in life; and nearly all the states, including Nebraska, enforce this obligation by compulsory laws.

Practically, education of the young is only possible in schools conducted by especially qualified persons who devote themselves thereto. The calling always has been regarded as useful and honorable,—essential, indeed, to the public welfare. Mere knowledge of the German language cannot reasonably be regarded as harmful. Heretofore it has been commonly looked upon as helpful and desirable. Plaintiff in error taught this language in school as part of his occupation. His right thus to teach and the right of parents to engage him so to instruct their children, we think, are within the liberty of the Amendment.

. . . The supreme court of the state has held that "the so-called ancient or dead languages" are not "within the spirit or the purpose of the act." Nebraska District of Evangelical Lutheran Synod, etc. v. McKelvie, et al. (Neb.) 187 N.W. 927 (April 19, 1922). Latin, Greek, Hebrew are not proscribed; but German, French, Spanish, Italian, and every other alien speech are within the ban. Evidently the legislature has attempted materially to interfere with the calling of modern language teachers, with the opportunities of pupils to acquire knowledge, and with the power of parents to control the education of their own.

It is said the purpose of the legislation was to promote civic development by inhibiting training and education of the immature in foreign tongues and ideals before they could learn English and acquire American ideals; and "that the English language should be and become the mother tongue of all children reared in this state." It is also affirmed that the foreign-born population is very large, that certain communities commonly use foreign words, follow foreign leaders, move in a foreign atmosphere, and that the children are thereby hindered from becoming citizens of the most useful type, and the public safety is imperiled.

That the state may do much, go very far, indeed, in order to improve the quality of its citizens, physically, mentally, and morally, is clear; but the individual has certain fundamental rights which must be respected. The protection of the Constitution extends to all,—to those who speak other languages as well as to those born with English on the tongue. Perhaps it would be highly advantageous if all had ready understanding of our ordinary speech, but this cannot be coerced by methods which conflict with the Constitution,—a desirable end cannot be promoted by prohibited means.

For the welfare of his Ideal Commonwealth, Plato suggested a law which should provide: "That the wives of our guardians are to be common, and their children are to be common, and no parent is to know his own child nor any child his parent. . . . The proper officers will take the offspring of the good parents to the pen or fold, and there they will deposit them with certain nurses who dwell in a separate quarter; but the offspring of the inferior, or of the better when they chance to be deformed, will be put away in some mysterious, unknown place, as they should be." In order to submerge the individual and develop ideal citizens, Sparta assembled the males at seven into barracks and intrusted their subsequent education and training to official guardians. Although such measures have been deliberately approved by men of great genius, their ideas touching the relation between individual and state were wholly different from those upon which our institutions rest; and it hardly will be affirmed that any legislature could impose such restrictions upon the people of a state without doing violence to both letter and spirit of the Constitution.

The desire of the legislature to foster a homogeneous people with American ideals, prepared readily to understand current discussions of civic matters, is easy to appreciate. Unfortunate experiences during the late war, and aversion toward every characteristic of truculent adversaries, were certainly enough to quicken that aspiration. But the means adopted, we think, exceed the limitations upon the power of the state, and conflict with rights assured to plaintiff in error. The interference is plain enough, and no adequate reason therefor in time of peace and domestic tranquility has been shown.

The power of the state to compel attendance at some school and to make reasonable regulations for all schools, including a requirement that they shall give instructions in English, is not questioned. Nor has challenge been made of the state's power to prescribe a curriculum for institutions which it supports. Those matters are not within the present controversy. Our concern is with the prohibition approved by the supreme court. Adams v. Tanner, 244 U.S. 594, 61 L.Ed. 1342 pointed out that mere abuse incident to an occupation ordinarily useful is not enough to justify its abolition, although regulation may be entirely proper. No emergency has arisen which renders knowledge by a child of some language other than English so clearly harmful as to justify its inhibition, with the consequent infringement of rights long freely enjoyed. We are constrained to conclude that the statute as applied is arbitrary, and without reasonable relation to any end within the competency of the state.

As the statute undertakes to interfere only with teaching which involves a modern language, leaving complete freedom as to other matters, there seems no adequate foundation for the suggestion that the purpose was to protect the child's health by limiting his mental activities. It is well known that proficiency in a foreign language seldom comes to one not instructed at an early age, and experience shows that this is not injurious to the health, morals, or understanding of the ordinary child.

. . .

Reversed.

■ [The dissenting opinion of Mr. Justice Holmes, concurred in by Mr. Justice Sutherland, is omitted.]

Pierce v. Society of Sisters of The Holy Names of Jesus and Mary

Supreme Court of the United States, 1925.
268 U.S. 510, 45 S.Ct. 571, 69 L.Ed. 1070.

■ MR. JUSTICE MCREYNOLDS delivered the opinion of the Court.

These appeals are from decrees, based upon undenied allegations, which granted preliminary orders restraining appellants from threatening or attempting to enforce the Compulsory Education Act. . . .

The challenged act, effective September 1, 1926, requires every parent, guardian, or other person having control or charge or custody of a child between 8 and 16 years to send him "to a public school for the period of time a public school shall be held during the current year" in the district where the child resides; and failure so to do is declared a misdemeanor. There are exemptions—not specially important here—for children who are not normal, or who have completed the eighth grade, or whose parents or private teachers reside at considerable distances from any public school, or who hold special permits from the county superintendent. The manifest purpose is to compel general attendance at public schools by normal children, between 8 and 16, who have not completed the eighth grade....

Appellee the Society of Sisters is an Oregon corporation, organized in 1880, with power to care for orphans, educate and instruct the youth, establish and maintain academies or schools, and acquire necessary real and personal property. It has long devoted its property and effort to the secular and religious education and care of children, and has acquired the valuable good will of many parents and guardians. It conducts interdependent primary and high schools and junior colleges, and maintains orphanages for the custody and control of children between 8 and 16. In its primary schools many children between those ages are taught the subjects usually pursued in Oregon public schools during the first eight years. Systematic religious instruction and moral training according to the tenets of the Roman Catholic Church are also regularly provided. All courses of study, both temporal and religious, contemplate continuity of training under appellee's charge; the primary schools are essential to the system and the most profitable.... The Compulsory Education Act of 1922 has already caused the withdrawal from its schools of children who would otherwise continue, and their income has steadily declined. The appellants, public officers, have proclaimed their purpose strictly to enforce the statute.

... [T]he Society's bill alleges that the enactment conflicts with the right of parents to choose schools where their children will receive appropriate mental and religious training, the right of the child to influence the parents' choice of a school, the right of schools and teachers therein to engage in a useful business or profession, and is accordingly repugnant to the Constitution and void. And, further, that unless enforcement of the measure is enjoined the corporation's business and property will suffer irreparable injury.

Appellee Hill Military Academy is a private corporation organized in 1908 under the laws of Oregon, engaged in owning, operating, and conducting for profit an elementary, college preparatory, and military training school for boys between the ages of 5 and 21 years. The average attendance is 100, and the annual fees received for each student amount to some $800. The elementary department is divided into eight grades, as in the public schools; the college preparatory department has four grades, similar to those of the public high schools; the courses of study conform to the requirements of the state board of education. Military instruction and training are also given, under the supervision of an army officer.... By reason of the statute and threat of enforcement appellee's business is being destroyed and its property depreciated; parents and guardians are refusing to make contracts for the future instruction of their sons, and some are being withdrawn.

The Academy's bill ... alleges that the challenged act contravenes the corporation's rights guaranteed by the Fourteenth Amendment and that unless appellants are restrained from proclaiming its validity and threatening to enforce it irreparable injury will result. The prayer is for an appropriate injunction.

No answer was interposed in either cause, and after proper notices they were heard by three judges on motions for preliminary injunctions.... The court ruled that the Fourteenth Amendment guaranteed appellees against the deprivation of their property without due process of law consequent upon the unlawful interference by appellants with the free choice of patrons, present and prospective. It declared the right to conduct schools was property and that parents and guardians, as a part of their liberty, might direct the education of children by selecting reputable teachers and places....

No question is raised concerning the power of the state reasonably to regulate all schools, to inspect, supervise and examine them, their teachers and pupils; to require that all children of proper age attend some school, that teachers shall be of good moral character and patriotic disposition, that certain studies plainly essential to good citizenship must be taught, and that nothing be taught which is manifestly inimical to the public welfare.

The inevitable practical result of enforcing the act under consideration would be destruction of appellees' primary schools, and perhaps all other private primary schools for normal children within the state of Oregon. Appellees are engaged in a kind of undertaking not inherently harmful, but long regarded as useful and meritorious. Certainly there is nothing in the present records to indicate that they have failed to discharge their obligations to patrons, students, or the state.[And there are no peculiar circumstances or present emergencies which demand extraordinary measures relative to primary education.]

emergency exception here

Under the doctrine of Meyer v. Nebraska, 262 U.S. 390, we think it entirely plain that the Act of 1922 unreasonably interferes with the liberty of parents and guardians to direct the upbringing and education of children under their control. As often heretofore pointed out, rights guaranteed by the Constitution may not be abridged by legislation which has no reasonable relation to some purpose within the competency of the state. The fundamental theory of liberty upon which all governments in this Union repose excludes any general power of the state to standardize its children by forcing them to accept instruction from public teachers only. The child is not the mere creature of the state; those who nurture him and direct his destiny have the right, coupled with the high duty, to recognize and prepare him for additional obligations.

. . .

The decrees below are affirmed.

SOME REFLECTIONS ON *MEYER* AND *PIERCE*

(1) *Meyer* and *Pierce* represent the first statements by the United States Supreme Court that the authority of parents to rear their children as they see fit is constitutionally protected. The cases arose at a time when states were defining a new role for government by enacting progressive social legislation, of which compulsory school attendance laws were only one example. In some sense, in these opinions the Supreme Court was simply articulating principles that had been implicit in the state's relationship to the family in an earlier era. In the climate of enthusiasm for an active state role to promote the betterment of society, it became important to define the boundaries of this relationship, since governmental overreaching was always a risk.

(2) The disputes in *Meyer* and *Pierce* reflect a tension that continues to play itself out in our society. The "melting pot" metaphor has been a powerful symbol of American society and yet, heterogeneity is also an important cultural value. Ethnic, racial, and cultural subgroups have an interest in preserving their unique identities, and are vulnerable to majoritarian politics. Note that the Nebraska law that was struck down in *Meyer* was enacted in the wake of the First World War, when anti-German sentiments were strong. Moreover, it seems likely that the Oregon statute in *Pierce* reflected widespread hostility toward Roman Catholics.

This issue is as important in educational policy today as it was in the 1920s. The recent interest in multiculturalism in education reflects an emphasis on diversity and on the importance to minority and subordinated groups of preserving racial, gender, and ethnic identity. Critics have focused on the extent to which the curriculum in American schools reflects a "Eurocentric" and masculine perspective. In recent years, educators have examined the public school curriculum with a goal of including the perspectives of women and of racial, religious and cultural minority groups. The reexamination has been far-reaching and includes an increased focus on Africa and African history and an emphasis on the contribution to American history and culture of women and minorities. Critics of the multicultural perspective emphasize the importance to a well-functioning society of shared values and common goals among its members. They argue that the risks of emphasizing cultural diversity can be seen in countries such as India and the former Yugoslavia that are torn apart by ethnic strife.

(3) **Bilingual Education.** Consider the Nebraska statute struck down in *Meyer*. Does the state have a legitimate policy objective in requiring that instruction be in English and that other languages be taught only in high school? What social costs are incurred if some Nebraska schoolchildren grow up only speaking German? Are these costs negligible? Did the legislature simply go too far? Was the Court perhaps responding to a perception that xenophobia against Germans played an important role in shaping the legislation?

Under *Meyer*, how would you analyze a state law prohibiting the use of any foreign language for general public school instruction, enacted in response to the practice of bilingual education in metropolitan districts with large Spanish populations? The Federal response to bilingual education has been relatively neutral. Congress enacted the Equal Educational Opportunities Act of 1974[1] requiring states to take "appropriate action to overcome language barriers that impede equal protection by its students in its instructional programs." The statute does not mandate nor does it even mention bilingual education. However, Congress also enacted the Federal Bilingual Education Act of 1974[2] in order to support Limited

---

1. 20 U.S.C. § 1701 (2001).   **2.** 20 U.S.C. § 880b, et seq. (1976).

English Proficient (LEP) students by pledging federal funding for school districts that use bilingual education, though it also does not mandate such programs.

Prior to 1998, bilingual education in California involved teaching LEP students in their native language while they were taught English with the ultimate goal of English or bilingual fluency. However, criticism of bilingual education in California rose in response to the high drop out rates and low English literacy levels of many immigrant children. In 1998, 61% of California voters approved Proposition 227, which was entitled "English Language in Public Schools." Providing that children "shall be taught English by being taught in English," Proposition 227 establishes an educational program known as "sheltered English immersion" where LEP students of similar English proficiency are taught together "during a temporary transition period not normally intended to exceed one year." After they "acquire a good working knowledge of English," they are to be placed in English-only class-rooms. The Proposition also provides that LEP children may receive a waiver from the immersion program and be transferred to a bilingual classroom under limited circumstances at the request and consent of the parents alone. Additionally, there is a parental enforcement provision, which allows a parent to sue a teacher or other school official "who willfully and repeatedly refuses to implement the terms of this statute." Proposition 227 declares that English is "the language of economic opportunity" and "Immigrant parents are eager to have their children acquire a good knowledge of English, thereby allowing them to fully participate in the American Dream of economic and social advancement."[3]

The day after Proposition 227's approval, LEP students enrolled in California public schools sued to enjoin its implementation in *Valeria G. v. Wilson*.[4] The students' broad-based facial challenge claimed that Proposition 227 violated the Equal Educational Opportunities Act and the First Amendment and Equal Protection clauses of the Constitution. The district court began by explaining that both sides of the debate shared the same objective, which was the education of LEP students and the argument is only "about which system will provide LEP children with the best education to enable them to function as American citizens and enjoy the opportunities of life in the United States." However, the court asserts, "It is not the province of this court to impose on the people of California its view of which is the better education policy. The voters of California expressed their policy prefer-ence by enacting Proposition 227." The district court thus held, "the fact that Proposition 227 *might* in the future operate in violation of a federal law or the constitution under some scenario is insufficient to render it facially invalid." It also went on to explain that Proposition 227 does not require any particular curriculum, but leaves schools free to implement curricula of their choosing. Finally, the district court rejected the students' Equal Protection claim that the proposition created a "political structure" burdening any attempts to modify the system later.

The students ultimately appealed the Equal Protection claim to the Ninth Circuit in *Valeria G. v. Davis*.[5] In affirming the District Court's holding, the Court of Appeals for the Ninth Circuit explained, "Proposition 227 ... does not obstruct minorities from seeking protection against unequal treatment." It went on to assert, "While Proposition 227 surely reallocated political authority, placing control over bilingual education at the state (rather than local) level, the reallocation of political authority ... operated solely to address an educational issue, *not* a racial one."

3.   Cal. Educ. Code §§ 300(a) and (b).   **5.**   307 F.3d 1036 (9th Cir.2002).
4.   12 F.Supp.2d 1007 (N.D.Cal.1998).

Proposition 227 was also challenged by other groups. In *McLaughlin v. State Board of Education*,[6] several school districts challenged Proposition 227's waiver provision that allowed only parents, and not school districts to file for waiver from inclusion in the English immersion program for their children. The school districts claimed that the proposition conflicted with California Education Code § 33050, which allowed school districts to apply for waivers from educational legislation.[7] The court explained, "Among other things, [Proposition 227's] ballot materials reveal that voters were promised passage of Proposition 227 would establish an LEP method of instruction which would heavily favor use of English-only, and would bestow bilingual education 'choice' to parents only." The court concluded, "voters believed Proposition 227 would ensure school districts could not escape the obligation to provide English language public education for LEP students in the absence of parental waivers." Ultimately, the court could "see no way that the guarantee of English-only instruction subject solely to parental waiver can be accomplished if school boards are allowed to avoid compliance ... by seeking waivers, no matter how well intentioned administrators may be in doing so," and "the failure to specifically amend section 33050 to add the core provisions of [the proposition] was due to an oversight by the initiative's drafters."

Other states have followed California's lead in the elimination of bilingual education by English-only legislation. In 2000, 63% of Arizona voters approved Proposition 203, which is a very similar though slightly stricter version of California's Proposition 227. Interestingly, this English-only legislation passed despite the fact that bilingual education in Arizona was more successful than in California. Sixty-eight percent of the voters in Massachusetts, which was the first state to mandate bilingual education in 1971, approved Question 2, a similar anti-bilingual-education measure in 2002.[8] The English-only initiative in Colorado, was rejected by a vote of 54.8 percent to 45.2 percent. While the trend seems to be moving toward more English-only legislation by other states, it remains to be seen whether English-only curriculum is superior to bilingual education programs. In California, proponents of the new system point to higher test scores since Proposition 227's implementation as evidence of its success, while opponents claim that there are numerous other factors that have contributed to the higher scores. Is the assumption underlying these English-only initiatives—that, English is the language of "economic opportunity"—correct? Does such English-only legislation have any impact on the psychological and cultural perceptions of immigrant families? For more discussion on Proposition 227 and its "offspring," see William Ryan, The Unz Initiatives and the Abolition of Bilingual Education, 43 B.C. L.Rev. 487 (2002).

(4) Do you understand *Meyer* and *Pierce* to protect any constitutional interest of the involved children—to learn German or attend a private school? If children and parents were in conflict on these matters, would children's preferences carry any legal weight? Professor Barbara Woodhouse has argued that *Meyer* and *Pierce,* although they appear to be liberal responses to legislation that was conceived in prejudice, reflected a conception of children as the property of their parents. The two opinions, in Woodhouse's view, clarified that parents, and not the state, own their children, in an era in which parents' ownership interest was challenged by the progressive child labor laws. Barbara Woodhouse, "Who Owns the Child?" *Meyer* and *Pierce* and the Child as Property, 33 Wm. & Mary L.Rev. 995 (1992).

For a discussion of compulsory education requirements in America generally, see pages 18, 32, infra.

6. 75 Cal.App.4th 196, 89 Cal.Rptr.2d 295 (1999).

7. See *McLaughlin*, at 206–7.

8. Jim Boulet Jr., *Win Some, Lose Some*, National Review Online, *at* http://www.nationalreview.com/comment/comment-boulet110702.asp (Nov. 7, 2002).

Prince v. Massachusetts

Supreme Court of the United States, 1944.
321 U.S. 158, 64 S.Ct. 438, 88 L.Ed. 645.

■ MR. JUSTICE RUTLEDGE delivered the opinion of the Court.

The case brings for review another episode in the conflict between Jehovah's Witnesses and state authority. This time Sarah Prince appeals from convictions for violating Massachusetts' child labor laws, by acts said to be a rightful exercise of her religious convictions.

When the offenses were committed she was the aunt and custodian of Betty M. Simmons, a girl nine years of age. Originally there were three separate complaints. They were, shortly, for (1) refusal to disclose Betty's identity and age to a public officer whose duty was to enforce the statutes; (2) furnishing her with magazines, knowing she was to sell them unlawfully, that is, on the street; and (3) as Betty's custodian, permitting her to work contrary to law. The complaints were made, respectively, pursuant to Sections 79, 80 and 81 of Chapter 149, Gen.Laws of Mass. (Ter.Ed.). The Supreme Judicial Court reversed the conviction under the first complaint on state grounds;[1] but sustained the judgments founded on the other two. 313 Mass. 223, 46 N.E.2d 755. They present the only questions for our decision. These are whether Sections 80 and 81, as applied, contravene the Fourteenth Amendment by denying or abridging appellant's freedom of religion and by denying to her the equal protection of the laws.

Sections 80 and 81 form parts of Massachusetts' comprehensive child labor law. They provide methods for enforcing the prohibitions of Section 69, which is as follows:

"No boy under twelve and no girl under eighteen shall sell, expose or offer for sale any newspapers, magazines, periodicals or any other articles of merchandise of any description, or exercise the trade of bootblack or scavenger, or any other trade, in any street or public place."

Sections 80 and 81, so far as pertinent, read:

"Whoever furnishes or sells to any minor any article of any description with the knowledge that the minor intends to sell such article in violation of any provision of sections sixty-nine to seventy-three, inclusive, or after having received written notice to this effect from any officer charged with the enforcement thereof, or knowingly procures or encourages any minor to violate any provisions of said sections, shall be punished by a fine of not less than ten nor more than two hundred dollars or by imprisonment for not more than two months, or both." [Section 80]

"Any parent, guardian or custodian having a minor under his control who compels or permits such minor to work in violation of any provision of sections sixty to seventy-four, inclusive, . . . shall for a first offence be

---

1. The court found there was no evidence that appellant was asked Betty's age. It then held that conviction for refusal to disclose the child's name, based on the charge under Section 79, would violate Article 12 of the Declaration of Rights of the Common- wealth, which provides in part: "No subject shall be held to answer for any crimes or offence, until the same is fully and plainly, substantially and formally, described to him; or be compelled to accuse, or furnish evidence against himself."

punished by a fine of not less than two nor more than ten dollars or by imprisonment for not more than five days, or both; ... " [Section 81]

The story told by the evidence has become familiar. It hardly needs repeating, except to give setting to the variations introduced through the part played by a child of tender years. Mrs. Prince, living in Brockton, is the mother of two young sons. She also has legal custody of Betty Simmons who lives with them. The children too are Jehovah's Witnesses and both Mrs. Prince and Betty testified they were ordained ministers. The former was accustomed to go each week on the streets of Brockton to distribute "Watchtower" and "Consolation," according to the usual plan. She had permitted the children to engage in this activity previously, and had been warned against doing so by the school attendance officer, Mr. Perkins. But, until December 18, 1941, she generally did not take them with her at night.

That evening, as Mrs. Prince was preparing to leave her home, the children asked to go. She at first refused. Childlike, they resorted to tears and, motherlike, she yielded. Arriving downtown, Mrs. Prince permitted the children "to engage in the preaching work with her upon the side- walks." That is, with specific reference to Betty, she and Mrs. Prince took positions about twenty feet apart near a street intersection. Betty held up in her hand, for passersby to see, copies of "Watch Tower" and "Consola- tion." From her shoulder hung the usual canvas magazine bag, on which was printed "Watchtower and Consolation 5 per copy." No one accepted a copy from Betty that evening and she received no money. Nor did her aunt. But on other occasions, Betty had received funds and given out copies.

Mrs. Prince and Betty remained until 8:45 p.m. A few minutes before this Mr. Perkins approached Mrs. Prince. A discussion ensued. He inquired and she refused to give Betty's name. However, she stated the child attended the Shaw School. Mr. Perkins referred to his previous warnings and said he would allow five minutes for them to get off the street. Mrs. Prince admitted she supplied Betty with the magazines and said, "[N]ei- ther you nor anybody else can stop me.... This child is exercising her God- given right and her constitutional right to preach the gospel, and no creature has a right to interfere with God's commands." However, Mrs. Prince and Betty departed. She remarked as she went, "I'm not going through this any more. We've been through it time and time again. I'm going home and put the little girl to bed." It may be added that testimony, by Betty, her aunt and others, was offered at the trials, and was excluded, to show that Betty believed it was her religious duty to perform this work and failure would bring condemnation "to everlasting destruction at Arma- geddon."

As the case reaches us, the questions are no longer open whether what the child did was a "sale" or an "offer to sell" within Section 69[5] or was "work" within Section 81. The state court's decision has foreclosed them adversely to appellant as a matter of state law. The only question remain- ing therefore is whether, as construed and applied, the statute is valid.

---

5. In this respect the Massachusetts de- cision is contrary to the trend in other states....

Upon this the court said: "We think that freedom of the press and of religion is subject to incidental regulation to the slight degree involved in the prohibition of the selling of religious literature in streets and public places by boys under twelve and girls under eighteen and in the further statutory provisions herein considered, which have been adopted as a means of enforcing that prohibition." 313 Mass. 223, 229, 46 N.E.2d 755, 758.

Appellant does not stand on freedom of the press. . . . [S]he rests squarely on freedom of religion under the First Amendment, applied by the Fourteenth to the states. She buttresses this foundation, however, with a claim of parental right as secured by the due process clause of the latter Amendment. Cf. Meyer v. Nebraska, 262 U.S. 390. These guaranties, she thinks, guard alike herself and the child in what they have done. Thus, two claimed liberties are at stake. One is the parent's, to bring up the child in the way he should go, which for appellant means to teach him the tenets and the practices of their faith. The other freedom is the child's, to observe these; and among them is "to preach the gospel . . . by public distribution" of "Watchtower" and "Consolation," in conformity with the scripture: "A little child shall lead them."

. . .

To make accommodation between these freedoms and an exercise of state authority always is delicate. It hardly could be more so than in such a clash as this case presents. On one side is the obviously earnest claim for freedom of conscience and religious practice. With it is allied the parent's claim to authority in her own household and in the rearing of her children. The parent's conflict with the state over control of the child and his training is serious enough when only secular matters are concerned. It becomes the more so when an element of religious conviction enters. Against these sacred private interests, basic in a democracy, stand the interests of society to protect the welfare of children, and the state's assertion of authority to that end, made here in a manner conceded valid if only secular things were involved. The last is no mere corporate concern of official authority. It is the interest of youth itself, and of the whole community, that children be both safeguarded from abuses and given opportunities for growth into free and independent well-developed men and citizens. Between contrary pulls of such weight, the safest and most objective recourse is to the lines already marked out, not precisely but for guides, in narrowing the no man's land where this battle has gone on.

The rights of children to exercise their religion, and of parents to give them religious training and to encourage them in the practice of religious belief, as against preponderant sentiment and assertion of state power voicing it, have had recognition here, most recently in West Virginia State Board of Education v. Barnette, 319 U.S. 624. Previously in Pierce v. Society of Sisters, 268 U.S. 510, this Court had sustained the parent's authority to provide religious with secular schooling, and the child's right to receive it, as against the state's requirement of attendance at public schools. And in Meyer v. Nebraska, 262 U.S. 390, children's rights to receive teaching in languages other than the nation's common tongue were guarded against the state's encroachment. It is cardinal with us that the custody, care and nurture of the child reside first in the parents, whose primary function and freedom include preparation for obligations the state can neither supply nor hinder. Pierce v. Society of Sisters, supra. And it is in recognition of this that these decisions have respected the private realm of family life which the state cannot enter.

But the family itself is not beyond regulation in the public interest, as against a claim of religious liberty. Reynolds v. United States, 98 U.S. 145; Davis v. Beason, 133 U.S. 333. And neither rights of religion nor rights of parenthood are beyond limitation. Acting to guard the general interest in youth's well being, the state as parens patriae may restrict the parent's control by requiring school attendance, regulating or prohibiting the child's labor, and in many other ways. Its authority is not nullified merely because the parent grounds his claim to control the child's course of conduct on religion or conscience. Thus, he cannot claim freedom from compulsory vaccination for the child more than for himself on religious grounds. The right to practice religion freely does not include liberty to expose the community or the child to communicable disease or the latter to ill health or death. People v. Pierson, 176 N.Y. 201, 68 N.E. 243. The catalogue need not be lengthened. It is sufficient to show what indeed appellant hardly disputes, that the state has a wide range of power for limiting parental freedom and authority in things affecting the child's welfare; and that this includes, to some extent, matters of conscience and religious conviction.

But it is said the state cannot do so here. This, first, because when state action impinges upon a claimed religious freedom, it must fall unless shown to be necessary for or conducive to the child's protection against some clear and present danger, cf. Schenck v. United States, 249 U.S. 47; and, it is added, there was no such showing here. The child's presence on the street, with her guardian, distributing or offering to distribute the magazines, it is urged, was in no way harmful to her, nor in any event more so than the presence of many other children at the same time and place, engaged in shopping and other activities not prohibited. Accordingly, in view of the preferred position the freedoms of the First Article occupy, the statute in its present application must fall. It cannot be sustained by any presumption of validity. And, finally, it is said, the statute is, as to children, an absolute prohibition, not merely a reasonable regulation, of the denounced activity.

Concededly a statute or ordinance identical in terms with Section 69, except that it is applicable to adults or all persons generally, would be invalid. But the mere fact a state could not wholly prohibit this form of adult activity, whether characterized locally as a "sale" or otherwise, does not mean it cannot do so for children. Such a conclusion granted would mean that a state could impose no greater limitation upon child labor than upon adult labor. Or, if an adult were free to enter dance halls, saloons, and disreputable places generally, in order to discharge his conceived religious duty to admonish or dissuade persons from frequenting such places, so would be a child with similar convictions and objectives, if not alone then in the parent's company, against the state's command.

The state's authority over children's activities is broader than over like actions of adults. This is peculiarly true of public activities and in matters of employment. A democratic society rests, for its continuance, upon the healthy, well-rounded growth of young people into full maturity as citizens, with all that implies. It may secure this against impeding restraints and dangers, within a broad range of selection. Among evils most appropriate for such action are the crippling effects of child employment, more especially in public places, and the possible harms arising from other activities subject to all the diverse influences of the street. It is too late now to doubt that legislation appropriately designed to reach such evils is within the state's police power, whether against the parent's claim to control of the child or one that religious scruples dictate contrary action.

It is true children have rights, in common with older people, in the primary use of highways. But even in such use streets afford dangers for them not affecting adults. And in other uses, whether in work or in other things, this difference may be magnified. This is so not only when children are unaccompanied but certainly to some extent when they are with their parents. What may be wholly permissible for adults therefore may not be so for children, either with or without their parents' presence.

Street preaching, whether oral or by handing out literature, is not the primary use of the highway, even for adults. While for them it cannot be wholly prohibited, it can be regulated within reasonable limits in accommodation to the primary and other incidental uses. But, for obvious reasons, notwithstanding appellant's contrary view, the validity of such a prohibition applied to children not accompanied by an older person hardly would seem open to question. The case reduces itself therefore to the question whether the presence of the child's guardian puts a limit to the state's power. That fact may lessen the likelihood that some evils the legislation seeks to avert will occur. But it cannot forestall all of them. The zealous though lawful exercise of the right to engage in propagandizing the community, whether in religious, political or other matters, may and at times does create situations difficult enough for adults to cope with and wholly inappropriate for children, especially of tender years, to face. Other harmful possibilities could be stated, of emotional excitement and psychological or physical injury. Parents may be free to become martyrs themselves. But it does not follow they are free, in identical circumstances, to make martyrs of their children before they have reached the age of full and legal discretion when they can make that choice for themselves. Massachusetts has determined that an absolute prohibition, though one limited to streets and public places and to the incidental uses proscribed, is necessary to accomplish its legitimate objectives. Its power to attain them is broad enough to reach these peripheral instances in which the parent's supervision may reduce but cannot eliminate entirely the ill effects of the prohibited conduct. We think that with reference to the public proclaiming of religion, upon the streets and in other similar public places, the power of the state to control the conduct of children reaches beyond the scope of its authority over adults, as is true in the case of other freedoms, and the rightful boundary of its power has not been crossed in this case.

. . .

Our ruling does not extend beyond the facts the case presents. We neither lay the foundation "for any [that is, every] state intervention in the indoctrination and participation of children in religion" which may be done "in the name of their health and welfare" nor give warrant for "every limitation on their religious training and activities." The religious training and indoctrination of children may be accomplished in many ways, some of which, as we have noted, have received constitutional protection through decisions of this Court. These and all others except the public proclaiming of religion on the streets, if this may be taken as either training or indoctrination of the proclaimer, remain unaffected by the decision.

The judgment is affirmed.

[Mr. Justice Jackson, in a separate opinion in which Mr. Justice Roberts and Mr. Justice Frankfurter, joined, dissented from the grounds for affirmance, stating the view that the judgment "was rightly decided, and upon right grounds, by the Supreme Judicial Court of Massachusetts. 313 Mass. 223, 46 N.E.2d 755."]

■ MR. JUSTICE MURPHY, dissenting.

This attempt by the state of Massachusetts to prohibit a child from exercising her constitutional right to practice her religion on the public streets cannot, in my opinion, be sustained.

The record makes clear the basic fact that Betty Simmons, the nine-year-old child in question, was engaged in a genuine religious, rather than commercial, activity.

... [T]he human freedoms enumerated in the First Amendment and carried over into the Fourteenth Amendment are to be presumed to be invulnerable and any attempt to sweep away those freedoms is prima facie invalid. It follows that any restriction or prohibition must be justified by those who deny that the freedoms have been unlawfully invaded. The burden was therefore on the state of Massachusetts to prove the reasonableness and necessity of prohibiting children from engaging in religious activity of the type involved in this case.

The burden in this instance, however, is not met by vague references to the reasonableness underlying child labor legislation in general. The great interest of the state in shielding minors from the evil vicissitudes of early life does not warrant every limitation on their religious training and activities. The reasonableness that justifies the prohibition of the ordinary distribution of literature in the public streets by children is not necessarily the reasonableness that justifies such a drastic restriction when the distribution is part of their religious faith. Murdock v. Pennsylvania, supra, 319 U.S. 111. If the right of a child to practice its religion in that manner is to be forbidden by constitutional means, there must be convincing proof that such a practice constitutes a grave and immediate danger to the state or to the health, morals or welfare of the child. West Virginia State Board of Education v. Barnette, 319 U.S. 624, 639. The vital freedom of religion, which is "of the very essence of a scheme of ordered liberty," Palko v. Connecticut, 302 U.S. 319, 325, cannot be erased by slender references to the state's power to restrict the more secular activities of children.

The state, in my opinion, has completely failed to sustain its burden of proving the existence of any grave or immediate danger to any interest which it may lawfully protect....

. . .

PRINCE v. MASSACHUSETTS IN PERSPECTIVE

(1) **Child Labor Laws and Parental Authority.** In *Prince*, the Supreme Court upholds the application of a Massachusetts child labor statute that implicitly restricts parental authority. The Court balances the state's interests that are promoted by the statute against the interest of parents in guiding the religious upbringing of their children. In general, what state interests are furthered by child labor laws? Enacted during the Progressive era, these laws were conceived as part of a comprehensive policy that also included compulsory school attendance requirements. Why are the two policies related? The primary purpose of imposing age restrictions on the employment of children is to restrict employers from hiring underage children, and thereby to protect children from employers who might be inclined to exploit this source of cheap labor. In doing so, the restrictions preempt parental authority as well. Another approach would be to prohibit the employment of underage children, *unless* parents give their consent. Such a scheme would allow parents to exercise their judgment in deciding whether their child should seek employment. That this approach is not adopted suggests that exploitation by parents is as much a concern as exploitation by employers. Why might this be true? Do parents and children have a conflict of interest in this context that justifies restricting the authority that received such deference in *Meyer* and *Pierce*?

Has the Court in *Prince* accurately weighed the conflicting state and parental interests in reaching its conclusion that enforcement of the statute did not unconstitutionally infringe on parental authority? First, are you persuaded that activities in which Mrs. Prince and Betty engaged were of the type contemplated by the legislation? Assuming that the state's interest in enacting and enforcing child labor legislation is substantial, to what extent is that interest implicated under the facts of *Prince*? Would the Court have found the activity of street preaching less offensive had Mrs. Prince and Betty not sold Watchtower magazine? If the sale of the magazine in itself was not the primary concern, then why did the police arrest Mrs. Prince for violating the statute?

What interests does Mrs. Prince assert? If you were her attorney, what argument would you make that her parental interest is more deserving of protection than that of the parents in *Meyer*? Why does the Court seem to discount this interest?

(2) **The Child's Interest.** The opinion reports that 9–year-old Betty was an ordained minister of the Jehovah's Witness faith, a status accorded all members of the congregation. Does she have an independent First Amendment interest in the free exercise of religion that the Court should have recognized? Is her age relevant to your response? For example, would a 15–year-old have a more substantial (and a 6–year-old less substantial) interest? Why?

(3) **Police Power and *Parens Patriae* Authority.** The state's power to override parental authority to protect children and promote their welfare derives from two sources. The first is the police power, which is based on the state's inherent power to promote the interest of society as a whole in the health, safety, education and welfare of its members. The second basis of state intervention in the family is the state's *parens patriae* authority. Chancery courts in England developed *parens patriae* authority to protect the welfare of vulnerable members of society— the poor, the infirm, the incompetent and children. As parens patriae doctrine evolved in this country in the nineteenth century, it served as the basis for state authority to promote the welfare of individual children when their parents failed to do so, either because of poverty or neglect. For an interesting historical account of parens patriae doctrine, see Douglas Rendleman, *Parens Patriae*: From Chancery to Juvenile Court, 23 S.C.L.Rev. 205 (1972).

Is the court in *Prince* more concerned with the welfare of the individual child or with the social costs and benefits at issue?

Wisconsin v. Yoder

Supreme Court of the United States, 1972.
406 U.S. 205, 92 S.Ct. 1526, 32 L.Ed.2d 15.

■ MR. CHIEF JUSTICE BURGER delivered the opinion of the Court.

[We granted certiorari to review a] Wisconsin Supreme Court holding that respondents' convictions for violating the State's compulsory school-attendance law were invalid under the Free Exercise Clause of the First Amendment to the United States Constitution made applicable to the States by the Fourteenth Amendment.... [W]e affirm the judgment of the Supreme Court of Wisconsin.

[Respondents were Wisconsin residents and members of either the Old Order Amish religion or the Conservative Amish Mennonite Church. Their children, ages 14 and 15 were not enrolled in any public or private school, although Wisconsin's compulsory school-attendance law requires parents to cause their children to attend school until they reach age 16. Respondents were convicted of violating the law and fined $5 each.]

... The trial testimony showed that respondents believed, in accordance with the tenets of Old Order Amish communities generally, that their children's attendance at high school, public or private, was contrary to the Amish religion and way of life. They believed that by sending their children to high school, they would not only expose themselves to the danger of the censure of the church community, but, as found by the county court, also endanger their own salvation and that of their children. The State stipulated that respondents' religious beliefs were sincere.

In support of their position, respondents presented as expert witnesses scholars on religion and education whose testimony is uncontradicted. They expressed their opinions on the relationship of the Amish belief concerning school attendance to the more general tenets of their religion, and described the impact that compulsory high school attendance could have on the continued survival of Amish communities as they exist in the United States today....

Formal high school education beyond the eighth grade is contrary to Amish beliefs, not only because it places Amish children in an environment hostile to Amish beliefs with increasing emphasis on competition in class work and sports and with pressure to conform to the styles, manners, and ways of the peer group, but also because it takes them away from their community, physically and emotionally, during the crucial and formative adolescent period of life. During this period, the children must acquire Amish attitudes favoring manual work and self-reliance and the specific skills needed to perform the adult role of an Amish farmer or housewife. They must learn to enjoy physical labor. Once a child has learned basic reading, writing, and elementary mathematics, these traits, skills, and attitudes admittedly fall within the category of those best learned through example and "doing" rather than in a classroom. And, at this time in life, the Amish child must also grow in his faith and his relationship to the Amish community if he is to be prepared to accept the heavy obligations imposed by adult baptism. In short, high school attendance with teachers who are not of the Amish faith—and may even be hostile to it—interposes a serious barrier to the integration of the Amish child into the Amish religious community. Dr. John Hostetler, one of the experts on Amish society, testified that the modern high school is not equipped, in curriculum or social environment, to impart the values promoted by Amish society.

The Amish do not object to elementary education through the first eight grades as a general proposition because they agree that their children must have basic skills in the "three R's" in order to read the Bible, to be good farmers and citizens, and to be able to deal with non-Amish people when necessary in the course of daily affairs. They view such a basic education as acceptable because it does not significantly expose their children to worldly values or interfere with their development in the Amish community during the crucial adolescent period. While Amish accept compulsory elementary education generally, wherever possible they have established their own elementary schools in many respects like the small local schools of the past. In the Amish belief higher learning tends to develop values they reject as influences that alienate man from God.

On the basis of such considerations, Dr. Hostetler testified that compulsory high school attendance could not only result in great psychological harm to Amish children, because of the conflicts it would produce, but would also, in his opinion, ultimately result in the destruction of the Old Order Amish church community as it exists in the United States. . . .

I

. . . [A] State's interest in universal education, however highly we rank it, is not totally free from a balancing process when it impinges on fundamental rights and interests, such as those specifically protected by the Free Exercise Clause of the First Amendment, and the traditional interest of parents with respect to the religious upbringing of their children so long as they, in the words of Pierce [v. Society of Sisters], "prepare [them] for additional obligations." 268 U.S., at 535.

It follows that in order for Wisconsin to compel school attendance beyond the eighth grade against a claim that such attendance interferes with the practice of a legitimate religious belief, it must appear either that the State does not deny the free exercise of religious belief by its requirement, or that there is a state interest of sufficient magnitude to override the interest claiming protection under the Free Exercise Clause. Long before there was general acknowledgment of the need for universal formal education, the Religion Clauses had specifically and firmly fixed the right to free exercise of religious beliefs, and buttressing this fundamental right was an equally firm, even if less explicit, prohibition against the establishment of any religion by government. The values underlying these two provisions relating to religion have been zealously protected, sometimes even at the expense of other interests of admittedly high social importance. The invalidation of financial aid to parochial schools by government grants for a salary subsidy for teachers is but one example of the extent to which courts have gone in this regard, notwithstanding that such aid programs were legislatively determined to be in the public interest and the service of sound educational policy by States and by Congress. Lemon v. Kurtzman, 403 U.S. 602 (1971); ...

The essence of all that has been said and written on the subject is that only those interests of the highest order and those not otherwise served can overbalance legitimate claims to the free exercise of religion. We can accept it as settled, therefore, that, however strong the State's interest in universal compulsory education, it is by no means absolute to the exclusion or subordination of all other interests.

II

We come then to the quality of the claims of the respondents concerning the alleged encroachment of Wisconsin's compulsory school-attendance statute on their rights and the rights of their children to the free exercise of the religious beliefs they and their forbears have adhered to for almost three centuries. In evaluating those claims we must be careful to determine whether the Amish religious faith and their mode of life are, as they claim, inseparable and interdependent....

... [T]he record in this case abundantly supports the claim that the traditional way of life of the Amish is not merely a matter of personal preference, but one of deep religious conviction, shared by an organized group, and intimately related to daily living....

... [T]he unchallenged testimony of acknowledged experts in education and religious history, almost 300 years of consistent practice, and strong evidence of a sustained faith pervading and regulating respondents' entire mode of life support the claim that enforcement of the State's requirement of compulsory formal education after the eighth grade would gravely endanger if not destroy the free exercise of respondents' religious beliefs.

III

. . .

We turn ... to the State's broader contention that its interest in its system of compulsory education is so compelling that even the established religious practices of the Amish must give away.

. . .

The State advances two primary arguments in support of its system of compulsory education. It notes, as Thomas Jefferson pointed out early in our history, that some degree of education is necessary to prepare citizens to participate effectively and intelligently in our open political system if we are to preserve freedom and independence. Further, education prepares individuals to be self-reliant and self-sufficient participants in society. We accept these propositions.

However, the evidence adduced by the Amish in this case is persuasively to the effect that an additional one or two years of formal high school for Amish children in place of their long-established program of informal vocational education would do little to serve those interests. Respondents' experts testified at trial, without challenge, that the value of all education must be assessed in terms of its capacity to prepare the child for life. It is one thing to say that compulsory education for a year or two beyond the eighth grade may be necessary when its goal is the preparation of the child for life in modern society as the majority live, but it is quite another if the goal of education be viewed as the preparation of the child for life in the separated agrarian community that is the keystone of the Amish faith. See Meyer v. Nebraska, 262 U.S., at 400.

The State attacks respondents' position as one fostering "ignorance" from which the child must be protected by the State. No one can question the State's duty to protect children from ignorance but this argument does not square with the facts disclosed in the record. Whatever their idiosyncrasies as seen by the majority, this record strongly shows that the Amish community has been a highly successful social unit within our society, even if apart from the conventional "mainstream." Its members are productive and very law-abiding members of society; they reject public welfare in any of its usual modern forms. The Congress itself recognized their self-sufficiency by authorizing exemption of such groups as the Amish from the obligation to pay social security taxes.[11]

It is neither fair nor correct to suggest that the Amish are opposed to education beyond the eighth grade level. What this record shows is that they are opposed to conventional formal education of the type provided by a certified high school because it comes at the child's crucial adolescent period of religious development. Dr. Donald Erickson, for example, testified that their system of learning-by-doing was an "ideal system" of education in terms of preparing Amish children for life as adults in the Amish community, ...

We must not forget that in the Middle Ages important values of the civilization of the Western World were preserved by members of religious orders who isolated themselves from all worldly influences against great obstacles. There can be no assumption that today's majority is "right" and the Amish and others like them are "wrong." A way of life that is odd or even erratic but interferes with no rights or interests of others is not to be condemned because it is different.

The State, however, supports its interest in providing an additional one or two years of compulsory high school education to Amish children because of the possibility that some such children will choose to leave the Amish community, and that if this occurs they will be ill-equipped for life.

---

11. Title 26 U.S.C. § 1402(h) authorizes the Secretary of Health, Education, and Welfare to exempt members of "a recognized religious sect" existing at all times since December 31, 1950, from the obligation to pay social security taxes if they are, by reason of the tenets of their sect, opposed to receipt of such benefits and agree to waive them, provided the Secretary finds that the sect makes reasonable provision for its dependent members. The history of the exemption shows it was enacted with the situation of the Old Order Amish specifically in view. H.R.Rep. No.213, 89th Cong., 1st Sess., 101–102 (1965).

The record in this case establishes without contradiction that the Green County Amish had never been known to commit crimes, that none had been known to receive public assistance, and that none were unemployed.

The State argues that if Amish children leave their church they should not be in the position of making their way in the world without the education available in the one or two additional years the State requires. However, on this record, that argument is highly speculative. There is no specific evidence of the loss of Amish adherents by attrition, nor is there any showing that upon leaving the Amish community Amish children, with their practical agricultural training and habits of industry and self-reliance, would become burdens on society because of educational shortcomings. Indeed, this argument of the State appears to rest primarily on the State's mistaken assumption, already noted, that the Amish do not provide any education for their children beyond the eighth grade, but allow them to grow in "ignorance." To the contrary, not only do the Amish accept the necessity for formal schooling through the eighth grade level, but continue to provide what has been characterized by the undisputed testimony of expert educators as an "ideal" vocational education for their children in the adolescent years.

There is nothing in this record to suggest that the Amish qualities of reliability, self-reliance, and dedication to work would fail to find ready markets in today's society. Absent some contrary evidence supporting the State's position, we are unwilling to assume that persons possessing such valuable vocational skills and habits are doomed to become burdens on society should they determine to leave the Amish faith, nor is there any basis in the record to warrant a finding that an additional one or two years of formal school education beyond the eighth grade would serve to eliminate any such problem that might exist.

. . .

The requirement for compulsory education beyond the eighth grade is a relatively recent development in our history. Less than 60 years ago, the educational requirements of almost all of the States were satisfied by completion of the elementary grades, at least where the child was regularly and lawfully employed. The independence and successful social functioning of the Amish community for a period approaching almost three centuries and more than 200 years in this country are strong evidence that there is at best a speculative gain, in terms of meeting the duties of citizenship, from an additional one or two years of compulsory formal education. Against this background it would require a more particularized showing from the State on this point to justify the severe interference with religious freedom such additional compulsory attendance would entail.

We should also note that compulsory education and child labor laws find their historical origin in common humanitarian instincts, and that the age limits of both laws have been coordinated to achieve their related objectives. In the context of this case, such considerations, if anything, support rather than detract from respondents' position. The origins of the requirement for school attendance to age 16, an age falling after the completion of elementary school but before completion of high school, are not entirely clear. But to some extent such laws reflected the movement to prohibit most child labor under age 16 that culminated in the provisions of the Federal Fair Labor Standards Act of 1938. It is true, then, that the 16-year child labor age limit may to some degree derive from a contemporary impression that children should be in school until that age. But at the same time, it cannot be denied that, conversely, the 16–year education limit reflects, in substantial measure, the concern that children under that age not be employed under conditions hazardous to their health, or in work that should be performed by adults.

The requirement of compulsory schooling to age 16 must therefore be viewed as aimed not merely at providing educational opportunities for children, but as an alternative to the equally undesirable consequence of unhealthful child labor displacing adult workers, or, on the other hand, forced idleness. The two kinds of statutes—compulsory school attendance and child labor laws—tend to keep children of certain ages off the labor market and in school; this regimen in turn provides opportunity to prepare for a livelihood of a higher order than that which children could pursue without education and protects their health in adolescence.

In these terms, Wisconsin's interest in compelling the school attendance of Amish children to age 16 emerges as somewhat less substantial than requiring such attendance for children generally. For, while agricultural employment is not totally outside the legitimate concerns of the child labor laws, employment of children under parental guidance and on the family farm from age 14 to age 16 is an ancient tradition that lies at the periphery of the objectives of such laws. There is no intimation that the Amish employment of their children on family farms is in any way deleterious to their health or that Amish parents exploit children at tender years. Any such inference would be contrary to the record before us. Moreover, employment of Amish children on the family farm does not present the undesirable economic aspects of eliminating jobs that might otherwise be held by adults.

IV

Finally, the State, on authority of Prince v. Massachusetts, argues that a decision exempting Amish children from the State's requirement fails to recognize the substantive right of the Amish child to a secondary education, and fails to give due regard to the power of the State as *parens patriae* to extend the benefit of secondary education to children regardless of the wishes of their parents. Taken at its broadest sweep, the Court's language in *Prince*, might be read to give support to the State's position. However, the Court was not confronted in *Prince* with a situation comparable to that of the Amish as revealed in this record; this is shown by the Court's severe characterization of the evils that it thought the legislature could legitimately associate with child labor, even when performed in the company of an adult. 321 U.S., at 169–170. The Court later took great care to confine *Prince* to a narrow scope in Sherbert v. Verner, when it stated:

"On the other hand, the Court has rejected challenges under the Free Exercise Clause to governmental regulation of certain overt acts prompted by religious beliefs or principles, for 'even when the action is in accord with one's religious convictions, [it] is not totally free from legislative restrictions.' Braunfeld v. Brown, 366 U.S. 599, 603, 81 S.Ct. 1144, 1146, 6 LED.2d 563. The conduct or actions so regulated have invariably posed some substantial threat to public safety, peace or order. See, e.g., Reynolds v. United States, 98 U.S. 145; Jacobson v. Massachusetts, 197 U.S. 11; Prince v. Massachusetts, 321 U.S. 158...." 374 U.S., at 402–403.

This case, of course, is not one in which any harm to the physical or mental health of the child or to the public safety, peace, order, or welfare has been demonstrated or may be properly inferred. The record is to the contrary, and any reliance on that theory would find no support in the evidence.

Contrary to the suggestion of the dissenting opinion of Mr. Justice Douglas, our holding today in no degree depends on the assertion of the religious interest of the child as contrasted with that of the parents. It is the parents who are subject to prosecution here for failing to cause their children to attend school, and it is their right of free exercise, not that of their children, that must determine Wisconsin's power to impose criminal penalties on the parent. The dissent argues that a child who expresses a desire to attend public high school in conflict with the wishes of his parents should not be prevented from doing so. There is no reason for the Court to consider that point since it is not an issue in the case. The children are not parties to this litigation. The State has at no point tried this case on the theory that respondents were preventing their children from attending school against their expressed desires, and indeed the record is to the contrary. The State's position from the outset has been that it is empowered to apply its compulsory-attendance law to Amish parents in the same manner as to other parents—that is, without regard to the wishes of the child. That is the claim we reject today.

Our holding in no way determines the proper resolution of possible competing interests of parents, children, and the State in an appropriate state court proceeding in which the power of the State is asserted on the theory that Amish parents are preventing their minor children from attending high school despite their expressed desires to the contrary. Recognition of the claim of the State in such a proceeding would, of course, call into question traditional concepts of parental control over the religious upbringing and education of their minor children recognized in this Court's past decisions. It is clear that such an intrusion by a State into family decisions in the area of religious training would give rise to grave questions of religious freedom comparable to those raised here and those presented in Pierce v. Society of Sisters, 268 U.S. 510 (1925). On this record we neither reach nor decide those issues.

The State's argument proceeds without reliance on any actual conflict between the wishes of parents and children. It appears to rest on the potential that exemption of Amish parents from the requirements of the compulsory-education law might allow some parents to act contrary to the best interests of their children by foreclosing their opportunity to make an intelligent choice between the Amish way of life and that of the outside world. The same argument could, of course, be made with respect to all church schools short of college. There is nothing in the record or in the ordinary course of human experience to suggest that non-Amish parents generally consult with children of ages 14–16 if they are placed in a church school of the parents' faith.

Indeed it seems clear that if the State is empowered, as *parens patriae*, to "save" a child from himself or his Amish parents by requiring an additional two years of compulsory formal high school education, the State will in large measure influence, if not determine, the religious future of the child. Even more markedly than in *Prince*, therefore, this case involves the fundamental interest of parents, as contrasted with that of the State, to guide the religious future and education of their children. The history and culture of Western civilization reflect a strong tradition of parental concern for the nurture and upbringing of their children. This primary role of the parents in the upbringing of their children is now established beyond debate as an enduring American tradition. If not the first, perhaps the most significant statements of the Court in this area are found in Pierce v. Society of Sisters, in which the Court observed:

> "Under the doctrine of Meyer v. Nebraska, 262 U.S. 390, we think it entirely plain that the Act of 1922 unreasonably interferes with the liberty of parents and guardians to direct the upbringing and education of children under their control. As often heretofore pointed out, rights guaranteed by the Constitution may not be abridged by legislation which has no reasonable relation to some purpose within the competency of the State. The fundamental theory of liberty upon which all governments in this Union repose excludes any general power of the State to standardize its children by forcing them to accept instruction from public teachers only. The child is not the mere creature of the State; those who nurture him and direct his destiny have the right, coupled with the high duty, to recognize and prepare him for additional obligations." 268 U.S., at 534–535.

The duty to prepare the child for "additional obligations," referred to by the Court, must be read to include the inculcation of moral standards, religious beliefs, and elements of good citizenship. *Pierce*, of course, recognized that where nothing more than the general interest of the parent in the nurture and education of his children is involved, it is beyond dispute that the State acts "reasonably" and constitutionally in requiring education to age 16 in some public or private school meeting the standards prescribed by the State.

However read, the Court's holding in *Pierce* stands as a charter of the rights of parents to direct the religious upbringing of their children. And, when the interests of parenthood are combined with a free exercise claim of the nature revealed by this record, more than merely a "reasonable relation to some purpose within the competency of the State" is required to sustain the validity of the State's requirement under the First Amendment. To be sure, the power of the parent, even when linked to a free exercise claim, may be subject to limitation under *Prince* if it appears that parental decisions will jeopardize the health or safety of the child, or have a potential for significant social burdens. But in this case, the Amish have introduced persuasive evidence undermining the arguments the State has advanced to support its claims in terms of the welfare of the child and society as a whole. The record strongly indicates that accommodating the religious objections of the Amish by forgoing one, or at most two, additional years of compulsory education will not impair the physical or mental health of the child, or result in an inability to be self-supporting or to discharge the duties and responsibilities of citizenship, or in any other way materially detract from the welfare of society.

In the face of our consistent emphasis on the central values underlying the Religion Clauses in our constitutional scheme of government, we cannot accept a *parens patriae* claim of such all-encompassing scope and with such sweeping potential for broad and unforeseeable application as that urged by the State.

V

For the reasons stated we hold, with the Supreme Court of Wisconsin, that the First and Fourteenth Amendments prevent the State from compelling respondents to cause their children to attend formal high school to age 16. Our disposition of this case, however, in no way alters our recognition of the obvious fact that courts are not school boards or legislatures, and are ill-equipped to determine the "necessity" of discrete aspects of a State's program of compulsory education. This should suggest that courts must move with great circumspection in performing the sensitive and delicate task of weighing a State's legitimate social concern when faced with religious claims for exemption from generally applicable educational requirements. It cannot be overemphasized that we are not dealing with a way of life and mode of education by a group claiming to have recently discovered some "progressive" or more enlightened process for rearing children for modern life.

Aided by a history of three centuries as an identifiable religious sect and a long history as a successful and self-sufficient segment of American society, the Amish in this case have convincingly demonstrated the sincerity of their religious beliefs, the interrelationship of belief with their mode of life, the vital role that belief and daily conduct play in the continued survival of Old Order Amish communities and their religious organization, and the hazards presented by the State's enforcement of a statute generally valid as to others. Beyond this, they have carried the even more difficult burden of demonstrating the adequacy of their alternative mode of continuing informal vocational education in terms of precisely those overall interests that the State advances in support of its program of compulsory high school education. In light of this convincing showing, one that probably few other religious groups or sects could make, and weighing the minimal difference between what the State would require and what the Amish already accept, it was incumbent on the State to show with more particularity how its admittedly strong interest in compulsory education would be adversely affected by granting an exemption to the Amish. Sherbert v. Verner, supra.

Nothing we hold is intended to undermine the general applicability of the State's compulsory school-attendance statutes or to limit the power of the State to promulgate reasonable standards that, while not impairing the free exercise of religion, provide for continuing agricultural vocational education under parental and church guidance by the Old Order Amish or others similarly situated. The States have had a long history of amicable and effective relationships with church-sponsored schools, and there is no basis for assuming that, in this related context, reasonable standards cannot be established concerning the content of the continuing vocational education of Amish children under parental guidance, provided always that state regulations are not inconsistent with what we have said in this opinion.

Affirmed.

■ Mr. Justice White, with whom Mr. Justice Brennan and Mr. Justice Stewart join, concurring.

. . . In the present case, the State is not concerned with the maintenance of an educational system as an end in itself, it is rather attempting to nurture and develop the human potential of its children, whether Amish or non-Amish: to expand their knowledge, broaden their sensibilities, kindle their imagination, foster a spirit of free inquiry, and increase their human understanding and tolerance. It is possible that most Amish children will wish to continue living the rural life of their parents, in which case their training at home will adequately equip them for their future role. Others, however, may wish to become nuclear physicists, ballet dancers, computer programmers, or historians, and for these occupations, formal training will be necessary. . . . [A]lthough the question is close, I am unable to say that the State has demonstrated that Amish children who leave school in the eighth grade will be intellectually stultified or unable to acquire new academic skills later. . . .

. . . I join the Court because the sincerity of the Amish religious policy here is uncontested, because the potentially adverse impact of the state requirement is great, and because the State's valid interest in education has already been largely satisfied by the eight years the children have already spent in school.

■ Mr. Justice Powell and Mr. Justice Rehnquist took no part in the consideration or decision of this case.

■ [The concurring opinion of Mr. Justice Stewart, with whom Mr. Justice Brennan joins, is omitted.]

■ Mr. Justice Douglas, dissenting in part.

. . . The Court's analysis assumes that the only interests at stake in the case are those of the Amish parents on the one hand, and those of the State on the other. The difficulty with this approach is that, despite the Court's claim, the parents are seeking to vindicate not only their own free exercise claims, but also those of their high-school-age children.

It is argued that the right of the Amish children to religious freedom is not presented by the facts of the case, as the issue before the Court involves only the Amish parents' religious freedom to defy a state criminal statute imposing upon them an affirmative duty to cause their children to attend high school.

First, respondents' motion to dismiss in the trial court expressly asserts, not only the religious liberty of the adults, but also that of the children, as a defense to the prosecutions. It is, of course, beyond question that the parents have standing as defendants in a criminal prosecution to assert the religious interests of their children as a defense.[1] Although the lower courts and a majority of this Court assume an identity of interest between parent and child, it is clear that they have treated the religious interest of the child as a factor in the analysis.

Second, it is essential to reach the question to decide the case, not only because the question was squarely raised in the motion to dismiss, but also because no analysis of religious-liberty claims can take place in a vacuum. If the parents in this case are allowed a religious exemption, the inevitable effect is to impose the parents' notions of religious duty upon their children. Where the child is mature enough to express potentially conflicting desires, it would be an invasion of the child's rights to permit such an imposition without canvassing his views. As in Prince v. Massachusetts, 321 U.S. 158, it is an imposition resulting from this very litigation. As the child has no other effective forum, it is in this litigation that his rights should be considered. And, if an Amish child desires to attend high school, and is mature enough to have that desire respected, the State may well be able to override the parents' religiously motivated objections. Religion is an individual experience. It is not necessary, nor even appropriate, for every Amish child to express his views on the subject in a prosecution of a single adult. Crucial, however, are the views of the child whose parent is the subject of the suit. Frieda Yoder has in fact testified that her own religious views are opposed to high-school education. I therefore join the judgment of the Court as to respondent Jonas Yoder. But Frieda Yoder's views may not be those of Vernon Yutzy or Barbara Miller. I must dissent, therefore, as to respondents Adin Yutzy and Wallace Miller as their motion to dismiss also raised the question of their children's religious liberty.

II

This issue has never been squarely presented before today. Our opinions are full of talk about the power of the parents over the child's education. See Pierce v. Society of Sisters, 268 U.S. 510; Meyer v. Nebraska, 262 U.S. 390. And we have in the past analyzed similar conflicts between parent and State with little regard for the views of the child. See Prince v. Massachusetts, supra. Recent cases, however, have clearly held that the children themselves have constitutionally protectible interests.

These children are "persons" within the meaning of the Bill of Rights. We have so held over and over again. . . .

. . .

1. Thus, in Prince v. Massachusetts, 321 U.S. 158, a Jehovah's Witness was convicted for having violated a state child labor law by allowing her nine-year-old niece and ward to circulate religious literature on the public streets. There, as here, the narrow question was the religious liberty of the adult. There, as here, the Court analyzed the problem from the point of view of the State's conflicting interest in the welfare of the child. But, as Mr. Justice Brennan, speaking for the Court, has so recently pointed out, "The Court [in Prince] implicitly held that the custodian had standing to assert alleged freedom of religion ... rights of the child that were threatened in the very litigation before the Court and that the child had no effective way of asserting herself." Eisenstadt v. Baird, 405 U.S. 438, 446 n. 6. Here, as in Prince, the children have no effective alternate means to vindicate their rights. The question, therefore, is squarely before us.

On this important and vital matter of education, I think the children should be entitled to be heard. While the parents, absent dissent, normally speak for the entire family, the education of the child is a matter on which the child will often have decided views. He may want to be a pianist or an astronaut or an oceanographer. To do so he will have to break from the Amish tradition.

It is the future of the student, not the future of the parents, that is imperiled by today's decision. If a parent keeps his child out of school beyond the grade school, then the child will be forever barred from entry into the new and amazing world of diversity that we have today. The child may decide that that is the preferred course, or he may rebel. It is the student's judgment, not his parents', that is essential if we are to give full meaning to what we have said about the Bill of Rights and of the right of students to be masters of their own destiny.[3] If he is harnessed to the Amish way of life by those in authority over him and if his education is truncated, his entire life may be stunted and deformed. The child, therefore, should be given an opportunity to be heard before the State gives the exemption which we honor today.

The views of the two children in question were not canvassed by the Wisconsin courts. The matter should be explicitly reserved so that new hearings can be held on remand of the case.[4]

NOTES

(1) *Yoder* **and** *Prince*. *Yoder* is another in the series of Supreme Court opinions that define the constitutional limits of state and parental authority over children. In determining these boundaries, the Court balances the parental interest against the state's interest in the welfare of children when the two are in conflict. Can you reconcile the Court's striking of this balance in *Yoder* with the opinion in *Prince*? The Court distinguishes the two cases on the ground that *Prince* dealt with the "evil" of child labor, while *Yoder* does not involve a threat of harm to the child

---

3. The court below brushed aside the students' interests with the offhand comment that "[w]hen a child reaches the age of judgment, he can choose for himself his religion." 49 Wis.2d 430, 440, 182 N.W.2d 539, 543. But there is nothing in this record to indicate that the moral and intellectual judgment demanded of the student by the question in this case is beyond his capacity. Children far younger than the 14– and 15–year–olds involved here are regularly permitted to testify in custody and other proceedings. Indeed, the failure to call the affected child in a custody hearing is often reversible error. See, e.g., Callicott v. Callicott, 364 S.W.2d 455 (Tex. Civ.App.) (reversible error for trial judge to refuse to hear testimony of eight-year-old in custody battle). Moreover, there is substantial agreement among child psychologists and sociologists that the moral and intellectual maturity of the 14–year-old approaches that of the adult. See, e.g., J. Piaget, The Moral

Judgment of the Child (1948); D. Elkind, Children and Adolescents 75–80 (1970); Kohlberg, Moral Education in the Schools: A Development View, in R. Muuss, Adolescent Behavior and Society 193, 199–200 (1971); W. Kay, Moral Development 172–183 (1968); A. Gesell & F. Ilg, Youth: The Years From Ten to Sixteen 175–182 (1956). The maturity of Amish youth, who identify with and assume adult roles from early childhood, see M. Goodman, The Culture of Childhood 92–94 (1970), is certainly not less than that of children in the general population.

4. Canvassing the views of all school-age Amish children in the State of Wisconsin would not present insurmountable difficulties. A 1968 survey indicated that there were at that time only 256 such children in the entire State. Comment, 1971 Wis.L.Rev. 832, 852 n. 132.

or to public welfare. Is this persuasive? Is the parental interest in *Yoder* more compelling than in *Prince*? Remember that Ms. Prince and Betty both believed that street preaching and the sale of *Watchtower* magazine were necessary to their salvation.

Is the difference between the two cases that the Court is persuaded that the *state's* interest in *Yoder* is less important than the state's interest in *Prince* (rather than that the Yoders' interest is more significant than is that of Ms. Prince)? Are the Amish parents in *Yoder* arguing that education does not serve an important state interest? As a general matter, education clearly serves the interest of the individual child in preparing her for adult life. What other interests of the state does it serve? Perhaps the Court is persuaded that the otherwise legitimate interest of the state in an educated populace is simply not that important as applied to these Old Order Amish children. Why?

One view is that *Meyer v. Nebraska*, *Pierce v. Society of Sisters*, and *Yoder* present a coherent account of the constitutional parameters of parental authority and that *Prince* is an aberration. The Court in *Prince* seems hostile to the Jehovah's Witness sect (and the Court in *Yoder* expresses great admiration for the Old Order Amish). Do these different subjective responses shed light on the different outcomes in the two cases?

(2) **An Amish Exception to Child Labor Laws**. On January 23, 2004, President Bush signed into law the following woodworking exemption to the Fair Labor Standards Act:

Section 13(c) of the Fair Labor Standards Act of 1938 (29 U.S.C. 213(c)) is amended by adding at the end the following:

"(7)(A)

(i) Subject to subparagraph (B), in the administration and enforcement of the child labor provisions of this Act, it shall not be considered oppressive child labor for a new entrant into the workforce to be employed inside or outside places of business where machinery is used to process wood products.

(ii) In this paragraph, the term 'new entrant into the workforce' means an individual who

(I) is under the age of 18 and at least the age of 14, and

(II) by statute or judicial order is exempt from compulsory school attendance beyond the eighth grade.

(B) The employment of a new entrant into the workforce under subparagraph (A) shall be permitted—

(i) if the entrant is supervised by an adult relative of the entrant or is supervised by an adult member of the same religious sect or division as the entrant;

(ii) if the entrant does not operate or assist in the operation of power-driven woodworking machines;

(iii) if the entrant is protected from wood particles or other flying debris within the workplace by a barrier appropriate to the potential hazard of such wood particles or flying debris or by maintaining a sufficient distance from machinery in operation; and

(iv) if the entrant is required to use personal protective equipment to prevent exposure to excessive levels of noise and saw dust."

This title may be cited as the "Department of Labor Appropriations Act, 2004".

One impetus for this legislative exception is that many of Old Order Amish no longer work in agriculture. The soaring land values in many areas have led many Amish families to leave their farms. Instead, many Amish run wood shops making a variety of wooden items from gazebos to toys. Woodworking is relatively dangerous work, often resulting in injuries. The U.S. Department of Labor had assessed fines against Amish wood shop owners for employing underage workers. The purpose of this legislation is to allow children of sects that are exempted from the compulsory school attendance laws to work in wood shops. *See The Economist*, February 7, 2004, p. 33.

Is this exception applicable to anyone other than children of Old Order Amish parents? Do you think such legislation uniquely tailored to the needs of a particular religious sect is appropriate? To what extent do you believe that *Yoder* is predicated on the assumption that the Amish children removed from school at age fourteen would only be employed in traditional agricultural jobs? How is the child labor exemption for Amish children justifiable in light of *Prince v. Massachusetts*?

(3) In *Yoder* the Supreme Court emphasized that in order for a parent's claim to have the protection of the Free Exercise clause, it must be firmly rooted in religious faith rather than in philosophical or social belief. What if the claim arises out of cultural belief? *In re McMillan*, 30 N.C.App. 235, 226 S.E.2d 693 (1976), a North Carolina appeals court upheld a decision that Native American children were neglected for the reason that their parents had failed to send them to the public schools. The court so held over the parental argument that their decision was based on the failure of the public schools to present adequate instruction in American Indian heritage and culture, and that their deeply rooted cultural convictions, like religious beliefs, were entitled to constitutional protection. In rejecting this argument the court distinguished *Yoder*: "There is no showing that Shelby and Abe Macmillan receive any mode of educational programs alternative to those in the public school. There is also no showing that the Indian heritage or culture of these children will be endangered or threatened in any way by their attending school." In a similar case, although no constitutional question was presented, a New York Court reached the same result based on a finding that no alternative instruction was being provided. See *In re Baum*, 61 A.D.2d 123, 401 N.Y.S.2d 514 (1978).

(4) The state's interest in the education of its citizens is based in part on the importance of an educated informed citizenry as participants in democratic government. Is this interest compromised by the Court in *Yoder*? Like *Meyer* and *Pierce*, the case suggests a tension, which the Court ignores, between important political values. On the one hand, political participation by citizens is essential for a democracy to operate. It is hard to imagine how a society could function if the Old Order Amish traditions of withdrawal and isolation were widespread. The "melting pot" metaphor posits a process of assimilation through which diverse cultural and religious sub-groups come to share a common culture and values. On the other hand, in our political tradition, an important norm is respect for cultural, religious and ethnic diversity and a belief that sub-groups in our society should maintain their identity and not be submerged in the mainstream.

(5) How important to the Court's analysis in *Yoder* was the claim by the parents that to require the Amish children to continue to attend school would threaten the existence of the Amish community itself? Do communities have protectible legal interests separate from the individual members? In a political and legal system based on liberal principles, the law generally focuses on protection of individual rights and the interest of the community is discounted. Nonetheless, the Court in *Yoder* seems to defer to the parents' desire for an exemption from the school attendance requirement in part because this course protects and supports the Amish community.

(6) Justice Douglas's dissent is almost as well known as the majority opinion. It may be the first suggestion in a Supreme Court opinion (albeit a dissent) that children may have a legally protected interest in participating in important decisions affecting their welfare. The dissent is discussed further in Chapter III (page 164).

PARENTS' AUTHORITY OVER THE EDUCATION OF THEIR CHILDREN

(1) **Compulsory School Attendance Laws.** Although the New England colonies, and particularly Massachusetts, regarded education in the basics as essential, the movement toward universal education and comprehensive compulsory attendance laws began in the late nineteenth century as part of a broad social reform movement and during a period of social, cultural, and economic upheaval and adjustment.[1] As the *Yoder* Court points out, the enactment of school attendance laws and child labor laws were parallel developments, as evidenced both by their timing and the fact that they commonly defined an age level, 16, below which children should be in school rather than at work. Although opposition to child labor was motivated in part by humanitarian concerns about exploitation of children, it was not entirely altruistic. Support for both child labor and compulsory school attendance laws came from organized labor at least partly because cheap child labor tended to depress wages generally and displace adult workers. Compulsory school attendance requirements carried with them a ready means of enforcement that worked equally well to enforce the child labor laws.[2]

School attendance laws preempt parental authority by requiring parents to send their children to school and by prohibiting them from deciding that the child should work to contribute to the family's income. Underlying these laws is a policy conclusion that parents may have a conflict of interest with their children on these matters. The assumption is that education until age 16 promotes children's welfare, and parents who would choose to have their children enter the labor market at an earlier age are pursuing their own interest to the detriment of that of their children. In other words, parental decisionmaking discretion is preempted because only one choice promotes the child's interest.

All states and the District of Columbia now have compulsory attendance laws. (Mississippi, after repealing its compulsory school attendance statute in 1956, rejoined the rest of the country by enacting a new statute in 1977.) Implicit in decisions such as *Yoder* and *Pierce v. Society of Sisters* is the conclusion that a state has the authority to compel children to attend school, unless to do so infringes on a protected constitutional interest. Indeed, the Court in *Yoder* referred to the "paramount responsibility" of states to educate their citizens, an obligation that permits states "to impose reasonable regulations for the control and duration of basic education." However equal emphasis was given to the fact that a state's interest in universal education "is not totally free from a balancing process when it impinges on fundamental rights and interests."

---

1. For a detailed and thoughtful history of the development of education in America generally as well as the development of compulsory school attendance provisions, see R. Freeman Butts and Lawrence Arthur Cremin, A History of Education In American Culture (1953), and Newton Edwards and Herman Glenn Richey, The School In the American Social Order (2d ed. 1963).

2. See Molly Ray Carroll, Labor and Politics 81–84 (1923); Newton Edwards and Herman Glenn Richey, supra n. (1), at 489; Raymond Fuller, The Meaning of Child Labor 62–64 (1922).

Yoder involved use of the criminal sanction against parents for failure to send their children to public school. Other cases, such as *In re McMillan*, supra, often involved neglect or similar proceedings as a means of enforcing compulsory attendance requirements. Suppose the child is proceeded against as a delinquent for failure to attend school. In *In re Peters*, 14 N.C.App. 426, 188 S.E.2d 619 (1972), the North Carolina Court of Appeals reversed an adjudication of delinquency and institutional commitment of a 15–year-old boy based on his truancy. In so holding the court observed: "Eddie obviously is a child who should be afforded some technical training where he can use his hands and develop his aptitudes along that line and have some motivation. He obviously does not take to book learning. Forcing him into a classical schoolroom introduces a disruptive element which is not good for the school, the teachers, the other students and likewise is not good for Eddie." 14 N.C.App. at 430, 188 S.E.2d at 621. A number of states now permit vocational training as an alternative to the regular classroom for children who are so inclined. See, e.g., 24 Pa.Cons.Stat.Ann. § 13–1327(a) (Purdon).

All compulsory attendance laws allow parents to educate their children through means other than enrollment in the public schools. Although private school enrollment now often is specifically allowed by statute, *Pierce v. Society of Sisters* makes clear that parents have a constitutionally protected right to educate their children in private schools. This is not to say of course that the state cannot regulate private schools and require conformity to state standards.

(2) **Home Schooling.** As this chapter demonstrates, state and federal courts have been forced to strike a balance between the state's interest in ensuring and regulating the education of its future citizens and the parents' right to direct the upbringing and education of their children. This competition becomes palpable when parents choose to remove their children from public schools and educate them at home. Home schooling, of course was historically the predominant form of education, but yielded to institutional school settings due to rapid urbanization as well as the political goal of achieving national cohesion and political participation in a country made up of immigrant populations. Recent years have seen an upsurge in home schooling by parents as well as the development of an organized movement that has sought to challenge state regulation of parents who want to educate their children at home. Many parents who decide to educate their children at home today are somewhat similar in their motivation to the Amish parents in *Yoder*. They are fundamentalist Christians who believe that public school education will undermine their efforts to convey the religious and moral values that they want their children to learn. A smaller group of parents who are part of a modern home schooling movement are not motivated by religious belief but by a conviction that public schools fail to provide academic challenge and hamper the natural creativity and curiosity of children.

Religious indoctrination and lack of confidence in the efficacy of institutional schooling continue to be the main reasons parents choose to home school their children, but recent images of violence like the murders at Columbine High School in 1999 have reinforced the exodus from public schools. Whatever the reasons for their departures, the number of home schooled students has increased from a few thousand in the early 1980s, to almost 2 million by 2003. Homeschooling parents are generally married with larger than average families. They have more formal education than other parents, with higher median incomes, and the mothers are typically homemakers or work at home.

It is settled that the state maintains a compelling interest in ensuring that citizens are being adequately educated. Indeed, each state constitution includes the provision of a public educational system. Despite numerous cases discussing the state's interest, *Wisconsin v. Yoder*,[3] is the first and only time that the United States Supreme Court has addressed a parents' right to home school their children, seeking an exemption from the state's compulsory school attendance statute. Since then, state courts and legislatures have dealt with the vast majority of home-school issues. While courts have been somewhat less sympathetic to home school students, generally evaluating whether a school district's policy or regulation has a rational basis, home schooling parents have found considerable success lobbying state legislatures. Since 1986, all 50 states have provided a home schooling exemption to their compulsory school attendance laws, recognizing it as a legal alternative to public schooling.

Regulation varies considerably among states as to whether the efforts of parents to educate their children at home are facilitated, tolerated, or discouraged. Under some statutes, home schooling is subject to the same regulation and standards as non-public schools. For example, parents who provide instruction may be required to meet teacher certification requirements.[4] At the other end of the continuum, some states give a broad latitude to parents who remove their children from school because of religious conviction. Many states require prior approval by local school authorities, often without setting standards for the evaluation of parents' plans for instruction.[5] This broad discretion allows local agents to impose their own values regarding education on parental choices.

Most states require that children who are educated at home be subject to standardized evaluation of their educational progress. How should performance of home-schooled children be measured to evaluate the adequacy of their educational progress? Against the mean performance of public school students? Against their own prior performance? Should the adequacy of performance be based on each student's aptitude? Should state officials be permitted to conduct visits to monitor home schooling? In *Brunelle v. Lynn Public Schools*, 428 Mass. 512, 702 N.E.2d 1182 (1998), the Massachusetts Supreme Court struck down a statutory requirement of home visits as a condition of approval of a home schooling program. The court stated that alternative and less intrusive methods, including requesting periodic progress reports or student testing, would satisfy the school system's purposes of ensuring that the plan was being implemented in a satisfactory manner.

Recently, courts have recognized the authority of school districts to distinguish between private schools and home schools in making decisions about appropriations for special education funding and services. In *Hooks v. Clark County School District*, 228 F.3d 1036 (9th Cir.2000), *cert. denied*, 532 U.S. 971, 121 S.Ct. 1602, 149 L.Ed.2d 468 (2001), for example, a Federal appellate court upheld the denial of special education services to a home schooled student because states have discretionary power to determine what constitutes a "private school" under federal law. Similarly a New Jersey court held that home schooling did not fall within the definition of a "non public school" and therefore participants in home schooling program were not mandated recipients of special education services under federal or state statutory requirements. *Forstrom v. Byrne*, 341 N.J.Super. 45, 775 A.2d 65 (App.Div.2001).

Courts have recognized the authority of the state to approve of curriculum plans and to monitor the quality of education that children receive when they are taught at home. In *Care and Protection of Charles*, 399 Mass. 324, 504 N.E.2d 592

---

3. 406 U.S. 205, 92 S.Ct. 1526, 32 L.Ed.2d 15 (1972).

4. See State v. Anderson, 427 N.W.2d 316 (N.D.1988) (upholding teacher certification requirement). But see People v. De-Jonge, 501 N.W.2d 127 (Mich. 1993) (holding that statutory teacher certification requirement violates Free Exercise Clause as applied to families whose religious beliefs were offended by the use of certified teachers).

5. Mass.Gen. Laws Ann. ch. 76, § 1 (West).

(1987), the Massachusetts Supreme Judicial Court rejected a statutory challenge by parents who wanted to educate their children at home due to their religious convictions, but who refused to comply with the statutory requirements for obtaining approval from the local school committee. Massachusetts law requires that parents seeking to educate their children at home must submit a proposed plan of instruction and provide other information to a local school committee, which was directed to approve the plan if it was equal "in thoroughness and efficiency" to that provided in the local public school. The parents refused to supply information to the school committee regarding their educational background and proposed schedule of instruction, and they objected to monitoring and evaluation of their children's progress by the school system. After the school committee refused to approve the parents' home schooling plan, the parents began to educate their children at home, resulting in a truancy petition alleging that the children were "without necessary educational care and discipline".

The parents defended in part on the ground that the approval process infringed upon their right, protected under the Fourteenth Amendment of the Constitution, to direct the education of their children. The court rejected this claim, although it acknowledged the importance of the parental interest. Neither the school committee nor the court questioned the parents' right to educate their children at home. The court, however, citing *Pierce*, *Meyer*, and *Yoder*, found that the parental interest was limited by the legitimate state interest in the education of children. Although the state's authority does not extend to the precise definition of the manner in which children are educated, the court found the approval process and monitoring used by the locality to be a means to assure that home schooling parents fulfill "certain reasonable educational requirements similar to those required for public and private schools." Factors that could be considered in the decision about approval included the curriculum, planned hours of instruction, and the competence of the parents to teach their children. The school committee could also require that it have access to textbooks and teaching materials used. Finally, the child's educational progress could be monitored through periodic evaluation.

Home schooling opponents have voiced numerous concerns relating to the inherent lack of institutional structure. One apprehension is that parents are not qualified to teach their children, especially older students with subjects like advanced math and foreign languages. Other opponents claim that the choice to home school represents a failure of the parents' civic duty by choosing not to expose their children's unique abilities to other students from the community. Perhaps the most compelling argument is that home-schooled students will not be adequately socialized because they are not exposed to a diverse set of people, ideals and experiences. Does a liberal policy of exemption from compulsory education requirements for home tutoring defeat a major social goal of compulsory education—that is, exposing children to new values? Will children who are removed from school so as to protect them from learning about the perspectives of other people who think differently from their parents be prepared to participate in a heterogenous society? Unlike the parents of the Amish children in *Yoder*, most parents seeking to educate their children at home do not anticipate that their children will live and work in a community that is separate from mainstream society. Should this difference be a factor in weighing the state's and parents' respective interests? Emily Buss argues that exposure to different peers is critically important to adolescent development in a heterogenous society, and that home schooling is undesirable in ways that have not been acknowledged. See Emily Buss, The Adolescents' Stake in the Allocation of Educational Control Between Parent and State, 67 U.Chi.L.Rev. 1233 (2000).

Children who are home schooled also may not get the benefit of classes, programs and resources that are available in schools, but beyond the financial resources or instructional capacities of home schooling parents. These would include science labs, orchestras and bands, and athletic programs. Some public schools and colleges have voluntarily cooperated[6] with home-schooled students and at least 12 states have enacted legislation guaranteeing home-schooled student access to public school activities and classes. However, many school districts have refused to collaborate with home educators and their requests for part-time enrollment. Should public schools be required to accommodate home schooled children who seek to enroll in courses or programs that they can not otherwise obtain? Most courts say "no."

In *Swanson v. Guthrie Independent School District No. I–L*, 135 F.3d 694 (10th Cir.1998), for example, a Federal appellate court rejected the claim that the school board's prohibition of part-time school attendance indirectly burdened the parents' and child's rights under the Free Exercise Clause or the parent's right to direct their child's education. The Swansons home schooled their child, Annie, for religious reasons. However, by the time Annie reached the seventh grade, they felt that the public school's classes in foreign language, vocal music and science were "superior to their instructional capability in those areas ... and would better prepare Annie for college."

In response to Annie's request to register for two courses, the school board adopted an attendance policy that prohibited part-time attendance. The policy was justified on the ground that part-time students could not be counted by the district for state financial-aid purposes.

The court rejected the Swansons' request that the school board demonstrate a compelling governmental interest and show that the policy was narrowly tailored to meet that interest. The court explained that the policy is facially neutral since it "applies to all persons who might wish to attend public school on a part-time basis, and prohibits such part-time attendance." Further, "it applies to students who are home-schooled for secular reasons as well as those home-schooled for religious reasons." The court noted that the Swansons could not claim that their right to free expression was directly burdened because "the policy does not prohibit them from home-schooling Annie in accordance with their religious beliefs, and does not force them to do anything that is contrary to those beliefs."

Although parents have a constitutional right to guide their children's education, the court explained that the right was limited in scope. "Parents simply do not have a constitutional right to control each and every aspect of their children's education and oust the state's authority over that subject." Parents cannot "pick and choose which courses their children will take from the public school," nor can they "override the local school board's explicit decision to disallow such part-time attendance." On the contrary, "decisions as to how to allocate scarce resources, as well as what curriculum to offer or require, are uniquely committed to the discretion of local school authorities."

In a 2008 opinion, *In re Rachel L.*, a California appellate court expressed little sympathy for home schooling parents in directing a trial court to order home schooling parents to send their children to public or private school.[7] Reversing the trial court's holding that the parents had a constitutional right to home school their children, the court expressed skepticism that the parents' First Amendment Free Exercise argument provided a basis for an exemption under *Yoder* from the California compulsory education statute. The court also concluded that the parents failed to meet either of the exemptions from full time public education under the statute. First, the mother did not qualify as a "credentialed tutor." The court also

---

6. Jane Duffy, *Home Schooling: A Controversial Alternative*, Principal, May 1998, at 23.

7. In re Rachel L., 160 Cal.App.4th 624, 73 Cal.Rptr.3d 77 (2008).

rejected the parents' argument that the mother was affiliated with a private Christian school in which the children were "enrolled." The school director's occasional visits with the children and monitoring of the mother's instruction was of no legal significance; nor was the fact that the children sometimes took tests at the school.

Proponents of home schooling point out that in numerous tests of academic performance and studies of social behavior, home-schooled students have outperformed their public and even private school counterparts. They do significantly better than the public school students on college entrance exams. Home-schooled students appear to be academically successful regardless of racial, economic, or even the educational background of the parents. Supporters also explain that there are numerous teaching aides available to home schooling parents in the form of books, CD–ROM programs, public libraries, and online assistance. Home schooling, its proponents argue, provides individualized, attentive and flexible learning environment to meet the unique needs of the student, whereas public schools are often overcrowded. Regarding socialization, proponents contend that home schooled students are actually more adequately socialized since they engage in other extracurricular activities like church, scouting and other social organizations, community service programs and home schooling support groups, which can offer field trips, dances and even athletic competition. Is this responsive to the concern raised by Buss and others that home schooled students will not be ready to participate in a heterogenous society? For more discussion regarding proponents' arguments in support of home schooling, *see generally* National Home Education Research Institute, www.nheri.org (last visited Mar. 24, 2003).

For further discussion of home schooling and related issues, see Michael Brian Dailey, Home Schooled Children Gaining Limited Access to Public Schools, 28 J.L. & Educ. 25 (1999); William Grob, Access Denied: Prohibiting Homeschooled Students from Participating in Public–School Athletics and Activities, 16 Ga.St. U.L.Rev. 823 (2000); Jeff Prather, Part–Time Public School Attendance and the Freedom of Religion: Yoder's Impact Upon Swanson, 29 J.L. & Educ. 553 (2000); Darryl C. Wilson, Home Field Disadvantage: The Negative Impact of Allowing Home–Schoolers to Participate in Mainstream Sports, 3 Va.J.Sports & L. 1 (2001). See Jon S. Lerner, Comment, Protecting Home Schooling through the Casey Undue Burden Standards, 62 U. CHI. L. REV. 363 (1995) (applying undue burden standard from abortion rights context to state regulation of home schooling); Ira C. Lupu, Home Education, Religious Liberty, and the Separation of Powers, 67 B.U.L. Rev. 971 (1987) (arguing against home education statutes).

(3) **Charter Schools.** Charter schools are public schools that operate with freedom from many of the regulations that apply to traditional public schools. Charter schools are created under a contract theory. The state grants these schools freedom to make educational choices in exchange for their promise of academic accountability. Charter schools are accountable to their sponsor—usually the state or local school board—to produce positive academic results for their students. Each charter may be different in its terms.

The charter school movement began in Minnesota in 1991. California followed in 1992. By 2002, thirty-nine states, Puerto Rico, and the District of Columbia had enacted legislation authorizing the creation of charter schools. In his 1997 State of the Union Address, President Clinton called for the creation of 3,000 charter schools and, later, President Bush called for $200 million to support charter schools.

There is considerable debate about how successful these educationally innovative public schools have been. See, e.g., Kate Zernike, "A Second Look: Charting the Charter Schools," in the New York Times, March 25, 2001, Section 4, p. 3, column 1, pointing out that some charter schools have out-performed comparable public schools on standardized student tests while other charter school students have scored lower than analogous public school students. There is perhaps more agreement about the value to parents of charter schools being smaller and perceived as a safer environment for their children than the larger local public schools. Safety and personalized attention may mean more to many parents than standardized test scores.

For a general discussion of the legal issues surrounding charter schools, see Jessica P. Driscoll, Charter Schools, 8 Georgetown J. Poverty L. & Pol'y 505 (2001). An even more complex and hotly debated issue is charter schools in cyberspace—the granting of charters to conduct distance learning by cyber charter schools. For a modern discussion, see Christian F. Rhodes, Razing the Schoolhouse: Whether Cyber Charter Schools Can Overcome Statutory Restrictions, 167 Ed. Law Reporter 561 (2002). See also Purdon's Pennsylvania Statutes and Consolidated Statutes Annotated, 24 P. S. § 17–1745–A creating cyber charter schools in Pennsylvania. Finally, for a positive British perspective on American charter schools, see James Tooley, Charter Schools, in Economic Affairs, September 2000, p. 54.

(4) **Special Accommodations and Vouchers—The Establishment Clause.** If the state accommodates requests for special treatment in recognition of parents' religious beliefs, it may be vulnerable to challenges under the Establishment Clause. The Supreme Court dealt with this tension in a case involving New York's creation of a separate school district for Hasidic Jews, to provide a religiously acceptable setting for Hasidic students who needed special education services. The Hasidic village of Kiryas Joel is located entirely within the Monroe–Woodbury Central School District. The private Hasidic schools that most children attended could could not provide special education services. The school district took the position (in response to several Supreme Court opinions dealing with the provision of services to the parochial schools) that it could only provide special education services to the Hasidic students in the public schools, and the Hasidim would not send their children to public school. The legislature, in an effort to resolve the conflict, created a separate school district in the village, and action which the Supreme Court concluded was a violation of the Establishment Clause of the First Amendment. *Board of Educ. of Kiryas Joel Village School District v. Grumet*, 512 U.S. 687, 114 S.Ct. 2481, 129 L.Ed.2d 546 (1994). Although the Court suggested that the state could accommodate religious groups by alleviating particular burdens, the New York legislature had gone too far, because it conferred a special benefit on the community of Kiryas Joel that it was unlikely to make available generally to other religious groups. The legislature's response—to make the benefit potentially available to other groups who wanted to establish a separate school district—was struck down by a New York appellate court because, although the criteria were formally neutral, in fact only the village of Kiryas Joel would qualify. *Grumet v. Cuomo*, 225 A.D.2d 4, 647 N.Y.S.2d 565 (N.Y.App.Div.1996), *aff'd* 90 N.Y.2d 57, 659 N.Y.S.2d 173, 681 N.E.2d 340 (1997). See Abner S. Greene, *Kiryas Joel* and Two Mistakes about Equality, 96 Colum.L.Rev. 1 (1996) (criticizing the Court and defending special school district as an example of "group exit" and the village's incorporation as an exercise of "appropriate public power"); Christopher L. Eisgruber, The Constitutional Value of Assimilation, 96 Colum.L.Rev. 87 (1996) (criticizing the districts as "government-sponsored segregation"); Ira C. Lupu, Uncovering the Village of Kiryas Joel, 96 Colum.L.Rev. 104 (1996) (criticizing Greene's accommodation argument).

In recent years, some cities have initiated voucher programs with the goal of offering low income parents an educational alternative for their children attending inferior inner city schools. In 2002, the Supreme Court upheld a Cleveland, Ohio, program that provided tuition aid to children to attend participating public or private schools against an Establishment Clause challenge. *Zelman v. Simmons–*

Harris, 536 U.S. 639, 122 S.Ct. 2460, 153 L.Ed.2d 604 (2002). In an opinion by Justice Rehnquist, a divided Court rejected the argument that the program effectively was a tax benefit to religious schools because 96% of the children receiving aid attended such schools. The program was enacted for a secular purpose, to provide educational aid to poor children in a failing school system, and the funds were provided directly to parents who then directed the aid to religious schools. The Court held the program was neutral toward religion and could not be interpreted as an endorsement of a religious message. Parents were making a "true private choice," and the constitutionality of the program did not, in the Court's view, depend on the fact that most private schools in Cleveland (and in most cities) happened to be religious schools. Justice Souter dissented, arguing that parents receiving aid did not have a "genuine choice" because few non-religious schools were available and were too expensive for voucher recipients. Thus, the program had the impermissible effect of advancing religious education.

School voucher programs and the implications of *Zelman* have generated a great deal of academic commentary. Consider the following observations by Dean Kathleen Sullivan:

> The Court in *Zelman* upheld as constitutional under the Establishment Clause one type of school voucher program that included religious provider;, but in so doing left many questions unanswered. Are voucher programs permissible for social services provision in such areas as soup kitchens or drug treatment where, unlike in the school context, there are no guaranteed government providers and few affordable nonreligious providers? How much practical and economic compulsion is enough to negate the "genuine" choice that was the watchword of the *Zelman* Court? Is even direct government funding of religious service provision constitutional as long as the government's funding criteria neutrally include both religious and nonreligious recipients alike? If government chooses to set up a voucher program that deliberately excludes religious schools, will the First Amendment's freedoms of speech and association require their inclusion? Are nondiscrimination and anti-hate provisions such as those that Cleveland adopted constitutionally permissible as a matter of free speech or free exercise? Compelled to avoid establishment?*

Kathleen M. Sullivan, The New Religion and the Constitution, 116 Harv.L.Rev. 1397, 1419, 1420 (2003). See also James Dwyer, Religious Schools v. Children's Rights (1998); James E. Ryan, Schools, Race, and Money, 109 Yale L.J. 249 (1999) (arguing that only policies that promote integration (including vouchers) will lead to enhanced academic achievement of poor urban children); For an analysis of *Zelman*, see Charles Fried, Five to Four: Reflections on the School Voucher Case, 116 Harv. L. Rev. 163 (2002).

Brown v. Hot, Sexy and Safer Productions

United States Court of Appeals, 1st Circuit, 1995.
68 F.3d 525.

■ TORRUELLA, CHIEF JUDGE.

The plaintiffs are two minors and their parents. . . .

. . . On April 8, 1992, [plaintiffs] Mesiti and Silva attended a mandatory, school-wide "assembly" at Chelmsford High School. Both students were

---

* Copyright © 2003 by the Harvard Law Review Association. Reprinted with permission.

fifteen years old at the time. The assembly consisted of a ninety-minute presentation characterized by the defendants as an AIDS awareness program (the "Program"). The Program was staged by defendant Suzi Landolphi ("Landolphi"), contracting through defendant Hot, Sexy, and Safer, Inc., a corporation wholly owned by Landolphi.

Plaintiffs allege that Landolphi gave sexually explicit monologues and participated in sexually suggestive skits with several minors chosen from the audience. Specifically, the complaint alleges that Landolphi: 1) told the students that they were going to have a "group sexual experience, with audience participation"; 2) used profane, lewd, and lascivious language to describe body parts and excretory functions; 3) advocated and approved oral sex, masturbation, homosexual sexual activity, and condom use during promiscuous premarital sex; 4) simulated masturbation; 5) characterized the loose pants worn by one minor as "erection wear"; 6) referred to being in "deep sh—" after anal sex; 7) had a male minor lick an oversized condom with her, after which she had a female minor pull it over the male minor's entire head and blow it up; 8) encouraged a male minor to display his "orgasm face" with her for the camera; 9) informed a male minor that he was not having enough orgasms; 10) closely inspected a minor and told him he had a "nice butt"; and 11) made eighteen references to orgasms, six references to male genitals, and eight references to female genitals.

Plaintiffs maintain that the sexually explicit nature of Landolphi's speech and behavior humiliated and intimidated Mesiti and Silva. Moreover, many students copied Landolphi's routines and generally displayed overtly sexual behavior in the weeks following the Program, allegedly exacerbating the minors' harassment. The complaint does not allege that either of the minor plaintiffs actually participated in any of the skits, or were the direct objects of any of Landolphi's comments.

The complaint names eight co-defendants along with Hot, Sexy, and Safer, and Landolphi, alleging that each played some role in planning, sponsoring, producing, and compelling the minor plaintiffs' attendance at the Program. [These included the chairperson and other members of the P.T.O. who negotiated the agreement, members of the school committee, the Superintendent and Assistant Superintendent of the school system and the Principal of Chelmsford High School] . . .

Plaintiffs allege that all the defendants participated in the decisions to hire Landolphi, and to compel the students to attend the Program. All the defendants were physically present during the Program.

A school policy adopted by the School Committee required "[p]ositive subscription, with written parental permission" as a prerequisite to "instruction in human sexuality." The plaintiffs allege, however, that the parents were not given advance notice of the content of the Program or an opportunity to excuse their children from attendance at the assembly.

. . .

The plaintiffs seek both declaratory and monetary relief, alleging that the school sponsored program deprived the minor plaintiffs of: their privacy rights under the First and Fourteenth Amendments; . . . and their First Amendment rights under the Free Exercise Clause (in conjunction with a

deprivation of the parent plaintiffs' right to direct and control the upbringing of their children)....

I.   *Privacy Rights and Substantive Due Process*

. . .

The Supreme Court has held that the Fourteenth Amendment encompasses a privacy right that protects against significant government intrusions into certain personal decisions. *See Roe v. Wade,* 410 U.S. 113 (1973).
This right of privacy "has some extension to activities relating to marriage,
procreation, contraception, family relationships, and child rearing and
education." *Id.* Nevertheless, the Supreme Court has explained that only
those rights that "can be deemed 'fundamental' or 'implicit in the concept
of ordered liberty' are included in this guarantee of personal privacy." *Id.*
Regulations limiting these "fundamental rights" may be justified "only by
a 'compelling state interest' ... [and] must be narrowly drawn to express
only the legitimate interests at stake." *Id.* (citations omitted)....

Parent-plaintiffs allege that the defendants violated their privacy right
to direct the upbringing of their children and educate them in accord with
their own views. This, they maintain, is a constitutionally protected "fundamental right" and thus can only be infringed upon a showing of a
"compelling state interest" that cannot be achieved by any less restrictive
means.

The genesis of the right claimed here can be found in *Meyer v.
Nebraska,*and *Pierce v. Society of Sisters*....

. . . . The *Meyer* and *Pierce* decisions have since been interpreted by the
Court as recognizing that, under our Constitutional scheme, "the custody,
care and nurture of the child reside first in the parents." *Prince v.
Massachusetts, see Wisconsin v. Yoder* [citations omitted]....

The *Meyer* and *Pierce* cases, we think, evince the principle that the
state cannot prevent parents from choosing a specific educational program—whether it be religious instruction at a private school or instruction
in a foreign language. That is, the state does not have the power to
"standardize its children" or "foster a homogenous people" by completely
foreclosing the opportunity of individuals and groups to choose a different
path of education. [Citation omitted.] We do not think, however, that this
freedom encompasses a fundamental constitutional right to dictate the
curriculum at the public school to which they have chosen to send their
children. We think it is fundamentally different for the state to say to a
parent, "You can't teach your child German or send him to a parochial
school," than for the parent to say to the state, "You can't teach my child
subjects that are morally offensive to me." The first instance involves the
state proscribing parents from educating their children, while the second
involves parents prescribing what the state shall teach their children. If all
parents had a fundamental constitutional right to dictate individually what
the schools teach their children, the schools would be forced to cater a
curriculum for each student whose parents had genuine moral disagree-
ments with the school's choice of subject matter. We cannot see that the
Constitution imposes such a burden on state educational systems, and
accordingly find that the rights of parents as described by *Meyer* and *Pierce*

do not encompass a broad-based right to restrict the flow of information in the public schools.

[The court rejected the plaintiffs claim that they had a privacy right to be free from "exposure to vulgar and offensive language and obnoxiously debasing portrayals of human sexuality." It also rejected the procedural due process claim based on the school's failure to get parental permission. The court concluded that this failure was "random and unauthorized" and could not have been predicted by the state; therefore, under relevant precedent, there was no due process violation.]

. . .

Plaintiffs' [also allege] that the defendants' endorsement and encouragement of sexual promiscuity at a mandatory assembly "imping[ed] on their sincerely held religious values regarding chastity and morality," and thereby violated the Free Exercise Clause of the First Amendment. . . .

[P]laintiffs allege that their case falls within the "hybrid" exception . . . for cases that involve "the Free Exercise Clause in conjunction with other constitutional protections." *Employment Div., Oregon Dep't of Human Resources v. Smith,* 494 U.S. 872 at 881. The most relevant of the so-called hybrid cases is *Wisconsin v. Yoder,* 406 U.S. 205 (1972), in which the Court invalidated a compulsory school attendance law as applied to Amish parents who refused on religious grounds to send their children to school. In so holding, the Court explained that

> *Pierce* stands as a charter of the rights of parents to direct the religious upbringing of their children. And, when combined with a free exercise claim of the nature revealed by this record, more than merely a "reasonable relation to some purpose within the competency of the State" is required to sustain the validity of the State's requirement under the First Amendment. *Id.* at 232–33 (discussing *Pierce,* 268 U.S. 510).

We find that the plaintiffs allegations do not bring them within the sweep of *Yoder* for two distinct reasons.

First, as we explained, the plaintiffs' allegations of interference with family relations and parental prerogatives do not state a privacy or substantive due process claim. Their free exercise challenge is thus not conjoined with an independently protected constitutional protection. Second, their free exercise claim is qualitatively distinguishable from that alleged in *Yoder*. . . . .

Here, the plaintiffs do not allege that the one-time compulsory attendance at the Program threatened their entire way of life. Accordingly, the plaintiffs' free exercise claim for damages was properly dismissed.

. . .

Mozert v. Hawkins County Board of Education

United States Court of Appeals, 6th Circuit, 1987.
827 F.2d 1058, cert. denied, 484 U.S. 1066, 108 S.Ct. 1029, 98 L.Ed.2d 993 (1988).

[Plaintiffs were a group of Christian parents and their children who objected to the Holt, Rinehart and Winston reading series used in grades one to eight in the Hawkins County school system. The objections to the textbook series were wide ranging. The parents were offended, inter alia, by descriptions of mental telepathy, the power of imagination and of occult, by discussion of the theory of evolution, and by stories that depicted egalitarian gender roles. They argued that their right of free expression (and right to inculcate their children in their religious beliefs) was undermined by the presentation in the books of concepts and perspectives that were inconsistent with their religious beliefs, without a clear statement that these ideas were wrong. The complaining parents sought an exemption for their children from participating in classes using the textbooks, arguing that the policy requiring the use of the textbook forced parents to choose between a free public education and their children's exposure to ideas that were offensive to their religious beliefs. The court found no unconstitutional burden under the Free Exercise Clause.]

.   .   .

The first question to be decided is whether a governmental requirement that a person be exposed to ideas he or she finds objectionable on religious grounds constitutes a burden on the free exercise of that person's religion as forbidden by the First Amendment. This is precisely the way the superintendent of the Hawkins County schools framed the issue in an affidavit filed early in this litigation. In his affidavit the superintendent set forth the school system's interest in a uniformity of reading texts. The affidavit also countered the claims of the plaintiffs that the schools were inculcating values and religious doctrines contrary to their religious beliefs, stating: "Without expressing an opinion as to the plaintiffs' religious beliefs, I am of the opinion that plaintiffs misunderstand the fact that exposure to something does not constitute teaching, indoctrination, opposition or promotion of the things exposed. While it is true that these textbooks expose the student to varying values and religious backgrounds, neither the textbooks nor the teachers teach, indoctrinate, oppose or promote any particular value or religion."

.   .   .

It is also clear that exposure to objectionable material is what the plaintiffs objected to albeit they emphasize the repeated nature of the exposure. . . . The plaintiffs did not produce a single student or teacher to testify that any student was ever required to affirm his or her belief or disbelief in any idea or practice mentioned in the various stories and passages contained in the Holt series. However, the plaintiffs appeared to assume that materials clearly presented as poetry, fiction and even "make-believe" in the Holt series were presented as facts which the students were required to believe. Nothing in the record supports this assumption.

Vicki Frost testified that an occasional reference to role reversal, pacifism, rebellion against parents, one-world government and other objectionable concepts would be acceptable, but she felt it was the repeated references to such subjects that created the burden. The district court suggested that it was a matter of balance, id. at 1199, apparently believing that a reading series that presented ideas with which the plaintiffs agree in juxtaposition to those with which they disagree would pass constitutional muster. While balanced textbooks are certainly desirable, there would be serious difficulties with trying to cure the omissions in the Holt series, as plaintiffs and their expert witnesses view the texts.

However, the plaintiffs' own testimony casts serious doubt on their claim that a more balanced presentation would satisfy their religious views. Mrs. Frost testified that it would be acceptable for the schools to teach her children about other philosophies and religions, but if the practices of other religions were described in detail, or if the philosophy was "profound" in that it expressed a world view that deeply undermined her religious beliefs, then her children "would have to be instructed to [the] error [of the other philosophy]." It is clear that to the plaintiffs there is but one acceptable view—the Biblical view, as they interpret the Bible. Furthermore, the plaintiffs view every human situation and decision, whether related to personal belief and conduct or to public policy and programs, from a theological or religious perspective. Mrs. Frost testified that many political issues have theological roots and that there would be "no way" certain themes could be presented without violating her religious beliefs. She identified such themes as evolution, false supernaturalism, feminism, telepathy and magic as matters that could not be presented in any way without offending her beliefs. The only way to avoid conflict with the plaintiffs' beliefs in these sensitive areas would be to eliminate all references to the subjects so identified. However, the Supreme Court has clearly held that it violates the Establishment Clause to tailor a public school's curriculum to satisfy the principles or prohibitions of any religion. Epperson v. Arkansas, 393 U.S. 97, 106 (1968).

. . .

In this case the district court erroneously applied decisions based on governmental requirements that objecting parties make some affirmation or take some action that offends their religious beliefs. In Sherbert the burden on the plaintiff's right of free exercise consisted of a governmental requirement that she either work on her Sabbath Day or forfeit her right to benefits. Similarly, in Thomas the plaintiff was denied a benefit for refusing to engage in the production of armaments. In each case the burden on the plaintiff's free exercise of religion consisted of being required to perform an act which violated the plaintiffs' religious convictions or forego benefits. Ms. Sherbert was not merely exposed to the view that others in the work force had no religious scruples against working on Saturdays and Mr. Thomas was not merely exposed to government publications designed to encourage employees to produce armaments. In each case there was compulsion to do an act that violated the plaintiffs' religious convictions.

. . . . In Spence this court upheld a conscientious objector's right not to be required to participate in his high school's ROTC program. The court found that Spence's claim resembled Sherbert's "since it compels the conscientious objector either to engage in military training contrary to his religious beliefs, or to give up his public education." 465 F.2d at 799. It is clear that it was being compelled to engage in military training, not being exposed to the fact that others do so, that was found to be an unconstitutional burden.

In Sherbert, Thomas and Hobbie there was governmental compulsion to engage in conduct that violated the plaintiffs' religious convictions. That element is missing in the present case. The requirement that students read the assigned materials and attend reading classes, in the absence of a showing that this participation entailed affirmation or denial of a religious belief, or performance or non-performance of a religious exercise or practice, does not place an unconstitutional burden on the students' free exercise of religion.

. . .

Board of Education v. Barnette, 319 U.S. 624 (1943), grew out of a school board rule that required all schools to make a salute to the flag and a pledge of allegiance a regular part of their daily program. All teachers and students were required to participate in the exercise and refusal to engage in the salute was considered an act of insubordination which could lead to expulsion and possible delinquency charges for being unlawfully absent. The plaintiff was a Jehovah's Witness who considered the flag an "image" which the Bible forbids worshiping in any way. Justice Jackson, writing for the Court, stated:

> Here, . . . we are dealing with a compulsion of students to declare a belief. They are not merely made acquainted with the flag salute so that they may be informed as to what it is or even what it means.

Id. at 631. Further, explaining the basis of the decision, Justice Jackson wrote:

> Here it is the State that employs a flag as a symbol of adherence to government as presently organized. It requires the individual to communicate by word and sign his acceptance of the political ideas it thus bespeaks.
>
> . . . It is also to be noted that the compulsory flag salute and pledge requires affirmation of a belief and attitude of mind.

Id. at 633. It is abundantly clear that the exposure to materials in the Holt series did not compel the plaintiffs to "declare a belief," "communicate by word and sign [their] acceptance" of the ideas presented, or make an "affirmation of a belief and an attitude of mind." In Barnette the unconstitutional burden consisted of compulsion either to do an act that violated the plaintiff's religious convictions or communicate an acceptance of a particular idea or affirm a belief. No similar compulsion exists in the present case.

It is clear that governmental compulsion either to do or refrain from doing an act forbidden or required by one's religion, or to affirm or disavow a belief forbidden or required by one's religion, is the evil prohibited by the Free Exercise Clause. In Abington School District v. Schempp, 374 U.S. 203, 223 (1963), the Court described the Free Exercise Clause as follows:

> Its purpose is to secure religious liberty in the individual by prohibiting any invasions thereof by civil authority. Hence it is necessary in a free exercise case for one to show the coercive effect of the enactment as it operates against him in the practice of his religion. The distinction between the two clauses is apparent—a violation of the Free

Exercise Clause is predicated on coercion while the Establishment Clause violation need not be so attended.

See also Engel v. Vitale, 370 U.S. 421, 430 (1962) ("The Establishment Clause, unlike the Free Exercise Clause, does not depend upon any showing of direct governmental compulsion....")

The plaintiffs appear to contend that the element of compulsion was supplied by the requirement of class participation in the reading exercises. As we have pointed out earlier, there is no proof in the record that any plaintiff student was required to engage in role play, make up magic chants, read aloud or engage in the activity of haggling. In fact, the Director of Education for the State of Tennessee testified that most teachers do not adhere to the suggestions in the teachers' manuals and a teacher for 11 years in the Hawkins County system stated that she looks at the lesson plans in the teachers' editions, but "does her own thing." Being exposed to other students performing these acts might be offensive to the plaintiffs, but it does not constitute the compulsion described in the Supreme Court cases, where the objector was required to affirm or deny a religious belief or engage or refrain from engaging in a practice contrary to sincerely held religious beliefs.

D.

The third Supreme Court decision relied upon by the plaintiffs is the only one that might be read to support the proposition that requiring mere exposure to materials that offend one's religious beliefs creates an unconstitutional burden on the free exercise of religion. Wisconsin v. Yoder, 406 U.S. 205 (1972). However, Yoder rested on such a singular set of facts that we do not believe it can be held to announce a general rule that exposure without compulsion to act, believe, affirm or deny creates an unconstitutional burden. The plaintiff parents in Yoder were Old Order Amish and members of the Conservative Amish Mennonite Church, who objected to their children being required to attend either public or private schools beyond the eighth grade. Wisconsin school attendance law required them to cause their children to attend school until they reached the age of 16. Unlike the plaintiffs in the present case, the parents in Yoder did not want their children to attend any high school or be exposed to any part of a high school curriculum. The Old Order Amish and the Conservative Amish Mennonites separate themselves from the world and avoid assimilation into society, and attempt to shield their children from all worldly influences. The Supreme Court found from the record that—

> [C]ompulsory school attendance to age 16 for Amish children carries with it a very real threat to undermining the Amish community and religious practice as they exist today; they must either abandon belief and be assimilated into society at large, or be forced to migrate to some other and more tolerant region.

Id. at 218 (footnote omitted).

As if to emphasize the narrowness of its holding because of the unique 300 year history of the Old Amish Order, the Court wrote:

It is one thing to say that compulsory education for a year or two beyond the eighth grade may be necessary when its goal is the preparation of the child for life in modern society as the majority live, but it is quite another if the goal of education be viewed as the preparation of the child for life in the separated agrarian community that is the keystone of the Amish faith.

Id. at 222 (citation omitted). This statement points up dramatically the difference between Yoder and the present case. The parents in Yoder were required to send their children to some school that prepared them for life in the outside world, or face official sanctions. The parents in the present case want their children to acquire all the skills required to live in modern society. They also want to have them excused from exposure to some ideas they find offensive. Tennessee offers two options to accommodate this latter desire. The plaintiff parents can either send their children to church schools or private schools, as many of them have done, or teach them at home. Tennessee law prohibits any state interference in the education process of church schools:

The state board of education and local boards of education are prohibit- ed from regulating the selection of faculty or textbooks or the estab- lishment of a curriculum in church-related schools.

TCA 49–50–801(b). Similarly the statute permitting home schooling by parents or other teachers prescribes nothing with respect to curriculum or the content of class work.

Yoder was decided in large part on the impossibility of reconciling the goals of public education with the religious requirement of the Amish that their children be prepared for life in a separated community. As the Court noted, the requirement of school attendance to age 16 posed a "very real threat of undermining the Amish community and religious practice as they exist today...." 406 U.S. at 218. No such threat exists in the present case, and Tennessee's school attendance laws offer several options to those parents who want their children to have the benefit of an education which prepares for life in the modern world without being exposed to ideas which offend their religious beliefs.

. . .

The Supreme Court has recently affirmed that public schools serve the purpose of teaching fundamental values "essential to a democratic society." These values "include tolerance of divergent political and religious views" while taking into account "consideration of the sensibilities of others." Bethel School Dist. No. 403 v. Fraser, 106 S.Ct. 3159, 3164 (1986). The Court has noted with apparent approval the view of some educators who see public schools as an "assimilative force" that brings together "diverse and conflicting elements" in our society "on a broad but common ground." Ambach v. Norwick, 441 U.S. 68, 77 (1979), citing works of J. Dewey, N. Edwards and H. Richey. The critical reading approach furthers these goals. Mrs. Frost stated specifically that she objected to stories that develop "a religious tolerance that all religions are merely different roads to God." Stating that the plaintiffs reject this concept, presented as a recipe for an ideal world citizen, Mrs. Frost said, "We cannot be tolerant in that we accept other religious views on an equal basis with ours." While probably not an uncommon view of true believers in any religion, this statement graphically illustrates what is lacking in the plaintiffs' case.

The "tolerance of divergent ... religious views" referred to by the Supreme Court is a civil tolerance, not a religious one. It does not require a person to accept any other religion as the equal of the one to which that person adheres. It merely requires a recognition that in a pluralistic society we must "live and let live." If the Hawkins County schools had required the plaintiff students either to believe or say they believe that "all religions are merely different roads to God," this would be a different case. No instrument of government can, consistent with the Free Exercise Clause, require such a belief or affirmation. However, there was absolutely no showing that the defendant school board sought to do this; indeed, the school board agreed at oral argument that it could not constitutionally do so. Instead, the record in this case discloses an effort by the school board to offer a reading curriculum designed to acquaint students with a multitude of ideas and concepts, though not in proportions the plaintiffs would like. While many of the passages deal with ethical issues, on the surface at least, they appear to us to contain no religious or anti-religious messages. Because the plaintiffs perceive every teaching that goes beyond the "three Rs" as inculcating religious ideas, they admit that any value-laden reading curriculum that did not affirm the truth of their beliefs would offend their religious convictions.

Although it is not clear that the plaintiffs object to all critical reading, Mrs. Frost did testify that she did not want her children to make critical judgments and exercise choices in areas where the Bible provides the answer. There is no evidence that any child in the Hawkins County schools was required to make such judgments. It was a goal of the school system to encourage this exercise, but nowhere was it shown that it was required. When asked to comment on a reading assignment, a student would be free to give the Biblical interpretation of the material or to interpret it from a different value base. The only conduct compelled by the defendants was reading and discussing the material in the Holt series, and hearing other students' interpretations of those materials. This is the exposure to which the plaintiffs objected. What is absent from this case is the critical element of compulsion to affirm or deny a religious belief or to engage or refrain from engaging in a practice forbidden or required in the exercise of a plaintiff's religion.

. . .

Judge Boggs concludes that the majority reverses the district court because it found the plaintiffs' claims of First Amendment protection so extreme as obviously to violate the Establishment Clause. This is not the holding of the majority. We do point out that under certain circumstances the plaintiffs, by their own testimony, would only accept accommodations that would violate the Establishment Clause. However, this is not the holding. What we do hold is that the requirement that public school students study a basal reader series chosen by the school authorities does not create an unconstitutional burden under the Free Exercise Clause when the students are not required to affirm or deny a belief or engage or refrain from engaging in a practice prohibited or required by their religion. There was no evidence that the conduct required of the students was forbidden by their religion. Rather, the witnesses testified that reading the Holt series "could" or "might" lead the students to come to conclusions that were contrary to teachings of their and their parents' religious beliefs. This is not sufficient to establish an unconstitutional burden.

. . .

NOTE ON PARENTS' EFFORTS TO INFLUENCE CURRICULUM

(1) **Parental Objections to Sex Education/Family Life Programs**. Parents whose children attend public school have attempted to challenge parts of the curriculum that offend their religious values. The most prominent target has been sex education programs, which became a standard part of the public school curriculum in the 1960s. School boards have initiated instruction in sex education in response to increasing sexual activity among adolescents and the rise in teen pregnancy and venereal disease. Parents object to the programs on the ground that in educating children about sex, the school is usurping parent authority to guide the moral development of their children (and specifically to instruct them about sexual morality) in accordance with parents' religious beliefs.

In *Smith v. Ricci*, 89 N.J. 514, 446 A.2d 501 (1982), New Jersey parents offered a constitutional challenge to a State Board of Education regulation requiring local school districts to implement a family life education program. The parents claimed that the regulation violated the Free Exercise and Establishment Clauses of the First Amendment and the Due Process Clause of the Fourteenth Amendment. They argued that the program violated the Free Exercise rights of both the complaining parents and their children by exposing the children to values and attitudes contrary to their religious beliefs. The program at issue, like most public school sex education programs, contained an "excusal policy" permitting parents who objected to the program to remove their children. However, the parents argued that the excusal policy did not make the program acceptable, because children would be required affirmatively to assert their objection and would be subject to peer pressure. They also claimed that the regulation violated the Establishment Clause, because it established secularism as a religion and thus had the primary effect of inhibiting religion. Finally, they argued that the state failed to establish that the family life education program was a reasonable means to pursue the goal of preventing teenage pregnancy and venereal disease.

The Supreme Court of New Jersey rejected the parents' claims. It followed a number of courts in other states in finding the Free Exercise claim to be without merit because children could be excused from the program—even though it acknowledged that exercising this right might be difficult for some children. In fact, the court found that the state would be open to a challenge to its curriculum under the Establishment Clause were it to tailor its curriculum to avoid conflict with the beliefs of particular religious groups. The court also was not persuaded by the parents' Establishment Clause challenge, finding that the regulation was neutral toward different religious and moral viewpoints and secular in its purpose. The court also rejected the Due Process claim, accepting the state's argument that the program was a reasonable means to combat the societal problems at which it was directed, since the parents presented no evidence to support their challenge to the reasonableness of the program.

Most sex education programs in public schools permit parents to remove their children from the classes and many courts have emphasized these exemption policies in rejecting constitutional challenges to sex education programs. Should the state be required to demonstrate a more substantial interest if it seeks to require students to participate in a compulsory sex education program? Some courts have suggested that the state must demonstrate that the compulsory program is essential to promote the state's interest.[1] However, other courts disagree. Although excusal policies may be politically advisable, *Brown* would suggest that they are not constitutionally mandated. Why did the court uphold the mandatory program in *Brown?* The court emphasized the burden that would be created if parents had a right to require that the school curriculum be tailored to fit their moral and religious values.

Other courts have followed *Brown.* The Ninth Circuit Court of Appeals recently rejected a constitutional claim by parents that the school district had violated their "right to control the upbringing of their children by introducing them to matters of and relating to sex." *Fields v. Palmdale School District,* 427 F.3d 1197 (9th Cir.2005). After obtaining general consent from parents, the school district had distributed a psychological questionnaire that included questions about sex, among other questions about experiences and feelings, to elementary school children. The court found that parents had no fundamental right under *Meyer* and *Pierce* to be the *exclusive* provider of such information or to override the school district in determining the information to which their children would be exposed while they were enrolled as students. Drawing on *Brown,* the court emphasized that while the state could not prevent parents from choosing a specific educational program under *Meyer* and *Pierce,* parents in turn could not dictate the public school curriculum or restrict the state from teaching subjects morally offensive to them. Like *Brown,* the *Fields* court focused on the burden on the state of tailoring the curriculum to meet the moral objections of individual parents.

Along the same lines, another federal Court of Appeals declared,

> While parents may have a fundamental right to decide *whether* to send their child to a public school, they do not have a fundamental right generally to direct *how* a public school teaches their child. Whether it is the school curriculum, the hours of the school day, school discipline, the timing and content of examinations, the individuals hired to teach at the school, the extracurricular activities offered at the school or, as here, a dress code, these issues of public education are generally "committed to the control of state and local authorities."

Blau v. Fort Thomas Pub. Sch. Dist., 401 F.3d 381, 395–96 (6th Cir.2005).

Courts are generally reluctant to expand sex education accommodations in response to parental objections based on religious belief. For example, a federal appellate court rejected a father's objection to his 7th grade son's participating in the school's health education classes, based on his view that "parents should be responsible for teaching their children about 'health, morals, ethical and personal behavior.'" *Leebaert v. Fairfield Board of Education,* 332 F.3d 134 (2d Cir.2003). Under a state statute, children could not be required to participate in a public school family life program. Pursuant to this law, the school policy provided that students could be excused from the 6 days of health education class that dealt with family life and AIDS education. However, the father also objected, on the basis of his religious belief, to the school teaching his child about tobacco and drugs, alcohol, self-esteem, setting personal goals and feelings about death. Citing *Brown,* the court held that the parental right to control the upbringing and education of their

1. *Valent v. New Jersey State Board of Education,* 114 N.J.Super. 63, 274 A.2d 832, 839 (Ch.Div.1971).

children did not include the right to exempt the child from public school requirements.

(2) **Textbook and Other School Program Challenges.** The *Mozert* parents sought to have their child excused from a core curriculum requirement, offering a common claim of Christian parents—that public school textbooks promote the "religion" of secular humanism in violation of the Establishment Clause. Although what is meant by secular humanism is subject to some debate, at a minimum it emphasizes rationality and tolerance of and neutrality toward different religious and cultural perspectives. Although this neutrality is precisely the quality that is offensive to the protesting parents, it clarifies why courts have not accepted this constitutional challenge.

The textbooks that are the subject of controversy in *Mozert* are the foundation of an integrated curriculum that includes social studies and other subjects as well as literature and language. Does this suggest that the burden that the parents' demands would place on the school system is substantial? In this regard, compare *Mozert* with *Yoder*. Was the accommodation of the parents' demands in *Yoder* less burdensome?

Two threads run through the cases dealing with the conflict between parents and public schools, when parents object to standard curriculum and attendance requirements on grounds of personal belief. First, courts emphasize the state's interest in educating children and the importance of educators having control over curriculum. A legal framework that required the public school curriculum to accommodate parents' preferences would be unworkable. This interest generally prevails absent some superior right of parents entitled to protection. Second, courts as well as legislatures are respectful of parents' role in child rearing and attempt to be responsive to parents' concerns, particularly when they are based on religious objections. An example of this effort to be flexible, of course, is excusal policies applied to family life programs. However, ultimately, accommodation takes the form of the freedom that parents have to pursue alternatives to public education. Do you think the court in *Mozert* rejected the parents' claims in part because alternatives were available to the accommodation that they were seeking?

Courts have also addressed challenges by parents and their children of mandatory community service requirements in public high schools. Parents object to these requirements on the basis of their values and ideology, arguing that community service must be a matter of individual choice and that a mandatory requirement interferes with their right to guide their child's upbringing. In rejecting these claims, courts have emphasized that the parents' objections are not based on religious beliefs, and thus get less constitutional weight. A federal appellate court upheld a graduation requirement of 50 hours of community service in a North Carolina high school against a parental challenge, finding that the regulation needed only to survive rational basis review where the parent's objection had no religious basis. *Herndon v. Chapel Hill–Carrboro City Board of Education*, 89 F.3d 174 (4th Cir.1996). The Court distinguished *Yoder*, quoting from Supreme Court opinion. "A way of life ... may not be interposed as a barrier to reasonable state regulation of education if it is based on purely secular considerations." 406 U.S. 205 at 207.

A few state legislatures have expanded parental authority to influence their children's education. Texas has recently enacted a statute, the Parents' Rights and Responsibilities Act, Tex. Educ. Code Ann. §§ 26.003–26.010 (Vernon 2000), which gives rights to parents in dealing with their children's school, including the right to petition ("with the expectation that the request will not be unreasonably denied") on behalf of their children to add or change a course, graduate early, and to withdraw from a class or other school activity that conflicts with their religious beliefs.

The extent to which parents should have authority to control children's education has been the focus of academic interest. Stephen Gilles has argued for strong parental authority to make educational choices for their children. Stephen Gilles, On Educating Children: A Parentalist Manifesto, 63 U.Chi.L.Rev. 937 (1996). Other scholars are more critical of broad recognition of parental authority. James Dwyer argues that parents have no right to right to inculcate their children generally or to school them at home. James G. Dwyer, Parents' Religion and Children's Welfare: Debunking the Doctrine of Parents' Rights, 82 Cal.L.Rev.1371 (1994).

Troxel v. Granville

Supreme Court of the United States, 2000.
530 U.S. 57, 120 S.Ct. 2054, 147 L.Ed.2d 49.

■ JUSTICE O'CONNOR announced the judgment of the Court and delivered an opinion, in which THE CHIEF JUSTICE, JUSTICE GINSBURG, and JUSTICE BREYER join. . . .

Tommie Granville and Brad Troxel shared a relationship that ended in June 1991. The two never married, but they had two daughters, Isabelle and Natalie. Jenifer and Gary Troxel are Brad's parents, and thus the paternal grandparents of Isabelle and Natalie. After Tommie and Brad separated in 1991, Brad lived with his parents and regularly brought his daughters to his parents' home for weekend visitation. Brad committed suicide in May 1993. Although the Troxels at first continued to see Isabelle and Natalie on a regular basis after their son's death, Tommie Granville informed the Troxels in October 1993 that she wished to limit their visitation with her daughters to one short visit per month.

In December 1993, the Troxels commenced the present action by filing, in the Washington Superior Court for Skagit County, a petition to obtain visitation rights with Isabelle and Natalie. The Troxels filed their petition under . . . Wash. Rev. Code 26.10.160(3) (1994) . . . Section 26.10.160(3) provides: "Any person may petition the court for visitation rights at any time including, but not limited to, custody proceedings. The court may order visitation rights for any person when visitation may serve the best interest of the child whether or not there has been any change of circum-stances." At trial, the Troxels requested two weekends of overnight visita-tion per month and two weeks of visitation each summer. Granville did not oppose visitation altogether, but instead asked the court to order one day of visitation per month with no overnight stay. In 1995, the Superior Court issued an oral ruling and entered a visitation decree ordering visitation one weekend per month, one week during the summer, and four hours on both of the petitioning grandparents' birthdays. . . .

[The Washington Court of Appeals reversed the visitation order and dismissed the Troxels' petition on statutory grounds. 940 P.2d 698 (Wash. Ct.App.1997). The Washington Supreme Court affirmed, 969 P.2d 21 (Wash.1998), rejecting the statutory ground, but agreeing with the lower court that the Troxels could not obtain visitation pursuant to

§ 26.10.160(3). During the appeal process, Granville married and her husband adopted the children.]

The [Washington Supreme] [C]ourt rested its decision on the Federal Constitution, holding that § 26.10.160(3) unconstitutionally infringes on the fundamental right of parents to rear their children. . . .

We granted certiorari, and now affirm the judgment. . . .

The demographic changes of the past century make it difficult to speak of an average American family. . . . While many children may have two married parents and grandparents who visit regularly, many other children are raised in single-parent households. In 1996, children living with only one parent accounted for 28 percent of all children under age 18 in the United States. . . . Understandably, in these single-parent households, persons outside the nuclear family are called upon with increasing frequency to assist in the everyday tasks of child rearing. In many cases, grandparents play an important role. . . .

The nationwide enactment of nonparental visitation statutes is assuredly due, in some part, to the States' recognition of these changing realities of the American family. Because grandparents and other relatives undertake duties of a parental nature in many households, States have sought to ensure the welfare of the children therein by protecting the relationships those children form with such third parties. The States' nonparental visitation statutes are further supported by a recognition. . . . that children should have the opportunity to benefit from relationships with . . . their grandparents. The extension of statutory rights in this area to persons other than a child's parents, however, comes with an obvious cost. For example, the State's recognition of an independent third-party interest in a child can place a substantial burden on the traditional parent-child relationship. . . .

The Fourteenth Amendment provides that no State shall "deprive any person of life, liberty, or property, without due process of law." . . . The Clause . . . includes a substantive component that "provides heightened protection against government interference with certain fundamental rights and liberty interests."

The liberty interest at issue in this case—the interest of parents in the care, custody, and control of their children—is perhaps the oldest of the fundamental liberty interests recognized by this Court. . . . *Meyer v. Nebraska*, 262 U.S. 390 (1923) . . . *Pierce v. Society of Sisters*, 268 U.S. 510, 534–535 (1925) . . . *Stanley v. Illinois*, 405 U.S. 645 (1972) . . . *Wisconsin v. Yoder*, 406 U.S. 205 (1972) . . . *Quilloin v. Walcott*, 434 U.S 246 (1978) . . . *Parham v. J. R.*, 442 U.S. 584, 602 (1979) . . . *Santosky v. Kramer*, 455 U.S. 745, 753 (1982). . . .

Section 26.10.160(3), as applied to Granville and her family in this case, unconstitutionally infringes on that fundamental parental right. The Washington nonparental visitation statute is breathtakingly broad. According to the statute's text, "*[a]ny person* may petition the court for visitation rights *at any time*," and the court may grant such visitation rights whenever "visitation may serve *the best interest of the child*." § 26.10.160(3) (emphases added). That language effectively permits any third party seeking visitation to subject any decision by a parent concerning visitation of the parent's children to state-court review ... [in which] a parent's decision that visitation would not be in the child's best interest is accorded no deference. Section 26.10.160(3) contains no requirement that a court accord the parent's decision any presumption of validity or any weight whatsoever.... Should the judge disagree with the parent's estimation of the child's best interests, the judge's view necessarily prevails. Thus, in practical effect, in the State of Washington a court can disregard and overturn any decision by a fit custodial parent concerning visitation whenever a third party affected by the decision files a visitation petition, based solely on the judge's determination of the child's best interests. The Washington Supreme Court had the opportunity to give § 26.10.160(3) a narrower reading, but it declined to do so. See, *e.g.*, 969 P.2d, at 23....

Turning to the facts of this case, the record reveals that the Superior Court's order was based on precisely the type of mere disagreement we have just described and nothing more. The Superior Court's order was not founded on any special factors that might justify the State's interference with Granville's fundamental right to make decisions concerning the rearing of her two daughters.... [The combination of several factors here compels our conclusion that Sect. 26.10160(3), as applied, exceeded the demands of the Due Process Clause ...].

First, the Troxels did not allege, and no court has found, that Granville was an unfit parent. That aspect of the case is important, for there is a presumption that fit parents act in the best interests of their children. As this Court explained in Parham:

> "[O]ur constitutional system long ago rejected any notion that a child is the mere creature of the State and, on the contrary, asserted that parents generally have the right, coupled with the high duty, to recognize and prepare [their children] for additional obligations.... [I]t has recognized that natural bonds of affection lead parents to act in the best interests of their children." 442 U.S., at 602 (alteration in original) (internal quotation marks and citations omitted).

Accordingly, so long as a parent adequately cares for his or her children (*i.e.*, is fit), there will normally be no reason for the State to inject itself into the private realm of the family to further question the ability of that parent to make the best decisions concerning the rearing of that parent's children....

The problem here is not that the Washington Superior Court intervened, but that when it did so, it gave no special weight at all to Granville's determination of her daughters' best interests. More importantly, it appears that the Superior Court applied exactly the opposite presumption....

The judge's comments suggest that he presumed the grandparents' request should be granted unless the children would be "impact[ed] adversely." In effect, the judge placed on Granville, the fit custodial parent, the burden of *disproving* that visitation would be in the best interest of her daughters....

The decisional framework employed by the Superior Court directly contravened the traditional presumption that a fit parent will act in the best interest of his or her child. In that respect, the court's presumption failed to provide any protection for Granville's fundamental constitutional right to make decisions concerning the rearing of her own daughters.... In an ideal world, parents might always seek to cultivate the bonds between grandparents and their grandchildren. Needless to say, however, our world is far from perfect, and in it the decision whether such an intergenerational relationship would be beneficial in any specific case is for the parent to make in the first instance. And, if a fit parent's decision of the kind at issue here becomes subject to judicial review, the court must accord at least some special weight to the parent's own determination.

Finally, we note that there is no allegation that Granville ever sought to cut off visitation entirely.... Granville did not oppose visitation but instead asked that the duration of any visitation order be shorter than that requested by the Troxels.... The Superior Court gave no weight to Granville's having assented to visitation even before the filing of any visitation petition or subsequent court intervention.... Significantly, many other States expressly provide by statute that courts may not award visitation unless a parent has denied (or unreasonably denied) visitation to the concerned third party. See, *e.g*.... Ore. Rev. Stat. § 109.121(1)(a)(B) (1997) (court may award visitation if the "custodian of the child has denied the grandparent reasonable opportunity to visit the child")....

Considered together with the Superior Court's reasons for awarding visitation to the Troxels, the combination of these factors demonstrates that the visitation order in this case was an unconstitutional infringement on Granville's fundamental right to make decisions concerning the care, custody, and control of her two daughters. The Washington Superior Court failed to accord the determination of Granville, a fit custodial parent, any material weight. In fact, the Superior Court made only two formal findings in support of its visitation order. First, the Troxels "are part of a large, central, loving family, all located in this area, and the [Troxels] can provide opportunities for the children in the areas of cousins and music." App. 70a. Second, "[t]he children would be benefitted from spending quality time with the [Troxels], provided that that time is balanced with time with the childrens' [sic] nuclear family." *Ibid*. These slender findings ... show that this case involves nothing more than a simple disagreement between the Washington Superior Court and Granville concerning her children's best interests.... As we have explained, the Due Process Clause does not permit a State to infringe on the fundamental right of parents to make childrearing decisions simply because a state judge believes a "better" decision could be made.... Accordingly, we hold that § 26.10.160(3), as applied in this case, is unconstitutional.

Because we rest our decision on the sweeping breadth of § 26.10.160(3) and the application of that broad, unlimited power in this case, we do not consider the primary constitutional question passed on by the Washington Supreme Court—whether the Due Process Clause requires all nonparental visitation statutes to include a showing of harm or potential harm to the child as a condition precedent to granting visitation. We do not, and need not, define today the precise scope of the parental due process right in the visitation context.... Because much state-court adjudication in this context occurs on a case-by-case basis, we would be hesitant to hold that specific nonparental visitation statutes violate the Due Process Clause as a *per se* matter....

There is ... no reason to remand the case for further proceedings in the Washington Supreme Court.... [I]t is apparent that the entry of the visitation order in this case violated the Constitution. We should say so now, without forcing the parties into additional litigation that would further burden Granville's parental right. We therefore hold that the application of § 26.10.160(3) to Granville and her family violated her due process right to make decisions concerning the care, custody, and control of her daughters.

Accordingly, the judgment of the Washington Supreme Court is affirmed.

■ JUSTICE SOUTER, concurring in the judgment.

I concur in the judgment affirming the decision of the Supreme Court of Washington, whose facial invalidation of its own state statute is consistent with this Court's prior cases addressing the substantive interests at stake. I would say no more....

[T]he state court authoritatively read [the statutory] provision as placing hardly any limit on a court's discretion to award visitation rights. As the court understood it, the specific best-interests provision in the statute would allow a court to award visitation whenever it thought it could make a better decision than a child's parent had done....

■ JUSTICE THOMAS, concurring in the judgment.

.... [I] agree with the plurality that this Court's recognition of a fundamental right of parents to direct the upbringing of their children resolves this case.... The opinions of the plurality, Justice KENNEDY, and Justice SOUTER recognize such a right, but curiously none of them articulates the appropriate standard of review. I would apply strict scrutiny to infringements of fundamental rights. Here, the State of Washington lacks even a legitimate governmental interest—to say nothing of a compelling one—in second-guessing a fit parent's decision regarding visitation with third parties. On this basis, I would affirm the judgment below.

■ JUSTICE STEVENS, dissenting.

.... The second key aspect of the Washington Supreme Court's holding—that the Federal Constitution requires a showing of actual or potential "harm" to the child before a court may order visitation continued over a parent's objections—finds no support in this Court's case law. While, as the Court recognizes, the Federal Constitution certainly protects the parent-child relationship from arbitrary impairment by the State, we have never held that the parent's liberty interest in this relationship is so inflexible as to establish a rigid constitutional shield, protecting every arbitrary parental decision from any challenge absent a threshold finding of harm. The presumption that parental decisions generally serve the best interests of their children is sound, and clearly in the normal case the parent's interest is paramount. But even a fit parent is capable of treating a child like a mere possession.

Cases like this do not present a bipolar struggle between the parents and the State over who has final authority to determine what is in a child's best interests. There is at a minimum a third individual, whose interests are implicated in every case to which the statute applies—the child.

. . .

A parent's rights with respect to her child have thus never been regarded as absolute, but rather are limited by the existence of an actual, developed relationship with a child, and are tied to the presence or absence of some embodiment of family. These limitations have arisen, not simply out of the definition of parenthood itself, but because of this Court's assumption that a parent's interests in a child must be balanced against the State's long-recognized interests as *parens patriae*, see, *e.g.*, . . . *Prince v. Massachusetts*, 321 U.S. 158, 166 (1944), and, critically, the child's own complementary interest in preserving relationships that serve her welfare and protection, *Santosky*, 455 U.S., at 760.

While this Court has not yet had occasion to elucidate the nature of a child's liberty interests in preserving established familial or family-like bonds, it seems to me extremely likely that, to the extent parents and families have fundamental liberty interests in preserving such intimate relationships, so, too, do children have these interests, and so, too, must their interests be balanced in the equation. At a minimum, our prior cases recognizing that children are, generally speaking, constitutionally protected actors require that this Court reject any suggestion that when it comes to parental rights, children are so much chattel. The constitutional protection against arbitrary state interference with parental rights should not be extended to prevent the States from protecting children against the arbitrary exercise of parental authority that is not in fact motivated by an interest in the welfare of the child.

This is not, of course, to suggest that a child's liberty interest in maintaining contact with a particular individual is to be treated invariably as on a par with that child's parents' contrary interests. Because our substantive due process case law includes a strong presumption that a parent will act in the best interest of her child, it would be necessary, were the state appellate courts actually to confront a challenge to the statute as applied, to consider whether the trial court's assessment of the "best interest of the child" incorporated that presumption. Neither would I decide whether the trial court applied Washington's statute in a constitutional way in this case. . . . For the purpose of a facial challenge like this, I think it safe to assume that trial judges usually give great deference to parents' wishes, and I am not persuaded otherwise here.

But presumptions notwithstanding, we should recognize that there may be circumstances in which a child has a stronger interest at stake than mere protection from serious harm caused by the termination of visitation by a "person" other than a parent. The almost infinite variety of family relationships that pervade our ever-changing society strongly counsel against the creation by this Court of a constitutional rule that treats a biological parent's liberty interest in the care and supervision of her child as an isolated right that may be exercised arbitrarily. It is indisputably the business of the States, rather than a federal court employing a national standard, to assess in the first instance the relative importance of the conflicting interests that give rise to disputes such as this. Far from guaranteeing that parents' interests will be trammeled in the sweep of cases arising under the statute, the Washington law merely gives an individual—with whom a child may have an established relationship—the procedural right to ask the State to act as arbiter, through the entirely well-known best-interests standard, between the parent's protected interests and the child's. It seems clear to me that the Due Process Clause of the Fourteenth Amendment leaves room for States to consider the impact on a child of possibly arbitrary parental decisions that neither serve nor are motivated by the best interests of the child. . . .

■ JUSTICE SCALIA, dissenting.

. . . . Only three holdings of this Court rest in whole or in part upon a substantive constitutional right of parents to direct the upbringing of their children—two of them from an era rich in substantive due process holdings that have since been repudiated. See *Meyer v. Nebraska*, 262 U.S. 390 (1923); *Pierce v. Society of Sisters*, 268 U.S. 510 (1925); *Wisconsin v. Yoder*, 406 U.S. 205 (1972). . . . The sheer diversity of today's opinions persuades me that the theory of unenumerated parental rights underlying these three cases has small claim to *stare decisis* protection. . . . While I would not now overrule those earlier cases (that has not been urged), neither would I extend the theory upon which they rested to this new context. . . .

[The dissenting opinion of Justice Kennedy is omitted.]

NOTES ON *TROXEL v. GRANVILLE*

(1) **Grandparents Visitation Rights—The Background.** *Troxel* deals with grandparent visitation, an issue that became the subject of legislative reform in the 1980s and 1990s. The common law rule gave grandparents no legal right to continue their relationship with their grandchildren when their own child (the grandchild's parent) died, divorced, or had her parental rights terminated, a position that is compatible with the general authority of custodial parents to decide who (including relatives) can associate with their child. Through successful lobbying efforts by grandparent groups, virtually all state legislatures enacted statutes authorizing courts to order grandparent visitation under some circumstances. Many of these statutes limited visitation to compelling claims by grandparents who had cared for their grandchildren as de facto parents, or whose relationships with grandchildren were severed when their own children died (as happened in *Troxel*) or lost parental rights. Others, however, gave grandparents standing to sue parents in intact families (including the grandparent's own child). The sweeping Washington statute at issue in *Troxel* contained few limits, allowing the trial judge to order visitation in favor any third party.

Despite its popularity in the period before *Troxel*, grandparent visitation has always had its critics. Many observers have challenged the wisdom of courts' overriding the decisions of responsible custodial parents who may have good reasons not to allow the contact. The issue, of course, is not whether it is generally beneficial to children to have contact with their grandparents, but whether courts or parents should make that decision. The broad authority given courts under many statutes to mandate visitation against the wishes of fit parents was not compatible with conventional notions of parents' rights as articulated by the Supreme Court.

Moreover, grandparent visitation can also be also challenged on fairness grounds. Unlike non-custodial parents, most grandparents (like the Troxels) have never lived with the children or taken responsibility for their upbringing—and they have no ongoing support obligation. See Emily Buss, "Parental" Rights, 88 Va.L.Rev. 635 (2002); Elizabeth S. Scott, Parental Autonomy and Children's Welfare, 11 Wm. & Mary Bill Rts. J. 1071 (2003). For an early critique by a child psychiatrist, see Andre P. Derdeyn, Grandparent Visitation Rights: Rendering Family Dissension More Pronounced, 55(2) Amer.J. Orthopsychiatry 277 (1985).

The most direct effects of *Troxel* are on grandparent visitation statutes, of course, and statutes in virtually every state have come under scrutiny post-*Troxel*. See below. The opinion also is important as a contemporary affirmation of the constitutional importance of parental rights, and it has broader (if somewhat uncertain) implications in other areas of law. For example, *Troxel* raises a question about the authority of courts to order visitation by a parent after adoption, and thus makes open adoptions less certain. See Chapter VIII.

(2) **The Judicial and Legislative Response to *Troxel*.** *Troxel* has generated a flood of litigation and courts across the country have sought to evaluate state statutes in light of the Supreme Court's somewhat cryptic opinion. Justice O'Connor's plurality opinion did not find the Washington statute to be unconstitutional *on its face*, but only as applied in the *Troxel* case itself. Given the sweeping breadth of the Washington statute, it would seem that every contemporary statute would pass facial constitutional muster. However, after *Troxel* a number of lower courts have ruled various state provisions facially unconstitutional. For example, the Michigan Supreme Court held that state's statute to be unconstitutional because it failed to require deference to a fit parent's objection to visitation. In that court's view, the Supreme Court in fact had found the Washington statute to be unconstitutional despite the failure of the O'Connor plurality to acknowledge this directly. *DeRose v. DeRose*, 469 Mich. 320, 666 N.W.2d 636 (2003). The Illinois Supreme Court also struck down that state's statute because it put non-parent and parent on equal footing, and contravened the presumption that parents are fit and act in the best interest of their children. In language that is far broader than *Troxel*, the court stated, "A fit parent's constitutionally protected liberty interest to direct the care, custody and control of his or her children mandates that parents—not judges—should be the ones to decide with whom their children will and will not associate". *Wickham v. Byrne*, 199 Ill.2d 309, 263 Ill.Dec. 799, 769 N.E.2d 1 (2002). The Arkansas Supreme Court adopted a strict scrutiny standard of review, a position advocated only by Justice Thomas in his *Troxel* concurrence, and found grandparent visitation to be a major intrusion on the fundamental right of parents to rear their children. *Linder v. Linder*, 348 Ark. 322, 72 S.W.3d 841 (2002).

Some courts have required a showing that the parent's denial of visitation was harmful to the child, before the court could justify ordering the parents to permit visitation. This question was expressly left undecided by the O'Connor plurality. *Roth v. Weston*, 259 Conn. 202, 789 A.2d 431 (2002) (party seeking visitation must have a parent-like relationship with the child and demonstrate by clear and convincing evidence that denial of visitation would cause significant harm to the child, of a kind that is contemplated by the neglect/dependency statute). Other courts have explicitly rejected the claim that a showing of harm to the child was constitutionally required before visitation can be ordered over a parent's objections. *Kansas Dep't of Soc. and Rehab. Serv. v. Paillet*, 270 Kan. 646, 16 P.3d 962 (2001) (petitioner must rebut presumption that a fit parent acts in child's best interest, by showing that visitation is in child's best interest).

Lower courts also have wrestled, post-*Troxel*, with custody decisions rendered under narrower statutes. These statutes are interpreted to give special weight to the parents' decision and/or restrict visitation that substantially interferes with the parent-child relationship. Thus, in a case involving a grandmother who had been a de facto parent to the child, the Supreme Court of Maine upheld a visitation order under a statute that includes a threshold standing requirement that the grandparent must have a sufficient existing relationship with the child; the statute then directs the court to consider the parent's objection and order visitation only if it does not significantly interfere with the parent-child relationship. *Rideout v. Riendeau,* 761 A.2d 291 (Me.2000). Some grandparent visitation statutes have been upheld on the basis of narrowing interpretations, although trial courts are left with considerable discretion. The Mississippi Supreme Court approved a statute that restricts petitioners seeking visitation to grandparents (unlike *Troxel*), but gives courts rather broad authority to order visitation. *Zeman v. Stanford,* 789 So.2d 798 (Miss.2001).

A number of state legislatures have revised grandparent visitation statutes, narrowing the authority of courts to order visitation over parents' objections. For example, the new North Dakota statute permits grandparent visitation only where a finding is made that it would be in the best interests of the minor and would not interfere with the parent-child relationship. The statute also removes the presumption that grandparent visitation is in the best interests of the child. N.D. Cent. Code § 14–09–05.1.

The recently adopted American Law Institute Principles of the Law of Family Dissolution does not deal specifically with grandparent visitation. Under the A.L.I. custody Principles, grandparents would only have standing to seek a portion of custodial responsibility if they qualify as de facto parents or parents by estoppel— i.e., they must have resided with the child and performed many parenting functions with the parent's acquiescence. § 2.03(1). Because the Principles abolish the conventional "visitation" category, and limit custodial access to adults who have lived with and cared for the child, most grandparents would lack standing.

(3) **Emily Buss, *"Parental" Rights,* 88 Va.L.Rev. 635 (2002).** Some academic critics have been very critical of *Troxel*, on the ground that it provides insufficient protection of parental rights. Consider the following analysis by Emily Buss, which generally offers an interesting view about the allocation between parents and the state of authority over child rearing.

> ... [T]he Constitution should be read to afford strong protection to parents' exercise of child-rearing authority but considerably weaker protection to any individual's claim to parental identity. This means that a state has broad authority to identify nontraditional caregivers as parents, and, if it does so, it must afford their child-rearing decisions the same strong protection afforded more traditional parental figures. It also means, however, that if a state chooses not to recognize these nontraditional figures as parents, the Constitution prevents the state from offering these figures some more limited right of contact or custodial control.

> . . .

> While a majority of the [*Troxel*] Court voted to strike down the challenged visitation order as a violation of the mother's constitutional rights, the scope of the Court's ruling and an analysis of the various opinions reveals a Court scrupulously avoiding any strong endorsement of parental rights ... Justice ... O'Connor's plurality opinion noted that affording legal protection to a child's relationship with nontraditional caregivers would come at a cost to the traditional parent-child relationship protected by the Constitution.... [T]he plurality tepidly concluded that the Due Process Clause entitled parents'

decisions about their children's associations and activities to "at least some special weight."

. . .

. . . [A] legal system that shows strong deference to parents' child-rearing decisions serves children well. Parents' strong emotional attachment to their children and considerable knowledge of their particular needs make parents the child-specific experts most qualified to assess and pursue their children's best interests in most circumstances. In contrast, the state's knowledge of and commitment to any particular child is relatively thin. A scheme of strong constitutional rights shields the parent expert from the intrusive second-guessing of the less expert state.

. . .

The state can legitimately claim at least two sorts of child-rearing expertise superior to that of individual parents. First, the state has the advantage in overseeing what we might call the child's "public development." Because the state is the relative expert on its own design and function, it is in a better position than a parent to judge what education and experiences are most likely to prepare a child for participation in the state's economy and government. At least where parents share the ultimate aim of public participation, the state's expertise in public development offers special justification for state intrusions designed to achieve this aim.

Second, the democratic process makes the state the relative expert in identifying community consensus about the appropriateness of particular child-rearing practices, including practices that have only private developmental effects. . . .

. . .

. . . [E]ven good state decisions about child-rearing practices are likely to produce bad results when the state relies on resistant parents to carry them out, and the self-interested or overstressed parent can be expected to do a particularly bad job of coping with these intrusions.

. . . State intervention, therefore, should be limited to those circumstances in which the state deems intervention necessary to protect a child from harm and, again, only from harm the state has some special expertise to assess. In the public realm, for example, the state has special expertise to assess risks associated with certain educational decisions. In the private realm, the state's expertise allows it to prohibit child abuse and neglect as a child-generic harm condemned by the community.

But where the choices to be made concern a child's intimate associations as they do in our context, both the private and child-specific nature of the inquiry make the state a particularly ill-qualified decisionmaker. Because the parent knows herself, her child, and her entire household better than the state knows them, and stands in a position of greater influence than the state over the behavior of all three, the parent is best situated to decide what private relationships should be fostered. Under a competence-based regime of parental rights, protection against state intervention to compel the child's contact with non-parents should be especially strong.

The legal scheme best designed to keep primary child-rearing authority in the hands of parents is a scheme of strong constitutional rights. As a matter of definition, a scheme that affords parents no constitutional protection shifts the ultimate allocation of child-rearing authority to the state. Perhaps less obviously, a scheme that affords parents a weaker or less crisply defined constitutional protection is likely to shift that allocating authority as well—this time to the courts interpreting the murky constitutional protection. In contrast to both, a strongly protective constitutional right reduces the role of the courts to enforcer of the strong protection, a reader of the scales tipped heavily in the parent's favor. Stated another way, a move to weaken the protection afforded parents under the Constitution is at least as threatening to parental autonomy as a move to eliminate the protection. Both moves threaten to shift decisionmaking to a state actor with considerably less child-specific competence than a parent and with the power to cause harm through the process and outcomes of its decisionmaking.

Buss, 88 Va.L.Rev. At 636, 639, 647–50.*

(4) **More Literature on *Troxel***. Much has been written about *Troxel* and its implications. For two excellent analyses and critiques of the opinion, see Emily Buss, Adrift in the Middle: Parental Rights After Troxel v. Granville, 2000 Sup.Ct. Rev. 279 (2000) and Stephen Gilles, Parental (and Grandparental) Rights after Troxel v. Granville, 9 Sup.Ct.Econ.Rev. 69 (2001). See also Janet Dolgin, The Constitution as Family Arbiter: A Moral in the Mess?, 102 Colum.L.Rev. 337 (2002) (arguing that constitutional jurisprudence is inadequate to the task of determining the proper scope of familial relationships, because constitutional law presumes individual autonomy). An excellent symposium on *Troxel* appears in 32 Rutgers L.J. 695 et. seq. and includes articles by Earl M. Maltz, David Meyer, Margaret Brinig, Sally Goldfarb, and Nancy Polikoff.

B. PARENTAL RIGHTS: THE CASE OF UNMARRIED FATHERS

The preceding section dealt with the constitutional parameters of state authority to intervene in the family under its *parens patriae* and police powers and with the freedom of parents to rear their children according to their own values and beliefs. In a legal system based on liberal principles, the state is constrained from excessive interference in the family unit by the same principles that generally limit interference in the lives of individual citizens. Thus, a presumption favoring family privacy supports relatively broad parental authority, and legal policies that restrict state authority are based on both deference to family privacy and on recognition of parental rights. When the state seeks to regulate parents in the intact family, the two constraints on state authority are hard to separate.

In this section, we turn to cases involving unmarried fathers, who often do not live in a family unit with their children. Historically, the relationship between unmarried fathers and their children received no legal protection. Unmarried fathers had no parental rights; perhaps more importantly, they were not held financially or legally responsible for their children, and children born outside of marriage received none of the benefits and privileges of legitimate children (such as inheritance rights). This has changed in recent years. Courts and legislatures have struggled to define the criteria for recognition of biological fathers' claims of parental rights. The cases dealing with the parental rights of unmarried fathers provide an opportunity to analyze the substantive dimensions of parental rights separate from authority based on family privacy, and to explore those elements besides genetic parenthood that are important when fathers seek legal recognition of their relationship with their children.

1.   The Supreme Court and Fathers' Rights

Stanley v. Illinois

Supreme Court of the United States, 1972.
405 U.S. 645, 92 S.Ct. 1208, 31 L.Ed.2d 551.

■ Mr. Justice White delivered the opinion of the Court.

Joan Stanley lived with Peter Stanley intermittently for 18 years, during which time they had three children. When Joan Stanley died, Peter Stanley lost not only her but also his children. Under Illinois law, the children of unwed fathers become wards of the State upon the death of the mother. Accordingly, upon Joan Stanley's death, in a dependency proceeding instituted by the State of Illinois, Stanley's children were declared wards of the State and placed with court-appointed guardians. Stanley appealed, claiming that he had never been shown to be an unfit parent and that since married fathers and unwed mothers could not be deprived of their children without such a showing, he had been deprived of the equal protection of the laws guaranteed him by the Fourteenth Amendment. The Illinois Supreme Court accepted the fact that Stanley's own unfitness had not been established but rejected the equal protection claim, holding that Stanley could properly be separated from his children upon proof of the single fact that he and the dead mother had not been married. Stanley's actual fitness as a father was irrelevant. In re Stanley, 45 Ill.2d 132, 256 N.E.2d 814 (1970).

Stanley presses his equal protection claim here. The State continues to respond that unwed fathers are presumed unfit to raise their children and that it is unnecessary to hold individualized hearings to determine whether particular fathers are in fact unfit parents before they are separated from their children. . . .

I

At the outset we reject any suggestion that we need not consider the propriety of the dependency proceeding that separated the Stanleys because Stanley might be able to regain custody of his children as a guardian or through adoption proceedings. The suggestion is that if Stanley has been treated differently from other parents, the difference is immaterial and not legally cognizable for the purposes of the Fourteenth Amendment. This Court has not, however, embraced the general proposition that a wrong may be done if it can be undone. Surely, in the case before us, if there is delay between the doing and the undoing petitioner suffers from the deprivation of his children, and the children suffer from uncertainty and dislocation.

It is clear, moreover, that Stanley does not have the means at hand promptly to erase the adverse consequences of the proceeding in the course of which his children were declared wards of the State. It is first urged that Stanley could act to adopt his children. . . . Insofar as we are informed, Illinois law affords him no priority in adoption proceedings. It would be his burden to establish not only that he would be a suitable parent but also that he would be the most suitable of all who might want custody of the children. Neither can we ignore that in the proceedings from which this action developed, the "probation officer," the assistant state's attorney, and the judge charged with the case, made it apparent that Stanley, unmarried and impecunious as he is, could not now expect to profit from adoption proceedings. . . .

Before us, the State focuses on Stanley's failure to petition for "custody and control"—the second route by which, it is urged, he might regain authority for his children. Passing the obvious issue whether it would be futile or burdensome for an unmarried father—without funds and already once presumed unfit—to petition for custody, this suggestion overlooks the fact that legal custody is not parenthood or adoption. A person appointed guardian in an action for custody and control is subject to removal at any time without such cause as must be shown in a neglect proceeding against a parent. He may not take the children out of the jurisdiction without the court's approval. He may be required to report to the court as to his disposition of the children's affairs. Obviously then, even if Stanley were a mere step away from "custody and control," to give an unwed father only "custody and control" would still be to leave him seriously prejudiced by reason of his status.

We must therefore examine the question that Illinois would have us avoid: Is a presumption that distinguishes and burdens all unwed fathers constitutionally repugnant? We conclude that, as a matter of due process of law, Stanley was entitled to a hearing on his fitness as a parent before his children were taken from him and that, by denying him a hearing and extending it to all other parents whose custody of their children is challenged, the State denied Stanley the equal protection of the laws guaranteed by the Fourteenth Amendment.

II

Illinois has two principal methods of removing nondelinquent children from the homes of their parents. In a dependency proceeding it may demonstrate that the children are wards of the State because they have no surviving parent or guardian. In a neglect proceeding it may show that children should be wards of the State because the present parent(s) or guardian does not provide suitable care.

The State's right—indeed, duty—to protect minor children through a judicial determination of their interests in a neglect proceeding is not challenged here. Rather, we are faced with a dependency statute that empowers state officials to circumvent neglect proceedings on the theory that an unwed father is not a "parent" whose existing relationship with his children must be considered. "Parents," says the State, "means the father and mother of a legitimate child, or the survivor of them, or the natural mother of an illegitimate child, and includes any adoptive parent," Ill.Rev. Stat., c. 37, § 701–14, but the term does not include unwed fathers.

.   .   .

The private interest here, that of a man in the children he has sired and raised, undeniably warrants deference and, absent a powerful counter-vailing interest, protection. It is plain that the interest of a parent in the companionship, care, custody, and management of his or her children "come[s] to this Court with a momentum for respect lacking when appeal is made to liberties which derive merely from shifting economic arrange-ments." Kovacs v. Cooper, 336 U.S. 77, 95 (1949) (Frankfurter, J., concur-ring).

The Court has frequently emphasized the importance of the family. The rights to conceive and to raise one's children have been deemed "essential," Meyer v. Nebraska, 262 U.S. 390, 399 (1923), "basic civil rights of man," Skinner v. Oklahoma, 316 U.S. 535, 541 (1942), and "[r]ights far more precious ... than property rights," May v. Anderson, 345 U.S. 528, 533 (1953). "It is cardinal with us that the custody, care and nurture of the child reside first in the parents, whose primary function and freedom include preparation for obligations the state can neither supply nor hin-der." Prince v. Massachusetts, 321 U.S. 158, 166 (1944). The integrity of the family unit has found protection in the Due Process Clause of the Fourteenth Amendment, Meyer v. Nebraska, supra, 262 U.S. at 399, the Equal Protection Clause of the Fourteenth Amendment, Skinner v. Okla-homa, supra, 316 U.S., at 541, and the Ninth Amendment, Griswold v. Connecticut, 381 U.S. 479, 496 (1965) (Goldberg, J., concurring).

Nor has the law refused to recognize those family relationships not legitimized by a marriage ceremony. The Court has declared unconstitu-tional a state statute denying natural, but illegitimate, children a wrongful-death action for the death of their mother, emphasizing that such children cannot be denied the right of other children because familial bonds in such cases were often as warm, enduring, and important as those arising within a more formally organized family unit. Levy v. Louisiana, 391 U.S. 68, 71–72 (1968). "To say that the test of equal protection should be the 'legal' rather than the biological relationship is to avoid the issue. For the Equal Protection Clause necessarily limits the authority of a State to draw such 'legal' lines as it chooses." Glona v. American Guarantee & Liability Ins. Co., 391 U.S. 73, 75–76 (1968).

.   .   .

For its part, the State has made its interest quite plain: Illinois has declared that the aim of the Juvenile Court Act is to protect "the moral, emotional, mental, and physical welfare of the minor and the best interests of the community" and to "strengthen the minor's family ties whenever possible, removing him from the custody of his parents only when his welfare or safety or the protection of the public cannot be adequately safeguarded without removal ..." Ill.Rev.Stat., c. 37, § 701–2. These are legitimate interests, well within the power of the State to implement. We do not question the assertion that neglectful parents may be separated from their children.

But we are here not asked to evaluate the legitimacy of the state ends, rather, to determine whether the means used to achieve these ends are constitutionally defensible. What is the state interest in separating children from fathers without a hearing designed to determine whether the father is unfit in a particular disputed case? We observe that the State registers no gain towards its declared goals when it separates children from the custody of fit parents. Indeed, if Stanley is a fit father, the State spites its own articulated goals when it needlessly separates him from his family.

.   .   .

It may be, as the State insists, that most unmarried fathers are unsuitable and neglectful parents. It may also be that Stanley is such a parent and that his children should be placed in other hands. But all unmarried fathers are not in this category; some are wholly suited to have custody of their children. This much the State readily concedes, and nothing in this record indicates that Stanley is or has been a neglectful father who has not cared for his children. Given the opportunity to make his case, Stanley may have been seen to be deserving of custody of his offspring. Had this been so, the State's statutory policy would have been furthered by leaving custody in him.

.   .   .

Procedure by presumption is always cheaper and easier than individualized determination. But when, as here, the procedure forecloses the determinative issues of competence and care, when it explicitly disdains present realities in deference to past formalities, it needlessly risks running roughshod over the important interests of both parent and child. It therefore cannot stand.[9]

We think the Due Process Clause mandates a similar result here. The State's interest in caring for Stanley's children is *de minimis* if Stanley is shown to be a fit father. It insists on presuming rather than proving Stanley's unfitness solely because it is more convenient to presume than to prove. Under the Due Process Clause that advantage is insufficient to justify refusing a father a hearing when the issue at stake is the dismemberment of his family.

III

The State of Illinois assumes custody of the children of married parents, divorced parents, and unmarried mothers only after a hearing and

---

9. We note in passing that the incremental cost of offering unwed fathers an opportunity for individualized hearings on fitness appears to be minimal. If unwed fathers, in the main, do not care about the disposition of their children, they will not appear to demand hearings. If they do care, under the scheme here held invalid, Illinois would admittedly at some later time have to afford them a properly focused hearing in a custody or adoption proceeding.

. . . . The Illinois law governing procedure in juvenile cases, Ill.Rev.Stat., c. 37, § 704–1 et seq., provides for personal service, notice by certified mail, or for notice by publication when personal or certified mail service cannot be had or when notice is directed to unknown respondents under the style of "All whom it may Concern." Unwed fathers who do not promptly respond cannot complain if their children are declared wards of the State. Those who do respond retain the burden of proving their fatherhood.

proof of neglect. The children of unmarried fathers, however, are declared dependent children without a hearing on parental fitness and without proof of neglect. Stanley's claim in the state courts and here is that failure to afford him a hearing on his parental qualifications while extending it to other parents denied him equal protection of the laws. We have concluded that all Illinois parents are constitutionally entitled to a hearing on their fitness before their children are removed from their custody. It follows that denying such a hearing to Stanley and those like him while granting it to other Illinois parents, is inescapably contrary to the Equal Protection Clause.

. . .

Reversed and remanded.

■ Mr. Chief Justice Burger, with whom Mr. Justice Blackmun concurs, dissenting.

. . .

The Illinois Supreme Court correctly held that the State may constitutionally distinguish between unwed fathers and unwed mothers. . . . In almost all cases, the unwed mother is readily identifiable, generally from hospital records, and alternatively by physicians or others attending the child's birth. Unwed fathers, as a class, are not traditionally quite so easy to identify and locate. Many of them either deny all responsibility or exhibit no interest in the child or its welfare; and, of course, many unwed fathers are simply not aware of their parenthood.

Furthermore, I believe that a State is fully justified in concluding, on the basis of common human experience, that the biological role of the mother in carrying and nursing an infant creates stronger bonds between her and the child than the bonds resulting from the male's often casual encounter. This view is reinforced by the observable fact that most unwed mothers exhibit a concern for their offspring either permanently or at least until they are safely placed for adoption, while unwed fathers rarely burden either the mother or the child with their attentions or loyalties. Centuries of human experience buttress this view of the realities of human conditions and suggest that unwed mothers of illegitimate children are generally more dependable protectors of their children than are unwed fathers. . . .

Stanley depicts himself as a somewhat unusual unwed father, namely, as one who has always acknowledged and never doubted his fatherhood of these children. He alleges that he loved, cared for, and supported these children from the time of their birth until the death of their mother. . . . Even assuming the truth of Stanley's allegations, I am unable to construe the Equal Protection Clause as requiring Illinois to tailor its statutory definition of "parents" so meticulously as to include such unusual unwed fathers, while at the same time excluding those unwed, and generally unidentified, biological fathers who in no way share Stanley's professed desires.

Indeed, the nature of Stanley's own desires is less than absolutely clear from the record in this case. Shortly after the death of the mother, Stanley turned these two children over to the care of a Mr. and Mrs. Ness; he took no action to gain recognition of himself as a father, through adoption, or as a legal custodian, through a guardianship proceeding. Eventually it came to the attention of the State that there was no living adult who had any legally enforceable obligation for the care and support of the children; it was only then that the dependency proceeding here under review took place and that Stanley made himself known to the juvenile court in connection with these two children. Even then, however, Stanley did not ask to be charged with the legal responsibility for the children. He asked only that such legal responsibility be given to no one else. He seemed, in particular, to be concerned with the loss of the welfare payments he would suffer as a result of the designation of others as guardians of the children.

Not only, then, do I see no ground for holding that Illinois' statutory definition of "parents" on its face violates the Equal Protection Clause; I see no ground for holding that any constitutional right of Stanley has been denied in the application of that statutory definition in the case at bar . . .

SOME IMPLICATIONS OF *STANLEY*

(1) In *Stanley,* the United States Supreme Court analyzed the rights of unmarried fathers for the first time. The Illinois statute struck down in the opinion was typical in excluding unmarried fathers from the definition of "parent." Can you suggest a rationale for the statutory provision that the child of an unmarried mother automatically becomes a ward of the state when the mother dies? The provision seems to reflect an assumption that in the typical situation in which the parents are not married, the biological father is not a part of the family unit and not likely to step forward as a suitable substitute for the mother should she be unable to care for the child. Is this a reasonable assumption in many cases? If so, the statutory procedure may serve the interests of some children. Why does the Court conclude that it violates Stanley's constitutional rights?

The Court holds that, under the Due Process Clause of the Fourteenth Amendment, unmarried fathers cannot be deprived of parental rights without the opportunity for a hearing to prove their parental fitness. What would constitute fitness? The Court seems to assume that if the father demonstrates fitness, his parental rights cannot be terminated, a conclusion that makes sense under the circumstances of *Stanley*. Are there other situations in which the desirability of this outcome is less clear? What if the "fit" father has had no contact with the child who has established a relationship with a stepfather who wants to adopt her? As we will see shortly, eleven years after *Stanley*, the Court dealt with this situation in *Lehr v. Robertson*.

Although the facts seem to be disputed, Stanley described himself as a father whose role, before the children's mother died, had been more akin to that of a married father than to the "typical" unmarried father. By his account, he lived with his children and their mother as a family until the mother's death, providing them with love, care and support. Assuming that this is the case, one interpretation of *Stanley* is that it stands for the proposition that a biological father who *functions* in the parental role cannot be denied parental rights simply because he is not formally married to the children's mother.

This interpretation fits well into an important trend in modern family law under which the formal status of marriage, with obligations and rights decreed by the state, has become less important in defining the legal scope of family relationships. Traditional family law was grounded in the belief that the only morally acceptable intimate relationship was formal marriage. Thus, "meretricious" relationships outside of marriage received no legal protection and generated no enforce-able rights and obligations between the parties. Children whose parents were not married were illegitimate; their relationship with their parents (particularly the father) received little legal protection. Modern family law has tended to give greater weight both to the understandings between unmarried couples[1] and to functional family roles. An example of the growing importance attached to family function can be seen in the trend toward greater legal protection of the relationship between children and involved stepparents. We will return to this topic below.

(2) *Stanley* **and Adoption.** The greatest immediate impact of the *Stanley* decision came from interpretation and attempts at application of the Court's remarks in footnote 9. It was common for states at that time to permit the natural mother of a child born out of wedlock to relinquish the child for adoption without consent from or notice to the natural father if he had neither legitimated nor formally acknowledged the child. *Stanley* was construed by many state legal officials as requiring notice to an unwed father regardless of his contacts with the child, in order to satisfy due process. Lawyers are quick to equate "notice" with publication in cases in which the whereabouts of a party is unknown, and not surprisingly it was urged that this would be the way to accomplish the goal. This argument was reinforced by the Supreme Court's mention of publication in footnote 9. Is the Court correct that the cost of providing unmarried fathers with the opportunity of a hearing to demonstrate that they are fit parents is likely to be "minimal"?

Because a large number of the children then being placed for adoption by licensed placement agencies were illegitimate and had been relinquished only by their mothers, the adoption process was thrown into turmoil in many states after *Stanley*. Agencies were reluctant to advertise for fathers to come forward for fear that this would discourage mothers from relinquishing their children, perhaps even diverting babies to the illicit market for them that flourishes from time to time.

State legislative responses to *Stanley* have varied from establishment of a system in Michigan (Mich.Comp.Laws Ann., § 710.33–.39 (West)) and New York (N.Y. Soc. Law § 372–c); (see *Lehr v. Robertson,* below) whereby a possible putative father could register his claim to fatherhood at a child's birth, to methods for effecting notice through certified mail unless there is evidence to show that the father's identity cannot be ascertained. Illustrative of the latter group of statutes, Va. Code Ann. § 63.1–225 requires consent to adoption by both living parents of an illegitimate as well as a legitimate child. However subsection D(2) of the statute states:

> The consent of the birth father of a child born to parents who were not married to each other at the time of the child's conception or birth shall not be required (i) if the identity of the birth father is not reasonably ascertainable, or (ii) if the identity of such birth father is ascertainable and his whereabouts are known, such birth father is given notice of the adoption proceeding by registered or certified mail to his last known address and such birth father fails to object to the adoption proceeding within twenty-one days of the mailing of such notice....

Subsection F of the statute permits a court to grant an adoption petition in instances in which the identity of the party is unobtainable and this fact is certified on the record. The statute provides:

> ... an affidavit of the birth mother that the identity of the birth father is not reasonably ascertainable shall be sufficient evidence of this fact, provided there is no other evidence before the court which would refute such an affidavit. The absence of such an affidavit shall not be deemed evidence that the identity of

---

1. See *Marvin v. Marvin,* 18 Cal.3d 660, 134 Cal.Rptr. 815, 557 P.2d 106 (1976).

the birth father is reasonably ascertainable. For purposes of determining whether the identity of the birth father is reasonably ascertainable, the standard of what is reasonable under the circumstances shall control, taking into account the relative interests of the child, the birth mother and the birth father.

The New York statute at issue in *Lehr* represents an effort to categorize the circumstances under which unmarried fathers are entitled to notice of adoption.

Was footnote 9 necessary to the decision by the Court in *Stanley*?

(3) One also can view *Stanley* as a case in which the rights of children—particularly those children affected by its impact on adoption generally—were never briefed or presented to the Court. If you had been called on to file an *amicus curiae* brief with the Supreme Court as attorney for an organization dedicated to the protection of children's rights, what would you have urged the Court to do or not to do in reaching its decision? Should there be some mechanism through which the interests of children in general can be raised in cases of such potential magnitude?

Lehr v. Robertson

Supreme Court of the United States, 1983.
463 U.S. 248, 103 S.Ct. 2985, 77 L.Ed.2d 614.

■ JUSTICE STEVENS delivered the opinion of the Court.

The question presented is whether New York has sufficiently protected an unmarried father's inchoate relationship with a child whom he has never supported and rarely seen in the two years since her birth. The appellant, Jonathan Lehr, claims that the Due Process and Equal Protection Clauses of the Fourteenth Amendment, as interpreted in Stanley v. Illinois, 405 U.S. 645 (1972), and Caban v. Mohammed, 441 U.S. 380 (1979), give him an absolute right to notice and an opportunity to be heard before the child may be adopted. We disagree.

Jessica M. was born out of wedlock on November 9, 1976. Her mother, Lorraine Robertson, married Richard Robertson eight months after Jessica's birth. On December 21, 1978, when Jessica was over two years old, the Robertsons filed an adoption petition in the Family Court of Ulster County, New York. The court heard their testimony and received a favorable report from the Ulster County Department of Social Services. On March 7, 1979, the court entered an order of adoption. In this proceeding, appellant contends that the adoption order is invalid because he, Jessica's putative father, was not given advance notice of the adoption proceeding.[3]

The State of New York maintains a "putative father registry."[4] A man who files with that registry demonstrates his intent to claim paternity of a

3. Appellee has never conceded that appellant is Jessica's biological father, but for purposes of analysis In this opinion it will be assumed that he is.

4. At the time Jessica's adoption order was entered, N.Y.Soc.Serv. Law § 372–c (McKinney Supp. 1982–1983) provided:

"1. The department shall establish a putative father registry which shall record

the names and addresses of ... any person who has filed with the registry before or after the birth of a child out-of-wedlock, a notice of intent to claim paternity of the child....

"2. A person filing a notice of intent to claim paternity of a child shall ... include therein his current address and shall notify the registry of any change of address pursu-

child born out of wedlock and is therefore entitled to receive notice of any proceeding to adopt that child. Before entering Jessica's adoption order, the Ulster County Family Court had the putative father registry examined. Although appellant claims to be Jessica's natural father, he had not entered his name in the registry.

In addition to the persons whose names are listed on the putative father registry, New York law requires that notice of an adoption proceeding be given to several other classes of possible fathers of children born out of wedlock—those who have been adjudicated to be the father, those who have been identified as the father on the child's birth certificate, those who live openly with the child and the child's mother and who hold themselves out to be the father, those who have been identified as the father by the mother in a sworn written statement, and those who were married to the child's mother before the child was six months old.[5] Appellant admittedly was not a member of any of those classes. He had lived with appellee prior to Jessica's birth and visited her in the hospital when Jessica was born, but his name does not appear on Jessica's birth certificate. He did not live with appellee or Jessica after Jessica's birth, he has never provided them with any financial support, and he has never offered to marry appellee. Nevertheless, he contends that the following special circumstances gave him a constitutional right to notice and a hearing before Jessica was adopted.

ant to procedures prescribed by regulations of the department.

"3. A person who has filed a notice of intent to claim paternity may at any time revoke a notice of intent to claim paternity previously filed therewith and, upon receipt of such notification by the registry, the revoked notice of intent to claim paternity shall be deemed a nullity nunc pro tunc.

"4. An unrevoked notice of intent to claim paternity of a child may be introduced In evidence by any party, other than the person who filed such notice, In any proceeding In which such fact may be relevant.

"5. The department shall, upon request, provide the names and addresses of persons listed with the registry to any court or authorized agency, and such information shall not be divulged to any other person, except upon order of a court for good cause shown."

5. At the time Jessica's adoption order was entered, N.Y.Dom.Rel. Law §§ 111–a(2) and (3) (McKinney 1977 and Supp. 1982–1983) provided:

"2. Persons entitled to notice, pursuant to subdivision one of this section, shall include:

"(a) any person adjudicated by a court In this state to be the father of the child;

"(b) any person adjudicated by a court of another state or territory of the United States to be the father of the child, when a certified copy of the court order has been filed with the putative father registry, pursuant to section three hundred seventy-two-c of the social services law;

"(c) any person who has timely filed an unrevoked notice of intent to claim paternity of the child, pursuant to section three hundred seventy-two of the social services law;

"(d) any person who is recorded on the child's birth certificate as the child's father;

"(e) any person who is openly living with the child and the child's mother at the time the proceeding is initiated and who is holding himself out to be the child's father;

"(f) any person who has been identified as the child's father by the mother In written, sworn statement; and

"(g) any person who was married to the child's mother within six months subsequent to the birth of the child and prior to the execution of a surrender instrument or the initiation of a proceeding pursuant to section three hundred eighty-four-b of the social services law.

"3. The sole purpose of notice under this section shall be to enable the person served pursuant to subdivision two to present evidence to the court relevant to the best interests of the child."

On January 30, 1979, one month after the adoption proceeding was commenced in Ulster County, appellant filed a "visitation and paternity petition" in the Westchester County Family Court. In that petition, he asked for a determination of paternity, an order of support, and reasonable visitation privileges with Jessica. Notice of that proceeding was served on appellee on February 22, 1979. Four days later appellee's attorney informed the Ulster County Court that appellant had commenced a paternity proceeding in Westchester County; the Ulster County judge then entered an order staying appellant's paternity proceeding until he could rule on a motion to change the venue of that proceeding to Ulster County. On March 3, 1979, appellant received notice of the change of venue motion and, for the first time, learned that an adoption proceeding was pending in Ulster County.

On March 7, 1979, appellant's attorney telephoned the Ulster County judge to inform him that he planned to seek a stay of the adoption proceeding pending the determination of the paternity petition. In that telephone conversation, the judge advised the lawyer that he had already signed the adoption order earlier that day. According to appellant's attorney, the judge stated that he was aware of the pending paternity petition but did not believe he was required to give notice to appellant prior to the entry of the order of adoption.

Thereafter, the Family Court in Westchester County granted appellee's motion to dismiss the paternity petition, holding that the putative father's right to seek paternity "must be deemed severed so long as an order of adoption exists." Appellant did not appeal from that dismissal. On June 22, 1979, appellant filed a petition to vacate the order of adoption on the ground that it was obtained by fraud and in violation of his constitutional rights. The Ulster County Family Court received written and oral argument on the question whether it had "dropped the ball" by approving the adoption without giving appellant advance notice. After deliberating for several months, it denied the petition. . . .

Appellant has now invoked our appellate jurisdiction.[9] He offers two alternative grounds for holding the New York statutory scheme unconstitutional. First, he contends that a putative father's actual or potential relationship with a child born out of wedlock is an interest in liberty which may not be destroyed without due process of law; he argues therefore that he had a constitutional right to prior notice and an opportunity to be heard before he was deprived of that interest. Second, he contends that the gender-based classification in the statute, which both denied him the right to consent to Jessica's adoption and accorded him fewer procedural rights than her mother, violated the Equal Protection Clause.[10]

---

9. We postponed consideration of our jurisdiction until after hearing argument on the merits. 456 U.S. 970 (1982). Our review of the record persuades us that appellant did in fact draw into question the validity of the New York statutory scheme on the ground of its being repugnant to the Federal Constitution, that the New York Court of Appeals upheld that scheme, and that we therefore have jurisdiction pursuant to 28 U.S.C. § 1257(2).

10. The question whether the Family Court abused its discretion in not requiring notice to appellant before the adoption order was entered and in not reopening the proceeding is, of course, not before us. That

The Due Process Claim.

. . .

I

The intangible fibers that connect parent and child have infinite variety. They are woven throughout the fabric of our society, providing it with strength, beauty, and flexibility. It is self-evident that they are sufficiently vital to merit constitutional protection in appropriate cases. In deciding whether this is such a case, however, we must consider the broad framework that has traditionally been used to resolve the legal problems arising from the parent-child relationship.

In the vast majority of cases, state law determines the final outcome. Rules governing the inheritance of property, adoption, and child custody are generally specified in statutory enactments that vary from State to State. Moreover, equally varied state laws governing marriage and divorce affect a multitude of parent-child relationships. The institution of marriage has played a critical role both in defining the legal entitlements of family members and in developing the decentralized structure of our democratic society. In recognition of that role, and as part of their general overarching concern for serving the best interests of children, state laws almost universally express an appropriate preference for the formal family.

In some cases, however, this Court has held that the Federal Constitution supersedes state law and provides even greater protection for certain formal family relationships. In those cases, as in the state cases, the Court has emphasized the paramount interest in the welfare of children and has noted that the rights of the parents are a counterpart of the responsibilities they have assumed. . . . This Court has examined the extent to which a natural father's biological relationship with his child receives protection under the Due Process Clause in precisely three cases: Stanley v. Illinois, 405 U.S. 645 (1972), Quilloin v. Walcott, 434 U.S. 246 (1978), and Caban v. Mohammed, 441 U.S. 380 (1979).

Stanley involved the constitutionality of an Illinois statute that conclusively presumed every father of a child born out of wedlock to be an unfit person to have custody of his children. The father in that case had lived with his children all their lives and had lived with their mother for 18 years. There was nothing in the record to indicate that Stanley had been a neglectful father who had not cared for his children. Under the statute, however, the nature of the actual relationship between parent and child was completely irrelevant. Once the mother died, the children were automatically made wards of the State. Relying in part on a Michigan case recognizing that the preservation of "a subsisting relationship with the

issue was presented to and decided by the New York courts purely as a matter of state law. Whether we might have given such notice had we been sitting as the trial court, or whether we might have considered the failure to give such notice an abuse of discretion had we been sitting as state appellate judges, are questions on which we are not authorized to express an opinion. The only question we have jurisdiction to decide is whether the New York statutes are unconstitutional because they inadequately protect the natural relationship between parent and child or because they draw an impermissible distinction between the rights of the mother and the rights of the father.

child's father" may better serve the child's best interest than "uprooting him from the family which he knew from birth," the Court held that the Due Process Clause was violated by the automatic destruction of the custodial relationship without giving the father any opportunity to present evidence regarding his fitness as a parent.

Quilloin involved the constitutionality of a Georgia statute that authorized the adoption, over the objection of the natural father, of a child born out of wedlock. The father in that case had never legitimated the child. It was only after the mother had remarried and her new husband had filed an adoption petition that the natural father sought visitation rights and filed a petition for legitimation. The trial court found adoption by the new husband to be in the child's best interests, and we unanimously held that action to be consistent with the Due Process Clause.

Caban involved the conflicting claims of two natural parents who had maintained joint custody of their children from the time of their birth until they were respectively two and four years old. The father challenged the validity of an order authorizing the mother's new husband to adopt the children; he relied on both the Equal Protection Clause and the Due Process Clause. Because this Court upheld his equal protection claim, the majority did not address his due process challenge. The comments on the latter claim by the four dissenting Justices are nevertheless instructive, because they identify the clear distinction between a mere biological relationship and an actual relationship of parental responsibility.

Justice Stewart correctly observed:

"Even if it be assumed that each married parent after divorce has some substantive due process right to maintain his or her parental relationship, cf. Smith v. Organization of Foster Families, 431 U.S. 816, 862–863 (opinion concurring in judgment), it by no means follows that each unwed parent has any such right. *Parental rights do not spring full-blown from the biological connection between parent and child. They require relationships more enduring.*" 441 U.S., at 397 (emphasis added).[16]

16. In the balance of that paragraph Justice Stewart noted that the relation between a father and his natural child may acquire constitutional protection if the father enters into a traditional marriage with the mother or if "the actual relationship between father and child" is sufficient.

"The mother carries and bears the child, and in this sense her parental relationship is clear. The validity of the father's parental claims must be gauged by other measures. By tradition, the primary measure has been the legitimate familial relationship he creates with the child by marriage with the mother. By definition, the question before us can arise only when no such marriage has taken place. In some circumstances the actual relationship between father and child may suffice to create in the unwed father parental interests comparable to those of the married father. Cf. *Stanley v. Illinois,* supra. But here we are concerned with the rights the unwed father may have when his wishes and those of the mother are in conflict, and the child's best interests are served by a resolution in favor of the mother. It seems to me that the absence of a legal tie with the mother may in such circumstances appropriately place a limit on whatever substantive constitutional claims might otherwise exist by virtue of the father's actual relationship with the children." 441 U.S., at 397.

In a similar vein, the other three dissenters in *Caban* were prepared to "assume that, *if and when one develops,* the relationship between a father and his natural child is entitled to protection against arbitrary state action as a matter of due process." Caban v. Mohammed, supra, 441 U.S., at 414 (emphasis added).

The difference between the developed parent-child relationship that was implicated in *Stanley* and *Caban,* and the potential relationship involved in *Quilloin* and this case, is both clear and significant. When an unwed father demonstrates a full commitment to the responsibilities of parenthood by "com[ing] forward to participate in the rearing of his child," *Caban,* 441 U.S., at 392, his interest in personal contact with his child acquires substantial protection under the Due Process Clause. At that point it may be said that he "act[s] as a father toward his children." But the mere existence of a biological link does not merit equivalent constitutional protection. The actions of judges neither create nor sever genetic bonds. "[T]he importance of the familial relationship, to the individuals involved and to the society, stems from the emotional attachments that derive from the intimacy of daily association, and from the role it plays in 'promot[ing] a way of life' through the instruction of children ... as well as from the fact of blood relationship." Smith v. Organization of Foster Families for Equality and Reform, 431 U.S. 816, 844 (1977) (quoting *Wisconsin v. Yoder,* 406 U.S. 205, 231–233 (1972)).

The significance of the biological connection is that it offers the natural father an opportunity that no other male possesses to develop a relationship with his offspring. If he grasps that opportunity and accepts some measure of responsibility for the child's future, he may enjoy the blessings of the parent-child relationship and make uniquely valuable contributions to the child's development.[18] If he fails to do so, the Federal Constitution will not automatically compel a State to listen to his opinion of where the child's best interests lie.

In this case, we are not assessing the constitutional adequacy of New York's procedures for terminating a developed relationship. Appellant has never had any significant custodial, personal, or financial relationship with Jessica, and he did not seek to establish a legal tie until after she was two years old.[19] We are concerned only with whether New York has adequately protected his opportunity to form such a relationship.

18. Of course, we need not take sides in the ongoing debate among family psychologists over the relative weight to be accorded biological ties and psychological ties, in order to recognize that a natural father who has played a substantial role in rearing his child has a greater claim to constitutional protection than a mere biological parent. New York's statutory scheme reflects these differences, guaranteeing notice to any putative father who is living openly with the child, and providing putative fathers who have never developed a relationship with the child the opportunity to receive notice simply by mailing a postcard to the putative father registry.

19. This case happens to involve an adoption by the husband of the natural mother, but we do not believe the natural father has any greater right to object to such an adoption than to an adoption by two total strangers. If anything, the balance of equities tips the opposite way in a case such as this. In denying the putative father relief in Quilloin v. Walcott, 434 U.S. 246 (1978), we made an observation equally applicable here:

"Nor is this a case in which the proposed adoption would place the child

II

The most effective protection of the putative father's opportunity to develop a relationship with his child is provided by the laws that authorize formal marriage and govern its consequences. But the availability of that protection is, of course, dependent on the will of both parents of the child. Thus, New York has adopted a special statutory scheme to protect the unmarried father's interest in assuming a responsible role in the future of his child.

After this Court's decision in *Stanley,* the New York Legislature appointed a special commission to recommend legislation that would accommodate both the interests of biological fathers in their children and the children's interest in prompt and certain adoption procedures. The commission recommended, and the legislature enacted, a statutory adoption scheme that automatically provides notice to seven categories of putative fathers who are likely to have assumed some responsibility for the care of their natural children.[20] If this scheme were likely to omit many responsible fathers, and if qualification for notice were beyond the control of an interested putative father, it might be thought procedurally inadequate. Yet, as all of the New York courts that reviewed this matter observed, the right to receive notice was completely within appellant's control. By mailing a postcard to the putative father registry, he could have guaranteed that he would receive notice of any proceedings to adopt Jessica. The possibility that he may have failed to do so because of his ignorance of the law cannot be a sufficient reason for criticizing the law itself. The New York Legislature concluded that a more open-ended notice requirement would merely complicate the adoption process, threaten the privacy interests of unwed mothers, create the risk of unnecessary controversy, and

with a new set of parents with whom the child had never before lived. Rather, the result of the adoption in this case is to give full recognition to a family unit already in existence, a result desired by all concerned, except appellant. Whatever might be required in other situations, we cannot say that the State was required in this situation to find anything more than that the adoption, and denial of legitimation, were in the 'best interests of the child.' " Id., at 255.

20. In a report explaining the purpose of the 1976 amendments to § 111–a of the New York Domestic Relations Law, the temporary state commission on child welfare that was responsible for drafting the legislation stated, in part:

"The measure will dispel uncertainties by providing clear constitutional statutory guidelines for notice to fathers of out-of-wedlock children. It will establish a desired finality in adoption proceedings and will provide an expeditious method for child placement agencies of identifying those fathers who are entitled

to notice through the creation of a registry of such fathers within the State Department of Social Services. Conversely, the bill will afford to concerned fathers of out-of-wedlock children a simple means of expressing their interest and protecting their rights to be notified and have an opportunity to be heard. It will also obviate an existing disparity of Appellate Division decisions by permitting such fathers to be petitioners in paternity proceedings.

"The measure is intended to codify the minimum protections for the putative father which *Stanley* would require. In so doing it reflects policy decisions to (a) codify constitutional requirements; (b) clearly establish, as early as possible in a child's life, the rights, interests and obligations of all parties; (c) facilitate prompt planning for the future of the child and permanence of his status; and (d) through the foregoing, promote the best interest of children." A.P. to Brief for Appellant C–15.

impair the desired finality of adoption decrees. Regardless of whether we would have done likewise if we were legislators instead of judges, we surely cannot characterize the State's conclusion as arbitrary.

Appellant argues, however, that even if the putative father's opportunity to establish a relationship with an illegitimate child is adequately protected by the New York statutory scheme in the normal case, he was nevertheless entitled to special notice because the court and the mother knew that he had filed an affiliation proceeding in another court. This argument amounts to nothing more than an indirect attack on the notice provisions of the New York statute. The legitimate state interests in facilitating the adoption of young children and having the adoption proceeding completed expeditiously that underlie the entire statutory scheme also justify a trial judge's determination to require all interested parties to adhere precisely to the procedural requirements of the statute. The Constitution does not require either a trial judge or a litigant to give special notice to nonparties who are presumptively capable of asserting and protecting their own rights. Since the New York statutes adequately protected appellant's inchoate interest in establishing a relationship with Jessica, we find no merit in the claim that his constitutional rights were offended because the Family Court strictly complied with the notice provisions of the statute.

The Equal Protection Claim.

The concept of equal justice under law requires the State to govern impartially. The sovereign may not draw distinctions between individuals based solely on differences that are irrelevant to a legitimate governmental objective. Specifically, it may not subject men and women to disparate treatment when there is no substantial relation between the disparity and an important state purpose.

The legislation at issue in this case is intended to establish procedures for adoptions. Those procedures are designed to promote the best interests of the child, to protect the rights of interested third parties, and to ensure promptness and finality. To serve those ends, the legislation guarantees to certain people the right to veto an adoption and the right to prior notice of any adoption proceeding. The mother of an illegitimate child is always within that favored class, but only certain putative fathers are included. Appellant contends that the gender-based distinction is invidious.

As we have already explained, the existence or nonexistence of a substantial relationship between parent and child is a relevant criterion in evaluating both the rights of the parent and the best interests of the child. In *Quilloin v. Walcott,* we noted that the putative father, like appellant, "ha[d] never shouldered any significant responsibility with respect to the daily supervision, education, protection, or care of the child. Appellant does not complain of his exemption from these responsibilities. . . ." 434 U.S., at 256. We therefore found that a Georgia statute that always required a mother's consent to the adoption of a child born out of wedlock, but required the father's consent only if he had legitimated the child, did not violate the Equal Protection Clause. Because appellant, like the father in *Quilloin,* has never established a substantial relationship with his daughter, see supra, at 2993 the New York statutes at issue in this case did not operate to deny appellant equal protection.

We have held that these statutes may not constitutionally be applied in that class of cases where the mother and father are in fact similarly situated with regard to their relationship with the child. In *Caban v. Mohammed,* the Court held that it violated the Equal Protection Clause to grant the mother a veto over the adoption of a four-year-old girl and a six-year-old boy, but not to grant a veto to their father, who had admitted paternity and had participated in the rearing of the children. The Court made it clear, however, that if the father had not "come forward to participate in the rearing of his child, nothing in the Equal Protection Clause [would] preclude[ ] the State from withholding from him the privilege of vetoing the adoption of that child." 441 U.S., at 392.

Jessica's parents are not like the parents involved in *Caban.* Whereas appellee had a continuous custodial responsibility for Jessica, appellant never established any custodial, personal, or financial relationship with her. If one parent has an established custodial relationship with the child and the other parent has either abandoned or never established a relationship, the Equal Protection Clause does not prevent a state from according the two parents different legal rights.

The judgment of the New York Court of Appeals is

Affirmed.

■ JUSTICE WHITE, with whom JUSTICE MARSHALL and JUSTICE BLACKMUN join, dissenting.

. . .

It is axiomatic that "[t]he fundamental requirement of due process is the opportunity to be heard 'at a meaningful time and in a meaningful manner.'" Mathews v. Eldridge, 424 U.S. 319, 333 (1976), quoting Armstrong v. Manzo, 380 U.S. 545, 552 (1965). As Jessica's biological father, Lehr either had an interest protected by the Constitution or he did not. If the entry of the adoption order in this case deprived Lehr of a constitutionally protected interest, he is entitled to notice and an opportunity to be heard before the order can be accorded finality.

According to Lehr, he and Jessica's mother met in 1971 and began living together in 1974. The couple cohabited for approximately two years, until Jessica's birth in 1976. Throughout the pregnancy and after the birth, Lorraine acknowledged to friends and relatives that Lehr was Jessica's father; Lorraine told Lehr that she had reported to the New York State Department of Social Services that he was the father. Lehr visited Lorraine and Jessica in the hospital every day during Lorraine's confinement. According to Lehr, from the time Lorraine was discharged from the hospital until August 1978, she concealed her whereabouts from him. During this time Lehr never ceased his efforts to locate Lorraine and Jessica and achieved sporadic success until August 1977, after which time he was unable to locate them at all. On those occasions when he did determine Lorraine's location, he visited with her and her children to the extent she was willing to permit it. When Lehr, with the aid of a detective agency, located Lorraine and Jessica in August 1978, Lorraine was already married to Mr. Robertson. Lehr asserts that at this time he offered to provide financial assistance and to set up a trust fund for Jessica, but that Lorraine refused. Lorraine threatened Lehr with arrest unless he stayed away and refused to permit him to see Jessica. Thereafter Lehr retained counsel who wrote to Lorraine in early December 1978, requesting that she permit Lehr to visit Jessica and threatening legal action on Lehr's behalf. On December 21, 1978, perhaps as a response to Lehr's threatened legal action, appellees commenced the adoption action at issue here.

. . .

The "nature of the interest" at stake here is the interest that a natural parent has in his or her child, one that has long been recognized and accorded constitutional protection. We have frequently "stressed the importance of familial bonds, whether or not legitimized by marriage, and accorded them constitutional protection." Little v. Streater, 452 U.S. 1, 13 (1981). If "both the child and the [putative father] in a paternity action have a compelling interest" in the accurate outcome of such a case, ibid., it cannot be disputed that both the child and the putative father have a compelling interest in the outcome of a proceeding that may result in the termination of the father-child relationship. "A parent's interest in the accuracy and justice of the decision to terminate his or her parental status is . . . a commanding one." Lassiter v. Department of Social Services, 452 U.S. 18, 27 (1981). It is beyond dispute that a formal order of adoption, no less than a formal termination proceeding, operates to permanently terminate parental rights.

Lehr's version of the "facts" paints a far different picture than that portrayed by the majority. The majority's recitation, that "[a]ppellant has never had any significant custodial, personal, or financial relationship with Jessica, and he did not seek to establish a legal tie until after she was two years old," ante, at 2994, obviously does not tell the whole story. Appellant has never been afforded an opportunity to present his case. The legitimation proceeding he instituted was first stayed, and then dismissed, on appellees' motions. Nor could appellant establish his interest during the adoption proceedings, for it is the failure to provide Lehr notice and an opportunity to be heard there that is at issue here. We cannot fairly make a judgment based on the quality or substance of a relationship without a complete and developed factual record. This case requires us to assume that Lehr's allegations are true—that but for the actions of the child's mother there would have been the kind of significant relationship that the majority concedes is entitled to the full panoply of procedural due process protections.[3]

3. In response to our decision in Caban v. Mohammed, 441 U.S. 380 (1979), the statute governing the persons whose consent is necessary to an adoption has been amended to include certain unwed fathers. The State has recognized that an unwed father's failure to maintain an actual relationship or to communicate with a child will not deprive him of his right to consent if he was "prevented from doing so by the person or authorized agency having lawful custody of the child." N.Y.Dom.Rel.Law § 111(1)(d) (McKinney Supp. 1982–1983) (as amended by Ch. 575, 1980 N.Y.Laws). Thus, even the State recognizes that before a lesser standard can be applied consistent with due process require-

I reject the peculiar notion that the only significance of the biological connection between father and child is that "it offers the natural father an opportunity that no other male possesses to develop a relationship with his offspring." A "mere biological relationship" is not as unimportant in determining the nature of liberty interests as the majority suggests.

"[T]he usual understanding of 'family' implies biological relationships, and most decisions treating the relation between parent and child have stressed this element." Smith v. Organization of Foster Families, supra, 431 U.S., at 843, 97 S.Ct., at 2109. The "biological connection" is itself a relationship that creates a protected interest. Thus the "nature" of the interest is the parent-child relationship; how well developed that relationship has become goes to its "weight," not its "nature." Whether Lehr's interest is entitled to constitutional protection does not entail a searching inquiry into the quality of the relationship but a simple determination of the *fact* that the relationship exists—a fact that even the majority agrees must be assumed to be established.

Beyond that, however, because there is no established factual basis on which to proceed, it is quite untenable to conclude that a putative father's interest in his child is lacking in substance, that the father in effect has abandoned the child, or ultimately that the father's interest is not entitled to the same minimum procedural protections as the interests of other putative fathers. Any analysis of the adequacy of the notice in this case must be conducted on the assumption that the interest involved here is as strong as that of *any* putative father. That is not to say that due process requires actual notice to every putative father or that adoptive parents of the State must conduct an exhaustive search of records or an intensive investigation before a final adoption order may be entered. The procedures adopted by the State, however, must at least represent a reasonable effort to determine the identity of the putative father and to give him adequate notice.

II

In this case, of course, there was no question about either the identity or the location of the putative father. The mother knew exactly who he was and both she and the court entering the order of adoption knew precisely where he was and how to give him actual notice that his parental rights were about to be terminated by an adoption order. Lehr was entitled to due process, and the right to be heard is one of the fundamentals of that right, which " 'has little reality or worth unless one is informed that the matter is pending and can choose for himself whether to appear or default, acquiesce or contest.' " Schroeder v. City of New York, 371 U.S. 208, 212 (1962), quoting Mullane v. Central Hanover Trust Co., 339 U.S. 306, 314 (1950).

The State concedes this much but insists that Lehr has had all the process that is due to him. It relies on § 111–a, which designates seven categories of unwed fathers to whom notice of adoption proceedings must be given, including any unwed father who has filed with the State a notice

ments, there must be a determination that there was no significant relationship and that the father was not prevented from forming such a relationship.

of his intent to claim paternity. The State submits that it need not give notice to anyone who has not filed his name, as he is permitted to do, and who is not otherwise within the designated categories, even if his identity and interest are known or are reasonably ascertainable by the State.

I am unpersuaded by the State's position. In the first place, § 111–a defines six categories of unwed fathers to whom notice must be given even though they have not placed their names on file pursuant to the section. Those six categories, however, do not include fathers such as Lehr who have initiated filiation proceedings, even though their identity and interest are as clearly and easily ascertainable as those fathers in the six categories. Initiating such proceedings necessarily involves a formal acknowledgment of paternity, and requiring the State to take note of such a case in connection with pending adoption proceedings would be a trifling burden, no more than the State undertakes when there is a final adjudication in a paternity action. Indeed, there would appear to be more reason to give notice to those such as Lehr who acknowledge paternity than to those who have been adjudged to be a father in a contested paternity action.

The State asserts that any problem in this respect is overcome by the seventh category of putative fathers to whom notice must be given, namely, those fathers who have identified themselves in the putative fathers' register maintained by the State. Since Lehr did not take advantage of this device to make his interest known, the State contends, he was not entitled to notice and a hearing even though his identity, location, and interest were known to the adoption court prior to entry of the adoption order. I have difficulty with this position. First, it represents a grudging and crabbed approach to due process. The State is quite willing to give notice and a hearing to putative fathers who have made themselves known by resorting to the putative fathers' register. It makes little sense to me to deny notice and hearing to a father who has not placed his name in the register but who has unmistakably identified himself by filing suit to establish his paternity and has notified the adoption court of his action and his interest. I thus need not question the statutory scheme on its face. Even assuming that Lehr would have been foreclosed if his failure to utilize the register had somehow disadvantaged the State, he effectively made himself known by other means, and it is the sheerest formalism to deny him a hearing because he informed the State in the wrong manner.

No state interest is substantially served by denying Lehr adequate notice and a hearing. The State no doubt has an interest in expediting adoption proceedings to prevent a child from remaining unduly long in the custody of the State or foster parents. But this is not an adoption involving a child in the custody of an authorized state agency. Here the child is in the custody of the mother and will remain in her custody. Moreover, had Lehr utilized the putative fathers' register, he would have been granted a prompt hearing, and there was no justifiable reason, in terms of delay, to refuse him a hearing in the circumstances of this case.

The State's undoubted interest in the finality of adoption orders likewise is not well served by a procedure that will deny notice and a hearing to a father whose identity and location are known. As this case well illustrates, denying notice and a hearing to such a father may result in

years of additional litigation and threaten the reopening of adoption proceedings and the vacation of the adoption. Here, the Family Court's
unseemly rush to enter an adoption order after ordering that cause be
shown why the filiation proceeding should not be transferred and consolidated with the adoption proceeding can hardly be justified by the interest
in finality. To the contrary, the adoption order entered in March 1979 has
remained open to question until this very day.

Respectfully, I dissent.

THE PRECEDENTS FOR *LEHR*

The Supreme Court considered the objections by unmarried biological fathers
to stepfather adoption in two earlier cases that are discussed in *Lehr v. Robertson*.

Quilloin v. Walcott, 434 U.S. 246, 98 S.Ct. 549, 54 L.Ed.2d 511 (1978).

In *Quilloin*, the Supreme Court considered a challenge to a Georgia
law by a biological father seeking to prevent the adoption of his 11–year-old
son by the child's stepfather. In an opinion by Justice Marshall, the Court
stated:

> Generally speaking, under Georgia law a child born in wedlock
> cannot be adopted without the consent of each living parent who has
> not voluntarily surrendered rights in the child or been adjudicated an
> unfair parent.... In contrast, only the consent of the mother is
> required for adoption of an illegitimate child. Ga. Code § 74–403(3)
> (1975) To acquire the same veto authority possessed by other parents,
> the father of a child born out of wedlock must legitimate his offspring,
> either by marrying the mother and acknowledging the child as his own,
> § 74–101, or by obtaining a court order declaring the child legitimate
> and capable of inheriting from the father, § 74–103. But unless and
> until the child is legitimated, the mother is the only recognized parent
> and is given exclusive authority to exercise all parental prerogatives,
> § 74–203, including the power to veto adoption of the child.

> Appellant did not petition for legitimation of his child at any time
> during the 11 years between the child's birth and the filing of Randall
> Walcott's adoption petition.[6] ... After receiving extensive testimony
> from the parties and other witnesses, the trial court found that,
> although the child had never been abandoned or deprived, appellant
> had provided support only on an irregular basis. Moreover, while the
> child previously had visited with appellant on "many occasions," and
> had been given toys and gifts by appellant "from time to time," the
> mother had recently concluded that these contacts were having a
> disruptive effect on the child and on appellees' entire family. The child
> himself expressed a desire to be adopted by Randall Walcott and to

---

6. It does appear the appellant consented to entry of his name on the child's birth
certificate....

take on Walcott's name, and the court found Walcott to be a fit and proper person to adopt the child.

. . .

Appellant took an appeal to the Supreme Court of Georgia, claiming that §§ 74–203 and 74–403(3), as applied by the trial court to his case, violated the Equal Protection and Due Process Clauses of the Fourteenth Amendment. In particular, appellant contended that he was entitled to the same power to veto an adoption as is provided under Georgia law to married or divorced parents and to unwed mothers . . .

. . .

We have little doubt that the Due Process Clause would be offended "[i]f a State were to attempt to force the breakup of a natural family, over the objections of the parents and their children, without some showing of unfitness and for the sole reason that to do so was thought to be in the children's best interest." Smith v. Organization of Foster Families, 431 U.S. 816, 862–863, 97 S.Ct. 2094, 2119, 53 L.Ed.2d 14 (1977) (Stewart, J., concurring in judgment). But this is not a case in which the unwed father at any time had, or sought, actual or legal custody of his child. Nor is this a case in which the proposed adoption would place the child with a new set of parents with whom the child had never before lived. Rather, the result of the adoption in this case is to give full recognition to a family unit already in existence, a result desired by all concerned, except appellant. Whatever might be required in other situations, we cannot say that the State was required in this situation to find anything more than that the adoption, and denial of legitimation, were in the "best interests of the child."

B

Appellant contends that even if he is not entitled to prevail as a matter of due process, principles of equal protection require that his authority to veto an adoption be measured by the same standard that would have been applied to a married father. In particular, appellant asserts that his interests are indistinguishable from those of a married father who is separated or divorced from the mother and is no longer living with his child, and therefore the State acted impermissibly in treating his case differently. We think appellant's interests are readily distinguishable from those of a separated or divorced father, and accordingly believe that the State could permissibly give appellant less veto authority than it provides to a married father.

Although appellant was subject, for the years prior to these proceedings, to essentially the same child-support obligation as a married father would have had, compare § 74–202 with § 74–105 and § 30–301, he has never exercised actual or legal custody over his child, and thus has never shouldered any significant responsibility with respect to the daily supervision, education, protection, or care of the child. Appellant does not complain of his exemption from these responsibilities and, indeed, he does not even now seek custody of his child. In contrast, legal custody of children is, of course, a central aspect of the marital relationship, and even a father whose marriage has broken apart will have borne full responsibility for the rearing of his children during the period of the marriage. Under any standard of review, the State was not foreclosed from recognizing this difference in the extent of commitment to the welfare of the child.

. . .

Caban v. Mohammed, 441 U.S. 380, 99 S.Ct. 1760, 60 L.Ed.2d 297 (1979).

In *Caban v. Mohammed*, the Supreme Court was called on to review the predecessor of N.Y.Dom.Rel.Law § 111, which provides that:

> Consent to adoption shall be required as follows: . . . (b) Of the parents or surviving parent, whether adult or infant, of a child born in wedlock; [and] (c) Of the mother, whether adult or infant, of a child born out of wedlock . . .

Appellant Caban was living with appellee Maria at the time she gave birth to two children in 1969 and 1971; he was identified as the father on their birth certificates. Appellee later married Kazim Mohammed in 1974. The children resided with them until they went to Puerto Rico with Maria Mohammed's mother at the Mohammeds' request; appellees planned to join the children there when they had saved enough money to start a business. Appellant went to Puerto Rico and was permitted by the grandmother to have the children visit with him for several days with the understanding that he would then return them. Instead, appellant took the children back to New York with him. Appellees instituted a custody proceeding in New York and the Family Court awarded temporary custody to the Mohammeds with visiting rights to appellant and his new wife. Thereafter appellees filed a petition to adopt the children, and appellant filed a similar cross-petition. (N.Y.Dom.Rel.Law § 110 provides that a husband and wife "together may adopt a child of either of them born out of wedlock and [a husband or wife] may adopt such a child of the other spouse.") The New York courts permitted the adoption by appellees, thus cutting off appellant Caban's parental rights. He appealed, arguing that the New York law drew an impermissible distinction between adoption rights of an unwed father and those of other parents, and that Quilloin v. Walcott "recognized the due process right of natural fathers to maintain a parental relationship with their children absent a finding that they are unfit as parents."

The United States Supreme Court reversed a lower court decision allowing appellees to adopt, finding § 111 of the N.Y.Dom.Rel.Law to be an overbroad generalization of a gender-based classification:

> . . . Even if the special difficulties attendant upon locating and identifying unwed fathers at birth would justify a legislative distinction between mothers and fathers of newborns, these difficulties need not persist past infancy. When the adoption of an older child is sought, the State's interest in proceeding with adoption cases can be protected by means that do not draw such an inflexible gender-based distinction as that made in § 111. In those cases where the father never has come forward to participate in the rearing of his child, nothing in the Equal

Protection Clause precludes the State from withholding from him the privilege of vetoing the adoption of that child. Indeed, under the statute as it now stands the surrogate may proceed in the absence of consent when the parent whose consent otherwise would be required never has come forward or has abandoned the child. See, *e.g., In re Orlando F.,* 40 N.Y.2d 103, 386 N.Y.S.2d 64, 351 N.E.2d 711 (1976). But in cases such as this, where the father has established a substantial relationship with the child and has admitted his paternity,[14] a State should have no difficulty in identifying the father even of children born out of wedlock. Thus, no showing has been made that the different treatment afforded unmarried fathers and unmarried mothers under § 111 bears a substantial relationship to the proclaimed interest of the State in promoting the adoption of illegitimate children.

. . .

... The effect of New York's classification is to discriminate against unwed fathers even when their identity is known and they have manifested a significant paternal interest in the child. The facts of this case illustrate the harshness of classifying unwed fathers as being invariably less qualified and entitled than mothers to exercise a concerned judgment as to the fate of their children. Section 111 both excludes some loving fathers from full participation in the decision whether their children will be adopted and, at the same time, enables some alienated mothers arbitrarily to cut off the paternal rights of fathers. We conclude that this undifferentiated distinction between unwed mothers and unwed fathers, applicable in all circumstances where adoption of a child of theirs is at issue, does not bear a substantial relationship to the State's asserted interests.

. . .

EQUAL PROTECTION AFTER *LEHR*

Nguyen v. Immigration and Naturalization Service, 533 U.S. 53, 121 S.Ct. 2053, 150 L.Ed.2d 115 (2001).

In *Nguyen,* the Supreme Court examined the differential treatment of unmarried fathers and mothers in the immigration context. The Court considered the constitutionality under the Equal Protection Clause of a federal statute that treated the citizenship status of children born abroad to an unmarried U.S. citizen and a noncitizen differently depending on whether the citizen parent was the mother or father. Under 8 U.S.C. § 1409, the child born abroad to a woman who is a U.S. citizen and a noncitizen father automatically becomes a citizen on birth, whereas the child of an unmarried citizen father and a noncitizen mother does not. In a 5–4 opinion authored by Justice Kennedy, the Court upheld the discriminatory statutory requirements. Justice Stephens, the author of the Court's opinion in *Lehr,* joined the majority opinion which relied heavily on an assumption

14. In *Quilloin v. Walcott,* 434 U.S. 246, 98 S.Ct. 549, 54 L.Ed.2d 511 (1978), we noted the importance in cases of this kind of the relationship that in fact exists between the parent and child.

that biological differences between mothers and fathers in reproduction were closely linked to behavioral differences that the government legitimately could take into account through a gender-based classification.

The case involved Tuan Anh Nguyen, born in Saigon in 1969 to a Vietnamese mother and an American father, Joseph Boulais. After his parents' relationship ended, Tuan moved to the United States at age 6 and was raised by his father. In 1992, at age 22, Nguyen was convicted of two counts of sexual assault on a child and sentenced to eight years in prison for each count. Three years later, the INS initiated deportation proceedings against Nguyen as a noncitizen on the basis of his criminal offenses. In 1998, while Nguyen's appeal to the Board of Immigration Appeals was pending, his father obtained an order of parentage from a state court, based on DNA testing. The Board rejected Nguyen's claim to United States citizenship because he had failed to establish compliance with 8 U.S.C. § 1409(a). Under the statute, citizenship was conferred "where the father is the citizen parent and the mother is an alien," only if, when the child is a minor, he is legitimated, the father acknowledges paternity in writing under oath, or paternity is established through a court proceeding.

The Court reviewed this gender-based classification and concluded that it withstood equal protection scrutiny, under the prevailing standard because it "served important governmental objectives and the discriminatory means employed" were "substantially related to the achievement of those objectives."

The first governmental objective to be served by the statutory scheme was the assurance that a biological parent-child relationship exists. According to the Court, in the case of the mother, the relation is verifiable from the birth itself. This is not the case with fathers and thus a different (and more burdensome) requirement to establish biological parenthood was justified.

> Petitioners argue that the requirement of 1409(a)(1), that a father provide clear and convincing evidence of parentage, is sufficient to achieve the end of establishing paternity, given the sophistication of modern DNA tests. Section 1409(a)(1) does not actually mandate a DNA test, however. The Constitution, moreover, does not require that Congress elect one particular mechanism from among many possible methods of establishing paternity, even if that mechanism arguably might be the most scientifically advanced method. . . .

The Court described the second important governmental interest furthered by the statute as "the determination to ensure that the child and the citizen parent have some demonstrated opportunity or potential to develop . . . the real, everyday ties that provide a connection between child and citizen parent and, in turn, the United States," and not just a formal legal relationship. Again, the Court viewed the "event of birth" as providing this opportunity for the mother. "The mother knows that the child is in being and is hers and has an initial point of contact with him. There is at least an opportunity for the mother to develop a real meaningful relationship." This is not the case for the father, who may not be present at the child's birth or even aware of its existence.

... There is nothing irrational or improper in recognizing that at the moment of birth ... the mother's knowledge of the child and the fact of parenthood have been established in a way not guaranteed in the case of the unwed father. This is not a stereotype. . . .

. . .

... The distinction embodied in the statutory scheme here at issue is not marked by misconception and prejudice, nor does it show disrespect for either class. The difference between men and women in relation to the birth process is a real one, and the principle of equal protection does not forbid Congress to address the problem at hand in a manner specific to each gender.

Justice O'Connor wrote a dissenting opinion, joined by Justices Breyer, Ginsburg, and Souter. The dissent argued that the INS failed to demonstrate that the different requirements for unmarried citizen mothers and fathers satisfied the heightened scrutiny standard applied in Equal Protection sex discrimination cases. The INS justified the requirements primarily as a means of satisfying its goal of determining biological parenthood, which, the dissent pointed out could be ascertained more accurately for both mothers and fathers through DNA testing. The dissent noted that while the mother's parental status was established by the child's birth, the INS, not present on that occasion, had no direct means under the statute of verifying the presumed biological connection.

... And to the extent Congress might seek simply to ensure an "opportunity" for a relationship, little administrative inconvenience would seem to accompany a sex-neutral requirement of presence at birth, knowledge of birth, or contact between parent and child prior to a certain age.

The claim that § 1409(a)(4) substantially relates to the achievement of the goal of a "real, practical relationship" thus finds support not in biological differences but instead in a stereotype—*i.e.,* "the generalization that mothers are significantly more likely than fathers ... to develop caring relationships with their children."

Justice O'Connor pointed out that, contrary to the stereotype, Nguyen had been raised by his father and had no relationship with his mother.

NOTES

(1) The Supreme Court found that statutes that distinguished between unmarried fathers and other parents (mothers, adoptive parents, and married or divorced fathers) infringed upon a constitutionally protected interest of the fathers in *Stanley* and *Caban*, but not in *Quilloin* and *Lehr*. Since the statutes in *Quilloin* and *Caban* are similar, the difference in the outcomes of these cases cannot be explained on the basis of statutory language. On what basis does the Court distinguish among the claims made by each of these fathers? Is it fair to say that biological fathers are more likely to receive legal protection if they play a role in rearing their children, fulfilling the responsibilities of parenthood by providing financial support and care and establishing a bond with their child? If so, how can *Nguyen* be explained?

(2) **Substantive or Procedural Rights.** It is sometimes hard to say whether the Supreme Court in the opinions dealing with fathers' rights is concerned with procedural rights—the opportunity of fathers to be heard—or with substantive parental rights. *Lehr*, for example, technically involves only a claim by a father that he had a right to notice and to the opportunity to be heard when the child's stepfather sought to adopt Lehr's child (and thus terminate Lehr's parental rights). Lehr claimed that the New York statute creating the putative father registry did not protect this right. The opinion also offers insights, however, about the Court's understanding of the content of substantive parental rights—although translating the Court's pronouncements into guidelines for future cases might prove difficult. Suppose a father who had registered as a putative father received notice of an adoption hearing. At the hearing, how should the court decide whether evidence offered by the father is sufficient to block termination of his parental rights and adoption by the stepfather? It seems likely, given the Court's analysis in *Lehr*, that a showing by the father that he is a fit parent would be insufficient. Should he be required to show that his continued relationship with the child is in her best interest? Would it generally be in the child's interest to continue an established relationship with her biological father (assuming that there is no abuse)?

(3) **The "Biological Connection".** What importance does the Supreme Court attach to the "mere biological relationship" as a basis of unmarried fathers' parental rights, given its emphasis on the father's efforts in creating a parent-child relationship as the basis of a legally protected interest? Clearly, genetic parenthood is not irrelevant. As the Court puts it in *Lehr*, "the biological connection . . . offers the natural father an opportunity that no other male possesses to develop a relationship with his offspring." This opportunity is not available indefinitely, however. It will be extinguished if the father does not act expeditiously and another man steps in to fill the role of father to the child.

Some critics challenge the law's protection of biological fathers' rights as antithetical to the interests of children, and as a vestige of an era when parents had a property-like interest in their children. Although the most controversial and publicized cases have involved infants whose fathers have come forward to challenge adoption by an unrelated couple, critics also argue that the law is ready to sacrifice relationships between children and devoted stepparents because of undue deference to biological parents. In the line of cases beginning with *Stanley*, does the Supreme Court afford undue constitutional protection to the rights of biological parents?

(4) In *Caban* and *Stanley*, the fathers who were successful in asserting their parental claims before the Supreme Court, developed their relationships with their children by living with them in a family unit. *Quilloin* and *Lehr*, in contrast, never lived with their children. How important do you think this factor is in distinguishing the cases? Is it important in itself or simply as evidence of the nature of the father-child relationship? Suppose an unmarried father never lives with his child but spends time with him and consistently provides financial support? Should his interest receive legal protection if the child's stepfather seeks to adopt him at age four? This question as yet is unanswered by the Supreme Court. Janet Dolgin suggests that under existing Supreme Court doctrine, the father who has not lived in an acceptable family unit with the child and her mother is unlikely to succeed in asserting parental rights. Janet Dolgin, Just a Gene: Judicial Assumptions about Parenthood, 40 U.C.L.A.L.Rev. 637 (1993). Do you agree?

(5) Did the Court in *Lehr* reach the correct result? If the account in Justice White's dissent is accurate, and Lehr was unable to establish a relationship with his daughter because her mother interfered, is it fair to extinguish his parental rights? What incentive does this create for the mother who wants to discourage the

unmarried father from maintaining a relationship with their child? Is the Court's decision based on a best-interest-of-the-child analysis? Given the child's age and the duration of her relationship with her stepfather, it is reasonable to assume that her interest would be harmed if her father's theoretical interest in the relationship was recognized. Perhaps, on the other hand, the Court concluded that the New York statute provides ample opportunity for fathers to assert their interest, and Lehr's failure to do so at a minimum demonstrated considerable ineptitude.

(6) Does *Nguyen* seem like an outlier among the cases dealing with unmarried father's rights in that the Court seems to ignore the established parent-child relationship of Boulais and Nguyen and the reality that Boulais stepped forward to fulfill his parental responsibilities, like the fathers whose interests were protected in *Stanley* and *Caban*? Like Stanley, Boulais had raised his child (and thus, when he was a minor, the state could not have taken custody without a hearing to establish unfitness). Is the *Nguyen* Court, as Justice O'Connor charges, relying on a gender stereotype—that unmarried mothers care for their children and fathers do not—which it assumes fits most cases, even if it doesn't fit the petitioners? Is there an administratively simple gender neutral mechanism to identify children born abroad to unmarried parents, only one of whom is a U.S. citizen, and to establish citizenship status? Evidence that the child has lived with the citizen parent or that the parent provided support are two possibilities. As the Court noted in *Caban*, in rejecting a gender-based classification, "where the father has established a substantial relationship with the child and has admitted his paternity, a State should have no difficulty in identifying the father ... of children born out of wedlock."

(7) **Parental Rights In a Fiduciary Framework.** Elizabeth Scott and Robert Scott argue that the line of Supreme Court cases dealing with the rights of unmarried fathers can be understood as fitting in a fiduciary framework, under which the law seeks to encourage parents diligently to serve the interests of their children. In this framework, parental rights and responsibilities have a reciprocal relationship. Scott and Scott challenge critics who complain that the law gives undue weight to the rights of biological fathers to the detriment of their children. They posit that rights can be seen as a form of reward or compensation (in a context in which monetary compensation is not available), designed to encourage parents to invest in the relationship with their child and to fulfill child-rearing responsibilities, with the assurance that the investment will receive legal protection. Elizabeth S. Scott & Robert E. Scott, Parents as Fiduciaries, 81 Va.L.Rev. 2401, 2456–62 (1995).

Lehr can be understood in this framework as well. The authors suggest that motivating fathers requires signaling that the benefits of paternal attachment may be lost if not initiated early in the child's life. Unmarried fathers understand their role as parent to be one that requires an expeditious commitment. "The failure to initiate a relationship until after a stepfather functionally becomes father to the child justifies treating the biological father's relationship claim as forfeited [because at this point the father's further involvement is more disruptive than beneficial.] Tolerating the father's ineffectual efforts to establish a relationship would encourage strategic behavior and undermine informal incentives to assume the role of parent." Id. at 2460.

Michael H. v. Gerald D., 491 U.S. 110, 109 S.Ct. 2333, 105 L.Ed.2d 91 (1989).

In this case, the United States Supreme Court confronted a claim of parental rights by a biological father, whose child was born to the wife of another man. Michael H., according to blood tests, was almost certainly the father of the child and had lived with her mother and her as a family unit during periods when the mother was separated from her husband. After the mother and her husband (Gerald D.) reconciled, Michael H. sought visitation rights. Gerald D. sought summary judgment under a California statute that creates a presumption that a child born to a married woman living with her husband is the child of the marriage. Michael H. argued that the presumption, which was not subject to challenge by third parties, denied him procedural and substantive due process rights under the Fourteenth Amendment. A claim was also brought on behalf of the child that the statute violated her due process right to maintain a relationship with her father.

In a splintered opinion (and over a vigorous dissent by Justice Brennan), the Supreme Court rejected the constitutional challenge to the statutory presumption. Justice Scalia, joined by three other justices, concluded that California committed no constitutional violation by privileging marriage in a way that denied the parental status of unmarried biological fathers, even those who had established relationships with their children.

Justice Scalia rejects Michael's claim that he had a constitutionally protected liberty interest in his relationship with his child:

> Michael contends as a matter of substantive due process that because he has established a parental relationship with Victoria, protection of Gerald's and Carole's marital union is an insufficient state interest to support termination of that relationship. This argument is, of course, predicated on the assertion that Michael has a constitutionally protected liberty interest in his relationship with Victoria.

> . . . In an attempt to limit and guide interpretation of the Clause, we have insisted not merely that the interest denominated as a "liberty" be "fundamental" (a concept that, in isolation, is hard to objectify), but also that it be an interest traditionally protected by our society. As we have put it, the Due Process Clause affords only those protections "so rooted in the traditions and conscience of our people as to be ranked as fundamental." Snyder v. Massachusetts, 291 U.S. 97, 105 (1934) (Cardozo, J.). Our cases reflect "continual insistence upon respect for the teachings of history [and] solid recognition of the basic values that underlie our society. . . ." Griswold v. Connecticut, 381 U.S. 479, 501 (1965) (Harlan, J., concurring in judgment).

> This insistence that the asserted liberty interest be rooted in history and tradition is evident, as elsewhere, in our cases according constitutional protection to certain parental rights. Michael reads the landmark case of Stanley v. Illinois, 405 U.S. 645 (1972), and the subsequent cases of Quilloin v. Walcott, 434 U.S. 246 (1978), Caban v. Mohammed, 441 U.S. 380 (1979) and Lehr v. Robertson, 463 U.S. 248 (1983), as establishing that a liberty interest is created by biological fatherhood plus an established parental relationship—factors that exist in the present case as well. We think that distorts the rationale of those cases. As we view them, they rest not upon such isolated factors but upon the historic respect—indeed, sanctity would not be too strong

a term—traditionally accorded to the relationships that develop within the unitary family.

.   .   .

Thus, the legal issue in the present case reduces to whether the relationship between persons in the situation of Michael and Victoria has been treated as a protected family unit under the historic practices of our society, or whether on any other basis it has been accorded special protection. We think it impossible to find that it has. In fact, quite to the contrary, our traditions have protected the marital family (Gerald, Carole, and the child they acknowledge to be theirs) against the sort of claim Michael asserts.

The presumption of legitimacy was a fundamental principle of the common law. Traditionally, that presumption could be rebutted only by proof that a husband was incapable of procreation or had had no access to his wife during the relevant period. . . . The primary policy rationale underlying the common law's severe restrictions on rebuttal of the presumption appears to have been an aversion to declaring children illegitimate, see Schouler, supra, § 225, at 306–307; M. Grossberg, Governing the Hearth 201 (1985), thereby depriving them of rights of inheritance and succession, 2 Kent's Commentaries 175 (1827), and likely making them wards of the state. A secondary policy concern was the interest in promoting the "peace and tranquility of States and families," Schouler, supra, § 225, at 304, quoting Boullenois, Traité des Status, bk. 1, p. 62, a goal that is obviously impaired by facilitating suits against husband and wife asserting that their children are illegitimate. Even though, as bastardy laws became less harsh, "[j]udges in both [England and the United States] gradually widened the acceptable range of evidence that could be offered by spouses, and placed restraints on the 'four seas rule' . . . [,] the law retained a strong bias against ruling the children of married women illegitimate." Grossberg, supra, at 202.

We have found nothing in the older sources, nor in the older cases, addressing specifically the power of the natural father to assert parental rights over a child born into a woman's existing marriage with another man. Since it is Michael's burden to establish that such a power (at least where the natural father has established a relationship with the child) is so deeply embedded within our traditions as to be a fundamental right, the lack of evidence alone might defeat his case. But the evidence shows that even in modern times—when, as we have noted, the rigid protection of the marital family has in other respects been relaxed—the ability of a person in Michael's position to claim paternity has not been generally acknowledged. . . .

In Lehr v. Robertson, a case involving a natural father's attempt to block his child's adoption by the unwed mother's new husband, we observed that "[t]he significance of the biological connection is that it offers the natural father an opportunity that no other male possesses to develop a relationship with his offspring," 463 U.S., at 262, and we assumed that the Constitution might require some protection of that opportunity. Where, however, the child is born into an extant marital family, the natural father's unique opportunity conflicts with the similarly unique opportunity of the husband of the marriage; and it is not unconstitutional for the State to give categorical preference to the latter. In *Lehr* we quoted approvingly from Justice Stewart's dissent in Caban v. Mohammed, 441 U.S., at 397, to the effect that although " '[i]n some circumstances the actual relationship between father and child may suffice to create in the unwed father parental interests comparable to those of the married father,' " " 'the absence of a legal tie with the mother may in such circumstances appropriately place a limit on whatever substantive constitutional claims might otherwise exist.' " 463 U.S., at 260, n. 16. In accord with our traditions, a limit is also imposed by the circumstance that the mother is, at the time of the child's conception and birth, married to and cohabiting with another man, both of whom wish to raise the child as the offspring of their union. It is a question of legislative policy and not constitutional law whether California will allow the presumed parenthood of a couple desiring to retain a child conceived within and born into their marriage to be rebutted . . . .

Justice Brennan, in dissent, challenges Justice Scalia's emphasis on tradition as the basis for defining protected liberty interests. [Indeed, even Justices O'Connor and Kennedy, who concur in Scalia's opinion, have some trouble with his historical analysis.] In Brennan's view, *Stanley*, *Quilloin*, *Caban*, and *Lehr* dictate that the parental rights of Michael H. should receive legal protection:

> On four prior occasions, we have considered whether unwed fathers have a constitutionally protected interest in their relationships with their children. See Stanley v. Illinois, supra; Quilloin v. Walcott, 434 U.S. 246 (1978); Caban v. Mohammed, 441 U.S. 380 (1979); and Lehr v. Robertson, 463 U.S. 248 (1983). Though different in factual and legal circumstances, these cases have produced a unifying theme: although an unwed father's biological link to his child does not, in and of itself, guarantee him a constitutional stake in his relationship with that child, such a link combined with a substantial parent-child relationship will do so. "When an unwed father demonstrates a full commitment to the responsibilities of parenthood by 'com[ing] forward to participate in the rearing of his child,' . . . his interest in personal contact with his child acquires substantial protection under the Due Process Clause. At that point it may be said that he 'act[s] as a father toward his children.' " Lehr v. Robertson, supra, at 261, quoting Caban v. Mohammed, supra, at 392, 389, n. 7. This commitment is why Mr. Stanley and Mr. Caban won; why Mr. Quilloin and Mr. Lehr lost; and why Michael H. should prevail today. Michael H. is almost certainly Victoria D.'s natural father, has lived with her as her father, has contributed to her support, and has from the beginning sought to strengthen and maintain his relationship with her.

Brennan challenges Scalia's conception of the "unitary family." The earlier cases, he argues, provide no basis for privileging marriage, and indeed, support Michael H's claim, since he lived with Victoria and her mother as a family. "[T]he very premise of *Stanley* and the cases following it is that marriage is not decisive in answering the question whether the Constitution protects the parental relationship under consideration.... [I]in *Quilloin, Caban,* and *Lehr,* the putative father's demands would have disrupted a 'unitary family' as the plurality defines it; in each case, the husband of the child's mother sought to adopt the child over the objections of the natural father."

NOTES

(1) **Questions on Michael H.** Is *Michael H.* simply an anomaly that cannot be reconciled with the Supreme Court's earlier pronouncements on the rights of unmarried fathers? Does Justice Brennan's dissent conform to the reasoning of the Court's earlier opinions better than the majority opinion? Do the circumstances that distinguish this case provide an adequate basis for rejecting the father's claims?

Justice Scalia brushes aside the child's claim to an interest in a continued relationship with her biological father. Should her interest be recognized? Would it be promoted by granting visitation to her biological father?

It has been asserted by some that the holding of this case (to the extent that there is a holding with any *stare decisis* meaning) is that states are free to determine who will have standing to question paternity (or maternity) of a child during wedlock—or at least whether it can be raised by other than a party to the marriage. If this is correct, then the decision may have little practical effect unless other states adopt statutes like the somewhat unusual California provision.

(2) **Parental Identity vs. Parental Authority.** It is important to distinguish between the Supreme Court's concern in the cases dealing with unmarried fathers, which could be described as issues of parental *identity*, and its focus in cases like *Meyer, Prince,* and *Yoder,* which deal with the scope of parental *authority*. Emily Buss has clarified this difference usefully in "Parental" Rights, 88 Va.L.Rev. 635, 651–52, 657–58 (2002):

> We should, then, avoid assigning distinct constitutional identity rights to any set of individuals based on their particular characteristics. Rather, we should conceive of identity rights as a form of familial right, the right of the family to control its child-rearing structure free from state interference. This is not to suggest that a parental right of identity is not an individual right, but rather that the assignment of that right derives from family status. This also suggests that the authority of private individuals to self-identify as parents depends upon the clarity of their familial claim. Where familial relationships do not offer clear answers to the question of parental identity, deferring to private arrangements may prevent any individuals from exercising child-rearing authority effectively. In such circumstances, the state facilitates rather than compromises parental authority by resolving the disputes that stand in the way.

> As with parental authority rights, we can justify state intervention in the assignment of parental identity where the state brings some superior competence to the decisionmaking process.... [T]he state can claim special competence to establish default rules of parental identity around which private parties can bargain.... [T]he state can [also] claim special competence as the resolver of disputes over parental identity. These ... forms of expertise bear most directly on the state's authority to identify nontraditional caregivers as parents.

While the state cannot justify reassignment of parental identity in the absence of conflict, it can help to avoid these conflicts by establishing identity default rules. . . .

. . .

In a string of five "unwed father" cases, biological fathers asserted the right to be legally identified as their children's fathers and to be afforded the authority associated with that legal identity. These men asserted parental rights not, as in the core cases, to prevent the state from interfering with the choices made by familial child rearers, but rather to prevent the state from depriving them of the status and authority of parents altogether. Where these biological fathers faced paternal competitors, however, the Court refused to afford their identity claims any due process protection and left the states with considerable latitude to assign parental identity among competing claimants. Acknowledging the link between clarity in lines of parental authority and the successful fulfillment of parental responsibilities, the Court suggested that such a state definitional role may serve precisely those interests protected by the Due Process Clause.

While the only parental claims rejected by the Court in the unwed father cases were *identity* claims, these cases have been misconstrued to support a diminution of parental *authority*, particularly authority over a child's associations. Justice Stevens, for example, cited these cases in *Troxel* for the proposition that "(d)espite this Court's repeated recognition of these significant parental liberty interests, these interests have never been seen to be without limits." . . . But these cases neither embrace the rights of non-parents nor call for any qualification of parental rights to accommodate these non-parents' claims. Rather, they simply recognize the state's legitimate role in resolving disputes among multiple parental contenders.*

2.   ADOPTION PLACEMENT AND FATHERS' RIGHTS

The preceding cases dealing with the rights of unmarried fathers have involved stepfathers' efforts to adopt older children in the custody of their mothers. The Supreme Court has not directly dealt with the very thorny issues surrounding the rights of biological fathers of infants whose mothers consent to adoption placement and the limits of state authority to terminate those rights in the child's interest. In these cases, the father has yet to establish a relationship with his child. The following opinion deals with such a case.

In re B.G.C.

Supreme Court of Iowa, 1992.
496 N.W.2d 239.

■ LARSON, JUSTICE.

[Cara Clausen, an unmarried woman, gave birth to B.G.C. (Baby Girl Clausen) in February, 1991, and within 48 hours consented in writing to the child's adoption, naming "Scott" (who also consented) as the father. On February 25, 1991, the child was placed in the temporary custody of Roberta and Jan DeBoer, the prospective adoptive parents, who named her

Jessica. Within 10 days, Cara sought to set aside the termination of her parental rights in juvenile court, and acknowledged for the first time that Daniel Schmidt was the child's father. On March 12, Schmidt filed an affidavit of paternity and a petition for custody, which was rejected by the juvenile court. On March 27, he intervened in the adoption case in district court to assert his parental rights. The juvenile court denied Cara's petition and she appealed. The district court denied the adoption and ordered the DeBoers to surrender the baby to Daniel, finding that he was the real father, that he had not released his parental rights and that he had not abandoned the child. The DeBoers appealed. Eventually the appeals in the two cases were considered together by the Iowa Supreme Court. The part of the opinion dealing with Cara's case is omitted.]

. . .

As tempting as it is to resolve this highly emotional issue with one's heart, we do not have the unbridled discretion of a Solomon. Ours is a system of law, and adoptions are solely creatures of statute. As the district court noted, without established procedures to guide courts in such matters, they would "be engaged in uncontrolled social engineering." This is not permitted under our law; "[c]ourts are not free to take children from parents simply by deciding another home offers more advantages." In re Burney, 259 N.W.2d 322, 324 (Iowa 1977).[1] We point out that this case does not invalidate an adoption decree. Adoption of the baby was denied by the district court because the father's rights were not terminated.

. . .

II. The Adoption Case.

R.D. and J.D., as prospective adoptive parents petitioned to terminate the parental rights of Daniel, the "second" father. The district court heard the petition for termination in conjunction with its hearing on the petition for adoption. The district court therefore acted in a joint role as juvenile court and district court. According to the order of Judge Kilburg, the adoption proceedings by J.D. and R.D. were fatally defective because Daniel established that he was the real father and his rights had not been terminated as required by Iowa Code section 600.3(2) ("An adoption petition shall not be filed until a termination of parental rights has been

---

1. It has been urged that the court should uphold this proposed adoption on the ground that the father had abandoned his rights by failing to protect them, beginning at the time the pregnancy became known. In other words, it is suggested that this father should have acted to protect his parental rights immediately when the pregnancy became known, even though he had no indication from her that he was the father and even though she was dating another man at the time. This, of course, is totally unrealistic; it would require a potential father to become involved in the pregnancy on the mere speculation that he might be the father because he was one of the men having sexual relations with her at the time in question. Iowa Code § 600A.8 requires that abandonment be shown by clear and convincing evidence. To hold that Daniel's action was required immediately on knowledge of the pregnancy, at the risk of losing his parental rights, would fly in the face of that standard. These facts would fall far short of clear and convincing evidence. More important, a finding of abandonment under these circumstances would deprive a father of a meaningful right, protected by the Constitution, to develop a parent-child relationship.

accomplished except [in adoptions of adults and stepchildren]."). The court concluded that the ground of abandonment had not been established and that the adoption petition must therefore be denied.

R.D. and J.D. challenge this ruling on the grounds that (1) the best interests of the child dictate that she remain with R.D. and J.D., (2) Daniel did not prove his paternity, and (3) he had abandoned the baby.

A.   Best interests of the child. The argument that the best interests of the baby are best served by allowing her to stay with R.D. and J.D. is a very alluring argument. Daniel has had a poor performance record as a parent. He fathered two children prior to this child, a son, age fourteen, and a daughter born out of wedlock, now age twelve. The record shows that Daniel has largely failed to support these children financially and has failed to maintain meaningful contact with either of them.

In contrast, as the district court found, R.D. and J.D. "have provided exemplary care for the child [and] view themselves as the parents of this child in every respect." What R.D. and J.D. ask us to do, however, is to bypass the termination requirements of chapter 600A and order the granting of the adoption without establishment of any of the grounds for termination specified in section 600A.8 because it would be in the baby's best interest. Their argument is that, although Daniel was not a party to the original termination hearing under chapter 600A (in which Scott was named as father), his rights could, and should, have been terminated by the court in the chapter 600 adoption proceeding. Under chapter 600, they argue, specific grounds for termination need not be established; the best interest of the child determines the issue of termination in an adoption case. We do not believe that our law is capable of this interpretation. Whatever our adoption law was prior to 1976, it is clear that since 1976 termination of parental rights "shall be accomplished only according to the provisions of this division [now chapter 600A]." 1976 Iowa Acts ch. 1229, § 3 (now Iowa Code § 600A.3).

The intention of the legislature to link the termination provisions of chapter 600 and 600A is apparent from the fact that the same 1976 Act that made chapter 600A the exclusive vehicle for termination also amended the adoption statute, ch. 600, to require a termination of parental rights prior to the filing of an adoption petition. 1976 Iowa Acts ch. 1229, § 12 (now codified in Iowa Code § 600.3(2)).

The general rule is that [t]he state cannot interfere with the rights of natural parents simply to better the moral and temporal welfare of the child as against an unoffending parent, and, as a general rule, the court may not consider whether the adoption will be for the welfare and best interests of the child where the parents have not consented to an adoption or the conditions which obviate the necessity of their consent do not exist. However, where a parent by his conduct forfeits the right to withhold consent, but nevertheless contests the adoption, the welfare of the child is the paramount issue. 2 C.J.S. Adoption of Persons § 67, at 491 (1972).

Our case law is in accord with this view; statutory grounds for termination must be established in addition to establishing the child's best interests in order to terminate. In re L.H., 480 N.W.2d 43, 47 (Iowa 1992); In re B.L.A., 357 N.W.2d 20, 23 (Iowa 1984).

We agree with the district court that under section 600.3(2) parental rights may not be terminated solely on consideration of the child's best interest but that specific grounds for termination under chapter 600A must also be established. Daniel's parental rights had not been terminated, and the adoption proceedings were therefore fatally flawed.

. . .

C. Abandonment. R.D. and J.D. contend that the court should have terminated the parental rights of Daniel on the ground that he had abandoned the child (one of the grounds for termination under chapter 600A). We agree with the district court that the evidence falls short of establishing abandonment.

While it is true that Daniel has not shared in any of the expenses in connection with the birth, he was never requested to do so. Nor was there any need to pay the expenses until he learned that the child was his. Abandonment is defined as the relinquishment or surrendering of parental rights and includes both the intention to abandon and the acts by which the intention is evidenced. Iowa Code § 600A.2(16). Abandonment is said to be a relinquishment of parental rights and responsibilities with an intent to forego them. In re Goettsche, 311 N.W.2d 104, 105 (Iowa 1981).

Abandonment must be shown by clear and convincing proof. Iowa Code § 600A.9. In this case, the mother informed Daniel on February 27, 1991, that she suspected that Daniel was the father. Daniel, a truck driver, was due to leave town the next day with his truck and asked the mother to see what she could do to "retrieve" the baby. Daniel testified that the mother called him while he was on the road trip and told him that she had located an attorney who would take the case. The next Saturday, ten days after he learned that the mother thought he was the father, Daniel met with the attorney to discuss how he might assert his parental rights. He still did not know for sure that he was the father because the blood tests that ultimately confirmed that fact came later. Nevertheless, he immediately filed a request to vacate the termination order on March 12, 1991, and an affidavit on March 18, 1991. He then filed his petition to intervene in the adoption case on March 27, 1991, one month after he first learned that he might be the father.

[handwritten margin note: found by mom →]

We agree with the district court that abandonment was not established by clear and convincing evidence. In fact, virtually all of the evidence regarding Daniel's intent regarding this baby suggests just the opposite: Daniel did everything he could reasonably do to assert his parental rights, beginning even before he actually knew that he was the father.

III. Conclusion.

We empathize with the district court, which observed that: The court had an opportunity to observe [R.D. and J.D.] at the time of hearing and the court is under no illusion that this tragic case is other than an unbelievably traumatic event.... While cognizant of the heartache which this decision will ultimately cause, this court is presented with no other option than that dictated by the law in this state. Purely equitable principles cannot be substituted for well-established principles of law. The parental rights of this father may not be dismissed without compliance with our termination statute, and the court correctly ordered that the petition for adoption be dismissed. We therefore affirm the adoption case. In the termination case, we affirm the decision of the court of appeals, reversing the order of the juvenile court, and remanding for further proceedings in respect to the post-trial motions filed by Cara.

■ SNELL, JUSTICE, dissenting . . .

The evidence is sufficient to show abandonment of the baby by Daniel. The record shows he has previously failed to raise or support his other two children. He quit supporting his son, born in 1976, after two years. From 1978 to 1990 he saw him three times. He has another daughter whom he has never seen and has failed to support. He stated he just never took any interest in her. In every meaningful way, he abandoned them.

Daniel knew that Cara was pregnant in December 1990. He saw her in the building where they worked for the same employer. The child was born in February 1991. Having knowledge of the facts that support the likelihood that he was the biological father, nevertheless, he did nothing to protect his rights. The mother, Cara, who knew better than anyone who the father was, named Scott as the father. The legal proceedings logically and reasonably were based on these representations. The termination of parental rights as known to exist at the time were legally completed and an adoption process was commenced.

Daniel's sudden desire to assume parental responsibilities is a late claim to assumed rights that he forfeited by his indifferent conduct to the fate of Cara and her child. The specter of newly named genetic fathers, upsetting adoptions, perhaps years later, is an unconscionable result. Such a consequence is not driven by the language of our statutes, due process concerns or the facts of this case. . . .

NOTES

(1) This case received an extraordinary amount of media attention before it was finally resolved when the United States Supreme Court denied the DeBoers' application for a stay of an order of the Michigan Supreme Court directing them to return the child to her biological parents. Television cameras captured the moment when sobbing 2–year-old Jessica was carried from the DeBoers' Ann Arbor home to begin her life with the Schmidts (who had married in the interim). After the Iowa Supreme Court ruled against them in *B.G.C.*, the DeBoers had sought to have the case decided in Michigan (where they lived with the child). Although the Michigan trial court asserted jurisdiction and ordered custody in the DeBoers, the Michigan Supreme Court ultimately concluded that, under the Federal Kidnaping Prevention Act, Michigan courts lacked jurisdiction and were bound to enforce the order of the Iowa Supreme Court stripping the DeBoers of custody. See *In re Clausen*, 442 Mich. 648, 502 N.W.2d 649 (1993).

In denying the application for a stay of the Michigan court order, Supreme Court Justice Stevens, sitting as Circuit Justice, said the following:

... Applicants' claim that Jessica's best interests will be served by allowing them to retain custody rests in part on the relationship that they have been able to develop with the child after it became clear that they were not entitled to adopt her. Neither [state] law ... nor federal law authorizes unrelated persons to retain custody of a child whose natural parents have not been found to be unfit simply because they may be better able to provide for her future and her education. As the Iowa Supreme Court stated: "[C]ourts are not free to take children from parents simply by deciding another home appears more advantageous."

DeBoer v. DeBoer, 509 U.S. 1301, 1302, 114 S.Ct. 1, 125 L.Ed.2d 755 (1993).

Do you agree with Justice Stevens? Suppose the law gave no protection to the rights of biological parents, but resolved every custody dispute by placing the child with the adult or couple whose custody was more likely to promote the child's interest. Parents of newborns in hospital nurseries might lose their infants to prospective adoptive parents who demonstrate that they were more deserving, because of education, income, character, etc. Such a legal regime is not likely to find much support. Is *B.G.C.* different from this case?

The outcome of this case, and the return of Jessica to her biological parents, was harshly criticized, in part because Schmidt was viewed as a deficient parent, while the DeBoers seemed to provide an exemplary home and family for Jessica. Moreover, many predicted that serious psychological harm to Jessica would inevitably result from her separation at age two from the DeBoers, the only parents she knew. However, the delay in reaching a final outcome in this case was caused by the litigation and appeal process, which continued for well over two years—and which was prolonged largely by the DeBoers. Under these circumstances, should the fact that the child and biological parents have been separated for an extended period be relevant to the outcome? What incentive would this create for prospective adoptive parents? Can you suggest procedural reforms that might mitigate the problem?

(2) *In re B.G.C.* in some regards is similar to *Lehr v. Robertson*. [Coincidentally the children in both cases are named Jessica!] Both fathers unsuccessfully sought to initiate a relationship with their children and both were thwarted by the efforts of others to keep child and parent apart. In both cases, other adults fulfilled the responsibilities of parenthood and became social parents of the child. In both cases, a strong argument could be made that an outcome that denied the biological father's parental rights would serve the child's interest. Yet, in *B.G.C.*, the state's interest in promoting the child's welfare is subordinated to the father's parental rights, while in *Lehr*, the father's rights are extinguished. How do you explain the difference? Consider the fact that Schmidt initiated legal action to assert his parental rights a short time after the child's birth, while Lehr acted informally and only sought legal recourse when the stepfather initiated an adoption action of 2–year-old Jessica. This seems to be a critical difference between the two cases.

(3) *Petition of Doe*, **159 Ill.2d 347, 202 Ill.Dec. 535, 638 N.E.2d 181 (1994).** In evaluating the unmarried father's rights, should it matter that the mother or prospective adoptive parents interfered with the father's ability to claim parental rights by withholding information about the child from him? In this case, Daniella Janikova consented to the adoption of her baby four days after his birth, telling the adoptive parents and their attorney that she knew who the father was but would not furnish his name. Meanwhile, she told the father, Otakar Kirchner, from whom she was estranged at the time (though he had supported her during the pregnancy), that the baby had died. Kirchner began an inquiry for information about his child, and learned that the child was alive 57 days after the child's birth. He immediately contested the adoption of his son. The trial court ruled that Kirchner was an unfit parent, because he had failed to show "a reasonable degree of

interest in the child in the first 30 days of life" as required by the Illinois Adoption Act. Because he was found to be unfit, his consent was not required. The appellate court affirmed.

The Illinois Supreme Court reversed and ordered that the child, age three, be returned to the father. It concluded that no evidence supported the finding that the father had not shown a reasonable degree of interest in his child in the first 30 days of life. The court pointed out that the burden was on the adoptive parents to prove that this requirement had been met before the father's parental rights could be terminated. The court criticized the appellate court for focusing on the child's best interest. The threshold issue in the case was whether the father's parental rights should have been terminated. "Since ... the father's parental interest was improperly terminated, there was no occasion to reach the factor of the child's best interests."

The court expressed regret for the fact that more than three years had elapsed since the birth of the baby, and that under its order, the child would be awarded to biological parents who he had never seen and knew nothing about. However, it faulted the mother for seeking to deprive the father of his rights, and the adoptive parents and their attorney. The attorney failed to make any effort to ascertain the identity of the father. Further, the court observed that the protracted litigation and appeal process was the cause of the delay, and criticized the adoptive parents for persevering in the face of clear Illinois law supporting the biological father.

In a concurring opinion, Justice McMorrow elaborated on the latter point. The appellate court below, in holding that no finding of the biological parent's unfitness was needed if the termination of parental rights was in the best interest of the child, had ignored recent precedent. In *In re Adoption of Syck* (138 Ill.2d 255, 149 Ill.Dec. 710, 562 N.E.2d 174 (1990)), the Illinois Supreme Court had interpreted a similar requirement for establishing parental unfitness in another section of the Adoption Act. In *Syck*, the court held that the court must determine the parent's unfitness (based on failure to show a reasonable degree of interest) *before* it could consider the child's best interests. "The child's welfare and whether the child's potential adoption by the petitioners would improve his future financial, social and emotional atmosphere is not relevant in judging the fitness of the natural parent ..." (159 Ill.2d 347, at 363, 202 Ill.Dec. 535, 638 N.E.2d 181, at 188), nor are these factors relevant in deciding whether the parent had failed to demonstrate sufficient interest in the child—the basis for termination of parental rights. In short, contrary to the view of the appellate court in *Petition of Doe*, *Syck* made clear that the child's best interests could not be used to justify extinguishing parental rights.

In denying the petition for rehearing, Justice Heiple hotly challenged critics of the opinion and of the law's rejection of a best interests test for termination of parental rights:

> If ... the best interests of the child is to be the determining factor in child custody cases, ... persons seeking babies to adopt might profitably frequent grocery stores and snatch babies from carts when the parent is looking the other way. Then, if custody proceedings can be delayed long enough, they can assert that they have a nicer home, a superior education, a better job or whatever, and that the best interests of the child are with the baby snatchers. Children of parents living in public housing ... and children of single parents might be considered particularly fair game. The law, thankfully, is otherwise.

159 Ill.2d 347, 363, 202 Ill.Dec. 535, 542, 638 N.E.2d 181, 188.

(4) ***Robert O. v. Russell K.***, **80 N.Y.2d 254, 590 N.Y.S.2d 37, 604 N.E.2d 99 (1992).** In this opinion, the New York Court of Appeals dealt with the question of how extensive is the opportunity of the father who is unaware of his parental status

to come forward to assert his parental rights. Carol A. became pregnant by Robert O., to whom she was engaged. Before he knew about the pregnancy, the couple separated. On October 1, 1988, the baby was born. Thereafter, Carol consented to the child's adoption by Russell K. and Joanne K., friends whom she had approached to adopt the child. The adoption was finalized in May 1989.

Carol was not required under New York law to identify the father, and Robert O. did not qualify under the New York statute as a father entitled to notice of adoption. [This is the notice statute at issue in *Lehr*.] From March 1988 until January 1990 Robert did not contact Carol. The couple reconciled in January 1990 and in March 1990, Carol informed Robert about the birth of the child. The couple petitioned to vacate the adoption, which had been finalized 10 months earlier. At that time, the child was 18 months old.

The court rejected the father's argument that the statute denied a constitutionally protected liberty interest to biological fathers who are ignorant of their parental status. Robert proposed that before adoption could be finalized, the issue of paternity must be resolved, by requiring the mother to testify, if necessary. The court was unsympathetic to Robert's claim that he had done "everything possible" to manifest his willingness to assume parental responsibility and that he was unable to act more promptly because he was unaware of his child's existence. The most important element in evaluating the fathers' interest was the timing of his actions:

> States' determination of the rights of unwed fathers need not be blind to the "vital importance" of adoption procedures possessed of "promptness and finality" promoting the best interests of the child.... Promptness is measured in terms of the baby's life, not by the onset of the father's awareness. The demand for prompt action by the father at the child's birth is neither arbitrary nor punitive, but instead a logical and necessary outgrowth of the child's need for the early permanence and stability.

Can you reconcile *Robert O.* with the other cases in this section? Would the New York court have reached a different result in *B.G.C.* from that reached by the Iowa court? In all three cases (*B.G.C.*, *Petition of Doe*, and *Robert O.*), the biological father's pursuit of parental rights followed a reconciliation between the parents, after the mother alone consented to adoption. Do decisions like *Doe* and *B.G.C.* open the door to strategic behavior by biological parents?

(5) ***Adoption of Kelsey S.*, 1 Cal.4th 816, 4 Cal.Rptr.2d 615, 823 P.2d 1216 (1992).** In adoption placement situations, fathers who object to adoption must be prepared to take custody of the child. In this regard, these cases are different from step-parent adoption, where the non-custodial parent may be able to block adoption by the spouse of the custodial parent without demonstrating that he is prepared to take custody of the child. In adoption placement cases, of course, the mother wants to place the child, and the child's future could be imperiled if the father could block the adoption without being ready to assume full parental responsibilities. Where the father *is* ready to take custody, however, he need only demonstrate that he is a fit parent. As the courts in Petition of Doe and B.G.C. indicate, courts generally do not apply the best interest standard in these cases.

California's highest court rejected the decision of the trial court in terminating the parental rights under the best interest standard of a father who did not qualify as a "presumed father" under the state's statutory scheme (which would have required him to attempt to marry the child's mother or to take the child into his home and hold her out as his own). *Adoption of Kelsey S.*, 1 Cal.4th 816, 4 Cal.Rptr.2d 615, 823 P.2d 1216 (1992). In this case, the mother had prevented the father from taking custody of the child after her birth, despite his expressed desire to raise her. The Court held that the state was required to recognize the father's "reasonable and meaningful attempt to establish a relationship" with his child, and that the application of the best interest standard in this situation was unconstitutional.

> [The] statutory scheme violates the federal constitutional guarantees of equal protection and due process *to the extent that* the statutes allow a mother unilaterally to preclude her child's biological from becoming a presumed father and thereby allowing the state to terminate his parental rights on nothing more than a showing of the child's best interest. If an unwed father promptly comes forward and demonstrates a full commitment to his parental responsibilities ... his federal constitutional right to due process prohibits the termination of his parental relationship absent a showing of his unfitness as a parent. Similarly, when the father comes forward to grasp his parental responsibilities, his parental rights are entitled to equal protection as those of the mother.

> ... Once the father knows or reasonably should know of the pregnancy, he must promptly attempt to assume his parental responsibilities as fully as the mother will allow and his circumstances will permit. In particular, the father the father must demonstrate "a willingness himself to assume full custody of the child—not merely to block adoption by others." ....

(6) **The Uniform Adoption Act.** Under Section 3–504 of the Uniform Adoption Act, a court considering an adoption petition is directed to respond to the assertion of parental rights by the parent opposing adoption as follows:

> (c) ... If the court finds, upon clear and convincing evidence, that one of the following grounds exists, and, by a preponderance of the evidence, that termination is in the best interest of the minor, the court shall terminate any relationship of parent and child between the respondent and the minor:

> (1) in the case of a minor who has not attained six months of age at the time the petition for adoption is filed, unless the respondent proves by a preponderance of the evidence a compelling reason for not complying with this paragraph, the respondent has failed to:

>> (i) pay reasonable prenatal, natal, and postnatal expenses in accordance with the respondent's financial means;

>> (ii) make reasonable and consistent payments, in accordance with the respondent's financial means, for the support of the minor;

>> (iii) visit regularly with the minor; and

>> (iv) manifest an ability and willingness to assume legal and physical custody of the minor, if, during this time, the minor was not in the physical custody of the other parent;

> (2) in the case of a minor who has attained six months of age at the time a petition for adoption is filed, unless the respondent proves by a preponderance of the evidence a compelling reason for not complying with this paragraph, the respondent, for a period of at least six consecutive months immediately preceding the filing of the petition, has failed to:

>> (i) make reasonable and consistent payments, in accordance with the respondent's means, for the support of the minor;

>> (ii) communicate or visit regularly with the minor; and

>> (iii) manifest an ability and willingness to assume legal and physical custody of the minor, if, during this time, the minor was not in the physical custody of the other parent;

> (3) the respondent has been convicted of a crime of violence or of violating a restraining or protective order, and the facts of the crime or violation and the

respondent's behavior indicate that the respondent is unfit to maintain a relationship of parent and child with the minor;

(4) the respondent is a man who was not married to the minor's mother when the minor was conceived or born and is not the genetic or adoptive father of the minor; or

(5) termination is justified on a ground specified in [the State's statute for involuntary termination of parental rights].

The Uniform Act further provides that, even if the parent proves that she has a compelling reason for not complying with the above section, the court may terminate parental rights if the parent is unable to immediately assume custody of the child or is unfit. In the case of an adoption petition by a stepparent, termination may be ordered if the parent is unwilling or unable to maintain contact with the child or to pay child support.

(7) Mary Shanley has analyzed the rights of unmarried fathers from a feminist perspective in an interesting article that discusses most of the cases in this section. Mary Shanley, Unmarried Fathers' Rights, Adoption and Sex Equality: Gender Neutrality and the Perpetuation of Patriarchy, 95 Colum.L.Rev. 60 (1995). She points out that the traditional common law response, which did not extend parental status to unmarried fathers, was grounded in patriarchal policies of protecting men from the claims of their illegitimate children. In this regard consider the following.

THE CONSTITUTIONAL STATUS OF ILLEGITIMATE CHILDREN

The law historically discriminated against illegitimate children, who were denied the right to inherit from their parents and were excluded from other entitlements accorded to legitimate children. During the 1968 term the United States Supreme Court surprised many observers when they held in *Levy v. Louisiana*[1] that it was unconstitutional for a state to create a right of action in favor of children for the wrongful death of a parent and exclude illegitimate children from its benefits. Describing illegitimate children as "clearly 'persons' within the meaning of the Equal Protection Clause", the Court concluded that it "is invidious to discriminate against them when no action, conduct, or demeanor of theirs is possibly relevant to the harm that was done to the mother." In a companion case, *Glona v. American Guarantee & Liability Insurance Company*,[2] the Court invalidated another Louisiana law that provided that a mother had no right of action for the death of her illegitimate son even though such an action would have been available had the child been legitimate.

Since *Levy* and *Glona* the Supreme Court has produced a flow of decisions dealing with the application of the Equal Protection Clause in cases involving inheritance, support and worker's compensation benefits for illegitimate children. In *Labine v. Vincent*,[3] an illegitimate child attacked the constitutionality of a Louisiana statute that disqualified her from sharing in the intestate distribution of her father's estate. Justice Black, writing for the Court, found illegitimacy not to be a suspect classification; thus, the state needed only a rational basis to sustain the succession provision. He also found the exclusion of acknowledged illegitimate children to be rationally related to the state's desire to promote family life and the need to supervise the distribution of estates without onerous problems of proof regarding paternity.

1. 391 U.S. 68, 88 S.Ct. 1509, 20 L.Ed.2d 436 (1968).

2. 391 U.S. 73, 88 S.Ct. 1515, 20 L.Ed.2d 441 (1968).

3. 401 U.S. 532, 91 S.Ct. 1017, 28 L.Ed.2d 288 (1971).

Some thought that the scope of *Levy* and *Glona* had been severely limited by *Labine* in definite contrast to developments that were taking place on the legislative front. Section 2 of the Uniform Parentage Act (1973), for example, was based on the premise that

> The parent and child relationship extends equally to every child and to every parent, regardless of the marital status of the parents.

Others regarded *Labine* as peculiar to the problems of Louisiana's inheritance law, which differs considerably from that of all the other states. Such doubts were justified. In *Weber v. Aetna Casualty and Surety Co.*,[4] the Court held that a blanket exclusion of illegitimate children from bringing a worker's compensation claim on behalf of their deceased father was an unconstitutional denial of both due process and equal protection. Nothing about the child's illegitimate status was seen to justify such a bar. The Court found that condemning a child to show disapproval of the parent's relationship "is illogical and unjust. Moreover, imposing disabilities on the illegitimate child is contrary to the basic concept of our system that legal burdens should bear some relationship to individual responsibility or wrongdoing. Obviously, no child is responsible for his birth and penalizing the illegitimate child is an ineffectual—as well as an unjust—way of deterring the parent."

In a short Per Curiam decision the following year, 1973, the Supreme Court held that a state could not constitutionally grant legitimate children a right of support from their natural fathers and at the same time deny such a right to illegitimate children.[5]

In contrast, the Supreme Court in *Mathews v. Lucas*[6] upheld a requirement of the Federal Social Security Act that unacknowledged, illegitimate children make a special proof of dependency on the father as a prerequisite to receiving his death benefits under the Act. Legitimate children and even acknowledged illegitimate children were given the benefit of a statutory presumption of dependency and were, therefore, exempted from proving the dependent relationship. In upholding the differential treatment, the Court found the classification rationally related to problems of proof. In *Mathews* the Court again determined that illegitimacy is not entitled to strict scrutiny because:

> [W]hile the law has long placed the illegitimate child in an inferior position relative to the legitimate in certain circumstances, particularly in regard to obligations of support or other aspects of family law, perhaps in part because the roots of the discrimination rest in the conduct of the parents rather than the child, and perhaps in part because illegitimacy does not carry an obvious badge, as race or sex do, this discrimination against illegitimates has never approached the severity or pervasiveness of the historic legal and political discrimination against women and Negroes.
>
> We therefore adhere to our earlier view, see Labine v. Vincent, 401 U.S. 532 (1971) that the Act's discrimination between individuals on the basis of their legitimacy does not command extraordinary protection from the majoritarian political process ... which our most exacting scrutiny would entail.[7]

Applying the rational basis standard, the majority found the challenged statutory requirement reasonably related to the likelihood of dependency at death. Since the purpose of the Act is to pay death benefits to dependent children, Congress was free to put the burden of case-by-case proof on unacknowledged illegitimates while

---

4. 406 U.S. 164, 92 S.Ct. 1400, 31 L.Ed.2d 768 (1972).

5. *Gomez v. Perez*, 409 U.S. 535, 93 S.Ct. 872, 35 L.Ed.2d 56 (1973).

6. 427 U.S. 495, 96 S.Ct. 2755, 49 L.Ed.2d 651 (1976).

7. Id. at 505–06, 96 S.Ct. at 2762.

exempting all children whose relationship to the decedent was more clearly established during his life.

One year later in *Trimble v. Gordon*[8] Mr. Justice Powell delivered an opinion of the Court which stated again that illegitimacy is not a suspect classification but nevertheless (in something of an upset given the overwhelming evidence that whoever bears the burden of proof usually loses in such challenges) struck down § 12 of the Illinois Probate Act, which barred illegitimates from sharing in the distribution of intestate property. In an opinion that some have read as according illegitimacy "quasi-suspect" status entitled to an intermediate level of scrutiny,[9] Justice Powell rejected all the government's purported bases for the statutory bar. As to the promotion of family life by penalizing the status of illegitimacy, which had been persuasive to Justice Black in *Labine*, Justice Powell followed *Weber*'s analysis and stated:

> In subsequent decisions [after *Labine*] we have expressly considered and rejected the argument that a State may attempt to influence the actions of men and women by imposing sanctions on the children born of their illegitimate relationships.
>
>   . . .
>
> The parents have the ability to conform their conduct to societal norms, but their illegitimate children can affect neither their parents' conduct nor their own status.[10]

The Court, echoing *Mathews v. Lucas*, acknowledged the appropriateness of upholding statutory distinctions closely related to the problem of proof and the need for orderly administration of decedents' estates, but nevertheless struck down Illinois' blanket disinheritance of illegitimates.

Finally the Court addressed the state's argument that the intestate succession statutes should be written to reflect what most people would do if they were to write a will; according to the state, most people would not include illegitimate children in their wills and the Illinois Probate Act merely reflected this presumed intent. However, Justice Powell found it unnecessary to resolve the issue of "presumed intent" because the Court did not think that the provision of the Illinois statute had been adopted for such a purpose. In a footnote, however, he pointed out that:

> The issue . . . becomes one of where the burden of inertia in writing a will is to fall. At least when the disadvantaged group has been a frequent target of discrimination, as illegitimates have, we doubt that a State constitutionally may place the burden on that group by invoking the theory of "presumed intent."[11]

It seemed almost inevitable that a case like *Lalli v. Lalli*[12] would appear before the Court after *Trimble*. In *Lalli* illegitimate children of a decedent attacked a New York statute[13] that required a filiation order declaring paternity during the father's lifetime before an illegitimate could share in the intestate distribution of his father's estate. The Court upheld the New York statute as specifically related to the state's legitimate concern—the problems of proving the relationship of putative

---

8. 430 U.S. 762, 97 S.Ct. 1459, 52 L.Ed.2d 31 (1977).

9. Justice Rehnquist's dissent in *Trimble* noted for example that the Court's opinion gave illegitimacy classification greater scrutiny than mere rationality, but they have never held those classifications to be "suspect". 430 U.S. at 781, 97 S.Ct. at 1470–71.

10. 430 U.S. at 769, 770.

11. Id. at 775, n. 16.

12. 439 U.S. 259, 99 S.Ct. 518, 58 L.Ed.2d 503 (1978).

13. N.Y. Decedent's Estates Law § 4–1.2.

illegitimates to the decedent and the difficulty of exposing spurious claims. The Court next analyzed the legislative means the state had chosen to further these legitimate legislative goals:

As the State's interests are substantial, we now consider the means adopted by New York to further these interests. . . . [T]he Commission recommended a requirement designed to ensure the accurate resolution of claims of paternity and to minimize the potential for disruption of estate administration. Accuracy is enhanced by placing paternity disputes in a judicial forum during the lifetime of the father. As the New York Court of Appeals observed in its first opinion in this case, the "availability [of the putative father] should be a substantial factor contributing to the reliability of the fact-finding process." *In re Lalli*, 38 N.Y.2d at 82, 340 N.E.2d at 724. In addition, requiring that the order be issued during the father's lifetime permits a man to defend his reputation against "unjust accusations in paternity claims," which was a secondary purpose of § 4–1.2.

The administration of an estate will be facilitated, and the possibility of delay and uncertainty minimized, where the entitlement of an illegitimate child to notice and participation is a matter of judicial record before the administration commences. Fraudulent assertions of paternity will be much less likely to succeed, or even to arise, where the proof is put before a court of law at a time when the putative father is available to respond, rather than first brought to light when the distribution of the assets of an estate is in the offing.

Appellant contends that § 4–1.2, like the statute at issue in Trimble, excludes "significant categories of illegitimate children" who could be allowed to inherit, "without jeopardizing the orderly settlement" of their intestate fathers' estates. He urges that those in his position—"known" illegitimate children who, despite the absence of an order of filiation obtained during their fathers' lifetimes, can present convincing proof of paternity—cannot rationally be denied inheritance as they pose none of the risks § 4–1.2 was intended to minimize.

We do not question that there will be some illegitimate children who would be able to establish their relationship to their deceased fathers without serious disruption of the administration of estates and that, as applied to such individuals § 4–1.2 appears to operate unfairly. But few statutory classifications are entirely free from the criticism that they sometimes produce inequitable results. Our inquiry under the Equal Protection Clause does not focus on the abstract "fairness" of a state law, but on whether the statute's relation to the state interests it is intended to promote is so tenuous that it lacks the rationality contemplated by the Fourteenth Amendment.

The Illinois statute in *Trimble* was constitutionally unacceptable because it effected a total statutory disinheritance of children born out of wedlock who were not legitimated by the subsequent marriage of their parents. The reach of the statute was far in excess of its justifiable purposes. Section 4–1.2 does not share this defect. Inheritance is barred only where there has been a failure to secure evidence of paternity during the father's lifetime in the manner prescribed by the State. This is not a requirement that inevitably disqualifies an unnecessarily large number of children born out of wedlock.[14]

Later cases dealt with the question of how a state might limit the period of time in which an action to establish paternity could be brought by a child born out of wedlock. In *Mills v. Habluetzel*[15] the Supreme Court struck down a Texas statute

14. 439 U.S. at 271–73, 99 S.Ct. at 526–527.

15. See 456 U.S. 91, 102 S.Ct. 1549, 71 L.Ed.2d 770 (1982).

providing a one-year limitation for actions to establish paternity as violative of Equal Protection guarantees. Soon afterward a Tennessee statute providing a two-year limitation period was invalidated,[16] and a similar fate was met by a Pennsylvania statute's six-year limitation period.[17]

The following principles have emerged from this series of cases: (1) The Court does not regard illegitimacy as a suspect classification for equal protection analysis but does suggest illegitimacy is entitled to the heightened scrutiny accorded a "quasi-suspect" classification; (2) statutes making distinctions between legitimate and illegitimate children must be narrowly drawn and closely related to real problems of proof in order to be on sound constitutional footing.

---

16. See *Pickett v, Brown*, 462 U.S. 1, 103 S.Ct. 2199, 76 L.Ed.2d 372 (1983).

17. *Clark v. Jeter*, 486 U.S. 456, 108 S.Ct. 1910, 100 L.Ed.2d 465 (1988).

CHAPTER II

Children as Legal Persons

A. Introduction

By this point, it is clear that children have a special status under the law. First, as Chapter I suggests, the legal framework defining the contours of parental and state authority over children is premised on the general assumption that children are subject to the legal authority of *some* adult (either parent or state agent). The important decisions affecting children's lives generally will be made by others. Subject to some state supervision, parents decide where children will live, where they will go to school, what religious practice they will follow and what medical treatment they will receive. Indeed, parents have the legal authority to control even trivial decisions affecting their children, although in practice, they may have difficulty enforcing this authority.

An important part of children's special legal status is that many of the rights and privileges accorded to adults are withheld from children, and their freedom is restricted in ways that would be intolerable if the restrictions were applied to adults. Thus, minors cannot vote, drive motor vehicles (until age 16), purchase and drink alcoholic beverages (until age 21), or purchase and smoke cigarettes. They must remain in school until a designated age under compulsory attendance laws and may also be subject to curfew laws that limit their freedom to be out at night. Legal restrictions on minors can affect interests of constitutional importance. We will see shortly (in *Tinker v. Des Moines Independent School District*) that the Supreme Court has made clear that minors have an interest in free expression that is protected under the First Amendment. It is also clear, however, that the Court has found that interest to be much more limited than is that of adults.

Restrictions on the freedom of minors are justified on several grounds. Minors are viewed as being unable to make competent decisions because of their immature understanding and judgment, and lack of experience. Younger children are limited in their decisionmaking ability simply because of immaturity in their cognitive development. The cognitive abilities of adolescents are more like those of adults, but they may lack maturity of judgment. Traditional law presumes that if minors were given the freedom that adults have, they would often make choices that are harmful to themselves or others, or that generally undermine social welfare. Moreover, minors may be vulnerable to coercion and undue influence in making choices, and thus may be taken advantage of by adults who do not have their interests at heart. Finally, to accord minors the rights and privileges of adults could directly and indirectly undermine parental authority, which in some sense is a quid pro quo for the burden of legal responsibility that parents are given.

Another dimension of minors' special legal status is that youthful conduct and choices are held to reduced standards of accountability and responsibility. This is embodied most importantly in the traditional legal response to juvenile crime. Most youthful offenders are adjudicated and sanctioned in a separate juvenile justice system (which is examined in Chapters IX & X). The premise of this legal framework—which in recent years has significantly eroded—is that minors are less culpable and more responsive to rehabilitation than are adults who commit crimes, and that rehabilitation rather than punishment is the appropriate goal of intervention. In the civil context, a policy of reduced accountability can be discerned in contract law. Under the infancy doctrine, most contracts are not enforceable against minors. These responses reflect some of the same assumptions about youthful immaturity as do policies that limit privileges and restrict youthful freedom: that minors, for developmental reasons will exercise poor judgment in making choices and will be vulnerable to influence. Society's interest, as well as that of young persons, may be served by protecting them from the harsh consequences of youthful choices.

The traditional conception of childhood and adulthood as dichotomous legal categories has been subject to challenge in recent years. Particularly, critics have observed that younger children and adolescents are very different in their capacities and need for protection, and that paternalistic policies ignore these differences in ways that result in burdensome restrictions and unwarranted protection for adolescents. A vigorous debate has developed about the extent to which adolescents should be treated like adults under the law. Procedures have long been available in many states by which individual minors can become generally emancipated from parental custody, either on the child's or parents' initiative. The current policy debate is far broader in its potential impact. One important arena of policy reform has been juvenile justice policy, with many critics arguing that juvenile offenders should be subject to the same procedures—and punishment—as are adults. (This debate and the issues it raises are discussed in Chapter X.) Also significant are questions that are examined in this chapter about whether certain constitutional rights and privileges should be extended to minors. The Supreme Court in the past generation has examined whether minors facing involuntary commitment in a psychiatric hospital have a liberty interest that is protected under the Due Process clause of the Fourteenth Amendment. The Court also has explored whether a pregnant minor seeking abortion without parental consent has an interest in reproductive autonomy. These high-profile issues have focused attention on whether the legal boundaries between adulthood and childhood should be redrawn in general or in certain contexts. This raises questions about the usefulness of having only two age-based classifications at all.

B.   PATERNALISTIC POLICIES OF RESTRICTION AND PROTECTION

1.   LIMITED ACCOUNTABILITY IN CONTRACTING

Dodson v. Shrader

Supreme Court of Tennessee, 1992.
824 S.W.2d 545.

■ O'BRIEN, JUSTICE.

This is an action to disaffirm the contract of a minor for the purchase of a pick-up truck and for a refund of the purchase price. The issue is whether the minor is entitled to a full refund of the money he paid or whether the seller is entitled to a setoff for the decrease in value of the pick-up truck while it was in the possession of the minor.

In early April of 1987, Joseph Eugene Dodson, then 16 years of age, purchased a used 1984 pick-up truck from Burns and Mary Shrader. The Shraders owned and operated Shrader's Auto Sales in Columbia, Tennessee. Dodson paid $4,900 in cash for the truck, using money he borrowed from his girlfriend's grandmother. At the time of the purchase there was no inquiry by the Shraders, and no misrepresentation by Mr. Dodson, concerning his minority. However, Mr. Shrader did testify that at the time he believed Mr. Dodson to be 18 or 19 years of age.

In December 1987, nine months after the date of purchase, the truck began to develop mechanical problems. A mechanic diagnosed the problem as a burnt valve, but could not be certain without inspecting the valves inside the engine. Mr. Dodson did not want, or did not have the money, to effect these repairs. He continued to drive the truck despite the mechanical problems. One month later, in January, the truck's engine "blew up" and the truck became inoperable.

Mr. Dodson parked the vehicle in the front yard at his parents' home where he lived. He contacted the Shraders to rescind the purchase of the truck and requested a full refund. The Shraders refused to accept the tender of the truck or to give Mr. Dodson the refund requested.

Mr. Dodson then filed an action in general sessions court seeking to rescind the contract and recover the amount paid for the truck. The general sessions court dismissed the warrant and Mr. Dodson perfected a de novo appeal to the circuit court. At the time the appeal was filed in the circuit court Mr. Shrader, through counsel, declined to accept the tender of the truck without compensation for its depreciation. Before the circuit court could hear the case, the truck, while parked in Dodson's front yard, was struck on the left front fender by a hit-and-run driver. At the time of the circuit court trial, according to Shrader, the truck was worth only $500 due to the damage to the engine and the left front fender.

The case was heard in the circuit court in November 1988. The trial judge, based on previous common-law decisions and, under the doctrine of stare decisis reluctantly granted the rescission. The Shraders were ordered, upon tender and delivery of the truck, to reimburse the $4,900 purchase price to Mr. Dodson. The Shraders appealed.

The Court of Appeals . . . affirmed. . . .

The earliest recorded case in this State, on the issue involved, appears to be in Wheaton v. East, 13 Tenn. 35 (5 Yeager 41) (1833). In pronouncing the rule to apply governing infant's contracts, the court said:

> We do not perceive that any general rule, as to contracts which are void and voidable, can be stated with more precision that is done by Lord Ch. J. Eyre in Keane v. Boycott, 2 H. Black, 511, and quoted with approbation by Judge Story, 1 Mason's Rep. 82, and by Chancellor Kent, 2 Com. 193, which is this: "that when the court can pronounce the contract to be to the infant's prejudice, it is void, and when to his benefit, as for necessaries, it is good; and when the contract is of any uncertain nature, as to benefit or prejudice, it is voidable only, at the election of the infant." . . .

The law on the subject of the protection of infant's rights has been slow to evolve. However, in Human v. Hartsell, 24 Tenn.App. 678, 148 S.W.2d 634, 636 (1940) the Court of Appeals noted:

> In Tuck v. Payne, 159 Tenn. 192, 17 S.W.2d 8, in an opinion by Mr. Justice McKinney, the modern rule that contracts of infants are not void but only voidable and subject to be disaffirmed by the minor either before or after attaining majority appears to have been favored.

> Under this rule the efforts of early authorities to classify contracts as beneficial or harmful and determine whether they are void or only voidable upon the basis of such classification are abandoned in favor of permitting the infant himself when he has become of age to determine what contracts are and what are not to his interest and liking. He is thus permitted to assume the burden of a contract, clearly disadvantageous to him, if he deems himself under a moral obligation to do so. The adoption of this rule does not lead to any retrenchment of the infant's rights but gives him the option of invoking contracts found to be advantageous but which, if held void, could not be enforced against the other party to the contract. Thus the minor can secure the advantage of contracts advantageous to himself and be relieved of the effect of an injudicious contract.

In Tuck, supra, 17 S.W.2d at p. 9, the court applied the rule based upon the maxims that he who seeks equity must do equity, that he who comes into equity must come with clean hands, that no one can take advantage of his own wrong, that he that has committed inequity shall not have equity, and that minors will not be permitted to use the shield of infancy as a cover, or turn it into a sword with which to injure others dealing with them in good faith.

As noted by the Court of Appeals, the rule in Tennessee, as modified, is in accord with the majority rule on the issue among our sister states. This rule is based upon the underlying purpose of the "infancy doctrine" which is to protect minors from their lack of judgment and "from squandering their wealth through improvident contracts with crafty adults who would take advantage of them in the marketplace." Halbman v. Lemke, 99 Wis.2d 241, 245, 298 N.W.2d 562, 564 (1980).

There is, however, a modern trend among the states, either by judicial action or by statute, in the approach to the problem of balancing the rights of minors against those of innocent merchants. As a result, two (2) minority rules have developed which allow the other party to a contract with a minor to refund less than the full consideration paid in the event of rescission.

The first of these minority rules is called the "Benefit Rule." E.g., Hall v. Butterfield, 59 N.H. 354 (1879); Johnson v. Northwestern Mut. Life Insurance Co., 56 Minn. 365, 59 N.W. 992 (1894); Berglund v. American Multigraph Sales Co., 135 Minn. 67, 160 N.W. 191 (1916); Porter v. Wilson, 106 N.H. 270, 209 A.2d 730 (1965); Valencia v. White, 134 Ariz. 139, 654 P.2d 287 (Ariz.App.1982). The rule holds that, upon rescission, recovery of the full purchase price is subject to a deduction for the minor's use of the merchandise. This rule recognizes that the traditional rule in regard to necessaries has been extended so far as to hold an infant bound by his contracts, where he failed to restore what he has received under them to the extent of the benefit actually derived by him from what he has received from the other party to the transaction.

The other minority rule holds that the minor's recovery of the full purchase price is subject to a deduction for the minor's "use" of the consideration he or she received under the contract, or for the "depreciation" or "deterioration" of the consideration in his or her possession. See Carter v. Jays Motors, 3 N.J.Super. 82, 65 A.2d 628 (N.J.S.Ct., App.Div. 1949); Creer v. Active Automobile Exch., 99 Conn. 266, 121 A. 888 (Conn.1923); Rodriguez v. Northern Auto Auction, 225 N.Y.S.2d 107 (N.Y.App.Div.1962); Pettit v. Liston, 97 Or. 464, 191 P. 660 (1920).

We are impressed by the statement made by the Arizona Appeals Court in Valencia v. White, supra, citing the Court of Appeals of Ohio in Haydocy Pontiac, Inc. v. Lee, 19 Ohio App.2d 217, 250 N.E.2d 898 (1969):

> At a time when we see young persons between 18 and 21 years of age demanding and assuming more responsibilities in their daily lives; when we see such persons emancipated, married, and raising families; when we see such persons charged with the responsibility for committing crimes; when we see such persons being sued in tort claims for acts of negligence; when we see such persons subject to military service; when we see such persons engaged in business and acting in almost all other respects as an adult, it seems timely to re-examine the case law pertaining to contractual rights and responsibilities of infants to see if the law as pronounced and applied by the courts should be redefined.

In Pettit v. Liston, supra, the Oregon court, endeavoring to resolve issues similar to those at hand in this case noted that in dealing with the right of the minor to rescind his contract and the conditions under which he may do so, the decisions of the courts in the different states have not only conflicted upon the main question involved, but many of the decisions of the same court in the same state seem to be inconsistent with each other; and often times one court has made its decision turn upon a distinction or difference not recognized by the courts of other states as a distinguishing feature. As a result rules have been promulgated which are considered to be suitable and appropriate upon considerations of principal and public policy.

Upon serious reflection we are convinced that a modified form of the Oregon rule should be adopted in this State concerning the rights and responsibilities of minors in their business dealings.

. . .

We state the rule to be followed hereafter, in reference to a contract of a minor, to be where the minor has not been overreached in any way, and there has been no undue influence, and the contract is a fair and reasonable one, and the minor has actually paid money on the purchase price, and taken and used the article purchased, that he ought not to be permitted to recover the amount actually paid, without allowing the vender of the goods reasonable compensation for the use of, depreciation, and willful or negligent damage to the article purchased, while in his hands. If there has been any fraud or imposition on the part of the seller or if the contract is unfair, or any unfair advantage has been taken of the minor inducing him to make the purchase, then the rule does not apply. Whether there has been such an overreaching on the part of the seller, and the fair market value of the property returned, would always, in any case, be a question for the trier of fact. This rule will fully and fairly protect the minor against injustice or imposition, and at the same time it will be fair to a business person who has dealt with such minor in good faith.

This rule is best adapted to modern conditions under which minors are permitted to, and do in fact, transact a great deal of business for themselves, long before they have reached the age of legal majority. Many young people work and earn money and collect it and spend it oftentimes without any oversight or restriction. The law does not question their right to buy if they have the money to pay for their purchases. It seems intolerably burdensome for everyone concerned if merchants and business people cannot deal with them safely, in a fair and reasonable way. Further, it does not appear consistent with practice of proper moral influence upon young people, tend to encourage honesty and integrity, or lead them to a good and useful business future, if they are taught that they can make purchases with their own money, for their own benefit, and after paying for them, and using them until they are worn out and destroyed, go back and compel the vendor to return to them what they have paid upon the purchase price. Such a doctrine can only lead to the corruption of principles and encourage young people in habits of trickery and dishonesty.

In view of the foregoing considerations, we conclude that the rule, as we have indicated, and which we have paraphrased from that adopted in the State of Oregon, will henceforth be the rule to be utilized in this State.

We note that in this case, some nine months after the date of purchase, the truck purchased by the plaintiff began to develop mechanical problems. Plaintiff was informed of the probable nature of the difficulty which apparently involved internal problems in the engine. He continued to drive the vehicle until the engine "blew up" and the truck became inoperable. Whether or not this involved gross negligence or intentional conduct on his part is a matter for determination at the trial level. It is not possible to determine from this record whether a counterclaim for tortious damage to the vehicle was asserted. After the first tender of the vehicle was made by plaintiff, and refused by the defendant, the truck was damaged by a hit-and-run driver while parked on plaintiff's property. The amount of that damage and the liability for that amount between the purchaser and the vendor, as well as the fair market value of the vehicle at the time of tender, is also an issue for the trier of fact.

The case is remanded to the trial court for further proceedings in accordance with this judgment. The costs on appellate review are assessed equally between the parties.

DODSON AND THE INFANCY DOCTRINE

(1) **The Infancy Doctrine and the Improvidence of Youth.** The infancy doctrine, with deep roots in English common law, has remained remarkably unchanged over the centuries. *Dodson* is representative of a modest reform trend. Under the traditional (and still majority) rule, minors are free to disaffirm most contracts, at their option. Upon recision, the minor must return consideration in his possession, but is not obliged to compensate the other contracting party if he has used or damaged what he received.

The purpose of the doctrine is to protect minors who execute contracts with adults. A classic description is offered by the Wisconsin Supreme Court in *Kiefer v. Fred Howe Motors*, 39 Wis.2d 20, 158 N.W.2d 288 (1968):

> The underpinnings of the general rule allowing the minor to disaffirm his contracts were undoubtedly the protection of the minor. It was thought that the minor was immature in both mind and experience and that therefore he should be protected from his own bad judgments as well as from adults who would take advantage of him.

How might minors' immaturity lead them to make improvident contracts? What characteristics of youthful choice are implicated? Developmental psychology research suggests that adolescents tend to focus more on short-term (and less on long-term) consequences than do adults. A young person might be more tempted to purchase a coveted item that she cannot afford, perhaps because she is considering the immediate pleasure of possessing the item, rather than the burden of the debt incurred, which will be paid off over time. Perhaps it is not surprising that many modern cases deal with contracts for motor vehicles or stereo equipment.

(2) **Voidability by the Minor.** Under infancy doctrine, contracts with a minor are not void, but voidable at the option of the minor. Thus, the infancy doctrine, on its face, does not restrict the freedom of minors to contract. The Court in *Dodson* (citing *Tuck v. Payne*, an earlier Tennessee opinion) explains how minors in theory should always benefit from the rule: they can enforce contracts they like and be relieved of obligation under those that they conclude are not to their advantage. In practice, do you see why the infancy doctrine might limit the ability of minors to contract or make contracting more costly? Will merchants view the prospect of contracting with minors as a more risky undertaking than contracting with adults? Might they insure against this risk by charging minors a premium?

(3) **The "Necessaries" Doctrine.** Contracts for "necessaries" constitute a well established exception to the right of minors to disaffirm their contracts. For

example, contracts for food, clothing, rent, and medical treatment are enforceable against minors. What explains this exception? Minors may be less likely to enter contracts for necessaries improvidently, and overreaching or undue influence may be less of a risk in this context. Perhaps the exception also recognizes that minors' right to disaffirm contracts can constitute a disability for the minor. One desirable effect of the exception is that reluctance about entering contracts for necessaries will be reduced, allowing minors to obtain food, medical treatment etc.

The necessaries doctrine only imposes liability on a minor who either expressly or impliedly assumes the contractual obligation. In this regard, consider the case of the unmarried teenager living with her parents who is admitted to a hospital on an emergency basis to deliver a baby. Is she liable to the hospital for payment? Are her parents liable?

(4) **Entertainment Industry Contracts.** By statute, some states (notably New York and California) provide a mechanism for making contracts by youthful performers enforceable against the minor. The statutes require court approval of the contract and the establishment of a trust to protect the minor's earnings. A recent note criticized these laws as providing inadequate protection for minors. Erika Munro, Underage, Under Contract and Under Protected: An Overview of the Administration and Regulation of Contracts with Minors in the Entertainment Industry in New York and California, 20 Colum.J.L. & Arts 553 (1996).

MINORS' TORT LIABILITY: A DIFFERENT RESPONSE

Minors are liable for their torts at common law. The Restatement of Torts provides a modern statement of the standard of minors' liability.

RESTATEMENT (SECOND) OF TORTS (1977)*

§ 283.A.   Children

If the actor is a child, the standard of conduct to which he must conform to avoid being negligent is that of a reasonable person of like age, intelligence, and experience under like circumstances.

Comment

   a.   *Children.* A child is a person of such immature years as to be incapable of exercising the judgment, intelligence, knowledge, experience, and prudence demanded by the standard of the reasonable man applicable to adults. The rule stated in this Section is commonly applied to children of tender years. In practice, it has seldom been applied to anyone over the age of sixteen, although situations may possibly arise where the rule might be applicable to persons above that age, and no definite line can be drawn....

   Most of the cases which have applied the rule stated in this Section have involved the contributory negligence of children, where the reason for special protection of them is readily apparent; but the rule is equally applicable to child defendants.

   b.   *Special standard for children.* The special standard to be applied in the case of children arises out of the public interest in their welfare and protection, together with the fact that there is a wide basis of community experience upon which it is possible, as a practical matter, to determine what is to be expected of them.

A child of tender years is not required to conform to the standard of behavior which it is reasonable to expect of an adult. His conduct is to be judged by the standard of behavior to be expected of a child of like age, intelligence, and experience. A child may be so young as to be manifestly and utterly incapable of exercising any of those qualities of attention, perception, knowledge, experience, intelligence, and judgment which are necessary to enable him to perceive a risk and to realize its unreasonable character. On the other hand, it is obvious that a minor who has not yet attained his majority may be quite as capable as an adult of exercising such qualities. Some courts have endeavored to lay down fixed rules as to a minimum age below which the child is incapable of being negligent, and a maximum age above which he is to be treated like an adult. Usually these rules have been derived from the old rules of the criminal law, by which a child under the age of seven was considered incapable of crime, and one over fourteen was considered to be as capable as an adult. The prevailing view is that in tort cases no such arbitrary limits can be fixed. Undoubtedly there is a minimum age, probably somewhere in the vicinity of four years, below which negligence can never be found; but with the great variation in the capacities of children and the situations which may arise, it cannot be fixed definitely for all cases.

Between the two extremes there are children whose capacities are infinitely various. The standard of conduct required of the child is that which it is reasonable to expect of children of like age, intelligence, and experience. "Intelligence" includes other mental capacities, but does not include judgment, which is an exercise of capacity rather than the capacity itself. The fact that the child is mentally retarded, or that he is unusually bright for his years, is to be taken into account; but once such account is taken, the child is still required to exercise the judgment of a reasonable person of that intelligence. Likewise to be taken into account are the circumstances under which the child has lived, and his experience in encountering particular hazards, or the education he has received concerning them. If the child is of sufficient age, intelligence, and experience to understand the risks of a given situation, he is required to exercise such prudence in protecting himself, and such caution for the safety of others, as is common to children similarly qualified.

It is impossible to lay down definite rules as to whether any child, or any class of children, should be able to appreciate and cope with the dangers of many situations. A child of ten may in one situation have sufficient capacity to appreciate the risk involved in his conduct, and to realize its unreasonable character, but in another situation he may lack the necessary mental capacity or experience to do so; and in the case of another child of ten of different mental capacity or experience a different conclusion may be reached in the same situation.

    c. Child engaging in adult activity. An exception to the rule stated in this Section may arise where the child engages in an activity which is normally undertaken only by adults, and for which adult qualifications are required. As in the case of one entering upon a professional activity which requires special skill (see § 299A), he may be held to the standard of adult skill, knowledge, and competence, and no allowance may be made for his immaturity. Thus, for example, if a boy of fourteen were to attempt to fly an airplane, his age and inexperience would not excuse him from liability for flying it in a negligent manner. The same may be true where the child drives an automobile. In this connection licensing statutes, and the examinations given to drivers, may be important in determining the qualifications required; but even if the child succeeds in obtaining a license he may thereafter be required to meet the standard established primarily for adults.

NOTE

At common law, parents were not liable for the torts of their children. In effect, this meant that recovery by victims of children's tortious acts usually was not possible. By statute, virtually all states impose tort liability on parents for the wilful and wanton acts of their children, usually specifying a ceiling limiting the extent of liability.

2.   RESTRICTION ON FREE MOBILITY: CURFEWS

Schleifer v. City of Charlottesville

United States Court of Appeals, 4th Circuit, 1998.
159 F.3d 843.

■ WILKINSON, CHIEF JUDGE:

This appeal involves a challenge to the constitutionality of a juvenile nocturnal curfew ordinance enacted by the City of Charlottesville. The district court held that the ordinance did not violate the constitutional rights of minors, their parents, or other affected parties and declined to enjoin its enforcement. We agree that the ordinance is constitutional and affirm the judgment of the district court.

I.

On December 16, 1996, the Charlottesville City Council, after several months of study and deliberation, amended Section 17–7 of the City Code to enact a new juvenile nocturnal curfew ordinance....

Effective March 1, 1997, the ordinance generally prohibits minors, defined as unemancipated persons under seventeen, from remaining in any public place, motor vehicle, or establishment within city limits during curfew hours. The curfew takes effect at 12:01 a.m. on Monday through Friday, at 1:00 a.m. on Saturday and Sunday, and lifts at 5:00 a.m. each morning.

The ordinance does not restrict minors' activities that fall under one of its eight enumerated exceptions. Minors may participate in any activity during curfew hours if they are accompanied by a parent; they may run errands at a parent's direction provided that they possess a signed note. The ordinance allows minors to undertake employment, or attend supervised activities sponsored by school, civic, religious, or other public organizations. The ordinance exempts minors who are engaged in interstate travel, are on the sidewalk abutting their parents' residence, or are involved in an emergency. Finally, the ordinance does not affect minors who are "exercising First Amendment rights protected by the United States Constitution, such as the free exercise of religion, freedom of speech and the right of assembly." *Id.* § 17–7(b)(8).

The ordinance sets forth a scheme of warnings and penalties for minors who violate it. For a first violation, a minor receives a verbal warning, followed by a written warning to the minor and the minor's parents. For subsequent violations, the minor is charged with a Class 4 misdemeanor. The ordinance also makes it unlawful for certain other individuals, including parents, knowingly to encourage a minor to violate the ordinance. The full text of the ordinance is included as an appendix to the opinion.

Plaintiffs are five minors under age seventeen who are subject to the ordinance, one eighteen-year-old, and two parents of minor children. The minors allege that, with their parents' permission, they occasionally wish to engage in lawful activities which the curfew will not permit.

These activities include attending late movies; getting a "bite to eat"; playing in a band; socializing with older siblings; and attending concerts in Richmond, which would bring them back through Charlottesville during curfew hours. The eighteen-year-old plaintiff alleges that he has been deprived of opportunities to associate with his younger friends by the ordinance. The parent plaintiffs allege that the ordinance interferes with their decisions on which activities, at what times, are appropriate for their children.

Plaintiffs brought this action for declaratory and injunctive relief, alleging that the ordinance violates their rights under the First, Fourth, Fifth and Fourteenth Amendments. At trial, plaintiffs dismissed their Fourth Amendment claims. Following trial, by order dated May 20, 1997, the district court rejected plaintiffs' remaining claims and denied their motion for a permanent injunction. Plaintiffs now appeal.

II.

Initially we must consider the level of scrutiny appropriate to this case. Plaintiffs contend that the ordinance infringes minors' constitutional liberties and therefore should be subject to strict scrutiny. It is true that "[a] child, merely on account of his minority, is not beyond the protection of the Constitution." *Bellotti v. Baird,* 443 U.S. 622, 633, 99 S.Ct. 3035, 61 L.Ed.2d 797 (1979) (plurality opinion) (*Bellotti II*).... At the same time, the Supreme Court has made abundantly clear that children's rights are not coextensive with those of adults [Citations omitted]....

In light of the case law, two things seem clear. First, children do possess at least qualified rights, so an ordinance which restricts their liberty to the extent that this one does should be subject to more than rational basis review. Second, because children do not possess the same rights as adults, the ordinance should be subject to less than the strictest level of scrutiny. *See Carey v. Population Servs. Int'l,* 431 U.S. 678, 693 n.

15, 97 S.Ct. 2010, 52 L.Ed.2d 675 (1977) (plurality opinion) (when minors are involved the level of scrutiny "is apparently less rigorous than the 'compelling state interest' test applied to restrictions on the privacy rights of adults") ... We thus believe intermediate scrutiny to be the most appropriate level of review and must determine whether the ordinance is "substantially related" to "important" governmental interests. [Citations omitted]. We also conclude, however, that the ordinance survives constitutional attack under either a substantial or a compelling state interest standard. The narrow means chosen by the City in the ordinance serve strong and indeed compelling public needs.

III.

A.

The text of the Charlottesville curfew ordinance identifies three legislative purposes: (1) to reduce juvenile violence and crime within the city; (2) to protect juveniles themselves from being swept up in unlawful drug activities and from becoming prey to older perpetrators of crime; and (3) to strengthen parental responsibility for children. These enumerated purposes represent important and compelling governmental interests. . . .

The City contends that its curfew ordinance was passed to combat the marked growth in the rate of juvenile crime both nationwide and within Virginia. . . . [T]he City produced evidence of a twenty-five percent increase in the delinquency caseload of Charlottesville's Juvenile and Domestic Relations Court between 1991 and 1996. Given the projected increase in the nation's juvenile population between 1995 and 2005, the problem of juvenile crime was unlikely to abate.

In addition, the City has documented two troubling features of the juvenile crime phenomenon. First, the City's evidence on nationwide trends indicated a high rate of recidivism among juveniles and a correlation between juvenile delinquency and adult criminal activity. Thus reducing juvenile crime was a pressing first step in reducing the overall impact of crime on the community. Second, Charlottesville's City Council was concerned about the marked increase in the violence associated with juvenile crime. . . . In light of this evidence, Charlottesville's first stated purpose is undeniably compelling.

Likewise, the City's strong interest in fostering the welfare of children and protecting the youngest members of society from harm is well-established. . . . Courts have recognized "the peculiar vulnerability of children," *Bellotti II*, 443 U.S. at 634, and the Supreme Court long ago observed that "streets afford dangers for [children] not affecting adults." *Prince*, 321 U.S. at 169, 64 S.Ct. 438. Those dangers have not disappeared; they simply have assumed a different and more insidious form today. Each unsuspecting child risks becoming another victim of the assaults, violent crimes, and drug wars that plague America's cities. Given the realities of urban life, it is not surprising that courts have acknowledged the special vulnerability of children to the dangers of the streets. [Citations omitted.] Charlottesville, unfortunately, has not escaped these troubling realities. Two experienced City police officers confirmed to the district court that the children they observe on the streets after midnight are at special risk of harm.

Charlottesville's third purpose—strengthening parental responsibility for children—is also a significant interest. The City shares with parents and guardians a responsibility to protect children. [Citations omitted.] State authority complements parental supervision, and "the guiding role of parents in the upbringing of their children justifies limitations on the freedoms of minors." *Bellotti II,* 443 U.S. at 637, 99 S.Ct. 3035.... Therefore, like the City's two preceding interests in reducing the incidence of juvenile crime and juvenile victimization, the City's third aim constitutes an important governmental purpose.

B.

Conceding for the sake of argument that the curfew's stated ends are sufficiently compelling, plaintiffs train their attack on the means by which the ordinance seeks to achieve its goals....

Charlottesville was constitutionally justified in believing that its curfew would materially assist its first stated interest—that of reducing juvenile violence and crime. The City Council acted on the basis of information from many sources, including records from Charlottesville's police department, a survey of public opinion, news reports, data from the United States Department of Justice, national crime reports, and police reports from other localities. On the basis of such evidence, elected bodies are entitled to conclude that keeping unsupervised juveniles off the streets late at night will make for a safer community. The same streets may have a more volatile and less wholesome character at night than during the day. Alone on the streets at night children face a series of dangerous and potentially life-shaping decisions. Drug dealers may lure them to use narcotics or aid in their sale. Gangs may pressure them into membership or participation in violence. "[D]uring the formative years of childhood and adolescence, minors often lack the experience, perspective, and judgment to recognize and avoid choices that could be detrimental to them." *Bellotti II,* 443 U.S. at 635, 99 S.Ct. 3035. Those who succumb to these criminal influences at an early age may persist in their criminal conduct as adults. Whether we as judges subscribe to these theories is beside the point. Those elected officials with their finger on the pulse of their home community clearly did. In attempting to reduce through its curfew the opportunities for children to come into contact with criminal influences, the City was directly advancing its first objective of reducing juvenile violence and crime.

Plaintiffs contend that the exclusion of seventeen-year-olds from the curfew is a fatal flaw in the ordinance. They argue that this group is responsible for one-third of all crimes committed by juveniles nationwide and that excluding seventeen-year-olds from the curfew thus renders the ordinance impermissibly underinclusive. However, the City's evidence documents a serious problem of crime among younger juveniles. In Charlottesville in 1995 eighty percent of juvenile arrests for the most serious crimes were of children aged ten to sixteen, and in 1996 eighty-five percent of such crimes were committed by this group. Furthermore, the City's decision to exclude seventeen-year-olds from coverage under the curfew is a legislative judgment that we are loath to second-guess.... In exercising its legislative judgment, the City was forced to balance the law enforcement benefit of subjecting seventeen-year-olds to the curfew against the greater law enforcement burden of doing so. Weighing benefits and burdens is what legislatures are about.

Plaintiffs also dispute the effectiveness of the curfew in reducing juvenile crime. They say that the real problem of juvenile crime is not at night, but in the after school hours. Plaintiffs make much of a report entitled *Juvenile Offenders and Victims: 1996 Update on Violence,* Office of Juvenile Justice and Delinquency Prevention, U.S. Dep't of Justice 27 (1996), which asserts that only seventeen percent of violent juvenile crime occurs during typical curfew hours, while twenty-two percent happens between 2:00 p.m. and 6:00 p.m. on school days. The City responds that the lower rate of late-night crime may reflect the fact that several of the South Carolina cities in the study actually had late-night curfews in effect. And with respect to conditions in Charlottesville before the curfew, City police officers and Charlottesville's Commonwealth's Attorney confirmed that the most serious crimes committed by juveniles occurred during curfew hours. Further, the City Council considered evidence that juvenile offenses occurring in Charlottesville between 11:00 p.m. and 6:00 a.m. increased by thirty-eight percent during 1995 and a further ten percent during 1996. Thus the City had reason to believe that, in both volume and severity, nighttime juvenile crime was a serious, growing problem in Charlottesville.

Charlottesville's City Council concluded that a nighttime curfew might help curb this rising trend of juvenile crime. In making this decision, the City relied on the experience of cities like Lexington, Kentucky, where eight months of enforcing a nighttime juvenile curfew effected an almost ten percent decrease in juvenile arrests for the serious crimes of homicide, assault, robbery, rape, burglary, larceny, auto theft and arson. And the district court heard testimony that a curfew has the greatest chance of reducing juvenile crime in a smaller city like Charlottesville, where juvenile crime, though a serious problem, has not yet become totally uncontrollable. Fundamentally, however, this dispute about the desirability or ultimate efficacy of a curfew is a political debate, not a judicial one.... [L]ocal legislative bodies are entitled to draw their conclusions in light of experience with a curfew's operation, and not have their efforts at reducing juvenile violence shut down by a court before they even have a chance to make a difference.

Plaintiffs also dispute that the curfew will contribute much, if anything, to protecting juveniles from crime, the City's second objective. They ... [contend] that the majority of crimes committed against children are committed by family members or acquaintances rather than by strangers on the street. The fact that children may be at risk at home or during the day.... does nothing to undermine the City's evidence that children remain at risk of crime in the street—in fact, the City points out that in 1991 thirty-three percent of the violent crimes reported by juvenile victims nationwide occurred on the street. *Juvenile Offenders & Victims: A National Report,* Office of Juvenile Justice and Delinquency Prevention, U.S. Dep't of Justice 22 (1995). The Constitution certainly does not put legislatures to the choice of solving the entirety of a social problem or no part of it at all.

Further, the evidence presented by the City identified several special
dangers of the nighttime hours: a vigorous street-level drug trade that
flourishes during the late evening and early morning hours and that
routinely uses children to facilitate drug transactions, thereby exposing
them to a high degree of danger; the difficulties of apprehending perpetrators of crime at night, as criminal activity is less visible and less subject to
monitoring by concerned neighbors and passers-by; and the increased
degree of violence and seriousness of the crimes that are committed at
night. The record documents that in Charlottesville in 1996 aggravated
assaults were almost one and one-half times as likely to occur during
curfew hours as non-curfew hours, robberies more than twice as likely to
occur at these times, forcible rapes more than three times as likely during
curfew hours.... By keeping children off the streets a few hours each
night, the curfew reduces the exposure of children to these well-known, and
well-documented harms.

Finally, plaintiffs dispute the City's claim that the curfew will support
the parental role in child-rearing, its third stated goal. They focus exclusively on the testimony of the parent plaintiffs, who clearly do not appreciate the curfew and do not welcome it as an enhancement of their authority.
The City was entitled to believe, however, that a nocturnal curfew would
promote parental involvement in a child's upbringing. A curfew aids the
efforts of parents who desire to protect their children from the perils of the
street but are unable to control the nocturnal behavior of those children.
And a curfew encourages parents who ignore their children's nighttime
activities to take a more active role in their children's lives. Finally, the
curfew assists the efforts of parents who prefer their children to spend time
on their studies rather than on the streets.... [T]he City Council acted on
the basis of surveys and testimony at public hearings reflecting widespread
approval of the curfew and the support it offers to parents' efforts to
discipline their children.

C.

The Charlottesville curfew is not only "substantially related" to its
stated purposes. The limited scope of the curfew and its numerous exceptions would satisfy even the strict scrutiny requirement of narrow tailoring.

[The court then distinguishes the Charlottesville ordinance from a
broader San Diego ordinance, which was struck down by the 9th Circuit
Court of Appeals.(see note following opinion). Instead, the court finds the
Charlottesville ordinance to mirror the narrower Dallas, Texas, ordinance
found to satisfy strict scrutiny by the 5th Circuit Court of Appeals in *Qutb
v. Strauss*, 11 F.3d 488 (5th Cir.1993). Like the Dallas ordinance, the
Charlottesville ordinance includes numerous exceptions, including one for
First Amendment activities.]

IV.

We next address plaintiffs' claims that the Charlottesville ordinance
violates the constitutional rights of parents.... The ordinance interferes
with this right, [plaintiffs] conclude, by prohibiting children's activities that

have the parents' full approval but do not fall under one of the ordinance's eight exceptions.

... The Supreme Court has rejected the view that parents possess an unqualified right to raise children that trumps any government regulation of their children's conduct. In *Prince,* the Court recognized "that the state has a wide range of power for limiting parental freedom and authority in things affecting the child's welfare." 321 U.S. at 167, 64 S.Ct. 438. Furthermore, were we to accept plaintiffs' argument, future litigants could simply artfully plead violations of parental rights to avoid the Supreme Court's determination that children do not possess all the freedoms of adults....

We are mindful that the Supreme Court has suggested in other contexts that parents may possess a fundamental right against undue, adverse interference by the state. [citing *Yoder* and Meyer] We do not believe, however, that cases involving a parent's custodial rights or authority to direct a child's education support plaintiffs' claim. The Charlottesville ordinance, prohibiting young children from remaining unaccompanied on the streets late at night, simply does not implicate the kinds of intimate family decisions considered in the above cases.

Finally, several of the exceptions to the Charlottesville curfew do accommodate the rights of parents These include the exception for minors accompanied by a parent and the exception for minors running an errand at the direction of a parent.... The limited curtailment of juvenile liberty in the ordinance violates neither a minor's nor a parent's rights.

V.

[Finally, the court rejected the plaintiff's claim that the ordinance's exception for exercise of 1st Amendment rights was unconstitutionally vague, because it gave "standardless discretion to law enforcement officers to decide whether or not the exception applies."]

.... Plaintiffs basically attempt to place city councils between a rock and a hard place. If councils draft an ordinance with exceptions, those exceptions are subject to a vagueness challenge. If they neglect to provide exceptions, then the ordinance is attacked for not adequately protecting First Amendment freedoms. It hardly seems fitting, however, for courts to chastise elected bodies for protecting expressive activity. The Charlottesville ordinance is constitutionally stronger with that protection than without....

Plaintiffs' vagueness claims threaten to make the drafting of a curfew ordinance an impossible task. The practical exceptions to the City's curfew shall not provide the cause of its demise.

The Charlottesville curfew serves not only to head off crimes before they occur, but also to protect a particularly vulnerable population from being lured into participating in such activity.... [W]e do not hold that every such curfew ordinance would pass constitutional muster. The means adopted by a municipality must bear a substantial relationship to significant governmental interests; the restrictiveness of those means remains the subject of judicial review. As the district court noted, however, the curfew law in Charlottesville is "among the most modest and lenient of the myriad curfew laws implemented nationwide." Charlottesville's curfew, compared to those in other cities, is indeed a mild regulation: it covers a limited age group during only a few hours of the night. Its various exceptions enable minors to participate in necessary or worthwhile activities during this time. We hold that Charlottesville's juvenile curfew ordinance comfortably satisfies constitutional standards.

APPENDIX

1. Section 17–7 of the Code of the City of Charlottesville, 1990, as amended, is hereby amended and reordained, as follows:

The purpose of this section is to: (*i*) promote the general welfare and protect the general public through the reduction of juvenile violence and crime within the City; (*ii*) promote the safety and well-being of the City's youngest citizens, persons under the age of seventeen (17), whose inexperience renders them particularly vulnerable to becoming participants in unlawful activities, particularly unlawful drug activities, and to being victimized by older perpetrators of crime; and (*iii*) foster and strengthen parental responsibility for children.

(a) Definitions.

As used within this section 17–7, the following words and phrases shall have the meanings ascribed to them below:

"Curfew hours" refers to the hours of 12:01 a.m. through 5:00 a.m. on Monday through Friday, and 1:00 a.m. through 5:00 a.m. on Saturday and Sunday.

"Emergency" refers to unforeseen circumstances, or the status or condition resulting therefrom, requiring immediate action to safeguard life, limb or property. The term includes, but is not limited to, fires, natural disasters, automobile accidents, or other similar circumstances.

"Establishment" refers to any privately-owned place of business within the City operated for a profit, to which the public is invited, including, but not limited to any place of amusement or entertainment. With respect to such Establishment, the term "Operator" shall mean any person, and any firm, association, partnership (and the members or partners thereof) and/or any corporation (and the officers thereof) conducting or managing that Establishment.

"Minor" refers to any person under seventeen (17) years of age who has not been emancipated by court order entered pursuant to Section 16.1–333 of the Code of Virginia, 1950, as amended.

"Officer" refers to a police or other law enforcement officer charged with the duty of enforcing the laws of the Commonwealth of Virginia and/or the ordinances of the City of Charlottesville.

"Parent" refers to:

(1) a person who is a minor's biological or adoptive parent and who has legal custody of a minor (including either parent, if custody is shared under a court order or agreement);

(2) a person who is the biological or adoptive parent with whom a minor regularly resides;

(3) a person judicially appointed as a legal guardian of the minor; and/or

(4) a person eighteen (18) years of age or older standing *in loco parentis*....

"Public Place" refers to any place to which the public or a substantial group of the public has access, including, but not limited to: streets, highways, roads, sidewalks, alleys, avenues, parks, and/or the common areas of schools, hospitals, apartment houses, office buildings, transportation facilities and shops.

"Remain" refers to the following actions:

(1) to linger or stay at or upon a place; and/or

(2) to fail to leave a place when requested to do so by an officer or by the owner, operator or other person in control of that place....

"Temporary care facility" refers to a non-locked, non-restrictive shelter at which minors may wait, under visual supervision, to be retrieved by a parent. No minors waiting in such facility shall be handcuffed and/or secured (by handcuffs or otherwise) to any stationary object.

(b) It shall be unlawful for a minor, during curfew hours, to remain in or upon any Public Place within the City, to remain in any motor vehicle operating or parked therein or thereon, or to remain in or upon the premises of any Establishment within the City, unless:

(1) the minor is accompanied by a parent; or

(2) the minor is involved in an emergency; or

(3) the minor is engaged in an employment activity, or is going to or returning home from such activity, without detour or stop; or

(4) the minor is on the sidewalk directly abutting a place where he or she resides with a parent; or

(5) the minor is attending an activity sponsored by a school, religious, or civic organization, by a public organization or agency, or by another similar organization or entity, which activity is supervised by adults, and/or the minor is going to or returning from such an activity without detour or stop; or

(6) the minor is on an errand at the direction of a parent, and the minor has in his or her possession a writing signed by the parent containing the following information: the name, signature, address and telephone number of the parent authorizing the errand, the telephone number where the parent may be reached during the errand, the name of the minor, and a brief description of the errand, the minor's destination(s) and the hours the minor is authorized to be engaged in the errand; or

(7) the minor is involved in interstate travel through, or beginning or terminating in, the City of Charlottesville; or

(8) the minor is exercising First Amendment rights protected by the United States Constitution, such as the free exercise of religion, freedom of speech and the right of assembly.

(c) It shall be unlawful for a minor's parent to knowingly permit, allow or encourage such minor to violate 17–7(b).

(d) It shall be unlawful for a person who is the owner or operator of any motor vehicle to knowingly permit, allow or encourage a violation of 17–7(b).

(e) It shall be unlawful for the Operator of any Establishment, or for any person who is an employee thereof, to knowingly permit, allow or encourage a minor to remain upon the premises of the Establishment during curfew hours. It shall be a defense to prosecution under this subsection that the Operator or employee of an Establishment promptly notified the police department that a minor was present at the Establishment after curfew hours and refused to leave. . . .

(g) Enforcement.

(1) Minors. Before taking any enforcement action hereunder, an officer shall make an immediate investigation for the purpose of ascertaining whether or not the presence of a minor in a public place, motor vehicle and/or Establishment within the City during Curfew hours is in violation of 17–7(b).

(A) If such investigation reveals that the presence of such minor is in violation of 17–7(b), then:

(1) if the minor has not previously been issued a warning for any such violation, then the officer shall issue a verbal warning to the minor, which shall be followed by a written warning mailed by the police department to the minor and his or her parent(s), or

(2) if the minor has previously been issued a warning for any such violation, then the officer shall charge the minor with a violation of this ordinance and shall issue a summons requiring the minor to appear in court (*Ref. Va.Code § 16.1–260(H)(1)*). And

(B) As soon as practicable, the officer shall:

(1) release the minor to his or her parent(s); or

(2) place the minor in a temporary care facility for a period not to exceed the remainder of the curfew hours, so that his or her parent(s) may retrieve the minor; or

(3) if a minor refuses to give an officer his or her name and address, refuses to give the name and address of his or her parent(s), or if no parent can be located prior to the end of the applicable curfew hours, or if located, no parent appears to accept custody of the minor, the minor may be taken to a nonsecure crisis center or juvenile shelter and/or may be taken to a judge or intake officer of the juvenile court to be dealt with in the manner and pursuant to such procedures as required by law. (*Ref. Va.Code § 16.1–260(H)(1); § 16.1–278.6; §§ 16.1–241(A)(1)*).

(2) Others. If an investigation by an officer reveals that a person has violated 17–7(c), (d) and/or (e), and if the person has not previously been issued a warning with respect to any such violation, an officer shall issue a verbal warning to the person, which shall be followed by a written warning mailed by the police department to the person. . . .

(h) Each violation of this section 17–7 shall constitute a Class 4 Misdemeanor.

CURFEWS AND RELATED RESTRICTIONS

(1) **Judicial Responses to Curfew Ordinances.** Nocturnal juvenile curfew laws (which are usually city ordinances) are not a new phenomenon. However, many municipalities have enacted curfews in recent years, mostly in response to public outcry over juvenile crime. Curfew laws have always been controversial; they have been challenged as unconstitutional on vagueness grounds, on equal protection grounds and as excessive restrictions of minors' fundamental rights. They also have been challenged as infringements on parental autonomy. These ordinances have met with a mixed judicial response. Some courts have viewed these restrictions on the freedom of minors more skeptically than the Fifth Circuit Court of Appeals in *Qutb*.

As early as 1898 such an ordinance was held unconstitutional by the Texas Court of Criminal Appeals in *Ex parte McCarver*, 39 Tex.Cr.R. 448, 46 S.W. 936 (1898). The court said:

> The rule laid down here is as rigid as under military law, and makes the tolling of the curfew bell equivalent to the drum taps of the camp. In our opinion, it is an undue invasion of the personal liberty of the citizen, as the boy or girl (for it applies equally to both) have the same rights of ingress and egress that citizens of mature years enjoy. We regard this character of legislation as an attempt to usurp the parental functions, and as unreasonable, and we therefore hold the ordinance in question as illegal and void. Id. at 937.

A more modern Honolulu ordinance prohibiting any person under 18 from loitering about public streets, parks or other places between 10 p.m. and sunrise was invalidated by the Supreme Court of Hawaii in 1973 because it was "so vague and overbroad as to violate due process standards." *In re Doe*, 54 Hawaii 647, 513 P.2d 1385, 1388 (1973). Loitering ordinances that applied to adults were routinely struck down on vagueness grounds. The Hawaii court stated that the United States Supreme Court opinion of *In re Gault* (see page 862), which extended due process protections to juveniles in delinquency proceedings, "greatly circumscribes distinctions between adults and juveniles in terms of constitutional protections."

Other modern ordinances have been found to be constitutionally deficient. A San Diego ordinance was struck down by the 9th Circuit Court of Appeals. *Nunez v. San Diego*, 114 F.3d 935 (9th Cir.1997). Applying a strict scrutiny standard, the court found that the exceptions to the San Diego ordinance were not sufficiently detailed and comprehensive to make the curfew the least restrictive means of serving San Diego's compelling ends. Most importantly, perhaps the ordinance provided no exceptions for attending supervised activities sponsored by school, religious, public, civic or other similar organizations, for undertaking interstate travel, or for engaging in activities protected by the First Amendment. *Nunez,* 114 F.3d at 938–39. The *Schiefer* court compared the Charlottesville ordinance to the San Diego ordinance, noting the more extensive and detailed exceptions in the Charlottesville ordinance, and also pointing out that the San Diego ordinance extended from 10 pm to "daylight immediately following."

Schleifer follows the recent trend in upholding juvenile curfew laws against constitutional challenge. The ordinance enacted by the City of Charlottesville (much of which appears as an Appendix to the opinion) is representative of the modern legislative efforts to design a reasonably narrow curfew rule with many exemptions. See also *Qutb v. City of Dallas*, 11 F.3d 488 (5th Cir.1993).

For general critiques of curfew ordinances, see Katherine Hunt Federle, Children, Curfews, and the Constitution, 73 Wash.U.L.Q. 1315 (1995); Note, Assessing the Scope of Minors' Fundamental Rights: Juvenile Curfews and the Constitution, 97 Harv.L.Rev. 1163 (1984); Note, Curfew Ordinances and the Control of Nocturnal Juvenile Crime, 107 U.Pa.L.Rev. 66 (1958).

(2) **Justifying the Curfew Restriction.** What are the basic justifications for restricting the freedom of minors through a nocturnal curfew? Two purposes emphasized in *Schiefer* are often mentioned—protection of the public from juvenile crime and protection of vulnerable youths from the dangers and temptations of the streets. Politically, the first purpose seems to be the most important. Recent enthusiasm for curfew ordinances reflects in part public alarm at perceived increases in juvenile crime, particularly crime committed by gangs. The City of Charlottesville in *Schiefer* presented evidence that crimes occurred disproportionately during the nighttime hours. Is protection of the public an adequate basis for restricting juveniles, if such restrictions would be unconstitutional if applied to adults? What would be the judicial response if the City of Charlottesville extended its ordinance to adults? Beginning in the mid–1990s, juvenile crime rates began to steadily decline. Does this weaken the rationale for juvenile curfew ordinances?

Curfews often are justified as a means to promote children's welfare. Children who are out at night (who do not qualify for exemption from the ordinance) may be directly and indirectly vulnerable to the risk of harm. Since more crime occurs at night, minors who are out may be harmed by others. Also, they may be tempted to engage in activities that will get them in trouble. The primary threat in this regard may be from the immature judgment of youth that makes minors vulnerable to antisocial peer influence. Minors who commit crimes are subject to punishment, and their future life prospects could be damaged. If parents fail to impose their own curfews to protect their children from these dangers, state intervention to limit youthful freedom may be warranted.

(3) **Parents and Curfew Ordinances.** *Schliefer* also notes that the curfew ordinance was justified as a means to assist parents in their efforts to control their children. The idea seems to be that most parents do not want their children to be out late at night, but that they are unable to impose discipline in the face of peer pressure. Thus, the state, by restricting the child's activity through the curfew, is simply reinforcing parental authority. Does this rationale reduce the burden on the state to justify an intervention that is otherwise vulnerable to constitutional challenge? This rationale is offered in other contexts in which minors are legally restricted from engaging in activities that implicate constitutional rights. In *Ginsberg v. New York*, (page 137) for example, a New York statute restricting minors' access to pornographic materials was upheld in part on the ground that it reinforced parental authority. What about parents like the plaintiffs, who object to the ordinance?

Note that under the Charlottesville curfew ordinance in *Schiefer*, parents of juveniles who violate the curfew ordinance can themselves be liable. Indeed, the court notes that an additional justification is that the sanction will encourage parents who may not care about their children's nocturnal activities to take an interest. We have seen that parents have considerable freedom to rear their children as they see fit. Yet, under curfew ordinances, they not only do not have the authority to permit their children to stay out late at night, but can be held liable if they give such permission. What is the basis for this liability? Are parents negligent per se if their children are out at night in violation of the ordinance? Can parental liability under curfew laws be reconciled with the rationale that the ordinances reinforce parental authority?

(4) **Aladdin's Castle, Inc. v. City of Mesquite, 630 F.2d 1029 (5th Cir. 1980).** This case involved a city ordinance prohibiting certain amusement center operators from allowing children under age 17 to play coin-operated games unless accompanied by a parent or guardian. An amusement center operator challenged the limitation along with the city's licensure provision directing investigation of the license applicant's character and conduct as a law abiding person and considering "connection with criminal elements. . . ." The United States Court of Appeals for the Fifth Circuit upheld a district court finding that the latter restriction (§ 6 of the ordinance) was void for vagueness, and also held that the constitutionality of the age restriction (§ 5) had been improperly sustained. As to § 5, the court first responded with regard to the argument that the ordinance was designed to prevent truancy:

> The decision to bar all people under seventeen years of age, whether or not they are required to be in a school, from all coin-operated amusement centers at all times is patently irrational. See, e.g., Stanley v. Illinois, 405 U.S. at 652–59. Barring young people from using coin-operated amusement devices at times and on days when school is closed simply bears no relation whatever to the city's alleged interest in eliminating truancy. See Eisenstadt v. Baird, 405 U.S. at 447–52 (contrived purpose evidenced by irrationality). The regulation instead evidences the city's disapproval of such centers in general or of Aladdin's owners in particular. See Orr v. Orr, 440 U.S. 268, 280 n. 10 (1979). Such disapproval may justify private action, such as the withholding of patronage, but mere disapproval is not enough constitutionally to justify bringing the full weight of the municipality's regulatory apparatus into play.
>
> By the same token, the regulation denies Aladdin's equal protection of the laws. Just as the "all hours" restriction is grossly overinclusive, the limitation of that restriction to coin-operated amusement centers is equally underinclusive. Before such centers existed, children found places and opportunities for truancy, and they would find places were such centers to become extinct. Singling out coin-operated amusement centers from all other establishments is an act of discrimination, not policy.

Id. at 1039–40.

As to the regulation of minors generally, the court stated:

> We do not doubt that the state may have a legitimate interest in protecting young people from certain unhealthy influences. Yet "a governmental purpose to control or prevent activities constitutionally subject to state regulation may not be achieved by means which sweep unnecessarily broadly and thereby invade the area of protected freedoms." NAACP v. Alabama, 377 U.S. 288, 307 (1964); Sawyer v. Sandstrom, 615 F.2d at 316 (association as one such protected freedom).
>
> Mesquite's interest in shielding young people from undesirable influences may be achieved in other ways. Activities such as gambling with children or selling them drugs can be criminalized and vigorously prosecuted.[17] The ordinance before us, however, sweeps too broadly and cannot be justified under our

---

17. We do not intimate by our holding that Mesquite cannot appropriately restrict minors in connection with establishments which dispense alcoholic beverages or illicit drugs.

Constitution. "[T]he deterrents ordinarily to be applied to prevent crime or education and punishment for violations of the law, not abridgement of the rights of free speech and assembly." Whitney v. California, 274 U.S. 357, 378 (1927) (Brandeis, J., concurring).

The standard that the ordinance must meet is not reduced because minors are involved. "A child, merely on account of his minority, is not beyond the protection of the Constitution." Bellotti v. Baird, 443 U.S. 622, 633 (1979) (Powell, J., joined by Burger, C. J. & Stewart & Rehnquist, JJ.). Minors "are possessed of fundamental rights which the State must respect." Tinker v. Des Moines Independent Community School District, 393 U.S. 503, 511 (1969). "[N]either the Fourteenth Amendment nor the Bill of Rights is for adults alone." In re Gault, 387 U.S. 1, 13 (1967). Accord, Planned Parenthood v. Danforth, 428 U.S. 52, 74 (1976).

In some cases to be sure, the state may have greater power to regulate conduct that is otherwise constitutionally protected if the regulation applies only to children. This "somewhat broader authority to regulate the activities of children than adults," Planned Parenthood v. Danforth, 428 U.S. at 74, is warranted only if a special circumstance of youth creates a unique danger to minors which presents the state with an interest in regulating their activities that does not exist in the case of adults. Ginsberg v. New York, 390 U.S. 629, 638–41 (1968); Prince v. Massachusetts, 321 U.S. 158, 169–70 (1944). Control and restraint by the state, which would otherwise be intolerable under our Constitution, may be justified if the regulation serves a " 'significant state interest . . . that is not present in the case of an adult,' " which arises from the fact of youthful vulnerability to harm. Carey v. Population Services International, 431 U.S. 678, 693 (1977) (citing Planned Parenthood v. Danforth, 428 U.S. at 75).

In Bellotti v. Baird, 443 U.S. at 633–39, Justice Powell set out for himself and three other Justices three reasons which in some circumstances might permit the state to restrain minors in a way which would be unconstitutional if applied to adults:

> the peculiar vulnerability of children; their inability to make critical decisions in an informed, mature manner; and the importance of the parental role in child-rearing.

Id. at 634. These reasons may be viewed as threshold criteria. If Mesquite's ordinance were based on any of them, we would be required to determine the strength of the support provided, its relation to the ordinance as a whole, and the extent, if any, to which it might serve to justify any special restraints on the associational rights of minors. Neither the Supreme Court nor this circuit has set forth the appropriate standards under which such an inquiry would be conducted. We need not undertake to resolve this matter here, since none of Justice Powell's factors even remotely apply to the present ordinance.

There is no issue of special vulnerability presented in this case. Justice Powell limited his discussion of this factor to juvenile criminal proceedings, where the special needs of children have served as a basis for distinguishing certain aspects of procedural due process from adult cases. Compare In re Gault, 387 U.S. 1 (1967) with McKeiver v. Pennsylvania, 403 U.S. 528 (1971). Even extending the vulnerability rationale to its broadest extent, it is impossible to conclude that a coin-operated amusement device presents a physical, mental, or moral threat under which "the State is entitled to adjust its legal system to account for children's vulnerability and their needs for 'concern, . . . sympathy, and . . . paternal attention.' " Bellotti v. Baird, 443 U.S. at 635, citing McKeiver v. Pennsylvania, 403 U.S. at 550 (plurality opinion). That

Mesquite may disapprove of Aladdin's Castle is hardly a sufficient justification for invoking "the peculiar vulnerability of children." Associations "cannot be suppressed solely to protect the young from ideas or images that a legislative body thinks unsuitable for them." Erznoznik v. City of Jacksonville, 422 U.S. 205, 213–14 (1975).

The irrelevance of the "critical decision" rationale is manifest on its face. To suggest that minors be permitted to express their views on divisive public issues, Tinker v. Des Moines Independent School District, and to secure abortions without parental consent, Bellotti v. Baird, Planned Parenthood v. Danforth, but that they can be barred from making the "critical decision" of whether or not to deposit a quarter in a coin-operated amusement device is not a proposition that deserves serious consideration.

As for Justice Powell's third element, the role of parents, clearly this concern militates against the ordinance, not for it. Even if youthfulness is relevant in the case before us, parents, not the state, should decide whether their children are to enter coin-operated amusement centers. The state may not burden parents who decide to allow their children to enter the centers by requiring these parents to accompany their children. If a parent would rather shop or work and decides to trust Aladdin's personnel or the child, that is the parent's prerogative.

> The history and culture of Western civilization reflect a strong tradition of parental concern for the nurture and upbringing of their children. This primary role of the parents in the upbringing of their children is now established beyond debate as an enduring American tradition.

Wisconsin v. Yoder, 406 U.S. 205, 232 (1972). Accord, Parham v. J. R., 442 U.S. 584, 602 (1979). Thus for minors as for adults, the ordinance impermissibly and unconstitutionally infringes on freedom of association.

Id. at 1042–44.

On appeal, the U.S. Supreme Court held that the ordinance was not unconstitutionally vague, reversing the finding as to § 6. However the Court declined to decide on the validity of § 5, remanding the case for clarification as to whether the issue had been decided under the Texas Constitution possibly based on language in that document differing from and broader than that of corresponding federal provisions. Ostensibly, the purpose of the remand was to avoid the Court's unnecessary adjudication of federal questions. 455 U.S. 283, 102 S.Ct. 1070, 71 L.Ed.2d 152 (1982), judgment recall denied, 464 U.S. 927, 104 S.Ct. 329, 78 L.Ed.2d 300 (1983). On remand, the Fifth Circuit Court of Appeals clarified that no Texas constitutional issue had been addressed. 713 F.2d 137 (5th Cir.1983).

3. The Right to Vote and the Age of Majority

> "The right of citizens of the United States, who are eighteen years of age or older, to vote shall not be denied or abridged by the United States or by any state on account of age."

> Amendment XXVI
> United States Constitution

The right to vote traditionally has been the defining marker of legal adulthood. Although minors are accorded the legal status of adults for some purposes (driving privileges, for example) before they have the right to vote, the age of majority has been closely linked with this right of political participation. Thus, until 1971, citizens could vote upon their twenty-first birthday; this also marked the point at which the legal status of childhood ended and the restrictions, entitlements, and protections associated with that status were set aside. With the passage of the Twenty–Sixth Amendment in 1971, the voting age was lowered to age 18. In the period that followed, the age of majority was lowered to 18 years for other purposes under Federal and State law.

The Case For 18–Year–Old Voting

Senate Committee on the Judiciary, Report on Lowering the Voting Age to 18, S. Rep. No. 26, 92nd Congress, 1st Session 5 (1971).

In recent years, we have achieved a nationwide political consensus favoring a lowering of the voting age to 18. In the extensive hearings of the Senate Subcommittee on Constitutional Amendments in the 91st Congress, the objective was agreed to by Senator Barry Goldwater and Senator Edward M. Kennedy, by Deputy Attorney General Richard Kleindienst and former Attorney General Ramsey Clark. This consensus has emerged from a series of arguments supporting an extension of the franchise to younger voters, arguments the Committee finds convincing.

First, these younger citizens are fully mature enough to vote. There is no magic to the age of 21. The 21 year age of maturity is derived only from historical accident. In the eleventh century 21 was the age at which most males were physically capable of carrying armor. But the physical ability to carry armor in the eleventh century clearly has no relation to the intellectual and emotional qualifications to vote in twentieth century America. And even if physical maturity were the crucial determinant of the right to vote, 18–year-olds would deserve that right: Dr. Margaret Mead and others have shown that the age of physical maturity of American youth has dropped more than three years since the eighteenth century. As Vice President Agnew said recently in endorsing a lowered voting age, "young people today are better educated and they mature physically much sooner than they did even 50 years ago."

The Committee believes that our younger citizens today are mentally and emotionally capable of full participation in our democratic form of government. Today more than half of the 18– to 21–year olds are receiving some type of higher education. Today nearly 80 percent of these young people are high school graduates. It is interesting to compare these recent statistics with some from 1920, when less than 10 percent went on to college and less than 20 percent of our youngsters actually graduated from high school.

Second, our 18–year-old citizens have earned the right to vote because they bear all or most of an adult citizen's responsibilities. Of the nearly 11 million 18– to 21–year-olds today, about half are married and more than 1 million of them are responsible for raising families. Nearly 1 million are serving their country in the Armed Forces. And tens of thousands of young people have paid the supreme sacrifice in the Indo–China War over the past five years.

Today more than 3 million young people, ages 18 to 21, are full-time employees and taxpayers. As former Attorney General Ramsey Clark has pointed out:

> We subject 10–12 million young citizens between 17 and 21 years of age to taxation without representation. This is four times the population of the Colonies the night the tea was dumped in Boston harbor. . . . It Exceeds the population of all but several of the States of the Union.

In 26 States, persons at the age of 18 can make wills. In 49 States, they are treated as adults in criminal courts of law. It is difficult to justify holding a person legally responsible for his or her actions in a criminal court of law when we continue to refuse to consider that same person responsible enough to take action in a polling booth. Our younger citizens have willingly shouldered the responsibilities we have put on them, and the Committee believes it is wrong to deprive these citizens of the vote. By their actions, they clearly have earned the right to vote.

Third, these younger voters should be given the right to full participation in our political system because they will contribute a great deal to our society. Although some of the student unrest of recent years has led to deplorable violence and intolerance, much of this unrest reflects the interest and concern of today's youth over the important issues of our day. The deep commitment of those 18 to 21 years old is often the idealism which Senator Barry Goldwater has said "is exactly what we need more of in the country. . . . more citizens who are concerned enough to pose high social and moral goals for the nation." Professor Paul Freund of the Harvard Law School recently wrote:

> I believe that the student movement around the world is nothing less than the herald of an intellectual and moral revolution, which can portend a new enlightenment and a wider fraternity, or if repulsed and repressed can lead to a new cynicism and even deeper cleavages. The student generation, disillusioned with absolutist slogans and utopian dogmas, has long since marked the end of ideology: wars of competing isms are as intolerable to them as wars of religion became centuries ago. Youth turned to pragmatism, to the setting of specific manageable tasks and getting them done. But that has proved altogether too uninspiring and youth has been restless for a new vision, a new set of ideals to supplant the discarded ideologies.

The Committee believes that we must channel these energies into our political system and give young people the real opportunity to influence our society in a peaceful and constructive manner. The President's Commission on the Causes and Prevention of Violence explored the relationships between campus unrest and the ability of our younger citizens to take a constructive part in the political process:

> The nation cannot afford to ignore lawlessness. . . . It is no less permissible for our nation to ignore the legitimate needs and desires of the young . . .

... We have seen the dedication and conviction they brought to the Civil Rights movement and the skill and enthusiasm they have infused into the political process, even though they lack the vote.

The anachronistic voting-age limitation tends to alienate them from systematic political processes and to drive them into a search for an alternative, sometimes violent, means to express their frustrations over the gap between the nation's deals and actions. Lowering the voting age will provide them with a direct, constructive and democratic channel for making their views felt and for giving them a responsible stake in the future of the nation.

Thus the Committee is convinced that the time has come to extend the vote to 18–year-olds in all elections: because they are mature enough in every way to exercise the franchise; because they have earned the right to vote by bearing the responsibilities of citizenship; their idealism and concern and energy into the constructive mechanism of elective government.

Elizabeth Scott, The Legal Construction of Adolescence, 29 Hofstra L. Rev. 547, 558–64 (2000).*

... The common law age of majority was twenty-one.... Currently, legal adulthood begins at age eighteen. This milestone signals the end of parental authority and responsibility, as well as the withdrawal of the state from its protective parens patriae role. The financial support obligation of parents generally ends when children attain the age of majority, as does parents' common law right to their children's earnings. The safety net of government support and protection is also terminated; for the most part, federal and state financial support, medical services, and abuse and neglect jurisdiction end when children become legal adults at age eighteen.

On reaching the age of majority, individuals acquire most of the legal capacities necessary to function as citizens and members of society. Legal adults have the right to make decisions about domicile and medical treatment, and the legal capacity to enter binding contracts, sign leases, purchase real estate, and make wills. Upon attaining the age of majority, individuals are also accorded the rights and privileges of citizens, including the right to serve on juries and (perhaps of greatest symbolic importance) the right to vote.

The designation of a categorical legal age of majority can be understood as reflecting a crude judgment about maturity and competence. Individuals at the specified age are assumed to be mature enough to function in society as adults, to care for themselves, and to make their own self-interested decisions. Before this threshold is crossed, authority to make these decisions rests largely either with the parents, who can be assumed to act in the child's interest, or with the state. Empirical evidence from developmental psychology supports that by age eighteen (and certainly by age twenty-one), most individuals attain the presumed adult competence in many domains. Although the process of psychological development and maturing continues into the adult years, there are only modest differences between late adolescents and adults in decision-making capacity. . . .

The use of a bright line rule to designate the end of childhood ignores individual variations in developmental maturity as well as varying maturity demands across the range of legal rights and responsibilities. Nonetheless, it generally functions quite well. For most purposes, no great harm results from postponing adult legal status until the designated age, or from giving parents legal authority and thereby involving them in their adolescent children's lives. Most adolescents have no pressing need to execute contracts, and if they do, parental involvement is probably desirable in most cases. Moreover, an extended dependency period offers benefits in the form of entitlement to support and other protections of childhood. Indeed, if maintaining parents' enthusiasm for their obligations toward their children is important, retention of parental authority may be worthwhile—as long as parents have no serious conflict of interest with their children. Political support for special governmental benefits for children and adolescents may also be strengthened by maintaining the bright line between childhood and adulthood for most purposes.

A bright line age of majority is a clear signal; all who deal with the young person understand that he does—or does not—have legal capacity. A more tailored approach that attempts to confer adult status in different domains on the basis of a more targeted assessment of maturity is likely to generate uncertainty and error. Moreover, it almost certainly would be administratively less efficient. A strategy of customized age grading introduces complexity and cost to legal policy, as it involves multiple judgments about the appropriate maturity threshold for a broad range of tasks and functions. Most cumbersome of all would be an approach that confers adult legal rights or responsibilities on the basis of individualized assessments of maturity. Because such a strategy is costly and burdensome, predictably it is only employed when the stakes are high.

The upshot is that a categorical approach that treats individuals below a designated age as legal minors for most purposes works well, despite some inevitable distortion of the developmental capacities of young persons, as long as that age corresponds roughly to some threshold of developmental readiness to assume the responsibilities and privileges of adulthood. Because of the advantages of this categorical approach, variations that depart from the presumptive age should attract our interest. These variations can be explained as serving some political or social goal that would be undermined by adherence to the conventional boundary of childhood. . . .

What determines the location of the presumptive boundary between childhood and adulthood? Clearly, it is based on some rough assessment about the level of maturity required to function as an adult in society, but (also clearly) no single age is dictated by developmental considerations. In the past generation, the boundary has shifted downward, in response to the passage of the Twenty–Sixth Amendment, lowering the age at which citizens have a right to vote in federal and state elections. . . .

The right to vote has long been the defining marker of legal adulthood and the age of majority has been linked with this important symbol of full-fledged citizenship. Like many other legal rights, the right to vote is withheld from minors because of assumptions about developmental immaturity. It is assumed that education and an informed understanding of the issues are important to political participation in a democracy, and that adults are more likely to meet these criteria than children and adolescents. . . . [T]he withholding of the right to vote from minors has generated little controversy in recent years. This is probably because of a combination of two factors suggested above. The administrative cost of identifying minors who are "competent" to exercise their voting rights would be substantial, and the cost of postponing the opportunity to exercise voting rights does not seem to be a great deprivation.

If the latter point is true, how can we explain the extensive effort undertaken in the late 1960s to amend the United States Constitution to extend voting rights to eighteen-year-old citizens? First, the political context and climate were important. The Twenty–Sixth Amendment was enacted in the midst of the Vietnam War, when many legal minors between the ages of eighteen and twenty-one were drafted into military service and sent into battle. Moreover, across the country, college students involved in the civil rights and anti-war protest movements demonstrated an interest in political participation and a commitment to social change. The Senate committee that recommended the enactment of the Twenty–Sixth Amendment emphasized these political facts. It also emphasized that the young adults who would be enfranchised under the new amendment were "mentally and emotionally capable of full participation in our democratic form of government." Finally, the report noted that legal minors were treated as adults for the purposes of criminal responsibility and punishment in all states, and that many were engaged in adult roles as employees and taxpayers. . . .

Several points about this political initiative are interesting. First, the Amendment's supporters believed it was important to emphasize that the common law boundary between childhood and adulthood distorted developmental reality. The argument for lowering the age of majority was based in part on an empirical claim that, for most purposes, psychological maturity was achieved by age eighteen, suggesting a view that legal status should follow intuitions about developmental maturity. Another important theme is that parity should exist between rights and responsibilities. On this view, fairness required the extension of voting rights to eighteen-year-olds because they were subject to the most onerous responsibility of citizenship (military service) and were often held legally accountable for their behavior under criminal law. There is little question that the image of young persons dying for their country in Vietnam who were not deemed mature enough to participate in elections carried much symbolic weight in the political process. It goes a long way towards explaining the timing of this constitutional reform. Finally, this reform reveals the extent to which legal childhood and adulthood are social and political constructs, rather than simply products of scientific understanding of human development. One implicit goal of the reform was to reconceptualize college student protesters from immature troublemakers who were "outside the system" into citizens with a stake in democratic processes. The broader point, of course, is that young persons between eighteen and twenty-one years of age were recast as legal adults in large part because of circumstances in the social and political environment

C.   Minors' Right of Free Expression Under the First Amendment

1.   The Traditional Approach

Ginsberg v. New York

Supreme Court of the United States, 1968.
390 U.S. 629, 88 S.Ct. 1274, 20 L.Ed.2d 195.

■ Mr. Justice Brennan delivered the opinion of the Court.

This case presents the question of the constitutionality on its face of a New York criminal obscenity statute which prohibits the sale to minors under 17 years of age of material defined to be obscene on the basis of its appeal to them whether or not it would be obscene to adults.

Appellant and his wife operate "Sam's Stationery and Luncheonette" in Bellmore, Long Island. They have a lunch counter, and, among other things, also sell magazines including some so-called "girlie" magazines. Appellant was prosecuted under two informations, each in two counts, which charged that he personally sold a 16–year-old boy two "girlie" magazines on each of two dates in October, 1965, in violation of § 484–h of the New York Penal Law, McKinney's Consol.Laws, c. 40. He was tried before a judge without a jury in Nassau County District Court and was found guilty on both counts. The judge found (1) that the magazines contained pictures which depicted female "nudity" in a manner defined in subsection 1(b), that is "the showing of ... female ... buttocks with less than a full opaque covering, or the showing of the female breast with less than a fully opaque covering of any portion thereof below the top of the nipple ...," and (2) that the pictures were "harmful to minors" in that they had, within the meaning of subsection 1(f) "that quality of ... representation ... of nudity ... [which] ... (i) predominantly appeals to the prurient, shameful or morbid interest of minors, and (ii) is patently offensive to prevailing standards in the adult community as a whole with respect to what is suitable material for minors, and (iii) is utterly without redeeming social importance for minors." He held that both sales to the 16–year-old boy therefore constituted the violation under § 484–h of "knowingly to sell ... to a minor" under 17 of "(a) any picture ... which depicts nudity ... and which is harmful to minors," and "(b) any ... magazine ... which contains ... [such pictures] ... and which, taken as a whole, is harmful to minors." ... We affirm.

I.

The "girlie" picture magazines involved in the sales here are not obscene for adults.... § 484–h does not bar the appellant from stocking the magazines and selling them to persons 17 years of age or older, and therefore the conviction is not invalid under our decision in Butler v. State of Michigan, 352 U.S. 380.

Obscenity is not within the area of protected speech or press. Roth v. United States, 354 U.S. 476, 485. The three-pronged test of subsection 1(f) for judging the obscenity of material sold to minors under 17 is a variable from the formulation for determining obscenity under *Roth* stated in the plurality opinion in A Book Named "John Cleland's Memoirs of a Woman of Pleasure" v. Attorney General of Com. of Massachusetts, 383 U.S. 413, 418. Appellant's primary attack upon § 484–h is leveled at the power of the State to adapt this *Memoirs* formulation to define the material's obscenity on the basis of its appeal to minors, and thus exclude material so defined from the area of protected expression. He makes no argument that the magazines are not "harmful to minors" within the definition in subsection 1(f). Thus "[n]o issue is presented ... concerning the obscenity of the material involved." Roth, 354 U.S., at 481, n. 8.

The New York Court of Appeals "upheld the Legislature's power to employ variable concepts of obscenity"[4] in a case in which the same challenge to state power to enact such a law was also addressed to § 484–h. Bookcase, Inc. v. Broderick, 18 N.Y.2d 71, 271 N.Y.S.2d 947, 218 N.E.2d 668, appeal dismissed for want of a properly presented federal question, sub nom. Bookcase, Inc. v. Leary, 385 U.S. 12. In sustaining state power to enact the law, the Court of Appeals said:

"[M]aterial which is protected for distribution to adults is not necessarily constitutionally protected from restriction upon its dissemination to children. In other words, the concept of obscenity or of unprotected matter may vary according to the group to whom the questionable material is directed or from whom it is quarantined. Because of the State's exigent interest in preventing distribution to children of objectionable material, it can exercise its power to protect the health, safety, welfare and morals of its community by barring the distribution to children of books recognized to be suitable for adults."

Appellant's attack is not that New York was without power to draw the line at age 17. Rather, his contention is the broad proposition that the scope of the constitutional freedom of expression secured to a citizen to read or see material concerned with sex cannot be made to depend upon whether the citizen is an adult or a minor. He accordingly insists that the denial to minors under 17 of access to material condemned by § 484–h, insofar as that material is not obscene for persons 17 years of age or older, constitutes an unconstitutional deprivation of protected liberty.

4. People v. Tannenbaum, 18 N.Y.2d 268, 270, 274 N.Y.S.2d 131, 133, 220 N.E.2d 783, 785, dismissed as moot, 388 U.S. 439. The concept of variable obscenity is developed in Lockhart & McClure, Censorship of Obscenity: The Developing Constitutional Standards, 45 Minn.L.Rev. 5 (1960). At 85 the authors state:

"Variable obscenity ... furnishes a useful analytical tool for dealing with the problem of denying adolescents access to material aimed at a primary audience of sexually mature adults. For variable obscenity focuses attention upon the make-up of primary and peripheral audiences in varying circumstances, and provides a reasonably satisfactory means for delineating the obscene in each circumstance."

We have no occasion in this case to consider the impact of the guarantees of freedom of expression upon the totality of the relationship of the minor and the State. . . . It is enough for the purposes of this case that we inquire whether it was constitutionally impermissible for New York, insofar as § 484–h does so, to accord minors under 17 a more restricted right than that assured to adults to judge and determine for themselves what sex material they may read or see. We conclude that we cannot say that the statute invades the area of freedom of expression constitutionally secured to minors.

Appellant argues that there is an invasion of protected rights under § 484–h constitutionally indistinguishable from the invasions under the Nebraska statute forbidding children to study German, which was struck down in Meyer v. State of Nebraska, 262 U.S. 390; the Oregon statute interfering with children's attendance at private and parochial schools, which was struck down in Pierce v. Society of Sisters of the Holy Names of Jesus and Mary, 268 U.S. 510; and the statute compelling children against their religious scruples to give the flag salute, which was struck down in West Virginia State Board of Education v. Barnette, 319 U.S. 624. We reject that argument. We do not regard New York's regulation in defining obscenity on the basis of its appeal to minors under 17 as involving an invasion of such minors' constitutionally protected freedoms. Rather § 484–h simply adjusts the definition of obscenity "to social realities by permitting the appeal of this type of material to be assessed in term of the sexual interests . . ." of such minors. Mishkin v. State of New York, 383 U.S. 502, 509; Bookcase, Inc. v. Broderick, supra. That the State has power to make that adjustment seems clear, for we have recognized that even where there is an invasion of protected freedoms "the power of the state to control the conduct of children reaches beyond the scope of its authority over adults. . . ." Prince v. Commonwealth of Massachusetts, 321 U.S. 158, 170.[6] . . .

The well-being of its children is of course a subject within the State's constitutional power to regulate, and, in our view, two interests justify the limitations in § 484–h upon the availability of sex material to minors under 17, at least if it was rational for the legislature to find that the minors' exposure to such material might be harmful. First of all, constitutional interpretation has consistently recognized that the parents' claim to authority in their own household to direct the rearing of their children is

6. Many commentators, including many committed to the proposition that "[n]o general restriction on expression in terms of 'obscenity' can . . . be reconciled with the first amendment," recognize that "the power of the state to control the conduct of children reaches beyond the scope of its authority over adults," and accordingly acknowledge a supervening state interest in the regulation of literature sold to children, Emerson, Toward a General Theory of the First Amendment, 72 Yale L.J. 877, 938, 939 (1963):

"Different factors come into play, also, where the interest at stake is the effect of erotic expression upon children. The world of children is not strictly part of the adult realm of free expression. The factor of immaturity, and perhaps other considerations, impose different rules. Without attempting here to formulate the principles relevant to freedom of expression for children, it suffices to say that regulations of communication addressed to them need not conform to the requirements of the first amendment in the same way as those applicable to adults."

. . .

basic in the structure of our society. "It is cardinal with us that the custody, care and nurture of the child reside first in the parents, whose primary function and freedom include preparation for obligations the state can neither supply nor hinder." Prince v. Commonwealth of Massachusetts, supra, at 166. The legislature could properly conclude that parents and others, teachers for example, who have this primary responsibility for children's well-being are entitled to the support of laws designed to aid discharge of that responsibility. Indeed, subsection 1(f)(ii) of § 484–h expressly recognizes the parental role in assessing sex-related material harmful to minors according "to prevailing standards in the adult community as a whole with respect to what is suitable material for minors." Moreover, the prohibition against sales to minors does not bar parents who so desire from purchasing the magazines for their children.[7]

The State also has an independent interest in the well-being of its youth. The New York Court of Appeals squarely bottomed its decision on that interest in Bookcase, Inc. v. Broderick, supra. Judge Fuld, now Chief Judge Fuld, also emphasized its significance in the earlier case of People v. Kahan, 15 N.Y.2d 311, 258 N.Y.S.2d 391, 206 N.E.2d 333, which had struck down the first version of § 484–h on grounds of vagueness. In his concurring opinion, 15 N.Y.2d, at 312, 258 N.Y.S.2d at 392, 206 N.E.2d, at 334, he said:

> "While the supervision of children's reading may best be left to their parents, the knowledge that parental control or guidance cannot always be provided and society's transcendent interest in protecting the welfare of children justify reasonable regulation of the sale of material to them. It is, therefore, altogether fitting and proper for a state to include in a statute designed to regulate the sale of pornography to children special standards, broader then those embodied in legislation aimed at controlling dissemination of such material to adults."

In Prince v. Commonwealth of Massachusetts, supra, 321 U.S., at 165, this Court, too, recognized that the State has an interest "to protect the welfare of children" and to see that they are "safeguarded from abuses" which might prevent their "growth into free and independent well-developed men and citizens." The only question remaining, therefore, is whether the New York Legislature might rationally conclude, as it has, that exposure to the materials proscribed by § 484–h constitutes such an "abuse."

Section 484–e of the law states a legislative finding that the material condemned by § 484–h is "a basic factor in impairing the ethical and moral

---

7. One commentator who argues that obscenity legislation might be constitutionally defective as an imposition of a single standard of public morality would give effect to the parental role and accept laws relating only to minors. Henkin, Morals and the Constitution: The Sin of Obscenity, 63 Col.L.Rev. 391, 413, n. 68 (1963):

> "One must consider also how much difference it makes if laws are designed to protect only the morals of a child.

While many of the constitutional arguments against morals legislation apply equally to legislation protecting the morals of children, one can well distinguish laws which do not impose a morality on children, but which support the right of parents to deal with the morals of their children as they see fit."

See also Elias, Sex Publications and Moral Corruption: The Supreme Court Dilemma, 9 Wm. & Mary L.Rev. 302, 320–321 (1967).

development of our youth and a clear and present danger to the people of the state." It is very doubtful that this finding expresses an accepted scientific fact. But obscenity is not protected expression and may be suppressed without a showing of the circumstances which lie behind the phrase "clear and present danger" in its application to protected speech. Roth v. United States, supra.[9] To sustain state power to exclude material defined as obscenity by § 484–h requires only that we be able to say that it was not irrational for the legislature to find that exposure to material condemned by the statute is harmful to minors. In Meyer v. State of Nebraska, supra, we were able to say that children's knowledge of the German language "cannot reasonably be regarded as harmful." That cannot be said by us of minors' reading and seeing sex material. To be sure, there is no lack of "studies" which purport to demonstrate that obscenity is or is not "a basic factor in impairing the ethical and moral development of ... youth and a clear and present danger to the people of the state." But the growing consensus of commentators is that "while these studies all agree that a causal link has not been demonstrated, they are equally agreed that a causal link has not been disproved either."[10] We do not demand of legislatures "scientifically certain criteria of legislation." Noble State Bank v. Haskell, 219 U.S. 104, 110. We therefore cannot say that § 484–h, in defining the obscenity of material on the basis of its appeal to minors under 17, has no rational relation to the objective of safeguarding such minors from harm.

[Appellant's arguments that the statute in question was void for vagueness and that it failed to meet the requirement of *scienter* also were rejected by the Court.]

Affirmed.

9. Our conclusion in Roth, 354 U.S., at 486–487, that the clear and present danger test was irrelevant to the determination of obscenity made it unnecessary in that case to consider the debate among the authorities whether exposure to pornography caused antisocial consequences. . . .

10. . . . [D]espite the vigor of the ongoing controversy whether obscene material will perceptibly create a danger of antisocial conduct, or will probably induce its recipients to such conduct, a medical practitioner recently suggested that the possibility of harmful effects to youth cannot be dismissed as frivolous. Dr. Gaylin of the Columbia University Psychoanalytic Clinic, reporting on the views of some psychiatrists in 77 Yale L.J., at 592–593, said:

"It is in the period of growth [of youth] when these patterns of behavior are laid down, when environmental stimuli of all sorts must be integrated into a workable sense of self, when sensuality is being defined and fears elaborated, when pleasure confronts security and impulse encounters control—it is in this period, undramatically and with time, that legalized pornography may conceivably be damaging."

Dr. Gaylin emphasizes that a child might not be as well prepared as an adult to make an intelligent choice as to the material he chooses to read:

"[P]sychiatrists ... made a distinction between the reading of pornography, as unlikely to be per se harmful, and the permitting of the reading of pornography, which was conceived as potentially destructive. The child is protected in his reading of pornography by the knowledge that it is pornographic, i.e., disapproved. It is outside of parental standards and not a part of his identification processes. To openly permit implies parental approval and even suggests seductive encouragement. If this is so of parental approval, it is equally so of societal approval—another potent influence on the developing ego." Id., at 594.

APPENDIX A TO OPINION OF THE COURT

New York Penal Law § 484–h as enacted by L.1965, c. 327, provides:

§ 484–h. Exposing minors to harmful materials

1. Definitions. As used in this section:

(a) "Minor" means any person under the age of seventeen years.

(b) "Nudity" means the showing of the human male or female genitals, pubic area or buttocks with less than a full opaque covering, or the showing of the female breast with less than a fully opaque covering of any portion thereof below the top of the nipple, or the depiction of covered male genitals in a discernibly turgid state.

(c) "Sexual conduct" means acts of masturbation, homosexuality, sexual intercourse, or physical contact with a person's clothed or unclothed genitals, pubic area, buttocks or, if such person be a female, breast.

(d) "Sexual excitement" means the condition of human male or female genitals when in a state of sexual stimulation or arousal.

(e) "Sado-masochistic abuse" means flagellation or torture by or upon a person clad in undergarments, a mask or bizarre costume, or the condition of being fettered, bound or otherwise physically restrained on the part of one so clothed.

(f) "Harmful to minors" means that quality of any description or representation, in whatever form, of nudity, sexual conduct, sexual excitement, or sadomasochistic abuse, when it:

(i) predominantly appeals to the prurient, shameful or morbid interest of minors, and

(ii) is patently offensive to prevailing standards in the adult community as a whole with respect to what is suitable material for minors, and

(iii) is utterly without redeeming social importance for minors.

(g) "Knowingly" means having general knowledge of, or reason to know, or a belief or ground for belief which warrants further inspection or inquiry of both:

(i) the character and content of any material described herein which is reasonably susceptible of examination by the defendant, and

(ii) the age of the minor, provided however, that an honest mistake shall constitute an excuse from liability hereunder if the defendant made a reasonable bona fide attempt to ascertain the true age of such minor.

2. It shall be unlawful for any person knowingly to sell or loan for monetary consideration to a minor:

(a) any picture, photograph, drawing, sculpture, motion picture film, or similar visual representation or image of a person or portion of the human body which depicts nudity, sexual conduct or sado-masochistic abuse and which is harmful to minors, or

(b) any book, pamphlet, magazine, printed matter however reproduced, or sound recording which contains any matter enumerated in paragraph (a) of subdivision two hereof, or explicit and detailed verbal descriptions or narrative accounts of sexual excitement, sexual conduct or sado-masochistic abuse and which, taken as a whole is harmful to minors.

3. It shall be unlawful for any person knowingly to exhibit for a monetary consideration to a minor or knowingly to sell to a minor an admission ticket or pass or knowingly to admit a minor for a monetary consideration to premises whereon there is exhibited, a motion picture, show or other presentation which, in whole or in part, depicts nudity, sexual conduct or sado-masochistic abuse and which is harmful to minors.

4. A violation of any provision hereof shall constitute a misdemeanor.

■ MR. JUSTICE STEWART, concurring in the result.

A doctrinaire, knee-jerk application of the First Amendment would, of course, dictate the nullification of this New York statute. But that result is not required, I think, if we bear in mind what it is that the First Amendment protects.

The First Amendment guarantees liberty of human expression in order to preserve in our Nation what Mr. Justice Holmes called a "free trade in ideas." To that end, the Constitution protects more than just a man's freedom to say or write or publish what he wants. It secures as well the liberty of each man to decide for himself what he will read and to what he will listen. The Constitution guarantees, in short, a society of free choice. Such a society presupposes the capacity of its members to choose.

When expression occurs in a setting where the capacity to make a choice is absent, government regulation of that expression may co-exist with and even implement First Amendment guarantees....

I think a State may permissibly determine that, at least in some precisely delineated areas, a child—like someone in a captive audience—is not possessed of that full capacity for individual choice which is the presupposition of First Amendment guarantees. It is only upon such a premise, I should suppose, that a State may deprive children of other rights—the right to marry, for example, or the right to vote—deprivations that would be constitutionally intolerable for adults.

I cannot hold that this state law, on its face, violates the First and Fourteenth Amendments.

■ [The dissenting opinion of Mr. Justice Douglas, with whom Mr. Justice Black concurs, is omitted.]

■ MR. JUSTICE FORTAS, dissenting.

   . . .

The Court avoids facing the problem whether the magazines in the present case are "obscene" when viewed by a 16–year-old boy, although not "obscene" when viewed by someone 17 years of age or older. It says that Ginsberg's lawyer did not choose to challenge the conviction on the ground that the magazines are not "obscene." He chose only to attack the statute on its face. Therefore, the Court reasons, we need not look at the magazines and determine whether they may be excluded from the ambit of the First Amendment as "obscene" for purposes of this case. . . .

In my judgment, the Court cannot properly avoid its fundamental duty to define "obscenity" for purposes of censorship of material sold to youths, merely because of counsel's position. By so doing the Court avoids the essence of the problem; for if the State's power to censor freed from the prohibitions of the First Amendment depends upon obscenity, and if obscenity turns on the specific content of the publication, how can we sustain the conviction here without deciding whether the particular magazines in question are obscene?

The Court certainly cannot mean that the States and cities and counties and villages have unlimited power to withhold anything and everything that is written or pictorial from younger people. But it here justifies the conviction of Sam Ginsberg because the impact of the Constitution, it says, is variable, and what is not obscene for an adult may be obscene for a child. This it calls "variable obscenity." I do not disagree with this, but I insist that to assess the principle—certainly to apply it—the Court must define it. . . .

I agree that the State in the exercise of its police power—even in the First Amendment domain—may make proper and careful differentiation between adults and children. But I do not agree that this power may be used on an arbitrary, free-wheeling basis. This is not a case where, on any standard enunciated by the Court, the magazines are obscene, nor one where the seller is at fault. Petitioner is being prosecuted for the sale of magazines which he had a right under the decisions of this Court to offer for sale, and he is being prosecuted without proof of "fault"—without even a claim that he deliberately, calculatedly sought to induce children to buy "obscene" material. Bookselling should not be a hazardous profession.

The conviction of Ginsberg on the present facts is a serious invasion of freedom. To sustain the conviction without inquiry as to whether the material is "obscene" and without any evidence of pushing or pandering, in face of this Court's asserted solicitude for First Amendment values, is to give the State a role in the rearing of children which is contrary to our traditions and to our conception of family responsibility. Cf. In re Gault, 387 U.S. 1 (1967). It begs the question to present this undefined, unlimited censorship as an aid to parents in the rearing of their children. This decision does not merely protect children from activities which all sensible parents would condemn. Rather, its undefined and unlimited approval of state censorship in this area denies to children free access to books and works of art to which many parents may wish their children to have uninhibited access. For denial of access to these magazines, without any standard or definition of their allegedly distinguishing characteristics, is also denial of access to great works of art and literature.

OBSCENITY AND MINORS

(1) **The Standard in *Ginsberg*.** As the Supreme Court in *Ginsberg* explains, obscene speech or written material, as defined under the three-prong test developed by the Supreme Court in *Roth v. United States*, is excluded from protection under

the First Amendment. The New York statute upheld in *Ginsberg* restricts minors' access to pornography to a greater degree by prohibiting the sale to minors of material that is "obscene" only on the basis of its appeal to minors—and that might well be protected from restriction under the First Amendment for adults under the *Roth* test. What kind of material do you think falls in this category?

(2) **The Harm of Pornography.** In *Ginsberg*, the Supreme Court acknowledges that little scientific evidence supports the New York legislature's finding that exposure to "obscene" materials, as defined in the statute, is harmful to minors' moral development. The Court concludes that, despite the failure of studies to establish any harmful effects of exposure to pornography, the legislature's finding was not "irrational", because "a causal link" between obscene materials and harm "has not been disproved." Does this suggest that the Court requires the state to offer very little justification for restricting the First Amendment rights of minors in a way that would be impermissible for adults?

(3) **Federal Pornography Commission Reports.** In 1970, two years after *Ginsberg*, the U.S. Commission on Obscenity and Pornography, appointed by President Johnson in 1967, issued its report. The Commission proposed the elimination of all restrictions on adults' access to obscene material because empirical research had found no evidence that exposure to such material is linked to criminal behavior or sexual deviancy. However, the Commission endorsed restriction of access to sexually explicit materials by minors "in order to aid parents in supervising and controlling the access of children to such materials." Id. at 66. Because of obvious ethical problems, only limited research had focused on the effects on minors of exposure to sexually explicit material. Thus, harmful effects could not be ruled out. What research had been conducted suggested that exposure to erotic materials was widespread among youth, and that there was no direct link between exposure and delinquent behavior. However, according to its investigation, most people believed that children should not have access to sexually explicit material. Therefore, the Commission concluded that parents should have the authority to decide about access. Id. at 57.

In 1985, President Reagan asked Attorney General Meese to establish a second Pornography Commission. In 1986, a Report of the Attorney General's Commission on Pornography concluded that research conducted since 1970 indicates that exposure to pornography is more harmful than had been realized previously. The Report described laboratory studies that found that exposure of male research subjects to sexually violent material (particularly of the type depicted in "slasher" films) was causally linked to aggression toward women. Id. at 324–25. Attitudinal changes were also observed. For example, research subjects who were exposed to a substantial amount of violent pornography were less sympathetic to rape victims and more likely to see the victim as responsible for the assault and as suffering less injury than were subjects not exposed to violent materials. In general, the Report concluded, such exposure leads to greater acceptance of the "rape myth"—that women enjoy forcible sexual acts. Id. at 326–27. The Report emphasized that the harmful effects that it described *"do not vary with the extent of sexual explicitness so long as the violence is presented in an undeniably sexual context."* Id. at 328 (emphasis in original). No link has been found by researchers between non-violent sexually explicit material and sexual violence, if the material is not degrading to women. Id. at 337.

Does the Attorney General's Report suggest that the state's interest may be more "rational" than the Court in *Ginsberg* recognized? Should New York reexamine the type of material that is defined as "obscene" under the statute, if the state's goal is to protect children from harm? Should access by adults be restricted?

In general, how important should empirical research evidence about the effects of pornography be in setting constitutional standards for access to erotic materials by minors? Does the changing picture of harmful effects as reflected in the two reports by federal pornography commissions argue for adapting the legal standard to conform to empirical knowledge? Or does it support the opposite conclusion? To what extent is this issue an empirical one? If claims about the harm to youth of sexually explicit material are set aside, do other justifications support restricting youthful access?

(4) **Youthful Incapacity for Choice—Justice Stewart's Concurrence.** Justice Stewart in his concurrence argues that an important purpose of the First Amendment is to preserve the "free trade of ideas" by protecting the right of individuals to choose what they read, free of state interference. Since minors lack "full capacity for individual choice", the state is justified in restricting their First Amendment rights. In essence, Stewart seems to be arguing that exercise of First Amendment free expression rights requires something akin to decisionmaking competence and that minors, due to their immature judgment, lack this competence. Are you persuaded by Stewart's argument? What is the nature of the capacity that is required to make choices in this context? Should minors who can demonstrate that they are mature and have the required capacity be exempt from the restriction of the statute? Should adults who clearly lack capacity (because of mental disability, for example) be restricted in their First Amendment freedom in the same way as minors?

(5) **The Role of Parents.** The Court in *Ginsberg* asserts that the New York statute not only furthers the state's independent interest in promoting children's welfare, but also supports parental authority, since most parents would not want their children exposed to obscene materials. The Court suggests that parents who feel differently can purchase the materials for their children. Given the shakiness of its empirical basis, would the state's proclaimed interest in protecting children from harm, standing alone, be inadequate as a basis for the restriction on minors' First Amendment rights? In effect, the Court is joining together two interests that usually are balanced against one another—the state's interest in protecting the welfare of children and parents' interest in rearing their children—and weighing these interests against the child's First Amendment interest. The Court's assertion that the state's restriction of minors reinforces parental authority should be familiar from the juvenile curfew cases. Is the state's independent interest stronger in that context?

If the State of New York is justified in concluding that exposure to sexually explicit material can impair the ethical and moral development of youth, shouldn't the state be authorized to intervene if parents provide such material to their child? Suppose a parent purchases a "girlie" magazine for his son which the boy takes to school and shares with friends. Can the state initiate a neglect proceeding? Suspend the boy from school? What if the boy is 10 years old? Fifteen?

(6) **American Booksellers Association, Inc. v. Virginia, 882 F.2d 125 (4th Cir.1989), cert. denied, 494 U.S. 1056, 110 S.Ct. 1525, 108 L.Ed.2d 764 (1990).** After *Ginsberg*, much uncertainty surrounded the question of how a court (or the owner of a newsstand) should decide that the sale of a particular magazine or book violates a statute restricting sale of sexually explicit material to minors. Do statutes like the New York statute upheld in *Ginsberg* put an unfair burden on merchants to monitor and evaluate the material that they sell, at the risk of criminal penalties?

The constitutional limits on the state's power to impose a burden on booksellers to prevent minors from having access to obscene materials was clarified somewhat in *American Booksellers Assn.*, a case that followed a complex course through the Federal court system, with a detour to the Virginia Supreme Court. The case involved a 1985 amendment to a Virginia statute modeled on the New York statute upheld in *Ginsberg*. The amendment made it unlawful to sell or "to knowingly display for commercial purpose in a manner whereby juveniles may examine and peruse" materials that are "harmful to juveniles" under the statute. Va. Code Ann. § 18.2–391 (1985). The statute defines "harmful to juveniles" similarly to the New York statute, except that instead of requiring that the material be "utterly without redeeming social importance," the Virginia statute provides that the material "when taken as a whole," must be "lacking in serious literary, artistic, political or scientific value for juveniles." Va. Code Ann. § 18.2–390(6)(c).

A federal district court found that between 5 and 25 percent of the books in a "general bookstore" were "harmful to juveniles" under the statute and that booksellers would be required to prevent access by juveniles to these books. *American Booksellers Ass'n. v. Strobel*, 617 F.Supp. 699 (E.D.Va.1985). In a holding that was affirmed by the Fourth Circuit Court of Appeals, the district court held that the statute was unconstitutional. The court found that despite the state's legitimate interest in shielding minors from obscene materials, it cannot do so by restricting access of adults to material protected under the First Amendment. *American Booksellers Ass'n. v. Virginia*, 792 F.2d 1261 (4th Cir.1986).

In 1988, the United States Supreme Court noted jurisdiction, 484 U.S. 383, 108 S.Ct. 636, 98 L.Ed.2d 782, and certified two questions to the Virginia Supreme Court.

The first question asked whether any of the 16 books offered as exhibits by the plaintiff booksellers were "harmful to juveniles" and "what general standard should be used to determine the statute's reach, in light of juveniles' differing ages and level of maturity?" Included in the list of books were the following:

R.   Bell, Changing Bodies, Changing Lives (1980)

J.   Betancourt, Am I Normal? (1983)

J.   Blume, Forever (1975)

J.   Collins, Hollywood Wives (1983)

A.   Comfort & J. Comfort, The Facts of Love (1979)

The Family of Woman (J. Mason ed. 1979)

J.   Joyce, Ulysses (1961)

J.   Lindsey, Tender is the Storm (1985)

The New Our Bodies, Ourselves (J. Pincus and W. Sanford ed. 1984)

The Penguin Book of Love Poetry (J. Stallworthy ed. 1973)

M.   Sheffield, Where Do Babies Come From? (1972)

J.   Updike, The Witches of Eastwick (1984)

The Virginia Supreme Court responded to the first question that none of the books listed in the plaintiffs' exhibit qualified as "harmful to juveniles." 236 Va. 168, 372 S.E.2d 618, 623 (1988). The court endorsed the state Attorney General's opinion that a book would "pass statutory muster if it has serious value for a legitimate minority of juveniles," which "may consist of older normal (not deviant) adolescents." Id.

The second question addressed the meaning of the disputed statutory provision. The Virginia Supreme Court responded by stating that the amendment "is not aimed at the method chosen by the bookseller to display his wares for sale, but at the opportunity that he may afford juveniles to take off the shelves books that they are unable to buy, and to read them in the store." Id. at 624. The Court emphasized the scienter requirement in the statute. "A violation must consist of proof . . . that the bookseller *knowingly* afforded juveniles an opportunity to peruse harmful materials, or took no reasonable steps to prevent such perusal when the juvenile's opportunity was reasonably apparent to the bookseller." Id. at 624–25.

On appeal, the Fourth Circuit Court of Appeals upheld the constitutionality of the statute as interpreted by the Virginia Supreme Court, rejecting the plaintiff's vagueness argument. 882 F.2d 125 (4th Cir.1989). The United States Supreme Court denied certiorari. 494 U.S. 1056, 110 S.Ct. 1525, 108 L.Ed.2d 764 (1990).

(7) **Regulation of Broadcasting—F.C.C. v. Pacifica Foundation, 438 U.S. 726, 98 S.Ct. 3026, 57 L.Ed.2d 1073 (1978).** Pacifica Foundation, in an afternoon radio program, broadcast a monologue by George Carlin entitled "Filthy Words." A father, driving with his young son, heard the broadcast on his car radio, and complained to the Federal Communications Commission. The F.C.C. issued an order granting the complaint against Pacifica for using "patently offensive" and indecent, although not obscene, language in a radio broadcast. The Supreme Court upheld the order and the Commission's authority to regulate broadcasting more restrictively than would be acceptable for other media. The Court concluded that offensive speech receives less protection under the First Amendment when it is broadcast, because it intrudes into the home and may be hard for the recipient to avoid. Moreover, "broadcasting is uniquely accessible to children, even those too young to read . . . other forms of offensive expression may be withheld from the young without restricting the expression at its source." 438 U.S. at 749. Citing *Ginsberg*, the Court continued: "[T]he government's interest in the 'well being of its youth' and in supporting 'parents' claim to authority in their own household' justifies the regulation of otherwise protected expression." Id.

(8) **Minors' Access to Pornography on Television—*United States v. Playboy Entertainment Group, Inc.*, 529 U.S. 803, 120 S.Ct. 1878, 146 L.Ed.2d 865 (2000).** Appellee Playboy Entertainment Group produces programming for adult television networks. Cable operators receive programs from Appellee, and in turn, broadcast them to subscribers in scrambled form. Although all homes in a given area had received the signal, only customers who had paid for the adult programming had the converter box necessary to de-scramble the signal. In some instances, however, imperfections in the scrambling scheme allowed for portions of audio and/or video from these adult programs to "bleed through."

Section 505 of the Telecommunications Act of 1996 (Act) was enacted in order to deal with the problem of children hearing and seeing sexually explicit material on television because of signal bleed. This section required cable operators who provide channels "primarily dedicated to sexually-oriented programming" either to "fully scramble or otherwise block" those channels or to limit their transmission to hours when children are unlikely to be viewing, between 10 p.m. and 6 a.m. 47 U.S.C. § 561(a) (1994 ed., Supp. III).

Appellee brought suit challenging the constitutionality of § 505 under the First Amendment in the United States District Court for the District of Delaware after obtaining a temporary restraining order (TRO) enjoining the enforcement of the section. The court denied issuing a preliminary injunction, and the United States Supreme Court summarily affirmed. Subsequently, the TRO was lifted and the Federal Communications Commission (FCC) began enforcement of § 505. Fearful of possible violations of § 505 that might occur because of accidental signal bleed, the majority of cable operators opted to use the second, "time channeling," option in order to comply. Appellee thus lost a large portion of its potential market: the hours between 6 a.m. and 10 p.m. The District Court concluded that § 505 violates the First Amendment as an overly restrictive, content-based speech regulation. The

United States filed a direct appeal with the Supreme Court of the United States pursuant § 561 of the Act.

Justice Kennedy wrote for a divided Court, holding that § 505 violated the First Amendment because it was not the least restrictive means of accomplishing a legitimate government objective. Justices Scalia and Breyer filed dissenting opinions. Justice Breyer also filed a dissenting opinion joined by Chief Justice Rehnquist, as well as by Justices O'Connor and Scalia.

The Court noted that the material at issue was presumed to be offensive, while at the same time fully protected by the First Amendment. "The Speech in question is defined by its content; and a statute which seeks to restrict it is content based," explained Kennedy. "Not only does § 505 single out particular programming content for regulation, it also singles out particular programmers." Laws designed to suppress or restrict the expression of specific speakers contradict basic First Amendment principles. "In determining that § 505 is a content-based speech regulation, the Court explains that the statute . . . can stand only if it satisfies strict scrutiny." [citation omitted.]

The Court next analyzed the section under strict scrutiny. "If a statute regulates speech based on its content, it must be narrowly tailored to promote a compelling Government interest . . . [and] [i]f a less restrictive alternative would serve the Government's purpose, the government must use that alternative." The majority focused on the "less restrictive alternative" available to the government in this case. Following the reasoning of the three-judge District Court, the Court concluded that § 504 of the Act provided a less restrictive alternative. Section 504 allowed a cable subscriber to have any channel fully blocked by the cable provider, free of charge. The Court reasoned that, if properly publicized to cable customers, § 504 would provide the protection of children that the government desired without having to effectively block an entire category of protected speech during the daytime hours. Kennedy explains, "Simply put, targeted blocking is less restrictive than banning, and the Government cannot ban speech if targeted blocking is a feasible and effective means of furthering its compelling interests."

The Court then turned to the probable effectiveness of "targeted blocking, and stated that it was the Government's obligation to prove that the alternative would be ineffective to achieve its goals." During the time that § 504 was in effect, very few households made any request to have channels blocked in their homes. In looking at the "tepid" response that cable customers had towards § 504, the Court was unconvinced of the severity of the "signal bleed" problem; the Government's evidence was characterized as largely anecdotal. "If the number of children transfixed by even flickering pornographic images in fact reached into the millions we. . . . would have expected to be directed to more than a handful of complaints," noted Kennedy. Finding the evidentiary basis for the Government's assertion of § 504's ineffectiveness to be lacking, the Court stated, "There is no evidence that a well promoted voluntary blocking provision would not be capable at least of informing parents about signal bleed . . . and their rights to have the bleed blocked." Finding the Government's restriction of speech in the instant case to be impermissible under the First Amendment, the Court invalidated § 505.

(9) **Child Pornography.** While child pornography that uses real children has no constitutional protection, the Supreme Court in *Ashcroft v. Free Speech Coalition*, 535 U.S. 234, 122 S.Ct. 1389, 152 L.Ed.2d 403 (2002), ruled that using virtual children—computer-generated images of young-looking adults—in explicit sexual activity is nothing more than "visual depiction of an idea," a form of expression entitled to First Amendment protection. The Court struck down the Child Pornography Prevention Act of 1996. In his majority opinion, Justice Kennedy said the law

was unconstitutionally broad, so unlimited in its reach it chills expression with clear artistic merit.

Since Shakespeare's Juliet was only 13 years old, the law which prohibited "any visual depiction that is or appears to be of a minor engaging in sexually explicit conduct" could prohibit modern productions of Shakespeare's play, along with such Academy Award winning films as "Traffic" and "American Beauty," which depict teenagers in explicit sexual situations. Another section of the law struck down created a criminal prohibition of advertising or promoting material "in such a manner that conveys the impression" that it is real child pornography.

The law, wrote Justice Kennedy, "prohibits speech that records no crime and creates no victims by its production." Further, "the statute prohibits the visual depiction of an idea—that of teenagers engaging in sexual activity—that is a fact of modern society and has been a theme in art and literature throughout the ages."

United States v. Williams, **553 U.S. ___, 128 S.Ct. 1830, 170 L.Ed.2d 650 (2008).** In 2008, the Supreme Court upheld the statute enacted by Congress in response to *Ashcroft*. The new statute, titled Prosecutorial Remedies and Other Tools to end the Exploitation of Children Today (PROTECT) Act, makes it an offense knowingly to pander (offer to provide or request to obtain through advertising, solicitation, etc.) material, in a manner that the actor believes or intends to cause another to believe, that it depicts children engaged in sexually explicit conduct. Thus, the statute does not require proof of actual child pornography, but instead prohibits the "collateral speech that introduces such material into the child pornography distribution network." The Court, in an opinion by Justice Scalia, rejected the argument that the statute failed under the First Amendment overbreadth doctrine, finding that it did not prohibit a substantial amount of protected speech. The Court noted that offers to engage in illegal transactions are categorically excluded from First Amendment protection and concluded that this exclusion is not limited to commercial transactions. Although advocacy of illegal activity, including child pornography, would enjoy First Amendment protection, the statutory prohibition was directed instead at offers to provide or requests to obtain pornography and thus came within the exclusion. The Court rejected the reasoning that Congress could not criminalize a mistaken belief that material included real children when it was actually virtual pornography (the latter protected under *Ashcroft*), noting that factual impossibility is no defense to an attempt (to transact in pornography involving real children).

Justice Souter, joined by Justice Ginsburg, dissented on the ground that the statute prohibited transactions in virtual pornography; the dissenters rejected the Court's attempt analogy, arguing that, in contrast to the conduct in the typical factual impossibility case, purveying virtual pornography was protected speech.

FEDERAL REGULATION OF MINORS' ACCESS TO INTERNET PORNOGRAPHY

Children's access to pornographic material over the Internet became a policy focus in the late 1990s. The Internet has presented a greater challenge to regulators than other media sources. Congress has enacted several statutes to deal with this problem, both of which were ultimately reviewed by the Supreme Court. The first statute, the Communication Decency Act, was enacted in 1996. It criminalized the knowing transmission of indecent and obscene material to minors, or the knowing sending or displaying of patently offensive material in a way that was available to minors. The Supreme Court found this statute to be unconstitutional in *Reno v. ACLU*, below. The Child Online Protection Act, another effort to shield children from pornography on the internet barely survived an initial Supreme Court test in *Ashcroft v. American Civil Liberties Union, 535 U.S. 564, 122 S.Ct. 1700, 152*

L.Ed.2d 771 (2002). The Justices remanded the case to the Third Circuit which had held the law. Finally, Congress enacted the the Children's Internet Protection Act which was upheld by the Court in *United States v. American Library Association,* which follows *Reno* below.

Reno v. American Civil Liberties Union, 521 U.S. 844, 117 S.Ct. 2329, 138 L.Ed.2d 874 (1997)

Two provisions of the Communications Decency Act (CDA) were enacted by Congress as part of Title V of the Telecommunications Act of 1996 to address growing concerns about the accessibility of minors to sexually explicit material on the Internet. The first provision, 47 U.S.C.A. § 223(a), prohibits the "knowing transmission of obscene or indecent messages to any recipient under 18 years of age." The second, § 223(d), prohibits the "knowing sending or displaying of patently offensive messages in a manner that is available to a person under 18 years of age." The Act provided that violation of either of these provisions is punishable by fine, imprisonment, or both.

A Federal District Court held that the CDA violated both the First and Fifth Amendments and enjoined the Government from enforcing the prohibitions. The Government appealed directly to the Supreme Court under the Act's special review provisions, and the Court granted certiorari. Confining its analysis to the First Amendment issue, the Court held that the CDA abridges the freedom of speech protected by the First Amendment.

Justice Stevens, writing for the majority, rejected the Government's effort to establish the constitutionality of the CDA based on three of the Court's prior decisions: 1) *Ginsberg v. New York,* 390 U.S. 629, 88 S.Ct. 1274, 20 L.Ed.2d 195 (1968); 2) *FCC v. Pacifica Foundation,* 438 U.S. 726, 98 S.Ct. 3026, 57 L.Ed.2d 1073 (1978); and 3) *Renton v. Playtime Theatres, Inc.,* 475 U.S. 41, 106 S.Ct. 925, 89 L.Ed.2d 29 (1986). The Court rejected the comparison in each of the three cases, observing that the prohibitions in *Ginsberg, Pacifica,* and *Renton* were considerably narrower than the CDA. The "overbreadth" of the CDA, wrote Stevens, is partly attributable to the vagueness of its language. The Court found that Sect. 223(a)'s prohibition against "indecent" material and Sect. 223(d)'s prohibition against "patently offensive" material would have the effect of "provok[ing] uncertainty . . . about how the two standards relate to each other and just what they mean." Stevens argued that since the Act is a content-based regulation of speech, its vagueness "raises special First Amendment concerns because of its obvious chilling effect on free speech." The vagueness of the Act's language is also particularly troubling, wrote Stevens, since violation of the CDA is punishable by imprisonment.

The Court thus determined that the CDA "lacks the precision that the First Amendment requires when a statute regulates the content of speech." "In order to deny minors access to potentially harmful speech," wrote Stevens, "the CDA effectively suppresses a large amount of speech that adults have a constitutional right to receive and to address to one another." Although Stevens acknowledged that the Government has an interest in protecting minors from harmful materials, the Court agreed with the District Court's determination that a less restrictive alternative could be found in "user-based software" soon to be "widely available" which would allow parents to prevent their children from accessing sexually explicit and other inappropriate material on the Internet. Stevens concluded the opinion by stating that "[t]he interest in encouraging freedom of expression in a democratic society outweighs any theoretical but unproven benefit of censorship."

Justice O'Connor, joined by Chief Justice Rehnquist, wrote a separate opinion concurring in part and dissenting in part. In her view, the CDA was an attempt by Congress to create constitutionally permissible "adult zones" on the Internet.

However, O'Connor agreed with the Court that portions of the CDA are unconstitutional since they "stray from the blueprint our prior cases have developed for constructing a 'zoning law' that passes constitutional muster."

United States v. American Library Association, 539 U.S. 194, 123 S.Ct. 2297, 156 L.Ed.2d 221 (2003).

The Children's Internet Protection Act (CIPA) requires school and public libraries to install software that blocks or filters Internet access to material that constitutes obscenity or child pornography or that is harmful to children, as a condition to receiving federal funds or grants created to expand and support internet access. The American Library Association challenged the constitutionality of CIPA as abridging First Amendment rights of adult library patrons in *United States v. American Library Association*, 539 U.S. 194, 123 S.Ct. 2297, 156 L.Ed.2d 221 (2003).

Chief Justice Rehnquist announced the judgment of the court and delivered the plurality opinion, in which Justices O'Connor, Scalia, and Thomas joined. Justices Kennedy and Breyer filed concurring opinions.

CIPA ... provides that a library may not receive [federal] assistance unless it has "a policy of Internet safety for minors that includes the operation of a technology protection measure ... that protects against access" by all persons to "visual depictions" that constitute "obscenity" or "child pornography," and that protects against access by minors to "visual depictions" that are "harmful to minors." 20 U.S.C. §§ 9134(f)1(A)(i) and (B)(i)....

... [T]he District Court ruled that CIPA was facially unconstitutional and enjoined the relevant agencies and officials from withholding federal assistance for failure to comply with CIPA. The District Court held that Congress had exceeded its authority under the Spending Clause, U.S. Const., Art I, § 8. cl. 1, because, in the court's view, "any public library that complies with CIPA's conditions will necessarily violate the First Amendment." 201 F.Supp.2d, at 453. The court acknowledged that "generally the First Amendment subjects libraries' content-based decisions about which print materials to acquire for their collections to only rational [basis] review." *Id.* at 462. But it distinguished libraries' decisions to make certain Internet material inaccessible. "The central difference," the court stated, "is that by providing patrons with even filtered Internet access, the library permits patrons to receive speech on a virtually unlimited number of topics, from a virtually unlimited number of speakers, without attempting to restrict patrons' access to speech that the library, in the exercise of its professional judgment, determines to be particularly valuable." *Ibid.* Reasoning that "the provision of Internet access within a public library ... is for use by the public ... for expressive activity," the court analyzed such access as a "designated public forum." *Id.* at 471....

Based on both of these grounds, the [district] court held that the filtering software contemplated by CIPA was a content-based restriction on access to a public forum, and was therefore subject to strict scrutiny. *Ibid.* Applying this standard, the District Court held that, although the Government has a compelling interest "in preventing the dissemination of obscenity, child pornography, or, in the case of minors, material harmful to minors," *id.* at 471, the use of software filters is not narrowly tailored to further those interests. *Id.* at 479....

... To determine whether libraries violate the First Amendment by employing filtering software that CIPA requires, we must first examine the role of libraries in our society ...

Public libraries pursue the worthy missions of facilitating learning and cultural enrichment ... To fulfill their traditional missions, public libraries must have broad discretion to decide what material to provide to their patrons. Although they seek to provide a wide array of information, their goal has never been to provide "universal coverage." 201 F.Supp.2d at 421. Instead, public libraries seek to provide materials "that would be of the greatest direct benefit or interest to the community." *Ibid*....

We have held ... that the government has broad discretion to make content-based judgments in deciding what private speech to make available to the public. In *Arkansas Ed. Television Comm'n v. Forbes*, 523 U.S. 666, 118 S.Ct. 1633, 140 L.Ed.2d 875 (1998), we held that public forum principles do not generally apply to a public television station's editorial judgments regarding the private speech it presents to its viewers. "... Similarly, in *National Endowment for Arts v. Finley*, 524 U.S. 569 (1998), we upheld an art funding program that required the National Endowment for the Arts (NEA) to use content-based criteria in making funding decisions ..."

The principles underlying *Forbes* and *Finley* also apply to a public library's exercise of judgment in selecting the material it provides to its patrons. Just as forum analysis and heightened judicial scrutiny are incompatible with the role of public television stations and the role of the NEA, they are also incompatible with the discretion that public libraries must have to fulfill their traditional missions. Public library staffs necessarily consider content in making collection decisions and enjoy broad discretion in making them.

The public forum principles on which the District Court relied, 201 F.Supp.2d at 457–470, are out of place in the context of this case. Internet access in public libraries is neither a "traditional" nor a "designated" public forum.... First, this resource—which did not exist until quite recently—has not "immemorially been held in trust for the use of the public and, time out of mind, ... been used for purposes of assembly, communication of thoughts between citizens, and discussing public questions." *International Soc. For Krishna Consciousness v. Lee*, 505 U.S. 672, 112 S.Ct. 2701, 120 L.Ed.2d 541 (1992). We have "rejected the view that traditional public forum status extends beyond historic confines." *Forbes*, supra, at 678....

Nor does Internet access in a public library satisfy our definition of a "designated public forum." To create such a forum, the government must make an affirmative choice to open up its property for use as a public forum. *Cornelius v. NAACP Legal Defense & Ed. Fund*, 473 U.S. 788, 802–3, 105 S.Ct. 3439, 87 L.Ed.2d 567 (1985).... A public library does not acquire Internet terminals in order to create a public forum for Web publishers to express themselves, any more than it collects books in order to provide a public forum for the authors of books to speak. It provides Internet access, not to "encourage a diversity of views from private speakers," *Rosenberger v. Rector and Visitors of Univ. of Va.*, 515 U.S. 819, 834, 115 S.Ct. 2510, 132 L.Ed.2d 700 (1995), but for the same reasons it offers other library resources: to facilitate research, learning, and recreational pursuits by furnishing materials of requisite and appropriate quality....

... A library's failure to make quality-based judgments about all the material it furnishes from the Web does not somehow taint the judgment it does make. A library's need to exercise judgment in making collection decisions depends on its traditional role in identifying suitable and worthwhile material; it is no less entitled to play that role when it collects material from the Internet than when it collects material from any other source. Most libraries already exclude pornography from their print collections because they deem it inappropriate for inclusion. We do not subject these decisions to heightened scrutiny; it would make little sense to treat libraries' judgments to block online pornography any differently, when these judgments are made for just the same reason.

Moreover, because of the vast quantity of material on the Internet and the rapid pace at which it changes, libraries cannot possibly segregate, item by item, all the Internet material that is appropriate for inclusion from all that is not. While a library could limit its Internet collection to just those sites it found worthwhile, it could do so only at the cost of excluding an enormous amount of valuable information that it lacks the capacity to review. Given that tradeoff, it is entirely reasonable for public libraries to reject that approach and instead exclude certain categories of content, without making individualized judgments that everything they do make available has requisite and appropriate quality.

. . . The District Court viewed unblocking and disabling as inadequate because some patrons may be too embarrassed to request them. But the Constitution does not guarantee the right to acquire information at a public library without any risk of embarrassment.

[The plurality also rejected the argument that CIPA imposed an unconstitutional condition on the receipt of federal assistance.]

Congress may certainly insist that these [referring to the E-rate and LSTA programs] "public funds be spent for the purposes for which they were authorized." *Id.* Especially because public libraries have traditionally excluded pornographic material from their other collections, Congress could reasonably impose a parallel limitation on its Internet assistance programs. . . .

. . . CIPA does not "penalize" libraries that choose not to install such software, or deny them the right to provide their patrons with unfiltered Internet access. Rather, CIPA simply reflects Congress' decision not to subsidize their doing so. "[A] legislature's decision not to subsidize the exercise of a fundamental right does not infringe the right." *Id.* (*internal citation and quotation omitted*).

Justice Kennedy concurred in the judgment. Applying a strict scrutiny analysis, he concluded that the government's interest in protecting young library users from material inappropriate for minors was legitimate, and even compelling, and the plaintiffs had failed to show that the ability of adult library users to have access to the material was burdened in any significant degree.

Justice Breyer concurred in the judgment, applying a heightened scrutiny analysis. He also emphasized that the government interests were legitimate, and also pointed to the provision that adult patrons could get access to "overblocked" Web sites.

Two Justices wrote dissenting opinions. Justice Stevens wrote, "rather than allowing local decisionmakers to tailor their responses to local problems, [CIPA] operates as a blunt nationwide restraint on adult access to 'an enormous amount of valuable information' that individual librarians cannot possibly review." As a prior restraint on speech, he would find CIPA unconstitutional: "An abridgment of speech by means of a threatened denial of benefits can be just as pernicious as an abridgment by means of a threatened penalty." Justice Souter, agreed with Justice Stevens and also argued that CIPA violates the Spending Clause. He wrote, "the question for me, then, is whether the local library could itself constitutionally impose these restrictions on the content otherwise available to an adult patron through an Internet connection, at a library terminal provided for public use." He answered the question in the negative because "[a] library that chose to block an adult's Internet access to material harmful to children (and whatever else the undiscriminating filter might interrupt) would be imposing a content-based restriction on communication of material in the library's control that an adult could otherwise lawfully see." Although he recognized that a library has discretion in choosing books to put on its shelves, after providing patrons with Internet access, the library cannot then unconstitutionally limit the access.

Handwritten note (partially covering text): *First Amendment applied to public schools + that administrators would have to demonstrate constitutionally valid reasons for any specific regulation of speech in the classroom.*

2. ... RST AMENDMENT

Ti... ommunity School
Di...

Sup...
393 ...

■ M... Court.

Eck... nd petitioner Christopher
... Des Moines, Iowa. Petition... -year-old student in junior
high school.

In December 1965, a group of adults and students in Des Moines held a meeting at the Eckhardt home. The group determined to publicize their objections to the hostilities in Vietnam and their support for a truce by wearing black armbands during the holiday season and by fasting on December 16 and New Year's Eve. Petitioners and their parents had previously engaged in similar activities, and they decided to participate in the program.

The principals of the Des Moines schools became aware of the plan to wear armbands. On December 14, 1965, they met and adopted a policy that any student wearing an armband to school would be asked to remove it, and if he refused he would be suspended until he returned without the armband. Petitioners were aware of the regulation that the school authorities adopted.

On December 16, Mary Beth and Christopher wore black armbands to their schools. John Tinker wore his armband the next day. They were all sent home and suspended from school until they would come back without their armbands. They did not return to school until after the planned period for wearing armbands had expired—that is, until after New Year's Day.

This complaint was filed in the United States District Court by petitioners, through their fathers, under § 1983 of Title 42 of the United States Code. It prayed for an injunction restraining the respondent school officials and the respondent members of the board of directors of the school district from disciplining the petitioners, and it sought nominal damages. After an evidentiary hearing the District Court dismissed the complaint. It upheld the constitutionality of the school authorities' action on the ground that it was reasonable in order to prevent disturbance of school discipline. 258 F.Supp. 971 (1966). The court referred to but expressly declined to follow the Fifth Circuit's holding in a similar case that the wearing of symbols like the armbands cannot be prohibited unless it "materially and substantially interfere[s] with the requirements of appropriate discipline in the operation of the school." Burnside v. Byars, 363 F.2d 744, 749 (1966).[1]

---

1. In *Burnside*, the Fifth Circuit ordered that high school authorities be enjoined from enforcing a regulation forbidding stu- dents to wear "freedom buttons." It is instructive that in Blackwell v. Issaquena County Board of Education, 363 F.2d 749

demonstrate to the other students that the petitioners were mourning because of the death of United States soldiers in Vietnam and to protest that war which they were against. Ordered to refrain from wearing the armbands in school by the elected school officials and the teachers vested with state authority to do so, apparently only seven out of the school system's 18,000 pupils deliberately refused to obey the order. One defying pupil was Paul Tinker, 8 years old, who was in the second grade; another, Hope Tinker, was 11 years old and in the fifth grade; a third member of the Tinker family was 13, in the eighth grade; and a fourth member of the same family was John Tinker, 15 years old, an 11th grade high school pupil. Their father, a Methodist minister without a church, is paid a salary by the American Friends Service Committee. Another student who defied the school order and insisted on wearing an armband in school was Christopher Eckhardt, an 11th grade pupil and a petitioner in this case. His mother is an official in the Women's International League for Peace and Freedom.

. . .

Assuming that the Court is correct in holding that the conduct of wearing armbands for the purpose of conveying political ideas is protected by the First Amendment, the crucial remaining questions are whether students and teachers may use the schools at their whim as a platform for the exercise of free speech—"symbolic" or "pure"—and whether the courts will allocate to themselves the function of deciding how the pupils' school day will be spent....

While the record does not show that any of these armband students shouted, used profane language, or were violent in any manner, detailed testimony by some of them shows their armbands caused comments, warnings by other students, the poking of fun at them, and a warning by an older football player that other, nonprotesting students had better let them alone. There is also evidence that a teacher of mathematics had his lesson period practically "wrecked" chiefly by disputes with Mary Beth Tinker, who wore her armband for her "demonstration." Even a casual reading of the record shows that this armband did divert students' minds from their regular lessons, and that talk, comments, etc., made John Tinker "self-conscious" in attending school with his armband. While the absence of obscene remarks or boisterous and loud disorder perhaps justifies the Court's statement that the few armband students did not actually "disrupt" the classwork, I think the record overwhelmingly shows that the armbands did exactly what the elected school officials and principals foresaw they would, that is, took the students' minds off their classwork and diverted them to thoughts about the highly emotional subject of the Vietnam war. And I repeat that if the time has come when pupils of state-supported schools, kindergartens, grammar schools, or high schools, can defy and flout orders of school officials to keep their minds on their own schoolwork, it is the beginning of a new revolutionary era of permissiveness in this country fostered by the judiciary. The next logical step, it appears to me, would be to hold unconstitutional laws that bar pupils under 21 or 18

2. Children as Persons Under the First Amendment

Tinker v. Des Moines Independent Community School District

Supreme Court of the United States, 1969.
393 U.S. 503, 89 S.Ct. 733, 21 L.Ed.2d 731.

■ Mr. Justice Fortas delivered the opinion of the Court.

Petitioner John F. Tinker, 15 years old, and petitioner Christopher Eckhardt, 16 years old, attended high schools in Des Moines, Iowa. Petitioner Mary Beth Tinker, John's sister, was a 13–year-old student in junior high school.

In December 1965, a group of adults and students in Des Moines held a meeting at the Eckhardt home. The group determined to publicize their objections to the hostilities in Vietnam and their support for a truce by wearing black armbands during the holiday season and by fasting on December 16 and New Year's Eve. Petitioners and their parents had previously engaged in similar activities, and they decided to participate in the program.

The principals of the Des Moines schools became aware of the plan to wear armbands. On December 14, 1965, they met and adopted a policy that any student wearing an armband to school would be asked to remove it, and if he refused he would be suspended until he returned without the armband. Petitioners were aware of the regulation that the school authorities adopted.

On December 16, Mary Beth and Christopher wore black armbands to their schools. John Tinker wore his armband the next day. They were all sent home and suspended from school until they would come back without their armbands. They did not return to school until after the planned period for wearing armbands had expired—that is, until after New Year's Day.

This complaint was filed in the United States District Court by petitioners, through their fathers, under § 1983 of Title 42 of the United States Code. It prayed for an injunction restraining the respondent school officials and the respondent members of the board of directors of the school district from disciplining the petitioners, and it sought nominal damages. After an evidentiary hearing the District Court dismissed the complaint. It upheld the constitutionality of the school authorities' action on the ground that it was reasonable in order to prevent disturbance of school discipline. 258 F.Supp. 971 (1966). The court referred to but expressly declined to follow the Fifth Circuit's holding in a similar case that the wearing of symbols like the armbands cannot be prohibited unless it "materially and substantially interfere[s] with the requirements of appropriate discipline in the operation of the school." Burnside v. Byars, 363 F.2d 744, 749 (1966).[1]

1. In *Burnside*, the Fifth Circuit ordered that high school authorities be enjoined from enforcing a regulation forbidding stu- dents to wear "freedom buttons." It is instructive that in Blackwell v. Issaquena County Board of Education, 363 F.2d 749

On appeal, the Court of Appeals for the Eighth Circuit considered the case *en banc.* The court was equally divided, and the District Court's decision was accordingly affirmed. . . .

The District Court recognized that the wearing of an armband for the purpose of expressing certain views is the type of symbolic act that is within the Free Speech Clause of the First Amendment. As we shall discuss, the wearing of armbands in the circumstances of this case was entirely divorced from actually or potentially disruptive conduct by those participating in it. It was closely akin to "pure speech" which, we have repeatedly held, is entitled to comprehensive protection under the First Amendment.

First Amendment rights, applied in light of the special characteristics of the school environment, are available to teachers and students. It can hardly be argued that either students or teachers shed their constitutional rights to freedom of speech or expression at the schoolhouse gate. This has been the unmistakable holding of this Court for almost 50 years.

In West Virginia State Board of Education v. Barnette, 319 U.S. 624 (1943), this Court held that under the First Amendment, the student in public school may not be compelled to salute the flag. Speaking through Mr. Justice Jackson, the Court said:

"The Fourteenth Amendment, as now applied to the States, protects the citizen against the State itself and all of its creatures—Boards of Education not excepted. These have, of course, important, delicate, and highly discretionary functions, but none that they may not perform within the limits of the Bill of Rights. That they are educating the young for citizenship is reason for scrupulous protection of Constitutional freedoms of the individual, if we are not to strangle the free mind at its source and teach youth to discount important principles of our government as mere platitudes." 319 U.S., at 637.

On the other hand, the Court has repeatedly emphasized the need for affirming the comprehensive authority of the States and of school officials, consistent with fundamental constitutional safeguards, to prescribe and control conduct in the schools. Our problem lies in the area where students in the exercise of First Amendment rights collide with the rules of the school authorities.

The problem posed by the present case does not relate to regulation of the length of skirts or the type of clothing, to hair style, or deportment. It does not concern aggressive, disruptive action or even group demonstrations. Our problem involves direct, primary First Amendment rights akin to "pure speech."

The school officials banned and sought to punish petitioners for a silent, passive expression of opinion, unaccompanied by any disorder or disturbance on the part of petitioners. There is here no evidence whatever of petitioners' interference, actual or nascent, with the schools' work or of

(1966), the same panel on the same day reached the opposite result on different facts. It declined to enjoin enforcement of such a regulation in another high school where the students wearing freedom buttons harassed students who did not wear them and created much disturbance.

collision with the rights of other students to be secure and to be let alone. Accordingly, this case does not concern speech or action that intrudes upon the work of the schools or the rights of other students.

Only a few of the 18,000 students in the school system wore the black armbands. Only five students were suspended for wearing them. There is no indication that the work of the schools or any class was disrupted. Outside the classrooms, a few students made hostile remarks to the children wearing armbands, but there were no threats or acts of violence on school premises.

The District Court concluded that the action of the school authorities was reasonable because it was based upon their fear of a disturbance from the wearing of the armbands. But, in our system, undifferentiated fear or apprehension of disturbance is not enough to overcome the right to freedom of expression. Any departure from absolute regimentation may cause trouble. Any variation from the majority's opinion may inspire fear. Any word spoken, in class, in the lunchroom, or on the campus, that deviates from the views of another person may start an argument or cause a disturbance. But our Constitution says we must take this risk....

In order for the State in the person of school officials to justify prohibition of a particular expression of opinion, it must be able to show that its action was caused by something more than a mere desire to avoid the discomfort and unpleasantness that always accompany an unpopular viewpoint. Certainly where there is no finding and no showing that engaging in the forbidden conduct would "materially and substantially interfere with the requirements of appropriate discipline in the operation of the school," the prohibition cannot be sustained. Burnside v. Byars, supra, 363 F.2d at 749.

In the present case, the District Court made no such finding, and our independent examination of the record fails to yield evidence that the school authorities had reason to anticipate that the wearing of the armbands would substantially interfere with the work of the school or impinge upon the rights of other students. Even an official memorandum prepared after the suspension that listed the reasons for the ban on wearing the armbands made no reference to the anticipation of such disruption.[3]

On the contrary, the action of the school authorities appears to have been based upon an urgent wish to avoid the controversy which might result from the expression, even by the silent symbol of armbands, of opposition to this Nation's part in the conflagration in Vietnam. It is revealing, in this respect, that the meeting at which the school principals decided to issue the contested regulation was called in response to a student's statement to the journalism teacher in one of the schools that he wanted to write an article on Vietnam and have it published in the school paper. (The student was dissuaded.)

---

3. ... [T]he testimony of school authorities at trial indicates that it was not fear of disruption that motivated the regulation prohibiting the armbands; the regulation was directed against "the principle of the demonstration" itself. School authorities simply felt that "the schools are no place for demonstrations," and if the students "didn't like the way our elected officials were handling things, it should be handled with the ballot box and not in the halls of our public schools."

It is also relevant that the school authorities did not purport to prohibit the wearing of all symbols of political or controversial significance. The record shows that students in some of the schools wore buttons relating to national political campaigns, and some even wore the Iron Cross, traditionally a symbol of Nazism. The order prohibiting the wearing of armbands did not extend to these. Instead, a particular symbol—black armbands worn to exhibit opposition to this Nation's involvement in Vietnam—was singled out for prohibition. Clearly, the prohibition of expression of one particular opinion, at least without evidence that it is necessary to avoid material and substantial interference with schoolwork or discipline, is not constitutionally permissible.

In our system, state-operated schools may not be enclaves of totalitarianism. School officials do not possess absolute authority over their students. Students in school as well as out of school are "persons" under our Constitution. They are possessed of fundamental rights which the State must respect, just as they themselves must respect their obligations to the State. In our system, students may not be regarded as closed-circuit recipients of only that which the State chooses to communicate. They may not be confined to the expression of those sentiments that are officially approved. In the absence of a specific showing of constitutionally valid reasons to regulate their speech, students are entitled to freedom of expression of their views. . . .

. . . In Keyishian v. Board of Regents, 385 U.S. 589, 603, Mr. Justice Brennan, speaking for the Court, said:

> " 'The vigilant protection of constitutional freedoms is nowhere more vital than in the community of American schools.' Shelton v. Tucker, [364 U.S. 479], at 487. The classroom is peculiarly the 'marketplace of ideas.' The Nation's future depends upon leaders trained through wide exposure to that robust exchange of ideas which discovers truth 'out of a multitude of tongues, [rather] than through any kind of authoritative selection.' "

The principle of these cases is not confined to the supervised and ordained discussion which takes place in the classroom. The principal use to which the schools are dedicated is to accommodate students during prescribed hours for the purpose of certain types of activities. Among those activities is personal intercommunication among the students.[6] This is not only an inevitable part of the process of attending school; it is also an important part of the educational process. A student's rights, therefore, do not embrace merely the classroom hours. When he is in the cafeteria, or on the playing field, or on the campus during the authorized hours, he may express his opinions, even on controversial subjects like the conflict in Vietnam, if he does so without "materially and substantially interfer[ing] with the requirements of appropriate discipline in the operation of the

---

6. In Hammond v. South Carolina State College, 272 F.Supp. 947 (D.C.S.C.1967), District Judge Hemphill had before him a case involving a meeting on campus of 300 students to express their views on school practices. He pointed out that a school is not like a hospital or a jail enclosure. It is a public place, and its dedication to specific uses does not imply that the constitutional rights of persons entitled to be there are to be gauged as if the premises were purely private property.

school" and without colliding with the rights of others. Burnside v. Byars, supra, 363 F.2d at 749. But conduct by the student, in class or out of it, which for any reason—whether it stems from time, place, or type of behavior—materially disrupts classwork or involves substantial disorder or invasion of the rights of others is, of course, not immunized by the constitutional guarantee of freedom of speech.

. . .

As we have discussed, the record does not demonstrate any facts which might reasonably have led school authorities to forecast substantial disruption of or material interference with school activities, and no disturbances or disorders on the school premises in fact occurred. These petitioners merely went about their ordained rounds in school. Their deviation consisted only in wearing on their sleeve a band of black cloth, not more than two inches wide. They wore it to exhibit their disapproval of the Vietnam hostilities and their advocacy of a truce, to make their views known, and, by their example, to influence others to adopt them. They neither interrupted school activities nor sought to intrude in the school affairs or the lives of others. They caused discussion outside of the classrooms, but no interference with work and no disorder. In the circumstances, our Constitution does not permit officials of the State to deny their form of expression.

We express no opinion as to the form of relief which should be granted, this being a matter for the lower courts to determine. . . .

Reversed and remanded.

■ Mr. Justice Stewart, concurring.

Although I agree with much of what is said in the Court's opinion, and with its judgment in this case, I cannot share the Court's uncritical assumption that, school discipline aside, the First Amendment rights of children are co-extensive with those of adults. Indeed, I had thought the Court decided otherwise just last Term in Ginsberg v. New York, 390 U.S. 629. I continue to hold the view I expressed in that case: "[A] State may permissibly determine that, at least in some precisely delineated areas, a child—like someone in a captive audience—is not possessed of that full capacity for individual choice which is the presupposition of First Amendment guarantees." Id., at 649–650 (concurring in result). Cf. Prince v. Massachusetts, 321 U.S. 158.

■ [The concurring opinion of Mr. Justice White is omitted.]

■ Mr. Justice Black, dissenting.

The Court's holding in this case ushers in what I deem to be an entirely new era in which the power to control pupils by the elected "officials of state supported public schools . . ." in the United States is in ultimate effect transferred to the Supreme Court. The Court brought this particular case here on a petition for certiorari urging that the First and Fourteenth Amendments protect the right of school pupils to express their political views all the way "from kindergarten through high school." Here the constitutional right to "political expression" asserted was a right to wear black armbands during school hours and at classes in order to demonstrate to the other students that the petitioners were mourning because of the death of United States soldiers in Vietnam and to protest that war which they were against. Ordered to refrain from wearing the armbands in school by the elected school officials and the teachers vested with state authority to do so, apparently only seven out of the school system's 18,000 pupils deliberately refused to obey the order. One defying pupil was Paul Tinker, 8 years old, who was in the second grade; another, Hope Tinker, was 11 years old and in the fifth grade; a third member of the Tinker family was 13, in the eighth grade; and a fourth member of the same family was John Tinker, 15 years old, an 11th grade high school pupil. Their father, a Methodist minister without a church, is paid a salary by the American Friends Service Committee. Another student who defied the school order and insisted on wearing an armband in school was Christopher Eckhardt, an 11th grade pupil and a petitioner in this case. His mother is an official in the Women's International League for Peace and Freedom.

.   .   .

Assuming that the Court is correct in holding that the conduct of wearing armbands for the purpose of conveying political ideas is protected by the First Amendment, the crucial remaining questions are whether students and teachers may use the schools at their whim as a platform for the exercise of free speech—"symbolic" or "pure"—and whether the courts will allocate to themselves the function of deciding how the pupils' school day will be spent. . . .

While the record does not show that any of these armband students shouted, used profane language, or were violent in any manner, detailed testimony by some of them shows their armbands caused comments, warnings by other students, the poking of fun at them, and a warning by an older football player that other, nonprotesting students had better let them alone. There is also evidence that a teacher of mathematics had his lesson period practically "wrecked" chiefly by disputes with Mary Beth Tinker, who wore her armband for her "demonstration." Even a casual reading of the record shows that this armband did divert students' minds from their regular lessons, and that talk, comments, etc., made John Tinker "self-conscious" in attending school with his armband. While the absence of obscene remarks or boisterous and loud disorder perhaps justi- fies the Court's statement that the few armband students did not actually "disrupt" the classwork, I think the record overwhelmingly shows that the armbands did exactly what the elected school officials and principals foresaw they would, that is, took the students' minds off their classwork and diverted them to thoughts about the highly emotional subject of the Vietnam war. And I repeat that if the time has come when pupils of state- supported schools, kindergartens, grammar schools, or high schools, can defy and flout orders of school officials to keep their minds on their own schoolwork, it is the beginning of a new revolutionary era of permissiveness in this country fostered by the judiciary. The next logical step, it appears to me, would be to hold unconstitutional laws that bar pupils under 21 or 18 from voting, or from being elected members of the boards of education.[2]

. . .

I deny ... that it has been the "unmistakable holding of this Court for almost 50 years" that "students" and "teachers" take with them into the "schoolhouse gate" constitutional rights to "freedom of speech or expression." Even *Meyer* did not hold that. It makes no reference to "symbolic speech" at all; ...

. . .

In my view, teachers in state-controlled public schools are hired to teach there. Although Mr. Justice McReynolds may have intimated to the contrary in Meyer v. Nebraska, supra, certainly a teacher is not paid to go into school and teach subjects the State does not hire him to teach as a part of its selected curriculum. Nor are public school students sent to the schools at public expense to broadcast political or any other views to educate and inform the public. The original idea of schools, which I do not believe is yet abandoned as worthless or out of date, was that children had not yet reached the point of experience and wisdom which enabled them to teach all of their elders. It may be that the Nation has outworn the old-fashioned slogan that "children are to be seen not heard," but one may, I hope, be permitted to harbor the thought that taxpayers send children to school on the premise that at their age they need to learn, not teach.

. . .

Change has been said to be truly the law of life but sometimes the old and the tried and true are worth holding. The schools of this Nation have undoubtedly contributed to giving us tranquility and to making us a more law-abiding people. Uncontrolled and uncontrollable liberty is an enemy to domestic peace. We cannot close our eyes to the fact that some of the country's greatest problems are crimes committed by the youth, too many of school age. School discipline, like parental discipline, is an integral and important part of training our children to be good citizens—to be better citizens. Here a very small number of students have crisply and summarily refused to obey a school order designed to give pupils who want to learn the opportunity to do so. One does not need to be a prophet or the son of a prophet to know that after the Court's holding today some students in Iowa schools and indeed in all schools will be ready, able, and willing to defy their teachers on practically all orders. This is the more unfortunate for the schools since groups of students all over the land are already running loose, conducting break-ins, sit-ins, lie-ins, and smash-ins.... Students engaged in such activities are apparently confident that they know far more about

2. The following Associated Press article appeared in the Washington Evening Star, January 11, 1969, p. A–2, col. 1: "Bellingham, Mass. (AP)—Todd R. Hennessy, 16, has filed nominating papers to run for town park commissioner in the March election.

" 'I can see nothing illegal in the youth's seeking the elective office,' said Lee Ambler, the town counsel. 'But I can't overlook the possibility that if he is elected any legal contract entered into by the park commissioner would be void because he is a juvenile.'

"Todd is a junior in Mount St. Charles Academy, where he has a top scholastic record."

how to operate public school systems than do their parents, teachers, and elected school officials. It is no answer to say that the particular students here have not yet reached such high points in their demands to attend classes in order to exercise their political pressures. Turned loose with lawsuits for damages and injunctions against their teachers as they are here, it is nothing but wishful thinking to imagine that young, immature students will not soon believe it is their right to control the schools rather than the right of the States that collect the taxes to hire the teachers for the benefit of the pupils. This case, therefore, wholly without constitutional reasons in my judgment, subjects all the public schools in the country to the whims and caprices of their loudest-mouthed, but maybe not their brightest, students. I, for one, am not fully persuaded that school pupils are wise enough, even with this Court's expert held from Washington, to run the 23,390 public school systems in our 50 States. I wish, therefore, wholly to disclaim any purpose on my part to hold that the Federal Constitution compels the teachers, parents, and elected school officials to surrender control of the American public school system to public school students. I dissent.

■ MR. JUSTICE HARLAN, dissenting.

I certainly agree that state public school authorities in the discharge of their responsibilities are not wholly exempt from the requirements of the Fourteenth Amendment respecting the freedoms of expression and association. At the same time I am reluctant to believe that there is any disagreement between the majority and myself on the proposition that school officials should be accorded the widest authority in maintaining discipline and good order in their institutions. To translate that proposition into a workable constitutional rule, I would, in cases like this, cast upon those complaining the burden of showing that a particular school measure was motivated by other than legitimate school concerns—for example, a desire to prohibit the expression of an unpopular point of view, while permitting expression of the dominant opinion.

Finding nothing in this record which impugns the good faith of respondents in promulgating the armband regulation, I would affirm the judgment below.

NOTES ON *TINKER*

(1) **Children as Rights–Bearing Persons.** The Supreme Court in *Tinker* uses expansive language to describe the interest of high school students in Free Expression under the First Amendment. *Tinker* clarifies that public school students have a right under some circumstances to express their political views, but it raises more questions than it answers. First, can *Tinker* be reconciled with *Ginsberg*? The Court in *Ginsberg* seems quite ready to permit states to restrict minor's First Amendment rights. Should one conclude that children are accorded greater freedom to express themselves in political matters than to learn about sex? How important was it to the Court in *Tinker* that school authorities tolerated some forms of political expression (the Nazi insignias), while prohibiting others? If the school district prohibited *all* political expression by students, would it have been on sounder constitutional ground? One interpretation of *Tinker* is that the case is primarily about viewpoint discrimination by state authorities, and that the Court

suspected that the Des Moines School District authorities, in prohibiting demonstration against the Vietnam War, were motivated largely by a desire to discourage expression reflecting an unpopular point of view.

Another important question left unanswered by *Tinker* is whether the age and maturity of the student is relevant in determining the extent of her interest in political expression under the First Amendment. Realistically, do young children have First Amendment rights or do only adolescents and adults have a meaningful interest in expression? Certainly, adults' free speech rights are not contingent on maturity or rationality. Nonetheless, few would take seriously the idea that 5–year-old children have a constitutionally protected interest in expressing their political views. Along these lines, it is interesting that Paul Tinker, age 8, and Hope Tinker, age 11, although they participated in the anti-War demonstration, were not plaintiffs in the action against the school district. At least one Federal appellate court has questioned whether children in elementary school have First Amendment rights under *Tinker*. *Muller v. Jefferson Lighthouse School*, 98 F.3d 1530 (7th Cir.1996).

(2) ***Tinker* and Parents' Rights.** Was *Tinker* really a case about children's rights, or was the Court primarily upholding family expression or parental inculcation of values? For a discussion, see John Garvey, Child, Parent, State, and the Due Process Clause: An Essay on the Supreme Court's Recent Work, 51 So.Cal.L.Rev. 769, 785 (1978), in which the author asserts that *Tinker* was really about "family rights". Not inconsistent, it would seem, is Professor Hafen's statement that "*Tinker* is not an obstacle to the assertion that none of the Supreme Court's children's rights cases provide authority for upholding the exercise of minors' choice rights—particularly against contrary parental claims." Bruce Hafen, Children's Liberation and the New Egalitarianism: Some Reservations about Abandoning Youth to Their "Rights", 1976 B.Y.U.L.Rev. 605, 646. Do you think that the outcome would have been the same if the parents opposed their children's political expression?

Professor Robert Burt has written this sensitive appraisal:

> Even if *Tinker* is—as *Yoder* and *Prince* may be—a symbolic battle between adults, each using children as sacrificial pawns, the Constitution clearly constrains the state more than parents in this matter. If the Des Moines school officials, that is, insist on one brand of ideological conformity, the traditions of the First Amendment amply justify a court ruling that this is impermissible state action in itself.
>
> The *Tinker* Court erred not in its result, but in its failure to acknowledge the potential educational and constitutional relevance of the facts in the case suggesting that the children's armbands reflected more their parents' convictions than theirs. The Court ignored the possibility that school officials might exclude parental political views from school in order to free children to think through these questions for themselves. As noted, that motivation was implausible on the face of the *Tinker* record, but it is not an implausible educational goal, nor should that goal be prohibited by the Constitution. The *Tinker* Court should have acknowledged that the constitutional question would have changed complexion if the school officials had convincingly argued that they were acting not to impose their political views on students, but rather on behalf of the root values of the first amendment—tolerance, diversity of thought, individual autonomy—against parental impositions on children.

Robert Burt, Developing Constitutional Rights of, in, and for Children, 39 Law & Contemp. Probs. 118, 123–24 (1975).*

(3) **The Limits of School Authority after *Tinker*.** The Court described the students' wearing of the black armband in *Tinker* as "pure speech" that was "entirely divorced from . . . disruptive conduct by those participating in it." As such this expression was entitled to comprehensive protection under the First Amendment. The Court appears to dismiss the district's implicit concern that disruption and disturbance might come from the other students reacting hostilely to the demonstration. Does *Tinker* stand for the proposition that school authorities may never prohibit silent political expression that is not accompanied by disruptive conduct? First Amendment doctrine suggests that in other settings, "pure speech," however provocative and offensive to recipients, is protected. Thus, a municipal government could not prohibit a group of Nazis from marching through a Jewish community. (*Collin v. Smith*, 578 F.2d 1197 (7th Cir.1978)). Would school authorities be similarly constrained under *Tinker*?

The language of *Tinker* suggests a broad conception of the rights of minors in the school setting. It left many unanswered questions about the extent of students' right of Free Expression and the parameters of the constitutional constraints on school officials' ability to make rules to promote order and discipline and to further the state's educational objectives. Can schools impose student dress codes or have rules about grooming? Are student-edited school newspapers entitled to the same protection under the First Amendment as the press generally enjoys? These issues will be addressed in Chapter III, which clarifies that the Court after *Tinker* has not been inclined toward an expansive view of students' First Amendment right of Free Expression.

D.   CHILDREN'S PARTICIPATION IN DECISIONMAKING IN LEGAL CONTEXTS

1.   AN ARGUMENT FOR PARTICIPATION

Wisconsin v. Yoder

Supreme Court of the United States, 1972.
406 U.S. 205, 92 S.Ct. 1526, 32 L.Ed.2d 15.

■ MR. JUSTICE DOUGLAS, dissenting in part.

(The opinion (including Justice Douglas's dissent) is reproduced on page 18 supra.)

WISCONSIN v. YODER: THE DOUGLAS DISSENT

(1) **Children and Self–Determination.** Justice Douglas's dissent in *Yoder*, proposing that the affected Amish children had a right to be heard before their future education could be decided, represents a bold departure from conventional constitutional doctrine regulating authority over children. Douglas posits that allocating authority over children is not simply a matter of balancing the interests of the state and the parents; under his analysis, the mature minor has a constitutionally protected interest in self-determination that may be implicated when important matters affecting her life are at stake. Douglas's position was radical when *Yoder* was decided, not because he argued that minors have constitutional rights (*Tinker* had settled that), but because these rights might be in conflict with, and trump, the rights of parents to make decisions about child rearing. Douglas conceives of the child as an autonomous legal person, separate from her parents.

Justice Douglas's dissent has provided critically important authority (and inspiration) for advocates arguing for expanded rights of self-determination for minors. Douglas has been a patron saint of sorts of a "children's rights" movement that emerged in the 1970s and 80s. This movement was grounded in the liberal ideology of the civil rights movement; its target was paternalistic policies that categorically subjected minors to adult authority. Like Justice Douglas, advocates draw on developmental psychology to challenge paternalistic legal policies on empirical grounds, arguing that by early to mid-adolescence, minors are developmentally as mature as adults in their decisionmaking capacity. This argument has been important in the challenge to legal restrictions on adolescent abortion, to which we will return later in this chapter.

The issue confronting the Court in *Yoder* involves a decision regarding the future education of the Amish children, a decision in which Douglas asserts the affected children should have a voice. If the eighth graders in *Yoder* are competent to participate in a decision of this nature (and have a constitutionally protected interest in doing so), should this right be extended to all minors mature enough to make the decision? Would Douglas conclude that all compulsory school attendance laws are unconstitutional, in that students are categorically required to stay in school until age 16? If not, how would he distinguish the two situations?

(2) **Practical Issues in Providing a Voice for Children.** Assume that Justice Douglas is persuasive in his argument that the Amish children should be consulted in the decision of whether they should remain in school. How would their preferences be elicited and evaluated? Should the children be asked directly if they agree with their parents' decision to remove them from school? As a practical matter, is it feasible for most children to express a preference that is contrary to their parents on a matter of such importance to the parents? What implications might this confrontation have for the future relationship of the child with her parents? Should a psychologist or judge try to ascertain the child's "true" preference? This is sometimes done when the child's preference is solicited in a divorce custody proceeding.

2. MINORS' CONSENT TO MEDICAL TREATMENT

The authority to make decisions about medical treatment for minor children is generally given to parents, in part because minors generally are deemed incompetent to make their own decisions. Because legally valid consent to treatment must be informed and competent, it is generally assumed that parental consent is necessary to avoid a potential battery action against the treating health care provider for unlawful invasion of a protected bodily interest. Several exceptions to the requirement of parental consent have developed over the years. One is the "mature minor" doctrine, described below. Another is through emancipation, now more easy to accomplish definitively in many jurisdictions. A few states extend broad capacity for minors to consent to their own medical care, as exemplified by the Arkansas statute below. More prevalent are statutes similar to the Virginia provision below, giving minors authority to consent in specifically enumerated instances at any age or at some designated point before reaching majority. The Virginia statute is typical in allowing minors to consent to treatment for birth control, pregnancy, substance abuse, and venereal disease. Minors' consent to treatment statutes should not be taken as a recognition of the intellectual capacity of minors for rational decision-making in the medical context. Instead they are designed to encourage minors to seek certain kinds of treatment that they might not pursue if they must consult their parents.

A larger and more publicized group of cases dealing with minors and medical care focus on questions of parental refusal to give consent. This has spawned the concept of "medical neglect", which will be addressed in Chapter V.

Walter Wadlington, Minors and Health Care: The Age of Medical Consent

11 Osgoode Hall L.J. 115, 117–120 (1973).*

. . .

The "Mature Minor" Rule: A Creature of Necessity If Not Emergency

Judicial response to the harshness of a requirement of parental consent for all medical care to minors has come largely through development of what is widely labeled the "mature minor" rule. The effect of this rule is to allow a subjective appraisal of at least some cases in which physicians proceed with non-emergency medical care for minors with only the patient's consent. Two recent cases and two older ones provide good illustrations of the circumstances under which judges have been willing to invoke it.

In Johnston v. Wellesley Hospital,[11] no parental consent had been obtained by a dermatologist for non-emergency treatment of a 20 year old male to remove facial marks caused by acne. The claimant asserted both negligence and invasion of his body without appropriate consent. As to the latter claim, Addy, J., of the Ontario High Court, pointed out that:

> Although the common law imposes very strict limitations on the capacity of persons under 21 years of age to hold, or rather to divest themselves of, property, or to enter into contracts concerning matters other than necessities, it would be ridiculous in this day and age, where the voting age is being reduced generally to 18 years, to state that a person of 20 years of age, who is obviously intelligent and as fully capable of understanding the possible consequences of a medical or surgical procedure as an adult, would, at law, be incapable of consenting thereto.[12]

In short, the court was willing to look at the capacity of the particular "infant" under the given circumstances, here an elective operation performed on one only months away from majority.

In Younts v. St. Francis Hospital and School of Nursing, Inc.,[13] the Supreme Court of Kansas was asked to hold that taking a skin graft from the forearm of a 17–year-old girl to repair her injured finger was a battery because the surgeon had not first secured parental consent. The girl's

---

11.   (1970), 17 D.L.R. (3d) 139.

12.   Id., at 144.

13.   Younts v. St. Francis Hospital & School of Nursing, Inc., [205 Kan. 292, 469 P.2d 330 (1970)].

injury had occurred when her hand was caught accidentally in the door of the hospital room in which her mother had been placed following major surgery. The mother, still semi-conscious from a general anesthetic, was in no condition to consent. The girl's father, from whom the mother was divorced, lived in another city 200 miles away and his address was unknown and not immediately available. The daughter was taken to the hospital's emergency room where a repair operation and skin graft was effected.

Despite what apparently was a successful operation from a medical standpoint, the daughter later sued the hospital alleging that taking a pinch graft from her forearm was tortious because no parental consent had been obtained.[14] To some it might seem that the court could have denied recovery under the "emergency" exception. In any event, they elected not to do so, but held that given the particular circumstances this 17 year old "was mature enough to understand the nature and consequences and to knowingly consent to the beneficial surgical procedure made necessary by the accident." The court clearly took into consideration both the non-availability of either parent and the fact that before the skin graft was effected the treating surgeon had discussed the proposed procedure with the girl's regular family physician and had obtained his approval (even though he had no more legal authority to consent for the child than did the surgeon himself).

In dismissing the plaintiff's allegation of battery in the *Younts* case, the Kansas court cited with approval an earlier Ohio decision in which an 18–year-old girl had responded to a telephone directory advertisement which urged readers to reshape their noses through plastic surgery. At an initial interview with an agent of the defendant doctor the plaintiff stated that she had no money, but she was assured that a loan could be obtained for her to finance the cosmetic procedure. A date for the operation then was set and she returned to the doctor's office. The girl's testimony, which made the operation sound somewhat like an encounter with a mad acupuncturist, was met with the doctor's own statement that she had told him that she was 21 years of age and that following the operation she had called at his office on several occasions for follow-up treatment. An intermediate court reversed the judgment of a trial court which had awarded damages for assault and battery. The reversal was upheld on appeal to the Ohio Supreme Court, which affirmed *Per Curiam* but prepared an official syllabus.[15] Two concurring opinions also were written and variously joined in by members of the court, evidencing a split in views on the issue of the age of consent; an opinion joined in by four of the seven members, however, stressed that the trial court had erred "in charging that a minor of 18 could not consent to what the jury from the evidence might have determined was only a *simple operation*."[16] This view also was translated into the officially prepared syllabus.

---

14. The daughter also alleged that a nurse employed by the hospital had negligently closed the door on her finger, causing the injury in the first place. This, of course, had nothing to do with the question of consent.

15. Lacey v. Laird (1956), 166 Ohio St. 12, 139 N.E.2d 25 (Sup.Ct.). The plaintiff had also alleged malpractice (negligence) but lost on this count in a directed verdict.

16. (1956), 166 Ohio St. 12 at 26, 139 N.E.2d 25 at 34. [emphasis by the court].

A somewhat different problem was presented to the United States Court of Appeals for the District of Columbia in Bonner v. Moran,[17] the second of our "older" cases. The plaintiff male, at age fifteen, had been hospitalized for some two months and was permanently disfigured through serving as a tissue donor for a severely burned cousin.

The request for the boy's participation as a donor had come from an aunt of both children. At the time of the request, the boy's mother was ill and she was not advised of the proposed medical procedure. After the boy appeared at the hospital for a blood typing procedure he was admitted for the first of a series of operations in which "a tube of flesh was cut and formed from his arm pit to his waist line" and one end of the tube was attached to his cousin. Unfortunately, the procedure turned out to be a failure. The boy brought suit to recover for his disfigurement but the trial court refused to instruct the jury that consent of both the boy and his mother was necessary, instead telling them that "if they believed that [the plaintiff] himself was capable of appreciating and did appreciate the nature and consequences of the operation and actually consented, or by his conduct implicitly consented, their verdict must be for the defendant." The appellate court held this charge to be incorrect and reversed and remanded the case with the opinion that consent of the parent should have been considered necessary. The appeals court specifically noted its concern over the fact that the boy underwent the surgical operation for the benefit of another rather than for his own health needs.[20]

The preceding decisions, along with some half a dozen others, allow us to draw certain inferences about the type of situation in which courts which recognize the "mature minor" rule will be likely to apply it and dispense with the requirement of parental consent. The cases in which the rule has been applied generally have had the following factors in common:

(1) The treatment was undertaken for the benefit of the minor rather than a third party.

(2) The particular minor was near majority (or at least in the range of 15 years of age upward), and was considered to have sufficient mental capacity to understand fully the nature and importance of the medical steps proposed.

(3) The medical procedures could be characterized by the courts as something less than "major" or "serious" in nature.

In a good number of the cases, it also seemed that the situation at least bordered on one in which the emergency doctrine could have been invoked, and it may be of some significance that the allegation of a battery frequently accompanied a specific charge of negligence. As to the latter point, one may question whether suit would have been brought in the first place simply for the "technical" trespass unless a negligence action also were being filed.

17. (1941), 126 F.2d 121 (D.C.Cir.).

20. Id., at 123. Although they acknowledged that the question was not before them, the court pointed out that it was possible that the mother could have ratified the treatment by her conduct after learning of it.

NOTE

What are the policy purposes of the mature minor doctrine? First, it may facilitate medical treatment of minors in circumstances in which obtaining parental consent is difficult. Second, it shields physicians who treat mature minors from tort liability. Indeed, as the cases suggest, the doctrine is usually invoked as a defense by physicians whose youthful patients or their parents sue for failure to obtain parental consent. Finally, allowing mature minors to obtain treatment without parental consent extends legal privileges associated with adulthood to adolescents. This function was not central to the development of the mature minor doctrine, but it becomes important as the doctrine is applied to issues of reproductive autonomy.

VIRGINIA CODE ANNOTATED (Lexis)

CONSENT TO SURGICAL AND MEDICAL TREATMENT OF MINORS

§ 54.1–2969

. . .

E. A minor shall be deemed an adult for the purpose of consenting to:

1. Medical or health services needed to determine the presence of or to treat venereal disease or any infectious or contagious disease that the State Board of Health requires to be reported;

2. Medical or health services required in case of birth control, pregnancy or family planning except for the purposes of sexual sterilization;

3. Medical or health services needed in the case of outpatient care, treatment or rehabilitation for substance abuse as defined in § 37.2–100;

4. Medical or health services needed in the case of outpatient care, treatment or rehabilitation for mental illness or emotional disturbance; or

A minor shall also be deemed an adult for the purpose of accessing or authorizing the disclosure of medical records related to subdivisions 1 through 4.

F. Except for the purposes of sexual sterilization, any minor who is or has been married shall be deemed an adult for the purpose of giving consent to surgical and medical treatment.

G. A pregnant minor shall be deemed an adult for the sole purpose of giving consent for herself and her child to surgical and medical treatment relating to the delivery of her child when such surgical or medical treatment is provided during the delivery of the child or the duration of the hospital admission for such delivery; thereafter, the minor mother of such child shall also be deemed an adult for the purpose of giving consent to surgical and medical treatment for her child.

H. Any minor 16 years of age or older may, with the consent of a parent or legal guardian, consent to donate blood and may donate blood if such minor meets donor eligibility requirements. However, parental consent to donate blood by any minor 17 years of age shall not be required if such minor receives no consideration for his blood donation and the procurer of the blood is a nonprofit, voluntary organization.

I. Any judge, local director of social services, Director of the Department of Corrections, Director of the Department of Juvenile Justice, or principal executive officer of any state or other institution or agency who consents to surgical or medical treatment of a minor in accordance with this section shall make a reasonable effort to notify the minor's parent or guardian of such action as soon as practicable.

J. Nothing in subsection G shall be construed to permit a minor to consent to an abortion without complying with § 16.1–241.

K. Nothing in subsection E shall prevent a parent, legal guardian or person standing in loco parentis from obtaining (i) the results of a minor's nondiagnostic drug test when the minor is not receiving care, treatment or rehabilitation for substance abuse as defined in § 37.2–100 or (ii) a minor's other health records, except when the minor's treating physician or the minor's treating clinical psychologist has determined, in the exercise of his professional judgment, that the disclosure of health records to the parent, legal guardian, or person standing in loco parentis would be reasonably likely to cause substantial harm to the minor or another person pursuant to subsection B of Sect. 20–124.6.

ARKANSAS CODE ANNOTATED (Lexis)

20–9–602.   Consent generally.

It is recognized and established that, in addition to such other persons as may be so authorized and empowered, any one (1) of the following persons is authorized and empowered to consent, either orally or otherwise, to any surgical or medical treatment or procedure not prohibited by law which may be suggested, recommended, prescribed, or directed by a licensed physician:

. . .

(3) Any married person, whether an adult or a minor, for himself or herself;

(4) Any female, regardless of age or marital status, for herself when given in connection with pregnancy or childbirth, except the unnatural interruption of a pregnancy;

. . .

(6) Any emancipated minor, for himself or herself;

(7) Any unemancipated minor of sufficient intelligence to understand and appreciate the consequences of the proposed surgical or medical treatment or procedures, for himself;

. . .

(12) Any minor incarcerated in the Department of Corrections or the Department of Community Correction, for himself of herself.

In re E.G.

Supreme Court of Illinois, 1989.
133 Ill.2d 98, 139 Ill.Dec. 810, 549 N.E.2d 322.

■ JUSTICE RYAN delivered the opinion of the court:

Appellee, E.G., a 17–year–old woman, contracted leukemia and needed blood transfusions in the treatment of the disease. E.G. and her mother,

Rosie Denton, refused to consent to the transfusions, contending that acceptance of blood would violate personal religious convictions rooted in their membership in the Jehovah's Witness faith. Appellant, the State of Illinois, filed a neglect petition in juvenile court in the circuit court of Cook County. The trial court entered an order finding E.G. to be neglected, and appointed a guardian to consent to the transfusions on E.G.'s behalf.

The appellate court reversed the trial court in part. The court held that E.G. was a "mature minor," and therefore could refuse the blood transfusions through the exercise of her first amendment right to freely exercise her religion. Nevertheless, the court affirmed the finding of neglect against Denton. We granted the State's petition for leave to appeal and now affirm the appellate court's decision in part, but on other grounds. We also remand this case to the trial court for the purpose of expunging the finding of neglect.

In February of 1987, E.G. was diagnosed as having acute nonlymphatic leukemia, a malignant disease of the white blood cells. When E.G. and her mother, Rosie Denton, were informed that treatment of the disease would involve blood transfusions, they refused to consent to this medical procedure on the basis of their religious beliefs. As Jehovah's Witnesses, both E.G. and her mother desired to observe their religion's prohibition against the "eating" of blood. Mrs. Denton did authorize any other treatment and signed a waiver absolving the medical providers of liability for failure to administer transfusions.

As a result of Denton's and E.G.'s refusal to assent to blood transfusions, the State filed a neglect petition in juvenile court. At the initial hearing on February 25, 1987, Dr. Stanley Yachnin testified that E.G. had approximately one-fifth to one-sixth the normal oxygen-carrying capacity of her blood and consequently was excessively fatigued and incoherent. He stated that without blood transfusions, E.G. would likely die within a month. Dr. Yachnin testified that the transfusions, along with chemotherapy, achieve remission of the disease in about 80% of all patients so afflicted. Continued treatment, according to Dr. Yachnin, would involve the utilization of drugs and more transfusions. The long-term prognosis is not optimistic, as the survival rate for patients such as E.G. is 20 to 25%.

Dr. Yachnin stated that he discussed the proposed course of treatment with E.G. He testified that E.G. was competent to understand the consequences of accepting or rejecting treatment, and he was impressed with her maturity and the sincerity of her beliefs. Dr. Yachnin's observations regarding E.G.'s competency were corroborated by the testimony of Jane McAtee, the associate general counsel for the University of Chicago Hospital. At the conclusion of this hearing, the trial judge entered an order appointing McAtee temporary guardian, and authorizing her to consent to transfusions on E.G.'s behalf.

On April 8, 1987, further hearings were held on this matter. E.G., having received several blood transfusions, was strong enough to take the stand. She testified that the decision to refuse blood transfusions was her own and that she fully understood the nature of her disease and the consequences of her decision. She indicated that her decision was not based on any wish to die, but instead was grounded in her religious convictions. E.G. further stated that when informed that she would undergo transfusions, she asked to be sedated prior to the administration of the blood. She testified that the court's decision upset her, and said: "[I]t seems as if everything that I wanted or believe in was just being disregarded."

Several other witnesses gave their opinions extolling E.G.'s maturity and the sincerity of her religious beliefs. One witness was Dr. Littner, a psychiatrist who has special expertise in evaluating the maturity and competency of minors. Based on interviews with E.G. and her family, Dr. Littner expressed his opinion that E.G. had the maturity level of an 18 to 21 year old. He further concluded that E.G. had the competency to make an informed decision to refuse the blood transfusions, even if this choice was fatal.

On May 18, 1987, the trial court ruled that E.G. was medically neglected, and appointed a guardian to consent to medical treatment. The court felt this was in E.G.'s best interests. The court did state, however, that E.G. was "a mature 17–year-old individual," that E.G. reached her decision on an independent basis, and that she was "fully aware that death [was] assured absent treatment." The court noted that it considered E.G.'s maturity and the religion of her and her parents, and that it gave great weight to the wishes of E.G. Nevertheless, the court felt that the State's interest in this case was greater than the interest E.G. and her mother had in refusing to consent to treatment. The court concluded its ruling by encouraging E.G. to appeal.

On appeal, the order of the trial court pertaining to E.G.'s right to refuse treatment was vacated in part and modified in part. The appellate court observed that this court, in In re Estate of Brooks (1965), 32 Ill.2d 361, 205 N.E.2d 435, held that an adult Jehovah's Witness had a first amendment right to refuse blood transfusions. The appellate court then extended the holding in Brooks to include "mature minors," deriving this extension from cases in which the United States Supreme Court allowed "mature minors" to consent to abortions without parental approval through the exercise of constitutional privacy rights. (See City of Akron v. Akron Center for Reproductive Health, Inc. (1983), 462 U.S. 416; Bellotti v. Baird (1979), 443 U.S. 622.) Although the United States Supreme Court has not broadened this constitutional right of minors beyond abortion cases, the appellate court found such an extension "inevitable." Relying on our Emancipation of Mature Minors Act (Ill.Rev.Stat.1987, ch. 40, par. 2201 et seq.), the court held that a mature minor may exercise a constitutional right to refuse medical treatment.

The appellate court noted that E.G., at the time of trial, was only six months shy of her eighteenth birthday, and that the trial court believed E.G. to be a mature individual. Based on these facts, the appellate court declared that E.G. was partially emancipated and therefore had the right to refuse transfusions. The court, however, affirmed the finding of neglect against Denton, E.G.'s mother.

... Both parties agree that although this case is technically moot, it should not be dismissed. Normally, this court will not adjudicate an appeal where a live controversy no longer exists. Here, since E.G. has reached her eighteenth birthday, she can no longer be adjudged a neglected minor for the purpose of the Juvenile Court Act of 1987. We do not review cases merely to guide future litigation or establish precedent. Where no present controversy exists between the parties, a case should be dismissed as moot.

Nevertheless, there are exceptions to the mootness doctrine. One departure from the usual rule occurs when a case presents an issue of substantial public interest. (In re Estate of Brooks (1965), 32 Ill.2d 361, 364–65, 205 N.E.2d 435; People ex rel. Wallace v. Labrenz (1952), 411 Ill. 618, 622–23, 104 N.E.2d 769.) In determining whether a case exhibits the requisite degree of public interest, we look to "the public or private nature of the question presented, the desirability of an authoritative determination for the future guidance of public officers, and the likelihood of future recurrence of the question." We note that both Labrenz and Brooks involved Jehovah's Witness members who refused to consent to blood transfusions. In Labrenz and Brooks, this court concluded that significant public interest existed and, although the controversies were moot, decided the cases on the merits. Similarly, we find that the case before us meets the public interest exception criteria quoted above from Labrenz. Consequently, we will consider the issues raised by the parties in this case.

The paramount issue raised by this appeal is whether a minor like E.G. has a right to refuse medical treatment. In Illinois, an adult has a common law right to refuse medical treatment, even if it is of a life-sustaining nature. (See In re Estate of Longeway (1989), 133 Ill.2d 33, 139 Ill.Dec. 780, 549 N.E.2d 292.) This court has also held that an adult may refuse life-saving blood transfusions on first amendment free exercise of religion grounds. (In re Estate of Brooks (1965), 32 Ill.2d 361, 205 N.E.2d 435.) An infant child, however, can be compelled to accept life-saving medical treatment over the objections of her parents. (People ex rel. Wallace v. Labrenz (1952), 411 Ill. 618, 104 N.E.2d 769.) In the matter before us, E.G. was a minor, but one who was just months shy of her eighteenth birthday, and an individual that the record indicates was mature for her age. Although the age of majority in Illinois is 18, that age is not an impenetrable barrier that magically precludes a minor from possessing and exercising certain rights normally associated with adulthood. Numerous exceptions are found in this jurisdiction and others which treat minors as adults under specific circumstances.

In Illinois, our legislature enacted "An Act in relation to the performance of medical, dental or surgical procedures on and counseling for minors" (the Consent by Minors to Medical Operations Act), which grants minors the legal capacity to consent to medical treatment in certain situations. (See Ill.Rev.Stat.1987, ch. 111, par. 4501 et seq.) For example, a minor 12 years or older may seek medical attention on her own if she believes she has venereal disease or is an alcoholic or drug addict. Similarly, an individual under 18 who is married or pregnant may validly consent to treatment. Thus, if E.G. would have been married she could have consented to or, presumably, refused treatment. Also, a minor 16 or older may be declared emancipated under the Emancipation of Mature Minors Act, and thereby control his or her own health care decisions. These two acts, when read together in a complementary fashion, indicate that the legislature did not intend that there be an absolute 18–year-old age barrier prohibiting minors from consenting to medical treatment.

In an analogous area of law, no "bright line" age restriction of 18 exists either. Under the Juvenile Court Act, individuals much younger than 18 may be prosecuted under the Criminal Code, if circumstances dictate. Furthermore, to be convicted of many of the offenses in the Criminal Code, a trier of fact would have to find that a minor had a certain mental state at the time the alleged crime was committed. Implied in finding this mental state would be an acknowledgment that a minor was mature enough to have formulated this mens rea. Consequently, the Juvenile Court Act presupposes a "sliding scale of maturity" in which young minors can be deemed mature enough to possess certain mental states and be tried and convicted as adults. This act reflects the common law, which allowed infancy to be a defense to criminal acts. The infancy defense at common law was "based upon an unwillingness to punish those thought to be incapable of forming criminal intent and not of an age where the threat of punishment could serve as a deterrent." (Emphasis added.) (W. LaFave & A. Scott, Criminal Law § 46 (1972).) When a minor is mature enough to have the capacity to formulate criminal intent, both the common law and our Juvenile Court Act treat the minor as an adult.

Another area of the law where minors are treated as adults is constitutional law, including the constitutional right of abortion. The United States Supreme Court has adopted a mature minor doctrine, which allows women under the age of majority to undergo abortions without parental consent. (See City of Akron v. Akron Center for Reproductive Health, Inc. (1983), 462 U.S. 416; Bellotti v. Baird (1979), 443 U.S. 622.) In the abortion rights context, the Court has noted: "Constitutional rights do not mature and come into being magically only when one attains the state-defined age of majority. Minors, as well as adults, are protected by the Constitution and possess constitutional rights." (Planned Parenthood of Central Missouri v. Danforth (1976), 428 U.S. 52, 74.) Moreover, children enjoy the protection of other constitutional rights, including the right of privacy (Carey v. Population Services International (1977), 431 U.S. 678), freedom of expression (Tinker v. Des Moines Independent Community School District (1969), 393 U.S. 503), freedom from unreasonable searches and seizures (New Jersey v. T.L.O. (1985), 469 U.S. 325); and procedural due process (In re Application of Gault (1967), 387 U.S. 1). Nevertheless, the Supreme Court has not held that a constitutionally based right to refuse medical treatment exists, either for adults or minors. While we find the language from the cases cited above instructive, we do not feel, as the appellate court did, that an extension of the constitutional mature minor doctrine to the case at bar is "inevitable." These cases do show, however, that no "bright line" age restriction of 18 is tenable in restricting the rights of mature minors, whether the rights be based on constitutional or other grounds. Accordingly, we hold that in addition to these constitutionally based rights expressly delineated by the Supreme Court, mature minors may possess and exercise rights regarding medical care that are rooted in this State's common law.

The common law right to control one's health care was also the basis for the right of an incompetent patient to refuse life-sustaining treatment through a surrogate in In re Estate of Longeway (1989), 133 Ill.2d at 45–46, 139 Ill.Dec. 780, 549 N.E.2d 292. While the issue before us in this case is not exactly the same as in Longeway, the foundation of the common law right here and in Longeway is the same. We see no reason why this right of dominion over one's own person should not extend to mature minors. Furthermore, we find support for this conclusion in a decision of one of our sister States. In Cardwell v. Bechtol (Tenn.1987), 724 S.W.2d 739, the Tennessee Supreme Court held that a mature minor had the capacity to consent to medical procedures based on the common law of that State. The court noted that the mature minor doctrine is not a recent development in the law: "[R]ecognition that minors achieve varying degrees of maturity and responsibility (capacity) has been part of the common law for well over a century." 724 S.W.2d at 744–45.

In Cardwell, the Tennessee court held that a minor 17 years, 7 months old was mature enough to consent to medical treatment. We note that in other jurisdictions, courts have ordered health care for minors over the objections of the minors' parents. These cases, however, involve minors who were younger than E.G. or the minor in Cardwell. (See, e.g., In re Eric B. (1987), 189 Cal.App.3d 996, 235 Cal.Rptr. 22 (six-year-old boy); In the Interest of D.L.E. (Colo.1982), 645 P.2d 271 (16 year old); In re Ivey (Fla.App.1975), 319 So.2d 53 (one-month-old infant); Morrison v. State (Mo.App.1952), 252 S.W.2d 97 (12–day-old child); People v. Perricone (1962), 37 N.J. 463, 181 A.2d 751 (infant); In re Custody of a Minor (1978), 375 Mass. 733, 379 N.E.2d 1053 (two-year-old girl); In re Willmann (1986), 24 Ohio App.3d 191, 493 N.E.2d 1380 (seven-year-old boy); In re Hamilton (Tenn.App.1983), 657 S.W.2d 425 (12–year-old girl); Mitchell v. Davis (Tex.Civ.App.1947), 205 S.W.2d 812 (12–year-old boy).) Moreover, the issue in the above cases was not whether a minor could assert a right to control medical treatment decisions, but whether the minor's parents could refuse treatment on behalf of their child. Here, E.G. contends she was mature enough to have controlled her own health care. We find that she may have done so if indeed she would have been adjudged mature.

The trial judge must determine whether a minor is mature enough to make health care choices on her own. An exception to this, of course, is if the legislature has provided otherwise, as in the Consent by Minors to Medical Operations Act (Ill.Rev.Stat.1987, ch. 111, par. 4501 et seq.). We feel the intervention of a judge is appropriate for two reasons.

First, Illinois public policy values the sanctity of life. When a minor's health and life are at stake, this policy becomes a critical consideration. A minor may have a long and fruitful life ahead that an immature, foolish decision could jeopardize. Consequently, when the trial judge weighs the evidence in making a determination of whether a minor is mature enough to handle a health care decision, he must find proof of this maturity by clear and convincing evidence.

Second, the State has a parens patriae power to protect those incompetent to protect themselves. "[I]t is well-settled that the State as parens patriae has a special duty to protect minors and, if necessary, make vital decisions as to whether to submit a minor to necessary treatment where the condition is life threatening, as wrenching and distasteful as such actions may be." (In re Hamilton (Tenn.App.1983), 657 S.W.2d 425, 429.) The State's parens patriae power pertaining to minors is strongest when the minor is immature and thus incompetent (lacking in capacity) to make these decisions on her own. The parens patriae authority fades, however, as the minor gets older and disappears upon her reaching adulthood. The State interest in protecting a mature minor in these situations will vary depending upon the nature of the medical treatment involved. Where the health care issues are potentially life threatening, the State's parens patriae interest is greater than if the health care matter is less consequential.

Therefore, the trial judge must weigh these two principles against the evidence he receives of a minor's maturity. If the evidence is clear and convincing that the minor is mature enough to appreciate the consequences of her actions, and that the minor is mature enough to exercise the judgment of an adult, then the mature minor doctrine affords her the common law right to consent to or refuse medical treatment. As we stated in Longeway, however, this common law right is not absolute. The right must be balanced against four State interests: (1) the preservation of life; (2) protecting the interests of third parties; (3) prevention of suicide; and (4) maintaining the ethical integrity of the medical profession. (Longeway, 133 Ill.2d at 48, 139 Ill.Dec. 780, 549 N.E.2d 292, quoting Superintendent of Belchertown State School v. Saikewicz (1977), 373 Mass. 728, 741, 370 N.E.2d 417, 425.) Of these four concerns, protecting the interests of third parties is clearly the most significant here. The principal third parties in these cases would be parents, guardians, adult siblings, and other relatives. If a parent or guardian opposes an unemancipated mature minor's refusal to consent to treatment for a life-threatening health problem, this opposition would weigh heavily against the minor's right to refuse. In this case, for example, had E.G. refused the transfusions against the wishes of her mother, then the court would have given serious consideration to her mother's desires.

Nevertheless, in this case both E.G. and her mother agreed that E.G. should turn down the blood transfusions. They based this refusal primarily on religious grounds, contending that the first amendment free exercise clause entitles a mature minor to decline medical care when it contravenes sincerely held religious beliefs. Because we find that a mature minor may exercise a common law right to consent to or refuse medical care, we decline to address the constitutional issue. . . .

The final issue we must address is whether the finding of neglect entered against Rosie Denton, E.G.'s mother, should stand. If the trial judge had ruled that E.G. was a mature minor, then no finding of neglect would be proper. Although the trial judge was impressed with E.G.'s maturity and sincerity, the judge did not explicitly hold that E.G. was a mature minor. The trial judge, guided only by the law as it existed prior to this opinion, rightly felt that he must protect the minor's health and well-being. This case is one of first impression with this court. Therefore, the trial judge had no precedent upon which to base a mature minor finding.

Because E.G. is no longer a minor, nothing would be gained by remanding this case back to the trial court for an explicit determination of E.G.'s maturity. Nevertheless, since the trial judge did not have any clear guidance on the mature minor doctrine, we believe that the finding of neglect should not stand. Accordingly, we affirm the appellate court in part and reverse in part, and remand this case to the circuit court of Cook County for the sole purpose of expunging the finding of neglect against Denton.

■ Justice Ward, dissenting:

I must respectfully dissent. I consider the majority has made an unfortunate choice of situations to announce, in what it calls a case of first impression, that a minor may with judicial approval reject medical treatment, even if the minor's death will be a medically certain consequence. The majority cites decisions where a minor was permitted to exercise what was called a common law right to consent to medical treatment. The safeguarding of health and the preservation of life are obviously different conditions from one in which a minor will be held to have a common law right, as the majority puts it, to refuse medical treatment and sometimes in effect take his own life. That violates the ancient responsibility of the State as parens patriae to protect minors and to decide for them, as the majority describes, vital questions, including whether to consent to or refuse necessary medical treatment. The majority also cites the decision in In re Estate of Longeway (1989), 133 Ill.2d 33, 139 Ill.Dec. 780, 549 N.E.2d 292, for the proposition that an incompetent patient has a common law right to refuse life-sustaining treatment through a surrogate. As a dissent in Longeway points out, an incompetent person by definition lacks the capacity to refuse life-sustaining treatment and thereby chooses death. The dissent observes that commentators have commented that it is a self-satisfying fiction to say that the incompetent patient exercises a common law right to refuse treatment and die when the decision to refuse is obviously that of the surrogate guardian.

Unless the legislature for specific purposes provides for a different age, a minor is one who has not attained legal age. It is not disputed that E.G. has not attained legal age. It is fundamental that where language is clear there is no need to seek to interpret or depart from the plain language and meaning and read into what is clear exceptions or limitations. The majority nevertheless would in effect define a minor in these grave situations to be one who has not attained legal age unless it is a "mature" minor who is involved. If so this protection that the law gives minors has been lost and the child may make his own decision even at the cost of his life. The majority acknowledges that this is a case of first impression. It may now be critically described by some as a holding without precedent. I point out again that this is not a holding where consent to treatment is the question but rather a unique one where a minor's injury or very self-destruction may be involved.

I am sure that in a host of matters of far lesser importance it would not be held that a minor however mature could satisfy a requirement of being of legal age. It would not be held that a minor was eligible to vote, to obtain a driver's or a pilot's license, or to enlist in one of the armed services before attaining enlistment age.

The trial court appointed a guardian to consent to transfusions for the minor. The appellate court reversed as to this, stating the minor was a mature minor. This court affirms the appellate court in this regard but does not attempt to state a standard by which "mature" is to be measured by judges in making these important findings.

[The dissenting opinion of JUSTICE CLARK, arguing that the case does not fall into any exceptions to the mootness doctrine, is omitted.]

NOTES

(1) In *O.G. v. Baum*, 790 S.W.2d 839 (Tex.App.1990), a Texas court refused to apply the rationale of the Illinois court in *E.G.* in a case involving a 16–year-old who had signed a form refusing to consent to a transfusion and releasing his physician from liability. The court appointed a conservator to consent to blood transfusions, explaining that Texas had no mature minor doctrine and that no authority had been cited to show that the action violated state or federal rights to privacy or infringed on the free exercise of religion.

(2) Should a minor child of any age be permitted to refuse treatment if death will result from implementing such a decision? John E. Schowalter, Julian B. Ferhold, and Nancy M. Mann, in The Adolescent Patient's Decision to Die, 51 Pediatrics 97 (1973), relate the case of a 16–year-old girl who was permitted to withdraw from a program of hemodialysis necessary to keep her alive after rejection of a kidney transplant. Since that time most states have adopted some form of "living will", durable power of attorney for health care, or other provisions that allow a terminally ill person to appoint a decision maker or to specify the conditions under which no more than comfort care (as opposed to active treatment) will be continued for the patient. Those statutes generally do not extend their provisions to minors. However the Supreme Court of Maine, in *In re Swan*, 569 A.2d 1202 (Me.1990), permitted statements of a terminally ill patient made before reaching majority to be used as evidence of his wishes not to be kept alive subsequently when he was in a vegetative state.

(3) For additional discussion of the problems of determining the appropriate decision makers for children's medical care, see Walter Wadlington, Medical Decision Making For and By Children: Tensions Between Parent, State, and Child, 1994 U.Ill.L.Rev. 311; Robert Bennett, Allocation of Child Medical Care Decisionmaking Authority: A Suggested Interest Analysis, 62 Va.L.Rev. 285 (1976); Angela Roddey Holder, Legal Issues in Adolescent and Pediatric Medicine (2d ed. 1985).

Parham v. J. R.

Supreme Court of the United States, 1979.
442 U.S. 584, 99 S.Ct. 2493, 61 L.Ed.2d 101.

■ MR. CHIEF JUSTICE BURGER delivered the opinion of the Court.

The question presented in this appeal is what process is constitutionally due a minor child whose parents or guardian seek state administered institutional mental health care for the child and specifically whether an adversary proceeding is required prior to or after the commitment.

I

(a) Appellee, J. R., a child being treated in a Georgia state mental hospital, was a plaintiff in this class-action[2] suit based on 42 U.S.C. § 1983, in the District Court for the Middle District of Georgia. . . . Appellee sought a declaratory judgment that Georgia's voluntary commitment procedures for children under the age of 18, Ga.Code, §§ 88–503.1, 88–503.2,[3] violated the Due Process Clause of the Fourteenth Amendment and requested an injunction against its future enforcement.

. . . [A three-judge District Court] held that Georgia's statutory scheme was unconstitutional because it failed to protect adequately the appellees' due process rights.

To remedy this violation the court enjoined future commitments based on the procedures in the Georgia statute. It also commanded Georgia to appropriate and expend whatever amount was "reasonably necessary" to provide nonhospital facilities deemed by the appellant state officials to be the most appropriate for the treatment of those members of plaintiffs' class, n. 2, supra, who could be treated in a less drastic, nonhospital environment.

. . .

(b) J. L., a plaintiff before the District Court who is now deceased, was admitted in 1970 at the age of six years to Central State Regional Hospital in Milledgeville, Ga. Prior to his admission, J. L. had received outpatient treatment at the hospital for over two months. J. L.'s mother then requested the hospital to admit him indefinitely.

The admitting physician interviewed J. L. and his parents. He learned that J. L.'s natural parents had divorced and his mother had remarried. He also learned that J. L. had been expelled from school because he was uncontrollable. He accepted the parents' representation that the boy had been extremely aggressive and diagnosed the child as having a "hyperkinetic reaction to childhood."

J. L.'s mother and stepfather agreed to participate in family therapy during the time their son was hospitalized. Under this program J. L. was permitted to go home for short stays. Apparently his behavior during these visits was erratic. After several months the parents requested discontinuance of the program.

---

2. The class certified by the District Court, without objection by appellants, consisted "of all persons younger than 18 years of age now or hereafter received by any defendant for observation and diagnosis and/or detained for care and treatment at any 'facility' within the State of Georgia pursuant to Ga.Code § 88–503.1. Although one witness testified that on any given day there may be 200 children in the class, in December 1975 there were only 140."

3. Section 88–503.1 provides:

"The superintendent of any facility may receive for observation and diagnosis . . . any individual under 18 years of age for whom such application is made by his parent or guardian. . . . If found to show evidence of mental illness and to be suitable for treatment, such person may be given care and treatment at such facility and such person may be detained by such facility for such period and under such conditions as may be authorized by law."

Section 88–503.2 provides:

"The superintendent of the facility shall discharge any voluntary patient who has recovered from his mental illness or who has sufficiently improved that the superintendent determines that hospitalization of the patient is no longer desirable."

In 1972, the child was returned to his mother and stepfather on a furlough basis, i.e., he would live at home but go to school at the hospital. The parents found they were unable to control J. L. to their satisfaction which created family stress. Within two months they requested his readmission to Central State. J. L.'s parents relinquished their parental rights to the county in 1974.

Although several hospital employees recommended that J. L. should be placed in a special foster home with "a warm, supported, truly involved couple," the Department of Family and Children Services was unable to place him in such a setting. On October 24, 1975, J. L. filed this suit requesting an order of the court placing him in a less drastic environment suitable to his needs.

(c) Appellee, J. R., was declared a neglected child by the county and removed from his natural parents when he was three months old. He was placed in seven different foster homes in succession prior to his admission to Central State Hospital at the age of seven.

Immediately preceding his hospitalization, J. R. received out-patient treatment at a county mental health center for several months. He then began attending school where he was so disruptive and incorrigible that he could not conform to normal behavior patterns. Because of his abnormal behavior J. R.'s seventh set of foster parents requested his removal from their home. The Department of Family and Children Services then sought his admission at Central State. The agency provided the hospital with a complete sociomedical history at the time of his admission. In addition, three separate interviews were conducted with J. R. by the admission team of the hospital.

It was determined that he was borderline retarded, and suffered an "unsocialized, aggressive reaction to childhood." It was recommended unanimously that he would "benefit from the structured environment" of the hospital and would "enjoy living and playing with boys of the same age."

J. R.'s progress was re-examined periodically. In addition, unsuccessful efforts were made by the Department of Family and Children Services during his stay at the hospital to place J. R. in various foster homes. On October 24, 1975, J. R. filed this suit requesting an order of the court placing him in a less drastic environment suitable to his needs.

(d) Georgia Code, § 88–503.1 provides for the voluntary admission to a state regional hospital of children such as J. L. and J. R. Under that provision admission begins with an application for hospitalization signed by a "parent or guardian." Upon application the superintendent of each hospital is given the power to admit temporarily any child for "observation and diagnosis." If, after observation, the superintendent finds "evidence of mental illness" and that the child is "suitable for treatment" in the hospital, then the child may be admitted "for such period and under such conditions as may be authorized by law."

Georgia's mental health statute also provides for the discharge of voluntary patients. Any child who has been hospitalized for more than five days may be discharged at the request of a parent or guardian. § 88–

503.3(a). Even without a request for discharge, however, the superintendent of each regional hospital has an affirmative duty to release any child "who has recovered from his mental illness or who has sufficiently improved that the superintendent determines that hospitalization of the patient is no longer desirable." § 88–503.2.

Georgia's Mental Health Director has not published any statewide regulations defining what specific procedures each superintendent must employ when admitting a child under 18. Instead, each regional hospital's superintendent is responsible for the procedures in his or her facility. [Acknowledging that "substantial variation" exists between them, the court describes the procedures of different hospitals. It also notes that Georgia funds over 50 community mental health clinics and 13 specialized foster care homes.... Georgia ranks 22nd nationally in per capita expenditures for mental health.]

The District Court nonetheless rejected the State's entire system of providing mental health care on both procedural and substantive grounds. The District Court found that 46 children could be "optimally cared for in another, less restrictive, non-hospital setting if it were available." These "optimal" settings included group homes, therapeutic camps and home care services. [State officials testified that Georgia] could not justify enlarging its budget during fiscal year 1977 to provide the specialized treatment settings urged by appellees in addition to those then available.

.   .   .

II

In holding unconstitutional Georgia's statutory procedure for voluntary commitment of juveniles, the District Court first determined that commitment to any of the eight regional hospitals constitutes a severe deprivation of a child's liberty. The court defined this liberty interest both in terms of a freedom from bodily restraint and freedom from the "emotional and psychic harm" caused by the institutionalization.[7] Having determined that a liberty interest is implicated by a child's admission to a mental hospital, the court considered what process is required to protect that interest. It held that the process due "includes at least the right after notice to be heard before an impartial tribunal."

In requiring the prescribed hearing, the court rejected Georgia's argument that no adversary-type hearing was required since the State was merely assisting parents who could not afford private care by making available treatment similar to that offered in private hospitals and by private physicians. The court acknowledged that most parents who seek to have their children admitted to a state mental hospital do so in good faith. It, however, relied on one of appellees' witnesses who expressed an opinion that "some still look upon mental hospitals as a 'dumping ground.' " Id., at

---

7. In both respects the District Court found strong support for its holding in this Court's decision In re Gault, 387 U.S. 1 (1967). In that decision we held that a state cannot institutionalize a juvenile delinquent without first providing certain due process protections.

138.[8] No specific evidence of such "dumping," however, can be found in the record.

The District Court also rejected the argument that review by the superintendents of the hospitals and their staffs was sufficient to protect the child's liberty interest. The court held that the inexactness of psychiatry, coupled with the possibility that the sources of information used to make the commitment decision may not always be reliable, made the superintendent's decision too arbitrary to satisfy due process.

. . .

III

In an earlier day, the problems inherent in coping with children afflicted with mental or emotional abnormalities were dealt with largely within the family. See S. Brakel & R. Rock, The Mentally Disabled and the Law 4 (1971). Sometimes parents were aided by teachers or a family doctor. While some parents no doubt were able to deal with their disturbed children without specialized assistance, others, especially those of limited means and education, were not. Increasingly, they turned for assistance to local, public sources or private charities. Until recently most of the states did little more than provide custodial institutions for the confinement of persons who were considered dangerous. Id., at 5–6; Slovenko, Criminal Justice Procedures In Civil Commitment, 24 Wayne L.Rev. 1, 3 (1977) (hereinafter Slovenko).

. . . Ironically, as most states have expanded their efforts to assist the mentally ill, their actions have been subjected to increasing litigation and heightened constitutional scrutiny. . . .

The parties agree that our prior holdings have set out a general approach for testing challenged state procedures under a due process claim. Assuming the existence of a protectible property or liberty interest, the Court has required a balancing of a number of factors:

> "First, the private interest that will be affected by the official action; second, the risk of an erroneous deprivation of such interest through the procedures used, and the probable value, if any, of additional or substitute procedural safeguards; and finally, the Government's interest, including the function involved and the fiscal and administrative burdens that the additional or substitute procedural requirement would entail." Mathews v. Eldridge, 424 U.S. 319, 335 (1976), quoted in Smith v. Organization of Foster Families, 431 U.S. 816, 847–848 (1977).

8. In light of the District Court's holding that a judicial or quasi-judicial body should review voluntary commitment decisions, it is at least interesting to note that the witness who made the statement quoted in the text was not referring to parents as the people who "dump" children into hospitals. This witness opined that some juvenile court judges and child welfare agencies misused the hospitals. App. to Juris. Statement 768. See also Rolfe & MacClintock, The Due Process Rights of Minors "Voluntarily Admitted" to Mental Institutions, 4 J. Psych. & L. 333, 351 (1976) (hereinafter Rolfe & MacClintock).

In applying these criteria, we must consider first the child's interest in not being committed. Normally, however, since this interest is inextricably linked with the parents' interest in and obligation for the welfare and health of the child, the private interest at stake is a combination of the child's and parents' concerns. Next we must examine the State's interest in the procedures it has adopted for commitment and treatment of children. Finally, we must consider how well Georgia's procedures protect against arbitrariness in the decision to commit a child to a state mental hospital.

(a) It is not disputed that a child, in common with adults, has a substantial liberty interest in not being confined unnecessarily for medical treatment and that the State's involvement in the commitment decision constitutes state action under the Fourteenth Amendment. See Addington v. Texas, 441 U.S. 418, 425 (1979); In re Gault, 387 U.S. 1, 27 (1967). We also recognize that commitment sometimes produces adverse social consequences for the child because of the reaction of some to the discovery that the child has received psychiatric care.

This reaction, however, need not be equated with the community response resulting from being labeled by the state as delinquent, criminal, or mentally ill and possibly dangerous. The state through its voluntary commitment procedures does not "label" the child; it provides a diagnosis and treatment that medical specialists conclude the child requires. In terms of public reaction, the child who exhibits abnormal behavior may be seriously injured by an erroneous decision not to commit. Appellees overlook a significant source of the public reaction to the mentally ill, for what is truly "stigmatizing" is the symptomatology of a mental or emotional illness. The pattern of untreated, abnormal behavior—even if nondangerous—arouses at least as much negative reaction as treatment that becomes public knowledge. A person needing, but not receiving, appropriate medical care may well face even greater social ostracism resulting from the observable symptoms of an untreated disorder.

However, we need not decide what effect these factors might have in a different case. For purposes of this decision, we assume that a child has a protectible interest not only in being free of unnecessary bodily restraints but also in not being labeled erroneously by some because of an improper decision by the state hospital superintendent.

(b) We next deal with the interests of the parents who have decided, on the basis of their observations and independent professional recommendations, that their child needs institutional care. Appellees argue that the constitutional rights of the child are of such magnitude and the likelihood of parental abuse is so great that the parents' traditional interests in and responsibility for the upbringing of their child must be subordinated at least to the extent of providing a formal adversary hearing prior to a voluntary commitment.

Our jurisprudence historically has reflected Western Civilization concepts of the family as a unit with broad parental authority over minor children. Our cases have consistently followed that course; our constitutional system long ago rejected any notion that a child is "the mere creature of the State" and, on the contrary, asserted that parents generally "have the right, coupled with the high duty, to recognize and prepare [their children] for additional obligations." Pierce v. Society of Sisters, 268 U.S. 510, 535 (1924). See also Wisconsin v. Yoder, 406 U.S. 205, 213 (1972); Prince v. Massachusetts, 321 U.S. 158, 166 (1944); Meyer v. Nebraska, 262 U.S. 390, 400 (1923). Surely, this includes a "high duty" to recognize symptoms of illness and to seek and follow medical advice. The law's concept of the family rests on a presumption that parents possess what a child lacks in maturity, experience, and capacity for judgment required for making life's difficult decisions. More important, historically it has recognized that natural bonds of affection lead parents to act in the best interests of their children. 1 W. Blackstone, Commentaries * 447; 2 Kent, Commentaries on American Law * 190.

As with so many other legal presumptions, experience and reality may rebut what the law accepts as a starting point; the incidence of child neglect and abuse cases attests to this. That some parents "may at times be acting against the interests of their child" as was stated in Bartley v. Kremens, 402 F.Supp. 1039, 1047–1048 (E.D.Pa.1975), vacated, 431 U.S. 119 (1977), creates a basis for caution, but is hardly a reason to discard wholesale those pages of human experience that teach that parents generally do act in the child's best interests. See Rolfe & MacClintock 348–349. The statist notion that governmental power should supersede parental authority in *all* cases because *some* parents abuse and neglect children is repugnant to American tradition.

Nonetheless, we have recognized that a state is not without constitutional control over parental discretion in dealing with children when their physical or mental health is jeopardized. See Wisconsin v. Yoder, supra, 406 U.S., at 230; Prince v. Massachusetts, supra, 321 U.S., at 166. Moreover, the Court recently declared unconstitutional a state statute that granted parents an absolute veto over a minor child's decision to have an abortion. Planned Parenthood of Missouri v. Danforth, 428 U.S. 52 (1976). Appellees urge that these precedents limiting the traditional rights of parents, if viewed in the context of the liberty interest of the child and the likelihood of parental abuse, require us to hold that the parents' decision to have a child admitted to a mental hospital must be subjected to an exacting constitutional scrutiny, including a formal, adversary, preadmission hearing.

Appellees' argument, however, sweeps too broadly. Simply because the decision of a parent is not agreeable to a child or because it involves risks does not automatically transfer the power to make that decision from the parents to some agency or officer of the state. The same characterizations can be made for a tonsillectomy, appendectomy or other medical procedure. Most children, even in adolescence, simply are not able to make sound judgments concerning many decisions, including their need for medical care or treatment. Parents can and must make those judgments. Here there is no finding by the District Court of even a single instance of bad faith by any parent of any member of appellees' class. We cannot assume that the result of Meyer v. Nebraska, supra, and Pierce v. Society of Sisters, supra, would have been different if the children there had announced a preference to learn only English or a preference to go to a public, rather than a church, school. The fact that a child may balk at hospitalization or complain about a parental refusal to provide cosmetic surgery does not diminish the parents' authority to decide what is best for the child. See generally Goldstein, Medical Case for the Child at Risk: On State Supervention of Parental Autonomy, 86 Yale L.J. 645, 664–668 (1977). Bennett, Allocation of Child Medical Care Decision-making Authority: A Suggested Interest Analysis, 62 Va.L.Rev. 285, 308 (1976). Neither state officials nor federal courts are equipped to review such parental decisions.

Appellees place particular reliance on *Planned Parenthood*, arguing that its holding indicates how little deference to parents is appropriate when the child is exercising a constitutional right. The basic situation in that case, however, was very different; *Planned Parenthood* involved an absolute parental veto over the child's ability to obtain an abortion. Parents in Georgia in no sense have an absolute right to commit their children to state mental hospitals; the statute requires the superintendent of each regional hospital to exercise independent judgment as to the child's need for confinement.

In defining the respective rights and prerogatives of the child and parent in the voluntary commitment setting, we conclude that our precedents permit the parents to retain a substantial, if not the dominant, role in the decision, absent a finding of neglect or abuse, and that the traditional presumption that the parents act in the best interests of their child should apply. We also conclude, however, that the child's rights and the nature of the commitment decision are such that parents cannot always have absolute and unreviewable discretion to decide whether to have a child institutionalized. They, of course, retain plenary authority to seek such care for their children, subject to a physician's independent examination and medical judgment.

(c) The State obviously has a significant interest in confining the use of its costly mental health facilities to cases of genuine need. . . .

The State . . . also has a significant interest in not imposing unnecessary procedural obstacles that may discourage the mentally ill or their families from seeking needed psychiatric assistance. The *parens patriae* interest in helping parents care for the mental health of their children cannot be fulfilled if the parents are unwilling to take advantage of the opportunities because the admission process is too onerous, too embarrassing or too contentious. . . .

The State also has a genuine interest in allocating priority to the diagnosis and treatment of patients as soon as they are admitted to a hospital rather than to time-consuming procedural minuets before the admission. One factor that must be considered is the utilization of the time of psychiatrists, psychologists and other behavioral specialists in preparing for and participating in hearings rather than performing the task for which their special training has fitted them. Behavioral experts in courtrooms and hearings are of little help to patients.

The *amicus* brief of the American Psychiatric Association points out at page 20 that the average staff psychiatrist in a hospital presently is able to devote only 47% of his time to direct patient care. One consequence of increasing the procedures the state must provide prior to a child's voluntary admission will be that mental health professionals will be diverted even more from the treatment of patients in order to travel to and participate In—and wait for—what could be hundreds—or even thousands—of hearings each year. . . .

(d) We now turn to consideration of what process protects adequately the child's constitutional rights by reducing risks of error without unduly trenching on traditional parental authority and without undercutting "efforts to further the legitimate interests of both the state and the patient that are served by" voluntary commitments. Addington v. Texas, 441 U.S., at 430. We conclude that the risk of error inherent in the parental decision to have a child institutionalized for mental health care is sufficiently great that some kind of inquiry should be made by a "neutral fact finder" to determine whether the statutory requirements for admission are satisfied. That inquiry must carefully probe the child's background using all available sources, including, but not limited to, parents, schools and other social agencies. Of course, the review must also include an interview with the child. It is necessary that the decisionmaker have the authority to refuse to admit any child who does not satisfy the medical standards for admission. Finally, it is necessary that the child's continuing need for commitment be reviewed periodically by a similarly independent procedure.

We are satisfied that such procedures will protect the child from an erroneous admission decision in a way that neither unduly burdens the states nor inhibits parental decisions to seek state help.

Due process has never been thought to require that the neutral and detached trier of fact be law-trained or a judicial or administrative officer. Surely, this is the case as to medical decisions for "neither judges nor administrative hearing officers are better qualified than psychiatrists to render psychiatric judgments." In re Roger S., 19 Cal.3d 921, 942, 141 Cal.Rptr. 298, 311, 569 P.2d 1286, 1299 (1977) (Clark, J., dissenting). Thus, a staff physician will suffice, so long as he or she is free to evaluate independently the child's mental and emotional condition and need for treatment.

It is not necessary that the deciding physician conduct a formal or quasi-formal hearing. A state is free to require such a hearing, but due process is not violated by use of informal traditional medical investigative techniques. Since well-established medical procedures already exist, we do not undertake to outline with specificity precisely what this investigation must involve. The mode and procedure of medical diagnostic procedures is not the business of judges. What is best for a child is an individual medical decision that must be left to the judgment of physicians in each case. We do no more than emphasize that the decision should represent an independent judgment of what the child requires and that all sources of information that are traditionally relied on by physicians and behavioral specialists should be consulted.

What process is constitutionally due cannot be divorced from the nature of the ultimate decision that is being made. Not every determination by state officers can be made most effectively by use of "the procedural tools of judicial or administrative decisionmaking." Board of Curators of Univ. of Missouri v. Horowitz, 435 U.S. 78, 90 (1978).

Here the questions are essentially medical in character: whether the child is mentally or emotionally ill and whether he can benefit from the treatment that is provided by the state. While facts are plainly necessary for a proper resolution of those questions, they are only a first step in the process. In an opinion for a unanimous Court, we recently stated in Addington v. Texas, supra, 441 U.S., at 429, "whether [a person] is mentally ill ... turns on the *meaning* of the facts which must be interpreted by expert psychiatrists and psychologists."

Although we acknowledge the fallibility of medical and psychiatric diagnosis, we do not accept the notion that the shortcomings of specialists can always be avoided by shifting the decision from a trained specialist using the traditional tools of medical science to an untrained judge or administrative hearing officer after a judicial-type hearing. Even after a hearing, the nonspecialist decisionmaker must make a medical-psychiatric decision. Common human experience and scholarly opinions suggest that the supposed protections of an adversary proceeding to determine the appropriateness of medical decisions for the commitment and treatment of mental and emotional illness may well be more illusory than real.

Another problem with requiring a formalized, factfinding hearing lies in the danger it poses for significant intrusion into the parent-child relationship. Pitting the parents and child as adversaries often will be at odds with the presumption that parents act in the best interests of their child. It is one thing to require a neutral physician to make a careful review of the parents' decision in order to make sure it is proper from a medical standpoint; it is a wholly different matter to employ an adversary contest to ascertain whether the parents' motivation is consistent with the child's interests.

Moreover, it is appropriate to inquire into how such a hearing would contribute to the long range successful treatment of the patient. Surely, there is a risk that it would exacerbate whatever tensions already existed between the child and the parents. Since the parents can and usually do play a significant role in the treatment while the child is hospitalized and even more so after release, there is a serious risk that an adversary confrontation will adversely affect the ability of the parents to assist the child while in the hospital. Moreover, it will make his subsequent return home more difficult. These unfortunate results are especially critical with an emotionally disturbed child; they seem likely to occur in the context of an adversary hearing in which the parents testify. A confrontation over such intimate family relationships would distress the normal adult parents and the impact on a disturbed child almost certainly would be significantly greater.[18]

---

18. While not altogether clear, the District Court opinion apparently contemplated a hearing preceded by a written notice of the proposed commitment. At the hearing the child presumably would be given an opportunity to be heard and present evidence, and the right to cross-examine witnesses, including, of course, the parents. The court also required an impartial trier of fact who would render a written decision reciting the reasons for accepting or rejecting the parental application.

Since the parents in this situation are seeking the child's admission to the state institution, the procedure contemplated by the District Court presumably would call for some other person to be designated as a

It has been suggested that a hearing conducted by someone other than the admitting physician is necessary in order to detect instances where parents are "guilty of railroading their children into asylums" or are using "voluntary commitment procedures in order to sanction behavior of which they disapprove." Ellis, Volunteering Children: Parental Commitment of Minors to Mental Institutions, 62 Calif.L.Rev. 840, 850–851 (1974). Curiously it seems to be taken for granted that parents who seek to "dump" their children on the state will inevitably be able to conceal their motives and thus deceive the admitting psychiatrists and the other mental health professionals who make and review the admission decision. It is elementary that one early diagnostic inquiry into the cause of an emotional disturbance of a child is an examination into the environment of the child. It is unlikely if not inconceivable that a decision to abandon an emotionally normal, healthy child and thrust him into an institution will be a discrete act leaving no trail of circumstances. Evidence of such conflicts will emerge either in the interviews or from secondary sources. It is unrealistic to believe that trained psychiatrists, skilled in eliciting responses, sorting medically relevant facts and sensitive to motivational nuances will often be deceived about the family situation surrounding a child's emotional disturbance.[19] . . .

By expressing some confidence in the medical decisionmaking process, we are by no means suggesting it is error free. . . . That there may be risks of error in the process affords no rational predicate for holding unconstitutional an entire statutory and administrative scheme that is generally followed in more than 30 states. "[P]rocedural due process rules are shaped by the risk of error inherent in the truthfinding process as applied to the generality of cases, not the rare exceptions." Mathews v. Eldridge, 424 U.S. at 344 (1976). In general, we are satisfied that an independent medical decisionmaking process, which includes the thorough psychiatric investigation described earlier followed by additional periodic review of a child's condition, will protect children who should not be admitted; we do not believe the risks of error in that process would be significantly reduced by a more formal, judicial-type hearing. The issue remains whether the Georgia practices ... comport with these minimum due process requirements.

[In subpart (e) the opinion reviews Georgia's statutory procedure, which "envisions a careful diagnostic medical inquiry ... by the admitting physician at each regional hospital." The Court rejects the District Court's view that the medical decision constitutes "an exercise of 'unbridled

guardian *ad litem* to act for the child. The guardian, in turn, if not a lawyer, would be empowered to retain counsel to act as an advocate of the child's interest.

Of course, a state may elect to provide such adversary hearings in situations where it perceives that parents and a child may be at odds, but nothing in the Constitution compels such procedures.

19. In evaluating the problem of detecting "dumping" by parents, it is important to keep in mind that each of the regional hospi-

tals has a continuing relationship with the Department of Family and Children Services. The staffs at those hospitals refer cases to the Department when they suspect a child is being mistreated and thus are sensitive to this problem. In fact, J. L.'s situation is in point. The family conflicts and problems were well documented in the hospital records. Equally well documented, however, were the child's severe emotional disturbances and his need for treatment.

discretion.' '' The Court notes again that the superintendent of each hospital is charged statutorily "to discharge any child who is no longer mentally ill or in need of therapy." The Court also expressed its satisfaction with the conclusion that hospital admissions staffs "have acted in a neutral and detached fashion in making medical judgments in the best interests of the children." It notes that on remand, the District Court "is free to and should consider any individual claims that initial admissions did not meet the standards . . . described in this opinion."]

IV

. . . Some members of appellees' class, including J. R., were wards of the state of Georgia at the time of their admission. . . . While the determination of what process is due varies somewhat when the state, rather than a natural parent, makes the request for commitment, we conclude that the differences in the two situations do not justify requiring different procedures at the time of the child's initial admission to the hospital.

For a ward of the State, there may well be no adult who knows him thoroughly and who cares for him deeply. Unlike with natural parents where there is a presumed natural affection to guide their action, Blackstone * 447; Kent * 190, the presumption that the state will protect a child's general welfare stems from a specific state statute. Ga.Code Ann. § 24A 101. Contrary to the suggestion of the dissent, however, we cannot assume that when the State of Georgia has custody of a child it acts so differently from a natural parent in seeking medical assistance for the child. . . . Nor could such a challenge be mounted on the record before us. There is no evidence that the State, acting as guardian, attempted to admit any child for reasons unrelated to the child's need for treatment. . . .

Once we accept that the State's application of a child for admission to a hospital is made in good faith, then the question is whether the medical decisionmaking approach of the admitting physician is adequate to satisfy due process. We have already recognized that an independent medical judgment made from the perspective of the best interests of the child after a careful investigation is an acceptable means of justifying a voluntary commitment. We do not believe that the soundness of this decisionmaking is any the less reasonable in this setting. . . .

It is possible that the procedures required in reviewing a ward's need for continuing care should be different from those used to review a child with natural parents.

. . .

The absence of an adult who cares deeply for a child has little effect on the reliability of the initial admission decision, but it may have some effect on how long a child will remain in the hospital. We noted in Addington v. Texas, supra, 441 U.S., at 428, "the concern of family and friends generally will provide continuous opportunities for an erroneous commitment to be corrected." For a child without natural parents, we must acknowledge the risk of being "lost in the shuffle." Moreover, there is at least some indication that J. R.'s commitment was prolonged because the Department of Family and Children Services had difficulty finding a foster home for him. Whether wards of the State generally have received less protection than children with natural parents, and, if so, what should be done about it, however, are matters that must be decided in the first instance by the District Court on remand, if the Court concludes the issue is still alive.

V

It is important that we remember the purpose of Georgia's comprehensive mental health program. It seeks substantively and at great cost to provide care for those who cannot afford to obtain private treatment and procedurally to screen carefully all applicants to assure that institutional care is suited to the particular patient. The State resists the complex of procedures ordered by the District Court because in its view they are unnecessary to protect the child's rights, they divert public resources from the central objective of administering health care, they risk aggravating the tensions inherent in the family situation and they erect barriers that may discourage parents from seeking medical aid for a disturbed child.

On this record we are satisfied that Georgia's medical factfinding processes are reasonable and consistent with constitutional guarantees. Accordingly, it was error to hold unconstitutional the State's procedures for admitting a child for treatment to a state mental hospital. . . .

Reversed and remanded.

■ [The concurring opinion of Mr. Justice Stewart is omitted.]

■ [In a separate opinion MR. JUSTICE BRENNAN, joined by MR. JUSTICE MARSHALL and MR. JUSTICE STEVENS concurred in part and dissented in part.]
. . .

I

Rights of Children Committed To Mental Institutions

Commitment to a mental institution necessarily entails a "massive curtailment of liberty," *Humphrey v. Cady*, 405 U.S. 504, 509 (1972), and inevitably affects "fundamental right." *Baxstrom v. Herold*, 383 U.S. 107, 113 (1966). Persons incarcerated in mental hospitals are not only deprived of their physical liberty, they are also deprived of friends, family, and community. Institutionalized mental patients must live in unnatural surroundings under the continuous and detailed control of strangers. They are subject to intrusive treatment which, especially if unwarranted, may violate their right to bodily integrity. Such treatment modalities may include forced administration of psychotropic medication, aversive conditioning, convulsive therapy, and even psycho-surgery. Furthermore, as the Court recognizes, *see ante*, at 600, persons confined in mental institutions are stigmatized as sick and abnormal during confinement and, in some cases, even after release.

Because of these considerations, our cases have made clear that commitment to a mental hospital "is a deprivation of liberty which the State cannot accomplish without due process of law." *O'Connor v. Donaldson*, 422 U.S. 563, 580 (1975) (Burger, C.J., concurring). In the absence of a voluntary, knowing, and intelligent waiver, adults facing commitment to mental institutions are entitled to full land fair adversary hearings in which the necessity for their commitment is established to the satisfaction of a neutral tribunal. At such hearings they must be accorded the right to "be present with counsel, have an opportunity to be heard, be confronted with witnesses against [them], have the right to cross-examine, and to offer evidence of [their] own." *Specht v. Patterson, supra,* at 610.

These principles also govern the commitment of children. "Constitutional rights do not mature and come into being magically only when one attains the state-defined age of majority. Minors, as well as adults, are protected by the Constitution and possess constitutional rights." *Planned Parenthood of Central Missouri v. Danforth,* 428 U.S. 52, 74 (1976).

Indeed, it may well be argued that children are entitled to more protection than are adults. The consequences of an erroneous commitment decision are more tragic where children are involved. Children, on the average, are confined for longer periods than are adults. Moreover, childhood is a particularly vulnerable time of life and children erroneously institutionalized during their formative years may bear the scars for the rest of their lives.

. . .

In addition, the chances of an erroneous commitment decision are particularly great where children are involved. Even under the best of circumstances psychiatric diagnosis and therapy decisions are fraught with uncertainties. See *O'Connor v. Donaldson, supra,* at 584 (Burger, C.J., concurring). These uncertainties are aggravated when, as under the Georgia practice, the psychiatrist interviews the child during a period of abnormal stress in connection with the commitment, and without adequate time or opportunity to become acquainted with the patient.

. . .

These compounded uncertainties often lead to erroneous commitments since psychiatrists tend to err on the side of medical caution and therefore hospitalize patients for whom other dispositions would be more beneficial. The National Institute of Mental Health recently found that only 36% of patients below age 20 who were confined at St. Elizabeth's Hospital actually required such hospitalization. Of particular relevance to this case, a Georgia study Commission on Mental Health Services for Children and Youth concluded that more than half of the State's institutionalized children were not in need of confinement if other forms of care were made available or used. Cited in *J.L. v. Parham,* 412 F.Supp. 112, 122 (M.D.Ga. 1976).

II

Rights of Children Committed By Their Parents

A

Notwithstanding all this, Georgia denies hearings to juveniles institutionalized at the behest of their parents. Georgia rationalizes this practice on the theory that parents act in their children's best interests and therefore may waive their children's due process rights. Children incarcerated because their parents wish them confined, Georgia contends, are really voluntary patients. I cannot accept this argument.

In our society, parental rights are limited by the legitimate rights and interests of their children.

. . .

This principle is also reflected in constitutional jurisprudence. Notions of parental authority and family autonomy cannot stand as absolute and invariable barriers to the assertion of constitutional rights by children. States, for example, may not condition a minor's right to secure an abortion on attaining her parents' consent since the right to an abortion is an important personal right and since disputes between parents and children on this question would fracture family autonomy. *See Planned Parenthood of Central Missouri v. Danforth*, 428 U.S., at 75.

This case is governed by the rule of *Danforth*. The right to be free from wrongful incarceration, physical intrusion, and stigmatization has significance for the individual surely as great as the right to an abortion. Moreover, as in *Danforth*, the parent-child dispute at issue here cannot be characterized as involving only a routine child-rearing decision made within the context of an ongoing family relationship. Indeed, *Danforth* involved only a potential dispute between parent and child, whereas here a break in family autonomy has actually resulted in the parents' decision to surrender custody of their child to a state mental institution. In my view, a child who has been ousted from his family has even greater need for an independent advocate.

Additional considerations counsel against allowing parents unfettered power to institutionalize their children without cause or without any hearing to ascertain that cause. The presumption that parents act in their children's best interests, while applicable to most child-rearing decisions, is not applicable in the commitment context. Numerous studies reveal that potential decisions to institutionalize their children often are the results of dislocation in the family unrelated to the children's mental condition. Moreover, even well-meaning parents lack the expertise necessary to evaluate the relative advantages and disadvantages of inpatient as opposed to outpatient psychiatric treatment. Parental decisions to waive hearings in which such questions could be explored, therefore, cannot be conclusively deemed either informed or intelligent. In these circumstances, I respectfully suggest, it ignores reality to assume blindly that parents act in their children's best interest when making commitment decisions and when waiving their children's due process rights.

B

This does not mean States are obliged to treat children who are committed at the behest of their parents in precisely the same manner as other persons who are involuntarily committed. The demands of due process are flexible and the parental commitment decision carries with it practical implications that States may legitimately take into account. While as a general rule due process requires that commitment hearings precede involuntary hospitalization, when parents seek to hospitalize their children special considerations militate in favor of postponement of formal commitment proceedings and against mandatory adversary preconfinement commitment hearings.

First, the prospect of an adversary hearing prior to admission might deter parents from seeking needed medical attention for their children. Second, the hearings themselves might delay treatment of children whose home life has become impossible and who require some form of immediate state care. Furthermore, because adversary hearings at this juncture would necessarily involve direct challenges to parental authority, judgment, or veracity, preadmission hearings may well result in pitting the child and his advocate against the parents. This, in turn, might traumatize both parent and child and make the child's eventual return to his family more difficult.

.   .   .

C

I do not believe, however, that the present Georgia juvenile commitment scheme is constitutional in its entirety. Although Georgia may postpone formal commitment hearings, when parents seek to commit their children, the State cannot dispense with such hearings altogether.

.   .   .

The special considerations that militate against preadmission commitment hearings when parents seek to hospitalize their children do not militate against reasonably prompt postadmission commitment hearings. In the first place, post-admission hearings would not delay the commencement of needed treatment. Children could be cared for by the State pending the disposition decision.

Second, the interest in avoiding family discord would be less significant at this stage since the family autonomy already will have been fractured by the institutionalization of the child. In any event, postadmission hearings are unlikely to disrupt family relationships. At later hearings, the case for and against commitment would be based upon the observations of the hospital staff and the judgments of the staff psychiatrists, rather than upon parental observations and recommendations. The doctors urging commitment, and not the parents, would stand as the child's adversaries. As a consequence, postadmission commitment hearings are unlikely to involve direct challenges to parental authority, judgment, or veracity. To defend the child, the child's advocate need not dispute the parents' original decision to seek medical treatment for their child, or even, for that matter, their observations concerning the child's behavior. The advocate need only argue, for example, that the child had sufficiently improved during his hospital stay to warrant outpatient treatment or outright discharge. Conflict between doctor and advocate on this question is unlikely to lead to family discord.

As a consequence, the prospect of a postadmission hearing is unlikely to deter parents from seeking medical attention for their children and the hearing itself is unlikely so to traumatize parent and child as to make the child's eventual return to the family impracticable.

. . .

Nor can the good faith and good intentions of Georgia's psychiatrists and social workers, adverted to by the Court, *see ante*, at 615–616, excuse Georgia's *ex parte* procedures. Georgia's admitting psychiatrists, like the school disciplinarians described in *Goss v. Lopez*, 419 U.S. 565 (1975), "although proceeding in utmost good faith, frequently act on the reports and advice of others; and the controlling facts and the nature of the conduct under challenge are often disputed." *Id.*, at 580. See App. 188–190, testimony of Dr. Messinger. Here, as in *Goss*, the "risk of error is not at all trivial, and it should be guarded against if that may be done without prohibitive cost or interference with the . . . process. . . ."

PSYCHIATRIC HOSPITALIZATION OF MINORS

(1) **A Medical Decision with Constitutional Dimensions.** As *Parham* reveals, the law has distinguished the parents' decision to admit their child to a psychiatric hospital from more routine health care decisions, where generally treatment of the child requires only the parent's informed consent. How is psychiatric hospitalization different from other medical care? Justice Brennan, in his dissent, draws on the parallel to abortion. Like the minor seeking abortion, the child whose parents seek admission to a psychiatric hospital has a constitutionally protected liberty interest, and parental authority should be restricted. How similar are these issues? Both abortion and psychiatric hospitalization involve medical treatment decisions with a dimension that sets them apart from routine treatment and presents a challenge to traditional legal responses. What is it about psychiatric hospitalization that presents such a challenge and raises doubts about deference to parental authority?

(2) **Psychiatric Disorders in Children.** Researchers have pointed out that the psychiatric diagnoses of children and adolescents in psychiatric facilities are generally different from the mental disorders of institutionalized adults. Consider the following account by Lois Weithorn, a clinical psychologist. Lois Weithorn, Mental Hospitalization of Troublesome Youth: An Analysis of Skyrocketing Admission Rates, 40 Stan.L.Rev. 773, 788–91 (1988).*

. . .

1. The characteristics of hospitalized adolescents: Are they severely or actually mentally ill?

Fewer than one-third of those juveniles admitted for inpatient mental health treatment in recent years were diagnosed as having severe or acute mental disorders of the type typically associated with such admissions (such as psychotic, serious depressive, or organic disorders). By contrast, about one-half to two-thirds of adults admitted for inpatient mental health treatment were diagnosed as having such serious disorders. Yet, once hospitalized, juvenile psychiatric patients remain in the hospital approximately twice as long as do adults. And, children hospitalized in private facilities are both more likely to have longer stays and less likely to be severely disturbed than are children in public facilities.

About two-thirds of juvenile inpatients receive initial diagnoses of conduct disorder, personality or childhood disorder, or transitional disorder. An examination of the various "symptoms" that characterize each type of disorder reveals that, in general, these categories describe troublemakers, children with relatively mild psychological problems, and children who do not appear to suffer from anything more serious than normal developmental changes.

For example, in order to assign a conduct disorder diagnosis, a clinician must note a persistent pattern of antisocial conduct for at least six months. Depending upon which of the enumerated behavioral problems a child exhibits, a clinician might diagnose the child as demonstrating a more "aggressive" versus "nonaggressive" conduct disorder, or a more socially oriented (such as gang-directed) or "solitary" conduct disorder. The more aggressive constellations of behavior may manifest as physical violence against persons or property, or thefts involving personal confrontation. As such, this "disorder" may mirror the type of behavior that could lead to an adjudication of delinquency in the juvenile justice system. The nonaggressive manifestations of this behavior problem include chronic violations of rules at home or at school, truancy, running away, persistent lying, or stealing not involving personal confrontation. Thus, the conduct required for this category is virtually parallel to conduct that could lead a judge to find that a minor is a status offender. These parallels have not escaped researchers, who have studied the similarities among juveniles in psychiatric and correctional facilities. Several have posited that rising rates of juvenile psychiatric admission result from the transinstitutionalization of children from the juvenile justice to the mental health system.

A second class of diagnoses frequently assigned to adolescent inpatients is that of the "personality disorders." The category includes the "oppositional disorder," the "identity disorder," and the "avoidant disorder." Children exhibiting the behavior required for a diagnosis of one of these disorders also are unlikely to be seriously mentally ill. For example, the oppositional disorder diagnosis requires a six-month pattern of behavior such as stubbornness, violations of minor rules, argumentativeness, and temper tantrums. Yet developmental researchers often regard such nondangerous expressions of oppositional behavior as a normal aspect of the transition from childhood to adolescence. Similar claims as to the nonpathological nature of the identity disorder and avoidant disorder can be made. An identity disorder is defined by a pattern of "severe subjective distress regarding uncertainty about a variety of issues relating to identity" (such as long-term goals, career choice, and friendship patterns). Many psychologists, however, view an "identity crisis" as an essential step on the path to healthy psychological development. Finally, although the excessive shyness that characterizes an avoidant disorder can interfere with social functioning, it also may represent one end of a continuum of normal behavior. Research suggests that in a large percentage of cases, the presence of such behavior in childhood is transitory.

The symptoms associated with "adjustment disorders" also do not suggest the presence of a serious mental disorder. Adjustment disorders, also called "transitional disorders" or "situational disorders," are characterized by an "overreaction" of some sort to identifiable social stressors (such as parental fighting), leading to impairment in social or occupational functioning. Incorporated into the formal definition of these disorders, however, is a recognition that "the disturbance will eventually remit after the stressor ceases or, if the stressor persists, when a new level of adaptation is achieved." This acknowledgment directly contradicts the notion that the disorders in this category represent serious mental illnesses. Nonetheless, in 1975 they accounted for more than 30 percent of all juvenile admissions to public and private psychiatric hospitals, and to psychiatric units of private general hospitals.

. . .

(3) **Physical Illness v. Psychiatric Disorder.** Does Weithorn's description of the mental disorders of minors in psychiatric hospitals suggest important differences, not only from adult mental illness, but also from physical illness and other medical conditions in children for which parents seek treatment? Parental authority to make medical treatment decisions for their children reflects the law's assumption that parents will make decisions that promote their children's best health and welfare. Justice Burger is quite correct in asserting that historically, the law "has recognized that natural bonds of affection lead parents to act in the best interests of their children." 442 U.S. at 602. The issue is whether there is a substantial risk that parents might, perhaps because of the unique character of the "illness," seek to admit their children to psychiatric hospitals under circumstances in which this placement is not in the child's best interests. Put another way, will the decision to hospitalize a disruptive "troublesome" child sometimes further the interests of the parents (and other family members) rather than the child? Review the facts about J.L. reported by the Court in *Parham*. Were the parents motivated here primarily by a concern for J.L.'s welfare? Does their interest conflict with that of J.L.?

Weithorn argues that increases in the rates of psychiatric hospitalization of minors can[1] be linked in part to greater family disruption in recent years, as reflected in high divorce rate. Several studies suggest that a disproportionately high percentage of children in residential facilities are from families in which the biological parents no longer live together. Id. at 802. Single parents may lack the psychological and financial resources to deal with a troubled child within the family.

(4) **The Least Restrictive Alternative Requirement.** Critics of *Parham* and of policies that permit parents to admit their children to psychiatric facilities without an adversary proceeding do not argue that children who are admitted by their parents are not in need of any treatment, but rather that hospitalization is often an inappropriate intervention, because it severely disrupts the child's life, is stigmatic, restrictive, and often ineffective. Weithorn, among others, argues that community-based interventions, particularly those that allow the child to remain in the family, are less disruptive and more effective than hospitalization. Id. at 792–98. Parents may choose psychiatric hospitalization because community programs are not available, or because reimbursement is inadequate or unavailable. Medical insurance policies tend to provide a strong incentive to choose inpatient psychiatric treatment over other options. Id. at 814–15.

(5) **The Psychiatrist as Neutral Fact Finder.** The Court in *Parham* holds that, because of the child's interest in avoiding an erroneous decision, due process requires that a "neutral fact finder" review the parents' hospitalization decision so as to assure that the statutory requirements for admission are met. The Court concludes that a hospital staff physician can serve in this role "so long as he or she is in a position to evaluate independently the child's mental and emotional condition and need for treatment." Do you think a hospital physician is well situated to serve as a "neutral fact finder"? What factors might undermine the physician's neutrality in this context? Some observers have suggested that psychiatrists tend to interpret behavior as reflecting pathology to a greater extent than do other observers—including other mental health professionals. A serious question about

---

1. Weithorn focuses particularly on the rapidly increasing rate of private psychiatric hospitalization of minors in recent years. Ad- missions increased four fold from 1980 to 1984. Mental Hospitalization of Troublesome Youth, 40 Stan.L.Rev. at 783.

the impartiality of the admitting physician arises in any situation in which the hospital has a financial stake in filling its beds. This is certainly the case with private psychiatric facilities, in which profits are directly linked to the level of admissions. As Weithorn points out, today most juveniles are hospitalized in private facilities; adolescent inpatient units are "big business." Id. at 813.

VIRGINIA CODE ANNOTATED (Lexis)

PSYCHIATRIC INPATIENT TREATMENT OF MINORS ACT

§ 16.1–338. Parental admission of minors younger than 14 and nonobjecting minors 14 years of age or older.

A.   A minor younger than 14 years of age may be admitted to a willing mental health facility for inpatient treatment upon application and with the consent of a parent. A minor 14 years of age or older may be admitted to a willing mental health facility for inpatient treatment upon the joint application and consent of the minor and the minor's parent.

B.   Admission of a minor under this section shall be approved by a qualified evaluator who has conducted a personal examination of the minor within forty-eight hours after admission and has made the following written findings:

1.   The minor appears to have a mental illness serious enough to warrant inpatient treatment and is reasonably likely to benefit from the treatment; and

2.   The minor has been provided with a clinically appropriate explanation of the nature and purpose of the treatment; and

3.   If the minor is 14 years of age or older, that he has been provided with an explanation of his rights under this Act as they would apply if he were to object to admission, and that he has consented to admission; and

4.   All available modalities of treatment less restrictive than inpatient treatment have been considered and no less restrictive alternative is available that would offer comparable benefits to the minor.

. . .

C.   Within 10 days after the admission of a minor under this section, the director of the facility or the director's designee shall ensure that an individualized plan of treatment has been prepared by the provider responsible for the minor's treatment and has been explained to the parent consenting to the admission and to the minor. The minor shall be involved in the preparation of the plan to the maximum feasible extent consistent with his ability to understand and participate, and the minor's family shall be involved to the maximum extent consistent with the minor's treatment needs. The plan shall include a preliminary plan for placement and after-care upon completion of inpatient treatment and shall include specific behavioral and emotional goals against which the success of treatment may be measured. . . .

D.   If the parent who consented to a minor's admission under this section revokes his consent at any time, or if a minor 14 or older objects at any time to further treatment, the minor shall be discharged within 48 hours to the custody of such consenting parent unless the minor's continued hospitalization is authorized pursuant to §§ 16.1–339, 16.1–340, or § 16.1–345.

E.   Inpatient treatment of a minor hospitalized under this section may not exceed 90 consecutive days unless it has been authorized by appropriate hospital medical personnel, based upon their written findings that the criteria set forth in subsection B of this section continue to be met, after such persons have examined the minor and interviewed the consenting parent and reviewed reports submitted by members of the facility staff familiar with the minor's condition.

F.   Any minor admitted under this section while younger than 14 and his consenting parent shall be informed ... within 10 days of his fourteenth birthday that continued voluntary treatment under ... this section requires his consent.

G.   Any minor 14 years of age or older who joins in an application and consents to admission pursuant to subsection A, shall, in addition to his parent, have the right to access his health information....

§ 16.1–339.   Parental admission of an objecting minor 14 years of age or older.

A.   A minor 14 years of age or older who (i) objects to admission, or (ii) is incapable of making an informed decision may be admitted to a willing facility for up to 96 hours, pending the review required by subsections B and C of this section, upon the application of a parent....

B.   A minor admitted under this section shall be examined within 24 hours of his admission by a qualified evaluator ... who is not and will not be treating the minor and who has no significant financial interest in the minor's hospitalization. The evaluator shall prepare a report that shall include written findings as to whether:

1.   Because of mental illness, the minor (i) presents a serious danger to himself or others to the extent that severe or irremediable injury is likely to result, as evidenced by recent acts or threats or (ii) is experiencing a serious deterioration of his ability to care for himself in a developmentally age-appropriate manner, as evidenced by delusionary thinking or by a significant impairment of functioning in hydration, nutrition, self-protection, or self-control;

2.   The minor is in need of inpatient treatment for a mental illness and is reasonably likely to benefit from the proposed treatment; and

3.   Inpatient treatment is the least restrictive alternative that meets the minor's needs. The qualified evaluator shall submit his report to the juvenile and domestic relations district court for the jurisdiction in which the facility is located.

C.   Upon admission of a minor under this section, the facility shall immediately file a petition for judicial approval no sooner than 24 hours and no later than 96 hours after admission with the juvenile and domestic relations district court for the jurisdiction in which the facility is located. ...Upon receipt of the petition and of the evaluator's report submitted pursuant to subsection B, the judge shall appoint a guardian ad litem for the minor and counsel to represent the minor, unless it has been determined that the minor has retained counsel. The court and the guardian ad litem shall review the petition and evaluator's report and shall ascertain the views of the minor, the minor's consenting parent, the evaluator, and the attending psychiatrist.... Based upon its review and the recommendations of the guardian ad litem, the court shall order one of the following dispositions:

1. If the court finds that the minor does not meet the criteria for admission specified in subsection B, the court shall issue an order directing the facility to release the minor into the custody of the parent who consented to the minor's admission. However, nothing herein shall be deemed to affect the terms and provisions of any valid court order of custody affecting the minor.

2. If the court finds that the minor meets the criteria for admission specified in subsection B, the court shall issue an order authorizing continued hospitalization of the minor for up to ninety days on the basis of the parent's consent.

Within 10 days after the admission of a minor under this section, the director of the facility or the director's designee shall ensure that an individualized plan of treatment has been prepared by the provider responsible for the minor's treatment....

3. If the court determines that the available information is insufficient to permit an informed determination regarding whether the minor meets the criteria specified in subsection B, the court shall schedule a commitment hearing that shall be conducted in accordance with the procedures specified in §§ 16.1–341 through 16.1–345....

D. A minor admitted under this section who rescinds his objection may be retained in the hospital pursuant to § 16.1–338.

E. If the parent who consented to a minor's admission under this section revokes his consent at any time, the minor shall be released within 48 hours to the parent's custody unless the minor's continued hospitalization is authorized pursuant to § 16.1–340 or § 16.1–345....

. . .

§ 16.1–341. Involuntary commitment; petition; hearing scheduled; notice and appointment of counsel.

A. A petition for the involuntary commitment of a minor may be filed with the juvenile and domestic relations district court serving the jurisdiction in which the minor is located by a parent or, if the parent is not available or is unable or unwilling to file a petition, by any responsible adult, including the person having custody over a minor in detention or shelter care pursuant to an order of the juvenile and domestic relations district court....

B. Upon the filing of a petition for involuntary commitment of a minor, the juvenile and domestic relations district court ... may schedule a hearing which shall occur no sooner than 24 hours and no later than 96 hours from the time the petition was filed....

. . .

§ 16.1–342.   Involuntary commitment; clinical evaluation.

Upon the filing of a petition for involuntary commitment, the juvenile and domestic relations district court shall direct the community services board serving the area in which the minor is located to arrange for an evaluation, if one has not already been performed pursuant to subsection B of § 16.1–339, by a qualified evaluator who is not and will not be treating the minor and who has no significant financial interest in the facility to which the minor would be committed. . . .

§ 16.1–343.   Involuntary commitment; duties of attorney for the minor

. . . [T]he minor's attorney shall interview the minor; the minor's parent, if available; the petitioner; and the qualified evaluator. He shall interview all other material witnesses, and examine all relevant diagnostic and other reports.

Any state or local agency, department . . . shall permit the attorney . . . to inspect and copy, without the consent of the minor or his parents, any records relating to the minor whom the attorney represents.

The obligation of the minor's attorney during the hearing or appeal is to interview witnesses, obtain independent experts when possible, cross-examine adverse witnesses, present witnesses on behalf of the minor, articulate the wishes of the minor, and otherwise fully represent the minor in the proceeding. Counsel appointed by the court shall be compensated in an amount not to exceed $100.

§ 16.1–344.   Involuntary commitment; hearing.

The court shall summon to the hearing all material witnesses requested by either the minor or the petitioner. All testimony shall be under oath. The rules of evidence shall apply; however, the evaluator's report required by § 16.1–342 shall be admissible into evidence by stipulation of the parties. The petitioner, minor and, with leave of court for good cause shown, any other person shall be given the opportunity to present evidence and cross-examine witnesses. The hearing shall be closed to the public unless the minor and petitioner request that it be open. Within thirty days of any final order committing the minor or dismissing the petition, the minor or petitioner shall have the right to appeal de novo to the circuit court having jurisdiction where the minor was committed or where the minor is hospitalized pursuant to the commitment order. The juvenile and domestic relations district court shall appoint an attorney to represent any minor desiring to appeal who does not appear to be already represented.

§ 16.1–345.   Involuntary commitment; criteria.

The court shall order the involuntary commitment of the minor to a mental health facility for treatment for a period not to exceed 90 days if it finds, by clear and convincing evidence, that:

1. Because of mental illness, the minor (i) presents a serious danger to himself or others to the extent that severe or irremediable injury is likely to result, as evidenced by recent acts or threats or (ii) is experiencing a serious deterioration of his ability to care for himself in a developmentally age-appropriate manner, as evidenced by delusionary thinking or by a

significant impairment of functioning in hydration, nutrition, self-protection, or self-control;

2. The minor is in need of compulsory treatment for a mental illness and is reasonably likely to benefit from the proposed treatment; and

3. If inpatient treatment is ordered, such treatment is the least restrictive alternative that meets the minor's needs. If the court finds that inpatient treatment is not the least restrictive treatment, the court may order the minor to participate in outpatient or other clinically appropriate treatment.

. . .

NOTES

(1) **Comparing Two Statutory Approaches.** In what ways does the Virginia statutory framework differ from that of Georgia that was upheld by the Supreme Court in *Parham*? Note that the Virginia statute distinguishes between minors under 14 years of age and those who are 14 or older. Why do you think this distinction is drawn? Remember Justice Douglas's argument, based on developmental psychology, that the 14–year-old Amish children were mature minors.

(2) **The Legal Standard for Involuntary Commitment.** The standard for involuntary commitment of minors under § 16.1–339(B)(1) of the Virginia statute is far more elaborately defined than is the admission standard applied to minors as involuntary patients under Georgia law. [Under Georgia law, evidence of mental illness and suitability for treatment in the hospital are required.] Does the Virginia statute seriously restrict the discretion of the court deciding about commitment? Why does the statute require evidence of recent acts or threats to substantiate that the minor presents a serious danger to herself or others?

Compare the standard applied to minors under the Virginia statute with that applied to adults who face an involuntary commitment procedure under Virginia law. In the case of adults, the court must find that the person for whom involuntary commitment is proposed: (1) presents an imminent danger to himself or others because of mental illness, or (2) is so seriously mentally ill as to be substantially unable to care for himself, and that there is no less restrictive alternative treatment. The standard applied to adults is more restrictive of commitment authority, recognizing the greater liberty interest of adults.

(3) **The Attorney's Role.** Consider the duties of the attorney for the minor under the Virginia statute. Do you think the attorney's role is any different from that of an attorney representing an adult under similar circumstances? Should the attorney representing an unwilling minor argue against involuntary commitment regardless of her own view of the minor's need for hospitalization? Under Georgia's informal procedures, there would seem to be little role for attorneys. Is this the only alternative to the full adversarial role suggested by the Virginia statute?

3. Adolescent Reproductive Autonomy

Bellotti v. Baird

Supreme Court of the United States, 1979.
443 U.S. 622, 99 S.Ct. 3035, 61 L.Ed.2d 797.

■ Mr. Justice Powell announced the judgment of the Court and delivered an opinion, in which The Chief Justice, Mr. Justice Stewart, and Mr. Justice Rehnquist joined.

[This opinion (*Bellotti II*) was rendered on the second consideration by the United States Supreme Court of the parental consent provision in Massachusetts's 1974 abortion statute (Mass. Gen. Laws Ann., ch. 112, § 12S). The relevant provision reads as follows:

> If the mother is less than eighteen years of age and has not married, the consent of both the mother and her parents [to an abortion to be performed on the mother] is required. If one or both of the mother's parents refuse such consent, consent may be obtained by order of a judge of the superior court for good cause shown, after such hearing as he deems necessary. Such a hearing will not require the appointment of a guardian for the mother. If one of the parents has died or has deserted his or her family, consent by the remaining parent is sufficient. If both parents have died or have deserted their family, consent of the mother's guardian or other person having duties similar to a guardian, or any person who had assumed the care and custody of the mother is sufficient. The commissioner of public health shall prescribe a written form for such consent. Such form shall be signed by the proper person or persons and given to the physician performing the abortion who shall maintain it in his permanent files.

In 1975, a Massachusetts Federal District invalidated section 12S as unconstitutional. (*Baird v. Bellotti*, 393 F.Supp. 847 (Mass.1975)). The United States Supreme Court, responding to the state's argument that § 12S could be construed so as to avoid a federal constitutional challenge, vacated the judgment of the District Court, and directed that it certify to the Supreme Judicial Court of Massachusetts questions regarding the construction of the statute. On remand, the District Court certified nine questions to the Massachusetts Supreme Court and based on the response, again declared the statute to be unconstitutional (*Baird v. Bellotti*, 450 F.Supp. 997 (Mass.1978)). The state sought review by the United States Supreme Court for a second time.

The Court began by summarizing the construction of section 12S by the Supreme Judicial Court (*Baird v. Attorney General*, 371 Mass. 741, 360 N.E.2d 288 (1977)):]

Among the more important aspects of § 12S, as authoritatively construed by the Supreme Judicial Court, are the following:

1.   In deciding whether to grant consent to their daughter's abortion, parents are required by § 12S to consider exclusively what will serve her best interests. . . .

2.   The provision in § 12S that judicial consent for an abortion shall be granted, parental objections notwithstanding, "for good cause shown" means that such consent shall be granted if found to be in the minor's best interests. The judge "must disregard all parental objections, and other considerations, which are not based exclusively" on that standard . . .

3.   Even if the judge in a § 12S proceeding finds "that the minor is capable of making, and has made, an informed and reasonable decision to have an abortion," he is entitled to withhold consent "in circumstances where he determines that the best interests of the minor will not be served by an abortion." . . .

4.   As a general rule, a minor who desires an abortion may not obtain judicial consent without first seeking both parents' consent. Exceptions to the rule exist when a parent is not available or when the need for the abortion constitutes " 'an emergency requiring immediate action.' " ... *Exception* Unless a parent is not available, he must be notified of any judicial proceedings brought under § 12S ...

5.   The resolution of § 12S cases and any appeals that follow can be expected to be prompt. The name of the minor and her parents may be held in confidence. If need be, the Supreme Judicial Court and the superior courts can promulgate rules or issue orders to ensure that such proceedings are handled expeditiously....

. . .

II

A child, merely on account of his minority, is not beyond the protection of the Constitution. As the Court said *In re Gault*, 387 U.S. 1, 13 (1967), "whatever may be their precise impact, neither the Fourteenth Amendment nor the Bill of Rights is for adults alone." This observation, of course, is but the beginning of the analysis. The Court long has recognized that the status of minors under the law is unique in many respects. As Mr. Justice Frankfurter aptly put it: "[C]hildren have a very special place in life which law should reflect. Legal theories and their phrasing in other cases readily lead to fallacious reasoning if uncritically transferred to determination of a State's duty towards children." *May v. Anderson*, 345 U.S. 528, 536 (1953) (concurring opinion). The unique role in our society of the family, the institution by which "we inculcate and pass down many of our most cherished values, moral and cultural," *Moore v. East Cleveland*, 431 U.S. 494, 503–504 (1977) (plurality opinion), requires that constitutional principles be applied with sensitivity and flexibility to the special needs of parents and children. We have recognized three reasons justifying the conclusion that the constitutional rights of children cannot be equated with those of adults: the peculiar vulnerability of children; their inability to make critical decisions in an informed, mature manner; and the importance of the parental role in child rearing.

A

The Court's concern for the vulnerability of children is demonstrated in its decisions dealing with minors' claims to constitutional protection against deprivations of liberty or property interests by the State. With respect to many of these claims, we have concluded that the child's right is virtually coextensive with that of an adult. For example, the Court has held that the Fourteenth Amendment's guarantee against the deprivation of liberty without due process of law is applicable to children in juvenile delinquency proceedings. *In re Gault*, supra. In particular, minors involved in such proceedings are entitled to adequate notice, the assistance of counsel, and the opportunity to confront their accusers. They can be found guilty only upon proof beyond a reasonable doubt, and they may assert the privilege against compulsory self-incrimination. *In re Winship*, 397 U.S. 358 (1970); *In re Gault*, supra. Similarly, in *Goss v. Lopez*, 419 U.S. 565 (1975), the Court held that children may not be deprived of certain property interests without due process.

These rulings have not been made on the uncritical assumption that the constitutional rights of children are indistinguishable from those of adults. Indeed, our acceptance of juvenile courts distinct from the adult criminal justice system assumes that juvenile offenders constitutionally may be treated differently from adults. In order to preserve this separate avenue for dealing with minors, the Court has said that hearings in juvenile delinquency cases need not necessarily "conform with all of the requirements of a criminal trial or even of the usual administrative hearing." *In re Gault*, supra, 387 U.S. at 30. Viewed together, our cases show that although children generally are protected by the same constitutional guarantees against governmental deprivations as are adults, the State is entitled to adjust its legal system to account for children's vulnerability and their needs for "concern, ... sympathy, and ... paternal attention."

B

Second, the Court has held that the States validly may limit the freedom of children to choose for themselves in the making of important, affirmative choices with potentially serious consequences. These rulings have been grounded in the recognition that, during the formative years of childhood and adolescence, minors often lack the experience, perspective, and judgment to recognize and avoid choices that could be detrimental to them.

Ginsberg v. New York, 390 U.S. 629 (1968), illustrates well the Court's concern over the inability of children to make mature choices, as the First Amendment rights involved are clear examples of constitutionally protected freedoms of choice. At issue was a criminal conviction for selling sexually oriented magazines to a minor under the age of 17 in violation of a New York state law. It was conceded that the conviction could not have stood under the First Amendment if based upon a sale of the same material to an adult. *Id.* at 634. Notwithstanding the importance the Court always has attached to First Amendment rights, it concluded that "even where there is an invasion of protected freedoms 'the power of the state to control the conduct of children reaches beyond the scope of its authority over adults ... ,'" *Id.* at 638, quoting *Prince v. Massachusetts*, 321 U.S. 158, 170 (1944). The Court was convinced that the New York Legislature rationally could conclude that the sale to children of the magazines in question presented a danger against which they should be guarded. *Ginsberg, supra,* at 641. It therefore rejected the argument that the New York law violated the constitutional rights of minors.

C

Third, the guiding role of parents in the upbringing of their children justifies limitations on the freedoms of minors. The State commonly protects its youth from adverse governmental action and from their own immaturity by requiring parental consent to or involvement in important decisions by minors.[16] But an additional and more important justification for state deference to parental control over children is that "[t]he child is not the mere creature of the State; those who nurture him and direct his destiny have the right, coupled with the high duty, to recognize and prepare him for additional obligations." *Pierce v. Society of Sisters*, 268 U.S. 510, 535 (1925). "The duty to prepare the child for 'additional obligations' ... must be read to include the inculcation of moral standards, religious beliefs, and elements of good citizenship." *Wisconsin v. Yoder*, 406 U.S. 205, 233 (1972). This affirmative process of teaching, guiding, and inspiring by precept and example is essential to the growth of young people into mature, socially responsible citizens.

We have believed in this country that this process, in large part, is beyond the competence of impersonal political institutions. Indeed, affirmative sponsorship of particular ethical, religious, or political beliefs is something we expect the State *not* to attempt in a society constitutionally committed to the ideal of individual liberty and freedom of choice. Thus, "[i]t is cardinal with us that the custody, care and nurture of the child reside first in the parents, whose primary function and freedom include *preparation for obligations the state can neither supply nor hinder.*" *Prince v. Massachusetts, supra*, 321 U.S. at 166 (emphasis added).

Unquestionably, there are many competing theories about the most effective way for parents to fulfill their central role in assisting their children on the way to responsible adulthood. While we do not pretend any special wisdom on this subject, we cannot ignore that central to many of these theories, and deeply rooted in our Nation's history and tradition, is the belief that the parental role implies a substantial measure of authority over one's children. Indeed, "constitutional interpretation has consistently recognized that the parents' claim to authority in their own household to direct the rearing of their children is basic in the structure of our society." *Ginsberg v. New York, supra*, 390 U.S. at 639.

Properly understood, then, the tradition of parental authority is not inconsistent with our tradition of individual liberty; rather, the former is one of the basic presuppositions of the latter. Legal restrictions on minors, especially those supportive of the parental role, may be important to the child's chances for the full growth and maturity that make eventual participation in a free society meaningful and rewarding. Under the Constitution, the State can "properly conclude that parents and others, teachers for example, who have [the] primary responsibility for children's well-being are entitled to the support of laws designed to aid discharge of that responsibility." *Ginsberg v. New York*, 390 U.S. at 639.

III

With these principles in mind, we consider the specific constitutional questions presented by these appeals. In § 12S, Massachusetts has attempted to reconcile the constitutional right of a woman, in consultation

16. See, e. g., Mass.Gen.Laws Ann., ch. 207, §§ 7, 24, 25, 33, 33A (West 1958 and Supp.1979) (parental consent required for marriage of person under 18); Mass.Gen. Laws Ann., ch. 119, sect. 55A (West Supp. 1979) (waiver of counsel by minor in juvenile delinquency proceedings must be made through parent or guardian).

with her physician, to choose to terminate her pregnancy as established by *Roe v. Wade*, 410 U.S. 113 (1973), and *Doe v. Bolton*, 410 U.S. 179 (1973), with the special interest of the State in encouraging an unmarried pregnant minor to seek the advice of her parents in making the important decision whether or not to bear a child. As noted above, § 12S was before us in *Bellotti I*, 428 U.S. 132 (1976), where we remanded the case for interpretation of its provisions by the Supreme Judicial Court of Massachusetts. We previously had held in *Planned Parenthood of Central Missouri v. Danforth*, 428 U.S. 52 (1976), that a State could not lawfully authorize an absolute parental veto over the decision of a minor to terminate her pregnancy. *Id.* at 74. In *Bellotti I, supra,* we recognized that § 12S could be read as "fundamentally different from a statute that creates a 'parental veto,' " 428 U.S. at 145, thus "avoid[ing] or substantially modify[ing] the federal constitutional challenge to the statute." Id. at 148. The question before us—in light of what we have said in the prior cases—is whether § 12S, as authoritatively interpreted by the Supreme Judicial Court, provides for parental notice and consent in a manner that does not unduly burden the right to seek an abortion. See *id.* at 147.

Appellees and intervenors contend that even as interpreted by the Supreme Judicial Court of Massachusetts, § 12S does unduly burden this right. They suggest, for example, that the mere requirement of parental notice constitutes such a burden. As stated in Part II above, however, parental notice and consent are qualifications that typically may be imposed by the State on a minor's right to make important decisions. As immature minors often lack the ability to make fully informed choices that take account of both immediate and long-range consequences, a State reasonably may determine that parental consultation often is desirable and in the best interest of the minor.[19] It may further determine, as a general proposition, that such consultation is particularly desirable with respect to the abortion decision—one that for some people raises profound moral and religious concerns.[20] As MR. JUSTICE STEWART wrote in concurrence in *Planned Parenthood of Central Missouri v. Danforth,* supra, at 91:

> "There can be little doubt that the State furthers a constitutionally permissible end by encouraging an unmarried pregnant minor to seek the help and advice of her parents in making the very important decision whether or not to bear a child. That is a grave decision, and a girl of tender years, under emotional stress, may be ill-equipped to make it without mature advice and emotional support. It seems unlikely that she will obtain adequate counsel and support from the attending physician at an abortion clinic, where abortions for pregnant minors frequently take place." (Footnote omitted.)[21]

19. In *Planned Parenthood of Central Missouri v. Danforth*, 428 U.S., at 75, "[w]e emphasize[d] that our holding ... [did] not suggest that every minor, regardless of age or maturity, may give effective consent for termination of her pregnancy."

20. The expert testimony at the hearings in the District Court uniformly was to the effect that parental involvement in a mi-

nor's abortion decision, if compassionate and supportive, was highly desirable. The findings of the court reflect this consensus. See *Baird I*, 393 F.Supp., at 853.

21. MR. JUSTICE STEWART's concurring opinion in *Danforth* underscored the need for parental involvement in minors' abortion decisions by describing the procedures followed

But we are concerned here with a constitutional right to seek an abortion. The abortion decision differs in important ways from other decisions that may be made during minority. The need to preserve the constitutional right and the unique nature of the abortion decision, especially when made by a minor, require a State to act with particular sensitivity when it legislates to foster parental involvement in this matter.

A

The pregnant minor's options are much different from those facing a minor in other situations, such as deciding whether to marry. A minor not permitted to marry before the age of majority is required simply to postpone her decision. She and her intended spouse may preserve the opportunity for later marriage should they continue to desire it. A pregnant adolescent, however, cannot preserve for long the possibility of aborting, which effectively expires in a matter of weeks from the onset of pregnancy.

Moreover, the potentially severe detriment facing a pregnant woman, see *Roe v. Wade*, 410 U.S. at 153, is not mitigated by her minority. Indeed, considering her probable education, employment skills, financial resources, and emotional maturity, unwanted motherhood may be exceptionally burdensome for a minor. In addition, the fact of having a child brings with it adult legal responsibility, for parenthood, like attainment of the age of majority, is one of the traditional criteria for the termination of the legal disabilities of minority. In sum, there are few situations in which denying a minor the right to make an important decision will have consequences so grave and indelible.

Yet, an abortion may not be the best choice for the minor. The circumstances in which this issue arises will vary widely. In a given case, alternatives to abortion, such as marriage to the father of the child, arranging for its adoption, or assuming the responsibilities of motherhood with the assured support of family, may be feasible and relevant to the minor's best interests. Nonetheless, the abortion decision is one that simply cannot be postponed, or it will be made by default with far-reaching consequences.

For these reasons, as we held in *Planned Parenthood of Central Missouri v. Danforth*, "the State may not impose a blanket provision ... requiring the consent of a parent or person *in loco parentis* as a condition for abortion of an unmarried minor during the first 12 weeks of her pregnancy." Although, as stated in Part II, *supra*, such deference to

---

at the clinic operated by the Parents Aid Society and Dr. Gerald Zupnick:

"The counseling ... occurs entirely on the day the abortion is to be performed.... It lasts for two hours and takes place in groups that include both minors and adults who are strangers to one another.... The physician takes no part In this counseling process.... Counseling is typically limited to a description of abortion procedures, possible complications, and birth control techniques.... The abortion itself takes five to seven minutes.... The physician has no prior contact with the minor, and on the days that abortions are being performed at the [clinic], the physician ... may be performing abortions on many other adults and minors.... On busy days patients are scheduled in separate groups, consisting usually of five patients.... After the abortion [the physician] spends a brief period with the minor and others in the group in the recovery room...." 428 U.S., at 91–92, n. 2.

parents may be permissible with respect to other choices facing a minor, the unique nature and consequences of the abortion decision make it inappropriate "to give a third party an absolute, and possibly arbitrary, veto over the decision of the physician and his patient to terminate the patient's pregnancy, regardless of the reason for withholding the consent." 428 U.S. at 74. We therefore conclude that if the State decides to require a pregnant minor to obtain one or both parents' consent to an abortion, it also must provide an alternative procedure[22] whereby authorization for the abortion can be obtained.

A pregnant minor is entitled in such a proceeding to show either: (1) that she is mature enough and well enough informed to make her abortion decision, in consultation with her physician, independently of her parents' wishes;[23] or (2) that even if she is not able to make this decision independently, the desired abortion would be in her best interests. The proceeding in which this showing is made must assure that a resolution of the issue, and any appeals that may follow, will be completed with anonymity and sufficient expedition to provide an effective opportunity for an abortion to be obtained. In sum, the procedure must ensure that the provision requiring parental consent does not in fact amount to the "absolute, and possibly arbitrary, veto" that was found impermissible in *Danforth. Ibid.*

B

It is against these requirements that § 12S must be tested. We observe initially that as authoritatively construed by the highest court of the State, the statute satisfies some of the concerns that require special treatment of a minor's abortion decision. It provides that if parental consent is refused, authorization may be "obtained by order of a judge of the superior court for good cause shown, after such hearing as he deems necessary." A superior court judge presiding over a § 12S proceeding "must disregard all parental objections, and other considerations, which are not based exclusively on what would serve the minor's best interests." *Attorney General,* 371 Mass. at 748, 360 N.E.2d at 293. The Supreme Judicial Court also stated: "Prompt resolution of a [§ 12S] proceeding may be expected.... The proceeding need not be brought in the minor's name and steps may be taken, by impoundment or otherwise, to preserve confidentiality as to the minor and her parents.... [W]e believe that an early hearing and decision

22. As § 12S provides for involvement of the state superior court in minors' abortion decisions, we discuss the alternative procedure described in the text in terms of judicial proceedings. We do not suggest, however, that a State choosing to require parental consent could not delegate the alternative procedure to a juvenile court or an administrative agency or officer. Indeed, much can be said for employing procedures and a forum less formal than those associated with a court of general jurisdiction.

23. The nature of both the State's interest in fostering parental authority and the problem of determining "maturity" makes clear why the State generally may resort to objective, though inevitably arbitrary, criteria such as age limits, marital status, or membership in the Armed Forces for lifting some or all of the legal disabilities of minority. Not only is it difficult to define, let alone determine, maturity, but also the fact that a minor may be very much an adult in some respects does not mean that his or her need and opportunity for growth under parental guidance and discipline have ended. As discussed in the text, however, the peculiar nature of the abortion decision requires the opportunity for case-by-case evaluations of the maturity of pregnant minors.

on appeal from a judgment of a Superior Court judge may also be achieved." *Id.* at 757–758, 360 N.E.2d at 298. The court added that if these expectations were not met, either the superior court, in the exercise of its rulemaking power, or the Supreme Judicial Court would be willing to eliminate any undue burdens by rule or order. *Ibid.*[25]

Despite these safeguards, which avoid much of what was objectionable in the statute successfully challenged in *Danforth*, § 12S falls short of constitutional standards in certain respects. We now consider these.

(1)

Among the questions certified to the Supreme Judicial Court was whether § 12S permits any minors—mature or immature—to obtain judicial consent to an abortion without any parental consultation whatsoever. The state court answered that, in general, it does not. "[T]he consent required by [§ 12S must] be obtained for every nonemergency abortion where the mother is less than eighteen years of age and unmarried." *Attorney General*, supra, at 750, 360 N.E.2d at 294. The text of § 12S itself states an exception to this rule, making consent unnecessary from any parent who has "died or has deserted his or her family." The Supreme Judicial Court construed the statute as containing an additional exception: Consent need not be obtained "where no parent (or statutory substitute) is available." *Ibid.* The court also ruled that an available parent must be given notice of any judicial proceedings brought by a minor to obtain consent for an abortion.[27] *Id.* at 755–756, 360 N.E.2d at 297.

We think that, construed in this manner, § 12S would impose an undue burden upon the exercise by minors of the right to seek an abortion.

---

25. Intervenors take issue with the Supreme Judicial Court's assurances that judicial proceedings will provide the necessary confidentiality, lack of procedural burden, and speed of resolution. In the absence of any evidence as to the operation of judicial proceedings under § 12S—and there is none, since appellees successfully sought to enjoin Massachusetts from putting it into effect—we must assume that the Supreme Judicial Court's judgment is correct.

27. This reading of the statute requires parental consultation and consent more strictly than appellants themselves previously believed was necessary. In their first argument before this Court, and again before the Supreme Judicial Court, appellants argued that sect. 12S was not intended to abrogate Massachusetts' common-law "mature minor" rule as it applies to abortions. See 428 U.S. at 144. They also suggested that, under some circumstances, sect. 12S might permit even immature minors to obtain judicial approval for an abortion without any parental consultation. See 428 U.S. at 145; *Attorney General*, supra, 371 Mass. at 751, 360 N.E.2d at 294. The Supreme Judicial Court sketched the outlines of the mature minor rule that

would apply in the absence of § 12S: "The mature minor rule calls for an analysis of the nature of the operation, its likely benefit, and the capacity of the particular minor to understand fully what the medical procedure involves.... Judicial intervention is not required. If judicial approval is obtained, however, the doctor is protected from a subsequent claim that the circumstances did not warrant his reliance on the mature minor rule, and, of course, the minor patient is afforded advance protection against a misapplication of the rule." *Id.* at 752, 360 N.E.2d at 295. "We conclude that, apart from statutory limitations which are constitutional, where the best interests of a minor will be served by not notifying his or her parents of intended medical treatment and where the minor is capable of giving informed consent to that treatment, the mature minor rule applies in this Commonwealth." *Id.* at 754, 360 N.E.2d at 296. The Supreme Judicial Court held that the common-law mature minor rule was inapplicable to abortions because it had been legislatively superseded by § 12S.

As the District Court recognized, "there are parents who would obstruct, and perhaps altogether prevent, the minor's right to go to court." *Baird III,* 450 F.Supp., at 1001. There is no reason to believe that this would be so in the majority of cases where consent is withheld. But many parents hold strong views on the subject of abortion, and young pregnant minors, especially those living at home, are particularly vulnerable to their parents' efforts to obstruct both an abortion and their access to court. It would be unrealistic, therefore, to assume that the mere existence of a legal right to seek relief in superior court provides an effective avenue of relief for some of those who need it the most.

We conclude, therefore, that under state regulation such as that undertaken by Massachusetts, every minor must have the opportunity—if she so desires—to go directly to a court without first consulting or notifying her parents. If she satisfies the court that she is mature and well enough informed to make intelligently the abortion decision on her own, the court must authorize her to act without parental consultation or consent. If she fails to satisfy the court that she is competent to make this decision independently, she must be permitted to show that an abortion neverthe- less would be in her best interests. If the court is persuaded that it is, the court must authorize the abortion. If, however, the court is not persuaded by the minor that she is mature or that the abortion would be in her best interests, it may decline to sanction the operation.

There is, however, an important state interest in encouraging a family rather than a judicial resolution of a minor's abortion decision. Also, as we have observed above, parents naturally take an interest in the welfare of their children—an interest that is particularly strong where a normal family relationship exists and where the child is living with one or both parents. These factors properly may be taken into account by a court called upon to determine whether an abortion in fact is in a minor's best interests. If, all things considered, the court determines that an abortion is in the minor's best interests, she is entitled to court authorization without any parental involvement. On the other hand, the court may deny the abortion request of an immature minor in the absence of parental consulta- tion if it concludes that her best interests would be served thereby, or the court may in such a case defer decision until there is parental consultation in which the court may participate. But this is the full extent to which parental involvement may be required.[28] For the reasons stated above, the constitutional right to seek an abortion may not be unduly burdened by state-imposed conditions upon initial access to court.

(2)

Section 12S requires that both parents consent to a minor's abortion. The District Court found it to be "custom" to perform other medical and surgical procedures on minors with the consent of only one parent, and it concluded that "nothing about abortions ... requires the minor's interest to be treated differently." *Baird I,* 393 F.Supp. at 852.

---

28. Of course, if the minor consults with her parents voluntarily and they with- hold consent, she is free to seek judicial au- thorization for the abortion immediately.

We are not persuaded that, as a general rule, the requirement of obtaining both parents' consent unconstitutionally burdens a minor's right to seek an abortion. The abortion decision has implications far broader than those associated with most other kinds of medical treatment. At least when the parents are together and the pregnant minor is living at home, both the father and mother have an interest—one normally supportive—in helping to determine the course that is in the best interests of a daughter. Consent and involvement by parents in important decisions by minors long have been recognized as protective of their immaturity. In the case of the abortion decision, for reasons we have stated, the focus of the parents' inquiry should be the best interests of their daughter. As every pregnant minor is entitled in the first instance to go directly to the court for a judicial determination without prior parental notice, consultation, or consent, the general rule with respect to parental consent does not unduly burden the constitutional right. Moreover, where the pregnant minor goes to her parents and consent is denied, she still must have recourse to a prompt judicial determination of her maturity or best interests.[29]

(3)

Another of the questions certified by the District Court to the Supreme Judicial Court was the following: "If the superior court finds that the minor is capable [of making], and has, in fact, made and adhered to, an informed and reasonable decision to have an abortion, may the court refuse its consent based on a finding that a parent's, or its own, contrary decision is a better one?" *Attorney General*, 371 Mass. at 747 n. 5, 360 N.E.2d at 293 n. 5. To this the state court answered:

> "[W]e do not view the judge's role as limited to a determination that the minor is capable of making, and has made, an informed and reasonable decision to have an abortion. Certainly the judge must make a determination of those circumstances, but, if the statutory role of the judge to determine the best interests of the minor is to be carried out, he must make a finding on the basis of all relevant views presented to him. We suspect that the judge will give great weight to the minor's determination, if informed and reasonable, but in circumstances where he determines that the best interests of the minor will not be served by an abortion, the judge's determination should prevail, assuming that his conclusion is supported by the evidence and adequate findings of fact." *Id.* at 748, 360 N.E.2d at 293.

The Supreme Judicial Court's statement reflects the general rule that a State may require a minor to wait until the age of majority before being permitted to exercise legal rights independently. See n. 23, supra. But we are concerned here with the exercise of a constitutional right of unique character. As stated above, if the minor satisfies a court that she has attained sufficient maturity to make a fully informed decision, she then is entitled to make her abortion decision independently. We therefore agree

---

29. There will be cases where the pregnant minor has received approval of the abortion decision by one parent. In that event, the parent can support the daughter's request for a prompt judicial determination, and the parent's support should be given great, if not dispositive, weight.

with the District Court that § 12S cannot constitutionally permit judicial disregard of the abortion decision of a minor who has been determined to be mature and fully competent to assess the implications of the choice she has made.

IV

Although it satisfies constitutional standards in large part, § 12S falls short of them in two respects: First, it permits judicial authorization for an abortion to be withheld from a minor who is found by the superior court to be mature and fully competent to make this decision independently. Second, it requires parental consultation or notification in every instance, without affording the pregnant minor an opportunity to receive an independent judicial determination that she is mature enough to consent or that an abortion would be in her best interests. Accordingly, we affirm the judgment of the District Court insofar as it invalidates this statute and enjoins its enforcement.[32]

Affirmed.

[Justice Stevens, joined by Justices Brennan, Marshall and Blackmun, concurred in the judgment, on the ground that the Massachusetts statute was unconstitutional under the Court's earlier holding in *Planned Parenthood of Central Missouri v. Danforth*, 428 U.S. 52 (1976), which struck a provision under Missouri law requiring minors to obtain parental consent to abortion. In striking down the Missouri statute, the Court had stated:

> "[T]he State does not have the constitutional authority to give a third party an absolute, and possibly arbitrary, veto over the decision of the physician and his patient to terminate the patient's pregnancy, regardless of the reason for withholding the consent." Id. at 74.

In Justice Stevens's view, the Massachusetts statute, in giving an absolute veto over the minor's abortion decision to a judge, imposed at least as great a burden as the Missouri law, and was thus unconstitutional under *Danforth*. The concurring justices declined to join Justice Powell's opinion because they deemed it an advisory opinion "address[ing] the constitutionality of an abortion statute that Massachusetts has not enacted." 443 U.S. at 655.]

BELLOTTI v. BAIRD AND ADOLESCENT ABORTION

(1) **Abortion as a Medical Procedure.** In *Bellotti v. Baird*, the United States Supreme Court examined the right of a pregnant minor to make an autonomous decision about abortion that is not subject to the authority of either her parents or the state. We have seen that typically disputes about authority over the lives of

---

32. The opinion of MR. JUSTICE STEVENS, concurring in the judgment, joined by three Members of the Court, characterizes this opinion as "advisory" and the questions it addresses as "hypothetical." Apparently, this is criticism of our attempt to provide some guidance as to how a State constitutionally may provide for adult involvement—either by parents or a state official such as a judge—In the abortion decisions of minors. In view of the importance of the issue raised, and the protracted litigation to which these parties already have been subjected, we think it would be irresponsible simply to invalidate sect. 12S without stating our views as to the controlling principles. . . .

minors are contests between the parents and the state. *Meyer v. Nebraska* and *Wisconsin v. Yoder* present this conflict in the context of decisions about education.

Decisions about "ordinary" medical treatment conform to the principles that govern in other contexts. Parents have general authority to make decisions about their children's care, but when parents make a decision that seriously threatens their child's health, their traditional authority (sometimes) is superseded by the state, which then decides about appropriate treatment for the child. The mature minor doctrine and minor consent statutes create some limited exceptions to this approach, under which minors' consent to treatment is recognized. The policies behind these exceptions, however, are not shaped primarily by concerns about adolescent autonomy, per se. On the issue of access to abortion, in contrast, autonomy is very much the focus. In *Bellotti,* the Supreme Court announces that, under some circumstances, the minor herself has a constitutionally protectible interest in making her own decision about abortion. Why is abortion treated differently from other medical procedures? Think about the following possible explanations:

a. Parental authority is supported generally by the assumption that parents are motivated to promote their children's health and welfare, and will make medical decisions in their best interest. Parents are more likely to have a conflict of interest with their child on the issue of abortion. Why might this be so?

b. The decision about whether or not to carry a child to term is uniquely an "adult" decision. Thus, the traditional paternalistic legal response is not appropriate.

c. The right to make autonomous reproductive decisions is constitutionally protected under well developed doctrine announced by the Supreme Court. The same cannot be said about the right to make other medical decisions. This constitutional right should be extended to minors as well as adults. If this explanation seems persuasive, would it also support extending the right to vote to minors? How can the two rights be distinguished?

d. Teenage pregnancy and parenthood generate enormous social costs and personal hardship for young mothers and their children. Facilitating access to abortion for the minor who wants to end her pregnancy mitigates those costs and promotes her welfare.

One characterization of Justice Powell's opinion is that it represents an effort to recognize and accommodate the competing interests of parents, the state and the child herself in the minor's abortion decision. How does Powell's proposed regime seek to recognize each of these interests?

(2) **"Maturity" Under Abortion Law.** Justice Powell's opinion emphasizes that a minor who establishes that she is "mature enough and well enough informed" has the right to make the decision about terminating her pregnancy independently of her parents. What must she show to demonstrate the requisite maturity?

a. *Judicial Definitions of Maturity.* Several courts exploring this issue have suggested factors that might be considered relevant to the determination of whether an adolescent has the requisite maturity to make an autonomous decision about abortion. In *In re Jane Doe*, 57 Ohio St.3d 135, 566 N.E.2d 1181 (1991), the Ohio Supreme Court reviewed the conclusion of a trial court that a 17–year-old high school senior failed to establish that she was mature enough to make an independent abortion decision. The young woman was a good student who planned to go to college. Although she lived at home with her parents, she had worked at various jobs since she was 16. A physician testified that she understood the risks of the procedure. In upholding the trial court's decision, the court stated:

... [Appellant] testified that she had an abortion in June 1990, and is seeking to have another one performed less than a year later. Moreover, appellant testified that each pregnancy was the result of intercourse with a different man. In addition, Dr. Rauh testified that appellant was on a program of birth control, but discontinued it. In light of the foregoing testimony, it was not unreasonable, arbitrary or unconscionable for the trial judge to dismiss the complaint by essentially finding that appellant did not prove her "maturity" allegation by clear and convincing evidence.

In *H.B. v. Wilkinson*, a federal district court in Utah analyzed the meaning of maturity under *Bellotti* (639 F.Supp. 952 (D.Utah 1986)):

.... Manifestly, as related to a minor's abortion decision, maturity is not solely a matter of social skills, level of intelligence or verbal skills. More importantly, it calls for experience, perspective and judgment. As to experience, the minor's prior work experience, experience in living away from home, and handling personal finances are some of the pertinent inquiries. Perspective calls for appreciation and understanding of the relative gravity and possible detrimental impact of each available option, as well as realistic perception and assessment of possible short term and long term consequences of each of those options, particularly the abortion option. Judgment is of very great importance in determining maturity. The exercise of good judgment requires being fully informed so as to be able to weigh alternatives independently and realistically. Among other things, the minor's conduct is a measure of good judgment. Factors such as stress and ignorance of alternatives have been recognized as impediments to the exercise of proper judgment by minors, who because of those factors "may not be able intelligently to decide whether to have an abortion." *American College of Obstetricians & Gynecologists v. Thornburgh*, 737 F.2d 283, 296 (3d Cir.1984), jurisdiction postponed, 471 U.S. 1014, 105 S.Ct. 2015, 85 L.Ed.2d 297 (1985)....

In upholding the trial court's decision that the pregnant minor (who was 17 years old and a "very good" student) was "immature," and thus subject to a statutory requirement of parental notification, the court described several facts that were important to this conclusion: the young woman lived at home, was not regularly employed and was financially dependent on her parents (and expected this to continue through college); she engaged in sexual activity several times without using contraceptives, believing that if she became pregnant, she could obtain an abortion without her parents' knowledge; she believed that she could obtain abortion and deal with any complications without her parents' knowledge; she sought counsel from friends, rather than from family members or church or school officials; she did not consider marriage to be an option as a response to the pregnancy; her demeanor as a witness was initially characterized by nervousness and stress; and she failed to give due consideration to the possibility of post-abortion depression. Based on these facts, the court found the young woman to be "immature, lacking the experience, perspective and judgment to recognize and avoid choice that could be detrimental to herself." 639 F.Supp. at 958.

Do you agree with the court's conclusion? Would most adolescents be found "immature" under this court's analysis?

As these cases suggest, appellate courts allow judges to exercise a considerable amount of discretion in evaluating the pregnant minor's maturity. One consequence may be that judges' attitudes toward abortion and teenage sexual behavior could affect the decision about the pregnant teenager's decision. Do you see evidence of this in *Wilkinson* and *Jane Doe*? More recent cases raise the same issue. For example, in *Ex parte Anonymous*, 803 So.2d 542 (Ala.2001), the Alabama Supreme Court upheld a trial court decision denying abortion where the minor was 17 years old and a student who worked part time to save for college. She had considered alternatives to abortion and acquired information about the procedure from many sources. The judge denying the abortion indicated that he thought the minor did not fully consider the emotional consequences of abortion. In a Mississippi case, the state's highest court upheld a decision by the chancellor denying the abortion, despite the fact that the child's guardian agreed to the abortion decision, but refused to give consent for religious reasons. The 17–year-old minor reported that she had ideas of suicide and that she felt that having a baby would interfere with her plans for college. *In the Matter of A.W.,* 826 So.2d 1280 (Miss.2002). Courts will reverse decisions based on clearly illegitimate factors. In *Appeal of L.D.F.,* 820 A.2d 714 (Pa.Super.2003), for example, the trial court denied the minor's petition because she was 20 weeks pregnant. The appellate court reversed, holding that, in the first 24 weeks, the stage of pregnancy could not be considered, and the minor, who already had a child and was almost 18 years old, was mature.

b.   An Informed Consent Approach. Another approach to evaluating maturity is to apply the legal standard for competence to make medical decisions developed under informed consent doctrine to the adolescent making a decisions about abortion. Under such an approach, the minor who is competent to make an informed decision about the medical procedure would meet the requisite standard for maturity. Although legal tests for competence in this context vary, the focus is on capacity for understanding relevant information and for reasoning about the choice. Thus, a judge evaluating maturity would examine the minor's understanding of disclosed information about the procedure, its risks and benefits, and of available alternatives. She would also likely inquire into the minor's ability to use this information rationally in making a decision. Do you see how this approach for evaluating maturity to make the abortion decision differs from that adopted by the courts in *Wilkinson* and *Jane Doe*? What information considered by these courts would be excluded under an approach based on informed consent tests?

Are teenagers likely to be competent to make informed treatment decisions using tests developed under informed consent doctrine—and thus likely to be "mature" using this approach? A recent study suggests that adolescents choosing abortion are similar to adults in their decisionmaking process. Bruce Ambuel & Julian Rappaport, Developmental Trends in Adolescents' Psychological and Legal Competence to Consent to Abortion, 16 L. & Human Behav. 129 (1992). An American Psychological Association Committee on Adolescent Abortion has issued a policy statement challenging the empirical basis of legal restrictions on adolescent abortion. The statement asserts that psychological theory and empirical research indicate that by mid-adolescence, minors are as capable as are adults of conceptualizing and reasoning about medical decisions. Adolescent Abortion: Psychological and Legal Issues, Interdivisional Committee on Adolescent Abortion, 42 American Psychologist 73 (January, 1987). The APA submitted amicus curiae briefs arguing this position before the United States Supreme Court in *Hartigan v. Zbaraz* (85–683) and *Hodgson v. Minnesota* (88–1125, 88–1309, 88–805). (*Hodgson* is discussed below). For an excerpt from the *Hartigan v. Zbaraz* brief and further discussion of adolescent decisionmaking capability in legal contexts and the role of empirical research on policy formation in this area.

(3) **The Dilemma of Immaturity.** Under Justice Powell's proposed regime, a court that finds the petitioning minor to lack the requisite maturity can refuse to permit the abortion procedure without parental consent, unless the minor demonstrates that the abortion is in her best interest. Under what circumstances would it be in the best interest of a girl who is too immature to decide about the procedure not to terminate her pregnancy? Robert Mnookin, in a study of the operation of the Massachusetts statute enacted pursuant to *Bellotti v. Baird*, found that judicial authorization was a "rubber stamp"; in only a handful of the 1300 cases studied

was the judicial consent to abortion withheld. *Bellotti v. Baird*: A Hard Case, in In the Interest of Children: Advocacy, Law Reform and Public Policy, R. Mnookin, ed. 239–40 (1985). What might explain this response?

(4) **Minor's Refusal to Consent.** In *In re Mary P.*, 111 Misc.2d 532, 444 N.Y.S.2d 545 (Fam. Ct., Queens County 1981), a mother sought to have her 15½-year-old daughter declared a person in need of supervision because of her refusal to have an abortion. Instead of granting the mother's petition, the court issued an order of protection to the daughter, directing the mother not to interfere with the daughter's determination to deliver her child. The court explained:

> The court is well aware that parents may and should play a meaningful role in counseling their children on all matters involving their well-being. Moreover, a minor's decision on whether or not to abort is of such far reaching consequence and sensitivity as to cry out for the understanding counsel of parents who care. And yet, such counsel must originate from the premise that it is the child who has the ultimate right to decide. Children are not the chattel of their parents. Rather, they are citizens in their own right, endowed with certain fundamental freedoms of which they may not be divested by parental fiat. The right to give birth is among those freedoms.

> Inevitably, there comes a point in time when the child's decision making process reaches fruition, with or without parental input, and a firm choice is made. Mary has made her choice and it is, indeed, her choice to make. In deciding to give birth, she has exercised a personal liberty guaranteed to her by the fourteenth amendment. Her decision now requires parental forbearance. There is a very thin line between counsel and coercion, especially when they originate from a relationship as special as that of parent-child. A child's right to decide for herself whether or not to give birth, is particularly susceptible to subversion by a parent. Thus the free exercise of her will may be overcome by feelings of guilt, disloyalty, and even fear. Surely not every parental reaction to a child's pregnancy is as overt as that of the petitioner's herein. To the extent that parents, either directly or indirectly, fail to respect their child's right to make the ultimate decision on whether to give birth, their conduct may indeed be labeled "offensive" to the child within the meaning of section 759(a) of the Family Court Act. Id. at 548.

For an earlier case reversing a juvenile court's order that a minor submit to medical procedures to terminate her pregnancy see *In re Smith*, 16 Md.App. 209, 295 A.2d 238 (1972).

Martin Guggenheim, in a thoughtful analysis of *Bellotti* and other Supreme Court opinions on adolescent abortion, concludes that *Bellotti* effectively eviscerated the privacy rights of pregnant adolescents provided earlier by the Court in *Danforth* (discussed in the *Bellotti* opinion). Guggenheim challenges the coherency of adolescent abortion doctrine, with its emphasis on an intrusive by-pass procedure. Martin Guggenheim, Minor Rights: Adolescent Abortion Cases, 30 Hofstra L.Rev. 589 (2002).

THE SUPREME COURT AND ADOLESCENT ABORTION

The Supreme Court in *Roe v. Wade*, 410 U.S. 113, 93 S.Ct. 705, 35 L.Ed.2d 147 (1973), sketched the limits of constitutionally permissible restrictions on abortion practice by state legislatures. During the first trimester of pregnancy, the abortion decision is controlled by the woman and her physician. During a second stage before the fetus is viable, the abortion procedure can be regulated by the state "in ways that are reasonably related to maternal health." During a third stage after viability, the state may regulate and even proscribe abortion "except where it is necessary, in appropriate medical judgment, for the preservation of the life or health of the mother."

Since *Roe v. Wade*, the Supreme Court has examined several state statutes (and one municipal ordinance) restricting adolescents' access to abortion. In several opinions, the Court has struggled with the question of whether the fact that a pregnant woman is a minor justifies particular statutory constraints on her constitutional right to make a private independent decision about whether to carry a fetus to term. The following are summaries of and excerpts from several important opinions dealing with this issue.

Planned Parenthood of Central Missouri v. Danforth, 428 U.S. 52, 96 S.Ct. 2831, 49 L.Ed.2d 788 (1976).

In this opinion, the first consideration of state restrictions of adolescent access to abortion, the Supreme Court invalidated a provision of Missouri's statute requiring permission from a parent or one *in loco parentis* for a non-lifesaving abortion during the first 12 weeks of pregnancy on an unmarried woman who was less than 18 years old.

The Court rejected the argument that "providing a parent with absolute power to overrule a determination, made by the physician and his minor patient, to terminate the patient's pregnancy will serve to strengthen the family unit. Neither is it likely that such veto power will enhance parental authority or control where the minor and the nonconsenting parent are so fundamentally in conflict and the very existence of the pregnancy already has fractured the family structure." 428 U.S. at 75.

H.L. v. Matheson, 450 U.S. 398, 101 S.Ct. 1164, 67 L.Ed.2d 388 (1981).

At issue in *Matheson* was the constitutionality of a Utah statute (Utah Code Ann. 76–7–304 (1974)) requiring a physician to "notify, if possible" the parents of a "dependent, unmarried, minor girl," prior to performing an abortion on the girl. Parental consent was not required. In an opinion by Justice Burger, the Supreme Court upheld the statute and affirmed the constitutionality of the parental notification requirement. The Court emphasized that it was not deciding the constitutionality of the statute as applied to mature minors. Because the plaintiff did not claim to be a mature minor, she had no standing to represent the interests of this class.

> The Utah statute gives neither parents nor judges a veto power over the minor's abortion decision.... As applied to immature and dependent minors, the statute plainly serves the important considerations of family integrity and protecting adolescents which we identified in *Bellotti II*. In addition, as applied to that class, the statute serves a significant state interest by providing an opportunity for parents to supply essential medical and other information to a physician....
>
> Appellant intimates that the statute's failure to declare, in terms, a detailed description of what information parents may provide to physicians, or to provide for a mandatory period of delay after the

physician notifies the parents, renders the statute unconstitutional. The notion that the statute must itemize information to be supplied by parents finds no support in logic, experience, or our decisions. And as the Utah Supreme Court recognized, time is likely to be of the essence in an abortion decision. The Utah statute is reasonably calculated to protect minors in appellant's class by enhancing the potential for parental consultation concerning a decision that has potentially traumatic and permanent consequences.

Appellant also contends that the constitutionality of the statute is undermined because Utah allows a pregnant minor to consent to other medical procedures without formal notice to her parents if she carries the child to term. But a State's interests in full-term pregnancies are sufficiently different to justify the line drawn by the statutes. Cf. Maher v. Roe, 432 U.S. 464, 473–474 (1977). If the pregnant girl elects to carry her child to term, the *medical* decisions to be made entail few—perhaps none—of the potentially grave emotional and psychological consequences of the decision to abort.

That the requirement of notice to parents may inhibit some minors from seeking abortions is not a valid basis to void the statute as applied to appellant and the class properly before us. The Constitution does not compel a State to fine-tune its statutes so as to encourage or facilitate abortions. To the contrary, state action "encouraging childbirth except in the most urgent circumstances" is "rationally related to the legitimate governmental objective of protecting potential life." Harris v. McRae, (448 U.S. 297 (1980)).

As applied to the class properly before us, the statute plainly serves important state interests, is narrowly drawn to protect only those interests, and does not violate any guarantees of the Constitution. The judgment of the Supreme Court of Utah is Affirmed.

Justice Marshall, in a dissent joined by Justices Brennan and Blackmun, rejected the claim by the state that the notice requirement does not burden the young woman's abortion decision. Although, in the ideal family, a pregnant minor may seek the advice and support of her parents, the dissenting Justices asserted that "many families do not conform to this ideal." . . .

Many minor women will encounter interference from their parents after the state-imposed notification. In addition to parental disappointment and disapproval, the minor may confront physical or emotional abuse, withdrawal of financial support, or actual obstruction of the abortion decision. Furthermore, the threat of parental notice may cause some minor women to delay past the first trimester of pregnancy, after which the health risks increase significantly. Other pregnant minors may attempt to self-abort or to obtain an illegal abortion rather than risk parental notification. Still others may forsake an abortion and bear an unwanted child, which, given the minor's "probable education, employment skills, financial resources and emotional resources, . . . may be exceptionally burdensome." *Bellotti II*, 443 U.S. at 642 (Powell, J.). The possibility that such problems may not occur in particular cases does not alter the hardship created by the notice requirement on its face. And that hardship is not a mere disincentive created by the State, but is instead an actual state-imposed obstacle to the exercise of the minor woman's free choice. For the class of pregnant minors represented by appellant, this obstacle is so onerous as to bar the desired abortions. Significantly, the interference sanctioned by the statute does not operate in a neutral fashion. No notice is required for any pregnancy-related medical care, so only the minor women who wish to abort encounter the burden imposed by the notification statute.

The dissenting Justices also rejected the state's claim that the notice requirement furthered a "significant state interest," and thus should survive constitutional challenge. The state claimed that the notice requirement permits the parents to provide the physician with medical information, encourages consultation between the parents and the minor woman, and preserves parental rights. Justice Marshall pointed out that, since the statutory requirement could be satisfied by a letter or a brief phone call by the physician moments before the operation, it did not promote the transfer of information by the parents. Further, the claim that parental consultation is an important state interest is undermined in that the statute allows minors to consent to other pregnancy-related treatment, including the surgical procedure of Caesarian delivery, without notice to their parents. The dissent also challenged the state's claim that the notice requirement protects parental authority and family privacy, recalling the Court's words three years before in *Danforth* (above).

City of Akron v. Akron Center for Reproductive Health, 462 U.S. 416, 103 S.Ct. 2481, 76 L.Ed.2d 687 (1983).

At issue was a city ordinance regulating abortion, including a specific provision for minors that was addressed in the following portion of the Supreme Court's opinion.

> We turn next to § 1870.05(B), the provision prohibiting a physician from performing an abortion on a minor pregnant woman under the age of 15 unless he obtains "the informed written consent of one of her parents or her legal guardian" or unless the minor obtains "an order from a court having jurisdiction over her that the abortion be performed or induced." The District Court invalidated this provision because "[i]t does not establish a procedure by which a minor can avoid a parental veto of her abortion decision by demonstrating that her decision is, in fact, informed. Rather, it requires, in all cases, both the minor's informed consent and either parental consent or a court order." 479 F.Supp., at 1201. The Court of Appeals affirmed on the same basis. . . .

The Supreme Court affirmed the lower court rulings:

> Akron's ordinance does not create expressly the alternative procedure required by Bellotti II. But Akron contends that the Ohio Juvenile Court will qualify as a "court having jurisdiction" within the meaning of § 1870.05(B), and that "it is not to be assumed that during the course of the juvenile proceedings the Court will not construe the ordinance in a manner consistent with the constitutional requirement

of a determination of the minor's ability to make an informed consent."... . This suit, however, concerns a municipal ordinance that creates no procedures for making the necessary determinations. Akron seeks to invoke the Ohio statute governing juvenile proceedings, but that statute neither mentions minors' abortions nor suggests that the Ohio Juvenile Court has authority to inquire into a minor's maturity or emancipation. In these circumstances, we do not think that the Akron ordinance, as applied in Ohio juvenile proceedings, is reasonably susceptible of being construed to create an "opportunity for case-by-case evaluations of the maturity of pregnant minors." *Bellotti II*, supra, 443 U.S. at 643, n. 23 (plurality opinion). We therefore affirm the Court of Appeals' judgment that § 1870.05(B) is unconstitutional.

Hodgson v. Minnesota, 497 U.S. 417, 110 S.Ct. 2926, 111 L.Ed.2d 344 (1990).

In a splintered five-four opinion delivered in part by Justice Stevens, the Supreme Court upheld a Minnesota statute requiring that a minor wait 48 hours after both parents have been notified before obtaining an abortion. (Minn. Stat. § 144.343(2)–(7) (1988)). Other than in emergency situations, the statutory notice and waiting period are mandatory unless the young woman declares herself to be the victim of parental abuse, in which case notice to the proper authorities is required. The Court concluded that the waiting period requirement "would reasonably further the legitimate state interest in ensuring that the minor's decision is knowing and intelligent."

In the opinion of the Court's majority, the requirement that *both* parents be notified of the abortion was not reasonable and represented an unconstitutional burden on the minor's right to obtain an abortion. When the parents are divorced or the family is otherwise dysfunctional, this requirement, in the view of the majority, not only fails to serve any legitimate state interest, but could inflict harm on the pregnant minor. However, a different majority of five justices held that the constitutional objection to the two-parent notice requirement was removed by the availability of a judicial by-pass procedure that allowed the minor to avoid notifying one or both parents.

Ayotte v. Planned Parenthood of Northern New England, 546 U.S. 320, 126 S.Ct. 961, 163 L.Ed.2d 812 (2006).

In this opinion the Court dealt with the New Hampshire Parental Notification Prior to Abortion Act, which required a 48–hour waiting period after written notice to parents before an abortion could be performed. The Court of Appeals for the First Circuit had found the statute to be unconstitutional because it failed to provide an exception for medical emergencies. The Court noted that the state had conceded that it would be unconstitutional to apply the statute in a manner that created significant health risks for minors. Justice O'Connor, writing for the majority, concluded that a permanent injunction invalidating the entire statute was unnecessary in that only a few applications presented a constitutional problem. The Court directed the lower courts to issue a declaratory judgment and an injunction prohibiting the unconstitutional application on a finding that this was consistent with legislative intent.

In 2007, before the district court acted, the New Hampshire legislature repealed the Parental Notification Prior to Abortion Act. N.H. H.B. 184.

Minors' Abortion Rights under State Constitutions

Some courts have interpreted their state constitutions to provide more protection of minors' abortion rights than the federal Constitution has been interpreted to require. For example, the New Jersey Supreme Court struck down that state's parental notification statute under the equal protection provision in the New Jersey constitution, although it recognized that the statute was constitutional under the United States Constitution. *Planned Parenthood of Central N.J. v. Farmer*, 165 N.J. 609, 762 A.2d 620 (2000). Under the statute, a minor's right to obtain an abortion was conditioned on notification of her parents, unless she obtained a judicial waiver. The court concluded that the statute imposed substantial and unjustifiable burdens on one class of young women without an adequate government interest to justify the unequal burden. It found that the requirement of notification of parents was extremely costly to young women and waiver hearings were inadequate as a way of avoiding notification (due to delay, threat to anonymity, and awkward procedures). The court rejected the state's three justifications for notification: that it protects minors from their own immaturity, promotes family structure, and protects parental rights. As to the first, the court pointed out that state law recognized minors' maturity in matters relating to sexuality, and substance abuse, and noted that the collective opinion of health care professionals presented to the court supported the view that minors were mature enough to make abortion decisions. As to the claim that notification promotes family structure, the court pointed out that young women who sought abortion without telling their parents were often in dysfunctional or abusive families. The minor's relationship with her parents determined whether she told them about abortion, whether the law required notification or not. Finally, the court dismissed the parental rights argument on the ground that the minor seeking abortion is exercising her independent constitutionally protected rights.

The California Supreme Court, in contrast, decided that a statute requiring that minors get parental consent for abortion or petition a juvenile court for authorization did not violate the minors' right to privacy under that state's constitution, Cal. Const. Art. I, § 7. *American Academy of Pediatrics v. Lungren*, 16 Cal.4th 307, 66 Cal.Rptr.2d 210, 940 P.2d 797 (1997). Upholding the lower courts' rulings, the court concluded that, although the privacy right under the California constitution was independent of and broader than the federal right, the statute did not violate the minor's state constitutional right. Applying the standard previously established to analyze claims of invasion of the right of privacy under the California constitution, the court reasoned that minors have a more limited privacy interest than do adults and a reduced expectation of privacy. Further, the intrusion of the procedure was minimal and was justified because of the state's compelling countervailing interest in the minor's health.

Carey v. Population Services International

Supreme Court of the United States, 1977.
431 U.S. 678, 97 S.Ct. 2010, 52 L.Ed.2d 675.

[The opinion examines the constitutionality of a New York statute that, in relevant part, makes it a crime for anyone to distribute "any contraceptive of any kind" to a minor under the age of 16. N.Y. Educ. Law § 6811(8)(1). Justice Brennan delivered the opinion of the Court. Basing his opinion heavily on Planned Parenthood of Central Missouri v. Danforth, 428 U.S. 52 (1976), Justice Brennan, joined by Justices Stewart, Marshall, and Blackmun in Part IV of the opinion, concluded that "the right of privacy in connection with decisions affecting procreation extends to minors as well as to adults." 431 U.S. 693.]

. . . State restrictions inhibiting privacy rights of minors are valid only if they serve "any significant state interest . . . that is not present in the case of an adult." *Id.* at 75.[15] Planned Parenthood found that no such interest justified a state requirement of parental consent.

Since the State may not impose a blanket prohibition, or even a blanket requirement of parental consent, on the choice of a minor to terminate her pregnancy, the constitutionality of a blanket prohibition of the distribution of contraceptives to minors is a *fortiori* foreclosed. The State's interests in protection of the mental and physical health of the pregnant minor, and in protection of potential life are clearly more implicated by the abortion decision than by the decision to use a nonhazardous contraceptive.

Appellants argue, however, that significant state interests are served by restricting minors' access to contraceptives, because free availability to minors of contraceptives would lead to increased sexual activity among the young. In violation of the policy of New York to discourage such behavior. The argument is that minors' sexual activity may be deterred by increasing the hazards attendant on it. The same argument, however, would support a ban on abortions for minors, or indeed support a prohibition on abortions, or access to contraceptives, for the unmarried, whose sexual activity is also against the public policy of many States. Yet, in each of these areas, the Court has rejected the argument, noting in *Roe v. Wade*, that "no court or commentator has taken the argument seriously." 410 U.S. at 148. The reason for this unanimous rejection was stated in *Eisenstadt v. Baird*: "It

[handwritten margin note: State's argument →]

---

15. This test is apparently less rigorous than the "compelling state interest" test applied to restrictions on the privacy rights of adults. See, e.g., n. 16, *infra*. Such lesser scrutiny is appropriate both because of the States' greater latitude to regulate the conduct of children, *Prince v. Massachusetts*, 321 U.S. 158 (1944); *Ginsberg v. New York*, 390 U.S. 629 (1968), and because the right of privacy implicated here is "the interest in independence in making certain kinds of important decisions," *Whalen v. Roe*, 429 U.S. 589, 599–600 (1977), and the law has generally regarded minors as having a lesser capability for making important decisions. See, e.g., *Planned Parenthood*, 428 U.S., at 102 (STEVENS, J., concurring in part and dissenting in part).

would be plainly unreasonable to assume that [the State] has prescribed pregnancy and the birth of an unwanted child [or the physical and psychological dangers of an abortion] as punishment for fornication." 405 U.S. at 448. We remain reluctant to attribute any such "scheme of values" to the State.[18]

Moreover, there is substantial reason for doubt whether limiting access to contraceptives will in fact substantially discourage early sexual behavior. Appellants themselves conceded in the District Court that "there is no evidence that teenage extramarital sexual activity increases in proportion to the availability of contraceptives," 398 F.Supp., at 332, and n. 10, and accordingly offered none, in the District court or here. Appellees, on the other hand, cite a considerable body of evidence and opinion indicating that there is no such deterrent effect. Although we take judicial notice, as did the District Court, *id.* at 331–333, that with or without access to contraceptives the incidence of sexual activity among minors is high, and the consequences of such activity are frequently devastating, the studies cited by appellees play no part in our decision. It is enough that we again confirm the principle that when a State, as here, burdens the exercise of a fundamental right, its attempt to justify that burden as a rational means for the accomplishment of some significant state policy requires more than a bare assertion, based on a conceded complete absence of supporting evidence, that the burden is connected to such a policy.[22] . . .

[Mr. Justice Powell concurred in finding New York's prohibition to be unconstitutional, but strongly rejected the rationale that the statute in restricting minors' access to contraceptives violated a fundamental right of minors to make reproductive decisions. He stated:]

. . .

. . . [T]his provision prohibits parents from distributing contraceptives to their children, a restriction that unjustifiably interferes with parental interests in rearing their children. Cf. *Ginsberg v. New York*, 390 U.S. at 639 and n. 7. "[C]onstitutional interpretation has consistently recognized that the parents' claim to authority in their own household to direct the

---

18. We note, moreover, that other provisions of New York law argue strongly against any conclusion that the deterrence of illegal sexual conduct among minors was an objective of § 6811 (8). First, a girl in New York may marry as young as 14, with the consent of her parents and a family court judge. N.Y. Dom. Rel. Law §§ 15–a, 15 (2), 15 (3) (McKinney 1964 and Supp. 1976–1977). Yet although sexual intercourse by a married woman of that age violates no state law, § 6811 (8) prohibits distribution of contraceptives to her. Second, New York requires that birth control information and services be provided to recipients of certain welfare programs, provided only that they are "of childbearing age, including children who can be considered sexually active." N.Y. Soc.Serv. Law § 350(1)(e) (McKinney 1976); cf. 42 U.S.

C. § 602(a)(15)(A) (1970 ed., Supp. V). See also N.Y. Soc. Serv. Law § 365–a(3)(c) (McKinney 1976); cf. 42 U.S.C. § 1396d (a)(vii)(4)(C) (1970 ed., Supp. V).

22. Appellants argue that the statement In *Ginsberg v. New York*, 390 U.S., at 641, that "it was not irrational for the legislature to find that exposure to material condemned by the statute is harmful to minors," is authority that the burden is appellees' to prove that there is no connection between the statute and the asserted state policy. But *Ginsberg* concerned a statute prohibiting dissemination of obscene material that it held was not constitutionally protected. In contrast § 6811 (8) concerns distribution of material access to which is essential to exercise of a fundamental right.

rearing of their children is basic in the structure of our society. 'It is cardinal with us that the custody, care and nurture of the child reside first in the parents, whose primary function and freedom include preparation for obligations the state can neither supply nor hinder.' " *Ibid.*, quoting *Prince v. Massachusetts, supra*, at 166. See *Wisconsin v. Yoder*, 406 U.S. 205, 231–233 (1972); *Pierce v. Society of Sisters*, 268 U.S. 510, 534–535 (1925); *Meyer v. Nebraska*, 262 U.S. 390, 399–401 (1923). Moreover, this statute would allow the State "to enquire into, prove, and punish," *Poe v. Ullman*, 367 U.S. 497, 548 (1961) (Harlan, J., dissenting), the exercise of this parental responsibility. The State points to no interest of sufficient magnitude to justify this direct interference with the parental guidance that is especially appropriate in this sensitive area of child development.[2]

But in my view there is considerably more room for state regulation in this area than would be permissible under the plurality's opinion. It seems clear to me, for example, that the State would further a constitutionally permissible end if it encouraged adolescents to seek the advice and guidance of their parents before deciding whether to engage in sexual intercourse. *Planned Parenthood*, 428 U.S. at 91 (STEWART, J., concurring). The State justifiably may take note of the psychological pressures that might influence children at a time in their lives when they generally do not possess the maturity necessary to understand and control their responses. Participation in sexual intercourse at an early age may have both physical and psychological consequences. These include the risk of venereal disease and pregnancy, and the less obvious mental and emotional problems that may result from sexual activity by children. Moreover, society has long adhered to the view that sexual intercourse should not be engaged in promiscuously, a judgment that an adolescent may be less likely to heed than an adult.

[Mr. Justice Stevens also concurred in the judgment, but objected to the Court's reasoning:]

. . .

I

There are two reasons why I do not join Part IV. First, the holding in *Planned Parenthood of Missouri v. Danforth*, 428 U.S. 52, 72–75, that a minor's decision to abort her pregnancy may not be conditioned on parental consent, is not dispositive here. The options available to the already pregnant minor are fundamentally different from those available to non-

2. The particular provision at issue makes it a crime for "[a]ny person to sell or distribute any instrument or article, or any recipe, drug or medicine for the prevention of contraception to a minor under the age of sixteen years ..." Educ. Law § 6811(8) (McKinney 1972). For the reasons stated n the text, this provision unjustifiably infringes the constitutionally protected interests of parents and married female minors, and it is invalid in those two respects. Although the prohibition on distribution might be sustained as to other individuals if the restrictions on parental distribution and distribution to married female minors could be treated as severable, the result "would be to create a program quite different from the one the legislature actually adopted." *Sloan v. Lemon*, 413 U.S. 825, 834 (1973). I therefore agree with the Court that the entire provision must be invalidated. See *Dorchy v. Kansas*, 264 U.S. 286, 291 (1924); *Dollar Co. v. Canadian C. & F. Co.*, 220 N.Y. 270, 279, 115 N.E. 711, 713 (1917).

pregnant minors. The former must bear a child unless she aborts; but persons in the latter category can and generally will avoid childbearing by abstention. Consequently, even if I had joined that part of *Planned Parenthood*, I could not agree that the Constitution provides the same measure of protection to the minor's right to use contraceptives as to the pregnant female's right to abort.

Second, I would not leave open the question whether there is a significant state interest in discouraging sexual activity among unmarried persons under 16 years of age. Indeed, I would describe as "frivolous" appellees' argument that a minor has the constitutional right to put contraceptives to their intended use, notwithstanding the combined objection of both parents and the State.

. . .

The State's important interest in the welfare of its young citizens justifies a number of protective measures. See *Planned Parenthood of Central Missouri v. Danforth, supra*, at 102 (STEVENS, J., Concurring in part and dissenting in part). Such special legislation is premised on the fact that young persons frequently make unwise choices with harmful consequences; the State may properly ameliorate those consequences by providing, for example, that a minor may not be required to honor his bargain. It is almost unprecedented, however, for a State to require that an ill-advised act by a minor give rise to greater risk of irreparable harm than a similar act by an adult.

Common sense indicates that many young people will engage in sexual activity regardless of what the New York Legislature does; and further, that the incidence of venereal disease and premarital pregnancy is affected by the availability or unavailability of contraceptives. Although young persons theoretically may avoid those harms by practicing total abstention, inevitably many will not. The statutory prohibition denies them and their parents a choice which, if available, would reduce their exposure to disease or unwanted pregnancy.

. . .

Although the State may properly perform a teaching function, it seems to me that an attempt to persuade by inflicting harm on the listener is an unacceptable means of conveying a message that is otherwise legitimate. The propaganda technique used in this case significantly increases the risk of unwanted pregnancy and venereal disease. It is as though a State decided to dramatize its disapproval of motorcycles by forbidding the use of safety helmets. One need not posit a constitutional right to ride a motorcycle to characterize such a restriction as irrational and perverse.

Even as a regulation of behavior, such a statute would be defective. Assuming that the State could impose a uniform sanction upon young persons who risk self-inflicted harm by operating motorcycles, or by engaging in sexual activity, surely that sanction could not take the form of deliberately injuring the cyclist or infecting the promiscuous child. If such punishment may not be administered deliberately, after trial and a finding of guilt, it manifestly cannot be imposed by a legislature, indiscriminately and at random. This kind of government-mandated harm, is, in my judgment, appropriately characterized as a deprivation of liberty without due process of law.

ADOLESCENT ACCESS TO CONTRACEPTIVES

(1) **Whose Interest is Protected?** Although eight Justices in *Carey* agree that New York's flat statutory prohibition on adolescent access to contraceptives is unconstitutional, they are divided about why this is so. Characterize the positions of Justices Brennan, Powell, and Stevens. What constitutionally protected interest does each Justice find to be undermined by the statute? In the opinion of Justice Powell, how do the statutory restrictions violate the interests of parents? Compare this position with the Court's opinion in *Ginsberg v. New York* at page 137 above. (390 U.S. 629, 88 S.Ct. 1274, 20 L.Ed.2d 195 (1968)). Should parents decide about whether their children should use contraceptives? How closely analogous is this issue to that of minors' access to pornographic literature?

(2) **Abortion and Contraception.** Justice Brennan asserts that decisions about contraceptive use, like decisions about abortion, fit into the category of "decisions affecting procreation" and thus implicate the minor's constitutionally protected right of privacy. Do you agree that the two decisions are analogous? Is the argument that minors should have the authority to make independent decisions about contraceptive use without involving their parents stronger (or weaker) than the case for legal autonomy for adolescents to make decisions about abortion? Both decisions, of course, allow the minor to avoid the burden of an unwanted pregnancy. However, the decisions have some distinguishing dimensions. The urgency of the abortion decision is absent in the decision about contraceptive use, which, ideally, is "future oriented." Arguably (although perhaps unrealistically), parental consultation would be beneficial for some minors making the latter decision. On the other hand, contraceptive use is not complicated by the interest in fetal life. Free access to contraceptives, in this sense, provides a less costly response to the problem of teenage pregnancy. Franklin Zimring provides a thoughtful analysis of these issues in The Changing Legal World of Adolescence 65–69 (1982).

Under Justice Brennan's analysis, would a state policy discouraging sexual activity by minors be prohibited? There is little doubt that the state has broad authority in this area. This seems like something of a puzzle. Zimring asks, "If the 15 year old girl has privacy rights to contraceptives, why can she be classified as a juvenile delinquent if she puts contraceptives to their intended use?" Id. at 11. Is Zimring correct? If so, what is your response to his question? Do Justice Powell and Justice Stevens, in their concurrences, provide clues?

(3) **Minor Consent Statutes and Teenage Pregnancy.** In most states, minors are able to obtain contraceptive services without parental consultation, either from family planning clinics or, with somewhat less certainty, from private physicians. National Research Council, Risking the Future: Adolescent Sexuality, Pregnancy, and Childbearing (1986). Many states have minors' consent statutes, like the Virginia statute on page 169, that designate specific medical treatments which minors can obtain without involving their parents. These include treatment for venereal disease and substance abuse, psychotherapy, and contraceptive treatment. What is the policy behind these statutes? Justice Brennan in *Carey* emphasizes that New York's restrictive statute is an undue burden on minors' constitutional right of reproductive privacy. Is this the only basis for a policy of providing free access to contraceptive treatment for minors without parental consent? Consider the following.

Teenage pregnancy is a serious social and public health problem in this country. The teen pregnancy rate is higher in the United States than in any developed country except Russia; the U.S. rate is far higher than the rate in Canada and European countries, perhaps because of more conservative attitudes in this country about teen age sexuality and contraceptive use.[1] Birth rates among unmarried teens increased by over 60% in the 1980s, resulting in a rate of almost 50 births per 1000 women in the 15–19 year age group. Although there is some evidence that the rate of teen pregnancies has peaked and may be declining, the social costs continue to be enormous. Pregnancy carries greater health risks for adolescents than for adult women. Teenage mothers are less likely than are their peers to complete high school. Although pregnant students and teenage mothers can no longer be excluded from public high school, many young women find the dual responsibilities to be too burdensome. Teenage mothers (and fathers) have fewer employment opportunities than their peers as adults, and are over-represented in lower-paying unskilled jobs. Although some of the discrepancy is linked to pre-pregnancy academic aptitude, socioeconomic status and educational expectations, the pregnancy itself is an important factor. Children of teenage parents have more health problems than do comparable children of older mothers. These children (and their mothers) are more likely to require public assistance than children of older mothers.

(4) **Condom Distribution Programs.** Policies designed to reduce teenage pregnancy, by providing easy access to contraceptives, are based both on paternalism—protection of the welfare of individual minors—and efficiency—reduction of the enormous social cost of teenage pregnancy. For many who support such policies, the question of whether, and to what extent, minors have a right of reproductive privacy is irrelevant or of secondary concern.

A recent example of this type of policy is the effort of school systems in many cities to provide teenagers with direct access to contraceptives in public middle and high schools, usually through condom distribution programs. Despite the dual purposes of preventing pregnancy and AIDS, these initiatives have often been met with resistance from community, parents' and religious groups. Some courts have found that condom distribution programs that do not provide for parental consent or allow parents to opt out exceed the authority of the department of education and violate parental rights. A New York appellate court struck down a program for distributing condoms in New York City public schools on these grounds, concluding that the program involved a health service that the Department of Education was not authorized to provide either by statute or at common law. *Alfonso v. Fernandez*, 195 A.D.2d 46, 606 N.Y.S.2d 259 (App.Div.1993).

Other courts have upheld school authority to initiate condom distribution programs, particularly when parents are provided the opportunity to opt out. A Federal appellate court rejected a challenge by a parents' group of a condom distribution program created by the Philadelphia School Board. *Parents United For Better Schools, Inc. v. School District of Philadelphia Bd. of Education*, 148 F.3d 260 (3d Cir.1998). The court found that the board did not exceed its statutory authority in creating the program, despite the fact that condom distribution was not listed among the health services that public schools are authorized to provide in the School Code. The legislature, in the court's view had no intent to restrict school-

---

1. For national and international data on teen pregnancy, see Alan Guttmacher Institute, Can More Progress be Made? Teenage Sexual and Reproductive Behavior in Developed Countries (2001); Susheela Singh & Jacqueline E. Darroch, Adolescent Pregnancy and Childbearing: Levels and Trends in Developed Countries, 32 Fam. Planning Perspectives 14 (2000). Center for Disease Control, Teenage Births in the United States: State Trends, 1991–2000 (2002).

based health services. The court also rejected the argument that the program represented an unlawful interference with parents' authority to rear their children:

> We recognize the strong parental interest in deciding what is proper for the preservation of their childrens' health. But we do not believe the Board's policy intrudes on this right. Participation in the program is voluntary. The program specifically reserves to parents the option of refusing their child's participation. (*See* App. 39–40 ("Parents or guardians of students in schools taking part in the phase-in pilot program shall have the absolute right to veto their child's or children's participation in the program")). Once parents return the opt out form, their child will not be able to receive either counseling or condoms.

Is a parental opt-out provision necessary to insulate condom distribution programs from constitutional challenge by parents? Some courts decline to impose this requirement. In *Curtis v. School Committee of Falmouth*,[2] for example, the Massachusetts Supreme Court upheld a middle and high school program that did not contain an opt out provision. Under the program, middle and high school students were counseled and supplied with pamphlets on AIDS and other sexually transmitted diseases before receiving condoms. They could obtain condoms from the school nurse or purchase them in high school restrooms. The court determined that the program did not violate parents' constitutional rights.

> We discern no coercive burden on the plaintiffs' parental liberties in this case. No classroom participation is required of students. Condoms are available to students who request them and, in high school, may be obtained from vending machines. The students are not required to seek out and accept the condoms, read the literature accompanying them, or participate in counseling regarding their use. In other words, the students are free to decline to participate in the program. No penalty or disciplinary action ensues if a student does not participate in the program. For their part, the plaintiff parents are free to instruct their children not to participate.... Although exposure to condom vending machines and to the program itself may offend the moral and religious sensibilities of plaintiffs, mere exposure to programs offered at school does not amount to unconstitutional interference with parental liberties without the existence of some compulsory aspect of the program.

For an constitutional analysis of these programs, see Karl J. Sanders, Kids and Condoms: Constitutional Challenges to the Distribution of Condoms in Public Schools, 61 U.Cin.L.Rev. 1479 (1993).

E. EMANCIPATION: ADOLESCENTS AS LEGAL ADULTS

Accent Service Co., Inc. v. Ebsen

Supreme Court of Nebraska, 1981.
209 Neb. 94, 306 N.W.2d 575.

■ VAN PELT, DISTRICT JUDGE.

This is an appeal from a $2,555.01 judgment of the District Court of Knox County, Nebraska, entered in favor of the plaintiff appellee, as assignee, against the defendant-appellant for hospital expenses incurred by

2. 420 Mass. 749, 652 N.E.2d 580 (1995), *cert. denied*, 516 U.S. 1067, 116 S.Ct. 753, 133 L.Ed.2d 700 (1996).

defendant's son. The District Court, in affirming the judgment of the county court, found that the evidence was insufficient to establish emancipation by the minor, and that the evidence did establish a contractual liability on the part of the defendant to pay for her son's medical services.

Appellant's first assignment of error is that the trial court erred in finding that there was insufficient evidence of a complete emancipation. Violet Ebsen, a widow, and her 18–year-old son, Dwaine, lived together until approximately December 1976. Dwaine then began associating and staying overnight with people his mother did not like and of whom she did not approve. Arguments over his associations and conduct took place in December of 1976 and in January of 1977. As a result of one such argument, on February 1, 1977, Dwaine took his personal belongings and moved from his mother's home in Verdigre, Nebraska, to Orchard, Nebraska. Both the mother and son agreed that he should move out and support himself. After moving out, Dwaine received no further support from his mother. On February 24, 1977, while still living in Orchard, Dwaine was shot and taken to a hospital in Norfolk, Nebraska. There, the hospital expenses were incurred that are the subject of this litigation. After being hospitalized for 2 weeks, Dwaine returned to his mother's home for 3 days and then left. He has been self-supporting and has not returned to his mother's home since leaving.

Whether Dwaine Ebsen was emancipated at the time of his hospitalization is relevant, since the complete emancipation of a child relieves the parent from liability to those who furnish necessaries of life to that child. Brosius v. Barker, 154 Mo.App. 657, 136 S.W. 18 (1911); Poudre Valley Hospital District v. Heckart, 491 P.2d 984 (Colo.App.1971).

The emancipation of a child by a parent may be proved by circumstantial evidence or by an express agreement, or implied from the conduct of the parties. Although this court has not had an occasion to discuss the factors to be considered in determining whether a minor has become emancipated, they were recently analyzed in Annot., 98 A.L.R. 3rd 334, 335–36 (1980): "In general, even in the absence of statute, parents are under a legal as well as a moral obligation to support, maintain, and care for their children, the basis of such a duty resting not only upon the fact of the parent-child relationship, but also upon the interest of the state as parens patriae of children and of the community at large in preventing them from becoming a public burden. However, various voluntary acts of a child, such as marriage or enlistment in military service, have been held to terminate the parent's obligation of support, the issue generally being considered by the courts in terms of whether an emancipation of the child has been effectuated. In those cases involving the issue of whether a parent is obligated to support an unmarried minor child who has voluntarily left home without the consent of the parent, the courts, in actions to compel support from the parent, have uniformly held that such conduct on the part of the child terminated the support obligation.

"Correlative to a parent's obligation of support and maintenance of a minor child is the liability of a parent to others who have performed the support obligation for the parent by furnishing the child with necessaries. Generally, a parent's liability for necessaries furnished a minor child will

parent not liable if child living apart from parent w/ consent — vice versa for no consent.

ad on a variety of circumstances, but it appears clear that no liability s where the parent has been ready and willing at all times to supply ssaries himself and to otherwise fulfill his obligation to support the . Thus, it has been held that a parent was not liable to a third person shing necessaries to an unmarried minor child while voluntarily living apart from the parent with consent, the courts concluding that in such a case the parent was under no obligation to support the child and that the child carried with him no authority to bind the parent for the necessaries furnished. However, a parent has been held liable for necessaries furnished his unmarried minor child by a third person while the child was living apart from the parent without consent, where there was evidence that the parent authorized the sale of the goods to the child."

Where a child departed from the family home and the parent consented to the departure, the child was found to be emancipated in Holland v. Hartley, 171 N.C. 376, 88 S.E. 507 (1916); in Poudre Valley Hospital District v. Heckart, supra; and in Timmerman v. Brown, 268 S.C. 303, 233 S.E.2d 106 (1977).

In the instant case, after several months of arguing and the defendant in effect telling her son to either change his behavior or move out, he left his mother's home with her consent. From that time until the hospital expense was incurred, he furnished his own support and received nothing from his mother. Under these facts, Dwaine Ebsen became emancipated, and his mother became relieved of liability to those furnishing him necessaries.

Appellant's second assignment of error is that the trial court erred in finding that there was evidence of a contractual agreement by the defendant to pay her son's hospital expenses. If such an agreement existed, defendant would be liable, regardless of her son's emancipation, under general principles of contract law.

The county court was unable to make a finding that there was or was not a contractual agreement, but entered judgment for the plaintiff on the basis that Dwaine Ebsen was not emancipated. The District Court affirmed the judgment of the county court, with the following additional finding: "3. That Defendant authorized Plaintiff's assignor to furnish medical services of an emergency nature to her minor son, Dwaine Ebsen, orally and by the execution of Exhibit '3' in writing, immediately prior to the furnishing of the first of said services."

Exhibit 3, referred to, is a consent to operation, anesthetics, and other medical services. This document contains no language of a promise, express or implied, to pay for the services. Lucille Loberg, the hospital employee who was present when the defendant signed exhibit 3, testified that normally the hospital uses another document which specifies how the bill is to be paid. However, no such document signed by the defendant was ever produced or received in evidence.

Nor does the record reveal any oral promise to pay the hospital expenses. The closest testimony to such a promise was in the county court, where the defendant, under examination by the plaintiff's attorney, stated that by signing exhibit 3 she wanted her son attended to and wanted him to stay alive. Under examination by her own attorney, she testified that at no time did she say anything to anyone at the hospital that she could or would pay the bill. Plaintiff has the burden of proving any oral or written agreement by a preponderance of the evidence. There is no such evidence in the record. . . .

   Reversed and remanded with directions to dismiss.

NOTE

   Emancipation liberates the minor from parental authority and bestows many of the rights and privileges of legal adulthood. [The California statute below (§ 7050) describes the legal purposes for which an emancipated minor is treated as an adult, and provides a typical (if expansive) description of the rights and privileges that are extended.] However, as the statute and *Accent Service Company* make clear, emancipation also offers several benefits to parents. Among the most important is relief from the parental financial support obligation. Many emancipation cases deal with parents' efforts to avoid their obligation to financially support their children. For example, in *In re Marriage of George*, a non-custodial divorced father sought to terminate his child support obligation when his 16 year old daughter quit school, became pregnant and had a child. The appellate court found that these factors were considerations in determining whether a child is emancipated but they were not dispositive. Also important were the financial resources available to the child, and in this case, the minor lived with her mother and was financially dependent on her. 26 Kan.App.2d 336, 988 P.2d 251 (1999).

   Much litigation has focused on whether college students are unemancipated for the purpose of receiving continued child support from non-custodial parents while they are in school. The legal obligation of parents to provide financial support to their children usually ends at age eighteen when the minor becomes a legal adult. In intact families, of course, parents are usually happy to contribute to their children's support through college, to the extent that they are able to do so. Non-custodial parents who are subject to child support orders may be less willing to continue to provide support, without which their children may be unable to attend college. In some states, by statute or judicial opinion, non-custodial parents' support obligation continues while children attend college—thus, these children are treated as unemancipated for this purpose. However, college-age children may become emancipated, terminating the parents' support obligation, where they fail to meet minimum college attendance requirements or other conditions. For example, one court found a college student to be emancipated where she failed to take 12 credits per semester or to provide her father with a transcript. *Rogers v. Rogers,* 87 S.W.3d 368 (Mo.App.W.D.2002).

   Another benefit to parents of emancipation is removal of much vicarious tort liability for their children's conduct. This issue has become more salient in recent years with the statutory trend toward imposing vicarious liability on parents for their children's conduct. Under recent statutes, parents are held accountable for their children's truancy, curfew violations, gang activity, and for their children's unsupported children. Emancipation may be attractive to parents as a means to escape such liability.

   In some jurisdictions emancipation can be either partial or complete. Whether emancipation has been effected is a question of fact, but guidelines laid down by the courts to assist in the determination often are sparse. See, e.g., *Lawson v. Brown,* 349 F.Supp. 203 (W.D.Va.1972); *Brumfield v. Brumfield,* 194 Va. 577, 74 S.E.2d 170 (1953).

While some contend that widespread lowering of majority age to 18 has diminished the importance of emancipation considerably, others strongly reject this argument and today there is substantial legislative sentiment for adoption of comprehensive statutes on the subject, as illustrated by the material that follows. For further discussion of the history of common law emancipation see Francis C. Cady, Emancipation of Minors, 12 Conn.L.Rev. 62 (1979); Homer H. Clark, Jr., Law of Domestic Relations vol. 1, 548 (2d ed.1987); ABA–IJA Juvenile Justice Standards, Standards Relating to Rights of Minors 21 (1980); and Sanford N. Katz, William A. Schroeder, and Lawrence R. Sidman, Emancipating Our Children—Coming of Legal Age in America, 7 Fam.L.Q. 211 (1973).

CALIFORNIA FAMILY CODE. EMANCIPATION OF MINORS LAW (West)

Chapter 1. GENERAL PROVISIONS

§ 7001. Purpose of Part

It is the purpose of this part to provide a clear statement defining emancipation and its consequences and to permit an emancipated minor to obtain a court declaration of the minor's status. This part is not intended to affect the status of minors who may become emancipated under the decisional case law that was in effect before the enactment of Chapter 1059 of the Statutes of 1978.

§ 7002. Emancipated minor; description

A person under the age of 18 years is an emancipated minor if any of the following conditions is satisfied:

(a) The person has entered into a valid marriage, whether or not the marriage has been dissolved.

(b) The person is on active duty with the armed forces of the United States.

(c) The person has received a declaration of emancipation pursuant to Section 7122.

Chapter 2. EFFECT OF EMANCIPATION

§ 7050. Purposes for which emancipated minors are considered an adult

An emancipated minor shall be considered as being an adult for the following purposes:

(a) The minor's right to support by the minor's parents.

(b) The right of the minor's parents to the minor's earnings and to control the minor.

(c) The application of Sections 300 and 601 of the Welfare and Institutions Code.

(d) Ending all vicarious or imputed liability of the minor's parents or guardian for the minor's torts. Nothing in this section affects any liability of a parent, guardian, spouse, or employer imposed by the Vehicle Code, or any vicarious liability that arises from an agency relationship.

(e) The minor's capacity to do any of the following:

(1) Consent to medical, dental, or psychiatric care, without parental consent, knowledge, or liability.

(2) Enter into a binding contract or give a delegation of power.

(3) Buy, sell, lease, encumber, exchange, or transfer an interest in real or personal property, including, but not limited to, shares of stock in a domestic or foreign corporation or a membership in a nonprofit corporation.

(4) Sue or be sued in the minor's own name.

(5) Compromise, settle, arbitrate, or otherwise adjust a claim, action, or proceeding by or against the minor.

(6) Make or revoke a will.

(7) Make a gift, outright or in trust.

(8) Convey or release contingent or expectant interests in property, including marital property rights and any right of survivorship incident to joint tenancy, and consent to a transfer, encumbrance, or gift of marital property.

(9) Exercise or release the minor's powers as donee of a power of appointment unless the creating instrument otherwise provides.

(10) Create for the minor's own benefit or for the benefit of others a revocable or irrevocable trust.

(11) Revoke a revocable trust.

(12) Elect to take under or against a will.

(13) Renounce or disclaim any interest acquired by testate or intestate succession or by inter vivos transfer, including exercise of the right to surrender the right to revoke a revocable trust.

(14) Make an election referred to in Section 13502 of, or an election and agreement referred to in Section 13503 of, the Probate Code.

(15) Establish the minor's own residence.

(16) Apply for a work permit pursuant to Section 49110 of the Education Code without the request of the minor's parents.

(17) Enroll in a school or college.

§ 7051.   Insurance contracts

An insurance contract entered into by an emancipated minor has the same effect as if it were entered into by an adult, and with respect to that contract, the minor has the same rights, duties, and liabilities as an adult.

.   .   .

Chapter 3.   COURT DECLARATION OF EMANCIPATION

§ 7110.   Legislative intent

It is the intent of the Legislature that proceedings under this part be as simple and inexpensive as possible. To that end, the Judicial Council is requested to prepare and distribute to the clerks of the superior courts appropriate forms for the proceedings that are suitable for use by minors acting as their own counsel.

§ 7120.   Petition

(a) A minor may petition the superior court of the county in which the minor resides or is temporarily domiciled for a declaration of emancipation.

(b) The petition shall set forth with specificity all of the following facts:

(1) The minor is at least 14 years of age.

(2) The minor willingly lives separate and apart from the minor's parents or guardian with the consent or acquiescence of the minor's parents or guardian.

(3) The minor is managing his or her own financial affairs. As evidence of this, the minor shall complete and attach a declaration of income and expenses as provided in Judicial Council form FL–150.

(4) The source of the minor's income is not derived from any activity declared to be a crime by the laws of this state or the laws of the United States.

§ 7121.   Notice

(a) Before the petition for a declaration of emancipation is heard, notice the court determines is reasonable shall be given to the minor's parents, guardian, or other person entitled to the custody of the minor, or proof shall be made to the court that their addresses are unknown or that for other reasons the notice cannot be given.

(b) The clerk of the court shall also notify the local child support agency of the county in which the matter is to be heard of the proceeding. If the minor is a ward of the court, notice shall be given to the probation department. If the child is a dependent child of the court, notice shall be given to the county welfare department.

(c) The notice shall include a form whereby the minor's parents, guardian, or other person entitled to the custody of the minor may give their written consent to the petitioner's emancipation. The notice shall include a warning that a court may void or rescind the declaration of emancipation and the parents may become liable for support and medical insurance coverage pursuant to Chapter 2 (commencing with Section 4000) of Part 2 of Division 9 and Sections 17400, 17402, 17404, and 17422.

§ 7122.   Issuance of declaration of emancipation

(a) The court shall sustain the petition if it finds that the minor is a person described by Section 7120 and that emancipation would not be contrary to the minor's best interest.

(b) If the petition is sustained, the clerk shall forthwith issue a declaration of emancipation, which shall be filed by the clerk of the court.

(c) A declaration is conclusive evidence that the minor is emancipated.

NOTE

Professors Carol Sanger and Eleanor Willemson have conducted a study of the emancipation process under the California statute, which is reported in a thought-provoking article. Carol Sanger & Eleanor Willemsen, Minor Changes: Emancipating Children in Modern Times, 25 U.Mich.J.L. Reform 239 (1992). The statute, the authors report, was promoted by its legislative sponsors (including social service agencies serving youth and families) as a reform measure to free mature minors who were living independently from legal disabilities which impaired their ability to function on a day-to-day basis. However, the findings of the study present an account of the emancipation process and of the lives of the emancipated minors that might not conform to the aspirations of the statute's proponents.

The authors interviewed 18 emancipated minors in two California counties, (all that could be found through telephone numbers or relatives of the 90 minors emancipated during a two-year period). The subjects described as the important factors motivating them to seek emancipation the overcoming of legal obstacles and freedom from parental authority. In most of the families, a considerable amount of conflict existed between the parents and the child, and the emancipation was often a means to escape the conflict, for both parents and children. Many of the parents were divorced and the presence of a stepparent was sometimes a factor. The authors found that, although the process was technically initiated by the minor, emancipation was often urged upon the minor by parents.

The process itself was simple and quick, requiring no waiting period, counseling, or investigation. There was little judicial inquiry into whether emancipation was in the best interest of the minor. The authors conclude that, in cases involving parental consent, judges take the parent's signature as a proxy for a best interest determination and rubber stamp the petition.

The lives of emancipated minors generally was not easy. Most experienced economic stress and most dropped out of high school as a result of emancipation. Yet most did not have jobs. Many continued to have legal hassles, as landlords, employers and others did not recognize their new legal status. In summing up the response of the subjects to their adult status, the authors say: "Life after emancipation is often precarious and lonely, and the decision to become emancipated is regarded with ambivalence." Id. at 297.

The authors conclude that emancipation under the California statute serves as a ready tool to separate parents from children in dysfunctional families in a way that may disserve the interests of the affected children—an outcome that would surprise the law's sponsors.

> [E]mancipation now operates as the out-of-home placement of least procedural resistance and greatest substantive practical advantage. It differs from the traditional forms of out-of-home placement such as foster care and institutionalization in that only minors may officially invoke it. But that difference is offset by a larger similarity: whatever its form, placement of a child outside the family often reflects conflict or dysfunction in the family.

Id. at 305.

What legal responses could ameliorate the problems that Sanger and Willemson identify? Is emancipation simply a bad idea for most adolescents, who need the legal protection that minority status confers? On this question, consider the materials in the following section.

F. ADOLESCENCE: A SEPARATE LEGAL CATEGORY?

In recent years, the treatment of adolescence under the law has been a subject of considerable interest. On the one hand, the attention directed at adolescents' legal right to make decisions about abortion has sparked a broad challenge to traditional legal categories based on age. Some advocates argue that adolescents should be accorded a far greater array of adult rights and privileges than current law allows. Gary Melton, for example, challenges the entrenched tendency to assume that adolescents, like younger children, are incapable of self-determination and that they are thus appropriately subject to adult decisionmaking authority.

Other observers argue that, in some legal contexts, paternalistic policies serve the interests of adolescents. For example, minors charged with crimes are dealt with far more leniently, in general, when they are adjudicated in juvenile court. In recent years, reforms in criminal justice policy have eroded the boundaries between adult criminal court and juvenile court. Today, youths can be tried and punished as adults at younger ages and for a broader range of crimes than was the case in the traditional juvenile court. These policies are criticized by commentators who emphasize the immaturity and more limited culpability of young offenders. See Elizabeth Scott & Larry Steinberg, Blaming Youth, 81 Texas L. Rev. 799 (2003). These issues are examined in Chapters IX and X.

Many questions about the direction of policy regulating adolescence are unresolved. Perhaps most important is the extent to which the legal status of adolescents should differ from that of adults. Advocates for extending legal rights and privileges to young people emphasize their similarity to adults in decisionmaking competence. Others argue that legal protection and restrictions may be warranted in some areas, and that paternalistic policies should not be abandoned. This section presents some perspectives on this policy debate.

Elizabeth Scott, The Legal Construction of Adolescence
29 Hofstra L. Rev. 547, 555–57 (2000).

.   .   .

B.   Adolescence in Legal Rhetoric

No one thinks that adolescents are similar to toddlers in their reasoning and judgment, dependency, or vulnerability. The empirical assumptions about developmental immaturity that shape the legal images of childhood do not fit comfortably with conventional notions of adolescence. As compared with younger children, adolescents are close to adulthood. They are physically mature, and most have the cognitive capacities for reasoning and understanding necessary for making rational decisions. Yet, adolescents are not fully formed persons in many regards; they continue to be dependent on their parents and on society, and their inexperience and immature judgment may lead them to make poor choices, which threaten harm to themselves or others. Conventional wisdom about adolescence generally tracks scientific knowledge about human development—individuals in this group are proceeding through a developmental stage between childhood and adulthood—they are neither children nor adults.

Although lawmakers have occasionally recognized the distinctive character of adolescence, more typically this transitional stage is invisible, and adolescents are incorporated into the binary legal categories of childhood or adulthood. For many purposes—voting, military service, domicile, contracting, and entitlement to support—adolescents are legal children until a bright line age of majority transforms them into adults. For other purposes, adult status is attained either before the age of majority (driving), or after (drinking).

When extending legal rights or responsibilities to minors is the subject of policy debate, adolescents are usually described either as children or as mature adults—depending upon the desired classification. Abortion jurisprudence provides a good example of the elusiveness of adolescence in legal rhetoric. When the Supreme Court recognizes parental authority and other constraints on the rights of pregnant minors, teens are described as children. In Bellotti v. Baird, for example, Justice Powell points to the vulnerability of children, their lack of experience, perspective, and judgment, and the guiding role of parents in the upbringing of their children as the basis for limiting adolescent abortion rights. In contrast, advocates who favor conferring adult abortion rights on teens present quite a different image of pregnant adolescents. In H.L. v. Matheson, for example, Justice Marshall argued (in dissent) that Utah's statutory restrictions amounted to a state-created "obstacle to the exercise of the minor woman's free choice."

In general, both advocates and lawmakers ignore the developmental realities of adolescence, and endorse fictional accounts in which adolescents are either immature children (and thus dependant, incompetent, and vulnerable), or mature adults (and thus self-sufficient, competent, and responsible). This does not mean, however, that such binary classification is generally bad policy, or that it disserves the interests of adolescents. To the contrary, this approach works well for the most part. To a considerable extent, classification of adolescents as children (for most purposes) or adults (for some purposes) constitutes a coherent and socially beneficial scheme.

. . . . [C]hildren cross over the line to legal adulthood at different ages for different purposes. The baseline, of course, is the age of majority, the age at which presumptive adult legal status is attained. However, a complex regime of age grading defines childhood as a category with multiple boundaries. Youths charged with murder can be tried as adults at age ten or younger in many states, and high school students can obtain contraceptives without parental permission. On the other hand, non-custodial parents may be obliged to contribute to their children's college expenses and young adults cannot drink or run for Congress. What explains this variation?

The logic of the multiple boundaries of childhood is far from obvious. Most straightforwardly, age grading can be explained as a function of different maturity requirements in different legal domains. Both youths and society benefit if adult legal status is conferred when (and only when) young citizens are capable of fulfilling the law's expectations. Thus, no one would challenge that the maturity demanded to fulfill the role of president (currently limited to citizens age thirty-five or older) is greater than that needed to drive a car or vote. However, perusal of the scheme of regulations suggests that, although crude assumptions about maturity play an important role, age grading policies are often shaped by other considerations as well. Examination of specific policies suggests that lines are drawn on the basis of a number of diverse policy concerns. Concern about youth welfare, protection of parental authority, and societal benefit are all a part of the mix, as is straightforward administrative convenience. On issues such as abortion access, political controversy and compromise have played a powerful role in the way in which the boundary of childhood is set.

Gary B. Melton, Toward "Personhood" for Adolescents

38 American Psychologist 99 (January 1983).*

. . .

Competence and Autonomy

Although varying orientations toward children's rights are not necessarily mutually exclusive, the underlying theory of each of these broad orientations rests, in part, on a variant assumption of minors' *competence*—that is, whether children and adolescents are capable of competent independent decision making. The ambivalence in public policy flows from divergent views of whether minors can be considered, in view of their immaturity in decision making, to be true moral agents who are full and autonomous members of the community. This view of children's liberty as contingent upon their level of competence was articulated by Justice Stewart:

> I think a State may permissibly determine that, at least in some precisely delineated areas, a child—like someone in a captive audience—is not possessed of that full capacity for individual choice which is the presupposition of First Amendment guarantees. It is only upon such a premise, I should suppose, that a State may deprive children of other rights—the right to marry, for example, or the right to vote—deprivations that would be constitutionally intolerable for adults.[10]

Essentially, the argument is that minors are dependent beings who lack the capacity, at least in some circumstances, for mature, independent choice. Lacking evidence to the contrary, they are presumed to lack autonomy, and therefore to lack independent liberty interests. Moreover, to the extent that privacy is predicated on respect for the boundaries—both physical and psychological—of the person, minors' lack of status as autonomous persons also raises questions of whether they possess justifiable expectations of privacy.

Although showing no inclination to abandon the premise that minors do have *some* rights, the Supreme Court has generally been reluctant to concede that adolescents may in fact be competent decision makers in many contexts. Even in abortion cases, the Court has started with an apparently lower standard (i.e., significant state interests)[12] for abridgment of minors'

10. Ginsberg v. New York, 390 U.S. 629, 649–50, 88 S.Ct. 1274, 20 L.Ed.2d 195 (1968) (concurring opinion).

12. Planned Parenthood of Central Missouri v. Danforth, 428 U.S. 52, 75, 96 S.Ct. 2831, 49 L.Ed.2d 788 (1976).

rights to privacy than the strict scrutiny (i.e., compelling state interests) normally applied to attempts to infringe upon fundamental rights of a class for state purposes. Thus, besides doubting minors' capacity to make such judgments,[13] the Court has seemingly begun its analysis of minors' interests regarding privacy and liberty with a *presumption* that they lack autonomy.

In *Parham v. J.R.*,[14] for example, Chief Justice Burger noted a tradition in "Western Civilization" that "parents possess what a child lacks in maturity, experience, and capacity for judgment required for making life's difficult decisions" and that "natural bonds of affection lead parents to act in the best interests of their children."[15] Then, leaping from tradition to a finding of social "fact," the Chief Justice, writing for the majority, concluded:

> Most children, even in adolescence, simply are not able to make sound judgments concerning many decisions, including their need for medical care or treatment. Parents can and must make those judgements.[16]

Finding, then, that the child had minimal independent liberty interests at stake in the decision of whether to be hospitalized, the Court held that no formal preadmission hearing was necessary.

The way in which the Court leans in a particular context in its dualistic view of minors as both autonomous "persons" and as dependent beings had seemed to vary with the result that the Court wanted to reach.[17] The "facts" of which the Chief Justice took notice in *Parham* seemed to reflect a desire to support idyllic concepts of the family and the mental health system rather than a careful examination of the available evidence. The Court appeared to ignore both the case facts developed at trial and the available research.

Assuming, however, that the stated assumptions about competence really are the bases for the analysis used by the Court in cases concerning the breadth of minors' rights, psychologists could help to inform the Court as to the modal level of competence of minors in particular contexts. The existing literature clearly suggests that, for most purposes, adolescents cannot be distinguished from adults on the ground of competence in decision making alone.[18] Grisso and Vierling, for example, considered the

---

13. *See, e.g.,* Bellotti v. Baird, 443 U.S. 622, 640, 99 S.Ct. 3035, 61 L.Ed.2d 797 (1979); Planned Parenthood of Central Missouri v. Danforth, 428 U.S. 52, 91, 96 S.Ct. 2831, 49 L.Ed.2d 788 (Stewart, J., concurring); id. at 95 (White J., dissenting).

14. 442 U.S. 584, 99 S.Ct. 2493, 61 L.Ed.2d 101 (1979).

15. *Id.* at 602.

16. *Id.* at 603.

17. The area in which the Court has been most willing to recognize adolescents as competent has ironically been the type of

decision in which there is most reason to suspect that minors may be incompetent: waivers of rights in delinquency proceedings (Grisso, 1981; Melton, in press). *See,* Fare v. Michael C., 442 U.S. 707, 99 S.Ct. 2560, 61 L.Ed.2d 197 (1979).

18. Citing Piaget, Elkind, Kohlberg, Gesell, and other authorities on child and adolescent development, Justice Douglas reached a similar conclusion about 14–year-olds' decision-making prowess in his lone dissent in Wisconsin v. Yoder, 406 U.S. 205, 245, n. 3, 92 S.Ct. 1526, 32 L.Ed.2d 15 (1972), the only instance in which developmental research has been cited to support a Supreme

developmental literature on problem-solving activities and vulnerability to social influence and concluded that there was no basis in that literature for distinguishing adolescents aged 15 and older from adults. They suggested further that ages 11 to 14 should be viewed as a transition period in the development of important cognitive and social abilities; youth in this age group might be competent as decision makers in some contexts. Some caution about the junior-high-age group is particularly important, given C.C. Lewis' (1981) finding that seventh and eighth graders appear to be less likely than older adolescents to consider potential risks and potential future consequences of decisions.

Since Grisso and Vierling's review, a substantial literature on adolescents' decision making in specific legally relevant contexts has developed. In terms of competence to consent to psychotherapy, for example, there is evidence that adolescents have adult-like concepts of psychotherapy, mental health professionals, and mental disorder itself. In perhaps the best-designed study of this sort, Weithorn and Campbell presented hypothetical dilemmas about medical and psychological treatment decisions to 9–, 14–, 18–, and 21–year olds. The responses of the 14–year-olds could not be differentiated from those of the adult groups according to any of the major standards of competency: evidence of a choice; reasonable outcome of choice; reasonable decision making process; understanding of the facts.[19]

The evidence on specific decisional competencies of adolescents is not limited to treatment decisions. For example, even elementary schoolchildren are frequently competent to consent to research, at least when their reasons for or against participation are evaluated relative to those of adult populations. Similarly, C.C. Lewis found that the reasons given by pregnant minors for or against abortion are similar to the reasons given by pregnant adults. In short, the Supreme Court's assumption of adolescents' incompetence as decision makers cannot be supported by the available psychological research.

Autonomy: Other Justifications

It is, of course, arguable that recognition of autonomy should not rely on a finding of competence. It is typically assumed that adults are autonomous persons, unless there is evidence of gross mental disability. Even if adults meet criteria for civil commitment, their liberty and privacy interests are not extinguished by that fact.[20] In short, mental disability need not

Court justice's opinion about minors' competence.

19. Interestingly, the 9–year-olds in Weithorn and Campbell's study were competent according to standards of expression of a choice and reasonable outcome. That is, even though they did not reason as well as did the older groups, they did express a choice, and the choice made tended to be the one identified as "reasonable" by a panel of health care professionals. This evidence from laboratory interviews is corroborated by an evaluation of a program in which children were given the right to make routine health care decisions (e.g., whether to go to the school nurse; C.E. Lewis, in press). Perhaps because they model adult behavior, even elementary-school-age children may often be "reasonable" decision makers, if defined by the outcomes rather than the process of their decisions.

20. *See, e.g.,* Youngberg v. Romeo, 457 U.S. 307, 102 S.Ct. 2452, 2458, 73 L.Ed.2d 28 (1982); Rogers v. Okin, 634 F.2d 650 (1st Cir.1980), *remanded on other grounds sub nom.* Mills v. Rogers, 457 U.S. 291, 102 S.Ct. 2442, 73 L.Ed.2d 16 (1982).

obviate an adult's status as a person. Respect for adolescents' status as developing members of the community arguably demands similar recognition of their personhood.

There might also be utilitarian grounds, for doubting the wisdom of a competence standard in some situations. Regardless of one's basic position on abortion, it makes little sense to base independent access to abortions on "maturity," as the Supreme Court has done.[21] Can minors considered to be incompetent to make decisions about abortions be any more competent to care for a child?

Moreover, insofar as the concern with competence is based on a desire to protect minors from the consequences of bad decisions, there may be reason to support increased self-determination by minors, even if they are incompetent or marginally competent, if decision making per se can be shown to be beneficial. Although evaluation research on the effects of granting adolescents freedom in real life settings is scarce, there is ample reasons to believe that there would be psychological benefits from increased freedom. Legal socialization, for example, depends largely on actual participation in legal decision making and the experience of conflict of ideas. Such involvement is likely to be especially effective in enhancing perception of rights as entitlements applicable to oneself.

An increase in freedom may also increase a sense of efficacy. For example, Rosen evaluated an "open campus" high school in Georgia in which students were given the same freedoms as they would have in a community college. The program resulted in more internal locus of control, especially for black students, who may have had less previous experience of control. Moreover, the experience of choice itself is likely to reinforce academic performance. Presumably when students have made an affirmative decision to participate in an educational or treatment program, they will be more likely to complete the program and to be less resistant to it.

Respect for privacy would also be likely to have positive psychological effects. It would be consistent with adolescents' attempts at individuation and their developing concern about control over personal information. Respect for privacy may also be a necessary guarantee before some adolescents will seek treatment for "sensitive" problems.

Implications for Policy

Despite these potential psychological and social benefits, the argument here is not that adolescents should be granted rights equal to those of adults in every situation. In some instances, there may be compelling reasons to limit adolescents' liberty. The relationship between age and traffic accidents associated with the use of alcohol may, for example, provide sufficient evidence of state interests to limit access to alcoholic beverages even among adolescents who have passed the age of majority. Also, where parents bear financial liability for their adolescent children's decisions, fairness may

---

21. *E.g.*, Planned Parenthood of Central Missouri v. Danforth, 428 U.S. 52, 75, 96 S.Ct. 2831, 49 L.Ed.2d 788 (1976).

dictate deference to parental wishes or at least parental participation in making decisions.

I am arguing that adolescents' personhood should be recognized by policymakers. Insofar as denial of autonomy has been based on assumptions of incompetence, current psychological research does not support such an age-graded distinction. Moreover, as suggested above, recognition of personhood might facilitate adolescents' personal individuation. Psychologists might profitably examine the effects of such recognition in evaluations of programs designed to increase freedom for adolescents and of comparable changes in adolescents' rights in specific jurisdictions. In the meantime, there seems to be ample basis for reversal of current presumptions in favor of a view of adolescents as autonomous persons possessed of independent interests regarding liberty and privacy. Accordingly, psychologists should actively involve minors in decision making about treatment and research, and policy-makers should begin their analyses of issues involving adolescents with respect for their autonomy and privacy.

Such a reversal of presumptions would probably result in substantial changes in the scope of adolescents' liberty and privacy rights. Assuming that compelling state interests to the contrary could not be demonstrated, adolescents' independent interests in decisions relating to such matters as psychotherapy, medical treatment, psychiatric hospitalization, abortion, and contraception would have to be recognized. Indiscriminate searches of high school students could not be upheld on the ground that students have no expectation of privacy.

Recognition of rights in these contexts would obviously result in partial redistribution of authority among parents, children, and the state. It should be noted, however, that irrespective of the ethical demands for recognition of adolescents' personhood, there may actually be popular support for recognizing adolescents' rights in many contexts. In a survey of adolescents and parents in the Los Angeles area Feshbach and Tremper found that there was support among both groups for adolescents making many key decisions at ages at which they may be presumed in law to be incompetent. For example, both groups would defer to minors' wishes in custody decisions at about age 12, in decision about medical treatment and psychotherapy at about age 14, and in decisions about birth control at about age 15. Although Feshbach and Tremper's results may be of limited generalizability to other populations, there is at least the suggestion that there would be substantial support among both adults and youth themselves for recognition of adolescents' interests in matters that substantially affect their privacy and liberty, a point worthy of further investigation.

In conclusion, it may be useful to say a word about the role of psychology in the development of these policies. An underlying assumption of this article is that policies based on empirical assumptions could be best informed by examination of relevant evidence. If these assumptions are not the real bases for the policies at stake, then intellectual honesty demands that the actual rationales be made explicit. To the extent that the assumption of incompetence has led to the courts' ambivalence about the personhood of adolescents, then this ambivalence may be reduced by the kind of psychological evidence described here.

If that bridge is crossed (i.e., if adolescents are presumed to be autonomous persons), then ironically psychology may be of much less ultimate relevance. At present, when standards for not infringing on adolescents' rights are set at low levels, balancing tests inevitably result; these require examination of potential harms and benefits, many of which are psychological. If respect is given to the personhood of adolescents, these questions will not be reached in many circumstances. Rather, the process of policy formation will stop with normative judgments of requirements for human dignity.

NOTES

(1) Do you think that Justice Douglas, based on his dissenting opinion in *Wisconsin v. Yoder*, supra at pages 18, 27, would agree with Professor Melton's approach? Note particularly footnote 3 of Douglas's opinion. Justice Douglas has been heralded as a pioneer by advocates who argue that psychological research and theory support a legal policy of greater self-determination for minors.

(2) Does Melton conclude that adolescents should be subject to the same legal standards as adults? For all purposes? Melton proposes that adolescents be authorized to make autonomous decisions about abortion, contraception, psychiatric hospitalization, and other medical treatments, but suggests that their liberty to use alcohol might be restricted. On what basis can this distinction be made?

As we saw in the last section, many advocates for extending legal rights to adolescents have focused on independent access to abortion. Psychologist-advocates have argued that scientific knowledge about child development does not support the traditional legal restrictions, because adolescents are competent decisionmakers. In this regard consider the following:

Hartigan v. Zbaraz Brief for Amicus Curiae— American Psychological Association

Supreme Court of the United States No. 85–673 (1986).

[The American Psychological Association submitted this brief in support of Illinois physicians challenging the Illinois Parental Notice of Abortion Act (Ill. Rev. Stat. Ch. 38 § 81–64 (1983)) on behalf of themselves and their minor patients.]

. . .

II. OLDER ADOLESCENTS AND MANY YOUNGER ADOLESCENTS ARE AS ABLE AS ADULTS TO MAKE COMPETENT DECISIONS REGARDING ABORTION.

. . .

A. Psychological Theory About Cognitive, Social, and Moral Development Strongly Supports the Conclusion That Most Adolescents Are Competent to Make Informed Decisions About Abortion.

Developmental psychologists[21] have generated well-established and generally accepted theories concerning adolescents' capacities for understanding and reasoning as part of the process of decisionmaking, especially in comparison to the same capacities in adults. Cognitive capacity develops in a predictable sequence of stages, from simple reflexive reactions in infancy to the comprehension of abstractions and future consequences in early adolescence.[22] The ability to comprehend future consequences, called "formal operations," is most relevant to the decisions affected by the Act.

The cognitive ability developed in the period of formal operations is most closely akin to the "capacity to consent." in the period of formal operations children acquire the capacity to generate many possible solutions to a problem, to think about each possible solution hypothetically, to imagine its consequences before they occur, to consider both immediate and longer-range consequences, and to weigh and balance these various potential outcomes to reach a conclusion about the decision to be made. Once the period of formal operations is complete, an individual has the decisionmaking abilities of an adult.

In early adolescence (10–13) children move from the period in which they learn to organize their environment coherently and conceptually to the period of formal operations. By the onset of late adolescence (14–17), almost all minors with at least average intellectual ability possess the capacity for formal operations that characterizes the problem-solving process of adults. *See* Keating, *Thinking Processes in Adolescence in* HANDBOOK OF ADOLESCENT PSYCHOLOGY 211 (J. Adelson ed. 1980) and n.22, *supra*. A large body of empirical research supports these principles.

In addition to reaching the stage of formal operations, competent decisionmaking is dependent on social development and situational factors such as the emerging of one's identity, establishing autonomy, and forming personal values, processes that continue through early and late adolescence. One might speculate that the need to establish a separate identity and autonomy from parents might, at times, cause adolescents to make decisions based on their need to demonstrate independence from parental values rather than on the appreciation of objective consequences. The evidence suggests, to the contrary, that the majority of adolescents do not repudiate parental values during their search for autonomy.

To the extent that many decisions require the weighing of the moral consequences of options, moral development is another important factor in competent decisionmaking. Psychological theory and empirical research on adolescents' moral development reaches virtually the same conclusions as found in cognitive development. Early adolescence is marked by emergence of the adult's capacity to form moral principles against which to judge one's behavior and decisions, and this capacity is fully developed by ages 14–15.

---

21. Developmental psychologists are scientists who study cognitive, personality, and emotional development along the life span of individuals.

22. Jean Piaget is credited with documenting this growth and providing the no-

menclature for these states. See B. INHELDER & J. PIAGET, THE GROWTH OF LOGICAL THINKING FROM CHILDHOOD.

See generally Kohlberg, The Development of Children's Orientations Toward Moral Order, 6 Vita Humana 11 (1963).

Thus, it is now generally accepted that by mid-adolescence (14–15) the great majority of adolescents do not differ from adults in their capacities to understand and reason about medical and psychological treatment alternatives, or in their abilities to comprehend and consider risks and benefits regarding treatment alternatives.

B.   Research Confirms that Most Adolescents Have the Capacity to Make Sound Health Care Decisions, Including Decisions About Abortion.

Extensive empirical literature demonstrates that adolescent's actual decisionmaking performance when faced with various types of real-life practical problems involving treatment and non-treatment decisions accords with the principles and theories discussed in Point II (A). Many of these studies compare the performance of adolescents to that of adults in making such decisions.

[The brief goes on to describe the study by Lois Weithorn and Susan Campbell previously discussed by Melton and a study of unmarried adolescents and adults considering their options in response to an unplanned pregnancy. Catherine Lewis, A comparison of Minors' and Adults' Pregnancy Decisions, 50 Amer.J.Orthopsychiatry 446 (1980). The brief reported that Lewis found that "minors equaled adults in their 'competence to imagine the various ramifications of the pregnancy decision.' " (p.18)]

NOTES

(1) **Criticism of Social Science Advocacy In the *Zbaraz* Brief.** The scientific accuracy of the American Psychological Association brief in Hartigan v. Zbaraz has been subject to criticism by some observers who assert that the A.P.A. in advocating for adolescent rights, has overstepped the bounds of science. William Gardner and his colleagues have offered a critique of the brief as part of a more general call for caution in the use of science for advocacy purposes. The authors argue that the A.P.A. brief relies on an outmoded theory of cognitive development and that it exaggerates the empirical research evidence about adolescent decisionmaking that is offered in support of the claim that adolescents are indistinguishable from adults in their decisionmaking competence. William Gardner, David Scherer and Maya Tester, Asserting Scientific Authority: Cognitive Development and Adolescent Legal Rights, 44 American Psychologist 895 (June 1989).

The authors point out that Piaget's stage theory of cognitive development on which the brief relies has come under fire in recent years. Today, few psychologists believe that cognitive development is stagelike. Rather, recent research suggests that similar skills develop at different rates in different task domains. Thus, the authors argue, little evidence supports that there is a "single competence to consent to medical treatments." Id. at 898. A finding of competence to make one kind of decision cannot be generalized to other decisions in other contexts.

Gardner and his colleagues also criticize the empirical basis of the claim made in the brief that adolescent decisionmaking competence is equivalent to that of adults. Much of the literature cited to support the assertion of adolescent competence is secondary literature. Only a handful of studies compare the decisionmaking of minors and adults, and most have examined only a small number of subjects. A few other studies compare adolescents' and adults' understanding in legal settings, but do not examine decisionmaking. The deficiencies in the research are exaggerated by the fact that the asserted claim involves the confirmation of a null hypothesis—that no differences exist. A positive claim of this kind requires a great deal of empirical substantiation, using different methodologies. The fact that no differences have been observed might only mean that differences have yet to be uncovered, because researchers have not asked the right questions. In short, to date science offers only tentative support for the assertion that adolescents are similar to adults in their decisionmaking competence.

(2) **Adolescent Self–Determination and Abortion**. Some observers have expressed regret that attention to the issue of adolescents' legal status has arisen in the context of the debate about abortion. Abortion is a highly politicized (and polarized) issue; the debate about self-determination for adolescents seems to have as much to do with attitudes toward abortion as it does with views on adolescent competence to make the decision. As the Gardner critique suggests, those who support adolescent access to abortion may bolster their arguments with exaggerated claims about the similarity between adolescent and adult decisionmaking. Moreover, a careful and neutral inquiry into developmental influences on decisionmaking (as it may affect decisionmaking in other areas) may be less likely in this politically charged environment.

(3) **The Informed Consent Framework.** The argument in the *Zbaraz* brief focuses on the capacity of adolescents to make competent medical decisions under informed consent doctrine. [Remember, this is one proposed standard for measuring the "maturity" of the pregnant minor under Supreme Court abortion doctrine.] Competence under this legal standard involves two aspects of cognitive functioning: the ability to understand information and capacity for reasoning. Perhaps because of the salience of access to abortion in the debate about adolescent self-determination, this informed consent framework has had a broad impact on the more general discourse about policy toward adolescents and has provided the standard for comparing the capabilities of adolescents and adults. Thus, some observers take the observed (although not proven) cognitive similarities between adolescents and adults as the basis for arguing against differential legal treatment in general. This raises a question: Are there other developmental factors that affect decisionmaking that are relevant in evaluating the appropriateness of paternalistic policies that affect adolescents? In this regard, consider the following.

(4) **Decisionmaking Capacity in Other Contexts—The Case of Criminal Responsibility.** Claims about the maturity of adolescents and their competence to make abortion decisions need not have implications for all areas of law. Nonetheless, such claims can become a two-edged sword when advocates seek argue for protective policies directed toward youth. For example, if adolescents have adultlike decisionmaking capacities, as the amicus brief in *Hartigan v. Zbaraz* indicates, should they be held fully responsible for their criminal conduct? Although advocates such as Gary Melton are careful to emphasize that they do not argue for policies that treat adolescents like adults for all purposes, some might see an inconsistency in according adolescents the rights and privileges of adults, but not the responsibilities.

In recent years, juvenile justice policy has taken center stage as the focus of attention by child advocates. This is not surprising in light of the national trend toward more punitive policies, under which juveniles increasingly are tried and punished as adults. In light of these developments, the arguments for adolescent self determination have become more muted, and researchers and scholars have sought to present a more complex account of adolescent decisionmaking capacities. For example, consider the following excerpt.

Elizabeth Scott, N. D. Reppucci, & Jennifer Woolard, Evaluating Adolescent Decisionmaking in Legal Contexts

19 Law & Human Behavior 221, 226–29 (1995).*

. . .

Competence and Judgment

Even if further research confirms that adolescents and adults have similar abilities to understand disclosed information, to appreciate its meaning, and to make decisions through a rational process, this conclusion is not likely to resolve, in the minds of policymakers, the issue of whether adolescents should be accorded the same legal treatment as adults. Although the legal presumption that minors are incompetent and need legal protection rests in part on an intuition that their capacity for understanding and reasoning is less developed than is that of adults', it also rests on the belief that their judgment is less mature. In essence, the intuition behind paternalistic policies is that developmentally linked traits and responses systematically affect the decision making of adolescents in a way that may incline them to make choices that threaten harm to their own and others' health, life, or welfare, to a greater extent than do adults.

The view that minors need protection from the costs of immature youthful choices supported the establishment of a separate juvenile justice system in which adolescents who commit crimes are treated as less responsible than adults who engage in similar behavior. It also justifies the infancy doctrine in contract law under which contracts executed by minors are not enforceable. Finally, restrictions on adolescent liberty to make decisions about medical treatment, employment, marriage, and education can be explained as derived in part from these perceptions.

If our claim is correct, then the informed consent model is incomplete as a framework in which to compare the decision-making capacities of adolescents with adults. An approach that will be more useful to legal policymakers must incorporate a wide range of elements in the conceptual domain of decision making, including some that would be irrelevant or excluded under an informed consent framework. [A] judgment framework includes not only understanding and reasoning ability, but also such factors as conformity and compliance in relation to peers and parents, attitude toward and perception of risk, and temporal perspective. Focusing on these decisionmaking factors allows a comparison between the subjective values that drive the choices of adolescents and those of adults, a comparison that is excluded under even the most expansive test of competence in an informed consent framework.

A reasonable question, at this point, is whether policymakers' focus on adolescent judgment is justified, when the legal capacity of adults, by and large, is not evaluated in this way. For example, under the informed consent doctrine, adults (in theory at least) are free to make poor decisions (from the perspective of others) based on idiosyncratic values, as long as their understanding and reasoning are not greatly impaired. Second-guessing of individual choices in this context is deemed an unacceptable burden on personal autonomy.

Two arguments support the claim that the evaluation of adolescent legal capacity appropriately considers judgment as well as reasoning and understanding. The first is that a different response would carry a significant social cost. Informed consent policy reflects a conclusion that the importance of respecting adults' autonomy in the context of health care decisions outweighs the social cost of poor decisions by occasional "outliers", particularly given the substantial costs of any other approach. It is plausible to assume that most people are motivated to make health-promoting medical decisions (i.e., use good judgment), and thus that the social cost of respecting autonomy is tolerable. If adolescents *as a class* have poorer judgment (and choose different outcomes) than adults, then the social cost of according them freedom and of holding them to adult standards of responsibility might be significant. In fact, in many legal contexts, anticipated social cost of poor judgment by adults justifies restriction of freedom (e.g., seat belt and motorcycle helmet laws, product safety regulations) and reduced responsibility (e.g., laws allowing "cooling off periods" before enforcing door-to-door sales contracts). If immature adolescent decision making creates costs that fall primarily on minors themselves, then the societal interest in preventing harm to this group may be particularly acute.

The second argument for considering judgment hinges on an important distinction that can be drawn between the poor choices made by individuals and those that the law presumes are made by minors as a group. The adult's "poor" decision (to refuse recommended treatment, for example) is presumed to reflect the subjective values and preferences of the individual. In the case of the adolescent refusing treatment, the values and preferences are presumed to reflect common age-linked developmental characteristics that predictably will change. It is assumed that with maturity, most individuals will make a different choice. If this is so, then the autonomy claim seems less compelling than is that of adults. Moreover, implicit in the presumption that developmental factors affect judgment is a prediction (or hope, in the case of delinquent behavior) that the adolescent will become an adult with different values and preferences from her youthful self. If this is so, then the case of protecting the opportunities and prospects of that future adult from the costs of her immature youthful judgment and choices seems powerful.

Whether policymakers legitimately focus on minors' judgment is a political and moral question ... [W]hether arguments for paternalism are persuasive may largely depend on one's ideological leanings. The assumption that minors are developmentally inclined to use immature judgment is often explicitly invoked when courts endorse restrictive policies on such issues as adolescent abortion and psychiatric hospitalization; it is discounted or disputed when policymakers are urged to expand adolescents' rights or to get tough on juvenile crime. The debate about how adolescent decision making compares with that of adults mainly reflects ideology and intuition.

In this politically charged environment, the task for researchers is to analyze the components of decision making that are relevant in different legal contexts, so as to provide policymakers with a more precise empirically based understanding of the ways in which the decision making of adolescents compares with that of adults.

Franklin Zimring, The Changing Legal World of Adolescence

89–96 (1982).*

Adolescence as a Learner's Permit

Being mature takes practice. To know this is to suppose still another justification for extending privileges in public law and family life to those who have not yet reached full maturity. We gamble when we extend choices to the not-yet-adult. If we win, the experience gained in decision-making becomes an integral part of a process of achieving adulthood. If we lose, harm can come to the adolescent and the community. But in positing contemporary adolescence as a "learner's permit" period of life, we can learn much about the dimensions of public policy that this kind of gambling requires.

Choice, Change, and Adolescent Liberty

Today's high specialization and rapid change make training the young a more difficult and more specialized task. The skills of one generation are generally not those that will be required of the next. But the larger society can provide more centralized training for social change, particularly if the nature of the change in adult roles can be anticipated. If parents are "inappropriate role models," other adults can be used to program the young for a very different future. This strategy was part of the agenda of the compulsory public high school movement during the Progressive era. More recently, societies with less respect for individual liberty than ours have performed more radical experiments in training for change.

But how do we train young people to be *free*? If the exercise of independent choice is an essential element of maturity, part of the process of becoming mature is learning to make independent decisions. This type of liberty cannot be taught; it can only be learned. And learning to make independent judgments is inevitably a risky process for the pupil and the larger society.

As in any gambling enterprise, we wish to maximize our gains and keep our losses small. The stakes are high.

And the calculus for determining "gains" and "losses" is somewhat more complicated than cursory inspection would suggest. In blackjack, an ideal "career" is never to lose a hand. In the game of learning to make free choices, winning every hand is poor preparation for the modern world, just as winning every hand is a terrible way to learn to play blackjack. We want adolescents to make mistakes, but we hope they make the right kinds of mistakes. An unsuccessful date may teach our child important lessons about his or her relations with the opposite sex at a far lower cost than an unsuccessful marriage.

An important part of cutting our losses during this period of development is minimizing the harm young persons do themselves, and keeping to a minimum the harm we inflict on them when they have abused opportunities in ways that harm the community. Above almost all else, we seek a legal policy that preserves the life chances for those who make serious mistakes, as well as preserving choices for their more fortunate (and more virtuous) contemporaries.

This learner's permit perspective is a splendid illustration of the limits of law as an instrument of social change. Nothing I have said has addressed the question of *when* our children should grow up. That is a question, hotly contested by theoreticians, which is in an important sense beyond the control of the state legislature. At present, we endure enormous social costs because so much "learning by experience" is centered in adolescence. Some take this as evidence that youth is wasted on the young and learning experiences should be postponed. Others preach that the best way of dispersing the process of learning by experience is to teach some of life's lessons earlier. These two perspectives may in fact be consistent rather than contradictory. Some learning might occur earlier in a social universe that would postpone certain more permanent decisions until later in life.

But one cannot legislate maturity. And our opportunities to control legally when children begin to "commit experience" are extremely limited in the short run by the values of adult freedom and liberal western democracy. The previous discussion demonstrated that least harm reforms kept confronting those limits in areas such as the regulation of status offenders, and New York's quixotic crusade to render 15–year-olds celibate. Peer orientation, foolhardy attitudes toward risk, and the powerful combination of social immaturity and physical mobility make middle adolescence into a mine field. But the costs of attempting to defer learning periods beyond these years are also substantial, and just because many of the negative characteristics of adolescence are, in Arlene Skolnick's words, "merely social" does not make them all that susceptible to legal control.

.   .   .

This perspective provides general guidance on the goals pursued by legal policy toward youth, but no precise prescriptions for how these goals can be translated into effective programs or what price the general public should be willing to pay in the name of youth welfare. We want kids to participate in decisions about their education, but not at the price of sacrificing long term opportunities to avoid short term burdens. Similarly, we want to give young law violators the chance to survive our legal system with their life opportunities still intact, but at what price and for how long? At the tactical level, the implications of a learner's permit perspective are distressingly inexact. . . .

There is one issue, however, where this conception of adolescent development has decisive impact: the relationship between liberty and responsibility during the growing years. This can best be illustrated by analyzing the argument of Richard Kuh, objecting to a series of recommendations for sentencing young offenders: . . .

Mr. Kuh wants to be lenient with youngsters for three or four years past puberty but no later. Why?

> The fact that eighteen-year olds today can vote and those between eighteen and twenty-one both typically are working or able to work or completing college, are sexually and physically mature (and mentally as close to being mature as they ever will be), and are in many cases married or the equivalent.

The distinguished former district attorney of Manhattan is making one of two arguments. Either he is arguing that kids are fully mature by the time they reach their eighteenth birthday or he is proposing that those given rights and privileges should as a matter of *quid pro quo* pay the full price when they violate the law. To see adolescence as a learner's permit is to reject both the evidence and the analysis he provides.

First the evidence. Are kids fully mature at eighteen because they can vote, even if they don't vote? Is that why we passed the Twenty-sixth Amendment? Kids are "mentally as close to being mature as they will ever be." But doesn't it take more than an I.Q. to make decisions? Kids are married or "the equivalent." From the data we reviewed, heaven help them. Eighteen-year-olds go to college and work at least those lucky enough to find jobs or to finance an education. But, in my view, all of this is evidence that 18–year-olds are in the *process* of becoming adult. For that reason, using this kind of evidence to "prove" adulthood is like assuming a flight is over the moment the plane has left the ground. To impose full responsibility because adolescents have begun to make life choices is much like expecting every new bride to be an instant Betty Crocker. It isn't realistic and it isn't fair.

In Rights Begin Responsibilities?

But what about the *quid pro quo* argument: Since they can vote they should pay the full price for committing transgressions. . . . At the outset, we must recall the special danger of this kind of argument when dealing with "least harm" reforms. We should never use the constitutional right to vaginal foam as the basis for making any kind of judgment about the penal responsibility of 14–year olds.

Many adolescents are working or going to college or exercising their voting rights while they are in transition to full adulthood—while they are using their learner's permit. What sentence *is* appropriate for a 17–year-old burglar if his 25–year-old brother would receive one year in prison for the same offense? Equal treatment for wrong-doing seems inappropriate to the transitional status of the learner. Of course, no learning role is complete without, in some measure, learning responsibility for conduct. Thus, part of the initiation into the adult role is building toward adult responsibilities. Just as the learning theory of adolescence implies a transition toward adulthood, so too it also implies a progression toward adult levels of responsibility. The adolescent must be protected from the full burden of adult responsibilities, but pushed along by degrees toward the moral and legal accountability that we consider appropriate to adulthood.

————

Treating Adolescents as a Special Legal Category: The Case of Driving Privileges

Adolescence, as we have seen is a unique developmental stage between childhood and adulthood, but, with the possible exception of abortion doctrine, it is seldom given special treatment as an intermediate *legal* category. As Elizabeth Scott notes above, adolescents, for the most part are classified as legal minors and subject to the same treatment as young children; occasionally they are treated as legal adults. An exception to this use of binary categories is the approach that most states have adopted toward extending driving privileges to teenagers, one that is designed to expand the probationary period to allow young drivers to gain experience and maturity. Most states allow legal minors to drive motor vehicles at age 16 or 17, recognizing the benefits of mobility for both teenagers and their parents, but impose restrictions on teenage drivers that do not apply to adults. Under a system called Graduated Driver Licensing (GDL), lawmakers create special rules for young drivers through a system of multi-stage licensing. In the typical three-stage model, individuals can obtain a learner's permit, often at age 16, that allows them to learn to drive with an adult supervisor; adult supervision is required for some minimum number of hours (up to 60 hours in some states). Upon successfully completing the requirements of this stage and passing a driver's licensing examination, the teenage driver obtains an intermediate license that allows her to drive without supervision, but subject to some restrictions that do not apply to adults (even adults who have newly received licenses). Finally, the young driver can obtain full driving privileges after a period of time in the intermediate stage or, in some states, upon reaching age 18. The most common restrictions imposed on young drivers in the intermediate stage are prohibitions of night driving and limits on the number of non-adult passengers. Some states restrict the use of cell phones and mandate the use of seat belts only for teen age drivers. Insurance Institute of Highway Safety, *Licensing Systems for Young Drivers*, http://www.iihs.org/laws/laws/GraduatedLicenseIntro.aspx.

GDL systems are justified as a means of protecting other drivers and of protecting teenage drivers themselves. Teenage drivers tend to have high accident rates, due to inexperience and also due to their immature judgment. Policymakers reasonably conclude that teenagers are more likely to take risks or become distracted when they drive with friends in the car; hence the restriction on other passengers. Some research indicates that GDL systems have contributed to a reduction in accidents among teenage drivers, although some studies also suggest that cell phone bans have not been effective in deterring cell phone use. See *Licensing systems*, above. For a summary of state GDL laws, see http://www.iihs.org?law/pdf/us_licensing_dsystems.pdf.

CHILDREN'S RIGHTS AND SCHOOL AUTHORITY

A. INTRODUCTION

Outside of the family, the school is the most important institution that directly affects the lives of children. Further, because public school experience is such an important part of most children's lives, it indirectly affects their parents and limits their ability to influence and control their children's upbringing. Chapter III explores some of the conflicts that can arise between parents who are seeking to raise their children according to their values and religious beliefs, and public school authorities, whose concern is the education of all children. We saw that parents who seek to remove their children from school and teach them at home receive substantial accommodation, parents whose goal is to shape the school curriculum to conform to their own values are less successful.

The public school is also a setting in which children's rights have been defined. The first announcement by the Supreme Court that children are persons who are possessed of fundamental rights under the Constitution was *Tinker v. Des Moines Independent Community School District* (393 U.S. 503, 89 S.Ct. 733, 21 L.Ed.2d 731 (1969)). As you remember, *Tinker* described students' rights in very expansive terms. Indeed, the Court's pronouncement that students do not "shed their constitutional rights to speech or expression at the school house gate" has been the rallying cry of children's rights advocates, particularly in efforts to maximize the rights of public school students. In this chapter we will explore further the parameters of students' First Amendment rights. The issues are varied: the extent to which censorship of school-sponsored newspapers and theatrical productions by school officials is constitutionally permissible, the constitutional limits on students' right of political expression in the forum of student government, dress and hair codes as constraints on personal freedom, and the delicate relationship between students' right of religious expression and the constraints of the Establishment Clause on school policy. The Supreme Court also has sought to define the extent to which students enjoy other constitutional protections under the Fourth, Eighth, and Fourteenth Amendments, and how these rights are shaped by the school context.

In thinking about the issues in this Chapter, it may be useful to distinguish several factors that can affect the analysis, by asking the following questions. First, is the contested restriction on students' rights by state officials justified because the restriction is considered necessary in the educational setting or because the students are minors? This issue can be explored by asking two further questions. First, would the state be prohibited from imposing the same kind of restriction on minors outside of the context of the public school? For example, school officials may have far greater authority to supervise and censor a school newspaper than state agents would have outside of this context. Second, would the proposed restriction be unacceptable in the college setting, or in any educational context that did not involve minors? How much is the authority of school officials to restrict students linked to immaturity and vulnerability of public school students? Another question, which draws on the theme of earlier chapters, is what role parents play in defining the legal relationship between school authorities and students. Few students bring suit against school officials without the support of their parents. Does the parents' interest have any further importance?

B. THE FIRST AMENDMENT IN THE PUBLIC SCHOOL

1. FREE EXPRESSION

West Virginia State Bd. of Education v. Barnette

Supreme Court of the United States, 1943.
319 U.S. 624, 63 S.Ct. 1178, 87 L.Ed. 1628.

■ MR. JUSTICE JACKSON delivered the opinion of the Court.

. . .

The Board of Education on January 9, 1942, adopted a resolution containing recitals taken largely from the Court's [Minersville School District v.] Gobitis[, 310 U.S. 586] opinion and ordering that the salute to the flag become "a regular part of the program of activities in the public schools," that all teachers and pupils "shall be required to participate in the salute honoring the Nation represented by the Flag; provided, however, that refusal to salute the Flag be regarded as an Act of insubordination, and shall be dealt with accordingly."[2]

2. The text read in part:

WHEREAS, The West Virginia State Board of Education recognizes that the manifold character of man's relations may bring his conception of religious duty into conflict with the secular interests of his fellowman; . . . . that the mere possession of convictions which contradict the relevant concerns of political WHEREAS, The West Virginia State Board of Education holds that national unity is the basis of national security; that the flag of our Nation is the symbol of our National Unity transcending all internal differences, however large within the framework of the Constitution; . . . . that it signifies government resting on the consent of the governed, liberty regulated by law, protection of the weak against the strong, security against the exercise of arbitrary power, and

absolute safety for free institutions against foreign aggression, and

WHEREAS, The West Virginia State Board of Education maintains that the public schools, established by the legislature of the State of West Virginia under the authority of the Constitution of the State of West Virginia and supported by taxes imposed by legally constituted measures, are dealing with the formative period in the development in citizenship that the Flag is an allowable portion of the program of schools thus publicly supported.

Therefore, be it RESOLVED, That the West Virginia Board of Education does hereby recognize and order that the commonly accepted salute to the Flag of the United States. . . .

.... What is now required is the "stiff-arm" salute, the saluter to keep the right hand raised with palm turned up while the following is repeated: "I pledge allegiance to the Flag of the United States of America and to the Republic for which it stands; one Nation, indivisible, with liberty and justice for all."

Failure to conform is "insubordination" dealt with by expulsion. Readmission is denied by statute until compliance. Meanwhile the expelled child is "unlawfully absent" and may be proceeded against as a delinquent. His parents or guardians are liable to prosecution, and if convicted are subject to fine not exceeding $50 and jail term not exceeding thirty days.

Appellees, citizens of the United States and of West Virginia, brought suit in the United States District Court for themselves and others similarly situated asking its injunction to restrain enforcement of these laws and regulations against Jehovah's Witnesses.... Their religious beliefs include a literal version of Exodus, Chapter 20, verses 4 and 5, which says: "Thou shalt not make unto thee any graven image, or any likeness of anything that is in heaven above, or that is in the earth beneath, or that is in the water under the earth; thou shalt not bow down thyself to them nor serve them." They consider that the flag is an "image" within this command. For this reason they refuse to salute it.

Children of this faith have been expelled from school and are threatened with exclusion for no other cause. Officials threaten to send them to reformatories maintained for criminally inclined juveniles. Parents of such children have been prosecuted and are threatened with prosecutions for causing delinquency....

This case calls upon us to reconsider a precedent decision, as the Court throughout its history often has been required to do. Before turning to the *Gobitis* case, however, it is desirable to notice certain characteristics by which this controversy is distinguished.

The freedom asserted by these appellees does not bring them into collision with rights asserted by any other individual.... [T]he refusal of these persons to participate in the ceremony does not interfere with or deny rights of others to do so. Nor is there any question in this case that their behavior is peaceable and orderly. The sole conflict is between authority and rights of the individual. The State asserts power to condition access to public education on making a prescribed sign and profession and at the same time to coerce attendance by punishing both parent and child. The latter stand on a right of self-determination in matters that touch individual opinion and personal attitude.

As the present Chief Justice said in dissent in the *Gobitis* case, the State may "require teaching by instruction and study of all in our history and in the structure and organization of our government, including the guaranties of civil liberty which tend to inspire patriotism and love of country." 310 U.S. at page 604 ... Here, however, we are dealing with a compulsion of students to declare a belief. They are not merely made acquainted with the flag salute so that they may be informed as to what it is or even what it means. . . .

There is no doubt that, in connection with the pledges, the flag salute is a form of utterance. Symbolism is a primitive but effective way of communicating ideas. . . . Symbols of State often convey political ideas just as religious symbols come to convey theological ones. Associated with many of these symbols are appropriate gestures of acceptance or respect: a salute, a bowed or bared head, a bended knee. . . .

Over a decade ago Chief Justice Hughes led this Court in holding that the display of a red flag as a symbol of opposition by peaceful and legal means to organized government was protected by the free speech guaranties of the Constitution. [citation omitted] Here it is the State that employs a flag as a symbol of adherence to government as presently organized. It requires the individual to communicate by word and sign his acceptance of the political ideas it thus bespeaks. Objection to this form of communication when coerced is an old one, well known to the framers of the Bill of Rights.

It is also to be noted that the compulsory flag salute and pledge requires affirmation of a belief and an attitude of mind. . . . It is now a commonplace that censorship or suppression of expression of opinion is tolerated by our Constitution only when the expression presents a clear and present danger of action of a kind the State is empowered to prevent and punish. It would seem that involuntary affirmation could be commanded only on even more immediate and urgent grounds than silence. But here the power of compulsion is invoked without any allegation that remaining passive during a flag salute ritual creates a clear and present danger that would justify an effort even to muffle expression. To sustain the compulsory flag salute we are required to say that a Bill of Rights which guards the individual's right to speak his own mind, left it open to public authorities to compel him to utter what is not in his mind.

Whether the First Amendment to the Constitution will permit officials to order observance of ritual of this nature does not depend upon whether as a voluntary exercise we would think it to be good, bad or merely innocuous. . . .

Nor does the issue as we see it turn on one's possession of particular religious views or the sincerity with which they are held. . . . It is not necessary to inquire whether non-conformist beliefs will exempt from the duty to salute unless we first find power to make the salute a legal duty.

. . . The question which underlies the flag salute controversy is whether such a ceremony so touching matters of opinion and political attitude may be imposed upon the individual by official authority under powers committed to any political organization under our Constitution. We examine rather than assume existence of this power and, against this broader definition of issues in this case, re-examine specific grounds assigned for the *Gobitis* decision.

. . . It was said that the flag-salute controversy confronted the Court with "the problem which Lincoln cast in memorable dilemma: 'Must a government of necessity be too strong for the liberties of its people, or too

weak to maintain its own existence?' and that the answer must be in favor
of strength." Minersville School District v. Gobitis, supra, 310 U.S. at page
596.

We think these issues may be examined free of pressure or restraint
growing out of such considerations. . . .

Government of limited power need not be anemic government. Assurance that rights are secure tends to diminish fear and jealousy of strong
government, and by making us feel safe to live under it makes for its better
support. Without promise of a limiting Bill of Rights it is doubtful if our
Constitution could have mustered enough strength to enable its ratification. To enforce those rights today is not to choose weak government over
strong government. It is only to adhere as a means of strength to individual
freedom of mind in preference to officially disciplined uniformity for which
history indicates a disappointing and disastrous end.

The subject now before us exemplifies this principle. Free public
education, if faithful to the ideal of secular instruction and political
neutrality, will not be partisan or enemy of any class, creed, party, or
faction. If it is to impose any ideological discipline, however, each party or
denomination must seek to control, or failing that, to weaken the influence
of the educational system. Observance of the limitations of the Constitution
will not weaken government in the field appropriate for its exercise. . . .

The Fourteenth Amendment, as now applied to the States, protects the
citizen against the State itself and all of its creatures—Boards of Education
not excepted. These have, of course, important, delicate, and highly discretionary functions, but none that they may not perform within the limits of
the Bill of Rights. That they are educating the young for citizenship is
reason for scrupulous protection of Constitutional freedoms of the individual, if we are not to strangle the free mind at its source and teach youth to
discount important principles of our government as mere platitudes.

Such Boards are numerous and their territorial jurisdiction often
small. But small and local authority may feel less sense of responsibility to
the Constitution, and agencies of publicity may be less vigilant in calling it
to account. . . .

The *Gobitis* opinion reasoned that. . . . it is constitutionally appropriate
to "fight out the wise use of legislative authority in the forum of public
opinion and before legislative assemblies rather than to transfer such a
contest to the judicial arena," . . . 310 U.S. at page 597, 598, 600.

The very purpose of a Bill of Rights was to withdraw certain subjects
from the vicissitudes of political controversy, to place them beyond the
reach of majorities and officials and to establish them as legal principles to
be applied by the courts. One's right to life, liberty, and property, to free
speech, a free press, freedom of worship and assembly, and other fundamental rights may not be submitted to vote; they depend on the outcome of
no elections.

. . . [F]reedoms of speech and of press, of assembly, and of worship . . .
are susceptible of restriction only to prevent grave and immediate danger
to interests which the state may lawfully protect. . . .

Nor does our duty to apply the Bill of Rights to assertions of official authority depend upon our possession of marked competence in the field where the invasion of rights occurs.... We cannot, because of modest estimates of our competence in such specialties as public education, withhold the judgment that history authenticates as the function of this Court when liberty is infringed.

.... Lastly, ... *Gobitis* ... reasons that "National unity is the basis of national security," that the authorities have "the right to select appropriate means for its attainment," and hence reaches the conclusion that such compulsory measures toward "national unity" are constitutional. Id., 310 U.S. at page 595 ... Upon the verity of this assumption depends our answer in this case.

National unity as an end which officials may foster by persuasion and example is not in question. The problem is whether under our Constitution compulsion as here employed is a permissible means for its achievement.

Struggles to coerce uniformity of sentiment in support of some end thought essential to their time and country have been waged by many good as well as by evil men. Nationalism is a relatively recent phenomenon but at other times and places the ends have been racial or territorial security, support of a dynasty or regime, and particular plans for saving souls. As first and moderate methods to attain unity have failed, those bent on its accomplishment must resort to an ever-increasing severity.... Probably no deeper division of our people could proceed from any provocation than from finding it necessary to choose what doctrine and whose program public educational officials shall compel youth to unite in embracing. Ultimate futility of such attempts to compel coherence is the lesson of every such effort from the Roman drive to stamp out Christianity...., the Inquisition,.... down to the fast failing efforts of our present totalitarian enemies. Those who begin coercive elimination of dissent soon find themselves exterminating dissenters....

It seems trite but necessary to say that the First Amendment to our Constitution was designed to avoid these ends by avoiding these beginnings.... We set up government by consent of the governed, and the Bill of Rights denies those in power any legal opportunity to coerce that consent. Authority here is to be controlled by public opinion, not public opinion by authority.

... [W]e apply the limitations of the Constitution with no fear that freedom to be intellectually and spiritually diverse or even contrary will disintegrate the social organization. To believe that patriotism will not flourish if patriotic ceremonies are voluntary and spontaneous instead of a compulsory routine is to make an unflattering estimate of the appeal of our institutions to free minds. We can have intellectual individualism and the rich cultural diversities that we owe to exceptional minds only at the price of occasional eccentricity and abnormal attitudes. When they are so harmless to others or to the State as those we deal with here, the price is not too great. But freedom to differ is not limited to things that do not matter much. That would be a mere shadow of freedom. The test of its substance is the right to differ as to things that touch the heart of the existing order.

If there is any fixed star in our constitutional constellation, it is that no official, high or petty, can prescribe what shall be orthodox in politics, nationalism, religion, or other matters of opinion or force citizens to confess by word or act their faith therein. If there are any circumstances which permit an exception, they do not now occur to us.

We think the action of the local authorities in compelling the flag salute and pledge transcends constitutional limitations on their power and invades the sphere of intellect and spirit which it is the purpose of the First Amendment to our Constitution to reserve from all official control.

The decision of this Court in Minersville School District v. Gobitis and the holdings of those few per curiam decisions which preceded and foreshadowed it are overruled, and the judgment enjoining enforcement of the West Virginia Regulation is affirmed.

■ [Mr. Justice Roberts and Mr. Justice Reed dissented on the basis of Gobitis. The concurring opinion of Mr. Justice Black and Mr. Justice Douglas, and the concurring opinion of Mr. Justice Murphy are omitted.]

■ MR. JUSTICE FRANKFURTER, dissenting.

.... In the light of all the circumstances, including the history of this question in this Court, it would require more daring than I possess to deny that reasonable legislators could have taken the action which is before us for review. Most unwillingly, therefore, I must differ from my brethren with regard to legislation like this. I cannot bring my mind to believe that the "liberty" secured by the Due Process Clause gives this Court authority to deny to the State of West Virginia the attainment of that which we all recognize as a legitimate legislative end, namely, the promotion of good citizenship, by employment of the means here chosen....

Parents have the privilege of choosing which schools they wish their children to attend. And the question here is whether the state may make certain requirements that seem to it desirable or important for the proper education of those future citizens who go to schools maintained by the states, or whether the pupils in those schools may be relieved from those requirements if they run counter to the consciences of their parents. Not only have parents the right to send children to schools of their own choosing but the state has no right to bring such schools "under a strict governmental control" or give "affirmative direction concerning the intimate and essential details of such schools, intrust their control to public officers, and deny both owners and patrons reasonable choice and discretion in respect of teachers, curriculum and textbooks." [citation omitted]. Why should not the state likewise have constitutional power to make reasonable provisions for the proper instruction of children in schools maintained by it?....

Tinker v. Des Moines Independent Community School District

Supreme Court of the United States, 1969.
393 U.S. 503, 89 S.Ct. 733, 21 L.Ed.2d 731.

[The opinion of the Court is reproduced at p. 155 supra.]

NOTES ON FREE EXPRESSION IN SCHOOLS

(1) **The First Amendment in Schools—From Restricting State Authority to Protecting Individual Rights.** In 1943, when *Barnette*, was decided, courts did not talk about school children as rights-bearing individuals; indeed, that notion likely would have seemed strange. The "children's rights" movement was a quarter century in the future. Indeed, Justice Fortas' pronouncement in Tinker that "children do not leave their rights at the school house door" became a mantra of children's rights advocates, and is often cited as the Court's first explicit recognition that children have a right of free expression protected by the First Amendment. Notice that Justice Jackson's emphasis in *Barnette* is not on the rights held by the children, but rather on the coercive nature of the mandatory flag salute policy. Justice Jackson saw the state's effort to coerce political expression as a serious threat to the core values on which our country was founded.

> Struggles to coerce uniformity of sentiment in support of some end thought essential to their time and country have been waged by many good as well as by evil men.... As first and moderate methods to attain unity have failed, those bent on its accomplishment must resort to an ever-increasing severity.... Those who begin coercive elimination of dissent soon find themselves exterminating dissenters....

> It seems trite but necessary to say that the First Amendment to our Constitution was designed to avoid these ends by avoiding these beginnings....

Justice Fortas in *Tinker* focuses on students in school as individuals with First Amendment rights. It should be recognized, however, that *Tinker* is somewhat misleading as a basis for understanding the relationship between students as holders of legal and constitutional rights and school officials exercising authority to pursue educational goals. One might take from *Tinker* the lesson that school officials are quite restricted in their ability to discipline, instruct, and maintain order if constitutionally protected interests are implicated. This is certainly not an accurate account of the developments in constitutional and legal doctrine in the generation since *Tinker*, as we will see below. Today, it is clear that the Constitution imposes limits on the authority of public school officials, but that they are given considerable latitude to pursue the goals of education in light of the exigencies of the public school context. This probably should not be surprising. As Chapter II reveals, children generally are accorded rights and privileges to a more limited extent than adults. It would be curious if this were not true in the school setting as well. Moreover, the educational focus, and the fact that school officials are charged with responsibility for large numbers of minors, may justify giving these officials authority to create additional restraints on the freedom of students. Even the *Tinker* opinion recognizes—in passing—the need to maintain school authority.

Note that the conflicts between individual rights and state authority that arose in both *Tinker* and *Barnette* occurred during periods when the United States was engaged in armed conflict abroad—the Vietnam war and the Second World War respectively. In both instances, the official policy constraining free expression is directed toward discouraging dissident views (or reinforcing patriotic support of the government). Are political rights particularly vulnerable during such periods?

Also notice that the Supreme Court in *Barnette*, like the *Tinker* court, emphasized that the students were peaceable and orderly in their behavior. In refusing to salute the flag, they did not interfere with the assertion of rights by any other person. In later opinions, as we will see, the potential for speech to disrupt education or interfere with other students has often been cited as a basis for restricting speech.

(2) **Censorship of Library Books and Internet Access.** *Tinker* represents the high water mark for the Supreme Court's recognition of First Amendment rights. Although the Court occasionally, in the years since *Tinker*, has found decisions by school officials to be unduly restrictive of students' First Amendment right of free expression, even those opinions signal a reluctance to interpret students' rights expansively. For example, in *Board of Education v. Pico*, 457 U.S. 853, 102 S.Ct. 2799, 73 L.Ed.2d 435 (1982), the Court accepted the claim that the school board's decision to remove certain books from the library was a First Amendment violation. The board ordered several books removed from the shelves of the junior and senior high school libraries, justifying its action on the ground that the books were "anti-American, anti-Christian, anti-Semitic, and just plain filthy." The books included Eldridge Cleaver's Soul on Ice, Kurt Vonnegut's Slaughterhouse Five, and Richard Wright's Black Boy. A three-justice plurality of the Court disallowed the removal action on the ground that students "have a right to receive information and ideas." The opinion quoted *Tinker* freely and emphasized the importance of free access to ideas, access that the school board was seeking to suppress. The plurality acknowledged, however, the school board's authority to remove books that were vulgar or that lacked "educational suitability." More importantly, the opinion recognized the school board's "absolute discretion" in curricular matters, suggesting that great deference would be accorded to any decision relating to curriculum. It was very important to the Court that the books in question were not textbooks or required reading. The library is outside of the "compulsory environment of the classroom," and thus arbitrary or suppressive restrictions receive less deference. As the Court would soon clarify in *Hazelwood School District v. Kuhlmeier* (page 284 infra), school officials have broad latitude to restrict speech when the restriction is linked to a curricular objective.

The school board in *Pico* sought to remove books from the library that it deemed objectionable. Suppose that, instead, it gave the librarian a list of books not to purchase. Would this violate students' free expression rights? The plurality in *Pico* suggests that this is quite a different issue from that which it confronted. How so? What if the librarian herself simply had very conservative views, and chose not to acquire controversial volumes?

Regulation of students' access to the Internet is an issue that has emerged in recent years. In the late 1990s, Congress enacted the Children's Internet Protection Act (CIPA) which requires schools and public libraries to install software that blocks or filters Internet access to material that constitutes obscenity or child pornography, or that is harmful to children, as a condition to receiving federal funds or grants. Although the statute's application to schools was relatively uncontroversial, in public libraries, the filtering software restricted Internet access for adults as well as minors. The Supreme Court upheld the statute against a First Amendment challenge in *United States v. American Library Association*, 539 U.S. 194, 123 S.Ct. 2297, 156 L.Ed.2d 221 (2003). The opinion is summarized at p. 152.

(3) **Interpreting *Tinker*.** Lower courts have been conservative in applying *Tinker*, often emphasizing the importance of school officials' authority to maintain order and discipline. Student protests that involve any significant amount of noise or disruption (sit-ins) are routinely struck down. When pure speech is involved, however, students have often been successful in asserting their rights, unless the speech threatens violence or disruption. For example, students wearing "scab" buttons in support of a teachers' strike were found to be engaging in protected speech. *Chandler v. McMinnville School Dist.*, 978 F.2d 524 (9th Cir.1992). However, some courts have allowed school officials to regulate protected speech, simply on the ground that it is offensive. In *In the Interest of Douglas D.*, an eighth grade boy wrote a story for a creative writing assignment about the murder of his English teacher (who had just disciplined the boy). 243 Wis.2d 204, 626 N.W.2d 725 (2001)

The story was found to be protected First Amendment speech which could not be the basis of a disorderly conduct conviction, because, under the circumstances, the story did not represent a "true threat." However, because of the crass insulting nature of the story, the Court held that the *school* had sufficient reason to discipline the boy for its content. The Court emphasized that under *Tinker*, the "First Amendment does not require teachers, parents, and elected school officials to surrender control of the American public school system to public school students." *Id. at* 743.

During the 2003 Iraq war, public school children demonstrated both for and against the war in larger numbers. In contrast to the few students from a single family protesting the war in Tinker, in some schools, over half of the student body was involved in protests. "Students Stage Walkouts to Protest Fighting; Few Face Consequences After Negotiating Terms with School Officials," Linda Perlstein, *Washington Post*, March 21, 2003, 2003 WL 15467578. School officials varied in their responses to student protests, including organizing pre-emptive class discussions on the war topic, barring the exits of schools to students trying to leave, posting security guards to dissuade students from leaving, and threatening 25 day suspensions for students threatening to protest. Some students were disciplined for distributing fliers advertising a proposed student strike. "Students join peace walkout; Academic trouble risked by many," Courtney Flynn, *Chicago Tribune*, March 6, 2003, 2003 WL 14861689. One student was sent home by school officials for wearing a T-shirt with a picture of President Bush over the caption "International Terrorist." "Extracurricular Activity on the March; All Over USA and by the Thousands, Teens Gather in Protest." Greg Toppo, *USA Today*, March 25, 2003, 2003 WL 5307730. Was this "pure, passive speech" like the armbands in Tinker? Were any or all of the reactions by administrators permissible ways for schools to deal with these students? Does your answer depend on whether they sought to restrain students' actions prior to the protests or instead chose to punish students after they participated? What type of disruption would justify the school actions? Would students leaving classes early en masse be a sufficient disruption to allow punishment or prior restraint? Does the fact that students broke an attendance law make the choice to discipline students in some way deserving of deference generally given to schools? What if officials only punished anti-war protesters who walked out but not those who walked out in support of the war?

Guiles ex rel. Guiles v. Marineau, 461 F.3d 320 (2d Cir.2006), involved a student who wore an anti-war T-shirt describing President George W. Bush as "Chicken–Hawk-in-Chief." The shirt also showed an image of the President and three lines of cocaine, a razorblade, and a martini glass with an olive inside. Citing *Tinker*, the court affirmed the student's right to wear the shirt, despite its illegal drug content. In *Morse v. Frederick*, infra at p. 276, the Supreme Court underscores the broad authority of school officials to discourage illegal drug use. Would the analysis in *Marineau* be different after *Morse*?

(4) **Hair, Dress and Conduct Codes**. At the time *Tinker* was decided, many observers predicted that it would create a major burden on the ability of school officials to maintain order and discipline in public schools (despite the Court's statement quoted above). Would the next step be limits on teachers' authority to decide the subject matter of classroom discussions? The abolition of all regulation of dress and appearance?

Among the predictions made in the wake of *Tinker* was that school officials would be unable to enact regulations dictating limits on students' freedom to express themselves through dress and hair style. A flurry of litigation followed *Tinker*, challenging dress and (particularly) hair codes on various constitutional grounds, including the First, Eighth and Fourteenth Amendments. A primary target of concern was the length of male students' hair—an issue that generated a passion in the late 1960s and 1970s that is hard to understand today. Long hair was taken to be a political statement of disaffection with government policies in Vietnam, or more generally with mainstream societal norms. Thus, some courts took seriously students' First Amendment objections, and were sympathetic to the claim that hair and dress codes served no educational purpose and did little to promote discipline. Some of the arguments offered by school officials to justify the restrictions were unsupported by factual evidence. For example, see *Holsapple v. Woods*, 500 F.2d 49 (7th Cir.1974) (Boys with long hair were rowdy or performed poorly academically). Others were close to ludicrous. See *Copeland v. Hawkins*, 352 F.Supp. 1022 (E.D.Ill.1973) (Long hair on boys made restroom supervision difficult since boys and girls could not be readily distinguished).

Many courts (including five federal circuit courts) have rejected the students' claims, holding that hair style regulations are a legitimate exercise of school authority. The Supreme Court declined to consider the issue, despite the sharp split among the federal circuit courts. This might be taken to signal that the Court was not inclined to extend the concept of students as rights-bearers announced in *Tinker* into new areas. For a scholarly review, see Larry D. Bartlett, Hair and Dress Codes Revisited, 33 Educ.L.Rep. 7 (1986).

However, regulation of student dress and conduct has proved more complicated as the following discussion suggests.

   a. School Uniform Requirements. In the past decade, there has been a trend among the nation's public school districts toward increased dress code regulations as well as mandatory uniform policies. The trend toward mandatory uniform policies began in 1994 when Long Beach, California became the first school district in the country to implement such a policy. In subsequent years, other school districts in large cities like Miami, Cleveland, and Chicago also implemented mandatory uniform. As of 2001, at least 20 states authorize school districts to establish "dress code" policies while 21 states and the District of Columbia authorize districts or schools to require school uniforms.[1] In his 1997 State of the Union address, President Clinton explained his plan for education reform and called upon the nation to continue promoting order and discipline in schools as well as "supporting communities that introduce school uniforms."[2] He also "directed the Federal Department of Education to distribute information to the nation's 16,000 school districts advising them on how to create and enforce such policies."[3]

   In February of 1998, the president of New York City's Board of Education proposed a plan requiring the city's 550,000 elementary school students (in 670 schools) to wear uniforms. New York City's mandatory uniform policy allowed parents and school boards to opt out for specified reasons, and proposed providing financial aid to qualifying families. Specifically left out of the policy's reach were older students who were expected to resist wearing uniforms. Although there is no independent study linking uniforms to improved academic performance, "Proponents argue that uniforms can instill a sense of pride and discipline, save parents money and spare students the distraction and potential danger of competition over clothing."[4] Critics of the policy believed that the school board should pursue more

1. *See* http://www.ecs.org/clearinghouse/27/09/2709.htm (last visited June 23, 2008).

2. http://www.washingtonpost.com/wp-srv/politics/special/states/docs/sou97.htm (last visited Nov. 28, 2007).

3. Abby Goodnough, *Crew Supports Having Pupils Wear Uniforms*, N.Y. Times, Mar. 9, 1997, § 1, at 36.

4. William L. Hamilton, *Cracking the Dress Code; How a School Uniform Becomes a Fashion Statement*, N.Y. Times, Feb. 19, 1998, at B1.

pressing matters like improvement of school buildings and updating textbooks, while others believed the policy would stifle the individuality and creativity of the city's schoolchildren. By 2000, 75% of New York City's public elementary schools chose not to opt out, but instead followed the district's mandatory uniform policy.[5]

However, during this same period of time, a great number of schools across the nation have abandoned their mandatory uniform policies. One practical problem with mandatory uniform policies is enforcement, which many school officials saw as a continuing distraction. While the nation saw safety as the most legitimate goal of dress and uniform codes, many observers thought that the recent uniform codes were merely attempts "to rein in what schools [saw] as rampant sexualization of teenagers."[6] Ultimately, however, the primary reason for the recent retreat from uniform policies was that public school officials "found it too hard to get parents to go along."[7] Parents ultimately had the authority to allow or prevent their children from coming to school out of uniform.

Courts have generally upheld School uniform requirements against claims that such restrictions violate students' Free Expression and parental rights. In *Canady v. Bossier Parish School Board*, 240 F.3d 437 (5th Cir.2001) parents appealed the district court's holding that the enforcement of the school's mandatory uniform policy did not violate their children's First Amendment rights. The Court of Appeals stated, "While a person's choice of clothing may be predicated solely on considerations of style and comfort, an individual's choice of attire also may be endowed with sufficient levels of intentional expression to elicit First Amendment shelter." Id. at 440. The Court of Appeals ultimately assumed for the purpose of its decision that the First Amendment applied to the students' choice of clothing, but it noted that children's constitutional protection is not absolute and, further, "School boards, not federal courts, have the authority to decide what constitutes appropriate behavior and dress in public schools." Id. at 441.

The Court of Appeals stated, "The School Board's uniform policy will pass constitutional scrutiny if it furthers an important or substantial government interest; if the interest is unrelated to the suppression of student expression; and if the incidental restrictions on First Amendment activities are no more than is necessary to facilitate that interest." Id. At 443. It found that the uniform policy was enacted "to increase test scores and reduce disciplinary problems throughout the school system," Id. which "is in no way related to the suppression of student speech," and again reiterated that it is up to the school board and "not the job of federal courts to determine the most effective way to educate our nation's youth." Id. The court continued,

Although students are restricted from wearing clothing of their choice at school students remain free to wear what they want after school hours. Students may still express their views through other mediums during the school day. The uniform requirement does not bar the important "personal intercommunication among students" necessary to an effective educational process. Id. at 443.

The court rejected the parents' final contention that the uniform policy creates an unacceptable financial burden. It stated, "Because uniforms are available at inexpensive retail stores, it is hard to imagine how the purchase of uniforms consisting of a certain color of shirt and pants could be any more expensive than the normal cost of a student's school clothes." Id. at 444.

5. *See* Joseph P. Fried, *Hemlines Are Down but Business Is Up*, N.Y. Times, Aug. 29, 2000, at B7; *See* Kate Zernike, *Plaid's Out, Again, As Schools Give Up Requiring Uniforms*, N.Y. Times Sept. 13, 2002, at A1.

6. Kate Zernike, *School Dress Codes vs. a Sea of Bare Flesh*, N.Y. Times, Sept. 11, 2001, at A3.

7. *Id.*

Although the court accepted that students in fact express themselves through their clothing, it seems to retreat from this by upholding the school's mandatory uniform policy. Do you agree with the court's conclusion that the availability of "other mediums" for student expression is sufficient to permit the elimination of their ability to express themselves through their clothing? How far could such reasoning be taken? Further, was the court's assessment of the ease with which parents may purchase uniforms for their children accurate or presumptuous?

b.   Regulation of Speech to Deter Violence and Maintain Order. A number of school systems have enacted "dress" code regulations that are designed to deter conflict and violence. For example, the wearing of identifying clothing or insignia in school can be a means of announcing gang membership to fellow gang members and other students. Urban schools have often prohibited students from wearing gang attire and regalia on the grounds that they can contribute to violence in school, or, at a minimum, distract from learning and undermine discipline. Modern courts have tended to uphold this type of prohibition, as a legitimate exercise of school authority, against First Amendment challenges.

In *Olesen v. Board of Education*, 676 F.Supp. 820 (N.D.Ill.1987), the court upheld a school rule prohibiting male students from wearing gang symbols, a rule that school officials applied to Oleson's earring, which had a gang cross attached. The Court rejected Oleson's Equal Protection argument that only males were prohibited from wearing earrings, as well as his First Amendment free expression claim. The Court concluded that the student's only message was one of expressing his "individuality" and that such a message was "not within the protected scope of the First Amendment." Moreover, the Court was persuaded that the school board had based the rule on a legitimate policy of discouraging gang activity, a policy related to protecting the safety of students.

General regulations that are not targeted narrowly at violence-prevention have fared less well when challenged on First Amendment grounds, particularly where courts are concerned about viewpoint discrimination (which is not a concern with uniforms). A Federal Appellate court struck down as overbroad a middle school dress code that prohibited "messages on clothing, jewelry and personal belongings that relate to drugs, alcohol, tobacco, weapons, violence, sex ... or reflect adversely upon persons because of their race or ethnic group." *Newsom v. Albemarle Co. School Bd.*, 354 F.3d 249 (4th Cir.2003). A youth who wore several National Rifle Association T-shirts, including one depicting a sharpshooter and advertising a shooting camp, challenged the dress code. The court analyzed the case within the *Tinker* framework and concluded that the dress code was overbroad in that it reached too much expression protected by the First Amendment. First, the court noted that no evidence was presented indicating that clothing worn by students containing messages related to weapons ever disrupted school activities or interfered with the rights of others. Moreover, the code could be understood as reaching nonviolent, nonthreatening legitimate messages about important organizations, causes and ideals. [For example, the court noted that both the seal of Virginia and depictions of the mascot of the University of Virginia depicted weapons.] The code could also be interpreted to allow peace signs but not messages urging support of troops [in the Iraq war], if accompanied by a weapon.

Similarly, the court in *Grzywna ex rel. Doe v. Schenectady Central School Dist.*, 489 F.Supp.2d 139 (N.D.N.Y.2006), upheld, against a motion to dismiss, a student's right to wear a red, white, and blue beaded necklace in support of American troops, despite school administrators' claims that it could be considered gang related and in violation of school policy.

Some courts, however, have upheld dress regulation that comes close to viewpoint discrimination. For example, an Ohio high school student sued the school district after being told by school officials that he could not come to school wearing T-shirts promoting the goth rocker Marilyn Manson. *Boroff v. Van Wert City Bd. Of Education*, 220 F.3d 465 (6th Cir.2000), cert. denied, 532 U.S. 920, 121 S.Ct. 1355, 149 L.Ed.2d 286 (2001). One offending shirt, advertising the band's album, Anti–Christ Superstar, depicted a three-faced Jesus, with the words "See No Truth; Hear No Truth; Speak No Truth." The school system argued that the T-shirt was offensive because "mocking any religious figure is contrary to our educational mission, which is to be respectful of others and others' beliefs." The court accepted that the Marilyn Manson T-shirts were prohibited because "this particular rock group promotes disruptive and demoralizing values which are inconsistent with and counter-productive to education." The T-shirts were "vulgar, offensive and contrary to the educational mission of the school." The court found no evidence that the T-shirts were "perceived to express any political or religious viewpoint." A dissenting judge disagreed. "It appears unmistakable that the reason why the three-headed Jesus T-shirt was deemed 'offensive' was because it said something about a venerated religious figure, and because many people in Van Wert (presumably including Principal Clifton) . . . disagree vehemently with what they perceive the T-shirt as saying."

Contrast *Boroff* with *Nixon v. Northern Local School Dist. Bd. of Educ.*, 383 F.Supp.2d 965 (S.D.Ohio 2005), in which a student wore a T-shirt with a Christian Bible verse on the front and the following statements on the back: "Homosexuality is a sin! Islam is a lie! Abortion is murder! Some issues are just black and white!". The *Nixon* court found that the shirt's message was not communicated in a plainly offensive manner. The court distinguished *Boroff* because, unlike the student's Christian shirt, the Marilyn Manson shirt promoted suicide, drugs, and murder, values that were inconsistent with the schools' message. Instead, the court found the shirt to be protected speech under *Tinker* because it did not pose a reasonable likelihood of material disruption.

Moreover, courts tend to reject objections to dress codes that are based on taste and not on a desire to communicate a message. On this ground, a recent federal appellate court rejected a challenge by a student and her father that the school district's rather strict dress code violated their First Amendment rights. *Blau v. Fort Thomas Public School District,* 401 F.3d 381 (6th Cir.2005). The code, while not requiring a uniform, restricted students to wearing solid colors (pants limited to navy, black, khaki or white) and prohibited hats, jeans, sweatpants, baggy or form fitting pants and tops, and tops with writing or logos larger than a quarter. The district justified the code as contributing to "a safe and positive learning environment". School officials stated that they believed it would promote school safety, improve the learning environment, reduce discipline problems and reduce socio-economic differences between families. The student and her father objected to the code on the ground that it interfered with her desire to wear clothes that "look nice" on her and that she "feels good in," but did not claim that she desired to convey "any particular message" with her clothes.

The court held that "the First Amendment does not protect such vague and attenuated notions of expression—namely self-expression through any and all clothing that a 12 year old may wish to wear on a given day." At a minimum, for expression to come within the protection of the First Amendment, according to the court, the "claimant must show that the desired conduct (*e.g.* the desired clothing) can fairly be described as 'imbued with the element of communication' which 'convey[s] a particularized message' that will be 'understood by those who view it.' " *Id.* at 390.

A California court relied on *Tinker* and distinguished *Blau* in holding that a middle school dress policy violated students' First Amendment rights. *Scott v. Napa*

Valley Unified School Dist., Superior Ct., Napa Co., Case No: 26–37082 (July 2007). The policy was similar to that upheld in *Blau* in requiring plain clothing without logos or pictures. Student plaintiffs had been disciplined for wearing, among other things, American Cancer Society pink ribbons supporting breast cancer survivors, a t-shirt reading "Jesus Freak," a T-shirt with the words "D.A.R.E. to resist drugs," and socks depicting Tigger from Winnie the Pooh. The court found that some of the prohibited clothing did convey a "particularized message," and that, under *Tinker*, the burden was on the school district to justify the restrictions. The court rejected the district's claim that the code was justified as a means of identifying outsiders who didn't belong in the school.

c. Regulation of Speech to Reduce Racial Conflict. School policies that are designed to reduce racial conflict through restrictions on certain kinds of speech have been examined often by courts in recent years. Often dress codes prohibiting messages that reflect adversely on any racial or ethnic group are part of larger racial harassment codes. In evaluating these restrictions, when they are challenged by students, courts look to whether the policy is justified on the basis of a history of racial tensions in the school and whether the racial message at issue was likely to disrupt school operations. For example, in a case involving two boys suspended from a Kentucky high school for wearing T-shirts depicting the Confederate flag, the court found that the flag represented speech protected by the First Amendment, and directed that the case be remanded to determine whether the school had a history of racial conflict and disruption that would justify the restriction of racially divisive messages. *Castorina v. Madison Co. School Bd.*, 246 F.3d 536 (6th Cir. 2001). Courts also examine racial harassment policies for overbreadth. For example, one court upheld the school district's racial harassment policy, but concluded that the prohibition of written material that "creates ill will" would prohibit protected speech, in that it was not limited to speech that would lead to conflict. [For example, criticism of affirmative action might create ill will.] *Sypniewski v. Warren Hills Regional Bd. of Education*, 307 F.3d 243 (3d Cir.2002).

Where the school system can show a history of student racial tension and conflict and demonstrate even-handed application of the racial harassment policy, courts have upheld suspensions of students displaying (or drawing) racially divisive symbols. One court upheld the suspension of a student for drawing the Confederate flag, pointing to a history of racial fights over the flag in the district's schools, together with evidence that the school system applied the policy against racially divisive messages without viewpoint discrimination. *West v. Derby Unified School Dist. No. 260,* 206 F.3d 1358 (10th Cir.2000). The court concluded that a regulation prohibiting racial harassment by name-calling may be unconstitutional in the absence of racial tension, but upheld as a legitimate exercise of school authority where such tensions exist. This suggests, of course, that a legitimate policy may *become* an unconstitutional restriction of student speech if racial tensions subside.

Some students have challenged regulations that restrict only speech relating to racial themes, as involving prohibited content-discrimination. The argument is based on *R.A.V. v. City of St. Paul*, 505 U.S. 377, 112 S.Ct. 2538, 120 L.Ed.2d 305 (1992), in which the Supreme Court struck down an ordinance that prohibited fighting words that "arouse ... anger, alarm or resentment in others on the basis of race, color...." 505 U.S.at 382. In rejecting the application of *R.A.V.* to public schools, courts emphasize the importance of the school context and the limited scope of students' rights under *Tinker*. Because of the authority of school officials to regulate conduct that causes disruption of the educational process or undermines the school's educational mission, a focus on racial expression, although it is clearly content-discrimination, may be justified. As one court put it, "When a school has identified a class of speech that, because of its content, is subject to a well-founded fear of conflict, it should be allowed to prescribe clear rules that students are capable of following to the degree necessary to maintain order." *Sypniewski* at 266.

For an interesting discussion of the differing perspectives regarding dress codes and commentary on related forms of school regulation of student speech, see Todd A. DeMitchell, Richard Fossey & Casey Cobb, Dress Codes in the Public Schools: Principals, Policies, and Precepts, 29 J.L. & Educ. 31 (2000), Clay Weisenberger, Constitution or Conformity: When the Shirt Hits the Fan in Public Schools, 29 J.L. & Educ. 51 (2000), Karen A. Haase, School Regulation of Exotic Body Piercing, 79 Neb.L.Rev. 976 (2000), Ann Kordas, Losing My Religion: Controlling Gang Violence Through Limitations on Freedom of Expression, 80 B.U. L.Rev. 1451 (2000).

(5) **Fraternities and Sororities.** Another area in which school officials have asserted authority to regulate the private behavior of students involves membership in sororities and fraternities, an activity that implicates the right of association, which, like the right of free expression, is protected under the First Amendment. High school fraternal organizations have received increased criticism in recent years, as public attention has focused on incidents of violent hazing among high school students. A number of states have prohibited fraternities, sororities and secret societies in public high schools describing such organizations as "unlawful,"[8] and "inimical" to the "public good"[9] and "the democratic principles and ideals of public education."[10] One state makes membership to "fraternities, sororities, secret societies, and gangs" a misdemeanor.[11] Other states leave the prohibition to the district school boards.[12] Courts that have considered this issue have upheld the restrictions as not violative of student rights.[13] Can these opinions be reconciled with *Tinker*? If you were representing a school board facing a challenge by a group of students seeking to establish a fraternity, what arguments would you make to justify the restriction?

At the university level, early cases affirmed the authority of public colleges and universities to regulate (and prohibit) fraternities and sororities in pursuit of educational goals. Since the ratification of the Twenty–Sixth Amendment, lowering the voting age to 18 (and effectively transforming college students into legal adults (See page 131 et seq.)), courts have given greater recognition to college students' right of association, and generally have been hostile to efforts of public universities efforts to restrict students' right of free association. (*IOTA XI Chapter v. George Mason University*, 993 F.2d 386 (4th Cir.1993)). Why should a change in the right to vote have any relevance to this issue?

Bethel School Dist. No. 403 v. Fraser

Supreme Court of the United States, 1986.
478 U.S. 675, 106 S.Ct. 3159, 92 L.Ed.2d 549.

■ CHIEF JUSTICE BURGER delivered the opinion of the Court.

We granted certiorari to decide whether the First Amendment prevents a school district from disciplining a high school student for giving a lewd speech at a school assembly. . . .

8. *E.g.* Mississippi, Miss. Code Ann. § 37–11–41 (2002); Arkansas, Ark. Code Ann. § 6–18–603 (2002).

9. *E.g.* Illinois, 105 Ill. Comp. Stat. Ann. 5/31–2 (2003); Michigan, Mich. Comp. Laws Ann. § 380.1316 (2002).

10. *E.g.* New Jersey, N.J. Stat. Ann. § 18A:42–5 (2002).

11. *E.g.* Texas, Tex. Educ. Code Ann. § 37.121 (2001).

12. *E.g.* Missouri, Mo. Ann. Stat. § 171.141 (2002); Rhode Island, R.I. Gen. Laws § 16–38–4 (2002); Oregon, Or. Rev. Stat. § 339.885 (2001).

13. *Passel v. Fort Worth Independent School District*, 453 S.W.2d 888 (Tex.Civ.App. 1970).

On April 26, 1983, respondent Matthew N. Fraser, a student at Bethel High School in Bethel, Washington, delivered a speech nominating a fellow student for student elective office. Approximately 600 high school students, many of whom were 14–year-olds, attended the assembly. Students were required to attend the assembly or to report to the study hall. The assembly was part of a school-sponsored educational program in self-government. Students who elected not to attend the assembly were required to report to study hall. During the entire speech, Fraser referred to his candidate in terms of an elaborate, graphic, and explicit sexual metaphor.

Two of Fraser's teachers, with whom he discussed the contents of his speech in advance, informed him that the speech was "inappropriate and that he probably should not deliver it," and that his delivery of the speech might have "severe consequences."

During Fraser's delivery of the speech, a school counselor observed the reaction of students to the speech. Some students hooted and yelled; some by gestures graphically simulated the sexual activities pointedly alluded to in respondent's speech. Other students appeared to be bewildered and embarrassed by the speech. One teacher reported that on the day following the speech, she found it necessary to forgo a portion of the scheduled class lesson in order to discuss the speech with the class.

A Bethel High School disciplinary rule prohibiting the use of obscene language in the school provides:

> "Conduct which materially and substantially interferes with the educational process is prohibited, including the use of obscene, profane language or gestures."

The morning after the assembly, the Assistant Principal called Fraser into her office and notified him that the school considered his speech to have been a violation of this rule. Fraser was presented with copies of five letters submitted by teachers, describing his conduct at the assembly; he was given a chance to explain his conduct, and he admitted to having given the speech described and that he deliberately used sexual innuendo in the speech. Fraser was then informed that he would be suspended for three days, and that his name would be removed from the list of candidates for graduation speaker at the school's commencement exercises.

Fraser sought review of this disciplinary action through the School District's grievance procedures. The hearing officer determined that the speech given by respondent was "indecent, lewd, and offensive to the modesty and decency of many of the students and faculty in attendance at the assembly." The examiner determined that the speech fell within the ordinary meaning of "obscene," as used in the disruptive-conduct rule, and affirmed the discipline in its entirety. Fraser served two days of his suspension, and was allowed to return to school on the third day.

The Court of Appeals for the Ninth Circuit affirmed the judgment of the District Court, 755 F.2d 1356 (1985), holding that respondent's speech was indistinguishable from the protest armband in *Tinker v. Des Moines Independent Community School Dist.* The court explicitly rejected the School District's argument that the speech, unlike the passive conduct of wearing a black armband, had a disruptive effect on the educational process. The Court of Appeals also rejected the School District's argument that it had an interest in protecting an essentially captive audience of minors from lewd and indecent language in a setting sponsored by the school, reasoning that the school board's "unbridled discretion" to determine what discourse is "decent" would "increase the risk of cementing white, middle-class standards for determining what is acceptable and proper speech and behavior in our public schools." 755 F.2d, at 1363. Finally, the Court of Appeals rejected the School District's argument that, incident to its responsibility for the school curriculum, it had the power to control the language used to express ideas during a school-sponsored activity.

We granted certiorari. We reverse.

II

This Court acknowledged in *Tinker v. Des Moines Independent Community School Dist.,* supra, that students do not "shed their constitutional rights to freedom of speech or expression at the schoolhouse gate." The Court of Appeals read that case as precluding any discipline of Fraser for indecent speech and lewd conduct in the school assembly. That court appears to have proceeded on the theory that the use of lewd and obscene speech in order to make what the speaker considered to be a point in a nominating speech for a fellow student was essentially the same as the wearing of an armband in *Tinker* as a form of protest or the expression of a political position.

The marked distinction between the political "message" of the armbands in *Tinker* and the sexual content of respondent's speech in this case seems to have been given little weight by the Court of Appeals. In upholding the students' right to engage in a nondisruptive, passive expression of a political viewpoint in *Tinker,* this Court was careful to note that the case did "not concern speech or action that intrudes upon the work of the schools or the rights of other students." Id., at 508.

It is against this background that we turn to consider the level of First Amendment protection accorded to Fraser's utterances and actions before an official high school assembly attended by 600 students.

III

The role and purpose of the American public school system was well described by two historians, saying "public education must prepare pupils for citizenship in the Republic.... It must inculcate the habits and manners of civility as values in themselves conducive to happiness and as indispensable to the practice of self-government in the community and the nation." C. Beard & M. Beard, New Basic History of the United States 228 (1968). In Ambach v. Norwick, 441 U.S. 68, 76–77 (1979), we echoed the essence of this statement of the objectives of public education as the "inculcat[ion of] fundamental values necessary to the maintenance of a democratic political system."

These fundamental values of "habits and manners of civility" essential to a democratic society must, of course, include tolerance of divergent political and religious views, even when the views expressed may be unpopular. But these "fundamental values" must also take into account consideration of the sensibilities of others, and, in the case of a school, the sensibilities of fellow students. The undoubted freedom to advocate unpopular and controversial views in schools and classrooms must be balanced against the society's countervailing interest in teaching students the boundaries of socially appropriate behaviour. Even the most heated political discourse in a democratic society requires consideration for the personal sensibilities of the other participants and audiences.

In our Nation's legislative halls, where some of the most vigorous political debates in our society are carried on, there are rules prohibiting the use of expressions offensive to other participants in the debate. The Manual of Parliamentary Practice, drafted by Thomas Jefferson and adopted by the House of Representatives to govern the proceedings in that body, prohibits the use of "impertinent" speech during debate and likewise provides that "[n]o person is to use indecent language against the proceedings of the House." ... Can it be that what is proscribed in the halls of Congress is beyond the reach of school officials to regulate?

The First Amendment guarantees wide freedom in matters of adult public discourse. A sharply divided Court upheld the right to express an antidraft viewpoint in a public place, albeit in terms highly offensive to most citizens. See Cohen v. California, 403 U.S. 15 (1971). It does not follow, however, that simply because the use of an offensive form of expression may not be prohibited to adults making what the speaker considers a political point, that the same latitude must be permitted to children in a public school. In New Jersey v. T.L.O., 469 U.S. 325 (1985), we reaffirmed that the constitutional rights of students in public school are not automatically coextensive with the rights of adults in other settings....

Surely it is a highly appropriate function of public school education to prohibit the use of vulgar and offensive terms in public discourse. Indeed, the "fundamental values necessary to the maintenance of a democratic political system" disfavor the use of terms of debate highly offensive or highly threatening to others. Nothing in the Constitution prohibits the states from insisting that certain modes of expression are inappropriate and subject to sanctions. The inculcation of these values is truly the "work of the schools." Tinker, 393 U.S., at 508; see Ambach v. Norwick, supra. The determination of what manner of speech in the classroom or in school assembly is inappropriate properly rests with the school board.

The process of educating our youth for citizenship in public schools is not confined to books, the curriculum, and the civics class; schools must teach by example the shared values of a civilized social order. Consciously or otherwise, teachers—and indeed the older students—demonstrate the appropriate form of civil discourse and political expression by their conduct and deportment in and out of class. Inescapably, like parents, they are role models. The schools, as instruments of the state, may determine that the essential lessons of civil, mature conduct cannot be conveyed in a school that tolerates lewd, indecent, or offensive speech and conduct such as that indulged in by this confused boy.

The pervasive sexual innuendo in Fraser's speech was plainly offensive to both teachers and students—indeed to any mature person. By glorifying male sexuality, and in its verbal content, the speech was acutely insulting to teenage girl students. The speech could well be seriously damaging to its less mature audience, many of whom were only 14 years old and on the threshold of awareness of human sexuality. Some students were reported as bewildered by the speech and the reaction of mimicry it provoked.

This Court's First Amendment jurisprudence has acknowledged limitations on the otherwise absolute interest of the speaker in reaching an unlimited audience where the speech is sexually explicit and the audience may include children. In *Ginsberg v. New York*, this Court upheld a New York statute banning the sale of sexually oriented material to minors, even though the material in question was entitled to First Amendment protection with respect to adults. And in addressing the question whether the First Amendment places any limit on the authority of public schools to remove books from a public school library, all Members of the Court, otherwise sharply divided, acknowledged that the school board has the authority to remove books that are vulgar. *Board of Education v. Pico*, 457 U.S. 853 (1982) (plurality opinion). These cases recognize the obvious concern on the part of parents, and school authorities acting *in loco parentis* to protect children—especially in a captive audience—from exposure to sexually explicit, indecent, or lewd speech.

We have also recognized an interest in protecting minors from exposure to vulgar and offensive spoken language. [FCC v. Pacifica Foundation, 438 U.S. 726 (1978)]. . . .

. . .

We hold that petitioner School District acted entirely within its permissible authority in imposing sanctions upon Fraser in response to his offensively lewd and indecent speech. Unlike the sanctions imposed on the students wearing armbands in *Tinker,* the penalties imposed in this case were unrelated to any political viewpoint. The First Amendment does not prevent the school officials from determining that to permit a vulgar and lewd speech such as respondent's would undermine the school's basic educational mission. A high school assembly or classroom is no place for a sexually explicit monologue directed towards an unsuspecting audience of teenage students. Accordingly, it was perfectly appropriate for the school to disassociate itself to make the point to the pupils that vulgar speech and lewd conduct is wholly inconsistent with the "fundamental values" of public school education. Justice Black, dissenting in *Tinker,* made a point that is especially relevant in this case:

> "I wish therefore, . . . to disclaim any purpose . . . to hold that the federal Constitution compels the teachers, parents and elected school officials to surrender control of the American public school system to public school students." 393 U.S., at 522, 526.

IV

Respondent contends that the circumstances of his suspension violated due process because he had no way of knowing that the delivery of the speech in question would subject him to disciplinary sanctions. This argument is wholly without merit. We have recognized that "maintaining security and order in the schools requires a certain degree of flexibility in school disciplinary procedures, and we have respected the value of preserving the informality of the student-teacher relationship." New Jersey v. T.L.O., 469 U.S., at ___, 105 S.Ct., at 743. Given the school's need to be able to impose disciplinary sanctions for a wide range of unanticipated conduct disruptive of the educational process, the school disciplinary rules need not be as detailed as a criminal code which imposes criminal sanctions. Two days' suspension from school does not rise to the level of a penal sanction calling for the full panoply of procedural due process protections applicable to a criminal prosecution. Cf. Goss v. Lopez, 419 U.S. 565 (1975). The school disciplinary rule proscribing "obscene" language and the pre-speech admonitions of teachers gave adequate warning to Fraser that his lewd speech could subject him to sanctions.

The judgment of the Court of Appeals for the Ninth Circuit is

Reversed.

■ Justice Stevens, dissenting.

"Frankly, my dear, I don't give a damn."

When I was a high school student, the use of those words in a public forum shocked the Nation. Today Clark Gable's four-letter expletive is less offensive than it was then. Nevertheless, I assume that high school administrators may prohibit the use of that word in classroom discussion and even in extracurricular activities that are sponsored by the school and held on school premises. For I believe a school faculty must regulate the content as well as the style of student speech in carrying out its educational mission. It does seem to me, however, that if a student is to be punished for using offensive speech, he is entitled to fair notice of the scope of the prohibition and the consequences of its violation. The interest in free speech protected by the First Amendment and the interest in fair procedure protected by the Due Process Clause of the Fourteenth Amendment combine to require this conclusion.

This respondent was an outstanding young man with a fine academic record. The fact that he was chosen by the student body to speak at the school's commencement exercises demonstrates that he was respected by his peers. This fact is relevant for two reasons. It confirms the conclusion that the discipline imposed on him—a three-day suspension and ineligibility to speak at the school's graduation exercises—was sufficiently serious to justify invocation of the School District's grievance procedures. More importantly, it indicates that he was probably in a better position to determine whether an audience composed of 600 of his contemporaries would be offended by the use of a four-letter word—or a sexual metaphor—than is a group of judges who are at least two generations and 3,000 miles away from the scene of the crime.

The fact that the speech may not have been offensive to his audience—or that he honestly believed that it would be inoffensive—does not mean that he had a constitutional right to deliver it. For the school—not the student—must prescribe the rules of conduct in an educational institution. But it does mean that he should not be disciplined for speaking frankly in a school assembly if he had no reason to anticipate punitive consequences.

One might conclude that respondent should have known that he would be punished for giving this speech on three quite different theories: (1) It violated the "Disruptive Conduct" rule published in the student handbook; (2) he was specifically warned by his teachers; or (3) the impropriety is so obvious that no specific notice was required. I discuss each theory in turn.

The Disciplinary Rule

At the time the discipline was imposed, as well as in its defense of this lawsuit, the school took the position that respondent violated the following published rule:

> " 'In addition to the criminal acts defined above, the commission of, or participation in certain noncriminal activities or acts may lead to disciplinary action. Generally, these are acts which disrupt and interfere with the educational process.
>
> . . .
>
> " '*Disruptive Conduct.* Conduct which materially and substantially interferes with the educational process is prohibited, including the use of obscene, profane language or gestures.' " 755 F.2d 1356, 1357, n. 1 (C.A.9 1985).

Based on the findings of fact made by the District Court, the Court of Appeals concluded that the evidence did not show "that the speech had a materially disruptive effect on the educational process." Id., at 1361. The Court of Appeals explained the basis for this conclusion:

> "[T]he record now before us yields no evidence that Fraser's use of a sexual innuendo in his speech materially interfered with activities at Bethel High School. While the students' reaction to Fraser's speech may fairly be characterized as boisterous, it was hardly disruptive of the educational process. In the words of Mr. McCutcheon, the school counselor whose testimony the District relies upon, the reaction of the student body 'was not atypical to a high school auditorium assembly.' In our view, a noisy response to the speech and sexually suggestive movements by three students in a crowd of 600 fail to rise to the level of a material interference with the educational process that justifies impinging upon Fraser's First Amendment right to express himself freely.
>
> "We find it significant that although four teachers delivered written statements to an assistant principal commenting on Fraser's speech, none of them suggested that the speech disrupted the assembly or otherwise interfered with school activities. See, Finding of Fact No. 8. Nor can a finding of material disruption be based upon the evidence

that the speech proved to be a lively topic of conversation among students the following day." Id., at 1360–1361.

Thus, the evidence in the record, as interpreted by the District Court and the Court of Appeals, makes it perfectly clear that respondent's speech was not "conduct" prohibited by the disciplinary rule.[4] Indeed, even if the language of the rule could be stretched to encompass the nondisruptive use of obscene or profane language, there is no such language in respondent's speech. What the speech does contain is a sexual metaphor that may unquestionably be offensive to some listeners in some settings. But if an impartial judge puts his or her own views about the metaphor to one side, I simply cannot understand how he or she could conclude that it is embraced by the above-quoted rule. At best, the rule is sufficiently ambiguous that without a further explanation or construction it could not advise the reader of the student handbook that the speech would be forbidden.[5]

The Specific Warning by the Teachers

Respondent read his speech to three different teachers before he gave it. Mrs. Irene Hicks told him that she thought the speech "was inappropriate and that he probably should not deliver it." Steven DeHart told respondent "that this would indeed cause problems in that it would raise eyebrows." The third teacher, Shawn Madden, did not testify. None of the three suggested that the speech might violate a school rule.

The fact that respondent reviewed the text of his speech with three different teachers before he gave it does indicate that he must have been aware of the possibility that it would provoke an adverse reaction, but the teachers' responses certainly did not give him any better notice of the likelihood of discipline than did the student handbook itself. In my opinion, therefore, the most difficult question is whether the speech was so obviously offensive that an intelligent high school student must be presumed to have realized that he would be punished for giving it.

Obvious Impropriety

Justice Sutherland taught us that a "nuisance may be merely a right thing in the wrong place,—like a pig in the parlor instead of the barnyard." Euclid v. Ambler Realty Co., 272 U.S. 365, 388 (1926). Vulgar language,

---

4. The Court's reliance on the school's authority to prohibit "unanticipated conduct disruptive of the educational process," is misplaced. The findings of the District Court, which were upheld by the Court of Appeals, established that the speech was not "disruptive." Departing from our normal practice concerning factual findings, the Court's decision rests on "utterly unproven, subjective impressions of some hypothetical students." Bender v. Williamsport, 475 U.S., at ___, 106 S.Ct., at 1337 (Burger, C.J., dissenting).

5. The school's disruptive conduct rule is entirely concerned with "the educational process." It does not expressly refer to extracurricular activities in general, or to student political campaigns or student debates. In contrast, "[i]n our Nation's legislative halls, where some of the most vigorous political debates in our society are carried on, there are rules prohibiting the use of expressions offensive to other participants in the debate." If a written rule is needed to forewarn a United States Senator that the use of offensive speech may give rise to discipline, a high school student should be entitled to an equally unambiguous warning. Unlike the Manual of Parliamentary Practice drafted by Thomas Jefferson, this School District's rules of conduct contain no unequivocal prohibition against the use of "impertinent" speech or "indecent language."

like vulgar animals, may be acceptable in some contexts and intolerable in others. Indeed, even ordinary, inoffensive speech may be wholly unacceptable in some settings.

It seems fairly obvious that respondent's speech would be inappropriate in certain classroom and formal social settings. On the other hand, in a locker room or perhaps in a school corridor the metaphor in the speech might be regarded as rather routine comment. If this be true, and if respondent's audience consisted almost entirely of young people with whom he conversed on a daily basis, can we—at this distance—confidently assert that he must have known that the school administration would punish him for delivering it?

For three reasons, I think not. First, it seems highly unlikely that he would have decided to deliver the speech if he had known that it would result in his suspension and disqualification from delivering the school commencement address. Second, I believe a strong presumption in favor of free expression should apply whenever an issue of this kind is arguable. Third, because the Court has adopted the policy of applying contemporary community standards in evaluating expression with sexual connotations, this Court should defer to the views of the district and circuit judges who are in a much better position to evaluate this speech than we are.

I would affirm the judgment of the Court of Appeals.

Morse v. Frederick

Supreme Court of the United States, 2007.
___ U.S. ___, 127 S.Ct. 2618, 168 L.Ed.2d 290.

■ CHIEF JUSTICE ROBERTS delivered the

. . .

I

On January 24, 2002, the Olympic Torch Relay passed through Juneau, Alaska, on its way to the winter games in Salt Lake City, Utah. The torchbearers were to proceed along a street in front of Juneau–Douglas High School (JDHS) while school was in session. Petitioner Deborah Morse, the school principal, decided to permit staff and students to participate in the Torch Relay as an approved social event or class trip. Students were allowed to leave class to observe the relay from either side of the street.

Respondent Joseph Frederick, a JDHS senior, was late to school that day. When he arrived, he joined his friends (all but one of whom were JDHS students) across the street from the school to watch the event. As the torchbearers and camera crews passed by, Frederick and his friends unfurled a 14–foot banner bearing the phrase: "BONG HiTS 4 JESUS." Principal Morse immediately crossed the street and demanded that the banner be taken down. Everyone but Frederick complied. Morse confiscated the banner and told Frederick to report to her office, where she suspended him for 10 days. Morse later explained that she told Frederick to take the banner down because she thought it encouraged illegal drug use, in violation of established school policy. Juneau School Board Policy No. 5520 states: "The Board specifically prohibits any assembly or public expression that ... advocates the use of substances that are illegal to minors...."

Frederick administratively appealed his suspension, but the Juneau School District Superintendent upheld it, limiting it to time served (8 days). In a memorandum setting forth his reasons, the superintendent determined that Frederick had displayed his banner "in the midst of his fellow students, during school hours, at a school-sanctioned activity." The Juneau School District Board of Education upheld the suspension. Frederick then filed suit under 42 U.S.C. § 1983, alleging that the school board and Morse had violated his First Amendment rights. He sought declaratory and injunctive relief, unspecified compensatory damages, punitive damages, and attorney's fees.

We granted certiorari on two questions: whether Frederick had a First Amendment right to wield his banner, and, if so, whether that right was so clearly established that the principal may be held liable for damages. We resolve the first question against Frederick, and therefore have no occasion to reach the second.

II

At the outset, we reject Frederick's argument that this is not a school speech case—as has every other authority to address the question. The event occurred during normal school hours. It was sanctioned by Principal Morse "as an approved social event or class trip," and the school district's rules expressly provide that pupils in "approved social events and class trips are subject to district rules for student conduct." Frederick, standing among other JDHS students across the street from the school, directed his banner toward the school, making it plainly visible to most students. There is some uncertainty at the outer boundaries as to when courts should apply school-speech precedents, but not on these facts.

III

The message on Frederick's banner is cryptic. It is no doubt offensive to some, perhaps amusing to others. To still others, it probably means nothing at all. Frederick himself claimed "that the words were just nonsense meant to attract television cameras." But Principal Morse thought the banner would be interpreted by those viewing it as promoting illegal drug use, and that interpretation is plainly a reasonable one. As Morse later explained in a declaration, when she saw the sign, she thought that "the reference to a 'bong hit' would be widely understood by high school students and others as referring to smoking marijuana."

We agree with Morse. At least two interpretations of the words on the banner demonstrate that the sign advocated the use of illegal drugs. First, the phrase could be interpreted as an imperative: "[Take] bong hits ..."— a message equivalent, as Morse explained in her declaration, to "smoke marijuana" or "use an illegal drug." Alternatively, the phrase could be viewed as celebrating drug use—"bong hits [are a good thing]," or "[we take] bong hits"—and we discern no meaningful distinction between celebrating illegal drug use in the midst of fellow students and outright advocacy or promotion.

The dissent mentions Frederick's "credible and uncontradicted explanation for the message—he just wanted to get on television." But that is a description of Frederick's *motive* for displaying the banner; it is not an interpretation of what the banner says. The *way* Frederick was going to fulfill his ambition of appearing on television was by unfurling a pro-drug banner at a school event, in the presence of teachers and fellow students. Elsewhere in its opinion, the dissent emphasizes the importance of political speech and the need to foster "national debate about a serious issue," as if to suggest that the banner is political speech. But not even Frederick argues that the banner conveys any sort of political or religious message. Contrary to the dissent's suggestion, this is plainly not a case about political debate over the criminalization of drug use or possession.

IV

The question thus becomes whether a principal may, consistent with the First Amendment, restrict student speech at a school event, when that speech is reasonably viewed as promoting illegal drug use. We hold that she may.

In *Tinker* [*v. Des Moines Independent Community School Dist.*], this Court made clear that "First Amendment rights, applied in light of the special characteristics of the school environment, are available to teachers and students." 393 U.S. [503], at 506[, 89 S.Ct. 733, 21 L.Ed.2d 731 (1969)]. *Tinker* held that student expression may not be suppressed unless school officials reasonably conclude that it will "materially and substantially disrupt the work and discipline of the school." *Id.*, at 513, 89 S.Ct. 733.

. . . This Court's next student speech case was [*Bethel School Dist. No. 403 v.*] *Fraser*, 478 U.S. 675, 106 S.Ct. 3159, 92 L.Ed.2d 549. Matthew Fraser was suspended for delivering a speech before a high school assembly in which he employed what this Court called "an elaborate, graphic, and explicit sexual metaphor." *Id.*, at 678, 106 S.Ct. 3159. Analyzing the case under *Tinker,* the District Court and Court of Appeals found no disruption, and therefore no basis for disciplining Fraser. 478 U.S., at 679–680, 106 S.Ct. 3159. This Court reversed, holding that the "School District acted entirely within its permissible authority in imposing sanctions upon Fraser in response to his offensively lewd and indecent speech." *Id.*, at 685, 106 S.Ct. 3159.

. . . For present purposes, it is enough to distill from *Fraser* two basic principles. First, *Fraser's* holding demonstrates that "the constitutional rights of students in public school are not automatically coextensive with the rights of adults in other settings." *Id.*, at 682, 106 S.Ct. 3159. . . . Second, *Fraser* established that the mode of analysis set forth in *Tinker* is not absolute. Whatever approach *Fraser* employed, it certainly did not conduct the "substantial disruption" analysis prescribed by *Tinker, supra,* at 514, 89 S.Ct. 733.

. . . Drawing on the principles applied in our student speech cases, we have held in the Fourth Amendment context that "while children assuredly do not 'shed their constitutional rights . . . at the schoolhouse gate,' . . . the nature of those rights is what is appropriate for children in school." *Vernonia School Dist. 47J v. Acton,* 515 U.S. 646, 655–656, 115 S.Ct. 2386,

132 L.Ed.2d 564 (1995) (quoting *Tinker, supra,* at 506, 89 S.Ct. 733). In particular, "the school setting requires some easing of the restrictions to which searches by public authorities are ordinarily subject." *New Jersey v. T.L.O.,* 469 U.S. 325, 340, 105 S.Ct. 733, 83 L.Ed.2d 720 (1985). See *Vernonia, supra,* at 656, 115 S.Ct. 2386 ("Fourth Amendment rights, no less than First and Fourteenth Amendment rights, are different in public schools than elsewhere ..."); *Board of Ed. of Independent School Dist. No. 92 of Pottawatomie Cty. v. Earls,* 536 U.S. 822, 829–830, 122 S.Ct. 2559, 153 L.Ed.2d 735 (2002) (" 'special needs' inhere in the public school context"; "[w]hile schoolchildren do not shed their constitutional rights when they enter the schoolhouse, Fourth Amendment rights ... are different in public schools than elsewhere; the 'reasonableness' inquiry cannot disregard the schools' custodial and tutelary responsibility for children") (quoting *Vernonia,* 515 U.S., at 656, 115 S.Ct. 2386; citation and some internal quotation marks omitted).

... Even more to the point, these cases also recognize that deterring drug use by schoolchildren is an "important—indeed, perhaps compelling" interest. *Id.,* at 661, 115 S.Ct. 2386. Drug abuse can cause severe and permanent damage to the health and well-being of young people:

> "School years are the time when the physical, psychological, and addictive effects of drugs are most severe. Maturing nervous systems are more critically impaired by intoxicants than mature ones are; childhood losses in learning are lifelong and profound; children grow chemically dependent more quickly than adults, and their record of recovery is depressingly poor. And of course the effects of a drug-infested school are visited not just upon the users, but upon the entire student body and faculty, as the educational process is disrupted."

Id., at 661–662[, 115 S.Ct. 2386] (citations and internal quotation marks omitted).

Just five years ago, we wrote: "The drug abuse problem among our Nation's youth has hardly abated since *Vernonia* was decided in 1995. In fact, evidence suggests that it has only grown worse." *Earls, supra,* at 834, and n. 5, 122 S.Ct. 2559.

... The "special characteristics of the school environment," *Tinker,* 393 U.S., at 506, 89 S.Ct. 733, and the governmental interest in stopping student drug abuse—reflected in the policies of Congress and myriad school boards, including JDHS—allow schools to restrict student expression that they reasonably regard as promoting illegal drug use. *Tinker* warned that schools may not prohibit student speech because of "undifferentiated fear or apprehension of disturbance" or "a mere desire to avoid the discomfort and unpleasantness that always accompany an unpopular viewpoint." *Id.,* at 508, 509, 89 S.Ct. 733. The danger here is far more serious and palpable. The particular concern to prevent student drug abuse at issue here, embodied in established school policy, extends well beyond an abstract desire to avoid controversy.

... Petitioners urge us to adopt the broader rule that Frederick's speech is proscribable because it is plainly "offensive" as that term is used in *Fraser.* We think this stretches *Fraser* too far; that case should not be read to encompass any speech that could fit under some definition of "offensive." After all, much political and religious speech might be perceived as offensive to some. The concern here is not that Frederick's speech was offensive, but that it was reasonably viewed as promoting illegal drug use.

. . . Although accusing this decision of doing "serious violence to the First Amendment" by authorizing "viewpoint discrimination," the dissent concludes that "it might well be appropriate to tolerate some targeted viewpoint discrimination in this unique setting." Nor do we understand the dissent to take the position that schools are required to tolerate student advocacy of illegal drug use at school events, even if that advocacy falls short of inviting "imminent" lawless action. ("[I]t is possible that our rigid imminence requirement ought to be relaxed at schools"). And even the dissent recognizes that the issues here are close enough that the principal should not be held liable in damages, but should instead enjoy qualified immunity for her actions. Stripped of rhetorical flourishes, then, the debate between the dissent and this opinion is less about constitutional first principles than about whether Frederick's banner constitutes promotion of illegal drug use. We have explained our view that it does. The dissent's contrary view on that relatively narrow question hardly justifies sounding the First Amendment bugle.

* * *

. . . School principals have a difficult job, and a vitally important one. When Frederick suddenly and unexpectedly unfurled his banner, Morse had to decide to act—or not act—on the spot. It was reasonable for her to conclude that the banner promoted illegal drug use—in violation of established school policy—and that failing to act would send a powerful message to the students in her charge, including Frederick, about how serious the school was about the dangers of illegal drug use. The First Amendment does not require schools to tolerate at school events student expression that contributes to those dangers.

■ [The concurring opinion of Justice Thomas is omitted.]

■ JUSTICE ALITO, with whom JUSTICE KENNEDY joins, concurring.

I join the opinion of the Court on the understanding that (a) it goes no further than to hold that a public school may restrict speech that a reasonable observer would interpret as advocating illegal drug use and (b) it provides no support for any restriction of speech that can plausibly be interpreted as commenting on any political or social issue, including speech on issues such as "the wisdom of the war on drugs or of legalizing marijuana for medicinal use."

■ [The opinion of Justice Breyer concurring in the judgment in part and dissenting in part is omitted.]

■ JUSTICE STEVENS, with whom JUSTICE SOUTER and JUSTICE GINSBURG join, dissenting.

A significant fact barely mentioned by the Court sheds a revelatory light on the motives of both the students and the principal of Juneau–Douglas High School (JDHS). On January 24, 2002, the Olympic Torch

Relay gave those Alaska residents a rare chance to appear on national television. As Joseph Frederick repeatedly explained, he did not address the curious message—"BONG HiTS 4 JESUS"—to his fellow students. He just wanted to get the camera crews' attention. Moreover, concern about a nationwide evaluation of the conduct of the JDHS student body would have justified the principal's decision to remove an attention-grabbing 14–foot banner, even if it had merely proclaimed "Glaciers Melt!"

I agree with the Court that the principal should not be held liable for pulling down Frederick's banner. I would hold, however, that the school's interest in protecting its students from exposure to speech "reasonably regarded as promoting illegal drug use," cannot justify disciplining Frederick for his attempt to make an ambiguous statement to a television audience simply because it contained an oblique reference to drugs. The First Amendment demands more, indeed, much more.

The Court holds otherwise only after laboring to establish two uncontroversial propositions: first, that the constitutional rights of students in school settings are not coextensive with the rights of adults; and second, that deterring drug use by schoolchildren is a valid and terribly important interest. As to the first, I take the Court's point that the message on Frederick's banner is not *necessarily* protected speech, even though it unquestionably would have been had the banner been unfurled elsewhere. As to the second, I am willing to assume that the Court is correct that the pressing need to deter drug use supports JDHS's rule prohibiting willful conduct that expressly "advocates the use of substances that are illegal to minors." But it is a gross non sequitur to draw from these two unremarkable propositions the remarkable conclusion that the school may suppress student speech that was never meant to persuade anyone to do anything.

In my judgment, the First Amendment protects student speech if the message itself neither violates a permissible rule nor expressly advocates conduct that is illegal and harmful to students. This nonsense banner does neither, and the Court does serious violence to the First Amendment in upholding—indeed, lauding—a school's decision to punish Frederick for expressing a view with which it disagreed.

. . .

NOTES ON *FRASER* AND *MORSE*

(1) **The offending speech in *Fraser*.** In a separate opinion concurring in the judgment, Justice Brennan began by quoting the "objectionable" speech:

"I know a man who is firm—he's firm in his pants, he's firm in his shirt, his character is firm—but most . . . of all, his belief in you, the students of Bethel, is firm.

"Jeff Kuhlman is a man who takes his point and pounds it in. If necessary, he'll take an issue and nail it to the wall. He doesn't attack things in spurts—he drives hard, pushing and pushing until he finally—he succeeds.

"Jeff is a man who will go to the very end—even the climax, for each and every one of you.

"So vote for Jeff for A.S.B. vice-president—he'll never come between you and the best our high school can be."

Justice Brennan then adds that "having read the full text of respondent's remarks, I find it difficult to believe that it is the same speech the Court describes." 478 U.S. at 687. Justice Brennan concurred in the judgment, however, because of the authority of school officials "to restrict a high school student's use of disruptive language in a speech given to a high school assembly." Id. at 689.

Justice Marshall wrote a dissenting opinion stating that he agreed with the principles set forth in Justice Brennan's opinion but that in his view "the school district failed to demonstrate that respondent's remarks were indeed disruptive." Id.

(2) **Questions about *Fraser* and *Morse*.** To what extent are *Fraser* and *Morse* a substantial retrenchment from the Court's position in *Tinker*? Is the Court simply carving out an exception to students' right of free expression for vulgar offensive speech or for speech that promotes illegal activities? Is the *Fraser* Court persuasive in drawing the analogy to *Ginsberg*? Is the threat to younger students in the assembly audience of Fraser's comments comparable to the threat to minors of pornography that is created by adults? How important is it that the speech took place in a school sponsored assembly in which the students were a "captive audience?"

Does *Morse* represent a further restriction of students' First Amendment rights or is it compatible with *Fraser*? Do you agree with the Court that the only thing that separates the majority and dissent in *Morse* is disagreement on the narrow factual issue of whether it was reasonable for Principal Morse to think that Frederick's banner promoted illegal drug use? The Court cites several Supreme Court opinions, such as *New Jersey v. T.L.O.*, *Vernonia School Dist. 47J v. Acton*, and *Board of Ed. of Independent School Dist. No. 92 of Pottawatomie Cty. v. Earls*. These cases deal with Fourth Amendment search and seizure challenges by students of public school policies designed to deter and detect the use of illegal drugs. (These cases are discussed later in this chapter and also in Chapter X). These are not First Amendment cases, but they represent an important backdrop to *Morse*, as they underscore the view (adopted by the Court) that illegal drug use is a serious problem in public schools and that officials are authorized to discourage and detect such use, even though the policies undertaken with this goal may limit students' constitutional rights—and might not be acceptable in the non-school setting.

In fact, might Frederick have had a stronger claim if his banner had contained sexually suggestive language such as that in *Fraser*? *Morse* involves a school activity, but the link to curricular goals seems more attenuated than does the student assembly and election in *Fraser*. Are the circumstances of the two cases sufficiently different to warrant a different response? Consider the following case.

In *Anderson v. Milbank School District*, 197 F.R.D. 682, 2000 DSD 49 (D.S.D. 2000), a challenge was raised as to the constitutionality of a student handbook rule prohibiting the use of profanity or inappropriate language on school property. A student went to the principal's office to receive a note left by the student's mother and after reading the note said, "shit." The principal's secretary, the only other person in the office, informed the principal of the student's violation of the rule and the student ultimately received a two and one-half day in-school suspension. Granting the school district's motion for summary judgment, the court acknowledged that the student was "talking to herself," and the better course of valor would have been to remind the student of the rule and "show mercy." However, the court noted, "the rule was clear ... well known to the student and the student, without dispute, violated the rule."

In determining whether or not the student's expletive was protected "purely individual speech," the court concluded, "Clearly, in the present case, the speech was independent student speech and had no connection with any school-sponsored activity, other than using principal's office to obtain a personal message." Nevertheless, the court stated, "a school need not tolerate speech that is inconsistent with its pedagogical mission, even though the government could not suppress that speech outside of the schoolhouse." Accordingly, the court explained, "School authorities can regulate indecent language because its circulation on school grounds undermines their responsibility to try to promote standards of decency and civility among school children. The task may be difficult, perhaps unlikely ever to be more than marginally successful." Despite the fact that the student's utterance was "certainly not disruptive to the educational environment," the court asserts, "With its captive audience of children, many of whom, along with their parents, legitimately expect reasonable regulation, a school need not capitulate to a student's preference for vulgar expression."

(3) *Henerey v. City of St. Charles*, 200 F.3d 1128 (8th Cir.1999). In a case similar to *Fraser*, Adam Henerey asserted that his First Amendment right to free speech was violated when he was disqualified from running for junior class president after handing out condoms attached to stickers bearing his campaign slogan, "Adam Henerey, The Safe Choice." Student candidates were required to meet with the student council advisor and sign a contract agreeing to obey all school rules. Also, students (including Henerey), were informed that all campaign materials needed prior approval by the school administration before distribution. On the morning of the election, Henerey handed out the condoms with his campaign slogan to students in the hallways. He had given the administration no prior indication that he would hand out condoms or that his campaign would reference sex-related topics. As ballots were being counted, a student complained about the condom distribution. The advisor relayed the complaint to the school principal who then disqualified Henerey from the election for failing to "comply with School Board Rule KJ–R, which required students to get prior approval from the school before distributing any materials." Had he not been disqualified, Henerey would have won the election.

Henerey sued in district court alleging a First Amendment violation, but the district court granted the school district's (District) motion for summary judgment. The appellate court gestured to *Tinker,* but ruled in favor of the school district, relying heavily on *Fraser.* The court stated, "a school need not tolerate speech that is inconsistent with its pedagogical mission, even though the government could not suppress that speech outside of the schoolhouse." Although it may be on school premises, a student's purely individual speech is highly protected by the First Amendment. However, "when the expressive conduct at issue occurs in the context of a school-sponsored activity that is not also a public forum, the authority of schools to exercise control over the content of speech is at its greatest." In such instances, the school official's restriction of a student's speech must be "reasonably related to legitimate pedagogical concerns."

In determining whether the election was a forum for public expression, the court noted, "Although school facilities are traditionally deemed nonpublic fora, they may be designated public when school authorities have a policy or practice of opening them for indiscriminate use by the general public or by some segment of the public such as student organizations." However, the court concluded that the election was conducted within the context of a nonpublic forum because only enrolled students could run for office, they had to obey school rules, and their campaign materials had to be approved by the school prior to distribution.

The court explained, "although to be considered 'school-sponsored,' expressive activities must be 'curricular' in a broad sense, they need not 'occur in a traditional classroom setting, so long as they are supervised by faculty members and designed to impart particular knowledge or skills to student participation and audiences.'" Since the election was supervised, limited in time by and conducted under the auspices of the school administration, "any member of the public could reasonably have concluded that campaign materials were distributed with the implied approval of the school." Also, given that the election was intended to teach leadership skills and expose students to the democratic process, the election was a school-sponsored activity and part of the school's curriculum.

The court then asserted that even if it were to assume that handing out condoms is constitutionally protected speech and the principal's disqualification of Henerey was based on disagreement with that content, there may still be no First Amendment violation. The court went on to explain:

> School districts have an interest in maintaining decorum and in preventing the creation of an environment in which learning might be impeded, an interest that was particularly strong in the present case because the condom distribution occurred within the context of a school-sponsored election. Henerey's distribution of the condoms carried with it the implied imprimatur of the school [citation omitted] for the other students would most likely have assumed that Henerey had complied with Rule KJ–R and had secured approval for the distribution. The District has a legitimate interest in divorcing its extracurricular programs from controversial and sensitive topics, such as teenage sex.

The Eighth Circuit concluded its opinion by professing that it is up to parents, teachers, and state and local school officials to teach the Nation's youth, and not federal judges. However, "it is only when the decision to censor a school-sponsored . . . vehicle of student expression has no valid educational purpose that the First Amendment is so directly and sharply implicated as to require judicial intervention to protect students' constitutional rights."

The court explained, "Purely individual speech by students constituting 'personal expression that happens to occur on the school premises' is subjected to a high degree of First Amendment Protection," whereas expression in the context of a school-sponsored activity may be restricted as long as the restriction is "reasonably related to legitimate pedagogical concerns." *Hazelwood Sch. Dist. v. Kuhlmeier*, 484 U.S. 260, 108 S.Ct. 562, 98 L.Ed.2d 592 (1988). See below. Would an expletive uttered by a student in the principal's office be considered "purely individual speech" and thus be protected?

2. SCHOOL NEWSPAPERS AND THE FIRST AMENDMENT

Hazelwood School District v. Kuhlmeier

Supreme Court of the United States, 1988.
484 U.S. 260, 108 S.Ct. 562, 98 L.Ed.2d 592.

■ JUSTICE WHITE delivered the opinion of the Court.

This case concerns the extent to which educators may exercise editorial control over the contents of a high school newspaper produced as part of the school's journalism curriculum.

I

Petitioners are the Hazelwood School District in St. Louis County, Missouri; various school officials; Robert Eugene Reynolds, the principal of Hazelwood East High School; and Howard Emerson, a teacher in the school district. Respondents are three former Hazelwood East students who were staff members of Spectrum, the school newspaper. They contend that school officials violated their First Amendment rights by deleting two pages of articles from the May 13, 1983, issue of Spectrum.

Spectrum was written and edited by the Journalism II class at Hazelwood East. The newspaper was published every three weeks or so during the 1982–1983 school year. More than 4,500 copies of the newspaper were distributed during that year to students, school personnel, and members of the community.

The Board of Education allocated funds from its annual budget for the printing of Spectrum. These funds were supplemented by proceeds from sales of the newspaper. The printing expenses during the 1982–1983 school year totaled $4,668.50; revenue from sales was $1,166.84. The other costs associated with the newspaper—such as supplies, textbooks, and a portion of the journalism teacher's salary—were borne entirely by the Board. . . .

The practice at Hazelwood East during the spring 1983 semester was for the journalism teacher to submit page proofs of each Spectrum issue to Principal Reynolds for his review prior to publication. On May 10, Emerson delivered the proofs of the May 13 edition to Reynolds, who objected to two of the articles scheduled to appear in that edition. One of the stories described three Hazelwood East students' experiences with pregnancy; the other discussed the impact of divorce on students at the school.

Reynolds was concerned that, although the pregnancy story used false names "to keep the identity of these girls a secret," the pregnant students still might be identifiable from the text. He also believed that the article's references to sexual activity and birth control were inappropriate for some of the younger students at the school. In addition, Reynolds was concerned that a student identified by name in the divorce story had complained that her father "wasn't spending enough time with my mom, my sister and I" prior to the divorce, "was always out of town on business or out late playing cards with the guys," and "always argued about everything" with her mother. Reynolds believed that the student's parents should have been given an opportunity to respond to these remarks or to consent to their publication. He was unaware that Emerson had deleted the student's name from the final version of the article.

Reynolds believed that there was no time to make the necessary changes in the stories before the scheduled press run and that the newspaper would not appear before the end of the school year if printing were delayed to any significant extent. He concluded that his only options under the circumstances were to publish a four-page newspaper instead of the planned six-page newspaper, eliminating the two pages on which the offending stories appeared, or to publish no newspaper at all. Accordingly, he directed Emerson to withhold from publication the two pages containing the stories on pregnancy and divorce. He informed his superiors of the decision, and they concurred.

Respondents subsequently commenced this action in the United States District Court for the Eastern District of Missouri seeking a declaration that their First Amendment rights had been violated, injunctive relief, and monetary damages. After a bench trial, the District Court denied an injunction, holding that no First Amendment violation had occurred. 607 F.Supp. 1450 (1985).

[The Court of Appeals for the Eighth Circuit (795 F.2d 1368 (1986)) held that Spectrum was not only "a part of the school adopted curriculum," but also a public forum, because it was "intended to be and operated as a conduit for student viewpoint." Because Spectrum was a public forum, school officials could only censor material when " 'necessary to avoid material and substantial interference with school work or discipline . . . or the rights of others.' " Id., at 1374 (quoting Tinker v. Des Moines Independent Community School Dist., 393 U.S. 503, 511 (1969)).

The Court of Appeals found "no evidence in the record that the principal could have reasonably forecast that the censored articles or any materials in the censored articles would have materially disrupted classwork or given rise to substantial disorder in the school." Only if the school could be subject to tort liability if the articles were published, could the school censor the articles on the ground that they invaded the rights of others. In this case, the Court concluded that, since no tort action for libel or invasion of privacy could have been maintained against the school by the subjects of the two articles or by their families, school officials had violated respondents' First Amendment rights by deleting the two pages of the newspaper.]

We granted certiorari, and we now reverse.

II

Students in the public schools do not "shed their constitutional rights to freedom of speech or expression at the schoolhouse gate." *Tinker,* supra, at 506. They cannot be punished merely for expressing their personal views on the school premises—whether "in the cafeteria, or on the playing field, or on the campus during the authorized hours,"—unless school authorities have reason to believe that such expression will "substantially interfere with the work of the school or impinge upon the rights of other students."

We have nonetheless recognized that the First Amendment rights of students in the public schools "are not automatically coextensive with the rights of adults in other settings," Bethel School District No. 403 v. Fraser, 478 U.S. 675, 682 (1986), and must be "applied in light of the special characteristics of the school environment." *Tinker,* supra, at 506; cf. New Jersey v. T.L.O., 469 U.S. 325, 341–343 (1985). A school need not tolerate student speech that is inconsistent with its "basic educational mission," *Fraser,* supra, at 685, even though the government could not censor similar speech outside the school. Accordingly, we held in *Fraser* that a student could be disciplined for having delivered a speech that was "sexually explicit" but not legally obscene at an official school assembly, because the school was entitled to "disassociate itself" from the speech in a manner that would demonstrate to others that such vulgarity is "wholly inconsistent with the 'fundamental values' of public school education." We thus recognized that "[t]he determination of what manner of speech in the classroom or in school assembly is inappropriate properly rests with the school board," rather than with the federal courts. It is in this context that respondents' First Amendment claims must be considered.

A

We deal first with the question whether Spectrum may appropriately be characterized as a forum for public expression. The public schools do not possess all of the attributes of streets, parks, and other traditional public forums that "time out of mind, have been used for purposes of assembly, communicating thoughts between citizens, and discussing public questions." Hence, school facilities may be deemed to be public forums only if school authorities have "by policy or by practice" opened those facilities "for indiscriminate use by the general public...."

School officials did not deviate in practice from their policy that production of Spectrum was to be part of the educational curriculum and a "regular classroom activit[y]." The District Court found that Robert Stergos, the journalism teacher during most of the 1982–1983 school year, "both had the authority to exercise and in fact exercised a great deal of control over *Spectrum.*" For example, Stergos selected the editors of the newspaper, scheduled publication dates, decided the number of pages for each issue, assigned story ideas to class members, advised students on the development of their stories, reviewed the use of quotations, edited stories, selected and edited the letters to the editor, and dealt with the printing company. Many of these decisions were made without consultation with the Journalism II students. The District Court thus found it "clear that Mr. Stergos was the final authority with respect to almost every aspect of the production and publication of *Spectrum,* including its content." Moreover, after each Spectrum issue had been finally approved by Stergos or his successor, the issue still had to be reviewed by Principal Reynolds prior to publication. Respondents' assertion that they had believed that they could publish "practically anything" in Spectrum was therefore dismissed by the District Court as simply "not credible." These factual findings are amply supported by the record, and were not rejected as clearly erroneous by the Court of Appeals.

The evidence relied upon by the Court of Appeals in finding Spectrum to be a public forum, is equivocal at best. For example, Board Policy 348.51, which stated in part that "[s]chool sponsored student publications will not restrict free expression or diverse viewpoints within the rules of responsible journalism," also stated that such publications were "developed within the adopted curriculum and its educational implications." One might reasonably infer from the full text of Policy 348.51 that school officials retained ultimate control over what constituted "responsible journalism" in a school-sponsored newspaper. Although the Statement of Policy published in the September 14, 1982, issue of Spectrum declared that "*Spectrum,* as a student-press publication, accepts all rights implied by the First Amendment,'' this statement, understood in the context of the paper's role in the school's curriculum, suggests at most that the administration will not interfere with the students' exercise of those First Amendment rights that attend the publication of a school-sponsored newspaper. It does not reflect an intent to expand those rights by converting a curricular newspaper into a public forum. Finally, that students were permitted to exercise some authority over the contents of Spectrum was fully consistent with the Curriculum Guide objective of teaching the Journalism II students ''leadership responsibilities as issue and page editors.'' A decision to teach leadership skills in the context of a classroom activity hardly implies a decision to relinquish school control over that activity. In sum, the evidence relied upon by the Court of Appeals fails to demonstrate the ''clear intent to create a public forum,'' that existed in cases in which we found public forums to have been created. School officials did not evince either ''by policy or by practice,'' any intent to open the pages of Spectrum to ''indiscriminate use,'' by its student reporters and editors, or by the student body generally. Instead, they ''reserve[d] the forum for its intended purpos[e],'' as a supervised learning experience for journalism students. Accordingly, school officials were entitled to regulate the contents of Spectrum in any reasonable manner. It is this standard, rather than our decision in *Tinker,* that governs this case.

B

The question whether the First Amendment requires a school to tolerate particular student speech—the question that we addressed in *Tinker*—is different from the question whether the First Amendment requires a school affirmatively to promote particular student speech. The former question addresses educators' ability to silence a student's personal expression that happens to occur on the school premises. The latter question concerns educators' authority over school-sponsored publications, theatrical productions, and other expressive activities that students, parents, and members of the public might reasonably perceive to bear the imprimatur of the school. These activities may fairly be characterized as part of the school curriculum, whether or not they occur in a traditional classroom setting, so long as they are supervised by faculty members and designed to impart particular knowledge or skills to student participants and audiences.

Educators are entitled to exercise greater control over this second form of student expression to assure that participants learn whatever lessons the activity is designed to teach, that readers or listeners are not exposed to material that may be inappropriate for their level of maturity, and that the views of the individual speaker are not erroneously attributed to the school. Hence, a school may in its capacity as publisher of a school newspaper or producer of a school play ''disassociate itself,'' *Fraser,* 478 U.S., at 685, not only from speech that would ''substantially interfere with [its] work . . . or impinge upon the rights of other students,'' *Tinker,* 393 U.S., at 509, but also from speech that is, for example, ungrammatical, poorly written, inadequately researched, biased or prejudiced, vulgar or profane, or unsuitable for immature audiences. A school must be able to set high standards for the student speech that is disseminated under its auspices—standards that may be higher than those demanded by some newspaper publishers or theatrical producers in the "real" world—and may refuse to disseminate student speech that does not meet those standards. In addition, a school must be able to take into account the emotional maturity of the intended audience in determining whether to disseminate student speech on potentially sensitive topics, which might range from the existence of Santa Claus in an elementary school setting to the particulars of teenage sexual activity in a high school setting. A school must also retain the authority to refuse to sponsor student speech that might reasonably be perceived to advocate drug or alcohol use, irresponsible sex, or conduct otherwise inconsistent with "the shared values of a civilized social order," *Fraser,* supra, at 683, or to associate the school with any position other than neutrality on matters of political controversy. Otherwise, the schools would be unduly constrained from fulfilling their role as "a principal instrument in awakening the child to cultural values, in preparing him for later professional training, and in helping him to adjust normally to his environment." Brown v. Board of Education, 347 U.S. 483, 493 (1954).

Accordingly, we conclude that the standard articulated in *Tinker* for determining when a school may punish student expression need not also be the standard for determining when a school may refuse to lend its name and resources to the dissemination of student expression. Instead, we hold that educators do not offend the First Amendment by exercising editorial control over the style and content of student speech in school-sponsored expressive activities so long as their actions are reasonably related to legitimate pedagogical concerns.

III

We also conclude that Principal Reynolds acted reasonably in requiring the deletion from the May 13 issue of Spectrum of the pregnancy article, the divorce article, and the remaining articles that were to appear on the same pages of the newspaper.

The initial paragraph of the pregnancy article declared that "[a]ll names have been changed to keep the identity of these girls a secret." The principal concluded that the students' anonymity was not adequately protected, however, given the other identifying information in the article and the small number of pregnant students at the school. Indeed, a teacher at the school credibly testified that she could positively identify at least one of the girls and possibly all three. It is likely that many students at Hazelwood East would have been at least as successful in identifying the girls. Reynolds therefore could reasonably have feared that the article violated whatever pledge of anonymity had been given to the pregnant students. In addition, he could reasonably have been concerned that the article was not sufficiently sensitive to the privacy interests of the students' boyfriends and parents, who were discussed in the article but who were given no opportunity to consent to its publication or to offer a response. The article did not contain graphic accounts of sexual activity. The girls did comment in the article, however, concerning their sexual histories and their use or nonuse of birth control. It was not unreasonable for the principal to have concluded that such frank talk was inappropriate in a school-sponsored publication distributed to 14–year–old freshmen and pre-sumably taken home to be read by students' even younger brothers and sisters.

The student who was quoted by name in the version of the divorce article seen by Principal Reynolds made comments sharply critical of her father. The principal could reasonably have concluded that an individual publicly identified as an inattentive parent—indeed, as one who chose "playing cards with the guys" over home and family—was entitled to an opportunity to defend himself as a matter of journalistic fairness. These concerns were shared by both of Spectrum's faculty advisers for the 1982–1983 school year, who testified that they would not have allowed the article to be printed without deletion of the student's name.

Principal Reynolds testified credibly at trial that, at the time that he reviewed the proofs of the May 13 issue during an extended telephone conversation with Emerson, he believed that there was no time to make any changes in the articles, and that the newspaper had to be printed immediately or not at all. It is true that Reynolds did not verify whether the necessary modifications could still have been made in the articles, and that Emerson did not volunteer the information that printing could be delayed until the changes were made. We nonetheless agree with the District Court that the decision to excise the two pages containing the problematic articles was reasonable given the particular circumstances of this case. These circumstances included the very recent replacement of Stergos by Emerson, who may not have been entirely familiar with Spec-trum editorial and production procedures, and the pressure felt by Reyn-olds to make an immediate decision so that students would not be deprived of the newspaper altogether.

In sum, we cannot reject as unreasonable Principal Reynolds' conclu-sion that neither the pregnancy article nor the divorce article was suitable for publication in Spectrum. Reynolds could reasonably have concluded that the students who had written and edited these articles had not sufficiently mastered those portions of the Journalism II curriculum that pertained to the treatment of controversial issues and personal attacks, the need to protect the privacy of individuals whose most intimate concerns are to be revealed in the newspaper, and "the legal, moral, and ethical restrictions imposed upon journalists within [a] school community" that includes adolescent subjects and readers. Finally, we conclude that the principal's decision to delete two pages of Spectrum, rather than to delete only the offending articles or to require that they be modified, was reasonable under the circumstances as he understood them. Accordingly, no violation of First Amendment rights occurred.

The judgment of the Court of Appeals for the Eighth Circuit is therefore

Reversed.

■ JUSTICE BRENNAN, with whom JUSTICE MARSHALL and JUSTICE BLACKMUN join, dissenting.

When the young men and women of Hazelwood East High School registered for Journalism II, they expected a civics lesson. Spectrum, the newspaper they were to publish, "was not just a class exercise in which students learned to prepare papers and hone writing skills, it was a . . . forum established to give students an opportunity to express their views while gaining an appreciation of their rights and responsibilities under the First Amendment to the United States Constitution. . . ." "[A]t the beginning of each school year," the student journalists published a Statement of Policy—tacitly approved each year by school authorities—announcing their expectation that "*Spectrum,* as a student-press publication, accepts all rights implied by the First Amendment. . . . Only speech that 'materially and substantially interferes with the requirements of appropriate discipline' can be found unacceptable and therefore prohibited." App. 26 (quoting Tinker v. Des Moines Independent Community School Dist., 393 U.S. 503, 513 (1969)). The school board itself affirmatively guaranteed the students of Journalism II an atmosphere conducive to fostering such an appreciation and exercising the full panoply of rights associated with a free student press. "School sponsored student publications," it vowed, "will not restrict free expression or diverse viewpoints within the rules of responsible journalism." App. 22 (Board Policy § 348.51).

This case arose when the Hazelwood East administration breached its own promise, dashing its students' expectations. The school principal, without prior consultation or explanation, excised six articles—comprising two full pages—of the May 13, 1983, issue of Spectrum. He did so not because any of the articles would "materially and substantially interfere with the requirements of appropriate discipline," but simply because he considered two of the six "inappropriate, personal, sensitive, and unsuitable" for student consumption.

In my view the principal broke more than just a promise. He violated the First Amendment's prohibitions against censorship of any student expression that neither disrupts classwork nor invades the rights of others, and against any censorship that is not narrowly tailored to serve its purpose.

I

Public education serves vital national interests in preparing the Nation's youth for life in our increasingly complex society and for the duties of citizenship in our democratic Republic. . . .

Free student expression undoubtedly sometimes interferes with the effectiveness of the school's pedagogical functions. Some brands of student expression do so by directly preventing the school from pursuing its pedagogical mission: The young polemic who stands on a soapbox during calculus class to deliver an eloquent political diatribe interferes with the legitimate teaching of calculus. And the student who delivers a lewd endorsement of a student-government candidate might so extremely distract an impressionable high school audience as to interfere with the orderly operation of the school. See Bethel School Dist. No. 403 v. Fraser, 478 U.S. 675 (1986). Other student speech, however, frustrates the school's legitimate pedagogical purposes merely by expressing a message that conflicts with the school's, without directly interfering with the school's expression of its message: A student who responds to a political science teacher's question with the retort, "socialism is good," subverts the school's inculcation of the message that capitalism is better. Even the maverick who sits in class passively sporting a symbol of protest against a government policy, cf. Tinker v. Des Moines Independent Community School Dist., 393 U.S. 503 (1969), or the gossip who sits in the student commons swapping stories of sexual escapade could readily muddle a clear official message condoning the government policy or condemning teenage sex. Likewise, the student newspaper that, like Spectrum, conveys a moral position at odds with the school's official stance might subvert the administration's legitimate inculcation of its own perception of community values.

. . .

... [P]ublic educators must accommodate some student expression even if it offends them or offers views or values that contradict those the school wishes to inculcate. . . .

. . .

II

Even if we were writing on a clean slate, I would reject the Court's rationale for abandoning *Tinker* in this case. The Court offers no more than an obscure tangle of three excuses to afford educators "greater control" over school-sponsored speech than the *Tinker* test would permit: the public educator's prerogative to control curriculum; the pedagogical interest in shielding the high school audience from objectionable viewpoints and sensitive topics; and the school's need to dissociate itself from student expression. None of the excuses, once disentangled, supports the distinction that the Court draws. *Tinker* fully addresses the first concern; the second is illegitimate; and the third is readily achievable through less oppressive means.

A

. . .

I fully agree with the Court that the First Amendment should afford an educator the prerogative not to sponsor the publication of a newspaper article that is "ungrammatical, poorly written, inadequately researched, biased or prejudiced," or that falls short of the "high standards for ... student speech that is disseminated under [the school's] auspices. . . ." But we need not abandon *Tinker* to reach that conclusion; we need only apply it.

The same cannot be said of official censorship designed to shield the *audience* or dissociate the *sponsor* from the expression. Censorship so motivated might well serve (although, as I demonstrate, cannot legitimately serve) some other school purpose. But it in no way furthers the curricular purposes of a student *newspaper,* unless one believes that the purpose of the school newspaper is to teach students that the press ought never report bad news, express unpopular views, or print a thought that might upset its sponsors. Unsurprisingly, Hazelwood East claims no such pedagogical purpose.

The Court relies on bits of testimony to portray the principal's conduct as a pedagogical lesson to Journalism II students who "had not sufficiently mastered those portions of the ... curriculum that pertained to the treatment of controversial issues and personal attacks, the need to protect the privacy of individuals ..., and 'the legal, moral, and ethical restrictions imposed upon journalists....' " In that regard, the Court attempts to justify censorship of the article on teenage pregnancy on the basis of the principal's judgment that (1) "the [pregnant] students' anonymity was not adequately protected," despite the article's use of aliases; and (2) the judgment that "the article was not sufficiently sensitive to the privacy interests of the students' boyfriends and parents...." Similarly, the Court finds in the principal's decision to censor the divorce article a journalistic lesson that the author should have given the father of one student an "opportunity to defend himself" against her charge that (in the Court's words) he "chose 'playing cards with the guys' over home and family...."

But the principal never consulted the students before censoring their work. "[T]hey learned of the deletions when the paper was released...." Further, he explained the deletions only in the broadest of generalities. In one meeting called at the behest of seven protesting Spectrum staff members (presumably a fraction of the full class), he characterized the articles as " 'too sensitive' for 'our immature audience of readers,' " and in a later meeting he deemed them simply "inappropriate, personal, sensitive and unsuitable for the newspaper," ibid. The Court's supposition that the principal intended (or the protesters understood) those generalities as a lesson on the nuances of journalistic responsibility is utterly incredible. If he did, a fact that neither the District Court nor the Court of Appeals found, the lesson was lost on all but the psychic Spectrum staffer.

B

The Court's second excuse for deviating from precedent is the school's interest in shielding an impressionable high school audience from material whose substance is "unsuitable for immature audiences." Specifically, the majority decrees that we must afford educators authority to shield high school students from exposure to "potentially sensitive topics" (like "the particulars of teenage sexual activity") or unacceptable social viewpoints (like the advocacy of "irresponsible se[x] or conduct otherwise inconsistent with 'the shared values of a civilized social order' ") through school-sponsored student activities.

Tinker teaches us that the state educator's undeniable, and undeniably vital, mandate to inculcate moral and political values is not a general warrant to act as "thought police" stifling discussion of all but state-approved topics and advocacy of all but the official position. Otherwise educators could transform students into "closed-circuit recipients of only that which the State chooses to communicate," *Tinker,* 393 U.S., at 511, and cast a perverse and impermissible "pall of orthodoxy over the class-room." Thus, the State cannot constitutionally prohibit its high school students from recounting in the locker room "the particulars of [their] teen-age sexual activity," nor even from advocating "irresponsible se[x]" or other presumed abominations of "the shared values of a civilized social order." Even in its capacity as educator the State may not assume an Orwellian "guardianship of the public mind."

The mere fact of school sponsorship does not, as the Court suggests, license such thought control in the high school, whether through school suppression of disfavored viewpoints or through official assessment of topic sensitivity.

Official censorship of student speech on the ground that it addresses "potentially sensitive topics" is, for related reasons, equally impermissible. I would not begrudge an educator the authority to limit the substantive scope of a school-sponsored publication to a certain, objectively definable topic, such as literary criticism, school sports, or an overview of the school year.

The case before us aptly illustrates how readily school officials (and courts) can camouflage viewpoint discrimination as the "mere" protection of students from sensitive topics. Among the grounds that the Court advances to uphold the principal's censorship of one of the articles was the potential sensitivity of "teenage sexual activity." Yet the District Court specifically found that the principal "did not, as a matter of principle, oppose discussion of said topi[c] in *Spectrum*." That much is also clear from the same principal's approval of the "squeal law" article on the same page, dealing forthrightly with "teenage sexuality," "the use of contraceptives by teenagers," and "teenage pregnancy." If topic sensitivity were the true basis of the principal's decision, the two articles should have been equally objectionable. It is much more likely that the objectionable article was objectionable because of the viewpoint it expressed: It might have been read (as the majority apparently does) to advocate "irresponsible sex."

C

The sole concomitant of school sponsorship that might conceivably justify the distinction that the Court draws between sponsored and non-sponsored student expression is the risk "that the views of the individual speaker [might be] erroneously attributed to the school." Of course, the risk of erroneous attribution inheres in any student expression, including "personal expression" that, like the armbands in *Tinker*, "happens to occur on the school premises." Nevertheless, the majority is certainly correct that indicia of school sponsorship increase the likelihood of such attribution, and that state educators may therefore have a legitimate interest in dissociating themselves from student speech.

But " '[e]ven though the governmental purpose be legitimate and substantial, that purpose cannot be pursued by means that broadly stifle fundamental personal liberties when the end can be more narrowly achieved.' " Dissociative means short of censorship are available to the school. It could, for example, require the student activity to publish a disclaimer, such as the "Statement of Policy" that Spectrum published each school year announcing that "[a]ll ... editorials appearing in this newspaper reflect the opinions of the *Spectrum* staff, which are not necessarily shared by the administrators or faculty of Hazelwood East," or it could simply issue its own response clarifying the official position on the matter and explaining why the student position is wrong. Yet, without so much as acknowledging the less oppressive alternatives, the Court approves of brutal censorship.

III

Since the censorship served no legitimate pedagogical purpose, it cannot by any stretch of the imagination have been designed to prevent "materia[l] disrup[tion of] classwork," *Tinker,* 393 U.S., at 513. Nor did the censorship fall within the category that *Tinker* described as necessary to prevent student expression from "inva[ding] the rights of others." If that term is to have any content, it must be limited to rights that are protected by law. "Any yardstick less exacting than [that] could result in school officials curtailing speech at the slightest fear of disturbance," a prospect that would be completely at odds with this Court's pronouncement that the "undifferentiated fear or apprehension of disturbance is not enough [even in the public school context] to overcome the right to freedom of expression." *Tinker,* supra, at 508. And, as the Court of Appeals correctly reasoned, whatever journalistic impropriety these articles may have contained, they could not conceivably be tortious, much less criminal.

Finally, even if the majority were correct that the principal could constitutionally have censored the objectionable material, I would emphatically object to the brutal manner in which he did so. Where "[t]he separation of legitimate from illegitimate speech calls for more sensitive tools" the principal used a paper shredder. He objected to some material in two articles, but excised six entire articles. He did not so much as inquire into obvious alternatives, such as precise deletions or additions (one of which had already been made), rearranging the layout, or delaying publication. Such unthinking contempt for individual rights is intolerable from any state official. It is particularly insidious from one to whom the public entrusts the task of inculcating in its youth an appreciation for the cherished democratic liberties that our Constitution guarantees.

IV

. . .

. . . The young men and women of Hazelwood East expected a civics lesson, but not the one the Court teaches them today.

I dissent.

HAZELWOOD AND STUDENT EXPRESSION

(1) Do you think the Supreme Court majority or dissenting opinion in *Hazelwood* is more faithful to *Tinker*? Is the majority abandoning the *Tinker* test for determining when school authorities can restrict student speech without violating the students' right to free expression? What exactly is the test employed in *Hazelwood* to determine whether the censorship amounted to a violation of the students' speech rights? At the beginning of the opinion, the Court concludes that the school-sponsored newspaper is not a public forum. Why is this so important to its analysis? If the school newspaper were not part of the curriculum, but were wholly an extra-curricular activity, would the outcome have been different?

In general, the Court has emphasized that when state authorities are justified (because of the importance of the state interest that is implicated) in restricting individual's constitutional rights, the restriction must be narrowly tailored to accomplish the state's purpose, without unduly burdening the right. The Court in *Hazelwood* concludes that Principal Reynolds' response to the offending articles was reasonable under the circumstances. Can you think of other more limited responses that would have satisfied his concerns and perhaps better served the curricular purposes of the journalism class? What lesson did the students learn about responsible journalism in a society with a free press?

(2) Much litigation has followed in the wake of *Hazelwood*, and many of the themes emphasized in the opinion have been developed by lower courts. In general, courts have taken *Hazelwood* to mean that school authorities have broad discretion to regulate and censor student speech when it is related in any way to the curriculum or when the activity involved is sponsored by the school, or would appear to an outsider to be sponsored by the school. What would count as a school-sponsored activity? It seems that school publications such as literary magazines would be included, as well as theatrical productions. If the official reasonably concludes that the material could make the school vulnerable to a defamation suit, censorship is acceptable.

Although *Hazelwood* seems to grant school officials broad deference in censoring student speech, a court's application of *Hazelwood* does not automatically ensure a judgment in favor of the school regulations. In *Desilets v. Clearview Regional Board of Education*, 137 N.J. 585, 647 A.2d 150 (1994), the Supreme Court of New Jersey held that a school official's refusal to publish a student's review of R-rated films in the junior high school's extracurricular newspaper was a violation of the student's First Amendment rights, despite the finding that the newspaper was not a "public forum." The rejected movie reviews contained brief descriptions and recommendations of the movies "Mississippi Burning" and "Rain Man." Relying heavily on *Hazelwood*, the New Jersey Supreme Court first concluded that the student newspaper, the *Pioneer Press*, was not a public forum.

Since the junior high newspaper was not a public forum, the speech therein may be subject to reasonable restrictions. The New Jersey Supreme Court then cited *Hazelwood*'s explanation that "educators do not offend the First Amendment by exercising editorial control over the style and content of student speech in school-sponsored expressive activities so long as their actions are reasonably related to legitimate pedagogical concerns." Reciting the *Hazelwood* court's "examples of legitimate pedagogical interests, which included 'speech that is . . . ungrammatical, poorly written, inadequately researched, biased or prejudiced, vulgar or profane, or unsuitable for immature audiences,' " the court concluded, "the R-rated movie reviews in this case do not appear to raise educational concerns that call for the kinds of editorial control exemplified by the Supreme Court in *Hazelwood*." It explained,

> The [*Hazelwood*] Court's focus on the account of the girls' sexual histories and their use or nonuse of birth control—what was "written about"—indicates, at least indirectly or partially, that the subject-matter of the articles was also a relevant consideration determining the scope of the educational concerns over whether such communications should be allowed in a school setting.

The court was "satisfied that the evidence in this case concerning the school's educational policy was, at best, equivocal and inconsistent." Indeed, "the school board's position with respect to the policy that applied to student publications, specifically as related to matters such as movie reviews, was vague and highly conclusory." Although the school board "conceded that it had no specific policy regarding movie reviews of R-rated films . . . it argued that the action taken by the

principal and superintendent complied with that 'policy.' " The school board asserted that the R-rated movie reviews violated the official policy because they "constituted 'material which advocated the use or advertised the availability of any
substance believed to constitute a danger to student health,' but how the reviews
posed such a danger was never explained." Further, "the evidence strongly suggests
that the policy was often ignored or applied inconsistently because R-rated movies
were discussed in class, referred to and available in the school library, and, in fact,
reviewed and published by the student newspaper." For these reasons, the court
held, "under *Hazelwood*, defendants failed to establish a legitimate educational
policy that would govern the publication of the challenged materials and, as a
consequence, the school authorities, under these circumstances, did violate the
student's expressional rights under the First Amendment."

The dissenting judge agreed that the school's policy in this case was "at best,
equivocal and inconsistent," but suggested, "the holding of the United States
Supreme Court in [*Hazelwood*] requires that we accord more respect to the
decisions of school officials than does the majority." The judge believed, "School
officials could find an educational purpose in not permitting the use of the student
newspaper as a means of promoting R-rated films, which some parents do not want
their children to see." Is the dissenting judge correct in suggesting that *Hazelwood*
grants more deference to school officials than the New Jersey Supreme Court
offered? What level of specificity would the New Jersey court require of the policies
that school officials may rely on when restricting student speech? Does it seem
appropriate to require school officials to do more than offer an informal policy in
order to support its claim to a legitimate pedagogical interest?

A federal appellate court recently expounded on the authority of school officials
in regulating school-sponsored activities in a case involving Columbine High School,
where a 1999 shooting rampage left 14 students and a teacher dead (including the
perpetrators). *Fleming v. Jefferson County School District*, 298 F.3d 918 (10th
Cir.2002). School officials decided to undertake, as part of the building renovation, a
project in which students were invited to create artwork on 4″ by 4″ tiles that would
be affixed and displayed throughout the school building. Although the purpose of
the project was to assist in community healing, the officials did not want the display
to become a memorial to the tragedy. Thus, the guidelines for participation included
rules that there be "no references to the attacks, the date, to students' names, no
religious symbols and nothing obscene or offensive." Many students, as well as
hundreds of community members who had some relationship to the school or the
tragedy, participated in the project. Although participants were informed of the
guidelines, many painted tiles with symbols or words that had been disallowed
("Jesus wept on April 20"), and these tiles were not affixed to the walls. Several of
these individuals sued the school system, charging that the guidelines violated their
right of Free Expression as well as the Establishment Clause.

The court rejected the claims, analyzing them under *Hazelwood.* In the court's
view, the speech, although not related to the curriculum, was school-sponsored
speech, which "students, parents, and members of the community might reasonably
perceive to bear the imprimatur of the school." Unlike the "pure" student speech
involved in *Tinker*, the Columbine tile project, like the school newspaper in
Hazelwood, involved speech that the school was actively promoting. Messages and
symbols on tiles, permanently affixed to the school building, could be seen as
bearing the school's imprimatur. Further, the court stated, the level of involvement
of school officials in organizing and supervising the event affects whether the
activity bears the school's imprimatur, and here the involvement was extensive
from beginning to end. Next, the court examined whether the project promoted
pedagogical concerns. Where an activity involves school-sponsored speech, school
officials may exercise control as long as the "activity is reasonably related to

legitimate pedagogical concerns.'' The goals for the tile project, ensuring that the interior of the building remain a positive learning environment and not a memorial and avoiding religious debate on the walls, were legitimate pedagogical concerns. Finally, the court concluded that educators can make viewpoint-based decisions about school sponsored speech, although it acknowledged that Federal circuit courts have divided on the issue of whether *Hazelwood* requires viewpoint neutrality. Under *Hazelwood,* in the court's view, educators were given control over school-sponsored speech for reasons that would often turn on viewpoint-based judgments—such as determining the appropriateness of the message, or the sensitivity of the subject matter. If viewpoint neutrality were required, the court suggested, school officials might have to tolerate messages promoting drug or alcohol use or irresponsible sex.

(3) ***Hazelwood*'s Application to Universities.** A debate has arisen over the possible application of *Hazelwood* in the college setting. In *Hosty v. Carter*, 412 F.3d 731 (7th Cir.2005), one court concluded that *Hazelwood*'s framework applied in analyzing the censorship of a subsidized student newspaper at a state university. While some commentators argue that *Hazelwood* should be limited to the high school setting, Judge Easterbrook, writing for the majority, states that "*Hazelwood*'s framework applies to subsidized student newspapers at colleges as well as elementary and secondary schools." *Id.* at 735. The decision has created a fair amount of controversy. See e.g. Jeff Sklar, The Presses Won't Stop Just Yet: Shaping Student Speech Rights in the Wake of *Hazelwood*'s Application to Colleges, 80 S.Cal.L.Rev. 641 (2007); Laura Merritt, How the *Hosty* Court Muddled First Amendment Protections by Misapplying *Hazelwood* to University Student Speech, 33 J.C. & U.L. 473 (2007); Chris Sanders, Censorship 101: Anti–*Hazelwood* Laws and the Preservation of Free Speech at Colleges and Universities, 58 Ala.L.Rev. 159 (2006); Daniel A. Applegate, Stop the Presses: The Impact of *Hosty v. Carter* and *Pitt News v. Pappert* on the Editorial Freedom of College Newspapers, 56 Case W.Res.L.Rev. 247 (2005).

(4) **Underground Newspapers.** When school officials seek to exercise prior restraint over student-produced material that is not generated as part of a school-sponsored activity, courts have been less supportive. Today, this issue arises mostly when students use their home computers to post Web site messages related to school personnel or other students. See note 5 below. An earlier version of the problem involved school newspapers.

In *Burch v. Barker*, 861 F.2d 1149 (9th Cir.1988), student publishers of an underground newspaper challenged a school policy that all student-written material must be submitted to school officials for approval before it could be distributed at any official school function. The student petitioners were reprimanded for distributing their newspaper *Bad Astra* at the senior class picnic, without obtaining prior approval. The newspaper contained several articles that were critical of the school administration and that mocked individual teachers, but it contained no profanity or obscene or defamatory material. School officials stated that it would have been approved without change under the policy, had it been submitted for approval.

The Ninth Circuit Court of Appeals concluded that, because the newspaper was not a school sponsored activity, the application of the school's prior approval policy constituted a violation of the students' First Amendment rights. The Court noted that the prior restraint upheld in *Hazelwood* was justified on the ground that the newspaper in that case was school-sponsored and a part of the curriculum. Student speech that is not part of a school-sponsored expressive activity is subject to the *Tinker* test, and can only be restricted based on evidence that it represents a real threat of disruption. The *Burch* court concluded that there was no evidence in the case before it of such a threat:

The student distribution of non-school-sponsored material ... cannot be subjected to regulation on the basis of undifferentiated fears of possible disturbances or embarrassment to school officials.

861 F.2d at 1159.

Using the *Hazelwood* Court's analysis, explain the distinction between restrictions on a school-sponsored newspaper and an underground newspaper that is distributed in the school. Could prior restraint of an underground newspaper be justified?

Can students be suspended or expelled for articles in underground newspapers? In an Oregon case, a high school student was expelled for writing articles included in an unauthorized publication that he distributed to fellow students on the school's campus. One article included a list of ten "things that he would like to see happen at school ... to the people who run it," including bomb threats, depositing "disgusting smelling liquid," and "putting epoxy glue in locks." The student argued that the publication was protected expression. The court analyzed the statements and concluded that they were intended to disrupt school activities and cause personal injury and property damage. Thus, the school officials could have reasonably believed the publication would substantially interfere with the educational work of the school and interfere with the rights of others. Unlike the action by the school officials in *Tinker,* the censure of the publication was not based on undifferentiated fear. *Pangle v. Bend–Lapine School Dist.*, 169 Or.App. 376, 10 P.3d 275 (2000).

(5) **Home-Based Student Web sites.** More recently, school officials and courts have struggled more often with what might be described as the modern version of the underground newspaper—student-created home-based Web sites and postings on social networking sites such as MySpace and YouTube. Courts have not found the issue to be an easy one. Messages posted on these Web sites, not surprisingly, usually focus on the school and discuss matters of concern to students, school administrators and teachers. However, unlike the newspaper in *Hazelwood*, they are created off campus—and thus are more like underground newspapers. Remember, the *Hazelwood* Court emphasized that school authorities can control some speech that the government could not regulate out of school. Thus, a key threshold issue in evaluating the level of First Amendment protection is often whether the Web site speech is "off-campus" or "on-campus" speech. In analyzing this issue, courts often focus on whether the Web site was accessed from the school by the creator or others and whether the message was aimed at a particular school audience, rather than a broader or random audience. One court described the threshold test in the following terms:

> Where speech that is aimed at a specific school and/or its personnel and is brought onto the school campus or accessed at school by its originator, the speech will be considered on-campus speech.

J.S. v. Bethlehem Area School Dist., 569 Pa. 638, 807 A.2d 847 (2002).

Sometimes the line between protected and unprotected speech is hard to discern. For example, compare the following cases. *Requa v. Kent School Dist. No. 415*, 492 F.Supp.2d 1272 (W.D.Wash.2007), involved the posting on the Web site YouTube.com of a video filmed by students of a teacher during class without her knowledge. The edited footage showed a student behind the teacher making "rabbit ears" and pelvic thrusts in her direction. It also showed the teacher's buttocks as she bent over, with a "Caution Booty Ahead" caption overlaid. The students were suspended and brought suit, claiming that the school's actions violated their First Amendment rights. The court denied the students' request for a temporary restraining order that would enjoin the school from enforcing the suspensions.

Relying heavily on *Tinker*, the court found that the filming "constitutes a material and substantial disruption to the work and discipline of the school." *Id.* at 1280. In *Layshock v. Hermitage School Dist.*, 496 F.Supp.2d 587 (W.D.Pa.2007), in contrast, the court ruled that a student's First Amendment rights were violated after he was disciplined for creating a fake MySpace.com profile of his high school principal. The fake profile suggested that the principal used alcohol and marijuana and stated that he was a "big whore" and "big steroid freak." Students accessed this profile, and three other fake profiles of the principal, during school hours before the school cut off access to MySpace.com. The court found *Fraser* inapplicable because the offensive conduct did not take place on school grounds. Additionally, the court held that *Tinker*'s substantial disruption test was not satisfied by the student showing the website to other students during school hours because no serious disruption arose other than a teacher threatening to shut down computer access.

Not surprisingly, courts are supportive of school regulation and discipline where the Web site message threatens harm to other students or teachers. This concern gained salience when it was revealed that one of the Columbine perpetrators had created a Web site with violent threats against students and teachers. Here, courts focus on whether the message represents a "true threat" or an offensive attempt at humor. If the message represents a genuine threat, the off-campus/on campus inquiry becomes irrelevant and school officials can intervene. The court in *J.S.*, supra, undertook this analysis. J.S., a middle school student, was expelled from school after he created a Web site titled "Teacher Suks," on which he posted derogatory remarks about the principal and his math teacher, and solicited contributions to hire a hit man to kill the math teacher. [He did not include an address to which contributions could be sent.] Students and teachers accessed the web site from school. The math teacher, upon seeing the Web site, had to take medical leave for the rest of the school year. The Pennsylvania Supreme Court concluded that the posting was not a "true threat" which a reasonable listener might interpret as a serious expression of an intention to do harm, but rather a sophomoric attempt at humor. Many people (including the police and F.B.I.) did not take the threat seriously, and indeed, the school district did not initiate disciplinary proceedings against the student until after the school year was completed.

In a more recent case, the Second Circuit upheld the suspension of a student for using an instant messenger icon that he created on his home computer suggesting that a particular teacher should be shot and killed. *Wisniewski v. Board of Ed.*, 494 F.3d 34 (2d Cir.2007). The court stated, "[T]he fact that Aaron's creation and transmission of the IM icon occurred away from school property does not necessarily insulate him from school discipline." Since Aaron showed the icon to at least fifteen of his friends, including a number of classmates, it was "reasonably foreseeable that the icon would come to the attention of school authorities and of the teacher whom the icon depicted being shot ...." Once that happened, the court concluded, "a risk of substantial disruption within the school environment" was also reasonably foreseeable.

Even where student Web site messages do not represent a threat of harm, however, "on-campus" speech may not be protected by the First Amendment if it is vulgar or offensive under *Fraser* or disruptive of educational activities under *Tinker* In *J.S.*, supra, the court concluded that the school's disciplinary action was justified under *Fraser* and *Tinker*, even though the threat was not intended seriously. Under *Fraser*, the court found the vulgar and offensive language and personal attacks on the teacher and principal to be undermining of the function of the public school and offensive in the same way that Fraser's language in the assembly was offensive. Do you think the two situations are similar enough to apply the *Fraser* analysis in this case? Under *Tinker*, the court found that J.S.'s Web site communication was disruptive of the educational work of the school. First, the math teacher was unable to complete the school year, resulting in the use of several substitute teachers. Beyond this, the Web site adversely affected the morale of students and teachers, and raised concerns among parents about the safety of the school. Indeed, the court concluded, J.S. was successful at his apparent goal of creating disorder.

Yeo v. Town of Lexington

United States Court of Appeals, 1st Circuit, 1997.
131 F.3d 241.

■ LYNCH, CIRCUIT JUDGE.

. . .

The LHS *Musket* is a student-written and edited newspaper that is published four or five times a year. All editorial, operational, and staffing decisions are made by the student editors. . . . Students do not seek or obtain the approval of the faculty advisor for any editorial or operational decisions. [T]he *Musket* receives about $4,500 a year from the School Committee. The *Musket* has no physical facilities at LHS, other than a mail box; all the layout is done at editors' homes. The *Musket* typically includes news articles about the high school, features, editorials, letters to the editor, sports coverage, and humor columns, all written, edited, and produced by students. The *Musket* is described in literature distributed to the student body as being a "student run newspaper" which is "written, edited and distributed by students." The editorial page bears a legend stating expressly that the opinions stated there are those of the student editors or newspaper staff and not of school policy.

Not every issue of the *Musket* contains advertising. Those that do contain two or three small ads from businesses that cater to student tastes. . . . Pursuant to an unwritten policy, the *Musket* has never accepted advocacy or political advertising, including that from candidates for student government. The purpose of this policy was to prevent the *Musket* from becoming a "bulletin board" for warring political ideas. . . .

In 1992, the Lexington School Committee adopted a policy making condoms available to students at LHS without parental permission. . . . Douglas Yeo, a town resident and parent, emerged as a leading opponent of condom distribution and other "safe sex" policies.

On February 1, 1994, Yeo submitted an ad to the *Musket*.

[The ad copy read: "We know you can do it! ABSTINENCE: The Healthy Choice." Sponsored by: Lexington Parents Information Network (LEXNET)]

The student editors of the *Musket*. . . . decided that Yeo's ad constituted a political statement that they would not run as a matter of policy. On February 24, 1994, (the student editor) Shen wrote to Yeo:

After careful consideration of your advertisement from LEXNET, the Musket came to the difficult decision of not printing it. . . . [W]e could not accept a political statement as an advertisement. . . . If we were to accept a politically aligned advertisement, we at the Musket would feel obligated to accept other political statements that might come our way. We do not wish to put ourselves in such position....

The decision was made, and the reply written, by the student editors without consulting Kafrissen, the *Musket* faculty advisor, or requesting his, or any other adult's, approval. In fact, Kafrissen ... did not see the ad or the students' response until after the reply had been sent.

Sometime the next week, Principal Wilson called Kafrissen and informed him that ... Yeo's lawyer.... had threatened to sue the town and the school authorities if the ad was not run.... On March 1, 1994, the student editors of the *Musket* met with Kafrissen. Kafrissen informed them of Yeo's actions.... The editors once again decided to reject the ad. They asked Kafrissen to contact Yeo and to invite him to present his views in a "letter to the editor."

Kafrissen, on behalf of the *Musket,* wrote to Yeo that day. In the letter, Kafrissen suggested that Yeo write a letter to the editor....

Yeo declined the offer on March 7 in a letter to Kafrissen....

On March 11, 1994, LHS officials and student editors met in the office of the Superintendent of Schools, Jeffrey Young.... *Musket* editor-in-chief Chan, advisors Kafrissen and Mechem, Superintendent Young and Principal Wilson attended. Young asked questions to determine what the students' reasoning was, and to determine that they had engaged in a thoughtful process prior to the meeting. The administrators and faculty were impressed with the way the students outlined the issues....

On March 13 ... [T]he student staff unanimously opposed publication of Yeo's ad.

On March 18, a second meeting was held in Superintendent Young's office. In addition to the prior participants, Lexington School Committee members attended. The *Musket* ... editors reiterated their refusal to run Yeo's ads. The school officials and School Committee members warned the students of the possible consequences of their decision, including litigation, and described the potentially unpleasant media exposure the students could expect. Although the students felt that the school officials wanted them to print the ads, the officials maintained that it was the students' decision to make. The students were repeatedly advised that the ultimate decision about publication of the advertisement was theirs to make and the school administration would stand by their decision.

. . .

On April 11, 1994, the Superintendent again met with the Musket staff and again told them the decision was theirs. Throughout Young's tenure as Superintendent, the Musket has been operated as an independent student-run newspaper and he has never authorized any school official to interfere with the students' decision on what to publish. Yeo offers no evidence to the contrary.

This litigation followed....

Yeo's action under 42 U.S.C. § 1983 alleges that the refusal to print the advertisement violated his rights to free speech and equal protection under the U.S. Constitution and Art. 16 of the Massachusetts Declaration of Rights. Yeo sued the Town, School Committee, Superintendent, Principal, and faculty advisers but did not name the students as defendants.

The defendants moved for summary judgment on various grounds, including, inter alia, the lack of state action, that no public forum had been created, and qualified immunity. . . .

III.   State Action

The essential state action inquiry is whether the government has been sufficiently involved in the challenged actions that it can be deemed responsible for the plaintiff's claimed injury. If there is no state action, then the court may not impose constitutional obligations on (and thus restrict the freedom of) private actors.

This is a situation in which the government actors—the school officials acting under a statute[5] of the Commonwealth of Massachusetts—have chosen to grant editorial autonomy to these high school students. The state action analysis is thus placed squarely in a very complex and changing area of law.

The state action issue implicates a myriad of players, only some of whom are defendants. Yeo sued only those individuals who are public school administrators, teachers, or members of the Lexington School Committee. They are concededly state actors. He did not sue the student editors. But the "action" of which Yeo complains was an action taken by the students. The "actions" he assails were the editorial judgments not to publish his advertisement. Those judgments were made by the students, who are not parties.

There are expressive interests involved on both sides of this case. Yeo's are obvious. Those on the other side are perhaps less obvious. The identification of these interests puts the state action question in context.

If the actions by the students are themselves state action or may be attributed to the school officials and provide the basis for state action, the inevitable legal consequence will be some level of judicial scrutiny of the students' editorial judgments. The inevitable practical consequence will be greater official control of the students' editorial judgments. Both consequences implicate the students' First Amendment interests, which are far from negligible.

In addition, the defendant school officials themselves have an interest in their autonomy to make educational decisions. The officials have determined that the best way to teach journalism skills is to respect in the

---

5. Mass. Gen. Laws ch. 71 § 82 provides, in pertinent part:

The right of students to freedom of expression in the public schools of the commonwealth shall not be abridged, provided that such right shall not cause any disruption or disorder within the school. Freedom of expression shall include without limitation, the rights and responsibilities of students, collectively and individually, . . . to write, publish and disseminate their views. . . . No expression made by students in the exercise of such rights shall be deemed to be an expression of school policy and no school officials shall be held responsible in any civil or criminal action for any expression made or published by the students.

students' editorial judgments a degree of autonomy similar to that exercised by professional journalists. That choice by the officials parallels the allocation of responsibility for editorial judgments made by the First Amendment itself. The Supreme Court has "oft expressed [the] view that the education of the Nation's youth is primarily the responsibility of parents, teachers, and state and local school officials, and not of federal judges." *Hazelwood,* 484 U.S. at 272.

The leading Supreme Court decisions concerning high schools and students are all meaningfully different from this case, and thus provide little guidance on the state action question. Each of those cases involved a claim by students that the actions of public school administrators violated their constitutional rights. [The court cites and discusses *Hazelwood, Fraser*, and Tinker.] Here, in contrast, the question is whether the actions by *students* may fairly lead to a conclusion there is state action.

Each court of appeals which has considered the state action requirement in the context of attempts to attribute student-controlled editorial decisions in public institutions of higher education to public officials has found no state action. . . .

The theories for (and against) state action basically devolve here into three categories of analysis. First, is there state action because the decisions not to publish were actually made by or controlled by the school officials? (Even if the decisions were not directly made by the school officials, those officials, Yeo argues, exerted such influence as effectively to determine the outcome of the student decisions.) This is primarily a factual question.

Second, even if the state did not actively direct or control the decisions, was the state required to intervene, and to do so in such a way as to provide a basis for a state action finding? This is primarily an issue of law.

Third, even if the decisions were made independently by the students, may the decisions of the students fairly be attributable to the school officials because of the public school setting? The material facts are undisputed; the question is what conclusion to draw from these facts. We take each argument in turn.

A.

Yeo argues that the decisions were made or controlled in fact by the school officials, but the record does not support that conclusion. The students and each of the involved school officials say that the students, and not the school officials, made the decision. Yeo has offered nothing to contradict that . . .

Nonetheless, the state action cases recognize that government should not be shielded when it is the real actor behind the scenes or when it joins in a charade designed to evade constitutional prohibitions . . . [Citations omitted.] . . . . [T]here is no evidence the school officials tacitly endorsed or benefitted from the students' decisions not to run Yeo's ads.

The state action cases also consider "de-privatizing" and attributing to the government the actions of private persons where the state has been involved in the sense of delegating traditional governmental authority to a private actor. S.Ct. at 2083.... The publishing of a newspaper.... is most emphatically not a traditional function nor an exclusive prerogative of the government in this country.

B.

Secondly, while there may be rare occasions when a state has a duty to intervene in actions taken by private persons which could give rise to a state action finding, this is not one.... Here, the state statute, Mass. Gen. Laws ch. 71, § 82, appears to have been intended, in part, to express Massachusetts' policy judgment that student editors of high school publications generally have editorial autonomy from school officials and that their decisions are not state action. While the state statute cannot be determinative of the outcome of the federal constitutional question [citation omitted], no such duty to act is imposed by state law.

The First Amendment free speech and free press guarantees do not involve a duty by the government to act where there is otherwise no state action. Indeed, those guarantees are largely based on prohibitions against government action.... As a matter of law, we see no legal duty here on the part of school administrators to control the content of the editorial judgments of student editors of publications. Such a duty—which Yeo in his briefing suggested could be derived from the traditional government function of running schools and the "symbiotic relationship" between the publications and the school—does not exist and cannot support state action.

We are left with the third theory: that the actions by the students should be attributed to the school officials, despite the officials' lack of actual or effective control and the lack of any duty. The key issue is whether the conduct may be "fairly attributable to the state." ...

Of course, the fact that the newspaper editors are public school students does not, in itself, make them state actors. Persons do not become state actors because they are clients of government services, whether they are students, hospital patients, or prison inmates. Some, like the students, are government clients by compulsion ... They may not be converted to the status of government actors simply on such a basis.

Yeo argues ... that there is a sufficient nexus to attribute the students' actions to the state. But examining the nexus here between state regulation and financial support of the publications and the challenged decisions militates against a state action finding.... It is established that a private institution's receipt of state funding does not render that institution's decisions state action.... This can be so even when the institution's budget is almost entirely derived from public money. *Id.* Here, the publication [is] the institutions at issue.

.... The *Musket* does receive.... financial assistance. Much of its operating costs as well as its advisor's stipend are paid by the school system. However, these facts are far from conclusive. ...There was no interplay between the decision not to publish the advertisement and the state's provision of financial and faculty support. That the principal kept the checkbook for the school newspaper had nothing to do with the students' decisions whether or not to run the ads.

Yeo's "nexus" argument turns on context.... The newspaper is the newspaper of the public high school; its name is the *"Lexington High School Musket"* and it identifies itself with the high school in its communications and interactions with other students and the community. It does receive some financial support from the school and the faculty advisors may have some subtle influence. The newspaper exists in the form it does because the school authorities and state law permit it to do so. While not part of the for-credit educational curriculum, work on the *Musket* does have explicit educational value and provides an attractive credential for students. The student editors perform some of their functions on school grounds, perhaps even during school hours. All of these factors support Yeo's argument. It is a close question whether the injury caused here "is aggravated in a unique way by the incidents of government authority."

The Supreme Court has taught that the state action question may shift depending on the context and the question asked. A public defender is not a state actor in her representation of a criminal defendant, even though she may be one in the performance of other duties, such as hiring or firing decisions. *See Polk County,* 454 U.S. at 324–25, 102 S.Ct. at 453–54. Even acknowledging that the public defender is a state employee, *Polk County* considered it important that, in the actual function of defending the client, the public defender's relationship to the state was necessarily independent, and even adversarial, and that the defender exercised independent judgment in the same manner as did attorneys in the private sector. So too here.

Here, the students' relationship to the public school officials in the exercise of their editorial judgment was certainly independent. At times, it was close to adversarial. The school officials gained nothing but a lawsuit from the students' decision, and the officials might themselves, as they told the students, have made a different decision. It is not enough to create state action that the decisions took place in a public school setting, that there was some governmental funding of the publication, that teachers were acting as advisors, and that the state actors made an educational judgment to respect the autonomy of the students' editorial judgment.

Where, as here, there are First Amendment interests on both sides of the case, the analysis of whether there is state action must proceed with care and caution. Because the record establishes that the editorial judgment exercised was the independent judgment of the student editors ..., we resolve the question of state action against Yeo.

The decision of the district court is affirmed.

■ [Concurring opinions by Chief Judge Torruella and Circuit Judge Stahl are omitted.]

NOTE ON STATUTORY PROTECTION OF STUDENT SPEECH

As Yeo suggests, some states, by statute accord students broader rights of press and speech than is constitutionally required under *Hazelwood.* Consider the California statute below. How does it expand students' rights?

CALIFORNIA EDUCATION CODE

§ 48907.   Student exercise of free expression

Students of the public schools shall have the right to exercise freedom of speech and of the press including, but not limited to, the use of bulletin boards, the distribution of printed materials or petitions, the wearing of buttons, badges, and other insignia, and the right of expression in official publications, whether or not such publications or other means of expression are supported financially by the school or by use of school facilities, except that expression shall be prohibited which is obscene, libelous, or slanderous. Also prohibited shall be material which so incites students as to create a clear and present danger of the commission of unlawful acts on school premises or the violation of lawful school regulations, or the substantial disruption of the orderly operation of the school.

Each governing board of a school district and each county board of education shall adopt rules and regulations in the form of a written publications code, which shall include reasonable provisions for the time, place, and manner of conducting such activities within its respective jurisdiction.

Student editors of official school publications shall be responsible for assigning and editing the news, editorial, and feature content of their publications subject to the limitations of this section. However, it shall be the responsibility of a journalism adviser or advisers of student publications within each school to supervise the production of the student staff, to maintain professional standards of English and journalism, and to maintain the provisions of this section.

There shall be no prior restraint of material prepared for official school publications except insofar as it violates this section. School officials shall have the burden of showing justification without undue delay prior to any limitation of student expression under this section.

"Official school publications" refers to material produced by students in the journalism, newspaper, yearbook, or writing classes and distributed to the student body either free or for a fee.

Nothing in this section shall prohibit or prevent any governing board of a school district from adopting otherwise valid rules and regulations relating to oral communication by students upon the premises of each school.

NOTE

In *Lopez v. Tulare Joint Union High School District Board of Trustees,* 34 Cal.App.4th 1302, 40 Cal.Rptr.2d 762 (1995), a California Court of Appeals interpreted the statute after the *Hazelwood* decision. In that case, the high school principal, after reviewing a draft of the script of a film written and produced by students for a Film Arts class, directed the instructor to have the students remove profanity as "highly offensive and educationally unsuitable." Both the instructor and the students objected on the ground that the profanity contributed to the realism of the dialogue and was artistically important. They appealed unsuccessfully to the school board. The students brought suit, claiming that the school board's action violated the statute, as well as the California constitution.

Although the trial court granted the students' request for an injunction, the appellate court rejected their claim, concluding that school officials were permitted by the California statute to exercise prior restraint under these circumstances. The court acknowledged that the statute gave California students more extensive rights to freedom of speech and press than did the First Amendment as interpreted by the Supreme Court. It emphasized that prior restraint was authorized only under limited circumstances. Moreover, the court did not find the profanity to be "obscene" under the statute, one of the statutory exceptions to the prohibition against prior restraint of material in school-sponsored publications.... Rather it found that school officials in censoring profanity in the film were acting to "maintain professional standards of English and journalism," as authorized by the statute. Do you think the court's conclusion is supported by the statute? How well does this provision of the statute apply to the use of profanity in a dramatic production? Does it matter whether the students are correct in their assertion that the profane language was artistically appropriate?

The California statute expressly gives school officials limited authority to censor student speech that is slanderous, libelous, or obscene. In *Leeb v. Delong*, 198 Cal.App.3d 47, 243 Cal.Rptr. 494 (1988), student editors of the school sponsored newspaper submitted the proposed April Fools edition of the newspaper to the principal. The edition included a disclaimer that "All the stories and announcements in this issue are fabrications of the mind." One story reported that Playboy magazine was coming to photograph female students at the high school. The article included a picture of five female students who purportedly were standing in line to be photographed. The principal prohibited distribution of the paper, on the ground that the school could be liable in a defamation suit for damaging the reputations of the young women in the photograph—despite the disclaimer. The student editor sued, challenging the statute's authorization of censorship.

The appellate court rejected both of the constitutional challenges, and endorsed the authority of school officials to exercise prior restraint of a student-authored publication if the school otherwise would be vulnerable to a defamation action. The court acknowledged that the constraints on school officials under California law were more rigorous than the federal constitution demanded. California educators lack the power to censor expression in school-sponsored publications for pedagogical purposes. Nonetheless, the court emphasized, the school newspaper is not an open forum; if it were, prior restraint would not be permitted even to prevent publication of libelous material. Rather, the school-sponsored publication is a "limited forum" and, as such, could be subject to some prior restraint. However, school officials cannot censor material that they find offensive, solely because some litigious person might sue. The concern must be based on a rational determination that the "challenged speech ... contains a false statement ... likely to harm the reputation of another...." 198 Cal.App.3d at 62, 243 Cal.Rptr. at 503.

3. ISSUES OF RELIGIOUS EXPRESSION

Good News Club v. Milford Central School

Supreme Court of the United States, 2001.
533 U.S. 98, 121 S.Ct. 2093, 150 L.Ed.2d 151.

■ JUSTICE THOMAS delivered the opinion of the Court.

. . .

I

.... In 1992, respondent Milford Central School (Milford) enacted a community use policy adopting ... purposes for which its building could be used after school. Two of the stated purposes are relevant here. First, district residents may use the school for "instruction in any branch of education, learning or the arts." Second, the school is available for "social, civic and recreational meetings and entertainment events, and other uses pertaining to the welfare of the community, provided that such uses shall be nonexclusive and shall be opened to the general public."

Stephen and Darleen Fournier.... are sponsors of the local Good News Club, a private Christian organization for children ages 6 to 12. Pursuant to Milford's policy, in September 1996 the Fourniers submitted a request.... in which they sought permission to hold the Club's weekly afterschool meetings in the school cafeteria. The [superintendant] denied the Fourniers' request on the ground that the proposed use—to have "a fun time of singing songs, hearing a Bible lesson and memorizing scripture," was "the equivalent of religious worship.".... [and that] the community use policy, which prohibits use "by any individual or organization for religious purposes," foreclosed the Club's activities.

In response to a letter submitted by the Club's counsel, Milford's attorney requested information to clarify the nature of the Club's activities. The Club sent a set of materials used or distributed at the meetings and the following description of its meeting:

> "The Club opens its session with Ms. Fournier taking attendance. As she calls a child's name, if the child recites a Bible verse the child receives a treat. After attendance, the Club sings songs. Next Club members engage in games that involve, *inter alia*, learning Bible verses. Ms. Fournier then relates a Bible story and explains how it applies to Club members' lives. The Club closes with prayer. Finally, Ms. Fournier distributes treats and the Bible verses for memorization."

McGruder and Milford's attorney reviewed the materials and concluded that "the kinds of activities proposed to be engaged in by the Good News Club were not a discussion of secular subjects such as child rearing, development of character and development of morals from a religious perspective, but were in fact the equivalent of religious instruction itself." In February 1997, the Milford Board of Education adopted a resolution rejecting the Club's request to use Milford's facilities "for the purpose of conducting religious instruction and Bible study."

[The club filed an action against Milford in Federal District Court alleging].... that Milford's denial of its application violated its free speech rights under the First and Fourteenth Amendments, its right to equal protection under the Fourteenth Amendment, and its right to religious freedom under the Religious Freedom Restoration Act of 1993, 107 Stat. 1488, 42 U.S.C. § 2000bb et seq.

[The district Court and the Court of Appeals granted Milford's motion for summary judgment.]

. . .

II

The standards that we apply to determine whether a State has unconstitutionally excluded a private speaker from use of a public forum depend on the nature of the forum. [Citation omitted]. If the forum is a traditional or open public forum, the State's restrictions on speech are subject to stricter scrutiny than are restrictions in a limited public forum. ... Because the parties have agreed that Milford created a limited public forum when it opened its facilities in 1992, ... we need not resolve the issue here. Instead, we simply will assume that Milford operates a limited public forum.

When the State establishes a limited public forum, the State is not required to and does not allow persons to engage in every type of speech. The State may be justified "in reserving [its forum] for certain groups or for the discussion of certain topics." *Rosenberger v. Rector and Visitors of Univ. of Va.*, 515 U.S. 819, 829 (1995). The State's power to restrict speech, however, is not without limits. The restriction must not discriminate against speech on the basis of viewpoint, *Rosenberger, supra,* at 829, and the restriction must be "reasonable in light of the purpose served by the forum," [citation omitted.]

III

Applying this test, we first address whether the exclusion constituted viewpoint discrimination. We are guided in our analysis by two of our prior opinions, *Lamb's Chapel* and *Rosenberger*. In *Lamb's Chapel*, we held that a school district violated the Free Speech Clause of the First Amendment when it excluded a private group from presenting films at the school based solely on the films' discussions of family values from a religious perspective. Likewise, in *Rosenberger*, we held that a university's refusal to fund a student publication because the publication addressed issues from a religious perspective violated the Free Speech Clause. Concluding that Milford's exclusion of the Good News Club based on its religious nature is indistinguishable from the exclusions in these cases, we hold that the exclusion constitutes viewpoint discrimination. Because the restriction is viewpoint discriminatory, we need not decide whether it is unreasonable in light of the purposes served by the forum.

Milford has opened its limited public forum to activities that serve a variety of purposes, including events "pertaining to the welfare of the community." Milford interprets its policy to permit discussions of subjects such as child rearing, and of "the development of character and morals from a religious perspective...."

Just as there is no question that teaching morals and character development to children is a permissible purpose under Milford's policy, it is clear that the Club teaches morals and character development to children. For example, no one disputes that the Club instructs children to overcome feelings of jealousy, to treat others well regardless of how they treat the children, and to be obedient, even if it does so in a nonsecular way. Nonetheless, because Milford found the Club's activities to be religious in nature—"the equivalent of religious instruction itself," 202 F.3d, at 507—it excluded the Club from use of its facilities.

Applying *Lamb's Chapel*, we find it quite clear that Milford engaged in viewpoint discrimination when it excluded the Club from the afterschool forum. In *Lamb's Chapel*, ... [t]he school district also prohibited use "by any group for religious purposes." 508 U.S., at 387. Citing this prohibition, the school district excluded a church that wanted to present films teaching family values from a Christian perspective. We held that, because the films "no doubt dealt with a subject otherwise permissible" under the rule, the teaching of family values, the district's exclusion of the church was unconstitutional viewpoint discrimination. *Id.*, at 394.

Like the church in *Lamb's Chapel*, the Club seeks to address a subject otherwise permitted under the rule, the teaching of morals and character, from a religious standpoint. Certainly, one could have characterized the film presentations in *Lamb's Chapel* as a religious use.... The only apparent difference between the activity of *Lamb's Chapel* and the activities of the Good News Club is that the Club chooses to teach moral lessons from a Christian perspective through live storytelling and prayer, whereas *Lamb's Chapel* taught lessons through films. This distinction is inconsequential. Both modes of speech use a religious viewpoint. Thus, the exclusion of the Good News Club's activities, like the exclusion of *Lamb's Chapel*'s films, constitutes unconstitutional viewpoint discrimination.

Our opinion in *Rosenberger* also is dispositive. In *Rosenberger*, a student organization at the University of Virginia was denied funding for printing expenses because its publication, Wide Awake, offered a Christian viewpoint. Just as the Club emphasizes the role of Christianity in students' morals and character, Wide Awake " 'challenge[d] Christians to live, in word and deed, according to the faith they proclaim and ... encourage[d] students to consider what a personal relationship with Jesus Christ means.' " 515 U.S., at 826. Because the university "select[ed] for disfavored treatment those student journalistic efforts with religious editorial viewpoints," we held that the denial of funding was unconstitutional. *Id.*, at 831.... Given the obvious religious content of Wide Awake, we cannot say that the Club's activities are any more "religious" or deserve any less First Amendment protection than did the publication of Wide Awake in *Rosenberger*.

Despite our holdings in *Lamb's Chapel* and *Rosenberger*, the Court of Appeals, like Milford, believed that its characterization of the Club's activities as religious in nature warranted treating the Club's activities as different in kind from the other activities permitted by the school. The "Christian viewpoint" is unique.... the Club "is focused on teaching children how to cultivate their relationship with God through Jesus Christ," which it characterized as "quintessentially religious." *Id.*, at 510. With these observations, the court concluded that, because the Club's activities "fall outside the bounds of pure 'moral and character development,' " the exclusion did not constitute viewpoint discrimination. *Id.*, at 511.

We disagree that something that is "quintessentially religious" or "decidedly religious in nature" cannot also be characterized properly as the teaching of morals and character development from a particular viewpoint.... What matters for purposes of the Free Speech Clause is that we can see no logical difference in kind between the invocation of Christianity by the Club and the invocation of teamwork, loyalty, or patriotism by other associations to provide a foundation for their lessons.... According to the Court of Appeals, reliance on Christian principles taints moral and character instruction in a way that other foundations for thought or viewpoints do not. We, however, have never reached such a conclusion. Instead, we reaffirm our holdings in *Lamb's Chapel* and *Rosenberger* that speech discussing otherwise permissible subjects cannot be excluded from a limited public forum on the ground that the subject is discussed from a religious viewpoint. Thus, we conclude that Milford's exclusion of the Club from use of the school, pursuant to its community use policy, constitutes impermissible viewpoint discrimination.[4]

IV

Milford argues that, even if its restriction constitutes viewpoint discrimination, its interest in not violating the Establishment Clause outweighs the Club's interest in gaining equal access to the school's facilities. In other words, according to Milford, its restriction was required to avoid violating the Establishment Clause. We disagree.

.... [I]t is not clear whether a State's interest in avoiding an Establishment Clause violation would justify viewpoint discrimination.... We need not, however, confront the issue in this case, because we conclude that the school has no valid Establishment Clause interest.

We rejected Establishment Clause defenses similar to Milford's in two previous free speech cases, *Lamb's Chapel* and Widmar. In particular, in *Lamb's Chapel*, we explained that "[t]he showing of th[e] film series would not have been during school hours, would not have been sponsored by the school, and would have been open to the public, not just to church members." 508 U.S., at 395. Accordingly, we found that "there would have been no realistic danger that the community would think that the District was endorsing religion or any particular creed." Ibid. Likewise, in Widmar, where the university's forum was already available to other groups, this Court concluded that there was no Establishment Clause problem. 454 U.S., at 272–273, and n. 13, 102 S.Ct. 269.

The Establishment Clause defense fares no better in this case. As in *Lamb's Chapel*, the Club's meetings were held after school hours, not sponsored by the school, and open to any student who obtained parental consent, not just to Club members. As in Widmar, Milford made its forum available to other organizations. The Club's activities are materially indis-

---

4. Despite Milford's insistence that the Club's activities constitute "religious worship," the Court of Appeals made no such determination. It did compare the Club's activities to "religious worship," 202 F.3d, at 510, but ultimately it concluded merely that the Club's activities "fall outside the bounds of pure 'moral and character development,'" *id.*, at 511. In any event, we conclude that the Club's activities do not constitute mere religious worship, divorced from any teaching of moral values. Justice SOUTER's recitation of the Club's activities is accurate (dissenting opinion). But in our view, religion is used by the Club in the same fashion that it was used by *Lamb's Chapel* and by the students in *Rosenberger*. Religion is the viewpoint from which ideas are conveyed. We did not find the *Rosenberger* students' attempt to cultivate a personal relationship with Christ to bar their claim that religion was a viewpoint. And we see no reason to treat the Club's use of religion as something other than a viewpoint merely because of any evangelical message it conveys. According to Justice SOUTER, the Club's activities constitute "an evangelical service of worship." Regardless of the label Justice SOUTER wishes to use, what matters is the substance of the Club's activities, which we conclude are materially indistinguishable from the activities in *Lamb's Chapel* and *Rosenberger*.

tinguishable from those in *Lamb's Chapel* and Widmar. Thus, Milford's reliance on the Establishment Clause is unavailing.

Milford attempts to distinguish *Lamb's Chapel* and Widmar by emphasizing that Milford's policy involves elementary school children. According to Milford, children will perceive that the school is endorsing the Club and will feel coercive pressure to participate, because the Club's activities take place on school grounds, even though they occur during nonschool hours. This argument is unpersuasive.

First, we have held that "a significant factor in upholding governmental programs in the face of Establishment Clause attack is their *neutrality* towards religion.".... Milford's implication that granting access to the Club would do damage to the neutrality principle defies logic. For the "guarantee of neutrality is respected, not offended, when the government, following neutral criteria and evenhanded policies, extends benefits to recipients whose ideologies and viewpoints, including religious ones, are broad and diverse." *Rosenberger*, supra, at 839, 115 S.Ct. 2510. The Good News Club seeks nothing more than to be treated neutrally and given access to speak about the same topics as are other groups. Because allowing the Club to speak on school grounds would ensure neutrality, not threaten it, Milford faces an uphill battle in arguing that the Establishment Clause compels it to exclude the Good News Club.

Second, to the extent we consider whether the community would feel coercive pressure to engage in the Club's activities, cf. *Lee v. Weisman,* 505 U.S. 577, 592–593, 112 S.Ct. 2649, 120 L.Ed.2d 467 (1992), the relevant community would be the parents, not the elementary school children. It is the parents who choose whether their children will attend the Good News Club meetings. Because the children cannot attend without their parents' permission, they cannot be coerced into engaging in the Good News Club's religious activities. Milford does not suggest that the parents of elementary school children would be confused about whether the school was endorsing religion. Nor do we believe that such an argument could be reasonably advanced.

Third, whatever significance we may have assigned in the Establishment Clause context to the suggestion that elementary school children are more impressionable than adults, cf., e.g., *id.,* at 592, we have never extended our Establishment Clause jurisprudence to foreclose private religious conduct during nonschool hours merely because it takes place on school premises where elementary school children may be present.

None of the cases discussed by Milford persuades us that our Establishment Clause jurisprudence has gone this far. For example, Milford cites *Lee v. Weisman* for the proposition that "there are heightened concerns with protecting freedom of conscience from subtle coercive pressure in the elementary and secondary public schools," 505 U.S., at 592. In *Lee,* however, we concluded that attendance at the graduation exercise was obligatory. Id., at 586.... Here, where the school facilities are being used for a nonschool function and there is no government sponsorship of the Club's activities, *Lee* is inapposite.

Equally unsupportive is *Edwards v. Aguillard,* 482 U.S. 578, in which we held that a Louisiana law that proscribed the teaching of evolution as part of the public school curriculum, unless accompanied by a lesson on creationism, violated the Establishment Clause. In *Edwards,* we mentioned that students are susceptible to pressure in the classroom, particularly given their possible reliance on teachers as role models. See *id.,* at 584. . . . But we did not suggest that, when the school was not actually advancing religion, the impressionability of students would be relevant to the Establishment Clause issue. . . . *Edwards* involved the content of the curriculum taught by state teachers *during the school day* to children required to attend. Obviously, when individuals who are not schoolteachers are giving lessons after school to children permitted to attend only with parental consent, the concerns expressed in *Edwards* are not present.

Fourth, even if we were to consider the possible misperceptions by schoolchildren in deciding whether Milford's permitting the Club's activities would violate the Establishment Clause, the facts of this case simply do not support Milford's conclusion. . . . The meetings were held in a combined high school resource room and middle school special education room, not in an elementary school classroom. The instructors are not schoolteachers. And the children in the group are not all the same age as in the normal classroom setting; their ages range from 6 to 12. In sum, these circumstances simply do not support the theory that small children would perceive endorsement here.

Finally, even if we were to inquire into the minds of schoolchildren in this case, we cannot say the danger that children would misperceive the endorsement of religion is any greater than the danger that they would perceive a hostility toward the religious viewpoint if the Club were excluded from the public forum. This concern is particularly acute given the reality that Milford's building is not used only for elementary school children. Students, from kindergarten through the 12th grade, all attend school in the same building. There may be as many, if not more, upperclassmen as elementary school children who occupy the school after hours. . . .

We cannot operate, as Milford would have us do, under the assumption that any risk that small children would perceive endorsement should counsel in favor of excluding the Club's religious activity. We decline to employ Establishment Clause jurisprudence using a modified heckler's veto, in which a group's religious activity can be proscribed on the basis of what the youngest members of the audience might misperceive. . . . There are countervailing constitutional concerns related to rights of other individuals in the community. In this case, those countervailing concerns are the free speech rights of the Club and its members. And, we have already found that those rights have been violated, not merely perceived to have been violated, by the school's actions toward the Club.

We are not convinced that there is any significance in this case to the possibility that elementary school children may witness the Good News Club's activities on school premises, and therefore we can find no reason to depart from our holdings in *Lamb's Chapel* and *Widmar.* Accordingly, we conclude that permitting the Club to meet on the school's premises would not have violated the Establishment Clause.

. . .

The judgment of the Court of Appeals is reversed, and the case is remanded for further proceedings consistent with this opinion.

It is so ordered.

■ JUSTICE STEVENS, dissenting.

The Milford Central School has invited the public to use its facilities for educational and recreational purposes, but not for "religious purposes." Speech for "religious purposes" may reasonably be understood to encompass three different categories. First, there is religious speech that is simply speech about a particular topic from a religious point of view. The film in *Lamb's Chapel* . . . . illustrates this category. Second, there is religious speech that amounts to worship, or its equivalent. Our decision in *Widmar v. Vincent* concerned such speech. Third, there is an intermediate category that is aimed principally at proselytizing or inculcating belief in a particular religious faith.

A public entity may not generally exclude even religious worship from an open public forum. *Id.*, at 276, 102 S.Ct. 269. Similarly, a public entity that creates a limited public forum for the discussion of certain specified topics may not exclude a speaker simply because she approaches those topics from a religious point of view. Thus, in *Lamb's Chapel* we held that a public school that permitted its facilities to be used for the discussion of family issues and child rearing could not deny access to speakers presenting a religious point of view on those issues.

But, while a public entity may not censor speech about an authorized topic based on the point of view expressed by the speaker, it has broad discretion to "preserve the property under its control for the use to which it is lawfully dedicated." "A school's extracurricular activities constitute a part of the school's teaching mission, and the school accordingly must make 'decisions concerning the content of those activities' " (quoting *Widmar*, 454 U.S., at 278, 102 S.Ct. 269 (STEVENS, J., concurring in judgment)). Accordingly, "control over access to a nonpublic forum can be based on subject matter and speaker identity so long as the distinctions drawn are reasonable in light of the purpose served by the forum and are viewpoint neutral." The novel question that this case presents concerns the constitutionality of a public school's attempt to limit the scope of a public forum it has created. More specifically, the question is whether a school can, consistently with the First Amendment, create a limited public forum that admits the first type of religious speech without allowing the other two.

Distinguishing speech from a religious viewpoint, on the one hand, from religious proselytizing, on the other, is comparable to distinguishing meetings to discuss political issues from meetings whose principal purpose is to recruit new members to join a political organization. If a school decides to authorize afterschool discussions of current events in its classrooms, it may not exclude people from expressing their views simply because it dislikes their particular political opinions. But must it therefore allow organized political groups—for example, the Democratic Party, the Libertarian Party, or the Ku Klux Klan—to hold meetings, the principal purpose of which is not to discuss the current-events topic from their own unique point of view but rather to recruit others to join their respective groups? I think not. Such recruiting meetings may introduce divisiveness and tend to separate young children into cliques that undermine the school's educational mission.[Citation omitted.]

School officials may reasonably believe that evangelical meetings designed to convert children to a particular religious faith pose the same risk. And, just as a school may allow meetings to discuss current events from a political perspective without also allowing organized political recruitment, so too can a school allow discussion of topics such as moral development from a religious (or nonreligious) perspective without thereby opening its forum to religious proselytizing or worship.... Moreover, any doubt on a question such as this should be resolved in a way that minimizes "intrusion by the Federal Government into the operation of our public schools," *Mergens*, 496 U.S., at 290, 110 S.Ct. 2356 (STEVENS, J., dissenting)....

■ JUSTICE SOUTER, with whom JUSTICE GINSBURG joins, dissenting.

The majority rules on two issues. First, it decides that the Court of Appeals failed to apply the rule in *Lamb's Chapel*...., which held that the government may not discriminate on the basis of viewpoint in operating a limited public forum. The majority applies that rule and concludes that Milford violated *Lamb's Chapel* in denying Good News the use of the school. The majority then goes on to determine that it would not violate the Establishment Clause of the First Amendment for the Milford School District to allow the Good News Club to hold its intended gatherings of public school children in Milford's elementary school. The majority is mistaken on both points....

I

.... *Lamb's Chapel* held that the government could not "permit school property to be used for the presentation of all views about family issues and child rearing except those dealing with the subject matter from a religious standpoint." 508 U.S., at 393–394.

This case, like *Lamb's Chapel*, properly raises no issue about the reasonableness of Milford's criteria for restricting the scope of its designated public forum. Milford has opened school property for, among other things, "instruction in any branch of education, learning or the arts" and for "social, civic and recreational meetings and entertainment events and other uses pertaining to the welfare of the community, provided that such uses shall be nonexclusive and shall be opened to the general public." ... But Milford has done this subject to the restriction that "[s]chool premises shall not be used ... for religious purposes." As the District Court stated, Good News did "not object to the reasonableness of [Milford]'s policy that prohibits the use of [its] facilities for religious purposes."

The sole question before the District Court was, therefore, whether, in refusing to allow Good News's intended use, Milford was misapplying its unchallenged restriction in a way that amounted to imposing a viewpoint-based restriction on what could be said or done by a group entitled to use the forum for an educational, civic, or other permitted purpose. The question was whether Good News was being disqualified when it merely sought to use the school property the same way that the Milford Boy and Girl Scouts and the 4–H Club did. The District Court held on the basis of undisputed facts that Good News's activity was essentially unlike the presentation of views on secular issues from a religious standpoint held to be protected in *Lamb's Chapel*, and was instead activity precluded by Milford's unchallenged policy against religious use, even under the narrowest definition of that term. . . .

Good News's classes open and close with prayer. In a sample lesson considered by the District Court, children are instructed that "[t]he Bible tells us how we can have our sins forgiven by receiving the Lord Jesus Christ. It tells us how to live to please Him. . . . If you have received the Lord Jesus as your Saviour from sin, you belong to God's special group— His family." The lesson plan instructs the teacher to "lead a child to Christ," and, when reading a Bible verse, to "[e]mphasize that this verse is from the Bible, God's Word," and is "important—and true—because God said it." The lesson further exhorts the teacher to "[b]e sure to give an opportunity for the 'unsaved' children in your class to respond to the Gospel" and cautions against "neglect[ing] this responsibility."

While Good News's program utilizes songs and games, the heart of the meeting is the "challenge" and "invitation," which are repeated at various times throughout the lesson. During the challenge, "saved" children who "already believe in the Lord Jesus as their Savior" are challenged to " 'stop and ask God for the strength and the "want" . . . to obey Him.' " . . . .

During the invitation, the teacher "invites" the "unsaved" children " 'to trust the Lord Jesus to be your Savior from sin,' " and " 'receiv[e] [him] as your Savior from sin.' " The children are then instructed that "[i]f you believe what God's Word says about your sin and how Jesus died and rose again for you, you can have His forever life today. Please bow your heads and close your eyes. If you have never believed on the Lord Jesus as your Savior and would like to do that, please show me by raising your hand. If you raised your hand to show me you want to believe on the Lord Jesus, please meet me so I can show you from God's Word how you can receive His everlasting life." *Ibid*.

It is beyond question that Good News intends to use the public school premises not for the mere discussion of a subject from a particular, Christian point of view, but for an evangelical service of worship calling children to commit themselves in an act of Christian conversion. The majority avoids this reality only by resorting to the bland and general characterization of Good News's activity as "teaching of morals and character, from a religious standpoint." If the majority's statement ignores reality, as it surely does, then today's holding may be understood only in equally generic terms. Otherwise, indeed, this case would stand for the remarkable proposition that any public school opened for civic meetings must be opened for use as a church, synagogue, or mosque. . . .

THE ESTABLISHMENT CLAUSE IN THE PUBLIC SCHOOLS

(1) *Good News* presents a tension between two First Amendment protections that school officials have struggled with in recent years. Under the Establishment Clause, the state must be neutral toward religious groups and cannot take actions that have the primary effect of advancing religion. At the same time, the state cannot unduly burden individual's right of free expression, whether the speech involves religious expression or other content. Viewpoint discrimination, as we learned in *Tinker*, is an offensive burden on this right. Do you agree with the *Good News* court that the school district's decision not to permit the religious club to use the school facilities discriminated on the basis of the Club's religious viewpoint? Or, as the dissent suggests, was the school excluding the club under a reasonable restriction of a limited public forum prohibiting use "for religious purposes?" Does the Court's conclusion that the club can not be excluded effectively mean that public school facilities must be open for religious worship?

The Court in *Good News* relies heavily on two earlier opinions. *Lamb's Chapel v. Center Moriches Union Free School District*, 508 U.S. 384, 113 S.Ct. 2141, 124 L.Ed.2d 352 (1993) involved a school board policy that permitted the after-hours use of school property for several specified purposes, but prohibited use by any group for religious purposes. The petitioner was an evangelical church group that requested use of facilities to show a Christian film on family values and child rearing, which request was denied under the policy. The Supreme Court held that the policy and its application to this case was a denial of the petitioners' right of freedom of speech. The Court rejected the church's claim that the school district, in opening its property to civic and social organizations, had created a public forum. Thus, the district was free to control access to the non-public forum "based on subject matter and speaker identity, so long as the distinctions drawn are reasonable in light of the purpose served by the forum and are viewpoint neutral." Thus, although the school district could impose reasonable restrictions if it chose to open its property for after-hours use, it could not deny access based on the view point of the speaker. This, the Court concluded, was what the school district regulation did. The district would have permitted school property to be used to present views on child rearing and family values, as long as the speaker did not address the topic from a religious perspective.

The Court also rejected the school district's argument that for it to permit public property to be used for religious purposes would have been a violation of the Establishment Clause. The Court acknowledged that under some circumstances, the showing of a religious film on school property might violate the Establishment Clause. Under the circumstances in this case, however, "there would have been no realistic danger the community would think that the district was endorsing religion." 508 U.S. at 395.

Rosenberger v. Rector and Visitors of the University of Virginia, 515 U.S. 819, 115 S.Ct. 2510, 132 L.Ed.2d 700 (1995), another opinion relied upon by the Court in *Good News*, involved a University of Virginia policy that denied student activity funds to a Christian student group, Wide Awake, that published an evangelical newspaper. The Court applied the reasoning of *Lamb's Chapel* to funding issues and concluded that the University policy violated the students' freedom of speech. The fact that money rather than access to meeting space was at issue was irrelevant.

(2) **The Equal Access Act and *Board of Education v. Mergens.*** In the 1970s and 1980s, many school districts tried to avoid Establishment Clause violations by excluding all religious activities from public schools. These concerns led to the kinds of policies under which religious groups and subject matter were singled out for exclusion, while other groups and topics were permitted on school premises. Policies of this kind, of course, were struck down in *Rosenberger, Lambs' Chapel*

and *Good News.* In the late 1980s (before these opinions were decided), Congress responded to school policies that discriminated against religious expression by enacting the Equal Access Act. Under this statute, a public secondary school with a "limited public forum" is prohibited from denying, "on the basis of the 'religious, political, philosophical or other content' of their speech, 'equal access' to students who wanted to conduct a meeting within that forum." 20 U.S.C. §§ 4071–4074. Under the Act, a limited open forum is created when a school "grants an offering to or opportunity for one or more noncurriculum related student groups to meet on school premises during noninstructional time." § 4071(b). If even one non-curricular group is allowed to meet, other groups can not be excluded on the basis of the content of their speech, and must be given equal access to meet during noninstructional time on school premises. Under the statute, a fair opportunity to conduct meetings is provided if the meetings are voluntary, student-initiated, not school-sponsored, but also not directed, controlled, conducted, or regularly attended by "nonschool persons." §§ 4071(c)(1), (2), (4), and (5). A teacher or other school employee can be assigned for custodial purposes, but if the meeting is religious in nature, school employees can only attend in a "nonparticipatory capacity." § 4071(c)(3). The Act expressly does not limit the authority of the school to maintain order and discipline.

In *Board of Education v. Mergens,* 496 U.S. 226, 110 S.Ct. 2356, 110 L.Ed.2d 191 (1990), the Equal Access Act withstood a challenge that it violated the Establishment Clause. The case involved the denial by the principal of Westside High School of a request by a student, Bridget Mergens, to form a Christian club at the high school. At the time, the high school had. approximately 30 clubs and groups that met after school, which students could join on a voluntary basis. The school justified denying permission for Bridget to form a Christian club on two grounds: First, it claimed the Act's prohibition did not apply to Westside High School because it had only curricular clubs and no non-curricular clubs which triggered the statutory requirement; Second the school board claimed if the Act did apply to Westside High School, it violated the Establishment Clause.

The Court, in a divided opinion written by Justice O'Connor, concluded that several of Westside's student clubs and groups were non-curriculum related groups under the statute, which created a limited public forum. The statute did not define "non-curriculum related student group, although it defined 'meeting' as including 'those activities of student groups which are ... not *directly related* to the school curriculum.' " In light of Congress' antidiscriminatory purpose, the Court concluded that "noncurriculum related student group" should be interpreted broadly to mean "any student group that does not *directly* relate to the body of courses offered by the school." Thus, a chess club, a stamp collecting club, or a community service club would be "noncurriculum related student groups" for purposes of the Act, unless they were directly related to the curriculum, were required, or if students received academic credit. The existence of such groups would create a "limited open forum" under the Act; as a result, the school would be prohibited from denying equal access to any other student group on the basis of the content of that group's speech. "Whether a specific student group is a 'noncurriculum related student group' [would] depend on a particular school's curriculum." The Court rejected the school's effort to define groups such as the Subsurfers, Welcome to Westside Club, the National Honor Society, two Rotary-affiliated service organizations, and the Future Business Leaders of America as "curriculum-related." The statute would be meaningless, the Court suggested, if every group that abstractly promoted some educational goal was defined as "curriculum-related." Moreover, the Court pointed to other clubs such as Band, Dramatics, Choir, and Orchestra, which by the school's own description were part of the curriculum, unlike the contested clubs and groups.

The Court then turned to the question of whether the Equal Access Act violated the Establishment Clause, as claimed by the school board, because "official recognition of respondents' proposed club would effectively incorporate religious activities into the school's official program, endorse participation in the religious club, and provide the club with an official platform to proselytize other students." The Court rejected this argument, finding that the non-discrimination policy, which extended to philosophical and political as well as religious speech, had a secular purpose, and in fact would avoid entanglement with religion by providing equal access to both secular and religious speech. In the Court's view, objective observers would not perceive official school support for meetings by religious clubs. The court emphasized the maturity of high school students in reaching this conclusion. It also pointed to the restrictions on participation by school officials under the statute as further protection against perceptions of school endorsement.

Under the Equal Access Act as interpreted by the Supreme Court in *Mergens,* are school officials required to recognize any student group that does not engage in or advocate disruption? What if a White Supremacist group seeks recognition? Could the authorities refuse recognition on the ground that other students would react to this group in a way that could lead to disorder or disruption? Can this justification be reconciled with *Tinker*? Can you think of other justifications?

Several courts have found that, under the Equal Access Act, schools that allow non-curricular student groups to use school facilities can not exclude groups promoting tolerance of (and devoted to the concerns of interests of) gay and lesbian students. See e.g. *Straights and Gays for Equality (SAGE) v. Osseo Area Schools–District No. 279*, 471 F.3d 908 (8th Cir.2006); *Boyd Co. High School Gay Straight Alliance v. Board of Education*, 258 F.Supp.2d 667 (E.D.Ky.2003); *East High Gay/Straight Alliance v. Board of Education of Salt Lake City School District*, 81 F.Supp.2d 1166 (D.Utah 1999). Must schools recognize sororities and fraternities under the Equal Access Act? As discussed earlier, courts and legislatures generally have given school officials the authority to restrict these groups. Are restrictive policies more vulnerable in light of *Mergens*?

(3) **Establishment Clause Violations in the Public School Setting**. The Supreme Court opinions discussed thus far clarify that when students or others engage in private religious speech on school property, the threat of an Establishment Clause violation by the school district will probably be deemed insubstantial unless the school is likely to be seen as endorsing religion or the religious perspective of the speaker. Under what circumstances might this happen? What if the religious film was shown in an assembly during school hours? Would the age of the students make a difference? The Court in *Mergens* seemed to suggest that it might, emphasizing the ability of high school students to understand that permitting a Christian group to meet does not signal that the school endorses the viewpoint of the group. However, *Good News* dismisses the concern that elementary school students would be confused by the presence of the Christian club. Do you agree? Consider the following cases.

In *Lee v. Weisman*, 505 U.S. 577, 112 S.Ct. 2649, 120 L.Ed.2d 467 (1992), the parent of a student at Nathan Bishop Middle School challenged the tradition in Providence, Rhode Island, middle and high schools of inviting members of the clergy to offer invocation and benediction prayers at the graduation ceremonies. At Deborah Weisman's graduation, a rabbi, conforming to guidelines given by the school, offered "inclusive" non-sectarian prayers. Mr. Weisman sought a permanent injunction against such graduation prayers in the future as a violation of the Establishment Clause of the First Amendment.

The Supreme Court, in a divided opinion, concluded that the custom of including clergy as part of an official graduation ceremony was a clear violation of the Establishment Clause. Several aspects of the custom troubled the Court. School officials were directly involved in soliciting the performance of a religious exercise as part of a school ceremony, established guidelines for the performance, and controlled the substantive content of the prayer through the requirement that the prayer be non-sectarian. Moreover, in effect, participation by the students attending the ceremony was required. Most non-believing students would feel compelled by official and peer pressure to participate, to the extent of standing and remaining silent during the prayer. The Court was skeptical that objecting students would feel free to protest, citing psychological research regarding the importance of social conformity and peer influence for adolescents. Finally, the Court rejected the state's argument that participation in the graduation ceremony was voluntary, and thus that any inducement to participate in a religious exercise in the ceremony itself was excused because students could opt not to attend. The Court called this argument "formalistic in the extreme," given the importance of high school graduation as a life occasion for most people.

In a later opinion, the Supreme Court struck down on Establishment Clause grounds a policy initiated by a school district that provided for a student election to determine whether an invocation should be delivered at high school football games, and (following a positive vote), a second election to choose the student who would offer the invocation. *Sante Fe Independent School Dist. v. Doe,* 530 U.S. 290, 120 S.Ct. 2266, 147 L.Ed.2d 295 (2000). After the policy was announced, a group of students sued the District, seeking an injunction on the ground that the policy and invocation were in violation of the Establishment Clause. The Supreme Court agreed, rejecting the District's argument that the football game invocations were private student speech and not government-sponsored speech. The policies violated the Establishment Clause because the football game messages were public speech authorized by a policy initiated by the District and implemented through school-sponsored elections. Moreover, the speech took place on public school property at government-sponsored school-related events and was broadcast over the school public address system. Further, the District policy involved both perceived and actual government endorsement of prayer at school events. Under the school regulations, the invocation was to be conducted in a way that was consistent with the policy's goal of "solemnizing the event." The Court also rejected the school district's effort to distinguish *Weisman* on the ground that, in contrast to graduation, a football game was an extracurricular activity, and attendance was voluntary. The Court pointed out that for many students (football players, band members, cheerleaders), attendance was not voluntary. Moreover, many students might feel social pressure to attend football games, and should not be made to choose between social embarrassment and submitting to "a personally offensive religious ritual."

Would a student-initiated prayer ever be acceptable under the Establishment Clause? Suppose members of the senior class initiated the proposal for a graduation prayer and supervised a referendum on the question of whether to include a prayer in the ceremony—without any involvement of school officials. Courts have not agreed on whether this response to *Lee v. Weisman* is acceptable. See *Doe v. Duncanville Independent School District,* 70 F.3d 402 (5th Cir.1995) (student referendum acceptable) and *A.C.L.U. of New Jersey v. Black Horse Pike Regional Board of Education,* 84 F.3d 1471 (3d Cir.1996) (prayer by student referendum violates Establishment Clause).

(4) **School Authority to Restrict Students' Religious Expression.** In light of the recent developments in First Amendment doctrine as it applies to schools, one might ask whether school officials have any authority to regulate truly private student religious expression. Do the Establishment Clause concerns that once led school officials to restrict students' religious speech have any salience today?

In fact, school officials and teachers retain considerable authority to restrict religious speech in curricular settings. A federal appellate court rejected a student's claim that her right of free speech was violated where a teacher refused to allow her to write a research paper on "The Life of Jesus Christ." *Settle v. Dickson Co. School Board,* 53 F.3d 152 (6th Cir.1995). The teacher assigned the paper so that the students could learn to do research, synthesize the information gathered, and write the paper on the basis of the research. Each student was permitted to choose a topic. The plaintiff, after failing to get prior approval as required, submitted an outline for a paper on the life of Jesus. The teacher refused to accept the outline on the grounds that the student, a devout Christian, would be unlikely to write a dispassionate research paper on this topic or to do the necessary research. The teacher also felt that it would be difficult for her to criticize the paper. The court found no violation of the student's right of Free Expression. Citing *Tinker*, the court emphasized that school officials have substantial control over student speech where they are engaged in administering the curriculum. In this case, the teacher offered legitimate pedagogical reasons for refusing to accept the topic and no evidence was presented that she was hostile toward religion. Similarly, a teacher's refusal to allow a first grader to distribute candy canes with a religious message attached (describing the supposed Christian origins of candy canes) to his class mates was found not to be a violation of the student's free expression rights. *Walz v. Egg Harbor Township Board of Education*, 342 F.3d 271 (3d Cir.2003), cert. denied, 541 U.S. 936, 124 S.Ct. 1658, 158 L.Ed.2d 356 (2004). The gift distribution was part of a classroom seasonal party which was designed to teach social skills to the children, and the court found that excluding gifts with religious or political messages was consistent with the educational goals promoted by the activity. The court emphasized that the parties were highly structured, supervised and regulated by the school as a classroom activity. Would the outcome have differed if the P.T.O had organized the parties?

On the other hand, students are free to engage in private religious speech in school within the constraints of the *Tinker–Fraser–Hazelwood* framework, supra. *Westfield High School L.I.F.E. Club v. City of Westfield*, 249 F.Supp.2d 98 (D.Mass. 2003). Thus, a high school principal was found to violate students' right of Free Expression when he prohibited a Christian student group from distributing candy canes with a religious message attached. In this case, the students belonged to a student-run non-curricular club, which met after school in the school building. The candy distribution took place in the halls, cafeteria and on the grounds during non-instructional time. The court found that the candy distribution was private speech that threatened no disruption of school activities. Moreover, the activity was not school-sponsored and there was no likelihood that the distribution would be seen to bear the school's imprimatur by other students, who were all of high school age.

Could the school district be liable to a student graduation speaker, chosen on the basis of academic performance, when it censors his speech because of its religious content? The Ninth Circuit Court of Appeals addressed this issue in a case in which a Christian student submitted to the principal a draft of his proposed graduation speech which included many quotations from the Bible and urged his fellow graduates to "develop a personal relationship with God, through faith in Jesus Christ." *Lassonde v. Pleasanton Unified School Dist.,* 320 F.3d 979 (9th Cir.2003), cert. denied, 540 U.S. 817, 124 S.Ct. 78, 157 L.Ed.2d 34 (2003). The school principal informed the student that he was free to comment on his own religious beliefs, but that he must remove the proselytizing statements from the speech. The student sued the school for violating his right of Free Speech. The appellate court rejected the argument, finding that the school would have violated the Establishment Clause had it *not* censored the religious content of the speech. Censorship was necessary to avoid the appearance of school sponsorship of the religious speech, and also to avoid the coercive impact that the religious speech would have had on dissenters at the ceremony. The court distinguished *Good News Club*, supra, on the ground that, unlike the club involved in that case, the graduation ceremony, as the Court in *Lee v. Weisman* emphasized, was a school-sponsored activity and attendance was obligatory.

(5) The state regulation of home schooling and parents' efforts to control curriculum, discussed in Chapter II, also raise Establishment and Free Exercise Clause questions.

C. Constitutional Issues in School Discipline
1. Procedural Due Process

Goss v. Lopez

Supreme Court of the United States, 1975.
419 U.S. 565, 95 S.Ct. 729, 42 L.Ed.2d 725.

■ Mr. Justice White delivered the opinion of the Court.

[Public school students in Ohio who had been suspended for misconduct for up to 10 days without a hearing brought this class action against appellant school officials. They sought a declaration that Ohio's statute allowing such suspensions was unconstitutional and an order enjoining school officials to remove references to the suspensions from the students' records. A three-judge district court declared that the statute and its implementing regulations were unconstitutional, found that appellant students had been denied due process of law, and granted the injunction.]

. . .

At the outset, appellants contend that because there is no constitutional right to an education at public expense, the Due Process Clause does not protect against expulsions from the public school system. This position misconceives the nature of the issue and is refuted by prior decisions. The Fourteenth Amendment forbids the State to deprive any person of life, liberty, or property without due process of law. Protected interests in property are normally "not created by the Constitution. Rather, they are created and their dimensions are defined" by an independent source such as state statutes or rules entitling the citizen to certain benefits.

. . .

Here, on the basis of state law, appellees plainly had legitimate claims of entitlement to a public education. Ohio Rev.Code Ann. §§ 3313.48 and 3313.64 (1972 and Supp.1973) direct local authorities to provide a free education to all residents between five and 21 years of age, and a compulsory-attendance law requires attendance for a school year of not less than 32 weeks. It is true that § 3313.66 of the Code permits school principals to suspend students for up to 10 days; but suspensions may not be imposed without any grounds whatsoever. All of the schools had their own rules specifying the grounds for expulsion or suspension. Having chosen to extend the right to an education to people of appellees' class generally,

Ohio may not withdraw that right on grounds of misconduct, absent fundamentally fair procedures to determine whether the misconduct has occurred.

Although Ohio may not be constitutionally obligated to establish and maintain a public school system, it has nevertheless done so and has required its children to attend. Those young people do not "shed their constitutional rights" at the schoolhouse door. Tinker v. Des Moines School Dist., 393 U.S. 503, 506 (1969). "The Fourteenth Amendment, as now applied to the States, protects the citizen against the State itself and all of its creatures—Boards of Education not excepted." West Virginia Board of Education v. Barnette, 319 U.S. 624, 637 (1943). The authority possessed by the State to prescribe and enforce standards of conduct in its schools, although concededly very broad, must be exercised consistently with constitutional safeguards. Among other things, the State is constrained to recognize a student's legitimate entitlement to a public education as a property interest which is protected by the Due Process Clause and which may not be taken away for misconduct without adherence to the minimum procedures required by that Clause.

The Due Process Clause also forbids arbitrary deprivations of liberty. "Where a person's good name, reputation, honor, or integrity is at stake because of what the government is doing to him," the minimal requirements of the Clause must be satisfied. Wisconsin v. Constantineau, 400 U.S. 433, 437 (1971); ... School authorities here suspended appellees from school for periods of up to 10 days based on charges of misconduct. If sustained and recorded, those charges could seriously damage the students' standing with their fellow pupils and their teachers as well as interfere with later opportunities for higher education and employment. It is apparent that the claimed right of the State to determine unilaterally and without process whether that misconduct has occurred immediately collides with the requirements of the Constitution.

Appellants proceed to argue that even if there is a right to a public education protected by the Due Process Clause generally, the Clause comes into play only when the State subjects a student to a "severe detriment or grievous loss." The loss of 10 days, it is said, is neither severe nor grievous and the Due Process Clause is therefore of no relevance. Appellants' argument is again refuted by our prior decisions; for in determining "whether due process requirements apply in the first place, we must look not to the 'weight' but to the *nature* of the interest at stake." Board of Regents v. Roth, supra [408 U.S. 564 (1972)] at 570–571. Appellees were excluded from school only temporarily, it is true, but the length and consequent severity of a deprivation, while another factor to weigh in determining the appropriate form of hearing, "is not decisive of the basic right" to a hearing of some kind. Fuentes v. Shevin, 407 U.S. 67, 86 (1972). The Court's view has been that as long as a property deprivation is not *de minimis*, its gravity is irrelevant to the question whether account must be taken of the Due Process Clause. A 10–day suspension from school is not *de minimis* in our view and may not be imposed in complete disregard of the Due Process Clause.

A short suspension is, of course, a far milder deprivation than expulsion. But, "education is perhaps the most important function of state and local governments," Brown v. Board of Education, 347 U.S. 483, 493 (1954), and the total exclusion from the educational process for more than a trivial period, and certainly if the suspension is for 10 days, is a serious event in the life of the suspended child. Neither the property interest in educational benefits temporarily denied nor the liberty interest in reputation, which is also implicated, is so insubstantial that suspensions may constitutionally be imposed by any procedure the school chooses, no matter how arbitrary.

III

"Once it is determined that due process applies, the question remains what process is due." Morrissey v. Brewer, 408 U.S., at 481. We turn to that question, fully realizing as our cases regularly do that the interpretation and application of the Due Process Clause are intensely practical matters and that "[t]he very nature of due process negates any concept of inflexible procedures universally applicable to every imaginable situation." Cafeteria Workers v. McElroy, 367 U.S. 886, 895 (1961).

. . .

... At the very minimum ... students facing suspension and the consequent interference with a protected property interest must be given *some* kind of notice and afforded *some* kind of hearing. "Parties whose rights are to be affected are entitled to be heard; and in order that they may enjoy that right they must first be notified." Baldwin v. Hale, 1 Wall. 223, 233 (1864).

... [T]he timing and content of the notice and the nature of the hearing will depend on appropriate accommodation of the competing interests involved. Cafeteria Workers v. McElroy, supra, at 895; Morrissey v. Brewer, supra at 481. The student's interest is to avoid unfair or mistaken exclusion from the educational process, with all of its unfortunate consequences. The Due Process Clause will not shield him from suspensions properly imposed, but it disserves both his interest and the interest of the State if his suspension is in fact unwarranted. The concern would be mostly academic if the disciplinary process were a totally accurate, unerring process, never mistaken and never unfair. Unfortunately, that is not the case, and no one suggests that it is. Disciplinarians, although proceeding in utmost good faith, frequently act on the reports and advice of others; and the controlling facts and the nature of the conduct under challenge are often disputed. The risk of error is not at all trivial, and it should be guarded against if that may be done without prohibitive cost or interference with the educational process.

The difficulty is that our schools are vast and complex. Some modicum of discipline and order is essential if the educational function is to be performed. Events calling for discipline are frequent occurrences and sometimes require immediate, effective action. Suspension is considered not only to be a necessary tool to maintain order but a valuable educational device. The prospect of imposing elaborate hearing requirements in every suspension case is viewed with great concern, and many school authorities may well prefer the untrammeled power to act unilaterally, unhampered by rules about notice and hearing. But it would be a strange disciplinary system in an educational institution if no communication was sought by the disciplinarian with the student in an effort to inform him of his dereliction and to let him tell his side of the story in order to make sure that an injustice is not done. . . .

We do not believe that school authorities must be totally free from notice and hearing requirements if their schools are to operate with acceptable efficiency. Students facing temporary suspension have interests qualifying for protection of the Due Process Clause, and due process requires, in connection with a suspension of 10 days or less, that the student be given oral or written notice of the charges against him and, if he denies them, an explanation of the evidence the authorities have and an opportunity to present his side of the story. The Clause requires at least these rudimentary precautions against unfair or mistaken findings of misconduct and arbitrary exclusion from school.

There need be no delay between the time "notice" is given and the time of the hearing. In the great majority of cases the disciplinarian may informally discuss the alleged misconduct with the student minutes after it has occurred. We hold only that, in being given an opportunity to explain his version of the facts at this discussion, the student first be told what he is accused of doing and what the basis of the accusation is. Lower courts which have addressed the question of the *nature* of the procedures required in short suspension cases have reached the same conclusion. Since the hearing may occur almost immediately following the misconduct, it follows that as a general rule notice and hearing should precede removal of the student from school. We agree with the District Court, however, that there are recurring situations in which prior notice and hearing cannot be insisted upon. Students whose presence poses a continuing danger to persons or property or an ongoing threat of disrupting the academic process may be immediately removed from school. In such cases, the necessary notice and rudimentary hearing should follow as soon as practicable, as the District Court indicated.

. . .

We stop short of construing the Due Process Clause to require, countrywide, that hearings in connection with short suspensions must afford the student the opportunity to secure counsel, to confront and cross-examine witnesses supporting the charge, or to call his own witnesses to verify his version of the incident. Brief disciplinary suspensions are almost countless. To impose in each such case even truncated trial-type procedures might well overwhelm administrative facilities in many places and, by diverting resources, cost more than it would save in educational effectiveness. Moreover, further formalizing the suspension process and escalating its formality and adversary nature may not only make it too costly as a regular disciplinary tool but also destroy its effectiveness as part of the teaching process.

On the other hand, requiring effective notice and informal hearing permitting the student to give his version of the events will provide a meaningful hedge against erroneous action. At least the disciplinarian will be alerted to the existence of disputes about facts and arguments about cause and effect. He may then determine himself to summon the accuser, permit cross-examination, and allow the student to present his own witnesses. In more difficult cases, he may permit counsel. In any event, his discretion will be more informed and we think the risk of error substantially reduced.

. . .

We should also make it clear that we have addressed ourselves solely to the short suspension, not exceeding 10 days. Longer suspensions or expulsions for the remainder of the school term, or permanently, may require more formal procedures. Nor do we put aside the possibility that in unusual situations, although involving only a short suspension, something more than the rudimentary procedures will be required.

. . .

Affirmed.

■ Mr. Justice Powell, with whom The Chief Justice, Mr. Justice Blackmun, and Mr. Justice Rehnquist join, dissenting.

The Court today invalidates an Ohio statute that permits student suspensions from school without a hearing "for not more than ten days." The decision unnecessarily opens avenues for judicial intervention in the operation of our public schools that may affect adversely the quality of education. The Court holds for the first time that the federal courts, rather than educational officials and state legislatures, have the authority to determine the rules applicable to routine classroom discipline of children and teenagers in the public schools. It justifies this unprecedented intrusion into the process of elementary and secondary education by identifying a new constitutional right: the right of a student not to be suspended for as much as a single day without notice and a due process hearing either before or promptly following the suspension.

. . .

One of the more disturbing aspects of today's decision is its indiscriminate reliance upon the judiciary, and the adversary process, as the means of resolving many of the most routine problems arising in the classroom. In mandating due process procedures the Court misapprehends the reality of the normal teacher-pupil relationship. There is an ongoing relationship, one in which the teacher must occupy many roles—educator, adviser, friend, and, at times, parent-substitute. It is rarely adversary in nature except with respect to the chronically disruptive or insubordinate pupil whom the teacher must be free to discipline without frustrating formalities.

The Ohio statute, providing as it does for due notice both to parents and the Board, is compatible with the teacher-pupil relationship and the informal resolution of mistaken disciplinary action. We have relied for generations upon the experience, good faith and dedication of those who staff our public schools, and the nonadversary means of airing grievances that always have been available to pupils and their parents. One would have thought before today's opinion that this informal method of resolving differences was more compatible with the interests of all concerned than resort to any constitutionalized procedure, however blandly it may be defined by the Court.

In my view, the constitutionalizing of routine classroom decisions not only represents a significant and unwise extension of the Due Process Clause, but it also was quite unnecessary in view of the safeguards prescribed by the Ohio statute. This is demonstrable from a comparison of what the Court mandates as required by due process with the protective procedures it finds constitutionally insufficient.

The Ohio statute, limiting suspensions to not more than eight school days, requires *written* notice including the "reasons therefor" to the student's parents and to the Board of Education within 24 hours of any suspension. The Court only requires oral *or* written notice to the pupil, with no notice being required to the parents or the Board of Education. The mere fact of the statutory requirement is a deterrent against arbitrary action by the principal. The Board, usually elected by the people and sensitive to constituent relations, may be expected to identify a principal whose record of suspensions merits inquiry. In any event, parents placed on written notice may exercise their rights as constituents by going directly to the Board or a member thereof if dissatisfied with the principal's decision.

Nor does the Court's due process "hearing" appear to provide significantly more protection than that already available. The Court holds only that the principal must listen to the student's "version of the events," either before suspension or thereafter—depending upon the circumstances. Such a truncated "hearing" is likely to be considerably less meaningful than the opportunities for correcting mistakes already available to students and parents. Indeed, in this case all of the students and parents were offered an opportunity to attend a conference with school officials.

In its rush to mandate a constitutional rule, the Court appears to give no weight to the practical manner in which suspension problems normally would be worked out under Ohio law. One must doubt, then, whether the constitutionalization of the student-teacher relationship, with all of its attendant doctrinal and practical difficulties, will assure in any meaningful sense greater protection than that already afforded under Ohio law.

No one can foresee the ultimate frontiers of the new "thicket" the Court now enters. Today's ruling appears to sweep within the protected interest in education a multitude of discretionary decisions in the educational process. Teachers and other school authorities are required to make many decisions that may have serious consequences for the pupil. They must decide, for example, how to grade the student's work, whether a student passes or fails a course, whether he is to be promoted, whether he is required to take certain subjects, whether he may be excluded from interscholastic athletics or other extracurricular activities, whether he may be removed from one school and sent to another, whether he may be bused long distances when available schools are nearby, and whether he should be placed in a "general," "vocational," or "college-preparatory" track.

In these and many similar situations claims of impairment of one's educational entitlement identical in principle to those before the Court today can be asserted with equal or greater justification. . . .

. . .

Not so long ago, state deprivations of the most significant forms of state largesse were not thought to require due process protection on the ground that the deprivation resulted only in the loss of a state-provided "benefit." E.g., Bailey v. Richardson, 86 U.S.App.D.C. 248, 182 F.2d 46 (1950), aff'd by an equally divided Court, 341 U.S. 918 (1951). In recent years the Court, wisely in my view, has rejected the "wooden distinction between 'rights' and 'privileges,' " Board of Regents v. Roth, 408 U.S., at 571, and looked instead to the significance of the state-created or state-enforced right and to the substantiality of the alleged deprivation. Today's opinion appears to abandon this reasonable approach by holding in effect that government infringement of any interest to which a person is entitled, no matter what the interest or how inconsequential the infringement, requires *constitutional* protection. As it is difficult to think of any less consequential infringement than suspension of a junior high school student for a single day, it is equally difficult to perceive any principled limit to the new reach of procedural due process.[22]

. . .

DUE PROCESS RIGHTS IN SCHOOL

(1) Is the Court in *Goss,* in holding that a student who is subject to a short suspension is entitled to procedural due process, according students an important right to be used against school officials? Will what is required in *Goss* create a substantial burden to school administrators, or is it simply requiring that those officials treat students with minimal decency? What exactly is required of the official in this situation? If the accused child has a witness who will support his account of events, must the official hear this evidence? Does the child have a right to confront her accuser?

Courts have tended to be quite deferential to school authority, in the wake of *Goss,* in evaluating whether suspended students have been accorded sufficient due process. For example, in *Breeding v. Driscoll*, 82 F.3d 383 (11th Cir.1996), the court found a telephone conversation between the principal and the student and her mother to be a sufficient hearing for a nine-day suspension. The conversation took

---

22. Some half dozen years ago, the Court extended First Amendment rights under limited circumstances to public school pupils. Mr. Justice Black, dissenting, viewed the decision as ushering in "an entirely new era in which the power to control pupils by the elected 'officials of state supported public schools' . . . is in ultimate effect transferred to the Supreme Court." Tinker v. Des Moines School Dist., 393 U.S. 503, 515 (1969). There were some who thought Mr. Justice Black was unduly concerned. But his prophecy is now being fulfilled. In the few years since *Tinker* there have been literally hundreds of cases by schoolchildren alleging violation of their constitutional rights. This flood of litigation, between pupils and school authorities, was triggered by a narrowly written First Amendment opinion which I could well have joined on its facts. One can only speculate as to the extent to which public education will be disrupted by giving every schoolchild the power to contest in *court* any decision made by his teacher which arguably infringes the state-conferred right to education.

. . .

place a few hours after the student had been bodily removed from the school for fighting, shouting obscenities, and ignoring instructions by the principal. The court found that the removal before the hearing was appropriate because the student was disruptive. It also found it to be unimportant that the decision to suspend may have been made before the phone conversation, because at that point the decision was tentative and, based on the conversation, it could have been modified or reversed.

The school policy applied in *Breeding* was typical of those enacted by many school boards after *Goss*. School administrators were permitted to suspend students for up to nine days after a "conference." A longer suspension required a formal hearing before the Board of Education.

Courts also have deferred to school administrators in interpreting the sufficiency of due process when administrators add other sanctions to a ten-day suspension from school. The suspension from extracurricular, social, or athletic events does not trigger additional due process requirements beyond those outlined in *Goss. Donovan v. Ritchie*, 68 F.3d 14 (1st Cir.1995).

Courts have also held that reassigning a student to an alternative school, which may not have typical classroom instruction by teachers for forty-five days does not trigger due process concerns unless the quality of education provided by the alternative school is so inferior to regular public school that it amounts to a denial of public education equivalent to expulsion or suspension. *Marner v. Eufaula City School Bd.*, 204 F.Supp.2d 1318 (M.D.Ala.2002). However, the "extremely minimal" due process rights of students may be violated in some circumstances. Where the student "alleged actual bias of [the school principal], pursuing punishment against a student for a rumor that affected him personally," this was evidence of insufficient process to satisfy the student's due process rights. *Riggan v. Midland Indep. Sch. Dist.*, 86 F.Supp.2d 647 (W.D.Tex.2000). Conduct being disciplined may be "of such an obviously personal nature that any reasonable administrator would have deferred to another uninvolved individual to conduct any investigation or to mete out any discipline." The high school principal, Neil Richmond, was under investigation for sexual improprieties when he disciplined Casey Riggan, a senior at his school, for being involved when other students took pictures of the principal's vehicle on the street outside of a female teacher's home. Neither the exact charges leveled against the student nor the precise conduct being punished was ever made clear, even once the case was presented to the appeals court. As a result, the court found that the principal did not satisfy due process guarantees. Under such circumstances, "the entire punishment assessed against Riggan must be considered as a whole" to determine whether it implicated the state-created property interest in education. The court held that Riggan's property interest was infringed by the punishment consisting of three day suspension, reassignment to an alternative school for five days during the finals reviews of his senior year, exclusion from graduation ceremonies and two letters of apology.

(2) **Due Process and Academic Performance.** Questions have arisen about the scope of *Goss* and the extent to which due process must be accorded students when school officials make a decision that impairs a property interest of the student. What if the student believes that she has been wrongly placed in a vocational education track and should be in a college preparatory curriculum? What if she believes that a teacher has been irrationally or malevolently giving her poor grades. Is she entitled to a hearing in either of these cases?

In *Board of Curators of University of Missouri v. Horowitz*, 435 U.S. 78, 98 S.Ct. 948, 55 L.Ed.2d 124 (1978), the question of whether due process standards apply to academic grading reached the U.S. Supreme Court in the context of an adult student who had been dismissed from medical school. Although the special problems of the case, including the fact that decisions about clinical performance were involved, may make the case seem far afield from the situation of a middle or high school student, some of the language from the opinion of the Court by Justice Rehnquist set the tone for future cases. Upholding the district court's finding that due process requirements had been satisfied in the case, the opinion by Justice Rehnquist states:

> Since the issue first arose 50 years ago, state and lower federal courts have recognized that there are distinct differences between decisions to suspend or dismiss a student for disciplinary purposes and similar actions taken for academic reasons which may call for hearings in connection with the former but not the latter.
>
> . . .
>
> Academic evaluations of a student, in contrast to disciplinary determinations, bear little resemblance to the judicial and administrative fact-finding proceedings to which we have traditionally attached a full hearing requirement. In *Goss*, the school's decision to suspend the students rested on factual conclusions that the individual students had participated in demonstrations that had disrupted classes, attacked a police officer, or caused physical damage to school property. The requirement of a hearing, where the student could present his side of the factual issue, could under such circumstances "provide a meaningful hedge against erroneous action." The decision to dismiss respondent, by comparison, rested on the academic judgment of school officials that she did not have the necessary clinical ability to perform adequately as a medical doctor and was making insufficient progress toward that goal. Such a judgment is by its nature more subjective and evaluative than the typical factual questions presented in the average disciplinary decision. Like the decision of an individual professor as to the proper grade for a student in his course, the determination whether to dismiss a student for academic reasons requires an expert evaluation of cumulative information and is not readily adapted to the procedural tools of judicial or administrative decisionmaking.
>
> Under such circumstances, we decline to ignore the historic judgment of educators and thereby formalize the academic dismissal process by requiring a hearing. The educational process is not by nature adversarial; instead it centers around a continuing relationship between faculty and students, "one in which the teacher must occupy many roles—educator, adviser, friend, and at times, parent-substitute." Goss v. Lopez, 419 U.S. 565, 594 (1975) (POWELL, J., dissenting). This is especially true as one advances through the varying regimes of the educational system, and the instruction becomes both more individualized and more specialized. In *Goss*, this Court concluded that the value of some form of hearing in a disciplinary context outweighs any resulting harm to the academic environment. Influencing this conclusion was clearly the belief that disciplinary proceedings, in which the teacher must decide whether to punish a student for disruptive or insubordinate behavior, may automatically bring an adversarial flavor to the normal student-teacher relationship. The same conclusion does not follow in the academic context. We decline to further enlarge the judicial presence in the academic community and thereby risk deterioration of many beneficial aspects of the faculty-student relationship. . . .

435 U.S. at 87, 89–90.

(3) In *Wood v. Strickland*, 420 U.S. 308, 95 S.Ct. 992, 43 L.Ed.2d 214 (1975), the Supreme Court determined that while school officials are entitled to a qualified good-faith immunity from damages pursuant to 42 U.S.C.A. § 1983, they are not immune from liability if they knew or reasonably should have known that their official action would violate the constitutional rights of the students involved. Thus,

students have been provided with a means of enforcing the rights they were granted through *Goss*. However the scope of review of the federal courts is quite limited with respect to such disciplinary decisions of high school officials as are likely to spawn dispute:

> Given the fact that there was evidence supporting the charge against respondents, the contrary judgment of the Court of Appeals is improvident. It is not the role of the federal courts to set aside decisions of school administrators which the court may view as lacking a basis in wisdom or compassion. Public high school students do have substantive and procedural rights while at school.... But § 1983 does not extend the right to relitigate in federal court evidentiary questions arising in school disciplinary proceedings or the proper construction of school regulations. The system of public education that has evolved in this Nation relies necessarily upon the discretion and judgment of school administrators and school board members, and § 1983 was not intended to be a vehicle for federal court correction of errors in the exercise of that discretion which do not rise to the level of violations of specific constitutional guarantees.

420 U.S. at 326.

2.   CORPORAL PUNISHMENT

Ingraham v. Wright

Supreme Court of the United States, 1977.
430 U.S. 651, 97 S.Ct. 1401, 51 L.Ed.2d 711.

Court upheld the disciplinary corporal punishment policy of Florida's public schools by 5-4 vote

■ MR. JUSTICE POWELL delivered the opinion of the Court.

This case presents questions concerning the use of corporal punishment in public schools: First, whether the paddling of students as a means of maintaining school discipline constitutes cruel and unusual punishment in violation of the Eighth Amendment; and, second, to the extent that paddling is constitutionally permissible, whether the Due Process Clause of the Fourteenth Amendment requires prior notice and an opportunity to be heard.

I

Petitioners James Ingraham and Roosevelt Andrews filed the complaint in this case on January 7, 1971, in the United States District Court for the Southern District of Florida. At the time both were enrolled in the Charles R. Drew Junior High School in Dade County, Fla., Ingraham in the eighth grade and Andrews in the ninth. The complaint contained three counts, each alleging a separate cause of action for deprivation of constitutional rights, under 42 U.S.C. §§ 1981–1988. Counts one and two were individual actions for damages by Ingraham and Andrews based on paddling incidents that allegedly occurred in October 1970 at Drew Junior High School. Count three was a class action for declaratory and injunctive relief filed on behalf of all students in the Dade County schools....

. . .

Petitioners' evidence may be summarized briefly. In the 1970–1971 school year many of the 237 schools in Dade County used corporal punishment as a means of maintaining discipline pursuant to Florida legislation and a local School Board regulation. The statute then in effect authorized limited corporal punishment by negative inference, proscribing punishment which was "degrading or unduly severe" or which was inflicted without prior consultation with the principal or the teacher in charge of the school. Fla.Stat.Ann. § 232.27 (1961).[6] The regulation, Dade County School Board Policy 5144, contained explicit directions and limitations.[7] The authorized

6. In the 1970–1971 school year, § 232.27 provided:

"Each teacher or other member of the staff of any school shall assume such authority for the control of pupils as may be assigned to him by the principal and shall keep good order in the classroom and in other places in which he is assigned to be in charge of pupils, but he shall not inflict corporal punishment before consulting the principal or teacher in charge of the school, and in no case shall such punishment be degrading or unduly severe in its nature . . . ."

Effective July 1, 1976, the Florida Legislature amended the law governing corporal punishment. Section 232.27 now reads:

"Subject to law and to the rules of the district school board, each teacher or other member of the staff of any school shall have such authority for the control and discipline of students as may be assigned to him by the principal or his designated representative and shall keep good order in the class-room and in other places in which he is assigned to be in charge of students. If a teacher feels that corporal punishment is necessary, at least the following procedures shall be followed:

(1) The use of corporal punishment shall be approved in principle by the principal before it is used, but approval is not necessary for each specific instance in which it is used.

(2) A teacher or principal may administer corporal punishment only in the presence of another adult who is informed beforehand, and in the student's presence, of the reason for the punishment.

(3) A teacher or principal who has administered punishment shall, upon request, provide the pupil's parent or guardian with a written explanation of the reason for the punishment and the name of the other [adult] who was pres-

ent." Fla.Stat.Ann. § 232.27 (1977) (codifier's notation omitted).

Corporal punishment is now defined as "the moderate use of physical force or physical contact by a teacher or principal as may be necessary to maintain discipline or to enforce school rules." § 228.041(28). The local school boards are expressly authorized to adopt rules governing student conduct and discipline and are directed to make available codes of student conduct, § 230.23(6). Teachers and principals are given immunity from civil and criminal liability for enforcing disciplinary rules, "[e]xcept in the case of excessive force or cruel and unusual punishment. . . ." § 232.275.

7. In the 1970–1971 school year, Policy 5144 authorized corporal punishment where the failure of other means of seeking cooperation from the student made its use necessary. The regulation specified that the principal should determine the necessity for corporal punishment, that the student should understand the seriousness of the offense and the reason for the punishment, and that the punishment should be administered in the presence of another adult in circumstances not calculated to hold the student up to shame or ridicule. The regulation cautioned against using corporal punishment against a student under psychological or medical treatment, and warned that the person administering the punishment "must realize his own personal liabilities" in any case of physical injury.

While this litigation was pending in the District Court, the Dade County School Board amended Policy 5144 to standardize the size of the paddles used in accordance with the description in the text, to proscribe striking a child with a paddle elsewhere than on the buttocks, to limit the permissible number of "licks" (five for elementary and intermediate grades and seven for junior and senior grades), and to require a contemporaneous explanation of the need for the punishment to the student and a subsequent notification to the parents.

refusing to obey

punishment consisted of paddling the recalcitrant student on the buttocks with a flat wooden paddle measuring less than two feet long, three to four inches wide, and about one-half inch thick. The normal punishment was limited to one to five "licks" or blows with the paddle and resulted in no apparent physical injury to the student. School authorities viewed corporal punishment as a less drastic means of discipline than suspension or expulsion. Contrary to the procedural requirements of the statute and regulation, teachers often paddled students on their own authority without first consulting the principal.

Petitioners focused on Drew Junior High School. ... The evidence ... suggests that the regime at Drew was exceptionally harsh. The testimony of Ingraham and Andrews, in support of their individual claims for damages, is illustrative. Because he was slow to respond to his teacher's instructions, Ingraham was subjected to more than 20 licks with a paddle while being held over a table in the principal's office. The paddling was so severe that he suffered a hematoma requiring medical attention and keeping him out of school for several days. Andrews was paddled several times for minor infractions. On two occasions he was struck on his arms, once depriving him of the full use of his arm for a week.

. . .

We granted certiorari, limited to the questions of cruel and unusual punishment and procedural due process.

II

In addressing the scope of the Eighth Amendment's prohibition on cruel and unusual punishment this Court has found it useful to refer to "[t]raditional common-law concepts," Powell v. Texas, 392 U.S. 514, 535 (1968) (plurality opinion), and to the "attitude[s] which our society has traditionally taken." Id., at 531. So, too, in defining the requirements of procedural due process under the Fifth and Fourteenth Amendments, the Court has been attuned to what "has always been the law of the land," United States v. Barnett, 376 U.S. 681, 692 (1964), and to "traditional ideas of fair procedure." Greene v. McElroy, 360 U.S. 474, 508 (1959). We therefore begin by examining the way in which our traditions and our laws have responded to the use of corporal punishment in public schools.

The use of corporal punishment in this country as a means of disciplining school children dates back to the colonial period. It has survived the transformation of primary and secondary education from the colonials' reliance on optional private arrangements to our present system of compulsory education and dependence on public schools. Despite the general abandonment of corporal punishment as a means of punishing criminal offenders, the practice continues to play a role in the public education of school children in most parts of the country. Professional and public opinion is sharply divided on the practice, and has been for more than a century. Yet we can discern no trend toward its elimination.

At common law a single principle has governed the use of corporal punishment since before the American Revolution: Teachers may impose reasonable but not excessive force to discipline a child. Blackstone catalogued among the "absolute rights of individuals" the right "to security from the corporal insults of menaces, assaults, beating, and wounding," 1 W. Blackstone, Commentaries * 134, but he did not regard it a "corporal insult" for a teacher to inflict "moderate correction" on a child in his care. To the extent that force was "necessary to answer the purposes for which [the teacher] is employed," Blackstone viewed it as "justifiable or lawful." Id., at * 453; 3 id., at * 120. The basic doctrine has not changed. The prevalent rule in this country today privileges such force as a teacher or administrator "reasonably believes to be necessary for [the child's] proper control, training, or education." Restatement (Second) of Torts § 147(2) (1965); see id., § 153(2). To the extent that the force is excessive or unreasonable, the educator in virtually all States is subject to possible civil and criminal liability.

Although the early cases viewed the authority of the teacher as deriving from the parents, the concept of parental delegation has been replaced by the view—more consonant with compulsory education laws— that the State itself may impose such corporal punishment as is reasonably necessary "for the proper education of the child and for the maintenance of group discipline." 1 F. Harper & F. James, Law of Torts § 3.20, p. 292 (1956). All of the circumstances are to be taken into account in determining whether the punishment is reasonable in a particular case. Among the most important considerations are the seriousness of the offense, the attitude and past behavior of the child, the nature and severity of the punishment, the age and strength of the child, and the availability of less severe but equally effective means of discipline. Id., at 290–291; Restatement (Second) of Torts § 150, Comments *c–e*, p. 268 (1965).

Of the 23 States that have addressed the problem through legislation, 21 have authorized the moderate use of corporal punishment in public schools. Of these States only a few have elaborated on the common-law test of reasonableness, typically providing for approval or notification of the child's parents, or for infliction of punishment only by the principal or in the presence of an adult witness. Only two States, Massachusetts and New Jersey, have prohibited all corporal punishment in their public schools. Where the legislatures have not acted, the state courts have uniformly preserved the common-law rule permitting teachers to use reasonable force in disciplining children in their charge.

Against this background of historical and contemporary approval of reasonable corporal punishment, we turn to the constitutional questions before us.

III

The Eighth A[mendment provides: "Exc]ive bail shall not be required, nor excess[ive fines imposed, a]nd unusual punishments
inflicted." Bail, fir[es, and punishment traditio]lly have been associated
with the criminal [process, and by subjecting the] three to parallel limitations the text of th[e Amendment suggests an inten]tion to limit the power of
those entrusted wit[h the criminal-law function of] government. An examination of the history of the Amendment and the decisions of this Court

construing the proscription against cruel and unusual punishment confirms that it was designed to protect those convicted of crimes....

. . .

Petitioners acknowledge that the original design of the Cruel and Unusual Punishments Clause was to limit criminal punishments, but urge nonetheless that the prohibition should be extended to ban the paddling of schoolchildren. Observing that the Framers of the Eighth Amendment could not have envisioned our present system of public and compulsory education, with its opportunities for noncriminal punishments, petitioners contend that extension of the prohibition against cruel punishments is necessary lest we afford greater protection to criminals than to schoolchildren. It would be anomalous, they say, if schoolchildren could be beaten without constitutional redress, while hardened criminals suffering the same beatings at the hands of their jailers might have a valid claim under the Eighth Amendment. Whatever force this logic may have in other settings,[37] we find it an inadequate basis for wrenching the Eighth Amendment from its historical context and extending it to traditional disciplinary practices in the public schools.

The prisoner and the schoolchild stand in wholly different circumstances, separated by the harsh facts of criminal conviction and incarceration....

The schoolchild has little need for the protection of the Eighth Amendment. Though attendance may not always be voluntary, the public school remains an open institution. Except perhaps when very young, the child is not physically restrained from leaving school during school hours; and at the end of the school day, the child is invariably free to return home. Even while at school, the child brings with him the support of family and friends and is rarely apart from teachers and other pupils who may witness and protest any instances of mistreatment.

The openness of the public school and its supervision by the community afford significant safeguards against the kinds of abuses from which the Eighth Amendment protects the prisoner. In virtually every community where corporal punishment is permitted in the schools, these safeguards are reinforced by the legal constraints of the common law. Public school teachers and administrators are privileged at common law to inflict only such corporal punishment as is reasonably necessary for the proper education and discipline of the child; any punishment going beyond the privilege may result in both civil and criminal liability. See Part II, supra. As long as the schools are open to public scrutiny, there is no reason to believe that the common-law constraints will not effectively remedy and deter excesses such as those alleged in this case.

---

37. Some punishments, though not labeled "criminal" by the State, may be sufficiently analogous to criminal punishments in the circumstances in which they are administered to justify application of the Eighth Amendment. Cf. In re Gault, 387 U.S. 1 (1967). We have no occasion in this case, for example, to consider whether or under what circumstances persons involuntarily confined in mental or juvenile institutions can claim the protection of the Eighth Amendment.

We conclude that when public school teachers or administrators impose disciplinary corporal punishment, the Eighth Amendment is inapplicable. The pertinent constitutional question is whether the imposition is consonant with the requirements of due process.

IV

The Fourteenth Amendment prohibits any state deprivation of life, liberty, or property without due process of law. Application of this prohibition requires the familiar two-stage analysis: We must first ask whether the asserted individual interests are encompassed within the Fourteenth Amendment's protection of "life, liberty or property"; if protected interests are implicated, we then must decide what procedures constitute "due process of law." Morrissey v. Brewer, 408 U.S. at 481; . . . Following that analysis here, we find that corporal punishment in public schools implicates a constitutionally protected liberty interest, but we hold that the traditional common-law remedies are fully adequate to afford due process.

A

. . .

. . . The liberty [protected by the Due Process Clause of the Fourteenth Amendment] included the right "generally to enjoy those privileges long recognized at common law as essential to the orderly pursuit of happiness by free men." Meyer v. Nebraska, 262 U.S. 390, 399 (1923); . . . Among the historic liberties so protected was a right to be free from and to obtain judicial relief, for unjustified intrusions on personal security.

. . . It is fundamental that the state cannot hold and physically punish an individual except in accordance with due process of law.

This constitutionally protected liberty interest is at stake in this case. There is, of course a *de minimis* level of imposition with which the Constitution is not concerned. But at least where school authorities, acting under color of state law, deliberately decide to punish a child for misconduct by restraining the child and inflicting appreciable physical pain, we hold that Fourteenth Amendment liberty interests are implicated.

B

"[T]he question remains what process is due." Morrissey v. Brewer, supra, at 481. Were it not for the common-law privilege permitting teachers to inflict reasonable corporal punishment on children in their care, and the availability of the traditional remedies for abuse, the case for requiring advance procedural safeguards would be strong indeed. But here we deal with a punishment—paddling—within that tradition, and the question is whether the common-law remedies are adequate to afford due process. . . .

Whether in this case the common-law remedies for excessive corporal punishment constitute due process of law must turn on an analysis of the competing interests at stake, viewed against the background of "history, reason, [and] the past course of decisions." The analysis requires consideration of three distinct factors: "First, the private interest that will be affected . . . ; second, the risk of an erroneous deprivation of such interest

. . . and the probable value, if any, of additional or substitute procedural safeguards; and, finally, the [state] interest, including the function involved and the fiscal and administrative burdens that the additional or substitute procedural requirement would entail." Mathews v. Eldridge, 424 U.S. 319, 335 (1976).

1

Because it is rooted in history, the child's liberty interest in avoiding corporal punishment while in the care of public school authorities is subject to historical limitations. Under the common law, an invasion of personal security gave rise to a right to recover damages in a subsequent judicial proceeding. 3 W. Blackstone, Commentaries * 120–121. But the right of recovery was qualified by the concept of justification. Thus, there could be no recovery against a teacher who gave only "moderate correction" to a child. Id., at * 120. To the extent that the force used was reasonable in light of its purpose, it was not wrongful, but rather "justifiable or lawful." Ibid.

The concept that reasonable corporal punishment in school is justifiable continues to be recognized in the laws of most States. It represents "the balance struck by this country," Poe v. Ullman, 367 U.S. 497, 542 (1961) (Harlan, J., dissenting), between the child's interest in personal security and the traditional view that some limited corporal punishment may be necessary in the course of a child's education. Under that long-standing accommodation of interests, there can be no deprivation of substantive rights as long as disciplinary corporal punishment is within the limits of the common-law privilege.

This is not to say that the child's interest in procedural safeguards is insubstantial. The school disciplinary process is not "a totally accurate, unerring process, never mistaken and never unfair. . . ." Goss v. Lopez, 419 U.S. 565, 579–580 (1975). In any deliberate infliction of corporal punishment on a child who is restrained for that purpose, there is some risk that the intrusion on the child's liberty will be unjustified and therefore unlawful. In these circumstances the child has a strong interest in procedural safeguards that minimize the risk of wrongful punishment and provide for the resolution of disputed questions of justification.

We turn now to a consideration of the safeguards that are available under applicable Florida law.

2

Florida has continued to recognize, and indeed has strengthened by statute, the common-law right of a child not to be subjected to excessive corporal punishment in school. Under Florida law the teacher and principal of the school decide in the first instance whether corporal punishment is reasonably necessary under the circumstances in order to discipline a child who has misbehaved. But they must exercise prudence and restraint. For Florida has preserved the traditional judicial proceedings for determining whether the punishment was justified. If the punishment inflicted is later found to have been excessive—not reasonably believed at the time to be necessary for the child's discipline or training—the school authorities inflicting it may be held liable in damages to the child and, if malice is shown, they may be subject to criminal penalties.

Although students have testified in this case to specific instances of abuse, there is every reason to believe that such mistreatment is an aberration.... [B]ecause paddlings are usually inflicted in response to conduct directly observed by teachers in their presence, the risk that a child will be paddled without cause is typically insignificant....

In those cases where severe punishment is contemplated, the available civil and criminal sanctions for abuse—considered in light of the openness of the school environment—afford significant protection against unjustified corporal punishment. Teachers and school authorities are unlikely to inflict corporal punishment unnecessarily or excessively when a possible consequence of doing so is the institution of civil or criminal proceedings against them.[46]

It still may be argued, of course, that the child's liberty interest would be better protected if the common-law remedies were supplemented by the administrative safeguards of prior notice and a hearing. We have found frequently that some kind of prior hearing is necessary to guard against arbitrary impositions on interests protected by the Fourteenth Amendment. But where the State has preserved what "has always been the law of the land," United States v. Barnett, 376 U.S. 681 (1964), the case for administrative safeguards is significantly less compelling.

. . .

3

But even if the need for advance procedural safeguards were clear, the question would remain whether the incremental benefit could justify the cost. Acceptance of petitioners' claims would work a transformation in the law governing corporal punishment in Florida and most other States. Given the impracticability of formulating a rule of procedural due process that varies with the severity of the particular imposition, the prior hearing petitioners seek would have to precede *any* paddling, however moderate or trivial.

Such a universal constitutional requirement would significantly burden the use of corporal punishment as a disciplinary measure. Hearings—even informal hearings—require time, personnel, and a diversion of attention from normal school pursuits. School authorities may well choose to aban-

---

46. The low incidence of abuse, and the availability of established judicial remedies in the event of abuse, distinguish this case from Goss v. Lopez, 419 U.S. 565 (1975). The Ohio law struck down in *Goss* provided for suspensions from public school of up to 10 days without "any written procedure applicable to suspensions." Id., at 567. Although Ohio law provided generally for administrative review, Ohio Rev.Code Ann. § 2506.01 (Supp.1973), the Court assumed that the short suspensions would not be stayed pending review, with the result that the review proceeding could serve neither a deterrent nor a remedial function. 419 U.S., at 581 n. 10. In these circumstances, the Court held the law authorizing suspensions unconstitutional for failure to require "that there be at least an informal give-and-take between student and disciplinarian, preferably prior to the suspension...." Id., at 584. The subsequent civil and criminal proceedings available in this case may be viewed as affording substantially greater protection to the child than the informal conference mandated by *Goss*.

don corporal punishment rather than incur the burdens of complying with the procedural requirements. Teachers, properly concerned with maintaining authority in the classroom, may well prefer to rely on other disciplinary measures—which they may view as less effective—rather than confront the possible disruption that prior notice and a hearing may entail.[50] Paradoxically, such an alteration of disciplinary policy is most likely to occur in the ordinary case where the contemplated punishment is well within the common-law privilege.

Elimination or curtailment of corporal punishment would be welcomed by many as a societal advance. But when such a policy choice may result from this Court's determination of an asserted right to due process, rather than from the normal processes of community debate and legislative action, the societal costs cannot be dismissed as insubstantial. We are reviewing here a legislative judgment, rooted in history and reaffirmed in the laws of many States, that corporal punishment serves important educational interests. This judgment must be viewed in light of the disciplinary problems common-place in the schools. As noted in Goss v. Lopez, 419 U.S., at 580: "Events calling for discipline are frequent occurrences and sometimes require immediate, effective action." Assessment of the need for, and the appropriate means of maintaining, school discipline is committed generally to the discretion of school authorities subject to state law. "[T]he Court has repeatedly emphasized the need for affirming the comprehensive authority of the States and of school officials, consistent with fundamental constitutional safeguards, to prescribe and control conduct in the schools." Tinker v. Des Moines School Dist., 393 U.S. 503, 507 (1969).

"At some point the benefit of an additional safeguard to the individual affected . . . and to society in terms of increased assurance that the action is just, may be outweighed by the cost." Mathews v. Eldridge, 424 U.S., at 348. We think that point has been reached in this case. In view of the low incidence of abuse, the openness of our schools, and the common-law safeguards that already exist, the risk of error that may result in violation of a schoolchild's substantive rights can only be regarded as minimal. Imposing additional administrative safeguards as a constitutional requirement might reduce that risk marginally, but would also entail a significant intrusion into an area of primary educational responsibility. We conclude that the Due Process Clause does not require notice and a hearing prior to the imposition of corporal punishment in the public schools, as that practice is authorized and limited by the common law.

　　　.　.　.

Affirmed.

■ MR. JUSTICE WHITE, with whom MR. JUSTICE BRENNAN, MR. JUSTICE MARSHALL, and MR. JUSTICE STEVENS join, dissenting.

　　　.　.　.

50. If a prior hearing, with the inevitable attendant publicity within the school, resulted in rejection of the teacher's recommendation, the consequent impairment of the teacher's ability to maintain discipline in the classroom would not be insubstantial.

The Eighth Amendment places a flat prohibition against the infliction of "cruel and unusual punishments." This reflects a societal judgment that there are some punishments that are so barbaric and inhumane that we will not permit them to be imposed on anyone, no matter how opprobrious the offense. See Robinson v. California, 370 U.S. 660, 676 (1962) (Douglas, J., concurring). If there are some punishments that are so barbaric that they may not be imposed for the commission of crimes, designated by our social system as the most thoroughly reprehensible acts an individual can commit, then, *a fortiori,* similar punishments may not be imposed on persons for less culpable acts, such as breaches of school discipline. Thus, if it is constitutionally impermissible to cut off someone's ear for the commission of murder, it must be unconstitutional to cut off a child's ear for being late to class. Although there were no ears cut off in this case, the record reveals beatings so severe that if they were inflicted on a hardened criminal for the commission of a serious crime, they might not pass constitutional muster.

Nevertheless, the majority holds that the Eighth Amendment "was designed to protect [only] those convicted of crimes," relying on a vague and inconclusive recitation of the history of the Amendment. Yet the constitutional prohibition is against cruel and unusual *punishments*; nowhere is that prohibition limited or modified by the language of the Constitution. Certainly the fact that the Framers did not choose to insert the word "criminal" into the language of the Eighth Amendment is strong evidence that the Amendment was designed to prohibit all inhumane or barbaric punishments, no matter what the nature of the offense for which the punishment is imposed.

No one can deny that spanking of schoolchildren is "punishment" under any reasonable reading of the word, for the similarities between spanking in public schools and other forms of punishment are too obvious to ignore. Like other forms of punishment, spanking of schoolchildren involves an institutionalized response to the violation of some official rule or regulation proscribing certain conduct and is imposed for the purpose of rehabilitating the offender, deterring the offender and others like him from committing the violation in the future, and inflicting some measure of social retribution for the harm that has been done.

B

We are fortunate that in our society punishments that are severe enough to raise a doubt as to their constitutional validity are ordinarily not imposed without first affording the accused the full panoply of procedural safeguards provided by the criminal process. The effect has been that "every decision of this Court considering whether a punishment is 'cruel and unusual' within the meaning of the Eighth and Fourteenth Amendments has dealt with a criminal punishment." The Court would have us believe from this fact that there is a recognized distinction between criminal and noncriminal punishment for purposes of the Eighth Amendment. This is plainly wrong. "[E]ven a clear legislative classification of a statute as 'non-penal' would not alter the fundamental nature of a plainly penal statute." Trop v. Dulles, 356 U.S. 86, 95 (1958) (plurality opinion).

The relevant inquiry is not whether the offense for which a punishment is inflicted has been labeled as criminal, but whether the purpose of the deprivation is among those ordinarily associated with punishment, such as retribution, rehabilitation, or deterrence. Id., at 96.

If this purposive approach were followed in the present case, it would be clear that spanking in the Florida public schools is punishment within the meaning of the Eighth Amendment. The District Court found that "[c]orporal punishment is one of a variety of measures employed in the school system for the correction of pupil behavior and the preservation of order." App., at 146. Behavior correction and preservation of order are purposes ordinarily associated with punishment.

Without even mentioning the purposive analysis applied in the prior decisions of this Court, the majority adopts a rule that turns on the label given to the offense for which the punishment is inflicted. Thus, the record in this case reveals that one student at Drew Junior High School received 50 licks with a paddle for allegedly making an obscene telephone call. Brief for Petitioners 13. The majority holds that the Eighth Amendment does not prohibit such punishment since it was only inflicted for a breach of school discipline. However, that same conduct is punishable as a misdemeanor under Florida law, Fla.Stat.Ann. § 365.16 (Supp.1977) and there can be little doubt that if that same "punishment" had been inflicted by an officer of the state courts for violation of § 365.16, it would have had to satisfy the requirements of the Eighth Amendment.

C

.   .   .

The essence of the majority's argument is that school children do not need Eighth Amendment protection because corporal punishment is less subject to abuse in the public schools than it is in the prison system. However, it cannot be reasonably suggested that just because cruel and unusual punishments may occur less frequently under public scrutiny, they will not occur at all. The mere fact that a public flogging or a public execution would be available for all to see would not render the punishment constitutional if it were otherwise impermissible. Similarly, the majority would not suggest that a prisoner who is placed in a minimum-security prison and permitted to go home to his family on the weekends should be any less entitled to Eighth Amendment protections than his counterpart in a maximum-security prison. In short, if a punishment is so barbaric and inhumane that it goes beyond the tolerance of a civilized society, its openness to public scrutiny should have nothing to do with its constitutional validity.

Nor is it an adequate answer that schoolchildren may have other state and constitutional remedies available to them. Even assuming that the remedies available to public school students are adequate under Florida law, the availability of state remedies has never been determinative of the coverage or of the protections afforded by the Eighth Amendment. The reason is obvious. The fact that a person may have a state-law cause of action against a public official who tortures him with a thumbscrew for the commission of an antisocial act has nothing to do with the fact that such official conduct is cruel and unusual punishment prohibited by the Eighth Amendment. Indeed, the majority's view was implicitly rejected this Term in Estelle v. Gamble, 429 U.S. 97 (1976), when the Court held that failure to provide for the medical needs of prisoners could constitute cruel and unusual punishment even though a medical malpractice remedy in tort was available to prisoners under state law.

D

By holding that the Eighth Amendment protects only criminals, the majority adopts the view that one is entitled to the protections afforded by the Eighth Amendment only if he is punished for acts that are sufficiently opprobrious for society to make them "criminal." This is a curious holding in view of the fact that the more culpable the offender the more likely it is that the punishment will not be disproportionate to the offense, and consequently, the less likely it is that the punishment will be cruel and unusual. Conversely, a public school student who is spanked for a mere breach of discipline may sometimes have a strong argument that the punishment does not fit the offense, depending upon the severity of the beating, and therefore that it is cruel and unusual. Yet the majority would afford the student no protection no matter how inhumane and barbaric the punishment inflicted on him might be.

The issue presented in this phase of the case is limited to whether corporal punishment in public schools can *ever* be prohibited by the Eighth Amendment. I am therefore not suggesting that spanking in the public schools is in every instance prohibited by the Eighth Amendment. My own view is that it is not. I only take issue with the extreme view of the majority that corporal punishment in public schools, no matter how barbaric, inhumane, or severe, is never limited by the Eighth Amendment. Where corporal punishment becomes so severe as to be unacceptable in a civilized society, I can see no reason that it should become any more acceptable just because it is inflicted on children in the public schools.

II

. . .

... Although the respondent school authorities provide absolutely *no* process to the student before the punishment is finally inflicted, the majority concludes that the student is nonetheless given due process because he can later sue the teacher and recover damages if the punishment was "excessive."

This tort action is utterly inadequate to protect against erroneous infliction of punishment for two reasons. First, under Florida law, a student punished for an act he did not commit cannot recover damages from a teacher "proceeding in utmost good faith ... on the reports and advice of others,"; the student has no remedy at all for punishment imposed on the basis of mistaken facts, at least as long as the punishment was reasonable from the point of view of the disciplinarian, uninformed by any prior hearing. The "traditional common-law remedies" on which the majority relies, thus do nothing to protect the student from the danger that concerned the Court in *Goss*—the risk of reasonable, good-faith mistake in the school disciplinary process.

. . . [E]ven if the student could sue for good-faith error in the infliction of punishment, the lawsuit occurs after the punishment has been finally imposed. The infliction of physical pain is final and irreparable; it cannot be undone in a subsequent proceeding. There is every reason to require, as the Court did in *Goss*, a few minutes of "informal give-and-take between student and disciplinarian" as a "meaningful hedge" against the erroneous infliction of irreparable injury. 419 U.S., at 583–584.

. . .

■ [A separate dissenting opinion of Mr. Justice Stevens has been omitted.]

NOTE: CORPORAL PUNISHMENT

(1) **Corporal Punishment and Due Process**. An important issue before the courts since *Ingraham* is whether students have a substantive due process right to avoid excessive punishment. The Court in *Ingraham* was silent on this issue, conforming its attention to the Eighth Amendment and Procedural Due Process issues. In addressing the substantive due process question, some courts have applied a "shocking to the conscience" standard, refusing to find a constitutional violation even in cases of severe injury. *Brown v. Johnson*, 710 F.Supp. 183 (E.D.Ky.1989). Many courts, however, including five federal circuit courts of appeal, have found that a severe beating can amount to a constitutional violation of the student's right to substantive due process, giving rise to a federal cause of action under 42 U.S.C.A. § 1983 that is independent of any tort remedy available under state law. In *Hall v. Tawney*, the Fourth Circuit Court of Appeals found that severe punishment implicates "the right to ultimate bodily security—the most fundamental aspect of personal privacy." 621 F.2d 607, 613 (4th Cir.1980). *Hall* established a test, adapted from the police brutality context, to be used by courts in evaluating due process claims to determine whether a constitutional tort has occurred when a child is subjected to corporal punishment in school. The inquiry should focus on (1) the severity of the injury; (2) whether the force was disproportionate to the need; and (3) whether malice or sadism was involved. Similar tests have been adopted by other courts, although some courts have not required that malice or sadism be shown. Do you think this test sufficiently constrains school officials in imposing corporal punishment? Is it appropriate to apply the same test that is applied to police officers subduing criminal suspects?

The Eleventh Circuit Court of Appeals in *Neal v. Fulton County Bd. of Educ.*, 229 F.3d 1069 (2000) considered the case of a 14–year-old member of the public high school varsity football team who had an eye knocked completely out of its socket and lost sight in one eye when his coach hit him in the eye with a metal lock as punishment for fighting with another player. The court found that "corporal punishment that is intentional, obviously excessive, and creates a foreseeable risk of serious injury" may be a violation of a student's substantive due process rights. It observed that "almost all of the Courts of Appeals to address the issue squarely have said that a plaintiff alleging excessive corporal punishment may in certain circumstances state a claim under the substantive Due Process Clause." The court pointed out that the Fifth Circuit was the only circuit to deny such actions when "adequate state law remedies exist," a position which "[n]o other court has adopted" and has been "expressly rejected by other Circuits."

(2) **Punishment in Juvenile Correctional Facilities.** Under the reasoning of the Court in *Ingraham,* do you think that youngsters in a juvenile correctional facility have a stronger claim against a policy of corporal punishment? *Nelson v. Heyne,* 491 F.2d 352 (7th Cir.), cert. denied 417 U.S. 976, 94 S.Ct. 3183, 41 L.Ed.2d 1146 (1974), involved the issue of corporal punishment in a medium security correctional institution for boys aged 12 to 18. The court, while noting that the law seemed to be well settled that "reasonable and moderate" corporal punishment was not barred by the Eighth Amendment in academic institutions, pointed out that the school in this instance was correctional as well as academic. In that setting the disciplinary beatings were held to violate plaintiffs' Fourteenth Amendment right against cruel and unusual punishment. How can the different outcome be explained? At the time *Nelson* was decided, rehabilitation was the announced purpose for placing delinquent youth in juvenile correctional facilities (and, indeed, the opinion held that correctional facilities must provide confined youths with treatment for this reason). Today, many legislatures have amended their statutes to provide that punishment is an equally important purpose. Does that undermine or strengthen the *Nelson* rationale?

(3) **Baker v. Owen, 395 F.Supp. 294 (M.D.N.C.), affirmed 423 U.S. 907, 96 S.Ct. 210, 46 L.Ed.2d 137 (1975).** The Supreme Court affirmed in summary opinion this decision of a three-judge district court that corporal punishment of a sixth-grader against his mother's express wishes denied neither the mother nor the child federally protected constitutional rights. The mother asserted that administering such punishment after her specific objections was violative of her right to determine the appropriate disciplinary methods for her child. She urged that her right as a parent to make such choices was of a fundamental character. Although agreeing that "the fourteenth amendment concept of liberty embraces the right of a parent to determine and choose between means of discipline of children", the district court denied that the mother's right was "fundamental" in the sense that the state would be required to show a "compelling interest" that outweighed her parental right:

> We do not read *Meyer* and *Pierce* to enshrine parental rights so high in the hierarchy of constitutional values. In each case the parental right prevailed not because the Court termed it fundamental and the State's interest uncompelling, but because the Court considered the action to be arbitrary, without reasonable relation to an end legitimately within its power.

395 F.Supp. at 299.

The district court also rejected the Eighth Amendment claim:

> ... [T]his record does not begin to present a picture of punishment comparable to that in *Ingraham,* [498 F.2d 248,] at 255–59 [5th Cir.1974] or in Nelson v. Heyne, 491 F.2d 352 (7th Cir.1974), which we believe indicate the kinds of beatings that could constitute cruel and unusual punishment if the eighth amendment is indeed applicable.

Id. at 303.

The district court did indicate that the child had a liberty interest in avoiding corporal punishment, protectible under the Fourteenth Amendment. The net result of this finding was that certain procedural safeguards would be required:

> First, except for those acts of misconduct which are so anti-social or disruptive in nature as to shock the conscience, corporal punishment may never be used unless the student was informed beforehand that specific misbehavior could occasion its use, and, subject to this exception, it should never be employed as a first line of punishment for misbehavior. The requirements of an announced possibility of corporal punishment and an attempt to modify behavior by some

other means—keeping after school, assigning extra work, or some other punishment—will insure that the child has clear notice that certain behavior subjects him to physical punishment. Second, a teacher or principal must punish corporally in the presence of a second school official (teacher or principal), who must be informed beforehand and in the student's presence of the reason for the punishment. The student need not be afforded a formal opportunity to present his side to the second official; the requirement is intended only to allow a student to protest, spontaneously, an egregiously arbitrary or contrived application of punishment. And finally, an official who has administered such punishment must provide the child's parent, upon request, a written explanation of his reasons and the name of the second official who was present.

Id. at 302.

In *Hall v. Tawney*,[1] discussed in note 1 above, the precedential value of the United States Supreme Court's summary affirmation of *Baker* was challenged. Parents of Naomi Faye Hall complained that the school officials violated their rights to determine the means by which Naomi would be disciplined when she was paddled after her parents expressly told the school officials not to subject her to corporal punishment. In response to the parents' challenge, the *Hall* court explained, "The [United States Supreme] Court itself . . . has left little doubt as to the significance it attributes to its disposition of the case. In *Ingraham* it cites its summary affirmance of *Baker* as holding 'that parental approval of corporal punishment is not constitutionally required.'" Id. at 610. The *Hall* court further noted,

Even without the imprimatur of the Supreme Court, however, we would be inclined to accept the reasoning of *Baker*. The state interest in maintaining order in schools limits the rights of particular parents unilaterally to except their children from the regime to which other children are subject. Id.

The Halls suggested that the severity of the corporal punishment distinguished this case from *Baker*. The court explained,

We do not believe . . . that any constitutional right of parents to choose the means by which their child should be disciplined can be made to turn on the severity of the punishment. The reasons advanced in *Baker* for finding no parental constitutional rights implicated apply alike to all degrees of punishment. Id.

Although a school may provide procedures allowing parents to request that their child not be corporally punished, *Baker* has been cited in subsequent cases as standing for the proposition that parental approval of corporal punishment is, nevertheless, not constitutionally required.[2]

Can *Baker* be satisfactorily reconciled with constitutional doctrine defining the rights of parents to rear their children according to their own values? Is it consistent with *Yoder*? Can the outcome be understood based on some similarity to cases in which parents seek to exempt their children from curricular requirements? Remember that parents can usually exempt their children from sex education classes, on the ground that they do not want them subject to instruction that is inconsistent with the parents' values. Are policies regarding discipline different? Are the elaborate procedural safeguards required by the court in *Baker* an effort to accommodate the parents' interests? Which approach do you prefer, the guidelines of *Baker* or the rule in *Ingraham*?

1.   621 F.2d 607 (4th Cir.1980).

2.   *See, e.g., Campbell v. Gahanna–Jefferson Board of Education*, 129 Ohio App.3d 85, 717 N.E.2d 347 (1998).

(4) **Criticism of Corporal Punishment and the Legal Trend.** Corporal punishment, both by parents and by school officials, has been subject to widespread criticism. Numerous professional organizations have issued policy statements condemning corporal punishment in schools, including the American Medical Association, the American Academy of Pediatrics and American Psychiatric Association. Corporal punishment is banned in most European countries. It has been attacked on the grounds that it is inhumane, ineffective and imposed in a discriminatory manner. Physical punishment is viewed as inconsistent with a respect for human dignity. For public officials to engage in conduct that would be criminal assault if it took place on the street, or if adult victims were involved, denies the personhood of children. Moreover, psychologists and educators argue that other forms of discipline are more effective, without creating a response of anger and hostility in the child. Very troublesome also is the evidence that corporal punishment is more likely to be imposed on poor minority children whose parents are less likely to protest in a politically effective way than are middle class parents. This concern may clarify the prohibition of physical punishment by urban school boards, who are likely to be politically sensitive to this issue.

Corporal punishment also has been criticized as reinforcing a norm that violence against children is acceptable. Commenting on *Ingraham* not long after the decision had been announced, psychologists Edward Zigler and Susan Hunsinger stated that "It is difficult to imagine a more sweeping setback for child abuse prevention efforts because the decision makes a mockery of the entire prevention campaign." Zigler and Hunsinger, Supreme Court on Spanking: Upholding Discipline or Abuse?, Young Children, Sept. 1977, at 14. The authors point out that although it is assumed that corporal punishment is exercised for the sake of discipline rather than to vent teacher frustrations, most corporal punishment takes place in elementary and junior high schools rather than high schools, where the physical threat to school personnel presumably would be greatest.

In May, 2001, opponents of spanking lobbied the Congress successfully to change the wording of legislation protecting teachers from lawsuits to say explicitly it was not intended to reduce tort liability in excessive corporal punishment cases. An amendment was accepted to say, "Nothing in this section shall be construed to affect any state or local law (including a rule or regulation) or policy pertaining to the use of corporal punishment." "Paddling Foes Get Change In Amendment On Liability," *New York Times,* May 11, 2001, p. A22.

The legal trend has been to prohibit or restrict corporal punishment in schools. As Kathryn R. Urbonya has written:

> [W]hen the Ingraham Court looked at "modern" practices of corporal punishment in schools, the 1970s legal landscape still reflected the historical pattern of diminished personal security interests for children. The Court canvassed the states' corporal punishment policies in analyzing whether the Fourteenth Amendment required pre-hitting procedures:
>
>> Of the 23 States that have addressed the problem through legislation, 21 have authorized the moderate use of corporal punishment in public schools. Of these States only a few have elaborated on the common-law test of reasonableness, typically providing for approval or notification of the child's parents, or for infliction of punishment by the principal or in the presence of an adult witness. Only two States, Massachusetts and New Jersey, have prohibited all corporal punishment in their public schools. Where the legislatures have not acted, the state courts have uniformly preserved the common-law rule permitting teachers to use reasonable force in disciplining children in their charge.

In short, the Court found "contemporary approval of reasonable corporal punishment," and "discern[ed] no trend toward its elimination."

However, a survey of the same state laws today would reveal quite different results. In contrast to the 1970s, when twenty-one states authorized teachers to physically punish students, today only two states directly grant school officials the authority to use bodily punishment. Another state requires parents or guardians to consent before the striking of their children is permitted. And, in a dramatic reversal, nineteen states and the charter schools in the District of Columbia now expressly forbid corporal punishment.

Such statutes are analogous to the regulations of at least thirty-four states that ban foster parents from administering corporal punishment under any circumstances and provide further support for the notion that school officials serve as state-employed caregivers (like foster-parents) rather than as substitutes for biological parents. Though parents continue to assert a legal privilege to physically punish their children, a tradition with deep religious roots, many have begun to advocate the abolition of corporal punishment even in the home.

Fifteen states now give local school boards discretion to decide whether to authorize corporal punishment as a means of discipline and one state recently repealed its prior statute prohibiting corporal punishment. In addition, many states have enacted statutes that only generally refer to a school board's authority to discipline. Of these, eight authorize school officials to use reasonable force to foster a safe and educational environment. Only two states have failed to enact a statute addressing the use of force by school officials, whether to physically punish or to control students.

In addition, even in those states that either directly authorize physical punishment or that grant educational entities the discretion to do so, school officials may still lose immunity from state law claims challenging the use of force where: the force constitutes unreasonable discipline; the force used is not "administered in good faith . . . [and is] excessive or unduly severe"; the official "exhibit[s] a wanton and willful disregard of human rights or safety"; the force is "excessive . . . or [constitutes] cruel and unusual punishment"; the force used violates the local school board's disciplinary policy; or where school officials act with a "malicious purpose." In addition, one state limits school officials' immunity to punitive damages, as at commonlaw. Two others grant discretion to the board of education merely to "[i]nsure any employee of the school district . . . from an act . . . within the scope of employment; and others allow indemnification only if the actions do not constitute 'willful, wanton or malicious wrongdoing,' "; "gross negligence," or "intentional acts." Another state provides for state-funded legal representation of the challenged official only where the corporal punishment is administered in good faith.

Therefore, since *Ingraham*, states have increasingly recognized the importance of children's interest in personal security both in the classroom and at home by both limiting the authority of public school teachers to physically punish students and by increasing their scrutiny of the force parents use to discipline their children. These changes reflect an evolving society, one that understands protecting children from harm furthers the community interest as well as the child's individual interest.

Kathryn R. Urbonya, Determining Reasonableness Under the Fourth Amendment: Physical Force to Control and Punish Students, 10 Cornell J.L. & Pub. Pol'y 397, 426–434 (2001) (footnotes omitted).*

Given the direction of policy reform, should this form of punishment now be found to violate due process?

For a recent constitutional challenge of corporal punishment generally, see Deana Pollard, Banning Child Corporal Punishment, 77 Tulane L.Rev. 575 (2003).

Is the Court's emphasis on the historical use and acceptance of corporal punishment of children from Puritan times consistent with the trend toward according children greater individual rights and trying to uphold and maintain an educational system that will prepare them to enter a modern technological society? As Urbonya explains, at the time *Ingraham* was decided, almost all states permitted corporal punishment. Perhaps the opinion is not surprising in this light. Moreover, remember that four dissenting Justices were ready to hold that due process is required when school authorities use physical punishment. Are *Goss* and *Ingraham* simply inconsistent with one another? Perhaps the only puzzle is what motivated Justice Stewart, who was the only Justice to vote with the majority in both *Goss* and *Ingraham*.

(5) Through the efforts of a number of groups interested in school discipline problems, The National Center for the Study of Corporal Punishment and Alternatives in the Schools has been established. Based at the Department of Psychology, Temple University, Philadelphia, it maintains an extensive library on school discipline.

Much has been written on the topic of corporal punishment and its legal regulation. For a recent treatment, see Benjamin Shmueli, "Who's Afraid of Banning Corporal Punishment?" A Comparative View on Current and Desireable Models, 26 Penn.St. Int'l L.Rev. 57 (2007); David R. Hague, The Ninth Amendment: A Constitutional Challenge to Corporal Punishment in Public Schools, 55 U.Kan. L.Rev. 429 (2007); Lynn Roy, Corporal Punishment in American Public Schools and the Rights of the Child, 30 J.L. & Educ. 554 (2001); Whitney S. Wiedeman, Don't Spare the Rod: A Proposed Return to Public, Corporal Punishment of Convicts, 23 Amer.J.Crim.L. 651 (1996); Jerry R. Parkinson, Federal Court Treatment of Corporal Punishment in Public Schools: Jurisprudence that is Literally Shocking to the Conscience, 39 S.D.L.Rev. 278 (1994); John Dayton, Corporal Punishment in Public Schools: the Legal and Political Battle Continues, 89 Educ.L.Rep. 729 (1994); Mary Kate Kearney, Substantive Due Process and Parental Corporal Punishment: Democracy and the Excluded Child, 32 San Diego L.Rev. 1 (Winter 1995). For a book of readings on the general subject, see I. Hyman and J. Wise (eds.), Corporal Punishment in American Education: Readings in History, Practice, and Alternatives (1979).

NOTE: SCHOOL VIOLENCE AND ZERO TOLERANCE POLICIES

In the late 1990s, the public became alarmed about school violence, in part because of a number of highly publicized school shootings. The most prominent was probably the incident in Columbine High School in Littleton, Colorado in April of 1999, in which two high school seniors shot and killed 12 classmates and a teacher before killing themselves. See Matt Bai, *Anatomy of a Massacre*, Newsweek, May 3, 1999. In another case that got a great deal of attention, in part because of the youth of the perpetrators, two boys, ages 11 and 13, killed 5 classmates and a teacher and injured 10 other students in a middle school in Jonesboro, Arkansas. See Nadya Labi, *The Jonesboro Shootings*, Time, 28, April 6, 1998. In response to the perceived threat of school violence, many state legislatures (and some school systems without statutory support) have enacted "zero tolerance" policies. These policies are directed at violent behavior or threats by students, possession of weapons and drugs, and other misbehavior in school that is deemed dangerous. Many policies require mandatory suspension or expulsion from school of students who violate school rules covered by the policies. Under some regulations, school officials must call police to arrest violators. The key component of zero tolerance policies is that sanctions are mandatory; often, school officials have little discretion to exercise judgment or to consider mitigating circumstances in imposing one-size-fits-all punishments.

Although the term "zero tolerance" is derived from a federal statute regulating gun possession in schools (the Gun Free Schools Act of 1994), the reach of zero tolerance policies is far wider. Under many policies, for example, possession of weapons that triggers mandatory sanctions includes anything that could be used as a weapon. For example, an American Bar Association report that is highly critical of zero tolerance policies reports that a child who found a manicure kit with a one inch knife was suspended from school; a 17 year old was expelled for shooting a cafeteria worker with a paper clip shot from a rubber band, and two 10 year olds were suspended for putting soapy water in a teacher's drink. At the teacher's urging, police charged the boys with a felony. (The case was dismissed months later.) See ABA Opposition to Zero Tolerance Policy www//aba.net Feb. 19, 2001.

Moreover, mitigating circumstances (including the age of the child) and intent often are not considered. In Florida, a 5–year-old kindergarten student was suspended from school for telling a class mate, during a recess game of cops and robbers, that he was going to shoot him. *S.G. v. Sayreville Board of Education*, 333 F.3d 417 (3d Cir.2003). In a Loudoun County, Virginia, case, a 13–year-old middle school student, Benjamin Ratner, was expelled from school for possession of a knife that he had taken from a classmate. The girl who brought the knife to school told Benjamen that she had been suicidal the night before. Benjamin, who knew of the girl's previous suicide attempts, asked her for the knife and put it in his locker. He did not tell school officials, but planned to tell his parents and her parents. The official who intervened, Dean Fanny Kellogg, stated that she believed that Ratner acted in what he believed was the girl's best interest and "at no time did [he] pose a threat to harm to anyone with the knife." Nonetheless, Ratner was suspended for the remainder of the school term. The Fourth Circuit Court of Appeals rejected Ratner's Due Process claim on the ground that he was given notice and a hearing (of sorts) and thus received constitutionally sufficient due process under *Goss v. Lopez. Ratner v. Loudoun Co. Public Schools*, 16 Fed.Appx. 140 (4th Cir.2001). The court stated:

> However harsh the results in this case, the federal courts are not properly called upon to judge the wisdom of a zero tolerance policy.... [O]ur inquiry is limited to whether Ratner's complaint alleges sufficient facts, which, if proved, would show that the implementation of the school policy failed to comport with the ... Constitution. We conclude that the facts alleged in this case do not so demonstrate.

Some courts have found that zero tolerance policies or procedures fail to meet due process requirements. A Mississippi youth was expelled from school for one year after a miniature (2 inch) Swiss army knife fell out of his backpack. In *Colvin ex rel. Colvin v. Lowndes County School District*, 114 F.Supp.2d 504 (N.D.Miss.1999), the Court held that, before a student could be expelled for a year, the school board must independently consider the relevant facts and circumstances pertaining to the individual's case. The Court equated the right to education with an individual's property interest, and viewed expulsion as a serious deprivation "worthy of a higher degree of due process." Pointing out that the hearing officer had not recommended expulsion to the board, the Court commented, "It appears that the board simply knew that a weapon was found on school property and instituted a blanket penalty, absent review of relevant facts or circumstances." Another court held the statutory provision prohibiting "possession" of alcohol at school violated due process because it did not provide sufficient notice that the school interpreted "possession" to include "present within the body" upon arrival at a school function as well as bringing alcohol to school or consuming alcohol on school property. In *James P. v. Lemahieu*, 84 F.Supp.2d 1113 (D.Haw.2000), the student was suspended for consuming alcohol prior to a school function, which, the court found, an ordinary person might not interpret the language of the prohibition to include.

In some jurisdictions, school officials increasingly turn to the criminal and juvenile justice systems to deal with student misbehavior, in situations that in an earlier era would have been handled as a school disciplinary matter. According to one report, for example, in October, 2003, two dozen Toledo, Ohio, students were arrested in school and charged with such crimes as being loud and disruptive, cursing at school officials and violating the school dress code—all offenses under the city's safe school ordinance. Of about 1700 school-related delinquency cases heard in juvenile court in 2002, the Toledo court's intake officer estimated that about 2 involved serious incidents—the rest were unruly student conduct. Sara Rimer, Unruly Students Facing Arrest, Not Detention, N.Y. Times, January 4, 2004. Many critics argue that this practice, and sanctions under zero tolerance policies generally, have a disproportionate impact on minority youth.

Zero tolerance policies have generated much scholarly interest. See, e.g., Kim Fries & Todd A. DeMitchell, Zero Tolerance and the Paradox of Fairness: Viewpoints From the Classroom, 36 J.L. & Educ. 211 (2007); Elisabeth Frost, Zero Privacy: Schools are Violating Students' Fourteenth Amendment Right of Privacy Under the Guise of Enforcing Zero Tolerance Policies, 81 Wash.L.Rev. 391 (2006); Ruth Zweifler & Julia DeBeers, The Children Left Behind: How Zero Tolerance Impacts Our Most Vulnerable Youth, 8 Mich.J. Race & L. 191 (2002); Joan Wasser, Zeroing in on Zero Tolerance, 15 J.L. & Politics 747 (1999); Irene Rosenberg, Teen Violence and the Juvenile Court: A Plea for Reflection and Restraint, 37 Houston L.Rev. 75 (2000); Nan Stein, Bullying or Sexual Harassment? The Missing Discourse of Rights in an Era of Zero Tolerance, 45 Ariz.L.Rev. 783 (2003).

D.   THE FOURTH AMENDMENT AND PUBLIC SCHOOL

New Jersey v. T.L.O.

Supreme Court of the United States, 1985.
469 U.S. 325, 105 S.Ct. 733, 83 L.Ed.2d 720.

■ JUSTICE WHITE delivered the opinion of the Court.

We granted certiorari in this case to examine the appropriateness of the exclusionary rule as a remedy for searches carried out in violation of the Fourth Amendment by public school authorities. Our consideration of the proper application of the Fourth Amendment to the public schools, however, has led us to conclude that the search that gave rise to the case now before us did not violate the Fourth Amendment. Accordingly, we here address only the questions of the proper standard for assessing the legality of searches conducted by public school officials and the application of that standard to the facts of this case.

I

On March 7, 1980, a teacher at Piscataway High School in Middlesex County, N.J., discovered two girls smoking in a lavatory. One of the two girls was the respondent T.L.O., who at that time was a 14–year-old high school freshman. Because smoking in the lavatory was a violation of a school rule, the teacher took the two girls to the Principal's office, where they met with Assistant Vice Principal Theodore Choplick. In response to questioning by Mr. Choplick, T.L.O.'s companion admitted that she had violated the rule. T.L.O., however, denied that she had been smoking in the lavatory and claimed that she did not smoke at all.

Mr. Choplick asked T.L.O. to come into his private office and demanded to see her purse. Opening the purse, he found a pack of cigarettes, which he removed from the purse and held before T.L.O. as he accused her of having lied to him. As he reached into the purse for the cigarettes, Mr. Choplick also noticed a package of cigarette rolling papers. In his experience, possession of rolling papers by high school students was closely associated with the use of marihuana. Suspecting that a closer examination of the purse might yield further evidence of drug use, Mr. Choplick proceeded to search the purse thoroughly. The search revealed a small amount of marihuana, a pipe, a number of empty plastic bags, a substantial quantity of money in one-dollar bills, an index card that appeared to be a list of students who owed T.L.O. money, and two letters that implicated T.L.O. in marihuana dealing.

Mr. Choplick notified T.L.O.'s mother and the police, and turned the evidence of drug dealing over to the police. At the request of the police, T.L.O.'s mother took her daughter to police headquarters, where T.L.O. confessed that she had been selling marihuana at the high school. On the basis of the confession and the evidence seized by Mr. Choplick, the State brought delinquency charges against T.L.O. in the Juvenile and Domestic Relations Court of Middlesex County. Contending that Mr. Choplick's search of her purse violated the Fourth Amendment, T.L.O. moved to suppress the evidence found in her purse as well as her confession, which, she argued, was tainted by the allegedly unlawful search.

[The Juvenile Court denied the motion to suppress, concluding that the search of T.L.O. met the applicable standard:

"a school official may properly conduct a search of a student's person if the official has a reasonable suspicion that a crime has been or is in the process of being committed, *or* reasonable cause to believe that the search is necessary to maintain school discipline or enforce school policies." Id., 178 N.J.Super., at 341, 428 A.2d, at 1333 (emphasis in original).

The court found T.L.O. to be a delinquent and on January 8, 1982, sentenced her to a year's probation.

On appeal from the final judgment of the juvenile court, a divided Appellate Division affirmed the trial court's finding that there had been no Fourth Amendment violation. T.L.O. appealed, and the Supreme Court of New Jersey reversed the judgment of the Appellate Division and ordered the suppression of the evidence found in T.L.O.'s purse. The New Jersey

Supreme Court agreed with the lower courts that the Fourth Amendment applies to searches conducted by school officials. With respect to the question of the legality of the search before it, the court agreed with the juvenile court that a warrantless search by a school official does not violate the Fourth Amendment so long as the official "has reasonable grounds to believe that a student possesses evidence of illegal activity or activity that would interfere with school discipline and order." However, the court, with two justices dissenting, sharply disagreed with the Juvenile Court's conclusion that the search of the purse was reasonable, because possession of cigarettes, as opposed to smoking, was not a violation of school rules.

The United States Supreme Court granted the State of New Jersey's petition for certiorari. 464 U.S. 991 (1983). Although the State had argued in the Supreme Court of New Jersey that the search of T.L.O.'s purse did not violate the Fourth Amendment, the petition for certiorari raised only the question whether the exclusionary rule should operate to bar consideration in juvenile delinquency proceedings of evidence unlawfully seized by a school official without the involvement of law enforcement officers.

The Supreme Court originally granted certiorari to decide the issue of the appropriate remedy in juvenile court proceedings for unlawful school searches, but then declined to address that question in isolation from the broader question of what limits, if any, the Fourth Amendment places on the activities of school authorities.]

. . . . Having heard argument on the legality of the search of T.L.O.'s purse, we are satisfied that the search did not violate the Fourth Amendment.[3]

II

In determining whether the search at issue in this case violated the Fourth Amendment, we are faced initially with the question whether that Amendment's prohibition on unreasonable searches and seizures applies to searches conducted by public school officials. We hold that it does.

It is now beyond dispute that "the Federal Constitution, by virtue of the Fourteenth Amendment, prohibits unreasonable searches and seizures by state officers." Equally indisputable is the proposition that the Fourteenth Amendment protects the rights of students against encroachment by public school officials:

"The Fourteenth Amendment, as now applied to the States, protects the citizen against the State itself and all of its creatures—Boards of Education not excepted. These have, of course, delicate, and highly discretionary functions, but none that they may not perform within the

---

3. In holding that the search of T.L.O.'s purse did not violate the Fourth Amendment, we do not implicitly determine that the exclusionary rule applies to the fruits of unlawful searches conducted by school authorities. The question whether evidence should be excluded from a criminal proceeding involves two discrete inquiries: whether the evidence was seized in violation of the Fourth Amendment, and whether the exclusionary rule is the ap- propriate remedy for the violation. Neither question is logically antecedent to the other, for a negative answer to either question is sufficient to dispose of the case. Thus, our determination that the search at issue in this case did not violate the Fourth Amendment implies no particular resolution of the question of the applicability of the exclusionary rule.

limits of the Bill of Rights. That they are educating the young for citizenship is reason for scrupulous protection of Constitutional freedoms of the individual, if we are not to strangle the free mind at its source and teach youth to discount important principles of our government as mere platitudes." West Virginia State Bd. of Ed. v. Barnette, 319 U.S. 624, 637 (1943).

. . .

Notwithstanding the general applicability of the Fourth Amendment to the activities of civil authorities, a few courts have concluded that school officials are exempt from the dictates of the Fourth Amendment by virtue of the special nature of their authority over schoolchildren. See, e.g., R.C.M. v. State, 660 S.W.2d 552 (Tex.App.1983). Teachers and school administrators, it is said, act in loco parentis in their dealings with students: their authority is that of the parent, not the State, and is therefore not subject to the limits of the Fourth Amendment. Ibid.

Such reasoning is in tension with contemporary reality and the teachings of this Court. We have held school officials subject to the commands of the First Amendment, see Tinker v. Des Moines Independent Community School District, 393 U.S. 503 (1969), and the Due Process Clause of the Fourteenth Amendment, see Goss v. Lopez, 419 U.S. 565 (1975). If school authorities are state actors for purposes of the constitutional guarantees of freedom of expression and due process, it is difficult to understand why they should be deemed to be exercising parental rather than public authority when conducting searches of their students. More generally, the Court has recognized that "the concept of parental delegation" as a source of school authority is not entirely "consonant with compulsory education laws." Ingraham v. Wright, 430 U.S. 651, 662 (1977). Today's public school officials do not merely exercise authority voluntarily conferred on them by individual parents; rather, they act in furtherance of publicly mandated educational and disciplinary policies. See, e.g., the opinion in State ex rel. T.L.O., 94 N.J., at 343, 463 A.2d, at 934, 940, describing the New Jersey statutes regulating school disciplinary policies and establishing the authority of school officials over their students. In carrying out searches and other disciplinary functions pursuant to such policies, school officials act as representatives of the State, not merely as surrogates for the parents, and they cannot claim the parents' immunity from the strictures of the Fourth Amendment.

III

To hold that the Fourth Amendment applies to searches conducted by school authorities is only to begin the inquiry into the standards governing such searches. Although the underlying command of the Fourth Amendment is always that searches and seizures be reasonable, what is reasonable depends on the context within which a search takes place. The determination of the standard of reasonableness governing any specific class of searches requires "balancing the need to search against the invasion which the search entails." Camara v. Municipal Court, supra, 387 U.S., at 536–537. On one side of the balance are arrayed the individual's legitimate expectations of privacy and personal security; on the other, the government's need for effective methods to deal with breaches of public order.

We have recognized that even a limited search of the person is a substantial invasion of privacy.... A search of a child's person or of a closed purse or other bag carried on her person,[5] no less than a similar search carried out on an adult, is undoubtedly a severe violation of subjective expectations of privacy.

.... To receive the protection of the Fourth Amendment, an expectation of privacy must be one that society is "prepared to recognize as legitimate." [Citation omitted.] The State of New Jersey has argued that because of the pervasive supervision to which children in the schools are necessarily subject, a child has virtually no legitimate expectation of privacy in articles of personal property "unnecessarily" carried into a school. This argument has two factual premises: (1) the fundamental incompatibility of expectations of privacy with the maintenance of a sound educational environment; and (2) the minimal interest of the child in bringing any items of personal property into the school. Both premises are severely flawed.

Although this Court may take notice of the difficulty of maintaining discipline in the public schools today, the situation is not so dire that students in the schools may claim no legitimate expectations of privacy. We have recently recognized that the need to maintain order in a prison is such that prisoners retain no legitimate expectations of privacy.... We are not yet ready to hold that the schools and the prisons need be equated for purposes of the Fourth Amendment.

Nor does the State's suggestion that children have no legitimate need to bring personal property into the schools seem well anchored in reality. Students at a minimum must bring to school not only the supplies needed for their studies, but also keys, money, and the necessaries of personal hygiene and grooming. In addition, students may carry on their persons or in purses or wallets such nondisruptive yet highly personal items as photographs, letters, and diaries.... In short, schoolchildren may find it necessary to carry with them a variety of legitimate, noncontraband items, and there is no reason to conclude that they have necessarily waived all rights to privacy in such items merely by bringing them onto school grounds.

Against the child's interest in privacy must be set the substantial interest of teachers and administrators in maintaining discipline in the classroom and on school grounds.... Even in schools that have been spared the most severe disciplinary problems, the preservation of order and a proper educational environment requires close supervision of schoolchildren, as well as the enforcement of rules against conduct that would be perfectly permissible if undertaken by an adult.... Accordingly, we have

5. We do not address the question, not presented by this case, whether a schoolchild has a legitimate expectation of privacy in lockers, desks, or other school property provided for the storage of school supplies. Nor do we express any opinion on the standards (if any) governing searches of such areas by school officials or by other public authorities acting at the request of school officials....

recognized that maintaining security and order in the schools requires a certain degree of flexibility in school disciplinary procedures, and we have respected the value of preserving the informality of the student-teacher relationship.

How, then, should we strike the balance between the schoolchild's legitimate expectations of privacy and the school's equally legitimate need to maintain an environment in which learning can take place? It is evident that the school setting requires some easing of the restrictions to which searches by public authorities are ordinarily subject. The warrant requirement, in particular, is unsuited to the school environment: requiring a teacher to obtain a warrant before searching a child suspected of an infraction of school rules (or of the criminal law) would unduly interfere with the maintenance of the swift and informal disciplinary procedures needed in the schools.... [W]e hold today that school officials need not obtain a warrant before searching a student who is under their authority.

The school setting also requires some modification of the level of suspicion of illicit activity needed to justify a search. Ordinarily, a search—even one that may permissibly be carried out without a warrant—must be based upon "probable cause" to believe that a violation of the law has occurred. [Citation omitted]. However, "probable cause" is not an irreducible requirement of a valid search. The fundamental command of the Fourth Amendment is that searches and seizures be reasonable, and although "both the concept of probable cause and the requirement of a warrant bear on the reasonableness of a search, ... in certain limited circumstances neither is required." ... Where a careful balancing of governmental and private interests suggests that the public interest is best served by a Fourth Amendment standard of reasonableness that stops short of probable cause, we have not hesitated to adopt such a standard.

We join the majority of courts that have examined this issue in concluding that the accommodation of the privacy interests of schoolchildren with the substantial need of teachers and administrators for freedom to maintain order in the schools does not require strict adherence to the requirement that searches be based on probable cause to believe that the subject of the search has violated or is violating the law. Rather, the legality of a search of a student should depend simply on the reasonableness, under all the circumstances, of the search. Determining the reasonableness of any search involves a twofold inquiry: first, one must consider "whether the ... action was justified at its inception," Terry v. Ohio, 392 U.S., at 20; second, one must determine whether the search as actually conducted "was reasonably related in scope to the circumstances which justified the interference in the first place," ibid. Under ordinary circumstances, a search of a student by a teacher or other school official[7] will be "justified at its inception" when there are reasonable grounds for suspecting that the search will turn up evidence that the student has violated or is

7. We here consider only searches carried out by school authorities acting alone and on their own authority. This case does not present the question of the appropriate standard for assessing the legality of searches conducted by school officials in conjunction with or at the behest of law enforcement agencies, and we express no opinion on that question.

violating either the law or the rules of the school.[8] Such a search will be permissible in its scope when the measures adopted are reasonably related to the objectives of the search and not excessively intrusive in light of the age and sex of the student and the nature of the infraction.

This standard will, we trust, neither unduly burden the efforts of school authorities to maintain order in their schools nor authorize unrestrained intrusions upon the privacy of schoolchildren. By focusing attention on the question of reasonableness, the standard will spare teachers and school administrators the necessity of schooling themselves in the niceties of probable cause and permit them to regulate their conduct according to the dictates of reason and common sense. At the same time, the reasonableness standard should ensure that the interests of students will be invaded no more than is necessary to achieve the legitimate end of preserving order in the schools.

IV

There remains the question of the legality of the search in this case. We recognize that the "reasonable grounds" standard applied by the New Jersey Supreme Court in its consideration of this question is not substantially different from the standard that we have adopted today. Nonetheless, we believe that the New Jersey court's application of that standard to strike down the search of T.L.O.'s purse reflects a somewhat crabbed notion of reasonableness. Our review of the facts surrounding the search leads us to conclude that the search was in no sense unreasonable for Fourth Amendment purposes.

. . .

Reversed.

■ JUSTICE POWELL, with whom JUSTICE O'CONNOR joins, concurring.

I agree with the Court's decision, and generally with its opinion. I would place greater emphasis, however, on the special characteristics of elementary and secondary schools that make it unnecessary to afford students the same constitutional protections granted adults and juveniles in a nonschool setting.

In any realistic sense, students within the school environment have a lesser expectation of privacy than members of the population generally. They spend the school hours in close association with each other, both in

---

8. We do not decide whether individualized suspicion is an essential element of the reasonableness standard we adopt for searches by school authorities. In other contexts, however, we have held that although "some quantum of individualized suspicion is usually a prerequisite to a constitutional search or seizure[,] ... the Fourth Amendment imposes no irreducible requirement of such suspicion." [Citations omitted]. Exceptions to the requirement of individualized suspicion are generally appropriate only where the privacy interests implicated by a search are minimal and where "other safeguards" are available "to assure that the individual's reasonable expectation of privacy is not 'subject to the discretion of the official in the field.' " [citation omitted]. Because the search of T.L.O.'s purse was based upon an individualized suspicion that she had violated school rules, we need not consider the circumstances that might justify school authorities in conducting searches unsupported by individualized suspicion.

the classroom and during recreation periods. The students in a particular class often know each other and their teachers quite well. Of necessity, teachers have a degree of familiarity with, and authority over, their students that is unparalleled except perhaps in the relationship between parent and child. It is simply unrealistic to think that students have the same subjective expectation of privacy as the population generally. But for purposes of deciding this case, I can assume that children in school—no less than adults—have privacy interests that society is prepared to recognize as legitimate.

However one may characterize their privacy expectations, students properly are afforded some constitutional protections. In an often quoted statement, the Court said that students do not "shed their constitutional rights ... at the schoolhouse gate". Tinker v. Des Moines School District, 393 U.S. 503, 506 (1969). The Court also has "emphasized the need for affirming the comprehensive authority of the states and of school officials ... to prescribe and control conduct in the schools." Id., at 507. See also Epperson v. Arkansas, 393 U.S. 97, 104 (1968). The Court has balanced the interests of the student against the school officials' need to maintain discipline by recognizing qualitative differences between the constitutional remedies to which students and adults are entitled.

. . .

The special relationship between teacher and student also distinguishes the setting within which school children operate. Law enforcement officers function as adversaries of criminal suspects. These officers have the responsibility to investigate criminal activity, to locate and arrest those who violate our laws, and to facilitate the charging and bringing of such persons to trial. Rarely does this type of adversarial relationship exist between school authorities and pupils.[1] Instead, there is a commonality of interests between teachers and their pupils. The attitude of the typical teacher is one of personal responsibility for the student's welfare as well as for his education.

The primary duty of school officials and teachers, as the Court states, is the education and training of young people. A state has a compelling interest in assuring that the schools meet this responsibility. Without first establishing discipline and maintaining order, teachers cannot begin to educate their students. And apart from education, the school has the obligation to protect pupils from mistreatment by other children, and also to protect teachers themselves from violence by the few students whose conduct in recent years has prompted national concern. For me, it would be unreasonable and at odds with history to argue that the full panoply of constitutional rules applies with the same force and effect in the schoolhouse as it does in the enforcement of criminal laws.

1. Unlike police officers, school authorities have no law enforcement responsibility or indeed any obligation to be familiar with the criminal laws. Of course, as illustrated by this case, school authorities have a layman's familiarity with the types of crimes that occur frequently in our schools: the distribution

In sum, although I join the Court's opinion and its holding,[3] my emphasis is somewhat different.

. . .

■ [Justice Blackmun writes separately to emphasize that the lesser standard of reasonable suspicion that the Court adopts is a very limited exception to the requirement of a warrant and probable cause, an exception created by "a special law enforcement need for greater flexibility." (105 S.Ct. at 749) He objects to the majority's "implication that the balancing test is the rule rather than the exception." Id. The special need for immediate response, in Justice Blackmun's view, is created by the context of the public school. Teachers must have the ability to respond quickly to incidents of misbehavior to maintain order and safety among large numbers of young people. The educational process would suffer if teachers were required to obtain a warrant or to determine whether probable cause exists (a task for which they are not well qualified).]

■ JUSTICE BRENNAN, with whom JUSTICE MARSHALL joins, concurring in part and dissenting in part.

I fully agree with Part II of the Court's opinion. Teachers, like all other government officials, must conform their conduct to the Fourth Amendment's protections of personal privacy and personal security. . . .

I do not, however, otherwise join the Court's opinion. Today's decision sanctions school officials to conduct full-scale searches on a "reasonableness" standard whose only definite content is that it is *not* the same test as the "probable cause" standard found in the text of the Fourth Amendment. In adopting this unclear, unprecedented, and unnecessary departure from generally applicable Fourth Amendment standards, the Court carves out a broad exception to standards that this Court has developed over years of considering Fourth Amendment problems. Its decision is supported neither by precedent nor even by a fair application of the "balancing test" it proclaims in this very opinion. . . .

I . . . do not accept the majority's premise that "[t]o hold that the Fourth Amendment applies to searches conducted by school authorities is only to begin the inquiry into the standards governing such searches." For me, the finding that the Fourth Amendment applies, coupled with the observation that what is at issue is a full-scale search, is the end of the inquiry. But even if I believed that a "balancing test" appropriately replaces the judgment of the Framers of the Fourth Amendment, I would nonetheless object to the cursory and short-sighted "test" that the Court employs to justify its predictable weakening of Fourth Amendment protections. In particular, the test employed by the Court vastly overstates the social costs that a probable-cause standard entails and, though it plausibly

---

and use of drugs, theft, and even violence against teachers as well as fellow students.

3. The Court's holding is that "when there are reasonable grounds for suspecting that [a] search will turn up evidence that the student has violated or is violating either the law or the rules of the school," a search of the student's person or belongings is justified. This is in accord with the Court's summary of the views of a majority of the state and federal courts that have addressed this issue.

articulates the serious privacy interests at stake, inexplicably fails to accord them adequate weight in striking the balance.

The Court begins to articulate its "balancing test" by observing that "the government's need for effective methods to deal with breaches of public order" is to be weighed on one side of the balance. Of course, this is not correct. It is not the government's need for effective enforcement methods that should weigh in the balance, for ordinary Fourth Amendment standards—including probable cause—may well permit methods for maintaining the public order that are perfectly effective. If that were the case, the governmental interest in having effective standards would carry no weight at all as a justification for *departing* from the probable-cause standard. Rather, it is the costs of applying probable cause as opposed to applying some lesser standard that should be weighed on the government's side.

In order to tote up the costs of applying the probable-cause standard, it is thus necessary first to take into account the nature and content of that standard, and the likelihood that it would hamper achievement of the goal—vital not just to "teachers and administrators,"—of maintaining an effective educational setting in the public schools. . . .

. . .

A consideration of the likely operation of the probable-cause standard reinforces this conclusion. Discussing the issue of school searches, Professor LaFave has noted that the cases that have reached the appellate courts "strongly suggest that in most instances the evidence of wrongdoing prompting teachers or principals to conduct searches is sufficiently detailed and specific to meet the traditional probable cause test." 3 W. LaFave, Search and Seizure § 10.11, pp. 459–460 (1978). The problems that have caused this Court difficulty in interpreting the probable-cause standard have largely involved informants. However, three factors make it likely that problems involving informants will not make it difficult for teachers and school administrators to make probable-cause decisions. This Court's decision in *Gates* applying a "totality of the circumstances" test to determine whether an informant's tip can constitute probable cause renders the test easy for teachers to apply. The fact that students and teachers interact daily in the school building makes it more likely that teachers will get to know students who supply information; the problem of informants who remain anonymous even to the teachers—and who are therefore unavailable for verification or further questioning—is unlikely to arise. Finally, teachers can observe the behavior of students under suspicion to corroborate any doubtful tips they do receive.

As compared with the relative ease with which teachers can apply the probable-cause standard, the amorphous "reasonableness under all the circumstances" standard freshly coined by the Court today will likely spawn increased litigation and greater uncertainty among teachers and administrators. Of course, as this Court should know, an essential purpose of developing and articulating legal norms is to enable individuals to conform their conduct to those norms. A school system conscientiously attempting to obey the Fourth Amendment's dictates under a probable-cause standard could, for example, consult decisions and other legal materials and prepare a booklet expounding the rough outlines of the concept. Such a booklet could be distributed to teachers to provide them with guidance as to when a search may be lawfully conducted. I cannot but believe that the same school system faced with interpreting what is permitted under the Court's new "reasonableness" standard would be hopelessly adrift as to when a search may be permissible. The sad result of this uncertainty may well be that some teachers will be reluctant to conduct searches that are fully permissible and even necessary under the constitutional probable-cause standard, while others may intrude arbitrarily and unjustifiably on the privacy of students.[7]

. . .

■ JUSTICE STEVENS, with whom JUSTICE MARSHALL joins, and with whom JUSTICE BRENNAN joins as to Part I, concurring in part and dissenting in part.

. . .

I

The question the Court decides today—whether Mr. Choplick's search of T.L.O.'s purse violated the Fourth Amendment—was not raised by the State's petition for writ of certiorari. That petition only raised one question: "Whether the Fourth Amendment's exclusionary rule applies to searches made by public school officials and teachers in school." The State quite properly declined to submit the former question because "[it] did not wish to present what might appear to be solely a factual dispute to this Court." Since this Court has twice had the threshold question argued, I believe that it should expressly consider the merits of the New Jersey Supreme Court's ruling that the exclusionary rule applies.

The New Jersey Supreme Court's holding on this question is plainly correct. As the state court noted, this case does not involve the use of evidence in a school disciplinary proceeding; the juvenile proceedings brought against T.L.O. involved a charge that would have been a criminal offense if committed by an adult. Accordingly, the exclusionary rule issue decided by that court and later presented to this Court concerned only the use in a criminal proceeding of evidence obtained in a search conducted by a public school administrator.

---

7. A comparison of the language of the standard ("reasonableness under all the circumstances") with the traditional language of probable cause ("facts sufficient to warrant a person of reasonable caution in believing that a crime had been committed and the evidence would be found in the designated place") suggests that the Court's new standard may turn out to be probable cause under a new guise. If so, the additional uncertainty caused by this Court's innovation is surely unjustifiable; it would be naive to expect that the addition of this extra dose of uncertainty would do anything other than "burden the efforts of school authorities to maintain order in the schools." If, on the other hand, the new standard permits searches of students in instances when probable cause is absent—instances, according to this Court's consistent formulations, when a person of reasonable caution would not think it likely that a violation existed or that evidence of that violation would be found—the new standard is genuinely objectionable and impossible to square with the premise that our citizens have the right to be free from arbitrary intrusions on their privacy.

Having confined the issue to the law enforcement context, the New Jersey court then reasoned that this Court's cases have made it quite clear that the exclusionary rule is equally applicable "whether the public official who illegally obtained the evidence was a municipal inspector, ... or a school administrator or law enforcement official." It correctly concluded "that if an official search violates constitutional rights, the evidence is not admissible in criminal proceedings."

When a defendant in a criminal proceeding alleges that she was the victim of an illegal search by a school administrator, the application of the exclusionary rule is a simple corollary of the principle that "all evidence obtained by searches and seizures in violation of the Constitution is, by that same authority, inadmissible in a state court." Mapp v. Ohio, 367 U.S. 643, 655 (1961). The practical basis for this principle is, in part, its deterrent effect, and as a general matter it is tolerably clear to me, as it has been to the Court, that the existence of an exclusionary remedy does deter the authorities from violating the Fourth Amendment by sharply reducing their incentive to do so.[6] In the case of evidence obtained in school searches, the "overall educative effect"[7] of the exclusionary rule adds important symbolic force to this utilitarian judgment.

. . .

Schools are places where we inculcate the values essential to the meaningful exercise of rights and responsibilities by a self-governing citizenry. If the Nation's students can be convicted through the use of arbitrary methods destructive of personal liberty, they cannot help but feel that they have been dealt with unfairly. The application of the exclusionary rule in criminal proceedings arising from illegal school searches makes an important statement to young people that "our society attaches serious consequences to a violation of constitutional rights,"[10] and that this is a principle of "liberty and justice for all."[11]

Thus, the simple and correct answer to the question presented by the State's petition for certiorari would have required affirmance of a state court's judgment suppressing evidence. That result would have been dramatically out of character for a Court that not only grants prosecutors relief from suppression orders with distressing regularity, but also is prone to rely on grounds not advanced by the parties in order to protect evidence from exclusion. In characteristic disregard of the doctrine of judicial restraint, the Court avoided that result in this case by ordering reargument and directing the parties to address a constitutional question that the parties, with good reason, had not asked the Court to decide. Because judicial activism undermines the Court's power to perform its central mission in a legitimate way, I dissented from the reargument order. I have not modified the views expressed in that dissent, but since the majority has brought the question before us, I shall explain why I believe the Court has

6. See, e.g., Stone v. Powell, 428 U.S. 465, 492 (1976)....

7. Stone v. Powell, 428 U.S., at 493.

10. Stone v. Powell, 428 U.S., at 492.

11. 36 U.S.C. § 172 (pledge of allegiance to the flag).

misapplied the standard of reasonableness embodied in the Fourth Amendment.

II

The search of a young woman's purse by a school administrator is a serious invasion of her legitimate expectations of privacy. A purse "is a common repository for one's personal effects and therefore is inevitably associated with the expectation of privacy." Arkansas v. Sanders, 442 U.S. 753, 762 (1979). Although such expectations must sometimes yield to the legitimate requirements of government, in assessing the constitutionality of a warrantless search, our decision must be guided by the language of the Fourth Amendment: "The right of the people to be secure in their persons, houses, papers and effects against *unreasonable* searches and seizures, shall not be violated. . . ." In order to evaluate the reasonableness of such searches, "it is necessary 'first to focus upon the governmental interest which allegedly justifies official intrusion upon the constitutionally protected interests of the private citizens,' for there is 'no ready test for determining reasonableness other than by balancing the need to search [or seize] against the invasion which the search [or seizure] entails.' " Terry v. Ohio, 392 U.S. 1, 20–21 (1968) (quoting Camara v. Municipal Court, 387 U.S. 523, 528, 534–537 (1967)).

The "limited search for weapons" in Terry was justified by the "immediate interest of the police officer in taking steps to assure himself that the person with whom he is dealing is not armed with a weapon that could unexpectedly and fatally be used against him." 392 U.S., at 23, 25. When viewed from the institutional perspective, "the substantial need of teachers and administrators for freedom to maintain order in the schools," (majority opinion), is no less acute. Violent, unlawful, or seriously disruptive conduct is fundamentally inconsistent with the principal function of teaching institutions which is to educate young people and prepare them for citizenship. When such conduct occurs amidst a sizable group of impressionable young people, it creates an explosive atmosphere that requires a prompt and effective response.

Thus, warrantless searches of students by school administrators are reasonable when undertaken for those purposes. But the majority's statement of the standard for evaluating the reasonableness of such searches is not suitably adapted to that end. The majority holds that "a search of a student by a teacher or other school official will be 'justified at its inception' when there are reasonable grounds for suspecting that the search will turn up evidence *that the student has violated or is violating either the law or the rules of the school.*" This standard will permit teachers and school administrators to search students when they suspect that the search will reveal evidence of even the most trivial school regulation or precatory guideline for student behavior. The Court's standard for deciding whether a search is justified "at its inception" treats all violations of the rules of the school as though they were fungible. For the Court, a search for curlers and sunglasses in order to enforce the school dress code[16] is

---

16. Parent–Student Handbook of Piscataway [N.J.] H.S. (1979), Record Doc. S–1, p. 7. A brief survey of school rule books reveals that, under the majority's approach,

apparently just as important as a search for evidence of heroin addiction or violent gang activity.

The majority, however, does not contend that school administrators have a compelling need to search students in order to achieve optimum enforcement of minor school regulations. To the contrary, when minor violations are involved, there is every indication that the informal school disciplinary process, with only minimum requirements of due process,[18] can function effectively without the power to search for enough evidence to prove a criminal case. In arguing that teachers and school administrators need the power to search students based on a lessened standard, the United States as amicus curiae relies heavily on empirical evidence of a contemporary crisis of violence and unlawful behavior that is seriously undermining the process of education in American schools.[19] A standard better attuned to this concern would permit teachers and school administrators to search a student when they have reason to believe that the search will uncover *evidence that the student is violating the law or engaging in conduct that is seriously disruptive of school order, or the educational process.*

This standard is properly directed at "[t]he sole justification for the [warrantless] search."[20]

. . .

The logic of distinguishing between minor and serious offenses in evaluating the reasonableness of school searches is almost too clear for argument. In order to justify the serious intrusion on the persons and privacy of young people that New Jersey asks this Court to approve, the State must identify "some real immediate and serious consequences." McDonald v. United States, 335 U.S. 451, 460 (1948) (Jackson, J., concurring, joined by Frankfurter, J.). While school administrators have entirely

teachers and school administrators may also search students to enforce school rules regulating:

    (i) secret societies;

    (ii) students driving to school;

    (iii) parking and use of parking lots during school hours;

    (iv) smoking on campus;

    (v) the direction of traffic in the hallways;

    (vi) student presence in the hallways during class hours without a pass;

    (vii) profanity;

    . . .

    (ix) cafeteria use and cleanup

. . .

See id., 7–18; Student Handbook of South Windsor [Conn.] H.S. (1984); Fairfax County [Va.] Public Schools, Student Responsibilities and Rights (1980); Student Handbook of Chantilly [Va.] H.S. (1984).

18.   See Goss v. Lopez, 419 U.S. 565, 583–584 (1975).

19.   "The sad truth is that many classrooms across the country are not temples of learning teaching the lessons of good will, civility, and wisdom that are central to the fabric of American life. To the contrary, many schools are in such a state of disorder that not only is the educational atmosphere polluted, but the very safety of students and teachers is imperiled." Brief for United States as Amicus Curiae 23. See also Brief for National Education Association as Amicus Curiae 21 ("If a suspected violation of a rule threatens to disrupt the school or threatens to harm students, school officials should be free to search for evidence of it").

20.   Terry v. Ohio, 392 U.S. 1, 29 (1968); United States v. Brigoni–Ponce, 422 U.S., at 881–882.

legitimate reasons for adopting school regulations and guidelines for student behavior, the authorization of searches to enforce them "displays a shocking lack of all sense of proportion."

The majority offers weak deference to these principles of balance and decency by announcing that school searches will only be reasonable in scope "when the measures adopted are reasonably related to the objectives of the search and not excessively intrusive in light of the age and sex of the student, *and the nature of the infraction*." (emphasis added). The majority offers no explanation why a two-part standard is necessary to evaluate the reasonableness of the ordinary school search. Significantly, in the balance of its opinion the Court pretermits any discussion of the nature of T.L.O.'s infraction of the "no smoking" rule.

The "rider" to the Court's standard for evaluating the reasonableness of the initial intrusion apparently is the Court's perception that its standard is overly generous and does not, by itself, achieve a fair balance between the administrator's right to search and the student's reasonable expectations of privacy. The Court's standard for evaluating the "scope" of reasonable school searches is obviously designed to prohibit physically intrusive searches of students by persons of the opposite sex for relatively minor offenses. The Court's effort to establish a standard that is, at once, clear enough to allow searches to be upheld in nearly every case, and flexible enough to prohibit obviously unreasonable intrusions of young adults' privacy only creates uncertainty in the extent of its resolve to prohibit the latter. Moreover, the majority's application of its standard in this case—to permit a male administrator to rummage through the purse of a female high school student in order to obtain evidence that she was smoking in a bathroom—raises grave doubts in my mind whether its effort will be effective. Unlike the Court, I believe the nature of the suspected infraction is a matter of first importance in deciding whether *any* invasion of privacy is permissible.

III

[Justice Stevens concludes that the New Jersey Supreme Court determined that the search of T.L.O. was unreasonable, using a similar analysis that focused on "the trivial character of the activity that promoted the official search." 469 U.S. at 382. He continues, id. at 383:

> In the view of the state court, there is a quite obvious, and material difference between a search for evidence relating to violent or disruptive activity, and a search for evidence of a smoking rule violation. This distinction does not imply that a no smoking rule is a matter of minor importance. Rather, like a rule that prohibits a student from being tardy, its occasional violation in a context that poses no threat of disrupting school order and discipline offers no reason to believe that an immediate search is necessary to avoid unlawful conduct, violence, or a serious impairment of the educational process.

In Justice Stephens's view, the lower court (and Justice Stevens himself) would have reached a different decision had Assistant Principal Choplick, in initiating the search, had reason to believe that the purse contained evidence of criminal activity or activity that would disrupt school discipline. The fact that the search revealed unexpected evidence of serious wrongdoing could not be used ex post as justification.]

NOTES

(1) The Court in *T.L.O.* adopted a reasonable suspicion standard for school searches, as opposed to the more stringent probable cause standard. Following the *T.L.O.* decision lower courts have applied the reasonable suspicion standard with mixed results. Lowering the standard has not proved the equivalent of abolishing it altogether. For example, in *In re William G.*, 40 Cal.3d 550, 221 Cal.Rptr. 118, 709 P.2d 1287 (1985), the court invalidated a search because the school official lacked a reasonable suspicion of the student's involvement in either criminal activity or conduct in violation of school rules. Accord, *In re Dumas*, 357 Pa.Super. 294, 515 A.2d 984 (1986). In other cases, however, courts have found school searches reasonable under the *T.L.O.* test. *In re Bobby B.*, 172 Cal.App.3d 377, 218 Cal.Rptr. 253 (1985); *People in Interest of P.E.A.*, 754 P.2d 382 (Colo.1988); *In re Devon T.*, 85 Md.App. 674, 584 A.2d 1287 (1991); *Commonwealth v. Snyder*, 413 Mass. 521, 597 N.E.2d 1363 (1992); *State v. Joseph T.*, 175 W.Va. 598, 336 S.E.2d 728 (1985).

(2) The Court in *T.L.O.* left unanswered the question of what standards would apply to a search of a place, i.e., a locker, a desk or a car, as opposed to a search of a person as in *T.L.O.* See 469 U.S. at 337 n.5. In a post-*T.L.O.* case the Pennsylvania Superior Court held the standards of *T.L.O.* applicable to searches of lockers and held evidence unlawfully seized from a locker inadmissible. *In re Dumas*, 357 Pa.Super. 294, 515 A.2d 984 (1986); see *Commonwealth v. Snyder*, 413 Mass. 521, 597 N.E.2d 1363 (1992) (students have expectation of privacy in lockers, but search was reasonable based on reasonable suspicion); *S.C. v. State*, 583 So.2d 188 (Miss.1991) (students have expectation of privacy in lockers; applicable standard governing searches is reasonable suspicion).

A concurring opinion in *Dumas* argues that the expectation of privacy in lockers is not absolute, that had the school published regulations on what could and could not be kept in lockers, the student in this case would not have possessed an expectation of privacy and the search of his locker would have been reasonable. See *Isiah B. v. State*, 176 Wis.2d 639, 500 N.W.2d 637 (1993), where because such regulations had been published, the court concluded the students lacked any expectation of privacy and held random searches of lockers for firearms and seizure of a weapon found in appellant's locker reasonable. See also *People in Interest of P.E.A.*, 754 P.2d 382 (Colo.1988) (search of student's car on school grounds reasonable).

(3) A careful reading of all the school search cases, plus consideration of the principles announced in *In re Gault*, 387 U.S. 1, 87 S.Ct. 1428, 18 L.Ed.2d 527 (1967), reveals a tendency of courts to treat these cases differently from other search and seizure cases not because of a distinction between juveniles and adults but rather because of a perceived distinction between students and nonstudents, i.e., between the school environment and the outside world. In *State v. Young*, supra note (2), e.g., the court held that school searches are governed by a reasonableness standard and that the exclusionary rule is inapplicable even in the case of an unlawful search. The notable fact about this case is that the student involved was 17 years old and, therefore, under Georgia law, an adult for purposes of juvenile court jurisdiction. The perception in such cases is that students in public schools generally, whether juveniles or adults, are entitled to limited, perhaps even minimal, Fourth Amendment protection. This is not surprising, perhaps, given the limits on the other constitutional protections in schools. Is there an argument that Fourth Amendment protections should receive greater deference?

(4) At least one court has held that students are entitled to full Fourth Amendment protection, namely the probable cause requirement and perhaps even the warrant requirement. *State v. Mora*, 307 So.2d 317 (La.1975). Although decided prior to *T.L.O.*, the *Mora* holding may have survived *T.L.O.* because the stricter standards adopted in *Mora* were based in part on state law rather than solely on federal law. The state petitioned for certiorari in *Mora*, and the Supreme Court vacated the judgment and remanded for a determination of whether the court's holding was based on state or federal law. *Louisiana v. Mora*, 423 U.S. 809, 96 S.Ct. 20, 46 L.Ed.2d 29 (1975). On remand, the Louisiana court determined that its holding that the search was unreasonable was based on state and federal law and its holding that the illegally seized evidence was inadmissible was based on federal law. *State v. Mora*, 330 So.2d 900 (La.1976). The state's petition for certiorari was denied. *Louisiana v. Mora*, 429 U.S. 1004, 97 S.Ct. 538, 50 L.Ed.2d 616 (1976).

If a state court bases its decision on state law, of course, and requires stricter standards than those demanded under the U.S. Constitution, its judgment rests on an adequate and independent state ground and is immune from review by the Supreme Court. In *T.L.O.*, e.g., the Supreme Court observed: "Of course, New Jersey may insist on a more demanding standard under its own Constitution or statutes. In that case, its courts would not purport to be applying the Fourth Amendment when they invalidate a search." 469 U.S. at 343 n.10. Many state courts in recent years have based their requirement of stricter standards on state constitutional and statutory law and have avoided some of the more conservative decisions of the U.S. Supreme Court, particularly those of the Burger years. For a thorough discussion of this phenomenon see Developments in the Law—The Interpretation of State Constitutional Rights, 95 Harv.L.Rev. 1324 (1982); Donald E. Wilkes, Jr., The New Federalism in 1984: Death of the Phoenix?, in Developments in State Constitutional Law: The Williamsburg Conference (Bradley D. McGraw ed. 1984).

(5) Even if a court finds a search to be unreasonable, school officials may receive deference under § 1983. At least one court has granted a teacher and principal immunity for unconstitutionally strip searching an entire fifth grade class looking for $26 that was stolen from the teacher's desk. *Thomas ex rel. Thomas v. Roberts*, 323 F.3d 950 (11th Cir.2003) (reinstating *Thomas ex rel. Thomas v. Roberts*, 261 F.3d 1160 (11th Cir.2001)). The entire class was segregated according to sex and marched into their respective restrooms four or five at a time. The boys were searched by a male officer and forced to drop their pants (at least some dropped their underpants) and their bodies and clothes including underpants were searched for the money. The girls were searched by their female teacher and compelled to raise their shirts or dresses, remove their bras if worn and expose their breasts while being searched. The court found this search unreasonable and unconstitutional but granted the individuals immunity from suit. The school district was not granted immunity.

(6) Particularly since *Gault*, courts have tended to assume that, outside of the school setting, the law of search and seizure applies to juveniles in the same way it applies to adults. The leading case holding the Fourth Amendment applicable to juvenile proceedings is *State v. Lowry*, 95 N.J.Super. 307, 230 A.2d 907 (1967). Relying heavily on the rationale enunciated in *Mapp v. Ohio*, 367 U.S. 643, 81 S.Ct. 1684, 6 L.Ed.2d 1081 (1961), the *Lowry* court emphasized that:

> The historical development clearly indicates that the rule is not only a basic right to *all* persons to privacy, security and liberty, whether accused of a crime or not, but is fundamental to the concept of due process, a principle precluding adjudications based on methods that offend a sense of justice and one that must endure if our society is to remain free. To insure a fact-finding process which at

least measures up to the essentials of fair treatment, State v. Carlo, 48 N.J. 224, 236, 225 A.2d 110 (1966), the constitutional safeguard enunciated in the Fourth Amendment must be applicable to juveniles. 230 A.2d at 910–11.

For a thorough discussion of the issue of applicability of the law of search and seizure to juveniles see Samuel M. Davis, Rights of Juveniles: The Juvenile Justice System § 3.6 (2d ed.2008). This issue is explored further in Chapter X.

DISCUSSION PROBLEM

GIRARD SCHOOL

Students at Girard Middle School attend each of six daily classes in a different room. Students sit at assigned desks in every class and traditionally leave their textbooks and other school supplies inside their desks. When $50 belonging to one of the teachers is reported missing, a surprise desk check reveals the money hidden between the pages of Kerry Smith's geography book.

1. Assume that teachers performed the search. Is such a wide-ranging search valid? Would it matter whether or not the desk was locked? What if the desk was locked and the student who happened to be occupying it during the period of the search consented? Does the third-party consent validate the search? Can the evidence be used to suspend Kerry for two weeks?

2. Do you think the case law would support Kerry's claim that she had a reasonable expectation of privacy in an unlocked desk that she shared with five other students?

VERNONIA SCHOOL DISTRICT 47J v. ACTON, 515 U.S. 646, 115 S.Ct. 2386, 132 L.Ed.2d 564 (1995).

[A more complete version of this opinion appears at p. 1093 infra.]

In *Acton* the Court was called on to decide the constitutionality of a school district's policy authorizing random urinalysis drug testing of student athletes. After observing a sharp increase in drug use in the mid-to-late 80s, and discovering that student athletes were the drug culture leaders, the Vernonia School District (District) brought in speakers and offered classes in order to deter drug use. When the drug problems persisted, the District proposed a drug testing program for student athletes. The drug testing program received unanimous approval from parents who attended a parent "input night" on the proposal, and was subsequently approved by the school board in the fall of 1989. The drug testing program required all interscholastic athletes to sign a form consenting to drug testing, which would occur at the beginning of the season for their sport and at random during the season. Acton signed up for football when he was in seventh grade but was not allowed to play because he and his parents would not consent to the drug testing. The Actons filed suit in federal district court seeking declaratory and injunctive relief, claiming that the drug testing program violated the Fourth and Fourteenth Amendments. The district court denied the claims after a bench trial, but the United States Court of Appeals for the Ninth Circuit reversed, holding that the drug testing program violated the Fourth and Fourteenth Amendments.

The Supreme Court, after granting review to determine whether the drug testing program constituted an unreasonable search and seizure under the Fourth Amendment, held six to three, that the drug testing program, designed to curb district-wide drug use, was not an unreasonable search and seizure under the Fourth Amendment.

Justice Scalia, writing for the Court, noting the "special needs" for law enforcement in public schools, and the lowered expectation of privacy of students in an environment where they were routinely subject to physical examinations and vaccinations, claimed that the student athletes' expectation of privacy was further diminished by the communal environment in which they dress.

> Public school locker rooms, the usual sites for these activities, are not notable for the privacy they afford. The locker rooms in Vernonia are typical: no individual dressing rooms are provided; shower heads are lined up along a wall, unseparated by any sort of partition or curtain; not even all the toilet stalls have doors.

Justice Scalia argued further that student athletes subject themselves to a greater degree of regulation than that imposed on other students, and as such should be accustomed to intrusions on their privacy.

Justice Scalia rejected Acton's argument that drug testing based on suspicions was a less restrictive alternative and stated that the Fourth Amendment does not require "the 'least intrusive' search practicable." Moreover, he asserted that testing on suspicion may lead to administrative problems and could be used as a "badge of shame" placed on "troublesome but not drug-likely students." Justice Scalia cautioned, however, that this opinion does not mean that "suspicionless drug testing will readily pass constitutional muster in other contexts." He stated that when the school acts as guardian and tutor, "the relevant question is whether the search is one that a reasonable guardian and tutor might undertake." In this case, the only parental objection to the drug testing program came from the Actons, and this limited objection is an "insufficient basis to contradict the judgment of Vernonia's parents, its school board, and the district court, as to what was reasonably in the interest of these children under the circumstances."

Justice O'Connor, joined by Justice Stevens and Justice Souter, dissented, arguing that drug testing of student athletes can only be reasonable when justified by some level of suspicion. Suspicionless searches, according to Justice O'Connor, have historically been held to be unreasonable, but recently have been permitted only where "a suspicion-based regime would be ineffectual."

NOTES

(1) On remand, the Ninth Circuit affirmed the federal district court's original decision in *Acton*, observing that in its view, the Oregon Supreme Court would not offer any greater protection under the provisions of the Oregon Constitution than was available under the federal Constitution, thus obviating any need to certify that question to the Oregon Supreme Court. *Acton v. Vernonia School District 47J*, 66 F.3d 217 (9th Cir.1995). One judge dissented on the ground that the question should be certified to the Oregon Supreme Court.

(2) Is the search in *Acton* different in some respects from that conducted in *T.L.O.*? Do you agree with Justice Scalia in *Acton* that suspicionless drug testing was a "less restrictive alternative"?

BOARD OF EDUCATION OF INDEPENDENT SCHOOL DISTRICT NO. 92 OF POTTAWATOMIE COUNTY V. EARLS, 536 U.S. 822, 122 S.Ct. 2559, 153 L.Ed.2d 735 (2002).

[A more complete version of this opinion appears at p. 1105 infra.]

In *Earls,* the Supreme Court again addressed suspicionless drug searches by school officials. The Tecumseh, Oklahoma School District adopted a policy under which middle and high school students were required to consent to urinalysis drug testing in order to participate in any extracurricular activity. Students and parents challenging the policy distinguished it from the policy upheld in *Acton* on several grounds. First, the Tecumseh policy was not limited to athletes, a group that in *Acton* were identified as drug culture leaders. No evidence suggested that students who participated in extracurricular activities in Tecumseh County were more likely than other students to engage in drug use. Moreover, in the *Acton* opinion, Justice Scalia emphasized that members of school athletic teams have a reduced expectation of privacy because they frequently disrobe together. The Tecumseh policy applied broadly to all students involved in extracurricular activities.

Despite these differences, the Supreme Court reversed the Court of Appeals and upheld the policy, rejecting the argument that it represented an unreasonable intrusion on students' expectations of privacy. In an opinion by Justice Thomas, the Court applied the *Acton* test to the Tecumseh policy.

First, the Court concluded that students who participate in extracurricular activities have a limited expectation of privacy.

> Respondents argue that because children participating in nonathletic extracurricular activities are not subject to regular physicals and communal undress, they have a stronger expectation of privacy than the athletes tested in *Acton*. This distinction, however, was not essential to our decision in *Acton*, which depended primarily upon the school's custodial responsibility and authority.

> .... [S]tudents who participate in competitive extracurricular activities voluntarily subject themselves to many of the same intrusions on their privacy as do athletes. Some of these clubs and activities require occasional off-campus travel and communal undress. All of them have their own rules and requirements for participating students that do not apply to the student body as a whole. For example, each of the competitive extracurricular activities governed by the Policy must abide by the rules of the Oklahoma Secondary Schools Activities Association, and a faculty sponsor monitors the students for compliance with the various rules dictated by the clubs and activities. This regulation of extracurricular activities further diminishes the expectation of privacy among schoolchildren.... We therefore conclude that the students affected by this Policy have a limited expectation of privacy.

The Court then turned to the intrusiveness of the policy and found the method of urine collection to be virtually identical to that used in *Acton*, and thus, in this regard, was also "minimally intrusive." Moreover, the Court emphasized that the results of the test were to remain confidential and kept in a file separate from other educational records of the students. The results were not to be shared with law enforcement officials; nor would they result in discipline or academic sanctions. The only effect was exclusion of a student found to be using drugs from extracurricular activities.

The Court completed the *Acton* analysis by considering the importance of the government's concerns and the efficacy of the drug policy in meeting them. The court focused on the serious nature of the problem of drug use among "our nation's youth," and pointed out that the School District presented evidence of drug use in Tecumseh schools. The Court rejected the students' claim that

> "there is no 'real and immediate interest' to justify a policy of drug testing nonathletes".... We have recognized, however, that "[a] demonstrated problem of drug abuse ... [is] not in all cases necessary to the validity of a testing regime," but that some showing does "shore up an assertion of special need for a suspicionless general search program." [citation omitted.] The School District has provided sufficient evidence to shore up the need for its drug testing program.

> . . .

> Given the nationwide epidemic of drug use, and the evidence of increased drug use in Tecumseh schools, it was entirely reasonable for the School District to enact this particular drug testing policy. We reject the Court of Appeals' novel test that "any district seeking to impose a random suspicionless drug testing policy as a condition to participation in a school activity must demonstrate that there is some identifiable drug abuse problem among a sufficient number of those subject to the testing, such that testing that group of students will actually redress its drug problem. Among other problems, it would be difficult to administer such a test. As we cannot articulate a threshold level of drug use that would suffice to justify a drug testing program for schoolchildren, we refuse to fashion what would in effect be a constitutional quantum of drug use necessary to show a 'drug problem.' "

> Respondents also argue that the testing of nonathletes does not implicate any safety concerns, and that safety is a "crucial factor" in applying the special needs framework.... Respondents are correct that safety factors into the special needs analysis, but the safety interest furthered by drug testing is undoubtedly substantial for all children, athletes and nonathletes alike....

The Court rejected the "respondents' argument that drug testing must presumptively be based upon an individualized reasonable suspicion of wrongdoing because such a testing regime would be less intrusive." The Court drew on the *Acton* analysis to conclude that individualized suspicion was not necessary; nor was it necessarily less intrusive.

Finally, we find that testing students who participate in extracurricular activities is a reasonably effective means of addressing the School District's legitimate concerns in preventing, deterring, and detecting drug use. While in *Acton* there might have been a closer fit between the testing of athletes and the trial court's finding that the drug problem was "fueled by the 'role model' effect of athletes' drug use," such a finding was not essential to the holding. *Acton* did not require the school to test the group of students most likely to use drugs, but rather considered the constitutionality of the program in the context of the public school's custodial responsibilities. Evaluating the Policy in this context, we conclude that the drug testing of Tecumseh students who participate in extracurricular activities effectively serves the School District's interest in protecting the safety and health of its students. . . .

Justice Ginsburg wrote a dissenting opinion, joined by Justices Stevens, O'Connor, and Souter. She emphasized the differences between the circumstances in *Acton* and those before the court in *Earls*. Unlike athletic activities, extracurricular activities, although voluntary, are part of a school's educational program and, in fact, participation is essential for students who plan to apply to college. Moreover, most extracurricular activities also do not involve physical risk or safety concerns which justified intrusions into the privacy of athletes. Justice Ginsburg also rejected the notion that the expectations of privacy were similar, emphasizing that the communal undress that was a part of athletic participation was absent in extracurricular activities. Finally, the seriousness of the drug problem differed in the two contexts. Whereas athletes in *Acton* were described as leaders of the "drug culture," no evidence suggested that participants in extracurricular activities in *Earls* played a similar role. Indeed, Justice Ginsburg suggested, nationwide, students who are involved in extracurricular activities were probably less likely than other students to be involved with drugs.

DRUG SNIFFING DOGS IN THE CLASSROOM? A SPECIAL ISSUE

Acton and *Earls* have implications for the practice of school officials of using trained drug-sniffing dogs to conduct sweeping, pervasive searches of students, classrooms, desks, lockers, and automobiles to detect the presence of drugs. In *Doe v. Renfrow*,[1] for example, the federal district court held that use of trained dogs to detect drugs in the school did not constitute an unreasonable search. In so holding the court relied on the *in loco parentis* authority of school officials to respond to any problem, such as the presence of drugs, that could have a serious impact on the educational environment in the school. The *in loco parentis* doctrine, of course, has gained new credence as a result of the Supreme Court's decision in *Acton*.

On the other hand, in a similar case[2] another federal district court held that use of a trained dog to sweep through a school sniffing for drugs was

1. 475 F.Supp. 1012 (N.D.Ind.1979), aff'd in part, rev'd in part, 631 F.2d 91 (7th Cir.1980), cert. denied, 451 U.S. 1022, 101 S.Ct. 3015, 69 L.Ed.2d 395 (1981).

2. *Jones v. Latexo Independ. School Dist.*, 499 F.Supp. 223 (E.D.Tex.1980).

an unconstitutional search. While acknowledging the *in loco parentis* authority of school officials, the court was of the view that in order for a search to be reasonable, articulable facts must cause suspicion to focus on a particular student. The search in this instance, to the contrary, was sweeping and indiscriminate and, therefore, unreasonable. Recall that the Supreme Court in *T.L.O.* left open the question whether individualized suspicion is an "irreducible" requirement of the Fourth Amendment[3] and that in *Acton* it upheld, at least for a certain class of students, random, suspicionless searches in the school setting.[4]

In *Horton v. Goose Creek Independent School District*[5] the Fifth Circuit held searches of the persons of students unreasonable and, therefore, unconstitutional. On the other hand, the court held use of drug-sniffing dogs to search students' lockers and automobiles in public areas did not constitute a "search" within the meaning of the Fourth Amendment. Some state courts have disagreed, holding that use of dogs does constitute a search and in some cases holding searches of "places" unconstitutional in the absence of reasonable suspicion or belief that drugs were present.[6]

In the adult context, the Supreme Court has held that use of trained dogs to screen luggage does not constitute a "search" within the meaning of the Fourth Amendment.[7] Perhaps crucial to the Court's reasoning was its conclusion that government agents had a reasonable belief that the luggage contained drugs before they screened it with the trained dog. At least one lower court, however, has construed *Place* to mean that since such screening does not constitute a search at all, it can be undertaken without even reasonable suspicion.[8] Use of trained dogs to screen persons, however, is more invasive of one's right to personal privacy and might require at least reasonable suspicion.[9]

Returning to the juvenile context, if state courts are inclined to treat use of trained dogs to sniff lockers and automobiles as a search governed by the Fourth Amendment, they certainly would afford at least as much, and

3. 469 U.S. at 342 n.8.

4. In *Acton* the Court said, "we explicitly acknowledged [in *T.L.O.* that] 'the Fourth Amendment imposes no irreducible requirement of such suspicion.'" 515 U.S. at 653.

5. 690 F.2d 470 (5th Cir.1982), cert. denied, 463 U.S. 1207, 103 S.Ct. 3536, 77 L.Ed.2d 1387 (1983).

6. See, e.g, *State v. Juarez–Godinez*, 135 Or.App. 591, 900 P.2d 1044 (1995) (automobile); But see *Commonwealth v. Cass*, 551 Pa. 25, 709 A.2d 350 (1998), cert. denied 525 U.S. 833, 119 S.Ct. 89, 142 L.Ed.2d 70 (1998).

7. *United States v. Place*, 462 U.S. 696, 103 S.Ct. 2637, 77 L.Ed.2d 110 (1983). This view has been reinforced more recently by the Court in *Illinois v. Caballes*, 543 U.S. 405, 125 S.Ct. 834, 160 L.Ed.2d 842 (2005). Some state courts have concluded, however, that such screening does constitute a search under state law, although they have found

such searches reasonable when balancing the individual interests against the governmental interests involved. See, e.g., *People v. Dunn*, 77 N.Y.2d 19, 564 N.E.2d 1054, 563 N.Y.S.2d 388 (1990); *Commonwealth v. Johnston*, 515 Pa. 454, 530 A.2d 74 (1987).

8. *United States v. Beale*, 736 F.2d 1289 (9th Cir.), cert. denied, 469 U.S. 1072, 105 S.Ct. 565, 83 L.Ed.2d 506 (1984).

9. The court in *Beale* seemed to concede as much. See *Beale*, 736 F.2d at 1291 & ns. 1 & 2. In fact, some state courts, again in the adult context, have held that because searches of the person are more intrusive than searches of a place, such as luggage or a locker, probable cause is generally required before subjecting a person to a canine sniff. See, e.g., *Commonwealth v. Martin*, 534 Pa. 136, 626 A.2d 556 (1993).

likely greater, protection to students where dogs are used to conduct personal searches. The issue, yet to be explored, is whether *Acton* represents a sea-change in the way the Supreme Court views searches in the school context, and more importantly, in the kind of justification needed (if any) to sustain them.

NOTE

For a full discussion of dog sniffing in the schools (pre-*T.L.O.* and pre-*Acton*) see Martin R. Gardner, Sniffing for Drugs in the Classroom—Perspectives on Fourth Amendment Scope, 74 Nw.U.L.Rev. 803 (1980).

CHAPTER IV

CUSTODY

A. IN THE BEST INTERESTS OF THE CHILD?

Ireland v. Smith

Supreme Court of Michigan, 1996.
451 Mich. 457, 547 N.W.2d 686.

■ Per Curiam.

This is a custody dispute. Following a hearing, the circuit court ordered that the defendant father be given custody of the parties' minor child. The Court of Appeals set aside the circuit court order and remanded the case for further proceedings before a different judge. The Court of Appeals retained jurisdiction. We approve the remand ordered by the Court of Appeals, though we modify the accompanying directions.

I

In their mid-teens, plaintiff Jennifer Ireland and defendant Steven Smith conceived a child, Maranda, who was born in 1991. The parties did not marry, but continued living with their respective parents while they completed high school. After initially planning to put the baby up for adoption, Ms. Ireland decided instead to keep her. The child lived with Ms. Ireland and her mother in Mount Clemens.

After a time, Mr. Smith began visiting the child and providing a few items for her care. However, Maranda continued to live with her mother and maternal grandmother, who provided nearly all the necessary support.

In January 1993, Ms. Ireland began an action to obtain child-support payments from Mr. Smith. She also obtained an ex parte order that granted her continuing custody of Maranda.

Ms. Ireland enrolled as a scholarship student at the University of Michigan in Ann Arbor for the fall semester of 1993. She and Maranda lived in the university's family housing unit. On weekdays, Maranda attended a university-approved day-care center.

During this period, Mr. Smith remained at his parents' home. He evidently continues to live with them.

In May and June 1994, the circuit court conducted a trial regarding the issue of custody. It would be difficult to exaggerate the extent to which the parties disagreed with regard to the proper setting for Maranda. Each produced witnesses who spoke very disparagingly of the other, and there was little agreement about the facts of this matter.

Following the hearing, the circuit court issued an opinion in which it discussed each of the statutory factors for determining the best interests of the child.[1] The court found that each of the statutory factors weighed evenly between the parties, except factor e, which concerns:

The permanence, as a family unit, of the existing or proposed custodial home or homes.

The circuit court found that factor e "heavily" favored Mr. Smith. It contrasted the stability of continued residence with Mr. Smith and his parents with the occasional moves that were likely as Ms. Ireland continued her education. In an extended discussion of this factor, the court also noted the demands that would be imposed on Ms. Ireland as she sought both to raise a child and attend the university.

For those reasons, the circuit court ordered that Mr. Smith be given custody of Maranda. Ms. Ireland appealed, and the Court of Appeals entered a stay.

Issues concerning visitation remained in circuit court. Those proceedings included entry of an order denying Ms. Ireland's motion to disqualify the trial judge. From that order, she filed a second appeal.

... The Court of Appeals agreed with the circuit court that Ms. Ireland had provided an established custodial environment.[3] However, it found that the circuit court had erred in determining that factor e favored Mr. Smith. The Court of Appeals upheld the circuit court's determination that the other statutory factors favored neither party.

1. As used in this act, "best interests of the child" means the sum total of the following factors to be considered, evaluated, and determined by the court:

(a) The love, affection, and other emotional ties existing between the parties involved and the child.

(b) The capacity and disposition of the parties involved to give the child love, affection, and guidance and to continue the education and raising of the child in his or her religion or creed, if any.

(c) The capacity and disposition of the parties involved to provide the child with food, clothing, medical care or other remedial care recognized and permitted under the laws of this state in place of medical care, and other material needs.

(d) The length of time the child has lived in a stable, satisfactory environment, and the desirability of maintaining continuity.

(e) The permanence, as a family unit, of the existing or proposed custodial home or homes.

(f) The moral fitness of the parties involved.

(g) The mental and physical health of the parties involved.

(h) The home, school, and community record of the child.

(i) The reasonable preference of the child, if the court considers the child to be of sufficient age to express preference.

(j) The willingness and ability of each of the parties to facilitate and encourage a close and continuing parent-child relationship between the child and the other parent or the child and the parents.

(k) Domestic violence, regardless of whether the violence was directed against or witnessed by the child.

(*l*) Any other factor considered by the court to be relevant to a particular child custody dispute.

3. Where an established custodial environment exists, custody may not be changed unless there is "clear and convincing evidence that [a change] is in the best interest of the child." (M.C.L. § 722.27c); M.S.A. § 25.312(7)(c).

The Court of Appeals remanded the case for further consideration, retaining jurisdiction. The Court also disqualified the trial judge from further participation in this matter.

Mr. Smith has applied to this Court for leave to appeal.

II

In the central portion of its analysis, the Court of Appeals first explained its conclusion that the evidentiary record did not support a factual finding that factor e favored Mr. Smith:

> We find no support in the record for the trial court's speculation that there is "no way that a single parent, attending an academic program at an institution as prestigious as the University of Michigan, can do justice to their studies and to raising of an infant child." The evidence shows that the child has thrived in the university environment. Defendant concedes that he has no complaint about the university day care, and the trial court recognized that the child has had a "meaningful experience" there. The trial court found plaintiff's day-care arrangements "appropriate," but concluded that defendant's plan to have his mother baby-sit was better for the child because she was a "blood relative" rather than a "stranger." Both parties will necessarily need the help of other people to care for their child as they continue their education and employment, and eventually their careers. In light of undisputed evidence that plaintiff's child-care arrangements are appropriate and working well, the evidence does not support the trial court's judgment that defendant's proposed, but untested, plans for the child's care would be better. [214 Mich.App. at 245–246, 542 N.W.2d 344.]

The Court of Appeals then explained that the circuit court had committed an error of law in its application of factor e. Observing that the factor concerns "permanence" of the custodial home, not its "acceptability," the Court stated:

> Moreover, an evaluation of each party's arrangements for the child's care while her parents work to go to school is not an appropriate consideration under this factor. We find the trial court committed clear legal error in considering the "acceptability" of the parties' homes and child-care arrangements under this factor, which is directed to the "permanence, as a family unit," of the individual parties. "This factor exclusively concerns whether the family unit will remain intact, not an evaluation about whether one custodial home would be more acceptable than the other." See Fletcher v. Fletcher, 200 Mich.App. 505, 517, 504 N.W.2d 684 (1993). Our Supreme Court affirmed this Court's opinion on this issue, 447 Mich. 871, 884–885 [526 N.W.2d 889] (1994), stating, "We agree with the Court of Appeals. The facts relied upon and expressed by the judge relate to acceptability, rather than permanence, of the custodial unit." [214 Mich.App. at 246, 542 N.W.2d 344.]

Finally, the Court of Appeals provided direction for the proceedings on remand:

On remand, the trial court is to consider "up-to-date information" regarding this factor, as well as the fact that the child has "been living with the plaintiff during the appeal and any other changes in circumstances arising *since the trial court's original custody order.*" Id., emphasis added. The trial court is not, however, to entertain or revisit further "evidence" concerning events before the trial in May and June 1994. See id. [214 Mich.App. at 247, 542 N.W.2d 344.]

III

We affirm the decision of the Court of Appeals to remand this case, and we agree that the circuit court erred in finding that factor e heavily favored Mr. Smith. However, we write to clarify the analysis and modify the terms of the remand.

A

First, there is the issue how properly to understand factor e. As the Court of Appeals observed, we discussed this factor in Fletcher, where we explained:

> Factor e requires the trial court to consider "[t]he permanence, as a family unit, of the existing or proposed custodial home or homes." M.C.L. § 722.23(e); M.S.A. § 25.312(3)(e). In the instant case, the trial court focused on the "*acceptability* of the custodial home," as opposed to its permanence. It stated its findings as follows: "The Court is satisfied that either parent would provide permanence, as a family unit, and would offer acceptable custodial homes. It is undisputed that plaintiff as a father is accustomed to and willing to preform [sic] the day to day jobs to maintain a household. The Court feels that some weight should be assigned in favor of plaintiff because the evidence shows that defendant had been out of the home in the evening many times and thus not caring for the family while plaintiff has been present on those occasions." Because acceptability of the home is not pertinent to factor e, the panel found that it was legal error for the trial court to consider it. We agree with the Court of Appeals. The facts relied upon and expressed by the judge relate to acceptability, rather than permanence, of the custodial unit. Therefore, the trial court's error seems to go beyond mere word choice. [447 Mich. at 884–885, 526 N.W.2d 889.]

We adhere to that explanation. The Legislature has provided twelve statutory factors, of which the first eleven (a through k) concern specific aspects of the family situation. Among them are factors d and e:

(d) The length of time the child has lived in a stable, satisfactory environment, and the desirability of maintaining continuity.

(e) The permanence, as a family unit, of the existing or proposed custodial home or homes.

These factors are phrased somewhat awkwardly,[8] and there clearly is a degree of overlap between them. However, we are satisfied that the focus of

---

8. Factor d calls for a factual inquiry (how long has the child been in a stable, satisfactory environment?) and then states a value ("the desirability of maintaining conti-

factor e is the child's prospects for a stable family environment.[9]

In this instance, we discern no significant difference between the stability of the settings proposed by the two parties. Ms. Ireland likely will continue to spend time both at the University of Michigan and at her mother's home in Mount Clemens (two settings that are now familiar to the child). It is also possible that she will change residences at the university, and that she will move again after completing her education. Such changes, normal for a young adult at this stage of life, do not disqualify Ms. Ireland for custody.

Neither are such changes to be ignored, however. While a child can benefit from reasonable mobility and a degree of parental flexibility regarding residence, the Legislature has determined that "permanence, as a family unit, of the existing or proposed custodial home or homes" is a value to be given weight in the custodial determination.

In some respects, Mr. Smith's proposed custodial home appears more stable. However, that stability may be chimerical. He will not live with his parents forever, and until the likely path of his life becomes more apparent, it is difficult to determine accurately how stable a custodial home he can offer. It would be ironic indeed if the uncertainty of Mr. Smith's plans regarding education, employment, and the early years of adulthood worked to his benefit as a court considered factor e.

In all events, however, the best interests of Maranda, not of Ms. Ireland or Mr. Smith, are central. As in every case, the circuit judge is to give careful consideration to the whole situation. When the court turns to factor e, it must weigh all the facts that bear on whether Ms. Ireland or Mr. Smith can best provide Maranda the benefits of a custodial home that is marked by permanence, as a family unit.

B

Second, we need to confirm that actual and proposed child-care arrangements—whether in the custodial home or elsewhere—are a proper consideration in a custody case. Many children spend a significant amount of time in such settings, and no reasonable person would doubt the importance of child-care decisions. While not directly within the scope of factor e, a parent's intentions in this regard are related to several of the statutory factors:

> (b) The capacity and disposition of the parties involved to give the child love, affection, and guidance and to continue the education and raising of the child in his or her religion or creed, if any.

---

nuity"). Taken literally, factor e appears to direct an inquiry into the extent to which a "home" will serve as a permanent "family unit."

9. The stability of a child's home can be undermined in various ways. This might include frequent moves to unfamiliar settings, a succession of persons residing in the home, live-in romantic companions for the custodial parent, or other potential disruptions. Of course, every situation needs to be examined individually.

(c) The capacity and disposition of the parties involved to provide the child with food, clothing, medical care or other remedial care recognized and permitted under the laws of this state in place of medical care, and other material needs.

* * *

(h) The home, school, and community record of the child.

To the extent that these factors fail to capture this aspect of child-rearing, it certainly falls within the final factor:

(*l*) Any other factor considered by the court to be relevant to a particular child custody dispute.

Having said that child-care arrangements are a proper consideration, we then encounter the issue that brought sixty-one amici curiae to the Court of Appeals (all in support of Ms. Ireland): *How* are such arrangements to be considered? Does a parent seeking custody lose ground by proposing to place a child in a day-care center while the parent works or goes to school? Is in-home care from parents and other relatives better than day care with other children under the supervision of licensed care givers? Is day care better?

Such questions are not susceptible of a broad answer. Certainly, placement of a child in a good day-care setting can have many benefits and is in no sense a sign of parental neglect. Both single and married parents have many obligations, and day care generally is an entirely appropriate manner of balancing those obligations.

At the same time, it requires no stretch of imagination to produce hypothetical situations in which a parent's unwise choices in this regard would reflect poorly on the parent's judgment. More fundamentally, every child, every adult, and every custody case is unique. There can be no broad rules that dictate a preference for one manner of child care over another. The circuit court must look at each situation and determine what is in the best interests of the child.

C

Third, we offer a clarification with regard to the scope of the inquiry on remand. In Fletcher, we explained:

[U]pon a finding of error an appellate court should remand the case for reevaluation, unless the error was harmless. We further hold that on remand, the court should consider up-to-date information, including the children's current and reasonable preferences,[10] as well as the fact that the children have been living with the plaintiff during the appeal and any other changes in circumstances arising since the trial court's original custody order. [447 Mich. at 889, 526 N.W.2d 889.]

---

10. A court considers the reasonable preference of the child, *if the court considers the child to be of sufficient age* to express preference. M.C.L. § 722.23(I); M.S.A. § 25.312(3)(I).

In this case, the Court of Appeals opinion is not clear with regard to whether all twelve statutory factors—not just factor e—are to be considered on remand.

As the Court of Appeals likely intended, the circuit court is to review the entire question of custody on remand.[11] The court should consider all the statutory factors and conduct whatever hearings or other proceedings are necessary to allow it to make an accurate decision concerning a custody arrangement that is in the best interests of Maranda.[12] Fletcher, 447 Mich. at 888–890, 526 N.W.2d 889.

IV

With the clarifications and modifications noted in this opinion, we affirm the judgment of the Court of Appeals, remanding this case to the circuit court for further proceedings.

UNIFORM MARRIAGE AND DIVORCE ACT

Section 402.   [Best Interest of Child.]*

The court shall determine custody in accordance with the best interest of the child. The court shall consider all relevant factors including:

(1) the wishes of the child's parent or parents as to his custody;

(2) the wishes of the child as to his custodian;

(3) the interaction and interrelationship of the child with his parent or parents, his siblings, and any other person who may significantly affect the child's best interest;

(4) the child's adjustment to his home, school, and community; and

(5) the mental and physical health of all individuals involved.

The court shall not consider conduct of a proposed custodian that does not affect his relationship to the child.

Section 406.   [Hearings.]

(a) Custody proceedings shall receive priority in being set for hearing.

(b) The court may tax as costs the payment of necessary travel and other expenses incurred by any person whose presence at the hearing the court deems necessary to determine the best interest of the child.

---

11. As the Court of Appeals observed, the record can be closed with regard to events that happened before the mid–1994 evidentiary hearing. The circuit court should reconsider the facts adduced at that hearing in light of the clarified analysis of factor e, but additional proofs regarding events before June 1994 would not be appropriate.

12. As noted earlier, the Court of Appeals upheld the circuit court's determination that the other statutory factors (a-d and f-l)

favored neither party. We will not attempt to sort through the many conflicting charges, confident that the circuit court on remand will be far better positioned to consider the present circumstances of Maranda and of the parties, and to determine where the truth lies in this matter.

(c) The court without a jury shall determine questions of law and fact. If it finds that a public hearing may be detrimental to the child's best interest, the court may exclude the public from a custody hearing, but may admit any person who has a direct and legitimate interest in the particular case or a legitimate educational or research interest in the work of the court.

(d) If the court finds it necessary to protect the child's welfare that the record of any interview, report, investigation, or testimony in a custody proceeding be kept secret, the court may make an appropriate order sealing the record.

Section 408.   [Judicial Supervision.]

(a) Except as otherwise agreed by the parties in writing at the time of the custody decree, the custodian may determine the child's upbringing, including his education, health care, and religious training, unless the court after hearing, finds, upon motion by the noncustodial parent, that in the absence of a specific limitation of the custodian's authority, the child's physical health would be endangered or his emotional development significantly impaired.

(b) If both parents or all contestants agree to the order, or if the court finds that in the absence of the order the child's physical health would be endangered or his emotional development significantly impaired, the court may order the [local probation or welfare department, court social service agency] to exercise continuing supervision over the case to assure that the custodial or visitation terms of the decree are carried out.

Section 409.   [Modification.]

(a) No motion to modify a custody decree may be made earlier than 2 years after its date, unless the court permits it to be made on the basis of affidavits that there is reason to believe the child's present environment may endanger seriously his physical, mental, moral, or emotional health.

(b) If a court of this State has jurisdiction pursuant to the Uniform Child Custody Jurisdiction Act, the court shall not modify a prior custody decree unless it finds, upon the basis of facts that have arisen since the prior decree or that were unknown to the court at the time of entry of the prior decree, that a change has occurred in the circumstances of the child or his custodian, and that the modification is necessary to serve the best interest of the child. In applying these standards the court shall retain the custodian appointed pursuant to the prior decree unless:

(1) the custodian agrees to the modification;

(2) the child has been integrated into the family of the petitioner with consent of the custodian; or

(3) the child's present environment endangers seriously his physical, mental, moral, or emotional health, and the harm likely to be caused by a change of environment is outweighed by its advantages to him.

(c) Attorney fees and costs shall be assessed against a party seeking modification if the court finds that the modification action is vexatious and constitutes harassment.

CALIFORNIA FAMILY CODE

§ 3120.   Action for exclusive custody; order

Without filing a petition for dissolution of marriage or legal separation of the parties, the husband or wife may bring an action for the exclusive custody of the children of the marriage. The court may, during the pendency of the action, or at the final hearing thereof, or afterwards, make such order regarding the support, care, custody, education, and control of the children of the marriage as may be just and in accordance with the natural rights of the parents and the best interest of the children. The order may be modified or terminated at any time thereafter as the natural rights of the parties and the best interest of the children may require.

Palmore v. Sidoti

Supreme Court of the United States, 1984.
466 U.S. 429, 104 S.Ct. 1879, 80 L.Ed.2d 421.

■ Chief Justice Burger delivered the opinion of the Court.

We granted certiorari to review a judgment of a state court divesting a natural mother of the custody of her infant child because of her remarriage to a person of a different race.

When petitioner Linda Sidoti Palmore and respondent Anthony J. Sidoti, both Caucasians, were divorced in May 1980 in Florida, the mother was awarded custody of their three-year-old daughter.

In September 1981 the father sought custody of the child by filing a petition to modify the prior judgment because of changed conditions. The change was that the child's mother was then cohabiting with a Negro, Clarence Palmore, Jr., whom she married two months later. Additionally, the father made several allegations of instances in which the mother had not properly cared for the child.

After hearing testimony from both parties and considering a court counselor's investigative report, the court noted that the father had made allegations about the child's care, but the court made no findings with respect to these allegations. On the contrary, the court made a finding that "there is no issue as to either party's devotion to the child, adequacy of housing facilities, or respect[a]bility of the new spouse of either parent."

The court then addressed the recommendations of the court counselor, who had made an earlier report "in [another] case coming out of this circuit also involving the social consequences of an interracial marriage. Niles v. Niles, 299 So.2d 162." From this vague reference to that earlier case, the court turned to the present case and noted the counselor's recommendation for a change in custody because "[t]he wife [petitioner] has chosen for herself and for her child, a life-style unacceptable to her father *and to society*.... The child ... is, or at school age will be, subject to environmental pressures not of choice."

The court then concluded that the best interests of the child would be served by awarding custody to the father. The court's rationale is contained in the following:

> "The father's evident resentment of the mother's choice of a black partner is not sufficient to wrest custody from the mother. It is of some significance, however, that the mother did see fit to bring a man into her home and carry on a sexual relationship with him without being married to him. Such action tended to place gratification of her own desires ahead of her concern for the child's future welfare. *This Court feels that despite the strides that have been made in bettering relations between the races in this country, it is inevitable that Melanie will, if allowed to remain in her present situation and attains school age and thus more vulnerable to peer pressures, suffer from the social stigmatization that is sure to come.*" App. to Pet. for Cert. 26–27 (emphasis added).

The Second District Court of Appeal affirmed without opinion, thus denying the Florida Supreme Court jurisdiction to review the case. We granted certiorari, and we reverse.

The judgment of a state court determining or reviewing a child custody decision is not ordinarily a likely candidate for review by this Court. However, the court's opinion, after stating that the "father's evident resentment of the mother's choice of a black partner is not sufficient" to deprive her of custody, then turns to what it regarded as the damaging impact on the child from remaining in a racially-mixed household. This raises important federal concerns arising from the Constitution's commitment to eradicating discrimination based on race.

The Florida court did not focus directly on the parental qualifications of the natural mother or her present husband, or indeed on the father's qualifications to have custody of the child. The court found that "there is no issue as to either party's devotion to the child, adequacy of housing facilities, or respect[a]bility of the new spouse of either parent." This, taken with the absence of any negative finding as to the quality of the care provided by the mother, constitutes a rejection of any claim of petitioner's unfitness to continue the custody of her child.

The court correctly stated that the child's welfare was the controlling factor. But that court was entirely candid and made no effort to place its holding on any ground other than race. Taking the court's findings and rationale at face value, it is clear that the outcome would have been different had petitioner married a Caucasian male of similar respectability.

A core purpose of the Fourteenth Amendment was to do away with all governmentally imposed discrimination based on race. Classifying persons according to their race is more likely to reflect racial prejudice than legitimate public concerns; the race, not the person, dictates the category. Such classifications are subject to the most exacting scrutiny; to pass constitutional muster, they must be justified by a compelling governmental interest and must be "necessary ... to the accomplishment" of its legitimate purpose, McLaughlin v. Florida, 379 U.S. 184 (1964). See Loving v. Virginia, 388 U.S. 1, 11 (1967).

The State, of course, has a duty of the highest order to protect the interests of minor children, particularly those of tender years. In common with most states, Florida law mandates that custody determinations be made in the best interests of the children involved. Fla. Stat. § 61.13(2)(b)(1) (1983). The goal of granting custody based on the best interests of the child is indisputably a substantial governmental interest for purposes of the Equal Protection Clause.

It would ignore reality to suggest that racial and ethnic prejudices do not exist or that all manifestations of those prejudices have been eliminated. There is a risk that a child living with a step-parent of a different race may be subject to a variety of pressures and stresses not present if the child were living with parents of the same racial or ethnic origin.

The question, however, is whether the reality of private biases and the possible injury they might inflict are permissible considerations for removal of an infant child from the custody of its natural mother. We have little difficulty concluding that they are not.[2] The Constitution cannot control such prejudices but neither can it tolerate them. Private biases may be outside the reach of the law, but the law cannot, directly or indirectly, give them effect. "Public officials sworn to uphold the Constitution may not avoid a constitutional duty by bowing to the hypothetical effects of private racial prejudice that they assume to be both widely and deeply held." Palmer v. Thompson, 403 U.S. 217, 260–261 (1971) (White, J., dissenting).

. . .

Whatever problems racially-mixed households may pose for children in 1984 can no more support a denial of constitutional rights than could the stresses that residential integration was thought to entail in 1971. The effects of racial prejudice, however real, cannot justify a racial classification removing an infant child from the custody of its natural mother found to be an appropriate person to have such custody.

In re Marriage of Short

Supreme Court of Colorado, En Banc, 1985.
698 P.2d 1310.

■ Erickson, Chief Justice.

We granted certiorari to review the standard of admissibility for evidence of religious beliefs or practices in a child custody proceeding. The court of appeals held that evidence of a parent's religious practices is admissible in a custody proceeding only if the proponent of such evidence establishes that there is a substantial probability that the religious practice will result in actual harm or endangerment to the child's physical or mental health. In re Marriage of Short, 675 P.2d 323 (Colo.App.1983). We conclude that the standard adopted by the court of appeals is unduly restrictive, and therefore reverse and remand with directions.

---

2. In light of our holding based on the Equal Protection Clause, we need not reach or resolve petitioner's claim based on the Fourteenth Amendment's Due Process Clause.

I.

The marriage of Laramie Short (mother) and Carl Short (father) was dissolved in September 1980. The parties entered into a settlement agreement regarding property division, maintenance, and attorneys' fees, but disputed the custody of their two minor sons who were of the ages of two and four at the time of the hearing.

Prior to the hearing on the custody issue, the mother, an active Jehovah's Witness, filed a motion *in limine* to exclude "all evidence concerning the beliefs or the practices or any other facet of the Jehovah's Witness religion or any participants thereof." The district court initially stated that it would admit any evidence, whether religiously based or not, that bears directly on the physical or mental well-being of the children. However, the court later limited its ruling, stating that it would admit only that evidence relating to the mother's religious practices "which affects the children to the degree that would require the attention of a physician or mental health professional."

The district court accordingly permitted a limited inquiry into the mother's views regarding blood transfusions and whether she would comply with a court order requiring such a procedure to be initiated upon the children in the case of a medical emergency. The court refused, however, to admit evidence of the mother's other beliefs and practices as a Jehovah's Witness, which the father alleged were potentially harmful to the children's emotional health and welfare. The father attempted to introduce evidence, by way of offers of proof, of the mother's practices of proselytizing and door-to-door solicitation; the implications of the father's "disfellowship" from the Jehovah's Witness religion; various beliefs and practices of the mother which encourage disassociation of the children from persons who are not members of the Jehovah's Witness religion; and expert psychological testimony regarding the potential impact of such beliefs and practices on the mental and emotional development of the children.

Permanent custody of the two children was ultimately awarded to the mother, and substantial visitation rights were granted to the father. Following an unsuccessful appeal to the court of appeals, the father petitioned this court for a writ of certiorari.

II.

The father asserts that, while under the United States and Colorado Constitutions a court must generally remain neutral with respect to the religious tenets of the parties, such religious neutrality does not preclude the admission of evidence in a child custody proceeding of a party's religious beliefs or practices which are likely to result in physical or emotional harm to the child. We agree.

The right of all citizens to freely pursue the religious beliefs of their choice is guaranteed by the free exercise of religion clause of the first amendment of the United States Constitution, as applied to the states through the due process clause of the fourteenth amendment, and of article II, section 4 of the Colorado Constitution.[2] We have recognized that the

---

2. Article II, section 4 of the Colorado Constitution provides:

Section 4. Religious freedom. The free exercise and enjoyment of religious prostate and the courts bear a heavy burden in justifying any infringement of an individual's first amendment freedoms. People in the Interest of D.L.E. I, 200 Colo. 244, 614 P.2d 873 (1980); People in the Interest of D.L.E. II, 645 P.2d 271 (Colo.1982); see, e.g., Sherbert v. Verner, 374 U.S. 398 (1963). However, the rights guaranteed under the free exercise of religion clause are not without limits. We stated in D.L.E. II that the family itself is not beyond regulation in the public interest as against a claim of religious liberty, and neither the rights of religion nor rights of parenthood are beyond limitation. Prince v. Massachusetts, 321 U.S. 158 (1944); see also Reynolds v. United States [8 Otto 145], 98 U.S. 145 (1878). Acting to guard the general interest in the youth's well-being, the authority of the state, as parens patriae, is not nullified merely because a parent grounds his claim to control the child's course of conduct on religion or conscience.

The overriding concern in any custody proceeding must be the welfare and best interests of the child. Section 14–10–124, 6 C.R.S. (1984 Supp.);[3] Kelley v. Kelley, 161 Colo. 486, 423 P.2d 315 (1967). Colorado's statute governing child custody requires a broad inquiry into all relevant factors bearing on the welfare of the child, to ensure that the trial court's custody determination is most conducive to the child's best interests. See § 14–10–124, 6 C.R.S. (1984 Supp.).

Courts are precluded by the free exercise of religion clause from weighing the comparative merits of the religious tenets of the various faiths or basing its custody decisions solely on religious considerations. Compton v. Gilmore, 98 Idaho 190, 560 P.2d 861 (1977); Quiner v. Quiner, 59 Cal.Rptr. 503 (Cal.App.1967). However, the religious beliefs and practices of the parent may be a relevant factor, along with other circumstances, which bears upon the child's best interests and general welfare. Hilley v. Hilley, 405 So.2d 708 (Ala.1981); Morris v. Morris, 271 Pa.Super. 19, 412 A.2d 139 (1979); Sinclair v. Sinclair, 204 Kan. 240, 461 P.2d 750 (1969); . . .

---

fession and worship, without discrimination, shall forever hereafter be guaranteed; and no person shall be denied any civil or political right, privilege or capacity, on account of his opinions concerning religion; but the liberty of conscience hereby secured shall not be construed to dispense with oaths or affirmations, excuse acts of licentiousness or justify practices inconsistent with the good order, peace or safety of the state. No person shall be required to attend or support any ministry or place of worship, religious sect or denomination against his consent. Nor shall any preference be given by law to any religious denomination or mode of worship.

3. Section 14–10–124, 6 C.R.S. (1984 Supp.) provides in pertinent part:

14–10–124. Best interests of child. (1) The general assembly finds and declares that it is in the best interest of all parties to encourage frequent and continuing contact between each parent and the minor child of the marriage after the parents have separated or dissolved their marriage. In order to effectuate this goal, the general assembly urges parents to share the rights and responsibilities of child-rearing and to encourage the love, affection, and contact between the children and the parents. (1.5) The court shall determine custody in accordance with the best interests of the child. In determining the best interests of the child, the court shall consider all relevant factors, including:.... (c) The interaction and interrelationship of the child with his parents, his siblings, and any other person who may significantly affect the child's best interests; (d) The child's adjustment to his home, school, and community; (e) The mental and physical health of all individuals involved; and (f) The ability of the custodian to encourage the sharing of love, affection, and contact between the child and the noncustodial party.

Among the diverse religious faiths are philosophies and practices which might reasonably imperil the physical or mental health of a child. While courts must remain sensitive to first amendment concerns, a court in a custody proceeding must not blind itself to evidence of religious beliefs or practices of a party seeking custody which may impair or endanger the child's welfare. See Clift v. Clift, 346 So.2d 429 (Ala.Civ.App.1977).

The court of appeals recognized that religious decisions and acts affecting the mental health or physical safety of the child may be admitted in a custody proceeding, but only if there is a substantial probability that the religious belief or practice will result in actual harm or endangerment to the child's welfare. Short, 675 P.2d at 325. In our view, the standard adopted by the court of appeals is unduly restrictive and is inconsistent with the broad scope of review accorded to the trial court in child custody proceedings.

We hold that under C.R.E. 403, evidence of a party's religious beliefs or practices is relevant and admissible in a custody proceeding if it is shown that such beliefs or practices are reasonably likely to cause present or future harm to the physical or mental development of the child. While evidence of endangering religious beliefs or practices may not be based upon mere conjecture, the evidence need not be restricted to actual present harm or impairment. Given the necessarily uncertain nature of psychological evaluation and diagnosis and the potential for severe future psychological impairment to result from practices which do not have present demonstrable effects upon the child, we conclude that evidence of beliefs or practices which are reasonably likely to cause present or future harm to the child is admissible in a custody proceeding.

We reiterate that a court may not properly inquire into or make judgments regarding the abstract wisdom of a particular religious value or belief. Evidence of religious beliefs or practices is admissible only as it reasonably relates to potential mental or physical harm to the welfare of the child. Nor do we intend to restrict the broad discretion of the trial court in appraising the circumstances of the parties and determining which party is best suited to assume primary custody of a child. The ultimate determination of custody remains a matter largely within the sound discretion of the trial court.

The judgment of the court of appeals is reversed and the case is returned to the court of appeals with directions to remand to the district court for further proceedings.

Due to the passage of time since the evidentiary hearing was held, a new hearing should be held on the issue of custody based upon the current status of the parties and in light of the standards announced in this opinion.

NOTE

For further commentary on the role of religion in child custody proceedings, see Gary M. Miller, Balancing the Welfare of Children with the Rights of Parents: Petersen v. Rogers and the Role of Religion in Custody Disputes, 73 N.C. L.Rev. 1271 (1995); Nelson A. Mendez, Child Custody Entangled with Religion: *Osteraas v.*

Osteraas, 31 Idaho L.Rev. 339 (1994); and Carolyn R. Wah, Religion in Child Custody and Visitation Cases: Presenting the Advantage of Religious Participation, 28 Fam.L.Q. 269 (1994).

Bottoms v. Bottoms

Supreme Court of Virginia, 1995.
249 Va. 410, 457 S.E.2d 102.

■ COMPTON, JUSTICE.

This is a child custody dispute between a child's mother and maternal grandmother. The sole issue is whether the Court of Appeals erred in deciding that the child's best interests would be served by awarding custody to the mother. We conclude that the Court of Appeals erred, and reverse.

No novel questions of law are involved; the legal principles applicable under these circumstances to child custody cases are settled in the Commonwealth. We took jurisdiction of this appeal because we decided that the application of the law to the facts of this case involves a matter of significant precedential value. See Code § 17–116.07(B).

In March 1993, appellant Pamela Kay Bottoms filed a petition against her daughter, appellee Sharon Lynne Bottoms, in the Juvenile and Domestic Relations District Court of Henrico County seeking an award of custody of the daughter's son, born in July 1991. In the petition, the grandmother alleged that the "infant is currently living in an environment which is harmful to his mental and physical well being." Following a hearing, at which both parties were represented by counsel, the juvenile court awarded custody to the grandmother and granted the mother restricted visitation rights. The mother appealed to the circuit court.

In May 1993, because the mother stated she was not represented by an attorney at that time, the circuit court appointed a guardian ad litem "for the infant child to represent him in these proceedings." Following psychological evaluations of the parties and the child, and after studies of the homes of the parties, the trial court conducted a hearing *de novo* in September 1993 at which eight witnesses testified. Participating in the hearing were the grandmother's attorney, the guardian ad litem, and the mother's present counsel. At the conclusion of the hearing, the trial court ruled that custody of the child should be awarded to the grandmother, with restricted visitation rights granted the mother.

The mother appealed to the Court of Appeals. A three-judge panel unanimously reversed and vacated the trial court's order, remanding the case to the circuit court for entry of an order "effectuating the resumption of custody by the mother of her son." Bottoms v. Bottoms, 18 Va.App. 481, 495, 444 S.E.2d 276, 284 (1994). We awarded the grandmother this appeal from the Court of Appeals' June 1994 order.

"In all child custody cases, including those between a parent and a non-parent, 'the best interests of the child are paramount and form the lodestar for the guidance of the court in determining the dispute.' " Bailes v. Sours, 231 Va. 96, 99, 340 S.E.2d 824, 826 (1986) (quoting Walker v.

Brooks, 203 Va. 417, 421, 124 S.E.2d 195, 198 (1962)). In a custody dispute between a parent and non-parent, "the law presumes that the child's best interests will be served when in the custody of its parent." Judd v. Van Horn, 195 Va. 988, 996, 81 S.E.2d 432, 436 (1954).

Although the presumption favoring a parent over a non-parent is strong, it is rebutted when certain factors, such as parental unfitness, are established by clear and convincing evidence. Bailes, 231 Va. at 100, 340 S.E.2d at 827. The term "clear and convincing evidence" is defined as the measure or degree of proof that will produce in the mind of the trier of facts a firm belief or conviction upon the allegations sought to be established. It is intermediate, being more than a mere preponderance, but not to the degree of proof beyond a reasonable doubt as in criminal cases; it does not mean clear and *unequivocal*. The burden to show unfitness is upon the one seeking to alter the parent's right to custody.

In custody cases, the welfare of the child takes precedence over the rights of the parent. Malpass v. Morgan, 213 Va. 393, 399, 192 S.E.2d 794, 799 (1972). But, when the contest is between parent and non-parent, this rule is conditioned upon the principle that a parent's rights "are to be respected if at all consonant with the best interests of the child." Id. at 400, 192 S.E.2d at 799. Some of the foregoing principles have been codified recently by the General Assembly in Code §§ 20–124.1 to –124.6. Act 1994, ch. 769.

When the trial court hears the evidence *ore tenus*, its findings are entitled to the weight accorded a jury verdict, and these findings should not be disturbed by an appellate court unless they are plainly wrong or without evidence to support them. Bailes, 231 Va. at 100, 340 S.E.2d at 827. A reviewing court should never redetermine the facts on appeal.

Absent clear evidence to the contrary in the record, the judgment of a trial court comes to an appellate court with a presumption that the law was correctly applied to the facts. Yarborough v. Commonwealth, 217 Va. 971, 978, 234 S.E.2d 286, 291 (1977). And, the appellate court should view the facts in the light most favorable to the party prevailing before the trial court. Accordingly, we shall summarize the facts in the light most favorable to the grandmother, resolving all conflicts in the evidence in her favor.

This child's mother, born in February 1970, "dropped out" of school in the twelfth grade. Until she was 18 years of age, she resided at home with her mother, who is a divorcee, and her mother's boyfriend.

Upon leaving home, the child's mother was supported by and lived with a cousin, a friend, and a sister respectively. In December 1989, the child's mother married Dennis Doustou, whom she had been dating for several years. She left Doustou after eight months of marriage, and resumed living with the cousin for a while. The child was born during the separation in July 1991. The parties were divorced, and the mother was awarded custody of her child. The child's father has expressed little interest in his son and pays no child support.

The maternal grandmother, born in January 1951, resides in the Richmond area. Her boyfriend ceased living with her shortly before the juvenile court hearing, and has not returned. The grandmother did not complete her high school education, and has worked as a nurse's aide and manager of a shoe store. She currently is employed as a "nanny," taking care of two children.

During the two-year period before the trial court hearing, the child had spent 70 percent of the time with the grandmother and 30 percent with his mother. The grandmother has kept the child for "weeks at a time" and during "every weekend since he's been born." On at least three occasions during that period, the mother left the child with the grandmother without informing her of the mother's whereabouts or how she could be reached "in the event something happened to the child."

Following the mother's separation from Doustou, she continued a "relationship" with another man that had begun during her marriage. She contracted a venereal disease during this relationship that prevents her from having additional children. During the child's first year, the mother "slept with two or three different guys, maybe four, in the same room" with the child "where his crib was." At the time, the mother "lived two blocks away" from the grandmother, and the mother kept the child's "suitcase packed" for visits to the grandmother's home. The mother said that she has "had trouble" with her temper, and that when the child was about "a year" old, she "popped him on his leg too hard a couple of times," and left her fingerprints there. She has had "counseling" in an effort to control her temper.

At "some point subsequent to" the child's birth, the mother lived in a dwelling with yet another man who supported her for more than a year. After the mother "left" this man, she "lived with" a lesbian "couple."

Except for brief employment as a grocery store cashier, the mother had been unemployed during most of the three-year period prior to the trial court hearing. She was receiving "welfare money" which often was spent to "do her fingernails before the baby would get any food."

During May 1992, ten months before the juvenile court hearing, 16 months before the trial court hearing, and when her son was ten months old, the mother met April Wade, a lesbian. Wade, born in April 1966, had been discharged from the U.S. Army in 1986. Wade is a "recovering alcoholic."

The mother and Wade "moved in together" in September 1992. From that time, with the exception of a two-week period, the mother and Wade have lived in "a lesbian relationship." According to the mother, the relationship involves hugging and kissing, patting "on the bottom," sleeping in the same bed, "fondling," and "oral sex." The mother testified that she loves Wade and that they "have a lifetime commitment."

At the time of the juvenile court hearing, the mother, the child, and Wade were living in a two-bedroom apartment with "Evelyn," another lesbian. "At one time," the child's bed was in the room where the mother and Wade slept, having "sex in the same bed." At one point in her testimony, however, when asked "how many times did you do it when the child was sleeping in the same bedroom," the mother responded, "None." She said that she and Wade displayed other signs of affection "in front of" the child.

Wade, employed as a gift shop manager, supports the mother. The pair lives in an apartment complex in Western Henrico County. Wade has become "a parent figure" to the child, who calls Wade "Da Da."

Two months before the petition for custody was filed, the mother revealed her lesbian relationship to the grandmother. This disclosure alienated the two.

During the period after the juvenile court hearing, when regimented visitation with the mother began, the child demonstrated certain traits. For example, when the child returned to the grandmother from being with the mother, he would "stomp" his foot, tell himself to "go to the corner," and then would stand in the corner of a room, facing the wall. He curses, saying "shit" and "damn," language never used in the grandmother's home. On one occasion, when the mother and Wade "came to pick him up," the child "held his breath, turned purple. He didn't want to go with her," according to the grandmother. During a period in mid–1993, each time the mother "would come pick him up," the child would scream and cry.

Wade has admitted she "hit" the child. Also, on one occasion, when an argument developed between the mother and Wade, on the one hand, and the grandmother, on the other, about the timing of the exchange of the child for visitation, Wade said during the quarrel, "I might end up killing somebody." According to the grandmother, the child is "always neglected." For example, when the child returns to the grandmother's home, she testified that he "can't even sit down in the bathtub. That's neglect from changing his diaper. He is so red."

At the conclusion of the hearing, the guardian ad litem made a closing statement to the trial judge. Saying that he "took this appointment very seriously," the guardian ad litem stated he had "done extensive reading in many areas," including "the effect homosexuality will have on the rearing of children." He stated that he had "talked with psychiatrists in the field," and met "at length" with the mother, the grandmother, Wade, and the child, and "interviewed all of these parties as best I could." He asked another attorney, a woman, to assist him in order to obtain "another perspective." The guardian ad litem said that he and his associate "literally" spent the entire month before the hearing on the case.

In evaluating the case, the guardian ad litem said he is "a pretty open-minded guy" without any biases, "especially involving a homosexual issue." He stated that the child's father "should be ashamed of himself" for having no interest in the child and for contributing "nothing towards financial support of the child."

He stated that Wade is "a very nice person," but "she has a lot of baggage that she brings along with her" causing him to question her "stability." He observed that Wade genuinely "loves the child," but in view of her "rather sketchy" employment history, he was "curious as to how she will support the child if custody goes with" Wade and the mother.

Commenting on the mother, the guardian ad litem said he has "no question that she loves [the child] very much," but he found her to be a "very ... immature young lady." He noted that she has "never really completed anything," has "jumped from relationship to relationship, from one place to another," and has "never really put roots down." Observing that "she has no employment to speak of, no skills, no education" and that her "future in the job market ... is rather bleak," nevertheless, the guardian ad litem said, she is the child's natural mother, and "the love between a natural mother and child is something that's almost sacred." He stated that he "firmly" believed that the mother's love for the child "is an honest love" and "that she comes to this court with clean hands in that regard."

Referring to the grandmother, he said he found "her to be an equally very nice person, a very sincere person." He said he regarded her "as a bit more than" a third-party stranger, and that she has had "more than a typical grandmother relationship with the child." He noted she "has taken care of this child the majority of the child's life," and "has provided for the child financially, fed the child, clothed the child," and "taken the child to the doctor."

The guardian ad litem observed, "The homosexual issue does not alarm me," stating his belief "that a homosexual should be allowed to raise a child." One matter "did concern" him about the mother. He referred to evidence that the mother separated herself from Wade after the juvenile court hearing, on the advice of counsel, to "help ... with the custody fight," but returned to live with her two weeks later on the advice of new counsel. When asked why she is presently living with Wade if she thought living apart would help her regain custody, the mother responded, "I was taking a chance." The guardian ad litem observed that the mother felt her individual "rights" were as important as her child's.

Summarizing, and noting "that custody is something that's flexible and can change if the circumstances change," the guardian ad litem suggested to the court that the child's best interests, "at this time under this actual situation," would be served by awarding custody to the grand-mother.

The trial judge, announcing his decision from the bench at the conclusion of the hearing, said the dispute "presents the question ... whether the child's best interest is served by a transfer of the custody of the child from [his] mother to [his] maternal grandmother." Stating that the mother's conduct is "illegal," and constitutes a felony under the Commonwealth's criminal laws, and that "her conduct is immoral," the court recognized the "presumption in the law in favor of the custody being with the natural parent."

Mentioning the evidence of lesbianism and specified "other evidence" in the case not involving homosexual conduct, the trial court concluded from "all the facts and circumstances ... of the case," that "the custody will be with the grandmother."

The Court of Appeals concluded that "the evidence fails to prove" that the mother "abused or neglected her son, that her lesbian relationship with April Wade has or will have a deleterious effect on her son, or that she is an unfit parent." Bottoms, 18 Va.App. at 484, 444 S.E.2d at 278. "To the contrary," said the Court of Appeals, the evidence showed that the mother "is and has been a fit and nurturing parent who has adequately provided and cared for her son. No evidence tended to prove that the child will be harmed by remaining with his mother." Id. The court held "that the trial court abused its discretion by invoking the state's authority to take the child from the custody of his natural mother ... and by transferring custody to a non-parent, ... the child's maternal grandmother." Id.

We disagree. The Court of Appeals failed to give proper deference upon appellate review to the trial court's factual findings, and misapplied the law to the facts viewed from a proper appellate perspective.

The evidence plainly is sufficient, when applying the clear and convincing standard and when viewing the facts from the correct appellate perspective, to support the trial court's findings that the parental presumption has been rebutted, that the mother is an unfit custodian at this time, and that the child's best interests would be promoted by awarding custody to the grandmother.

Among the factors to be weighed in determining unfitness are the parent's misconduct that affects the child, neglect of the child, and a demonstrated unwillingness and inability to promote the emotional and physical well-being of the child. Other important considerations include the nature of the home environment and moral climate in which the child is to be raised. Brown v. Brown, 218 Va. 196, 199, 237 S.E.2d 89, 91 (1977).

We have held, however, that a lesbian mother is not per se an unfit parent. Doe v. Doe, 222 Va. 736, 748, 284 S.E.2d 799, 806 (1981). Conduct inherent in lesbianism is punishable as a Class 6 felony in the Commonwealth, Code § 18.2–361; thus, that conduct is another important consideration in determining custody.

And, while the legal rights of a parent should be respected in a custody proceeding, those technical rights may be disregarded if demanded by the interests of the child. Forbes v. Haney, 204 Va. 712, 716, 133 S.E.2d 533, 536 (1963).

In the present case, the record shows a mother who, although devoted to her son, refuses to subordinate her own desires and priorities to the child's welfare. For example, the mother disappears for days without informing the child's custodian of her whereabouts. She moves her residence from place to place, relying on others for support, and uses welfare funds to "do" her fingernails before buying food for the child. She has participated in illicit relationships with numerous men, acquiring a disease from one, and "sleeping" with men in the same room where the child's crib was located. To aid in her mobility, the mother keeps the child's suitcase packed so he can be quickly deposited at the grandmother's.

The mother has difficulty controlling her temper and, out of frustration, has struck the child when it was merely one year old with such force as to leave her fingerprints on his person. While in her care, she neglects to change and cleanse the child so that, when he returns from visitation with her, he is "red" and "can't even sit down in the bathtub."

Unlike Doe, 222 Va. at 747, 284 S.E.2d at 805, relied on by the mother, there is proof in this case that the child has been harmed, at this young age, by the conditions under which he lives when with the mother for any extended period. For example, he has already demonstrated some disturbing traits. He uses vile language. He screams, holds his breath until he turns purple, and becomes emotionally upset when he must go to visit the mother. He appears confused about efforts at discipline, standing himself in a corner facing the wall for no apparent reason.

And, we shall not overlook the mother's relationship with Wade, and the environment in which the child would be raised if custody is awarded the mother. We have previously said that living daily under conditions stemming from active lesbianism practiced in the home may impose a burden upon a child by reason of the "social condemnation" attached to such an arrangement, which will inevitably afflict the child's relationships with its "peers and with the community at large." Roe v. Roe, 228 Va. 722, 728, 324 S.E.2d 691, 694 (1985). We do not retreat from that statement; such a result is likely under these facts. Also, Wade has struck the child and, when there was a dispute over visitation, she has threatened violence when her views were not accepted.

Finally, the recommendation of the guardian ad litem in this case, while not binding or controlling, should not be disregarded. Contra Matter of Baby K, 832 F.Supp. 1022, 1031 n. 2 (E.D.Va.1993), aff'd on other grounds, 16 F.3d 590 (4th Cir.1994), cert. denied, 513 U.S. 825 (1994) (recommendation of court-appointed guardian ad litem "irrelevant" to disposition of declaratory judgment proceeding to authorize withholding by hospital of infant's ventilator treatment). The duty of a guardian ad litem in a child custody dispute is to see that the interest of the child is "represented and protected." Code § 8.01–9. See Rule 8:6 (describing role of guardian ad litem appointed for child in juvenile and domestic relations district courts). This child had no other independent participant in the proceeding, aside from the trial court, to protect his interests. Thus, this diligent guardian ad litem's recommendation that custody be awarded to the grandmother was entitled to be considered by the court in reaching a decision on the issue.

Accordingly, we hold that the trial court, based on all the facts and circumstances, correctly ruled on the custody question. And, the study of the grandmother's home by the Chesterfield–Colonial Heights Department of Social Services determined there was "no reason" why she should not be awarded custody should the trial court make such a ruling.

Thus, the judgment of the Court of Appeals will be reversed and the case will be remanded, with directions that the Court of Appeals remand the case to the Circuit Court of Henrico County for reinstatement of that court's order of September 21, 1993 awarding custody of the child to Pamela Kay Bottoms.

Reversed and remanded.

■ Keenan, Justice, with whom Whiting and Lacy, Justices, join, dissenting.

This Court has held, as the majority states, that a lesbian mother is not *per se* an unfit parent. Doe v. Doe, 222 Va. 736, 748, 284 S.E.2d 799, 806 (1981). Nevertheless, the majority ignores the trial court's refusal to follow this established law of the Commonwealth.

The record plainly shows that the trial court made a per se finding of unfitness based on the mother's homosexual conduct. The trial court stated:

> I will tell you first that the mother's conduct is illegal. It is a Class 6 felony in the Commonwealth of Virginia. I will tell you that it is the opinion of this Court that her conduct is immoral. And it is the opinion of this Court that the conduct of Sharon Bottoms renders her an unfit parent.

The trial court added to this statement only by citing two other factors to support its custody award. These factors were the "social condemnation" that would "inevitably" affect the child, and "other evidence of the child being affected or afflicted with the evidence [sic] which is unrebutted of the cursing, the evidence of the child standing in the corner."

As the Court of Appeals properly recognized, "adverse effects of a parent's homosexuality on a child cannot be assumed without specific proof." Bottoms v. Bottoms, 18 Va.App. 481, 493, 444 S.E.2d 276, 283 (1994); see also Doe, 222 Va. at 746, 284 S.E.2d at 805. Although there is no evidence in this record showing that the mother's homosexual conduct is harmful to the child, the majority improperly presumes that its own perception of societal opinion and the mother's homosexual conduct are germane to the issue whether the mother is an unfit parent. Thus, the majority commits the same error as the trial court by attaching importance to factors not shown by the evidence to have an adverse effect on the child.

Additionally, I believe that this appeal cannot be resolved by imposition of final judgment. Since the trial court applied the wrong rule of law in this custody determination, this case must be remanded to the trier of fact, pursuant to McEntire v. Redfearn, 217 Va. 313, 316–17, 227 S.E.2d 741, 744 (1976), for application of the correct principles of law to all the evidence.

The majority's award of final judgment is doubly inappropriate under the holding of McEntire, because approximately 19 months have passed since the last evidentiary hearing in this case. In McEntire, the trial court had applied the wrong rule of law, and almost 18 months had passed since the last evidentiary hearing. This Court held that, based on the passage of that amount of time, "we are unable at this time properly to determine the issue of custody from the record before us. Accordingly, we will remand the case to the circuit court with direction to hold forthwith another hearing ... applying the law in a manner consistent with this opinion." 217 Va. at 317, 227 S.E.2d at 744.

In the present case, the same disposition is required. Thus, I would affirm the Court of Appeals' holding that the trial court erred in applying a *per se* rule of parental unfitness based on the mother's homosexual conduct, but would reverse its imposition of final judgment and remand this matter to the trial court for further proceedings.

NOTES

(1) The *Bottoms* decision was widely publicized by the media. Despite the majority opinion's statement that "No novel questions of law are involved", it is

seen by some as a holding that will make it far easier to defeat custody claims of lesbian or homosexual parents based on their lifestyle alone. One reason for this is the great authority accorded the trial judge's findings as to issues of fact. This is not unusual; appellate courts generally seem reluctant to overrule trial court decisions unless there is some constitutional defect or a clear misapplication of legal rules or principles. Note, however, that the dissent in *Bottoms* suggests that the judge seemingly made a per se finding of unfitness based on the parent's lifestyle. In some other cases in which a trial judge's statement reflecting a strongly held personal bias or opposition to a life style was or seemingly could have been key to the decision, appellate courts have at least granted a new trial. See, e.g., *In re Marriage of Cabalquinto*, 100 Wn.2d 325, 669 P.2d 886 (1983). If a trial judge makes no such statement, however, an attack based on legal issues can be very difficult.

For further analysis and a critique of *Bottoms* throughout the judicial process, see Amy D. Ronner, *Bottoms v. Bottoms*: The Lesbian Mother and the Judicial Perpetuation of Damaging Stereotypes, 7 Yale J.L. & Feminism 341 (1995); Stephen B. Pershing, "Entreat Me Not to Leave Thee": *Bottoms v. Bottoms* and the Custody Rights of Gay and Lesbian Parents, 3 Wm. & Mary Bill of Rights J. 289 (1994).

(2) In *Taylor v. Taylor*, 353 Ark. 69, 110 S.W.3d 731 (2003), involved parents who were divorced in 1999. The mother was given custody of their two boys ages 5 and 9 at the time of the appeal from a trial court's decision to shift custody to the father. The evidence presented to support modification were (1) that he father was better prepared both financially and educationally to care for the boys, and (2) that an acknowledged lesbian was living with the mother and the children. As to the former, the father had been in better financial condition that the mother at the time of the divorce. As to the latter, there was no sexual relationship between the women (though they had slept in the same bed on occasion), but the concern of the father was that the appearance of an inappropriate relationship might subject the children to ridicule and embarrassment. The boys were described in the weight of the testimony as "happy, outgoing and well-parented children". The Arkansas Supreme Court reversed the trial court on the ground that neither of the allegations was sufficient to constitute a material change of circumstances warranting modification of custody from the mother to the father.

Painter v. Bannister

Supreme Court of Iowa, 1966.
258 Iowa 1390, 140 N.W.2d 152.

■ STUART, JUSTICE.

We are here setting the course for Mark Wendell Painter's future. Our decision on the custody of this 7 year old boy will have a marked influence on his whole life. The fact that we are called upon many times a year to determine custody matters does not make the exercising of this awesome responsibility any less difficult. Legal training and experience are of little practical help in solving the complex problems of human relations. However, these problems do arise and under our system of government, the burden of rendering a final decision rests upon us. It is frustrating to know we can only resolve, not solve, these unfortunate situations.

The custody dispute before us in this habeas corpus action is between the father, Harold Painter, and the maternal grandparents, Dwight and Margaret Bannister. Mark's mother and younger sister were killed in an automobile accident on December 6, 1962 near Pullman, Washington. The father, after other arrangements for Mark's care had proved unsatisfactory, asked the Bannisters to take care of Mark. They went to California and brought Mark to their farm home near Ames in July, 1963. Mr. Painter remarried in November, 1964 and about that time indicated he wanted to take Mark back. The Bannisters refused to let him leave and this action was filed in June, 1965. Since July, 1965 he has continued to remain in the Bannister home under an order of this court staying execution of the judgment of the trial court awarding custody to the father until the matter could be determined on appeal. For reasons hereinafter stated, we conclude Mark's better interests will be served if he remains with the Bannisters.

Mark's parents came from highly contrasting backgrounds. His mother was born, raised and educated in rural Iowa. Her parents are college graduates. Her father is agricultural information editor for the Iowa State University Extension Service. The Bannister home is in the Gilbert Community and is well kept, roomy and comfortable. The Bannisters are highly respected members of the community. Mr. Bannister has served on the school board and regularly teaches a Sunday school class at the Gilbert Congregational Church. Mark's mother graduated from Grinnell College. She then went to work for a newspaper in Anchorage, Alaska, where she met Harold Painter.

Mark's father was born in California. When he was 2½ years old, his parents were divorced and he was placed in a foster home. Although he has kept in contact with his natural parents, he considers his foster parents, the McNellys as his family. He flunked out of a high school and a trade school because of a lack of interest in academic subjects, rather than any lack of ability. He joined the navy at 17. He did not like it. After receiving an honorable discharge, he took examinations and obtained his high school diploma. He lived with the McNellys and went to college for 2½ years under the G.I. bill. He quit college to take a job on a small newspaper in Ephrata, Washington in November 1955. In May 1956, he went to work for the newspaper in Anchorage which employed Jeanne Bannister.

Harold and Jeanne were married in April, 1957. Although there is a conflict in the evidence on the point, we are convinced the marriage, overall, was a happy one with many ups and downs as could be expected in the uniting of two such opposites.

We are not confronted with a situation where one of the contesting parties is not a fit or proper person. There is no criticism of either the Bannisters or their home. There is no suggestion in the record that Mr. Painter is morally unfit. It is obvious the Bannisters did not approve of their daughter's marriage to Harold Painter and do not want their grandchild raised under his guidance. The philosophies of life are entirely different. As stated by the psychiatrist who examined Mr. Painter at the request of Bannisters' attorneys: "It is evident that there exists a large difference in ways of life and value systems between the Bannisters and Mr. Painter, but in this case, there is no evidence that psychiatric instability is involved. Rather, these divergent life patterns seem to represent alternative normal adaptations."

It is not our prerogative to determine custody upon our choice of one of two ways of life within normal and proper limits and we will not do so.

However, the philosophies are important as they relate to Mark and his particular needs.

The Bannister home provides Mark with a stable, dependable, conventional, middleclass, middlewest background and an opportunity for a college education and profession, if he desires it. It provides a solid foundation and secure atmosphere. In the Painter home, Mark would have more freedom of conduct and thought with an opportunity to develop his individual talents. It would be more exciting and challenging in many respects, but romantic, impractical and unstable.

·   ·   ·

Our conclusion as to the type of home Mr. Painter would offer is based upon his Bohemian approach to finances and life in general. We feel there is much evidence which supports this conclusion. His main ambition is to be a free lance writer and photographer. He has had some articles and picture stories published, but the income from these efforts has been negligible. At the time of the accident, Jeanne was willingly working to support the family so Harold could devote more time to his writing and photography. In the 10 years since he left college, he has changed jobs seven times. He was asked to leave two of them; two he quit because he didn't like the work; two because he wanted to devote more time to writing and the rest for better pay. He was contemplating a move to Berkeley at the time of trial. His attitude toward his career is typified by his own comments concerning a job offer:

"About the Portland news job, I hope you understand when I say it took guts not to take it; I had to get behind myself and push. It was very, very tempting to accept a good salary and settle down to a steady, easy routine. As I approached Portland, with the intention of taking the job, I began to ask what, in the long run, would be the good of this job: 1, it was not *really* what I wanted; 2, Portland is just another big farm town, with none of the stimulation it takes to get my mind sparking. Anyway, I decided Mark and myself would be better off if I went ahead with what I've started and the hell with the rest, sink, swim or starve."

There is general agreement that Mr. Painter needs help with his finances. Both Jeanne and Marilyn, his present wife, handled most of them. Purchases and sales of books, boats, photographic equipment and houses indicate poor financial judgment and an easy come easy go attitude. He dissipated his wife's estate of about $4300, most of which was a gift from her parents and which she had hoped would be used for the children's education.

The psychiatrist classifies him as "a romantic and somewhat of a dreamer". An apt example are the plans he related for himself and Mark in February 1963: "My thought now is to settle Mark and myself in Sausalito, near San Francisco; this is a retreat for wealthy artists, writers, and such aspiring artists and writers as can fork up the rent money. My plan is to do expensive portraits ($150 and up), sell prints ($15 and up) to the tourists who flock in from all over the world. . . . "

The house in which Mr. Painter and his present wife live, compared with the well kept Bannister home, exemplifies the contrasting ways of life.

In his words "it is a very old and beat up and lovely home ...". They live in the rear part. The interior is inexpensively but tastefully decorated. The large yard on a hill in the business district of Walnut Creek, California, is of uncut weeds and wild oats. The house "is not painted on the outside because I do not want it painted. I am very fond of the wood on the outside of the house."

The present Mrs. Painter has her master's degree in cinema design and apparently likes and has had considerable contact with children. She is anxious to have Mark in her home. Everything indicates she would provide a leveling influence on Mr. Painter and could ably care for Mark.

Mr. Painter is either an agnostic or atheist and has no concern for formal religious training. He has read a lot of Zen Buddhism and "has been very much influenced by it". Mrs. Painter is Roman Catholic. They plan to send Mark to a Congregational Church near the Catholic Church, on an irregular schedule.

He is a political liberal and got into difficulty in a job at the University of Washington for his support of the activities of the American Civil Liberties Union in the university news bulletin.

There were "two funerals" for his wife. One in the basement of his home in which he alone was present. He conducted the service and wrote her a long letter. The second at a church in Pullman was for the gratification of her friends. He attended in a sport shirt and sweater.

These matters are not related as a criticism of Mr. Painter's conduct, way of life or sense of values. An individual is free to choose his own values, within bounds, which are not exceeded here. They do serve however to support our conclusion as to the kind of life Mark would be exposed to in the Painter household. We believe it would be unstable, unconventional, arty, Bohemian, and probably intellectually stimulating.

Were the question simply which household would be the most suitable in which to raise a child, we would have unhesitatingly chosen the Bannister home. We believe security and stability in the home are more important than intellectual stimulation in the proper development of a child. There are, however, several factors which have made us pause.

First, there is the presumption of parental preference, which though weakened in the past several years, exists by statute.... We have a great deal of sympathy for a father, who in the difficult period of adjustment following his wife's death, turns to the maternal grandparents for their help and then finds them unwilling to return the child. There is no merit in the Bannister claim that Mr. Painter permanently relinquished custody. It was intended to be a temporary arrangement. A father should be encouraged to look for help with the children, from those who love them without the risk of thereby losing the custody of the children permanently. This fact must receive consideration in cases of this kind. However, as always, the primary consideration is the best interest of the child and if the return of custody to the father is likely to have a seriously disrupting and disturbing effect upon the child's development, this fact must prevail....

Second, Jeanne's will named her husband guardian of her children and if he failed to qualify or ceased to act, named her mother. The parent's wishes are entitled to consideration....

Third, the Bannisters are 60 years old. By the time Mark graduates from high school they will be over 70 years old. Care of young children is a strain on grandparents and Mrs. Bannister's letters indicate as much.

We have considered all of these factors and have concluded that Mark's best interest demands that his custody remain with the Bannisters. Mark was five when he came to their home. The evidence clearly shows he was not well adjusted at that time. He did not distinguish fact from fiction and was inclined to tell "tall tales" emphasizing the big "I". He was very aggressive toward smaller children, cruel to animals, not liked by his classmates and did not seem to know what was acceptable conduct. As stated by one witness: "Mark knew where his freedom was and he didn't know where his boundaries were." In two years he made a great deal of improvement. He now appears to be well disciplined, happy, relatively secure and popular with his classmates, although still subject to more than normal anxiety.

We place a great deal of reliance on the testimony of Dr. Glenn R. Hawks, a child psychologist. The trial court, in effect, disregarded Dr. Hawks' opinions stating: "The court has given full consideration to the good doctor's testimony, but cannot accept it at full face value because of exaggerated statements and the witness' attitude on the stand." We, of course, do not have the advantage of viewing the witness' conduct on the stand, but we have carefully reviewed his testimony and find nothing in the written record to justify such a summary dismissal of the opinions of this eminent child psychologist.

Dr. Hawks is head of the Department of Child Development at Iowa State University. However, there is nothing in the record which suggests that his relationship with the Bannisters is such that his professional opinion would be influenced thereby. Child development is his specialty and he has written many articles and a textbook on the subject. He is recognized nationally, having served on the staff of the 1960 White House Conference on Children and Youth and as consultant on a Ford Foundation program concerning youth in India. . . .

Between June 15th and the time of trial, he spent approximately 25 hours acquiring information about Mark and the Bannisters, including appropriate testing of and "depth interviews" with Mark. Dr. Hawks' testimony covers 70 pages of the record and it is difficult to pinpoint any bit of testimony which precisely summarizes his opinion. He places great emphasis on the "father figure" and discounts the importance of the "biological father". "The father figure is a figure that the child sees as an authority figure, as a helper, he is a nutrient figure, and one who typifies maleness and stands as maleness as far as the child is concerned."

His investigation revealed: ". . . the strength of the father figure before Mark came to the Bannisters is very unclear. Mark is confused about the father figure prior to his contact with Mr. Bannister." Now, "Mark used Mr. Bannister as his father figure. This is very evident. It shows up in the depth interview, and it shows up in the description of Mark's life given by Mark. He has a very warm feeling for Mr. Bannister."

Dr. Hawks concluded that it was not for Mark's best interest to be removed from the Bannister home. He is criticized for reaching this conclusion without investigating the Painter home or finding out more about Mr. Painter's character. He answered:

"I was most concerned about the welfare of the child, not the welfare of Mr. Painter, not about the welfare of the Bannisters. In as much as Mark has already made an adjustment and sees the Bannisters as his parental figures in his psychological make-up, to me this is the most critical factor. Disruption at this point, I think, would be detrimental to the child even tho Mr. Painter might well be a paragon of virtue. I think this would be a kind of thing which would not be in the best interest of the child. I think knowing something about where the child is at the present time is vital. I think something about where he might go, in my way of thinking is essentially untenable to me, and relatively unimportant. It isn't even helpful. The thing I was most concerned about was Mark's view of his own reality in which he presently lives. If this is destroyed I think it will have rather bad effects on Mark. I think then if one were to make a determination whether it would be the parents' household, or the McNelly household, or X-household, then I think the further study would be appropriate."

Dr. Hawks stated: "I am appalled at the tremendous task Mr. Painter would have if Mark were to return to him because he has got to build the relationship from scratch. There is essentially nothing on which to build at the present time. Mark is aware Mr. Painter is his father, but he is not very clear about what this means. In his own mind the father figure is Mr. Bannister. I think it would take a very strong person with everything in his favor in order to build a relationship as Mr. Painter would have to build at this point with Mark."

It was Dr. Hawks' opinion "the chances are very high (Mark) will go wrong if he is returned to his father". This is based on adoption studies which "establish that the majority of adoptions in children who are changed, from ages six to eight, will go bad, if they have had a prior history of instability, some history of prior movement. When I refer to instability I am referring to where there has been no attempt to establish a strong relationship." Although this is not an adoption, the analogy seems appropriate, for Mark who had a history of instability would be removed from the only home in which he has a clearly established "father figure" and placed with his natural father about whom his feelings are unclear.

We know more of Mr. Painter's way of life than Dr. Hawks. We have concluded that it does not offer as great a stability or security as the Bannister home. Throughout his testimony he emphasized Mark's need at this critical time is stability. He has it in the Bannister home.

Other items of Dr. Hawks' testimony which have a bearing on our decision follow. He did not consider the Bannisters' age anyway disqualifying. He was of the opinion that Mark could adjust to a change more easily later on, if one became necessary, when he would have better control over his environment.

He believes the presence of other children in the home would have a detrimental effect upon Mark's adjustment whether this occurred in the Bannister home or the Painter home.

The trial court does not say which of Dr. Hawks' statements he felt were exaggerated. We were most surprised at the inconsequential position to which he relegated the "biological father". He concedes "child psychologists are less concerned about natural parents than probably other professional groups are." We are not inclined to so lightly value the role of the natural father, but find much reason for his evaluation of this particular case.

Mark has established a father-son relationship with Mr. Bannister, which he apparently had never had with his natural father. He is happy, well adjusted and progressing nicely in his development. We do not believe it is for Mark's best interest to take him out of this stable atmosphere in the face of warnings of dire consequences from an eminent child psychologist and send him to an uncertain future in his father's home. Regardless of our appreciation of the father's love for his child and his desire to have him with him, we do not believe we have the moral right to gamble with this child's future. He should be encouraged in every way possible to know his father. We are sure there are many ways in which Mr. Painter can enrich Mark's life.

For the reasons stated, we reverse the trial court and remand the case for judgment in accordance herewith.

NOTES

(1) Mark rejoined his father after several visits to the latter's California home. Ultimately the son expressed a desire to stay with his father and in light of that the grandparents did not oppose the custody change. Mr. Painter was given temporary custody by a California court on Aug. 8, 1968. See Harold Painter, Mark, I Love You (1969).

(2) In Child–Custody Adjudication: Judicial Functions in the Face of Indeterminacy, 39 L. & Contemp.Prob. 226, 251 (1975) Professor Mnookin points out that "applying the best-interests standard requires an individualized prediction: with whom will this child be better off in the years to come?" However, adjudication ordinarily "requires the determination of past acts" rather than prediction of the future. Professor Mnookin stresses the "indeterminacy" of the "best interests standard." To judge rationally by the use of such a standard seemingly would require a judge to obtain considerable information about the child, his family and other persons who come in close contact. The judge should be informed about the possible outcomes and should assess the probabilities respecting these outcomes and be aware of the values that he or she uses to make a final selection among the possible choices. Given the knowledge that any judge is likely to possess and the limitations of the judicial process, in terms of time, would it be preferable to formulate some arbitrary rules rather than to embrace an amorphous or difficult to define "best interests" standard?

B. THE CONCEPT OF PSYCHOLOGICAL PARENTHOOD

Bennett v. Jeffreys

Court of Appeals of New York, 1976.
40 N.Y.2d 543, 387 N.Y.S.2d 821, 356 N.E.2d 277.

■ BREITEL, CHIEF JUDGE.

Petitioner is the natural mother of Gina Marie Bennett, now an eight-year-old girl. The mother in this proceeding seeks custody of her daughter from respondent, to whom the child had been entrusted since just after birth. Family Court ruled that, although the mother had not surrendered or abandoned the child and was not unfit, the child should remain with the present custodian, a former schoolmate of the child's grandmother. The Appellate Division reversed, one Justice dissenting, and awarded custody to the mother. Respondent custodian appeals.[1]

.   .   .

There should be a reversal and a new hearing before the Family Court. The State may not deprive a parent of the custody of a child absent surrender, abandonment, persisting neglect, unfitness or other like extraordinary circumstances. If any such extraordinary circumstances are present, the disposition of custody is influenced or controlled by what is in the best interest of the child. In the instant case extraordinary circumstances, namely, the prolonged separation of mother and child for most of the child's life, require inquiry into the best interest of the child. . . .

Some eight years ago, the mother, then 15 years old, unwed, and living with her parents, gave birth to the child. Under pressure from her mother, she reluctantly acquiesced in the transfer of the newborn infant to an older woman, Mrs. Jeffreys, a former classmate of the child's grandmother. The quality and quantity of the mother's later contacts with the child were disputed. The Family Court found, however, that there was no statutory surrender or abandonment. Pointedly, the Family Court found that the mother was not unfit. The Appellate Division agreed with this finding.

There was evidence that Mrs. Jeffreys intended to adopt the child at an early date. She testified, however, that she could not afford to do so and admitted that she never took formal steps to adopt.

The natural mother is now 23 and will soon graduate from college. She still lives with her family, in a private home with quarters available for herself and the child. The attitude of the mother's parents, however, is changed and they are now anxious that their daughter keep her child.

Mrs. Jeffreys, on the other hand, is now separated from her husband, is employed as a domestic and, on occasion, has kept the child in a motel. It is significant that Mrs. Jeffreys once said that she was willing to surrender the child to the parent upon demand when the child reached the age of 12 or 13 years.

.   .   .

[The court emphasizes that the case does not involve an attempted revocation of a voluntary surrender for adoption, abandonment, permanent termination of custody, or temporary placement into foster care by an authorized agency obliged to conduct an investigation and determine the

---

1.   The child is currently with her mother and will remain there pending final determination of this litigation, a stay of the Appellate Division order having been denied by that court.

qualification of foster parents before placement of a child in need of such care.]

Instead, this proceeding was brought by an unwed mother to obtain custody of her daughter from a custodian to whom the child had been voluntarily, although not formally, entrusted by the mother's parents when the mother was only 15 years old. Thus, as an unsupervised private placement, no statute is directly applicable, and the analysis must proceed from common-law principles.

Absent extraordinary circumstances, narrowly categorized, it is not within the power of a court, or, by delegation of the Legislature or court, a social agency, to make significant decisions concerning the custody of children, merely because it could make a better decision or disposition. The State is *parens patriae* and always has been, but it has not displaced the parent in right or responsibility. Indeed, the courts and the law would, under existing constitutional principles, be powerless to supplant parents except for grievous cause or necessity. Examples of cause or necessity permitting displacement of or intrusion on parental control would be fault or omission by the parent seriously affecting the welfare of a child, the preservation of the child's freedom from serious physical harm, illness or death, or the child's right to an education, and the like....

The parent has a "right" to rear its child, and the child has a "right" to be reared by its parent. However, there are exceptions created by extraordinary circumstances, illustratively, surrender, abandonment, persisting neglect, unfitness, and unfortunate or involuntary disruption of custody over an extended period of time. It is these exceptions which have engendered confusion, sometimes in thought but most often only in language.

The day is long past in this State, if it had ever been, when the right of a parent to the custody of his or her child, where the extraordinary circumstances are present, would be enforced inexorably, contrary to the best interest of the child, on the theory solely of an absolute legal right. Instead, in the extraordinary circumstance, when there is a conflict, the best interest of the child has always been regarded as superior to the right of parental custody. Indeed, analysis of the cases reveals a shifting of emphasis rather than a remaking of substance. This shifting reflects more the modern principle that a child is a person, and not a subperson over whom the parent has an absolute possessory interest. A child has rights too, some of which are of a constitutional magnitude.

Earlier cases emphasized the right of the parent, superior to all others, to the care and custody of the child. This right could be dissolved only by abandonment, surrender, or unfitness. Of course, even in these earlier cases, it was recognized that parental custody is lost or denied not as a moral sanction for parental failure, but because "the child's welfare compels awarding its custody to the nonparent".

Although always recognizing the parent's custodial rights, the concern in the later cases, given the extraordinary circumstances, was consciously with the best interest of the child.... [I]n People ex rel. Scarpetta v. Spence–Chapin Adoption Serv., 28 N.Y.2d 185, 269 N.E.2d 787, ... the court held "that the record before us supports the finding by the courts below that the surrender was improvident and that the child's best interests—moral and temporal—will be best served by its return to the natural mother", 321 N.Y.S.2d p. 72, 269 N.E.2d p. 792.

Finally in Matter of Spence–Chapin Adoption Serv. v. Polk, 29 N.Y.2d 196, 204, 324 N.Y.S.2d 937, 944, 274 N.E.2d 431, 436, the court rejected any notion of absolute parental rights. The court restated the abiding principle that the child's rights and interests are "paramount" and are not subordinated to the right of parental custody, as important as that right is, p. 204, 324 N.Y.S.2d p. 944, 274 N.E.2d p. 436. Indeed, and this is key, the rights of the parent and the child are ordinarily compatible, for "the generally accepted view [is] that a child's best interest is that it be raised by its parent unless the parent is disqualified by gross misconduct" p. 204, 324 N.Y.S.2d p. 944, 274 N.E.2d 436.

Recently enacted statute law, applicable to related areas of child custody such as adoption and permanent neglect proceedings, has explicitly required the courts to base custody decisions solely upon the best interest of the child (Social Services Law, § 383, subd. 5; Domestic Relations Law, § 115–b, subd. 3, par. [d], cl. [v]; Family Ct. Act, § 614, subd. 1, par. [e]; § 631); . . . Under these statutes, there is no presumption that the best interest of the child will be promoted by any particular custodial disposition. Only to this limited extent is there a departure from the pre-existing decisional rule, which never gave more than rebuttable presumptive status, however strongly, to the parent's "right."

. . .

But neither decisional rule nor statute can displace a fit parent because someone else could do a "better job" of raising the child in the view of the court (or the Legislature), so long as the parent or parents have not forfeited their "rights" by surrender, abandonment, unfitness, persisting neglect or other extraordinary circumstance. These "rights" are not so much "rights", but responsibilities which reflect the view, noted earlier, that, except when disqualified or displaced by extraordinary circumstances, parents are generally best qualified to care for their own children and therefore entitled to do so.

Indeed, as said earlier, the courts and the law would, under existing constitutional principles, be powerless to supplant parents except for grievous cause or necessity . . .

But where there is warrant to consider displacement of the parent, a determination that extraordinary circumstances exist is only the beginning, not the end, of judicial inquiry. Extraordinary circumstances alone do not justify depriving a natural parent of the custody of a child. Instead, once extraordinary circumstances are found, the court must then make the disposition that is in the best interest of the child.

Although the extraordinary circumstances trigger the "best interests of the child" test, this must not mean that parental rights or responsibilities may be relegated to a parity with all the other surrounding circumstances in the analysis of what is best for the child. So for one example only, while it is true that disruption of custody over an extended period of time is the touchstone in many custody cases, where it is voluntary the test is met more easily but where it is involuntary the test is met only with great difficulty, for evident reasons of humanity and policy.

The child's "best interest" is not controlled by whether the natural parent or the nonparent would make a "better" parent, or by whether the parent or the nonparent would afford the child a "better" background or superior creature comforts. Nor is the child's best interest controlled alone by comparing the depth of love and affection between the child and those who vie for its custody. Instead, in ascertaining the child's best interest, the court is guided by principles which reflect "considered social judgments in this society respecting the family and parenthood" (Matter of Spence–Chapin Adoption Serv. v. Polk, 29 N.Y.2d 196, 204, 324 N.Y.S.2d 937, 944, 274 N.E.2d 431, 436). These principles do not, however, dictate that the child's custody be routinely awarded to the natural parent.

.   .   .

To recapitulate: intervention by the State in the right and responsibility of a natural parent to custody of her or his child is warranted if there is first a judicial finding of surrender, abandonment, unfitness, persistent neglect, unfortunate or involuntary extended disruption of custody, or other equivalent but rare extraordinary circumstance which would drastically affect the welfare of the child. It is only on such a premise that the courts may then proceed to inquire into the best interest of the child and to order a custodial disposition on that ground.

In custody matters parties and courts may be very dependent on the auxiliary services of psychiatrists, psychologists, and trained social workers. This is good. But it may be an evil when the dependence is too obsequious or routine or the experts too casual. Particularly important is this caution where one or both parties may not have the means to retain their own experts and where publicly compensated experts or experts compensated by only one side have uncurbed leave to express opinions which may be subjective or are not narrowly controlled by the underlying facts.

The court's determination may be influenced by whether the child is in the present custody of the parent or the nonparent. Changes in conditions which affect the relative desirability of custodians, even when the contest is between two natural parents, are not to be accorded significance unless the advantages of changing custody outweigh the essential principle of continued and stable custody of children. . . .

Moreover, the child may be so long in the custody of the nonparent that, even though there has been no abandonment or persisting neglect by the parent, the psychological trauma of removal is grave enough to threaten destruction of the child. Of course, such a situation would offer no opportunity for the court, under the guise of determining the best interest of the child, to weigh the material advantages offered by the adverse parties. . . .

Before applying these principles to this case, a factor should be mentioned which, although not here present, often complicates custody dispositions. The resolution of cases must not provide incentives for those likely to take the law into their own hands. Thus, those who obtain custody of children unlawfully, particularly by kidnaping, violence, or flight from the jurisdiction of the courts, must be deterred. Society may not reward, except at its peril, the lawless because the passage of time has made correction inexpedient. Yet, even then, circumstances may require that, in the best interest of the child, the unlawful acts be blinked.

In this case, there were extraordinary circumstances present, namely, the protracted separation of mother from child, combined with the mother's lack of an established household of her own, her unwed state, and the attachment of the child to the custodian. Thus, application of the principles discussed required an examination by the court into the best interest of the child.

In reaching its conclusion that the child should remain with the nonparent custodian, the Family Court relied primarily upon the seven-year period of custody by the nonparent and evidently on the related testimony of a psychologist. The court did not, however, adequately examine into the nonparent custodian's qualifications and background. Also, the court apparently failed to consider the fact that, absent a finding of abandonment or neglect by the mother, or her consent, the nonparent cannot adopt the child. Family Court's disposition, if sustained, would therefore have left the child in legal limbo, her status indefinite until the attainment of her majority. For a single example, a question could arise as to whose consent, the parent's or the nonparent custodian's, would be necessary for the child to marry while underage (see Domestic Relations Law, § 15, subd. 2 [consent of "parent" or "guardian" required]). A similar question could arise with respect to many situations affecting employment and entry into occupations, an adoption, and any other matters requiring the consent of a parent or legal guardian.

On the other hand, the Appellate Division, in awarding custody to the mother, too automatically applied the primary principle that a parent is entitled to the custody of the child. This was not enough if there were extraordinary circumstances, as indeed there were. Other than to agree with Family Court that she was not "unfit", the court did not pursue a further analysis. Most important, no psychological or other background examination of the mother had ever been obtained. There was, therefore, no consideration of whether the mother is an adequate parent, in capacity, motivation, and efficacious planning. Nevertheless, the Appellate Division determination may well be right.

Thus, a new hearing is required because the Family Court did not examine enough into the qualifications and background of the long-time custodian, and the Appellate Division did not require further examination into the qualifications and background of the mother. Each court was excessive in applying abstract principles, a failing, however important those principles are.

At the cost of some repetition, perhaps unnecessary, it should be said, given the extraordinary circumstances present in this case, in determining the best interest of the child, the age of the child, and the fact and length of custody by the nonparent custodian are significant. Standing alone, these factors may not be sufficient to outweigh the mother's "right" to custody. However, taken together with the testimony of the psychologist that return to her mother would be "very traumatic for the child", the relatively lengthy period of nonparent custody casts the matter in sufficient doubt with respect to the best interest of the child to require a new hearing. At this hearing, the mother's adequacy may be explored and positively established, and if so, in connection with the parent's past visiting it might well weight the balance in her favor. Then too, the circumstances and environment of the custodian, the stability of her household, her inability to adopt, her age, and any other circumstances bearing upon the fitness or adequacy of a child's custodian over the whole period of childhood, are all relevant.

In all of this troublesome and troubled area there is a fundamental principle. Neither law, nor policy, nor the tenets of our society would allow a child to be separated by officials of the State from its parent unless the circumstances are compelling. Neither the lawyers nor Judges in the judicial system nor the experts in psychology or social welfare may displace the primary responsibility of child-raising that naturally and legally falls to those who conceive and bear children. Again, this is not so much because it is their "right", but because it is their responsibility. The nature of human relationships suggests over-all the natural workings of the child-rearing process as the most desirable alternative. But absolute generalizations do not fulfill themselves and multifold exceptions give rise to cases where the natural workings of the process fail, not so much because a legal right has been lost, but because the best interest of the child dictates a finding of failure.

Accordingly, the order of the Appellate Division should be reversed, without costs, and the proceeding remitted to Family Court for a new hearing.

■ FUCHSBERG, JUDGE (concurring).

I welcome the express recognition the court today gives to the concept that, under evolving child custody law in New York, circumstances other than the statutory and traditional ones of abandonment, surrender, permanent neglect and unfitness may form the basis for termination of a biological parent-child relationship, and I agree with the result it reaches. However, in concurring, the strength of my conviction that even greater movement in this area of the law is long overdue requires me to indicate the nature of some of my reservations.

Security, continuity and "long-term stability" ... in an on-going custodial relationship, whether maintained with a natural parent or a third party, are vital to the successful personality development of a child.... Indeed, that is one of the soundest justifications for the priority which our society accords natural parents when the continuance of their status as parents is under legal attack.

The same considerations, however, it seems to me, dictate that, where a natural parent has affirmatively brought about or acquiesced in the creation of a secure, stable and continuing parent-child relationship with a third party who has become the psychological parent,[1] there comes a point

1. (Goldstein, Freud and Solnit, Beyond the Best Interests of the Child [1973]; Erik-son, Growth and Crisis of the "Healthy Personality" in Personality, in Nature, Society

where the "rebuttable presumption" which, absent such a change, is employed to favor the natural parent, disappears, as evidentiary presumptions usually do in the face of facts. Accordingly, when that point is reached, the determination of whether the original parental relationship has terminated should proceed without such bolstering of the natural parent's position vis-à-vis that of the child, the custodial parent or any other proper parties in interest. Generally speaking, when displaced by a state of facts contraindicating their further utility in a fact-finding setting, presumptions can only get in the way of substance, and, as a practical matter, when that happens, the less they are relied upon the better. I would, therefore, that we had spelled out an evidentiary balance consistent with these principles for application in custody litigation, always bearing in mind that each custody case, dealing as it does with emotion-laden and highly sensitive human relationships, is unique.[2]

Further, I do not agree that inquiry into the best interests of a child must await a determination that, because of surrender, abandonment, neglect or "extraordinary" circumstances, a natural parent's "rights" to a child are at an end. Willy-nilly, concern for the best interests of the child must play a central and unavoidable role in the resolution of such questions.

Moreover, even under prior law, when only a finding of abandonment, surrender or neglect could defeat the presumption in favor of natural parents, the best interests of the child were involved from the very outset. Unfitness, for instance, cannot be determined abstractly or in isolation, but only relative to the psychological needs of a particular child, given its age, its mental health, its physical well-being and the like. And the very same conduct which constitutes clear neglect towards one child might not be so at all with regard to another child whose level of independence and emotional requirements are different. It follows that evidence offered to show that the State must intervene in a natural parent-child relationship is, by its very nature, evidence as to the best interests of the child. In short, termination or intervention, on the one hand, and best interests, on the other, are not discrete matters. Pragmatically, they are closely interrelated. Proof of one overlaps the other and I do not believe they should be considered separately.

and Culture [1955], 185–225; Bowley, Child Care and Growth of Love [1953]; Freud, Some Remarks on Infant Observation, 8 Psychoanalytic Study of the Child.)

2. Commentators point out that presumptions and the burden to rebut them should be allocated "on the basis of pragmatic considerations of fairness, convenience, and policy" (James, Burdens of Proof, 47 Va.L.Rev. 51, 60). Thus, where the burden of proof is allocated on policy grounds, it is most often done in order to "handicap" a party whose cause is disfavored (at p. 61). That was the historical basis for casting the entire bur-

den of rebutting the presumption in favor of natural parents on third parties in custody proceedings, the resulting substantive effect varying with the extent to which the "handicap", combined with other evidentiary strictures, rendered the nonparent's case difficult to maintain. In those jurisdictions where that policy was fully developed, it produced essentially the same results as were obtained under the old theory that children were the chattels of their parents (see Note, Alternatives to "Parental Right" in Child Custody Disputes Involving Third Parties, 73 Yale L.J. 151, 154, n. 18, and accompanying text).

I would add too that I am not completely convinced that there was not a sufficient basis for the decision of the Trial Judge, despite the unfortunate limitation on resources available to the Family Court and, often, the parties who appear before it. . . . Nevertheless, since painstaking fact finding is so far superior to presumptions and assumptions, and, therefore, should be encouraged, I join in the decision to remit this case for further information-gathering, noting, in doing so, that it is clear that it should not be controlling that Ms. Bennett, the natural mother, because she is now pursuing collegiate studies may at some time in the future be more likely to afford greater creature comforts for the child than is Mrs. Jeffreys, whose modest position on the vocational social scale did not prevent her from undertaking to act as surrogate mother and thus to form psychological bonds between the child and herself. And, needless to say, any profession by Mrs. Jeffreys that she would have been willing to return the child to her biological mother when she was older *if* it were in the best interests of the child for her to do so would be an evidence of altruistic maternal concern that would win the approval of every sound practitioner of child psychiatry from King Solomon on.

NOTE

The New York Court of Appeals has shown reluctance to expand the application of the *Bennett* rationale and has circumscribed its application in specific contexts such as abandonment or termination of parental rights. See, e.g., *Dickson v. Lascaris*, 53 N.Y.2d 204, 440 N.Y.S.2d 884, 423 N.E.2d 361 (1981); *In re Sanjivini K.*, 47 N.Y.2d 374, 418 N.Y.S.2d 339, 391 N.E.2d 1316 (1979); *Corey L. v. Martin L.*, 45 N.Y.2d 383, 408 N.Y.S.2d 439, 380 N.E.2d 266 (1978); *In re Michael B.*, infra at 714.

Bennett v. Marrow

New York Supreme Court, Appellate Division, Second Department, 1977.
59 A.D.2d 492, 399 N.Y.S.2d 697.

■ O'Connor, Justice.

There is here presented one of the most difficult and disturbing problems known to the law—the custody of a child. The problem is, of course, compounded when, as here, the conflict rages between the natural mother and a foster mother. The Family Court awarded custody of the child to the foster mother and, after carefully studying this meticulously compiled record, we conclude that the order should be affirmed.

[The court reviews the custody determination principles from the opinion in Bennett v. Jeffreys, which remitted this case to Family Court for a hearing.]

The new hearing extended over a four-week period and contains the testimony of some 26 witnesses; that record and the order entered thereon are now before us for review.

We are here concerned with an unsupervised, private placement and, hence, any analysis of the decision of the Family Court must be predicated not upon statute, but upon common law principles.

Fortunately, the hearing was held before the same Judge who had presided at the first hearing some two years before. Predicated upon his observations and findings at the 1975 hearing, the court was in a rather unique position to completely re-examine and re-evaluate the testimony of those witnesses who had testified at both hearings. In the light of his intimate knowledge of the background and history of the case, he was able to conduct a more in-depth examination of the psychiatrists, psychologists, social workers, teachers and other witnesses called by the parties. Most importantly, the court was enabled to clearly and closely observe for a second time the conduct and deportment of the principals, namely the petitioner-appellant (the natural parent), the respondent (the foster parent) and Gina Marie (the infant involved). His comments therefore concerning the changes he found in the personality and demeanor of Gina Marie become all the more significant and persuasive in view of the fact that the child, in the intervening 15 months, had been living in the home of the petitioner, her natural mother.

The trial court, after noting that during the first hearing Gina Marie appeared to be a well-adjusted, happy child, went on to say that "the fact is that notwithstanding a period of some 15 months spent in the home of her mother, Gina Marie has not settled into the household. She does not feel comfortable there, she is not happy there. She continues unswerving in her request to be restored to the custody of Mrs. Marrow."

These surface observations, while bearing some significance, are certainly not controlling; but the court's conclusions concerning the natural mother are perhaps more revealing. The court said: "To the extent that the petitioner has responded to Gina Marie's needs to be housed, to be clothed, to be fed, she could be considered to have performed adequately as a parent. But she has not begun to respond to Gina Marie's emotional needs." At another point the court observed: "I am constrained to consider that Miss Bennett's motivation in seeking custody of Gina Marie stems from a feeling that she is her child and should reside with her. That she has feeling for Gina Marie I am certainly prepared to believe, but in view of the testimony presented during the course of these proceedings, I have serious reservations that she is capable of giving Gina Marie the emotional support so vital to her well-being."

The court then concluded: "This Court was asked to determine whether the mother is an adequate parent. As stated previously, she has provided materially for Gina Marie. That is to say, she has made available to Gina Marie what Welfare has provided in the first instance. But that is virtually all she has given Gina Marie. She had not given significantly of herself. I find that an emotional void exists between mother and daughter that shows no signs of being bridged despite the time they have resided together. This child continues to mourn the loss of her 'mother.' "

Addressing itself then to the relationship between the respondent and Gina Marie, the court gave credence to the testimony of a witness called by the Law Guardian, Dr. Sally Provence, a child psychiatrist from Yale University. Finding her to be "certainly the most impressive expert witness who appeared in this proceeding", the hearing court accepted Dr. Provence's testimony that a psychological parent-child relationship had developed between respondent and the child and the court noted that such bond "appears as strong today as when this case was first heard."

It was Dr. Provence's further testimony, in substance, that to remove the child from such a relationship would endanger the development of the child in many ways and could affect her academic success and her motivation to learn.

This testimony is all the more significant in view of the record, which discloses that in January, 1977 an intelligence test was administered to Gina Marie resulting in a score of 84, in the low-normal range, whereas in April, 1975 she had scored 113. Despite efforts to explain away this rather disturbing pattern, it seems to be, at least to some extent, buttressed by the obvious and drastic decline in the physical, mental and emotional make-up of Gina Marie.

Reflection upon the totality of the testimony and careful consideration of all of the factors involved leads but to one conclusion, the order of the Family Court should be affirmed.

We note in closing that that order properly and fully protects petitioner's rights of visitation but, under the extraordinary circumstances here presented, the best interests of the child require that custody of Gina Marie be awarded to respondent.

NOTES

(1) A celebrated and somewhat controversial book by Joseph Goldstein, Anna Freud, and Albert Solnit, Beyond the Best Interests of the Child, (The Free Press 1973) had significant influence on the court's decision in Guardianship of Phillip B, which follows. The concepts in it also were important in the decision in Bennett v. Marrow. The key part of the book is a model statute, Selected Provisions for the Child Placement Code of Hampstead–Haven (hereinafter the Act). The remainder of the book is essentially an extended commentary to the statute. Strongly influenced by their psychoanalytic backgrounds, the authors place great weight on the values of continuity and stability in child placements. Para. 10.2 of the Act defines a wanted child as "one who receives affection and nourishment on a continuing basis from at least one adult and who feels that he or she is and continues to be valued by those who take care of him or her." A psychological parent is "one who, on a continuing, day-to-day basis, through interaction, companionship, interplay, and mutuality, fulfills the child's psychological needs for a parent, as well as the child's physical needs." Under Para. 10.3 a psychological parent can be "a biological, adoptive, foster, or common-law parent, or any other person"; after initial assignment of the child to the biological child at birth, there is no presumption in favor of any of them.

The Act specifically recognizes a "common-law parent-child relationship", defined as "a psychological parent-wanted child relationship" which developed outside of adoption, assignment by custody in separation or divorce proceedings, or the initial assignment at birth of child to his or her biological parents. Although some commentators and jurists cite the text as supportive of traditional "best interests of the child" approach, such a simplistic appraisal belies the fact that the Act basically establishes a new set of presumptions that heavily emphasize maintenance of continuity and stability and minimization of disruption of relationships between psychological parent and child. Key to this is the desire for the least detrimental child placement, defined as "that placement and procedure which maximizes, in accord with th child's sense of time, the child's opportunity for being wanted and for maintaining on a continuous, unconditional, and permanent basis a relationship with at least one child who is or will become the child's psychological parent." Para. 10.6.

Any entity, (person, state, or institution) wishing to disrupt a continuing relationship between psychological parent and child is designated an intervenor. Para. 30.2. There is a presumption in favor of the current placement, and to change this the intervenor must establish that the child is unwanted, and that the placement is not the least detrimental alternative. Para. 30.3. The child will be made a party to such proceedings and represented by independent counsel. Courts must conduct trials and appeals as rapidly as possible. All placements are "unconditional and final"; accordingly, a court will not retain continuing jurisdiction over a parent-child relationship and will not establish or enforce conditions such as visitation.

If such a statutory scheme had governed in *Painter v. Bannister* and *Bennett v. Marrow*, how might the courts' decisions have been affected?

(2) The debate over whether biological parentage should prime all other relationships continues today, heightened by widespread media coverage of surrogate parentage and several poignant cases in which biological parents regained children after adoptive placement or even after adoption. A special symposium issue on The Impact of Psychological Parenting on Child Welfare Decision–Making was published in Vol. XII, No. 3 of the N.Y.U. Rev.L. & Soc. Change (1984).

For an imaginative approach that separates custody disputes into several different categories in order to devise more predictable standards for guiding decision makers, see Carolyn Wilkes Kaas, Breaking Up a Family or Putting It Back Together Again: Refining the Preference of the Parent in Third–Party Custody Cases, 37 Wm. & Mary L.Rev. 2045 (1996).

Guardianship of Phillip B.

Court of Appeals, First District, Division 1, 1983.
139 Cal.App.3d 407, 188 Cal.Rptr. 781.

■ RACANELLI, PRESIDING JUSTICE.

Few human experiences evoke the poignancy of a filial relationship and the pathos attendant upon its disruption in society's effort to afford every child a meaningful chance to live life to its fullest promise. This appeal, posing a sensitive confrontation between the fundamental right of parental custody and the well being of a retarded child, reflects the deeply ingrained concern that the needs of the child remain paramount in the judicial monitoring of custody. In reaching our decision to affirm, we neither suggest nor imply that appellants' subjectively motivated custodial objectives affront conventional norms of parental fitness; rather, we determine only that on the unusual factual record before us, the challenged order of guardianship must be upheld in order to avert potential harm to the minor ward likely to result from appellants' continuing custody and to subserve his best interests.

. . .

On February 23, 1981, respondents Herbert and Patsy H. filed a petition for appointment as guardians of the person and estate of Phillip B., then 14 years of age. Phillip's parents, appellants Warren and Patricia B., appeared in opposition to the petition.

On August 7, 1981, following a 12–day trial, the trial court filed a lengthy memorandum of decision ordering—inter alia—1) the issuance of letters of guardianship to respondents with authority to permit a heart catheterization to be performed on Phillip, and 2) the immediate delivery (by appellants) of Phillip to the Sheriff and Juvenile Authority of Santa Clara County. That same day appellants filed a notice of appeal from both orders followed by a petition to this court for a writ of supersedeas which we summarily denied.

On August 20, 1981, the California Supreme Court granted appellants' petition for hearing, stayed the trial court's order authorizing heart catheterization and retransferred the cause to this court with directions to issue an order to show cause why a writ of supersedeas should not issue.

Meanwhile, on September 24, the trial court filed formal findings of fact and conclusions of law and entered a "final order" confirming issuance of letters of guardianship and authorizing a heart catheterization. A second notice of appeal specifying both orders was thereafter filed by appellants.

On October 19, 1981, we again denied supersedeas in an unpublished opinion.

On November 18, 1981, the California Supreme Court granted a second petition for hearing, issued its writ of supersedeas limited to the trial court's orders of August 7 and September 24 "insofar as they give authority for a heart catheterization upon Phillip B.," and retransferred the cause to this court for determination of the merits of the appeal upon the completed record and full briefing. Thereafter, the matter was duly argued and submitted for decision.

Appellants raise several claims of reversible error relating to the sufficiency of evidence to support the findings, the admissibility of certain evidence and procedural due process. For the reasons which we explain, we find no error as claimed and affirm the order or judgment appealed....

Phillip B. was born on October 16, 1966, with Down Syndrome, a chromosomal anomaly—usually the presence of an extra chromosome attached to the number 21 pair—resulting in varying degrees of mental retardation and a number of abnormal physical characteristics. Down Syndrome reportedly occurs in approximately 1/10 of 1 percent of live births.

Appellants, deeply distraught over Phillip's disability, decided upon institutionalization, a course of action recommended by a state social worker and approved by appellants' pediatrician. A few days later, Phillip was transferred from the hospital to a licensed board and care facility for disabled youngsters. Although the facility was clean, it offered no structured educational or developmental programs and required that all the children (up to 8 years of age) sleep in cribs. Appellants initially visited Phillip frequently; but soon their visits became less frequent and they became more detached from him.

When Phillip was three years old a pediatrician informed appellants that Phillip had a congenital heart defect, a condition afflicting half of Down Syndrome children. Open heart surgery was suggested when Phillip attained age six. However appellants took no action to investigate or remedy the suspected medical problem.

After the board and care facility had been sold during the summer of 1971, appellants discovered that the condition of the facility had seriously deteriorated under the new management; it had become dirty and cluttered with soiled clothing, and smelled strongly of urine. Phillip was very thin and listless and was being fed watery oatmeal from a bottle. At appellants' request, a state social worker arranged for Phillip's transfer in January, 1972, to We Care, a licensed residential facility for developmentally disabled children located in San Jose, where he remained up to the time of trial.

At that time, the facility—which cared for about 20 children more severely handicapped than Phillip—operated under very limited conditions: it had no programs of education or therapy; the children were not enrolled in outside programs; the facility lacked an outdoor play area; the building was in poor repair; and the kitchen had only a two-burner hot plate used to cook pureed food.

In April 1972, We Care employed Jeanne Haight (later to become program director and assistant administrator of the facility) to organize a volunteer program. Mrs. Haight quickly noticed Phillip's debilitated condition. She found him unusually small and thin for his age (five); he was not toilet trained and wore diapers, still slept in a crib, walked like a toddler, and crawled down stairs only inches high. His speech was limited and mostly unintelligible; his teeth were in poor condition.

Mrs. Haight, who undertook a recruitment program for volunteers, soon recruited respondent Patsy H., who had helped to found a school for children with learning disabilities where Mrs. Haight had once been vice-principal. Mrs. H. began working at We Care on a daily basis. Her husband, respondent Herbert H., and their children, soon joined in the volunteer activities.

Mrs. H., initially assigned to work with Phillip and another child, assisted Phillip in experimenting with basic sensory experiences, improving body coordination, and in overcoming his fear of steps. Mr. H. and one of the H. children helped fence the yard area, put in a lawn, a sandbox, and install some climbing equipment.

Mrs. Haight promptly initiated efforts to enroll Phillip in a preschool program for the fall of 1972, which required parental consent.[4] She contacted Mr. B. who agreed to permit Phillip to participate provided learning aptitude could be demonstrated. Mrs. H. used vocabulary cards to teach Phillip 25 to 50 new words and to comprehend word association. Although Mr. B. failed to appear at the appointed time in order to observe what

---

4. Apparently, Phillip had received no formal preschool education for the retarded even though such training programs were available in the community. Expert testimony established that early introduction to preschool training is of vital importance in preparing a retarded child for entry level public education.

Phillip had learned, he eventually gave his parental consent enabling Phillip to attend Hope Preschool in October, 1972.

Respondents continued working with Phillip coordinating their efforts with his classroom lessons. Among other things, they concentrated on development of feeding skills and toilet training and Mr. H. and the two eldest children gradually became more involved in the volunteer program.

Phillip subsequently attended a school for the trainable mentally retarded (TMR) where the children are taught basic survival words. They are capable of learning to feed and dress themselves appropriately, doing basic community activities such as shopping, and engaging in recreational activities. There is no attempt to teach them academics, and they are expected to live in sheltered settings as adults. In contrast, children capable of attending classes for the educable mentally retarded (EMR) are taught reading, writing, and simple computation, with the objective of developing independent living skills as adults.

A pattern of physical and emotional detachment from their son was developed by appellants over the next several years. In contrast, during the same period, respondents established a close and caring relationship with Phillip. Beginning in December, 1972, Phillip became a frequent visitor at respondents' home; with appellants' consent, Phillip was permitted to spend weekends with respondents, a practice which continued regularly and often included weekday evenings. At the same time respondents maintained frequent contact with Phillip at We Care as regular volunteer visitors. Meanwhile, appellants visited Phillip at the facility only a few times a year; however, no overnight home visits occurred until after the underlying litigation ensued.

Respondents played an active role in Phillip's behavioral development and educational training. They consistently supplemented basic skills training given Phillip at We Care.[5]

Phillip was openly accepted as a member of the H. family whom he came to love and trust. He eventually had his own bedroom; he was included in sharing household chores. Mr. H. set up a workbench for Phillip and helped him make simple wooden toys; they attended special Boy Scout meetings together. And Philip regularly participated in family outings. Phillip referred to the H. residence as "my house." When Phillip began to refer to the H. as "Mom" and "Dad," they initially discouraged the familiar reference, eventually succeeding in persuading Phillip to use the discriminate references "Mama Pat" and "Dada Bert" and "Mama B." and "Daddy B."[6] Both Mrs. Haight and Phillip's teacher observed significant improvements in Phillip's development and behavior. Phillip had developed, in Mrs. Haight's opinion, "true love and strong [emotional] feelings" for respondents.

5. In addition to their efforts to improve Phillip's communication and reading skills through basic sign language and word association exercises, respondents toilet-trained Phillip and taught him to use eating utensils and to sleep in a regular bed (the latter frequently monitored during the night).

6. At respondents' suggestion, Mrs. Haight requested a photograph of appellants to show Phillip who his parents were; but appellants failed to provide one.

Meanwhile, appellants continued to remain physically and emotionally detached from Phillip. The natural parents intellectualized their decision to treat Phillip differently from their other children. Appellants testified that Phillip, whom they felt would always require institutionalization, should not be permitted to form close emotional attachments which—upon inevitable disruption—would traumatize the youngster.

In matters of Phillip's health care needs, appellants manifested a reluctant—if not neglectful—concern. When Dr. Gathman, a pediatric cardiologist, diagnosed a ventricular septal defect[7] in Phillip's heart in early 1973 and recommended catheterization (a medically accepted pre-surgery procedure to measure pressure and to examine the interior of the heart), appellants refused their consent.

In the spring of 1977, Dr. Gathman again recommended heart catheterization in connection with the anticipated use of general anesthesia during Phillip's major dental surgery. Appellants consented to the preoperative procedure which revealed that the heart defect was surgically correctable with a maximum risk factor of 5 percent. At a conference attended by appellants and Mrs. Haight in June, 1977, Dr. Gathman recommended corrective surgery in order to avoid a progressively deteriorating condition resulting in a "bed-to-chair existence" and the probability of death before the age of 30.[8] Although Dr. Gathman—as requested by Mrs. B.—supplied the name of a parent of Down Syndrome children with similar heart disease, no contact was ever made. Later that summer, appellants decided—without obtaining an independent medical consultation—against surgery. Appellants' stated reason was that Dr. Gathman had "painted" an inaccurate picture of the situation. They felt that surgery would be merely life-prolonging rather than life-saving, presenting the possibility that they would be unable to care for Phillip during his later years.[9] A few months later, in early 1978, appellants' decision was challenged in a juvenile dependency proceeding initiated by the district attorney on the ground that the withholding of surgery constituted neglect within the meaning of Welfare and Institutions Code section 300 subdivision (b); the juvenile court's dismissal of the action on the basis of inconclusive evidence was ultimately sustained on appeal (In re Phillip B. (1979) 92 Cal.App.3d 796, 156 Cal.Rptr. 48, cert. den. sub nom. Bothman v. Warren B. (1980) 445 U.S. 949).

In September, 1978, upon hearing from a staff member of We Care that Phillip had been regularly spending weekends at respondents' home, Mr. B. promptly forbade Phillip's removal from the facility (except for medical purposes and school attendance) and requested that respondents be

---

7. The disease, found in a large number of Down Syndrome children, consists of an opening or "hole" between the heart chambers resulting in elevated blood pressure and impairment of vascular functions. The disease can become a progressive, and ultimately fatal, disorder.

8. Dr. Gathman's explicit description of the likely ravages of the disease created an-

ger and distrust on the part of appellants and motivated them to seek other opinions and to independently assess the need for surgery.

9. Oddly, Mr. B. expressed no reluctance in the hypothetical case of surgery for his other two sons if they had the "same problem," justifying the distinction on the basis of Phillip's retardation.

denied personal visits with Phillip at We Care. Although respondents continued to visit Phillip daily at the facility, the abrupt cessation of home visits produced regressive changes in Phillip's behavior: he began acting out violently when respondents prepared to leave, begging to be taken "home"; he resorted to profanity; he became sullen and withdrawn when respondents were gone; bed-wetting regularly occurred, a recognized symptom of emotional disturbance in children. He began to blame himself for the apparent rejection by respondents; he began playing with matches and on one occasion he set his clothes afire; on another, he rode his tricycle to respondents' residence a few blocks away proclaiming on arrival that he was "home." He continuously pleaded to return home with respondents. Many of the behavioral changes continued to the time of trial.

Appellants unsuccessfully pressed to remove Phillip from We Care notwithstanding the excellent care he was receiving. However, in January, 1981, the regional center monitoring public assistance for residential care and training of the handicapped, consented to Phillip's removal to a suitable alternate facility. Despite an extended search, none could be found which met Phillip's individualized needs. Meanwhile, Phillip continued living at We Care, periodically visiting at appellants' home. But throughout, the strong emotional attachment between Phillip and respondents remained intact.

Evidence established that Phillip, with a recently tested I.Q. score of 57,[11] is a highly functioning Down Syndrome child capable of learning sufficient basic and employable skills to live independently or semi-independently in a non-institutional setting.

Courts generally may appoint a guardian over the person or estate of a minor "if it appears necessary or convenient." (Prob.Code, § 1514, subd. (a).) But the right of parents to retain custody of a child is fundamental and may be disturbed " '. . . only in extreme cases of persons acting in a fashion incompatible with parenthood.' " (In re Angelia P. (1981) 28 Cal.3d 908, 916, 171 Cal.Rptr. 637, 623 P.2d 198, quoting In re Carmaleta B. (1978) 21 Cal.3d 482, 489, 146 Cal.Rptr. 623, 579 P.2d 514.) Accordingly, the Legislature has imposed the stringent requirement that before a court may make an order awarding custody of a child to a nonparent without consent of the parents, "it shall make a finding that an award of custody to a parent would be detrimental to the child and the award to a nonparent is required to serve the best interests of the child." (Civ.Code, § 4600, subd.(c)); see (In re B.G. (1974) 11 Cal.3d 679, 695–699, 114 Cal.Rptr. 444, 523 P.2d 244.)[12] That requirement is equally applicable to guardianship proceedings under Probate Code section 1514, subdivision (b). The legislative shift in emphasis from parental unfitness to detriment to the child did

11. A retarded child within an I.Q. range of 55–70 is generally considered as mildly retarded and classified as educable under California school standards.

12. Civil Code section 4600 was enacted in response to the celebrated case of Painter v. Bannister (1966) 258 Iowa 1390, 140 N.W.2d 152, cert. den. 385 U.S. 949, in which the state court awarded custody of a young boy to his grandparents because it disapproved of the father's "Bohemian" lifestyle in California (see In re B.G., supra, 11 Cal.3d at pp. 697–698, 114 Cal.Rptr. 444, 523 P.2d 244, citing Report of Assembly Judiciary Committee, 4 Assem.J. (1969 Reg.Sess. pp. 8060–8061)).

not, however, signal a retreat from the judicial practice granting custodial preference to nonparents "only in unusual or extreme cases." (In re B.G., supra, 11 Cal.3d 679, 698, 114 Cal.Rptr. 444, 523 P.2d 244, see Guardianship of Marino (1973) 30 Cal.App.3d 952, 958, 106 Cal.Rptr. 655.)

The trial court expressly found that an award of custody to appellants would be harmful to Phillip in light of the psychological or "de facto" parental relationship established between him and respondents. Such relationships have long been recognized in the fields of law and psychology. As Justice Tobriner has cogently observed, "The fact of biological parenthood may incline an adult to feel a strong concern for the welfare of his child, but it is not an essential condition; a person who assumes the role of parent, raising the child in his own home, may in time acquire an interest in the 'companionship, care, custody and management' of that child. The interest of the 'de facto parent' is a substantial one, recognized by the decision of this court in In re Shannon's Estate (1933) 218 Cal. 490 [23 P.2d 1020] and by courts of other jurisdictions and deserving of legal protection." (In re B.G., supra, 11 Cal.3d 679, 692–693, 114 Cal.Rptr. 444, 523 P.2d 244 [fns. omitted], citing the seminal study of Goldstein, Freud & Solnit, Beyond the Best Interests of the Child (1973) pp. 17–20, hereafter Goldstein.) Persons who assume such responsibility have been characterized by some interested professional observers as "psychological parents": "Whether any adult becomes the psychological parent of a child is based . . . on day-to-day interaction, companionship, and shared experiences. The role can be fulfilled either by a biological parent or by an adoptive parent or by any other caring adult—but never by an absent, inactive adult, whatever his biological or legal relationship to the child may be." (Goldstein, supra, p. 19, 114 Cal.Rptr. 444, 523 P.2d 244.)

Appellants vigorously challenge the evidence and finding that respondents have become Phillip's de facto or psychological parents since he did not reside with them full-time, as underscored in previous California decisions which have recognized de facto parenthood. They argue that the subjective concept of psychological parenthood, relying on such nebulous factors as "love and affection" is susceptible to abuse and requires the countervailing element of objectivity provided by a showing of the child's long-term residency in the home of the claimed psychological parent.

We disagree. Adoption of the proposed standard would require this court to endorse a novel doctrine of child psychology unsupported either by a demonstrated general acceptance in the field of psychology or by the record before us. Although psychological parenthood is said to result from "day-to-day attention to [the child's] needs for physical care, nourishment, comfort, affection, and stimulation" (Goldstein, supra, p. 17), appellants fail to point to any authority or body of professional opinion that equates daily attention with full-time residency. To the contrary, the record contains uncontradicted expert testimony that while psychological parenthood usually will require residency on a "24–hour basis," it is not an absolute requirement; further, that the frequency and quality of Phillip's weekend visits with respondents, together with the regular weekday visits at We Care, provided an adequate foundation to establish the crucial parent-child relationship.

Nor are we persuaded by appellants' suggested policy considerations concerning the arguably subjective inquiry involved in determining psychological parenthood. Trial fact-finders commonly grapple with elusive subjective legal concepts without aid of "countervailing" objective criteria.... Moreover, the suggested standard is itself vulnerable to a claim of undue subjectivity in its vague requirement of residency for a "considerable period of time."[15]

Appellants also challenge the sufficiency of the evidence to support the finding that their retention of custody would have been detrimental to Phillip. In making the critical finding, the trial court correctly applied the "clear and convincing" standard of proof necessary to protect the fundamental rights of parents in all cases involving a nonparent's bid for custody....

The record contains abundant evidence that appellants' retention of custody would cause Phillip profound emotional harm. Notwithstanding Phillip's strong emotional ties with respondents, appellants abruptly foreclosed home visits and set out to end all contact between them. When Phillip's home visits terminated in 1978, he displayed many signs of severe emotional trauma: he appeared depressed and withdrawn and became visibly distressed at being unable to return to "my house," a request he steadily voiced up until trial. He became enuretic, which a psychologist, Dr. Edward Becking, testified indicates emotional stress in children.... Dr. Becking testified to other signs of emotional disturbance which were present nearly three years after the termination of home visits.

Our law recognizes that children generally will sustain serious emotional harm when deprived of the emotional benefits flowing from a true parent-child relationship.

There was uncontroverted expert testimony that Phillip would sustain further emotional trauma in the event of total separation from respondents: that testimony indicated that, as with all children, Phillip needs love and affection, and he would be profoundly hurt if he were deprived of the existing psychological parental relationship with respondents in favor of maintaining unity with his biological parents.

Phillip's conduct unmistakably demonstrated that he derived none of the emotional benefits attending a close parental relationship largely as a result of appellants' individualized decision to abandon that traditional supporting role. Dr. Becking testified that no "bonding or attachment" has occurred between Phillip and his biological parents, a result palpably consistent with appellants' view that Phillip had none of the emotional needs uniquely filled by natural parents. We conclude that such substantial

---

15. Appellants also fear that, absent a full-time residency requirement, anyone who visits an institutionalized child can lay claim to psychological parenthood. As earlier discussed, development of a parent-child relationship requires long-term nurturing and fulfillment of the child's total needs which can rarely occur without full-time residency. But it was manifested here only as a direct result of respondents' unique relationship with Phillip as We Care volunteers, their previously uninterrupted weekend close contacts and appellants' physical and emotional detachment from the child. All of such important factors contributed to respondents' ability to devote the enormous amount of time and loving care essential to fill the tangible and emotional needs in Phillip's life.

evidence adequately supports the finding that parental custody would have resulted in harmful deprivation of these human needs contrary to Phillip's best interests.

Finally, there was also evidence that Phillip would experience educational and developmental injury if parental custody remains unchanged. At Phillip's functioning level of disability, he can normally be expected to live at least semi-independently as an adult in a supervised residential setting and be suitably trained to work in a sheltered workshop or even a competitive environment (e.g., performing assembly duties or custodial tasks in a fast-food restaurant). Active involvement of a parent figure during the formative stages of education and habilitation is of immeasurable aid in reaching his full potential. Unfortunately, appellants' deliberate abdication of that central role would effectively deny Phillip any meaningful opportunity to develop whatever skills he may be capable of achieving. Indeed, Dr. Becking testified that further separation from respondents would not only impair Phillip's ability to form new relationships but would "for a long while" seriously impair Phillip's development of necessary prevocational and independent-living skills for his future life.

Nor can we overlook evidence of potential physical harm to Phillip due to appellants' passive neglect in response to Phillip's medical condition. Although it appears probable that the congenital heart defect is no longer correctable by surgery,[18] the trial court could have reasonably concluded that appellants' past conduct reflected a dangerously passive approach to Phillip's future medical needs.[19]

It is a clearly stated legislative policy that persons with developmental disabilities shall enjoy—inter alia—the right to treatment and rehabilitation services, the right to publicly supported education, the right to social interaction, and the right to prompt medical care and treatment. (Welf. & Inst.Code, § 4502.) Moreover, the legislative purpose underlying Civil Code section 4600 is to protect the needs of children generally " '. . . to be raised with love, emotional security and physical safety.' " (In re D.L.C., supra, 54 Cal.App.3d 840, 851, 126 Cal.Rptr. 863.) When a trial court is called upon to determine the custody of a developmentally disabled or handicapped child, as here, it must be guided by such overriding policies rather than by the personal beliefs or attitudes of the contesting parties, since it is the child's interest which remains paramount. . . . Clearly, the trial court faithfully complied with such legislative mandate in exercising its sound discretion based upon the evidence presented. We find no abuse as contended by appellants.

18. A pediatric cardiologist estimated that the surgery now might have a one-third chance of harming him, a one-third chance of helping him and a one-third chance of causing no appreciable change in his condition. Dr. Gathman testified that it is "highly probable" that Phillip's condition is no longer correctable by surgery, but that a heart catheterization is required to be certain.

19. Notably, the failure to obtain competent medical advice concerning the heart disease and the admitted willingness to forego medical treatment solely by reason of Phillip's retarded condition. The gravity of such dangerous inaction was dramatically illustrated by Mr. B.'s reaction to Phillip's recent undiagnosed episodes of apparent semi-consciousness—discounting their existence without even the benefit of a medical consultation.

We strongly emphasize, as the trial court correctly concluded, that the fact of detriment *cannot* be proved solely by evidence that the biological parent has elected to institutionalize a handicapped child, or that nonparents are able and willing to offer the child the advantages of their home in lieu of institutional placement. Sound reasons may exist justifying institutionalization of a handicapped child. But the totality of the evidence under review permits of no rational conclusion other than that the detriment caused Phillip, and its possible recurrence, was due not to appellants' choice to institutionalize but their calculated decision to remain emotionally and physically detached—abdicating the conventional role of competent decisionmaker in times of demonstrated need—thus effectively depriving him of *any* of the substantial benefits of a true parental relationship. *It is the emotional abandonment of Phillip, not his institutionalization,* which inevitably has created the unusual circumstances which led to the award of limited custody to respondents. We do not question the sincerity of appellants' belief that their approach to Phillip's welfare was in their combined best interests. But the record is replete with substantial and credible evidence supporting the trial court's determination, tested by the standard of clear and convincing proof, that appellants' retention of custody has caused and will continue to cause serious detriment to Phillip and that his best interests will be served through the guardianship award of custody to respondents. In light of such compelling circumstances, no legal basis is shown to disturb that carefully considered determination.

    . . .

NOTE

In The Guardianship of Phillip B.: Jay Spears' Achievement, 40 Stan.L.Rev. 841 (1988), Professor Robert Mnookin provides a followup on Phillip Becker–Heath, who turned 21 years old a year before the article was published. Phillip by then had been adopted by the Heaths and had undergone successful open heart surgery. He enrolled in school, obtained a part-time job, and became a Joe Montana fan. The sensitive account of the case carries a sad message because it is one of a series of tributes to Jay Spears, the young lawyer whose efforts were key to the result in case, and who died in December 1986. See In Memory of Jay Spears, 40 Stan.L.Rev. 839 (1988).

C.   Using Past Caretaking Roles to Allocate Responsibility in Custody Decisions

Elizabeth S. Scott, Pluralism, Parental Preference and Child Custody

80 Cal.L.Rev. 615 (1992).*

    . . .

The current debate about custody is in large measure a conflict about the extent to which the custody decision should rest on the parents' participation in rearing their child during marriage. During an era in which parenting roles are in flux, families vary in the allocation of child care responsibilities. In response to this pluralism, the dominant best interests standard for deciding custody presumes that past patterns of care are inadequate as a guide to future custody. In different ways, both joint custody advocates and proponents of a primary caretaker preference object to the best interests standard because it obscures the importance of past parental involvement. Only a legal preference for the primary caretaker assures that the parent who has been principally responsible for rearing the child during the marriage will be her custodian after divorce. Only a joint custody rule assures that two parents who have fully shared in the care of their child will continue to do so after divorce. Both of these challenges contain a measure of truth. Each in its own way, however, also distorts past parental roles. A primary caretaker preference discounts the role of the "secondary" parent, while a joint custody rule accurately describes parental role allocation only when both parents fully participated in child care during marriage.

[T]he inquiry regarding future custody arrangements should focus on the past relationship of each parent to the child and do so in a more precise and individualized way than either the best interests standard or the reform alternatives require. The custody decision is an announcement and prescription of the future part each parent will play in the child's life over the years of her minority. There is ... no sounder basis for this prescription than past relationships. Therefore, in most cases the law's goal should be to approximate, to the extent possible, the predivorce role of each parent in the child's life.

. . .

Divorce, which by any measure is a period of upheaval in a child's life, should not be treated as an opportunity for restructuring parent-child relationships. Child development experts emphasize the harmful impact of the disruption associated with divorce, and the link between continuity of the parent-child relationship and healthy child development.[45] Custody law can minimize disruption of the child's habitual routines and relationships after divorce by perpetuating patterns of parental care established in the intact family. A rule that preserves the continuity of family relationships would seem to reflect the best interests of the child as accurately as this elusive concept permits.

The approximation approach ... accommodates two strands of child development research and theory that have been drawn into the policy debate over custody and are currently treated as irreconcilable. The first strand, attachment theory, emphasizes the importance of the mother-child relationship to the child's healthy development[47] and has been invoked to

45. *See* ROBERT E. EMERY, MARRIAGE, DIVORCE, AND CHILDREN'S ADJUSTMENT 48–104 (1988) (clinical findings on how the disruption from divorce impacts children).

47. As Michael Lamb has stated, "[M]ost theorists, whatever their orientation, support both the tender years presumption and the primary caretaker preference. Attachment theory would support the assertion that the gravest deficiency of the best interests standard is the risk of disrupting the relationship between the child and her primary caretaker. More recently, however, other researchers have suggested that the role of fathers in their children's lives has been undervalued and that attachment theory exaggerates the uniqueness and exclusiveness of the primary caretaker-child bond.[51] Some observers argue that this research supports a stronger claim for father custody or, at least, weakens the viability of a primary caretaker preference.[52] Taken together, these two psychological perspectives point to a legal response that does not choose between parents or split custody of the child but rather seeks to gauge the strength of existing bonds and to perpetuate them through the custody arrangement. Thus, for example, if both parents have been active caretakers, the child should not have to suffer from the disruptive effects of relegating one parent's status to that of visitor. On the other hand, if one parent's involvement and care for the child has been dominant, that strong bond should not be disturbed. The secondary role of the other parent, however, should also be recognized.

Structuring future custody as I propose could also mitigate the observed tension between two goals of custody law: encouraging the participation of both parents after divorce and avoiding exposure of the child to excessive interparental conflict. The joint custody debate demonstrates this tension, with advocates stressing the harm of lost parental contact while opponents emphasize the detriment to the child from exposure to interparental conflict. It is plausible to assume that basing custody roles on past patterns of caretaking would provide optimal parental involvement with minimal conflict. Joint physical custody, which provides the greatest oppor-

---

have assumed that the mother-infant relationship is unique and vastly more important than any contemporaneous, or indeed any subsequent, relationships." Michael E. Lamb, *The Role of the Father: An Overview, in* THE ROLE OF THE FATHER IN CHILD DEVELOPMENT 1, 2 (Michael E. Lamb ed., 1976) (citations omitted). According to attachment theory, disruption and separation from the mother during early childhood are associated with human attachment problems. *See* SELMA FRAIBERG, EVERY CHILD'S BIRTH RIGHT: IN DEFENSE OF MOTHERING 52 (1977). *See generally* Mary D.S. Ainsworth, *Infant-Mother Attachment*, 34 AM. PSYCHOLOGIST (1979) (overview of attachment theory); Chambers, Rethinking the Substantive Rules for Custody Disputes, 83 Mich. L.Rev. 477 (1984) 528–32 (same).

51. *See* Lamb, *supra* note 47, at 3–6. This claim has gained strength as fathers have assumed a more active family role. For two comprehensive presentations of research dealing with father-child relationships, see Chambers, *supra* note [47], at 532–37; Ross A. Thompson, *The Father's Case in Child Custody Disputes: The Contributions of Psychological Research, in* FATHERHOOD AND FAMILY POLICY 53 (Michael E. Lamb & Abraham Sagi eds., 1983).

52. In part, the research on fathers' role has been used to support the position that fathers are competent parents and could become primary caretakers without detriment to the child. *See* Thompson, *supra* note 51, at 91. This of course does not speak to whether there is a basis for choosing the primary over the secondary caretaker, given a choice between the two. Thompson supports a primary caretaker preference for very young children. *Id.* Chambers also adopts this approach with some hesitation, concluding after a review of the empirical research that the difference in the significance of children's relationships to their two parents is less than had been formerly believed. *See* Chambers, *supra* note [47], at 536–37. These findings suggest that the trauma from losing contact with the primary caretaker might be only marginally more severe than from losing contact with the other parent.

tunity for conflict, will be ordered under this approach only if it replicates the pattern of childrearing that occurred during the marriage. In such a situation, the couple's prior experience of shared responsibility increases the likelihood of mutual commitment, competency, and respect. Thus, the prospect of a cooperative adjustment is better than it would be were new roles thrust upon parents.[54] The resent of joint custody by primary caretaker mothers and the potential conflict that it could generate might be reduced if custody is formulated on the basis of past roles.

2.   Parental Preferences About Custody and Past Family Roles

Basing future custody on past parental performance has the potential not only to reduce instability for the child during the transition period, but also to better promote continuity in the reconstituted family over time. This is because predivorce roles may reflect the "true" preferences of parents for their future relationship to their child, and thus predict future performance more accurately than any alternative. Although contemporary families do not follow any single prescription regarding the allocation of parenting roles, the division of roles that a given couple adopts likely reflects internalized values and preferences, and may be intricately linked to personal and gender identity for each spouse. The child herself has expectations about the way that each parent participates in her life that can influence the parents' own preferences. Other factors reinforce predivorce roles as well. Each parent tacitly recognizes the other parent's competency in some spheres and asserts a proprietary claim in others. Moreover, the social context in which the family has lived—extended family, family, neighbors, and employers—creates expectations that promote conformity to these predivorce parental roles.[59] Diversity among families should not lead us to conclude that parental roles are casually assumed or changed. Dramatic change in the parent-child relationship can be disruptive for both the parents and the child.

Consider the following comparison between a joint custody arrangement involving parents who have fully shared parenting responsibilities during marriage and an arrangement in which a primary caretaker and an ambitious professional begin to share in the care of their children only after

54. One study found that parents are most likely to negotiate joint custody agreements when they both share a perception that the father is an "active and involved parent." Carol R. Lowery, *Maternal and Joint Custody: Differences in the Decision Process*, 10 LAW & HUM. BEHAV. 303, 312 (1986). The results of another study show that parents who share decisionmaking regarding childrearing during the separation are more likely to maintain this cooperative relationship two years later. William S. Coysh et al., *Parental Postdivorce Adjustment in Joint and Sole Physical Custody Families*, J. FAM. ISSUES, Mar. 1989, at 52, 68. Although the authors warned of potential limitations on the study's applicability to the general divorcing population, *id.* At 69, they

concluded that the dominant pattern of parental adjustment following divorce is characterized by a continuity of predivorce to postdivorce functioning, *id.* At 68.

59. Moreover, general societal expectations can be internalized and influence preferences for custody. One study noted social pressure on mothers to remain at home with their children. *See* Judith J. Fischer, *Mothers Living Apart from Their Children*, 32 FAM. REL. 351 (1983). The results of the same study suggest that mothers who live apart from their children are disapproved of by society and viewed as unusual, whereas noncustodial fathers are seen as typical and are not subject to disapproval. *Id.* At 356–57.

divorce. Common sense suggests differing prospects for success between the two arrangements. In the former case, both parents have invested heavily in their caretaking role, which can be assumed to be an important part of their lives. Each has likely adjusted to the other's participation in the family, and both function in a social and employment context that has adapted to their choice of role division. In this situation of shared caretaking, both parents might value the caretaking relationship equally and would consider any disproportionate diminishment of this role to be a serious loss. In contrast, a mother who was the primary caretaker during the marriage is likely to prefer a larger share of custody than does her professional husband.[61] Because most wives spend a greater proportion of their time doing domestic tasks, caring for the child plays a larger part in their lives and personal identities. The primary caretaker mother might find it difficult to adjust to a reduction in this role or to accept an expansion of the childbearing responsibilities of her former husband. Furthermore, the father who has been only peripherally involved with his children before divorce might contemplate strain in both the professional and domestic spheres of his life should he assume a greatly expanded role thereafter. Under these circumstances, both psychological factors and external stresses could interfere with a stable joint custody arrangement.

My contention that parents are generally inclined to track predivorce roles is consistent with the growing body of empirical research on custody. Children of divorce in single-parent homes are overwhelmingly in the custody of their mothers, an arrangement that is closer to patterns of parent-child relationships in most intact families than is the alternative of exclusive paternal custody. When the menu of custody arrangements expands to include joint custody, the importance of predivorce roles seems even clearer. Joint legal custody, which I have argued reflects typical role allocation more accurately than does sole custody, has been accepted by both mothers and fathers and is now the prevailing norm in some jurisdictions. In comparison, parents have been less receptive to joint physical custody,[66] suggesting that parents resist radically altering patterns of care

---

61. Mothers in general express a stronger desire to get custody than do fathers. *See* Mnookin et al., [*Private Ordering Revisited: What Custodial Arrangements are Parents Negotiating?*, in Divorce Reform at the Crossroads, Stephen Sugarman and Herma Kay, eds.] at 46–49 ("overwhelming majority" of mothers wish to be their children's main caretaker). This finding might be explained by the typical variance in each parent's child care responsibility during marriage. *See also* Chambers, *supra* note [47], at 542–43 (primary caretakers suffer more from losing custody than their secondary caretaker counterparts); Fischer, *supra* note 59, at 353 (non-controlled study of noncustodial mothers shows incidence of depression). Finally, the fact that noncustodial mothers have more continued contact with their children than do noncustodial fathers, *see* Frank F. Fursten-

berg et al., *The Life Course of Children of Divorce: Marital Disruption and Parental Contact*, 48 AM. SOC. REV. 656, 656–67 (1983), suggests that sustaining the parent-child relationship is more important to mothers than to fathers.

66. Studies indicate that joint legal custody is more popular than joint physical custody. Research in California and Massachusetts indicates that joint physical custody is relatively less popular in those states. A group led by Robert Mnookin and Eleanor Maccoby studied over one thousand California families who filed for divorce in the years 1984–85 and found that although 75.5% of the parents had joint legal custody, only 19.6% had court orders for joint physical custody. *See* Mnookin et al., *supra* note [61], at 60. A Massachusetts study of the records of 500 divorced families found that only 10% of

and authority established in the intact family. Moreover, researchers in California have found that, even in custody arrangements that began as joint physical custody, children of divorce tended over time to live primarily with their mothers.[67] This trend suggests that parents might be revealing their true preferences through their conduct, "drifting" toward arrangements that may reflect predivorce patterns of care.[68] Parental resistance to the transformation of established roles might also contribute to the poor adjustment and high relitigation rates associated with court-ordered joint custody in which one party, usually the mother, resists the arrangement.[69] In general, the experience with joint custody is consistent with my hypothesis that parents tend to accept and adapt to this innovation to the extent that it comports with past roles.

Implicit in this analysis is the conclusion that a rule that reflects parents' preferences for custody is also in the best interests of the child. This conclusion is dissonant with much rhetoric about custody, which rarely focuses on the impact of parental satisfaction on the success of future family relations. My analysis, however, argues that the premise upon which the law operates in dealing with intact families should not be forgotten upon divorce. Parents adopt roles and functions in the family according to complex sets of values and preferences and with little legal

those families with joint legal custody also had joint physical custody. *See* W.P.C. Phear et al., *An Empirical Study of Custody Arrangements: Joint Versus Sole Legal Custody, in* JOINT CUSTODY AND SHARED PARENTING 142, 147 (Jay Folberg ed., 1984); *cf.* Robert J. Racusin et al., *Factors Associated with Joint Custody Awards*, 28 J. AM. ACAD. CHILD ADOLESCENT PSYCHIATRY 164 (1989) (despite a judicial rule in Vermont that joint custody in general was to be disfavored and a statutory preference in New Hampshire for joint legal custody, a study found the incidence of joint physical custody in both states to be identically low).

67. This is true even though California is favorable to joint custody. The California custody study found a significant "drift" toward de facto mother custody, both in cases in which the father was awarded physical custody (drift of nearly 23%) and in joint physical custody cases (nearly 40%). Mnookin et al., *supra* note [61] at 67.

68. Because this drift is systematically in the direction of mother custody, it probably cannot be explained simply as resulting from a difficulty in maintaining joint custody arrangements.

69. Joint custody advocates initially argued that relitigation rates would be lower than in sole custody, and an early study confirmed this result under joint custody arrangements with the consent of both parents. Court-ordered joint custody in which one parent was forced to accept the arrangement had

relitigation rates comparable to those in sole custody. *See* Frederic W. Ilfeld, Jr., et al., *Does Joint Custody Work? A First Look at Outcome Data of Relitigation*, 139 AM. J. PSYCHIATRY 62, 64–65 (1982). Later studies have shown higher joint custody relitigation rates. Steinman and colleagues found that parents whose joint custody arrangement was court-ordered had the least successful relationships and were most likely to relitigate. Susan Steinman et al., *A Study of Parents Who Sought Joint Custody Following Divorce: Who Reaches Agreement and Sustains Joint Custody and Who Returns to Court*, 24 J. AM. ACAD. CHILD PSYCHIATRY 545 (1985). A study of 500 family records by Phear and colleagues found the instances of relitigation to be the same between joint and sole custody families. *See* W.P.C. Phear et al., *supra* note 66, at 151. California recently revised its joint custody statute to clarify the fact that it contains no presumption favoring joint custody. Act of Sept. 27, 1988, ch. 1442, § 1, 1988 Cal. Stat. 4927, 4927–28 (codified as amended at CAL. CIV. CODE § 4600(d) (West Supp. 1991)). Proponents of the statutory amendment cited research evidence finding harmful effects of court-ordered joint custody. *See Family Law Issues Relating to SB 1296, SB 1306, and SB 1341 (and SB 13), Public Hearing Before the Cal. Assembly Comm. On Judiciary*, 1987 Regular Sess. 49–87 (Dec. 14, 1987).

supervision. The law can look to these family patterns as the best reflection of the parents' true preferences and the best predictor of the future stability of custody arrangements. This analysis does not deny that substantial change in parent-child relationships occurs in many divorces. Nor do I argue that insurmountable barriers face parents when divorce signifies substantial reordering of their predivorce roles. Nevertheless, the law has been naive in assuming that substantially different family roles can be dictated by fiat. To the extent that custody arrangements involve a major restructuring of parental roles, the risk of instability might well be increased.

WEST VIRGINIA CODE (West)

§ 48–9–206. Allocation of custodial responsibility

(a) Unless otherwise resolved by agreement of the parents under section 9–201 or unless manifestly harmful to the child, the court shall allocate custodial responsibility so that the proportion of custodial time the child spends with each parent approximates the proportion of time each parent spent performing caretaking functions for the child prior to the parents' separation or, if the parents never lived together, before the filing of the action, except to the extent required under section 9–209 or necessary to achieve any of the following objectives:

(1) To permit the child to have a relationship with each parent who has performed a reasonable share of parenting functions;

(2) To accommodate the firm and reasonable preferences of a child who is fourteen years of age or older, and with regard to a child under fourteen years of age, but sufficiently matured that he or she can intelligently express a voluntary preference for one parent, to give that preference such weight as circumstances warrant;

(3) To keep siblings together when the court finds that doing so is necessary to their welfare;

(4) To protect the child's welfare when, under an otherwise appropriate allocation, the child would be harmed because of a gross disparity in the quality of the emotional attachments between each parent and the child or in each parent's demonstrated ability or availability to meet a child's needs;

(5) To take into account any prior agreement of the parents that, under the circumstances as a whole including the reasonable expectations of the parents in the interest of the child, would be appropriate to consider;

(6) To avoid an allocation of custodial responsibility that would be extremely impractical or that would interfere substantially with the child's need for stability in light of economic, physical or other circumstances, including the distance between the parents' residences, the cost and difficulty of transporting the child, the parents' and child's daily schedules, and the ability of the parents to cooperate in the arrangement;

(7) To apply the principles set forth in 9–403(d) of this article if one parent relocates or proposes to relocate at a distance that will impair the ability of a parent to exercise the amount of custodial responsibility that would otherwise be ordered under this section; and

(8) To consider the stage of a child's development.

(b) In determining the proportion of caretaking functions each parent previously performed for the child under subsection (a) of this section, the court shall not consider the divisions of functions arising from temporary arrangements after separation, whether those arrangements are consensual or by court order. The court may take into account information relating to the temporary arrangements in determining other issues under this section.

(c) If the court is unable to allocate custodial responsibility under subsection (a) of this section because the allocation under that subsection would be manifestly harmful to the child, or because there is no history of past performance of caretaking functions, as in the case of a newborn, or because the history does not establish a pattern of caretaking sufficiently dispositive of the issues of the case, the court shall allocate custodial responsibility based on the child's best interest, taking into account the factors in considerations that are set forth in this section and in section two hundred nine and 9–403(d) of this article and preserving to the extent possible this section's priority on the share of past caretaking functions each parent performed.

(d) In determining how to schedule the custodial time allocated to each parent, the court shall take account of the economic, physical and other practical circumstances such as those listed in subdivision (6), subsection (a) of this section.

§ 48–9–207. Allocation of significant decision-making responsibility

(a) Unless otherwise resolved by agreement of the parents under section 9–201, the court shall allocate responsibility for making significant life decisions on behalf of the child, including the child's education and health care, to one parent or to two parents jointly, in accordance with the child's best interest, in light of:

(1) The allocation of custodial responsibility under section 9–206 of this article;

(2) The level of each parent's participation in past decision-making on behalf of the child;

(3) The wishes of the parents;

(4) The level of ability and cooperation the parents have demonstrated in decision-making on behalf of the child;

(5) Prior agreements of the parties; and

(6) The existence of any limiting factors, as set forth in section 9–209 of this article.

(b) If each of the child's legal parents has been exercising a reasonable share of parenting functions for the child, the court shall presume that an allocation of decision-making responsibility to both parents jointly is in the child's best interests. The presumption is overcome if there is a history of domestic abuse, or by a showing that joint allocation of decision-making responsibility is not in the child's best interest.

(c) Unless otherwise provided or agreed by the parents, each parent who is exercising custodial responsibility shall be given sole responsibility for day-to-day decisions for the child, while the child is in that parent's care and control, including emergency decisions affecting the health and safety of the child.

NOTE

The preceding West Virginia statute was adopted in 2001 to replace the primary caretaker presumption announced by the Supreme Court of Appeals of West Virginia in *Garska v. McCoy*, 167 W.Va. 59, 278 S.E.2d 357 (1981) more than 20 years ago. It was assumed that one of the parents would be designated the "primary caretaker" based on past role playing, and most of the factors involved were based on who spent more time with the child in the home. They included

> (1) preparing and planning of meals; (2) bathing, grooming and dressing; (3) purchasing, cleaning, and care of clothes; (4) medical care, including nursing and trips to physicians; (5) arranging for social interaction among peers after school, i.e. transporting to friends' houses or, for example, to girl or boy scout meetings; (6) arranging alternative care, i.e. babysitting, day-care, etc. (7) putting child to bed at night, attending to child in the middle of the night, waking child in the morning; (8) disciplining, i.e. teaching general manners and toilet training; (9) educating, i.e. religious, cultural, social, etc.; and, (10) teaching elementary skills, i.e., reading, writing and arithmetic.

In a subsequent review of the primary caretaker doctrine in *David M. v. Margaret M.*, 182 W.Va. 57, 385 S.E.2d 912 (1989) some eight years after *Garska*, the Supreme Court of Appeals acknowledged that

> . . . This list of criteria usually, but not necessarily, spells "mother." That fact reflects social reality; the rule itself is neutral on its face and in its application. When women pursue lucrative and successful careers while their husbands take care of the children, those husbands receive the benefit of the presumption as strongly as do traditional mothers. Furthermore, where both parents share child-rearing responsibilities equally, our courts hold hearings to determine which parent would be the better single parent. This latter situation is rare, but is evidence of the actual gender-neutrality of the primary caretaker presumption.

> Our rule inevitably involves some injustice to fathers who, as a group, are usually not primary caretakers. There are instances when the primary caretaker will not be the better custodian in the long run. Yet there is no guarantee that the courts will be able to know, in advance and based on the deliberately distorted evidence that characterizes courtroom custody proceedings, when such is the case. And, notwithstanding its theoretical imperfections, the primary caretaker parent presumption acknowledges that exhaustive hearings on relative degrees of parenting ability rarely disclose any but the most gross variations in skill and suitability. Permitting such hearings inevitably has distortive effect on the parties' behavior, and is likely to lead to potentially disastrous emotional trauma for all concerned if the case goes to court.

Despite such a defense, many criticized the approach as little more than a revival of the discredited or discarded "tender years presumption". Under that approach children of "tender years" generally would be placed with a mother who requested custody unless she was legally "unfit". Fathers often refrained from seeking custody of their young children because it was seen as an exercise in futility. For a combination of reasons, including the decline of presumptions and increased concern about gender discrimination, the "tender years" presumption (or rule) has officially disappeared in most jurisdictions though vestiges of it may remain in practice. Also, the old rule that custody of an illegitimate child presumptively vests in the mother has eroded. See, e.g., *Rosero v. Blake*, 357 N.C. 193, 581 S.E.2d 41 (2003).

The current West Virginia approach is based on the A.L.I. Principles of the Law of Family Dissolution that were published in 2002. It also reflects some of the ideas set forth in the article by Professor Elizabeth Scott at p. 411. Under the A.L.I. approach the labels of "custody" and "visitation" are replaced by the term "custodial responsibility rather than what Dean Katherine Bartlett has described as" the more traditional concepts of "winner take all...." See Katherine T. Bartlett, U.S. Custody Law and Trends in the Context of the ALI Principles on the Law of Family Dissolution, 10 Virginia Journal of Social Policy and the Law 5, 25 (2002). For more discussion of the new West Virginia statute see John D. Athey, The Ramifications of West Virginia's codified Custody Law: A Departure From *Garska v. McCoy,* 106 W.Va.L.Rev. 389 (2004).

D. JOINT CUSTODY

CALIFORNIA FAMILY CODE (West)

§ 3003. Joint legal custody

"Joint legal custody" means that both parents shall share the right and the responsibility to make the decisions relating to the health, education, and welfare of a child.

§ 3004. Joint physical custody

"Joint physical custody" means that each of the parents shall have significant periods of physical custody. Joint physical custody shall be shared by the parents in such a way so as to assure a child of frequent and continuing contact with both parents....

§ 3006. Sole legal custody

"Sole legal custody" means that one parent shall have the right and the responsibility to make the decisions relating to the health, education, and welfare of a child.

§ 3007. Sole physical custody

"Sole physical custody" means that a child shall reside with and be under the supervision of one parent, subject to the power of the court to order visitation.

§ 3010. Custody of unemancipated children

(a) The mother of an unemancipated child and the father, if presumed to be the father under section 7611, are equally entitled to custody of the child.

(b) If one parent is dead, is unable or refuses to take custody, or has abandoned the child, the other parent is entitled to the child.

§ 3011. Best interest of child; considerations

In making a determination of the best interest of the child in a proceeding described in Section 3021, the court shall, among any other factors it finds relevant, consider all of the following:

(a) The health, safety, and welfare of the child.

(b) Any history of abuse by one parent or any other person seeking custody against any of the following:

(1) Any child to whom he or she is related by blood or affinity or with whom he or she has had a caretaking relationship, no matter how temporary.

(2) The other parent.

(3) A parent, current spouse, or cohabitant, of the parent or person seeking custody, or a person with whom the parent or person seeking custody has a dating or engagement relationship.

As a prerequisite to the consideration of allegations of abuse, the court may require substantial independent corroboration, including, but not limited to, written reports by law enforcement agencies, child protective services or other social welfare agencies, courts, medical facilities, or other public agencies or private nonprofit organizations providing services to victims of sexual assault or domestic violence. As used in this subdivision, "abuse against a child" means "child abuse" as defined in Section 11165.6 of the Penal Code and abuse against any of the other persons described in paragraph (2) or (3) means "abuse" as defined in Section 6203 of this code.

(c) The nature and amount of contact with both parents, except as provided in Section 3046.

(d) The habitual or continual illegal use of controlled substances or habitual or continual abuse of alcohol by either parent. Before considering these allegations, the court may first require independent corroboration, including, but not limited to, written reports from law enforcement agencies, courts, probation departments, social welfare agencies, medical facilities, rehabilitation facilities, or other public agencies or nonprofit organizations providing drug and alcohol abuse services. As used in this subdivision, "controlled substances" has the same meaning as defined in the California Uniform Controlled Substances Act, Division 10 (commencing with Section 11000) of the Health and Safety Code.

(e)(1) Where allegations about a parent pursuant to subdivision (b) or (d) have been brought to the attention of the court in the current proceeding, and the court makes an order for sole or joint custody to that parent, the court shall state its reasons in writing or on the record. In these circumstances, the court shall ensure that any order regarding custody or visitation is specific as to time, day, place, and manner of transfer of the child as set forth in subdivision (b) of Section 6323.

(2) The provisions of this subdivision shall not apply if the parties stipulate in writing or on the record regarding custody or visitation.

§ 3020. Legislative findings and declarations; health, safety, and welfare of children; continuing contact with parents

(a) The Legislature finds and declares that it is the public policy of this state to assure that the health, safety, and welfare of minor children shall be the court's primary concern in determining the best interest of children when making any orders regarding the legal or physical custody or visitation of children. The legislature further finds and declares that the perpetration of child abuse or domestic violence in a household where a child resides is detrimental to the child.

(b) The Legislature finds and declares that it is the public policy of this state to assure that children have frequent and continuing contact with both parents after the parents have separated or dissolved their marriage, or ended their relationship, and to encourage parents to share the rights and responsibilities of child rearing in order to effect this policy, except where the contact would not be in the best interest of the child, as provided in Section 3011.

(c) Where the policies set forth in subdivisions (a) and (b) of this section are in conflict, any court's order regarding legal or physical custody or visitation shall be made in a manner that ensures the health, safety, and welfare of the child and the safety of all family members.

§ 3022. Best interest of child; considerations

The court may, during the pendency of a proceeding or at any time thereafter, make an order for the custody of a child during minority that seems necessary or proper.

§ 3080. Presumption of joint custody

There is a presumption, affecting the burden of proof, that joint custody is in the best interest of a minor child, subject to Section 3011, where the parents have agreed to joint custody or so agree in open court at a hearing for the purpose of determining the custody of the minor child.

In re Marriage of Hickey

Court of Appeals of Iowa, 1986.
386 N.W.2d 141.

■ OXBERGER, CHIEF JUDGE.

The child custody and child support provisions of the parties' divorce decree are appealed by the petitioner, Sharon Hickey. We affirm as modified.

The petitioner and respondent, David, are parents of two children, Matthew, born March 14, 1979, and Jennifer, born February 3, 1981. . . . During the marriage, David's work resulted in him spending some nights away from home on business. Sharon was primarily responsible for the care of the children. In November 1982, she entered college and David took greater involvement in the daily care of the children. Sharon expects to receive a degree in pharmacy in August 1986.

. . .

The trial court awarded both joint legal and joint physical custody of the children to the parents. They are to spend one month with Sharon, the next month with David, alternating months throughout the year. Child support was ordered paid to Sharon of $250 per child for the six months of the year in which Sharon has physical custody. David was also ordered to pay $350 per month in alimony until August 1986, when Sharon will graduate from school. Sharon has appealed from the custody provision saying the joint physical custody will be unduly disruptive to the children, and from the child support award, claiming it is insufficient.

The Iowa Supreme Court has stated on several occasions that the primary goal of an award of physical care is to assure the child's best interest, and provide for as much stability in their lives as is possible following the breakup of a marriage. See In re Marriage of Winter, 223 N.W.2d 165, 166–67 (Iowa 1974). The recently enacted statute which encourages joint custody refers to an award of joint legal custody, not necessarily joint physical care. See Iowa Code § 598.41 (1985). It does not require joint physical care. Id. at § 598.41(5). In fact, an award of joint physical care is considered unusual by this court.

In another case this court has refused to expand visitation rights of the noncustodial parent to include midweek visitation with the five-year-old child because we believed "midweek visitation, in addition to visitation on alternate weekends would involve excessive shifting of the child between parents and could impair the child's sense of stability." In re Marriage of Fish, 350 N.W.2d 226, 231 (Iowa.Ct.App.1984).

Previously it has been found that a request that summer vacation visitation be provided for alternating two-week intervals instead of four weeks would not be granted because "such an arrangement would be confusing and upsetting to the children and would deprive them of the stability which they need at this stage of their development." In re Marriage of Weidner, 338 N.W.2d 351, 359 (Iowa 1983). The supreme court has also disapproved a decree granting visitation to the noncustodial parents on every weekend instead of alternating weekends because such visits would be "unduly disruptive." In re Marriage of Guyer, 238 N.W.2d 794, 797 (Iowa 1976).

If children were like chattels, it would seem eminently fair to divide their time as equally as possible between their parents. However, as the statements from the court we have referred to indicate, we must consider the children's best interests as well as those of the parents. If it were possible for one parent to care for the child during the week at a time in which the child would otherwise be with a third-party baby-sitter, division of the child's time between the parents' residences during the week or month would be justified for the child's best interest. In this manner, the child could spend the maximum time with parents and minimum time with third parties. In the more typical case which we find here, both parents work during the week. We find these young children need the stability of having a primary home, where they will be provided with consistency in environment, playmates, and scheduling. We hold an award of joint physical custody is not in the best interests of these children.

Both parents love their children and are capable of providing a good home. We are forced to choose between two people who both care for their children. A review of the evidence shows that although David began participating more in the care of the children when Sharon returned to school, Sharon remains the primary caretaker. In one incident, which is undisputed by David, the young daughter hurt her arm when Sharon and David were at home. Rather than accompanying Sharon and the child to the hospital, David chose to leave to go to a ball game. Instead, a neighbor accompanied Sharon and the child to the hospital. Neither does David seriously dispute that when he spends time with the children, he takes them to activities which he would enjoy, but the children might not appreciate. As an example, he takes the three-year-old daughter to football games and golfing. Without elaborating on the details reflected in the record, it is also noted by the court that David has difficulty controlling his hostility towards Sharon when he is in front of the children.

We repeat these facts not to disparage David as a parent but to support our conclusion that Sharon has been the person primarily responsible for care of the children and has shown superior parenting ability. We therefore award sole physical care of the children to Sharon. David shall be given liberal visitation as the parties shall agree upon. This will include, at a minimum, visitation on alternating weekends, and alternating holidays, and include a three-week visitation in the summer.

. . .

AFFIRMED AS MODIFIED.

NOTES

(1) Compare *Kaloupek v. Burfening*, 440 N.W.2d 496 (N.D.1989), in which the North Dakota Supreme Court affirmed a trial court's joint (actually divided) physical custody award in which the child would alternate between parents every six months until school age. Justice Levine, dissenting, stated:

> Poor Robert! In order to "assure" that his relationship with his father "survive[s] and grow[s]," he has been placed in a state of custodial schizophrenia—six months with one parent and six months with the other. In my view, the trial court's failure to bite the bullet and award custody to one parent or the other has placed a two-year-old child in a state of animated suspension, a custodial limbo. What we have is a probationary custody period of four years, to be reviewed when Robert is of school age. Obviously, that allows the court to defer making a tough decision, but it does not justify it and we ought not approve it. By condoning a practice that may provide instant gratification to a trial judge but real problems to a very young child for whom bonding and attachments to the primary caretaker are crucial, the majority avoids the horns of the dilemma that every trial court is faced with in a custody decision, and fails to provide any guidelines or benchmarks for trial courts to follow in

resolving disputes between equally fit and loving parents over the custody of young children.

. . .

    . . . I view divided custody as the antithesis of "Solomonic." I note that Solomon did not offer the contestants who appeared before him divided custody of the sought-after child and I assume he refrained from doing so for obvious reasons. It may have provided an easy out but it would have resolved neither the underlying contest of parenthood nor the source of continuing upheaval in the continuity of the child's life. Not that making a sandwich of the child is good for the child, but Solomon's acuity was in his recognition that not even combative parents would demand so much. Thus, Solomon avoided letting the parents off the hook by resorting to divided custody. Instead, he forced them into resolving the issue based upon the health and welfare (best interest?) of the child. I would require as much from the trial court.

    (2) Joint custody became popular at a time when the "tender years" and other presumptions were in a process of erosion. This also was a period of increased divorce between couples with minor children following widespread enactment of "no fault" divorce laws. Some initial proponents of joint custody then were fathers who had difficulty obtaining custody. Others favored it as a way of helping more children benefit from continued involvement in their upbringing by both parents after their marriages had broken up. Some critics of joint custody were concerned that a committee of two is often unsatisfactory in practice, with the likelihood of stalemate even higher for a committee of two former spouses whose marriage may have broken down because of disagreement on very basic issues. When enabling legislation on joint custody was first introduced, there were few studies about the possible impact on children other than in cases where both parents genuinely wanted to participate in the process. Not surprisingly, courts often have found most difficulty in situations where parents are divided over whether joint custody should be awarded. There is worry by some that a parent who in fact is opposed to joint custody might nevertheless at least acquiesce for fear that opposition might be deemed contrary to a child's best interests by a court that regards continuing participation by both parents as being of prime importance.

    As the California statute reflects, there can be variations in what is labeled joint custody.

E.   Visitation

UNIFORM MARRIAGE AND DIVORCE ACT*

Section 407. [Visitation.]

    (a) A parent not granted custody of the child is entitled to reasonable visitation rights unless the court finds, after a hearing, that visitation would endanger seriously the child's physical, mental, moral, or emotional health.

    (b) The court may modify an order granting or denying visitation rights whenever modification would serve the best interest of the child; but the court shall not restrict a parent's visitation rights unless it finds that the visitation would endanger seriously the child's physical, mental, moral, or emotional health.

CALIFORNIA FAMILY CODE (West)

§ 3101.   Stepparent's visitation rights

(a) Notwithstanding any other provision of law, the court may grant reasonable visitation to a stepparent, if visitation by the stepparent is determined to be in the best interest of the minor child.

(b) If a protective order, as defined in Section 6218, has been directed to a stepparent to whom visitation may be granted pursuant to this section, the court shall consider whether the best interest of the child requires that any visitation by the stepparent be denied.

(c) Visitation rights may not be ordered under this section that would conflict with a right of custody or visitation of a birth parent who is not a party to the proceeding.

(d) As used in this section:

(1) "Birth parent" means "birth parent" as defined in Section 8512.

(2) "Stepparent" means a person who is a party to the marriage that is the subject of the proceeding, with respect to a minor child of the other party to the marriage.

NOTE

(1) **Stepparents, Custody and Visitation.** More stepparents are now seeking visitation or custody of their stepchildren on divorce, and their chances of a favorable response in the courts seemingly has increased. Some states have enacted statutes specifically granting courts discretion to consider stepparents, grandparents and others, in making custody or visitation awards. Courts in some jurisdictions have recognized judicial authority to grant stepparent visitation rights even in the absence of such a statute. The usual rationale is that the stepparent has become a surrogate or psychological parent and thus stands in loco parentis. Thus it is not necessarily step parentage alone but the in loco parentis relationship that may control. For illustrations of this approach, see *Carter v. Brodrick*, 644 P.2d 850 (Alaska 1982), and *Gribble v. Gribble*, 583 P.2d 64 (Utah 1978). It should be noted, however, that while a parent typically will be accorded visitation rights unless it would be detrimental to a child (see, e.g., U.M.D.A. § 407(a) above), the issue with stepparents (and other persons with a nonbiological relationship) more often involves a question of standing, and the award of visitation rights is discretionary with the courts.

In *Stanley D. v. Deborah D.*, 124 N.H. 138, 467 A.2d 249 (1983), the New Hampshire Supreme Court upheld a trial court's authority to award joint legal custody of Sarah, a minor child, to her natural mother and her stepfather and physical custody to the stepfather. The applicable state statute provided that:

> In all cases where there shall be a decree of divorce or nullity, the court shall make such further decree in relation to the support, education and custody of the children as shall be most conducive to their benefit, and may order a reasonable provision for their support and education.

The court explained that

> Mr. D. is the only father that Sarah has known. She is apparently unaware that he is not her natural father. One can perceive that Mr. D. has treated Sarah at all times as if she were his child; he has loved and supported her and has formed a psychological parent-child relationship with her. Additionally, Sarah and Jacob [the child of both parties, whose custody was awarded to the father] have been raised as brother and sister.
>
> We hold that under these circumstances, when such a family unit has formed, the court has the power and the responsibility to make provision for the well-being of all children involved in the dissolution of the marriage. In so holding, we do not disturb the ruling of Ruben v. Ruben, 123 N.H. 358, 461 A.2d 733 (1983). In a divorce proceeding, a stepparent cannot be required after the divorce to support the children of his former spouse; however, the same stepparent may request custody of the stepchildren.

(2) **Wrongful Denial of Visitation Time.** A custodial parent's arbitrary or impermissible denial of visitation rights can produce ongoing disputes and delays to correct in timely fashion through the judicial process. The following statute shows how one state has designed a mechanism for dealing with such problems.

MICHIGAN COMPILED LAWS ANNOTATED

552.642. Makeup parenting time policy for wrongful denial of parenting time

Sec. 42. (1) Each circuit shall establish a makeup parenting time policy under which a parent who has been wrongfully denied parenting time is able to make up the parenting time at a later date. The policy does not apply until it is approved by the chief circuit judge. A makeup parenting time policy established under this section shall provide all of the following:

(a) That makeup parenting time shall be at least the same type and duration of parenting time as the parenting time that was denied, including, but not limited to, weekend parenting time for weekend parenting time, holiday parenting time for holiday parenting time, weekday parenting time for weekday parenting time, and summer parenting time for summer parenting time.

(b) That makeup parenting time shall be taken with 1 year after the wrongfully denied parenting time was to have occurred.

(c) That the wrongfully denied parent shall choose the time of the makeup parenting time.

(d) That the wrongfully denied parent shall notify both the office of the friend of the court and the other parent in writing not less than 1 week before making use of makeup weekend or weekday parenting time or not less than 28 days before making use of makeup holiday or summer parenting time.

(2) If wrongfully denied parenting time is alleged and the friend of the court determines that action should be taken, the office of the friend of the court shall send each party a notice containing the following statement in boldfaced type of not less than 12 points:

"FAILURE TO RESPOND IN WRITING TO THE OFFICE OF THE FRIEND OF THE COURT WITHIN 21 DAYS AFTER THIS NOTICE WAS SENT SHALL BE CONSIDERED AS AN AGREEMENT THAT

PARENTING TIME WAS WRONGFULLY DENIED AND THAT THE MAKEUP PARENTING TIME POLICY ESTABLISHED BY THE COURT WILL BE APPLIED.''

(3) If a party to the parenting time order does not respond in writing to the office of the friend of the court, within 21 days after the office sends the notice required under subsection (2), to contest the application of the makeup parenting time policy, the office of the friend of the court shall notify each party that the makeup parenting time policy applies. If a party makes a timely response to contest the application of the makeup parenting time policy, the office of the friend of the court shall utilize a procedure authorized under section 41* other than the application of the makeup parenting time policy.'

F.   LIMITATIONS ON A CHILD'S ROLE AND PREFERENCES

Miller v. Miller

Supreme Judicial Court of Maine, 1996.
677 A.2d 64.

■ LIPEZ, J.

This case is before us on report, pursuant to M.R. Civ. P. 72(c), of an interlocutory order entered in the Superior Court (Penobscot County, Mead, J.), granting the motion of three minor children to intervene as parties in the divorce action between their parents and be represented by legal counsel independently of the guardian ad litem appointed previously to represent their interests. We vacate the order of the Superior Court.

Eileen and Clark Miller were married on October 25, 1975. In December 1992, Eileen filed a complaint for a divorce. Shortly thereafter, Clark filed an answer and a counterclaim for a divorce. Both parties filed motions pending the divorce, with each seeking the primary residence of their three children: Carissa Noel Miller, age 14; Nicholas Russell Miller, age 11; and Dylan Patrick Miller, age 9. Following a contested hearing in June 1993, the court (MacInnes, A.R.J.) issued its order pending divorce and awarded the primary residence of all three children to Eileen.

Prior to its order pending the divorce, and by an agreement of the parties, the court appointed a guardian ad litem for the three children.[1]

---

* M.C.L.A. § 552.641.

1. The terms of the court's order provided, in relevant part:

ORDERED that the guardian ad litem shall act in pursuit of the best interest of the children and shall investigate the circumstances concerning the childrens' welfare as it relates to the disposition of parental rights and responsibilities under 19 M.R.S.A. § 752. The guardian ad litem shall have the authority to undertake any or all of the following

action [sic] which the guardian, in her discretion, deems appropriate including:

1. Review of relevant mental health records and materials of the parents and children;

2. Review of relevant medical records of the parents and children;

3. Review of relevant school records and other pertinent materials of the parents and children;

Pursuant to the terms of the order appointing the guardian, Charles L. Robinson, a psychologist, prepared a psychological evaluation of the parties and the children. In preparing his evaluation, Robinson had a joint ninety minute meeting with Clark and Eileen; one-time individual meetings with Clark and Eileen; one visit each at the homes of Clark and Eileen when the children were present; and finally, two meetings with each of the children individually, in the presence of the guardian. All three children rejected the opportunity to speak with Robinson or the guardian alone. In January 1994, Robinson submitted a report recommending that all three children's primary residence be with Clark. Robinson noted in his report Eileen's stated intention to move to Connecticut. He also noted that Nicholas had expressed a preference to live with his mother.

Less than one month after Robinson submitted his report, the guardian submitted her report, which also recommended that all three children maintain their primary residence with Clark. The guardian's investigation consisted of one interview separately with Clark and Eileen, and two interviews with each of the children in the presence of either Dr. Robinson or Clark. The guardian also accompanied Robinson on each, of the home visits mentioned above. The guardian noted in her report Eileen's stated intention to move to Connecticut, and Nicholas's expressed desire to move to Connecticut with his mother. According to the guardian's report, Dylan did not express a discernible preference about where he wished to reside.

Subsequent to the recommendations of Robinson and the guardian, Clark filed a motion to alter and amend the order pending the divorce to provide that the children's primary residence be with him. The motion was based primarily on his belief that Eileen was considering moving from Maine to Connecticut. At the hearing on Clark's motion, Eileen admitted that she was planning to move to Connecticut, and Carissa expressed a clear preference to live with Eileen.

In May 1994, attorney Margaret Semple received a phone call from Nicholas Miller seeking legal representation for himself and his siblings in his parents' pending divorce. Semple agreed to represent all three children on a pro bono basis. In July 1994, the Miller children filed a motion to intervene in their own names and to be represented by legal counsel. Clark opposed the children's motion, as did the guardian.

In August 1994, the court (Marsano, J.) granted Clark's motion to amend the order pending divorce by providing that the children's primary

---

4. Interviews with the children with or without other persons present;

5. Interviews with parents, grandparents. teachers, daycare providers, psychologists, and other persons who have been involved in caring for or treating the children or parents, or who may have knowledge of the children or family;

6. Request and arrange for psychological evaluations and/or counseling for the parents and/or children;

7. Appearance at any and all future proceedings, including pretrial conferences and trial;

8. Submission to the Court of a report in writing summarizing her position on behalf of the children with regard to the issues before the Court, provided that the guardian ad litem furnish copies to all parties reasonably in advance of hearing; and 9. Any other further and necessary authority as may be required to carry out her responsibilities.

residence be with him. In September 1994, the children's motion to intervene was granted. The order included the following directives:

> 1.   That Carissa, Nicholas and Dylan Miller are parties in interest in this matter, and may intervene in their own names as interested parties;
>
> 2.   That Margaret H. Semple, Attorney of Portland, shall serve as their Attorney of Record on a pro bono basis.

In response to Clark's motion pursuant to M.R.Civ.P. 72(c), the court ordered the report of its interlocutory ruling.

The claim of the children pursuant to the common law

There is no basis in the common law for the intervention of minor children as parties in the divorce action of their parents with an attorney of their choice. Although at common law minor children have a right to sue and be sued. Children do not possess the requisite legal capacity to participate in litigation in their own names. This incapacity is premised on age, inexperience, and immaturity. Due to their incapacity, children must bring or defend a legal proceeding through an adult representative, such as a next friend[2] or a guardian ad litem.[3] Similarly, intervention of minor children in an action may only be commenced by a guardian ad litem or a next friend. A person acting as either a next friend or a guardian ad litem is only a nominal party to the litigation; the child is the real party in interest. The next friend or guardian ad litem brings the minor child's claim or interest to the attention of a court.

The Maine Rules of Civil Procedure reflect this common law tradition. M.R.Civ.P. 17(b) provides in relevant part:

> (b) Guardians and Other Representatives. Whenever an infant or incompetent person has a representative, such as a general guardian, conservator, or other like fiduciary, the representative may sue or defend on behalf of the infant or incompetent person. An infant or

---

2.   The term "next friend" is of English origin. In re Beghtel's Estate, 20 N.W.2d 421.423 (Iowa 1945). According to Blackstone, a next friend is any adult person who volunteers to undertake a minor child's legal cause. Id. (citing William Blackstone Commentaries at 464 (Sharswood ed.)). A next friend represents a minor child in the absence of a regularly appointed guardian. Id.: Garcia v. Middle Rio Grande Conservancy District, 664 P.2d 1000, 1006 (N.M.App. 1983), cert. denied, 663 P.2d 1197 (1983), overruled on other grounds, 838 P.2d 971 (N.M.1992). There is no formal appointment required for a next friend. Dye v. Fremont County School District No. 24, 820 P.2d 982, 985 (Wyo.1991). A next friend is not a part to the suit that she prosecutes on behalf of a minor child, but is an officer of the court. Beghtel's Estate, 20 N.W.2d at 423. A next friend is under the control of the court and can be removed if the best Interest of the child so requires. Id. at 424.

3.   A guardian ad litem is a representative appointed by a court to represent a child in a specific legal matter. Historically, guardians ad litem represented children who were defendants to an action, see Dye, 820 P.2d at 985, Jones v. Cowan, 729 S.W.2d 188, 189 (Ky.Ct.App.1987), but today they also represent children who have an interest in litigation other than as a defendant. Such as in abuse and neglect proceedings, see e.g., 22 M.R.S.A. s 4005 (1992 & Supp.1995), and estate proceedings, see e.g., 18–A. M.R.S.A. § 1–403(4) (1981). A guardian ad litem is an officer of the court. The rights and duties of a guardian ad litem and a next friend are essentially the same. Missouri ex rel. Dep't of Social Services, Div. of Child Support Enforcement v. Kobusch, 908 S.W.2d 383, 385 (Mo.Ct.App.1995).

incompetent person who does not have a duly appointed representative may sue by a next friend or by a guardian ad litem. The court shall appoint a guardian ad litem for an infant or incompetent person not otherwise represented in an action or shall make such other order as it deems proper for the protection of the infant or incompetent person....

Pursuant to Rule 17(b), a minor child may only sue if the child has a representative, next friend, or guardian ad litem. The court is empowered to appoint such a representative for a child whenever protection of the child's interests demands it.

There is one exception to this rule in M.R.Civ.P. 80(e), that allows minor children who are themselves married and parties to a divorce to proceed in their own capacity, without the need for a next friend or guardian ad litem. M.R.Civ.P. 80(e).[4] With respect to the children of these divorcing parties, however, the second sentence of Rule 80(e) reverts to the common law approach, and allows a court to appoint a guardian ad litem to represent the interests of those children. Read together, Rule 17(b) and Rule 80(e) confirm that Maine subscribes to the common law view of the legal capacity of children. Except for the unique situation presented by a divorce that involves minor children as parties, minor children may not under Maine law sue or be sued unless they are represented by a guardian or next friend. The same rule applies when children seek, as they do here, to become parties to an action by intervention.

There is another obstacle to the claim of the Miller children that they have a right to intervene as parties in this divorce action with an attorney of their choice. Pursuant to Maine law, children have "no authority to appoint an attorney." 1 Field, McKusick & Wroth, Maine Civil Practice § 17.5 at 356 (1970) (citing Bernard v. Merrill, 91 Me. 358, 361 (1898)). We stated the rule emphatically in the Bernard case: "Even should the infant employ counsel, who procures the suit dismissed, the entry would be void, because the infant could not appear by attorney as the employment would be null." Bernard v. Merrill, 91 Me. at 361.[5] We see no reason to depart from this rule, which reflects the same concerns that account for the legal incapacity of children to sue or be sued—their age, inexperience and immaturity.

Although the law imposes procedural limitations on children, it does so to protect their interests. In the realm of divorce and other family litigation, this protective purpose finds expression in the best interest standard. In Maine, as in the multitude of other states which have adopted the best interest standard, courts faced with the task of rearranging parental rights

---

4. M.R.Civ.P. 80(e) provides: Notwithstanding the provisions of Rule 17(b), a minor party to any proceeding under this rule need not be represented by next friend, guardian ad litem, or other fiduciary, unless the court so orders. Whenever it shall appear to the court to be in the best interests of a minor child of the parties to a proceeding under this rule, the court may on its own motion or on motion of a party, appoint a guardian ad litem. The court may make such provision for payment of a guardian ad litem by the parties as it deems necessary and proper.

5. A Maryland case that is a precursor to remand reveals that this rule is borrowed from the English common law. See Deford v. State, Use of Keyser, 30 Md. 179, 199 (1869).

and responsibilities must strive for an outcome that will maximize the best interest of children. See 19 M.R.S.A. § 752 (Supp.1995). This standard protects children who lack the ability because of youth, inexperience, and immaturity to protect themselves. The protective purpose of this standard is also important in analyzing the constitutional claim of the Miller children.

The constitutional claim of the children

The remaining issue is whether the intervention of the children as parties in the divorce action of their parents with an attorney of their choice is constitutionally required. Relying on the procedural due process guarantees of the Fourteenth Amendment of the United States Constitution, the Miller children contend that they have a significant liberty interest in the outcome of their parents' divorce because of the custodial issues involved. Assuming, arguendo, that the Miller children have a liberty interest in the outcome of their parents' divorce,[6] we must determine whether representation by a court-appointed guardian ad litem responsible for advocating for their best interests satisfies the requirements of procedural due process.

The test we use for evaluating procedural due process claims was set forth by the United States Supreme Court in Mathews v. Eldridge, 424 U.S. 319 (1976).... It consists of three factors which must be balanced against each other: (1) the private interests affected by the chosen procedure; (2) the risk of erroneous deprivation of those interests by the chosen procedure and the probable value, if any, of additional or substitute procedural safeguards; and (3) the countervailing state interest(s) supporting use of the challenged procedure. Mathews, 424 U.S. at 335.

The interests involved in a divorce case include those of the divorcing parties and, if they have children, those of the children. The interests of the divorcing parents are financial, custodial, and emotional. As a result of divorce, financial and custodial rights and obligations are reconfigured. In addition, divorce terminates a legal partnership. For the children, there is an emotional fallout from the divorce, and an interest in the financial bargain struck by the divorcing parties, especially on child support. The most immediate interest of the children, however, is in the custodial outcome.[7] The position of the Miller children confirms this immediacy.

---

6. The Miller children read the landmark case of Stanley v. Illinois, 405 U.S. 645 (1972), and the subsequent cases of Smith v. Organization of Foster Families for Equality and Reform, 431 U.S. 816 (1977), and Duchesne v. Sugarman, 566 F.2d 817, 825 (2d Cir.1977), as establishing that the children of divorcing parents have a liberty interest in voicing their preferences on custody. This proposition is by no means undisputed. Although a number of Supreme Court cases have concluded that freedom of personal choice in matters of family life is protected by the Due Process Clause of the Fourteenth Amendment, see Smith v. Organization of Foster Families for Equality and Reform, 431 U.S. 816 (1977); Stanley v. Illinois, 405 U.S. 645 (1972), the Supreme Court has pointedly declined to state whether children have a liberty interest in maintaining a relationship with a parent. See Michael H. v. Gerald D., 491 U.S. 110, 130 (stating, "[w]e have never had occasion to decide whether a child has a liberty interest, symmetrical with that of her parent.") In maintaining her filial relationship. We also have no occasion in this case to decide whether minor children have a constitutionally protected liberty interest in the outcome of the divorce of their parents.

7. In Maine divorce law, the term "custody" has been replaced with the term "primary residence." See 19 M.R.S.A.

They do not want to intervene in their parents' divorce because of the potential impact on them of the property, alimony, or child support bargains that will be struck. Rather, the Miller children wish to participate in the reconfiguration of their family and advocate their preferences because their custody is at stake. They argue that this interest is not and cannot be met by the guardian ad litem, who is duty-bound to represent their best interests as she sees them.[8] They emphasize that the guardian ad litem's recommendations on custody are directly contrary to their wishes.[9]

In making this point, the Miller children link their custodial interest in the outcome of the divorce to forceful advocacy of their preference by independent counsel representing them as parties, and cite the absence of such advocacy as increasing the likelihood of an erroneous deprivation of their custodial interest. Implicit in that argument is the further contention that the preference of the children should have primacy when the court makes its custody determination. We reject that proposition. The best interest standard set forth in 19 M.R.S. § 752(5) appropriately makes the preference of the child only one of many factors that the court must consider.[10] The exclusion of children as parties in the divorce of their

§ 214(2)(A) & 752(5) (Supp.1995). In this opinion, the phrase "custodial outcome" therefore refers to the outcome of Clark and Eileen's divorce with respect to the primary residence of the children. The court awarded primary residence of the children to Eileen in its original order pending divorce: It Is further ORDERED that the primary residence of said minor children shall be with the Plaintiff [Eileen] and the Defendant [Clark] shall have reasonable rights of parent-child contact including visitation with Defendant. Subsequently, the court amended its order pending divorce and awarded primary residence of the children to Clark: The minor children of the parties, Carissa Noel Miller, Nicholas Russell Miller, and Dylan Patrick Miller shall maintain their primary residence with the Defendant, Clark Miller, with the Plaintiff. Eileen Miller, entitled to reasonable rights of parent/child contact including visitation with the Plaintiff.

8. The responsibilities of a guardian ad litem are currently embodied In 19 M.R.S.A. § 752–A (Supp.1995). At the time of the appointment of the guardian in this case, however, section 752–A had not been enacted. Instead, the responsibilities of guardians were elaborated in judicial opinions. According to those opinions, which formed the basis for the current statute, a guardian ad litem's central responsibility is to assist the court in its role as parens patriae to determine the best interests of the child(ren). Gerber v. Peters, 584 A.2d 605, 607 (Me.1990); Ziehm v. Ziehm, 433 A.2d 725, 729 (Me.1981).

9. In their brief, the children state that they have all expressed a preference for living with their mother. A review of the record, however, reveals that only Carissa and Nicholas have expressed a preference. According to the guardian ad litem, Dylan was "unable to express a meaningful preference" about where he wants to live. Dr. Robinson also did not report a preference on the part of Dylan.

10. 19 M.R.S.A. § 752(5)(Supp.1995) provides: The court, in making an award of parental rights and responsibilities with respect to a minor child, shall apply the standard of the best interest of the child. In making decisions regarding primary residence and parent-child contact, the court shall consider as primary the safety and well-being of the child. In applying this standard, the court shall consider the following factors: A. The age of the child; B. The relationship of the child with the child's parents and any other persons who may significantly affect the child's welfare; C. The preference of the child, if old enough to express a meaningful preference; D. The duration and adequacy of the child's current living arrangements and the desirability of maintaining continuity; E. The stability of any proposed living arrangements for the child; F. The motivation of the parties involved and their capacities to give the child love, affection and guidance; G. The child's adjustment to the child's present home, school and community; H. The capacity of each parent to allow and encourage frequent and continuing contact between the child and the other parent, including physical

parents, and the related possibility that there will be no forceful advocacy for the custodial preference of the children, does not increase the risk of erroneous custody determinations that disserve the best interests of children. The guardian ad litem is already an advocate for the best interest of the children in all of its complex dimensions.[11] The narrow focus of an attorney for the children, who would be obligated to carry out their preferences regardless of the wisdom of such a course, might well increase the likelihood of a custody determination that is not in the best interest of the children.

Finally, the State has a substantial interest in divorce proceedings that do not include children as parties represented by counsel. Divorce litigation would be complicated exponentially by the involvement of children as parties. Children could object to any settlement offer. They would have the right to participate in discovery and at hearings to present witnesses on their own behalf and cross-examine witnesses called by the other parties. Multiple children could insist on multiple representation. The occurrence of any or all of these probabilities would protract divorce litigation beyond current bounds, and result in a substantial additional financial burden on both the parties and our court system.[12]

In our view, the use of guardians ad litem to protect the best interests of children in divorce proceedings fully satisfies any federal constitutional requirements. Accordingly, the Miller children are not entitled to intervene in the divorce action of their parents and be represented by independent legal counsel.

.   .   .

NOTES

(1) For a discussion of theories on which it might be argued that children should have standing in cases such as *Miller*, see Ellen B. Wells, Unanswered Questions: Standing and Party Status of Children in Custody and Visitation Proceedings, 13 J.Am.Acad. Matrimonial Lawyers 95 (1995).

(2) Regardless of whether children have standing as parties, there are many instances when they might be entitled to independent representation. Determining

access; I. The capacity of each parent to cooperate or to learn to cooperate in child care; J. Methods for assisting parental cooperation and resolving disputes and each parent's willingness to use those methods; K. The effect on the child if one parent has sole authority over the child's upbringing; K–1. The existence of domestic abuse between the parents, in the past or currently, and how that abuse affects: (1) The child emotionally; and (2) The safety of the child; K–2. The existence of any history of child abuse by a parent; and L. All other factors having a reasonable bearing on the physical and psychological well-being of the child.

11. A guardian ad litem may also be made a full party in a divorce proceeding if the court concludes that it would be in the best interests of the children to do so. See 19 M.R.S.A. § 752–A. That determination was not made in this case.

12. The Miller children argue that this case involves only the "narrow" question of whether they, on the unique facts of this case, are entitled to intervene in the divorce action of their parents with an attorney of their choosing, and therefore we need not think about the implications of our decision for other divorce cases or custodial proceedings. We cannot Indulge that myopic view. None of the implications noted are fanciful once intervention is permitted.

exactly when counsel should be appointed and their has been the subject of increasing debate. See, e.g., Martin Guggenheim, The Right To Be Represented But Not Heard: Reflections on Legal Representation of Children, 59 N.Y.U. L.Rev. 76 (1984). At least nine states now have statutes that deal in part with the issues, and the American Academy of Matrimonial Lawyers in 1994 drafted a set of standards on the subject. Representing Children: Standards for Attorneys and Guardians ad Litem in Custody or Visitation Proceedings (With Commentary), 13 J.Am.Acad. Matrimonial Lawyers 1 (1995).* For a discussion of the project and its background, see Martin Guggenheim, The Making of Standards for Representing Children in Custody and Visitation Proceedings: The Reporter's Perspective, 13 J.Am.Acad. Matrimonial Lawyers 35 (1995). Section 1.1 of the Standards provides that:

> Courts should not routinely assign counsel or guardians ad litem for children in custody or visitation proceedings. Appointment of counsel or guardians should be preserved for those cases in which both parties request the appointment or the court finds after a hearing that appointment is necessary in light of the particular circumstances of the case.

Section 1.2 of the Standards provides that a person should be trained in representation of children in order to be eligible for appointment as counsel or guardian ad litem, and with regard to their roles Section 1.3 provides that:

> Whenever a court assigns counsel or a guardian ad litem for a child, the court should specify in writing the tasks expected of the representative. In the event the court does not specify the tasks expected of the representative, the representative's first action should be to seek clarification of the tasks expected of him or her.

(3) A special issue of the Fordham Law Review, Vol. 64, No. 4 is devoted to Ethical Issues in the Legal Representation of Children. It includes the Proceedings of The Conference on Ethical Issues in the Legal Representation of Children.

G.   Disputes Over Removal or Relocation

Baures v. Lewis

Supreme Court of New Jersey, 2001.
167 N.J. 91, 770 A.2d 214.

■ Long, J.

Ideally, after a divorce, parents cooperate and remain in close proximity to each other to provide access and succor to their children. But that ideal is not always the reality. In our global economy, relocation for employment purposes is common. On a personal level, people remarry and move away. Noncustodial parents may relocate to pursue other interests regardless of the strength of the bond they have developed with their children. Custodial parents may do so only with the consent of the former spouse. Otherwise, a court application is required.

Inevitably, upon objection by a noncustodial parent, there is a clash between the custodial parent's interest in self-determination and the non-

---

* Permission received from the American Academy of Matrimonial Lawyers to reprint excerpts from Representing Children.

custodial parent's interest in the companionship of the child. There is rarely an easy answer or even an entirely satisfactory one when a noncustodial parent objects. If the removal is denied, the custodial parent may be embittered by the assault on his or her autonomy. If it is granted, the noncustodial parent may live with the abiding belief that his or her connection to the child has been lost forever.

Courts throughout the country, grappling with the issue of relocation, have not developed a uniform approach. Ann M. Driscoll, Note, *In Search of a Standard: Resolving the Relocation Problem in New York*, 26 *Hofstra L.Rev.* 175, 176 (1997). Some use a presumption against removal as their point of departure; others use a presumption in favor of removal; still others presume nothing, but rely on a classic best-interests analysis. *Id.* at 178.

We have struggled to accommodate the interests of parents and children in a removal situation in our prior cases. *Holder v. Polanski*, 111 *N.J.* 344, 544 *A.*2d 852 (1988); *Cooper v. Cooper*, 99 *N.J.* 42, 491 *A.*2d 606 (1984). In so doing, we have developed something of a hybrid scheme. Although it is not based upon a presumption in favor of the custodial parent, it does recognize the identity of the interests of the custodial parent and the child, and, as a result, accords particular respect to the custodial parent's right to seek happiness and fulfillment. At the same time, it emphasizes the importance of the noncustodial parent's relationship with the child by guaranteeing regular communication and contact of a nature and quality to sustain that relationship. Further, it incorporates a variation on a best interests analysis by requiring proof that the child will not suffer from the move.

We revisit the issue in this appeal, not only to resolve the matter before us, but because of what we perceive as confusion among the bench, Bar, and litigants over the legal standards that should apply in addressing a removal application, and particularly over what role visitation plays in the calculus.

I

Carita Baures (Baures), a native of Wisconsin married Steven Lewis (Lewis), a native of Iowa and an officer in the United States Navy, on October 5, 1985, in Rothschild, Wisconsin. Their only child, Jeremy, was born on June 24, 1990. During the marriage, the couple lived in the various locations in which the Navy billeted them. In 1994, they moved to New Jersey when Lewis was stationed in Leonardo.

At age two, Jeremy began to exhibit developmental difficulties. By 1994, Jeremy, then aged four, was diagnosed with Pervasive Developmental Disorder (PDD), a form of autism.[1] Over the next few years, through trial

---

1. PDD is a lifelong disability and patients suffering from this disorder have difficulty with language and social communication. *The American Heritage Stedman's Medical Dictionary* 627 (1995). A cause has not been identified, but current research suggests that autism is caused by a biochemical or neurological disorder of the brain. Jeremy exhibits the following characteristics of autism: speech problems; repetition of what he hears; little interest in playing with others; no interest in being cuddled or

and error, the parents arranged an effective therapeutic and educational regimen for Jeremy through a combination of public school and the Douglass College Outreach Program.

In 1995, recognizing that their financial resources were being taxed to the limit, Baures and Lewis discussed moving to Wisconsin. Baures' parents live in Wisconsin and are retired school teachers who offered to help care for Jeremy while Baures and Lewis worked. According to both parties, the couple planned to move to Wisconsin after Lewis was discharged from the Navy in 1998. In anticipation of the discharge, Baures' parents sold their home in Schofield, Wisconsin and moved to Galesville because, according to them, it was a short distance to the Chileda Institute (Chileda), a Program for autistic children. Lewis flew to Wisconsin to research job opportunities.

In 1996, escalating marital discord brought the case to court. Lewis sought custody of Jeremy because he believed that Baures was going to remove the child to Wisconsin. One day before the hearing, Baures filed a complaint for divorce alleging extreme cruelty. In response to Lewis's application for custody, Baures denied that she had any intention of moving Jeremy out of New Jersey. The parties then entered into a consent order that provided for custody and visitation and restrained both parties from leaving New Jersey with Jeremy. Baures and Lewis separated in late 1996. In April 1997, Baures filed an amended complaint for divorce requesting permission to relocate to Wisconsin. A three-day trial was held to resolve the issue.

At trial, Baures claimed that she should be allowed to relocate to Wisconsin because the parties had limited funds and could no longer afford to live in New Jersey without the help of her parents. Without a vehicle (Lewis had taken the family car), Baures had no way to get Jeremy to his special programming or to his doctors. Moreover, because Jeremy is a child with special needs, he could not be admitted to regular day care. Baures testified that in Wisconsin, her parents would be able to provide child care and shelter for her and Jeremy so that she could work.

Although Baures holds a master's degree in human resources management that she obtained in 1989, she never worked in that field and has held only part-time cleaning and baby-sitting jobs since Jeremy was born. She attempted to find more suitable employment but, of the twenty-four jobs in her field that she researched, Baures testified that none was able to provide child care for Jeremy because of his special needs.

In June of 1996, Baures' parents came to New Jersey to help her care for Jeremy and remained for over a year after Lewis took Baures' name off the checkbook, credit cards and savings account, and denied her the use of the automobile. In that time, Baures' father transported Jeremy to and from his programming, and provided additional child care. In total, Baures' parents paid her in excess of one-thousand dollars per month to supple-

touched; limited interest in activities; insistence on following strict routines; prone to tantrums.

ment the court ordered child support she received in the amount of one-hundred dollars per week.

Baures testified that the Chileda Institute offers outreach programming to children who have been diagnosed with autism or PDD. The program is similar to the Douglas Program in that it provides trained professional therapy for the child at home. Chileda is located within twenty minutes of Baures' parents' house. Baures inquired whether Jeremy would be eligible for services at Chileda and faxed the school Jeremy's diagnostic materials and other documentation. A representative of Chileda responded that, based on the materials she had received, Jeremy would be eligible. She could not, however, say specifically what programming would be provided until there was an accurate assessment of Jeremy to determine what approach should be incorporated into the home program. Baures conceded that, although her father visited Chileda, she never did so, and that what she knew about the program was elicited from telephone calls, literature, and her father's visit. Baures offered no information regarding what services are available in the Wisconsin public schools.

Baures acknowledged that Lewis should have ongoing contact with Jeremy. To encourage the relationship, she stated that Lewis could visit Jeremy one week a month and stay in her parents' basement free of charge. That offer was reiterated by Baures' father. In addition, Baures agreed to pay half of the transportation costs from New Jersey to Wisconsin if Lewis could obtain an economical rate.

On cross-examination, Baures testified that Lewis was a good father to Jeremy, and that his presence in Jeremy's life is important to the child's progress. Moreover, she acknowledged that in the initial action instituted by Lewis to prevent her from moving to Wisconsin, she had stated that if Jeremy was to leave the State of New Jersey, he would lose his relationship with his father and would be prevented from attending the Douglass Program, the best available program, both of which would adversely affect his progress.

Joan Hurst, a coordinator at the Douglass Program, testified at trial on Baures' behalf. Hurst was offered and accepted as an expert in the field of autism and PDD. Hurst explained that a child with autism needs a highly structured, full-day program beyond normal school hours that teaches and applies behavior modification techniques throughout the day. Hurst explained that a strong family support system is important because:

> [i]t's really the basis of the child's program. The school and the professionals can lay the foundation and show the family what to do, but it needs follow through in all areas of their lives. And since home is really the most common place for them and in their security and where they are most of the time, everything needs to continue when they come home from school. And it needs to continue to go on with the family at home.

When asked what a family member might have to do to continue home programming, Hurst went on:

> every minute is a teaching minute ... especially with Jeremy having the diagnosis of autism, since language is such an issue, there should

be constant modeling of language. There should be constant modeling of appropriate reactions to situations.... There should be constant teaching on how to successfully complete daily activities of the day. And constant teaching and modeling and prompting of what is normal and acceptable to society of things that we go through each day.

Hurst made several recommendations with respect to Jeremy that include the following: that any program for Jeremy must be highly structured and staffed by professionals experienced in the field of autism; have a low student/teacher ratio; provide appropriate peer models; operate on a twelve month basis; support the family; offer a trained professional to assist Jeremy as a shadow,[2] and provide speech therapy sessions as needed. She did not render an opinion regarding whether the Wisconsin public schools and Chileda could provide those services.

At the time of the hearing, Lewis, who holds a bachelor's degree in economics, was employed in the United States Navy, and had been for over nineteen years. His rank was that of a chief petty officer, electronics technician. He indicated that his ultimate career goal is to be an electrical engineer, but that he will be required to take further courses. Further, he claimed, based on advertisements in the newspaper and talking with people in the area, Galesville, Wisconsin offered no jobs. He stated that he has no property or family in Wisconsin, however, his mother lives in Minnesota, about a five-hour distance from Wisconsin. At the time of the hearing, his visitation schedule was two afternoons a week from 4:30 p.m. until 7:30 p.m. and alternate weekends.

Lewis testified that his command would not let him travel to Wisconsin one week a month to visit his son. Regardless, he stressed that he could not visit at the Baures's house due to the estranged relationship with their daughter. Lewis stated that Jeremy will regress if he is separated from him for an extended period of time.

The trial court denied the removal. Although acknowledging that Baures had a good faith reason to move (financial and emotional stability and caregiving by her parents), the court held that the move would adversely affect Lewis' visitation with Jeremy; that Lewis could not visit regularly or relocate because of his Navy service; and that he does not have the financial resources to travel back and forth to Wisconsin. Further, the court held that Baures had not provided sufficient evidence that the educational opportunities for Jeremy in Wisconsin are comparable to that which he was receiving in New Jersey. Accordingly, the court held it was not in Jeremy's "best interests" to move to Wisconsin.

After being denied permission to remove Jeremy from New Jersey, Baures moved for reconsideration. The court entered a Judgment of Divorce in February 1998, and ordered a "best interests" evaluation by Dr. Amy Altenhaus. Although there was no issue as to custody, Dr. Altenhaus stated her opinion that it was in Jeremy's best interest that his mother continue as the primary custodial parent. However, Altenhaus found that

---

2. A "shadow" is a trained worker that follows the child around the classroom and encourages appropriate activities and re- sponses. Hurst was one of Jeremy's shadows from February 1997 to the end of the school year.

Baures and Lewis complemented each other's parenting styles. For example, Altenhaus observed that Baures attends to the everyday details of Jeremy's life, and is caring and supportive. In contrast, she found that Lewis wanted desperately for Jeremy to be "normal" and seemed "motivated to do whatever he can to help this boy be 'normal.'" Furthermore,

> [w]hile [Mr. Lewis] may need to have a more realistic picture of what is possible for Jeremy, nonetheless his style with Jeremy is certainly important as well. Mr. Lewis gives Jeremy more room to explore and to do rough and tumble play. Mr. Lewis will take him places and let him explore more on his own without some of the structure that Ms. Baures imposes. While this structure is very important for Jeremy's acquisition of skills, it is also important that children like this have a chance to explore their environment in a less structured manner as well ... Jeremy clearly loves and enjoys being with both of his parents.

She stated that a move to Wisconsin "does not seem" to be in Jeremy's interest because Jeremy was doing well in East Brunswick, and because he would be unable to sustain a long distance relationship with his father who could not relocate because of his Navy commitments. Reconsideration was denied.

Lewis was discharged from the Navy on July 31, 1998. He found a full-time job in Edison as an electronics technician at a starting salary of $26,500, and a part-time job as a quality assurance tester for $9 an hour. As a result of Lewis' discharge, Baures requested the trial court to conduct a hearing on the issue of whether Lewis could relocate to Wisconsin pursuant to the requirements of *Rampolla v. Rampolla,* 269 *N.J.Super.* 300, 307–08, 635 *A.*2d 539 (App.Div.1993). *Rampolla* holds that in a removal case, the court should inquire about the capacity of the noncustodial parent to relocate as a method of ensuring the vitality of a shared custody arrangement. *Id.* at 307, 635 *A.*2d 539. Lewis testified that he had investigated job opportunities in Wisconsin, but had no success. He said that the jobs that were available in Galesville, a very small town, were not in his area of expertise and were low paying. He identified only two jobs that were commensurate with his skill level, but claimed that they were located in Milwaukee, a six-hour drive from Galesville. Lewis said that he had considered working at IBM, located in nearby Rochester, Minnesota, but that he did not have the necessary digital electronics background or computer skills.

To counter Lewis's arguments, Baures offered the testimony of Arnold Gelfman, an employability and vocational expert from the Career Choice Institute of New Jersey. Gelfman testified in detail, concluding that Lewis had significant job opportunities as an electronics technician in Wisconsin and Minnesota at comparable or higher wages than in New Jersey and that the availability of such employment would increase at greater rates between 1994 and 2005 in Wisconsin and Minnesota than in New Jersey.

Lewis downplayed those statistics and said that they did not provide information about exactly where in Wisconsin and Minnesota those jobs could be found; did not identify any particular employer or industry in either state that had an immediate need for electronics' technicians; did not consider the fact that his expertise is limited to analog electronics; and did not recognize that not all electronics' technicians have the same skills. On cross-examination, Lewis acknowledged that his entire job search consisted of looking at classified ads on the Internet and that he never sent a letter or made a phone call to any potential employer in Wisconsin or went to that state to seek employment.

Based on the *Rampolla* hearing, and the testimony from the 1997 trial, the trial court affirmed its denial of Baures' motion. In so doing, the court stated that Baures was required to prove "the prospective advantages" of the move and that she had failed to do so. The court reaffirmed the conclusion that Baures' motion was made in good faith but noted that Jeremy is doing well in New Jersey; that the proximity of both parents is important to a special needs' child; and that there was insufficient evidence adduced to show that Lewis could obtain employment in Wisconsin at a location near Jeremy. Most importantly, in denying removal, the court relied on the fact that Baures did not provide adequate evidence of the comparability of educational and therapeutic facilities available to Jeremy in Wisconsin.

The Appellate Division affirmed the ruling in an unpublished decision. We granted certification.

II

Historically, courts throughout the country have disfavored removal of a child from the jurisdiction after divorce. Edwin J. Terry et al., *Relocation: Moving Forward or Moving Backward?*, 31 Tex. Tech. L.Rev. 983, 986 (2000). Some courts continue to adhere to that view and apply a presumption against removal based on the notion that it will necessarily destroy the relationship between the noncustodial parent and the child....

Recently, however, many courts have reassessed the burden cast on custodial parents who desire to relocate with their children. Reasons for the change include the geographic mobility of the United States population and post-divorce demands. Chris Ford, *Untying the Relocation Knot: Recent Developments and a Model for Change*, 7 Colum. J. Gender & L. 1, 7 (1997). For example, within four years of separation and divorce about one-fourth of mothers with custody move to a new location. *Ibid.* In addition, one in five Americans overall changes his or her residence each year. *Ibid.*

That the ability to communicate over long distances has been revolutionized during the years since the first removal cases is also undeniable. Computers, technology and competitive long-distance rates, among other things, essentially have changed the way people connect with each other when they are apart.

Most importantly, social science research links a positive outcome for children of divorce with the welfare of the primary custodian and the stability and happiness within that newly formed post-divorce household. *See* Judith S. Wallerstein & Tony J. Tanke, *To Move or Not to Move: Psychological and Legal Considerations in the Relocation of Children Following Divorce*, 30 *Fam. L.Q.* 305, 311–12 (1996) (stating that psychological adjustment of custodial parent consistently has been found to be related to child's adjustment); Marsha Kline et al., *Children's Adjustment in Joint and Sole Custody Families,* 25 *Develop. Psych.* 430, 431 (1989) (noting that research indicates that factor associated with good outcomes for children in post-divorce families includes a close, sensitive relationship with a psychologically intact custodial parent). Justice Garibaldi touched on that in *Cooper* sixteen years ago when she said:

> [T]he child's quality of life and style of life are provided by the custodial parent. That the interests of the child are closely interwoven with those of the custodial parent is consistent with psychological studies of children of divorced or separated parents. One researcher has concluded that [o]f all factors related to the child's way of coping with loss [of a parent because of divorce or death], the role of the home parent seemed most central. Some years after the divorce or death, the well-being of the child appeared closely related to the well-being of the [home]parent. [L. Tessman, *Children of Parting Parents* 516 (1978).]

Other investigators have found that there is an increased emotional dependence on the custodial parent after divorce and that children of all ages "were in trouble" when the home parent-child relationship was affected by stress on the home-parent, such as "loneliness and discouragement." J. Wallerstein & J. Kelly, *Surviving the Breakup* 114, 224–225 (1980). [*Cooper, supra,* 99 N.J. at 53–54,491 A.2d 606.]

Since that time, social science research has uniformly confirmed the simple principle that, in general, what is good for the custodial parent is good for the child.

To be sure, the research also affirms the importance of a loving and supportive relationship between the noncustodial parent and the child. Frank F. Furstenberg & Andrew J. Cherlin, *Divided Families: What Happens to Children When Parents Part* 72 (1991); Michael E. Lamb, *Fathers and Child Development: An Integrative View of the Role of the Father in Child Development* (rev. ed. 1981); Janet R. Johnson, *Children's Adjustment in Sole Compared to Joint Custody Families and Principles for Custody Decision Making,* 33 *Fam. & Conciliation Cts. Rev.* 415, 419 (1995); Marsha Kline et al., *Children's Adjustment in Joint and Sole Custody Families,* 25 *Develop. Psych.* 430, 431 (1989). What it does not confirm is that there is any connection between the duration and frequency of visits and the quality of the relationship of the child and the noncustodial parent. Wallerstein, *supra,* 30 *Fam. L.Q.* at 312 ("There is no evidence in Dr. Wallerstein's work of many years, including the ten and fifteen year longitudinal study, or in that of any other research, that frequency of visiting or amount of time spent with the noncustodial parent over the child's entire growing-up years is significantly related to good outcome in the child or adolescent."); *see also* Frank F. Furstenberg & Andrew J. Cherlin, *Divided Families: What Happens to Children When Parents Part* 72 (1991) (noting no connection between frequency of noncustodial visits and good outcomes for child). Although confidence that he or she is loved and supported by both parents is crucial to the child's well-being after a divorce, no particular visitation configuration is necessary to foster that belief. *Ibid.* According to scholars, so long as the child has regular communication and contact with the noncustodial parent that is extensive enough to sustain their relationship, the child's interests are served. *Ibid.;* Judith

S. Wallerstein et al., *The Unexpected Legacy of Divorce* 215(2000). In short, a happy, productive, supportive custodial household along with a loving, sustaining relationship with the noncustodial parent are what is necessary to the adjustment of a child of divorce. Eleanor E. Maccoby & Robert H. Mnookin, *Dividing the Child: Social and Legal Dilemmas of Custody* (1992); E. Mavis Hetherington et al., *Long-Term Effects of Divorce and Remarriage on the Adjustment of Children,* 24 *J. Amer. Acad. Child Psych.* 518, 518 (1985).

As a result of all those factors, many courts have significantly eased the burden on custodial parents in removal cases. . . .

The shift in relocation law is underscored in three fairly recent court decisions. In *Tropea v. Tropea,* 87 *N.Y.*2d 727, 642 *N.Y.S.*2d 575, 665 *N.E.*2d 145, 151 (1996), the New York Court of Appeals replaced the "exceptional circumstances" requirement with a general "best interests" test in relocation cases. Prior to *Tropea,* if a litigant could not prove exceptional circumstances justifying relocation, and the relocation would deprive the noncustodial parent of regular access, New York courts were compelled to deny the relocation request without considering the child's best interests. *Id.* at 149–50. *Tropea* changed direction and began a focus not on the needs and desires of the parents, but on the way those needs and desires relate to the child.

Likewise, in *In re Marriage of Burgess,* 13 *Cal.*4th 25, 51 *Cal.Rptr.*2d 444, 913 *P.*2d 473, 481 (1996), the California Supreme Court abandoned the prior hostile approach taken toward the custodial parent in relocation cases. The court rejected a rigid test that required a custodial parent to show a "necessity" for the move and said,

> the "necessity" of relocating frequently has little, if any, substantive bearing on the suitability of a parent to retain the role of a custodial parent. A parent who has been the primary caretaker for minor children is ordinarily no less capable of maintaining the responsibilities and obligations of parenting simply by virtue of a reasonable decision to change his or her geographical location. [*Id.* at 481.]

In place of the "necessity test," *Burgess* directed the lower courts to take into account the custodial parent's "presumptive right" to move.

The Colorado Supreme Court followed suit in *In re Marriage of Francis, supra,* 919 *P.*2d at 782. There, the custodial parent sought to move east to attend school. *Id.* at 778. The trial court ruled that if she enrolled in the school program, she would lose custody of her children. *Id.* at 779. The Colorado Supreme Court reversed and held that the child's interests are so interwoven with the new family unit that a court must consider the custodial parent's interests:

> [W]e find that the child's best interests are served by preserving the custodial relationship, by avoiding relitigation of custody decisions, and by recognizing the close link between the best interests of the custodial parent and the best interest of the child. In a removal dispute, this leads logically to a presumption that the custodial parent's choice to move with the children should generally be allowed. [*Id.* at 784.]

Those cases embody the growing trend in the law easing restrictions on the custodial parent's right to relocate with the children and recognizing the identity of interest of the custodial parent and child.

III

An analysis of New Jersey's removal scheme begins with *N.J.S.A.* 9:2–2. That act provides:

> When the Superior Court has jurisdiction over the custody and maintenance of the minor children of parents divorced, separated or living separate, and such children are natives of this State, or have resided five years within its limits, they shall not be removed out of its jurisdiction against their own consent, if of suitable age to signify the same, nor while under that age without the consent of both parents, unless the court, upon cause shown, shall otherwise order.

Several cases are instructive regarding the import of the "cause" provision of that statute. In *Cooper, supra,* 99 *N.J.* at 46, 491 *A.*2d 606, the trial court was faced with an application by a custodial parent (the mother) to move to California to take advantage of a business opportunity. Her former husband objected on the basis that the reasons for the move were frivolous; that the children had a deep connection to his close-knit east coast family; and that he could not arrange blocks of time in his schedule to make his former wife's visitation proposal realistic. *Id.* at 48, 491 *A.*2d 606. The trial court allowed the move and the Appellate Division reversed. *Id.* at 49, 491 *A.*2d 606.

We granted certification and began our opinion by emphasizing that the purpose underlying *N.J.S.A.* 9:2–2 is

> to preserve the rights of the noncustodial parent and the child to maintain and develop their familial relationship. This mutual right of the child and the noncustodial parent to develop and maintain their familial relationship is usually achieved by means of visitation between them. Because the removal of the child from the state may seriously affect the visitation rights of the noncustodial parent, the statute requires the custodial parent to show cause why the move should be permitted.

[*Id.* at 50–51, 491 *A.*2d 606.]

However, citing *D'Onofrio v. D'Onofrio,* 144 *N.J.Super.* 200, 365 *A.*2d 27 (Ch.Div.), *aff'd o.b.,* 144 *N.J.Super.* 352, 365 *A.*2d 716 (App.Div.1976) and *Helentjaris v. Sudano,* 194 *N.J.Super.* 220, 476 *A.*2d 828 (App.Div. 1984), we also recognized a countervailing interest:

> '[T]he family unity which is lost as a consequence of the divorce is lost irrevocably, and there is no point in judicial insistence on maintaining a wholly unrealistic simulation of unity.' [citations omitted]. The realities of the situation after divorce compel the realization that the child's quality of life and style of life are provided by the custodial parent. That the interests of the child are closely interwoven with those of the custodial parent is consistent with psychological studies of children of divorced or separated parents.

[*Cooper, supra,* 99 *N.J.* at 53–54, 491 A.2d 606.]

We further stated that

> [t]he custodial parent who bears the burden and responsibility for the child is entitled, to the greatest possible extent, to the same freedom to seek a better life for herself or himself and the children as enjoyed by the noncustodial parent. [*Id.* at 55, 491 A.2d 606.]

By those acknowledgments, we identified a fundamental tension that exists in a removal case: the interests of the custodial parent in self-governance are pitted against the interests of the noncustodial parent in maintaining his or her relationship with the child. Against that backdrop, we went on to set forth the methodology to be utilized in a removal case:

> When removal is challenged under *N.J.S.A.* 9:2–2, we hold that to establish sufficient cause for the removal, the custodial parent initially must show that there is a real advantage to that parent in the move and that the move is not inimical to the best interests of the children.... It is only after the custodial parent establishes these threshold requirements that the court should consider, based on evidence presented by both parties, visitation and other factors to determine whether the custodial parent has sufficient cause to permit removal under the statute....

* * *

> The first factor to be considered is the prospective advantages of the move in terms of its likely capacity for either maintaining or improving the general quality of life of both the custodial parent and the children. The second factor is the integrity of both the custodial parent's motives in seeking to move and the noncustodial parent's motives in seeking to restrain such a move (e.g., whether the custodial parent is motivated by a desire to defeat and frustrate the noncustodial parent's visitation rights and remove himself or herself from future visitation orders or whether the noncustodial parent is contesting the move mainly to impede the custodial parent's plans or to secure a financial advantage with respect to future support payments). And the third factor is whether, under the facts of the individual case, a realistic and reasonable visitation schedule can be reached if the move is allowed. In a given case, evidence of any of these factors may be used to militate against either the threshold showing of the custodial parent for removal, or the arguments of the noncustodial parent against removal.

* * *

> Since the noncustodial parent has the necessary information to demonstrate that an alternative visitation schedule is not feasible because of distance, time, or financial restraints, we place the burden on that parent to come forward with evidence that a proposed alternative visitation schedule would be impossible or so burdensome as to affect unreasonably and adversely his or her right to preserve his or her relationship with the child. [*Id.* at 56–58, 491 A.2d 606.]

In *Cooper,* we specifically noted that the advantages of the move should not be sacrificed solely to maintain the "same" visitation schedule where a reasonable alternative visitation scheme is available and the advantages of the move are substantial.

Four years later, we revisited the issue of removal. In *Holder, supra,* 111 *N.J.* at 347, 544 *A.*2d 852, the custodial parent (a mother) requested permission from the trial court to allow her to move to Connecticut because she wanted to live near family members who could provide her with emotional and financial support, she had a job offer in Connecticut and also planned to attend college there. The trial court denied the mother's request because she failed to make the threshold showing that there was a "real advantage" to the move. *Id.* at 351, 544 *A.*2d 852. Specifically, the court held that she failed to establish that the cost of living was lower in Connecticut or that superior housing, educational opportunities, job opportunities, or child care were available there. *Ibid.* Thus, even though the move was not inimical to the best interests of the children, the trial court held that the personal satisfaction and emotional support for the custodial parent were not enough to satisfy the "real advantage" test. *Ibid.* The Appellate Division affirmed.

We granted certification and began our analysis by underscoring what we had recognized in *Cooper*—that after divorce, the family unit is forever altered and that it is the reality of that changed family structure that must be accounted for in a removal case. *Id.* at 349, 544 *A.*2d 852. Focusing on the liberty interests of custodial parents and the fundamental inequity that emerges out of a scheme that holds a custodial parent in this state while allowing a noncustodial parent complete freedom of movement, we said:

> As men and women approach parity, the question arises when a custodial mother wants to move from one state to another, why not? Until today, our response has included the requirement that the custodial parent establish, among other things, a real advantage to that parent from the move. *Cooper v. Cooper,* 99 *N.J.* 42, 56, 491 *A.*2d 606 (1984). We now modify that requirement and hold that a custodial parent may move with the children of the marriage to another state as long as the move does not interfere with the best interests of the children or the visitation rights of the noncustodial parent. [*Id.* at 349, 544 *A.*2d 852.]

More particularly, we revisited *Cooper* and held that "any sincere, good-faith reason will suffice," and that a custodial parent need not establish a "real advantage from the move." *Id.* at 352–53, 544 *A.*2d 852.

Motives are relevant, but if the custodial parent is acting in good faith and not to frustrate the noncustodial parent's visitation rights, that should suffice. Maintenance of a reasonable visitation schedule by the noncustodial parent remains a critical concern, but in our mobile society, it may be possible to honor that schedule and still recognize the right of a custodial parent to move. In resolving the tension between a custodial parent's right to move and a noncustodial parent's visitation rights, the beacon remains the best interests of the children. [*Id.* at 353–54, 544 *A.*2d 852.]

That modification recognized that, because the real advantage test was too great a burden, the *Cooper* calculus had failed in its intent to allow custodial parents the same freedom enjoyed by noncustodial parents to seek a better life. Expressing the *Cooper* standard in *Holder* terms, removal should not be denied solely to maintain the same visitation schedule where a reasonable alternative visitation scheme is available and there are good faith reasons for the move.

Under *Holder* it is not any effect on visitation, but an adverse effect that is pivotal. 111 *N.J.* at 352, 544 *A.2d* 852. An adverse effect is not a mere change or even a lessening of visitation; it is a change in visitation that will not allow the noncustodial parent to maintain his or her relationship with the child. Such a change implicates what *Holder* describes as a best interest analysis, although not the classic one: "The emphasis ... should be not on whether the children or the custodial parent will benefit from the move, but on whether the children will suffer from it." *Id.* at 353, 544 *A.2d* 852. Implicit in that aspect of *Holder* is the notion that a visitation schedule that will not maintain the relationship of the noncustodial parent and the child would cause the child to suffer.

It would be fair to say that together *Cooper* and *Holder* elucidated the general philosophy underpinning the removal scheme of *N.J.S.A.* 9:2–2. It is equally fair to say that those decisions left open questions. For example, although the cases following *Cooper* and *Holder* are clear about the custodial parent's burden of proving good faith, they are unclear and at variance regarding the burden of going forward, the ultimate burden of proof, and the elements of the burden in determining whether the move would be inimical to the interests of the child.

That is particularly true when visitation is the nub of the noncustodial parent's objection. Thus, *Cerminara v. Cerminara*, 286 *N.J.Super.* 448, 669 *A.2d* 837 (App.Div.1996), *Winer v. Winer*, 241 *N.J.Super.* 510, 575 *A.2d* 518 (App.Div.1990), and *Murnane v. Murnane*, 229 *N.J.Super.* 520, 552 *A.2d* 194 (App.Div.1989), all declared that it is the burden of the custodial parent to prove a good faith reason for the move. However, *Murnane* then added to the custodial parent's burden the obligation to "offer evidence" of a practical alternative visitation schedule and held that the noncustodial parent has the burden of "coming forward" with evidence that the proposed schedule would be unworkable and would "adversely affect" his relationship with the child. *Murnane, supra,* 229 *N.J.Super.* at 531, 552 *A.2d* 194.

In *Winer,* a different panel of the Appellate Division held that once the party seeking removal establishes a good faith reason for the move, "[t]he burden remains with the noncustodial parent *to prove* that as a result of relocation, *visitation will be affected in a way that will prove harmful to the child[ren]*." *Winer, supra,* 241 *N.J.Super.* at 518, 575 *A.2d* 518 (emphasis added).

In *Cerminara,* the court set forth the scheme this way:

Under the *Holder* test, "a custodial parent may move with the children of the marriage to another state as long as the move does not interfere with the best interests of the children or the visitation rights of the noncustodial parent." *Id.* at 349, 544 A.2d 852. *All the custodial parent need establish is that he or she has a "good-faith reason" for making the move. Id.* at 353, 544 A.2d 852. In short, absent "an adverse effect on the noncustodial parent's visitation rights or other aspects of a child's best interests, the custodial parent should enjoy the same freedom of movement as the noncustodial parent." *Id.* at 352, 544 A.2d 852. [*Cerminara, supra,* 286 *N.J.Super.* at 454–55, 669 A.2d 837 (*emphasis added*).]

Again, although each of the cited decisions is clear regarding the burden of the party seeking removal to prove a good faith reason, a clear paradigm for trying a removal case cannot be distilled from them, especially when a change in visitation is the crux of the objection advanced by the noncustodial parent.

Roiling the waters, *McMahon v. McMahon,* 256 *N.J.Super.* 524, 528, 607 A.2d 696 (Ch.Div.1991) has held that the *Cooper/Holder* removal scheme applies in a joint physical custody situation while *Voit v. Voit,* 317 *N.J.Super.* 103, 106, 721 A.2d 317 (Ch.Div.1998), has held that it does not. *See also Chen v. Heller,* 334 *N.J.Super.* 361, 378–79, 759 A.2d 873 (App.Div. 2000) (upholding the *Voit* analysis). Further, at least one commentator writing on the subject of removal in New Jersey has characterized our cases as creating a "rebuttable presumption" in favor of relocation. Carol S. Bruch & Janet M. Bowermaster, *The Relocation of Children and Custodial Parents: Public Policy Past and Present,* 30 *Fam. L.Q.* 245, 283 (1996). Our task is to clarify those matters.

IV

In order to describe the template for a removal case, some preliminary observations are in order. A removal case is entirely different from an initial custody determination. When initial custody is decided, either by judicial ruling or by settlement, the ultimate judgment is squarely dependent on what is in the child's best interests. *N.J.S.A.* 9:2–4; . . . Whoever can better advance the child's interests will be awarded the status of custodial parent.

Removal is quite different. In a removal case, the parents' interests take on importance. However, although the parties often do not seem to realize it, the conflict in a removal case is not purely between the parents' needs and desires. Rather, it is a conflict based on the extent to which those needs and desires can be viewed as intertwined with the child's interests. *Cooper,* and more particularly, *Holder,* recognize that subtlety by according special respect to the liberty interests of the custodial parent to seek happiness and fulfillment because that parent's happiness and fulfillment enure to the child's benefit in the new family unit. At the same time those cases underscore the importance of the child's relationship with the noncustodial parent and require a visitation schedule sufficient to support and nurture that relationship. The critical path to a removal disposition therefore is not necessarily the one that satisfies one parent or even splits the difference between the parents, but the one that will not cause detriment to the child.

One final important point is that the *Cooper/Holder* scheme is entirely inapplicable to a case in which the noncustodial parent shares physical custody either *de facto* or *de jure* or exercises the bulk of custodial responsibilities due to the incapacity of the custodial parent or by formal or informal agreement. In those circumstances, the removal application effectively constitutes a motion for a change in custody and will be governed initially by a changed circumstances inquiry and ultimately by a simple best interests analysis. *Chen, supra,* 334 *N.J.Super.* at 381–82, 759 *A.2d* 873. Obviously then, the preliminary question in any case in which a parent seeks to relocate with a child is whether it is a removal case or whether by virtue of the arrangement between the parties, it is actually a motion for a change in custody.

V

With those principles in mind, in assessing whether to order removal, the court should look to the following factors relevant to the plaintiff's burden of proving good faith and that the move will not be inimical to the child's interest: (1) the reasons given for the move; (2) the reasons given for the opposition; (3) the past history of dealings between the parties insofar as it bears on the reasons advanced by both parties for supporting and opposing the move; (4) whether the child will receive educational, health and leisure opportunities at least equal to what is available here; (5) any special needs or talents of the child that require accommodation and whether such accommodation or its equivalent is available in the new location; (6) whether a visitation and communication schedule can be developed that will allow the noncustodial parent to maintain a full and continuous relationship with the child; (7) the likelihood that the custodial parent will continue to foster the child's relationship with the noncustodial parent if the move is allowed; (8) the effect of the move on extended family relationships here and in the new location; (9) if the child is of age, his or her preference; (10) whether the child is entering his or her senior year in high school at which point he or she should generally not be moved until graduation without his or her consent; (11) whether the noncustodial parent has the ability to relocate; (12) any other factor bearing on the child's interest.

Obviously not all factors will be relevant and of equal weight in every case. For example, in a case in which the parties have no extended family in either location, that factor will not be considered. Likewise, when the children are not of the age of reason, consent will not come into play. Contrariwise, if the focus of the challenge to removal is the inadequacy of the out-of-state health or educational facilities, that factor will take on greater significance. It is likely that the main objection that will be lodged by the majority of noncustodial parents will be the change in the visitation structure thus; that will be the primary factor for consideration in most cases.

Again, a mere change, even a reduction, in the noncustodial parent's visitation is not an independent basis on which to deny removal. It is one important consideration relevant to the question of whether a child's interest will be impaired, although not the only one. It is not the alteration in the visitation schedule that is the focus of the inquiry. Indeed, alterations in the visitation scheme when one party moves are inevitable and acceptable. If that were not the case, removal could never occur and what *Cooper* and *Holder* attempted to achieve would be illusory.

We reiterate, however, the importance of mutual efforts to develop an alternative visitation scheme that can bridge the physical divide between the noncustodial parent and the child. By mutual is meant that the noncustodial parent is not free to reject every scheme offered by the custodial parent without advancing other suggestions. Innovative technology should be considered where applicable, along with traditional visitation initiatives. In many cases, vacations, holidays, school breaks, daily phone calls, and E-mail, for example, may sustain a parent-child relationship as well as alternate weekends. No set scheme can ever guarantee a relationship. What is necessary is that communication and visitation is extensive enough to maintain and nurture the connection between the noncustodial parent and the child.

VI

That said, the template for a removal case becomes clearer. As we have indicated, under *Cooper* and *Holder,* the moving party ultimately bears a two-pronged burden of proving a good faith reason for the move and that the child will not suffer from it.

In terms of the burden of going forward, the party seeking to move, who has had an opportunity to contemplate the issues, should initially produce evidence to establish *prima facie* that (1) there is a good faith reason for the move and (2) that the move will not be inimical to the child's interests. Included within that *prima facie* case should be a visitation proposal. By *prima facie* is meant evidence that, if unrebutted, would sustain a judgment in the proponent's favor.

The initial burden of the moving party is not a particularly onerous one. It will be met, for example, by a custodial parent who shows that he is seeking to move closer to a large extended family that can help him raise his child; that the child will have educational, health and leisure opportunities at least equal to that which is available here, and that he has thought out a visitation schedule that will allow the child to maintain his or her relationship with the noncustodial parent. If, for some reason, the custodial parent fails to produce evidence on the issues to which we have referred, the noncustodial parent will have no duty to go forward and a judgment denying removal should be entered.

Once that *prima facie* case has been adduced, however, the burden of going forward devolves upon the noncustodial parent who must produce evidence opposing the move as either not in good faith or inimical to the child's interest. She might, for example, challenge the move as pretextual and show that the custodial parent's past actions reveal a desire to stymie her relationship with the child, thus bearing on good faith. She might also offer proof that the move will take the child away from a large extended family that is a mainstay in the child's life. Alternatively, she could adduce evidence that educational, avocational or health care available in the new location are inadequate for the child's particular needs. She might also proffer evidence that because of her work schedule, neither relocation nor reasonable visitation is possible, and that those circumstances will cause the child to suffer. Where visitation is the issue, in order to defeat the custodial parent's proofs, the burden is on the noncustodial parent to produce evidence, not just that the visitation will change, but that the change will negatively affect the child.

Indeed, there are powerful visitation related issues that can defeat a removal application. For example, if the child has an emotional disorder and the noncustodial parent has provided a needed safety net, the impact of a move, with concomitant irregularity in visitation, might well cause the child to suffer. Likewise, as in this case, the proofs may reveal that because of the child's developmental disorder, a change in visitation will be harmful. But a child need not be ill or disabled for removal to cause harm because of diminished visitation. For example, if the child has a particular talent or skill, a noncustodial parent who has driven him or her to early and late practices, assisted the teacher or coach, organized road trips, attended competitions, and is the constant support in the child's dedication to the talent, can advance a persuasive argument that the inability to fulfill that role and pursue that connection with the child will be the kind of harm that should tip the scales against removal.

Although children are generally resilient and can adapt to removal so long as their relationship with the noncustodial parent is fully sustained through a new visitation scheme, the noncustodial parent remains free to adduce evidence that for particular reasons, and in light of the unique facts surrounding his or her relationship with the child, such a conclusion should not be drawn. The possible evidential proffers in a case like this are as varied as human nature itself.

It goes without saying that a noncustodial parent who is lackadaisical or sporadic in his or her visitation ordinarily will be unable to prevail in a removal case. That is not by way of retaliation for past inadequacies but because he or she will not be able to show that particularized harm will occur from removal.

After the noncustodial parent has gone forward, the moving party may rest or adduce additional evidence regarding the noncustodial parent's motives, the visitation scheme or any other matter bearing on the application. The trial court must then apply the burden of proof and the standards to which we have previously adverted.

VII

As we have indicated, in order for Baures to prevail on her removal application the trial judge must be satisfied that she has a good faith reason for the move and that Jeremy will not suffer from it. Because there was confusion at trial over the details of the standard, and because, with the passage of time, the evidence adduced in the earlier proceedings may have changed, we reverse and remand for further proceedings consistent with this opinion.

Plainly Baures met the burden of establishing that she has a good faith reason for the move—the help and support of her parents. Further she has offered Lewis financial and logistical help to ameliorate visitation problems. However, she fell short in adducing sufficient evidence of the comparability of the special education program available in Wisconsin's public schools and private agencies.[3] Jeremy has a serious developmental disorder. Fine tuning a program for him is not an easy task. Indeed the program coordinator from Douglass, an expert in the field of PDD who testified on Baures' behalf, made a number of specific recommendations at the hearing regarding what kind of a full-day program is necessary for Jeremy. She did not address Chileda nor did she comment on Wisconsin's public school program. Baures needs to produce evidence of the comparability of Wisconsin's public and private accommodations and that Jeremy will be accepted and not just placed on a wait list. The best program in the world is of no value if access is lacking.

Further, the record does not contain any specific information regarding Jeremy's current level of PDD including projections for improvement or current programming. The most recent information available is child study team evaluations conducted in 1997 by the East Brunswick public school system. Jeremy's level of functioning is directly related to the programming issue. If his functioning is very low and unlikely to change, the considerations regarding comparability of program would be entirely different than if he was functioning at a high level and continuing to make progress.

Assuming that Baures is able to adduce that proof, then Lewis may produce evidence about the particularized harm that would occur to Jeremy if removal is allowed. He may challenge the comparability of accommodations for Jeremy in Wisconsin. In terms of visitation, he may offer evidence that because of his disorder, Jeremy needs his regular visitation with Lewis, that Jeremy is incapable of maintaining any long distance relationship, that Jeremy's incapacity precludes meaningful computer, telephonic and written communication, and that other modes of communication cannot compensate for loss of visitation. On that score, expert testimony will likely be required. Baures may counter with an expert of her own on all the aforementioned issues, and because Jeremy's deficit is at least in part in the nature of an attachment disorder, on the question of whether he would suffer less than the average child if his visitation with his father became irregular.

If sporadic visitation with Lewis would be problematic for Jeremy, Lewis's ability to relocate with his family to Wisconsin becomes a question. As far as the record reveals, his connections with New Jersey are tenuous at best, and he should produce evidence regarding his capacity to move. We note that the evidence he adduced at the *Rampolla* hearing was entirely inadequate to sustain his position that he could not obtain employment in Wisconsin. Indeed, he made no legitimate effort to seek employment there. That of course is not the sole determinant. *Rampolla* itself recognizes that relocation by the noncustodial parent is likely to occur only in unusual cases. We note, also, that Lewis failed to offer any evidence that his ties to

3. Under the Individuals with Disabilities Education Act (IDEA), 20 U.S.C. § 1400, handicapped children are entitled to a free and appropriate education. New Jersey has complied with this mandate, N.J.S.A. 18A:46–19.1, as has Wisconsin, Wis. Stat. Ann. § 115.81 (West 2001).

New Jersey are such that he should not be viewed as able to relocate. Finally, inquiry should be made regarding Baures' parents' willingness to remain with her in New Jersey. To be sure they have no duty to do so. But if they are amenable, that is a factor to be considered.

After all the evidence is in, in order to warrant removal, the trial court will have to be satisfied by a preponderance of credible evidence that Baures has proved a good faith reason to move and that Jeremy will not suffer therefrom. The matter should be scheduled for trial expeditiously.

VIII

In a removal case, the burden is on the custodial parent, who seeks to relocate, to prove two things: a good faith motive and that the move will not be inimical to the interests of the child. Visitation is not an independent prong of the standard, but an important element of proof on the ultimate issue of whether the child's interest will suffer from the move.

IX

The judgment under review is reversed and the matter remanded for further proceedings consonant with this opinion.

NOTES

(1) Custody decrees generally are modifiable prospectively, based on changed circumstances since the time of the original decree. While an outright ban on a parent's changing residence would impinge on the right to travel, at the least, a court's power to modify custody based on changed circumstances effectively can veto by forcing the custodial parent to leave the child behind. The approaches and results of courts have varied considerably, as the court's discussion in *Baures* reveals. For example, In *Mize v. Mize*, 621 So.2d 417 (Fla.1993), the Supreme Court of Florida followed an approach set forth in a prior District Court of Appeals decision, *Hill v. Hill*, 548 So.2d 705 (Fla. 3d DCA 1989), review denied, 560 So.2d 233 (Fla.1990). The court explained:

> [So] long as the parent who has been granted the primary custody of the child desires to move for a well-intentioned reason and founded belief that the relocation is best for that parent's—and, it follows, the child's—well-being, rather than from a vindictive desire to interfere with the visitation rights of the other parent, the change in residence should ordinarily be approved. However, Judge Schwartz recognized that circumstances may exist that would justify a departure from the general rule. For example, when older children are involved, the trauma of leaving friends, other family members, and school may outweigh the trauma in separating from the primary residential parent. Thus, in making the ultimate decision, trial courts must consider and weigh factors discussed by Judge Nesbitt, such as:
>
> 1.   Whether the move would be likely to improve the general quality of life for both the primary residential spouse and the children.
>
> 2.   Whether the motive for seeking the move is for the express purpose of defeating visitation.
>
> 3.   Whether the custodial parent, once out of the jurisdiction, will be likely to comply with any substitute visitation arrangements.

4.   Whether the substitute visitation will be adequate to foster a continuing meaningful relationship between the child or children and the noncustodial parent.

5.   Whether the cost of transportation is financially affordable by one or both of the parents.

6.   Whether the move is in the best interests of the child. (This sixth requirement we believe is a generalized summary of the previous five.)

Shaw, J., concurring only in the result, added:

The majority's liberal standard favoring removal will work no inequity in those cases where the noncustodial parent has failed to exercise decisionmaking and visitation rights or has done so in a negative manner. However, where the noncustodial parent has exercised extensive parenting and visitation rights, perhaps at great personal sacrifice, and has worked hard to create a loving bond with the child, the majority opinion will invite clear injustice—as well as immeasurable heartbreak—for that parent and child, in case after case within our state. To my mind, when a parent is granted the great benefits of primary physical residence he or she may reasonably be expected to shoulder the responsibilities as well, and this may at times include reasonable geographical limitations during the child's minority.

Half a century ago in Fields v. Fields, 143 Fla. 886, 890, 197 So. 530, 531 (1940), this Court embraced the then-popular "tender years" doctrine, ruling: "Other things being equal ... the mother of infants of tender years [is] best fitted to bestow the motherly affection, care, companionship, and early training suited to their needs." Today's majority opinion is a throwback to those days— in fact, today's opinion actually expands the "tender years" doctrine to hold that the convenience of the custodial parent is tantamount to the best interests of the child. This mindset ignores virtually the entire weight of social and psychological data in the intervening half century, summarized above, which indicates that the interests of the child are best served by shared parenting and "frequent and continuing contact with both parents"—a fact long recognized by our Legislature.

(2) In Scott v. Scott, 276 Ga. 372, 578 S.E.2d 876 (2003), the question before the Georgia Supreme Court was the legality of a self-executing provision of a divorce decree that would automatically transfer child custody from the mother to the father is she were to leave the county of residence without regard for whether this would be in the best interests of the children. Reversing the trial court's decision that had upheld the provision, the appellate court explained:

... [S]elf-executing change of custody provisions are not rendered valid merely because the initial award of custody may have been based upon the child's best interests. It is not the factual situation at the time of the divorce decree that determines whether a change of custody is warranted but rather the factual situation at the time the custody modification is sought.

(3) As seen in the West Virginia statute which follows, some states have sought to codify provisions dealing with relocation or removal.

WEST VIRGINIA CODE (West)

§ 48–9–403.   Relocation of a parent

(a) The relocation of a parent constitutes a substantial change in the circumstances under subsection 9–401(a) of the child only when it significantly impairs either parent's ability to exercise responsibilities that the parent has been exercising.

(b) Unless otherwise ordered by the court, a parent who has responsibility under a parenting plan who changes, or intends to change, residences for more than ninety days must give a minimum of sixty days' advance notice, or the most notice practicable under the circumstances, to any other parent with responsibility under the same parenting plan. Notice shall include:

(1) The relocation date;

(2) The address of the intended new residence;

(3) The specific reasons for the proposed relocation;

(4) A proposal for how custodial responsibility shall be modified, in light of the intended move; and

(5) Information for the other parent as to how he or she may respond to the proposed relocation or modification of custodial responsibility.

Failure to comply with the notice requirements of this section without good cause may be a factor in the determination of whether the relocation is in good faith under subsection (d) of this section and is a basis for an award of reasonable expenses and reasonable attorney's fees to another parent that are attributable to such failure.

The supreme court of appeals shall make available through the offices of the circuit clerks and the secretary-clerks of the family courts a form notice that complies with the provisions of this subsection. The supreme court of appeals shall promulgate procedural rules that provide for an expedited hearing process to resolve issues arising from a relocation or proposed relocation.

(c) When changed circumstances are shown under subsection (a) of this section, the court shall, if practical, revise the parenting plan so as to both accommodate the relocation and maintain the same proportion of custodial responsibility being exercised by each of the parents. In making such revision, the court may consider the additional costs that a relocation imposes upon the respective parties for transportation and communication, and may equitably allocate such costs between the parties.

(d) When the relocation constituting changed circumstances under subsection (a) of this section renders it impractical to maintain the same proportion of custodial responsibility as that being exercised by each parent, the court shall modify the parenting plan in accordance with the child's best interests and in accordance with the following principles:

(1) A parent who has been exercising a significant majority of the custodial responsibility for the child should be allowed to relocate with the child so long as that parent shows that the relocation is in good faith for a legitimate purpose and to a location that is reasonable in light of the purpose. The percentage of custodial responsibility that constitutes a significant majority of custodial responsibility is seventy percent or more. A relocation is for a legitimate purpose if it is to be close to significant family or other support networks, for significant health reasons, to protect the safety of the child or another member of the child's household from significant risk of harm, to pursue a

significant employment or educational opportunity or to be with one's spouse who is established, or who is pursuing a significant employment or educational opportunity, in another location. The relocating parent has the burden of proving of the legitimacy of any other purpose. A move with a legitimate purpose is reasonable unless its purpose is shown to be substantially achievable without moving or by moving to a location that is substantially less disruptive of the other parent's relationship to the child.

(2) If a relocation of the parent is in good faith for legitimate purpose and to a location that is reasonable in light of the purpose and if neither has been exercising a significant majority of custodial responsibility for the child, the court shall reallocate custodial responsibility based on the best interest of the child, taking into account all relevant factors including the effects of the relocation on the child.

(3) If a parent does not establish that the purpose for that parent's relocation is in good faith for a legitimate purpose into a location that is reasonable in light of the purpose, the court may modify the parenting plan in accordance with the child's best interests and the effects of the relocation on the child. Among the modifications the court may consider is a reallocation of primary custodial responsibility, effective if and when the relocation occurs, but such a reallocation shall not be ordered if the relocating parent demonstrates that the child's best interests would be served by the relocation.

(4) The court shall attempt to minimize impairment to a parent-child relationship caused by a parent's relocation through alternative arrangements for the exercise of custodial responsibility appropriate to the parents' resources and circumstances and the developmental level of the child.

(e) In determining the proportion of caretaking functions each parent previously performed for the child under the parenting plan before relocation, the court may not consider a division of functions arising from any arrangements made after a relocation but before a modification hearing on the issues related to relocation.

. . .

NOTE

Professor Merle H. Weiner, in her article Inertia and Inequality: Reconceptualizing Disputes Over Parental Relocation, 40 U.C. Davis L.Rev. 1747 (2007), sensitively proposes a practical way of better reconciling many of the disputes over reconciliation in a way that would better maintain relationships between children and both parents. This would be to encourage noncustodial parents to relocate with the child and the custodial parent.

In re Amberley D.

Supreme Judicial Court of Maine, 2001.
775 A.2d 1158.

■ ALEXANDER, J.

Joann R., mother of Amberley D., appeals the judgment of the Waldo County Probate Court (*Mailloux, J.*) appointing Diana and Richard B.

coguardians of Amberley pursuant to 18–A M.R.S.A. § 5–204 (1998 & Supp.2000). On appeal, Joann contends that: (1) the court erred by appointing temporary guardians without notice to her; (2) the court lacked jurisdiction and venue over the guardianship petition; (3) no clear and convincing evidence supported the petition; and (4) the guardianship statute is unconstitutional as applied. We affirm the judgment.

I. CASE HISTORY

Amberley D. was born on January 19, 1985, and grew up with her mother, Joann R., her stepfather, Charles R., and her two siblings, moving many times and living in Maine, Vermont and several other states.[4] Joann and Charles separated several times, during which Joann and the children utilized various temporary living arrangements, including friends' homes, motels, and a shelter.

In the spring of 1999, Joann and Charles separated and filed for divorce in Vermont. Joann and the children then moved to New Hampshire, staying in motels and with friends. Amberley, who was in the eighth grade, stopped going to school. By this time, she had been enrolled in approximately twenty-seven different schools. Amberley testified that Joann was abusing drugs and alcohol, providing them to her, staying out all night drinking, and engaging in sexual activity in front of her. Amberley also testified that she had been sexually molested several times, and that she reported this to Joann, who had done nothing.

In late 1999, Amberley ran away on two occasions. She was found at her boyfriend's home and then at Charles' home, and returned to Joann. In January 2000, Amberley ran away again to Charles' home in Vermont. Charles drove her to a friend's place in Massachusetts. From there, Amberley took a bus to Augusta to meet Charles' parents, Diana and Richard B., who reside in Stockton Springs. Joann notified law enforcement agencies that Amberley was missing, then departed for a California vacation. Upon her return, she was informed by the Waldo County Sheriff's Office that Amberley was with Diana and Richard B.

Shortly after Amberley's arrival, Diana and Richard B. filed a petition requesting appointment as temporary coguardians of a minor pursuant to 18–A M.R.S.A. § 5–207(c) (Supp.2000).[5] After a hearing, the court granted a temporary, six-month guardianship, finding that Amberley was in an intolerable living situation at her mother's, inadequately cared for, and subject to abuse by others. Joann was served with notice of the appointment and, representing herself, filed a motion to dismiss the temporary guardianship. Subsequently, through counsel, she filed another motion to dismiss the guardianship and an answer to the petition. After a hearing, the court denied the motion.

---

4. Amberley's biological father, Mark M., never developed a relationship with her and did not participate in the proceedings.

5. Section 5–207(c) states that "[i]f necessary, the court may appoint a temporary guardian, with the status of an ordinary guardian of a minor, but the authority of a temporary guardian may not last longer than 6 months."

A hearing on full guardianship was held, which Joann had notice of and participated in. The court found by clear and convincing evidence a history of abuse, neglect, and mistreatment, and a living situation that was at least temporarily intolerable for Amberley, and that the guardians would provide a living situation in her best interest. *See* 18–A M.R.S.A. § 5–204(c). The court then entered an order appointing Diana and Richard B. full coguardians of Amberley pursuant to 18–A M.R.S.A. § 5–204.[6]

The record does not indicate that there was any other prior or pending order from any other court in any state addressing custody or parental rights for Amberley during this time.

Joann brought this appeal from the Probate Court's order.

II. NOTICE

The Probate Court, in appointing Diana and Richard B. temporary guardians of Amberley, waived notice of hearing to Amberley's parents pursuant to 18–A M.R.S.A. § 5–207, which states that "[u]pon a showing of good cause, the court may waive service of the notice of hearing on any person, other than the minor, if the minor is at least 14 years of age." Joann contends that the Uniform Child Custody Jurisdiction, and Enforcement Act (UCCJEA), 19–A M.R.S.A. §§ 1731–1783 (Supp.2000), which defers to state notice provisions for child custody determinations, is preempted by the Parental Kidnapping Prevention Act (PKPA), 28 U.S.C. § 1738A (1994 & Supp.2000), and that she was entitled to notice of the emergency guardianship hearing under the PKPA.

The UCCJEA provides that notice to persons outside the state "may be given in a manner prescribed by the law of this State for service of process or by the law of the state in which the service is made." 19–A M.R.S.A. § 1738(1). In the event of a conflict, the PKPA preempts the UCCJEA. *See Barclay v. Eckert*, 2000 ME 10, ¶ 8, 743 A.2d 1259, 1262; *Guardianship of Gabriel W.*, 666 A.2d 505, 508 (Me.1995). However, the PKPA addresses jurisdictional issues only when existing orders have been entered by courts of other states concerning the custody or visitation of a child. *See Thompson v. Thompson*, 484 U.S. 174, 177, 108 S.Ct. 513, 98 L.Ed.2d 512 (1988) ("[a]s the legislative scheme suggests, and as Congress explicitly specified, one of the chief purposes of the PKPA is to avoid jurisdictional competition and conflict between State courts") (citation omitted). The PKPA is not

---

6. Section 5–204 states in relevant part:

The court may appoint a guardian or coguardians for an unmarried minor if:

(a) All parental rights of custody have been terminated or suspended by circumstance or prior court order;

(b) Each living parent whose parental rights and responsibilities have not been terminated or the person who is the legal custodian of the unmarried minor consents to the guardianship and the court finds that the consent creates a condition that is in the best interest of the child; or

(c) The person or persons whose consent is required under subsection (b) do not consent, but the court finds by clear and convincing evidence that the person or persons have failed to respond to proper notice or a living situation has been created that is at least temporarily intolerable for the child even though the living situation does not rise to the level of jeopardy required for the final termination of parental rights, and that the proposed guardian will provide a living situation that is in the best interest of the child.

applicable in this case because no competing custody order regarding Amberley was pending or entered in another state.[7]

III. DUE PROCESS

Joann also contends that 18–A M.R.S.A. § 5–207, as applied, violates due process by depriving her of fundamental parental rights. In assessing what process is due, we apply the *Mathews* factors:

First, the private interest that will be affected by the official action; second, the risk of an erroneous deprivation of such interest through the procedures used, and the probable value, if any, of additional or substitute procedural safeguards; and finally, the Government's interest, including the function involved and the fiscal and administrative burdens that the additional or substitute procedural requirement would entail.

In re Heather C., 2000 ME 99, ¶ 22, 751 A.2d 448, 454 (citing *Mathews v. Eldridge,* 424 U.S. 319, 335, 96 S.Ct. 893, 47 L.Ed.2d 18 (1976)). *See also Rideout v. Riendeau,* 2000 ME 198, ¶ 14, 761 A.2d 291, 297–98 ("[i]f we can reasonably interpret a statute as satisfying those constitutional requirements, we must read it in such a way, notwithstanding other possible unconstitutional interpretations of the same statute").

Joann has a fundamental parental right, and the government has a significant interest in protecting children. *See Heather C.,* 2000 ME 99, ¶ ¶ 23–28, 751 A.2d at 454–56. The risk of a due process violation occurs when an emergency guardian may be appointed without notice to parents, temporarily depriving them of parental rights, before a hearing takes place. However, section 5–207(c) limits the emergency guardianship to six months. Further, upon notice that a guardian has been appointed, a parent can petition for removal of the guardian pursuant to 18–A M.R.S.A. § 5–212 (1998),[8] [FN5] entitling them to a hearing. At the hearing, the guardian has the burden of demonstrating that continuation of the guardianship is in the child's best interest. 18–A M.R.S.A. § 5–212(d). Joann received notice of the six-month guardianship appointment, filed a motion to dismiss, and a prompt hearing was held on her motion, at which her attorneys were present. She also received notice of and participated in the hearing on full guardianship. Thus, the guardianship statute, providing for waiver of notice in limited circumstances, but with subsequent opportunity to be heard, did not violate Joann's due process rights.

IV. JURISDICTION

Joann contends that New Hampshire has jurisdiction over the guardianship petition pursuant to the PKPA and the UCCJEA. As set forth

---

7. However, the PKPA is relevant to initial custody determinations by providing guidelines to prevent jurisdictional disputes. *See Wambold v. Wambold,* 651 A.2d 330, 332 (Me.1994).

8. Section 5–212 reads in relevant part:

(a) Any person interested in the welfare of a ward, or the ward, if 14 or more years of age, may petition for removal of a guardian on the ground that removal would be in the best interest of the ward.

A guardian may petition for permission to resign. A petition for removal or for permission to resign may, but need not, include a request for appointment of a successor guardian.

(b) After notice and hearing on a petition for removal or for permission to resign, the court may terminate the guardianship and make any further order that may be appropriate.

above, the PKPA is not directly at issue where no competing court order is involved. However, the jurisdictional requirements of the PKPA, which are similar but not identical to the UCCJEA, must be met, or the decree risks being denied full faith and credit by courts of other states. *See Wambold v. Wambold,* 651 A.2d 330, 333 (Me.1994).

Both the PKPA and the UCCJEA provide that a state has jurisdiction over a child custody proceeding if the state is the "home state" of the child on the date the proceeding is commenced, or was the home state within six months before the date the proceeding is commenced.[9] *See* 28 U.S.C. § 1738A(c); 19–A M.R.S.A. § 1745. The PKPA and the UCCJEA define the home state as the state in which the child lived with a parent, or a person acting as a parent, for at least six consecutive months immediately before the commencement of a child custody proceeding, and include periods of temporary absence as part of the period. 28 U.S.C. § 1738A(b)(4); 19–A M.R.S.A. § 1732(7).

Immediately prior to the filing of the temporary guardianship petition, Amberley lived in New Hampshire, but for less than six months. Nevertheless, Joann contends that New Hampshire is Amberley's home state because she lived there for almost six months, last attended school there, and had contacts with individuals providing services in the state, such as her physician and the New Hampshire Department of Health and Human Services' workers concerning her truancy. However, this evidence is inadequate because the six-month requirement was not met, due to Joann and Amberley's transitory living situation. New Hampshire cannot be considered Amberley's home state.

When the child has no home state, the PKPA and the UCCJEA require the court to examine whether a sufficiently significant connection and substantial evidence exists to exercise jurisdiction. Pursuant to the PKPA, in the absence of a home state, a state can exercise jurisdiction when it is in the child's best interest because "the child and his parents, or the child and at least one contestant, have a significant connection with such State other than mere physical presence," and "substantial evidence" is available in the state concerning the child's care. 28 U.S.C. § 1738A(c)(2)(B). The corresponding UCCJEA provision, which does not include the "best interest" language, states that jurisdiction is proper when "the child and at least one parent or a person acting as a parent" has a significant connection with the state. 19–A M.R.S.A. § 1745(1)(B)(1).

Diana and Richard B. are residents of Maine. They have had physical custody and care of Amberley since her arrival in this state, and they are the parents of her stepfather. The record indicates that Amberley has visited them on a regular basis in the past, and that she lived and attended school in Maine for periods during 1991–97. Consequently, the significant connection and substantial evidence requirements were satisfied under the UCCJEA and the PKPA, and the Probate Court has jurisdiction over the guardianship petition. *See Gabriel W.,* 666 A.2d at 509–10.

---

9. The UCCJEA's child custody juris-diction provisions generally track the PKPA's, although they differ slightly in some respects. *See Wambold,* 651 A.2d at 332–33; 19–A M.R.S.A. § 1745 comment (2000); 19–A M.R.S.A. § 1748 comment (2000).

Regarding Joann's claim that venue did not exist, under 18–A M.R.S.A. § 5–205 (1998), venue for guardianship proceedings for minors is "in the place where the minor resides or is present." Amberley's presence within Maine was determinative in establishing venue. *See Guardianship of Zachary Z.,* 677 A.2d 550, 552–53 (Me.1996).

V. SUFFICIENCY OF THE EVIDENCE

Pursuant to 18–A M.R.S.A. § 5–204(c), absent the consent of a parent or legal custodian to the guardianship appointment, the Probate Court must find by clear and convincing evidence that "a living situation has been created that is at least temporarily intolerable for the child even though the living situation does not rise to the level of jeopardy required for the final termination of parental rights, and that the proposed guardian will provide a living situation that is in the best interest of the child." Neither the child protective statute, 22 M.R.S.A. §§ 4001–4091 (1992 & Supp.2000), nor the protection from abuse statute, 19–A M.R.S.A. §§ 4001–4014 (1998 & Supp.2000), prohibits the Probate Court from appointing emergency guardians for minors, absent parental consent, when the requisite findings are made.

On a direct appeal from the Probate Court, we review the court's findings for clear error. *See Conservatorship of Justin R.,* 662 A.2d 232, 234 (Me.1995) (citing *Estate of Paine,* 609 A.2d 1150, 1152 (Me.1992)). In its guardianship order, the court found that the testimony established a history of abuse, neglect and mistreatment of Amberley by her mother. Among the evidence cited by the court was the unstable living arrangement involving multiple moves, and Amberley's fear for her own safety. The court further cited the testimony that Joann used alcohol and marijuana and provided them to Amberley, and that she engaged in sexual activity in Amberley's presence. In addition, the court cited Joann's apparent disregard for Amberley's well-being in taking a vacation when she was missing. The court determined that Diana and Richard B., with whom Amberley had spent considerable time during her life, offer her a stable, loving home and have met her physical, educational, emotional, and social needs.

The evidence is sufficient to support the court's findings that a living situation was created that was at least temporarily intolerable for Amberley and that Diana and Richard B. provide a living situation in her best interests. Joann claims that the testimony presented at the hearing was self-interested and conflicting. However, it is the factfinder's responsibility to assess the credibility of witnesses and the weight and significance of the evidence. *Guardianship of Boyle,* 674 A.2d 912, 913 (Me.1996) (citation omitted). Absent clear error, we defer to that assessment. *Id.*

Amberley's age and her participation in the proceedings further supports the court's best interest determination. Amberley was fifteen at the time the petition was filed and granted, and the record indicates she nominated Diana and Richard B. to be her guardians pursuant to 18–A M.R.S.A. § 5–206 (1998).[10] Minors who are older are permitted, under

---

10. Section 5–206 states in relevant part that "[t]he court shall appoint a person nominated by the minor, if the minor is 14 years of age or older, unless the court finds

certain circumstances, to exercise a greater degree of choice. *See, e.g.,* 15 M.R.S.A. § 3506–A (Supp.2000) (allowing sixteen-year-olds to seek emancipation). The court did not err in appointing guardians based on this evidence.

VI. CONSTITUTIONALITY

Apart from her notice claim, Joann challenges the constitutionality of the guardianship statute by contending her parental rights have effectively been terminated, but that unlike a child protective termination proceeding, no home study was made, and no agency or individual will work with Joann towards reunification. However, guardianship determinations are not final. Under 18–A M.R.S.A. § 5–212(a), any person who is interested in the welfare of the ward, or the ward if over fourteen years old, may petition for removal of the guardian. When the guardian does not consent to removal, the guardian has the burden of showing, by a preponderance of the evidence, that continuation of the guardianship is in the best interest of the ward pursuant to 18–A M.R.S.A. § 5–212(d).[11] Because the parent retains the right to regain custody, the same degree of procedural safeguards as in termination proceedings is not constitutionally required. *See, e.g., In re Sabrina M.,* 460 A.2d 1009, 1015–16 (Me.1983) ("the nature of the interests concerned in a child protection proceeding significantly differs from that in a proceeding to terminate parental rights").

Finally, we do not address the question of visitation. The record does not indicate that Joann has made an effort to obtain contact with Amberley, or that Diana and Richard B. attempted to restrict visitation between them. As a result, this issue is not reached.

The entry is:

Judgment affirmed.

NOTES

(1) Family law traditionally has been within the province of the states. This has lead to many problems involving conflicting provisions. In 1958 the National Conference of Commissioners on Uniform Laws, facing an increasingly transient population, attempted to deal with problems of custody decree recognition and modification through a Uniform Child Custody Jurisdiction Act. Their product was widely accepted among the states; its basic approach was to maintain custody jurisdiction in the original or rendering state (the "home" state) so long as significant contacts with it remain. Also provided in the various versions of the At which followed were provisions for interstate cooperation, and also for voluntary relinquishment of jurisdiction based on *forum non conveniens.*

In 1980 the U.S. Congress adopted the Parental Kidnaping Prevention Act. This federal act, passed rather quietly as an adjunct to the Pneumococcal Vaccine Act, nailed down the provision for "home state" jurisdiction over custody decrees in order to deter interstate abduction in child custody disputes. As a federal law

the appointment contrary to the best interests of the minor."

11. Because Joann has not yet petitioned for removal of the guardian, we do not reach her claims that the process for such a petition would violate her due process rights.

enacted under the Full Faith and Credit Clause of the U.S. Constitution, it has primacy over the state provisions and the Uniform Laws.

In 1997 the Uniform Child Custody Jurisdiction and Enforcement Act (UC-CJEA) became the latest in the long line of UCCJA revisions. Its ostensible purpose was to harmonize state efforts in the enforcement of the PKPA and disputes stemming from the UCCJA. It adopts the strict federal provisions for home state jurisdiction. It did not solve all the problems, as the previous case illustrates. The full text of the UCCJEA can be found in 9 (part 1A) U.L.A. 649 (1999), and in Walter Wadlington and Raymond O'Brien, Family Law Statutes, International Conventions and Uniform Laws (3d Ed. 2007, Foundation Press).

(2) The key provision of the PKPA is 28 USCA § 1738A:

Full faith and credit given to child custody determinations

(a) The appropriate authorities of every State shall enforce according to its terms, and shall not modify except as provided in subsections (f), (g) and (h), of this section, any custody determination or visitation determination made consistently with the provisions of this section by a court of another State.

(b) As used in this section, the term—

(1) "child" means a person under the age of eighteen;

(2) "contestant" means a person, including a parent, who claims a right to custody or visitation of a child;

(3) "custody determination" means a judgment, decree, or other order of a court providing for the custody of a child, and includes permanent and temporary orders, and initial orders and modifications;

(4) "home State" means the State in which, immediately preceding the time involved, the child lived with his parents, a parent, or a person acting as parent, for at least six consecutive months, and in the case of a child less than six months old, the State in which the child lived from birth with any of such persons. Periods of temporary absence of any of such persons are counted as part of the six-month or other period;

(5) "modification" and "modify" refer to a custody or visitation determination which modifies, replaces, supersedes, or otherwise is made subsequent to, a prior custody or visitation determination concerning the same child, whether made by the same court or not;

(6) "person acting as a parent" means a person, other than a parent, who has physical custody of a child and who has either been awarded custody by a court or claims a right to custody;

(7) "physical custody" means actual possession and control of a child; and

(8) "State" means a State of the United States, the District of Columbia, the Commonwealth of Puerto Rico, or a territory or possession of the United States.

(c) A child custody or visitation determination made by a court of a State is consistent with the provisions of this section only if—

(1) such court has jurisdiction under the law of such State; and

(2) one of the following conditions is met:

(A) such State (i) is the home State of the child on the date of the commencement of the proceeding, or (ii) had been the child's home State within six months before the date of the commencement of the proceeding and the child is absent from such State because of his removal or retention by a contestant or for other reasons, and a contestant continues to live in such State;

(B)(i) it appears that no other State would have jurisdiction under subparagraph (A), and (ii) it is in the best interest of the child that a court of such State assume jurisdiction because (I) the child and his parents, or the child and at least one contestant, have a significant connection with such State other than mere physical presence in such State, and (II) there is available in such State substantial evidence concerning the child's present or future care, protection, training, and personal relationships;

(C) the child is physically present in such State and (i) the child has been abandoned, or (ii) it is necessary in an emergency to protect the child because the child, a sibling, or parent of the child has been subjected to or threatened with mistreatment or abuse;

(D)(i) it appears that no other State would have jurisdiction under subparagraph (A), (B), (C), or (E), or another State has declined to exercise jurisdiction on the ground that the State whose jurisdiction is in issue is the more appropriate forum to determine the custody or visitation of the child, and (ii) it is in the best interest of the child that such court assume jurisdiction; or

(E) the court has continuing jurisdiction pursuant to subsection (d) of this section.

(d) The jurisdiction of a court of a State which has made a child custody or visitation determination consistently with the provisions of this section continues as long as the requirement of subsection (c)(1) of this section continues to be met and such State remains the residence of the child or of any contestant.

(e) Before a child custody determination is made, reasonable notice and opportunity to be heard shall be given to the contestants, any parent whose parental rights have not been previously terminated and any person who has physical custody of a child.

(f) A court of a State may modify a determination of the custody of the same child made by a court of another State, if—

(1) it has jurisdiction to make such a child custody determination; and

(2) the court of the other State no longer has jurisdiction, or it has declined to exercise such jurisdiction to modify such determination.

(g) A court of a State shall not exercise jurisdiction in any proceeding for a custody determination commenced during the pendency of a proceeding in a court of another State where such court of that other State is exercising jurisdiction consistently with the provisions of this section to make a custody or visitation determination.

(h) A court of a State may not modify a visitation determination made by a court of another State unless the court of the other State no longer has jurisdiction to modify such determination or has declined to exercise jurisdiction to modify such determination.

The PKPA also provides for use of the Federal Parent Locator Service in determination of child custody in cases involving parental kidnaping of a child.

(3) Among the types of cases which ultimately lead to widespread state adoption of the UCCJA in its various iterations were those in which a noncustodial parent removed a child to another jurisdiction in the hope of making the custodial parent relitigate a custody proceeding (or at least a modification request) there. These were sometimes described as "seize and run" cases. Professor Russell

Coombs has suggested that the new provisions in the UCCJA replacing the former definition of "home state" have the potential to encourage the use of self help by non-parents. See Russell M. Coombs, Child Custody and Visitation By Non–Parents Under the New Uniform Child Custody Jurisdiction and Enforcement Act: A Re–Run of Seize-and-Run, 16 J.Am.Acad. Matrimonial Lawyers 1 (1999).

Thompson v. Thompson

Supreme Court of the United States, 1988.
484 U.S. 174, 108 S.Ct. 513, 98 L.Ed.2d 512.

■ JUSTICE MARSHALL delivered the opinion of the Court.

We granted certiorari in this case to determine whether the Parental Kidnaping Prevention Act of 1980, 28 U.S.C. § 1738A, furnishes an implied cause of action in federal court to determine which of two conflicting state custody decisions is valid.

The Parental Kidnaping Prevention Act (PKPA or Act) imposes a duty on the States to enforce a child custody determination entered by a court of a sister State if the determination is consistent with the provisions of the Act. In order for a state court's custody decree to be consistent with the provisions of the Act, the State must have jurisdiction under its own local law and one of five conditions set out in § 1738(c)(2) must be met. Briefly put, these conditions authorize the state court to enter a custody decree if the child's home is or recently has been in the State, if the child has no home State and it would be in the child's best interest for the State to assume jurisdiction, or if the child is present in the State and has been abandoned or abused. Once a State exercises jurisdiction consistently with the provisions of the Act, no other State may exercise concurrent jurisdiction over the custody dispute, § 1738A(g), even if it would have been empowered to take jurisdiction in the first instance,[2] and all States must accord full faith and credit to the first State's ensuing custody decree.

As the legislative scheme suggests, and as Congress explicitly specified, one of the chief purposes of the PKPA is to "avoid jurisdictional competition and conflict between State courts." This case arises out of a jurisdictional stalemate that came to pass notwithstanding the strictures of the Act. In July 1978, respondent Susan Clay (then Susan Thompson) filed a petition in Los Angeles Superior Court asking the court to dissolve her marriage to petitioner David Thompson and seeking custody of the couple's infant son, Matthew. The court initially awarded the parents joint custody of Matthew, but that arrangement became infeasible when respondent decided to move from California to Louisiana to take a job. The court then entered an order providing that respondent would have sole custody of Matthew once she left for Louisiana. This state of affairs was to remain in effect until the court investigator submitted a report on custody, after which the court intended to make a more studied custody determination.

Respondent and Matthew moved to Louisiana in December of 1980. Three months later, respondent filed a petition in Louisiana state court for

---

2. The sole exception to this constraint occurs where the first State either has lost jurisdiction or has declined to exercise continuing jurisdiction. See § 1738A(f).

enforcement of the California custody decree, judgment of custody, and modification of petitioner's visitation privileges. By order dated April 7, 1981, the Louisiana court granted the petition and awarded sole custody of Matthew to respondent. Two months later, however, the California court, having received and reviewed its investigator's report, entered an order awarding sole custody of Matthew to petitioner. Thus arose the current impasse.

In August 1983, petitioner brought this action in the District Court for the Central District of California. Petitioner requested an order declaring the Louisiana decree invalid and the California decree valid, and enjoining the enforcement of the Louisiana decree. Petitioner did not attempt to enforce the California decree in a Louisiana state court before he filed suit in federal court. The District Court granted respondent's motion to dismiss the complaint for lack of subject matter and personal jurisdiction. The Court of Appeals for the Ninth Circuit affirmed.... 798 F.2d 1547 (C.A.9 1986). Canvassing the background, language, and legislative history of the PKPA, the Court of Appeals held that the Act does not create a private right of action in federal court to determine the validity of two conflicting custody decrees.

In determining whether to infer a private cause of action from a federal statute, our focal point is Congress' intent in enacting the statute....

We examine initially the context of the PKPA with an eye toward determining Congress' perception of the law that it was shaping or reshaping. At the time Congress passed the PKPA, custody orders held a peculiar status under the full faith and credit doctrine, which requires each State to give effect to the judicial proceedings of other States, see U.S. Const., Art. IV, § 1; 28 U.S.C. § 1738. The anomaly traces to the fact that custody orders characteristically are subject to modification as required by the best interests of the child. As a consequence, some courts doubted whether custody orders were sufficiently "final" to trigger full faith and credit requirements, see e.g., Hooks v. Hooks, 771 F.2d 935, 948 (C.A.6 1985); McDougald v. Jenson, 596 F.Supp. 680, 684–685 (N.D.Fla.1984), aff'd 786 F.2d 1465 (C.A.11), cert. denied, 479 U.S. 860 (1986), and this Court had declined expressly to settle the question. See Ford v. Ford, 371 U.S. 187, 192 (1962). Even if custody orders were subject to full faith and credit requirements, the Full Faith and Credit Clause obliges States only to accord the same force to judgments as would be accorded by the courts of the State in which the judgment was entered. Because courts entering custody orders generally retain the power to modify them, courts in other States were no less entitled to change the terms of custody according to their own views of the child's best interest. See New York ex rel. Halvey v. Halvey, 330 U.S. 610 (1947). For these reasons, a parent who lost a custody battle in one State had an incentive to kidnap the child and move to another State to relitigate the issue. This circumstance contributed to widespread jurisdictional deadlocks like this one, and more importantly, to a national epidemic of parental kidnaping. At the time the PKPA was enacted, sponsors of the Act estimated that between 25,000 and 100,000 children were kidnaped by parents who had been unable to obtain custody in a legal forum.

A number of States joined in an effort to avoid these jurisdictional conflicts by adopting the Uniform Child Custody Jurisdiction Act. The UCCJA prescribed uniform standards for deciding which State could make a custody determination and obligated enacting States to enforce the determination made by the State with proper jurisdiction. The project foundered, however, because a number of States refused to enact the UCCJA while others enacted it with modifications. In the absence of uniform national standards for allocating and enforcing custody determinations, noncustodial parents still had reason to snatch their children and petition the courts of any of a number of haven States for sole custody.

The context of the PKPA therefore suggests that the principal problem Congress was seeking to remedy was the inapplicability of full faith and credit requirements to custody determinations. Statements made when the Act was introduced in Congress forcefully confirm that suggestion. The sponsors and supporters of the Act continually indicated that the purpose of the PKPA was to provide for nationwide enforcement of custody orders made in accordance with the terms of the UCCJA. . . .

The significance of Congress' full faith and credit approach to the problem of child snatching is that the Full Faith and Credit Clause, in either its constitutional or statutory incarnations, does not give rise to an implied federal cause of action. . . . Because Congress' chief aim in enacting the PKPA was to extend the requirements of the Full Faith and Credit Clause to custody determinations, the Act is most naturally construed to furnish a rule of decision for courts to use in adjudicating custody disputes and not to create an entirely new cause of action. It thus is not compatible with the purpose and context of the legislative scheme to infer a private cause of action.

The language and placement of the statute reinforce this conclusion. The PKPA is an addendum to the full faith and credit statute, 28 U.S.C. § 1738. This fact alone is strong proof that the Act is intended to have the same operative effect as the full faith and credit statute. Similarly instructive is the heading to the PKPA: "Full faith and credit given to child custody determinations." As for the language of the Act, it is addressed entirely to States and state courts. Unlike statutes that explicitly confer a right on a specified class of persons, the PKPA is a mandate directed to state courts to respect the custody decrees of sister States. We agree with the Court of Appeals that "[i]t seems highly unlikely Congress would follow the pattern of the Full Faith and Credit Clause and section 1738 by structuring section 1738A as a command to state courts to give full faith and credit to the child custody decrees of other states, and yet, without comment, depart from the enforcement practice followed under the Clause and section 1738." 798 F.2d, at 1556.

Finally, the legislative history of the PKPA provides unusually clear indication that Congress did not intend the federal courts to play the enforcement role that petitioner urges. Two passages are particularly revealing. The first of these is a colloquy between Congressmen Conyers and Fish. Congressman Fish had been the sponsor of a competing legislative proposal—ultimately rejected by Congress—that would have extended the District Courts' diversity jurisdiction to encompass actions for enforcement of state custody orders. In the following exchange, Congressman Conyers questioned Congressman Fish about the differences between his proposal and "the Bennett proposal," which was a precursor to the PKPA.

"Mr. Conyers: Could I just interject, the difference between the Bennett proposal and yours: You would have, enforcing the full faith and credit provision, the parties removed to a Federal court. Under the Bennett provision, his bill would impose the full faith and credit enforcement on the State court.

"It seems to me that that is a very important difference. The Federal jurisdiction, could it not, Mr. Fish, result in the Federal court litigating between two State court decrees; whereas, in an alternate method previously suggested, we would be imposing the responsibility of the enforcement upon the State court, and thereby reducing, it seems to me, the amount of litigation.

"Do you see any possible merit in leaving the enforcement at the State level, rather than introducing the Federal judiciary?

"Mr. Fish: Well, I really think that it is easier on the parent that has custody of the child to go to the nearest Federal district court. . . .

"Mr. Conyers: Of course you know that the Federal courts have no experience in these kinds of matters, and they would be moving into this other area. I am just thinking of the fact that they have [many areas of federal concern and] on the average of a 21–month docket, you would now be imposing custody matters which it seems might be handled in the courts that normally handle that. . . ." Parental Kidnaping: Hearing on H.R. 1290 Before the Subcommittee on Crime of the House Committee on the Judiciary, 96th Cong., 2d Sess., 14 (1980).

This exchange suggests that Congress considered and rejected an approach to the problem that would have resulted in a "[f]ederal court litigating between two State court decrees." Ibid.

The second noteworthy entry in the legislative history is a letter from then Assistant Attorney General Patricia Wald to the Chairman of the House Judiciary Committee, which was referred to extensively during the debate on the PKPA. The letter outlined a variety of solutions to the child-snatching problem. It specifically compared proposals that would "grant jurisdiction to the federal courts to enforce state custody decrees" with an approach, such as was proposed in the PKPA, that would "impose on states a federal duty, under enumerated standards derived generally from the UCCJA, to give full faith and credit to the custody decrees of other states." The letter endorsed the full faith and credit approach that eventually was codified in the PKPA. More importantly, it "strongly oppose[d] . . . the creation of a federal forum for resolving custody disputes." Id., at 108. Like Congressman Conyers, the Justice Department reasoned that federal enforcement of state custody decrees would increase the workload of the federal courts and entangle the federal judiciary in domestic relations disputes with which they have little experience and which traditionally have been the province of the States. That the views of the Justice

Department and Congressman Conyers prevailed, and that Congress explicitly opted for a full faith and credit approach over reliance on enforcement by the federal courts, provide strong evidence against inferring a federal cause of action.

Petitioner discounts these portions of the legislative history. He argues that the cause of action that he asks us to infer arises only in cases of an actual conflict between two State custody decrees, and thus is substantially narrower than the cause of action proposed by Congressman Fish and rejected by Congress. The Fish bill would have extended federal-diversity jurisdiction to permit federal courts to enforce custody orders in the first instance, before a second State had created a conflict by refusing to do so. This cause of action admittedly is farther reaching than that which we reject today. But the considerations that prompted Congress to reject the Fish bill also militate against the more circumscribed role for the federal courts that petitioner proposes. Instructing the federal courts to play Solomon where two State courts have issued conflicting custody orders would entangle them in traditional state-law questions that they have little expertise to resolve.[4] This is a cost that Congress made clear it did not want the PKPA to carry.[5]

In sum, the context, language, and history of the PKPA together make out a conclusive case against inferring a cause of action in federal court to determine which of two conflicting state custody decrees is valid. Against this impressive evidence, petitioner relies primarily on the argument that failure to infer a cause of action would render the PKPA nugatory. We note, as a preliminary response, that ultimate review remains available in this Court for truly intractable jurisdictional deadlocks. In addition, the unspoken presumption in petitioner's argument is that the States are either unable or unwilling to enforce the provisions of the Act. This is a

---

4. Petitioner argues that determining which of two conflicting custody decrees should be given effect under the PKPA would not require the federal courts to resolve the merits of custody disputes and thus would not offend the long-standing tradition of reserving domestic-relations matters to the States. Petitioner contends that the cause of action he champions would require federal courts only to analyze which of two States is given exclusive jurisdiction under a federal statute, a task for which the federal courts are well-qualified. We cannot agree with petitioner that making a jurisdictional determination under the PKPA would not involve the federal courts in substantive domestic-relations determinations. Under the Act, jurisdiction can turn on the child's "best interest" or on proof that the child has been abandoned or abused. See §§ 1738A(c)(2)(B), (C), and (D). In fact, it would seem that the jurisdictional disputes that are sufficiently complicated as to have provoked conflicting state-court holdings are the most likely to require resolution of these traditional domestic-relations inquiries. See Rogers v. Platt, 259 U.S.App.D.C. 154, 162, 814 F.2d 683, 691 (1987). Cf. Cort v. Ash, 422 U.S. 66, 84 (1975) (possibility that implied federal cause of action *may* in certain instances turn on state-law issues counsels against inferring such an action).

5. Moreover, petitioner's argument serves to underscore the extraordinary nature of the cause of action he urges us to infer. Petitioner essentially asks that federal district courts exercise appellate review of state-court judgments. This is an unusual cause of action for Congress to grant, either expressly or by implication. Petitioner's proposal is all the more remarkable in the present case, in which he seeks to have a California District Court enjoin enforcement of a Louisiana state-court judgment before the intermediate and supreme courts of Louisiana even have had an opportunity to review that judgment.

presumption we are not prepared, and more importantly, Congress was not prepared, to indulge. State courts faithfully administer the Full Faith and Credit Clause every day; now that Congress has extended full faith and credit requirements to child custody orders, we can think of no reason why the courts' administration of federal law in custody disputes will be any less vigilant. Should state courts prove as obstinate as petitioner predicts, Congress may choose to revisit the issue. But any more radical approach to the problem will have to await further legislative action; we "will not engraft a remedy on a statute, no matter now salutary, that Congress did not intend to provide." The judgment of the Court of Appeals is affirmed.

NOTES

(1) Under what circumstances would the Supreme Court ever be likely to hear a case on the issue of applicability of one state's custody law over another? For a critique of the UCCJA and the PKPA and suggestions about further reform, see Anne B. Goldstein, The Tragedy of the Interstate Child: A Critical Reexamination of the Uniform Child Custody Jurisdiction Act and the Parental Kidnaping Prevention Act, 25 U.C. Davis L.Rev. 845 (1992).

(2) **Custodial Interference as a Crime.** In *State v. Carver*, 113 Wn.2d 591, 781 P.2d 1308 (1989), the Supreme Court of Washington held the state's custodial interference statute constitutionally valid, overcoming arguments that it was vague and defined the offense in a manner that would encourage arbitrary or discriminatory enforcement. The statute, Wash.Rev. Code Ann. § 9A.40.060 (Lexis), provides that:

(1) A relative of a child under the age of eighteen or of an incompetent person is guilty of custodial interference in the first degree if, with the intent to deny access to the child or incompetent person by a parent, guardian, institution, agency, or other person having a lawful right to physical custody of such person, the relative takes, entices, retains, detains, or conceals the child or incompetent person from a parent, guardian, institution, agency, or other person having a lawful right to physical custody of such person and:

(a) Intends to hold the child or incompetent person permanently or for a protracted period; or

(b) Exposes the child or incompetent person to a substantial risk of illness or physical injury; or

(c) Causes the child or incompetent person to be removed from the state of usual residence; or

(d) Retains, detains, or conceals the child or incompetent person in another state after expiration of any authorized visitation period with intent to intimidate or harass a parent, guardian, institution, agency, or other person having lawful right to physical custody or to prevent a parent, guardian, institution, agency, or other person with lawful right to physical custody from regaining custody

(2) A parent of a child is guilty of custodial interference in the first degree if the parent takes, entices, retains, detains, or conceals the child, with the intent to deny access, from the other parent having the lawful right to time with the child pursuant to a court-ordered parenting plan, and:

(a) Intends to hold the child permanently or for a protracted period; or

(b) Exposes the child to a substantial risk of illness or physical injury; or

(c) Causes the child to be removed from the state of usual residence.

(3) A parent or other person acting under the directions of the parent is guilty of custodial interference in the first degree if the parent or other person intentionally takes, entices, retains, or conceals a child, under the age of eighteen years and for whom no lawful custody order or parenting plan has been entered by a court of competent jurisdiction, from the other parent with intent to deprive the other parent from access to the child permanently or for a protracted period.

(4) Custodial interference in the first degree is a class C felony.

Custodial interference in the second degree is defined in Wash.Rev.Code Ann. § 9A.40.070 (Lexis).

Friedrich v. Friedrich

United States Court of Appeals, Sixth Circuit, 1996.
78 F.3d 1060.

■ BOGGS, CIRCUIT JUDGE.

For the second time, we address the application of the Hague Convention on the Civil Aspects of International Child Abduction ("the Convention") and its implementing legislation, the International Child Abduction Remedies Act ("the Act"), 42 U.S.C. §§ 11601–11610, to the life of Thomas Friedrich, now age six. We affirm the district court's order that Thomas was wrongfully removed from Germany and should be returned.

I

Thomas was born in Bad Aibling, Germany, to Jeana Friedrich, an American servicewoman stationed there, and her husband, Emanuel Friedrich, a German citizen. When Thomas was two years old, his parents separated after an argument on July 27, 1991. Less than a week later, in the early morning of August 2, 1991, Mrs. Friedrich took Thomas from Germany to her family home in Ironton, Ohio, without informing Mr. Friedrich. Mr. Friedrich sought return of the child in German Family Court, obtaining an order awarding him custody on August 22. He then filed this action for the return of his son in the United States District Court for the Southern District of Ohio on September 23.

We first heard this case three years ago. Friedrich v. Friedrich, 983 F.2d 1396 (6th Cir.1993) ("Friedrich I"). At that time, we reversed the district court's denial of Mr. Friedrich's claim for the return of his son to Germany pursuant to the Convention. We outlined the relevant law on what was then an issue of first impression in the federal appellate courts, and remanded with instructions that the district court determine whether, as a matter of German law, Mr. Friedrich was exercising custody rights to Thomas at the time of removal. We also asked the district court to decide if Mrs. Friedrich could prove any of the four affirmative defenses provided by the Convention and the Act. Thomas, meanwhile, remained with his mother and his mother's parents in Ohio.

On remand, the district court allowed additional discovery and held a new hearing. The court eventually determined that, at the time of Thomas's removal on August 1, 1991, Mr. Friedrich was exercising custody rights to Thomas under German law, or would have been exercising such rights but for the removal. The court then held that Mrs. Friedrich had not established any of the affirmative defenses available to her under the Convention. The court ordered Mrs. Friedrich to return Thomas to Germany "forthwith," but later stayed the order, upon the posting of a bond by Mrs. Friedrich, pending the resolution of this appeal.[1]

Mrs. Friedrich's appeal raises two issues that are central to the young jurisprudence of the Hague Convention. First, what does it mean to "exercise" custody rights? Second, when can a court refuse to return a child who has been wrongfully removed from a country because return of the abducted child would result in a "grave" risk of harm?

In answering both these questions, we keep in mind two general principles inherent in the Convention and the Act, expressed in Friedrich I, and subsequently embraced by unanimous federal authority. First, a court in the abducted-to nation has jurisdiction to decide the merits of an abduction claim, but not the merits of the underlying custody dispute. Hague Convention, Article 19; 42 U.S.C. § 11601(b)(4); Friedrich I, 983 F.2d at 1400; Rydder v. Rydder, 49 F.3d 369, 372 (8th Cir.1995); Feder v. Evans–Feder, 63 F.3d 217, 221 (3d Cir.1995); Journe v. Journe, 911 F.Supp. 43 (D.P.R.1995). Second, the Hague Convention is generally intended to restore the pre-abduction status quo and to deter parents from crossing borders in search of a more sympathetic court. Pub. Notice 957, 51 Fed.Reg. 10494, 10505 (1986); Friedrich I, 983 F.2d at 1400; Rydder, 49 F.3d at 372; Feder, 63 F.3d at 221; Wanninger v. Wanninger, 850 F.Supp. 78, 80 (D.Mass.1994).

II

The removal of a child from the country of its habitual residence is "wrongful" under the Hague Convention if a person in that country is, or would otherwise be, exercising custody rights to the child under that country's law at the moment of removal. Hague Convention, Article 3. The plaintiff in an action for return of the child has the burden of proving the exercise of custody rights by a preponderance of the evidence. 42 U.S.C. § 11603(e)(1)(A). We review the district court's findings of fact for clear error and review its conclusions about American, foreign, and international law de novo. See Fed.R.Civ.P. 44.1 (a district court's determination of foreign law should be reviewed as a ruling on a question of law)....

The district court held that a preponderance of the evidence in the record established that Mr. Friedrich was exercising custody rights over Thomas at the time of Thomas's removal. Mrs. Friedrich alleges that the district court improperly applied German law. Reviewing de novo, we find no error in the court's legal analysis. Custody rights "may arise in particular by operation of law or by reason of a judicial or administrative

---

1. The stay of the judge's order pending appeal, hotly contested below, is not now challenged by Mr. Friedrich. It may have been improvident. Staying the return of a child in an action under the Convention should hardly be a matter of course. The aim of the Convention is to secure prompt return of the child to the correct jurisdiction, and any unnecessary delay renders the subsequent return more difficult for the child, and subsequent adjudication more difficult for the foreign court.

decision, or by reason of an agreement having legal effect under the law of the State." Hague Convention, Article 3. German law gives both parents equal de jure custody of the child, German Civil Code 1626(1), and, with a few exceptions, this de jure custody continues until a competent court says otherwise. See Currier v. Currier, 845 F.Supp. 916, 920 (D.N.H.1994) ("under German law both parents retain joint rights of custody until a decree has been entered limiting one parent's rights"); Wanninger, 850 F.Supp. at 78 (D.Mass.1994).

Mrs. Friedrich argues that Mr. Friedrich "terminated" his custody rights under German law because, during the argument on the evening of July 27, 1991, he placed Thomas's belongings and hers in the hallway outside of their apartment. The district court properly rejected the claim that these actions could end parental rights as a matter of German law. We agree. After examining the record, we are uncertain as to exactly what happened on the evening of July 27, but we do know that the events of that night were not a judicial abrogation of custody rights. Nor are we persuaded by Mrs. Friedrich's attempts to read the German Civil Code provisions stipulated to by the parties in such a way as to create the ability of one parent to terminate his or her custody rights extrajudicially.[2]

Mrs. Friedrich also argues that, even if Mr. Friedrich had custody rights under German law, he was not exercising those custody rights as contemplated by the Hague Convention. She argues that, since custody rights include the care for the person and property of the child, Mr. Friedrich was not exercising custody rights because he was not paying for or taking care of the child during the brief period of separation in Germany.

The Hague Convention does not define "exercise." As judges in a common law country, we can easily imagine doing so ourselves. One might look to the law of the foreign country to determine if custody rights existed de jure, and then develop a test under the general principles of the Hague Convention to determine what activities—financial support, visitation— constitute sufficient exercise of de jure rights. The question in our immediate case would then be: "was Mr. Friedrich's single visit with Thomas and plans for future visits with Thomas sufficient exercise of custodial rights for us to justify calling the removal of Thomas wrongful?" One might even approach a distinction between the exercise of "custody" rights and the exercise of "access" or "visitation" rights.[3] If Mr. Friedrich, who has de

---

2. Mrs. Friedrich cites German Civil Code s 1629, which says that a parent who exercises parental care alone can also represent the child in legal matters alone. Obviously, the ability of one parent to "represent" the child does not imply that the other parent has no custody rights. Mrs. Friedrich also cites German Civil Code s 1631, which says that the Family Court, if petitioned, can assist the parents in providing parental care. We have no idea how this provision, which is essentially no more than a grant of jurisdiction to appoint and direct a family services

officer, can support Mrs. Friedrich's claim that "a German parent can certainly relinquish custody or parental rights absent a judicial determination." Defendants–Appellants' Brief at 15.

3. Article 21 of the Hague Convention instructs signatory countries to protect the "rights of access" of non-custodial parents to their children. Courts have yet to address the question whether Article 21 implies that a custodial parent can remove a child from its country of habitual residence without the permission of a parent whose rights that

jure custody, was not exercising sufficient de facto custody, Thomas's removal would not be wrongful.

We think it unwise to attempt any such project. Enforcement of the Convention should not to be made dependent on the creation of a common law definition of "exercise." The only acceptable solution, in the absence of a ruling from a court in the country of habitual residence, is to liberally find "exercise" whenever a parent with de jure custody rights keeps, or seeks to keep, any sort of regular contact with his or her child.

We see three reasons for this broad definition of "exercise." First, American courts are not well suited to determine the consequences of parental behavior under the law of a foreign country. It is fairly easy for the courts of one country to determine whether a person has custody rights under the law of another country. It is also quite possible for a court to determine if an order by a foreign court awards someone "custody" rights, as opposed to rights of "access."[4] Far more difficult is the task of deciding, prior to a ruling by a court in the abducted-from country, if a parent's custody rights should be ignored because he or she was not acting sufficiently like a custodial parent. A foreign court, if at all possible, should refrain from making such policy-oriented decisions concerning the application of German law to a child whose habitual residence is, or was, Germany.

Second, an American decision about the adequacy of one parent's exercise of custody rights is dangerously close to forbidden territory: the merits of the custody dispute. The German court in this case is perfectly capable of taking into account Mr. Friedrich's behavior during the August 1991 separation, and the German court presumably will tailor its custody order accordingly. A decision by an American court to deny return to Germany because Mr. Friedrich did not show sufficient attention or concern for Thomas's welfare would preclude the German court from addressing these issues—and the German court may well resolve them differently.

Third, the confusing dynamics of quarrels and informal separations make it difficult to assess adequately the acts and motivations of a parent. An occasional visit may be all that is available to someone left, by the vagaries of marital discord, temporarily without the child. Often the child may be avoided, not out of a desire to relinquish custody, but out of anger, pride, embarrassment, or fear, vis a vis the other parent.[5] Reading too much into a parent's behavior during these difficult times could be inaccurate and unfair. Although there may be situations when a long period of

country's courts have expressly limited to "visitation." See infra n. 4.

4. For a particularly difficult situation, ably resolved, see David S. v. Zamira, 151 Misc.2d 630, 574 N.Y.S.2d 429 (Fam.Ct. 1991), aff'd In re Schneir, 17 F.L.R. 1237 (N.Y.App.Div.2d Dep't). The court here held that an order giving the non-custodial parent visitation rights and restricting the custodial parent from leaving the country constitutes an order granting "custodial" rights to both parents under the Hague Convention.

5. When Mrs. Friedrich took Thomas and her belongings from the family apartment on the morning of July 28, she was accompanied by some friends from work: soldiers of the United States Army. Mr. Friedrich testified that he was "intimidated" by the presence of the soldiers, and discouraged from making a stronger objection to the removal of his child.

unexplainable neglect of the child could constitute non-exercise of otherwise valid custody rights under the Convention, as a general rule, any attempt to maintain a somewhat regular relationship with the child should constitute "exercise." This rule leaves the full resolution of custody issues, as the Convention and common sense indicate, to the courts of the country of habitual residence.

We are well aware that our approach requires a parent, in the event of a separation or custody dispute, to seek permission from the other parent or from the courts before taking a child out of the country of its habitual residence. Any other approach allows a parent to pick a "home court" for the custody dispute ex parte, defeating a primary purpose of the Convention. We believe that, where the reason for removal is legitimate, it will not usually be difficult to obtain approval from either the other parent or a foreign court. Furthermore, as the case for removal of the child in the custody of one parent becomes more compelling, approval (at least the approval of a foreign court) should become easier to secure.

Mrs. Friedrich argues that our approach cannot adequately cope with emergency situations that require the child and parent to leave the country. In her case, for example, Mrs. Friedrich claims that removal of Thomas to Ohio was necessary because she could no longer afford to have the child stay at the army base, and Mr. Friedrich refused to provide shelter. Examining the record, we seriously doubt that Mr. Friedrich would have refused to lodge Thomas at his expense in Germany. In any event, even if an emergency forces a parent to take a child to a foreign country, any such emergency cannot excuse the parent from returning the child to the jurisdiction once return of the child becomes safe. Nor can an emergency justify a parent's refusal to submit the child to the authority of the foreign court for resolution of custody matters, including the question of the appropriate temporary residence of the child. See Viragh v. Foldes, 415 Mass. 96, 612 N.E.2d 241 (1993) (child removed to America by one parent without notification to other parent may remain in America in light of decision by Hungarian court in parallel proceeding that best interests of the child require exercise of sole custody by parent in America).

We therefore hold that, if a person has valid custody rights to a child under the law of the country of the child's habitual residence, that person cannot fail to "exercise" those custody rights under the Hague Convention short of acts that constitute clear and unequivocal abandonment of the child.[6] Once it determines that the parent exercised custody rights in any manner, the court should stop—completely avoiding the question whether the parent exercised the custody rights well or badly. These matters go to the merits of the custody dispute and are, therefore, beyond the subject matter jurisdiction of the federal courts. 42 U.S.C. § 11601(b)(4).

---

6. The situation would be different if the country of habitual residence had a legal rule regarding the exercise of custody rights clearly tied to the Hague concept of international removal. If, for example, Germany had a law stating that, for the purposes of the Convention, mere visitation without financial support during a period of informal separation does not constitute the "exercise" of custody rights, we would, of course, be bound to apply that law in this case.

In this case, German law gave Mr. Friedrich custody rights to Thomas. The facts before us clearly indicate that he attempted to exercise these rights during the separation from his wife. Mr. and Mrs. Friedrich argued during the evening of July 27, 1991, and separated on the morning of July 28. Mrs. Friedrich left with her belongings and Thomas. She stayed on the army base with the child for four days. Mr. Friedrich telephoned Mrs. Friedrich on July 29 to arrange a visit with Thomas, and spent the afternoon of that day with his son. Mr. and Mrs. Friedrich met on August 1 to talk about Thomas and their separation. The parties dispute the upshot of this conversation. Mrs. Friedrich says that Mr. Friedrich expressed a general willingness that Thomas move to America with his mother. Mr. Friedrich denies this. It is clear, however, that the parties did agree to immediate visitations of Thomas by Mr. Friedrich, scheduling the first such visit for August 3. Shortly after midnight on August 2, Mrs. Friedrich took her son and, without informing her husband,[7] left for America by airplane.

Because Mr. Friedrich had custody rights to Thomas as a matter of German law, and did not clearly abandon those rights prior to August 1, the removal of Thomas without his consent was wrongful under the Convention, regardless of any other considerations about Mr. Friedrich's behavior during the family's separation in Germany.

III

Once a plaintiff establishes that removal was wrongful, the child must be returned unless the defendant can establish one of four defenses. Two of these defenses can be established by a preponderance of the evidence, 42 U.S.C. § 11603(e)(2)(B): the proceeding was commenced more than one year after the removal of the child and the child has become settled in his or her new environment, Hague Convention, Article 12; or, the person seeking return of the child consented to or subsequently acquiesced in the removal or retention, Hague Convention, Article 13a. The other two defenses must be shown by clear and convincing evidence, 42 U.S.C. § 11603(e)(2)(A): there is a grave risk that the return of the child would expose it to physical or psychological harm, Hague Convention, Article 13b; or, the return of the child "would not be permitted by the fundamental principles of the requested State relating to the protection of human rights and fundamental freedoms," Hague Convention, Article 20.[8]

All four of these exceptions are "narrow," 42 U.S.C. § 11601(a)(4). They are not a basis for avoiding return of a child merely because an American court believes it can better or more quickly resolve a dispute. See Rydder, 49 F.3d at 372 (citing Friedrich I, 983 F.2d at 1400). In fact, a federal court retains, and should use when appropriate, the discretion to return a child, despite the existence of a defense, if return would further

7. Q. You didn't call your husband, Mrs. Friedrich, because you didn't want him to know you were leaving; isn't that the reason? A. Yes it is. Transcript of October 16, 1991, Proceedings at 36.

8. The situation changes somewhat when the child is older. The Hague Conven-tion allows a court in the abducted-to country to "refuse to order the return of the child if it finds that the child objects to being returned and has attained an age and degree of maturity at which it is appropriate to take account of its views." Hague Convention, Article 13.

the aims of the Convention. Feder, 63 F.3d at 226 (citing Pub. Notice 957, 51 Fed.Reg. 10494, 10509 (1986)).

Mrs. Friedrich alleges that she proved by clear and convincing evidence in the proceedings below that the return of Thomas to Germany would cause him grave psychological harm. Mrs. Friedrich testified that Thomas has grown attached to family and friends in Ohio. She also hired an expert psychologist who testified that returning Thomas to Germany would be traumatic and difficult for the child, who was currently happy and healthy in America with his mother. [Thomas] definitely would experience the loss of his mother ... if he were to be removed to Germany. Than that would be a considerable loss. And there then would be the probabilities of anger both towards his mother, who it might appear that she has abandoned him [sic], and towards the father for creating that abandonment. [These feelings] could be plenty enough springboard for other developmental or emotional restrictions which could include nightmares, antisocial behavior, a whole host of anxious-type behavior. Blaske Deposition at 28–29.

If we are to take the international obligations of American courts with any degree of seriousness, the exception to the Hague Convention for grave harm to the child requires far more than the evidence that Mrs. Friedrich provides. Mrs. Friedrich alleges nothing more than adjustment problems that would attend the relocation of most children. There is no allegation that Mr. Friedrich has ever abused Thomas. The district court found that the home that Mr. Friedrich has prepared for Thomas in Germany appears adequate to the needs of any young child. The father does not work long hours, and the child's German grandmother is ready to care for the child when the father cannot. There is nothing in the record to indicate that life in Germany would result in any permanent harm or unhappiness.

Furthermore, even if the home of Mr. Friedrich were a grim place to raise a child in comparison to the pretty, peaceful streets of Ironton, Ohio, that fact would be irrelevant to a federal court's obligation under the Convention. We are not to debate the relevant virtues of Batman and Max und Moritz, Wheaties and Milchreis. The exception for grave harm to the child is not license for a court in the abducted-to country to speculate on where the child would be happiest. Than that decision is a custody matter, and reserved to the court in the country of habitual residence.

Mrs. Friedrich advocates a wide interpretation of the grave risk of harm exception that would reward her for violating the Convention. A removing parent must not be allowed to abduct a child and then—when brought to court—complain that the child has grown used to the surroundings to which they were abducted.[9] Under the logic of the Convention, it is the abduction that causes the pangs of subsequent return. The disruption of the usual sense of attachment that arises during most long stays in a single place with a single parent should not be a "grave" risk of harm for the purposes of the Convention.

---

9. We forgo the temptation to compare this behavior to the standard definition of "chutzpah." See A. Kozinski & E. Volokh, Lawsuit, Shmawsuit, 103 Yale L.J. 463, 467 (1993).

In thinking about these problems, we acknowledge that courts in the abducted-from country are as ready and able as we are to protect children. If return to a country, or to the custody of a parent in that country, is dangerous, we can expect that country's courts to respond accordingly. Cf. Nunez–Escudero v. Tice–Menley, 58 F.3d 374, 377 (8th Cir.1995) (if parent in Mexico is abusive, infant returned to Mexico for custody determination can be institutionalized during pendency of custody proceedings). And if Germany really is a poor place for young Thomas to grow up, as Mrs. Friedrich contends, we can expect the German courts to recognize that and award her custody in America. When we trust the court system in the abducted-from country, the vast majority of claims of harm—those that do not rise to the level of gravity required by the Convention—evaporate.

The international precedent available supports our restrictive reading of the grave harm exception. In Thomson v. Thomson, 119 D.L.R.4th 253 (Can.1994), the Supreme Court of Canada held that the exception applies only to harm "that also amounts to an intolerable situation." Id. at 286. The Court of Appeal of the United Kingdom has held that the harm required is "something greater than would normally be expected on taking a child away from one parent and passing him to another." In re A., 1 F.L.R. 365, 372 (Eng.C.A.1988). And other circuit courts in America have followed this reasoning in cases decided since Friedrich I. See Nunez–Escudero, 58 F.3d at 377 (citing Thomson, 119 D.L.R.4th at 286, and In re A., 1 F.L.R. at 372); Rydder, 49 F.3d at 373 (affirming district court order for return of child over abducting parent's objection that return would cause grave harm). Finally, we are instructed by the following observation by the United States Department of State concerning the grave risk of harm exception. This provision was not intended to be used by defendants as a vehicle to litigate (or relitigate) the child's best interests. Only evidence directly establishing the existence of a grave risk that would expose the child to physical or emotional harm or otherwise place the child in an intolerable situation is material to the court's determination. The person opposing the child's return must show that the risk to the child is grave, not merely serious. A review of deliberations on the Convention reveals that "intolerable situation" was not intended to encompass return to a home where money is in short supply, or where educational or other opportunities are more limited than in the requested State. An example of an "intolerable situation" is one in which a custodial parent sexually abuses the child. If the other parent removes or retains the child to safeguard it against further victimization, and the abusive parent then petitions for the child's return under the Convention, the court may deny the petition. Such action would protect the child from being returned to an "intolerable situation" and subjected to a grave risk of psychological harm. Public Notice 957, 51 FR 10494, 10510 (March 26, 1986) (emphasis added).

For all of these reasons, we hold that the district court did not err by holding that "[t]he record in the instant case does not demonstrate by clear and convincing evidence that Thomas will be exposed to a grave risk of harm." Although it is not necessary to resolve the present appeal, we believe that a grave risk of harm for the purposes of the Convention can exist in only two situations. First, there is a grave risk of harm when return of the child puts the child in imminent danger prior to the resolution of the custody dispute—e.g., returning the child to a zone of war, famine, or disease. Second, there is a grave risk of harm in cases of serious abuse or neglect, or extraordinary emotional dependence, when the court in the country of habitual residence, for whatever reason, may be incapable or unwilling to give the child adequate protection. Psychological evidence of the sort Mrs. Friedrich introduced in the proceeding below is only relevant if it helps prove the existence of one of these two situations.[10]

IV

Mrs. Friedrich also claims that the district court erred in ordering Thomas's return because Mrs. Friedrich proved by a preponderance of the evidence that Mr. Friedrich (I) consented to, and (ii) subsequently acquiesced in, the removal of Thomas to America.[11]

Mrs. Friedrich bases her claim of consent to removal on statements that she claims Mr. Friedrich made to her during their separation. Mr. Friedrich flatly denies that he made these statements. The district court was faced with a choice as to whom it found more believable in a factual dispute. There is nothing in the record to suggest that the court's decision to believe Mr. Friedrich, and hold that he "did not exhibit an intention or a willingness to terminate his parental rights," was clearly erroneous. In fact, Mr. Friedrich's testimony is strongly supported by the circumstances of the removal of Thomas—most notably the fact that Mrs. Friedrich did not inform Mr. Friedrich that she was departing. Supra n. 7. The deliberately secretive nature of her actions is extremely strong evidence that Mr. Friedrich would not have consented to the removal of Thomas. For these reasons, we hold that the district court did not abuse its discretion in finding that Mrs. Friedrich took Thomas to America without Mr. Friedrich's consent.

Mrs. Friedrich bases her claim of subsequent acquiescence on a statement made by Mr. Friedrich to one of her commanding officers, Captain Michael Farley, at a cocktail party on the military base after Mrs. Friedrich had left with Thomas. Captain Farley, who cannot date the conversation exactly, testified that: During the conversation, Mr. Friedrich indicated that he was not seeking custody of the child, because he didn't have the means to take care of the child. Farley Deposition at 13. Mr. Friedrich denies that he made this statement. The district court made no specific finding regarding this fact.

We believe that the statement to Captain Farley, even if it was made, is insufficient evidence of subsequent acquiescence. Subsequent acquiescence requires more than an isolated statement to a third-party. Each of the words and actions of a parent during the separation are not to be

10. The only other circuit addressing the issue had its own doubts about whether a psychological report concerning the difficulty that a child would face when separated from the abducting parent is ever relevant to a Hague Convention action. Nunez–Escudero, 58 F.3d at 378 (such reports are not per se irrelevant, but they are rarely dispositive).

11. Article 13a provides a defense to an action for return if the petitioner "consented to or subsequently acquiesced in the removal or retention" of the child. The Convention does not define consent or acquiescence in any more definite manner, and there is no statement to guide us in the text or legislative history of the Act.

scrutinized for a possible waiver of custody rights. See Wanninger, 850 F.Supp. at 81–82 (refusing to construe father's personal letters to wife and priest as sufficient evidence of acquiescence where father consistently attempted to keep in contact with child). Although we must decide the matter without guidance from previous appellate court decisions, we believe that acquiescence under the Convention requires either: an act or statement with the requisite formality, such as testimony in a judicial proceeding;[12] a convincing written renunciation of rights;[13] or a consistent attitude of acquiescence over a significant period of time.

By August 22, 1991, twenty-one days after the abduction, Mr. Friedrich had secured a German court order awarding him custody of Thomas. He has resolutely sought custody of his son since that time. It is by these acts, not his casual statements to third parties, that we will determine whether or not he acquiesced to the retention of his son in America. Since Mrs. Friedrich has not introduced evidence of a formal renunciation or a consistent attitude of acquiescence over a significant period of time, the judgment of the district court on this matter was not erroneous.

V

The district court's order that Thomas be immediately returned to Germany is AFFIRMED, and the district court's stay of that order pending appeal is VACATED. Because Thomas's return to Germany is already long-overdue, we order, pursuant to Fed.R.App.P. 41(a), that our mandate issue forthwith.

NOTE

In *Walsh v. Walsh*, 221 F.3d 204 (1st Cir.2000), the U.S. Court of Appeals for the First Circuit partially overruled a U.S. District Court decision involving interpretation and application of Hague Convention Article 13(b) regarding extraordinary threats to children's health and safety. The husband had absconded from the U.S. to Ireland, his native home, after being charged with criminal offenses in the United States. The children were then living in Massachusetts, having been brought there by their mother. He sought their return to Ireland.

In an opinion by Lynch, J., the court stated

> ... [T]he district court erroneously required a showing of an "immediate, serious threat." *Id.* at 206; *see also id.* at 208 (concluding that "the Court [only] may act [under article 13(b)] to avert truly extraordinary threats to [the children's] health and safety"). Article 13(b) of the Convention requires a showing that there be a "grave risk that his or her return would expose the

---

12. In Journe v. Journe, 911 F.Supp. 43 (D.P.R.1995), a French father instituted custody proceedings in France after the mother took the children to Puerto Rico. The mother returned to France, presumably without the children, to participate in the proceedings. The father voluntarily dismissed the French custody proceedings, but continued to pursue Hague Convention remedies The district court held that the father had waived his rights to have a French court determine custody issues by virtue of the voluntary dismissal of his French case. Id. at 48. The court reached that decision because of "its equitable powers," not because the dismissal constituted "acquiescence" for the purposes of the Convention.

13. A hastily-drafted and soon-rued written agreement was found insufficient indication of consent in Currier v. Currier, 845 F.Supp. 916 (D.N.H.1994).

child to physical or psychological harm or otherwise place the child in an intolerable situation." The Convention does not require that the risk be "immediate"; only that it be grave.

The text of the article requires only that the harm be "physical or psychological," but context makes it clear that the harm must be a great deal more than minimal. *See Nunez–Escudero v. Tice–Menley,* 58 F.3d 374, 377 (8th Cir.1995).[12] Not any harm will do nor may the level of risk of harm be low. The risk must be "grave," and when determining whether a grave risk of harm exists, courts must be attentive to the purposes of the Convention. *See* Hague Convention, art. 1. For example, the harm must be "something greater than would normally be expected on taking a child away from one parent and passing him to another"; otherwise, the goals of the Convention could be easily circumvented. *Re A. (a Minor) (Abduction)* [1988] 1 F.L.R. 365, 372 (Eng.C.A.); *see also Friedrich,* 78 F.3d at 1067–68; *Re C. (Abduction: Grave Risk of Psychological Harm)* [1999] 1 F.L.R. 1145 (Eng.C.A.); *C. v. C. (Minor: Abduction: Rights of Custody Abroad)* [1989] 1 F.L.R. 403, 410 (Eng.C.A.). Courts are not to engage in a custody determination, so "[i]t is not relevant . . . who is the better parent in the long run, or whether [the absconding parent] had good reason to leave her home . . . and terminate her marriage." *Nunez-Escudero,* 58 F.3d at 377; *see also* Department of State, Hague International Child Abduction Convention: Text and Legal Analysis, 51 Fed.Reg. 10,494, 10,510 (1986) ("[Article 13(b)] was not intended to be used by defendants as a vehicle to litigate . . . the child's best interests."). We return to the issue of risk and harm, and how it applies to this case, below, but we first discuss the role that undertakings play in article 13(b) determinations.

A potential grave risk of harm can, at times, be mitigated sufficiently by the acceptance of undertakings and sufficient guarantees of performance of those undertakings. Necessarily, the "grave risk" exception considers, inter alia, where and how a child is to be returned. The undertakings approach allows courts to conduct an evaluation of the placement options and legal safeguards in the country of habitual residence to preserve the child's safety while the courts of that country have the opportunity to determine custody of the children within the physical boundaries of their jurisdiction. Given the strong presumption that a child should be returned, many courts, both here and in other countries, have determined that the reception of undertakings best allows for the achievement of the goals set out in the Convention while, at the same time, protecting children from exposure to grave risk of harm. *See, e.g., Blondin v. Dubois,* 189 F.3d 240, 248 (2d Cir.1999) *(Blondin II); Turner v. Frowein,* 253 Conn. 312, 752 A.2d 955 (2000); *Thomson v. Thomson* [1994] 3 S.C.R. 551, 599 (Can.); *P. v. B.* [1994] 3 I.R. 507, 521 (Ir.S.C.). *See generally* Paul R. Beaumont & Peter E. McEleavy, *The Hague Convention on International Child Abduction* 156–72 (1999).

A good example of this approach is the Second Circuit's recent decision in *Blondin II.* The district court had denied the father's petition to return the children to France because the mother had established that returning the children to their father's custody would pose a grave risk of harm. *See Blondin v. Dubois,* 19 F.Supp.2d 123, 127–29 (S.D.N.Y.1998) *(Blondin I).* The Court of Appeals vacated the district court's judgment and remanded the case to allow the district court to consider "remedies that would allow the children's safety

---

12.   There is disagreement as to whether the "the physical or psychological harm contemplated by the first clause of Article 13(b) is harm to a degree that also amounts to an intolerable situation." *Thomson v. Thomson* [1994] 3 S.C.R. 551, 596 (Can.). The Supreme Court of Canada has said that it does. *See id.* We are doubtful about this.

to be protected [in France] pending a final adjudication of custody." *Blondin II,* 189 F.3d at 250.

Yet, there may be times when there is no way to return a child, even with undertakings, without exposing him or her to grave risk. Thus, on remand in *Blondin,* the district court found that the "return of [the children] to France, *under any arrangement,* would present a 'grave risk' "because "removal . . . from their presently secure environment would interfere with their recovery from the trauma they suffered in France; . . . returning them to France, where they would encounter the uncertainties and pressures of custody proceedings, would cause them psychological harm; and . . . [one of the children] objects to being returned to France." *Blondin v. Dubois,* 78 F.Supp.2d 283, 294 (S.D.N.Y. 2000) (*Blondin III*), *appeal filed,* No. 00–6066 (2d Cir. Jan. 20, 2000) (emphasis added).

Against this background, we consider this case. In our view, the district court committed several fundamental errors: it inappropriately discounted the grave risk of physical and psychological harm to children in cases of spousal abuse; it failed to credit John's more generalized pattern of violence, including violence directed at his own children; and it gave insufficient weight to John's chronic disobedience of court orders. The quantum here of risked harm, both physical and psychological, is high. There is ample evidence that John has been and can be extremely violent and that he cannot control his temper. There is a clear and long history of spousal abuse, and of fights with and threats against persons other than his wife. These include John's threat to kill his neighbor in Malden, for which he was criminally charged, and his fight with his son Michael.

The district court distinguished these acts of violence because they were not directed at M.W. and E.W. *See Walsh I,* 31 F.Supp.2d at 206–07. Setting aside, for now, Jacqueline's allegations of John's direct physical and psychological abuse of the children, the district court's conclusions are in error, whatever the initial validity of the distinction. First, John has demonstrated an uncontrollably violent temper, and his assaults have been bloody and severe. His temper and assaults are not in the least lessened by the presence of his two youngest children, who have witnessed his assaults—indeed, M.W. was forced by him to witness the aftermath of his assault on Michael. Second, John has demonstrated that his violence knows not the bonds between parent and child or husband and wife, which should restrain such behavior. Third, John has gotten into fights with persons much younger than he, as when he attempted to assault the young man in Malden. Fourth, credible social science literature establishes that serial spousal abusers are also likely to be child abusers. *See, e.g.,* Jeffrey L. Edleson, *The Overlap Between Child Maltreatment and Woman Battering,* 5 Violence Against Women 134 (1999); Anne E. Appel & George W. Holden, *The Co–Occurrence of Spouse and Physical Child Abuse: A Review and Appraisal,* 12 J. Fam. Psychol. 578 (1998); Lee H. Bowker et al., *On the Relationship Between Wife Beating and Child Abuse,* in Kersti Yllo & Michele Bograd, *Feminist Perspectives on Wife Abuse* 158 (1988); Susan M. Ross, *Risk of Physical Abuse to Children of Spouse Abusing Parents,* 20 Child Abuse & Neglect 589 (1996). *But cf. Nunez–Escudero,* 58 F.3d at 376–77; *K. v. K.* [1997] 3 F.C.R. 207 (Eng.Fam.). Fifth, both state and federal law have recognized that children are at increased risk of physical and psychological injury themselves when they are in contact with a spousal abuser.

. . . The question remains whether John's undertakings, or even a potential barring order from the Irish courts, are sufficient to render any risk less than grave. John's undertakings require him to obey the orders of the district court and the courts of Ireland. We do not believe the undertakings received by the district court,[15] or even a potential barring order, are sufficient to protect the children from the exposure to grave risk in this case. We have no doubt that the Irish courts would issue appropriate protective orders. That is not the issue. The issue is John's history of violating orders issued by any court, Irish or American.

Courts, when confronted with a grave risk of physical harm, have allowed the return of a child to the country of habitual residence, provided sufficient protection was afforded. *See, e.g., Re K. (Abduction: Child's Objections)* [1995] 1 F.L.R. 977 (Eng.Fam.); *N. v. N. (Abduction: Article 13 Defence)* [1995] 1 F.L.R. 107 (Eng.Fam.); *cf. Friedrich*, 78 F.3d at 1069 (finding that the grave risk exception only applies when the child is in "danger *prior* to the resolution of the custody dispute—*e.g.,* returning the child to a zone of war, famine, or disease . . . [or when] there is a grave risk of harm in cases of serious abuse or neglect, or extraordinary emotional dependence, when the court in the country of habitual residence, for whatever reason, may be incapable . . . to give the child adequate protection"). Such an approach has little chance of working here. John's past acts clearly show that he thinks little of court orders. He has violated the orders of the courts of Massachusetts, and he has violated the orders of the courts of Ireland. There is every reason to believe that he will violate the undertakings he made to the district court in this case and any barring orders from the Irish courts.

Our conclusion here is similar to that of the English Court of Appeal in *Re F. (a Minor) (Abduction: Rights of Custody Abroad)* [1995] 3 All E.R. 641 (Eng.C.A.). In that case, the father, an American citizen, petitioned for the return of his son. *See id.* at 341. The father had abused the mother and was harsh with the son, including pinching his legs so hard as to leave bruises and other forms of abuse. *See id.* at 347. After the mother obtained a temporary restraining order, the father "engaged in a campaign of intimidation and harassment directed at the mother." *Id.* Granting the father's petition, the lower court held that the mother did not make out a case under article 13(b). *See id.* at 342. The Court of Appeal allowed the appeal (thus reversing the lower court). *See id.* at 352. The Court of Appeal was particularly concerned that the child would have been returned to the "very same surroundings and potentially the very same situation as that which has had such a serious effect upon him," and noted, in particular, that "[t]here has to be concern as to whether the father would take any notice of future orders of the court or comply with the undertakings he has given to the judge." *Id.* at 347–48.

While this case is not entirely one-sided,[16] we believe that the district court underestimated the risks to the children and overestimated the strength of the undertakings in this case. The article 13(b) exception must be applied and the petition must be dismissed.[17]

---

15.   The district court attempted to reduce the potential harm by making its order self-executing. Thus, the court's order provided that it would be of no force and effect if any of the undertakings were violated. *See Walsh I*, 31 F.Supp.2d at 207. As laudable as the attempt was, it necessarily falls short in this case, because the undertakings themselves are unlikely to be obeyed.

16.   The district court also found significant lapses on Jacqueline's part. *See Walsh I*, 31 F.Supp.2d at 204.

17.   The Convention says that the return of the child is not mandatory if grave risk is shown. John correctly urges that the district court nonetheless has discretion to order the return. *See* Hague Convention, art. 18; *Friedrich*, 78 F.3d at 1067; *Feder v. Evans–Feder*, 63 F.3d 217, 226 (3d Cir.1995). From this, John argues that the order should

We do not come to this conclusion lightly. International child abduction is a serious problem. Further, a court's interpretation of a treaty will have consequences not only for the family immediately involved but also for the way in which other courts—both here and abroad—interpret the treaty. *See United States v. Kin–Hong,* 110 F.3d 103, 106 (1st Cir.1997); W. Michael Reisman, *Necessary and Proper: Executive Competence to Interpret Treaties,* 15 Yale J. Int'l L. 316, 325 (1990). In the United States, the vast majority of Hague Convention petitions result in the return of children to their country of habitual residence, and rightly so. But the Convention provides for certain limited exceptions to this general rule. The clearly established facts of this case—including the father's flight after indictment for threatening to kill another person in a separate case and a documented history of violence and disregard for court orders going well beyond what one usually encounters even in bitter divorce and custody contexts—lead us to conclude that this case fits within one of these.

The judgments of the district court are *affirmed in part* and *reversed in part* and the case is remanded with instructions that John's petition be dismissed.

International Child Abduction Remedies Act of 1988

42 U.S.C.A. § 11601 et seq.

§ 11601.   Findings and declarations

(a) Findings

The Congress makes the following findings:

(1) The international abduction or wrongful retention of children is harmful to their well-being.

(2) Persons should not be permitted to obtain custody of children by virtue of their wrongful removal or retention.

(3) International abductions and receptions of children are increasing, and only concerted cooperation pursuant to an international agreement can effectively combat this problem.

(4) The Convention on the Civil Aspects of International Child Abduction, done at The Hague on October 25, 1980, establishes legal rights and procedures for the prompt return of children who have been wrongfully removed or retained, as well as for securing the exercise of visitation rights. Children who are wrongfully removed or retained within the meaning of the Convention are to be promptly returned unless one of the narrow exceptions set forth in the Convention applies. The Convention provides a sound treaty framework to help resolve the problem of international abduction and retention of children and will deter such wrongful removals and receptions.

be upheld as a reasonable exercise of the district court's discretion. Plainly, though, this misdescribes the basis for the court's order. We have no reason to think that the district court would have ordered the return of the children had it found that Jacqueline had made an article 13(b) showing. Moreover, even if it had, on these facts, such an order would have been an abuse of discretion.

(b) Declarations

The Congress makes the following declarations:

(1) It is the purpose of this chapter to establish procedures for the implementation of the Convention in the United States.

(2) The provisions of this chapter are in addition to and not in lieu of the provisions of the Convention.

(3) In enacting this chapter the Congress recognizes—

(A) the international character of the Convention; and

(B) the need for uniform international interpretation of the Convention.

(4) The Convention and this chapter empower courts in the United States to determine only rights under the Convention and not the merits of any underlying child custody claims.

§ 11602. Definitions

For the purposes of this chapter—

(1) the term "applicant" means any person who, pursuant to the Convention, files an application with the United States Central Authority or a Central Authority of any other party to the Convention for the return of a child alleged to have been wrongfully removed or retained or for arrangements for organizing or securing the effective exercise of rights of access pursuant to the Convention;

(2) the term "Convention" means the Convention on the Civil Aspects of International Child Abduction, done at The Hague on October 25, 1980;

(3) the term "Parent Locator Service" means the service established by the Secretary of Health and Human Services under section 653 of this title;

(4) the term "petitioner" means any person who, in accordance with this chapter, files a petition in court seeking relief under the Convention;

(5) the term "person" includes any individual, institution, or other legal entity or body;

(6) the term "respondent" means any person against whose interests a petition is filed in court, in accordance with this chapter, which seeks relief under the Convention;

(7) the term "rights of access" means visitation rights;

(8) the term "State" means any of the several States, the District of Columbia, and any commonwealth, territory, or possession of the United States; and

(9) the term "United States Central Authority" means the agency of the Federal Government designated by the President under section 11606(a) of this title.

§ 11603.   Judicial remedies

(a) Jurisdiction of the courts

The courts of the States and the United States district courts shall have concurrent original jurisdiction of actions arising under the Convention.

(b) Petitions

Any person seeking to initiate judicial proceedings under the Convention for the return of a child or for arrangements for organizing or securing the effective exercise of rights of access to a child may do so by commencing a civil action by filing a petition for the relief sought in any court which has jurisdiction of such action and which is authorized to exercise its jurisdiction in the place where the child is located at the time the petition is filed.

(c) Notice

Notice of an action brought under subsection (b) of this section shall be given in accordance with the applicable law governing notice in interstate child custody proceedings.

(d) Determination of case

The court in which an action is brought under subsection (b) of this section shall decide the case in accordance with the Convention.

(e) Burdens of proof

(1) A petitioner in an action brought under subsection (b) of this section shall establish by a preponderance of the evidence—

(A) in the case of an action for the return of a child, that the child has been wrongfully removed or retained within the meaning of the Convention; and

(B) in the case of an action for arrangements for organizing or securing the effective exercise of rights of access, that the petitioner has such rights.

(2) In the case of an action for the return of a child, a respondent who opposes the return of the child has the burden of establishing—

(A) by clear and convincing evidence that one of the exceptions set forth in article 13b or 20 of the Convention applies; and

(B) by a preponderance of the evidence that any other exception set forth in article 12 or 13 of the Convention applies.

(f) Application of the Convention

For purposes of any action brought under this chapter—

(1) the term "authorities", as used in article 15 of the Convention to refer to the authorities of the state of the habitual residence of a child, includes courts and appropriate government agencies;

(2) the terms "wrongful removal or retention" and "wrongfully removed or retained", as used in the Convention, include a removal or retention of a child before the entry of a custody order regarding that child; and

(3) the term "commencement of proceedings", as used in article 12 of the Convention, means, with respect to the return of a child located in the

United States, the filing of a petition in accordance with subsection (b) of this section.

(g) Full faith and credit

Full faith and credit shall be accorded by the courts of the States and the courts of the United States to the judgment of any other such court ordering or denying the return of a child, pursuant to the Convention, in an action brought under this chapter.

(h) Remedies under the Convention not exclusive

The remedies established by the Convention and this chapter shall be in addition to remedies available under other laws or international agreements.

§ 11604.   Provisional remedies

(a) Authority of courts

In furtherance of the objectives of article 7(b) and other provisions of the Convention, and subject to the provisions of subsection (b) of this section, any court exercising jurisdiction of an action brought under section 11603(b) of this title may take or cause to be taken measures under Federal or State law, as appropriate, to protect the well-being of the child involved or to prevent the child's further removal or concealment before the final disposition of the petition.

(b) Limitation on authority

No court exercising jurisdiction of an action brought under section 11603(b) of this title may, under subsection (a) of this section, order a child removed from a person having physical control of the child unless the applicable requirements of State law are satisfied.

§ 11605.   Admissibility of documents

With respect to any application to the United States Central Authority, or any petition to a court under section 11603 of this title, which seeks relief under the Convention, or any other documents or information included with such application or petition or provided after such submission which relates to the application or petition, as the case may be, no authentication of such application, petition, document, or information shall be required in order for the application, petition, document, or information to be admissible in court.

§ 11606.   United States Central Authority

(a) Designation

The President shall designate a Federal agency to serve as the Central Authority for the United States under the Convention.

(b) Functions

The functions of the United States Central Authority are those ascribed to the Central Authority by the Convention and this chapter.

(c) Regulatory authority

The United States Central Authority is authorized to issue such regulations as may be necessary to carry out its functions under the Convention and this chapter.

(d) Obtaining information from Parent Locator Service

The United States Central Authority may, to the extent authorized by the Social Security Act [42 U.S.C.A. § 301 et seq.], obtain information from the Parent Locator Service.

(e) Grant Authority

The United States Central Authority is authorized to make grants to, or enter into contracts or agreements with, any individual, corporation, other Federal, State, or local agency, or private entity or organization in the United States for purposes of accomplishing its responsibilities under the Convention and this Act.

. . .

§ 11607.   Costs and fees

(a) Administrative costs

No department, agency, or instrumentality of the Federal Government or of any State or local government may impose on an applicant any fee in relation to the administrative processing of applications submitted under the Convention.

(b) Costs incurred in civil actions

(1) Petitioners may be required to bear the costs of legal counsel or advisors, court costs incurred in connection with their petitions, and travel costs for the return of the child involved and any accompanying persons, except as provided in paragraphs (2) and (3).

(2) Subject to paragraph (3), legal fees or court costs incurred in connection with an action brought under section 11603 of this title shall be borne by the petitioner unless they are covered by payments from Federal, State, or local legal assistance or other programs.

(3) Any court ordering the return of a child pursuant to an action brought under section 11603 of this title shall order the respondent to pay necessary expenses incurred by or on behalf of the petitioner, including court costs, legal fees, foster home or other care during the course of proceedings in the action, and transportation costs related to the return of the child, unless the respondent establishes that such order would be clearly inappropriate.

§ 11608.   Collection, maintenance, and dissemination of information

(a) In general

In performing its functions under the Convention, the United States Central Authority may, under such conditions as the Central Authority prescribes by regulation, but subject to subsection (c) of this section, receive from or transmit to any department, agency, or instrumentality of the Federal Government or of any State or foreign government, and receive from or transmit to any applicant, petitioner, or respondent, information necessary to locate a child or for the purpose of otherwise implementing the

Convention with respect to a child, except that the United States Central Authority—

(1) may receive such information from a Federal or State department, agency, or instrumentality only pursuant to applicable Federal and State statutes; and

(2) may transmit any information received under this subsection notwithstanding any provision of law other than this chapter.

(b) Requests for information

Requests for information under this section shall be submitted in such manner and form as the United States Central Authority may prescribe by regulation and shall be accompanied or supported by such documents as the United States Central Authority may require.

(c) Responsibility of government entities

Whenever any department, agency, or instrumentality of the United States or of any State receives a request from the United States Central Authority for information authorized to be provided to such Central Authority under subsection (a) of this section, the head of such department, agency, or instrumentality shall promptly cause a search to be made of the files and records maintained by such department, agency, or instrumentality in order to determine whether the information requested is contained in any such files or records. If such search discloses the information requested, the head of such department, agency, or instrumentality shall immediately transmit such information to the United States Central Authority, except that any such information the disclosure of which—

(1) would adversely affect the national security interests of the United States or the law enforcement interests of the United States or of any State; or

(2) would be prohibited by section 9 of Title 13;

shall not be transmitted to the Central Authority. The head of such department, agency, or instrumentality shall, immediately upon completion of the requested search, notify the Central Authority of the results of the search, and whether an exception set forth in paragraph (1) or (2) applies. In the event that the United States Central Authority receives information and the appropriate Federal or State department, agency, or instrumentality thereafter notifies the Central Authority that an exception set forth in paragraph (1) or (2) applies to that information, the Central Authority may not disclose that information under subsection (a) of this section.

(d) Information available from Parent Locator Service

To the extent that information which the United States Central Authority is authorized to obtain under the provisions of subsection (c) of this section can be obtained through the Parent Locator Service, the United States Central Authority shall first seek to obtain such information from the Parent Locator Service, before requesting such information directly under the provisions of subsection (c) of this section.

(e) Record keeping

The United States Central Authority shall maintain appropriate records concerning its activities and the disposition of cases brought to its attention.

[EDITORS' NOTE: Sections 11609 and 11610 are omitted. The first provides for designation of persons (some of whom may be private citizens) to monitor operation of the Convention and to provide advice on its implementation. The latter section authorizes annual appropriations.]

NOTES

(1) The Hague Convention on the Civil Aspects of International Child Abduction was adopted by the Hague Conference on Private International Law in 1980 and was ratified by the United States in 1988. *See* Westbrook, Law and Treaty Responses to International Child Abduction, 20 Va.J.Int.Law 669 (1980). It was implemented in the United States in 1988 through adoption of the International Child Abduction Remedies Act. The text of the Hague Convention can be found in 32 I.L.M. 1134, and in Walter Wadlington and Raymond O'Brien, Family Law Statutes, International Conventions and Uniform Laws 344 (Foundation Press 2007). For a thorough analysis of the Convention, see Merle H. Weiner, 33 Colum. Hum. Rts. L. Rev. 275 (2002)

There are some important practical problems regarding the Hague Convention. Not all countries adopting it have adequately implemented it. The cost and availability of counsel also can serve as impediments. *See* Christopher B. Whitman, Recent Development. The Second Circuit Limits "Custody Rights" Under the Hague Convention on the Civil Aspects of International Child Abduction. 9 Tul. J. Int'l & Comp. L. 605 (2001); Peter Pfund, The Hague Convention on International Child Abduction, the International Child Abduction Remedies Act, and the Need for Availability of Counsel for All Petitioners, 24 Fam.L.Q. 35 (1990). For more details about the convention, *see* THE LEGAL ANALYSIS OF THE HAGUE CONVENTION ON THE CIVIL ASPECTS OF INTERNATIONAL CHILD ABDUCTION, 51 Fed. Reg. 10,503, 10,505 (1993).

(2) Section 23 of the UCCJA provides:

The general policies of this Act extend to the international area. The provisions of this Act relating to the recognition and enforcement of custody decrees of other states apply to custody decrees and decrees involving legal institutions similar in nature to custody, rendered by appropriate authorities of other nations if reasonable notice and opportunity to be heard were given to all affected persons.

This section was generally included in the laws of states which have adopted the Act, though at least one jurisdiction (Ohio) omitted it. Several state appeals courts used their versions of the UCCJA provision in reconciling disputes across national borders. *See, e.g., Middleton v. Middleton*, 227 Va. 82, 314 S.E.2d 362 (1984); *Miller v. Superior Court of Los Angeles County*, 22 Cal.3d 923, 151 Cal.Rptr. 6, 587 P.2d 723 (1978).

Sections 301 and 302 of the UCCJEA provide that a state may enforce an order for return of a child made under the Hague Convention on the Civil Aspects of International Child Abduction.

International Parental Kidnapping Crime Act of 1993

18 U.S.C.A. § 1204

§ 1204. International parental kidnapping

(a) Whoever removes a child from the United States, or attempts to do so, or retains a child (who has been in the United States) outside the

United States with intent to obstruct the lawful exercise of parental rights shall be fined under this title or imprisoned not more than 3 years, or both.

(b) As used in this section—

(1) the term "child" means a person who has not attained the age of 16 years; and

(2) the term "parental rights", with respect to a child, means the right to physical custody of the child—

(A) whether joint or sole (and includes visiting rights); and

(B) whether arising by operation of law, court order, or legally binding agreement of the parties.

(c) It shall be an affirmative defense under this section that—

(1) the defendant acted within the provisions of a valid court order granting the defendant legal custody or visitation rights and that order was obtained pursuant to the Uniform Child Custody Jurisdiction Act and was in effect at the time of the offense;

(2) the defendant was fleeing an incidence or pattern of domestic violence;

(3) the defendant had physical custody of the child pursuant to a court order granting legal custody or visitation rights and failed to return the child as a result of circumstances beyond the defendant's control, and the defendant notified or made reasonable attempts to notify the other parent or lawful custodian of the child of such circumstances within 24 hours after the visitation period had expired and returned the child as soon as possible.

(d) This section does not detract from The Hague Convention on the Civil Aspects of International Parental Child Abduction, done at The Hague on October 25, 1980.

NOTE

The principal mechanism by which abducted children may be returned to the United States is the Hague Convention on the Civil Aspects of International Law. If a child is taken to a non-signatory country, however, the treaty may not be implemented. To fill this vacuum in the Hague Convention's coverage, Congress enacted the preceding statute.

CHAPTER V

INTERVENTION IN THE FAMILY TO PROTECT CHILDREN

A. THE CHILD PROTECTION UMBRELLA

CALIFORNIA WELFARE AND INSTITUTIONS CODE (WEST)

ARTICLE 6. DEPENDENT CHILDREN—JURISDICTION

§ 300. **Children subject to jurisdiction; legislative intent and declarations; guardian defined**

Any child who comes within any of the following descriptions is within the jurisdiction of the juvenile court which may adjudge that person to be a dependent child of the court:

(a) The child has suffered, or there is a substantial risk that the child will suffer, serious physical harm inflicted nonaccidentally upon the child by the child's parent or guardian. For the purposes of this subdivision, a court may find there is a substantial risk of serious future injury based on the manner in which a less serious injury was inflicted, a history of repeated inflictions of injuries on the child or the child's siblings, or a combination of these and other actions by the parent or guardian which indicate the child is at risk of serious physical harm. For purposes of this subdivision, "serious physical harm" does not include reasonable and age-appropriate spanking to the buttocks where there is no evidence of serious physical injury.

(b) The child has suffered, or there is a substantial risk that the child will suffer, serious physical harm or illness, as a result of the failure or inability of his or her parent or guardian to adequately supervise or protect the child, or the willful or negligent failure of the child's parent or guardian to adequately supervise or protect the child from the conduct of the custodian with whom the child has been left, or by the willful or negligent failure of the parent or guardian to provide the child with adequate food, clothing, shelter, or medical treatment, or by the inability of the parent or guardian to provide regular care for the child due to the parent's or guardian's mental illness, developmental disability, or substance abuse. No child shall be found to be a person described by this subdivision solely due to the lack of an emergency shelter for the family. Whenever it is alleged that a child comes within the jurisdiction of the court on the basis of the parent's or guardian's willful failure to provide adequate medical treatment or specific decision to provide spiritual treatment through prayer, the court shall give deference to the parent's or guardian's medical treatment, nontreatment, or spiritual treatment through prayer alone in accordance with the tenets and practices of a recognized church or religious denomination, by an accredited practitioner thereof, and shall not assume jurisdiction unless necessary to protect the child from suffering serious physical harm or illness. In making its determination, the court shall consider (1) the nature of the treatment proposed by the parent or guardian, (2) the risks to the child posed by the course of treatment or nontreatment proposed by the parent or guardian, (3) the risk, if any, of the course of treatment being proposed by the petitioning agency, and (4) the likely success of the courses of treatment or nontreatment proposed by the parent or guardian and agency. The child shall continue to be a dependent child pursuant to this subdivision only so long as is necessary to protect the child from risk of suffering serious physical harm or illness.

(c) The child is suffering serious emotional damage, or is at substantial risk of suffering serious emotional damage, evidenced by severe anxiety, depression, withdrawal, or untoward aggressive behavior toward self or others, as a result of the conduct of the parent or guardian or who has no parent or guardian capable of providing appropriate care. No child shall be found to be a person described by this subdivision if the willful failure of the parent or guardian to provide adequate mental health treatment is based on a sincerely held religious belief and if a less intrusive judicial intervention is available.

(d) The child has been sexually abused, or there is a substantial risk that the child will be sexually abused, as defined in Section 11165.1 of the Penal Code, by his or her parent or guardian or a member of his or her household, or the parent or guardian has failed to adequately protect the child from sexual abuse when the parent or guardian knew or reasonably should have known that the child was in danger of sexual abuse.

(e) The child is under the age of five years and has suffered severe physical abuse by a parent, or by any person known by the parent, if the parent knew or reasonably should have known that the person was physically abusing the child. For the purposes of this subdivision, "severe physical abuse" means any of the following: any single act of abuse which causes physical trauma of sufficient severity that, if left untreated, would cause permanent physical disfigurement, permanent physical disability, or death; any single act of sexual abuse which causes significant bleeding, deep bruising, or significant external or internal swelling; or more than one act of physical abuse, each of which causes bleeding, deep bruising, significant external or internal swelling, bone fracture, or unconsciousness; or the willful, prolonged failure to provide adequate food. A child may not be removed from the physical custody of his or her parent or guardian on the basis of a finding of severe physical abuse unless the social worker has made an allegation of severe physical abuse pursuant to Section 332.

(f) The child's parent or guardian caused the death of another child through abuse or neglect.

(g) The child has been left without any provision for support; physical custody of the child has been voluntarily surrendered pursuant to Section 1255.7 of the Health and Safety Code and the child has not been reclaimed within the 14–day period specified in subdivision (e) of that section; the child's parent has been incarcerated or institutionalized and cannot arrange for the care of the child; or a relative or other adult custodian with whom the child resides or has been left is unwilling or unable to provide care or support for the child, the whereabouts of the parent are unknown, and reasonable efforts to locate the parent have been unsuccessful.

(h) The child has been freed for adoption by one or both parents for 12 months by either relinquishment or termination of parental rights or an adoption petition has not been granted.

(i) The child has been subjected to an act or acts of cruelty by the parent or guardian or a member of his or her household, or the parent or guardian has failed to adequately protect the child from an act or acts of cruelty when the parent or guardian knew or reasonably should have known that the child was in danger of being subjected to an act or acts of cruelty.

(j) The child's sibling has been abused or neglected, as defined in subdivision (a), (b), (d), (e), or (i), and there is a substantial risk that the child will be abused or neglected, as defined in those subdivisions. The court shall consider the circumstances surrounding the abuse or neglect of the sibling, the age and gender of each child, the nature of the abuse or neglect of the sibling, the mental condition of the parent or guardian, and any other factors the court considers probative in determining whether there is a substantial risk to the child.

It is the intent of the Legislature that nothing in this section disrupt the family unnecessarily or intrude inappropriately into family life, prohibit the use of reasonable methods of parental discipline, or prescribe a particular method of parenting. Further, nothing in this section is intended to limit the offering of voluntary services to those families in need of assistance but who do not come within the descriptions of this section. To the extent that savings accrue to the state from child welfare services funding obtained as a result of the enactment of the act that enacted this section, those savings shall be used to promote services which support family maintenance and family reunification plans, such as client transportation, out-of-home respite care, parenting training, and the provision of temporary or emergency in-home caretakers and persons teaching and demonstrating homemaking skills. The Legislature further declares that a physical disability, such as blindness or deafness, is no bar to the raising of happy and well-adjusted children and that a court's determination pursuant to this section shall center upon whether a parent's disability prevents him or her from exercising care and control.

As used in this section "guardian" means the legal guardian of the child.

B.   NEGLECT, DEPENDENCY AND ENDANGERMENT

In re B.K.

District of Columbia Court of Appeals, 1981.
429 A.2d 1331.

■ Before KELLY, FERREN and PRYOR, ASSOCIATE JUDGES.

■ PER CURIAM:

The District of Columbia has the authority pursuant to D.C.Code 1973, §§ 16–2301, –2320, to protect a "neglected child" by removing that child from the custody of his or her parents. In this appeal, the father of a child found to be "neglected" challenges both the finding below and the constitutionality of the D.C. Statute. . . .

The young girl, B.K., whose present and future well-being is the central concern of this proceeding, was born on September 19, 1978, at the Georgetown University Hospital. Both her parents have been diagnosed as suffering from undifferentiated paranoid schizophrenia. Although appellant argues that the court below incorrectly focused on the parents' mental illness rather than the well-being of the child, it is clear from the record that the parents' condition was considered relevant only insofar as it pertained to their ability to provide proper care for B.K. The evidence showed that they were unable to do so, and that when in their care, B.K.'s physical and emotional health was threatened.

During the period while she was in the hospital delivering her baby, B.K.'s mother exhibited strange behavior which prompted further examination by staff psychiatrists. The mother's condition was diagnosed as a "classic case of schizophrenia" and the prediction was that she would be unable to comprehend her child's emotional and physical needs. Although the Child Protective Services Division of the Department of Human Resources was apprised of the situation by doctors at Georgetown, there was no direct intervention by the Division at that time. On February 16, 1979, the Child Protective Services Division was again contacted about this unfortunate situation when the father of B.K.'s mother informed the Division that his daughter and appellant had been arrested while standing in the middle of the street, apparently under the influence of drugs. The events which finally caused intervention by the Protective Services Division began on March 23, 1979, when pedestrians observed appellant and B.K.'s mother, with B.K. in a stroller, walking downtown at about 11:00 p.m. According to the pedestrians, appellant and B.K.'s mother appeared to be disoriented and intoxicated, and B.K. was screaming. This alarmed the pedestrians who approached the couple. At that point, B.K.'s mother walked away and, after arguing with the pedestrians, appellant also left. The pedestrians, then took B.K., who was clad only in a thin cloth pajama, into the Embassy Row Hotel where they called the police. After police arrived on the scene, B.K.'s mother appeared at the hotel. Since she appeared to be intoxicated, the officers transported her to the detoxification unit of the D.C. General Hospital. Meanwhile, B.K. was taken into custody by the Youth Division of the Metropolitan Police Department.

That night, a police officer and an investigator for the Protective Services Division visited the Kalorama Road house where appellant lived with B.K. and B.K.'s mother. According to their testimony, and the testimony of an inspector for the Housing and Community Development Department who inspected the house on March 27, 1979, the premises were, to put it mildly, not very pleasant. There was plaster falling from holes in the ceiling, cracks in the walls, no adequate kitchen facilities, dirty pampers strewn all over the floor, profuse odors, human and animal feces on the first and second floors, broken windows in the bathroom and, due to a structural defect, water was leaking on exposed wiring. According to the housing inspector, these conditions were dangerous and constituted a health hazard.

When he was visited on the night of March 23, 1979, by the police officer and the housing inspector, appellant agreed to permit the Child Protective Services Division to provide emergency care for B.K. However, on March 27, 1979, B.K. was released into the custody of her mother, who at that time expressed her willingness to cooperate with Protective Services. Only a few days later, during the evening of April 3, 1979, B.K. was again taken into protective custody. Customers and employees in a restaurant had observed B.K.'s mother, seated at a table, swinging B.K. through the air. With each swing, B.K.'s head came perilously close to colliding with the table top. The acting manager of the restaurant, after talking to B.K.'s mother, became concerned for the safety of the child and called the police. All the while, appellant was seated at the bar, apparently oblivious to the situation. When the police arrived, B.K. and her mother were taken into custody. B.K. was placed in shelter care at St. Ann's Infant Home.

At this point, the Protective Services Division began a more thorough investigation of the circumstances surrounding B.K.'s care and both parents underwent physical and mental examinations. On April 10, 1979, a petition was filed in Superior Court alleging that B.K. was a "neglected child" under D.C.Code 1973, § 16–2301(9)(B) & (C).[1]

A lengthy factfinding hearing was conducted in the Superior Court Family Division beginning on October 15, 1979. Extensive testimony was heard from case workers and psychiatrists regarding B.K. and her parents. Appellant's landlady and a Catholic priest testified on behalf of B.K.'s parents. At the conclusion of the evidence, the court issued its findings of fact and ruled that the government had shown, by a preponderance of the evidence, that B.K. was neglected within the meaning of the statute. A dispositional hearing ... was held on December 18, 1979, and B.K. was placed in the custody of her maternal grandparents.

We emphasize at the outset that the order below does not terminate parental rights but merely determines custody of the neglected child for a period of two years, at which time further proceedings must be held.

The trial court correctly stated that in a neglect proceeding the government must prove its case by a "preponderance of the evidence." This is clear from the statute itself. Appellant, however, argues that because the ruling below separated him from his child, and thus threatens the sanctity of his family, see Moore v. City of East Cleveland, 431 U.S. 494 (1977), the

---

1. The term "neglected child" means a child—

. . .

(B) who is without proper parental care or control, subsistence, education as required by law, or other care or control necessary for his physical, mental, or emotional health, and the deprivation is not due to the lack of financial means of his parent, guardian, or other custodian;

(C) whose parent, guardian, or other custodian is unable to discharge his responsibilities to and for the child because of incarceration, hospitalization, or other physical or mental incapacity; ... [D.C.Code 1973, § 16–2301(9)(B) & (C).]

Constitution requires that the standard of proof be "clear and convincing evidence." In In re: J.S.R., D.C.App., 374 A.2d 860 (1977), we stated that the consequences of a finding that parental consent to an adoption was being withheld contrary to the best interests of the child are "far more severe than those of a finding of neglect." Id. at 864. Nonetheless, we held that, although the higher standard of "clear and convincing evidence" was warranted in the adoption case, it was not constitutionally required. Therefore, it follows that in a neglect proceeding the Constitution does not require the "clear and convincing evidence" standard.

Our holding in In re: J.S.R. is not altered by Addington v. Texas, 441 U.S. 418 (1979), in which the Supreme Court held that due process requires the "clear and convincing" standard of proof in a civil proceeding brought to commit an individual involuntarily for an indefinite period of time to a state mental hospital. The individual's liberty interest at stake in *Addington* is greater than appellant's interest in retaining custody of his child, particularly when balanced against the interest of the state in protecting neglected children.

On the basis of the record in this case, we are satisfied the child was shown to be neglected by a preponderance of the evidence. We note also that the trial court stated in its findings that even under the "clear and convincing" standard the government had made its case. That exemplifies both the solicitousness of the trial court for the interests involved and the great weight of the evidence presented by the government.

Appellant also challenges the constitutionality of the neglect statute pursuant to which the petition was brought. We cannot quarrel with appellant's assertion that the state must tread carefully when it intrudes upon the integrity of the family unit. This court recognized that fundamental proposition in In re: J.S.R.:

> The right of a natural parent to raise one's child is a fundamental and essential one which is constitutionally protected. However, it is not an absolute one. The state has both the right and the duty to protect minor children through judicial determinations of their interest. To this end, the state has a substantial range of authority to protect the welfare of a child, and the state's legitimate interest in the child's welfare may be implemented by separating the child from the parent. [Supra at 863 (citations omitted).]

Appellant contends the statutory definition of a "neglected" child is vague, and therefore unconstitutional. In order to withstand a vagueness challenge the statute must state its standard with adequate clarity and make sufficiently distinct boundaries for the law to be fairly administered. Roth v. United States, 354 U.S. 476 (1957). The Supreme Court has reminded us that in considering vagueness, statutes which do not involve First Amendment freedoms must be evaluated in light of the facts of the case at hand. United States v. Mazurie, 419 U.S. 544 (1975); ... The statute in question here may be broad in its coverage, but we are not persuaded that it is vague. We point out that "proceedings under this type statute demand and provide a certain amount of elasticity to the court." Matter of C.M.S., 609 P.2d 240, 244 (Mont.1979). The statute requires an investigation into the circumstances of the particular case and provides clear guidelines for determining whether a child is neglected. On the facts of this case, there is no question that such a finding was proper.

Affirmed.

In re Jeannette S.

California Court of Appeals, Fifth District, 1979.
94 Cal.App.3d 52, 156 Cal.Rptr. 262.

■ FRANSON, ASSOCIATE JUSTICE.

STATEMENT OF THE CASE

Appellant Margery S. appeals from a judgment of the juvenile court declaring her five-year old daughter Jeannette S. a dependent child of the juvenile court under section 300, subdivisions (a) and (b) of the Welfare and Institutions Code and removing the child from her custody and control under section 361, subdivisions (a) and (b) of that code. (All further statutory references are to the Welfare and Institutions Code unless otherwise specified.)

On January 5, 1978, representatives of the Merced County Department of Human Resources (hereinafter Department) went to appellant's home where Jeannette resided to investigate problems which appellant had mentioned to a Department representative earlier that day. As a result of that investigation, Jeannette was taken into protective custody. On January 6, 1978, Sheila Callan, a Department social worker, filed a petition in the juvenile court alleging that Jeannette was a person described under section 300, subdivisions (a) and (b).

At the detention hearing both appellant and Frank S., the minor's father, were present. The father requested that Jeannette be placed in his custody pending the jurisdictional hearing. The court denied the request, found probable cause to detain Jeannette and ordered her detained. The court appointed separate counsel to represent Jeannette's mother and father at the jurisdictional and dispositional hearings.

At the jurisdictional hearing which commenced on January 25 and was completed after several continued hearings on February 22, 1978, the court found that Jeannette was a person within the provisions of section 300, subdivisions (a) and (b) since she had no parent capable of exercising the necessary care and control or of providing her with a suitable home; she was accordingly declared a dependent child of the court.

The parties agreed to proceed with the dispositional hearing immediately. The judge stated that he had reviewed the dispositional reports and had concluded that the minor should be placed in the custody of the Department for suitable placement. The court found that the allegations of the petition were true; that the award of custody to the parents would be detrimental to the minor; and that the award to the Department would serve the best interests of the child. It was ordered that Jeannette be placed in the custody of the Department for suitable placement. It was further ordered that the matter be continued for a review hearing on

January 10, 1979, and that during the interim both parents would have the right to visit Jeannette without supervision.

Appellant filed a timely notice of appeal.

THE EVIDENCE

Jeannette was born to appellant and Frank on July 23, 1972. They were divorced in 1976, and appellant was awarded custody of Jeannette. Jeannette lived with appellant in Merced until she was detained by the Department on January 5. Frank had regularly exercised visitation rights on weekends during the two-year period since the divorce.

Appellant's psychological profile reveals that she is of above average intelligence; that she suffers from chronic anxiety and has a somewhat schizoid personality. Appellant attended a mental health clinic on a daily basis from 9 a.m. to 3 p.m. where she participated in group therapy and other activities. She demonstrates a concern for her child and her relationship with Jeannette is a close and loving one.

Appellant has a limited income and has been active in seeking aid from social agencies. She requested and received visits from a public health nurse who instructed her on child care. She also received assistance from a homemaker assigned by the welfare department for the two weeks preceding January 5, 1978. The homemaker apparently reported to her supervisor that the assignment was "unsuccessful," but the homemaker did not testify at the hearings to explain what the problem was about. Appellant testified that the homemaker merely transported Jeannette to the doctor and to the day-care school while appellant was at the mental health clinic. Other than one time for a five-minute period, the homemaker did not assist appellant in cleaning the house. Appellant acknowledged that it was difficult for her to take criticism but "If it is made in a suggestive way, I can cope with it." Except for the homemaker service for the two weeks preceding January 5, appellant had received no assistance in the care of her home for the past one and a half years. On the afternoon of January 5, appellant went to the Department's office and told one of the supervisors that she had several problems with her home situation and that she needed help, thereby triggering the instant proceedings.

When the Department representatives went to appellant's house on January 5, they found it dirty and cluttered with debris. There were extensive dog feces on the kitchen floor and cat feces in the bathroom. The house smelled of urine and there was spoiled food on the stove. Jeannette had been forced to sleep on the couch in the living room because her bedroom was such a mess.

Appellant kept three dogs and two cats at her residence.

Jeannette was in apparent good health and good spirits on January 5. There was no evidence of trauma or abuse. However, Jeannette's kindergarten teacher testified that the child was frequently dirty when she came to school and her clothing was extremely odoriferous which caused some teasing by the other children. Although Jeannette behaved in a distracted manner at school and had difficulty communicating due to a speech defect, her behavior was not particularly deviant. A psychological evaluation of

Jeannette by the school psychologist reveals that she is mildly hyperactive and sometimes has difficulty concentrating in class, but her academic progress is good. She is bright and gets along well with others.

There was some evidence that on occasions appellant did not prepare breakfast or other meals for Jeannette; however, she did not appear undernourished. Frequently appellant was not home when Jeannette returned from school.

Mr. Stutsman, a social worker for the Department, testified at the jurisdictional hearing that he had visited appellant's home on several occasions from January 1976 to August of 1977 because of complaints by school authorities about Jeannette's unclean appearance at school. On one occasion in February 1976, he went into the house and found it to be extremely dirty with animal feces on the floor.

Jeannette's father Frank appeared at both the jurisdictional and dispositional hearings and requested custody of Jeannette. He testified that he loved Jeannette and had a good relationship with her. He had regularly exercised his visitation rights with Jeannette during the two years since his divorce from appellant. Frank lived in a small two-bedroom single-bath house in Merced with Robert and Helen Christiansen (his former brother-in-law and his wife). The Christiansens had moved into Frank's house to provide a home for Jeannette if she should be removed from the custody of her mother. Mr. Christiansen is employed full time as a truck driver, and his wife Helen would care for Jeannette at Frank's home. Frank testified that he would give Jeannette his room and would sleep on the couch in the living room.

Sheila Callan, a social worker, investigated Frank's home and filed a supplemental report at the jurisdictional hearing. The report states that because Frank's house has only two bedrooms and one bath that the sleeping arrangements proposed by Frank if he should obtain custody of Jeannette would be unsatisfactory in that he would have to go through Jeannette's bedroom to reach the bathroom. The report states, "This action appears to be antithetical to the well-being of Jeannette because of the crowded living arrangements." The report also noted that Frank has an unstable employment record and receives welfare and unemployment benefits. He also has a serious problem with alcohol and lacks the knowledge and skills required for child rearing.[1] On the basis of her investigation, Ms. Callan opined that Frank was incapable of providing a suitable home for Jeannette due to his alcoholism, financial instability and lack of "parenting skills." She recommended that Jeannette be placed in the custody of the Department for suitable placement.

At no time did the Department in its dispositional reports to the court recommend a plan for reuniting Jeannette with her mother or father as required by California Rule of Court 1376, subdivision (b). The disposition-

[1]. The report also notes that Frank "has an arrest record of contributing to the delinquency of a minor; he molested a six-year old female in December 1965." However, apparently neither the Department nor the juvenile court place any emphasis on the arrest record in making the recommendation and decision not to place Jeannette with Frank. Mrs. Christiansen's presence at Frank's home should have obviated any concern in this regard.

al report recommended that the parents' visits with Jeannette be supervised by a social worker "to insure that Jeannette will not be upset by false promises, threats and demands [by the parents]." The court rejected the recommendation.

THERE IS SUFFICIENT EVIDENCE TO SUPPORT THE JURISDICTIONAL FINDING OF DEPENDENCY

The standard of proof required to establish that a minor is a dependent child under section 300 is the "preponderance of the evidence." (§ 355.) If there is any substantial evidence to support the findings of the juvenile court, a reviewing court must uphold the trial court's findings. All reasonable inferences must be drawn in support of the findings and the record must be viewed in the light most favorable to the juvenile court's order.

In the present case, the report prepared by the Department for presentation at the jurisdictional hearing details the condition of Jeannette's inadequate home environment. That report states that Jeannette was sent to school in clothes which were soiled with urine, she was not given breakfast at home, and she frequently returned from school to an empty house. The home was "filthy" and there was no adequate place for Jeannette to sleep because of clutter. The jurisdictional report also stated that appellant had not provided a stable mother role and was unable to place her child's needs above her own. Testimony of witnesses verified the allegations in the report and established that the condition of the home on January 5 was not an isolated occurrence. Thus, there was substantial evidence to support the trial court's order that Jeannette be declared a dependent child of the court.[2]

We have considered and reject the various contentions of appellant that she was deprived of constitutional and statutory procedural due process requirements by lack of notice of the jurisdictional charges under section 300. We also reject her contention regarding the lack of written findings of fact.

THERE IS INSUFFICIENT EVIDENCE TO SUPPORT THE DISPOSITIONAL ORDER REMOVING JEANNETTE FROM THE CUSTODY OF HER MOTHER AND FATHER UNDER SECTION 361

It is a cardinal rule of our society that the custody, care and nurture of a child resides first in the parents rather than in a public agency. As stated in In re Carmaleta (1978) 21 Cal.3d 482 at page 489, 146 Cal.Rptr. 623 at page 627, 579 P.2d 514 at page 518:

"Parenting is a fundamental right, and accordingly, is disturbed only in extreme cases of persons acting in a fashion incompatible with

---

2. We acknowledge that the dependency order is highly questionable insofar as Frank's ability to provide effective care and control of Jeannette (§ 300, subd. (a)) and to provide Jeannette with the necessities of life and with a suitable place of abode (§ 300, subd. (b)). It is difficult to justify the dependency finding in light of Frank's willingness to accept Jeannette in his home under the care and supervision of Mrs. Christiansen. The crowded living conditions together with Frank's alcoholism and dependence upon welfare services clearly are insufficient, standing alone, to support a finding of dependence. However, Frank has not appealed the dependency order, and we believe that the reversal of the disposition order and a remand for another dispositional hearing will adequately protect Jeannette's interests.

parenthood. Thus, . . ." [t]he relationship of . . . natural parent . . . [and] . . . children is a vital human relationship which has far-reaching implications for the growth and development of the child. (See Kay & Phillips, Poverty and the Law of Child Custody (1966) 54 Cal.L.R. 717.) . . . [T]he involuntary termination of that relationship by state action must be viewed as a drastic remedy which should be resorted to only in extreme cases of neglect or abandonment [citations]. . . . "[S]evering the parental relationship [must be] the least detrimental alternative for the child."

In furtherance of these principles, the courts have imposed a standard of *clear and convincing* proof of parental inability to provide proper care for the child and resulting detriment to the child if it remains with the parent, before custody can be awarded to a nonparent.

The clear and convincing standard was not met in the instant case. First, the juvenile court had two reasonable alternatives available to it short of awarding custody to the Department. It could have returned Jeannette to her mother under stringent conditions of supervision by the welfare department with the warning that if she again let her house get filthy or failed to keep Jeannette in clean clothes and to properly care for her that appellant would lose custody of the child. Moreover, the trial court could have ordered the removal of some or all of the animals at appellant's residence as a condition of returning Jeannette to her mother. It could have ordered homemaker service to assist appellant in keeping her home clean; the fact that she had received some assistance for the two weeks preceding the January 5 incident does not demonstrate a total incapacity to benefit from future homemaking service in light of the fact that she had received no such assistance in the preceding one and half year period. Moreover, the trial court should have ascertained the cause of the difficulty between appellant and the homemaker which triggered appellant's request for help from the Department on January 5. Perhaps, another homemaker would have been successful in getting appellant to clean her house—at least the possibility that this could be accomplished should have been explored. If stringent supervision of appellant's activities with reference to Jeannette did not provide a suitable home environment, then the court could remove Jeannette from the custody of her mother.

Second, assuming the trial court had a reasonable basis for concluding that appellant was incapable of providing a suitable home for Jeannette, it could have placed Jeannette with her father and the Christiansens. Frank offered an alternative home to Jeannette. The fact that the home was small, that Frank was unemployed and that he had a drinking problem does not support a finding that it would be detrimental to Jeannette for her to be with her father and the Christiansens rather than the Department. The presence of Mrs. Christiansen in the home would have alleviated any concern arising from Frank's alcoholism and arrest for child molesting 13 years earlier. Apparently, Frank recognized this when he asked the Christiansens to move in with him. Again, under the trial court's broad powers of supervision over Jeannette and her home environment (§ 362), it could have monitored Jeannette's progress in her father's home to assure her protection.

We observe that none of the social reports filed by the Department at the dispositional hearing included a "recommended plan for reuniting the minor with the family," as required by California Rule of Court rule 1376, subdivision (b). It is readily apparent that the Department had "given up" insofar as appellant and Frank's ability to properly care for Jeannette. While this attitude is understandable, it is contrary to the policy of the law. We deem it appropriate to quote from Judge Homer Thompson's California Juvenile Court Deskbook (2d ed. Cont.Ed.Bar 1978) at page 184:

> "Although placement in the parents' home is utilized at times in all kinds of section 300 cases, it is most frequently used in filthy home cases. These cases are the most responsive to supervision, and are usually referred to the probation department by social workers in the welfare department. Many of these cases involve families on welfare, and a social worker is already working with the family. Frequently the welfare department has a home-services unit or officer who will enter a filthy home and help the mother with the problems that have produced the condition.

> "Filthy home cases are sometimes those in which it is most difficult to remove the children, *and often it could be the most damaging to the children to do so.* Even though the home is a health hazard for the children, the mother is often a good, loving, and attentive mother in other respects. The children have responded to their mother's love and are very close to her. *Removal of such children can be a shattering experience for them.*" (Emphasis added.)

The judgment is reversed as to the dispositional order placing Jeannette in the custody of the Department of Human Resources. The trial court is directed to conduct another dispositional hearing in accordance with the principles expressed herein.

NOTE

A typical neglect or dependency proceeding is instituted through filing a form petition by a child case worker. Allegations forming the basis for two such petitions filed in a California juvenile court under § 300 of the California Welfare and Institutions Code are shown below.

The first petition involved an 11-year-old boy:

PARAGRAPH I SUBDIVISION A: Said minor has no parent and/or guardian capable of and actually exercising proper and effective parental care and control and is in need of such care and control, in that: Minor normally resides in the home of his mother and on or about April 6, 1977 minor's home was in an unfit condition and a danger to minor due to the following conditions: The electricity and water being shut off since approximately February 1, 1977, a leaking inoperative gas stove in the kitchen, which filled the home with gas fumes, the family using candles for light; trash, litter, papers, soiled clothing scattered throughout the floors of the home; inoperative toilets filled with fecal matter and animal fecal matter on the floors throughout home, no edible food in home, no clean clothing, the entire home being in a state of disarray having trash and debris scattered throughout; the yard area around home being in a similar condition including having human feces along with soiled toilet paper.

The second petition involved a 6-year-old girl:

PARAGRAPH I SUBDIVISION A: Said minor has no parent and/or guardian capable of and actually exercising proper and effective parental care and control and is in need of such care and control, in that: Minor normally resides in the home of her mother and mother's male companion, and approximately one month ago and on a prior occasion during the past year, minor's mother's male companion performed various sex acts on minor's sister, including sexual intercourse. Further, minor's mother was aware of said sex incidents and failed to and/or was unwilling to protect minor's sister.

In re Dubreuil

Supreme Court of Florida, 1993, Rehearing denied 1994.
629 So.2d 819.

■ BARKETT, CHIEF JUDGE.

We review In re Dubreuil, 603 So.2d 538 (Fla. 4th DCA 1992), which held that a married but separated woman who chose not to receive a blood transfusion for religious reasons could be compelled to receive medical treatment because her death would cause the abandonment of four minor children. We quash the district court's decision because there was no abandonment proved in this case to override the patient's constitutional rights.[1]

I.   The Facts

The parties have agreed on the essential facts in this case. In the late evening of Thursday, April 5, 1990, Patricia Dubreuil was admitted to Memorial Hospital in Hollywood, Florida, through its emergency room.[2] Patricia was in an "advanced stage" of pregnancy. At the time of her admission, she did not have a private attending physician, so Memorial Hospital assigned an obstetrician from its staff to render necessary obstetrical services. Upon admission, Patricia signed a standard consent form agreeing to the infusion of blood if it were to become necessary.

By the early morning hours of April 6, physicians determined that Patricia was ready to deliver her child and that a Caesarean section delivery would be appropriate. She consented to the Caesarean section, but notwithstanding the routine consent form she had signed, she withheld consent to the transfusion of blood on the basis of her values and religious convictions as a Jehovah's Witness.[3] Michael Dubreuil was subsequently delivered by Caesarean section at approximately 5:30 a.m. on April 6.

At the time of delivery Patricia experienced a significant loss of blood because of a severe blood condition that prevents her blood from clotting properly. Attending physicians determined that a blood transfusion was

1. We have jurisdiction pursuant to article V, section 3(b)(3) of the Florida Constitution to review the district court's express construction of the Florida Constitution.

2. Memorial Hospital is a public health care facility owned and operated by the South Broward Hospital District, a special taxing district established under Florida law.

3. Neither party has suggested that Patricia was incapacitated when she withheld her consent to the transfusion, nor do the parties question that her refusal of treatment was unambiguous despite her earlier written consent.

required to save her life, but Patricia still refused to consent. Because of the extreme medical emergency that existed on the morning of April 6, medical authorities, with police assistance, contacted Luc Dubreuil, Patricia's estranged husband. He had not accompanied Patricia when she went to the hospital hours earlier. When Luc arrived shortly thereafter, he consented to the blood transfusion. Physicians relied upon Luc's written consent and transfused a quantity of blood into Patricia during the morning of April 6.

Luc and Patricia were still married but were separated and living apart when this incident arose. They are the natural parents of the newborn infant, Michael, and three other minor children, Cary, Tina, and Tracy, who at the time, respectively, were twelve, six, and four years old and living with their mother. Luc was not a Jehovah's Witness. Luc's consent was supported by Patricia's two brothers, who were not Jehovah's Witnesses, while Patricia's mother, who is a Jehovah's Witness, backed her daughter's decision.

After the transfusion early on April 6, physicians apparently believed that transfusions would continue to be needed. Unsure of its legal obligations and responsibilities under these circumstances, the hospital petitioned the circuit court for an emergency declaratory judgment hearing to determine the hospital's authority or duty to administer blood transfusions to Patricia over her objections.[4] A hearing was scheduled for 3 p.m. on April 6. The parties do not know whether the trial court was aware that a transfusion had already been given at the time of the hearing, but they believe the trial court was aware that transfusions would continue to be needed throughout the day.

The trial court conducted the hearing as scheduled, attended by counsel representing Patricia and the hospital. No testimony was taken, but during the hearing the hospital's counsel received a telephone call advising that Patricia, who had been unconscious, had just become conscious, appeared lucid, and was able to communicate. When asked at that time whether she would consent to a blood transfusion, Patricia again refused.

At 3:30 p.m. on April 6, the trial court orally announced judgment in favor of the hospital, allowing it to administer blood as physicians deemed necessary. Subsequently, according to an affidavit later executed by Patricia, the hospital continued to administer blood, and Patricia survived.

The trial court issued a written order on April 11, concluding that there has been no suggestion as to the means or methods of caring for the four minor children of Patricia Dubreuil, if she should die. In the absence of some suggestion or showing as to the availability of proper care and custody of the four minor children, in the event of the death of Patricia Dubreuil, this court believes that the demands of the state (and society) outweigh the wishes of Patricia Dubreuil and that every medical effort should be made to prolong her life so that she can care for her four minor

---

4. The Petition was filed in the circuit court by the South Broward Hospital District on behalf of the hospital, and the District is the Respondent in the action in this Court. For clarity, we refer to Respondent as the hospital throughout this opinion.

children until their respective majorities. Patricia moved for rehearing, indicating that she continued to object to blood transfusion and that she had an "extended family as well as friends who are willing to assist in the rearing of [her] minor children in the event of her demise." The Circuit Court denied rehearing on April 12. The Fourth District affirmed by a 2–1 vote.

Patricia sought discretionary review here, arguing that the decision below violates her state and federal constitutional rights of privacy, bodily self-determination, and religious freedom. We recognize that the present case is moot given that Patricia received blood and was released from the hospital. However, we accept jurisdiction because the issue is one of great public importance, is capable of repetition, and otherwise might evade review.

II.   The Rights of Privacy and Free Exercise of Religion

We begin our analysis with the overarching principle that article I, section 23 of the Florida Constitution guarantees that "a competent person has the constitutional right to choose or refuse medical treatment, and that right extends to all relevant decisions concerning one's health." In re Guardianship of Browning, 568 So.2d 4, 11 (Fla.1990); see also In re T.W., 551 So.2d 1186 (Fla.1989); Public Health Trust of Dade County v. Wons, 541 So.2d 96 (Fla.1989). In cases like this one, the privacy right overlaps with the right to freely exercise one's religion to protect the right of a person to refuse a blood transfusion because of religious convictions. Art. I, §§ 3, 23, Fla. Const.; Wons.[5]

In cases where these rights are litigated, a party generally seeks to invoke the power of the State, through the exercise of the court's judicial power, either to enforce the patient's rights or to prevent the patient from exercising those rights. We have set forth the following guiding principles: The state has a duty to assure that a person's wishes regarding medical treatment are respected. That obligation serves to protect the rights of the individual from intrusion by the state unless the state has a compelling interest great enough to override this constitutional right. The means to carry out any such compelling state interest must be narrowly tailored in the least intrusive manner possible to safeguard the rights of the individual. Browning, 568 So.2d at 13–14 (footnote omitted); see also Wons, 541 So.2d at 96; In re T.W., 551 So.2d at 1192–93. Among the factors we have identified that could be considered in determining whether to give force to a patient's right to refrain from medical treatment is the protection of innocent third parties, see, e.g., Browning, 568 So.2d at 14, often discussed in terms of "abandonment." See, e.g., Wons, 541 So.2d at 97 (Ehrlich, C.J., concurring specially).[6]

5. We adhere to the doctrine of primacy enunciated in Traylor v. State, 596 So.2d 957, 962–63 (Fla.1992), deciding this case under express provisions of the state constitution rather than the federal constitution.

6. Although we have recognized other state interests that may be considered, see

Browning, 568 So.2d at 14; Wons, 541 So.2d at 97, only the protection of innocent third parties has been argued in this case, and that issue was dispositive in the decision below. Moreover, as we previously have stated, these state interests are merely factors to consider and "are 'by no means a bright-line test,

The arguments made in this Court present two basic issues. First, we must determine whether it is appropriate for a hospital to assert the state interests in an attempt to defeat a patient's decision to forgo emergency medical treatment. Second, assuming the state interests were properly presented in this case, we must decide whether Patricia's rejection of a blood transfusion constituted, as the district court found, abandonment of the couple's minor children and amounted to a state interest that was compelling enough to override her constitutional rights of privacy and religious freedom, by the least intrusive means available.

III. Asserting the State Interests

[The court rejects the argument that Memorial Hospital should not have intervened in a private decision to refuse a blood transfusion and the claim that the "State" has never been a party in the action, has not asserted any interest, and that the hospital has no authority to assume the State's responsibilities. They explain that:]

In most prior Florida decisions where state interests were asserted under analogous medical emergency situations, the State Attorney joined as a party at some point in the proceedings. See In re Guardianship of Browning, 568 So.2d 4 (Fla.1990); John F. Kennedy Memorial Hosp., Inc. v. Bludworth, 452 So.2d 921 (Fla.1984); Satz v. Perlmutter, 379 So.2d 359 (Fla.1980); In re Guardianship of Barry, 445 So.2d 365 (Fla. 2d DCA 1984); St. Mary's Hosp. v. Ramsey, 465 So.2d 666 (Fla. 4th DCA 1985).

One noteworthy exception is Public Health Trust of Dade County v. Wons, 541 So.2d 96 (Fla.1989), where, as in this case, the state interests were argued by a public health care provider without further intervention of the State. In discussing the need for court proceedings and the requisite burden of proof, we said "it will be necessary for hospitals that wish to contest a patient's refusal of treatment to commence court proceedings and sustain the heavy burden of proof that the state's interest outweighs the patient's constitutional rights." Id. at 98. We merely assumed, based on the facts in that case, that the health care provider would raise the state interests. Until today, we were not asked to determine whether it is appropriate for a health care provider, as opposed to another party, to assert the state interests in the first instance.

We conclude that a health care provider must not be forced into the awkward position of having to argue zealously against the wishes of its own patient, seeking deference to the wishes or interests of nonpatients—in this case Patricia's husband, her brothers, the children, and the State itself. Patients do not lose their right to make decisions affecting their lives simply by entering a health care facility. Despite concededly good intentions, a health care provider's function is to provide medical treatment in accordance with the patient's wishes and best interests, not as a "substitute parent" supervening the wishes of a competent adult. Accordingly, a health care provider must comply with the wishes of a patient to refuse medical treatment unless ordered to do otherwise by a court of competent

capable of resolving every dispute regarding the refusal of medical treatment.' " Brown-

ing, 568 So.2d at 14 (quoting Wons, 541 So.2d at 97).

jurisdiction. A health care provider cannot act on behalf of the State to assert the state interests in these circumstances. This is an appropriate role for the State to play directly, not through the legal artifice of a special taxing district.

"Additionally, it should be recognized that in many instances, the hospital's agents will understandably be primarily interested in protecting the hospital's interests, and may not represent all of the factors recognized in Wons." Dubreuil, 603 So.2d at 541. Moreover, placing the State's burden on the health care provider would be even more inappropriate where the health care provider is a private, rather than public, entity.

Therefore, we recede from Wons to the extent that it may be read to put any burden of proof on the health care provider with respect to asserting the state interests. That heavy burden must be borne directly by the State.

We recognize that in situations like these, health care providers generally have sought judicial intervention to determine their rights and obligations to avoid liability. In John F. Kennedy Memorial Hospital, Inc. v. Bludworth, 452 So.2d 921, 926 (Fla.1984), we held that health care providers, when terminating life support in accordance with their patient's wishes, are relieved of potential civil and criminal liability as long as they act in good faith, and that no prior court approval of the health care provider's action is required. We believe the same principles apply here. When a health care provider, acting in good faith, follows the wishes of a competent and informed patient to refuse medical treatment, the health care provider is acting appropriately and cannot be subjected to civil or criminal liability.

Although this procedure absolves the health care facility of any obligation to go to court, we recognize the need for the State and interested parties to have the opportunity to seek judicial intervention if appropriate. Accordingly, a health care provider wishing to override a patient's decision to refuse medical treatment must immediately provide notice to the State Attorney presiding in the circuit where the controversy arises, and to interested third parties known to the health care provider. The extent to which the State Attorney chooses to engage in a legal action, if any, is discretionary based on the law and facts of each case. This procedure should eliminate needless litigation by health care providers while honoring the patient's wishes and giving other interested parties the right to intervene if there is a good faith reason to do so. Cf. In re Guardianship of Browning, 568 So.2d 4, 16 (Fla.1990) (courts are open to adjudicate legitimate questions pertaining to written or oral instructions expressing a patient's wishes).

Even though the State did not properly join this action, the hospital followed Wons and stood in the State's shoes, assuming the heavy burden of proving that the prevention of abandonment outweighed Patricia Dubreuil's constitutional right to refuse medical treatment. The court below accepted the hospital's argument and adjudicated the case on the merits. Accordingly, we address the merits of the district court's decision.

IV. Protecting Innocent Third Parties

The state interest raised in this case is the protection of innocent third parties, which the parties and courts in other jurisdictions under similar circumstances have termed the prevention of abandonment of minor children. Until Dubreuil, no other reported Florida appellate decision had found abandonment in this context. The case most closely on point in this Court's jurisprudence is Wons, where abandonment was discussed but not found.[8]

8. Perhaps the closest Florida appellate decision is St. Mary's Hospital v. Ramsey, 465 So.2d 666 (Fla. 4th DCA 1985). There, a 27–year-old divorced man was deemed not to have abandoned his minor daughter when he refused a transfusion upon evidence that (1) the daughter's primary residence was in Michigan with Ramsey's former wife, and as a result the father seldom saw the child; (2) the mother and both families pledged their help to support the child; and (3) Ramsey owned a small annuity that named the child as a beneficiary. Appellate courts in other jurisdictions have looked at abandonment in the general context of a parent refusing medical treatment, and most have found no abandonment. In Fosmire v. Nicoleau, 75 N.Y.2d 218, 551 N.Y.S.2d 876, 551 N.E.2d 77 (N.Y. 1990), Denise Nicoleau refused a blood transfusion after hemorrhaging when she gave birth prematurely by Caesarean section. She and her husband were Jehovah's Witnesses, and she made her intention to refuse treatment clear. The court held that an asserted state interest in preventing a parent from intentionally abandoning a child did not outweigh the patient's statutory and common law right to refuse medical treatment. The court's analysis focused exclusively on the nature of the rights and interests at issue, and did not include any reference to whether there was evidence of the circumstances of the father or extended family. In Norwood Hospital v. Munoz, 409 Mass. 116, 564 N.E.2d 1017, 1024–25 (1991), the court followed Wons to conclude that "the State does not have an interest in maintaining a two-parent household in the absence of compelling evidence that the child will be abandoned if he is left under the care of a one-parent household." 564 N.E.2d at 1025. The court found no compelling interest in protecting the minor child of Yolanda and Ernesto Munoz when Yolanda refused on religious grounds to receive a blood transfusion because there was no evidence that the father, who supported his wife's decision, was unwilling to take care of the child, although there was no plan to take care of the youth in

Yolanda's absence; Ernesto had financial resources to take care of the child; and Ernesto's sister and brother-in-law, who supported Yolanda's decision, said they would assist in caring for the child. See also In re Farrell, 108 N.J. 335, 529 A.2d 404 (1987) (woman suffering from debilitating disease had right to terminate life support even though she would leave behind husband and two teenage children where they had a close loving family, she had expressed concern for their welfare, and guardian ad litem believed the children would not be harmed); In re Osborne, 294 A.2d 372 (D.C.1972) (approving trial court's refusal to appoint a guardian to consent to blood transfusion for father of two minor children where both patient and wife were Jehovah's Witnesses, the family had sufficient financial resources to meet the children's material needs, and the extended family was prepared to help care for the children). Two cases that we know of have found abandonment. In Application of the President & Directors of Georgetown College, Inc., 331 F.2d 1000 (D.C.Cir.) (one-judge decision), rehearing en banc denied with opinions, 331 F.2d 1010 (D.C.Cir.), cert. denied, 377 U.S. 978, 84 S.Ct. 1883, 12 L.Ed.2d 746 (1964), a Jehovah's Witness, who was the mother of seven-month-old child, was "in extremis." Although physicians believed she needed a transfusion, both she and her husband refused to consent on religious grounds. The hospital asked the federal district court to permit it to administer blood, but the court denied the petition. The hospital then "appealed" that decision to a single member of the United States Circuit Court, Judge J. Skelly Wright. Judge Wright went to the hospital and spoke to the patient, but she was incapacitated and could only mutter the words "against my will." When the judge asked if she would consent to the transfusion, "[s]he indicated, as best I could make out, that it would not then be her responsibility." 331 F.2d at 1007. The judge then "reversed" the district court and permitted the hospital to administer blood, reasoning in part that

Norma Wons, a 38–year-old woman, had been suffering from dysfunctional uterine bleeding, and physicians said she could die without a blood transfusion. However, she refused based on her religious convictions as a Jehovah's Witness. Norma lived with her husband Henrich and their two minor children, who were twelve and fourteen years of age. Henrich was also a Jehovah's Witness and supported Norma's decision. Henrich worked to support the family, and during Norma's illness the children had been cared for in Henrich's absence by Norma's sixty-two-year-old mother, who was in good health. Testimony established that if Norma were to die, her mother and two brothers, who also were Jehovah's Witnesses, would assist in taking care of the children. The trial court ruled that Norma's refusal would deny the children the intangible right to be reared by two loving parents, and the state interest in protecting the two minor children overrode Norma's right to refuse lifesaving medical treatment. The Third District reversed, finding that there was no showing of an abandonment of the minor children to override Norma's constitutional rights. The district court said that the societal interest in protecting Mrs. Wons' two minor children as recognized in [Satz v. Perlmutter, 379 So.2d 359 (Fla.1980), adopting 362 So.2d 160 (Fla. 4th DCA 1978) and St. Mary's Hospital v. Ramsey, 465 So.2d 666 (Fla. 4th DCA 1985)]—although a vital and troubling consideration in this case—cannot, in our view, override Mrs. Wons' constitutional right to refuse a blood transfusion under the circumstances of this case. This is so because, simply put, Mrs. Wons' probable, but not certain, demise by refusing the subject blood transfusions will not result in an abandonment of her two minor children. According to the undisputed testimony below, she has a tightly knit family unit, all practicing Jehovah's Witnesses, all of whom fully support her decision to refuse a blood transfusion, all of whom will care for and rear the two minor children in the event she dies. Her husband will, plainly, continue supporting the two children with the aid of her two brothers; her mother, a sixty-two-year-old woman in good health, will also care for the children while her husband is at work. Without dispute, these children will not become wards of the state and will be reared by a loving family. Wons, 500 So.2d at 688.

This Court generally approved the district court's rationale and held that the state interest in maintaining a home with two parents for the minor children does not override a patient's constitutional rights of privacy

the state had a parens patriae interest in preventing abandonment of a minor child and the patient had a responsibility to her community to care for the infant. In re Winthrop University Hospital, 128 Misc.2d 804, 490 N.Y.S.2d 996 (Sup.Ct.1985) followed Georgetown to order the mother of two minor children to receive blood transfusions during kidney stone removal surgery despite the religious objections of the patient and her husband. Although the reasoning of Fosmire, Munoz, Farrell, Osborne, Winthrop and Georgetown lends some guidance to this Court, all are more similar to Wons than Dubreuil in that there was no question that spouses or others would assume responsibility for the children when treatment was refused. Georgetown is further distinguishable because the mother was incapacitated when asked to consent. Moreover, that decision has little precedential value given that most of the judges on the circuit court disagreed with Judge Wright, albeit for a variety of reasons, when they were asked to rehear the case en banc. Georgetown, 331 F.2d at 1010–1018 (opinions of Washington, J., Danaher, J., Miller, J., Burger, J.). Winthrop is undermined by its reliance on Georgetown, and by the New York Court of Appeals' subsequent decision in Fosmire. Moreover, Georgetown and Winthrop may well conflict with Florida constitutional law as expressed in Wons.

and religion to refuse a potentially lifesaving blood transfusion. Wons, 541 So.2d at 98.

Significantly, as then-Chief Justice Ehrlich noted, there was no abandonment proved in that case, so the protection of innocent third parties could not have been a "compelling interest sufficient to override the competent patient's right to refuse treatment." Id. at 99 (Ehrlich, C.J., concurring specially). Because there was no abandonment in Wons, we did not decide in that case "whether evidence of abandonment alone would be sufficient in itself to override the competent patient's constitutional rights." Id. at 99 n. 2 (Ehrlich, C.J., concurring specially).

The trial court in Dubreuil found abandonment and held it to be an overriding state interest. The court distinguished Wons, noting that Luc no longer lived with Patricia and the children; Luc was not a Jehovah's Witness and consented to the transfusion; and Patricia presented no evidence of how the children would be cared for in the event of her death.

In a split decision, the district court affirmed by reasoning that Wons put the burden on the hospital to prove abandonment, and under the emergency circumstances and limited evidence presented, the hospital carried its burden. The district court focused on the fact that no evidence was presented about Luc, his ability to care for the couple's children, or the ability or willingness of any others to help care for the children in the event of Patricia's death. The court rejected the argument that a presumption against finding abandonment should exist in the absence of firsthand evidence to the contrary, suggesting that if any presumption were to apply, it would be a presumption in favor of finding abandonment given the ages of the children and the preexisting custody conditions.

The district court concluded that because there was no showing that the children of tender years would be protected in the event of their parent's death, the trial court did not abuse its discretion by concluding that "there was an overriding interest in the state as parens patriae that out-balances the mother's free exercise and privacy right to reject the transfusion." Dubreuil, 603 So.2d at 541.

In dissent, Judge Warner observed that Luc, as the natural father, is the children's legal guardian and is responsible for their care as a matter of Florida law under section 744.301, Florida Statutes (1991). Judge Warner relied on our decision in Wons to conclude that because the hospital failed to present compelling evidence that abandonment would result from the rejection of medical treatment, no compelling state interest was established to override Patricia's decision. 603 So.2d at 546.

In her argument to this Court, Patricia urges us to eliminate from this line of cases any consideration given to the state interest in protecting innocent third parties from abandonment, claiming that it is inherently unsound and dangerous and cannot be consistently applied. She argues, for example, that it will lead beyond blood transfusions to major medical procedures ranging from Caesarean sections to heart bypass surgery; or it will allow courts to compel a pregnant Catholic woman who is the single parent of a minor child to have an abortion against her religious beliefs if taking the pregnancy to term would endanger the mother's life. She also argues that the rule eventually will go well beyond the protection of minor children, compelling a single adult, who cares for her dependent elderly parent or grandparent, to receive unwanted medical treatment in order to advance the state interest in protecting the elderly dependent.

Patricia's argument has some merit. Parenthood, in and of itself, does not deprive one of living in accord with one's own beliefs. Society does not, for example, disparage or preclude one from performing an act of bravery resulting in the loss of that person's life simply because that person has parental responsibilities.[9]

Nonetheless, we decline at this time to rule out the possibility that some case not yet before us may present a compelling interest to prevent abandonment.[10] Therefore, we think the better course is the one we took in Wons, where we held that "these cases demand individual attention" and cannot be covered by a blanket rule. Wons, 541 So.2d at 98.

Next, Patricia argues that even if the prevention of abandonment may be a valid state interest, there was no proof in this record that an abandonment would have occurred had Patricia died after refusing medical treatment. We agree.

Both the circuit and district courts failed to properly consider the father of the four children, Luc Dubreuil. Under Florida law, as Judge Warner's dissent correctly observed, a child with two living natural parents has two natural guardians who share equally the responsibilities of parenting. "If one parent dies, the natural guardianship shall pass to the surviving parent, and the right shall continue even though the surviving parent remarries. If the marriage between the parents is dissolved, the natural guardianship shall belong to the parent to whom the custody of the child is awarded." § 744.301(1), Fla.Stat. (1991). Thus, Florida law unambiguously presumes that had Patricia died under these circumstances, Luc would have become the sole legal guardian of the couple's four minor children and would have been given full responsibility for their care in the absence of any contravening legal agreement or order.

The State could rebut this strong legal presumption only by presenting clear and convincing evidence that Luc would not properly assume responsibility for the children under the circumstances.[12] . . . However, there was absolutely no such evidence presented in this case, as the record is silent as to Luc's ability or desire to care for the children. The record shows only that Luc and Patricia were married but separated, their minor children were under Patricia's care, Luc did not accompany his wife to the hospital,

9. See also Alan Meisel, The Right to Die § 4.15 (1989) (noting the possibility that the state interest in protecting innocent third parties may not be limited to minor children because "[o]ther close relatives, including adult offspring of the patient and perhaps even persons emotionally close to the patient but not related by blood or marriage, might be able to assert a substantial interest in the patient's continued life").

10. The district court termed this interest as a parens patriae interest of the State. Dubreuil, 603 So.2d at 541. We, however, do not view the state interest to protect innocent third parties as a parens patriae interest because the State is looking to protect society, not just children, from all of the consequences of abandonment.

12. The State's only concern is that the children would be cared for and would not be a burden on the State.

he was readily available when called to Patricia's bedside on the morning of April 6, and he was available to "consent"[13] to an emergency treatment for Patricia.

Likewise, there was no evidence presented as to whether anyone else, including the families of Luc and Patricia, would take responsibility for the children. To the contrary, Patricia said in an affidavit on rehearing that extended family members and friends were willing to assist in raising the children in the event of Patricia's death.

Moreover, we do not know if Luc or any other interested party was given the opportunity to address these issues. According to the parties' stipulation, neither Luc nor any other family members attended the emergency hearing, and the record contains no evidence that notice of the hearing was provided. . . .

We conclude that the district court erred in holding that sufficient evidence was presented to satisfy the heavy burden required to override the patient's constitutional right to refuse medical treatment. The State alone bore that burden, which the hospital, standing in the State's shoes, did not carry.

Moreover, the district court erred by suggesting that absent firsthand proof, the law should presume abandonment under these circumstances. To the contrary, the law presumes that when one parent is no longer able to care for the couple's children, the other parent will do so. The district court's decision effectively presumed that Luc had abandoned his children when he separated from his wife. That presumption is unacceptable. The state cannot disparage a person's parental rights nor excuse a person's parental responsibilities based on martial status alone. See Stanley v. Illinois, 405 U.S. 645, 651 (1972).

Likewise, although not intended by the district court, its rationale could be read by some to perpetuate the damaging stereotype that a mother's role is one of caregiver, and the father's role is that of an apathetic, irresponsible, or unfit parent. See, e.g., Sylvia A. Law, Rethinking Sex and the Constitution, 132 U.Pa.L.Rev. 955, 995–98 (1984); . . . The law has evolved to move away from inappropriate gender-based distinctions. See, e.g., Caban v. Mohammed, 441 U.S. 380 (1979) (holding unconstitutional a state statute that treated parental rights of unwed men and unwed women differently); Frontiero (holding unconstitutional a federal statute that treated husbands and wives of military service personnel

13. We note that marriage does not destroy one's constitutional right to personal autonomy. In In re Guardianship of Browning, 568 So.2d 4 (Fla.1990), we held in relevant part that "when the patient has left instructions regarding life-sustaining treatment, the surrogate must make the medical choice that the patient, if competent, would have made, and not one that the surrogate might make for himself or herself, or that the surrogate might think is in the patient's best interests." Id. at 13 (emphasis supplied). The majority below said it looked to the husband's consent as "relevant only for the purpose of considering whether alternative care for the surviving children is available, in weighing the overriding interest of the state, and in determining whether or not the spouse's decision to refuse the transfusion constitutes an abandonment." Dubreuil, 603 So.2d at 542. However, implicit in the decision of the trial court, and in its approval by the district court, is acceptance of the hospital's decision to allow Luc to assert his own views over Patricia's wishes. This is impermissible. See Browning.

differently). We do not want the district court's rationale misinterpreted to reinforce these outdated ideas in a manner that effectively denies a woman her constitutional right to refuse medical treatment as guaranteed by article I, sections 3 and 23 of the Florida Constitution. Such an interpretation would also undermine the principle of shared parental responsibility, to which this state adheres. § 61.13(2)(b), Fla.Stat. (1991); see, e.g., Mize v. Mize, 621 So.2d 417 (Fla.1993).

For the foregoing reasons, we quash the district court's decision.

■ McDONALD, J., dissents with an opinion, in which OVERTON, J., concurs.

■ OVERTON, JUSTICE, dissenting.

... [I]n my view, this innocent newborn child should have some rights, particularly when (1) the mother sought the medical treatment and consented to the birth by Caesarean section; (2) the mother could be and was restored to full health in a short period of time after the birth and blood transfusion; and (3) the family disagreed as to whether the blood transfusion should be administered (Dubreuil's estranged husband and two brothers believed she should receive full medical treatment, while her mother agreed with her decision not to have the blood transfusion).

Clearly, a newborn does have a significant special need for his or her natural mother. The majority opinion, however, eliminated this need as a factor in this life-or-death-decision process. Further, and as important, the majority has effectively denied the State an opportunity to protect the interests of this newborn child and has effectively condoned child abandonment, if the mother's decision is made for religious reasons. I adhere to my dissent in Public Health Trust v. Wons, 541 So.2d 96 (Fla.1989).

■ McDONALD, JUSTICE, dissenting.

Admittedly, the courts travel in treacherous waters when they place any restrictions upon the free exercise of a person's religious beliefs. Such restriction should occur only when there is another compelling interest great enough to override this strong constitutional right. The trial judge found that the circumstances of this case meet this test. I agree with him.

There is no controversy or contest to the fact that unless Mrs. Dubreuil received blood transfusions she would die. The majority holds that this is a choice she can make if done in the exercise of her religious belief. The trial judge found, and I agree, that the children's right to have a mother outweighs the mother's right to observe her religious beliefs. Considering the age of these children, as opposed to the age of the children in Wons v. Public Health Trust, 541 So.2d 96 (Fla.1989), this would be true whether Mr. Dubreuil faithfully performed all of his parental responsibilities or not.

Children of tender age desperately need the nurturing of a mother. Mrs. Dubreuil, according to all reports, is a fit and loving mother. It would be a legal mistake to let her expire because of the observance of her religious beliefs and leave these children motherless. I firmly place myself in the camp of In re President & Directors of Georgetown College, Inc., 331 F.2d 1000 (D.C.Cir.), cert. denied, 377 U.S. 978 (1964), and In re Winthrop University Hospital, 128 Misc.2d 804, 490 N.Y.S.2d 996 (Sup.Ct.1985). Children need, and are entitled to have, their mothers; this need is sufficiently great to outweigh one's free exercise of religious beliefs. The majority states: "Parenthood in and of itself does not deprive one of living in accord with one's own beliefs." Majority op. at 826. I suggest that parenthood, under some circumstances at least, can indeed deprive one of the right to live in accord with one's own beliefs. Parenthood requires many adjustments and often great sacrifice for the welfare of a person's children. Nearly every living creature of every species recognizes the duty to nurture its offspring. Their lives are changed in doing so. Humans should not allow religious beliefs, no matter how deeply seated or appropriately held, to neglect this fundamental duty. Mothers do not abandon the nest.

Were this less than a life or death decision, or involved adolescents as opposed to young children, I would feel less fervent. Under the facts here, a compelling interest great enough to override Mrs. Dubreuil's exercise of her religious beliefs or right of privacy clearly exists. I believe the majority makes a tragic mistake.

C. Special Problems of Child Abuse

State v. Wilkerson

Supreme Court of North Carolina, 1978.
295 N.C. 559, 247 S.E.2d 905.

■ Exum, Justice.

The homicide victim in this tragic affair was Kessler Wilkerson, the two-year-old son of defendant and his wife, Nancy. The state's evidence tended to show, and the jury apparently believed, that the child's death was the result of physical abuse inflicted upon him by his father. On his appeal defendant contends the trial court erred in (1) admitting into evidence expert medical opinion having to do with the "battered child" syndrome; (2) permitting cross-examination of defendant's mother as to acts of misconduct earlier committed by defendant; and (3) improperly instructing the jury, principally by failing properly to define the crimes of second degree murder, voluntary manslaughter and involuntary manslaughter. With regard to the first contention, we find no error. We agree with defendant that the cross-examination of his mother was improper; but we also conclude under the circumstances that no prejudice resulted. As to the third contention the error committed was favorable to defendant.

The state's evidence, in summary, is as follows: On 16 October 1976 around 10:30 a.m., neighbors heard loud sounds "like something was being thrown inside the trailer" coming from the Wilkersons' mobile home, the voice of a little boy crying, and defendant shouting at him to shut up. Mrs. Wilkerson appeared at the door of the trailer, said, "Hurry up, Kenny, hurry up," and slammed the door closed. Pursuant to a call an ambulance arrived at the Wilkerson trailer at 12:42 p.m. Defendant delivered the child's limp body to ambulance attendants and told them he had choked on some cereal, swallowed some water, and stopped breathing. Cardiopulmonary resuscitation was applied unsuccessfully en route to the hospital. The child was dead on arrival there. The emergency room physician who examined the child found no fluid in his lungs or other signs of drowning. Bruises were present on his chest, shoulders, upper arm and forearm. Upon being informed that his son was dead, defendant appeared "quite calm and told his wife something to the effect that it's done, it's over, there's nothing we can do about it now." An autopsy revealed, externally, multiple bruises all over the child's body and, internally, significant bleeding and a deep laceration of the liver. Cause of death was abdominal hemorrhage from a ruptured liver.

Other evidence for the state, consisting of defendant's pre-trial statement made to investigating officers and the testimony of other witnesses who had observed defendant in his relationship with his son, tended to show the kind of disciplinary methods defendant customarily used with the child. According to this evidence defendant frequently kicked the child and on occasion made him stand "spread eagle" against a wall for long periods of time. One such occasion was 14 October 1976, two days before the boy died. Defendant at that time kicked him with such force that his chest hit the wall. One witness testified that defendant had said the little boy had no manners and that he was determined to teach him some manners and bring him up to be a man the way that "his [defendant's] mother has raised him, that his mother put him through hell." When asked why he wanted to repeat his mother's treatment, defendant "said that he didn't really approve of it or like it but it made him a man, and that's the way his son was going to be."

Defendant testified that his relationship with his son had been close. Although admitting disciplining his son and occasionally spanking him with a belt, defendant denied ever hitting or kicking him. He also denied that he was punished excessively as a child or that he ever talked with state's witnesses about his childhood. He said that on the morning of October 16 the child had wet himself on the floor. Defendant spanked him with his wife's belt and then ran some water in a tub and made him get in whereupon the child began "gasping for air and choking." Defendant searched his throat for possible obstructions, patted him on his back, and applied mouth-to-mouth resuscitation, all without any success. On cross-examination defendant admitted spanking his son on 16 October "hard enough to make him cry as long as I beat him."

Several witnesses testified that the relationship between defendant and his son was good and that they had never seen defendant abuse the child in any way. Defendant's mother testified that defendant treated his younger brothers and sisters in a kind manner while growing up in Philadelphia and that she had never beaten defendant severely or seen him abuse any child.

Defendant first assigns as error the testimony of two medical witnesses—Dr. Casey John Jason, a pediatrician who first examined the child at the emergency room of Womack Army Hospital, and Dr. John Edward Grauerholz, who performed the autopsy. Specifically, defendant complains of Dr. Jason's testimony that the bruises he observed on the child were not "the typical bruising pattern that is normally sustained by children in [their] normal day-to-day life." Defendant likewise complains of the testimony of Dr. Grauerholz, a pathologist, who after describing at some length his findings on autopsy testified in part as follows:

"DR. GRAUERHOLZ: All right, I made a diagnosis.

MR. GREGORY: And what was that diagnosis, Doctor?

MR. DOWNING: Object.

COURT: Overruled.

DR. GRAUERHOLZ: Battered child.

MR. DOWNING: Move to strike.

. . .

MR. GREGORY: Dr. Grauerholz, what do you mean by the term 'battered child'?

DR. GRAUERHOLZ: I mean a child who died as a result of multiple injuries of a non-accidental nature.

MR. GREGORY: Can you explain what you mean by 'non-accidental nature'?

DR. GRAUERHOLZ: Yes. That these injuries were inflicted by someone other than the child upon the child.

MR. DOWNING: Move to strike.

COURT: Denied.

. . .

MR. GREGORY: Is the term 'battered child' a relatively new term in the field of medicine?

MR. DOWNING: Objection.

COURT: Overruled.

DR. GRAUERHOLZ: It's been around for a while. I think probably in the last ten years or so it has become very well established.

MR. GREGORY: Dr. Grauerholz, without referring to any particular person, can you describe for us about the battered child?

MR. DOWNING: Objection.

COURT: Overruled. You are seeking an explanation of the term 'battered child'?

MR. GREGORY. Yes sir.

COURT: Overruled. You may give your explanation, Doctor.

DR. GRAUERHOLZ: These are children who suffer multiple injuries inflicted by others. The injuries are multiple in terms of distribution on the body and in time of infliction in certain cases. They are seen in children who have been perhaps over-zealously disciplined or have in other ways upset or run afoul of their guardians or their caretakers or usually some adult who is in relation to the child. By 'relation' I mean physical relation.

MR. DOWNING: Move to strike.

COURT: Denied.

. . .

DR. GRAUERHOLZ: They show essentially such things as abdominal injuries or fractures or other damage that is inconsistent with an accidental origin by virtue of the distribution of the injury. There are certain places where children classically do injure themselves when they fall, they run along and they fall, they bang their knees, they fall on their hands and so forth and these children, however, show injuries in noncharacteristic places, across the back, places where they could not spontaneously fall with sufficient force to produce that sort of injury, deep injuries in the abdomen, again which would necessitate a force being directed to the abdomen. One of the classic findings in a lot of these children are multiple fractures of varying ages. The bruising I observed in the chest area of the child were not bruises characteristic of the everyday life of a child, of being a child from day to day and falling. In my opinion an external striking or compressive force of some sort applied to the abdomen would produce the laceration to the liver.

. . .

MR. GREGORY: My question is, without all the paraphrasing, Your Honor, under what circumstances does the battered child syndrome occur?

COURT: Overruled. You may move to strike. The ruling of the Court does not foreclose you opportunity to move to strike. Go ahead, Doctor.

DR. GRAUERHOLZ: The syndrome usually occurs in a disciplinary situation involving the child and some guardian or custodian, a parent, a relative, a babysitter, someone who has physical custody of the child at that time. The injuries are usually inflicted as a disciplinary measure upon the child.

MR. DOWNING: Move to strike.

COURT: Denied.

. . .

MR. GREGORY: Now when you say in disciplining the child, what are you talking about, Dr. Grauerholz?

MR. DOWNING: Objection.

COURT: Overruled.

. . .

DR. GRAUERHOLZ: I am talking about punishment in the sense that one might spank a child for misbehaving. In that sort of situation. A question of corporal punishment. In these cases the punishment is excessive in its result if not necessarily in its intent."

Defendant contends that to permit Dr. Grauerholz to give an opinion that the child was a victim of the battered child syndrome, to explain what this syndrome means, and "to theorize ... that the child was killed by a parent, a guardian or caretaker who used more force than was called for in a disciplinary situation" was, in effect, to permit the doctor to testify "as to the ultimate fact of the defendant's guilt or innocence" and therefore was improper. Defendant makes no argument in his brief to support his assignment of error with regard to Dr. Jason's testimony. We conclude that all of this testimony was properly admitted.

Defendant relies on the principle that an expert witness should not express an opinion on the very issue to be decided by the jury and thereby invade the jury's province. As this Court has noted before, this principle "is not inflexible, is subject to many exceptions, and is open to criticism." Patrick v. Treadwell, 222 N.C. 1, 4, 21 S.E.2d 818, 821 (1942), ... "It is frequently relaxed in the admission of evidence as to ultimate facts in regard to matters of science, art or skill." State v. Powell, 238 N.C. 527, 530, 78 S.E.2d 248, 251 (1953)....

. . .

Expert medical opinion has been allowed on a wide range of facts, the existence or non-existence of which is ultimately to be determined by the trier of fact....

We conclude, therefore, that in determining whether expert medical opinion is to be admitted into evidence the inquiry should not be whether it invades the province of the jury, but whether the opinion expressed is really one based on the special expertise of the expert, that is, whether the witness because of his expertise is in a better position to have an opinion on the subject than is the trier of fact. The test is as stated in State v. Powell, supra, 238 N.C. at 530, 78 S.E.2d at 250, whether the "opinion required expert skill or knowledge in the medical or pathologic field about which a person of ordinary experience would not be capable of satisfactory conclusions, unaided by expert information from one learned in the medical profession."

The opinions expressed by the physicians in this case fall well within the bounds of permissible medical expert testimony. The basis for Dr. Jason's opinion, that the bruises on the child's chest did not form the typical bruising pattern normally sustained by children in day to day activities, was given in his earlier testimony in which he said:

"In my work in pediatrics I have had the occasion to work with numerous children. At Johns Hopkins I would say somewhere in the neighborhood of five hundred children total. Many times I have had occasion to observe lesions or bruises about children that have occurred in the normal course of events. A child frequently falls on his knees or bangs what we call the tibial surfaces, the area underneath the knee, and, of course, bangs their elbows, and skin their hands and occasionally even fall and hit their heads and in that case get a bruise similar to the one that Kessler had on the front of his head.

MR. GREGORY: Have you had a chance in your work in pediatrics to observe the chests of children?

DR. JASON: Oh, of course, of course."

Likewise, Dr. Grauerholz' opinion that this child was a "battered child" and his explanation of that term were based on his experience as a physician and a pathologist who had at the time of the trial performed over 150 autopsies, and on the fact that the "battered child" syndrome has been a recognized medical diagnosis for over ten years.... Dr. Grauerholz' opinion regarding the usual cause of the syndrome, again, was based on his expertise in the area and his knowledge of the subject as contained in the medical literature.

Contrary to what defendant seems to argue, neither physician testified, nor should he have been permitted to do so, that the battered child syndrome from which this victim suffered was in fact caused by any particular person or class of persons engaging in any particular activity or class of activities. Nowhere in the record did either physician express or purport to express an opinion as to defendant's guilt or innocence. On these kinds of factual questions the physicians would have been in no better position to have an opinion than the jury.

Upholding the admission of similar testimony, the California Court of Appeals in People v. Jackson, 18 Cal.App.3d 504, 507, 95 Cal.Rptr. 919, 921 (1971) said:

"A finding, as in this case, of the 'battered child syndrome' is not an opinion by the doctor as to whether any particular person has done anything, but, as this doctor indicated, 'it would take thousands of children to have the severity and number and degree of injuries that this child had over the span of time that we had' by accidental, means. In other words, the 'battered child syndrome' simply indicates that a child found with the type of injuries outlined above has not suffered those injuries by accidental means. This conclusion is based upon an extensive study of the subject by medical science. The additional finding that the injuries were probably occasioned by someone who is ostensibly caring for the child is simply a conclusion based upon logic and reason. Only someone regularly 'caring' for the child has the continuing opportunity to inflict these types of injuries; an isolated contact with a vicious stranger would not result in this pattern of successive injuries stretching through several months."

As far as our research reveals, all courts which have considered the question, including our own Court of Appeals, have concluded that such expert medical testimony concerning the battered child syndrome as was offered in this case is properly admitted into evidence. State v. Periman, 32 N.C.App. 33, 230 S.E.2d 802 (1977); State v. Loss, 295 Minn. 271, 204 N.W.2d 404 (1973); People v. Henson, 33 N.Y.2d 63, 304 N.E.2d 358 (1973); State v. Best, 232 N.W.2d 447 (S.D.1975).

The cases relied on by defendant are readily distinguishable. In each of these cases the difficulty was that the medical expert was permitted to testify that a certain event had in fact caused the injuries complained of. The court in each case pointed out that it would have been proper to have asked the expert whether the event could or might have caused the injury, but not whether it in fact did cause it. (There may be questions of cause and effect, however, about which an expert should be permitted to give, if he has one, a positive opinion.) ...

Defendant's first assignment of error is overruled.

. . .

NOTES

(1) In *Commonwealth v. Day*, 409 Mass. 719, 569 N.E.2d 397 (1991), the Supreme Judicial Court of Massachusetts held that admission of testimony regarding a profile of persons who abuse children constituted reversible error in a conviction of manslaughter. The court pointed out that:

> The Commonwealth's case closed with the testimony of Dr. Eli Newberger, who testified as an expert on the so-called "battered child syndrome." Dr. Newberger testified about how it is possible to differentiate between injuries which are the result of child abuse, and injuries which are the result of accidents. Dr. Newberger reviewed the victim's medical records and concluded that the child died as a result of child abuse.

> As part of his testimony on battered child syndrome, Dr. Newberger testified, over repeated and strenuous objections by defense counsel, that five "family characteristics" are sometimes associated with child abuse: (1) stress derived from economic hardship and conflict between the parents; (2) isolation of the family; (3) violence against the mother; (4) obtaining medical care from different physicians and hospitals; and (5) singling out of a particular child for abuse. Dr. Newberger also testified, over repeated objections by defense counsel, about the presence of "risk factors" in child abuse cases such as a "repeated pattern" of partners of single mothers who sometimes "offend against [the] children" while the mothers are at work. Dr. Newberger added that another "pattern" recognized in child abuse cases is when a single parent, usually the mother, has several partners who bring alcohol and drugs into the household. Dr. Newberger stated that more than 60% of the cases of child abuse reported to the department "involved" the use of drugs. A criminal trial is by its very nature an individualized adjudication of a defendant's guilt or legal innocence. Testimony regarding a criminal profile is nothing more than an expert's opinion as to certain characteristics which are common to some or most of the individuals who commit particular crimes. Evidence of a "child battering profile" does not meet the relevancy test, because the mere fact that a defendant fits the profile does not tend to prove that a particular defendant physically abused the victim. See State v. Brown, 370 So.2d 547, 554 (La.1979) (drug courier profile "does not tend to prove that this defendant is guilty of the offense charged, nor does it explain any relevant fact with regard to guilt or innocence"); Duley v. State, 56 Md.App. 275, 281, 467 A.2d 776 (1983) (child battering profile "totally irrelevant because it does not tend to prove that [the defendant] committed the acts of abuse attributed to him"); State v. Maule, 35 Wash.App. 287, 293, 667 P.2d 96 (1983) ("relevancy of [such] evidence is not discernible").

> The use of criminal profiles as substantive evidence of guilt is inherently prejudicial to the defendant.... Evidence of a "[child battering profile] is highly prejudicial since it invites a jury to conclude that because an expert experienced in child abuse cases identifies an accused as someone fitting a particular profile, it is more likely than not that this individual committed the crime." Sloan v. State, 70 Md.App. 630, 638, 522 A.2d 1364 (1987). We conclude that the admission in evidence of a "child battering profile" is reversible error due to its irrelevance and its inherent prejudicial impact on the defendant.

The court nevertheless found important differences between a "child battering profile" and the "battered child syndrome", explaining that:

> Testimony involving a "child battering profile" must be distinguished from testimony describing the "battered child syndrome," which both parties in the instant case agree is a proper subject for expert testimony. "[Battered child] syndrome has come to be a well recognized medical diagnosis, dependent on inferences, not a matter of common knowledge, but within the area of expertise of physicians whose familiarity with numerous instances of injuries accidentally caused qualifies them to express with reasonable probability that a particular injury or group of injuries is not accidental or is not consistent with the explanation offered therefor but is instead the result of physical abuse by a person of mature strength" (footnote omitted.) Commonwealth v. Labbe, 6 Mass.App.Ct. 73, 77, 373 N.E.2d 227 (1978).

(2) The phenomenon of child abuse was first labeled the "battered child syndrome" by Dr. Henry Kempe and his associates in 1962. C.H. Kempe, F.N. Silverman, B.F. Steele, W. Droegemuller, and H.K. Silver, The Battered–Child Syndrome, 181 J.A.M.A. 17 (1962).* They described their use of the term in order "to characterize a clinical condition in young children who have received serious physical abuse, generally from a parent or foster parent," and explained that:

> The clinical manifestations of the battered-child syndrome vary widely from those cases in which the trauma is very mild and is often unsuspected and unrecognized, to those who exhibit the most florid evidence of injury to the soft tissues and skeleton. In the former group, the patients' signs and symptoms may be considered to have resulted from failure to thrive from some other cause or to have been produced by a metabolic disorder, an infectious process, or some other disturbance. In these patients specific findings of trauma such as bruises or characteristic roentgenographic changes as described below may be misinterpreted and their significance not recognized.

> The battered child syndrome may occur at any age, but, in general, the affected children are younger than 3 years. In some instances the clinical manifestations are limited to those resulting from a single episode of trauma, but more often the child's general health is below par, and he shows evidence of neglect including poor skin hygiene, multiple soft tissue injuries, and malnutrition. One often obtains a history of previous episodes suggestive of parental neglect or trauma. A marked discrepancy between clinical findings and historical data as supplied by the parents is a major diagnostic feature of the battered-child syndrome. The fact that no new lesions either of the soft tissue or of the bone, occur while the child is in the hospital or in a protected environment lends added weight to the diagnosis and tends to exclude many diseases of the skeletal or hemopoietic systems in which lesions may occur spontaneously or after minor trauma. Subdural hematoma, with or without fracture of the skull is in our experience, an extremely frequent finding even in the absence of fractures of the long bones. In an occasional case the parent or parent-substitute may also have assaulted the child by administering an overdose of a drug or by exposing the child to natural gas or other toxic substances. The characteristic distribution of these multiple fractures and the observation that the lesions are in different stages of healing are of additional value in making the diagnosis.

The following year Dr. Vincent Fontana and his associates attempted to persuade physicians and others that the designation "battered child syndrome"— with its vivid connotations of physical violence—was under inclusive, and that there

---

* Copyright © 1962, American Medical Association. Reprinted with permission.

were other kinds of abuse inflicted on children with harmful results. They proposed the more inclusive label "maltreatment syndrome." V.J. Fontana, D. Donovan, and R.J. Wong, The "Maltreatment Syndrome" in Children, 269 N.Eng.J.Med. 1389 (1963). They also noted that this pediatric syndrome had often gone unrecognized, and that there was little information on the subject in medical literature. Since that time there has been a flood of literature as professionals have sought to determine the scope of the problem of child abuse and to determine its etiology. An international journal, Child Abuse and Neglect, now is published quarterly. Mary Edna Helfer, Ruth S. Kempe and Richard S. Krugman, The Battered Child, is now in a fifth edition (1999).

Dr. Kempe and his colleagues were not the first to recognize the phenomenon of child abuse. Other physicians earlier had called attention to the increasing incidence of nonaccidental injuries to children, particularly trauma to the long bones. The developmental history of efforts to diagnose and publicize the problem is chronicled in McCoid, The Battered Child and Other Assaults Upon the Family: Part One, 50 Minn.L.Rev. 1 (1965). For an account of the legislative response to revelations of the seriousness and substantial incidence of child abuse, see Paulsen, Parker, and Adelman, Child Abuse Reporting Laws: Some Legislative History, 34 Geo.Wash.L.Rev. 482 (1966).

The recent tendency has been to broaden the definition of child abuse as a medical phenomenon, which in turn has resulted in a broadening of its definition in reporting statutes, criminal statutes, juvenile court statutes, and for other purposes under the law.

Numerous legal questions are presented by expansion of the definition of abuse. Under what circumstances should the state be authorized to intervene in the lives and relationships of a family? Are there due process limitations on defining abuse, particularly if it extends to acts other than physical abuse or inadequate parenting? What special problems of proof are encountered in attempting to prove that a parent has abused a child?

D.   THE SPECIAL CASE OF MUNCHAUSEN SYNDROME BY PROXY

Consider the following facts:

By nearly all accounts, Priscilla Phillips was a kind, helpful and loving person, a dutiful wife to her husband and a devoted mother to their two sons, who at the time of trial were nine and six years of age. Highly educated, with a master's degree in social work, she was employed in the Marin County Health and Human Services Department. After the birth of her sons, she turned her attention increasingly to religious and civil volunteer work, and became active in a variety of community organizations. Among the many organizations to which she volunteered time and energy was the Child Protective Services Unit of the Marin County child abuse agency.

After the birth of her second son in 1973, [Ms. Phillips] developed physical symptoms which led to a hysterectomy in 1975. Deeply upset that she could not have another child, especially a daughter, [Ms. Phillips] and her husband decided to adopt a Korean infant who had been found abandoned on the streets of Seoul. They called her Tia.

Tia arrived at the Phillips' household in November 1975. [Ms. Phillips] promptly took her to Dr. Aimy Taniguchi, a pediatrician at the Kaiser clinic in San Rafael, for examination. Dr. Taniguchi found Tia to be in good health except for a diaper rash and an ear infection, and prescribed treatment for both. By late November the rash and the infection appeared to have been successfully treated.

On January 26, 1976, [Ms. Phillips] brought Tia into the clinic and informed Dr. Taniguchi that Tia had a low-grade fever. A urine specimen revealed a urinary tract infection for which Dr. Taniguchi prescribed first a sulfur-based antibiotic, which did not appear to help, and then a different antibiotic, which worked successfully. Tia's ear infection recurred, however, and was twice treated in February.

On February 27, 1976, [Ms. Phillips] brought Tia into the clinic and told Dr. Taniguchi that Tia had a fever and had vomited violently in the morning. The source of the fever could not be determined.

On March 2, 1976, [Ms. Phillips] brought Tia to the clinic again and reported that she had been vomiting off and on since the last visit. The doctor believed that the ear infection might be persisting, and added another antibiotic. Later that day, [Ms. Phillips] brought Tia into the Kaiser Hospital at San Rafael and told the doctor on call that Tia was having brief "staring spells," and Tia was admitted for observation.

Dr. William Leider, a pediatric neurologist from San Francisco Kaiser, was called in to evaluate Tia's condition, and a variety of tests were performed, including blood sugar and blood calcium tests, a urine culture, a lumbar puncture, X-rays, and an intravenous pyelogram, but the tests revealed no abnormalities. Dr. Al Baumann, an ear, nose and throat specialist, examined Tia, found evidence of a low-grade infection, and because of her previous ear infection recommended an operation called a myringotomy, which entails removal of fluid from the ear drums. The operation was performed on March 5. On March 6, Dr. Taniguchi informed [Ms. Phillips] that all of the diagnostic tests were complete, that the results were normal, that the ear operation was successful, and that she planned to discharge Tia within 48 hours.

During the evening of March 6, however, while Tia was still in the hospital, she began to cry and was unable to be comforted. The next day she began to vomit and have diarrhea. Her diet was changed from regular baby formula to clear liquid, but she did not improve. By March 9 feeding by mouth was discontinued and Tia was given intravenous fluids. She improved and was given clear fluids by mouth, but on the evening of March 10 the diarrhea attacks recurred. Feeding by mouth was again discontinued, and the diarrhea stopped abruptly.

Tia remained hospitalized, and the pattern continued. Further diagnostic tests revealed no abnormality, and the doctors were baffled. In April 1976 she was transferred to Kaiser Hospital in San Francisco, where a central venous hyperalimentation device was implanted through a catheter to permit introduction of nutritious fluids. She remained in San Francisco until June 8, 1976, and was then returned to Kaiser San Rafael to monitor her progress on naso-gastric feeding. On July 7, 1976, she was taken to

Stanford Medical Center for an intestinal biopsy. Although playful and alert when admitted, by the evening of July 8 she had developed cramps, acute diarrhea, and projectile vomiting. The diarrhea stopped abruptly the next morning. On July 10 Tia was transferred to a San Francisco hospital for the performance of a laparotomy to explore for tumors. Two days later, while at that hospital, Tia had another bout of diarrhea. Her doctors found this "inexplicable." On July 14 or 15, while still at the San Francisco hospital, [Ms. Phillips] suggested that Tia be given solid foods. The doctors agreed to try her suggestion, and it appeared to work. Tia "really did very well" and had normal body functions. On July 28 she was discharged. The laparotomy was not performed.

On August 6 [Ms. Phillips] called Dr. Taniguchi and told her that Tia's illness had recurred, that she was very sick with vomiting and diarrhea. Upon examination at the hospital, Tia was found to be severely dehydrated, lethargic, and unresponsive to stimulation. Tests revealed she was suffering from an extreme level of sodium in her blood. This finding coincided with prior readings, taken during periods when Tia was having attacks of diarrhea and vomiting; these findings also showed abnormally high levels of blood serum sodium, and of bicarbonate. The doctors had no explanation for this phenomenon.

Tia was admitted to the hospital, improved rapidly, and was released on August 9. On August 23, however, she was again hospitalized with the same symptoms. Abdominal X-rays showed no obstruction of the intestinal tract. She was discharged on August 28 but the symptoms reappeared and she was hospitalized twice in September and twice in October. Electrolyte readings continued to fluctuate, but again, all diagnostic tests were normal. In November 1976 a laparotomy was performed at Kaiser Hospital in San Francisco, but it revealed no abnormalities. Tia was discharged on November 26.

On December 3, 1976, Tia was examined by her pediatrician and was found to be doing well. Three days later she was back in the emergency room in shock, vomiting convulsively, and displaying elevated sodium and bicarbonate levels. On December 11, having improved to the point that she could take formula, she was discharged. Less than three hours later she was back with the same symptoms, and was discharged again on December 22. A similar episode occurred in January 1977.

On February 2, 1977, [Ms. Phillips] brought Tia to the emergency room for the last time. The child was in critical condition. She was having generalized seizures. She had an extreme level of sodium in her blood. An X-ray showed aspiration of vomit into her right lung. She was unable to eliminate carbon dioxide from her body, and she began to demonstrate abnormal posturings which indicated damage to her central nervous system. She died on February 3.

Several months after Tia's death, [Ms. Phillips] and her husband adopted another Korean infant whom they named Mindy. On February 3, 1979—the anniversary of Tia's death—[Ms. Phillips] brought Mindy to the hospital. The child had been vomiting, and she had diarrhea. Mindy was admitted to the hospital; her symptoms eventually subsided; and she was discharged on February 10. On February 16 Mindy was hospitalized again with the same symptoms. Her sodium level was elevated. Dr. Taniguchi began to note similarities between Mindy's case and Tia's case: "[T]hinking about it as objectively as possible, I realized that these two girls were not related in any way and ... it just seemed incredible that they could even possibly have the same type of problem...." At a pediatric staff conference on February 22, all doctors present agreed that "it was important to consider the possibility that this child was being poisoned."

The following day Dr. Arnhold, a pediatrician at Kaiser, gave Dr. Taniguchi a copy of an article from the Journal of the American Medical Association concerning a form of child abuse which had been reported in the British Medical Journal, Lancet, by a physician named Meadow. The article noted Meadow's observations of a case in which one little girl underwent innumerable manipulative, anesthetic, radiologic and surgical procedures during the six years of her life because her parents provided false information about her symptoms, tampered with her urine specimens, and otherwise interfered with observation by physicians and nurses; and of a second case in which a 14-month-old infant died of hypernatremia after repeated hospital admissions for vomiting and drowsiness that were precipitated by ingestion of large quantities of salt given to her surreptitiously by her mother. Both mothers appeared to be loving, cooperative, and appreciative of the care given to their children. Dr. Meadow had denominated the phenomena "Munchausen syndrome by proxy," after the so-called "Munchausen syndrome" in which a patient beguiles a physician into performing unnecessary diagnostic and surgical procedures on the basis of false reports of symptoms.

Dr. Taniguchi proceeded with a series of tests to determine a medical cause for Mindy's symptoms: "Again, I was faced with the puzzling finding of an elevated sodium; and for the first time [I] began to look at it in terms of what was going into the patient and what was coming out of the patient. And, it did not add up. There was much more coming out than was going in." Mindy continued to have diarrhea. Sodium levels were abnormally high.

On February 24, around 2:45 p.m., Leslie McCarcy, a pediatric nurse at the hospital, arrived on duty and received a report from Cathy Place, the outgoing nurse. The question of Mindy's formula came up. Appellant was in Mindy's hospital room at the time. According to Nurse McCarcy, "Mrs. Phillips came out to the desk and Cathy asked her if she had made up the formula and Mrs. Phillips said yes, she had. It was in the refrigerator."

The next morning, February 25, the pediatrician on duty checked Mindy's intake and output charts. "I found that indeed, there was a large amount of unaccountable sodium in Mindy's stool and urine.... She was losing about five times the amount of sodium she was receiving." The doctor then went to the nurse on duty and asked her where Mindy's formula was kept. He took a sample of the formula and had it analyzed. The sodium content was 448 milliequivalents per liter. According to the manufacturer's specification, the sodium content should have been only 15 milliequivalents per liter. The doctor had Mindy's formula replaced and transferred her to the intensive care unit.

[Ms. Phillips] was forbidden to feed Mindy, and was forbidden to visit the child except in the presence of a nurse. She was told that sodium appeared to be the cause of Mindy's illness, and that some sort of laxative salt might be a cause of the diarrhea. [Ms. Phillips] said, "I don't know anything about things like that," and asked what the doctor was going to do. When he told her that under the circumstances it was his obligation to call the Child Protective Services, [Ms. Phillips] became downcast and said, "Then I'll be a suspect."

Once Mindy was placed in the ICU unit, she recovered quickly. She "seemed fine. . . . She did not have any more diarrhea at all. . . . She ate well, she was happy. . . ."

Dr. Boyd Stephens, Coroner of the City and County of San Francisco, testified on the basis of his observations that the cause of Tia's death was sodium poisoning, and that the amount of the sodium was so high that it had to have been administered into the gastrointestinal tract. Dr. Malcolm Holliday, Professor of Pediatrics at the University of California, concurred, and concluded that since Tia's chloride levels were normal, and her bicarbonate level was high, that the form of the salt was sodium bicarbonate. He testified that two to three teaspoons of sodium bicarbonate, dissolved in liquid, would have been sufficient to produce the symptoms which Tia and Mindy displayed.

At each of the hospitals to which Tia was admitted, parents were encouraged to participate in the care of their infants and young children; and mothers were permitted to remain overnight and to feed their babies. Throughout Tia's hospitalizations, [Ms. Phillips] visited frequently and for prolonged periods of time. Because of her dedication, she won the admiration, sympathy, and respect of hospital staff members. Because of her obvious intelligence, her frequent presence, and her willingness to help, she was allowed to perform "minor nursing chores," including administration of formula through the nasogastric tube. The pediatric facility at each hospital had a small room or kitchen area not visible from the nursing station, which contained an unlocked refrigerator for formulas and other foods. [Ms. Phillips] had access to those areas.

What could explain Ms. Phillips' possible motivation to poison her adopted daughters? Why would anyone do something like this to their child?

A criminal prosecution of Ms. Phillips would be virtually doomed to failure unless the prosecutor can present the jury with some motive for such aberrant and unusual behavior by a parent.

The motive may be supplied by presenting the jury evidence of the disorder called Munchausen Syndrome by Proxy (MSBP). The syndrome is one in which an individual either directly or through a child feigns, simulates, or actually fabricates a physical illness, usually a dramatic or life threatening one. By "proxy" simply means instead of the person making themselves ill, they go through the psychodynamic process in another. As one expert testified in the trial of the above set of facts:

> In order to suggest a motive for appellant's alleged conduct, the prosecution, over the objections of defense counsel, presented evidence

relating to the so-called "Munchausen's syndrome by proxy" through the testimony of Dr. Martin Blinder, a psychiatrist. Dr. Blinder had not examined appellant, nor had he treated patients who displayed the syndrome which was the subject of his testimony. Rather, his testimony was based upon various reports in professional journals, copies of which were made available to the jury.

In response to a hypothetical question, Dr. Blinder theorized that a mother who repeatedly and surreptitiously administered a cathartic sodium compound to her adopted children, under circumstances identical to those presented by this case, displayed symptoms consistent with Munchausen's syndrome by proxy. He testified that the syndrome "is one in which an individual either directly or through the vehicle of a child feigns, simulates, or actually fabricates a physical illness.... Typically, the illness is a dramatic one." "And 'by proxy' simply means instead of the person making themselves ill, they go through the psychodynamic process in another. It's usually the mother.... She's outwardly devoted to the child and invariably, the child is very small, less than two years of age.... The mothers who perpetrate a child abuse or Munchausen's form of child abuse typically will transfer their own unmet parental needs ... onto pediatricians, nurses, spouses, maybe even the community and get from these people through their child's illness the attention and sympathy they never got from their own parents."

Describing the syndrome, Dr. Blinder continued: "The mother will flourish on the ward. She seems almost to blossom in the medical drama of the hospital.... The concern, competence and intelligence of these mothers ... makes it hard for the doctors to suspect them as the possible cause of their child's illness.... When the mother is confronted with evidence that she in fact is responsible for the illness, [she] cannot accept responsibility, even when the evidence is incontrovertible.... The literature describes some mothers who are frankly psychotic.... But a great number of the mothers who do this to their children are not overtly mentally ill."

People v. Phillips, 122 Cal.App.3d 69, 175 Cal.Rptr. 703 (1981).

Would this medical testimony persuade you of the mother's guilt in the above facts? What about the fact that no one ever saw her tampering with the baby's formula? Do you think the mother is guilty? How about the responsibility of the hospital or the attending physicians? How would your conclusions be affected if the expert noted that a further symptom of MSBP is the mother's inability to accept any responsibility for her abusive behavior or any mental illness?

Reid v. State

Court of Appeals of Texas, Amarillo, 1998.
964 S.W.2d 723.

■ BOYD, CHIEF JUSTICE.

In eight points of error, appellant Tanya Thaxton Reid contends her conviction of murder and the consequent jury-assessed punishment of 40 years confinement in the Institutional Division of the Department of Criminal Justice must be reversed. In the first four of those points, she argues the trial court abused its discretion in admitting testimony regarding Munchausen Syndrome by Proxy because 1) it is not relevant and not scientific knowledge, 2) it is not relevant and would not assist the trier of fact, 3) the probative value of the evidence is substantially outweighed by its prejudicial effect, and 4) it is impermissible character evidence.... In her next four points, she posits the trial court abused its discretion in admitting 5) evidence of extraneous offenses allegedly committed by appellant against Morgan Reid, her child, 6) evidence of extraneous offenses allegedly committed by appellant against Robert Matthew Reid (Matthew), another of her children, 7) evidence that Matthew was removed from her custody in a prior judicial proceeding, and 8) in admitting expert testimony regarding Munchausen Syndrome by Proxy to prove appellant committed the extraneous offenses against Matthew and Morgan and, as well, to prove that appellant committed the charged offense. We affirm the judgment of the trial court.

Because the questions presented by this appeal are primarily legal, and the factual record is lengthy, other than a background statement, we will refer to the factual evidence as it becomes necessary to a proper discussion of appellant's challenges. Parenthetically, there is a paucity of cases which have considered and discussed Munchausen Syndrome by Proxy.

. . .

As background, suffice it to say that on February 7, 1984, Deaf Smith County Emergency (EMS) personnel were summoned to the home of Tanya and Raymond Reid because their infant daughter, Morgan Reid, had suffered an apnea[2] episode. When the EMS personnel arrived, appellant was attempting to resuscitate Morgan. After an initial visit to the hospital in Hereford, Morgan was taken to Northwest Texas Hospital in Amarillo. Efforts to revive her were unsuccessful and, after it was learned the child was brain dead, she was removed from the ventilator and she died some fourteen hours later. After an autopsy, her cause of death was determined, and is shown on her death certificate, as brain death secondary to cardiorespiratory arrest of undetermined etiology.

The Reids also had another child, Robert Matthew Reid, who had apnea episodes beginning in 1985 and continuing until March of 1988. In March 1988 in Des Moines, Iowa, by court order, Matthew was adjudicated a child in need of assistance, removed from the Reid home, and placed in foster care. After that time, Matthew suffered no further apnea episodes.

In our discussion, as did the parties, we will refer to Munchausen Syndrome by Proxy by its initials, *i.e.,* MSBP. Appellant's challenges present four basic questions to be decided by us. The first is whether MSBP has attained a sufficient degree of scientific reliability to be admissible in a

---

2. Apnea, in a pathological sense, is defined as "a suspension of respiration, partial or entire; suffocation." Reader's Digest Great Encyclopedic Dictionary (including Funk & Wagnalls Standard College Dictionary) 1975 Edition.

proper case. A subset of that question, assuming the diagnosis is sufficiently reliable to be received into evidence, is whether it is relevant in this particular case. The second question, assuming affirmative answers to the first question and its subset, is whether, in this case, the probative value of the MSBP testimony is exceeded by its prejudicial effect. The third question is whether the trial court erred in admitting evidence of extraneous offenses allegedly committed by appellant against Matthew and Morgan, as well as admitting expert MSBP testimony to establish appellant committed these extraneous offenses and, by extension, that she committed the offense charged. The fourth question is if the trial court reversibly erred in admitting evidence that custody of Matthew, Morgan's brother, was removed from appellant in a prior judicial proceeding.

Texas Rule of Criminal Evidence 702 provides:

> If scientific, technical, or other specialized knowledge will assist the trier of fact to understand the evidence or to determine a fact in issue, a witness qualified as an expert by knowledge, skill, experience, training, or education, may testify thereto in the form of an opinion or otherwise.

Prior to the adoption of Rule 702,[3] the standard for admissibility of expert testimony as to scientific evidence was whether the subject matter "had gained general acceptance in the particular field in which it belongs."
. . .

The seminal case in interpreting the threshold requirements for admissibility of expert testimony under Rule 702 is *Kelly v. State, supra.* In *Kelly,* the court held that to be admissible under the rule, proffered scientific expert testimony must be "sufficiently reliable and relevant to help the jury in reaching accurate results." *Kelly v. State,* 824 S.W.2d at 572. In order to meet that reliability standard, the evidence must meet three criteria: a) the underlying scientific theory must be valid; b) the technique applying the theory must be valid; and c) the technique must have been properly applied on the occasion in question. *Id.* at 573. In its analysis, the *Kelly* court applied Rule 104(a) and (c), in conjunction with Rule 702, and determined that prior to its receipt into evidence, the proponent must satisfy the trial court in a preliminary hearing outside the presence of the jury, that the expert testimony meets all three criteria. *Id.* at 573. In doing so, the *Kelly* court also listed several non-exclusive factors that might affect a determination as to whether those criteria had been met. Those non-exclusive factors are: 1) the extent to which the underlying scientific theory and technique are accepted as valid by the relevant scientific community, if such a community can be ascertained; 2) the qualifications of the expert(s) testifying; 3) the existence of literature supporting or rejecting the underlying scientific theory and technique; 4) the potential rate of error of the technique; 5) the availability of other experts to test and evaluate the technique; 6) the clarity with which the underlying scientific theory and

---

3. Later references to rule numbers are to those Rules of Criminal Evidence unless   otherwise specifically denominated.

technique can be explained to the court; and 7) the experience and skill of the person(s) who applied the technique on the occasion in question. . . .

Needless to say, the careful trial judge held the requisite pretrial hearing before making his determination that the MSBP testimony was admissible. At the preliminary hearing, the State's expert witness was Dr. Thomas Bennett, the Iowa State Medical Examiner. Because of the importance of his testimony in determining whether the trial court properly decided to admit MSBP testimony, it is necessary to recount relevant portions of that testimony. Appellant does not challenge Dr. Bennett's expertise in the field of pathology and child abuse, therefore it is not necessary in this opinion to address his qualifications. Dr. Bennett described MSBP as a "fairly recently" developed term for "a medical diagnosis that has been accepted to encompass, what we found is some rather unexplainable otherwise signs and symptoms" in children. He said he had seen "probably" a dozen or more cases over the years and he has consulted on "numerable others, numerous others."

Dr. Bennett noted that he had personally performed around 4,000 autopsies over the years, and reviewed "thousands" by virtue of his responsibilities as the state medical examiner, and even others on a consultive basis. Additionally, Dr. Bennett had testified as an expert on MSBP in four or five cases and, basically, had been an expert in almost every case that has been presented in Iowa. Dr. Bennett defined MSBP as "a series of unexplained incongruous signs and symptoms the child presents with but after you do further testing or remove them from the caretaker's control the signs and symptoms tend to disappear or they resolve otherwise." He also opined that because the signs and symptoms do not otherwise fit into a classic medical diagnosis, the children are victimized otherwise over the years "in an ongoing pattern of medical intervention studies diagnostic tests which are in themselves even abusive because they involve invasion into the body for blood work, other tests through the looking at various orifices and so on, and again is one that carries with it, and unfortunately, a very significant percentage of cases to make more percent of cases a fatality risk." He concluded that about ten percent of MSBP cases do result in fatalities, and "it's a very severe form of child abuse."

When queried about the diagnosis's acceptance in medical circles, Dr. Bennett averred, "[t]his theory has been studied, it has been written up in dozens and dozens of articles, and it has in my opinion achieved widespread acceptance, and it is now being taught in the schools, because if you don't teach of it—if you don't teach it the doctor won't think of it; if you don't think of it you won't diagnose it because it is such a severe form of child abuse. It has been taught and it is recognized and accepted, it's even in the latest addition of the diagnostical manual, the DSM–4 has recognized it, it's finally made that recognized entity." The DSM–4, he explained, is a book prepared over the years primarily for psychiatric disorders. The book, he said, has a special chapter for fictitious disorders by proxy which "is another way of saying" MSBP.

In his testimony, Dr. Bennett also reviewed State's pretrial exhibit 10 consisting of six photocopies of complete articles and a med-line database search covering the period from 1922 to May 1996 which showed 122 articles in their abstract form. The search also contained the citations by which those articles could be located if it was desired to read them in their entirety. The doctor also identified State's pretrial exhibit 11, which was another bibliography containing articles relating to MSBP going back to 1977. The State also offered its pretrial exhibit 12 which was a compilation of some 17 legal articles dealing with MSBP. The witness also commented there were "many" books or publications which discussed MSBP. He specifically identified a book written by Robert Reese as one of the publications dealing with child abuse medical diagnosis and which contained a chapter dealing specifically with MSBP, although the book itself was not introduced into evidence. Dr. Bennett also opined that there were "dozens and dozens and dozens"[5] of experts who would be available to testify concerning MSBP. It was Dr. Bennett's conclusion that a diagnosis of MSBP was "universally accepted." After an examination of Morgan and Matthew's medical records, it was his conclusion that the children were victims of MSBP. With regard to Morgan, the child whose death appellant was accused of causing, the doctor's conclusion was that the underlying cause of death was MSBP. The medical records of Morgan and Matthew were also properly verified and introduced at the pretrial hearing.

The evidence introduced at the pretrial hearing was sufficient to sustain the trial court's "gatekeeper" decision that it was sufficient to meet all three criteria explicated in the *Kelly* case. . . .

At trial, expert witnesses Drs. Carol Rosen, Randall Alexander, Austin Colman, and Thomas Kelly testified for the State. Parenthetically, appellant does not challenge the expertise of any of these witnesses. As each expert witness was tendered by the State at trial, appellant's trial counsel objected to the receipt of any MSBP testimony for reasons similar to those she advanced at the pretrial hearing and is also advanced in this appeal. Accordingly, a voir dire examination of each witness was conducted outside the presence of the jury and prior to the receipt of the witness's testimony before the jury. Thus, the issues were consensually relitigated by the parties at trial. Because that is true, the exception to the general rule is applicable and the experts' trial testimony may also be considered in determining the admissibility of the MSBP testimony. Distilled, the testimony of the expert witnesses was that: MSBP is an identifiable, reliable, generally accepted medical diagnosis (Dr. Bennett in pretrial testimony) (Dr. Rosen at trial) (Dr. Alexander at trial); MSBP is a form of child abuse in which a caretaker either makes up illness symptoms or is actively creating or causing those symptoms (Dr. Bennett in pretrial testimony) (Dr. Rosen at trial) (Dr. Alexander at trial); the illnesses are usually extraordinary or bizarre, result in multiple hospitalizations, and extensive medical evaluations never seem to reveal explanations for the child's illness (Dr. Rosen at trial); the MSBP diagnosis is recognized in medical schools and is taught in those schools (Dr. Bennett in pretrial testimony) (Dr. Alexander at trial) (Dr. Colman at trial); MSBP is the subject of medical literature (Dr. Bennett at pretrial) (Dr. Rosen at trial); information about MSBP was helpful in determining a medical diagnosis or treatment of

---

5. He commented there were 20 such experts in the State of Iowa alone.

Morgan (Dr. Rosen at trial). Dr. Rosen also opined that the MSBP diagnosis would be helpful in determining intent, motive, plan, pattern, absence of illness, mistake or accidents in the apnea episodes suffered by Morgan. Thus, the expert testimony at trial reinforces the trial judge's pretrial conclusion that the MSBP diagnosis is one generally recognized and accepted in the medical community and meets the three-prong reliability test articulated by the *Kelly* court. We also note that appellant's medical expert, Dr. Stephen L. Linder, although disagreeing that the diagnosis was applicable to appellant, admitted that MSBP was "a medical diagnosis and it falls in this category of medical and psychiatric."

Rule 702 also requires that the trial court, before admitting expert testimony, must be satisfied that another three conditions are met: 1) that the expert witness qualifies as an expert by reason of his knowledge, skill, experience, training or education; 2) the subject matter is an appropriate one for expert testimony; and 3) that admitting the expert testimony will actually assist the jury. The trial court's decision as to those three conditions may not be disturbed on appeal absent an abuse of discretion.

Here, as the expert testimony was received at trial, the jury was instructed that if there was any testimony from the witnesses that appellant had committed "offenses, wrongs, or acts other than the offense alleged here in the indictment," it could not consider them unless they believed beyond a reasonable doubt appellant committed them and then might only consider them in determining "intent, motive, plan, pattern, absence of illness, mistake or accident, if any" in connection with the offense alleged against her in the indictment. With regard to MSBP testimony, the judge orally instructed that it might be considered:

> * * * only for the limited purpose or purposes of assisting you in considering the motive of the defendant, if any; the intent of the defendant, if any; the plan of the defendant, if any; the pattern, if any, of apneic episodes, if any, involving Morgan Reid or Robert (Matthew) Reid, if any, or both of them, if any;
>
> The absence of illness, mistake or accident, if any; the state of mind of the defendant on the occasion in question, if any; the medical diagnosis of Morgan Reid, if any; the relationship between the defendant and Morgan Reid, if any;
>
> The cause of death of Morgan Reid, if any, in connection with the offense, if any, alleged against the defendant in the indictment in this case and no other purpose or purposes.

A similar instruction was given the jury in the court's charge with the addendum that they "could not consider evidence of Munchausen Syndrome by Proxy, if any, as a substitute for proof that the defendant committed the crime charged nor as proof that the defendant has a criminal personality, if any, or bad character, if any."

Having made the decision that the trial court did not err in determining the scientific reliability of the MSBP testimony, it becomes necessary to determine appellant's next challenge. She argues that even if it is found the expert MSBP testimony meets the *Kelly* test, the trial court abused its discretion in admitting the testimony because "it is not relevant and would not assist the jury; and, even if relevant, its probative value is substantially outweighed by the danger of unfair prejudice, confusion of issues, or misleading the jury."

In considering this challenge, again we must bear in mind the rule that a trial court is vested with the discretion to admit or exclude evidence and an appellate court should not reverse a trial court unless that court has abused its discretion in admitting the evidence. It is also the rule that if evidence is relevant to a matter or issue in the case, our evidentiary rules now require the party opposing the proffered evidence not only to demonstrate the negative attributes of the evidence but also show how those negative attributes substantially outweigh its probative value.

In Rule 401, relevant evidence is defined as "evidence having any tendency to make the existence of any fact that is of consequence to the determination of the action more probable or less probable than it would be without the evidence." In considering the question of relevancy, it is worthy of note that although a prosecutor ordinarily need not prove motive as an element of a crime, the absence of an apparent motive may make proof of the essential elements of a crime less persuasive. That is certainly the case here. In the absence of a motivational hypothesis, and in the light of other information which was before the jury concerning appellant's demeanor, personality and character, including the fact that she was the mother of the child, without other relevant and reliable evidence, the conduct ascribed to appellant was incongruous and apparently inexplicable. MSBP testimony would, if accepted by the jury, bridge that gap.

. . .

However, appellant continues, even assuming *arguendo,* that if the expert testimony is deemed relevant, reliable, and otherwise admissible, the trial court "crossed the line" of admissibility by allowing the experts to testify that in his or her opinion, appellant repeatedly suffocated the children. That testimony was improper, reasons appellant, because in so testifying, the experts impermissively decided for the jury the ultimate issue of appellant's guilt.

Morgan was born on May 17, 1983, and died on February 8, 1984. The State introduced evidence of approximately 13 apnea episodes suffered by Morgan prior to her death. The State's evidence was that the apnea episodes were similar in that they usually occurred on weekdays between 1:00 p.m. and 4:00 p.m., Morgan was usually awake before the episodes began, appellant was the only one present who observed the onset of an apnea episode and she was the one who had to revive Morgan by the use of mouth-to-mouth or cardiopulmonary resuscitation. The State also presented testimony that Morgan had undergone tests without a satisfactory physiological explanation for the apnea episodes.

With regard to Matthew, the State's evidence showed he was born on May 2, 1985, and had his first of approximately 15 apnea episodes some 26 days later. Appellant was the only one who witnessed the onset of the severe apnea episodes; they only occurred when Matthew was awake; appellant performed mouth or cardiopulmonary resuscitation upon him; Matthew underwent numerous tests without a satisfactory physiological explanation for the tests. The State also produced evidence that he never had another apnea episode after he was removed from appellant.

In responding to this challenge, the State initially contends the question was not preserved for our review. This follows, it says, because appellant's objections and requests for running objections were merely directed at the admission of testimony about MSBP, *per se,* and did not specifically address the issue of identification of appellant as the perpetrator.

. . .

In advancing her proposition, appellant acknowledges the provision of Rule 704 that expert testimony, which is otherwise admissible, is not objectionable because it embraces an ultimate fact to be decided by the trier of fact. However, she argues, while an expert witness may possess scientific, technical, or other specialized knowledge concerning MSBP as a form of child abuse, "that same person does not possess 'scientific, technical, or other specialized knowledge' beyond the realm of the jury in making a determination of Appellant's guilt or innocence," and the effect of the challenged testimony was to invade that realm.

. . .

In this case, . . . the testimony about appellant's conduct with her minor children was part and parcel of the diagnosis of MSBP, a diagnosis which could not be made without application to the facts of the case. The testimony was about a mental condition, the understanding of which is beyond the comprehension and understanding of the average person. Under the peculiar and special circumstances of the psychiatric condition known as MSBP and its diagnosis, the experts' use of the facts, *i.e.,* the apnea episodes and appellant's relation to them, in pursuing and determining their medical diagnosis, in explaining the diagnosis to the jury, and giving their opinion as to the cause of Morgan's death was within the permissible range of Rule 702 testimony as an aid to the jury in determining the guilt or innocence of appellant. As such, it did not preempt or invade the peculiar and special right to determine guilt.

In homicide cases, it has long been established in this state that the cause of death may be shown by either or both expert and circumstantial evidence, and such evidence is admissible for that purpose. . . . With the limiting instruction he gave, the trial judge did not abuse his discretion in admitting the MSBP to aid the jury in making its determination as to the cause of Morgan's death.

Our preceding discussion foreshadows our disposition of appellant's rather conclusory argument that the probative value of the expert testimony was substantially outweighed by its prejudicial effect. As we have discussed above, by its very nature, the MSBP diagnosis depends upon expert testimony such as was received here and is necessary to aid the jury in deciding the ultimate issue of guilt or innocence in cases such as this. Under this record, appellant has not met her burden of demonstrating that the negative attributes of the MSBP testimony substantially outweighed its probative value. Thus, we hold the trial court did not abuse its discretion in reaching that conclusion.

. . .

We must now consider appellant's contention that the trial court erred in admitting testimony that Matthew was removed from appellant's custody. We note that during his direct examination, State's witness Dr. Thomas Kelly twice made reference to Matthew's removal, and during re-direct examination again referred to the child's removal, all without objection. Additionally, during direct examination by counsel, defense witness Raymond Reid was asked about Matthew's removal from his home in Iowa and about his well being when in foster care. Assuming, *arguendo,* that evidence about this removal was inadmissible, it is the rule that inadmissible evidence can be rendered harmless if other evidence at trial is admitted without objection and it establishes the same fact that the inadmissible evidence sought to prove. *Stoker v. State,* 788 S.W.2d 1, 14 (Tex.Crim.App. 1989), *cert. denied,* 498 U.S. 951, 111 S.Ct. 371, 112 L.Ed.2d 333 (1990); *Willis v. State,* 785 S.W.2d 378, 383 (Tex.Crim.App.1989); *Russell v. State,* 904 S.W.2d 191, 202 (Tex.App.—Amarillo 1995, pet. ref'd).

. . . The State's case was purely circumstantial. The fact that until Matthew was removed from appellant's custody he suffered the same symptoms as Morgan but they did not reoccur after he left her custody was admissible as evidence of a system or scheme and as bearing upon appellant's intent. It was also admissible to aid the jury in determining whether Morgan died as a result of some defect or disease of an unknown origin. In sum, the evidence was admissible for the purposes for which it was admitted, given the trial court's limiting instructions both at the time of the receipt of the evidence and in its written jury charge.

In final summary, all of appellant's points are overruled and the judgment of the trial court affirmed.

NOTES

(1) From 1981 and the pioneering work of the California court in *Phillips* to the present, there has been geometrically escalating popular and scholarly attention devoted to Munchausen Syndrome by Proxy. It appears that the medical, legal, and popular understanding and familiarity with the mental disorder is now wide-spread. See, for example, Kathleen R. Miller, Detecting the Undetectable: An Examination of the Intersection Between Sudden Infant Death Syndrome and Munchausen Syndrome By Proxy, 5 Conn. Pub. Int. L.J. 287 (2006); Melinda Cleary, Mothering Under the Microscope: Gender Bias in Law and Medicine and the Problem of Munchausen Syndrome By Proxy, 7 T.M. Cooley J. Prac. & Clinical L. 183 (2005); Melissa A. Prentice, Prosecuting Mothers Who Maim and Kill: The Profile of Munchausen Syndrome by Proxy Litigation in the Late 1990s, 28 Am. J. Crim. L. 373 (2001).

There are now several web sites devoted to discussion of Munchausen Syndrome by Proxy: http://www.vachss.com/help_text/msp.html. Indeed, there is at least one web site for the organization called Mothers Against Munchausen Syndrome by Proxy Allegations: http://www.msbp.com. M.A.M.A., as it styles itself, was "begun in response to the fast growing number of false allegations of Munchausen Syndrome by Proxy.... Families ... are being destroyed by doctors and other professionals who make false and even malicious allegations against desperate mothers of chronically/critically ill children.''

In addition to these web sites, there have been several portrayals of Munchausen Syndrome by Proxy in movies and television shows such as *The X–Files* (''The Calusari,'' 1995); ''A Child's Cry for Help''; *ER* (''Abby Road,'' Season 6, Episode 12, 2000); and, perhaps best known, *The Sixth Sense,* released in 1999, in which star Bruce Willis plays a child psychologist helping a young boy who claims spirit visions. The film contains some intriguing references to Munchausen Syndrome by Proxy.

(2) May the conduct of parents toward other children be introduced in a criminal prosecution whose allegations relate only to one child? See *State v. Hocevar,* 300 Mont. 167, 7 P.3d 329 (2000). In this case, the mother (Susan) was charged with attempted homicide and criminal endangerment of one child (Wesley) who suffered a drug overdose of Benadryl and felony assault, felony murder, and deliberate homicide of a second child (Mathew) who had died one year earlier. The state introduced evidence of the death of a third child (Zachary) and the mother objected on appeal:

Issue 8

Whether evidence concerning Zachary Hocevar's death was properly admitted pursuant to Rule 404(b), M.R.Evid.

A district court has broad discretion to determine whether other crimes, wrongs or acts evidence is relevant and admissible. . . . Absent a showing of an abuse of discretion, we will not overturn a district court's determinations on evidentiary matters. . . .

The State gave pretrial notice of its intent to introduce evidence of Zachary's death pursuant to Rule 404(b), M.R.Evid., for the purposes of proving:

(1) that Susan engaged in a common plan or modus operandi pursuant to which she unlawfully caused the deaths of Zachary and Mathew;

(2) that the death of Mathew and the poisoning of Wesley were neither natural nor accidental; and

(3) that Susan's affliction with MSBP gave her motive to smother Mathew.

Susan filed a motion *in limine* to prohibit the State from introducing this other crimes, wrongs or acts evidence. The District Court denied the motion following a hearing. Susan renewed her objection to this evidence in her motion for a new trial. In denying the motion, the District Court held that Zachary's and Wesley's medical histories bore remarkable similarities regarding the phenomenon of MSBP and that Zachary's death was thus admissible to show motive . . .

Susan argues that, contrary to the State's Notice, the evidence of Zachary's death was not intended to prove common plan or modus operandi, but to show Susan's ''character,'' i.e., MSBP, and that she acted in conformity with that character. Susan asserts that the State used the evidence of Zachary's death to show that she suffered from MSBP and then used MSBP as the common plan or motive for her actions against Mathew and Wesley.

Susan analogizes the introduction of evidence of Zachary's death to a situation where the State seeks to introduce evidence of past burglaries to show a that defendant charged with burglary is a kleptomaniac and acted in conformity with that diagnosis. We agree with the State that this analogy is not apt. As the District Court noted in allowing the MSBP evidence, MSBP is not a psychiatric diagnosis of a mental disorder, such as kleptomania. Rather, MSBP is a pediatric diagnosis of a form of child abuse, where the "disorder" consists of the behavior of the person suffering from it. Unlike in the case of a mental disorder, there is no distinction between the disorder and the behavior associated with that disorder. As such, MSBP does not describe Susan's character, but her behavior toward her children.

The Modified Just Rule guides the District Court's discretion in admitting other crimes, wrongs or acts evidence under Rules 404(b) and 403, M.R.Evid.:

(1) The other crimes, wrongs or acts must be similar.

(2) The other crimes, wrongs or acts must not be remote in time.

(3) The evidence of other crimes, wrongs or acts is not admissible to prove the character of a person in order to show that he acted in conformity with such character; but may be admissible for other purposes, such as proof of motive, opportunity, intent, preparation, plan, knowledge, identity, or absence of mistake or accident.

(4) Although relevant, evidence may be excluded if its probative value is substantially outweighed by the danger of unfair prejudice, confusion of the issues, misleading of the jury, considerations of undue delay, waste of time, or needless presentation of cumulative evidence.

Matt, 249 Mont. at 142, 814 P.2d at 56. Applying the Modified Just Rule to the evidence of Zachary's death, we conclude that the District Court did not abuse its discretion in allowing the evidence.

We limit our discussion to the third and fourth requirements of the Modified Just rule. Susan does not raise the second requirement in her briefs and cites no legal authority in support of her argument that Zachary's death was not similar to Wesley's overdose. Because Susan cites to no authority as required by Rule 23(a)(4), M.R.App.P., and recognizing that she bears the burden of establishing error by the trial court ... we decline to address her argument: regarding the first requirement of the Modified *Just* rule.

The evidence of Zachary's death was introduced to show motive and not, as Susan contends, that she acted in conformity with her character—MSBP—in causing Mathew's death and Wesley's overdose. The evidence was thus properly admitted under the third requirement of the Modified Just rule because it was introduced to establish MSBP as Susan's motive for smothering Mathew and poisoning Wesley, not to establish MSBP as Susan's character and that she acted in conformity therewith.

Finally, Susan argues that the evidence of Zachary's death was inadmissible under the fourth requirement because its probative value was substantially outweighed by the danger of unfair prejudice, confusion of the issues, misleading the jury, considerations of undue delay, and waste of time. With regard to counts I and II, concerning Wesley's overdose, Susan contends that the evidence of Zachary's death caused undue prejudice and that, because Alexander did not testify with certainty that Wesley's overdose was consistent with MSBP, the evidence only served to mislead the jury, cause undue delay, waste of time, and confusion of the issues. With regard to counts III, IV, and V, concerning Mathew's death, Susan contends that the evidence of Zachary's death caused undue prejudice because the State wanted the jury to be aware that two of the Hocevar children had died, leaving them to question how this could happen absent some wrongdoing.

This Court has previously recognized that other crimes evidence will inevitably have some prejudicial effect on a defendant ... The evidence of Zachary's death had great probative weight because it tended to establish the diagnosis of MSBP, which the State alleged as Susan's motive for smothering Mathew and poisoning Wesley. While it is possible that the jury could have viewed the deaths of two Hocevar children with suspicion, such inevitable prejudice does not rise to the level of outweighing the probative weight of the evidence of Zachary's death.

The District Court did not abuse its discretion in admitting evidence of Zachary's death pursuant to Rule 404(b), M.R.Evid.

(3) Should the evidence of a profile of the Munchausen Syndrome by Proxy caretaker be admitted into evidence? With the battered child syndrome and the battering parent profile, the syndrome is admissible as expert scientific evidence and the profile is inadmissible as a mere attempt to portray a particular parent in a negative way by using a form of guilt by association. Should the same be true of Munchausen Syndrome by Proxy? See In *the Matter of Patrick GG* et al., 286 A.D.2d 540, 729 N.Y.S.2d 215 (2001), where the court stated at page 544:

> Yet a MSP diagnosis is not typically based upon these factors alone; rather, it becomes an assessment of "the total picture presented", Notably, within that picture the parent or caretaker of an MSP child is typically described as:

> "articulate and bright, and possesses a high degree of medical knowledge and/or fascination with medical details and hospital gossip, and seems to enjoy the hospital environment. Normally the mother seems almost unperturbed by the serious nature of her child's medical course and is highly supportive and/or encouraging of the physician and medical staff. She is a highly attendant parent who is reluctant to leave her child's side and is often perceived as very needy herself. The parent-child relationship is so intimate as to be described as 'symbiotic' ...

> "[and] [t]he suspected parent may be a health care professional, have a nursing degree or nursing training"....

> Respondent exhibits none of these characteristics. Her testimony revealed that she is a farm worker with a ninth grade education, lacking any medical training or knowledge; the record fails to establish that she developed any particular rapport or relationship of trust with either the attending physicians, nurses or other hospital staff and, in fact, testified to a confrontational relationship with Kjolhede from its inception. Neither was it established that she had an especially close or symbiotic relationship with Caroline nor had sought out an unreasonable number of medical providers. Notably, no psychiatric evidence was proffered ...

See again, Melissa A. Prentice, Prosecuting Mothers Who Maim and Kill: The Profile of Munchausen Syndrome by Proxy Litigation in the Late 1990s, 28 Am.J Crim.L. 373 (2001).

(4) Given the fact that, in may cases, it appears the parent with Munchausen Syndrome by Proxy may be accused of tampering with the infant child's diet in the hospital itself, would you encourage the use of covert surveillance cameras and techniques to monitor contacts between parents and children in hospitals? For a thorough discussion of this topic, see Michael T. Flannery, First, Do No Harm: The Use of Covert Video Surveillance to Detect Munchausen Syndrome by Proxy—An Unethical Means of 'Preventing' Child Abuse, 32 U.Mich.J.L.Ref. 105 (1998).

(5) Recent scholarly literature has suggested the possibility of a diminished capacity defense for the parent based on the mental disorder MSBP. See, e.g., E. Selene Steelman, A Question of Revenge: Munchausen Syndrome by Proxy and a

Proposed Diminished Capacity Defense for Homicidal Mothers, 8 Cardozo Women's L.J. 261 (2002).

(6) Other child abuse cases have involved allegations of a parent suffering from Munchausen's Syndrome by Proxy. Kathy Bush, a Florida woman whose daughter Jennifer had been hospitalized 200 times and had 40 surgeries in eight years, was accused in April 1996 of aggravated child abuse and fraud for allegedly receiving unnecessary medical services. The prosecution argued that hers was a case of Munchausen's Syndrome by Proxy, but the mother denied inflicting any of the illnesses ostensibly involving the daughter's gall bladder, appendix, and part of an intestine that were removed by doctors. Kathy Bush was convicted of aggravated child abuse and in 2002 lost her appeal. *Bush v. State*, 809 So.2d 107 (Fla.Dist.Ct. App. 2002). In July 2002 she commenced serving a five-year prison term. She was released on parole in 2005 after serving three years, and requested contact with Jennifer, whom she had not seen since 1999. Jennifer, who earlier had been a poster child for the Clinton administration's charge that health care costs were out of control, had been placed in state custody following the trial. By 2005 she was 18 years old and agreed to the visit with her mother. See http://www.nbc6.net/news/4766539/detail.html. Kathy Bush and her prosecution for child abuse were the subjects of an episode of "American Justice" on the Arts and Entertainment television channel.

Prior to the Bush case, Yvonne Eldridge, a foster mother in Oregon who was nationally honored in 1988 by Nancy Reagan for outstanding care of sick children, was accused of abusing two medically fragile babies between 1987 and 1991 by "continually making them ill and then pressing for unnecessary medical treatment, in part by falsifying symptoms." San Francisco Chronicle, July 11, 1996, A13. It was asserted by the state attorney general's office that Eldridge suffered from Munchausen's Syndrome by Proxy, but Eldridge denied she suffered from the syndrome or that she had engaged in any wrongdoing. The judge in Eldridge's trial did not allow mention of the syndrome. Eldridge was convicted of the charges and sentenced in June 1996 to four years in state prison.

Another woman, Angela Kelley, recently was convicted in Ohio of misdemeanor child endangering and ordered to serve 30 days in a work-release program. The county prosecutor claimed that Kelley suffered from Munchausen's Syndrome by Proxy. Kelley, who had taken her son (by that time two years old) to the hospital 88 times in 18 months, denied having fabricated illnesses. She was ordered by a judge to undergo psychological treatment.

(7) In *Commonwealth v. Robinson*, 30 Mass.App.Ct. 62, 565 N.E.2d 1229 (1991), the Massachusetts Appeals Court upheld the conviction of a mother of involuntary manslaughter in connection with the death of her hospitalized child, which resulted from poisoning caused by massive salt intoxication. The trial court had granted the defendant's request that the Commonwealth be prohibited from introducing evidence concerning Munchausen by Proxy or any profile evidence of the character, education, socio-economic condition, etc. of defendant on the failure to thrive syndrome. However, the judge did not preclude introduction of evidence of the physical condition of the child that led to his admission to Children's Hospital. The court also held that the Commonwealth could introduce evidence concerning the course of the child's treatment at that institution. In finding that circumstantial evidence was sufficient "to warrant a rational trier of fact to find beyond a reasonable doubt that the defendant placed large amounts of salt in the child's formula, causing his death" the appellate court noted that:

> Here, there was evidence that the defendant had the means and the opportunity to commit the crime. Salt in large amounts was available to her, and she had access to the child's formula while it was being refrigerated. She

was observed in and around the kitchen, the location of the refrigerator, on several occasions, including the relevant times that the two salt loads were added to the formula. A nurser containing salt-tainted formula was found secreted in the defendant's belongings. There was evidence which could indicate that on the morning of March 3 the defendant knew that the child's crisis was the result of salt ingestion before that fact was known to anyone else outside of the treatment room. Further, the defendant could have been found to have been motivated, however irrationally, to add salt to the child's formula. She suspected that the authorities were directing an investigation to her as the possible source of the child's failure to gain weight. She was aware that salt ingestion gave an appearance of added weight to the body. A reasonable inference could be drawn that the defendant added the salt to the formula to have the child give the appearance of weight gain, have him released from the hospital, and thereby deflect the investigation from herself.

It is possible, of course, that the salt was added to the child's formula by accident during the course of his stay at the hospital. There was, however, considerable evidence of painstaking investigations conducted by the hospital personnel to locate the source of the toxic amount of salt found in the formula. The results of those investigations, by a process of elimination, pointed to the defendant as the source.

(8) For a case in which Munchausen Syndrome by Proxy is discussed by a court in the context of a proceeding to terminate parental rights, see *In re S.R.*, 157 Vt. 417, 599 A.2d 364 (1991), reproduced infra at 766.

E.   Defining "Abuse" and Determining When and How to Intervene

VIRGINIA CODE ANNOTATED

CHILD ABUSE REPORTING ACT

§ 63.2–1509.   Physicians, nurses, teachers, etc., to report certain injuries to children; penalty for failure to report

A.   The following persons who, in their professional or official capacity, have reason to suspect that a child is an abused or neglected child, shall report the matter immediately to the local department of the county or city wherein the child resides or wherein the abuse or neglect is believed to have occurred or to the Department's toll-free child abuse and neglect hotline:

1.   Any person licensed to practice medicine or any of the healing arts;

2.   Any hospital resident or intern, and any person employed in the nursing profession;

3.   Any person employed as a social worker;

4.   Any probation officer;

5.   Any teacher or other person employed in a public or private school, kindergarten or nursery school;

6.   Any person providing full-time or part-time child care for pay on a regularly planned basis;

7.   Any mental health professional;

8.   Any law-enforcement officer or animal control officer;

9.   Any mediator eligible to receive court referrals pursuant to § 8.01–576.8;

10.   Any professional staff person, not previously enumerated, employed by a private or state-operated hospital, institution or facility to which children have been committed or where children have been placed for care and treatment;

11.   Any person associated with or employed by any private organization responsible for the care, custody or control of children; and

12.   Any person who is designated a court-appointed special advocate pursuant to Article 5 (§ 9.1–151 et seq.) of Chapter 1 of Title 9.1.

13.   Any person, over the age of 18 years, who has received training approved by the Department of Social Services for the purpose of recognizing and reporting child abuse and neglect; and

14.   Any person employed by a local department as defined in § 63.2–100 who determines eligibility for public assistance; and

15.   Any emergency medical services personnel certified by the Board of Health pursuant to § 32.1–111.5, unless such personnel immediately reports the matter directly to the attending physician at the hospital to which the child is transported, who shall make such report forthwith.

[subsection A(15) to become effective March 31, 2009]

This subsection shall not apply to any regular minister, priest, rabbi, imam, or duly accredited practitioner of any religious organization or denomination usually referred to as a church as it relates to (i) information required by the doctrine of the religious organization or denomination to be kept in a confidential manner or (ii) information that would be subject to § 8.01–400 or 19.2–271.3 if offered as evidence in court.

If neither the locality in which the child resides nor where the abuse or neglect is believed to have occurred is known, then such report shall be made to the local department of the county or city where the abuse or neglect was discovered or to the Department's toll-free child abuse and neglect hotline.

If an employee of the local department is suspected of abusing or neglecting a child, the report shall be made to the court of the county or city where the abuse or neglect was discovered. Upon receipt of such a report by the court, the judge shall assign the report to a local department that is not the employer of the suspected employee for investigation or family assessment. The judge may consult with the Department in selecting a local department to respond to the report or the complaint.

If the information is received by a teacher, staff member, resident, intern or nurse in the course of professional services in a hospital, school or similar institution, such person may, in place of said report, immediately notify the person in charge of the institution or department, or his designee, who shall make such report forthwith.

The initial report may be an oral report but such report shall be reduced to writing by the child abuse coordinator of the local department on a form prescribed by the Board. Any person required to make the report pursuant to this subsection shall disclose all information that is the basis for his suspicion of abuse or neglect of the child and, upon request, shall make available to the child-protective services coordinator and the local department, which is the agency of jurisdiction, any information, records or reports that document the basis for the report. All persons required by this subsection to report suspected abuse or neglect who maintain a record of a child who is the subject of such a report shall cooperate with the investigating agency and shall make related information, records and reports available to the investigating agency unless such disclosure violates the federal Family Educational Rights and Privacy Act (20 U.S.C. § 1232g). Provision of such information, records and reports by a health care provider shall not be prohibited by § 8.01–399. Criminal investigative reports received from law-enforcement agencies shall not be further disseminated by the investigating agency nor shall they be subject to public disclosure.

B. For purposes of subsection A, "reason to suspect that a child is abused or neglected" shall include (i) a finding made by an attending physician within seven days of a child's birth that the results of a blood or urine test conducted within 48 hours of the birth of the child indicate the presence of a controlled substance not prescribed for the mother by a physician; (ii) a finding by an attending physician made within 48 hours of a child's birth that the child was born dependent on a controlled substance which was not prescribed by a physician for the mother and has demonstrated withdrawal symptoms; (iii) a diagnosis by an attending physician made within seven days of a child's birth that the child has an illness, disease or condition which, to a reasonable degree of medical certainty, is attributable to in utero exposure to a controlled substance which was not prescribed by a physician for the mother or the child; or (iv) a diagnosis by an attending physician made within seven days of a child's birth that the child has fetal alcohol syndrome attributable to in utero exposure to alcohol. When "reason to suspect" is based upon this subsection, such fact shall be included in the report along with the facts relied upon by the person making the report.

C. Any person who makes a report or provides records or information pursuant to subsection A or who testifies in any judicial proceeding arising from such report, records or information shall be immune from any civil or criminal liability or administrative penalty or sanction on account of such report, records, information or testimony, unless such person acted in bad faith or with malicious purpose.

D. Any person required to file a report pursuant to this section who fails to do so within 72 hours of his first suspicion of child abuse or neglect shall be fined not more than $500 for the first failure and for any subsequent failures not less than $100 nor more than $1,000.

§ 63.2–1510. Complaints by others of certain injuries to children

Any person who suspects that a child is an abused or neglected child may make a complaint concerning such child, except as hereinafter provided, to the local department of the county or city wherein the child resides or wherein the abuse or neglect is believed to have occurred or to the

Department's toll-free child abuse and neglect hotline. If an employee of the local department is suspected of abusing or neglecting a child, the complaint shall be made to the court of the county or city where the abuse or neglect was discovered. Upon receipt of such a report by the court, the judge shall assign the report to a local department that is not the employer of the suspected employee for investigation or family assessment; or, if the judge believes that no local department in a reasonable geographic distance can be impartial in responding to the reported case, the judge shall assign the report to the court service unit of his court for evaluation. The judge may consult with the Department in selecting a local department to respond to the report or complaint. Such a complaint may be oral or in writing and shall disclose all information which is the basis for the suspicion of abuse or neglect of the child.

§ 63.2–1512. Immunity of person making report, etc., from liability

Any person making a report pursuant to § 63.2–1509, a complaint pursuant to § 63.2–1510, or who takes a child into custody pursuant to § 63.2–1517, or who participates in a judicial proceeding resulting therefrom shall be immune from any civil or criminal liability in connection therewith, unless it is proven that such person acted in bad faith or with malicious intent.

§ 63.2–1514. Retention of records in all reports; procedures regarding unfounded reports alleged to be made in bad faith or with malicious intent

A.   The local department shall retain the records of all reports or complaints made pursuant to this chapter, in accordance with regulations adopted by the Board.

B.   The Department shall maintain a child abuse and neglect information system that includes a central registry of founded complaints, pursuant to § 63.2–1515. The Department shall maintain all (i) unfounded investigations, (ii) family assessments, and (iii) reports or complaints determined to be not valid in a record which is separate from the central registry and accessible only to the Department and to local departments for child-protective services. The purpose of retaining these complaints or reports is to provide local departments with information regarding prior complaints or reports. In no event shall the mere existence of a prior complaint or report be used to determine that a subsequent complaint or report is founded. The subject of the complaint or report is the person who is alleged to have committed abuse or neglect. The subject of the complaint or report shall have access to his own record. The record of unfounded investigations, and complaints and reports determined to be not valid shall be purged one year after the date of the complaint or report if there are no subsequent complaints or reports regarding the same child or the person who is the subject of the complaint or report in that one year. The local department shall retain such records for an additional period of up to two years if requested in writing by the person who is the subject of such complaint or report. The record of family assessments shall be purged three years after the date of the complaint or report if there are no subsequent complaints or reports regarding the same child or the person who is the subject of the report in that three-year period. The child-protective services records regarding the petitioner which result from such complaint or report shall be purged immediately by any custodian of such records upon presentation to the custodian of a certified copy of a court order that there has been a civil action that determined that the complaint or report was made in bad faith or with malicious intent. After purging the records, the custodian shall notify the petitioner in writing that the records have been purged.

C. At the time the local department notifies a person who is the subject of a complaint or report made pursuant to this chapter that such complaint or report is either an unfounded investigation or a completed family assessment, it shall notify him how long the record will be retained and of the availability of the procedures set out in this section regarding reports or complaints alleged to be made in bad faith or with malicious intent. Upon request, the local department shall advise the person who was the subject of an unfounded investigation if the complaint or report was made anonymously. However, the identity of a complainant or report shall not be disclosed.

D. Any person who is the subject of an unfounded report or complaint made pursuant to this chapter who believes that such report or complaint was made in bad faith or with malicious intent may petition the circuit court in the jurisdiction in which the report or complaint was made for the release to such person of the records of the investigation or family assessment. Such petition shall specifically set forth the reasons such person believes that such report or complaint was made in bad faith or with malicious intent. Upon the filing of such petition, the circuit court shall request and the local department shall provide to the circuit court its records of the investigation or family assessment for the circuit court's in camera review. The petitioner shall be entitled to present evidence to support his petition. If the circuit court determines that there is a reasonable question of fact as to whether the report or complaint was made in bad faith or with malicious intent and that disclosure of the identity of the complainant would not be likely to endanger the life or safety of the complainant, it shall provide to the petitioner a copy of the records of the investigation or family assessment. The original records shall be subject to discovery in any subsequent civil action regarding the making of a complaint or report in bad faith or with malicious intent.

§ 63.2–1515. Central registry; disclosure of information

The central registry shall contain such information as shall be prescribed by Board regulation; however, when the founded case of abuse or neglect does not name the parents or guardians of the child as the abuser or neglector, and the abuse or neglect occurred in a licensed or unlicensed child day center, a licensed, registered or approved family day home, a private or public school, or a children's residential facility, the child's name shall not be entered on the registry without consultation with and permission of the parents or guardians. If a child's name currently appears on the registry without consultation with and permission of the parents or guardians for a founded case of abuse and neglect that does not name the parents or guardians of the child as the abuser or neglector, such parents or guardians may have the child's name removed by written request to the Department. The information contained in the central registry shall not be open to inspection by the public. However, appropriate disclosure may be made in accordance with Board regulations.

The Department shall respond to requests for a search of the central registry made by (i) local departments and (ii) local school boards regarding applicants for employment, pursuant to § 22.1–296.4, in cases where there is no match within the central registry within 10 business days of receipt of such requests. In cases where there is a match within the central registry regarding applicants for employment, the Department shall respond to requests made by local departments and local school boards within 30 business days of receipt of such requests. The response may be by first-class mail or facsimile transmission.

Any central registry check of a person who has applied to be a volunteer with a (a) Virginia affiliate of Big Brothers/Big Sisters of America, (b) Virginia affiliate of Compeer, (c) Virginia affiliate of Childhelp USA; (d) volunteer fire company or volunteer rescue squad, or (e) with a court-appointed special advocate program pursuant to § 9.1–153 shall be conducted at no charge.

§ 63.2–1516.   Tape recording child abuse investigations

Any person who is suspected of abuse or neglect of a child and who is the subject of an investigation or family assessment pursuant to this chapter may tape record any communications between him and child-protective services personnel that take place during the course of such investigation or family assessment, provided all parties to the conversation are aware the conversation is to be recorded. The parties' knowledge of the recording shall be demonstrated by a declaration at the beginning of the recorded portion of the conversation that the recording is to be made. If a person who is suspected of abuse or neglect of a child and who is the subject of an investigation or family assessment pursuant to this chapter elects to make a tape recording as provided in this section, the child-protective services personnel may also make such a recording.

§ 63.2–1518.   Authority to talk to child or sibling

Any person required to make a report or conduct an investigation or family assessment, pursuant to this chapter may talk to any child suspected of being abused or neglected or to any of his siblings without consent of and outside the presence of his parent, guardian, legal custodian, or other person standing in loco parentis, or school personnel.

§ 63.2–1519.   Physician-patient and husband-wife privileges inapplicable

In any legal proceeding resulting from the filing of any report or complaint pursuant to this chapter, the physician-patient and husband-wife privileges shall not apply.

§ 63.2–1520. Photographs and X-rays of child; use as evidence

In any case of suspected child abuse, photographs and X-rays of the child may be taken without the consent of the parent or other person responsible for such child as a part of the medical evaluation. Photographs of the child may also be taken without the consent of the parent or other person responsible for such child as a part of the investigation or family assessment of the case by the local department or the court; however, such photographs shall not be used in lieu of medical evaluation. Such photographs and X-rays may be introduced into evidence in any subsequent proceeding.

The court receiving such evidence may impose such restrictions as to the confidentiality of photographs of any minor as it deems appropriate.

§ 63.2–1525. Prima facie evidence for removal of child custody

In the case of a petition in the court for removal of custody of a child alleged to have been abused or neglected, competent evidence by a physician that a child is abused or neglected shall constitute prima facie evidence to support such petition.

NOTE

All the states now have child abuse reporting laws. Initially they were enacted largely over a four-year period following revelations about the "battered child syndrome" in the early and mid–60s. Many were based on models proposed in 1963 by the Children's Bureau (The Abused Child—Principles and Suggested Language for Legislation on Reporting of the Physically Abused Child) and the Children's Division of the American Humane Association (Guidelines for Legislation to Protect the Battered Child). Although many statutes share basic features, they can differ considerably in language and detail. Definitions of what constitutes abuse vary, as do descriptions of who must report, to whom reports must be made, and what responses must be made to reports. There also is inconsistency about sanctions for nonreporting.

Today's typical statute defines the class of persons who must report to include at least health care professionals, teachers and social workers. Most statutes provide for civil immunity for one who reports in good faith, and for a waiver of the husband-wife and physician-patient privileges. Many statutes specifically authorize physicians to take photographs without parental permission.

There is still controversy concerning central registries of reports that have been made, the question of who should have access to such information, and whether there should be a provision for purging it. Some fear that the introduction of popularized procedures such as "hot lines" through which anonymous reports can be made poses a serious threat to civil liberties while offering only marginally incremental effectiveness for the reporting system. In a nation that has shown little favor for informer statutes generally, it seems somewhat surprising that such issues have been slow to draw public dissent.

Albert Solnit, in his article Too Much Reporting, Too Little Service, published in Child Abuse: An Agenda For Action, 135 (George Gerbner et al. eds., 1980), proposes that child abuse statutes generally place too much emphasis on reporting all types of child abuse, regardless of how trivial or serious, while failing to give enough resources to servicing the complaints made. Solnit proposes remedying this by allowing greater familial privacy in cases not involving serious bodily harm to the child by eliminating the requirement to report such cases. The scarce resources could then be focused on servicing more serious cases. Statutes should also aim to prevent additional cases of child abuse. Often abuse is preceded by unfulfilled requests by parents for help from community services to provide for their children. Requests range from parents who are unable to cope with children requesting adoption to asking for assistance in providing preventative health care, food or other needs of their child. Statutes should address these needs by tracking the types of services requested by parents who have abused their children and ensure that the types of services that would have prevented the abuse are available to the community in future.

For a discussion of the clergy exception to mandatory reporting statutes given by many states, see Shannon O'Malley, At All Costs: Mandatory Child Abuse Reporting Statutes and the Clergy–Communicant Privilege, 21 Rev. Litig. 701 (2002). For a discussion of the shortcomings of reporting statutes because of vagueness, see Scott A. Davidson, When Is Parental Discipline Child Abuse? The Vagueness of Child Abuse Laws, 34 U. Louisville J. Fam. L. 403 (1995–96); and Douglas J. Besharov & Lisa A. Laumann, Child Abuse Reporting, 33 Society 40 (1996).

For further history of the development of child abuse reporting statutes and summaries of their content, see V. DeFrancis and C.L. Lucht, Child Abuse Legislation in the 1970s (Rev. ed. 1974); Monrad G. Paulsen, The Legal Framework for Child Protection, 66 Colum.L.Rev. 679 (1966); Paulsen, Parker and Adelman, Child Abuse Reporting Laws: Some Legislative History, 34 Geo.Wash.L.Rev. 482 (1966). Ellen Marrus, Please Keep My Secret: Child Abuse Reporting Statutes, Confidentiality, and Juvenile Delinquency, 11 Geo. J. Legal Ethics 509 (1998); Curt Richardson, 23 J. Legal Med. 131 (2002); Brian G. Fraser, A Glance At The Past, A Gaze At The Present, A Glimpse At The Future: A Critical Analysis Of The Development Of Child Abuse Reporting Statutes, 54 Chi.-Kent L. Rev. 641, 649–50 (1977).

DeShaney v. Winnebago County Dept. Social Services

Supreme Court of the United States, 1989.
489 U.S. 189, 109 S.Ct. 998, 103 L.Ed.2d 249.

■ CHIEF JUSTICE REHNQUIST delivered the opinion of the Court.

. . .

The facts of this case are undeniably tragic. Petitioner Joshua DeShaney was born in 1979. In 1980, a Wyoming court granted his parents a divorce and awarded custody of Joshua to his father, Randy DeShaney. The father shortly thereafter moved to Neenah, a city located in Winnebago County, Wisconsin, taking the infant Joshua with him. There he entered into a second marriage, which also ended in divorce.

The Winnebago County authorities first learned that Joshua DeShaney might be a victim of child abuse in January 1982, when his father's second wife complained to the police, at the time of their divorce, that he had previously "hit the boy causing marks and [was] a prime case for child abuse." The Winnebago County Department of Social Services (DSS) interviewed the father, but he denied the accusations, and DSS did not pursue them further. In January 1983, Joshua was admitted to a local hospital with multiple bruises and abrasions. The examining physician suspected child abuse and notified DSS, which immediately obtained an order from a

Wisconsin juvenile court placing Joshua in the temporary custody of the hospital. Three days later, the county convened an ad hoc "Child Protection Team"—consisting of a pediatrician, a psychologist, a police detective, the county's lawyer, several DSS caseworkers, and various hospital personnel—to consider Joshua's situation. At this meeting, the Team decided that there was insufficient evidence of child abuse to retain Joshua in the custody of the court. The Team did, however, decide to recommend several measures to protect Joshua, including enrolling him in a preschool program, providing his father with certain counselling services, and encouraging his father's girlfriend to move out of the home. Randy DeShaney entered into a voluntary agreement with DSS in which he promised to cooperate with them in accomplishing these goals.

Based on the recommendation of the Child Protection Team, the juvenile court dismissed the child protection case and returned Joshua to the custody of his father. A month later, emergency room personnel called the DSS caseworker handling Joshua's case to report that he had once again been treated for suspicious injuries. The caseworker concluded that there was no basis for action. For the next six months, the caseworker made monthly visits to the DeShaney home, during which she observed a number of suspicious injuries on Joshua's head; she also noticed that he had not been enrolled in school and that the girlfriend had not moved out. The caseworker dutifully recorded these incidents in her files, along with her continuing suspicions that someone in the DeShaney household was physically abusing Joshua, but she did nothing more. In November 1983, the emergency room notified DSS that Joshua had been treated once again for injuries that they believed to be caused by child abuse. On the caseworker's next two visits to the DeShaney home, she was told that Joshua was too ill to see her. Still DSS took no action.

In March 1984, Randy DeShaney beat 4–year–old Joshua so severely that he fell into a life-threatening coma. Emergency brain surgery revealed a series of hemorrhages caused by traumatic injuries to the head inflicted over a long period of time. Joshua did not die, but he suffered brain damage so severe that he is expected to spend the rest of his life confined to an institution for the profoundly retarded. Randy DeShaney was subsequently tried and convicted of child abuse.

Joshua and his mother brought this action under 42 U.S.C. § 1983 . . . against respondents Winnebago County, its Department of Social Services, and various individual employees of the Department. . . . The District Court granted summary judgment for respondents.

The Court of Appeals for the Seventh Circuit affirmed, 812 F.2d 298 (1987), holding that petitioners had not made out an actionable § 1983 claim for two alternative reasons. First, the court held that the Due Process Clause of the Fourteenth Amendment does not require a state or local governmental entity to protect its citizens from "private violence, or other mishaps not attributable to the conduct of its employees." Id., at 301. In so holding, the court specifically rejected the position endorsed by a divided panel of the Third Circuit in Estate of Bailey by Oare v. County of York, 768 F.2d 503, 510–511 (C.A.3 1985), and by dicta in Jensen v. Conrad, 747 F.2d 185, 190–194 (C.A.4 1984), cert. denied, 470 U.S. 1052 (1985), that once the State learns that a particular child is in danger of abuse from third parties and actually undertakes to protect him from that danger, a "special relationship" arises between it and the child which imposes an affirmative constitutional duty to provide adequate protection. Second, the court held, in reliance on our decision in Martinez v. California, 444 U.S. 277, 285 (1980), that the causal connection between respondents' conduct and Joshua's injuries was too attenuated to establish a deprivation of constitutional rights actionable under § 1983. The court therefore found it unnecessary to reach the question whether respondents' conduct evinced the "state of mind" necessary to make out a due process claim after Daniels v. Williams, 474 U.S. 327 (1986), and Davidson v. Cannon, 474 U.S. 344 (1986).

Because of the inconsistent approaches taken by the lower courts in determining when, if ever, the failure of a state or local governmental entity or its agents to provide an individual with adequate protective services constitutes a violation of the individual's due process rights, and the importance of the issue to the administration of state and local governments, we granted certiorari. We now affirm.

The Due Process Clause of the Fourteenth Amendment provides that "[n]o State shall ... deprive any person of life, liberty, or property, without due process of law." Petitioners contend that the State deprived Joshua of his liberty interest in "free[dom] from ... unjustified intrusions on personal security," by failing to provide him with adequate protection against his father's violence. The claim is one invoking the substantive rather than procedural component of the Due Process Clause; petitioners do not claim that the State denied Joshua protection without according him appropriate procedural safeguards, but that it was categorically obligated to protect him in these circumstances.

But nothing in the language of the Due Process Clause itself requires the State to protect the life, liberty, and property of its citizens against invasion by private actors. The Clause is phrased as a limitation on the State's power to act, not as a guarantee of certain minimal levels of safety and security. It forbids the State itself to deprive individuals of life, liberty, or property without "due process of law," but its language cannot fairly be extended to impose an affirmative obligation on the State to ensure that those interests do not come to harm through other means. Nor does history support such an expansive reading of the constitutional text. Like its counterpart in the Fifth Amendment, the Due Process Clause of the Fourteenth Amendment was intended to prevent government "from abusing [its] power, or employing it as an instrument of oppression," Davidson v. Cannon, supra, at 348; ... Its purpose was to protect the people from the State, not to ensure that the State protected them from each other. The Framers were content to leave the extent of governmental obligation in the latter area to the democratic political processes.

Consistent with these principles, our cases have recognized that the Due Process Clauses generally confer no affirmative right to governmental aid, even where such aid may be necessary to secure life, liberty, or property interests of which the government itself may not deprive the individual. ...

Petitioners contend, however, that even if the Due Process Clause imposes no affirmative obligation on the State to provide the general public with adequate protective services, such a duty may arise out of certain "special relationships" created or assumed by the State with respect to particular individuals. Petitioners argue that such a "special relationship" existed here because the State knew that Joshua faced a special danger of abuse at his father's hands, and specifically proclaimed, by word and by deed, its intention to protect him against that danger. Having actually undertaken to protect Joshua from this danger—which petitioners concede the State played no part in creating—the State acquired an affirmative "duty," enforceable through the Due Process Clause, to do so in a reasonably competent fashion. Its failure to discharge that duty, so the argument goes, was an abuse of governmental power that so "shocks the conscience," Rochin v. California, 342 U.S. 165, 172 (1952), as to constitute a substantive due process violation.

We reject this argument. It is true that in certain limited circumstances the Constitution imposes upon the State affirmative duties of care and protection with respect to particular individuals. In Estelle v. Gamble, 429 U.S. 97 (1976), we recognized that the Eighth Amendment's prohibition against cruel and unusual punishment, made applicable to the States through the Fourteenth Amendment's Due Process Clause, Robinson v. California, 370 U.S. 660 (1962), requires the State to provide adequate medical care to incarcerated prisoners. 429 U.S., at 103–104.[5] We reasoned that because the prisoner is unable " 'by reason of the deprivation of his liberty [to] care for himself,' " it is only " 'just' " that the State be required to care for him. Ibid., quoting Spicer v. Williamson, 191 N.C. 487, 490, 132 S.E. 291, 293 (1926).

In Youngberg v. Romeo, 457 U.S. 307 (1982), we extended this analysis beyond the Eighth Amendment setting, holding that the substantive component of the Fourteenth Amendment's Due Process Clause requires the State to provide involuntarily committed mental patients with such services as are necessary to ensure their "reasonable safety" from themselves and others. As we explained, "[i]f it is cruel and unusual punishment to hold convicted criminals in unsafe conditions, it must be unconstitutional [under the Due Process Clause] to confine the involuntarily committed—who may not be punished at all—in unsafe conditions."

But these cases afford petitioners no help. Taken together, they stand only for the proposition that when the State takes a person into its custody and holds him there against his will, the Constitution imposes upon it a corresponding duty to assume some responsibility for his safety and general well-being.... The rationale for this principle is simple enough: when the State by the affirmative exercise of its power so restrains an individual's

---

5. To make out an Eighth Amendment claim based on the failure to provide adequate medical care, a prisoner must show that the state defendants exhibited "deliberate indifference" to his "serious" medical needs; the mere negligent or inadvertent failure to provide adequate care is not enough. Estelle v. Gamble, 429 U.S., at 105–106. In Whitley v. Albers, 475 U.S. 312 (1986), we suggested that a similar state of mind is required to make out a substantive due process claim in the prison setting. Id., at 326–327.

liberty that it renders him unable to care for himself, and at the same time fails to provide for his basic human needs—e.g., food, clothing, shelter, medical care, and reasonable safety—it transgresses the substantive limits on state action set by the Eighth Amendment and the Due Process Clause. The affirmative duty to protect arises not from the State's knowledge of the individual's predicament or from its expressions of intent to help him, but from the limitation which it has imposed on his freedom to act on his own behalf.... In the substantive due process analysis, it is the State's affirmative act of restraining the individual's freedom to act on his own behalf—through incarceration, institutionalization, or other similar restraint of personal liberty—which is the "deprivation of liberty" triggering the protections of the Due Process Clause, not its failure to act to protect his liberty interests against harms inflicted by other means.

The ... analysis simply has no applicability in the present case. Petitioners concede that the harms Joshua suffered did not occur while he was in the State's custody, but while he was in the custody of his natural father, who was in no sense a state actor. While the State may have been aware of the dangers that Joshua faced in the free world, it played no part in their creation, nor did it do anything to render him any more vulnerable to them. That the State once took temporary custody of Joshua does not alter the analysis, for when it returned him to his father's custody, it placed him in no worse position than that in which he would have been had it not acted at all; the State does not become the permanent guarantor of an individual's safety by having once offered him shelter. Under these circumstances, the State had no constitutional duty to protect Joshua.

It may well be that, by voluntarily undertaking to protect Joshua against a danger it concededly played no part in creating, the State acquired a duty under state tort law to provide him with adequate protection against that danger.... But the claim here is based on the Due Process Clause of the Fourteenth Amendment, which, as we have said many times, does not transform every tort committed by a state actor into a constitutional violation. A State may, through its courts and legislatures, impose such affirmative duties of care and protection upon its agents as it wishes. But not "all common-law duties owed by government actors were ... constitutionalized by the Fourteenth Amendment." Daniels v. Williams, supra, 474 U.S. at 335. Because, as explained above, the State had no constitutional duty to protect Joshua against his father's violence, its failure to do so—though calamitous in hindsight—simply does not constitute a violation of the Due Process Clause.[10]

Judges and lawyers, like other humans, are moved by natural sympathy in a case like this to find a way for Joshua and his mother to receive

---

10. Because we conclude that the Due Process Clause did not require the State to protect Joshua from his father, we need not address respondents' alternative argument that the individual state actors lacked the requisite "state of mind" to make out a due process violation. See Daniels v. Williams, 474 U.S., at 334, n. 3. Similarly, we have no occasion to consider whether the individual respondents might be entitled to a qualified immunity defense, see Anderson v. Creighton, 483 U.S. 635 (1987), or whether the allegations in the complaint are sufficient to support a § 1983 claim against the county and its Department of Social Services under Monell v. New York City Dept. of Social Services, 436 U.S. 658 (1978), and its progeny.

adequate compensation for the grievous harm inflicted upon them. But before yielding to that impulse, it is well to remember once again that the harm was inflicted not by the State of Wisconsin, but by Joshua's father. The most that can be said of the state functionaries in this case is that they stood by and did nothing when suspicious circumstances dictated a more active role for them. In defense of them it must also be said that had they moved too soon to take custody of the son away from the father, they would likely have been met with charges of improperly intruding into the parent-child relationship, charges based on the same Due Process Clause that forms the basis for the present charge of failure to provide adequate protection.

The people of Wisconsin may well prefer a system of liability which would place upon the State and its officials the responsibility for failure to act in situations such as the present one. They may create such a system, if they do not have it already, by changing the tort law of the State in accordance with the regular law-making process. But they should not have it thrust upon them by this Court's expansion of the Due Process Clause of the Fourteenth Amendment.

■ JUSTICE BRENNAN, with whom JUSTICE MARSHALL and JUSTICE BLACKMUN join, dissenting.

"The most that can be said of the state functionaries in this case," the Court today concludes, "is that they stood by and did nothing when suspicious circumstances dictated a more active role for them." Because I believe that this description of respondents' conduct tells only part of the story and that, accordingly, the Constitution itself "dictated a more active role" for respondents in the circumstances presented here, I cannot agree that respondents had no constitutional duty to help Joshua DeShaney.

It may well be, as the Court decides, that the Due Process Clause as construed by our prior case creates no general right to basic governmental services. That, however, is not the question presented here; indeed, that question was not raised in the complaint, urged on appeal, presented in the petition for certiorari, or addressed in the briefs on the merits. No one, in short, has asked the Court to proclaim that, as a general matter, the Constitution safeguards positive as well as negative liberties.

This is more than a quibble over dicta; it is a point about perspective, having substantive ramifications. In a constitutional setting that distinguishes sharply between action and inaction, one's characterization of the misconduct alleged under § 1983 may effectively decide the case. Thus, by leading off with a discussion (and rejection) of the idea that the Constitution imposes on the States an affirmative duty to take basic care of their citizens, the Court foreshadows—perhaps even preordains—its conclusion that no duty existed even on the specific facts before us. This initial discussion establishes the baseline from which the Court assesses the DeShaneys' claim that, when a State has—"by word and by deed,"— announced an intention to protect a certain class of citizens and has before it facts that would trigger that protection under the applicable state law, the Constitution imposes upon the State an affirmative duty of protection.

The Court's baseline is the absence of positive rights in the Constitution and a concomitant suspicion of any claim that seems to depend on such rights. From this perspective, the DeShaneys' claim is first and foremost about inaction (the failure, here, of respondents to take steps to protect Joshua), and only tangentially about action (the establishment of a state program specifically designed to help children like Joshua). And from this perspective, holding these Wisconsin officials liable—where the only difference between this case and one involving a general claim to protective services is Wisconsin's establishment and operation of a program to protect children—would seem to punish an effort that we should seek to promote.

I would begin from the opposite direction. I would focus first on the action that Wisconsin *has* taken with respect to Joshua and children like him, rather than on the actions that the State failed to take. Such a method is not new to this Court. Both Estelle v. Gamble, 429 U.S. 97 (1976), and Youngberg v. Romeo, 457 U.S. 307 (1982), began by emphasizing that the States had confined J.W. Gamble to prison and Nicholas Romeo to a psychiatric hospital. This initial action rendered these people helpless to help themselves or to seek help from persons unconnected to the government. . . . Cases from the lower courts also recognize that a State's actions can be decisive in assessing the constitutional significance of subsequent inaction. For these purposes, moreover, actual physical restraint is not the only State action that has been considered relevant. See, e.g., White v. Rochford, 592 F.2d 381 (C.A.7 1979) (police officers violated due process when, after arresting the guardian of three young children, they abandoned the children on a busy stretch of highway at night). . . .

Wisconsin has established a child-welfare system specifically designed to help children like Joshua. Wisconsin law places upon the local departments of social services such as respondent (DSS or Department) a duty to investigate reported instances of child abuse. See Wis.Stat.Ann. § 48.981(3) (1987 and Supp.1988–1989). While other governmental bodies and private persons are largely responsible for the reporting of possible cases of child abuse, see § 48.981(2), Wisconsin law channels all such reports to the local departments of social services for evaluation and, if necessary, further action. § 48.981(3). Even when it is the sheriff's office or police department that receives a report of suspected child abuse, that report is referred to local social services departments for action, see § 48.981(3)(a); the only exception to this occurs when the reporter fears for the child's immediate safety. § 48.981(3)(b). In this way, Wisconsin law invites—indeed, directs—citizens and other governmental entities to depend on local departments of social services such as respondent to protect children from abuse.

The specific facts before us bear out this view of Wisconsin's system of protecting children. Each time someone voiced a suspicion that Joshua was being abused, that information was relayed to the Department for investigation and possible action. When Randy DeShaney's second wife told the police that he had " 'hit the boy causing marks and [was] a prime case for child abuse,' " the police referred her complaint to DSS. When, on three separate occasions, emergency room personnel noticed suspicious injuries on Joshua's body, they went to DSS with this information. When neighbors informed the police that they had seen or heard Joshua's father or his father's lover beating or otherwise abusing Joshua, the police brought these reports to the attention of DSS. And when respondent Kemmeter, through these reports and through her own observations in the course of nearly 20 visits to the DeShaney home, compiled growing evidence that Joshua was being abused, that information stayed within the Department—chronicled by the social worker in detail that seems almost eerie in light of her failure to act upon it. (As to the extent of the social worker's involvement in and knowledge of Joshua's predicament, her reaction to the news of Joshua's last and most devastating injuries is illuminating: "I just knew the phone would ring some day and Joshua would be dead." 812 F.2d 298, 300 (C.A.7 1987).)

Even more telling than these examples is the Department's control over the decision whether to take steps to protect a particular child from suspected abuse. While many different people contributed information and advice to this decision, it was up to the people at DSS to make the ultimate decision (subject to the approval of the local government's Corporation Counsel) whether to disturb the family's current arrangements. When Joshua first appeared at a local hospital with injuries signaling physical abuse, for example, it was DSS that made the decision to take him into temporary custody for the purpose of studying his situation—and it was DSS, acting in conjunction with the Corporation Counsel, that returned him to his father. Unfortunately for Joshua DeShaney, the buck effectively stopped with the Department.

In these circumstances, a private citizen, or even a person working in a government agency other than DSS, would doubtless feel that her job was done as soon as she had reported her suspicions of child abuse to DSS. Through its child-welfare program, in other words, the State of Wisconsin has relieved ordinary citizens and governmental bodies other than the Department of any sense of obligation to do anything more than report their suspicions of child abuse to DSS. If DSS ignores or dismisses these suspicions, no one will step in to fill the gap. Wisconsin's child-protection program thus effectively confined Joshua DeShaney within the walls of Randy DeShaney's violent home until such time as DSS took action to remove him. Conceivably, then, children like Joshua are made worse off by the existence of this program when the persons and entities charged with carrying it out fail to do their jobs.

It simply belies reality, therefore, to contend that the State "stood by and did nothing" with respect to Joshua. Through its child-protection program, the State actively intervened in Joshua's life and, by virtue of this intervention, acquired ever more certain knowledge that Joshua was in grave danger. These circumstances, in my view, plant this case solidly within the tradition of cases like *Youngberg* and *Estelle*.

It will be meager comfort to Joshua and his mother to know that, if the State had "selectively den[ied] its protective services" to them because they were "disfavored minorities," ante, at 1004, n. 3, their § 1983 suit might have stood on sturdier ground. Because of the posture of this case, we do not know why respondents did not take steps to protect Joshua; the Court, however, tells us that their reason is irrelevant so long as their inaction was not the product of invidious discrimination. Presumably, then, if respondents decided not to help Joshua because his name began with a "j," or because he was born in the spring, or because they did not care enough about him even to formulate an intent to discriminate against him based on an arbitrary reason, respondents would not be liable to the DeShaneys because they were not the ones who dealt the blows that destroyed Joshua's life.

I do not suggest that such irrationality was at work in this case; I emphasize only that we do not know whether or not it was. I would allow Joshua and his mother the opportunity to show that respondents' failure to help him arose, not out of the sound exercise of professional judgment that we recognized in *Youngberg* as sufficient to preclude liability, see 457 U.S., at 322–323, but from the kind of arbitrariness that we have in the past condemned.... *Youngberg's* deference to a decisionmaker's professional judgment ensures that once a caseworker has decided, on the basis of her professional training and experience, that one course of protection is preferable for a given child, or even that no special protection is required, she will not be found liable for the harm that follows. (In this way, *Youngberg's* vision of substantive due process serves a purpose similar to that served by adherence to procedural norms, namely, requiring that a State actor stop and think before she acts in a way that may lead to a loss of liberty.) Moreover, that the Due Process Clause is not violated by merely negligent conduct, means that a social worker who simply makes a mistake of judgment under what are admittedly complex and difficult conditions will not find herself liable in damages under § 1983.

As the Court today reminds us, "the Due Process Clause of the Fourteenth Amendment was intended to prevent government 'from abusing [its] power, or employing it as an instrument of oppression.' " My disagreement with the Court arises from its failure to see that inaction can be every bit as abusive of power as action, that oppression can result when a State undertakes a vital duty and then ignores it. Today's opinion construes the Due Process Clause to permit a State to displace private sources of protection and then, at the critical moment, to shrug its shoulders and turn away from the harm that it has promised to try to prevent. Because I cannot agree that our Constitution is indifferent to such indifference, I respectfully dissent.

■ Justice Blackmun, dissenting.

Today, the Court purports to be the dispassionate oracle of the law, unmoved by "natural sympathy." But, in this pretense, the Court itself retreats into a sterile formalism which prevents it from recognizing either the facts of the case before it or the legal norms that should apply to those facts. As Justice Brennan demonstrates, the facts here involve not mere passivity, but active state intervention in the life of Joshua DeShaney— intervention that triggered a fundamental duty to aid the boy once the State learned of the severe danger to which he was exposed.

The Court fails to recognize this duty because it attempts to draw a sharp and rigid line between action and inaction. But such formalistic reasoning has no place in the interpretation of the broad and stirring clauses of the Fourteenth Amendment. Indeed, I submit that these clauses were designed, at least in part, to undo the formalistic legal reasoning that infected antebellum jurisprudence, which the late Professor Robert Cover analyzed so effectively in his significant work entitled *Justice Accused* (1975).

Like the antebellum judges who denied relief to fugitive slaves, the Court today claims that its decision, however harsh, is compelled by existing legal doctrine. On the contrary, the question presented by this case is an open one, and our Fourteenth Amendment precedents may be read more broadly or narrowly depending upon how one chooses to read them. Faced with the choice, I would adopt a "sympathetic" reading, one which comports with dictates of fundamental justice and recognizes that compassion need not be exiled from the province of judging. . . .

Poor Joshua! Victim of repeated attacks by an irresponsible, bullying, cowardly, and intemperate father, and abandoned by respondents who placed him in a dangerous predicament and who knew or learned what was going on, and yet did essentially nothing except, as the Court revealingly observes, ante, at 1001, "dutifully recorded these incidents in [their] files." It is a sad commentary upon American life, and constitutional principles— so full of late of patriotic fervor and proud proclamations about "liberty and justice for all," that this child, Joshua DeShaney, now is assigned to live out the remainder of his life profoundly retarded. Joshua and his mother, as petitioners here, deserve—but now are denied by this Court— the opportunity to have the facts of their case considered in the light of the constitutional protection that 42 U.S.C. § 1983 is meant to provide.

Town of Castle Rock, Colo. v. Gonzales

Supreme Court of the United States, 2005.
545 U.S. 748, 125 S.Ct. 2796, 162 L.Ed.2d 658.

■ JUSTICE SCALIA delivered the opinion of the Court.

We decide in this case whether an individual who has obtained a state-law restraining order has a constitutionally protected property interest in having the police enforce the restraining order when they have probable cause to believe it has been violated.

The horrible facts of this case are contained in the complaint that respondent Jessica Gonzales filed in Federal District Court. . . . Respondent alleges that petitioner, the town of Castle Rock, Colorado, violated the Due Process Clause of the Fourteenth Amendment to the United States Constitution when its police officers, acting pursuant to official policy or custom, failed to respond properly to her repeated reports that her estranged husband was violating the terms of a restraining order.

The restraining order had been issued by a state trial court several weeks earlier in conjunction with respondent's divorce proceedings. The original form order, issued on May 21, 1999, and served on respondent's husband on June 4, 1999, commanded him not to "molest or disturb the peace of [respondent] or of any child," and to remain at least 100 yards from the family home at all times. 366 F.3d 1093, 1143 (C.A.10 2004) (en banc) (appendix to dissenting opinion of O'Brien, J.).

... On June 4, 1999, the state trial court modified the terms of the restraining order and made it permanent. The modified order gave respondent's husband the right to spend time with his three daughters (ages 10, 9, and 7) on alternate weekends, for two weeks during the summer, and, " 'upon reasonable notice,' " for a mid-week dinner visit " 'arranged by the parties' "; the modified order also allowed him to visit the home to collect the children for such "parenting time."

According to the complaint, at about 5 or 5:30 p.m. on Tuesday, June 22, 1999, respondent's husband took the three daughters while they were playing outside the family home. No advance arrangements had been made for him to see the daughters that evening. When respondent noticed the children were missing, she suspected her husband had taken them. At about 7:30 p.m., she called the Castle Rock Police Department, which dispatched two officers. The complaint continues: "When [the officers] arrived ... , she showed them a copy of the TRO and requested that it be enforced and the three children be returned to her immediately. [The officers] stated that there was nothing they could do about the TRO and suggested that [respondent] call the Police Department again if the three children did not return home by 10:00 p.m."

At approximately 8:30 p.m., respondent talked to her husband on his cellular telephone. He told her "he had the three children [at an] amusement park in Denver." She called the police again and asked them to "have someone check for" her husband or his vehicle at the amusement park and "put out an [all points bulletin]" for her husband, but the officer with whom she spoke "refused to do so," again telling her to "wait until 10:00 p.m. and see if" her husband returned the girls.

At approximately 10:10 p.m., respondent called the police and said her children were still missing, but she was now told to wait until midnight. She called at midnight and told the dispatcher her children were still missing. She went to her husband's apartment and, finding nobody there, called the police at 12:10 a.m.; she was told to wait for an officer to arrive. When none came, she went to the police station at 12:50 a.m. and submitted an incident report. The officer who took the report "made no reasonable effort to enforce the TRO or locate the three children. Instead, he went to dinner."

At approximately 3:20 a.m., respondent's husband arrived at the police station and opened fire with a semiautomatic handgun he had purchased earlier that evening. Police shot back, killing him. Inside the cab of his pickup truck, they found the bodies of all three daughters, whom he had already murdered.

On the basis of the foregoing factual allegations, respondent brought an action under Rev. Stat. § 1979, 42 U.S.C. § 1983, claiming that the town violated the Due Process Clause because its police department had "an official policy or custom of failing to respond properly to complaints of restraining order violations" and "tolerate[d] the non-enforcement of restraining orders by its police officers." The complaint also alleged that the town's actions "were taken either willfully, recklessly or with such gross negligence as to indicate wanton disregard and deliberate indifference to" respondent's civil rights....

A panel of the Court of Appeals affirmed [a] rejection of a substantive due process claim, but found that respondent had alleged a cognizable procedural due process claim. 307 F.3d 1258 (C.A.10 2002). On rehearing en banc, a divided court reached the same disposition, concluding that respondent had a "protected property interest in the enforcement of the terms of her restraining order" and that the town had deprived her of due process because "the police never 'heard' nor seriously entertained her request to enforce and protect her interests in the restraining order." 366 F.3d, at 1101, 1117. We granted certiorari. 543 U.S. 955, 125 S.Ct. 417, 160 L.Ed.2d 316 (2004).

The Fourteenth Amendment to the United States Constitution provides that a State shall not "deprive any person of life, liberty, or property, without due process of law." Amdt. 14, § 1. In 42 U.S.C. § 1983, Congress has created a federal cause of action for "the deprivation of any rights, privileges, or immunities secured by the Constitution and laws." Respondent claims the benefit of this provision on the ground that she had a property interest in police enforcement of the restraining order against her husband; and that the town deprived her of this property without due process by having a policy that tolerated nonenforcement of restraining orders.

As the Court of Appeals recognized, we left a similar question unanswered in *DeShaney v. Winnebago County Dept. of Social Servs.*, 489 U.S. 189, 109 S.Ct. 998, 103 L.Ed.2d 249 (1989), another case with "undeniably tragic" facts.... We held that the so-called "substantive" component of the Due Process Clause does not "requir[e] the State to protect the life, liberty, and property of its citizens against invasion by private actors." *Id.*, at 195, 109 S.Ct. 998. We noted, however, that the petitioner had not properly preserved the argument that—and we thus "decline[d] to consider" whether—state "child protection statutes gave [him] an 'entitlement' to receive protective services in accordance with the terms of the statute, an entitlement which would enjoy due process protection." *Id.*, at 195, n. 2, 109 S.Ct. 998.

The procedural component of the Due Process Clause does not protect everything that might be described as a "benefit": "To have a property interest in a benefit, a person clearly must have more than an abstract need or desire" and "more than a unilateral expectation of it. He must, instead, have a legitimate claim of entitlement to it." *Board of Regents of State Colleges v. Roth,* 408 U.S. 564, 577, 92 S.Ct. 2701, 33 L.Ed.2d 548 (1972). Such entitlements are " 'of course, ... not created by the Constitution. Rather, they are created and their dimensions are defined by existing rules or understandings that stem from an independent source such as state law.' " *Paul v. Davis,* 424 U.S. 693, 709, 96 S.Ct. 1155, 47 L.Ed.2d 405 (1976) (quoting *Roth, supra,* at 577, 92 S.Ct. 2701); see also *Phillips v. Washington Legal Foundation,* 524 U.S. 156, 164, 118 S.Ct. 1925, 141 L.Ed.2d 174 (1998).

Our cases recognize that a benefit is not a protected entitlement if government officials may grant or deny it in their discretion. See, *e.g., Kentucky Dept. of Corrections v. Thompson,* 490 U.S. 454, 462–463, 109 S.Ct. 1904, 104 L.Ed.2d 506 (1989). The Court of Appeals in this case determined that Colorado law created an entitlement to enforcement of the restraining order because the "court-issued restraining order . . . specifically dictated that its terms must be enforced" and a "state statute command[ed]" enforcement of the order when certain objective conditions were met (probable cause to believe that the order had been violated and that the object of the order had received notice of its existence). 366 F.3d, at 1101, n. 5. . . . Respondent contends that we are obliged "to give deference to the Tenth Circuit's analysis of Colorado law on" whether she had an entitlement to enforcement of the restraining order.

. . . We have said that a "presumption of deference [is] given the views of a federal court as to the law of a State within its jurisdiction." *Phillips, supra,* at 167, 118 S.Ct. 1925. That presumption can be overcome, however, see *Leavitt v. Jane L.,* 518 U.S. 137, 145, 116 S.Ct. 2068, 135 L.Ed.2d 443 (1996) *(per curiam),* and we think deference inappropriate here. [Discussion omitted]. We proceed, then, to our own analysis of whether Colorado law gave respondent a right to enforcement of the restraining order.

The critical language in the restraining order came not from any part of the order itself (which was signed by the state-court trial judge and directed to the restrained party, respondent's husband), but from the preprinted notice to law-enforcement personnel that appeared on the back of the order. That notice effectively restated the statutory provision describing "peace officers' duties" related to the crime of violation of a restraining order. At the time of the conduct at issue in this case, that provision read as follows:

"(a) Whenever a restraining order is issued, the protected person shall be provided with a copy of such order. *A peace officer shall use every reasonable means to enforce a restraining order.*

"(b) *A peace officer shall arrest, or, if an arrest would be impractical under the circumstances, seek a warrant for the arrest of a restrained person* when the peace officer has information amounting to probable cause that:

"(I) The restrained person has violated or attempted to violate any provision of a restraining order; and

"(II) The restrained person has been properly served with a copy of the restraining order or the restrained person has received actual notice of the existence and substance of such order.

"(c) In making the probable cause determination described in paragraph (b) of this subsection (3), a peace officer shall assume that the information received from the registry is accurate. *A peace officer shall enforce a valid restraining order whether or not there is a record of the restraining order in the registry.*" Colo.Rev.Stat. § 18–6–803.5(3) . . . (emphases added).

The Court of Appeals concluded that this statutory provision-especially taken in conjunction with a statement from its legislative history, and with another statute restricting criminal and civil liability for officers making arrests-established the Colorado Legislature's clear intent "to alter the fact that the police were not enforcing domestic abuse retraining orders," and thus its intent "that the recipient of a domestic abuse restraining order have an entitlement to its enforcement." 366 F.3d, at 1108. Any other result, it said, "would render domestic abuse restraining orders utterly valueless." *Id.,* at 1109.

. . . We do not believe that these provisions of Colorado law truly made enforcement of restraining orders *mandatory.* A well established tradition of police discretion has long coexisted with apparently mandatory arrest statutes.

. . . Against that backdrop, a true mandate of police action would require some stronger indication from the Colorado Legislature than "shall use every reasonable means to enforce a restraining order" (or even "shall arrest . . . or . . . seek a warrant"), §§ 18–6–803.5(3)(a), (b). That language is not perceptibly more mandatory than the Colorado statute which has long told municipal chiefs of police that they "shall pursue and arrest any person fleeing from justice in any part of the state" and that they "shall apprehend any person in the act of committing any offense . . . and, forthwith and without any warrant, bring such person before a . . . competent authority for examination and trial." Colo.Rev.Stat. § 31–4–112 (Lexis 2004). It is hard to imagine that a Colorado peace officer would not have some discretion to determine that-despite probable cause to believe a restraining order has been violated-the circumstances of the violation or the competing duties of that officer or his agency counsel decisively against enforcement in a particular instance. The practical necessity for discretion is particularly apparent in a case such as this one, where the suspected violator is not actually present and his whereabouts are unknown. Cf. *Donaldson v. Seattle,* 65 Wash.App. 661, 671–672, 831 P.2d 1098, 1104 (1992) ("There is a vast difference between a mandatory duty to arrest [a violator who is on the scene] and a mandatory duty to conduct a follow up investigation [to locate an absent violator]. . . . A mandatory duty to investigate . . . would be completely open-ended as to priority, duration and intensity").

. . . Respondent does not specify the precise means of enforcement that the Colorado restraining-order statute assertedly mandated-whether her interest lay in having police arrest her husband, having them seek a warrant for his arrest, or having them "use every reasonable means, up to and including arrest, to enforce the order's terms,". . . . Such indeterminacy is not the hallmark of a duty that is mandatory. Nor can someone be safely deemed "entitled" to something when the identity of the alleged entitlement is vague. See *Roth,* 408 U.S., at 577, 92 S.Ct. 2701 (considering whether "certain benefits" were "secure[d]" by rule or understandings); cf. *Natale v. Ridgefield,* 170 F.3d 258, 263 (C.A.2 1999) ("There is no reason . . . to restrict the 'uncertainty' that will preclude existence of a federally protectable property interest to the uncertainty that inheres in the exercise of discretion").

. . . Even if the statute could be said to have made enforcement of restraining orders "mandatory" because of the domestic-violence context of the underlying statute, that would not necessarily mean that state law gave *respondent* an entitlement to *enforcement* of the mandate. Making the actions of government employees obligatory can serve various legitimate ends other than the conferral of a benefit on a specific class of people. See, *e.g., Sandin v. Conner,* 515 U.S. 472, 482, 115 S.Ct. 2293, 132 L.Ed.2d 418 (1995) (finding no constitutionally protected liberty interest in prison regulations phrased in mandatory terms, in part because "[s]uch guidelines are not set forth solely to benefit the prisoner"). The serving of public rather than private ends is the normal course of the criminal law because criminal acts, "besides the injury [they do] to individuals, ... strike at the very being of society; which cannot possibly subsist, where actions of this sort are suffered to escape with impunity." 4 W. Blackstone, Commentaries on the Laws of England 5 (1769); see also *Huntington v. Attrill,* 146 U.S. 657, 668, 13 S.Ct. 224, 36 L.Ed. 1123 (1892).

... Respondent's alleged interest stems only from a State's *statutory* scheme-from a restraining order that was authorized by and tracked precisely the statute on which the Court of Appeals relied. She does not assert that she has any common-law or contractual entitlement to enforcement. If she was given a statutory entitlement, we would expect to see some indication of that in the statute itself. Although Colorado's statute spoke of "protected person[s]" such as respondent, it did so in connection with matters other than a right to enforcement. It said that a "protected person shall be provided with a copy of [a restraining] order" when it is issued, § 18–6–803.5(3)(a); that a law enforcement agency "shall make all reasonable efforts to contact the protected party upon the arrest of the restrained person," § 18–6–803.5(3)(d); and that the agency "shall give [to the protected person] a copy" of the report it submits to the court that issued the order, § 18–6–803.5(3)(e). Perhaps most importantly, the statute spoke directly to the protected person's power to "initiate contempt proceedings against the restrained person if the order [was] issued in a civil action or request the prosecuting attorney to initiate contempt proceedings if the order [was] issued in a criminal action." § 18–6–803.5(7). The protected person's express power to "initiate" civil contempt proceedings contrasts tellingly with the mere ability to "request" initiation of criminal contempt proceedings-and even more dramatically with the complete silence about any power to "request" (much less demand) that an arrest be made.

The creation of a personal entitlement to something as vague and novel as enforcement of restraining orders cannot "simply g[o] without saying." *Post,* at 2821, n. 16 (STEVENS, J., dissenting). We conclude that Colorado has not created such an entitlement.

Even if we were to think otherwise concerning the creation of an entitlement by Colorado, it is by no means clear that an individual entitlement to enforcement of a restraining order could constitute a "property" interest for purposes of the Due Process Clause. Such a right would not, of course, resemble any traditional conception of property. Although that alone does not disqualify it from due process protection, as *Roth* and its progeny show, the right to have a restraining order enforced does not "have some ascertainable monetary value," as even our "*Roth*-type property-as-entitlement" cases have implicitly required. Merrill, The Landscape of Constitutional Property, 86 Va. L.Rev. 885, 964 (2000). Perhaps most radically, the alleged property interest here arises *incidentally,* not out of some new species of government benefit or service, but out of a function that government actors have always performed-to wit, arresting people who they have probable cause to believe have committed a criminal offense.

... We conclude, therefore, that respondent did not, for purposes of the Due Process Clause, have a property interest in police enforcement of the restraining order against her husband.

... In light of today's decision and that in *DeShaney,* the benefit that a third party may receive from having someone else arrested for a crime generally does not trigger protections under the Due Process Clause, neither in its procedural nor in its "substantive" manifestations. This result reflects our continuing reluctance to treat the Fourteenth Amendment as " 'a font of tort law,' " *Parratt v. Taylor,* 451 U.S. 527, 544, 101 S.Ct. 1908, 68 L.Ed.2d 420 (1981) (quoting *Paul v. Davis,* 424 U.S., at 701, 96 S.Ct. 1155), but it does not mean States are powerless to provide victims with personally enforceable remedies. Although the framers of the Fourteenth Amendment and the Civil Rights Act of 1871, 17 Stat. 13 (the original source of § 1983), did not create a system by which police departments are generally held financially accountable for crimes that better policing might have prevented, the people of Colorado are free to craft such a system under state law. Cf. *DeShaney,* 489 U.S., at 203, 109 S.Ct. 998....

■ [The concurring opinion of Justice Souter, joined by Justice Breyer, is omitted.]

■ Justice Stevens, with whom Justice Ginsburg joins, dissenting.

The issue presented to us is much narrower than is suggested by the far-ranging arguments of the parties and their *amici.* Neither the tragic facts of the case, nor the importance of according proper deference to law enforcement professionals, should divert our attention from that issue. That issue is whether the restraining order entered by the Colorado trial court on June 4, 1999, created a "property" interest that is protected from arbitrary deprivation by the Due Process Clause of the Fourteenth Amendment.

It is perfectly clear, on the one hand, that neither the Federal Constitution itself, nor any federal statute, granted respondent or her children any individual entitlement to police protection. See *DeShaney v. Winnebago County Dept. of Social Servs.,* 489 U.S. 189, 109 S.Ct. 998, 103 L.Ed.2d 249 (1989). Nor, I assume, does any Colorado statute create any such entitlement for the ordinary citizen. On the other hand, it is equally clear that federal law imposes no impediment to the creation of such an entitlement by Colorado law. Respondent certainly could have entered into a contract with a private security firm, obligating the firm to provide protection to respondent's family; respondent's interest in such a contract would unquestionably constitute "property" within the meaning of the Due Process Clause. If a Colorado statute enacted for her benefit, or a valid order entered by a Colorado judge, created the functional equivalent of such a private contract by granting respondent an entitlement to mandatory individual protection by the local police force, that state-created right would also qualify as "property" entitled to constitutional protection.

... The central question in this case is therefore whether, as a matter of Colorado law, respondent had a right to police assistance comparable to the right she would have possessed to any other service the government or a private firm might have undertaken to provide. See *Board of Regents of State Colleges v. Roth,* 408 U.S. 564, 577, 92 S.Ct. 2701, 33 L.Ed.2d 548 (1972) ("Property interests, of course, are not created by the Constitution. Rather, they are created and their dimensions are defined by existing rules or understandings that stem from an independent source such as state law-rules or understandings that secure certain benefits and that support claims of entitlement to those benefits").

There was a time when our tradition of judicial restraint would have led this Court to defer to the judgment of more qualified tribunals in seeking the correct answer to that difficult question of Colorado law. Unfortunately, although the majority properly identifies the "central state-law question" in this case as "whether Colorado law gave respondent a right to police enforcement of the restraining order," it has chosen to ignore our settled practice by providing its *own* answer to that question.

... Three flaws in the Court's rather superficial analysis of the merits highlight the unwisdom of its decision to answer the state-law question *de novo*. First, the Court places undue weight on the various statutes throughout the country that seemingly mandate police enforcement but are generally understood to preserve police discretion. As a result, the Court gives short shrift to the unique case of "mandatory arrest" statutes in the domestic violence context; States passed a wave of these statutes in the 1980's and 1990's with the unmistakable goal of eliminating police discretion in this area. Second, the Court's formalistic analysis fails to take seriously the fact that the Colorado statute at issue in this case was enacted for the benefit of the narrow class of persons who are beneficiaries of domestic restraining orders, and that the order at issue in this case was specifically intended to provide protection to respondent and her children. Finally, the Court is simply wrong to assert that a citizen's interest in the government's commitment to provide police enforcement in certain defined circumstances does not resemble any "traditional conception of property,"; in fact, a citizen's property interest in such a commitment is just as concrete and worthy of protection as her interest in any other important service the government or a private firm has undertaken to provide.

... Police enforcement of a restraining order is a government service that is no less concrete and no less valuable than other government services, such as education. The relative novelty of recognizing this type of property interest is explained by the relative novelty of the domestic violence statutes creating a mandatory arrest duty; before this innovation, the unfettered discretion that characterized police enforcement defeated any citizen's "legitimate claim of entitlement" to this service. Novel or not, respondent's claim finds strong support in the principles that underlie our due process jurisprudence. In this case, Colorado law *guaranteed* the provision of a certain service, in certain defined circumstances, to a certain class of beneficiaries, and respondent reasonably relied on that guarantee. As we observed in *Roth,* "[i]t is a purpose of the ancient institution of property to protect those claims upon which people rely in their daily lives, reliance that must not be arbitrarily undermined." 408 U.S., at 577, 92 S.Ct. 2701. Surely, if respondent had contracted with a private security firm to provide her and her daughters with protection from her husband, it would be apparent that she possessed a property interest in such a contract. Here, Colorado undertook a comparable obligation, and respondent-with restraining order in hand-justifiably relied on that undertaking. Respondent's claim of entitlement to this promised service is no less legitimate than the other claims our cases have upheld, and no less concrete than a hypothetical agreement with a private firm. The fact that it is based on a statutory enactment and a judicial order entered for her special protection, rather than on a formal contract, does not provide a principled basis for refusing to consider it "property" worthy of constitutional protection.

Because respondent had a property interest in the enforcement of the restraining order, state officials could not deprive her of that interest without observing fair procedures. Her description of the police behavior in this case and the department's callous policy of failing to respond properly to reports of restraining order violations clearly alleges a due process violation. At the very least, due process requires that the relevant state decisionmaker *listen* to the claimant and then *apply the relevant criteria* in reaching his decision. The failure to observe these minimal procedural safeguards creates an unacceptable risk of arbitrary and "erroneous deprivation[s]," *Mathews,* 424 U.S., at 335, 96 S.Ct. 893. According to respondent's complaint-which we must construe liberally at this early stage in the litigation, see *Swierkiewicz v. Sorema N. A.,* 534 U.S. 506, 514, 122 S.Ct. 992, 152 L.Ed.2d 1 (2002)-the process she was afforded by the police constituted nothing more than a " 'sham or a pretense.' " *Joint Anti–Fascist Refugee Comm. v. McGrath,* 341 U.S. 123, 164, 71 S.Ct. 624, 95 L.Ed. 817 (1951) (Frankfurter, J., concurring).

. . .

NOTES

(1) In *McComb v. Wambaugh,* 934 F.2d 474 (3d Cir.1991), the court followed *DeShaney* in holding that Philadelphia social workers were not liable to a child for injury based on malnutrition after the child was returned from foster care by a Virginia court to the mother in Pennsylvania. The court also found that the Interstate Compact on Placement of Children did not apply where the Virginia court had directed that the child be taken from foster care and sent to the natural mother in Pennsylvania, and that the Compact did not create a special relationship between the child and Philadelphia social workers. Recently, courts outside the Third Circuit have had differing views as to the applicability of the Interstate Compact on the Placement of Children (*see, e.g., Department of Children and Families v. Benway,* 745 So.2d 437 (Fla.Dist.Ct.App.1999); *Arizona Dept. of Economic Security v. Leonardo,* 200 Ariz. 74, 22 P.3d 513 (Ariz.Ct.App.2001)). The facts, as stated by the Court of Appeals, follow:

> Khemsu Walton [the injured child and plaintiff] was born in Philadelphia in 1980. Two weeks later he, his siblings, and mother, Marie Walton, were all injured in an automobile accident in Virginia. When taken to the hospital, the children were found to be suffering from malnutrition. After an investigation by Virginia social welfare agencies, the Domestic Relations Court of Halifax County, Virginia removed the children from their mother's custody and placed them in the temporary custody of the Halifax County Department of Social

Services. Following partial recovery from her injuries, Marie Walton, but not the children, returned to her Philadelphia home. The Halifax Court later placed Khemsu in foster care with his aunt and uncle in Virginia.

Ms. Walton maintained contact with the Halifax court and petitioned for the return of her children or, in the alternative, maintenance of the children's previous diet. One year after the automobile accident, Halifax County sought information for a forthcoming hearing on Ms. Walton's petitions. Pursuant to the Interstate Compact on the Placement of Children, to which Pennsylvania and Virginia are parties, the County social workers submitted a request for information through the Commonwealth of Virginia's Interstate Placement Specialist. In turn, that official requested that her counterpart in the Pennsylvania Department of Welfare contact the appropriate Philadelphia agency for an evaluation of the Walton home after an unannounced visit.

The Philadelphia Department of Public Welfare was given the responsibility for providing the necessary information. Defendant Jean Summons, a social worker employed by the Department, interviewed Marie Walton and according to Department procedure, but contrary to Virginia's wishes, made an announced visit to the Walton home. After that investigation, Summons and her supervisor, defendant Rosita Wambaugh, reported to Pennsylvania's Compact Administrator that they "would approve of the children being returned to their mother."

On October 20, 1981 the Halifax Court directed that "custody" of Khemsu's three oldest siblings be "returned" to Marie Walton "but under supervision of the Department of Social Services for the City of Philadelphia, which department shall make at least bi-monthly unannounced visitations of the home." The order also asked Philadelphia to file a progress report within six months so that the court could determine whether to return custody of the two youngest children to their mother.

Although the Virginia authorities had requested unannounced visits to the Walton home, the Philadelphia Department's policy called for prearranged home visitation. Over the next eight months, Summons made two announced visits and found the home in satisfactory condition, the children healthy and attending school. In April 1982, Summons wrote to the Virginia Court stating that she had spoken with Marie Walton and that because she had demonstrated the capability to care for her children, Philadelphia would support the mother in her desire to reunite her family.

On April 27, 1982 the Halifax Court ordered that custody of Khemsu and his brother "is hereby returned to their mother, Maria[sic] Walton, but under continuing supervision of the appropriate Department of Social Services in Philadelphia, Pa." On the same day, the judge signed an Interstate Compact Application Child Placement Request for each of the five children. The documents purported to "place" the children with their mother and requested quarterly reports from the receiving agency. A social worker from Virginia then accompanied Khemsu and his brother on the trip to Philadelphia and left them with Ms. Walton at her home.

On May 27, 1982, the Pennsylvania Compact Administrator advised her Virginia counterpart that Pennsylvania had approved the placement requests. She noted, however, that Pennsylvania would provide a six-month report on the Walton children instead of the quarterly reports Virginia had requested.

On October 22, 1982 and February 24, 1983 the Halifax County social worker asked for the Compact Administrator's progress reports. In response to these requests, defendant Summons notified Pennsylvania's Compact Administrator that Ms. Walton refused to cooperate and would not permit a home visit. In her letter, Ms. Summons concluded "if Virginia wants us to make another attempt to investigate Ms. Walton, please have them notify us in writing."

A copy of the letter was also sent to the social worker in Halifax County. Apparently nothing further was done by either the Philadelphia or Virginia authorities.

On August 17, 1984 Ms. Walton brought four-year old Khemsu to a hospital in Philadelphia. He weighed 13 pounds and was in a comatose condition. As a result of malnutrition, he has suffered irreversible brain damage.

Ms. Walton plead guilty to criminal charges arising out of her failure to provide properly for Khemsu. The child now lives in foster care.

Khemsu's hospitalization occurred more than two years after he was returned to his mother, and more than fifteen months after Philadelphia's last correspondence with Virginia.

The plaintiff urged that rather than apply the *DeShaney* rationale, the court's determination should be controlled by *Stoneking v. Bradford Area School Dist.*, 882 F.2d 720 (3d Cir.1989), cert. denied, 493 U.S. 1044, 110 S.Ct. 840, 107 L.Ed.2d 835 (1990), in which the court of appeals had held that a school district could be liable for its policies of deliberate indifference toward alleged abuse by one of its teachers. However the court held that DeShaney's injuries resulted at the hands of a private actor and Stoneking's resulted from the actions of a state employee, critical distinction because the harm done to the plaintiff was by his mother. After analyzing the history and scope of the Interstate Compact on the Placement of Children, adopted by both Virginia and Pennsylvania, the court determined that:

> We are persuaded that read as a whole the Compact was intended only to govern placing children in substitute arrangements for parental care. Thus, the Compact does not apply when a child is returned by the sending state to a natural parent residing in another state.

(2) In *Baltimore City Dept. Social Services v. Bouknight*, 493 U.S. 549, 110 S.Ct. 900, 107 L.Ed.2d 992 (1990), the Supreme Court held that a mother, the custodian of a child pursuant to a court order, could not invoke the Fifth Amendment privilege against self-incrimination to resist a juvenile court's order to produce the child. At issue was the location (and condition) of an abused child who had been hospitalized at three months of age with a fractured left femur. An examination also revealed several partially healed bone fractures along with other indications of severe physical abuse. The mother's conduct in the hospital led personnel there to make a report of suspected child abuse, and the department of social services secured a court order removing the child from his mother's control and placing him in shelter care. According to the Supreme Court opinion, several months later the shelter care order was "inexplicably modified" to return the child to his mother's custody temporarily. After a hearing soon thereafter, the juvenile court declared him to be a "child in need of assistance," thus asserting jurisdiction and placing him under continuing oversight of the Baltimore City Department of Social Services (BCDSS), setting forth extensive conditions in a protective supervision order with which the mother was bound to comply. According to the Supreme Court:

> Eight months later, fearing for Maurice's safety, BCDSS returned to Juvenile Court. BCDSS caseworkers related that Bouknight would not cooperate with them and had in nearly every respect violated the terms of the protective order. BCDSS stated that Maurice's father had recently died in a shooting incident and that Bouknight, in light of the results of a psychological examination and her history of drug use, could not provide adequate care for

the child. On April 20, 1988, the Court granted BCDSS's petition to remove Maurice from Bouknight's control for placement in foster care. BCDSS officials also petitioned for judicial relief from Bouknight's failure to produce Maurice or reveal where he could be found. The petition recounted that on two recent visits by BCDSS officials to Bouknight's home, she had refused to reveal the location of the child or had indicated that the child was with an aunt whom she would not identify. The petition further asserted that inquiries of Bouknight's known relatives had revealed that none of them had recently seen Maurice and that BCDSS had prompted the police to issue a missing persons report and referred the case for investigation by the police homicide division. Also on April 20, the Juvenile Court, upon a hearing on the petition, cited Bouknight for violating the protective custody order and for failing to appear at the hearing. Bouknight had indicated to her attorney that she would appear with the child, but also expressed fear that if she appeared the State would "snatch the child." The court issued an order to show cause why Bouknight should not be held in civil contempt for failure to produce the child. Expressing concern that Maurice was endangered or perhaps dead, the court issued a bench warrant for Bouknight's appearance.

When the child was not produced at subsequent hearings, the court directed that the mother be imprisoned until she "purge[d] herself of contempt by either producing [Maurice] before the court or revealing to the court his exact whereabouts." Her subsequent claim that the order violated the Fifth Amendment's guarantee against self-incrimination was rejected by the court. The Maryland Court of Appeals reversed, holding that the contempt order unconstitutionally compelled the mother to admit to a measure of continuing control and dominion over the child's person when she was under reasonable apprehension that she would be prosecuted.

On *certiorari*, the U.S. Supreme Court reversed the Maryland appeal court, explaining:

> The possibility that a production order will compel testimonial assertions that may prove incriminating does not, in all contexts, justify invoking the privilege to resist production. Even assuming that this limited testimonial assertion is sufficiently incriminating and "sufficiently testimonial for purposes of the privilege," Bouknight may not invoke the privilege to resist the production order because she has assumed custodial duties related to production and because production is required as part of a noncriminal regulatory regime.

> The Court has on several occasions recognized that the Fifth Amendment privilege may not be invoked to resist compliance with a regulatory regime constructed to effect the State's public purposes unrelated to the enforcement of its criminal laws....

> These principles readily apply to this case. Once Maurice was adjudicated a child in need of assistance, his care and safety became the particular object of the State's regulatory interests.... Maryland first placed Maurice in shelter care, authorized placement in foster care, and then entrusted responsibility for Maurice's care to Bouknight. By accepting care of Maurice subject to the custodial order's conditions (including requirements that she cooperate with BCDSS, follow a prescribed training regime, and be subject to further court orders), Bouknight submitted to the routine operation of the regulatory system and agreed to hold Maurice in a manner consonant with the State's regulatory interests and subject to inspection by BCDSS. Cf. Shapiro v. United States, 335 U.S. 1 (1948). In assuming the obligations attending custody, Bouknight "has accepted the incident obligation to permit inspection." Wilson, 221 U.S. at 382. The State imposes and enforces that obligation as part of a broadly directed,

noncriminal regulatory regime governing children cared for pursuant to custodial orders. See Md.Cts. & Jud.Proc. Code Ann. § 3–802(a) (1984)....

. . .

Similarly, BCDSS's efforts to gain access to children, as well as judicial efforts to the same effect, do not "focu[s] almost exclusively on conduct which was criminal." Many orders will arise in circumstances entirely devoid of criminal conduct. Even when criminal conduct may exist, the court may properly request production and return of the child, and enforce that request through exercise of the contempt power, for reasons related entirely to the child's well-being and through measures unrelated to criminal law enforcement or investigation. See Maryland Cts. & Jud.Proc.Code Ann. § 3–814(c) (1984). This case provides an illustration: concern for the child's safety underlay the efforts to gain access to and then compel production of Maurice. Finally, production in the vast majority of cases will embody no incriminating testimony, even if in particular cases the act of production may incriminate the custodian through an assertion of possession, the existence, or the identity of the child. These orders to produce children cannot be characterized as efforts to gain some testimonial component of the act of production. The government demands production of the very public charge entrusted to a custodian, and makes the demand for compelling reasons unrelated to criminal law enforcement and as part of a broadly applied regulatory regime. In these circumstances, Bouknight cannot invoke the privilege to resist the order to produce Maurice.

. . .

Justice Marshall was joined by Justice Brennan in a dissent, stating:

> ... The State's goal of protecting children from abusive environments through its juvenile welfare system cannot be separated from criminal provisions that serve the same goal. When the conduct at which a civil statute aims—here, child abuse and neglect—is frequently the same conduct subject to criminal sanction, it strikes me as deeply problematic to dismiss the Fifth Amendment concerns by characterizing the civil scheme as "unrelated to criminal law enforcement investigation". A civil scheme that inevitably intersects with criminal sanctions may not be used to coerce, on pain of contempt, a potential criminal defendant to furnish evidence crucial to the success of her own prosecution.

. . .

(3) **The aftermath of _DeShaney_ and _Castle Rock_.** Do you agree with the decisions in _DeShaney_ and _Castle Rock_? Note the Court's mention in _Castle Rock_ of a state's right to adopt legislation that would hold police departments "financially accountable for crimes that better policing might have prevented." The same could theoretically apply with respect to social workers. What might be the advantages and disadvantages of such frameworks? What other possibilities are there for encouraging stronger enforcement by police and social workers? For a recent treatment of this issue with regard to domestic violence restraining orders, see Mandeep Talwar, Improving the Enforcement of Restraining Orders After _Castle Rock v. Gonzales_, 45 Fam.Ct.Rev. 322 (2007). See also, Kathryn E. Litchman, Mentorship Article, Punishing the Protectors: The Illinois Domestic Violence Act Remedy For Victims of Domestic Violence Against Police Misconduct, 38 Loy.U.Chi. L.J. 765 (2007); Sarah Metusalem, Note, Should There Be a Public Duty to Respond to Private Violence? The Effect of _Town of Castle Rock v. Gonzales_ on Restraining Orders, 38 U.Tol.L.Rev. 1037 (2007).

Doe v. Holt

Supreme Court of North Carolina, 1992.
332 N.C. 90, 418 S.E.2d 511.

■ MITCHELL, JUSTICE.

The issue before this Court is whether this suit by two minor plaintiffs against their father for damages allegedly resulting from his having repeatedly raped and sexually molested them is barred by the parent-child immunity doctrine. We conclude that the complaint states a claim upon which relief can be granted and that the parent-child immunity doctrine does not bar this suit.

In their complaint, the plaintiffs allege that they are both unemancipated minors. They resided with the defendant, their natural father, from 5 August 1978 until June 1989. Beginning in 1980, when the plaintiffs were five and six years old respectively, the defendant raped and sexually molested both plaintiffs repeatedly; these acts continued until 1989. The defendant pled guilty, in a separate criminal action, to charges of second-degree rape and second-degree sexual offense; those charges and convictions involved some of the same acts against the plaintiffs forming the basis of the tort claims presented in this case. At the time the complaint was filed, the defendant was serving an active prison sentence for those acts.

The plaintiffs brought this tort action by and through their guardian ad litem to recover damages for permanent physical, mental and emotional injuries they suffered as a result of being raped and sexually molested by the defendant, their father.

[The trial court's dismissal of the action was reversed by the Court of Appeals in Doe v. Holt, 103 N.C.App. 516, 405 S.E.2d 807 (1991).]

The doctrine of parent-child immunity was first recognized in the case of Hewlett v. George, 68 Miss. 703, 9 So. 885 (1891). In North Carolina, the doctrine was first applied in Small v. Morrison, 185 N.C. 577, 118 S.E. 12 (1923). In denying a minor child's action to recover damages against her father for his negligence resulting in an automobile collision, this Court stated: [T]he government of a well ordered home is one of the surest bulwarks against the forces that make for social disorder and civic decay. It is the very cradle of civilization, with the future welfare of the commonwealth dependent, in a large measure, upon the efficacy and success of its administration. Under these conditions, the State will not and should not permit the management of the home to be destroyed by the individual members thereof, unless and until the interests of society are threatened.

We are well aware of the fact that some appellate courts and legislatures have abolished or significantly eroded the parent-child immunity doctrine in other jurisdictions. See generally Dean, It's Time to Abolish North Carolina's Parent–Child Immunity, But Who's Going to Do It? 68 N.C.L.Rev. 1317, 1328 n. 123 (1990) (listing states where the doctrine has been abolished or modified); ... But since our decision in Small, this Court has consistently applied the rule enunciated in that case; "an unemancipated minor child may not maintain an action based on ordinary negligence against his parents." Lee v. Mowett Sales Co., 316 N.C. 489, 491, 342 S.E.2d 882, 884 (1986). See Redding v. Redding, 235 N.C. 638, 70 S.E.2d

676 (1952). The parent-child immunity doctrine was abrogated in part, however, when the General Assembly enacted a statute making it inapplicable to actions "arising out of the operation of a motor vehicle owned or operated by the parent or child." N.C.G.S. § 1–539.21 (1991 Cum.Supp.). After the enactment of this statute, we were asked to judicially abolish what remained of the parent-child immunity doctrine. We declined to do so because "[t]o judicially abolish the parent-child immunity after the legislature has considered and retained the doctrine would be to engage in impermissible judicial legislation." Lee, 316 N.C. at 494, 342 S.E.2d at 885. We stated that "[t]he doctrine will continue to be applied as it now exists in North Carolina until it is abolished or amended by the legislature." Id. at 495, 342 S.E.2d at 886. We adhere to that statement in this case.

We do not deviate from the position we took in Lee, to the effect that the parent-child immunity doctrine as first enunciated in Small continues to apply in North Carolina, except to the extent it has been specifically abolished or amended by the legislature. Id. However, the case before us is not one in which we are asked to modify or abolish the parent-child immunity doctrine. The question before us here is whether the parent-child immunity doctrine, as it has existed in North Carolina since Small, bars tort claims for injuries unemancipated minors have suffered as a result of a parent's willful and malicious conduct. We conclude that the doctrine does not bar such claims. . . .

The defendant argues in the present case that the parent-child immunity doctrine, as it has been recognized and applied in North Carolina since our decision in Small, operates as a complete bar to all tort suits by unemancipated children against their parents unless specifically authorized by statute. We disagree.

The history of the parent-child immunity doctrine in North Carolina reveals that maintenance of family harmony was foremost among the public policies the doctrine was intended to serve. Lee, 316 N.C. at 492, 342 S.E.2d at 884; Skinner v. Whitley, 281 N.C. 476, 480, 189 S.E.2d 230, 232 (1972). It was feared that suits by children against their parents for negligent injury would "tend to destroy parental authority and to undermine the security of the home." Small, 185 N.C. at 584, 118 S.E. at 15. For such reasons, the doctrine has been applied in North Carolina to bar actions between unemancipated children and their parents based on ordinary negligence.

[The court explained that in prior cases they had determined the question raised by an intentional, willful or malicious tort inflicted on a child by a parent or person in loco parentis would be passed on when it arises in a case properly before them. They then stated that "The present case is just such a case. . . ."]

. . . Faced as we are here with a case requiring us to decide the issue with finality, we . . . conclude that the parent-child immunity doctrine in North Carolina has never applied to, and may not be applied to, actions by unemancipated minors to recover for injuries resulting from their parent's willful and malicious acts.

In reviewing the propriety of the trial court's dismissal of the plaintiff's complaint for failure to state a claim upon which relief can be granted, we must next resolve the issue of whether the plaintiffs' complaint alleged "willful and malicious acts" sufficient to withstand the defendant's motion to dismiss under Rule 12(b)(6) of the North Carolina Rules of Civil Procedure. An act is "willful" "when it is done purposely and deliberately in violation of law ... or when it is done knowingly and of set purpose...." Foster v. Hyman, 197 N.C. 189, 191, 148 S.E. 36, 37 (1929).... "Malice in law" is "presumed from tortious acts, deliberately done without just cause, excuse or justification, which are reasonably calculated to injure another or others." Betts v. Jones, 208 N.C. 410, 411, 181 S.E. 334, 335 (1935), quoted in McKeel v. Armstrong, 96 N.C.App. 401, 406, 386 S.E.2d 60, 63 (1989). It is clear in light of such definitions that the plaintiffs' complaint in the present case alleged conduct against the plaintiffs by their father which was both "willful" and "malicious."

It would be unconscionable if children who were injured by heinous acts of their parents such as alleged here should have no avenue by which to recover damages in redress of those wrongs. Where a parent has injured his or her child through a willful and malicious act, any concept of family harmony has been destroyed. Thus, the foremost public purpose supporting the parent-child immunity doctrine is absent, and there is no reason to extend the doctrine's protection to such acts.

We wish to make it clear that no issue involving reasonable chastisement of children by their parents is before us in the present case, and we expressly do not intend to be understood as commenting on situations involving such issues. Furthermore, our opinion in the present case is not intended to permit interference in the proper scope of discretion parents must utilize in rearing their children. As the Supreme Court of New Jersey recognized in Foldi, there is no universally correct philosophy on how to raise one's child. Foldi, 93 N.J. at 546, 461 A.2d at 1152. In no way do we intend to indicate that reasonable parental decisions concerning children should be reviewed in the courts of this state. Such decisions make up the essence of parental discretion, discretion which allows parents to shape the views, beliefs and values their children carry with them into adulthood. These decisions are for the parents to make, and will be protected as such.

Here, we have addressed a different concern; when a parent steps beyond the bounds of reasonable parental discretion and commits a willful and malicious act which injures his or her child, the parent negates the public policies which led to recognition of the parent-child immunity doctrine in North Carolina, and the doctrine does not shield the parent. In the present case, the defendant's rapes and sexual abuses of his two minor daughters certainly constituted "willful and malicious acts" against them. Therefore, the plaintiffs' complaint alleged a proper claim for relief and should not have been dismissed....

■ MEYER, JUSTICE, concurring in result....

Though the majority says otherwise, it is clearly recognizing an exception to the immunity rule, and an exception to the rule by any other name is still an exception. Because of the peculiar nature of these cases, the recognition of an exception would be a far better solution. Some states that have made an exception have limited the exception to cases of sexual abuse, which I believe is all that is called for here.

While I agree with the majority that the plaintiff should recover on the facts alleged here, the same result could be reached with far less damage to existing law. My reticence to join the majority opinion arises not from its result, but from my fear of how the law it announces will be applied in future cases in this particular area, and surely many will be spawned by this case.

In addition to limiting our holding in this case to cases of sexual abuse, I would prefer that this Court erect some hurdles that would weed out the truly marginal cases. One method would be to raise the standard of proof required for recovery from a preponderance of the evidence to clear, cogent, and convincing evidence. Such a course of action by this Court would not be without precedent. Only recently in recognizing a cause of action for unintentional infliction of emotional distress, and because of similar concerns, we took the extraordinary step of imposing a high standard of proof of the injury claimed. *Johnson v. Ruark Obstetrics*, 327 N.C. 283, 395 S.E.2d 85 (plaintiff may not recover damages where mere fright or temporary anxiety does not amount to severe emotional distress; "severe emotional distress" means any emotional or mental disorder, such as, for example, neurosis, psychosis, chronic depression, phobia, or any other type of severe and disabling emotional or mental condition that may be generally recognized and diagnosed by professionals trained to do so; factors to be considered on the question of foreseeability include the plaintiff's proximity to the negligent act, the relationship between the plaintiff and the other person for whose welfare the plaintiff is concerned, and whether the plaintiff personally observed the negligent act), *reh'g denied*, 327 N.C. 644, 399 S.E.2d 133 (1990).

For the foregoing reasons, I concur only in the result reached by the majority.

NOTES

(1) Statutes of limitation can pose a bar to delayed actions for childhood sexual abuse. Virginia Code Ann. § 8.01–249 was amended in the 1990s and more recently in 2005 to provide:

> The cause of action in the actions herein listed shall be deemed to accrue as follows:
>
> . . .
>
> 6. In actions for injury to the person, whatever the theory of recovery, resulting from sexual abuse occurring during the infancy or incapacity of the person, upon removal of the disability of infancy or incapacity . . . or, if the fact of the injury or its causal connection to the sexual abuse is not then known, when the fact of the injury and its causal connection to the sexual abuse is first communicated to the person by a licensed physician, psychologist, or clinical psychologist. As used in this subdivision, "sexual abuse" means sexual abuse as defined in subdivision 6 of § 18.2–67.10 and acts constituting rape, sodomy, object sexual penetration or sexual battery . . . .

(2) For a wide ranging group of articles focusing on child sexual abuse, see Sexual Abuse of Children, in The Future of Children, Vol. 4, No. 2 (Summer/Fall 1994). In an article on Responding to Child Sexual Abuse: The Need for a Balanced Approach, Douglas J. Besharov addresses problems of reporting and the importance of interviewing. Id. at 135.

Johnson v. State

Supreme Court of Florida, 1992.
602 So.2d 1288.

■ HARDING, JUSTICE.

We have for review Johnson v. State, 578 So.2d 419, 420 (Fla. 5th DCA 1991), in which the Fifth District Court of Appeal certified the following question as one of great public importance: WHETHER THE INGESTION OF A CONTROLLED SUBSTANCE BY A MOTHER WHO KNOWS THE SUBSTANCE WILL PASS TO HER CHILD AFTER BIRTH IS A VIOLATION OF FLORIDA LAW?

. . .

The issue before the court is whether section 893.13(1)(c)(1), Florida Statutes (1989), permits the criminal prosecution of a mother, who ingested a controlled substance prior to giving birth, for delivery of a controlled substance to the infant during the thirty to ninety seconds following the infant's birth, but before the umbilical cord is severed.

Johnson presents four arguments attacking the applicability of section 893.13(1)(c)(1) to her conviction: 1) the district court's interpretation of the statute violates the legislature's intent; 2) the plain language of the statute prevents her conviction; 3) the conviction violates her constitutional rights of due process and privacy; and 4) the State presented insufficient evidence to show that she intentionally delivered cocaine to a minor.... The State contends that the district court correctly found that the statute's plain language prohibits the delivery of the controlled substance to a minor, and that the conviction does not violate Johnson's constitutional rights.

We adopt Judge Sharp's analysis concerning the insufficiency of the evidence to support Johnson's conviction and her analysis concerning the legislature's intent in section 893.13(1)(c)(1). However, we note that Judge Sharp's analysis did not clearly state the rules of statutory construction in the criminal context. Although Judge Sharp correctly applied the rule of strict construction, she failed to apply the other paramount rule of criminal statutory construction, the rule of lenity. § 775.021(1), Fla. Stat. (1989).

The rules of statutory construction require courts to strictly construe criminal statutes, and that "when the language is susceptible to differing constructions, [the statute] shall be construed most favorably to the accused." § 775.021(1). In strictly construing criminal statutes, we have held that only those terms which are " 'clearly and intelligently described in [a penal statute's] very words, as well as manifestly intended by the Legislature' " are to be considered as included in the statute. State v. Wershow, 343 So.2d 605, 608 (Fla.1977), quoting Ex parte Amos, 93 Fla. 5, 112 So. 289 (1927). We find that the legislative history does not show a manifest intent to use the word "delivery" in the context of criminally prosecuting mothers for delivery of a controlled substance to a minor by way of the umbilical cord. This lack of legislative intent coupled with uncertainty that the term "delivery" applies to the facts of the instant case, compels this Court to construe the statute in favor of Johnson. The text of Judge Sharp's dissent is as follows:

Johnson appeals from two convictions for delivering a controlled substance to her two minor children in violation of section 893.13(1)(c)1., Florida Statutes (1989).[1] The state's theory of the case was that Johnson "delivered" cocaine or a derivative of the drug to her two children via blood flowing through the children's umbilical cords in the sixty-to-ninety second period after they were expelled from her birth canal but before their cords were severed. The application of this statute to this concept of "delivery" presents a case of first impression in this state. Because I conclude that section 893.13(1)(c)1. was not intended to apply to these facts, I would vacate the convictions and remand for the entry of a judgment of acquittal.

The record in this case establishes the following facts. On October 3, 1987, Johnson delivered a son. The birth was normal with no complications. There was no evidence of fetal distress either within the womb or during the delivery. About one and one-half minutes elapsed from the time the son's head emerged from his mother's birth canal to the time he was placed on her stomach and the cord was clamped.

The obstetrician who delivered Johnson's son testified he presumed that the umbilical cord was functioning normally and that it was delivering blood to the baby after he emerged from the birth canal and before the cord was clamped. Johnson admitted to the baby's pediatrician that she used cocaine the night before she delivered. A basic toxicology test performed on Johnson and her son was positive for benzoylecgonine, a metabolite or "breakdown" product of cocaine.

In December 1988, Johnson, while pregnant with a daughter, suffered a crack overdose. Johnson told paramedics that she had taken $200 of crack cocaine earlier that evening and that she was concerned about the effects of the drug on her unborn child. Johnson was then taken to the hospital for observation.

Johnson was hospitalized again on January 23, 1989, when she was in labor. Johnson told Dr. Tompkins, an obstetrician, that she had used rock cocaine that morning while she was in labor. With the exception of finding meconium stain fluid in the amniotic sac,[2] there were no other complications with the birth of Johnson's baby daughter. Approximately sixty-to-

---

1. Section 893.13(1)(c)1., Florida Statutes (1989) provides as follows: 893.13 Prohibited acts; penalties.—

* * *

(c) Except as authorized by this chapter, it is unlawful for any person 18 years of age or older to deliver any controlled substance to a person under the age of 18 years, or to use or hire a person under the age of 18 years as an agent or employee in the sale or delivery of such a substance, or to use such person to assist in avoiding detection or apprehension for a violation of this chapter. Any person who violates this provision with respect to: 1. A controlled substance ... is guilty of a felony of the first degree....

2. This condition may indicate that the baby is normal or that its neurological function has been compromised.

ninety seconds elapsed from the time the child's head emerged from her mother's birth canal until her umbilical cord was clamped.

The following day, the Department of Health and Rehabilitative Services investigated an abuse report of a cocaine baby concerning Johnson's daughter. Johnson told the investigator that she had smoked pot and crack cocaine three to four times every-other-day throughout the duration of her pregnancy with her daughter. Johnson's mother acknowledged that Johnson had been using cocaine for at least three years during the time her daughter and son were born.

At Johnson's trial, Dr. Tompkins testified that a mother's blood passes nutrients, oxygen and chemicals to an unborn child by a diffusion exchange at the capillary level from the womb to the placenta. The umbilical cord then circulates the baby's blood (including the exchange from its mother) between the placenta and the child. Metabolized cocaine derivatives in the mother's blood thus diffuse from the womb to the placenta, and then reach the baby through its umbilical cord. Although the blood flow is somewhat restricted during the birthing process, a measurable amount of blood is transferred from the placenta to the baby through the umbilical cord during delivery and after birth.

Dr. Shashi Gore, a pathologist and toxicologist, testified that cocaine has a half life of about one hour. This means that half of the amount of the drug remains in a person's blood stream for about one hour. The remainder gradually decreases over a period of forty-eight to seventy-two hours. The liver metabolizes the cocaine into benzoylecgonine which travels through the kidneys and into the urine until it is voided.

When Dr. Gore was asked whether a woman who had smoked cocaine at 10:00 p.m. and again between 6:00 and 7:00 a.m. the following morning and delivered a child at 1:00 p.m. that afternoon would still have cocaine or benzoylecgonine present in her blood stream at the time of delivery, the response was yes. When asked whether a woman who had smoked cocaine sometime the night before delivering a child at 8:00 in the morning would still have cocaine or benzoylecgonine in her system at the time of the child's birth, the response again was yes.

Dr. Stephen Kandall, a neonatologist, testified for the defense that it was impossible to tell whether the cocaine derivatives which appeared in these children's urine shortly after birth were the result of the exchange from the mother to her children before or after they were born because most of it took place from womb to the placenta before the birth process was complete.

He also testified that blood flow to the infant from the placenta through the umbilical cord to the child is restricted during contractions. Cocaine also constricts the passage of blood dramatically but benzoylecgonine does not. Dr. Kandall admitted that it is theoretically possible that cocaine or other substances can pass between a mother and her baby during the thirty-to-sixty-second period after the child is born and before the umbilical cord is cut, but that the amount would be tiny.

I submit there was no medical testimony adequate to support the trial court's finding that a "delivery" occurred here during the birthing process, even if the criminal statute is applicable. The expert witnesses all testified about blood flow from the umbilical cord to child. But that blood flow is the child's and the placenta through which it flows, is not part of the mother's body. No witness testified in this case that any cocaine derivatives passed from the mother's womb to the placenta during the sixty-to-ninety seconds after the child was expelled from the birth canal. That is when any "delivery" would have to have taken place under this statute, from one "person" to another "person."

Further, there was no evidence that Johnson timed her dosage of cocaine so as to be able to transmit some small amount after her child's birth. Predicting the day or hour of a child's birth is difficult to impossible even for experts. Had Johnson given birth one or two days later, the cocaine would have been completely eliminated, and no "crime" would have occurred. But since she went into labor which progressed to birth after taking cocaine when she did, the only way Johnson could have prevented the "delivery" would have been to have severed the cord before the child was born which, of course, would probably have killed both herself and her child. This illustrates the absurdity of applying the delivery-of-a-drug statute to this scenario.

However, in my view, the primary question in this case is whether section 893.13(1)(c)1. was intended by the Legislature to apply to the birthing process. Before Johnson can be prosecuted under this statute, it must be clear that the Legislature intended for it to apply to the delivery of cocaine derivatives to a newborn during a sixty-to-ninety second interval, before severance of the umbilical cord. I can find no case where "delivery" of a drug was based on an involuntary act such as diffusion and blood flow. Criminal statutes must be strictly—not loosely—construed.

Further, in construing a statute, we must consider its history, the evil to be corrected, the intention of the Legislature, the subject to be regulated and the objects to be attained. Legislative intent is the polestar by which the courts must be guided. Legislative intent may be express or it may be gathered from the purpose of the act, the administrative construction of it, other legislative acts bearing upon the subject, and all the circumstances surrounding and attendant upon it. My review of other pertinent legislative enactments, specifically chapter 415, leads me to conclude in this case that the Legislature expressly chose to treat the problem of drug dependent mothers and newborns as a public health problem and that it considered but rejected imposing criminal sanctions, via section 893.13(1)(c)1.

In 1982, sections 415.501–514 were enacted to deal with the problem of child abuse and neglect. The Legislature determined that because of the impact that abuse or neglect has on a victimized child, siblings, family structure, and inevitably on all citizens of the state, the prevention of child abuse and neglect is a priority of this state. § 415.501, Fla. Stat. (1989). To further this end, the Legislature required that a comprehensive approach for the prevention of abuse and neglect of children be developed for the state. Id. The statute defined an "abused or neglected child" as a child whose physical or mental health or welfare was harmed, or threatened with harm, by the acts of omissions of the parent or other person responsible for the child's welfare. As originally defined, "harm" included physical or mental injury, sexual abuse, exploitation, abandonment, and neglect. § 415.503(7), Fla. Stat. (1983).

In 1987, a bill was proposed to broaden the definition of "harm" to include physical dependency of a newborn infant upon certain controlled drugs. However, there was a concern among legislators that this language might authorize criminal prosecutions of mothers who give birth to drug-dependent children. Comment, A Response to "Cocaine Babies"—Amendment of Florida's Child Abuse and Neglect Laws to Encompass Infants Born Drug Dependent, 15 Fla.S.U.L.Rev. 865, 877 (1987).[3] The bill was then amended to provide that no parent of a drug-dependent newborn shall be subject to criminal investigation solely on the basis of the infant's drug dependency. In the words of the sponsor of the House bill:

> This clearly states that the individual would not be subject to any investigation solely upon the basis of the infant's drug dependency.

> The prime purpose of this bill is to keep the families intact. It's not for the purpose of investigation.

* * *

Again, there is a well-founded anxiety that we are looking to arrest Moms. We're not looking to do that. What we are looking to do is we're looking to intervene on behalf of many different state policies. . . . The bill was passed by the Legislature and the changes were codified in section 415.503(9)(a)2.

From this legislative history, it is clear that the Legislature considered and rejected a specific statutory provision authorizing criminal penalties against mothers for delivering drug-affected children who received transfer of an illegal drug derivative metabolized by the mother's body, in utero. In light of this express legislative statement, I conclude that the Legislature never intended for the general drug delivery statute to authorize prosecutions of those mothers who take illegal drugs close enough in time to childbirth that a doctor could testify that a tiny amount passed from mother to child in the few seconds before the umbilical cord was cut. Criminal prosecution of mothers like Johnson will undermine Florida's express policy of "keeping families intact" and could destroy the family by incarcerating the child's mother when alternative measures could protect the child and stabilize the family. Comment, A Response to "Cocaine Babies", 15 Fla.S.U.L.Rev. at 881.

In similar cases in which charges have been brought against mothers after delivery of drug-affected newborns, those charges have been dismissed. See People v. Hardy, 188 Mich.App. 305, 469 N.W.2d 50 (1991); People v. Bremer, No. 90–32227–FH (Mich.Cir.Ct. January 31, 1991); State v. Gray, 1990 WL 125695, No. L–89–239 (Ohio Ct.App. August 31, 1990), jurisdictional motion allowed, 57 Ohio St.3d 711, 568 N.E.2d 695 (1991). In People v. Bremer, the defendant was charged with delivery of cocaine to her newborn daughter after urine samples from the defendant and child

3. The staff analysis of this bill noted that the legislation, as written, provided a likelihood that a parent could be criminally prosecuted under chapter 893 for delivering a drug dependent child.

following birth tested positive for benzoylecgonine. The circuit court concluded that the Michigan Legislature never intended to include the action of the defendant under the delivery statute: To interpret this section to cover ingestion of cocaine by a pregnant woman would be a radical incursion upon existing law. A person may not be punished for a crime unless her acts fall clearly within the language of the statute. The specific language of this act does not allow the strained construction advanced by the prosecution. Neither judges nor prosecutors can make criminal laws. This is the purview of the Legislature. If the Legislature wanted to punish the uterine transfer of cocaine from a mother to her fetus, it would be up to the Legislature to consider the attending public policy and constitutional arguments and then pass its legislation. The Legislature has not done so and the court has no power to make such a law.

The Michigan court also rejected the prosecutor's argument that charging women with delivery of controlled substances to their newborns provides a strong deterrent against unlawful use of drugs by pregnant women and prompts them to drug treatment. The court noted that prosecution of these women would likely have the opposite effect. A woman may abort her child or avoid prenatal care or treatment out of fear of prosecution. Thus the court concluded that the state's interest was better served by making treatment programs available to pregnant addicts rather than driving them away from treatment by criminal sanctions.

In State v. Gray, the defendant was indicted for child endangering based on her use of cocaine during the last trimester of pregnancy. The trial court concluded that the child endangering statute did not apply to this situation and dismissed the charge against her. On appeal, the state of Ohio argued that the trial court had failed to consider the time the fetus is a child and still attached to the mother and the duty of care created at that point. The appellate court concluded that the Ohio General Assembly did not intend to criminalize the passage of harmful substances from a mother to a child in the brief moments from birth to the severance of the umbilical cord. "To construe the statute in this manner would mean that every expectant woman who ingested a substance with the potential of harm to her child, e.g., alcohol or nicotine, would be criminally liable under [the child endangering statute]. We do not believe such result was intended by the General Assembly."

There can be no doubt that drug abuse is one of the most serious problems confronting our society today. Of particular concern is the alarming rise in the number of babies born with cocaine in their systems as a result of cocaine use by pregnant women. Some experts estimate that as many as eleven percent of pregnant women have used an illegal drug during pregnancy, and of those women, seventy-five percent have used cocaine. Report of the American Medical Association Board of Trustees, Legal Interventions During Pregnancy, 264 JAMA 2663 (Nov. 28, 1990). Others estimate that 375,000 newborns per year are born to women who are users of illicit drugs. American Public Health Association 1990 Policy Statement.

It is well-established that the effects of cocaine use by a pregnant woman on her fetus and later on her newborn can be severe. On average, cocaine-exposed babies have lower birth weights, shorter body lengths at birth, and smaller head circumferences than normal infants. 264 JAMA at 2666. Cocaine use may also result in sudden infant death syndrome, neural-behavioral deficiencies as well as other medical problems and long-term developmental abnormalities. American Public Health Association 1990 Policy Statement. The basic problem of damaging the fetus by drug use during pregnancy should not be addressed piecemeal, however, by prosecuting users who deliver their babies close in time to use of drugs and ignoring those who simply use drugs during their pregnancy.

Florida could possibly have elected to make *in utero* transfers criminal. But it chose to deal with this problem in other ways. One way is to allow evidence of drug use by women as a ground for removal of the child to the custody of protective services, as was done in this case. Some states have responded to this crisis by charging women with child abuse and neglect. See In re Baby X, 97 Mich.App. 111, 293 N.W.2d 736 (1980) (newborn suffering from narcotics withdrawal symptoms due to prenatal maternal drug addiction is neglected and within jurisdiction of the probate court); In re Smith, 128 Misc.2d 976, 492 N.Y.S.2d 331 (N.Y.Fam.Ct.1985) (person under Family Court Act includes unborn child who is neglected as the result of mother's conduct); In re Ruiz, 27 Ohio Misc.2d 31, 27 O.B.R. 350, 500 N.E.2d 935 (Com.Pl.1986) (mother's use of heroin close to baby's birth created substantial risk to the health of the child and constituted child abuse).

However, prosecuting women for using drugs and "delivering" them to their newborns appears to be the least effective response to this crisis.[4] Rather than face the possibility of prosecution, pregnant women who are substance abusers may simply avoid prenatal or medical care for fear of being detected. Yet the newborns of these women are, as a group, the most fragile and sick, and most in need of hospital neonatal care. A decision to

---

4. As the AMA Board of Trustees Report notes, possession of illicit drugs already results in criminal penalties and pregnant women who use illegal substances obviously are not deterred by existing sanctions. Thus the goal of deterrence is not served. To punish a person for substance abuse ignores the impaired capacity of these individuals to make rational decisions concerning their drug use. "In all but a few cases, taking a harmful substance such as cocaine is not meant to harm the fetus but to satisfy an acute psychological and physical need for that particular substance. If a pregnant woman suffers from a substance dependency, it is the physical impossibility of avoiding an impact on fetal health that causes severe damage to the fetus, not an intentional or malicious wish to cause harm." 264 JAMA at 2667–2668. Punishment is simply not an effective way of curing a dependency or preventing future substance abuse. Id. at 2667. See also National Treasury Employees Union, 109 S.Ct. at 1396 ("Addicts may be unable to abstain even for a limited period of time, or may be unaware of the 'fade-away affect' of certain drugs."). Stated another way: However the initial use of a drug might be characterized, its continued use by addicts is rarely, if any, truly voluntarily. Drug addiction tends to obliterate rational, autonomous decision making about drug use. Drugs become a necessity for dependent users, even when they would much prefer to escape their addiction. In virtually all instances, a user specifically does not want to harm her fetus, yet she cannot resist the drive to use the drug. Thus it is not plausible to attribute to drug-using women a motive of causing harm to the fetus. Mariner, Glantz and Annas, Pregnancy, Drugs and the Perils of Prosecution, 9 Criminal Justice Ethics 30, 36 (Winter/Spring 1990).

deliver these babies "at home" will have tragic and serious consequences. As the Board of Trustees Reports notes:

> [C]riminal penalties may exacerbate the harm done to fetal health by deterring pregnant substance abusers from obtaining help or care from either the health or public welfare professions, the very people who are best able to prevent future abuse. The California Medical Association has noted:
>
> > While unhealthy behavior cannot be condoned, to bring criminal charges against a pregnant woman for activities which may be harmful to her fetus is inappropriate. Such prosecution is counter-productive to the public interest as it may discourage a woman from seeking prenatal care or dissuade her from providing accurate information to health care providers out of fear of self-incrimination. This failure to seek proper care or to withhold vital information concerning her health could increase the risks to herself and her baby.
>
> > Florida's Secretary of Health and Rehabilitative Services has also observed that potential prosecution under existing child abuse or drug use statutes already "makes many potential reporters reluctant to identify women as substance abusers." (footnotes omitted)

264 JAMA at 2669. See also Commonwealth v. Pellegrini, No. 87970 (Mass. Superior Court Oct. 15, 1990) (by imposing criminal sanctions, women may turn away from seeking prenatal care for fear of being discovered, undermining the interests of the state in protecting potential human life). Prosecution of pregnant women for engaging in activities harmful to their fetuses or newborns may also unwittingly increase the incidence of abortion.[5]

Such considerations have led the American Medical Association Board of Trustees to oppose criminal sanctions for harmful behavior by a pregnant woman toward her fetus and to advocate that pregnant substance abusers be provided with rehabilitative treatment appropriate to their specific psychological and physiological needs. 264 JAMA at 2670. Likewise, the American Public Health Association has adopted the view that the use of illegal drugs by pregnant women is a public health problem. It also recommends that no punitive measures be taken against pregnant women who are users of illicit drugs when no other illegal acts, including drug-related offenses, have been committed. See 1990 Policy Statement.

In summary, I would hold that section 893.13(1)(c)1. does not encompass "delivery" of an illegal drug derivative from womb to placenta to umbilical cord to newborn after a child's birth. If that is the intent of the Legislature, then this statute should be redrafted to clearly address the basic problem of passing illegal substances from mother to child in utero, not just in the birthing process.

---

5. See 264 JAMA at 2667; Rush, Prenatal Care Taking: Limits of State Intervention With and Without Roe, 39 Univ.Fla.L.Rev. 55, 68 n. 38 (1986). A woman could simply "opt out" of the scope of any criminal regulations by terminating the pregnancy through abortion. 39 Univ.Fla.L.Rev. at 68 n. 38.

. . . At oral argument the State acknowledged that no other jurisdiction has upheld a conviction of a mother for delivery of a controlled substance to an infant through either the umbilical cord or an *in utero* transmission; nor has the State submitted any subsequent authority to reflect that this fact has changed. The Court declines the State's invitation to walk down a path that the law, public policy, reason and common sense forbid it to tread. Therefore, we quash the decision below, answer the certified question in the negative, and remand with directions that Johnson's two convictions be reversed.

NOTES

(1) In *In re Valerie D.*, 223 Conn. 492, 613 A.2d 748 (1992), the Supreme Court of Connecticut held that its state law allowing termination of parental rights if a child has been denied care necessary for its well being by acts of parental commission or omission did not authorize termination of a mother's parental rights based on her injecting cocaine several hours before onset of labor. The court added that the state could not terminate parental rights where assertion of custody over the child immediately after birth led directly to the condition. For further discussion, see Jennifer M. Mone, Has Connecticut Thrown out the Baby with the Bath Water? Termination of Parental Rights and *Valerie D.*, 19 Fordham Urb.L.J. 535 (1992).

(2) How to cope with what is described by some as "fetal abuse" is a subject of increasing controversy. The term describes maternal conduct during pregnancy that would endanger a child's health or development. Most prominent is substance abuse leading to fetal alcohol syndrome or impairment from cocaine.

A few states have modified their child protection laws to provide greater latitude in dealing with substance abuse affected children immediately after birth. See, e.g., 10 Okla.Stat.Ann. § 7001–1.3, which includes under the definition of "injury" the following:

> a child who at birth tests positive for alcohol or a controlled dangerous substance and who, pursuant to a drug or alcohol screen of the child and an assessment of the parent, is determined to be at risk for future exposure to such substances. . . .

Provisions such as these may be used to intervene after birth for the protection of such children. However, some persons would like to take measures to protect the fetus before birth at least in cases of extreme or well defined danger. This obviously raises serious legal and ethical questions about the extent to which the state can intervene to regulate maternal life styles and habits. In a widely publicized case in the District of Columbia during 1988, a pregnant woman was convicted of forging some $700 in checks and sentenced to jail during the remainder of her pregnancy. The checks were against an account of her employer, who previously had paid for a private rehabilitation program to help the employee deal with cocaine addiction. The judge explained that even though the offense normally might not have resulted in a jail term, the purpose was to protect the fetus against the mother's cocaine use. See Washington Post, July 23, 1988, page 1, col. 1. The mother remained in jail until she went to the hospital and gave birth to a normal child.

Authority to take affirmative action before birth has been asserted by some courts in requiring a Caesarean section over a mother's objection—cases that remain controversial. See, e.g., *Jefferson v. Griffin Spalding County Hospital Authority*, 247 Ga. 86, 274 S.E.2d 457 (1981). However, in *In re A.C.*, 573 A.2d 1235 (1990), the D.C. Court of Appeals held that when a pregnant patient with a viable fetus is near death, the decision whether to undergo a Caesarean is for the patient to make unless she is incompetent or unable to give informed consent. In the latter instance, according to the court, her decision must be ascertained through substituted judgment. The court explained their view of such a process:

> . . . [T]o determine the subjective desires of the patient, the court must consider the totality of the evidence, focusing particularly on written or oral directions concerning treatment to family, friends, and health-care professionals. The court should also take into account the patient's past decisions regarding medical treatment, and attempt to ascertain from what is known about the patient's value system, goals, and desires what the patient would decide if competent.
>
> After considering the patient's prior statements, if any, the previous medical decisions of the patient, and the values held by the patient, the court may still be unsure what course the patient would choose. In such circumstances the court may supplement its knowledge about the patient by determining what most persons would likely do in a similar situation. When the patient is pregnant, however, she may not be concerned exclusively with her own welfare. Thus it is proper for the court, in a case such as this, to weigh (along with all the other factors) the mother's prognosis, the viability of the fetus, the probable result of treatment or non-treatment for both mother and fetus, and the mother's likely interest in avoiding impairment for her child together with her own instincts for survival.
>
> Additionally, the court should consider the context in which prior declarations, treatment decisions, and expressions of personal values were made, including whether statements were made casually or after contemplation, or in accordance with deeply held beliefs. Finally, in making a substituted judgment, the court should become as informed about the patient's condition, prognosis, and treatment options as one would expect any patient to become before making a treatment decision. Obviously, the weight accorded to all of these factors will vary from case to case.

573 A.2d at 1251.

For more detailed review of some of the medical, social, and legal issues, see Fetal Alcohol Syndrome: Diagnosis, Epidemiology, Prevention, and Treatment, Institute of Medicine (National Academy Press 1966); Bonnie I. Robin–Vergeer, Note, The Problem of the Drug–Exposed Newborn: A Return to Principled Intervention, 42 Stan.L.Rev. 745 (1990); and Note, Maternal Rights and Fetal Wrongs: The Case Against the Criminalization of "Fetal Abuse", 101 Harv.L.Rev. 994 (1988).

F.   Special Evidentiary Problems

Steward v. State

Supreme Court of Indiana, 1995.
652 N.E.2d 490.

■ DICKSON, JUSTICE.

In prosecutions for child molesting, is child sexual abuse syndrome, profile, or pattern evidence admissible to prove that child abuse occurred? To address this important question, we grant transfer.

Defendant Bobby Joe Steward was convicted of two counts of child molesting, one involving victim S.M. and the other involving victim A.M. In his appeal from the convictions, the defendant presented multiple issues. Our Court of Appeals affirmed the defendant's conviction for molesting A.M. but reversed the conviction relating to S.M. because the trial court unconstitutionally excluded evidence of allegations claimed to have been made by S.M. that she had been molested by others, proffered by the defendant to offer an alternative explanation for the State's evidence that her behavior was consistent with that of a victim of sexual abuse. Steward v. State (1994), Ind.App., 636 N.E.2d 143. As to those issues addressed by the Court of Appeals, we summarily affirm pursuant to Indiana Appellate Rule 11(B)(3).

In his briefs to this Court and the Court of Appeals, the defendant argues that expert testimony regarding the child sexual abuse syndrome is unreliable and unscientific and thus inadmissible, citing, inter alia, Indiana Evidence Rule 702; Daubert v. Merrell Dow Pharmaceuticals, Inc. (1993), 113 S.Ct. 2786 (1992), 529 Pa. 168, 602 A.2d 830; and State v. Rimmasch (1989), Utah, 775 P.2d 388. In his transfer petition, the defendant asserts that the Court of Appeals failed to address this argument.

The Court of Appeals discussed the possible problems with the use of such syndrome evidence for the purpose of vouching for a victim's credibility, correctly noting that a witness may not testify that another is or is not telling the truth, Steward, 636 N.E.2d at 146–47; see Ind.Evidence Rule 704(b), but finding that the defendant waived this claim of error by failing to make a timely objection. Steward, 636 N.E.2d at 147. We grant transfer solely to address the defendant's further argument that, regardless of the resolution of the vouching issue, such syndrome testimony is scientifically unreliable evidence and is thus inadmissible. This is an important question likely to arise in future cases, including the retrial of this defendant.[1]

The defendant, a 52–year-old police officer and family friend of the alleged victims, was convicted of one count of child molesting, a class C felony, for performing sexual intercourse with S.M. when she was 15 years of age;[2] acquitted of three other counts of child molesting as to S.M.; and convicted of child molesting, a class D felony, for touching and/or fondling S.M.'s 13–year-old sister, A.M., with the intent to arouse sexual desires.[3]

As noted by the Court of Appeals, the State presented evidence at trial that S.M.'s behavior was consistent with that of other victims of child

---

1. In support of this transfer petition, the defendant further contends that his conviction for the child molesting of A.M. should be reversed because the child sexual abuse syndrome evidence, although directly relating only to S.M., generally prejudiced the defendant by bolstering the credibility of the State's witnesses, impliedly bolstering S.M.'s testimony, and strengthening the State's portrayal of the defendant as a sexual deviant. As to his conviction for molesting A.M., we agree with the Court of Appeals's finding that by failing to object to the testimony, the

defendant waived his claim, Steward, 636 N.E.2d at 147; and we find that no fundamental error occurred.

2. Ind.Code Ann. § 35–42–4–3(c) (West 1986). This statute was substantially amended in 1994. See Ind.Code Ann. § 35–42–4–3 (West Supp.1994).

3. Ind.Code Ann. § 35–42–4–3(d) (West 1986). This section was substantially amended in 1994. See Ind.Code Ann. § 35–42–4–3 (West Supp.1994).

sexual abuse in order to prove that sexual contact occurred. Steward, 636 N.E.2d at 149–50. The State called Betty Watson, Ph.D., a licensed clinical psychologist with considerable professional experience who had provided treatment for S.M. After stating that common traits or behavioral symptoms are found in teenagers who have experienced sexual abuse, Record at 1276, Dr. Watson testified that S.M. exhibited such symptoms, identifying poor self-esteem, "family problems," association with an older peer group, depression, leaving home without permission, and problems with school behavior and performance. Record at 1277–83.

The State also presented testimony from Michael S. Girton, a minister and executive director of a licensed group residential treatment facility, and his wife, Katherine R. Girton, a caseworker at the facility. After establishing that Rev. Girton had taken courses in "sexual abuse work," including "being able to identify sexual abuse," the State asked him whether, based upon his personal experience, "kids who have known incidents of sexual abuse exhibit certain traits or characteristics or behavior patterns." Record at 1378. Rev. Girton answered, "Yes," and described the following types of behavior that he looks for "in the characterization of sexual abuse": Anything for medical reasons, from bladder infections to abnormal medical problems, and more of the characteristics, the girls can be anything from promiscuous, they can be very timid, they can come in with extremely low esteem. Almost exclusively, that is going to be a major characteristic. Some of the different cues can range in areas from being really over timid to different kind of touches and approaches, where you would approach them in different directions or from different manners or methods. You might even put your hand on their shoulder and that might freak them out or something. There is a lot of different areas where just working with them it becomes really quite evident. You can see that behavior demonstrated quite plainly. Record at 1378–79. Both Rev. and Mrs. Girton testified that there was a marked change in S.M.'s behavior immediately after S.M. disclosed to them and to Dr. Watson that she had had a sexual relationship with the defendant. Record at 1322, 1324–26, 1400–01.

The defendant argues that testimony concerning similarities between S.M.'s behaviors and those of known child abuse victims is not scientifically reliable evidence to prove S.M. was sexually abused and is therefore inadmissible.

1. The Problem

The admissibility of expert testimony regarding child sexual abuse syndrome evidence is controversial and has received substantial criticism. Recognition of the prevalence of child sexual abuse and intensive study of the problem by behavioral scientists did not begin until the mid–1970s. David McCord, Expert Psychological Testimony About Child Complainants in Sexual Abuse Prosecutions: A Foray Into the Admissibility of Novel Psychological Evidence, 77 J.Crim.L. & Criminology 1, 2–3 (1986). The Child Sexual Abuse Accommodation Syndrome (CSAAS) was first identified by Dr. Roland Summit in a 1983 article in which he described five experiences typically occurring in sexually abused children: (1) secrecy about the sexual abuse, often ensured by threats of negative consequences of disclosure; (2) emotional helplessness to resist or complain; (3) entrapment and accommodation, where the child sees no way to escape ongoing abuse and thus learns to adapt; (4) delayed, conflicted, and unconvincing disclosure of the abuse; and (5) retraction of the child's allegations in an attempt to restore order to the family structure when the disclosure threatens to destroy it. Roland C. Summit, The Child Sexual Abuse Accommodation Syndrome, 7 Child Abuse & Neglect 177, 181–88 (1983). [hereinafter Summit, The CSAAS]. Summit has noted that, since his original identification and description of CSAAS, which he refers to as "a clinical observation," it "has become both elevated as gospel and denounced as dangerous pseudoscience." Roland C. Summit, Abuse of the Child Sexual Abuse Accommodation Syndrome, 1 J. of Child Sexual Abuse 153, 153 (1992) [hereinafter Summit, Abuse of the CSAAS]. The syndrome was not intended as a diagnostic device and does not detect sexual abuse. John E.B. Myers et al.,[4] Expert Testimony in Child Sexual Abuse Litigation, 68 Neb.L.Rev. 1, 67 (1989). Rather, the syndrome was designed for purposes of treating child victims and offering them more effective assistance "within the family and within the systems of child protection and criminal justice," Summit, The CSAAS, supra, at 179–80, and helps to explain reactions—such as recanting or delayed reporting—of children assumed to have experienced abuse. Myers et al., supra, at 67–68.

Because children's responses to sexual abuse vary widely, and because many of the characteristics identified by CSAAS, or by similar victim behavior groupings, may result from causes unrelated to abuse, diagnostic use of syndrome evidence in courtrooms poses serious accuracy problems. See State v. Foret (1993), La., 628 So.2d 1116, 1124–27; State v. J.Q. (1991), App.Div., 252 N.J.Super. 11, 599 A.2d 172, 181–82 [hereinafter "J.Q. I"], aff'd (1993), 130 N.J. 554, 617 A.2d 1196 [hereinafter "J.Q. II"]; Dunkle, 602 A.2d at 833–35; Rimmasch, 775 P.2d at 401–02. See also Josephine Bulkley, Legal Proceedings, Reforms, and Emerging Issues in Child Sexual Abuse Cases, 6 Behavioral Sci. & L. 153, 174–75; David Finkelhor, Early and Long–Term Effects of Child Sexual Abuse: An Update, 21 Prof.Psych.Res. & Prec. 325, 328–29 (1990); McCord, supra, at 18–24; Myers et al., supra, at 67–68. The syndrome's discoverer has noted, "Adversarial rivals seem determined to enhance it or to destroy it according to their designated role." Summit, Abuse of the CSAAS, supra, at 156. Summit explains that: some criticism has been a legitimate defense against

4. Myers is listed as a Professor of Law at the McGeorge School of Law, University of the Pacific, in Sacramento, California. The expertise of his co-authors is widespread and varied. At the time of publication, their credentials included: Jan Bays, M.D. and F.A.A.P., Medical Director of Child Abuse Programs at Emmanuel Hospital and Health Center, Portland, Oregon; Judith Becker, Ph. D., Professor of Clinical Psychology at Columbia University's College of Physicians and Surgeons and Director of the Sexual Behavior Clinic, New York Psychiatric Institute; Lucy Berliner, M.S.W., Assistant Clinical Professor of Social Work at the University of Washington's College of Social Work, and Research Director of Harborview Sexual Assault Center in Seattle, Washington; David L. Corwin, M.D., psychiatric consultant to the Multidisciplinary Child Abuse Team at Children's Hospital, Oakland, California, and a child psychiatrist in private practice; and Karen J. Saywitz, Ph.D., Assistant Professor of Psychiatry at UCLA School of Medicine and the Director of Child and Adolescent Psychology Services in the Division of Child and Adolescent Psychiatry, Harbor/UCLA Medical Center, Los Angeles.

improper use by prosecutors and expert witnesses called by prosecution. There has been some tendency to use the CSAAS as an offer of proof that a child has been abused. A child may be said to be suffering from or displaying the CSAAS, as if it is a malady that proves the alleged abuse. Or a child's conspicuous helplessness or silence might be said to be consistent with the CSAAS, as if not complaining proves the complaint. Some have contended that a child who retracts is a more believable victim than one who has maintained a consistent complaint. Summit, Abuse of the CSAAS, supra, at 159–60. Our discussion today encompasses not only CSAAS but also similar descriptions of "typical" behavior profiles or patterns, whether or not termed "syndromes," all of which we shall refer to generally as "child sexual abuse syndrome," or "syndrome evidence."[5]

Courts have witnessed the presentation of child sexual abuse syndrome evidence for three major purposes: (1) to prove directly—through either implication or explicit testimony of the expert's conclusion—the fact that abuse actually occurred; (2) to counter claims that the testimony or behavior of alleged victims is inconsistent with abuse or otherwise not credible; and (3) to opine that, because the behavioral characteristics of the child comport with the syndrome profile, the child is likely to be telling the truth. In this opinion we explore the first and second of these applications and summarily affirm the Court of Appeals decision as to the third.

Trial and appellate courts face the challenge of determining under what circumstances, if any, such evidence is admissible, acutely aware of the potentially severe consequences of error in either direction. This challenge is heightened by the distinctive evidentiary problems posed by prosecutions for child sexual abuse: Often these cases pit the word of a traumatized child against that of an adult. Child sexual abuse typically occurs in private, when the abuser is confident that there will be no witnesses. Therefore, the child victim is usually the only eyewitness. The prosecution's case is severely hampered if the court finds the child to be too young to be a witness or incompetent to testify. Even if the child does testify, several factors often limit the effectiveness of this testimony. The child's cognitive and verbal abilities may not enable her to give consistent, spontaneous, and detailed reports of her sexual abuse. A child who must testify against a trusted adult, such as a parent or relative, may experience feelings of fear and ambivalence, and may retract her story because of family pressures or insensitivities in the legal process. Prosecutors face another dilemma when offering the child victim as a witness if the child has delayed reporting the abuse. Jurors may interpret delayed disclosure as evidence of fabrication, especially if defense counsel suggests this conclusion during cross-examination of the child. Further, jurors may hold misconceptions that the child has memory deficits, is suggestible, cannot distinguish between fact or fantasy, or is likely to fabricate sexual experi-

---

5. The Pennsylvania Supreme Court, for instance, grouped together with CSAAS syndrome phenomena known as "Sexually Abused Child Syndrome" and "the Child Abuse Syndrome." Dunkle, 602 A.2d at 832. It should be noted that our analysis today is not applicable to battered child syndrome, which identifies signs—including various physical symptoms and their inconsistency with a story about accidental injury—of physical child abuse and is generally considered a sound diagnostic tool. See id. at 835–36; Rimmasch, 775 P.2d at 400–01; Myers et al., supra, at 67.

ences with adults. These problems are compounded by the lack of corroborative physical or mental evidence in many child sexual abuse cases. Lisa R. Askowitz, Comment, Restricting the Admissibility of Expert Testimony in Child Sexual Abuse Prosecutions: Pennsylvania Takes it to the Extreme, 47 U.Miami L.Rev. 201, 201–03 (1992) (footnotes omitted).

The utilization of innovative methodologies to address these problems must be balanced with "the preservation of the constitutional right to presumption of innocence in a criminal case." See People v. Leon (1989), Cal.Ct.App., 263 Cal.Rptr. 77, 86. As the Supreme Court of Utah has noted: the fact that child sexual abuse has emerged as a critical problem about which the public is seriously concerned does not mean all legal rules that may constitute obstacles to increasing the conviction and incarceration rates of those accused of such crimes, as opposed to those actually guilty, can properly be brushed aside. Rimmasch, 775 P.2d at 390. Similarly, the Delaware Supreme Court has observed: a sexual abuse charge by itself imposes a stigma on the accused and conviction provides a serious penalty. In interpreting our rules of evidence, we must be aware not only of the needs of society in general but also the defendant's right to a fair trial. Wheat v. State (1987), Del., 527 A.2d 269, 275. The particular dilemma expert testimony poses in these emotionally charged cases has been aptly described by the Supreme Court of Michigan: Given the nature of the offense and the terrible consequences of a miscalculation—the consequences when an individual, on many occasions a family member, is falsely accused of one of society's most heinous offenses, or, conversely, when one who commits such a crime would go unpunished and a possible reoccurrence of the act would go unprevented—appropriate safeguards are necessary. To a jury recognizing the awesome dilemma of whom to believe, an expert will often represent the only seemingly objective source, offering it a much sought-after hook on which to hang its hat. People v. Beckley (1990), 434 Mich. 691, 456 N.W.2d 391, 404.

2. Other States' Approaches

A few decisions from other states have held child sexual abuse syndrome evidence inadmissible for any purpose, and some cases have permitted expert testimony opining that, because of the correlation between a child's behavior and the syndrome, the child has been sexually abused. Most jurisdictions, however, have settled somewhere between these two extremes.

A significant number of state courts have recognized as a misuse of the syndrome the admission of child sexual abuse syndrome testimony as substantive proof that abuse has been detected in a particular case. Wisconsin courts, for instance, have rejected the use of testimony that the defendant's daughter was "a typical case of intrafamilial sexual abuse" and thus an incest victim, State v. Haseltine (1984), Wis.Ct.App., 120 Wis.2d 92, 352 N.W.2d 673, 675, and have held to be error the admission of expert testimony that a complainant's behavior following an alleged sexual assault was proof that the assault occurred, State v. Jensen (1987), Wis.Ct.App., 141 Wis.2d 333, 415 N.W.2d 519 (requiring evidence of abuse and of seemingly contradictory behavior by complainant as a foundation for admitting syndrome evidence), aff'd (1988), 147 Wis.2d 240, 432 N.W.2d 913. The Arkansas Supreme Court held that a trial court erred in permitting an expert to testify that, in part because the victim's history was consistent with the doctor's experiences dealing with child abuse, he believed that abuse had occurred. Johnson v. State (1987), 292 Ark. 632, 732 S.W.2d 817.

Other cases that have likewise rejected the use of syndrome evidence as affirmative proof of the occurrence of abuse include: People v. Bowker (1988), 203 Cal.App.3d 385, 249 Cal.Rptr. 886; Leon, 263 Cal.Rptr. 77; Lantrip v. Commonwealth (1986), Ky., 713 S.W.2d 816; State v. York (1989), Me., 564 A.2d 389; State v. Lawrence (1988), Me., 541 A.2d 1291; State v. Black (1988), Me., 537 A.2d 1154; Goodson v. State (1990), Miss., 566 So.2d 1142; J.Q. II, 617 A.2d 1196; State v. Michaels (1993), App.Div., 264 N.J.Super. 579, 625 A.2d 489, aff'd (1994), 136 N.J. 299, 642 A.2d 1372; People v. Duell (1990), 163 A.D.2d 866, 558 N.Y.S.2d 395; State v. Schimpf (1989), Tenn.Crim.App., 782 S.W.2d 186; Rimmasch, 775 P.2d 388; State v. Gokey (1990), 154 Vt. 129, 574 A.2d 766; State v. Jones (1993), 71 Wash.App. 798, 863 P.2d 85, review denied (1994), 124 Wash.2d 1018, 881 P.2d 254.

Additional disagreement exists on the issue of the admissibility of syndrome evidence where the expert merely describes certain behavioral characteristics as being consistent with sexual abuse, thereby offering direct proof through implication, rather than where the expert explicitly draws the conclusion for the jury. Numerous cases have ruled such implication evidence inadmissible as proof that an assault occurred. In contrast, other jurisdictions have ruled in favor of admissibility where the expert presents evidence of abuse through implication but refrains from giving an explicit opinion on whether abuse occurred.

It is important to recognize that syndrome evidence is not similarly problematic in all situations. The reliability of syndrome evidence, although highly questionable for purposes of affirmatively proving sexual abuse, is generally accepted for purposes of helping the jury to understand that a complainant's reactions are not atypical of a young sexual assault victim. As the Myers article notes: The accommodation syndrome has a place in the courtroom. The syndrome helps explain why many sexually abused children delay reporting their abuse, and why many children recant allegations of abuse and deny that anything occurred. If use of the syndrome is confined to these rehabilitative functions, the confusion clears, and the accommodation syndrome serves a useful forensic purpose. Myers et al., supra, at 67–68. Thus, behavioral characteristics of child abuse victims, even where inadmissible to prove abuse, are far less controversial when offered to rebut a claim by the defense that a child complainant's behavior—such as delayed reporting or retracting allegations—is inconsistent with her claim of abuse. This more limited, but nonetheless important, purpose is in harmony with the syndrome's original mission. Indeed, "[a] myriad of expert writings in the psychology field have countenanced" such use of the evidence, which has "received nearly universal judicial approval." J.Q. I, 599 A.2d at 183; see also Myers et al., supra, at 68.

The following cases, for example, have allowed expert testimony to explain failures to report or delays in reporting incidents of abuse or sexual assault; Bostic v. State (1989), Alaska Ct.App., 772 P.2d 1089, rev'd on other grounds (1991), Alaska, 805 P.2d 344; People v. Hampton (1987), Colo., 746 P.2d 947; People v. Matlock (1986), 153 Mich.App. 171, 395 N.W.2d 274; State v. Sandberg (1987), Minn., 406 N.W.2d 506; Smith v. State (1984), 100 Nev. 570, 688 P.2d 326; State v. Garfield (1986), 34 Ohio App.3d 300, 518 N.E.2d 568, 571; State v. Hicks (1987), 148 Vt. 459, 535 A.2d 776, 777–78; Scadden v. State (1987), Wyo., 732 P.2d 1036, 1047. Several state decisions have allowed such expert testimony to explain recantations or other apparent inconsistencies in children's reports or behavior. See Moran, 728 P.2d at 251–52, 254; Black, 537 A.2d at 1156; State v. Rogers (1987), 293 S.C. 505, 362 S.E.2d 7, 8, overruled in part by State v. Schumpert (1993), S.C., 435 S.E.2d 859, 862 n. 1; Griego v. State (1988), Wyo., 761 P.2d 973. Other cases permitting syndrome testimony to be utilized for rehabilitation purposes include: Bowker, 249 Cal.Rptr. at 891–92; Wheat, 527 A.2d at 273–75; Beckley, 456 N.W.2d at 399; State v. Myers (1984), Minn., 359 N.W.2d 604, 609–10; J.Q. II, 617 A.2d at 1209; State v. Middleton (1983), 290 Or. 427, 657 P.2d 1215, 1221; State v. Hudnall (1987), 293 S.C. 97, 359 S.E.2d 59, overruled in part by State v. Schumpert (1993), S.C., 435 S.E.2d 859, 862; Jones, 863 P.2d at 98–99.

Many of these courts have differentiated between admitting such evidence to explain the victim's seemingly suspicious behaviors and admitting it to prove that abuse occurred. See, e.g., Moran, 728 P.2d at 251–52 (approving expert testimony to rehabilitate child but not testimony that the alleged victim is telling the truth); Bowker, 249 Cal.Rptr. at 891–92 (permitting expert testimony's use to rehabilitate witness concerning delays and recantation but directing that jury be instructed not to use the testimony to determine whether the victim was molested); Matlock, 395 N.W.2d at 277–78 (limiting expert testimony to rehabilitation concerning delays while precluding it to prove abuse or confirm truthfulness of witness).

The use of syndrome evidence for rehabilitative purposes has not met with universal approval. In Dunkle, the Pennsylvania Supreme Court prohibited from admission in child sexual abuse cases essentially all expert testimony concerning behavior patterns. Dunkle, 602 A.2d 830.[6] Dunkle's approach is noteworthy because much of the expert testimony excluded seems to have been offered for rehabilitative, not diagnostic, purposes. The evidence sought to explain in general terms, without reference to the alleged victim, "why a victim would delay reporting an offense, why a victim might be unable to recall exact dates and times of an alleged offense, and why victims of sexual abuse omitted details of the incident when they first told their stor[ies]." Dunkle, 602 A.2d at 831. Permitting such evidence, the Dunkle court believed, "would infringe upon the jury's right to determine credibility," because the reasons for delay, inconsistencies, and omissions in victims' allegations "are easily understood by lay people and do not require expert analysis." Id. at 836–37. Such a complete exclusion of child sexual abuse syndrome evidence for any purpose is generally not

6. See also Hester v. Commonwealth, Ky., 734 S.W.2d 457, cert. denied (1987), 484 U.S. 989, 108 S.Ct. 510, 98 L.Ed.2d 508; Mitchell v. Commonwealth (1989), Ky., 777 S.W.2d 930.

favored. See Myers et al., supra, at 89, 92–93 (recognizing need for expert testimony to counteract jurors' commonly held misconceptions about sexual abuse and to explain emotional reactions that cause children's seemingly self-impeaching behavior).

A contrasting approach has been taken by the Michigan Supreme Court. While finding syndrome evidence admissible when a victim's behavior becomes an issue in a case, it noted that: the evidence has a very limited use and should be admitted cautiously because of the danger of permitting an inference that as a result of certain behavior sexual abuse in fact occurred, when evidence of the syndrome is not a conclusive finding of abuse. Although syndrome evidence may be appropriate as a tool for purposes of treatment, we hold that it is unreliable as an indicator of sexual abuse. Beckley, 456 N.W.2d at 406. The Michigan court allowed the testimony "to give the jury a framework of possible alternatives for the behaviors of the victim at issue," and to assist the jury in "dispelling any popular misconception commonly associated with the demonstrated reaction." Id. The court cautioned that: to assist the jury in understanding the unique reactions of victims of sexual assault, the testimony should be limited to whether the behavior of this particular victim is common to the class of reported child abuse victims. The expert's evaluation of the individual behavior traits at issue is not centered on what was observed in this victim, but rather whether the behavioral sciences recognize this behavior as being a common reaction to a unique criminal act. Id. at 406–07. The Beckley court warned: Given the abhorrence of the crime, it is inevitable that those who treat a child victim will have an emotional inclination toward protecting the child victim. The expert who treats a child victim may lose some objectivity concerning a particular case. Therefore to avoid the pitfall of the treating professional being inclined to give an opinion regarding whether the complaining witness had been sexually abused, we caution the trial court to carefully scrutinize the treating professional's ability to aid the trier of fact when exercising discretion and qualifying such an expert witness. Beckley, 456 N.W.2d at 408. The Michigan Supreme Court concluded that it was unwilling to have "the so-called child sexual abuse syndrome . . . introduced as a scientific tool, standing on its own merits as a doctrine or benchmark for determining causality in child sexual abuse cases." Id. at 409. However, it also held that: persons otherwise properly qualified as experts in dealing with sexually abused children should be permitted to rely on their own experience and their knowledge of the experience of others to rebut an inference that specific behavioral patterns attributed to the victim are not [sic] uncharacteristic of the class of child sexual abuse victims. Such witnesses should be permitted to testify regarding characteristics of sexually abused children so long as it is without reference to a fixed set of behaviors constituting a "syndrome." Id.

Commentators have embraced judicial decisions rejecting the use of CSAAS to prove abuse and advocating limiting its use to explaining victim behaviors that are seemingly inconsistent with their allegations. See, e.g., Marian D. Hall, The Role of Psychologists as Experts in Cases Involving Allegations of Child Sexual Abuse, 23 Fam.L.Q. 451, 463 (1989) (noting that behavioral science research does not demonstrate the existence of an accurate method of identifying an individual child as having been sexually abused); McCord, supra, at 67 (advocating that the admissibility of expert opinion testimony be limited to explaining the complainant's unusual actions); Myers et al., supra, at 68 (identifying the utility of expert testimony on child sexual abuse syndrome to rehabilitate the credibility of victims whose behavior may appear self-impeaching).

3. Conclusion

The admissibility of child sexual abuse syndrome evidence will be primarily determined in the courts of this state in accordance with the provisions in the Indiana Rules of Evidence defining "relevant evidence," Evid.R. 401; declaring its general admissibility, Evid.R. 402; permitting exclusion due to the danger of unfair prejudice, Evid.R. 403; prohibiting opinions concerning witness truthfulness, Evid.R. 704(b); and, most particularly, prescribing the requirements for expert scientific testimony, Evid.R. 702.

Federal Rule of Evidence 702 was adopted as subsection (a) of the Indiana rule. Subsection (b) of the Indiana rule is unique in its express requirement that expert testimony must be based upon reliable scientific principles. (a) If scientific, technical, or other specialized knowledge will assist the trier of fact to understand the evidence or to determine a fact in issue, a witness qualified as an expert by knowledge, skill, experience, training, or education, may testify thereto in the form of an opinion or otherwise. (b) Expert scientific testimony is admissible only if the court is satisfied that the scientific principles upon which the expert testimony rests are reliable. Evid.R. 702.

The United States Supreme Court's Daubert decision, coincidentally handed down just weeks after Indiana's Rule 702(b) was adopted, interpreted Federal Rule of Evidence 702 as requiring that expert testimony "be supported by appropriate validation—i.e., 'good grounds,' based on what is known," and as "establish[ing] a standard of evidentiary reliability." Daubert, 509 U.S. at ___, 113 S.Ct. at 2795, 125 L.Ed.2d at 481. The concerns driving Daubert coincide with the express requirement of Indiana Rule of Evidence 702(b) that the trial court be satisfied of the reliability of the scientific principles involved. Thus, although not binding upon the determination of state evidentiary law issues, the federal evidence law of Daubert and its progeny is helpful to the bench and bar in applying Indiana Rule of Evidence 702(b). Of particular relevance to our inquiry here are Daubert's statements that "scientific validity for one purpose is not necessarily scientific validity for other, unrelated purposes," and that Federal Rule of Evidence 702 "requires a valid scientific connection to the pertinent inquiry as a precondition to admissibility." Id. at ___, 113 S.Ct. at 2796.

Child sexual abuse syndrome evidence must satisfy the reliability requirement of Rule 702(b) as well as the Rule 403 balancing test. Although relevant, evidence may be excluded if its probative value is substantially outweighed by the danger of unfair prejudice, confusion of the issues, misleading the jury, or by considerations of undue delay or needless presentation of cumulative evidence. Evid.R. 403. If determined to be sufficiently reliable to be eligible for admission into evidence as expert testimony, its probative value must also outweigh the danger that it will unfairly prejudice the defendant. As the U.S. Supreme Court pointed out in Daubert, Conjectures that are probably wrong are of little use ... in the project of reaching a quick, final, and binding legal judgment—often of great consequence—about a particular set of events in the past. We recognize that in practice, a gatekeeping role for the judge, no matter how flexible, inevitably on occasion will prevent the jury from learning of authentic insights and innovations. That, nevertheless, is the balance that is struck by Rules of Evidence designed not for the exhaustive search for cosmic understanding but for the particularized resolution of legal disputes. Daubert, 509 U.S. at ___, 113 S.Ct. at 2798.

Under Indiana Evidence Rule 702(b), expert scientific testimony is admissible only if reliability is demonstrated to the trial court. We agree with the Utah Supreme Court's observation in Rimmasch that reliability may be established either by judicial notice or, in its absence, by the proponent of the scientific testimony providing sufficient foundation to convince the trial court that the relevant scientific principles are reliable. Rimmasch, 775 P.2d at 403. This sort of inquiry is generally more appropriate for trial courts than for appellate resolution. While we, like the Utah Supreme Court, "do not mean to imply that [syndrome] testimony is unreliable as a matter of law," Rimmasch, 775 P.2d at 403, the reliability of such evidence for the purpose of proving abuse is at present extremely doubtful and the subject of substantial and widespread repudiation by courts and scientists. Accord Rimmasch, 775 P.2d at 403.

It is possible that foundational support may be discovered in the future which will expand the purposes for which such expert testimony may be deemed reliable. We echo the Mississippi Supreme Court in noting that "what should be emphasized about this view is that it renders dynamic the realm of expert opinion testimony. Should subsequent empirical research and scientific investigation yield a [diagnostic] child sexual abuse profile or syndrome." Goodson, 566 So.2d at 1146 n. 6, our trial courts may consider admitting that evidence for any use to which it may reliably be put.

Furthermore, we decline to distinguish between expert testimony which offers an unreserved conclusion that the child in question has been abused and that which merely uses syndrome evidence to imply the occurrence of abuse. Where a jury is confronted with evidence of an alleged child victim's behaviors, paired with expert testimony concerning similar syndrome behaviors, the invited inference—that the child was sexually abused because he or she fits the syndrome profile—will be as potentially misleading and equally as unreliable as expert testimony applying the syndrome to the facts of the case and stating outright the conclusion that a given child was abused. The danger of the jury misapplying syndrome evidence thus remains the same whether an expert expresses an explicit opinion that abuse has occurred or merely allows the jury to draw the final conclusion of abuse. Exclusion of such evidence is authorized by Indiana Rule of Evidence 403.

However, we recognize that, once a child's credibility is called into question, proper expert testimony may be appropriate. Daubert notes the importance of "a valid scientific connection to the pertinent inquiry as a precondition to admissibility." Daubert, 509 U.S. at ___, 113 S.Ct. at 2796 (emphasis added). Because research generally accepted as scientifically reliable recognizes that child victims of sexual abuse may exhibit unexpected behavior patterns seemingly inconsistent with the claim of abuse, such evidence may be permissible under Indiana Evidence Rule 702(a)'s authorization of "specialized knowledge [which] will assist the trier of fact to understand the evidence." Therefore, if the defense discusses or presents evidence of such unexpected behavior by the child, or if during trial testimony the child recants a prior allegation of abuse, a trial court may consider permitting expert testimony, if based upon reliable scientific principles, regarding the prevalence of the specific unexpected behavior within the general class of reported child abuse victims. To be admissible, such scientific evidence must assist the finder of fact in understanding a child's responses to abuse and satisfy the requirements of both Rule 702(b) and the Rule 403 balancing test.

We agree with the Arizona Supreme Court's assessment that when the relevant inquiry is the syndrome's reliability and probative value for rehabilitative and related purposes, "[s]uch evidence may harm defendant's interests, but we cannot say it is unfairly prejudicial; it merely informs jurors that commonly held assumptions are not necessarily accurate and allows them to fairly judge credibility." Moran, 728 P.2d at 251–52.

Transfer is granted. As to the issues addressed therein, the opinion of the Court of Appeals is summarily affirmed. We affirm, as did the Court of Appeals, the defendant's conviction for Child Molesting, a class D felony, and reverse his conviction for Child Molesting, a class C felony, and remand this cause for a new trial on the latter charge consistent with this opinion.

■ SHEPARD, C.J., and DEBRULER and SELBY, JJ., concur.

■ SULLIVAN, JUSTICE, dissenting.

Cases of alleged child abuse provide a particular challenge for the criminal justice system. If trials are genuine searches for truth, that truth must be sought in light of society's modern understanding of children.... Adults who assume that their own perceptions, motivations, and fears are universal cannot empathize with children caught between the horrors of sexual abuse and the criminal justice system. Adults who doubt children because of false assumptions about their perception, memory, suggestibility, and truthfulness cannot fairly evaluate their testimony in the courtroom. Billie W. Dziech and Charles B. Schudson, On Trial: America's Courts and Their Treatment of Sexually Abused Children 53 (1991). Expert testimony has proved to be helpful in meeting this challenge. Recognizing that most jurors will not have experience that allows for a fully informed evaluation of a child's behavior and credibility, courts have thus permitted experts to help juries by testifying in three areas: (1) factors affecting credibility of children, (2) factors affecting behavior of child sexual abuse victims, (3) interpretations of special forms of child communication. Id. at 157.

I believe our rules of evidence provide a fair yet flexible regime for determining whether any particular expert testimony proffered on the subject of sexual abuse is admissible. Assuming that the proffered testimony is relevant and will assist the jury in understanding the evidence or a fact at issue, [and that the witness is properly qualified as an expert (issues not implicated by this case or by the majority opinion), the trial court must determine whether the scientific principles upon which the expert testimony rests are reliable.] As to the reliability of expert testimony concerning child sexual abuse accommodation syndrome and similar evidence, the majority sets general rules for the following three situations:

(1) Child sexual abuse accommodation syndrome evidence is presently not scientifically reliable enough to permit an expert to offer "an unreserved conclusion that the child in question has been abused."

(2) Child sexual abuse accommodation syndrome is also presently[5] not scientifically reliable enough to permit the use of expert testimony "merely . . . to imply the occurrence of abuse."

(3) However, child sexual abuse accommodation syndrome is presently scientifically reliable enough to permit the use of expert testimony to assist the factfinder in understanding a child's response to abuse when, but only when, the defense asserts or implies that the alleged child victim's conduct was inconsistent with the claim of abuse, or if the child recanted a prior allegation of abuse.

As to situation (1), I certainly agree that an expert may not comment directly on whether the child has been sexually abused or whether the child has testified truthfully. Ind.Evidence Rule 704. But as to situation (2), the Court of Appeals correctly pointed out that our rule has been that expert testimony that a putative rape victim's behavior was consistent with that of one who had in fact been raped merely tended to show that the victim had been raped and was not a direct opinion that the victim was telling the truth. Steward v. State (1994), Ind.App., 636 N.E.2d 143, 146–47 (citing Henson v. State (1989), Ind., 535 N.E.2d 1189, 1192–93). I see no basis for having different rules for child sexual abuse and for rape. And I also think that banning expert testimony because the "danger of the jury misapplying [the evidence] remains the same whether an expert expresses an explicit opinion . . . or merely allows the jury to draw the final conclusion" has very restrictive implications for expert testimony generally.

I acknowledge the majority's citation of Daubert's observation that scientific evidence can be reliable for one purpose but not another, Daubert v. Merrell Dow Pharmaceuticals, Inc., 113 S.Ct. 2786, 2796 (1993). It seems clear to me, however, that the purposes of the testimony in situations (2) and (3) are the same—to aid the jury in assessing the credibility of the child witness. While the former may be more prejudicial than the latter, that does not make the scientific principles upon which the former is based less reliable than the latter's.

I do not think we can say that the scientific principles upon which child sexual abuse accommodation syndrome is based are not reliable as direct evidence but are reliable as rebuttal evidence. In logic, either those

---

5. While the majority says that such evidence is not "unreliable as a matter of law," the majority would permit trial courts to consider admitting the evidence only if future empirical research and scientific investigation resolves present doubts about reliability.

principles are reliable for purposes of aiding the jury in assessing the child victim's credibility or they are not. The majority cites dozens of opinions where such evidence was found to be reliable, at least for rebuttal purposes, and I would hold that to the extent that that authority establishes its reliability for rebuttal evidence, it establishes it for direct evidence as well.

Once the trial court determines that expert testimony is admissible under Evidence Rule 702(b), the proffered testimony is still subject to challenge under Indiana Evidence Rule 403 which, as the majority points out, provides: Although relevant, evidence may be excluded if its probative value is substantially outweighed by the danger of unfair prejudice, confusion of the issues, misleading the jury, or by consideration of undue delay or needless presentation of cumulative evidence.

It is here, rather than under the rubric of scientific or expert testimony, that I think the real battle over the admissibility of child sexual abuse accommodation syndrome should be fought in most cases. We recently observed that scientific evidence is subject to particular scrutiny under Evidence Rule 403. Harrison v. State (1995), Ind., 644 N.E.2d 1243, 1252 (quoting Daubert, 509 U.S. at ___, 113 S.Ct. at 2798, and Cornett v. State (1983), Ind., 450 N.E.2d 498, 503). But whether any particular evidence violates Evidence Rule 403 is a matter first and foremost for the trial court to decide: we review only for an abuse of discretion. Evans v. State (1994), Ind., 643 N.E.2d 877, 880. While Daubert's progeny suggest some heightened scrutiny of such determinations is appropriate when scientific evidence is involved, In re: Paoli Railroad Yard PCB Litigation, 35 F.3d 717, 749–750 (3d Cir.1994), cert. denied sub nom. General Elec. Co. v. Ingram, 513 U.S. 1190, 115 S.Ct. 1253 (1995), I agree with the analysis given this evidence in this case by Judge Najam and concur in his view that it was not erroneous for the trial court to admit Dr. Watson's testimony.[6] More generally, I would hold that, while Evidence rule 704 prohibits the use of child sexual abuse accommodation syndrome evidence in situation (1), the reliability test of Evidence Rule 702(b) applies in the same way to such evidence in both situations (2) and (3), and that the admissibility of such evidence under Evidence Rule 403 is committed to the sound discretion of the trial court.

I would make one final observation. In Henson v. State, supra, this court reversed the conviction of an appellant convicted of rape on grounds that he was denied due process of law when the trial court refused to permit him to introduce evidence that the putative victim's conduct was not consistent with that which would have been predicted were she suffering from rape trauma syndrome. Henson, 504 N.E.2d at 1193–94. I cannot avoid the conclusion that today's opinion prohibits a defendant from offering child sexual abuse accommodation syndrome evidence in his own defense.

NOTES ON EVIDENCE OF CHILD ABUSE

(1) Is there a logical difference between (a) allowing an expert to testify that a child's behavior is evidence of abuse and (b) allowing an expert to testify that a

---

6. The majority does not explicitly conclude that Dr. Watson's testimony was erroneously admitted but that is the only inference I can draw from its opinion.

child's behavior is not inconsistent with abuse? The majority thinks there is a difference, and disapproves (a). The court approves (b), at least when the defense attacks the child's testimony or the child recants abuse. The dissent thinks there is no difference, and would allow both (a) and (b). Imagine that an expert testifies that children often recant abuse and that a recantation does not disprove abuse. Is this the same as testimony that a recantation increases the likelihood that abuse occurred? See See Thomas D. Lyon & Jonathan J. Koehler, The Relevance Ratio: Evaluating the Probative Value of Expert Testimony in Child Sexual Abuse Cases, 82 Cornell L.Rev. 43 (1996) (explaining the difference between proof of abuse and rehabilitative testimony, and noting a number of other errors in judicial reasoning).

(2) A number of studies have found that sexualized behavior is more common among abused children than among non-abused children. See, e.g., William N. Friedrich, et al., Child Sexual Behavior Inventory: Normative, Psychiatric, and Sexual Abuse Comparisons, 6 Child Maltreatment 37 (2001). Would the court in Steward allow expert testimony on the significance of sexualized behavior, or would it bar such testimony because such problems "may result from causes unrelated to abuse"? Can you think of any evidence of sexual abuse that couldn't "result from causes unrelated to abuse"? For example, imagine that the child testifies that abuse occurred. Couldn't the child be lying, or mistaken? Perhaps what the court in *Steward* is concerned about is behavior that is very common among nonabused children (such as the low self-esteem of the alleged victim), and commentary on such behavior by experts who may be very persuasive to the jury.

(3) Recently, the courts have seen an increasing number of expert witnesses offered by the defense to prove that children are highly suggestible. The experts will cite a large body of recent research documenting how children can be led to report and even believe events that never occurred. See e.g., Stephen J. Ceci & Richard D. Friedman, The Suggestibility of Children: Scientific Research and Legal Implications, 86 Cornell L.Rev. 33 (2000). Would expert testimony on the suggestibility of children violate the prohibition of opinions concerning the witness' truthfulness? Although some courts have excluded such testimony on this ground, many have allowed experts to testify about the suggestibility of children as a class, or to testify about the suggestibility of the questioner rather than the child. See Thomas D. Lyon, Expert Testimony on the Suggestibility of Children: Does it Fit? In Children, Social Science, and the Law 378 (Bette L. Bottoms, Margaret B. Kovera, Bradley D. McAuliff, Eds., 2002) How do you think the court in *Steward* would respond to these distinctions? One potentially important difference is that testimony on suggestibility is offered by the defense, and the courts will give criminal defendants more leeway than prosecutors to offer testimony on the credibility of prosecution witnesses.

Maryland v. Craig

Supreme Court of the United States, 1990.
497 U.S. 836, 110 S.Ct. 3157, 111 L.Ed.2d 666.

■ JUSTICE O'CONNOR delivered the opinion of the Court.

This case requires us to decide whether the Confrontation Clause of the Sixth Amendment categorically prohibits a child witness in a child abuse case from testifying against a defendant at trial, outside the defendant's physical presence, by one-way closed circuit television.

I

In October 1986, a Howard County grand jury charged respondent, Sandra Ann Craig, with child abuse, first and second degree sexual offenses, perverted sexual practice, assault, and battery. The named victim in each count was Brooke Etze, a six-year-old child who, from August 1984 to June 1986, had attended a kindergarten and prekindergarten center owned and operated by Craig.

In March 1987, before the case went to trial, the State sought to invoke a Maryland statutory procedure that permits a judge to receive, by one-way closed circuit television, the testimony of a child witness who is alleged to be a victim of child abuse.[1] To invoke the procedure, the trial judge must first "determin[e] that testimony by the child victim in the courtroom will result in the child suffering serious emotional distress such that the child cannot reasonably communicate." Md.Cts. & Jud.Proc. Code Ann. § 9–102(a)(1)(ii) (1989). Once the procedure is invoked, the child witness, prosecutor, and defense counsel withdraw to a separate room; the judge, jury, and defendant remain in the courtroom. The child witness is then examined and cross-examined in the separate room, while a video monitor records and displays the witness' testimony to those in the courtroom. During this time the witness cannot see the defendant. The defendant remains in electronic communication with defense counsel, and objections may be made and ruled on as if the witness were testifying in the courtroom.

In support of its motion invoking the one-way closed circuit television procedure, the State presented expert testimony that Brooke, as well as a number of other children who were alleged to have been sexually abused by Craig, would suffer "serious emotional distress such that [they could not]

---

1. Section 9–102 of the Courts and Judicial Proceedings Article of the Annotated Code of Maryland (1989) provides in full:

"(a)(1) In a case of abuse of a child as defined in § 5–701 of the Family Law Article or Article 27, § 35A of the Code, a court may order that the testimony of a child victim be taken outside the courtroom and shown in the courtroom by means of a closed circuit television if:

"(i) The testimony is taken during the proceeding; and

"(ii) The judge determines that testimony by the child victim in the courtroom will result in the child suffering serious emotional distress such that the child cannot reasonably communicate.

"(2) Only the prosecuting attorney, the attorney for the defendant, and the judge may question the child.

"(3) The operators of the closed circuit television shall make every effort to be unobtrusive.

"(b)(1) Only the following persons may be in the room with the child when the child testifies by closed circuit television:

"(i) The prosecuting attorney;

"(ii) The attorney for the defendant;

"(iii) The operators of the closed circuit television equipment; and

"(iv) Unless the defendant objects, any person whose presence, in the opinion of the court, contributes to the well-being of the child, including a person who has dealt with the child in a therapeutic setting concerning the abuse.

"(2) During the child's testimony by closed circuit television, the judge and the defendant shall be in the courtroom.

"(3) The judge and the defendant shall be allowed to communicate with the persons in the room where the child is testifying by any appropriate electronic method.

"(c) The provisions of this section do not apply if the defendant is an attorney pro se.

"(d) This section may not be interpreted to preclude, for purposes of identification of a defendant, the presence of both the victim and the defendant in the courtroom at the same time."

For a detailed description of the § 9–102 procedure, see Wildermuth v. State, 310 Md. 496, 503–504, 530 A.2d 275, 278–279 (1987).

reasonably communicate," § 9–102(a)(1)(ii), if required to testify in the courtroom. The Maryland Court of Appeals characterized the evidence as follows:

> "The expert testimony in each case suggested that each child would have some or considerable difficulty in testifying in Craig's presence. For example, as to one child, the expert said that what 'would cause him the most anxiety would be to testify in front of Mrs. Craig....' The child 'wouldn't be able to communicate effectively.' As to another, an expert said she 'would probably stop talking and she would withdraw and curl up.' With respect to two others, the testimony was that one would 'become highly agitated, that he may refuse to talk or if he did talk, that he would choose his subject regardless of the questions' while the other would 'become extremely timid and unwilling to talk.' " 316 Md. 551, 568–569, 560 A.2d 1120, 1128–1129 (1989).

Craig objected to the use of the procedure on Confrontation Clause grounds, but the trial court rejected that contention, concluding that although the statute "take[s] away the right of the defendant to be face to face with his or her accuser," the defendant retains the "essence of the right of confrontation," including the right to observe, cross-examine, and have the jury view the demeanor of the witness. App. 65–66. The trial court further found that, "based upon the evidence presented ... the testimony of each of these children in a courtroom will result in each child suffering serious emotional distress ... such that each of these children cannot reasonably communicate." Id., at 66, 560 A.2d 1120. The trial court then found Brooke and three other children competent to testify and accordingly permitted them to testify against Craig via the one-way closed circuit television procedure. The jury convicted Craig on all counts, and the Maryland Court of Special Appeals affirmed the convictions, 76 Md.App. 250, 544 A.2d 784 (1988).

The Court of Appeals of Maryland reversed and remanded for a new trial. 316 Md. 551, 560 A.2d 1120 (1989). The Court of Appeals rejected Craig's argument that the Confrontation Clause requires in all cases a face-to-face courtroom encounter between the accused and his accusers, id., at 556–562, 560 A.2d, at 1122–1125, but concluded:

> "[U]nder § 9–102(a)(1)(ii), the operative 'serious emotional distress' which renders a child victim unable to 'reasonably communicate' must be determined to arise, at least primarily, from face-to-face confrontation with the defendant. Thus, we construe the phrase 'in the courtroom' as meaning, for sixth amendment and [state constitution] confrontation purposes, 'in the courtroom in the presence of the defendant.' Unless prevention of 'eyeball-to-eyeball' confrontation is necessary to obtain the trial testimony of the child, the defendant cannot be denied that right." Id., at 566, 560 A.2d, at 1127.

. . .

We granted certiorari to resolve the important Confrontation Clause issues raised by this case. 493 U.S. 1041 (1990).

II

The Confrontation Clause of the Sixth Amendment, made applicable to the States through the Fourteenth Amendment, provides: "In all criminal prosecutions, the accused shall enjoy the right . . . to be confronted with the witnesses against him."

We observed in *Coy v. Iowa* that "the Confrontation Clause guarantees the defendant a face-to-face meeting with witnesses appearing before the trier of fact." [487 U.S. 1012, 1016 (1988)] (citing Kentucky v. Stincer, 482 U.S. 730, 748, 749–750 (1987) (Marshall, J., dissenting)). . . .

We have never held, however, that the Confrontation Clause guarantees criminal defendants the *absolute* right to a face-to-face meeting with witnesses against them at trial. Indeed, in *Coy v. Iowa,* we expressly "le[ft] for another day . . . the question whether any exceptions exist" to the "irreducible literal meaning of the Clause: 'a right to *meet face to face* all those who appear and give evidence *at trial.*' " 487 U.S., at 1021 (quoting [California v. Green, 399 U.S. 149, 175 (1970)] (Harlan, J., concurring)). The procedure challenged in *Coy* involved the placement of a screen that prevented two child witnesses in a child abuse case from seeing the defendant as they testified against him at trial. See 487 U.S., at 1014–1015. In holding that the use of this procedure violated the defendant's right to confront witnesses against him, we suggested that any exception to the right "would surely be allowed only when necessary to further an important public policy"—i.e., only upon a showing of something more than the generalized, "legislatively imposed presumption of trauma" underlying the statute at issue in that case. Id., at 1021; see also id., at 1025 (concurring opinion). We concluded that "[s]ince there ha[d] been no individualized findings that these particular witnesses needed special protection, the judgment [in the case before us] could not be sustained by any conceivable exception." Id., at 1021. Because the trial court in this case made individualized findings that each of the child witnesses needed special protection, this case requires us to decide the question reserved in *Coy.*

The central concern of the Confrontation Clause is to ensure the reliability of the evidence against a criminal defendant by subjecting it to rigorous testing in the context of an adversary proceeding before the trier of fact. The word "confront," after all, also means a clashing of forces or ideas, thus carrying with it the notion of adversariness. As we noted in our earliest case interpreting the Clause:

> "The primary object of the constitutional provision in question was to prevent depositions or *ex parte* affidavits, such as were sometimes admitted in civil cases, being used against the prisoner in lieu of a personal examination and cross-examination of the witness in which the accused has an opportunity, not only of testing the recollection and sifting the conscience of the witness, but of compelling him to stand face to face with the jury in order that they may look at him, and judge by his demeanor upon the stand and the manner in which he gives his testimony whether he is worthy of belief." [Mattox v. United States, 156 U.S. 237, 242–243 (1895).]

As this description indicates, the right guaranteed by the Confrontation Clause includes not only a "personal examination," id., at 242, but also "(1) insures that the witness will give his statements under oath—thus impressing him with the seriousness of the matter and guarding against the lie by the possibility of a penalty for perjury; (2) forces the witness to submit to cross-examination, the 'greatest legal engine ever invented for the discovery of truth'; [and] (3) permits the jury that is to decide the defendant's fate to observe the demeanor of the witness in making his statement, thus aiding the jury in assessing his credibility." *Green,* 399 U.S., at 158 (footnote omitted).

The combined effect of these elements of confrontation—physical presence, oath, cross-examination, and observation of demeanor by the trier of fact—serves the purposes of the Confrontation Clause by ensuring that evidence admitted against an accused is reliable and subject to the rigorous adversarial testing that is the norm of Anglo–American criminal proceedings. See *Stincer,* supra, at 739 ("[T]he right to confrontation is a functional one for the purpose of promoting reliability in a criminal trial").

. . .

We have recognized, for example, that face-to-face confrontation enhances the accuracy of factfinding by reducing the risk that a witness will wrongfully implicate an innocent person. See *Coy,* 487 U.S., at 1019–1020 ("It is always more difficult to tell a lie about a person 'to his face' than 'behind his back.' . . . That face-to-face presence may, unfortunately, upset the truthful rape victim or abused child; but by the same token it may confound and undo the false accuser, or reveal the child coached by a malevolent adult"); Ohio v. Roberts, 448 U.S., 56, 63, n. 6 (1980).

. . .

Although face-to-face confrontation forms, "the core of the values furthered by the Confrontation Clause," *Green,* supra, at 157, we have nevertheless recognized that it is not the *sine qua non* of the confrontation right. See Delaware v. Fensterer, 474 U.S. 15, 22 (1985) *(per curiam)* ("[T]he Confrontation Clause is generally satisfied when the defense is given a full and fair opportunity to probe and expose [testimonial] infirmities [such as forgetfulness, confusion, or evasion] through cross-examination, thereby calling to the attention of the factfinder the reasons for giving scant weight to the witness' testimony"); *Roberts,* supra, at 69 (oath, cross-examination, and demeanor provide "all that the Sixth Amendment demands: 'substantial compliance with the purposes behind the confrontation requirement' ").

. . .

For this reason, we have never insisted on an actual face-to-face encounter at trial in *every* instance in which testimony is admitted against a defendant. Instead, we have repeatedly held that the Clause permits, where necessary, the admission of certain hearsay statements against a defendant despite the defendant's inability to confront the declarant at trial. See, e.g., *Mattox,* 156 U.S., at 243.

. . .

In sum, our precedents establish that "the Confrontation Clause reflects a *preference* for face-to-face confrontation at trial," *Roberts,* supra, at 63 (emphasis added; footnote omitted), a preference that "must occasionally give way to considerations of public policy and the necessities of the case," *Mattox,* supra, at 243.

. . .

That the face-to-face confrontation requirement is not absolute does not, of course, mean that it may easily be dispensed with. As we suggested in *Coy,* our precedents confirm that a defendant's right to confront accusatory witnesses may be satisfied absent a physical, face-to-face confrontation at trial only where denial of such confrontation is necessary to further an important public policy and only where the reliability of the testimony is otherwise assured. See *Coy,* 487 U.S., at 1021 (citing *Roberts,* supra, at 64; [Chambers v. Mississippi, 410 U.S. 284, 295 (1973)]; *Coy,* supra, at 1025 (concurring opinion)).

III

Maryland's statutory procedure, when invoked, prevents a child witness from seeing the defendant as he or she testifies against the defendant at trial. We find it significant, however, that Maryland's procedure preserves all of the other elements of the confrontation right: the child witness must be competent to testify and must testify under oath; the defendant retains full opportunity for contemporaneous cross-examination; and the judge, jury, and defendant are able to view (albeit by video monitor) the demeanor (and body) of the witness as he or she testifies. Although we are mindful of the many subtle effects face-to-face confrontation may have on an adversary criminal proceeding, the presence of these other elements of confrontation—oath, cross-examination, and observation of the witness' demeanor—adequately ensures that the testimony is both reliable and subject to rigorous adversarial testing in a manner functionally equivalent to that accorded live, in-person testimony. These safeguards of reliability and adversariness render the use of such a procedure a far cry from the undisputed prohibition of the Confrontation Clause: trial by *ex parte* affidavit or inquisition, see *Mattox,* 156 U.S., at 242; see also *Green,* 399 U.S., at 179 (Harlan, J., concurring) ("[T]he Confrontation Clause was meant to constitutionalize a barrier against flagrant abuses, trials by anonymous accusers, and absentee witnesses"). Rather, we think these elements of effective confrontation not only permit a defendant to "confound and undo the false accuser, or reveal the child coached by a malevolent adult," *Coy,* 487 U.S., at 1020, but may well aid a defendant in eliciting favorable testimony from the child witness. Indeed, to the extent the child witness' testimony may be said to be technically given out-of-court (though we do not so hold), these assurances of reliability and adversariness are far greater than those required for admission of hearsay testimony under the Confrontation Clause. See *Roberts,* 448 U.S., at 66. We are therefore confident that use of the one-way closed-circuit television procedure, where necessary to further an important state interest, does not impinge upon the truth-seeking or symbolic purposes of the Confrontation Clause.

The critical inquiry in this case, therefore, is whether use of the procedure is necessary to further an important state interest. The State contends that it has a substantial interest in protecting children who are allegedly victims of child abuse from the trauma of testifying against the alleged perpetrator and that its statutory procedure for receiving testimony from such witnesses is necessary to further that interest.

We have of course recognized that a State's interest in "the protection of minor victims of sex crimes from further trauma and embarrassment" is a "compelling" one. Globe Newspaper Co. v. Superior Court, 457 U.S. 596, 607 (1982).

. . .

We ... conclude today that a State's interest in the physical and psychological well-being of child abuse victims may be sufficiently important to outweigh, at least in some cases, a defendant's right to face his or her accusers in court. That a significant majority of States has enacted statutes to protect child witnesses from the trauma of giving testimony in child abuse cases attests to the widespread belief in the importance of such a public policy. See *Coy,* 487 U.S., at 1022–1023 (concurring opinion) ("Many States have determined that a child victim may suffer trauma from exposure to the harsh atmosphere of the typical courtroom and have undertaken to shield the child through a variety of ameliorative measures"). Thirty-seven States, for example, permit the use of videotaped testimony of sexually abused children;[2] 24 States have authorized the use of one-way closed circuit television testimony in child abuse cases;[3] and 8 States authorize the use of a two-way system in which the child-witness is permitted to see the courtroom and the defendant on a video monitor and in which the jury and judge is permitted to view the child during the testimony.[4]

The statute at issue in this case, for example, was specifically intended "to safeguard the physical and psychological well-being of child victims by avoiding, or at least minimizing, the emotional trauma produced by testifying." ... Given the State's traditional and " 'transcendent interest in protecting the welfare of children.' " [Ginsberg v. New York, 390 U.S. 629, 640 (1968)], and buttressed by the growing body of academic literature documenting the psychological trauma suffered by child abuse victims who must testify in court, see Brief for American Psychological Association as *Amicus Curiae* 7–13; G. Goodman et al., Emotional Effects of Criminal Court Testimony on Child Sexual Assault Victims, Final Report to the National Institute of Justice (presented as conference paper at annual convention of American Psychological Assn., Aug. 1989), we will not second-guess the considered judgment of the Maryland Legislature regarding the importance of its interest in protecting child abuse victims from the emotional trauma of testifying. Accordingly, we hold that, if the State

2. See Ala.Code § 15–25–2 (Supp.1989); ...; Wis.Stat.Ann. § 967.04(7) to (10) (West Supp.1989); Wyo.Stat. § 7–11–408 (1987).

3. See Ala.Code § 15–25–3 (Supp.1989); . . .

4. See Cal.Penal Code Ann. § 1347 (West Supp.1990); ...

makes an adequate showing of necessity, the state interest in protecting child witnesses from the trauma of testifying in a child abuse case is sufficiently important to justify the use of a special procedure that permits a child witness in such cases to testify at trial against a defendant in the absence of face-to-face confrontation with the defendant.

The requisite finding of necessity must of course be a case-specific one: the trial court must hear evidence and determine whether use of the one-way closed circuit television procedure is necessary to protect the welfare of the particular child witness who seeks to testify. See Globe Newspaper Co., 457 U.S., at 608–609 (compelling interest in protecting child victims does not justify a *mandatory* trial closure rule)....

Denial of face-to-face confrontation is not needed to further the state interest in protecting the child witness from trauma unless it is the presence of the defendant that causes the trauma. In other words, if the state interest were merely the interest in protecting child witnesses from courtroom trauma generally, denial of face-to-face confrontation would be unnecessary because the child could be permitted to testify in less intimidating surroundings, albeit with the defendant present. Finally, the trial court must find that the emotional distress suffered by the child witness in the presence of the defendant is more than *de minimis,* i.e., more than "mere nervousness or excitement or some reluctance to testify," [Wildermuth v. State, 310 Md. 496, 524, 530 A.2d 275, 289 (1987)]; see also State v. Mannion, 19 Utah 505, 511–512, 57 P. 542, 543–544 (1899). We need not decide the minimum showing of emotional trauma required for use of the special procedure, however, because the Maryland statute, which requires a determination that the child witness will suffer "serious emotional distress such that the child cannot reasonably communicate," § 9–102(a)(1)(ii), clearly suffices to meet constitutional standards.

To be sure, face-to-face confrontation may be said to cause trauma for the very purpose of eliciting truth, cf. *Coy,* supra, at 1019–1020, but we think that the use of Maryland's special procedure, where necessary to further the important state interest in preventing trauma to child witnesses in child abuse cases, adequately ensures the accuracy of the testimony and preserves the adversary nature of the trial. See supra, at 11–12. Indeed, where face-to-face confrontation causes significant emotional distress in a child witness, there is evidence that such confrontation would in fact *disserve* the Confrontation Clause's truth-seeking goal. See e.g., *Coy,* supra, at 1032.

. . .

IV

The Maryland Court of Appeals held, as we do today, that although face-to-face confrontation is not an absolute constitutional requirement, it may be abridged only where there is a "case-specific finding of necessity." 316 Md., at 564, 560 A.2d, at 1126 (quoting *Coy,* supra, at 1025 (concurring opinion)). Given this latter requirement, the Court of Appeals reasoned that "[t]he question of whether a child is unavailable to testify ... should not be asked in terms of inability to testify in the ordinary courtroom setting, but in the much narrower terms of the witness's inability to testify in the presence of the accused." 316 Md., at 564, 560 A.2d, at 1126. . . .

In addition, however, the Court of Appeals interpreted our decision in *Coy* to impose two subsidiary requirements. First, the court held that "§ 9–102 ordinarily cannot be invoked unless the child witness initially is questioned (either in or outside the courtroom) in the defendant's presence." Id., at 566, 560 A.2d 1120, 560 A.2d, at 1127; see also *Wildermuth*, 310 Md., at 523–524, 530 A.2d, at 289 (personal observation by the judge should be the rule rather than the exception). Second, the court asserted that, before using the one-way television procedure, a trial judge must determine whether a child would suffer "severe emotional distress" if he or she were to testify by *two*-way closed circuit television. 316 Md., at 567, 560 A.2d, at 1128.

. . .

The Court of Appeals appears to have rested its conclusion at least in part on the trial court's failure to observe the children's behavior in the defendant's presence and its failure to explore less restrictive alternatives to the use of the one-way closed circuit television procedure. Although we think such evidentiary requirements could strengthen the grounds for use of protective measures, we decline to establish, as a matter of federal constitutional law, any such categorical evidentiary prerequisites for the use of the one-way television procedure. The trial court in this case, for example, could well have found, on the basis of the expert testimony before it, that testimony by the child witnesses in the courtroom in the defendant's presence "will result in [each] child suffering serious emotional distress such that the child cannot reasonably communicate," § 9–102(a)(1)(ii). So long as a trial court makes such a case-specific finding of necessity, the Confrontation Clause does not prohibit a State from using a one-way closed circuit television procedure for the receipt of testimony by a child witness in a child abuse case. Because the Court of Appeals held that the trial court had not made the requisite finding of necessity under its interpretation of "the high threshold required by [*Coy*] before § 9–102 may be invoked," 316 Md., at 554–555, 560 A.2d, at 1121 (footnote omitted), we cannot be certain whether the Court of Appeals would reach the same conclusion in light of the legal standard we establish today. We therefore vacate the judgment of the Court of Appeals of Maryland and remand the case for further proceedings not inconsistent with this opinion. . . .

■ Justice Scalia, with whom Justice Brennan, Justice Marshall, and Justice Stevens join, dissenting.

Seldom has this Court failed so conspicuously to sustain a categorical guarantee of the Constitution against the tide of prevailing current opinion. The Sixth Amendment provides, with unmistakable clarity, that "[i]n all criminal prosecutions, the accused shall enjoy the right . . . to be confronted with the witnesses against him." The purpose of enshrining this protection in the Constitution was to assure that none of the many policy interests from time to time pursued by statutory law could overcome a defendant's right to face his or her accusers in court.

. . .

I

According to the Court, "we cannot say that [face-to-face] confrontation [with witnesses appearing at trial] is an indispensable element of the Sixth Amendment's guarantee of the right to confront one's accusers." That is rather like saying "we cannot say that being tried before a jury is an indispensable element of the Sixth Amendment's guarantee of the right to jury trial." The Court makes the impossible plausible by recharacterizing the Confrontation Clause, so that confrontation (redesignated "face-to-face confrontation") becomes only one of many "elements of confrontation." The reasoning is as follows: The Confrontation Clause guarantees not only what it explicitly provides for—"face-to-face" confrontation—but also implied and collateral rights such as cross-examination, oath, and observation of demeanor (TRUE); the purpose of this entire cluster of rights is to ensure the reliability of evidence (TRUE); the Maryland procedure preserves the implied and collateral rights (TRUE), which adequately ensure the reliability of evidence (perhaps TRUE); therefore the Confrontation Clause is not violated by denying what it explicitly provides for—"face-to-face" confrontation (unquestionably FALSE). This reasoning abstracts from the right to its purposes, and then eliminates the right. It is wrong because the Confrontation Clause does not guarantee reliable evidence; it guarantees specific trial procedures that were thought to *assure* reliable evidence, undeniably among which was "face-to-face" confrontation. Whatever else it may mean in addition, the defendant's constitutional right "to be confronted with the witnesses against him" means, always and everywhere, at least what it explicitly says: the " 'right to meet face to face all those who appear and give evidence at trial.' " Coy v. Iowa, 487 U.S. 1012, 1016 (1988), quoting California v. Green, 399 U.S. 149, 175 (1970)(Harlan, J., concurring).

The Court supports its antitextual conclusion by cobbling together scraps of dicta from various cases that have no bearing here. It will suffice to discuss one of them, since they are all of a kind: Quoting Ohio v. Roberts, 448 U.S. 56, 63 (1980), the Court says that "[i]n sum, our precedents establish that 'the Confrontation Clause reflects a *preference* for face-to-face confrontation at trial,' " ante, at 10 (emphasis added by the Court). But *Roberts,* and all the other "precedents" the Court enlists to prove the implausible, dealt with the *implications* of the Confrontation Clause, and not its literal, unavoidable text. When *Roberts* said that the Clause merely "reflects a preference for face-to-face confrontation at trial," what it had in mind as the nonpreferred alternative was not (as the Court implies) the appearance of a witness at trial without confronting the defendant. That has been, until today, not merely "nonpreferred" but utterly unheard of. What *Roberts* had in mind was the receipt of *other-than-first-hand testimony* from witnesses at trial—that is, witnesses' recounting of hearsay statements by absent parties who, *since they did not appear at trial,* did not have to endure face-to-face confrontation. Rejecting that, I agree, was merely giving effect to an evident constitutional preference; there are, after all, many exceptions to the Confrontation Clause's hearsay rule. But that the defendant should be confronted by the witnesses who appear at trial is not a preference "reflected" by the Confrontation Clause; it is a constitutional right unqualifiedly guaranteed.

. . .

II

Much of the Court's opinion consists of applying to this case the mode of analysis we have used in the admission of hearsay evidence. The Sixth Amendment does not literally contain a prohibition upon such evidence, since it guarantees the defendant only the right to confront "the witnesses against him." As applied in the Sixth Amendment's context of a prosecution, the noun "witness"—in 1791 as today—could mean either (a) one "who knows or sees any thing; one personally present" or (b) "one who gives testimony" or who "testifies," *i.e.,* "[i]n *judicial proceedings,* [one who] make[s] a solemn declaration under oath, for the purpose of establishing or making proof of some fact to a court." 2 N. Webster, An American Dictionary of the English Language (1828) (emphasis added). See also J. Buchanan, Linguae Britannicae Vera Pronunciatio (1757). The former meaning (one "who knows or sees") would cover hearsay evidence, but is excluded in the Sixth Amendment by the words following the noun: "witnesses *against him.*" The phrase obviously refers to those who give testimony against the defendant at trial. We have nonetheless found implicit in the Confrontation Clause some limitation upon hearsay evidence, since otherwise the Government could subvert the confrontation right by putting on witnesses who know nothing except what an absent declarant said. And in determining the scope of that implicit limitation, we have focused upon whether the reliability of the hearsay statements (which are not *expressly* excluded by the Confrontation Clause) "is otherwise assured." Ante, at 11. The same test cannot be applied, however, to permit what is explicitly forbidden by the constitutional text; there is simply no room for interpretation with regard to "the irreducible literal meaning of the Clause." *Coy,* supra, at 1020–1021.

Some of the Court's analysis seems to suggest that the children's testimony here was itself hearsay of the sort permissible under our Confrontation Clause cases. See ante, at 12. That cannot be. Our Confrontation Clause conditions for the admission of hearsay have long included a "general requirement of unavailability" of the declarant. Idaho v. Wright, ante, p. 8. "In the usual case . . . , the prosecution must either produce or demonstrate the unavailability of, the declarant whose statement it wishes to use against the defendant." Ohio v. Roberts, 448 U.S., at 65. We have permitted a few exceptions to this general rule—e.g., for co-conspirators' statements, whose effect cannot be replicated by live testimony because they "derive [their] significance from the circumstances in which [they were] made," United States v. Inadi, 475 U.S. 387, 395 (1986). "Live" closed-circuit television testimony, however—if it can be called hearsay at all—is surely an example of hearsay as "a weaker substitute for live testimony," id., at 394, which can be employed only when the genuine article is unavailable. "When two versions of the same evidence are available, longstanding principles of the law of hearsay, applicable as well to Confrontation Clause analysis, favor the better evidence." Ibid. See also

Roberts, supra (requiring unavailability as precondition for admission of prior testimony); Barber v. Page, 390 U.S. 719 (1968) (same).

The Court's test today requires unavailability only in the sense that the child is unable to testify in the presence of the defendant. That cannot possibly be the relevant sense. If unconfronted testimony is admissible hearsay when the witness is unable to confront the defendant, then presumably there are other categories of admissible hearsay consisting of unsworn testimony when the witness is unable to risk perjury, uncross-examined testimony when the witness is unable to undergo hostile questioning, etc. California v. Green, 399 U.S. 149 (1970), is not precedent for such a silly system. That case held that the Confrontation Clause does not bar admission of prior testimony when the declarant is sworn as a witness but refuses to answer. But in *Green,* as in most cases of refusal, we could not know *why* the declarant refused to testify. Here, by contrast, we know that it is precisely because the child is unwilling to testify in the presence of the defendant. That unwillingness cannot be a valid excuse under the Confrontation Clause, whose very object is to place the witness under the sometimes hostile glare of the defendant. "That face-to-face presence may, unfortunately, upset the truthful rape victim or abused child; but by the same token it may confound and undo the false accuser, or reveal the child coached by a malevolent adult." *Coy,* 487 U.S., at 1020. To say that a defendant loses his right to confront a witness when that would cause the witness not to testify is rather like saying that the defendant loses his right to counsel when counsel would save him, or his right to subpoena witnesses when they would exculpate him, or his right not to give testimony against himself when that would prove him guilty.

III

The Court characterizes the State's interest which "outweigh[s]" the explicit text of the Constitution as an "interest in the physical and psychological well-being of child abuse victims," ante, at 13, an "interest in protecting" such victims "from the emotional trauma of testifying," ante, at 16. That is not so. A child who meets the Maryland statute's requirement of suffering such "serious emotional distress" from confrontation that he "cannot reasonably communicate" would seem entirely safe. Why would a prosecutor want to call a witness who cannot reasonably communicate? And if he did, it would be the State's own fault. Protection of the child's interest—as far as the Confrontation Clause is concerned—is entirely within Maryland's control. The State's interest here is in fact no more and no less than what the State's interest always is when it seeks to get a class of evidence admitted in criminal proceedings: more convictions of guilty defendants. That is not an unworthy interest, but it should not be dressed up as a humanitarian one.

And the interest on the other side is also what it usually is when the State seeks to get a new class of evidence admitted: fewer convictions of innocent defendants—specifically, in the present context, innocent defendants accused of particularly heinous crimes. The "special" reasons that exist for suspending one of the usual guarantees of reliability in the case of children's testimony are perhaps matched by "special" reasons for being particularly insistent upon it in the case of children's testimony. Some studies show that children are substantially more vulnerable to suggestion than adults, and often unable to separate recollected fantasy (or suggestion) from reality.

. . .

In the last analysis, however, this debate is not an appropriate one. I have no need to defend the value of confrontation, because the Court has no authority to question it. It is not within our charge to speculate that, "where face-to-face confrontation causes significant emotional distress in a child witness," confrontation might "in fact *disserve* the Confrontation Clause's truth-seeking goal." Ante, at 17. If so, that is a defect in the Constitution—which should be amended by the procedures provided for such an eventuality, but cannot be corrected by judicial pronouncement.

. . .

The Court today has applied "interest-balancing" analysis where the text of the Constitution simply does not permit it. We are not free to conduct a cost-benefit analysis of clear and explicit constitutional guarantees, and then to adjust their meaning to comport with our findings. The Court has convincingly proved that the Maryland procedure serves a valid interest, and gives the defendant virtually everything the Confrontation Clause guarantees (everything, that is, except confrontation). I am persuaded, therefore, that the Maryland procedure is virtually constitutional. Since it is not, however, actually constitutional I would affirm the judgment of the Maryland Court of Appeals reversing the judgment of conviction.

NOTES

(1) *Craig*, and in the Supreme Court's earlier opinion in *Coy v. Iowa*, which is discussed by the Court in *Craig*, together suggest the constitutional boundaries limiting statutes enacted in many states that are designed to respond to the problems of obtaining evidence from child witnesses in child sexual abuse cases. Generally the reform statutes allow the child to avoid testimony in open court during the trial. Some alternatives are statutory provisions that the child's testimony at a deposition or preliminary hearing may be videotaped and introduced as evidence at trial, and provisions for out-of-courtroom testimony by the child at the time of the trial.

(2) In *Kentucky v. Stincer*, 482 U.S. 730, 107 S.Ct. 2658, 96 L.Ed.2d 631 (1987), an opinion that preceded *Coy* and *Craig*, the Court examined a related issue, the constitutionality of excluding a defendant from the pre-trial hearing to determine the child's competency to testify as a witness. The Court upheld the exclusion of the defendant, but emphasized that it did so only because defendant's right of confrontation was clearly protected. The defendant's attorney was present at the competency hearing, and the defendant later had an opportunity to cross-examine the child. In the following excerpt from *Stincer,* how does the Court's analysis of defendant's confrontation rights differ from that in *Coy?*

> Instead of attempting to characterize a competency hearing as a trial or pretrial proceeding, it is more useful to consider whether excluding the defendant from the hearing interferes with his opportunity for effective cross-examination. No such interference occurred when respondent was excluded from the competency

hearing of the two young girls in this case. After the trial court determined that the two children were competent to testify, they appeared and testified in open court. At that point, the two witnesses were subject to full and complete cross-examination, and were so examined. Respondent was present throughout this cross-examination and was available to assist his counsel as necessary. There was no Kentucky rule of law, nor any ruling by the trial court, that restricted respondent's ability to cross-examine the witnesses at trial. Any questions asked during the competency hearing, which respondent's counsel attended and in which he participated, could have been repeated during direct examination and cross-examination of the witnesses in respondent's presence. See California v. Green, 399 U.S., at 159 ("[T]he inability to cross-examine the witness at the time he made his prior statement cannot easily be shown to be of crucial significance as long as the defendant is assured of full and effective cross-examination at the time of trial").

In this case both T.G. and N.G. were asked several background questions during the competency hearing, as well as several questions directed at what it meant to tell the truth. Some of the questions regarding the witnesses' backgrounds were repeated by the prosecutor on direct examination, while others—particularly those regarding the witnesses' ability to tell the difference between truth and falsehood—were repeated by respondent's counsel on cross-examination. At the close of the children's testimony, respondent's counsel, had he thought it appropriate, was in a position to move that the court reconsider its competency rulings on the ground that the direct and cross-examination had elicited evidence that the young girls lacked the basic requisites for serving as competent witnesses. Thus, the critical tool of cross-examination was available to counsel as a means of establishing that the witnesses were not competent to testify, as well as a means of undermining the credibility of their testimony.

Because respondent had the opportunity for full and effective cross-examination of the two witnesses during trial, and because of the nature of the competency hearing at issue in this case, we conclude that respondent's rights under the Confrontation Clause were not violated by his exclusion from the competency hearing of the two girls.

. . .

482 U.S. at 743, 744.

(3) The United States Supreme Court's decision in *Crawford v. Washington*, 541 U.S. 36, 124 S.Ct. 1354, 158 L.Ed.2d 177 (2004) could lead to a reexamination of the Court's position in the principal case *Maryland v. Craig*. While not in the child abuse or child testimony context, *Crawford* said the Constitution gives defendants the right to confront their accusers in court and makes it more difficult for prosecutors to introduce statements at trial from absent witnesses who are not available for cross examination by the defense.

The ruling overturns the assault conviction of a Washington state man who was found guilty after the jury heard a tape recorded statement his wife had given the police. The wife could not be compelled to testify against her husband, and refused to testify at his trial. The judge however permitted the prosecutor to introduce her taped statement in lieu of her live testimony.

Justice Scalia writing for the 7–2 majority in *Crawford* set a high bar for use of out-of-court statements at trial. "The Framers [of the Constitution] would not have allowed admission of testimonial statements of witness" without the opportunity to confront and cross-examine that witness.

Further, Scalia wrote: "Admitting [out-of-court] statements deemed reliable by a judge is fundamentally at odds with the right of confrontation." He added,

"Dispensing with confrontation because testimony is obviously reliable is akin to dispensing with jury trial because a defendant is obviously guilty. This is not what the Sixth Amendment prescribes."

The Court stated further: "Where testimonial evidence is at issue . . . the Sixth Amendment demands what the common law required: unavailability and a prior opportunity for cross-examination. We leave for another day any effort to spell out a comprehensive definition of 'testimonial'."

One likely ramification of *Crawford* in child abuse cases might be exclusion of out-of-court statements made by a child to a therapist or counselor. It is not clear under *Crawford* whether a child's statement made to an abuse counselor could be considered testimony.

The issue of the use of out-of-court statements by children in child abuse cases has arisen frequently and courts have been divided over whether prosecutors may use a child's statement to a counselor or the police if the child is too young to testify in court.

Crawford throws considerable doubt over the admissibility of such out-of-court statements.

For further discussion of the *Crawford* case and more recent Supreme Court decisions clarifying its meaning and scope, see infra page 630 infra.

(4) A flood of legal commentary has examined the constitutionality of statutory reforms designed to protect child witnesses. See, e.g., Note, The Constitutionality of the Use of Two–Way Closed Circuit Television to Take Testimony of Child Victims of Sex Crimes, 53 Fordham Urb.L.J. 995 (1985); Note, The Testimony of Child Victims in Sex Abuse Prosecutions: Two Legislative Innovations, 98 Harv.L.Rev. 806 (1985); Note, The Use of Videotaped Testimony of Victims in Cases Involving Child Sexual Abuse: A Constitutional Dilemma, 14 Hofstra L.Rev. 261 (1985); Comment, Use of Videotaping to Avoid Traumatization of Child Sexual Abuse Victim–Witnesses, 21 Land & Water L.Rev. 565 (1986); Videotaping the Testimony of an Abused Child: Necessary Protection for the Child or Unwarranted Compromise of the Defendant's Constitutional Rights?, 1986 Utah L.Rev. 461. Susan B. Apel, Custodial Parents, Child Sexual Abuse, and the Legal System: Beyond Contempt, 38 Am. U. L. Rev. 491 (1989); Comment, Randal C. Shaffer, Protecting the Innocent: Confrontation, Coy v. Iowa, and Televised Testimony in Child Sexual Abuse Cases, 78 Ky. L.J. 803 (1990); Note, Marianne T. Bayardi, Balancing the Defendant's Confrontation Clause Rights with the State's Public Policy Goal of Protecting Child Witnesses from Undue Traumatization: Arizona Law in Light of Maryland v. Craig and Coy v. Iowa, 32 Ariz. L. Rev. 1029 (1990); Jean Montoya, On Truth and Shielding in Child Abuse Trials, 43 Hastings L.J. 1259 (1992); Note, Jacqueline Miller Beckett, The True Value of the Confrontation Clause: A Study of Child Sex Abuse Trials, 82 Geo. L.J. 1605 (1994); Penny J. White, Rescuing the Confrontation Clause, 54 S.C. L. Rev. 537 (2003); Thomas D. Lyon & Raymond LaMagna, The History of Children's Hearsay: From Old Bailey to Post–Davis, 82 Ind.L.J. 1029 (2007).

UNITED STATES CODE ANNOTATED

TITLE 18. CRIMES AND CRIMINAL PROCEDURE

§ 3509.   Child victims' and child witnesses' rights

. . .

(b) Alternatives to live in-court testimony.—

(1) Child's live testimony by 2–way closed circuit television.—

(A) In a proceeding involving an alleged offense against a child, the attorney for the Government, the child's attorney, or a guardian ad litem appointed under subsection (h) may apply for an order that the child's testimony be taken in a room outside the courtroom and be televised by 2–way closed circuit television. The person seeking such an order shall apply for such an order at least 5 days before the trial date, unless the court finds on the record that the need for such an order was not reasonably foreseeable.

(B) The court may order that the testimony of the child be taken by closed-circuit television as provided in subparagraph (A) if the court finds that the child is unable to testify in open court in the presence of the defendant, for any of the following reasons:

(i) The child is unable to testify because of fear.

(ii) There is a substantial likelihood, established by expert testimony, that the child would suffer emotional trauma from testifying.

(iii) The child suffers a mental or other infirmity.

(iv) Conduct by defendant or defense counsel causes the child to be unable to continue testifying.

(C) The court shall support a ruling on the child's inability to testify with findings on the record. In determining whether the impact on an individual child of one or more of the factors described in subparagraph (B) is so substantial as to justify an order under subparagraph (A), the court may question the minor in chambers, or at some other comfortable place other than the courtroom, on the record for a reasonable period of time with the child attendant, the prosecutor, the child's attorney, the guardian ad litem, and the defense counsel present.

(D) If the court orders the taking of testimony by television, the attorney for the Government and the attorney for the defendant not including an attorney pro se for a party shall be present in a room outside the courtroom with the child and the child shall be subjected to direct and cross-examination. The only other persons who may be permitted in the room with the child during the child's testimony are—

(i) the child's attorney or guardian ad litem appointed under subsection (h);

(ii) Persons necessary to operate the closed-circuit television equipment;

(iii) A judicial officer, appointed by the court; and

(iv) Other persons whose presence is determined by the court to be necessary to the welfare and well-being of the child, including an adult attendant.

The child's testimony shall be transmitted by closed circuit television into the courtroom for viewing and hearing by the defendant, jury, judge, and public. The defendant shall be provided with the means of private, contemporaneous communication with the defendant's attorney during the testimony. The closed circuit television transmission shall relay into the room in which the child is testifying the defendant's image, and the voice of the judge.

(2) Videotaped deposition of child.—(A) In a proceeding involving an alleged offense against a child, the attorney for the Government, the child's attorney, the child's parent or legal guardian, or the guardian ad litem appointed under subsection (h) may apply for an order that a deposition be taken of the child's testimony and that the deposition be recorded and preserved on videotape.

(B)(i) Upon timely receipt of an application described in subparagraph (A), the court shall make a preliminary finding regarding whether at the time of trial the child is likely to be unable to testify in open court in the physical presence of the defendant, jury, judge, and public for any of the following reasons:

(I) The child will be unable to testify because of fear.

(II) There is a substantial likelihood, established by expert testimony, that the child would suffer emotional trauma from testifying in open court.

(III) The child suffers a mental or other infirmity.

(IV) Conduct by defendant or defense counsel causes the child to be unable to continue testifying.

(ii) If the court finds that the child is likely to be unable to testify in open court for any of the reasons stated in clause (i), the court shall order that the child's deposition be taken and preserved by videotape.

(iii) The trial judge shall preside at the videotape deposition of a child and shall rule on all questions as if at trial. The only other persons who may be permitted to be present at the proceeding are—

(I) the attorney for the Government;

(II) the attorney for the defendant;

(III) the child's attorney or guardian ad litem appointed under subsection (h);

(IV) persons necessary to operate the videotape equipment;

(V) subject to clause (iv), the defendant; and

(VI) other persons whose presence is determined by the court to be necessary to the welfare and well-being of the child.

The defendant shall be afforded the rights applicable to defendants during trial, including the right to an attorney, the right to be confronted with the witness against the defendant, and the right to cross-examine the child.

(iv) If the preliminary finding of inability under clause (i) is based on evidence that the child is unable to testify in the physical presence of the defendant, the court may order that the defendant, including a defendant represented pro se, be excluded from the room in which the deposition is conducted. If the court orders that the defendant be excluded from the deposition room, the court shall order that 2–way closed circuit television equipment relay the defendant's image into the room in which the child is testifying, and the child's testimony into the room in which the defendant is viewing the proceeding, and that the defendant be provided with a means of private, contemporaneous communication with the defendant's attorney during the deposition.

(v) Handling of videotape.—The complete record of the examination of the child, including the image and voices of all persons who in any way participate in the examination, shall be made and preserved on video tape in addition to being stenographically recorded. The videotape shall be transmitted to the clerk of the court in which the action is pending and shall be made available for viewing to the prosecuting attorney, the defendant, and the defendant's attorney during ordinary business hours.

(C) If at the time of trial the court finds that the child is unable to testify as for a reason described in subparagraph (B)(i), the court may admit into evidence the child's videotaped deposition in lieu of the child's testifying at the trial. The court shall support a ruling under this subparagraph with findings on the record.

. . .

(e) Closing the courtroom.—When a child testifies the court may order the exclusion from the courtroom of all persons, including members of the press, who do not have a direct interest in the case. Such an order may be made if the court determines on the record that requiring the child to testify in open court would cause substantial psychological harm to the child or would result in the child's inability to effectively communicate. Such an order shall be narrowly tailored to serve the Government's specific compelling interest.

. . .

(i) Adult attendant.—A child testifying at or attending a judicial proceeding shall have the right to be accompanied by an adult attendant to provide emotional support to the child. The court, at its discretion, may allow the adult attendant to remain in close physical proximity to or in contact with the child while the child testifies. The court may allow the adult attendant to hold the child's hand or allow the child to sit on the adult attendant's lap throughout the course of the proceeding. An adult attendant shall not provide the child with an answer to any question directed to the child during the course of the child's testimony or otherwise prompt the child. The image of the child attendant, for the time the child is testifying or being deposed, shall be recorded on videotape.

(j) Speedy trial.—In a proceeding in which a child is called to give testimony, on motion by the attorney for the Government or a guardian ad litem, or on its own motion, the court may designate the case as being of special public importance. In cases so designated, the court shall, consistent with these rules, expedite the proceeding and ensure that it takes precedence over any other. The court shall ensure a speedy trial in order to minimize the length of time the child must endure the stress of involvement with the criminal process. When deciding whether to grant a continuance, the court shall take into consideration the age of the child and the potential adverse impact the delay may have on the child's well-being. The court shall make written findings of fact and conclusions of law when granting a continuance in cases involving a child.

. . .

NOTE

The preceding statute was enacted after *Maryland v. Craig*, and it represents Congress's effort to follow the Court's prescription about the constitutional requirements for children's testimony. The statute contains several other provisions dealing comprehensively with the treatment of child witnesses and victims in legal proceedings. It details the procedures for evaluating the competency to testify of child witnesses (although children are presumed under the statute to be competent witnesses). The statute also includes guidelines for protecting the child's privacy, limiting the disclosure of information about the child's identity to parties with an interest in the proceeding. In another section, the statute directs the court to cooperate with multi-disciplinary child abuse teams to assist child victims and witnesses in jurisdictions that have established such teams. The court also may appoint a guardian for the child victim or witness.

VIRGINIA CODE ANNOTATED

§ 63.2–1521.   Testimony by child using two-way closed-circuit television

A.   In any civil proceeding involving alleged abuse or neglect of a child pursuant to this chapter or pursuant to §§ 16.1–241, 16.1–251, 16.1–252, 16.1–253, 16.1–283 or § 20–107.2, the child's attorney or guardian ad litem or, if the child has been committed to the custody of a local department, the attorney for the local department may apply for an order from the court that the testimony of the alleged victim or of a child witness be taken in a room outside the courtroom and be televised by two-way closed-circuit television. The person seeking such order shall apply for the order at least seven days before the trial date.

B.   The provisions of this section shall apply to the following:

1.   An alleged victim who was fourteen years of age or under on the date of the alleged offense and is sixteen or under at the time of the trial; and

2.   Any child witness who is fourteen years of age or under at the time of the trial.

C.   The court may order that the testimony of the child be taken by closed-circuit television as provided in subsections A and B if it finds that the child is unavailable to testify in open court in the presence of the defendant, the jury, the judge, and the public, for any of the following reasons:

1.   The child's persistent refusal to testify despite judicial requests to do so;

2.   The child's substantial inability to communicate about the offense; or

3.   The substantial likelihood, based upon expert opinion testimony, that the child will suffer severe emotional trauma from so testifying.

Any ruling on the child's unavailability under this subsection shall be supported by the court with findings on the record or with written findings in a court not of record.

D.   In any proceeding in which closed-circuit television is used to receive testimony, the attorney for the child and the defendant's attorney and, if the child has been committed to the custody of a local board, the attorney for the local board shall be present in the room with the child, and the child shall be subject to direct and cross examination. The only other persons allowed to be present in the room with the child during his testimony shall be the guardian ad litem, those persons necessary to operate the closed-circuit equipment, and any other person whose presence is determined by the court to be necessary to the welfare and well-being of the child.

E.   The child's testimony shall be transmitted by closed-circuit television into the courtroom for the defendant, jury, judge and public to view. The defendant shall be provided with a means of private, contemporaneous communication with his attorney during the testimony.

[§ 63.2–1522, dealing with admission of evidence of sexual acts with children is reproduced at p. 636 infra.]

§ 63.2–1523.   Use of videotaped statements of complaining witnesses as evidence

A.   In any civil proceeding involving alleged abuse or neglect of a child pursuant to this chapter or pursuant to §§ 16.1–241, 16.1–251, 16.1–252, 16.1–253, 16.1–283 or § 20–107.2, a recording of a statement of the alleged victim of the offense, made prior to the proceeding, may be admissible as evidence if the requirements of subsection B are met and the court determines that:

1.   The alleged victim is the age of twelve or under at the time the statement is offered into evidence;

2.   The recording is both visual and oral, and every person appearing in, and every voice recorded on, the tape is identified;

3.   The recording is on videotape or was recorded by other electronic means capable of making an accurate recording;

4.   The recording has not been altered;

5.   No attorney for any party to the proceeding was present when the statement was made;

6.   The person conducting the interview of the alleged victim was authorized to do so by the child-protective services coordinator of the local department;

7.   All persons present at the time the statement was taken, including the alleged victim, are present and available to testify or be cross examined at the proceeding when the recording is offered; and

8.   The parties or their attorneys were provided with a list of all persons present at the recording and were afforded an opportunity to view the recording at least ten days prior to the scheduled proceedings.

B.   A recorded statement may be admitted into evidence as provided in subsection A if:

1.   The child testifies at the proceeding, or testifies by means of closed-circuit television, and at the time of such testimony is subject to cross examination concerning the recorded statement or the child is found by the court to be unavailable to testify on any of these grounds:

a.   The child's death;

b.   The child's absence from the jurisdiction, provided such absence is not for the purpose of preventing the availability of the child to testify;

c.   The child's total failure of memory;

d.   The child's physical or mental disability;

e.   The existence of a privilege involving the child;

f.   The child's incompetency, including the child's inability to communicate about the offense because of fear or a similar reason;

g.   The substantial likelihood, based upon expert opinion testimony, that the child would suffer severe emotional trauma from testifying at the proceeding or by means of closed-circuit television; and

2.   The child's recorded statement is shown to possess particularized guarantees of trustworthiness and reliability.

C.   A recorded statement may not be admitted under this section unless the proponent of the statement notifies the adverse party of his intention to offer the statement and the substance of the statement sufficiently in advance of the proceedings to provide the adverse party with a reasonable opportunity to prepare to meet the statement, including the opportunity to subpoena witnesses.

D.   In determining whether a recorded statement possesses particularized guarantees of trustworthiness and reliability under subdivision B 2, the court shall consider, but is not limited to, the following factors:

1.   The child's personal knowledge of the event;

2.   The age and maturity of the child;

3.   Any apparent motive the child may have to falsify or distort the event, including bias, corruption, or coercion;

4.   The timing of the child's statement;

5.   Whether the child was suffering pain or distress when making the statement;

6.   Whether the child's age makes it unlikely that the child fabricated a statement that represents a graphic, detailed account beyond the child's knowledge and experience;

7.   Whether the statement has a "ring of verity," has internal consistency or coherence, and uses terminology appropriate to the child's age;

8.   Whether the statement is spontaneous or directly responsive to questions;

9.   Whether the statement is responsive to suggestive or leading questions; and

10.   Whether extrinsic evidence exists to show the defendant's opportunity to commit the act complained of in the child's statement.

E.   The court shall support with findings on the record, or with written findings in a court not of record, any rulings pertaining to the child's unavailability and the trustworthiness and reliability of the recorded statement.

ADMISSION AT TRIAL OF HEARSAY STATEMENTS MADE BY A CHILD AND THE CONFRONTATION CLAUSE OF THE 6TH AMENDMENT.

Until recently, out-of-court statements by children about abuse could be admitted into evidence through testimony by third parties, but only if the requirements established by the Supreme Court in *Ohio v. Roberts,* 448 U.S. 56, 100 S.Ct. 2531, 65 L.Ed.2d 597 (1980), were satisfied. The *Roberts* test, which was recently overruled by the Court, allowed hearsay statements to be admitted if the declarant was unavailable and the statements bore "particularized guarantees of trustworthiness." Id. at 65. In *Idaho v. Wright,* 497 U.S. 805, 110 S.Ct. 3139, 111 L.Ed.2d 638 (1990), the Court clarified what *Roberts* required when the prosecution sought to introduce hearsay statements by an allegedly abused child.

In *Idaho v. Wright,* respondent Laura Lee Wright was jointly charged with Robert L. Giles of two counts of lewd conduct with a minor child under sixteen. The alleged victims were respondent's two daughters, one of whom was 5½ and the other 2½ years old at the time the crimes were charged. Ms. Wright was convicted of the two counts. The trial court permitted the examining pediatrician to testify regarding certain statements made by the younger daughter in response to questions he asked about the alleged abuse. The Supreme Court of Idaho held that the admission of the inculpatory hearsay testimony violated respondent's federal constitutional right to confrontation because the testimony did not fall within a traditional hearsay exception and was based on an interview that lacked procedural safeguards.

The issue before the Supreme Court was whether the admission at trial of certain hearsay statements made by a child declarant to an examining pediatrician violated a defendant's rights under the Confrontation Clause of the Sixth Amendment. The Court affirmed the holding of the Supreme Court of Idaho agreeing that the State had failed to show that the younger daughter's incriminating statements to the pediatrician possessed sufficient "particularized guarantees of trustworthiness" under the Confrontation Clause to overcome the presumption of inadmissibility.

The Court reasoned that where the hearsay declarant's truthfulness is so clear from the surrounding circumstances that the test of cross-examination would be of marginal utility, then the hearsay rules do not bar admission of the statement at trial. The "particularized guarantees of trustworthiness" required for admission under the Confrontation Clause must likewise be drawn from the totality of circumstances that surround the making of the statement and that render the declarant particularly worthy of belief. The Court also deemed unacceptable the use of corroborating evidence to support the hearsay statements.

Justice O'Connor, writing for the Court in *Idaho v. Wright,* based the decision on the Court's previous analysis in *Ohio v. Roberts,* 448 U.S. 56, 100 S.Ct. 2531, 65 L.Ed.2d 597 (1980), stating:

> In *Ohio v. Roberts,* we set forth "a general approach" for determining when incriminating statements admissible under an exception to the hearsay rule also meet the requirements of the Confrontation Clause. [448 U.S. 56, 65 (1980).] We noted that the Confrontation Clause "operates in two separate ways to restrict the range of admissible hearsay." Ibid. "First, in conformance with the Framers' preference for face-to-face accusation, the Sixth Amendment establishes a rule of necessity. In the usual case . . ., the prosecution must either produce or demonstrate the unavailability of, the declarant whose statement it wishes to use against the defendant." Ibid. (citations omitted). Second, once a witness is shown to be unavailable, "his statement is admissible only if it bears adequate 'indicia of reliability.' Reliability can be inferred without more in a case where the evidence falls within a firmly rooted hearsay exception. In other cases, the evidence must be excluded, at least absent a showing of particularized guarantees of trustworthiness." Id., at 66 (footnote omitted); see also Mancusi v. Stubbs, 408 U.S. 204, 213 (1972).
>
> . . .
>
> Applying the *Roberts* approach to this case, we first note that this case does not raise the question whether, before a child's out-of-court statements are admitted, the Confrontation Clause requires the prosecution to show that a child witness is unavailable at trial—and, if so, what that showing requires. The trial court in this case found that respondent's younger daughter was incapable of communicating with the jury, and defense counsel agreed. App. 39. The court below neither questioned this finding nor discussed the general requirement of unavailability. For purposes of deciding this case, we assume without deciding that, to the extent the unavailability requirement applies in this case, the younger daughter was an unavailable witness within the meaning of the Confrontation Clause.
>
> The crux of the question presented is therefore whether the State, as the proponent of evidence presumptively barred by the hearsay rule and the Confrontation Clause, has carried its burden of proving that the younger daughter's incriminating statements to Dr. Jambura bore sufficient indicia of reliability to withstand scrutiny under the Clause.
>
> . . .
>
> In *Roberts,* we suggested that the "indicia of reliability" requirement could be met in either of two circumstances: where the hearsay statement "falls within a firmly rooted hearsay exception," or where it is supported by "a showing of particularized guarantees of trustworthiness."
>
> The Court also held that the indicia of reliability under *Roberts* must come from the circumstances surrounding the out-of-court statement, not from other corroborating evidence. The Court stated:

... [T]he use of corroborating evidence to support a hearsay statement's "particularized guarantees of trustworthiness" would permit admission of a presumptively unreliable statement by bootstrapping on the trustworthiness of other evidence at trial, a result we think at odds with the requirement that hearsay evidence admitted under the Confrontation Clause be so trustworthy that cross-examination of the declarant would be of marginal utility. . . .

This "particularized guarantees of trustworthiness" analysis from *Roberts* applied to a child abuse prosecution in *Wright* has been disapproved in the Supreme Court's decision in *Crawford v. Washington,* 541 U.S. 36, 124 S.Ct. 1354, 158 L.Ed.2d 177 (2004). In that case, the question presented was the admission into evidence of a witness's tape-recorded statement concerning defendant Crawford's violent behavior. There was no opportunity to cross-examine the witness's statements because she was Crawford's wife and invoked the spousal privilege to avoid testifying at his criminal trial. The Supreme Court concluded that the playing of the tape recording violated defendant's Sixth Amendment right to confront the witnesses against him.

In so doing, the *Crawford* Court overruled *Ohio v. Roberts* and its "particularized guarantees of trustworthiness" analysis. The *Crawford* Court stated:

Although the results of our decisions have generally been faithful to the original meaning of the Confrontation Clause, the same cannot be said of our rationales. *Roberts* conditions the admissibility of all hearsay evidence on whether it falls under a "firmly rooted hearsay exception" or bears "particularized guarantees of trustworthiness." 448 U.S., at 66, 100 S.Ct. 2531, 65 L.Ed.2d 597. This departs from the historical principles identified above in two respects. First, it is too broad: It applies the same mode of analysis whether or not the hearsay consists of *ex parte* testimony. This often results in close constitutional scrutiny in cases that are far removed from the core concerns of the Clause. At the same time, however, the test is too narrow: It admits statements that *do* consist of *ex parte* testimony upon a mere finding of reliability. This malleable standard often fails to protect against paradigmatic confrontation violations.

Crawford, 124 S.Ct. 1369. The Court went on to state:

Where testimonial statements are involved, we do not think the Framers meant to leave the Sixth Amendment's protection to the vagaries of the rules of evidence, much less to amorphous notions of "reliability." . . . Admitting statements deemed reliable by a judge is fundamentally at odds with the right of confrontation. To be sure, the Clause's ultimate goal is to ensure reliability of evidence, but that reliability be assessed in a particular manner: by testing in the crucible of cross-examination. The Clause thus reflects a judgment, not only about the desirability of reliable evidence (a point on which there could be little dissent), but about how reliability can best be determined.

. . .

> The *Roberts* test allows a jury to hear evidence, untested by the adversary process, based on a mere judicial determination of reliability. It thus replaces the constitutionality prescribed method of assessing reliability with a wholly foreign one.

Id. at 1370. Finally, the Court concluded:

> Where testimonial evidence is at issue ... the Sixth Amendment demands what the common law required: unavailability and a prior opportunity for cross-examination. We leave for another day any effort to spell out a comprehensive definition of "testimonial."

Ibid. at p. 1374.

To the extent *Ohio v. Roberts* has been overruled, the validity of the rationale underpinning *Idaho v. Wright* is in grave doubt. In the same way, the continued validity of the Supreme Court's holding in *White v. Illinois*, 502 U.S. 346, 112 S.Ct. 736, 116 L.Ed.2d 848 (1992), which admitted statements of a child victim to an investigating officer as spontaneous declarations, must also be questioned. See *Crawford* at p. 1370.

Prosecutors concerned about the impact of *Crawford* may have some tactical ways around the difficulties *Crawford* presents to successful child abuse prosecutions:

> 1) *Crawford* does not directly apply to child custody cases as they are civil proceedings. The Confrontation Clause applies to "criminal prosecutions". Although the Due Process Clause of the Fourteenth Amendment accords parents a right to confront accusatory witnesses in child custody cases, confrontation under the Due Process Clause does not have to be as extensive as the right guaranteed by the Sixth Amendment.

> 2) *Crawford* will not apply to criminal proceedings in which the child will testify. If the child is available for cross-examination, the evil *Crawford* is designed to eliminate does not arise.

> 3) It might be that some out-of-court statements by children will not be deemed "testimonial." While the *Crawford* Court chose to "leave for another day any effort to spell out a comprehensive definition of 'testimonial'," *Crawford* at p. 1374, trial courts may find some out-of-court statements by children made to investigators admissible as not being testimonial in nature. A child's casual remark to a friend might not be seen as testimonial and, therefore, might be admissible. Also, it is possible that statements made to a doctor or therapist may be viewed as statements made for the purpose of treatment, not for trial. If so, such out-of-court statements by the child might be deemed admissible under traditional hearsay rules even if the child does not testify. This outcome seems far less likely if the child's statements were made to a governmental investigator, such as a police officer, given the *Crawford* Court's disapproval of the admissibility of statements to the investigator in *White v. Illinois*, 502 U.S. 346 (1992).

In the companion cases of *Davis v. Washington* and *Hammon v. Indiana*, 547 U.S. 813, 126 S.Ct. 2266, 165 L.Ed.2d 224 (2006), the Court addressed what kinds of statements made to law enforcement personnel are "testimonial" and subject to the Sixth Amendment's Confrontation Clause.

In *Davis*, a call was made to 911, which was terminated prior to any conversation. The 911 operator returned the call and the operator, while speaking with Michelle McCottry, determined that McCottry was involved in a domestic disturbance with her former boyfriend, Adrian Davis. McCottry indicated that Davis was hitting her. Davis ran while McCottry was on the phone with the 911 operator. The operator told McCottry to stop talking and to answer her questions. The operator then solicited certain information from McCottry. The police arrived within four minutes of the 911 call.

Davis was charged with "felony violation of a domestic no-contact order." 126 S.Ct. at 2271. The police who responded to the call testified but McCottry did not. Therefore, to establish McCottry's injuries were caused by Davis, the prosecution, over Davis's objections, used the 911 tapes. Davis was convicted. The Washington Court of Appeals affirmed the conviction, as did the Washington Supreme Court. The latter concluded "that the portion of the 911 conversation in which McCottry identified Davis was not testimonial, and that if other portions of the conversation were testimonial, admitting them was harmless beyond a reasonable doubt." Id.

In *Hammon*, police responded to a reported domestic disturbance call. Amy Hammon was sitting on the porch when police arrived and, despite being visibly agitated, stated that nothing was the matter. She gave police permission to enter the house. Hershel Hammon stated that he and Amy, his wife, had an argument but there was no physical altercation. Hershel became angry when the police attempted to separate Amy and Hershel so they could speak with Amy. Amy then admitted to police and signed an affidavit to the effect that Hershel physically assaulted her.

Amy did not testify at trial. Over Hershel's objections, the officer testified to what Amy told him that night and authenticated Amy's affidavit. The trial court admitted the evidence under the present sense impression and excited utterance exceptions to the hearsay rule. Hershel was found guilty of both charges and his conviction was affirmed by both the Indiana Court of Appeals and Indiana Supreme Court. The latter determined that "Amy's statement was admissible for state-law purposes as an excited utterance." Id. at 2273. It also determined that " 'a "testimonial" statement is one given or taken in significant part for purposes of preserving it for potential future use in legal proceedings,' where 'the motivations of the questioner and declarant are the central concerns,' 829 N.E.2d, at 456, 457 ... and that Amy's oral statement was not 'testimonial' under these standards, *id.*, at 458." *Davis*, 126 S.Ct. 2273.

In an 8–1 decision, the Court held:

> Statements are nontestimonial when made in the course of police interrogation under circumstances objectively indicating that the primary purpose of the interrogation is to enable police assistance to meet an ongoing emergency. They are testimonial when the circumstances objectively indicate that there is no such ongoing emergency, and that

the primary purpose of the interrogation is to establish or prove past events potentially relevant to later criminal prosecution. Id.

Turning to *Davis* and the 911 call, the Court states that when it categorized police interrogation as testimonial in *Crawford*, the Court was considering "interrogations solely directed at establishing the facts of a past crime, in order to identify (or provide evidence to convict) the perpetrator." Id. at 2276. On the other hand, a 911 call "is ordinarily not designed primarily to 'establish or prove' some past fact, but to describe current circumstances requiring police assistance." Id. The Court views McCottry's statements as speaking to events as they occurred and that McCottry was facing an ongoing emergency. In addition, the Court concludes that, viewed objectively, "the elicited statements were necessary to be able to *resolve* the present emergency." Id. The final difference between the situation in *Davis* and *Crawford* is that while the interrogation in *Crawford* occurred in a police station, "McCottry's frantic answers were provided over the phone, in an environment that was not tranquil, or even (as far as any reasonable 911 operator could make out) safe." Id. at 2266. The Court concludes therefore, "that the circumstances of McCottry's interrogation objectively indicate its primary purpose was to enable police assistance to meet an ongoing emergency. She simply was not acting as a *witness*; she was not *testifying*." Id. at 2277.

The Court notes that nontestimonial statements to a 911 operator may evolve into testimonial statements. For instance, when Davis fled the premises, the 911 operator's barrage of questions could be considered an interrogation and McCottry's responses testimonial. However, the Court decided that it did not need to address this issue stating that trial courts, through a motion *in limine*, "should redact or exclude the portions of any statement that have become testimonial." Id.

The Court believed that characterizing the statements in *Hammon* as testimonial or nontestimonial is an easier task, "since they were not much different from the statements we found to be testimonial in *Crawford*." Id. at 2278. The Court writes, "[i]t is entirely clear from the circumstances that the interrogation was part of an investigation into possibly criminal past conduct—as, indeed, the testifying office expressly acknowledged." Id. While it is true that the interrogation in *Crawford* was more formal, that difference only makes it more objectively apparent that the statements obtained were testimonial in nature; it does not change the characterization of the statements made in *Hammon*. Although the Court implicitly rejects the Indiana Supreme Court's implication that "virtually any 'initial inquiries' at the crime scene will not be testimonial ... [it] do[es] not hold the opposite—that *no* questions at the scene will yield nontestimonial answers." As the Court already indicated, the police might need to obtain answers to "assess the situation, the threat to their own safety, and possible danger to the potential victim." Id. at 2279.

NOTE

The Court, in *Whorton v. Bockting*, ___ U.S. ___, 127 S.Ct. 1173, 167 L.Ed.2d 1 (2007), held that *Crawford* does not apply retroactively. In *Whorton*, the Court reversed a Ninth Circuit decision that held "that *Crawford* applies retroactively to cases on collateral review." Id. at 1180. The Court held "that *Crawford* announced a 'new rule' of criminal procedure and that this rule does not fall within the *Teague* exception for watershed rules. We therefore reverse the judgment of the Court of Appeals and remand the case for further proceedings consistent with this opinion."

VIRGINIA CODE ANNOTATED

§ 63.2–1522. Admission of evidence of sexual acts with children

A. In any civil proceeding involving alleged abuse or neglect of a child pursuant to this chapter or pursuant to §§ 16.1–241, 16.1–251, 16.1–252, 16.1–253, 16.1–283 or § 20–107.2, an out-of-court statement made by a child the age of twelve or under at the time the statement is offered into evidence, describing any act of a sexual nature performed with or on the child by another, not otherwise admissible by statute or rule, may be admissible in evidence if the requirements of subsection B are met.

B. An out-of-court statement may be admitted into evidence as provided in subsection A if:

1. The child testifies at the proceeding, or testifies by means of a videotaped deposition or closed-circuit television, and at the time of such testimony is subject to cross examination concerning the out-of-court statement or the child is found by the court to be unavailable to testify on any of these grounds:

a. The child's death;

b. The child's absence from the jurisdiction, provided such absence is not for the purpose of preventing the availability of the child to testify;

c. The child's total failure of memory;

d. The child's physical or mental disability;

e. The existence of a privilege involving the child;

f. The child's incompetency, including the child's inability to communicate about the offense because of fear or a similar reason; and

g. The substantial likelihood, based upon expert opinion testimony, that the child would suffer severe emotional trauma from testifying at the proceeding or by means of a videotaped deposition or closed-circuit television.

2. The child's out-of-court statement is shown to possess particularized guarantees of trustworthiness and reliability.

C. A statement may not be admitted under this section unless the proponent of the statement notifies the adverse party of his intention to offer the statement and the substance of the statement sufficiently in advance of the proceedings to provide the adverse party with a reasonable opportunity to prepare to meet the statement, including the opportunity to subpoena witnesses.

D. In determining whether a statement possesses particularized guarantees of trustworthiness and reliability under subdivision B 2, the court shall consider, but is not limited to, the following factors:

1.   The child's personal knowledge of the event;

2.   The age and maturity of the child;

3.   Certainty that the statement was made, including the credibility of the person testifying about the statement and any apparent motive such person may have to falsify or distort the event including bias, corruption or coercion;

4.   Any apparent motive the child may have to falsify or distort the event, including bias, corruption, or coercion;

5.   The timing of the child's statement;

6.   Whether more than one person heard the statement;

7.   Whether the child was suffering pain or distress when making the statement;

8.   Whether the child's age makes it unlikely that the child fabricated a statement that represents a graphic, detailed account beyond the child's knowledge and experience;

9.   Whether the statement has internal consistency or coherence, and uses terminology appropriate to the child's age;

10.   Whether the statement is spontaneous or directly responsive to questions;

11.   Whether the statement is responsive to suggestive or leading questions; and

12.   Whether extrinsic evidence exists to show the defendant's opportunity to commit the act complained of in the child's statement.

E.   The court shall support with findings on the record, or with written findings in a court not of record, any rulings pertaining to the child's unavailability and the trustworthiness and reliability of the out-of-court statement.

Court Appointed Special Advocates

The CASA movement was the brainchild of a Seattle, Washington Superior Court Judge in 1976. He wanted to ensure that courts received as much information as possible about the children coming before them in neglect, abuse and dependency proceedings. Today CASA is a vital part of the system for dealing with abused and neglected children in many places across the country. One basic thesis is that guardians ad litem and social case workers do not have adequate time to work with each child; the CASA complements these persons and reports directly to the court. Key to the success of the movement are committed groups of well trained volunteer advocates. Some state legislatures have formalized the structure, as the Virginia statute below illustrates.

VIRGINIA CODE ANNOTATED

§ 9.1–153.   Volunteer court-appointed special advocates; powers and duties; assignment; qualifications; training

A.   Services in each local court-appointed special advocate program shall be provided by volunteer court-appointed special advocates, hereinafter referred to as advocates. The advocate's duties shall include:

1.   Investigating the case to which he is assigned to provide independent factual information to the court.

2.   Submitting to the court of a written report of his investigation in compliance with the provisions of § 16.1–274. The report may, upon request of the court, include recommendations as to the child's welfare.

3.   Monitoring the case to which he is assigned to ensure compliance with the court's orders.

4.   Assisting any appointed guardian ad litem to represent the child in providing effective representation of the child's needs and best interests.

5.   Reporting a suspected abused or neglected child pursuant to § 63.2–1509.

B.   The advocate is not a party to the case to which he is assigned and shall not call witnesses or examine witnesses. The advocate shall not, with respect to the case to which he is assigned, provide legal counsel or advice to any person, appear as counsel in court or in proceedings which are part of the judicial process, or engage in the unauthorized practice of law. The advocate may testify if called as a witness.

C.   The program director shall assign an advocate to a child when requested to do so by the judge of the juvenile and domestic relations district court having jurisdiction over the proceedings. The advocate shall continue his association with each case to which he is assigned until relieved of his duties by the court or by the program director.

D.   The Department shall adopt regulations governing the qualifications of advocates who for purposes of administering this subsection shall be deemed to be criminal justice employees. The regulations shall require that an advocate be at least twenty-one years of age and that the program director shall obtain with the approval of the court (i) a copy of his criminal history record or certification that no conviction data are maintained on him and (ii) a copy of information from the central registry maintained pursuant to § 63.2–1515 on any investigation of child abuse or neglect undertaken on him or certification that no such record is maintained on him. Advocates selected prior to the adoption of regulations governing qualifications shall meet the minimum requirements set forth in this article.

E.   An advocate shall have no associations which create a conflict of interests or the appearance of such a conflict with his duties as an advocate. No advocate shall be assigned to a case of a child whose family has a professional or personal relationship with the advocate. Questions concerning conflicts of interests shall be determined in accordance with regulations adopted by the Department.

F.   No applicant shall be assigned as an advocate until successful completion of a program of training required by regulations. The Department shall set standards for both basic and ongoing training.

G. "Medical Neglect" and its Special Treatment

Walter Wadlington, Medical Decision Making for and by Children: Tensions Between Parent, State and Child
1994 U.Ill. L. Rev. 311, 314–18.*

. . .

I. A STEP BACK IN TIME

A good starting point for an historical review of how our law on medical decision making for children developed is the case of Tony Tuttendario, which reached a Pennsylvania court in 1912[17]. Tony, age seven, suffered from rickets which had caused his legs to be badly misshapen. Medical testimony indicated that an operation could remedy the problem and that without it Tony probably would be "a cripple for life and unable to provide for himself".[18] Despite that dire prospect, his parents refused their consent. Because a minor is legally incompetent to consent to medical care or enter into contracts, a parent, guardian or other legally authorized person must give consent or a physician performing non-emergency surgery risks a tort action for battery based on an unauthorized violation of a protected bodily interest. It is because of this that judicial approval or designation of a new legal representative to give consent long has been sought in such cases.[19]

After complaints from school authorities, the Society for the Prevention of Cruelty to Children[20] asked that Tony be committed to them in order to receive proper medical treatment. The court reviewed existing legislation, some of it dating from 1860, which attempted to protect children whose lives or health were endangered, including an 1893 Act specifically authorizing judicial commitment of such minors to charitable societies. The court next stated the question it considered to be before it:

> We are . . . asked to supersede the child's natural guardians on the sole ground that their judgement is impaired by natural love and affection, and that we should substitute for them a humane society whose judgment is untainted by such emotions.[21]

They concluded:

> We see no warrant in the statutes for granting this request. We have not yet adopted as a public policy the Spartan rule that children

* Copyright © 1994, Illinois Law Review. Reprinted with permission.

17. In re Tuttendario, 21 Pa. Dist. 561 (Q.S. Phila. 1912).

18. Id. at 562.

19. For more general discussion, see Walter Wadlington, Consent to Medical Care for Minors: The Legal Framework, in Children's Competence to Consent 57, 58 (Gary B. Melton et al. eds., 1983).

20. The SPCC was a benevolent society established in the late 1800s, a few years after the Society for Prevention of Cruelty to Animals was founded.

21. Tuttendario, 21 Pa.D. at 563.

belong, not to their parents, but to the state.... Even if the law had advanced so far as to consider defective judgment of parents in a critical case a good reason for depriving them of their guardianship, we would not be prepared to say that a clear case of defective judgment has been here made out. The science of medicine and surgery, notwithstanding its enormous advances, has not yet been able to insure an absolutely correct diagnosis in all cases, and still less an absolutely correct prognosis. There is always a residuum of the unknown, and it is this unknown residuum which scientists, by a necessary law for the development of science, disregard, but which parents, in their natural love for their children, regard with apprehension and terror.[22]

Important in the court's refusal to displace the natural parents from their decisional role was that the child's present condition involved "no danger to its life". The court also seemed to believe that under existing law it could intervene otherwise only on the ground of cruelty.[23]

Given the state of medicine in 1911, the decision may have been appropriate in any event. But in following the progression of legal responses in subsequent cases we should remember that it was a forceful statement in favor of parental decision making (almost a cry of parents *uber alles*) and it laid the groundwork for what was dubbed a "life threatening exception" that endured for half a century.

The typical cases invoking the "life threatening exception" involved requests for surgical intervention to obviate almost certain death for a minor whose parents refused consent to transfusion of whole blood. These cases posed special legal concern because parental objections typically were based on religious beliefs.[24] Because of the urgency in such situations, operations often were performed before appeals could be heard. But though the cases became technically moot, appellate courts were sufficiently concerned with providing guidelines for the future that appeals were heard under exceptions to the mootness doctrine.[25]

22. Id.

23. Id.

24. Genesis 9:4 ("I give you everything, with this exception: you must not eat flesh with life, that is to say blood, in it."); Leviticus 17:14 ("For the life of all flesh is its blood, and I have said to the sons of Israel: You must not eat the blood of any flesh, for the life of all flesh is in its blood, and anyone who eats it shall be outlawed from his people."); and Acts 15:19–20 (James's speech to the Pharisees at Jerusalem) ("I rule, then, that instead of making things more difficult for pagans who turn to God, we send them a letter telling them merely to abstain from anything polluted by idols, from fornication, from the meat of strangled animals and from blood.") are the most frequently cited sources of Biblical support for religious objections to transfusion of whole blood.

25. As the Illinois Supreme Court explained in People ex rel. Wallace v. Labrenz, 104 N.E.2d 769, 772 (1952):

> [W]hen the issue presented is of substantial public interest, a well-recognized exception exists to the general rule that a case which has become moot will be dismissed upon appeal. Among the criteria considered in determining the existence of the requisite degree of public interest are the public or private nature of the question presented, the desirability of an authoritative determination for the future guidance of public officers, and the likelihood of future recurrence of the question.

Applying these criteria, we find that the present case falls within that highly sensitive area in which governmental action comes into contact with the religious beliefs of individual citizens. Both the construction of the

In 1952 the Illinois Supreme Court[26] upheld such an intervention for an eight-day-old child with erythroblastosis after two physicians testified that they were certain she would die without transfusions. A third said that although there was a slim chance the child might live, she would suffer permanent mental impairment without the transfusion. The court upheld the constitutionality of the statute allowing intervention as well as the decision of the judge in applying it. The former was important because by this time the bases and procedures for state intervention to protect children had been further spelled out in legislation. Although courts in such cases were and still are wont to explain that they are acting for the state in the role of *parens patriae*, intervention usually is predicated specifically on a neglect, endangerment or other child protection statute. The sanctions or remedies may range from appointing a guardian with limited powers to removing a child from parents temporarily or even permanently.

In determining that the parents' First Amendment rights were not violated, the Illinois Supreme Court relied heavily on both the U.S. Supreme Court's 1878 *Reynolds*[27] decision, which upheld the bigamy conviction of a man who asserted that his acts were in furtherance of his religious beliefs and, not surprisingly, the 1944 *Prince* decision.[28] Similar cases reaching other state supreme courts around this time met with like results.[29] Sixteen years later a three-judge federal court, in a case initiated under 42 U.S.C.A. § 1983, upheld the constitutionality of a Washington state law construed to authorize judges to provide consent for a minor's necessary blood transfusions over a parent's refusal.[30] The U.S. Supreme Court upheld the decision in a one-sentence opinion, citing *Prince v. Massachusetts*.[31]

Two cases during this period illustrate the outer limits of the scope of the "life threatening exception". In 1942 an adult sibling of an eleven-year-

---

statute under which the trial court acted and its validity are challenged. In situations like this one, public authorities must act promptly if their action is to be effective, and although the precise limits of authorized conduct cannot be fixed in advance, no greater uncertainty should exist than the nature of the problems makes inevitable. In addition, the very urgency which presses for prompt action by public officials makes it probable that any similar case arising in the future will likewise become moot by ordinary standards before it can be determined by this court. For these reasons the case should not be dismissed as moot.

26. Id.

27. Reynolds v. United States, 98 U.S. 145 (1878).

28. The other major authorities cited by the court with minimal explanation were Meyer v. Nebraska, op. cit., supra at n. 5, and West Virginia Board of Education v. Barnette, 319 U.S. 624 (1943) (both dealing with the rights of parents to care for and train

their children); and Jacobson v. Massachusetts, 197 U.S. 11 (1905), which upheld the constitutionality of a compulsory vaccination ordinance. *Jacobson* seems strained as an authority because it refers to protecting the public health under the police power rather than protecting the health of a specific individual. On the other hand, there wasn't much else in the way of U.S. Supreme Court decisions to cite.

29. See, e.g., State v. Perricone, 181 A.2d 751 (N.J.1962).

30. Jehovah's Witnesses v. King County Hospital, 278 F.Supp. 488 (W.D.Wash. 1967).

31. Jehovah's Witnesses v. King County Hospital, 390 U.S. 598 (1968). The Court stated simply that: "The judgment is affirmed," relying without comment on its previous decision in Prince v. Massachusetts, 321 U.S. 158 (1944). Justice Douglas and Justice Harlan noted probable jurisdiction and would have set the case for oral argument.

old complained to a Washington juvenile court that her younger sister was not receiving adequate medical care.[32] The child was born with a congenitally oversized arm that was functionally "useless" and posed increasing danger to her system, though there was no suggestion that it would cause imminent death. Physicians recommended amputation and there was evidence that the child agreed with such an approach. Her mother refused,[33] explaining that she had no religious objection but "thought there was 'too much of a chance on her [the daughter's] life' ".[34] The Supreme Court of Washington declined to overrule the parental objection, holding that there was no basis for intervention unless the refusing parent were found unfit. They explained

> At the common law no court had jurisdiction, there is no authority granted by statute or constitution to any court nor has a court of equity inherent power, to deprive a natural guardian of custody and control of his or her minor child in the absence of a determination, after a hearing that such parent is unfit to have custody of the child.[35]

The opinion discloses a very limited view of the *parens patriae* powers of courts regarding child protection in such cases independent of some clear statutory mechanism for it. I doubt that such a view is widely prevalent among judges today, but this is problematical because the controlling statutes now are more broadly worded.

In another boundary-defining case, In re Seiferth,[36] the New York Court of Appeals refused to authorize a state agency to intervene[37] and overrule a father's refusal to consent to corrective surgery for his fourteen-year-old son's cleft palate and harelip[38]. The only risk of mortality in the procedure, the court noted, was a possible adverse anesthesia outcome. The father professed belief "in mental healing by letting 'the forces of the universe work on the body' " though he regarded that as his particular philosophy rather than part of a religion. Torn by concerns such as the need for cooperation by both child and parent, the court refused to intervene. In a dissenting opinion Judge Fuld, noting that the Children's Court Act defined a neglected child as one "whose parent, guardian or custodian neglects or refuses, when able to do so, to provide necessary

---

32. In re Hudson, 126 P.2d 765 (Wash. 1942).

33. The child lived with her mother and her invalid father. According to the court, the father,

> inappreciative of his paternal right of guardianship and unmindful of the obligation imposed on him by virtue of that sacred right, bowed to the will of his wife and testified, in effect, that while he would not of his own volition approve amputation of his child's left arm, he would like to shirk his responsibility as a father and leave the entire matter to the court.

Id. at 768.

34. Id.

35. Id. at 783.

36. 127 N.E.2d 820 (1955).

37. The agency sought to have custody transferred to the local Commissioner of Social Welfare for the specific purpose of consenting to whatever medical, surgical and dental services might be deemed necessary to remedy the problem. Id. at 821.

38. The court explained that the condition called for three operations, followed by an extended period of concentrated speech therapy. *Seiferth,* 127 N.E.2d at 821.

medical, surgical, institutional or hospital care for such child", expressed the view that the court had a duty to perform in such a case.[39]

By the late 1950s, the rules regulating state intervention may have seemed fairly clear, at least to the extent that rules can be discerned from judicial opinions. At this time, however, courts began to see major increases in constitutional litigation contesting state regulation of the family, as well as an ensuing spate of legislative reform. Although much of the latter focused on areas such as divorce and marital property, the scheme for child protection also was expanded. In retrospect, further disputes over medical neglect should have seemed almost inevitable.

. . .

In re Hofbauer

Court of Appeals of New York, 1979.
47 N.Y.2d 648, 419 N.Y.S.2d 936, 393 N.E.2d 1009.

■ JASEN, JUDGE.

This appeal involves the issue whether a child suffering from Hodgkin's disease whose parents failed to follow the recommendation of an attending physician to have their child treated by radiation and chemotherapy, but, rather, placed their child under the care of physicians advocating a nutritional or metabolic therapy, including injections of laetrile, is a "neglected child" within the meaning of section 1012 of the Family Court Act. This case does not involve the legality of the use of laetrile per se in this State inasmuch as neither party contends that a duly licensed New York physician may not administer laetrile to his or her own patients. Nor is this an action brought against a physician to test the validity of his determination to treat Hodgkin's disease by prescribing metabolic therapy and injections of laetrile. Rather, the issue presented for our determination is whether the parents of a child afflicted with Hodgkin's disease have failed to exercise a minimum degree of care in supplying their child with adequate medical care by entrusting the child's physical well-being to a duly licensed physician who advocates a treatment not widely embraced by the medical community.

The relevant facts are as follows: In October, 1977, Joseph Hofbauer, then a seven-year-old child, was diagnosed as suffering from Hodgkin's disease,[1] a disease which is almost always fatal if left untreated. The then attending physician, Dr. Arthur Cohn, recommended that Joseph be seen

---

39. Judge Fuld further explained that:

Neither by statute nor decision is the child's consent necessary or material, and we should not permit his refusal to agree, his failure to co-operate, to ruin his life and any chance for a normal, happy existence; normalcy and happiness, difficult of attainment under the most propitious conditions, will unquestionably be impossible if the disfigurement is not remedied.

Id. at 824 (Fuld, J., dissenting).

1. Hodgkin's disease is a "disease marked by chronic inflammatory enlargement of the lymph nodes, first the cervical and then the axillary, inguinal, mediastinal, mesenteric, etc., together with enlargement of the spleen, and often of the liver and kidneys, with lymphoid infiltration along the blood vessels; there is no pronounced leukocytosis." (Stedman's Medical Dictionary [19th ed.].)

by an oncologist or hematologist for further treatment which would have included radiation treatments and possibly chemotherapy, the conventional modes of treatment. Joseph's parents, however, after making numerous inquiries, rejected Dr. Cohn's advice and elected to take Joseph to Fairfield Medical Clinic in Jamaica where a course of nutritional or metabolic therapy, including injections of laetrile, was initiated.

Upon Joseph's return home to Saratoga County in November, 1977, the instant neglect proceeding was commenced, pursuant to article 10 of the Family Court Act, upon the filing of a petition in Family Court by the Saratoga County Commissioner of Social Services. The petition alleged, in substance, that Joseph's parents neglected their son by their failure to follow the advice of Dr. Cohn with respect to treatment and, instead, chose a course of treatment for Joseph in the form of nutritional therapy and laetrile. A preliminary hearing was held and the court, finding "that there exists the probability of neglect of [Joseph] by his parents," ordered that Joseph be temporarily removed from the custody of his parents and placed in St. Peter's Hospital in Albany.

Thereafter, Joseph's parents made an application to have Joseph returned to their custody. A hearing was duly commenced in December, 1977, but the proceeding was suspended for six months when a stipulation was entered into by the parties returning Joseph to the custody and care of his parents, and authorizing Joseph to come under the care of Dr. Michael Schachter, a physician duly licensed in New York who is a proponent of metabolic therapy. The stipulation further provided that at least one other physician would be consulted regularly, with medical reports to be submitted to the court periodically.[2]

At the direction of the Appellate Division, a fact-finding hearing on the merits of this case was conducted by Family Court in June, 1978. A review of the testimony adduced at the hearing reveals a sharp conflict in medical opinion as to the effectiveness of the treatment being administered to Joseph. The physicians produced by appellants testified, in substance, that radiation and chemotherapy were the accepted methods of treating Hodgkin's disease and that nutritional therapy was an inadequate and ineffective mode of treatment. In addition, two physicians, who by stipulation examined Joseph during the hearing, testified, in essence, that there had been a progression of the disease and denounced the treatment being rendered to Joseph as ineffective.

Two physicians produced by respondents, however, testified that they prescribed nutritional therapy for cancer patients and considered such therapy as a beneficial and effective mode of treatment, although they did

_____

2. In February, 1978, the New York Commissioners of Health and Social Services moved to intervene in the neglect proceeding. Although such motion was denied by Family Court, the Appellate Division reversed, and granted the motion to intervene. (61 A.D.2d 1102, 403 N.Y.S.2d 714.) Thereafter, the intervenors applied to vacate the stipulation and requested that a plenary hearing pursuant to article 10 of the Family Court Act be held immediately. The Family Court denied the requested relief and the Appellate Division affirmed such order (62 A.D.2d 508, 405 N.Y.S.2d 799). The Appellate Division, however, did direct Family Court, immediately upon expiration of the stipulation, to proceed with the requisite "fact-finding" and dispositional hearing on the merits.

not preclude the use of conventional therapy—radiation treatments and chemotherapy—in some cases. In addition, a biologist testified as to a study which had been conducted which demonstrated significant regression in cancerous tumors in mice which had been treated with amygdalin (laetrile), vitamin A, and proteolytic enzymes. Dr. Schachter, the attending physician, then testified that in his opinion Joseph was responding well to the nutritional therapy and that both his appetite and energy levels were good. Dr. Schachter further stated that he had consulted with numerous other physicians concerning Joseph's treatment, and that he never ruled out the possibility of conventional treatment if the boy's condition appeared to be deteriorating beyond control. Significantly, Joseph's father also testified that he would allow his son to be treated by conventional means if Dr. Schachter so advised. Both appellants' and respondents' witnesses testified as to the potentially dangerous side effects of radiation treatments and chemotherapy which could include, among other things, fibrosis of the body organs, swelling of the heart, impairment of the growth centers and leukemia.

Family Court, finding that Joseph's mother and father are concerned and loving parents who have employed conscientious efforts to secure for their child a viable alternative of medical treatment administered by a duly licensed physician, found that Joseph was not a neglected child within the meaning of section 1012 of the Family Court Act and dismissed the petitions. On appeal, a unanimous Appellate Division affirmed. Leave to appeal to this court was granted by the Appellate Division. There should be an affirmance.

. . . [O]ur scope of review is narrow in a case, such as this, coming to us with affirmed findings of fact. This is so because this court is without power to review the findings of fact if such findings are supported by evidence in the record. Thus, our review is confined solely to the legal issues raised by the parties.

Our threshold task in this case is, by necessity, the identification of the standard of neglect against which the facts of this case may be measured. So far as is material for the issue under consideration, a neglected child is defined, by statute, to "[mean] a child less than eighteen years of age whose physical . . . condition has been impaired or is in imminent danger of becoming impaired as a result of the failure of his parent . . . to exercise a minimum degree of care in supplying the child with adequate . . . medical . . . care, though financially able to do so."[3] (Family Ct.Act, § 1012 subd. [f], par. [I], cl. [A].)

A reading of this statutory provision makes it clear that the Legislature has imposed upon the parents of a child the non-delegable affirmative duty to provide their child with adequate medical care. What constitutes adequate medical care, however, cannot be judged in a vacuum free from external influences, but, rather, each case must be decided on its own

---

3. It was stipulated by the parties that Joseph's parents are financially able to provide medical care.

particular facts. In this regard, we deem certain factors significant in determining whether Joseph was afforded adequate medical care.

It is readily apparent that the phrase "adequate medical care" does not require a parent to beckon the assistance of a physician for every trifling affliction which a child may suffer for everyday experience teaches us that many of a child's ills may be overcome by simple household nursing. We believe, however, that the statute does require a parent to entrust the child's care to that of a physician when such course would be undertaken by an ordinarily prudent and loving parent, "solicitous for the welfare of his child and anxious to promote [the child's] recovery." (See People v. Pierson, 176 N.Y. 201, 206, 68 N.E. 243, 244.) This obligation, however, is not without qualification.

It surely cannot be disputed that every parent has a fundamental right to rear its child. While this right is not absolute inasmuch as the State, as *parens patriae*, may intervene to ensure that a child's health or welfare is not being seriously jeopardized by a parent's fault or omission, great deference must be accorded a parent's choice as to the mode of medical treatment to be undertaken and the physician selected to administer the same. . . .

In this regard, it is important to stress that a parent, in making the sensitive decision as how the child should be treated, may rely upon the recommendations and competency of the attending physician if he or she is duly licensed to practice medicine in this State, for "[i]f a physician is licensed by the State, he is recognized by the State as capable of exercising acceptable clinical judgment." (Doe v. Bolton, 410 U.S. 179, 199, 93 S.Ct. 739, 751, 35 L.Ed.2d 201, 217, . . .) Obviously, for all practical purposes, the average parent must rely upon the recommendations and competency of the attending physician since the physician is both trained and in the best position to evaluate the medical needs of the child.

Ultimately, however, the most significant factor in determining whether a child is being deprived of adequate medical care, and, thus, a neglected child within the meaning of the statute, is whether the parents have provided an acceptable course of medical treatment for their child in light of all the surrounding circumstances. This inquiry cannot be posed in terms of whether the parent has made a "right" or a "wrong" decision, for the present state of the practice of medicine, despite its vast advances, very seldom permits such definitive conclusions. Nor can a court assume the role of a surrogate parent and establish as the objective criteria with which to evaluate a parent's decision its own judgment as to the exact method or degree of medical treatment which should be provided, for such standard is fraught with subjectivity. Rather, in our view, the court's inquiry should be whether the parents, once having sought accredited medical assistance and having been made aware of the seriousness of their child's affliction and the possibility of cure if a certain mode of treatment is undertaken, have provided for their child a treatment which is recommended by their physician and which has not been totally rejected by all responsible medical authority.

With these considerations in mind and cognizant that the State has the burden of demonstrating neglect, we now examine the facts of this case. It is abundantly clear that this is not a case where the parents, for religious reasons, refused necessary medical procedures for their child (e.g., Matter of Sampson, 37 A.D.2d 668, 323 N.Y.S.2d 253, affd. 29 N.Y.2d 900, 328 N.Y.S.2d 686; . . .), nor is this a case where the parents have made an irreversible decision to deprive their child of a certain mode of treatment (Custody of a Minor, 379 N.E.2d 1053 [Mass.]). Indeed, this is not a case where the child is receiving no medical treatment, for the record discloses that Joseph's mother and father were concerned and loving parents who sought qualified medical assistance for their child.[4]

Rather, appellants predicate their charge of neglect upon the basis that Joseph's parents have selected for their child a mode of treatment which is inadequate and ineffective. Both courts below found, however—and we conclude that these findings are supported by the record—that numerous qualified doctors have been consulted by Dr. Schachter and have contributed to the child's care; that the parents have both serious and justifiable concerns about the deleterious effects of radiation treatments and chemotherapy; that there is medical proof that the nutritional treatment being administered Joseph was controlling his condition and that such treatment is not as toxic as is the conventional treatment; and that conventional treatments will be administered to the child if his condition so warrants. In light of these affirmed findings of fact, we are unable to conclude, as a matter of law, that Joseph's parents have not undertaken reasonable efforts to ensure that acceptable medical treatment is being provided their child.

By our decision today, we are by no means advocating the use of nutritional or metabolic therapy, including injections of laetrile, as a means to cure or control cancer, since this is not, in the context of this case, an issue for our resolution. . . .

. . . [T]he order of the Appellate Division should be affirmed. . . .

NOTES

(1) Joey Hofbauer died during 1980 at age 10. According to a story in the New York Times after his death, his father stated in an interview that the boy had been "a pioneer whose purpose was to establish the right of parents to make these decisions for their children and to keep [New York] Governor Carey and his faceless bureaucrats out of the family." N.Y. Times, July 18, 1980, at D13, col. 5.

(2) In a widely publicized Massachusetts case involving infant Chad Green, the Supreme Judicial Court of that state addressed the problem of medical care for a young boy with acute lymphocytic leukemia. His doctors had prescribed a course of chemotherapy that they believed would give him a substantial chance of cure or long-term remission of the disease. The parents wished to augment or replace such treatment with a regimen centering on use of laetrile. A trial judge found the minor to be in need of care and protection and issued an order requiring the parents to allow the child to undergo chemotherapy under a board certified hematologist of their choice in the state; legal custody of the child was vested in the Department of

---

4. We would note that it appears that no appropriate State agency has taken any disciplinary action against Dr. Schachter for his treatment of Joseph.

Public Welfare for the limited purpose of assuring that the medical treatment was administered. Affirming that order on appeal, the court stated that

> Essentially, the judge's findings, which we affirm here, are that there is a substantial chance for a cure and a normal life for the child if he undergoes chemotherapy treatment. The uncontradicted medical testimony supports those conclusions, and no evidence of any alternative treatment consistent with good medical practice was offered.

Custody of a Minor, 375 Mass. 733, 379 N.E.2d 1053, 1056 (1978).

The boy's parents later petitioned for a review and redetermination of the need for care and protection. The trial judge continued in effect the prior order requiring chemotherapy and further ordered that the parents cease administering laetrile, enzyme enemas, and certain other treatments to the child. When the appeal from that decision reached the Massachusetts Supreme Judicial Court in 1979, the boy was three years old. The court was informed at oral argument that the parents had taken the child from the state in violation of the trial judge's orders, but it nevertheless passed the issue of standing because it had not been argued before them and "particularly since a small child is concerned". *Custody of a Minor*, 378 Mass. 732, 393 N.E.2d 836 (1979). The court restated the relevant principles:

> The principles governing this case are set out fully in our prior opinion concerning this child. Custody of a Minor, 379 N.E.2d 1053 (1978).... Basically they place three sets of interests in competition: the natural rights of the parents, the responsibilities of the State, and the best interests of the child.

> While recognizing that there exists a private realm of family life which the State cannot enter, Prince v. Massachusetts, 321 U.S. 158 (1944), we think that family autonomy is not absolute, and may be limited where, as here, it appears that parental decisions will jeopardize the health or safety of a child. Custody of a Minor, 389 N.E.2d 68 (1979). Wisconsin v. Yoder, 406 U.S. 205, 234 (1972).

> It is well settled that parents are the "natural guardians of their children ... [with] the legal as well as the moral obligation to support ... educate" and care for their children's development and well-being. Richards v. Forrest, 278 Mass. 547, 553, 180 N.E. 508, 511 (1932). See Purinton v. Jamrock, 195 Mass. 187, 199, 80 N.E. 802 (1907). As such, it is they who have the primary right to raise their children according to the dictates of their own consciences. See Quilloin v. Walcott, 434 U.S. 246, 255 (1978), quoting from Prince v. Massachusetts, 321 U.S. 158, 166 (1944). Pierce v. Society of Sisters, 268 U.S. 510, 535 (1925). Meyer v. Nebraska, 262 U.S. 390, 399 (1923). Indeed, these "natural rights" of parents have been recognized as encompassing an entire private realm of family life which must be afforded protection from unwarranted State interference. Quilloin v. Walcott, supra. Smith v. Organization of Foster Families for Equality & Reform, 431 U.S. 816, 842 (1977). In light of these principles, this court and others have sought to treat the exercise of parental prerogative with great deference.

> It is also well established, however, that the parental rights described above do not clothe parents with life and death authority over their children. This court has stated that the parental right to control a child's nurture is grounded not in any absolute property right which can be enforced to the detriment of the child, but rather is akin to a trust, subject to a correlative duty to care for and protect the child, and terminable by the parents' failure to discharge their obligations. Richards v. Forrest, supra, 278 Mass. at 553, 180 N.E. 508. Purinton v. Jamrock, supra, 195 Mass. at 201, 80 N.E. 802. Donnelly v. Donnelly, 4 Mass.App. 162, 164, 344 N.E.2d 195 (1976). Thus we have stated that where a child's well-being is placed in issue, it is not the rights of parents

that are chiefly to be considered. The first and paramount duty is to consult the welfare of the child.

The standard to be applied in such circumstances is articulated in G.L. c. 119, § 24. Pursuant to this provision, a child may be taken from the custody of his parents on a showing that the child is without necessary and proper physical care and that the parents are unwilling to provide such care. The essential inquiry involves application of the "substituted judgment" or "best interests of the child" principles, ... On a proper showing that parental conduct threatens a child's well-being, the interests of the State and of the individual child may mandate intervention.

Because we are dealing with a child, we find little relevance in arguments which posit the existence of a fundamental right in competent adults to make personal health care decisions and to choose or reject medical treatment, whether orthodox or unorthodox, rational or foolish. We appreciate that the law presently appears to impose certain limitations on such rights in competent adults, and express no opinion as to whether there is such unfettered freedom of choice arising from the constitutional right of privacy and the right of bodily integrity, or whether such freedom of choice might be deemed a logical extension of the right to refuse life-prolonging and life-saving medical care in appropriate circumstances. Cf. Superintendent of Belchertown State School v. Saikewicz, 373 Mass. 728, 370 N.E.2d 417 (1977); Lane v. Candura, 376 N.E.2d 1232 (1978).

Even were we to assume that competent adults have the right to use controversial treatments without limitation, we are dealing here with a three year old child. The parents do not—and indeed cannot—assert on their own behalf the privacy rights of their child. Custody of a Minor, 379 N.E.2d 1053 (1978). On the other hand, the child's own rights of privacy and bodily integrity are fully recognized in principles set out in this opinion. "[T]he State must recognize the dignity and worth of [an incompetent] person and afford to that person the same panoply of rights and choices it recognizes in competent persons." *Saikewicz,* supra, 370 N.E.2d at 428. Such respect is manifested by use of the "substituted judgment" doctrine, according to which a court must seek to identify and effectuate the actual values and preferences of the incompetent individual. Id. at 370 N.E.2d 417. In the case of a child, however, the substituted judgment doctrine and the "best interests of the child" test are essentially coextensive, involving examination of the same criteria and application of the same basic reasoning. Custody of a Minor, supra, 379 N.E.2d 1053.

Applying these principles to the case before it, the court affirmed the trial judge's decision as "clearly warranted, and probably required, on the evidence before him." The trial court had found that none of the metabolic therapy components the parents wished to use were shown to have any curative or ameliorative effect in the treatment of acute lymphocytic anemia and that some posed the threat of damage. In concluding, the appellate court stated:

> It is with sadness that we review the entire history of this case. The child's disease under chemotherapy treatment has been in constant remission except for a period of months when the parents, without knowledge of the attending physician, discontinued the medication. Only after the first Superior Court hearing was completed, and was on appeal, did the parents make any mention of laetrile.
>
> Now the parents concede that chemotherapy must be continued, but they persist in their support of metabolic therapy, including laetrile, despite the proof that this regimen is not only useless but dangerous for their child.

This is not a case where, in either of the two hearings, conflicting testimony was weighed as to the merits of contesting theories or opinions. The evidence in the first hearing supportive of chemotherapy as the sole hope for amelioration or cure of the disease was undisputed. Likewise, in the second hearing, the evidence was essentially uncontested that metabolic therapy for this child is useless and dangerous. The decisions entered after both hearings were supported by convincing, even overwhelming, evidence.

The judgment of the parents has been consistently poor, from the child's standpoint, and his well-being seriously threatened as a result. Their persistence in pursuing for their child a course against all credible medical advice cannot be explained in terms of despair of a cure, or by the suffering of serious side effects of chemotherapy. The chance for cure with chemotherapy is good; the side effects of chemotherapy in this case have been minor and readily controllable. The parents' actions must be viewed with compassion, but beyond doubt their poor judgment has added immeasurably and unnecessarily to their difficulties, and to those of the child.

This case well illustrates that parents do not and must not have absolute authority over the life and death of their children. Under our free and constitutional government, it is only under serious provocation that we permit interference by the State with parental rights. That provocation is clear here. It is beyond argument that a drug or course of treatment is unsafe if its potential for inflicting death or physical injury is not offset by the possibility of therapeutic benefit. The position of the parents in this case, however well intentioned, is indefensible against the overwhelming weight of medical evidence.

Judgment affirmed.

As the Massachusetts court noted, Chad Green's parents had taken him from the state by the time the case was last heard on appeal. The boy died in October 1979 at age 3 in Mexico, where he had been receiving treatments using laetrile. The press continued its wide coverage of the case afterward, focusing on the question whether the parents might be held in criminal contempt for violating the Massachusetts judicial order. According to one newspaper report, California's Governor Jerry Brown said he would not approve any request for extradition of the Greens, criticizing the Massachusetts action as the medical establishment's attempt "to dictate a family choice." San Francisco Chronicle, Oct. 19, 1979, at 1, col. 1. The following year, after the Greens had returned to Massachusetts, a Superior Court Judge there did hold them in contempt but declined to impose either a fine or a jail sentence on them under the rationale that they had suffered enough. N.Y. Times, Dec. 9, 1980, sec. 2, at 21, col. 1.

In re Sampson

Family Court, Ulster County, 1970.
65 Misc.2d 658, 317 N.Y.S.2d 641.

■ HUGH R. ELWYN, JUDGE:

The Commissioner of Health of Ulster County brings this neglect proceeding pursuant to Article 10 of the Family Court Act charging that Kevin Sampson, a male child under sixteen years of age is neglected by reason of the failure of his mother, Mildred Sampson, to provide him with proper medical and surgical care. The mother is not opposed to having the recommended surgery performed upon her son, but because she is a member of the religious sect known as Jehovah's Witnesses she has steadfastly refused to give her consent to the administration of any blood transfusions during the course of the surgery, without which the proposed surgery may not safely be performed. After extensive hearings the Court finds that the following facts are established by the evidence.

The boy, Kevin Sampson, who is now fifteen years of age, having been born on January 25, 1955, suffers from extensive neurofibromatosis or Von Recklinghausen's disease which has caused a massive deformity of the right side of his face and neck. The outward manifestation of the disease is a large fold or flap of an overgrowth of facial tissue which causes the whole cheek, the corner of his mouth and right ear to drop down giving him an appearance which can only be described as grotesque and repulsive. Fortunately, however, the disease has not yet progressed to a point where his vision has been affected or his hearing impaired. Dr. Robert C. Lonergan, an eye doctor appointed by the Court to examine Kevin reported that "I do not believe ocular condition related to systemic disease—in any event it does not alter or require any change in treatment—the eye condition requires no treatment." Dr. Elbert Loughran, an ear doctor appointed by the Court to examine Kevin reported that he found "normal drum heads bilateral. Effect on hearing limited to occlusion of external ear canal on right by folds of skin. The left ear drum and canal are normal. Gross hearing normal on both sides."

Thus, insofar as the boy's sight and hearing are concerned, it appears from the doctor's reports that the neurofibromatosis poses no immediate threat to either and that there is, therefore, no need for treatment of either his eyes or his ears. However, the massive deformity of the entire right side of his face and neck is patently so gross and so disfiguring that it must inevitably exert a most negative effect upon his personality development, his opportunity for education and later employment and upon every phase of his relationship with his peers and others. Although the staff psychiatrist of the County Mental Health Center reports that "there is no evidence of any thinking disorder" and that "in spite of marked facial disfigurement he failed to show any outstanding personality aberration", this finding hardly justifies a conclusion that he has been or will continue to be wholly unaffected by his misfortune. Although Kevin was found to be not psychotic, a psychologist found him to be a "boy (who) is extremely dependent and (who) sees himself as an inadequate personality." The staff psychiatrist reports that "Kevin demonstrates inferiority feeling and low self concept. Such inadequate personality is often noted in cases of mental retardation, facial disfigurement and emotional deprivation."

If the boy exhibited to the psychologist some mental retardation it is hardly surprising in view of the fact that he has been exempted from school since November 24, 1964 and is currently exempted from school by reason of his facial disfigurement. As a result, although various tests administered by school authorities show him to be intellectually capable of being educated and trained to a reasonable level of self-sufficiency, he is, at 15 years of age, a virtual illiterate.

From all the information available to the Court as the result of extended hearings and various reports, particularly those supplied by those educators who have become familiar with the pattern of Kevin's development, or more accurately, the lack thereof, the conclusion is inescapable that the marked facial disfigurement from which this boy suffers constitutes such an overriding limiting factor militating against his future development that unless some constructive steps are taken to alleviate his condition, his chances for a normal, useful life are virtually nil.

The unanimous recommendation of all those who have dealt with the many problems posed by Kevin's affliction—educators, psychologists, psychiatrists, physicians and surgeons is that steps be taken to correct the condition through surgery. It is conceded, however, by the surgeons that, insofar as his health and his life is concerned, this is not a necessary operation. The disease poses no immediate threat to his life nor has it as yet seriously affected his general health. Moreover, the surgery will not cure him of the disease. In fact, for the condition from which he suffers there is no known cure. According to Dr. Brandon Maccomber, one of the highly qualified plastic surgeons who testified as to the need for surgery, "where (the disease) is interfering with function or appearance many times it can be excised partially, it never can be cured, but it can be excised, removed and by plastic procedures you may be able to improve not only the function but the appearance."

The surgery which the surgeons recommend for the alleviation of the diseased condition cannot, however, be performed without substantial risk. In the words of Dr. Ferdinand Stanley Hoffmeister, the other highly qualified surgeon who testified as to the need for corrective surgery and who had previously performed some limited surgery upon this boy, "I think it's a dangerous procedure. I think it involves considerable risk. It's a massive surgery of six to eight hours duration with great blood loss. This is a risky surgical procedure." When asked if the risk would be much above average he replied, "much, much, much." The surgeon repeatedly "emphasiz(ed) the surgery risk in operating on this patient even with blood."

Without the mother's permission to administer blood transfusions the risk becomes wholly unacceptable. According to Dr. Hoffmeister, "if this tumor had to be removed as extensively as it is desirable to improve his appearance, I think the loss of blood would be so extensive, that I personally would not dare to undertake such a procedure having only plasma expanders at my disposal". The surgeons are adamant in their refusal to operate upon Kevin unless they have permission to use blood and to administer during the surgery such blood transfusions as the patient's condition requires.

Mrs. Sampson, while not opposed to surgery as such, having already given permission for surgery limited to the use of plasma, is equally adamant in her refusal to give her consent to the use of blood. As previously noted, Mrs. Sampson is an adherent to the religious sect known as Jehovah's Witnesses who according to the minister of the Kingston Congregation of Jehovah's Witnesses "feel that the Bible is explicit on the matter of taking any form of blood into our system either by eating, through mouth, food, through the body, through the veins. This is specifically prohibited in the Scriptures for Christians". Although not opposed to medicine or surgery on religious grounds, Jehovah's Witnesses hold as a cardinal principle of their faith that the eating or ingestion of blood into the body by any means whatever, including modern surgical procedures for the transfusion of blood are explicitly forbidden by the law of God. According to Jehovah's Witnesses' doctrine the divine proscription dates back to God's pronouncement to Noah immediately after the global flood over 4300 years ago,[1] was reiterated and emphasized to the Jews when the Nation of Israel was brought into the covenant relationship with Jehovah,[2] applies to the eating of human blood as well as animal blood[3] and was made applicable to Christians by the new covenant made over the blood of Jesus Christ.[4] Jehovah's Witnesses regard the prohibition against the consumption of blood as more than a mere dietary law of the Jews—the eating of blood in any form is a sin against God[5] and draws upon the soul of the transgressor the enmity of God[6]. ("Blood, Medicine and the Law of God." Watchtower Bible and Tract Society, 1961; State v. Perricone, 37 N.J. 463, 181 A.2d 751).

While Jehovah's Witnesses emphasize that their refusal to submit to blood transfusions is based upon the law of God as recorded in their Bible, New World Translation of the Holy Scriptures, they find further support for their position in the substantial risk to health and even to life which medical science acknowledges to be inherent in the transfusion of human blood. In addition to the adverse reaction in a patient to be anticipated from the mismatching of incompatible blood types or the ofttime fatal consequences of a circulatory overload or an air embolism caused by inept procedures, the Court finds considerable support for the Witnesses' fear that the current widespread practice of using blood from commercial blood banks poses a serious risk to the patient's health through the transmission of such diseases as syphilis, malaria, hepatitis and a variety of allergic conditions.[7]

Finally, the Court finds that the child's parent has been offered the financial means with which to have the recommended surgery performed, but that for the reasons heretofore expressed she adamantly refuses to give her consent.

The Jurisdiction and Power of the Court

The Constitution of the State of New York provides in Article 6 § 13, subd. b that "The family court shall have jurisdiction over the following classes of actions and proceedings which shall be originated in such family court in the manner provided by law: (1) the protection, treatment, correction and commitment of those minors who are in need of the exercise of the authority of the court because of circumstances of neglect, delinquency or dependency, as the legislature may determine."

1. Genesis 9:3, 4.
2. Leviticus 3:17; 7:26, 27; 17:10—14 Deuteronomy 12:23.
3. I Chronicles 11:16–19; II Samuel 23:15–17.
4. Acts 15:28, 29; 21:25.
5. I Samuel 14:32, 33.
6. Leviticus 17:10.
7. The New York Times of July 1970, p. 6 in an article entitled "Why there is Peril from Some Blood Donors" reports that "a study carried out at the National Institutes of Health reveals that 51 percent of heart surgery patients receiving commercial blood came down with hepatitis, while those receiving voluntary blood rarely did"....

"The family court has exclusive original jurisdiction over (i) abuse and neglect proceedings, as set forth in article ten." (Family Court Act § 115).

"This article is designed to establish procedures to help protect children from injury or mistreatment and to help safeguard their physical, mental, and emotional well-being. It is designed to provide a due process of law for determining when the state, through its family court, may intervene against the wishes of a parent on behalf of a child so that his needs are properly met." (Family Court Act § 1011).

"The family court has exclusive original jurisdiction over proceedings under this article alleging abuse or neglect of a child." (Family Court Act § 1013). "When used in this article and unless the specific context indicates otherwise:

"(f) 'Neglected child' means a child less than eighteen years of age

"(i) whose physical, mental or emotional condition has been impaired or is in imminent danger of becoming impaired as a result of the failure of his parent or other person legally responsible for his care to exercise a minimum degree of care

"(A) in supplying the child with adequate food, clothing, shelter, education, medical or surgical care, though financially able to do so or offered financial or other reasonable means to do so." (Family Court Act § 1012)

"The Family Court (also) has jurisdiction over physically handicapped children" (Family Court Act s 232(a)), and over "proceedings concerning physically handicapped and mentally defective or retarded children" (Family Court Act § 115, subd. (b))

"(c) 'Physically handicapped child' means a person under twenty-one years of age who, by reason of physical defect or infirmity, whether congenital or acquired by accident, injury or disease, is or may be expected to be totally or partially incapacitated for education or for remunerative occupation, as provided in the education law, or is physically handicapped, as provided in section two thousand five hundred eighty-one of the public health law" (Family Court Act § 232, subd. (c)).

As defined in the Education Law "A 'handicapped child' is one who, because of mental, physical or emotional reasons, cannot be educated in regular classes but can benefit by special services and programs to include, but not limited to, transportation, the payment of tuition to boards of cooperative educational services and public school districts, home teaching, special classes, special teachers, and resource rooms." (Education Law § 4401, subd. 1).

"Physically handicapped children" are defined in the Public Health Law as [meaning persons] "under twenty-one years of age who are handicapped by reason of a defect or disability, whether congenital or acquired by accident, injury, or disease, or who are suffering from long-term disease, including but without limiting the generality of the foregoing, cystic fibrosis, muscular dystrophy, nephrosis, rheumatic fever and rheumatic heart disease, blood dyscrasias, cancer, brain injured, and chronic asthma, or from any disease or condition likely to result in a handicap in the absence of treatment, provided, however, no child shall be deprived of a service under the provisions of this chapter solely because of the degree of mental retardation." (Public Health Law § 2581).

"Whenever a child within the jurisdiction of the court appears to the court to be in need of medical, surgical, therapeutic, or hospital care or treatment, a suitable order may be made therefor." (Family Court Act § 232, subd. (b)).

Whether this child be deemed to be "neglected" or "Physically handicapped" there is plainly ample constitutional and statutory authority for this court to entertain this proceeding and to do whatever is necessary and appropriate to insure this child's welfare. The authority to act for the child's welfare includes the power to direct a surgical operation over the objection of parents (Matter of Seiferth, 309 N.Y. 80, 85, 127 N.E.2d 820, 823; Matter of Vasko, 238 App.Div. 128, 129, 263 N.Y.S. 552, 554; Matter of Rotkowitz, 175 Misc. 948, 25 N.Y.S.2d 624). The question is, however, whether the court should exercise the power which it undoubtedly has, to compel this boy to undergo a dangerous surgical procedure for the partial correction, but not a cure, of the facial deformity from which he suffers, over the sincerely held religious objection of his mother? The answer to this question requires a most careful balancing of the potential good to be attained against the risks to life necessarily involved in so dangerous a surgical procedure and consideration of the validity of the religious objections which have been raised to the administration of blood transfusions. These two facets of the question will be examined in inverse order.

The Religious Objections

The free exercise of religion is, of course, one of our most precious freedoms and is guaranteed by both the United States and New York State Constitution. The First Amendment to the United States Constitution made applicable to the States by virtue of the Fourteenth Amendment (Cantwell v. Connecticut, 310 U.S. 296, 303; Matter of Brown v. McGinnis, 10 N.Y.2d 531, 535, 225 N.Y.S.2d 497, 180 N.E.2d 791) provides that "Congress shall make no law respecting an establishment of religion or prohibiting the free exercise thereof."

Article 1, § 3 of the New York State Constitution provides that "the free exercise and enjoyment of religious profession and worship, without discrimination or preference, shall forever be allowed in this state to all mankind; * * * but the liberty of conscience hereby secured shall not be so construed as to excuse acts of licentiousness, or justify practices inconsistent with the peace or safety of this state."

The courts have, however, drawn a distinction between the free exercise of religious belief which is constitutionally protected against any infringement and religious practices that are inimical or detrimental to public health or welfare which are not (Reynolds v. United States, 98 U.S. 145; Davis v. Beason, 133 U.S. 333). In Reynolds v. United States, supra, a case which dealt with the power of the state to outlaw the Mormon's practice of polygamy in the name of religion, the United States, Supreme Court culled from the writings of Thomas Jefferson, a strong supporter of the inclusion of the First Amendment in the Bill of Rights, to draw a distinction between religious belief and religious practice. The Court said: "Laws are made for the government of actions, and while they cannot interfere with mere religious belief and opinions, they may with practice."

This distinction has been preserved and reaffirmed by the United States Supreme Court in subsequent decisions. In Cantwell v. Connecticut, 310 U.S. 296 306—304, the Court set forth the dimensions of the free exercise of religion stating: "The constitutional inhibition of legislation on the subject of religion has a double aspect. On the one hand, it forestalls compulsion by law of the acceptance of any creed or the practice of any form of worship. Freedom of conscience and freedom to adhere to such religious organization or form of worship as the individual may choose cannot be restricted by law. On the other hand, it safeguards the free exercise of the chosen form of religion. Thus the Amendment embraces two concepts,—freedom to believe and freedom to act. The first is absolute but, in the nature of things, the second cannot be. Conduct remains subject to regulation for the protection of society".

In Prince v. Massachusetts, 321 U.S. 158, the United States Supreme Court held that Massachusetts, acting to safeguard the general interest and well-being of its youth, could prohibit a child of a Jehovah's Witness parent from distributing religious pamphlets on the street even though the child was accompanied by her adult guardian. The Massachusetts statute which prohibited such activities by a minor was not violative of Jehovah's Witnesses' freedom of religion, nor a denial of the equal protection of the laws, under the Fourteenth Amendment of the Constitution.

While recognizing "the rights of children to exercise their religion, and of parents to give them religious training and to encourage them in the practice of religious belief" citing West Virginia State Board of Education v. Barnette, 319 U.S. 624 and Pierce v. Society of Sisters, 268 U.S. 510, the court in Prince v. Massachusetts, supra also said:

"But the family itself is not beyond regulation in the public interest, as against a claim of religious liberty. And neither rights of religion nor rights of parenthood are beyond limitation. Acting to guard the general interest in youth's well-being, the state as Parens patriae may restrict the parent's control by requiring school attendance, regulating or prohibiting the child's labor, and in many other ways. Its authority is not nullified merely because the parent grounds his claim to control the child's course of conduct on religion or conscience. Thus, he cannot claim freedom from compulsory vaccination for the child more than for himself on religious grounds (Jacobson v. Massachusetts, 197 U.S. 11). The right to practice religion freely does not include liberty to expose the community or the child to communicable disease or the latter to ill health or death. The catalogue need not be lengthened. It is sufficient to show what indeed appellant hardly disputes, that the state has a wide range of power for limiting parental freedom and authority in things affecting the child's welfare; and that this includes, to some extent, matters of conscience and religious conviction."

Specifically, the same issue presented here—i.e. the power of the state through its courts to order a necessary blood transfusion for a minor over the religious objections of a parent has been frequently contested by

Jehovah's Witnesses before. However, in every reported case that research has revealed in which the issue has been presented the courts have unequivocally upheld the power of the state to authorize the administration of a blood transfusion over the religious objections of the parent where the blood transfusion was shown to be necessary for the preservation of the minor's life or the success of needed surgery.

A cogent expression of the Civil authority's answer to the scriptural authority relied upon by Jehovah's Witnesses in support of their position may be found in the following excerpt from the Ohio Court's opinion in In re Clark, supra:

"To a layman unversed in the seemingly esoteric art of theological interpretation of the 17th century English version of ancient Hebrew and Greek Scriptures, these passages[8] are, to say the least, somewhat obscure. They have to do with blood and the eating or taking thereof. Blood transfusion as administered by modern medicine was unknown to the authors of these cryptic dicta. Had its beneficent effects been known to them, it is not unlikely some exception would have been made in its favor— especially be St. Luke who is said to have been a physician.

"But in our humble Civil Court we must confine ourselves to the civil law of the State. Religious doctrines and dogmas, be they obviously sound or curiously dubious, may not control. The parents in this case have a perfect right to worship as they please and believe what they please. They enjoy complete freedom of religion. The parents also have the right to use all lawful means to vindicate this right (and in the present instance they appear to have done their full duty by their religion).

"But this right of theirs ends where somebody else's right begins. Their child is a human being in his own right, with a soul and body of his own. He has rights of his own—*the right to live and grow up without disfigurement* (emphasis supplied).

"The child is a citizen of the State. While he 'belongs' to his parents, he belongs also to his State. Their rights in him entail many duties. Likewise the fact the child belongs to the State imposes upon the State many duties. Chief among them is the duty to protect *his right to live and to grow up with a sound mind in a sound body*, and to brook no interference with that right by any person or organization (emphasis supplied).

"When a religious doctrine espoused by the parents threatens to defeat or curtail such a right of their child, the State's duty to step in and preserve the child's right is immediately operative.

"To put it another way, when a child's right to live and his parents' religious belief collide, the former is paramount, and the religious doctrine must give way."

In the light of the foregoing authorities I conclude that although the mother's religious objections to the administration of a blood transfusion to her son in the event surgery is to be performed upon his face is founded upon the scriptures and is sincerely held, it must give way before the state's paramount duty to insure his right to live and grow up without

---

8. Genesis 9:3, 4 Leviticus 3:17; 17:14 Deuteronomy 12:23 Acts 15:28, 29.

disfigurement—the right to live and grow up with a sound mind in a sound body. "Parents may be free to become martyrs themselves. But it does not follow they are free, in identical circumstances, to make martyrs of their children before they have reached the age of full and legal discretion when they can make that choice for themselves" (Prince v. Massachusetts, 321 U.S. 158).

The Potential Good vs. The Risk to Life

In the opinion of the surgeons who are familiar with Kevin's condition the neurofibromatosis from which he suffers poses no immediate threat to his life or even to his general health and the proposed surgery for its excision would have no material effect upon his life expectancy. Fortunately, according to Dr. Maccomber, "To date there are no signs of any central nervous system, that is brain or spinal cord, involvement."

It is not necessary, however, that a child's life be in danger before this court may act to safeguard his health or general welfare. In Matter of Rotkowitz, 175 Misc. 948, 25 N.Y.S.2d 624 in which the Domestic Relations Court of New York ordered an operation for the correction of a deformity of the child's right lower extremity the Court said: "I must conclude that it was the intention of the Legislature to give power to the Justices of this Court to order an operation not only in an instance where the life of the child is to be saved but also in instances where the health, the limb, the person or the future of the child is at stake." And in Matter of Seiferth, 285 App.Div. 221, 224–225, 137 N.Y.S.2d 35, 38, reversed 309 N.Y. 80, 127 N.E.2d 820, the Appellate Division, referring to a twelve year old boy who was afflicted with congenital hair lip and cleft palate, said: "There need be no 'emergency'. * * * We believe that the infant respondent is both a neglected child and a physically handicapped child. He is neglected because his father refuses to furnish him with medical care which is needed. He is physically handicapped because, equally with the deaf and the crippled, he is partially incapacitated for education and remunerative occupation. It is immaterial that his physical life is not in danger. The statute contains no such requirement. What is in danger is his change for a normal useful life. It is a serious error to permit this twelve year old boy, a victim of his father's delusions, to make such a choice for himself."

This view of the Court's power and authority did not prevail, however, for the Court of Appeals (309 N.Y. 80, 127 N.E.2d 820) reversed the decision of the Appellate Division in Seiferth which had required the boy to submit to surgery, largely because it found no emergency which threatened his health or his life. While conceding that "the Children's Court has power in drastic situations to direct the operation over the objection of parents", the Court of Appeals, "nevertheless, [found that there] is no present emergency, [and] that time is less of the essence than it was a few years ago insofar as it concerns the physical prognosis * * * ". The decision was not, however, without a strong dissent[9] by Judge Fuld in which Judges Desmond and Burke concurred.

9. "Every child has a right, so far as is possible, to lead a normal life and, if his parents, through viciousness or ignorance, act in such a way as to endanger that right,

Matter of Seiferth was, moreover, decided fifteen years ago in 1955 and in the light of the broad powers and "wide discretion and grave responsibilities" (Family Court Act § 141) conferred upon the Judges of this Court by the enactment of the Family Court Act, it is of doubtful validity as a binding precedent upon this Court in the present situation. It is now, as it was at the time Seiferth was decided, declared to be "the policy of the state of New York to provide medical service for the treatment and rehabilitation of physically handicapped children" (Public Health Law § 2580). Although "medical service" as defined in subd. 2 of section 2581 of the Public Health Law does not include surgical treatment[10] section 232 of the Family Court Act which gives the Family Court jurisdiction over physically handicapped children provides that "Whenever a child within the jurisdiction of the court appears to the court to be in need of medical, Surgical, therapeutic, or hospital care or treatment, a suitable order may be made therefor." (emphasis supplied). There is no requirement in the statute that there be an emergency or danger to the child's life before the Court may act—only a requirement that the child be within the jurisdiction of the Court and appear to the Court to be in need. Furthermore, the recent revision of Article 10 of the Family Court which confers upon this Court exclusive jurisdiction and ample authority to deal with the abused and neglected child is a clear indication of the Legislature's concern for these unfortunate children and its intention to confer upon the Court the broadest power and discretion to deal with these matters. I therefore conclude that this court's authority to deal with the abused, neglected or physically handicapped child is not limited to "drastic situations" or to those which constitute a "present emergency", but that the Court has a "wide discretion" to order medical or surgical care and treatment for an infant even over parental objection, if in the Court's judgment the health, safety or welfare of the child requires it.

The question still remains, however, whether this Court should, under the circumstances of this case, order this boy to undergo a risky surgical procedure, which the surgeons concede will not cure him of the disease. Dr. Hoffmeister, one of the plastic surgeons who testified in this case concedes, "we would certainly leave a tumor behind. This is a non-resectable lesion." Dr. Maccomber, the other surgeon also was frank in admitting the limitations upon the surgeon's skill when he said: "well, you can remove—you can't get it all, this is for sure." Although the results of the surgery would be to change his physical appearance, Dr. Maccomber conceded that "he can't be returned to a normal face, impossible."

Counsel for Mrs. Sampson stresses the surgical risk involved in the contemplated procedure which the surgeons candidly concede is a "danger-

---

the courts should, as the legislature has provided, act on his behalf. Such is the case before us.

* * *

"It is quite true that the child's physical life is not at peril—as would be the situation if he had an infected appendix or a growth on the brain—but it may not be questioned, to quote from the opinion below, 'What is in danger is his chance for a normal, useful life.'" (Dissenting opinion Judge Fuld, Matter of Seiferth, 309 N.Y. 80, 86, 127 N.E.2d 820, 823).

10. The phrase, "surgical treatment" was eliminated from the definition of "medical service" contained in sect. 2581 of the Public Health Law by Laws 1963, c. 701.

ous procedure" and involves "considerable risk" even with the use of blood transfusions. Moreover, counsel points out with much persuasiveness that Dr. Hoffmeister expressed the opinion that, while the contemplated surgery would still be risky, it would be less risky if the operation were delayed for five or six years, because the boy's blood volume would then be larger and while the loss of blood would be about the same, the relative blood loss would be smaller than now.

Because of the high surgical risk inherent in the operation and the minimization of the risk as the boy grows older by reason of the lower relative blood loss to total blood supply, counsel for Mrs. Sampson and the Law Guardian counsel delay until the boy is old enough to make the decision for himself. In fact, even Dr. Hoffmeister counsels delay. He said: "I would suggest to the Court wait until the child is 21 years old and have him make his own decision because I feel we are not losing by waiting five or six years.

"Q. In other words you feel it is not increasing the degree of risk to wait five or six years?

"A. I think it's decreasing the degree of risk.

"Q. It's decreasing?

"A. Because of the blood volume we alluded to."

From the surgeon's point of view the fact that the surgical risk may decrease as the boy grows older is certainly a most persuasive reason for postponing the surgery. However, to postpone the surgery merely to allow the boy to become of age so that he may make the decision himself as suggested by the surgeon and urged by both counsel for the mother and the Law Guardian (Matter of Seiferth, supra) totally ignores the developmental and psychological factors stemming from his deformity which the Court deems to be of the utmost importance in any consideration of the boy's future welfare and begs the whole question.

This Court cannot evade the responsibility for a decision now by the simple expedient of foisting upon this boy the responsibility for making a decision at some later day, which by the time it is made, if at all, will be too late to undo the irreparable damage he will have suffered in the interim. This Court plainly has a duty to perform and though the responsibility for decision is awesome, the burden cannot be shared by transferring even a small part of it to another. Except for the difference in the degree of risk involved in the surgery, the words of Judge Fuld dissenting in Seiferth, supra 86, 127 N.E.2d 824, are an eloquent exposition of the "grave responsibilities" this Court must carry and are peculiarly apposite to this case. Judge Fuld wrote:

> "It would, of course, be preferable if the boy were to accede to the operation, and I am willing to assume that, if he acquiesces, he will the more easily and quickly react to the postoperative speech therapy. However, there is no assurance that he will, either next year, in five years or six, give his consent. Quite obviously, he is greatly influenced by his father, quite plainly a victim of the latter's unfortunate delusions. And, beyond that, it must be borne in mind that there is little if

any risk involved in the surgery and that, as time goes on, the operation becomes more difficult.

Be that as it may, though, it is the court which has a duty to perform, Children's Court Act, § 24, and it should not seek to avoid that duty by foisting upon the boy the ultimate decision to be made. Neither by statute nor decision is the child's consent necessary or material, and we should not permit his refusal to agree, his failure to co-operate, to ruin his life and any chance for a normal, happy existence; normalcy and happiness, difficult of attainment under the most propitious conditions, will unquestionably be impossible if the disfigurement is not remedied.

Moreover, it is the fact, and a vital one, that this is a proceeding brought to determine whether the parents are neglecting the child by refusing and failing to provide him with necessary surgical, medical and dental service [according to the Children's Court Act] Whether the child condones the neglect, whether he is willing to let his parents do as they choose, surely cannot be operative on the question as to whether or not they are guilty of neglect. They are not interested or concerned with whether he does or does not want the essential operation. They have arbitrarily taken the position that there is to be no surgery. What these parents are doing, by their failure to provide for an operation, however well-intentioned, is far worse than beating the child or denying him food or clothing. To the boy, and his future, it makes no difference that it may be ignorance rather than viciousness that will perpetuate his unfortunate condition. If parents are actually mistreating or neglecting a child, the circumstance that he may not mind it cannot alter the fact that they are guilty of neglect and it cannot render their conduct permissible.

. . .''

It is conceded that "there are important considerations both ways" and that the views expressed by the dissenting Judges in Seiferth have not been universally accepted.[11] Moreover, it must also be humbly acknowledged that under the circumstances of this case "one cannot be certain of being right."[12] (Matter of Seiferth, supra, 309 N.Y. at 87, 127 N.E.2d 820).

---

11. Cf. In re Hudson, 13 Wash.2d 673, 126 P.2d 765 (Sup.Ct.1942) in which the Supreme Court of Washington reversed an order of a Juvenile Court which had ordered surgery for the amputation of a child's left arm with this rebuke to judicial authority: "However, the mere fact that the court is convinced of the necessity of subjecting a minor child to a surgical operation will not sustain a court order which deprives a parent of the responsibility and right to decide respecting the welfare of the child. No court has authority to take a minor child, over objection of its parents who have not been deprived as unfit and unsuitable persons to have custody and control of the child, and subject it to a surgical operation."

12. I am keenly aware of the moral dilemma posed by the choice between an abdication of this court's responsibility for this boy's health and general welfare and the seeming assumption by the court of a power many would regard as the exclusive prerogative of God alone. In re Hudson, 13 Wash.2d 673, 126 P.2d 765 the Washington Supreme Court by a 5–4 decision chose the first horn of the dilemma rather than arrogate to itself such divine powers. In eschewing such powers the court said: "Implicit in their (the family's) position is their opinion that it would be preferable that the child die instead

Nevertheless, a decision must be made, and so, after much deliberation, I am persuaded that if this court is to meet its responsibilities to this boy it can neither shift the responsibility for the ultimate decision onto his shoulders nor can it permit his mother's religious beliefs to stand in the way of attaining through corrective surgery whatever chance he may have for a normal, happy existence, which, to paraphrase Judge Fuld, is difficult of attainment under the most propitious circumstances, but will unquestionably be impossible if the disfigurement is not corrected.

If this boy has any chance at all for a normal, happy existence, without a disfigurement so gross as to overshadow all else in his life, some risk must be taken. The surgeons acknowledge that in every case of surgery performed under anesthesia there is always a risk of cardiac arrest, but as Dr. Maccomber said, "if we worried about that all the time we wouldn't do any good for anybody." He acknowledged: "we know there's a risk and they have to have surgery." But then he added: "Here the risk shouldn't be too great with blood. In other words, we're not working on vital organs that can go haywire, but with this, we surely, if we didn't have blood, no one should touch him."

Thus, while the surgeons concede that there are risks inherent in the contemplated surgery, in their opinion that risk should not be too great if they have permission to use blood. In any event, when one considers the bleak prospect for this boy's future of the alternative of doing nothing, it is a risk which I believe must be taken. However, this conclusion must be qualified by stating that if in the judgment of those surgeons who have been consulted concerning Kevin's condition and who have the responsibility for the actual performance of the surgery, the contemplated procedures pose an unacceptable risk to his life, they ought not to undertake such surgery. This is a judgment that only the surgeons are qualified to make and nothing in this decision should be so construed as to require any surgeon to perform any surgery upon this boy if, in their judgment, such surgery ought not to be undertaken. The court wishes to leave the surgeons completely free to exercise their own professional judgment as to the nature, extend and timing of any surgery that may be required for the correction of Kevin's deformity.

For the reasons heretofore expressed the court finds the mother's religious objections to the administration of blood transfusions untenable. It is both illogical and impractical for Mrs. Sampson to consent to surgery for her son and then for religious reasons attempt to limit or circumscribe the surgeons in the employment of their surgical skills. In passing it should be noted, however, that this is not a case in which the mother resists medical or surgical treatment for her son because of her sole reliance upon the power of God to heal, for it does not appear that either Jehovah's Witnesses or Mrs. Sampson individually make any pretext of reliance upon

of going through life handicapped by the enlarged, deformed left arm. That may be to some today the humane, and in the future it may be the generally accepted, view. However, we have not advanced or retrograded to the stage where, in the name of mercy, we may lawfully decide that one shall be deprived of life rather than continue to exist crippled or burdened with some abnormality. That right of decision is a prerogative of the Creator."

divine power to heal through prayer. Consequently, since that issue is not presented, it is unnecessary to pass upon it.

Because of the refusal of Mrs. Mildred Sampson to give her consent to the blood transfusions essential for the safety of the surgical procedures necessary to insure the physical, mental and emotional well being of her son, the Court adjudicates Kevin Sampson to be a neglected child within the meaning of section 1012 of the Family Court Act. This adjudication, however, in no way imports a finding that the mother failed in her duty to the child in any other respect.

The court therefore orders that the child, Kevin Sampson, be released to the custody of his mother and pursuant to section 1054 of the Family Court Act further orders that Mrs. Mildred Sampson be placed under the supervision of the Commissioner of Social Services of Ulster County for the maximum period of one year upon the following terms and conditions: (a) that Mrs. Mildred Sampson cooperate with the Department of Social Services to remedy her omission to provide her son with such surgical care and treatment as may be necessary to remedy or alleviate the facial disfigurement from which he suffers; (b) report to the Department of Social Services as directed by the court or the Department of Social Services; (c) permit authorized representatives of the Department of Social Services to visit the home or any other place where the boy may be; (d) notify the Department of Social Services of any change of address or employment.

In addition, the court specifically orders and directs that the mother, Mrs. Mildred Sampson permit Kevin to undergo such surgery as, in the judgment of the Commissioner of Health of Ulster County upon the advice and recommendation of duly qualified surgeons, shall be necessary or required to remedy or correct the facial condition of neurofibromatosis or Von Recklinghausen's disease from which he suffers. During the course of such surgery the surgeons are authorized to administer from time to time such blood transfusions as in their judgment may be necessary. The cost of such surgical treatment ad hospital care as may be necessary shall be borne by the County of Ulster.

NOTES

(1) The order of the Family Court was upheld by the Supreme Court of New York, Appellate Division. *In re Sampson*, 37 A.D.2d 668, 323 N.Y.S.2d 253 (App.Div. 1971). The short Memorandum Decision synthesized the issue as follows:

> We are confronted here with two basic rights, i.e., the child's right to lead, as far as possible, a normal life and a mother's adherence to sincere religious beliefs. The mother's right to her religious beliefs is inviolate, but her right to practice them is subject to limitations. Initially a parent has the duty and obligation to provide medical care for a child, but if he neglects that duty the State is authorized to act in his stead. (*Matter of Vasko*, 238 App.Div. 128, 263 N.Y.S. 552.) Appellant argues that State intervention is permitted only where the life of the child is in danger by a failure to act. This, in our opinion, is a much too restricted approach. As things now exist, Kevin can never lead a normal life or be of much benefit to himself or society. From an examination of the testimony of the eminent surgeons, an operation will improve Kevin's appearance. Viewing this in light of the testimony of the psychiatrist, or a

psychologist, to the effect of the present condition on the boy's behavior it is reasonable to assume that an operation at the present time will have a beneficial effect. There is no guarantee as to the ultimate result of the operation or the effect it will have on Kevin's outlook in the future. On the record as a whole, however, and the reasonable probabilities, we are constrained to agree with the trial court that Kevin should have the operation, provided the surgeons at the time conclude it should be performed. In arriving at our decision we are not unmindful of the fact that the trial court talked with Kevin, saw and heard all of the witnesses and consequently, his discretion should not be lightly regarded. Under all the circumstances we conclude that Kevin is a neglected child within the meaning of the Family Court Act. We use the word "neglected" in its limited legal sense within the meaning of the Family Court Act and not that this mother has failed in her duty to her son in any other respect.

The court's language distinguishing medical neglect from other forms of neglect has been fairly typical of the view since taken in other jurisdictions. This seems to be that there usually is no sort of moral culpability, but rather a bad judgment call by the "neglecting" parent.

The decision was affirmed by the New York Court of Appeals. *In re Sampson*, 328 N.Y.S.2d 686, 29 N.Y.2d 900, 278 N.E.2d 918 (1972). The brief, per curiam decision sought to reconcile the case with earlier decisions:

> In affirming the qualified court direction to operate on the then 15–year-old child over the mother's religious objections two observations only need be added to the exhaustive opinion at the Family Court. The holding by this court in Matter of Seiferth, 127 N.E.2d 820, did not limit to drastic or mortal circumstances the statutory power of the Family Court or like court in neglect proceedings to order necessary surgery. In the Seiferth case the court was obliged to choose between the findings of the Children's Court and that of the Appellate Division on how best to exercise a court's discretionary powers in the circumstances. There was no disagreement over power, and that case, like this, involved a serious physiological impairment which did not threaten the physical life or health of the subject or raise the risk of contagion to the public. Indeed, the opinions in that case impliedly or expressly recognized the court's power to direct surgery even in the absence of risk to the physical health or life of the subject or to the public. Nor does the religious objection to blood transfusion present a bar at least where the transfusion is necessary to the success of required surgery. What doubt there may have been was laid to rest by the case of *Jehovah's Witnesses in State of Wash. v. King County Hosp.*, 390 U.S. 598, affg. 278 F.Supp. 488, rehearing den. 391 U.S. 961.

Sampson was a watershed case. Afterward, many courts were willing to intervene in non-life threatening situations. (Strictly speaking, the operation in *Sampson* probably was more life threatening than medical inaction.) Not all courts were ready to follow the rationale of the New York judiciary, however. In *In re Green*, 448 Pa. 338, 292 A.2d 387 (Pa.1972), a latter day *Tuttendario* case that even took place in Pennsylvania, Ricky Green, a 15–year-old boy suffering from paralytic scoliosis (with a 94 percent curvature of the spine), was the subject of a neglect petition by the Director of the State Hospital for Crippled Children. The petition sought appointment of a guardian to consent to corrective surgery to prevent Ricky from being bedridden for the rest of his life. The operation was dangerous and the condition was not life threatening. Ricky's mother, for religious reasons, refused to consent to the whole blood transfusions that the procedure would require. Depicting the potential problems that might stem from following the *Sampson* rationale as "endless", the Pennsylvania Supreme Court refused to appoint a guardian on the ground that "as between a parent and the state, the state does not have an interest of sufficient magnitude outweighing a parent's religious beliefs when the child's life *is not immediately imperiled* by his physical condition." 448 Pa. 338, 292 A.2d 387, 392 (Pa.1972). However, in a strong dissent, Judge Eagan took issue with the court's adherence to the life threatening exception, pointing out that the pertinent statute referred to neglect or refusal "to provide *proper or necessary* subsistence, education, *medical or surgical care, or other care necessary for his or her health....* [Emphasis supplied.]" Id. at 394, citing 11 Pa. Stat. § 243(5)(c).

Despite the court's unwillingness to expand the life threatening exception, the court was prompted by the dissent of Justice Douglas in *Wisconsin v. Yoder*, supra at pp. 18, 27, and remanded the case to learn the views of the child.[1] In an evidentiary hearing on remand, Ricky indicated that he did not wish to submit to the surgery. His view ostensibly was not based simply on religious tenets; he said he had been going to the hospital for a long time and no one had told him that "it is going to come out right." *In re Green*, 452 Pa. 373, 307 A.2d 279, 280 (Pa.1973).

(2) Child abuse reporting laws have had considerable impact on surfacing "medical neglect" issues. Among those usually required to report are physicians, hospitals, and teachers who learn of abuse through their official duties. Professionals such as physicians are encouraged to report by provisions protecting them from civil liability for good faith reporting. The statutes quickly became popular after their introduction in the mid–60s, and their scope has been expanded in many states since their initial adoption. The definition of what should be reported increasingly has been extended to apply to cases of medical neglect. This has occurred either through specific language to that effect in reporting statutes or through adoption of basic definitions of abuse, neglect, or endangerment laws as the operative key to what should be reported. In addition, hospitals have protective services groups to whom physicians may channel their reports. All this increases the likelihood of disputes about medical decisionmaking reaching the courts. One can ask, quite justifiably, whether a physician today would be required to report a Tony Tuttendario as medically neglected. Even so, one can appropriately ask whether this is the most effective way of surfacing issues of medical neglect in timely fashion.

Hermanson v. State

Supreme Court of Florida, 1992.
604 So.2d 775.

■ Overton, Justice.

. . .

In this tragic case, Amy Hermanson, the daughter of William and Christine Hermanson, died from untreated juvenile diabetes. The Herman-

---

1. 406 U.S. 205, 246, 92 S.Ct. 1526, 32 L.Ed.2d 15 (1972). The Pennsylvania court in *Green* noted that in *Yoder*

The majority opinion as well as the concurring opinion of Mr. Justice Stewart did not think it wise to reach this point for two principal reasons: (1) it was the parents, not the children, who were criminally prosecuted for their religious beliefs; and (2) the record did not indicate a parent-child conflict.... While the record before us gives no indication of Ricky's thinking, it is the child rather than the parents in this appeal who is

directly involved which thereby distinguishes *Yoder's* decision not to discuss the beliefs of the parents vis-a-vis the children.

448 Pa. 338, 292 A.2d 387, 392 (1972).

The court also noted that in *Sampson*, the trial judge felt that "foisting" the decision on the boy was unreasonable (a view they recognized had been expressed also by Judge Fuld in his dissent in *Seiferth*), but they nevertheless determined that Ricky Green should be heard.

sons, members of the First Church of Christ, Scientist, were charged and convicted of child abuse resulting in third-degree murder for failing to provide Amy with conventional medical treatment. The Hermansons received four-year suspended prison sentences on their murder convictions and were ordered to serve fifteen years' probation. The district court, finding that the spiritual treatment accommodation provision of section 415.503(7)(f), Florida Statutes (1985), did not prevent their prosecution and conviction, affirmed the trial court's sentence and certified the above question. In summary, we find that sections 827.04(1) and 415.503(7)(f), when considered together, are ambiguous and result in a denial of due process because the statutes in question fail to give parents notice of the point at which their reliance on spiritual treatment loses statutory approval and becomes culpably negligent. We further find that a person of ordinary intelligence cannot be expected to understand the extent to which reliance on spiritual healing is permitted and the point at which this reliance constitutes a criminal offense under the subject statutes. The statutes have created a trap that the legislature should address. Accordingly, we quash the decision of the district court.

Statutory History

The statutory provisions are critical to the legal and constitutional issues presented in this case. Florida's child abuse statute, section 827.04(1)–(2), Florida Statutes (1985), provides:

> (1) Whoever, willfully or by culpable negligence, deprives a child of, or allows a child to be deprived of, necessary food, clothing, shelter, or medical treatment, or who, knowingly or by culpable negligence, permits physical or mental injury to the child, and in so doing causes great bodily harm, permanent disability, or permanent disfigurement to such child, shall be guilty of a felony of the third degree....

> (2) Whoever, willfully or by culpable negligence, deprives a child of, or allows a child to be deprived of, necessary food, clothing, shelter, or medical treatment, or who, knowingly or by culpable negligence, permits physical or mental injury to the child, shall be guilty of a misdemeanor of the first degree....

The third-degree murder provision of section 782.04(4), Florida Statutes (1985), provides that the killing of a human being while engaged in the commission of child abuse constitutes murder in the third degree and is a felony of the second degree. Section 415.503 provides, in part, as follows:

> (1) "Abused or neglected child" means a child whose physical or mental health or welfare is harmed, or threatened with harm, by the acts or omissions of the parent or other person responsible for the child's welfare....

> (7) "Harm" to a child's health or welfare can occur when the parent or other person responsible for the child's welfare:

> . . .

(f) Fails to supply the child with adequate food, clothing, shelter, *or health care,* although financially able to do so or although offered financial or other means to do so; *however, a parent or other person responsible for the child's welfare legitimately practicing his religious beliefs, who by reason thereof does not provide specified medical treatment for a child, may not be considered abusive or neglectful for that reason alone,* but such an exception does not:

1. Eliminate the requirement that such a case be reported to the department;

2. Prevent the department from investigating such a case; or

3. Preclude a court from ordering, when the health of the child requires it, the provision of medical services by a physician, as defined herein, or treatment by a duly accredited practitioner who relies solely on spiritual means for healing in accordance with the tenets and practices of a well-recognized church or religious organization.

(Emphasis added)[1]

The religious accommodation provision in section 415.503(7)(f) was initially passed by the legislature in 1975 as section 827.07(2), Florida Statutes (1975), the same chapter that contained the child abuse provision under which the Hermansons were prosecuted. The senate staff analysis of the religious accommodation provision stated that these provisions were "a defense for parents who decline medical treatment for legitimate religious reasons." Staff of Fla. S. Comm. Crim. Just., SB 1186 (1975) Staff Analysis 1 (final May 26, 1975) (available at Fla. Dep't of State, Div. of Archives, Tallahassee, Fla.). In 1983, the Division of Statutory Revision moved the above religious accommodation provision from chapter 827 to chapter 415.

Facts

The facts of this case, as stipulated to by the parties in the trial court, are as follows:

1. The Defendant, William F. Hermanson, is 39 years of age. Mr. Hermanson is married to the Defendant, Christine Hermanson, who is 36 years of age. Since June of 1973, Mr. and Mrs. Hermanson have resided in Sarasota, Florida. At all times material to this case, they resided at.... Mr. Hermanson is a bank vice president, and Mrs. Hermanson is the director of the Sarasota Fine Arts Academy. Mr. and Mrs. Hermanson have graduate degrees from Grand Valley State College and the University of Michigan, respectively. Neither Mr. nor Mrs. Hermanson has ever been arrested for, or convicted of, a crime.

2. Mr. and Mrs. Hermanson were married on May 30, 1970. There have been two children born of this marriage: Eric Thomas Hermanson, date of birth 8/26/77 and Amy Kathleen Hermanson (deceased) date of birth 7/16/79. There are no facts indicating that Mr.

---

1. [The court lists statutes in 27 other states that provide some form of religious exemption.]

or Mrs. Hermanson ever deprived their children of necessary food, clothing or shelter as those terms are used in section 827.04, Florida Statutes.

3. According to the autopsy report of the Medical Examiner, James C. Wilson, M.D., on September 30, 1986, at approximately 1:55 p.m., Amy Hermanson died. Dr. Wilson found the cause of death to be diabetic ketoacidosis due to juvenile onset diabetes mellitus. Additional autopsy findings of dehydration and weight loss were consistent with the disease process. Dr. Wilson believes that the disease could have been diagnosed by a physician prior to death and, within the bounds of medical probability, Amy's death could have been prevented even up to several hours before her death with proper medical treatment.

4. At the time of Amy's death, the Hermanson family, including William, Christine, Eric and Amy, were regular attenders of the First Church of Christ, Scientist in Sarasota. William Hermanson has been a member of the Christian Science Church since childhood, and Christine Hermanson has been a member of the Church of Christ, Scientist since 1969. The Church of Christ, Scientist is a well-recognized church or religious organization, as that term is used in Section 415.503, Florida Statutes.

5. Christian Scientists believe in healing by spiritual means in accordance with the tenets and practices of the Christian Science Church. William and Christine Hermanson, at all times material to the facts in this case, followed the religious teachings of their church and relied upon Christian Science healing in the care and treatment of Amy Hermanson.

6. On or about September 22, 1986, the Hermansons became aware that something was particularly wrong with Amy Hermanson which they believed to be of an emotional nature. They contacted Thomas Keller, a duly-accredited practitioner of the First Church of Christ, Scientist for consultation and treatment in accordance with the religious tenets and beliefs of the Christian Science Religion. Thomas Keller treated Amy from September 22, 1986 until September 30, 1986.

7. On or about September 25, 1986, the Hermansons traveled to Indianapolis, Indiana to attend an annual Christian Science conference on healing and left their children in the care of one Marie Beth Ackerman, age 24, a Christian Scientist employed by the Christian Science Committee on Publications and who was residing with the Hermanson family in Sarasota County, Florida and assisting Mrs. Hermanson as an administrator at the Sarasota Fine Arts Academy. The Hermansons returned to their home in Sarasota County, Florida at approximately 2 a.m. on September 29, 1986.

8. After their arrival, the Hermansons noticed a worsening of Amy's condition. They decided to seek the assistance of a local Christian Science practitioner and at approximately 9 a.m. on September 29, 1986, the Hermansons contacted one Frederick Hillier, a duly-accredited Christian Science practitioner of the First Church of Christ, Scientist whom they secured as a practitioner for Amy. Thereafter, until

Amy's death, Hillier provided treatment for Amy relying solely on spiritual means for healing in accordance with the tenets and practices of the First Church of Christ, Scientist.

9. On Monday, September 29, 1986, William Hermanson had a discussion with Jack Morton, the father of Christine Hermanson, wherein Mr. Morton expressed his concern for the health of Amy and suggested the possibility that Amy had diabetes.

10. At approximately 9:30 a.m. on September 30, 1986, Hillier went to the Hermanson home to continue treatment and, due to the fact the Hermansons had been up all night with Amy, suggested that a Christian Science nurse be called to help care for Amy.

11. At approximately 10 a.m. on Tuesday, September 30, 1986, one Molly Jane Sellers was called to the Hermanson residence to assist in the care of Amy Hermanson. Molly Jane Sellers is recognized as a Christian Science nurse by the First Church of Christ, Scientist and has been so recognized for twenty years. In preparation for such accreditation by the Church, Sellers completed a three and one-half year training course. Her area of care primarily relates to the physical needs of the patients and would be closely related to the duties performed by a licensed practical nurse.

12. On September 30, 1986 at approximately 11 a.m., William Hermanson was contacted by a counselor from the Department of Health and Rehabilitative Services (Willy Torres) who informed him that they had received a complaint alleging child abuse of his daughter, Amy Hermanson and that a hearing pursuant to said allegation had been set before the Juvenile Court for 1:30 p.m. Torres further informed Mr. Hermanson that the purpose of the hearing was to determine if medical treatment would be court ordered or if treatment as prescribed by the Christian Science practitioner would be ordered at that time.

13. At approximately 12:30 p.m., Mr. Hermanson left his home and traveled to the Sarasota County Courthouse for the hearing pursuant to the notification from Willy Torres. While at the hearing, at approximately 1:27 p.m., Mr. Hermanson received a telephone call from an individual at the Hermanson home who reported that Amy had "taken a turn for the worse and an ambulance had been called." Such information was related to the Court and an order was entered which required that Amy Hermanson be examined by a licensed medical doctor. When paramedics arrived they found that Amy had died.

14. Prior to her death, Amy Hermanson continued under the care and treatment of Frederick Hillier with the assistance of Molly Jane Sellers until approximately 1:27 p.m. September 30, 1986 at which time Amy had died.

15. On or about October 7, 1986, the Department of Health and Rehabilitative Services notified Mr. and Mrs. William Hermanson that it had completed its investigation and had classified the report as unfounded.

Hermanson, 570 So.2d at 324–27.

The district court summarized the facts presented at trial as follows:

In the month or so before her death Amy was having a marked and dramatic weight loss, that she was almost skeletal in her thinness and this was a big change in her appearance. There were great dark circles under her eyes that had never been there before. Her behavior was very different from the usual; she was lethargic and complaining whereas previously she had been bubbly, vivacious, and outgoing. She was seen lying down on the floor to sleep during the day when accompanying her mother to visit music students and lying down on the floor after school at her mother's fine arts academy. She often complained of not feeling well, that her stomach hurt and that she wasn't sleeping well. She was too tired during the day to participate in gym class at school. There was a bluish tint to her skin. Her breath smelled funny, one observer called it a "fruity" odor. The pathologist who performed the autopsy testified to Amy's skeletal appearance, that her vertebrae and shoulder blades were prominent and her abdomen distended as if she were undernourished. Her eyes were quite sunken, due to the dehydration, although her parents had told the pathologist that on the day before her death she was drinking a lot of fluids but urinating frequently too. They also told him that they had noticed changes in Amy starting about a month previously. Amy had complained of constipation during the last week of her life but at no time seemed feverish although there was intermittent vomiting.

The pathologist opined that the illness was chronic, not acute. According to her parents' talk with the pathologist, Amy seemed incoherent on the evening before her death although the next morning she seemed better. The pathologist also testified that vomiting and dehydration are compatible with flu-like symptoms but these, added to a four-week-long history of weight loss with the more severe conditions reported, would not be indicative of flu. Finally, the jury was shown photographs of Amy taken shortly after she died before her body was removed from the home by the paramedics as well as some taken before the autopsy was performed.

Id. at 336–37.

The evidence and the stipulated facts established that the Hermansons treated Amy in accordance with their Christian Science beliefs. On the day of Amy's death, a Christian Science nurse had been summoned to the home to care for her. The nurse testified that Amy was unresponsive and that, when she began vomiting and her condition worsened, she recommended that an ambulance should be called. The Christian Science practitioner who was present advised the nurse that the church headquarters in Boston should be contacted before an ambulance was called. After placing a call to Boston, an ambulance was summoned.

In its argument to the jury, the State asserted that the Hermansons' reliance on Christian Science healing practices under these circumstances constituted culpable negligence. The basis of its argument was that the Hermansons were not legitimately practicing their religious beliefs. Drawing on the evidence that the Christian Science nurse had called an ambulance when Amy began vomiting, the State suggested that the Christian Science Church recognizes conventional medical care and, therefore, the Hermansons had not been legitimately practicing their religious beliefs when they failed to seek medical care before Amy's death. No specific evidence was introduced by either side on the question of when, if at all, the Christian Science faith allows its members to call for medical attention. The Hermansons, on the other hand, argued to the jury that they should not be convicted of a criminal offense because they were "legitimately" practicing their faith in accordance with the accommodation provision of section 415.503(7)(f).

The jury, after one and one-half hours of deliberation, sought the answer to three questions: "(1) As a Christian Scientist do they have a choice to go to a medical doctor if they want to? (2) Or if not, can they call a doctor at a certain point? (3) Do they need permission first?" In response, the court advised the jurors that they must look to the evidence presented during the trial to find the answers. Counsel for both parties had previously agreed to this response by the trial court. The jury found the Hermansons guilty of felony child abuse and third-degree murder, and they were sentenced to four-year suspended prison sentences, with fifteen years' probation, on condition that they provide regular medical examinations and treatment for their surviving children.

On appeal, the district court affirmed, finding that the statutory accommodation section in 415.503(7)(f) applied only to matters contained in chapter 415 and that that provision did not provide any protection from criminal penalties for actual child abuse or neglect in chapters 782 and 827, Florida Statutes (1985). The district court rejected the Hermansons' claim that the evidence did not establish that they had acted willfully or with culpable negligence under the circumstances of this case. The district court agreed with the trial court that, when they returned from Indiana thirty-six hours before Amy's death and had seen that her condition had worsened, the Hermansons were placed on notice "that their attempts at spiritual treatment were unavailing and [that] it was time to call in medical help." The district court concluded that those facts justified the issue's being submitted to the jury and the verdict finding the Hermansons guilty of culpable negligence. The district court also rejected the Hermansons' claim of a due process violation for lack of notice of when their conduct became criminal. In rejecting this contention, the district court relied on the decision of the California Supreme Court in Walker v. Superior Court, 47 Cal.3d 112, 253 Cal.Rptr. 1, 21, 763 P.2d 852, 872 (1988), cert. denied, 491 U.S. 905 (1989), in which that court stated:

> "[T]he law is full of instances where a man's fate depends on his estimating rightly, that is, as the jury subsequently estimates it, some matter of degree ... 'An act causing death may be murder, manslaughter, or misadventure according to the degree of danger attending it' by common experience in the circumstances known to the actor." (Nash v. United States (1913) 229 U.S. 373, 377; see also Coates v. City of Cincinnati, (1971) 402 U.S. 611, 614.) The "matter of degree" that persons relying on prayer treatment must estimate rightly is the point

at which their course of conduct becomes criminally negligent. In terms of notice, due process requires no more.

Hermanson, 570 So.2d at 352.

In this appeal, the Hermansons challenge the district court decision on the following four issues: (1) that the Florida Statutes under which they were convicted did not give them fair warning of the consequences of practicing their religious belief and their conviction was, therefore, a denial of due process; (2) that the Hermansons were entitled to a judgment of acquittal because the evidence presented at trial failed to establish culpable negligence beyond a reasonable doubt; (3) that permitting a jury to decide the reasonableness of the Hermansons in following their religious beliefs was a violation of the First Amendment freedom of religion; and (4) that the trial court erred in not granting a mistrial when the prosecutor stated in closing argument that Christian Science recognizes conventional medical treatment, which was not supported by any evidence in the record. We choose to discuss only the first issue because we find that it is dispositive.

Due Process

In asserting that they were denied due process, the Hermansons claim that the statutes failed to give them sufficient notice of when their treatment of their child in accordance with their religious beliefs became criminal. They argue that their position is supported by (1) the fact that it took the district court of appeal nine pages to explain how it arrived at its conclusion that the exemption for spiritual treatment was only part of the civil child abuse statute, not the criminal child abuse statute and (2) the trial court's construing the statute differently, holding that they were protected by the provision of section 415.503(7)(f) to the extent of making it a jury issue.

The United States Supreme Court, in United States v. Cardiff, 344 U.S. 174 (1952), stated that confusion in lower courts is evidence of vagueness which violates due process. Furthermore, in Linville v. State, 359 So.2d 450, 453–54 (Fla.1978), we held that due process is lacking where "a man of common intelligence cannot be expected to discern what activity the statute is seeking to proscribe." In State v. McKown, 461 N.W.2d 720 (Minn.Ct.App.1990), aff'd, 475 N.W.2d 63 (Minn.1991), cert. denied, 112 S.Ct. 882 (1992), a child's parents utilized a Christian Science practitioner and a Christian Science nurse, but did not seek conventional medical treatment. The McKowns were indicted for second-degree manslaughter when their child died of untreated diabetes. The issue in that case was whether the child abuse statute, which contained an exception for spiritual treatment similar to the Florida statute, was to be construed in conjunction with a manslaughter statute that was based on culpable negligence resulting in death. In finding a violation of due process, the Minnesota court concluded that there was a "lack of clarity in the relationship between the two statutes." Id. at 723.

> [T]he state would have us conclude that the choice of spiritual treatment, which has been put on legal footing equal to that of orthodox medical care by the child neglect statute, can result in a manslaughter

indictment, simply because of its outcome. That is unacceptably arbitrary, and a violation of due process.

Id. at 724. The court further stated:

Evidence before the trial court suggests that, due to the sensitive nature of this issue, many Christian Scientists, including the McKowns, were specifically aware of the statutory provisions relating to use of spiritual means and prayer. They may have indeed "mapped out" their behavior based upon the statute. While the cases in this area are more likely to involve reliance by the defendant on administrative pronouncements, there is nothing inherent in the concept which would make it inapplicable to an argument of reliance on a specific statutory enactment. The state in this instance has attempted to take away with the one hand—by way of criminal prosecution—that which it apparently granted with the other hand, and upon which defendants relied. This it cannot do, and meet constitutional requirements.

Id. at 724–25.

The State, in this instance, relies primarily on the decision of the Supreme Court of California in Walker. In Walker, a child died from untreated meningitis as a result of her mother's reliance on spiritual means in treating the child's illness. The mother, charged with manslaughter and felony child endangerment, argued that a religious accommodation provision found in a California misdemeanor child neglect statute, similar to chapter 415, barred her prosecution under the California manslaughter statute. The mother argued that "the statutory scheme violate[d] her right to fair notice by allowing punishment under sections 192(b) and 273(a)(1) for the same conduct that is assertedly accommodated under section 270." In rejecting this claim, the California Supreme Court explained that the statutes were clearly distinguishable and, in light of their differing objectives, the statutes could not be said to constitute inexplicably contradictory commands with respect to their respective requirements.

In addressing the lack of notice claim, the State relies on the previously quoted statements in the Walker decision, particularly the conclusion that "persons relying on prayer treatment must estimate rightly" to avoid criminal prosecution because "due process requires no more." Walker, 253 Cal.Rptr. at 20–21, 763 P.2d at 871–72. Pennsylvania and Indiana have taken a similar view and rejected similar due process arguments. See Commonwealth v. Barnhart, 345 Pa.Super. 10, 497 A.2d 616 (1985), cert. denied, 488 U.S. 817 (1988); Hall v. State, 493 N.E.2d 433 (Ind.1986). The State asserts that we should also reject the Minnesota court's reasoning in McKown in part because the spiritual treatment exception in that case was contained in a criminal child abuse statute, while the provision in the Florida statute is contained in the child dependency statute.

The United States Supreme Court has stated that one of the purposes of due process is "to insure that no individual is convicted unless 'a fair warning [has first been] given to the world in language that the common world will understand, of what the law intends to do if a certain line is passed.'" Mourning v. Family Publications Serv., Inc., 411 U.S. 356 (1973) (quoting McBoyle v. United States, 283 U.S. 25, 27 (1931)). In Linville, this

Court explained that a person of common intelligence must be able to determine what type of activity the statute is seeking to proscribe.

We disagree with the view of the Supreme Court of California in Walker that, in considering the application of this type of religious accommodation statute, persons relying on the statute and its allowance for prayer as treatment are granted only the opportunity to guess rightly with regard to their utilization of spiritual treatment. In commenting on this type of situation, one author has stated: "By authorizing conduct in one statute, but declaring that same conduct criminal under another statute, the State trapped the Hermansons, who had no fair warning that the State would consider their conduct criminal." Christine A. Clark, Religious Accommodation and Criminal Liability, 17 Fla.St.U.L.Rev. 559, 585 (1990) (footnotes omitted). We agree.

To say that the statutes in question establish a line of demarcation at which a person of common intelligence would know his or her conduct is or is not criminal ignores the fact that, not only did the judges of both the circuit court and the district court of appeal have difficulty understanding the interrelationship of the statutes in question, but, as indicated by their questions, the jurors also had problems understanding what was required.

In this instance, we conclude that the legislature has failed to clearly indicate the point at which a parent's reliance on his or her religious beliefs in the treatment of his or her children becomes criminal conduct. If the legislature desires to provide for religious accommodation while protecting the children of the state, the legislature must clearly indicate when a parent's conduct becomes criminal. As stated by another commentator: "Whatever choices are made ... both the policy and the letter of the law should be clear and clearly stated, so that those who believe in healing by prayer rather than medical treatment are aware of the potential liabilities they may incur." Catherine W. Laughran, Comment, Religious Beliefs and the Criminal Justice System: Some Problems of the Faith Healer, 8 Loy.L.A.L.Rev. 396, 431 (1975).

Accordingly, for the reasons expressed, we quash the decision of the district court of appeal and remand this case with directions that the trial court's adjudication of guilt and sentence be vacated and the petitioners discharged.

NOTES

(1) *Walker v. Superior Court*, 47 Cal.3d 112, 253 Cal.Rptr. 1, 763 P.2d 852, cert. den., 491 U.S. 905, 109 S.Ct. 3186, 105 L.Ed.2d 695 (1989), which was discussed but not followed by the Florida Supreme Court in *Hermanson*, carefully detailed the legislative provisions of California law that contained a religious exception in some statutes but not in those for involuntary manslaughter and felony child endangerment. The court first explained that imposing felony liability for failure to seek medical care for a seriously ill child is justified by a compelling state interest and then added that, even so, to survive a First Amendment challenge the policy also must represent "the least restrictive alternative available to the state." The court pointed out that:

Defendant and the Church argue that civil dependency proceedings advance the governmental interest in a far less intrusive manner. This is not evident. First, we have already observed the profoundly intrusive nature of such proceedings; it is not clear that parents would prefer to lose custody of their children pursuant to a disruptive and invasive judicial inquiry than to face privately the prospect of criminal liability. Second, child dependency proceedings advance the governmental interest only when the state learns of a child's illness in time to take protective measures, which quite likely will be the exception rather than the rule. . . . Finally, the imposition of criminal liability is reserved for the actual loss or endangerment of a child's life and thus is narrowly tailored to those instances when governmental intrusion is absolutely compelled.

We conclude that an adequately effective and less restrictive alternative is not available to further the state's compelling interest in assuring the provision of medical care to gravely ill children whose parents refuse such treatment on religious grounds. Accordingly, the First Amendment and its California equivalent do not bar defendant's criminal prosecution.

Accordingly, the court held that prosecution of the defendant for involuntary manslaughter and felony child endangerment did not violate statutory law or either the California or federal Constitution. In a separate concurring opinion, Justice Mosk notes that the majority chose not to reach the Attorney General's contention that extending the religious exemption of § 270 to the felony prosecution "would import into the proceeding a defense that offends the establishment clauses of the state and federal Constitutions." 763 P.2d 852, at 873. Noting that the issue had been "timely raised and thoroughly briefed, and its importance is manifest", he expressed the view that "the statutory exemption as it now reads plainly violates the establishment clauses." For further development of that argument, see footnote 8 in *Newmark v. Williams*, infra at 684. See also Felicia Strankman, Children's Medical Care in California: Conflicts Between Parent, Child, and State, 36 Santa Clara L.Rev. 899 (1996).

The preceding cases obviously point up the need for clarity in any statutory scheme for religious exemption from prosecution. However, they do not decide that statutes with no religious exemption are invalid or that there is a common law exemption.

(2) In *Matter of Appeal in Cochise County*, 133 Ariz. 157, 650 P.2d 459 (1982), the Supreme Court of Arizona was called on to determine whether there was sufficient evidence to justify "state interference with the fundamental right of a parent to the custody and control of his or her child, particularly to 'monitor' the health of the child when there is known medical danger and when providing medical care is contrary to the parent's religious beliefs." After death of one of her children from septicemia and peritonitis secondary to a strangulated inguinal hernia, the mother explained to the Department of Economic Security (D.E.S.) case workers that "she had faith that miracles would safeguard her children" and that she would not seek medical help if any of her other seven children became ill. A juvenile court judge declined to find the children "dependent" in light of their otherwise seemingly satisfactory home life, but that decision was reversed by the Court of Appeals. The latter based its finding of present abuse on the threatened passive conduct of the mother in possibly failing to provide medical care in the future. Reversing the Court of Appeals, the Supreme Court noted that the cases cited in justification of their decision were distinguishable because they upheld state intervention in cases in which there was present rather than future need of medical attention. However, the Supreme Court emphasized that the state continued to maintain broad supervisory powers and that the D.E.S. could "keep a close eye" on the children's progress.

Also, it might be prompted to investigate further based on something less than would be required in a more typical situation.

(3) In *Commonwealth v. Twitchell*, 416 Mass. 114, 617 N.E.2d 609 (1993), an involuntary manslaughter conviction was set aside and the case remanded for new trial at the prosecutor's discretion when the court decided that the parents apparently had relied on a manual that incorporated language from a State Attorney General's opinion (even though it later was established to be incorrect). The court also found that the indictment violated the parents' due process rights because the statute failed to give fair notice of the prohibited conduct. The parents had relied on spiritual treatment for dealing with a bone disorder from which their 2½–year-old son died.

In re M.L.G.

Court of Appeals of Georgia, 1984.
170 Ga.App. 642, 317 S.E.2d 881.

■ DEEN, PRESIDING JUDGE.

Leon Grizzle and Helen Grizzle separately appeal from the order of the Juvenile Court of Hall County, severing their parental rights to their daughter, M.L.G. On appeal, both parents contend that the evidence was insufficient to support the termination of their parental rights.

M.L.G., who is now 9 years old, has been in foster care since late 1977. The Department of Family and Children Services (the Department) began assisting the appellants in caring for M.L.G. before the child was 1 year old. On September 9, 1977, pursuant to an emergency shelter care order, the child was placed in the custody of the Department. By consent order of October 12, 1977, the Department retained custody of the child for 60 days. Subsequently, on December 14, 1977, the court found the child to be deprived and gave custody to the Department. Custody was continued in the Department by orders dated December 19, 1979, and January 9, 1980, the latter being a consent order which extended custody until January 2, 1981. Following a hearing on January 7, 1981, on a petition to terminate parental rights brought by the Department, the court found that the child was presently deprived but denied the petition on the basis that the deprivation was not likely to continue. That order also required Leon Grizzle to pay $20 per week for child support. The Department's second petition was heard in September 1982, and the order of severance was entered on March 7, 1983.

M.L.G. was born without a sacrum, which resulted in her paralyzed bladder. In June 1976 she underwent a cutaneous vesicotomy, a surgical procedure which re-routes urine from the bladder to empty out a stoma (or hole) in the abdomen to be collected in an ileostomy bag. Additional corrective surgery became necessary and was performed in August 1977.

Since that surgery, the child has required constant care and supervision in the maintenance, cleaning, and replacement of the ileostomy bag and in the stimulation of the stoma. If the bag, which requires emptying 3–4 times per day and daily cleaning, is not emptied as often as needed, the urine will back into the kidneys and possibly result in infection; the risk of infection also is increased by failure to clean or replace (every 3–4 days) the bag regularly. The stoma requires periodic dilating by someone placing a finger into the abdominal opening and stimulating the sphincter so that it will remain open; failure to dilate properly can result in contraction of the stoma and back pressure on the kidneys, again increasing the risk of kidney infection. Infection can damage the kidneys, and extended infection could eventually result in renal failure. While the medical testimony indicated that infection could occur even with proper maintenance and sanitary conditions, the lack thereof would increase the risk. There also was medical evidence that even though some infections developed, examination by a urologist and X-ray of the kidneys every 6 months would discover any problems and allow treatment before damage to the kidneys resulted. The child required regular medication to control the growth of bacteria, and needed to drink adequate amounts of liquids, especially fruit juices.

Leon Grizzle and Helen Grizzle have been separated most of the time during the child's foster care placement. Leon Grizzle is an alcoholic, and when intoxicated he often becomes violent. He has beaten Helen Grizzle several times, and on one occasion he struck M.L.G., knocking her off a couch onto the floor and causing the stoma to bleed. (He claimed that the child had fallen off the couch while dodging a slight disciplinary slap, but that the stoma did not bleed.) Leon's driver's license has been revoked for repeated convictions for driving under the influence. Prompted by his being ordered to seek treatment under the terms of probation, he participated in the alcohol program at the North Georgia Mental Health Center from November 1978 until October 1980; he also enrolled in the therapy sessions in August 1981 until March 1982, but his attendance during that time was poor. At the time of termination hearing in September 1982, he was not undergoing any treatment for his alcoholism, but he claimed not to have drunk anything in 6–7 months.

During the past several years, Leon, now 54 years old, has worked only sporadically. At the time of the hearing, he was living alone in a trailer park (although he hoped to find a 15–year-old to marry), was unemployed, and he considered himself disabled due to a back condition; he had applied for Social Security disability benefits, but the application had not yet been approved. He had never paid the court-ordered child support, at one point refusing to pay such because his visitation rights with the child had been restricted and at trial denying ever having been informed of that obligation. Caseworkers with the Department in the past had found his housing usually adequately maintained.

Leon Grizzle claimed that he knew how to and had in fact changed the ileostomy bag on M.L.G., but had never cleaned one, having disposed of the bag upon changing it; he also stated that he could hook up the night drainage bag to the child's ileostomy bag. Nevertheless, he had earlier indicated to one caseworker that he felt that it was inappropriate for him now to change the bag for M.L.G. because of the latter's age.

Helen Grizzle also has a past of excessive drinking, and despite her claim of not having drunk alcohol for 3 years, on May 7, 1982, while in a drunken condition she physically attacked a caseworker. (She denied this incident, explaining that she was not drunk and had only pushed the caseworker aside so that she could prevent her other child from falling off the porch.) Over the course of the last several years, the Department has provided Helen Grizzle with a variety of services, including transportation for doctor's appointments, grocery shopping, mental health clinics, parenting skills classes, and vocational counseling. These endeavors for the most part have been greeted by noncooperation. For years Helen Grizzle has failed to maintain even the minimum standards of housekeeping. At the time of the hearing, she was living with her mother and 6 others in a 2 bedroom house that was filthy, malodorous, and in disrepair, essentially the same conditions which had existed at all of her previous residences. She has persistently refused the Department's suggestion of and/or efforts to locate adequate public housing, and, instead, denies the uncleanliness of her residence. She has not worked in years, but her mother pays her $20 per month for household chores, including mowing the lawn with a swing blade; she claimed, however, to be disabled by a back condition.

Mrs. Grizzle similarly has failed to provide adequate care for M.L.G.'s medical needs. Over the past 4 years, M.L.G. has frequently returned from home visits with Helen Grizzle dirty and smelling of urine because of improper care of the ileostomy bag. The required medication for M.L.G., sent by the foster parents, would often not be administered to the child. On at least 2 occasions, the foster mother has had to pick up M.L.G. at school on Monday, following the child's weekend stay with Helen Grizzle, and take her home to change the bag and to bathe the child.

Dr. Norman Polanski, whose doctorate was in social psychology, testified as an expert witness on abusive and neglectful families. Conceding that his profession is a soft science where subjective philosophical interplay operates, he described a condition which he identified as the apathetic futile syndrome, characterized by a pervasive conviction that nothing is worth doing. It results in an emotional numbness, a lack of confidence, an expression of anger through hostile non-compliance, non-commitment to positive standards, verbal inaccessibility to others, and an uncanny skill in spreading the sense of futility to those who attempt to assist her. Dr. Polanski noted that this syndrome is statistically associated with mothers who are involved in the most chronic and severe cases of child neglect. Another psychologist testified that M.L.G. had regressed between 1980 and 1982 in her coping skills, and suggested that the child needed more stability.

Over the years, caseworkers with the Department have emphasized the goals of minimum standards of cleanliness, stable employment, and abstinence from alcohol. The child's court-appointed guardian ad litem felt that neither natural parent was able to care for the child. The juvenile court concluded that clear and convincing evidence demonstrated that M.L.G. was a deprived child because of the inability of each parent to care for the special needs of M.L.G., and that that deprivation was likely to continue, and that unless the parental rights were terminated the child would suffer serious physical and emotional harm.

Held:

OCGA § 15–11–51(a)(2) provides that the juvenile court may terminate parental rights if "[t]he child is a deprived child and the court finds that the conditions and causes of the deprivation are likely to continue or will not be remedied and that by reason thereof the child is suffering or will probably suffer serious physical, mental, moral, or emotional harm ..." Parental rights to a child, however, may not be terminated "without some required showing of parental unfitness, caused either by intentional or unintentional misconduct resulting in abuse or neglect of the child, or by what is tantamount to physical or mental incapability to care for the child." Ray v. Dept. of Human Resources, 155 Ga.App. 81, 88, 270 S.E.2d 303 (1980); ...

Both appellants contend that the circumstances as proved by the Department were simply insufficient to authorize a finding of unfitness and termination of their parental rights. Comparing the facts of this case with those detailed in Ray, Harper, and Chancey, this court would probably be in agreement with that contention, were it not for the peculiar medical condition borne by M.L.G. and the concomitant special care required. As both appellants emphasize, the child is more subject to the risk of kidney infection than is a normal child, because of the ileostomy apparatus, and that infection may develop even with proper care and maintenance. However, there is no dispute that exposure to unsanitary conditions and inadequate cleaning and changing of the ileostomy bag increases that risk of infection, an increased risk to which M.L.G. should not unnecessarily be subjected. Sustained infection could result in kidney damage and perhaps even renal failure; improper care of the ileostomy not only endangers the child's health, but it could also stigmatize her socially and emotionally.

We find that the Department proved by clear and convincing evidence that Helen Grizzle and Leon Grizzle are either physically or mentally incapable of taking care of M.L.G.'s special medical needs. Despite years of encouragement and services provided by the Department, Helen Grizzle has failed utterly to maintain a sanitary living environment. On several occasions, M.L.G. returned from her weekend visits with Helen Grizzle unbathed, smelling of urine, and in need of ileostomy maintenance; on one particular occasion, Helen Grizzle had applied a plastic sandwich bag rather than the appropriate ileostomy bag. During these scheduled weekend visits, Helen Grizzle also frequently failed to administer to M.L.G. the medication prescribed to curtail the growth of bacteria, despite adequate supplies having been furnished by the foster parents. In short, she clearly has failed to provide even minimum adequate care for the child. For the past 7 years, Helen Grizzle has demonstrated that she is content with squalor, and it defies the evidence and reality even to suggest that her performance will improve. Leon Grizzle has maintained a cleaner home, but he is an alcoholic with violent propensities when becoming drunk and intoxicated, and he currently is not seeking treatment for alcoholism nor does he appear to have made a choice to leave alcohol alone (although he claimed not to have drunk anything in several months). His professed concern over M.L.G.'s welfare was squarely contradicted by his wilful refusal to pay any child support. At the hearing, he claimed experience in changing the ileostomy bag, but not in cleaning them; prior to the hearing, he had admitted his reluctance or unwillingness now to change the bags because of the child's age.

A deprived child is defined as a child "without proper parental care or control, subsistence, education as required by law, or other care or control necessary for his physical, mental, or emotional health or morals." OCGA § 15–11–2(8)(A). We agree with the juvenile court that M.L.G. was a deprived child because of the parents' failure to provide the special care required by the child's peculiar medical condition. We also find that the Department demonstrated with clear and convincing evidence that both the natural parents were unfit because of their physical or mental inability to meet these special needs of the child, and that the deprivation of the child therefore was likely to continue. Accordingly, the court below properly ordered termination of the parental rights to M.L.G. of both Leon Grizzle and Helen Grizzle.

Newmark v. Williams

Supreme Court of Delaware, 1991.
588 A.2d 1108.

■ Moore, Justice.

Colin Newmark,[1] a three year old child, faced death from a deadly aggressive and advanced form of pediatric cancer known as Burkitt's Lymphoma. We were presented with a clash of interests between medical science, Colin's tragic plight, the unquestioned sincerity of his parents' religious beliefs as Christian Scientists, and the legal right of the State to protect dependent children from perceived neglect when medical treatment is withheld on religious grounds. The Delaware Division of Child Protective Services ("DCPS") petitioned the Family Court for temporary custody of Colin to authorize the Alfred I. duPont Institute ("duPont Institute"), a nationally recognized children's hospital, to treat Colin's condition with chemotherapy. His parents, Morris and Kara Newmark, are well educated and economically prosperous. As members of the First Church of Christ, Scientist ("Christian Science") they rejected medical treatment proposed for Colin, preferring instead a course of spiritual aid and prayer.[2] The parents rely upon provisions of Delaware law, which exempt those who treat their children's illnesses "solely by spiritual means" from the abuse and neglect statutes. Thus, they opposed the State's petition. See 10 Del.C. § 901(11) & 16 Del.C. § 907 (emphasis added). The Newmarks also claimed

1. We have used pseudonyms to protect the privacy of Colin and his family.

2. Mary Baker Eddy, the founder of the Christian Science Church, professed a deep belief in spirituality. She preached that sickness was a manifestation of a diseased mind. See Eddy, Sermon Subject Christian Science Healing 7–8 (Pamphlet 1886). Eddy therefore claimed that "[m]edicine will not arrive at the Science of treating disease until disease is treated mentally and man is healed morally and physically." Id. at 17. Accordingly, Christian Scientists do not treat most sicknesses with medical care. Rather, they rely on prac-

titioners who administer spiritual aid. See Schneider, Christian Science and the Law: Room for Compromise? 1 Colum.J.L. & Soc. Probs. 81, 81 (1965). Eddy also believed that childhood illnesses were more manifestations of their parents' own spiritual infirmities. She reasoned that "[t]he law of mortal mind and [parents'] own fears govern [their] own child more than the child's mind governs itself and they produce the very results which might have been prevented through the opposite." M. EDDY, SCIENCE AND HEALTH WITH KEY TO THE SCRIPTURES 154 (1934).

that removing Colin from their custody would violate their First Amendment right, guaranteed under the United States Constitution, to freely exercise their religion.

The Family Court rejected both of these arguments and awarded custody of Colin to DCPS. The trial court, however, issued a stay permitting the Newmarks to file an immediate appeal to this Court.

We heard this appeal on an emergency basis. After argument on September 14, 1990, we issued an order reversing the Family Court and returned custody of Colin to his parents. At that time we noted that this more detailed opinion would follow in due course.

We have concluded that Colin was not an abused or neglected child under Delaware law. Parents enjoy a well established legal right to make important decisions for their children. Although this right is not absolute, the State has the burden of proving by clear and convincing evidence that intervening in the parent-child relationship is necessary to ensure the safety or health of the child, or to protect the public at large. DCPS did not meet this heavy burden. This is especially true where the purpose of the custody petition was to administer, over the objections of Colin's parents, an extremely risky, toxic and dangerously life threatening medical treatment offering less than a 40% chance for "success".

I.

Colin was the youngest of the three Newmark children. In late August, 1990, the Newmarks noticed that he had lost most of his appetite and was experiencing frequent vomiting. The symptoms at first appeared occasionally but soon worsened.

The Newmarks reluctantly took Colin to the duPont Institute for examination. The parties stipulated that this violated the Newmarks' Christian Science beliefs in the effectiveness of spiritual healing. The parties further stipulated that the Newmarks acted out of concern for their potential criminal liability, citing a Massachusetts case which held parents liable for manslaughter for foregoing medical treatment and treating their minor child only in accordance with Christian Science tenets.

Dr. Charles L. Minor, a duPont Institute staff pediatric surgeon, examined Colin and ordered X-rays of his stomach. Dr. Minor found the X-rays inconclusive and suggested that Colin remain at the hospital for further testing. The Newmarks refused and took Colin home. Colin remained at home for approximately one week while receiving treatments under the care of a Christian Science practitioner. Colin's symptoms nonetheless quickly reappeared and the Newmarks returned him to the hospital.

Dr. Minor ordered a second set of X-rays and this time discovered an obstruction in Colin's intestines. The doctor suggested immediate surgery and, again, the Newmarks consented. The Newmarks considered the procedure "mechanical" and therefore believed that it did not violate their religious beliefs.

During the operation, Dr. Minor discovered a large mass 10 to 15 centimeters wide connecting Colin's large and small bowels. He also noticed that some of Colin's lymph nodes were unusually large. Dr. Minor removed the mass and submitted tissue samples for a pathological report. There were no complications from the surgery and Colin was recovering "well."

The pathology report confirmed that Colin was suffering from a non-Hodgkins Lymphoma. Five pathologists from Children's Hospital, Philadelphia, Pennsylvania, confirmed the diagnosis. Dr. Minor, after receiving the pathology report, contacted Dr. Rita Meek, a board certified pediatric hematologist-oncologist and an attending physician at the duPont Institute.

Dr. Meek ordered two blood tests which indicated the presence of elevated levels of uric acid and LHD in Colin's system. The presence of these chemicals indicated that the disease had spread. Dr. Meek then conducted an external examination and detected a firm mass growing above Colin's right testicle. She diagnosed Colin's condition as Burkitt's Lymphoma, an aggressive pediatric cancer.[3] The doctor recommended that the hospital treat Colin with a heavy regimen of chemotherapy.

Dr. Meek opined that the chemotherapy offered a 40% chance of "curing" Colin's illness. She concluded that he would die within six to eight months without treatment. The Newmarks, learning of Colin's condition only after the surgery, advised Dr. Meek that they would place him under the care of a Christian Science practitioner and reject all medical treatment for their son. Accordingly, they refused to authorize the chemotherapy. There was no doubt that the Newmarks sincerely believed, as part of their religious beliefs, that the tenets of their faith provided an effective treatment.

II.

We start with an overview of the relevant Delaware statutory provisions. Delaware law defines a neglected child as: [A] child whose physical, mental or emotional health and well-being is threatened or impaired because of inadequate care and protection by the child's custodian, who has the ability and financial means to provide for the care but does not or will not provide adequate care; or a child who has been abused or neglected as defined by § 902 of Title 16. 10 Del.C. § 901(11). Section 902 further defines abuse and neglect as: [P]hysical injury by other than accidental means, injury resulting in a mental or emotional condition which is a result of abuse or neglect, negligent treatment, sexual abuse, maltreatment, mistreatment, nontreatment, exploitation or abandonment, of a child under the age of 18. Sections of the Delaware Code, however, contain spiritual treatment exemptions which directly affect Christian Scientists. Specifically, the exemptions state: No child who in good faith is under treatment solely by spiritual means through prayer in accordance with the tenets and practices of a recognized church or religious denomination by a duly accredited practitioner thereof shall for that reason alone be considered a neglected child for purposes of this chapter. 10 Del.C. § 901(11) & 16 Del.C. § 907. These exceptions reflect the intention of the Delaware General Assembly to provide a "safe harbor" for parents, like the Newmarks, to

3. Dr. Meek testified that Burkitt's Lymphoma cancer cells double more rapidly than any other form of pediatric cancer which inevitably results in a fast growing tumor.

pursue their own religious beliefs. This is evident from the limited legislative history available on the subject.

As originally enacted in 1972, one of the spiritual healing exemptions appeared in the child abuse reporting section of the Code, under the general heading of "Immunity from liability." The statute included both the spiritual treatment exemption and an immunity provision applicable to reporting child abuse. See 58 Del. Laws 154 (1972). The General Assembly later amended this section of the Code in 1976 and placed the spiritual treatment exemption under a separate heading entitled "Child Under Treatment By Spiritual Means Not Neglected." See 60 Del. Laws 494 (1976); 16 Del.C. § 907. The amendment reflects the legislature's apparent intent to clarify the meaning of the exemption and to magnify its importance. The accuracy of this conclusion is less in doubt after considering the legislative history of the other identical exemption.

The General Assembly also amended the meaning of a "neglected child" in the section of the Code dealing with the Family Court. See 10 Del.C. § 901(11). The statute originally defined a neglected child as one "whose custodian refuses to provide him with adequate care." 58 Del. Laws 114 (1971). In 1978, the legislature changed the definition of a "neglected child" to include the spiritual treatment exemption found in 16 Del.C. § 907. See 61 Del. Laws 334 (1978). The amendment clearly reflects the General Assembly's intent to provide protection for parents who treat their children through statutorily defined spiritual means. Accordingly, our ruling from the bench noted that the spiritual treatment exemptions reflect, in part, "[t]he policy of this State with respect to the quality of life" a desperately ill child might have in the caring and loving atmosphere of his or her family, versus the sterile hospital environment demanded by physicians seeking to prescribe excruciating, and life threatening, treatments of doubtful efficacy.

With the considerable reflection that time has now permitted us in examining these issues, we recognize the possibility that the spiritual treatment exemptions[4] may violate the ban against the establishment of an official State religion guaranteed under both the Federal and Delaware Constitutions. Clearly, in both reality and practical effect, the language providing an exemption only to those individuals practicing "in accordance" with the "practices of a recognized church or religious denomination by a duly accredited practitioner thereof" is intended for the principal benefit of Christian Scientists.[7] Our concern is that it possibly forces us to

4. We express no view, and indeed, this case does not concern the good faith healing defense contained in the Delaware Criminal Code. See 11 Del.C. § 1104.

7. The terminology used in the spiritual treatment exemption indicates that the statute was enacted as a result of a Christian Science lobbying effort. See In Child Deaths, a Test for Christian Science, N.Y. Times, Aug. 6, 1990, at 1, col. 2 (exemptions to neglect statutes passed at behest of Christian Science Church in forty state legislatures).

Specifically, the requirement that a person must be a "duly accredited practitioner" mirrors the Christian Science belief that only "practitioners" receiving approval from the Christian Science Mother Church can conduct spiritual healing. See Schneider, Christian Science and the Law: Room for Compromise?, 1 Colum.J.L. & Soc.Probs. 81, 81 (1965); see also Walker v. Super. Ct. Sacramento Co., 47 Cal.3d 112, 147–48, 763 P.2d 852, 875, 253 Cal.Rptr. 1, 24 (1988) (Mosk, J., concurring), cert. denied, 491 U.S. 905 (1989)

impermissibly determine the validity of an individual's own religious beliefs.[8]

(Christian Scientists sponsored spiritual treatment exception to abuse and neglect law in California and therefore it is "more than a fortuity that the word 'practitioner'" appears in California spiritual healing statute). The influence of the Church of Christ Scientist on the Delaware exemptions is also apparent when those statutes are compared with the federal spiritual healing exemption, which the Department of Health, Education and Welfare ("HEW") adopted in response to the Child Abuse Prevention and Treatment Act of 1974. See 45 C.F.R. s 1340.1 (1990). The federal regulation provides that "[n]othing in this part should be construed as requiring or prohibiting a finding of negligent treatment or maltreatment when a parent practicing his or her religious beliefs does not, for that reason alone, provide medical treatment for a child...." 45 C.F.R. s 1340.2(d)(2)(ii)(1990). (Emphasis added). The states were required to enact statutes similar to the HEW regulations to qualify for federal funds. See Comment, Faith Healing and Religious Treatment Exemptions To Child Endangerment Laws: Should Parental Religious Practices Excuse The Failure To Provide Necessary Medical Care To Children?, 13 U.Dayton L.Rev. 79, 96 (1987) (written by LeClair). Tellingly, the statute the General Assembly enacted to adopt the Child Abuse Prevention and Treatment Act of 1974 in Delaware merely incorporated the prior version of the Delaware exemption including the language "duly accredited practitioner" and "recognized religion." See 16 Del.C. s 907; 60 Del.Laws 494 (1976) (synopsis). It is perhaps more than coincidental that the legislature merely carried over the exemption without amending it to conform with the new federal regulations. Certainly, any statute passed as the result of the efforts of one religious group to benefit that one particular group to the exclusion of others bears a strong presumption against its validity as a direct violation of the Establishment Clause.

8. At least one state court has ruled that a statutory exemption to a criminal abuse and neglect statute, containing identical language as the Delaware statutes, violated both the Establishment Clause and the Equal Protection Clause of the Fourteenth Amendment. See State v. Miskimens, 22 Ohio Misc.2d 43, 43–46, 490 N.E.2d 931, 933–36 (Ohio Ct.Com.Pl.1984); OHIO REV. CODE ANN. § 2919.22(A) (Page 1990) (no violation of "care, protection, or support" when parent treats child's infirmity "by spiritual means through prayer alone, in accordance with the tenets of a recognized religious body.") (Emphasis added). Miskimens found that the statute "hopelessly involved" the state in issues involving religious beliefs and served no "legitimate purpose." Id. at 45, 490 N.E.2d at 934–35. Justice Mosk, of the California Supreme Court, observed that a California statute, exempting parents from criminal child neglect if they treat their child "in accordance with the tenets and practices of a recognized church or religious denomination, by a duly accredited practitioner thereof" violated the Equal Protection Clause of the First Amendment. Walker, 47 Cal.3d at 144–51, 763 P.2d at 874–78, 253 Cal.Rptr. at 22–27 (Mosk, J., concurring). Justice Mosk recognized that the statute specifically excluded both parents who are not members of a recognized religion and parents of a recognized religion who nonetheless do not treat their children through an accredited practitioner. Id. at 146–47, 763 P.2d at 874–75, 253 Cal.Rptr. at 23–24. The Justice opined that the statute served no legitimate state function and agreed with the reasoning in Miskimens that the exemption would involve the court in a "troubling entanglement of church and state...." Id. at 150, 253 Cal.Rptr. 1, 763 P.2d 852, 763 P.2d at 877, 253 Cal.Rptr. at 26. The reasoning applied in Miskimens and the concurrence in Walker is a firmly rooted principle of constitutional law. Numerous state courts have already ruled that a statutory exemption violates the Establishment Clause when it only applies to members of a "recognized" church or religion. See Davis v. State, 294 Md. 370, 381, 451 A.2d 107, 113 (1982) (immunization exception for members of "recognized" religion "contravenes ... principle of governmental neutrality regarding different religious beliefs."); Maier v. Besser, 73 Misc.2d 241, 245, 341 N.Y.S.2d 411, 414 (N.Y.Sup.Ct. 1972) ("if the Legislature desires to exempt for religious grounds a certain class of persons, it must do so on a logical and non-discriminatory basis."); Dalli v. Bd. of Ed., 358 Mass. 753, 759, 267 N.E.2d 219, 222–23 (1971) (same); Kolbeck v. Kramer, 84 N.J.Super. 569, 574, 202 A.2d 889, 892 (1964) ("[t]here is no right in a state or an instrumentality thereof to determine that a cause is not a religious one."); Cf. Wilmington Housing Authority v. Greater St. John

Neither party challenged the constitutionality of the spiritual treatment exemptions in either the Family Court or on appeal. Thus, except to recognize that the issue is far more complicated than was originally presented to us, we must leave such questions for another day.

III.

Addressing the facts of this case, we turn to the novel legal question whether, under any circumstances, Colin was a neglected child when his parents refused to accede to medical demands that he receive a radical form of chemotherapy having only a forty percent chance of success. Other jurisdictions differ in their approaches to this important and intensely personal issue. Some courts resolved the question on an ad hoc basis, without a formal test, concluding that a child was neglected if the parents refused to administer chemotherapy in a life threatening situation. See In re Willmann, 24 Ohio App.3d 191, 199, 493 N.E.2d 1380, 1389 (1986); In re

Baptist Church, Del.Supr., 291 A.2d 282, 286 (1972) (any preference for religious organizations in determining applicability of depreciation statute "may encounter serious constitutional questions"). The Supreme Court of the United States has similarly ruled on numerous occasions that a statute violates the Establishment Clause of the First Amendment if it requires the State to act or refrain from acting on the basis of whether it recognizes a certain religious belief. See Cantwell v. Connecticut, 310 U.S. 296, 307, 60 S.Ct. 900, 904–05, 84 L.Ed. 1213 (1940) (statute which permits state to issue license only when convinced "cause is a religious ... lay[s] a forbidden burden upon the exercise of liberty protected by the Constitution"); U.S. v. Ballard, 322 U.S. 78, 86–87, 64 S.Ct. 882, 886, 88 L.Ed. 1148 (1944) (Establishment Clause "embraces the right to maintain theories of life and of death ... which are rank heresy to followers of the orthodox faiths ... [y]et the fact that [religious beliefs] may be beyond the ken of mortals does not mean that they can be made suspect before the law."); Larson v. Valente, 456 U.S. 228, 244, 102 S.Ct. 1673, 1683, 72 L.Ed.2d 33, reh'g denied, 457 U.S. 1111, 102 S.Ct. 2916, 73 L.Ed.2d 1323 (1982) ("clearest command of the Establishment Clause is that one religious denomination cannot be officially preferred over another.") The Court recognized in Larson that statutory provisions tending to discriminate "among religions" are subject to strict scrutiny requiring a "closely fitted" statute to "further a 'compelling governmental interest.'" Id. 456 U.S. at 251, 102 S.Ct. at 1687. (Emphasis in original). The Larson Court also recognized that the statute in that case would foster " 'an excessive governmental entangle-

ment with religion' " and thus violate one of three tests first announced in Lemon v. Kurtzman, 403 U.S. 602, 612–613, 91 S.Ct. 2105, 2111, 29 L.Ed.2d 745 reh'g denied, 404 U.S. 876, 92 S.Ct. 24, 30 L.Ed.2d 123 (1971), to determine whether a statute which applied equally to all religions violated the Establishment Clause. Id. 456 U.S. at 251, 102 S.Ct. at 1687. Although unnecessary to judge the constitutionality of statutes which discriminate among various religious beliefs, the Ohio Court of Common Pleas, in Miskimens, utilized the entanglement test to strike down its own spiritual treatment exemption to the neglect statutes. 22 Ohio Misc.2d at 47, 490 N.E.2d at 934. See Walker, 47 Cal.3d at 150, 763 P.2d at 877, 253 Cal.Rptr. at 26. Application of the Delaware exemption possibly raises the same concerns that Miskimens recognized. Most importantly, the Delaware statutes would require this Court to determine, as an initial matter, whether a certain religion is worthy of official recognition. This inquiry, as Miskimens understood, "hopelessly involves the State in a determination of questions which should not be the subject of governmental inquisition and potential public ridicule" which in turn violates the Lemon "excessive entanglement" test. 22 Ohio Misc.2d at 45, 490 N.E.2d at 934. It is noteworthy that at least in another context, the Delaware Superior Court has already refused the opportunity to decide whether to recognize a certain religious group. See State v. Cubbage, Del.Super., 210 A.2d 555, 562 (1965) (Black nationalist movement named "Black Muslims" considered religion for purposes of religious freedom suit because "this Court cannot or should not undertake to define or rule on what is or what is not a religion.")

Hamilton, 657 S.W.2d 425, 429 (Tenn.Ct.App.1983). The California Court of Appeals in In re Ted B., 189 Cal.App.3d 996, 235 Cal.Rptr. 22 (1987), employed the best interests test to determine if a child was neglected when his parents refused to permit treatment of his cancer with "mild" chemotherapy following more intense treatment. Id. at 1006, 235 Cal.Rptr. at 27. Ted B. weighed the gravity, or potential gravity of the child's illness, the treating physician's medical evaluation of the course of care, the riskiness of the treatment and the child's "expressed preferences" to ultimately judge whether his parents' decision to withhold chemotherapy served his "best interests." Finally, the Supreme Judicial Court of Massachusetts, in Custody Of A Minor, 375 Mass. 733, 379 N.E.2d 1053 (1978), utilized a tripartite balancing test which weighed the interests of the parents, their child and the State to determine whether a child was neglected when his parents refused to treat his leukemia with non-invasive chemotherapy.

In the present case, the Family Court did not undertake any formal interest analysis in deciding that Colin was a neglected child under Delaware law. Instead, the trial court used the same ad hoc approach as the Ohio and Tennessee courts respectively employed in Willmann and Hamilton. Specifically, the Family Court rejected the Newmarks' proposal to treat Colin by spiritual means under the care of a Christian Science practitioner. The trial judge considered spiritual treatment an inadequate alternative to chemotherapy. The court therefore concluded that "[w]ithout any other factually supported alternative" the Newmarks' decision to refuse chemotherapy "constitute[d] inadequate parental care for their son who is in a life threatening situation and constitute[d] neglect as defined in the Delaware statute."

This Court reviews the trial court's application of legal precepts involving issues of law de novo. While we do not recognize the primacy of any one of the tests employed in other jurisdictions, we find that the trial court erred in not explicitly considering the competing interests at stake. The Family Court failed to consider the special importance and primacy of the familial relationship, including the autonomy of parental decision making authority over minor children. The trial court also did not consider the gravity of Colin's illness in conjunction with the invasiveness of the proposed chemotherapy and the considerable likelihood of failure. These factors, when applied to the facts of this case, strongly militate against governmental intrusion.

A.

Any balancing test must begin with the parental interest. The primacy of the familial unit is a bedrock principle of law. See Stanley v. Illinois, 405 U.S. 645, 651 (1972) (citing cases); . . . ("State and society in general have a fundamental interest in preserving and protecting the family unit."); . . . We have repeatedly emphasized that the parental right is sacred which can be invaded for only the most compelling reasons. Indeed, the Delaware General Assembly has stated that the preservation of the family is "fundamental to the maintenance of a stable, democratic society. . . ." 10 Del.C. § 902(a); see 16 Del.C. § 901 (abuse, neglect reporting statute designed to ensure strength of "parental care.")

Courts have also recognized that the essential element of preserving the integrity of the family is maintaining the autonomy of the parent-child relationship. In Prince v. Commonwealth of Massachusetts, 321 U.S. 158, 166, reh'g denied, 321 U.S. 804 (1944), the United States Supreme Court announced: It is cardinal with us that the custody, care and nurture of the child reside first in the parents, whose primary function and freedom include preparation for obligations the state can neither supply nor hinder. Parental autonomy to care for children free from government interference therefore satisfies a child's need for continuity and thus ensures his or her psychological and physical well-being.

Parental authority to make fundamental decisions for minor children is also a recognized common law principle. A doctor commits the tort of battery if he or she performs an operation under normal circumstances without the informed consent of the patient. Tort law also assumes that a child does not have the capacity to consent to an operation in most situations. Thus, the common law recognizes that the only party capable of authorizing medical treatment for a minor in "normal" circumstances is usually his parent or guardian.

Courts, therefore, give great deference to parental decisions involving minor children. In many circumstances the State simply is not an adequate surrogate for the judgment of a loving, nurturing parent. See Baskin, supra, at 1386. As one commentator aptly recognized, the "law does not have the capacity to supervise the delicately complex interpersonal bonds between parent and child."

B.

We also recognize that parental autonomy over minor children is not an absolute right. Clearly, the State can intervene in the parent-child relationship where the health and safety of the child and the public at large are in jeopardy. Accordingly, the State, under the doctrine of parens patriae, has a special duty to protect its youngest and most helpless citizens. The parens patriae doctrine is a derivation of the common law giving the State the right to act on behalf of minor children in certain property and marital disputes. See In Re Hudson, 13 Wash.2d 673, 126 P.2d 765, 777 (1942). More recently, courts have accepted the doctrine of parens patriae to justify State intervention in cases of parental religious objections to medical treatment of minor children's life threatening conditions. The Supreme Court of the United States succinctly described the parens patriae concept in Prince, 321 U.S. at 170. The Court found that parental autonomy, under the guise of the parents' religious freedom, was not unlimited. Rather, the Court held: Parents may be free to become martyrs themselves. But it does not follow they are free, in identical circumstances, to make martyrs of their children before they have reached the age of full and legal discretion when they can make that choice for themselves.

The basic principle underlying the parens patriae doctrine is the State's interest in preserving human life. See Cruzan v. Director, Missouri Dept. of Health, 110 S.Ct. 2841, 2853 (1990) (State may "assert an unqualified interest in the preservation of human life....."); Custody Of A

Minor, 375 Mass at 755, 379 N.E.2d at 1066. Yet this interest and the parens patriae doctrine are not unlimited. In its recent Cruzan opinion, the Supreme Court of the United States announced that the state's interest in preserving life must "be weighed against the constitutionally protected interests of the individual." 110 S.Ct. 2841, 2853 (1990).

The individual interests at stake here include both the Newmarks' right to decide what is best for Colin and Colin's own right to life. We have already considered the Newmarks' stake in this case and its relationship to the parens patriae doctrine. The resolution of the issues here, however, is incomplete without a discussion of Colin's interests.

C.

All children indisputably have the right to enjoy a full and healthy life. Colin, a three year old boy, unfortunately lacked the ability to reach a detached, informed decision regarding his own medical care.[9] This Court must therefore substitute its own objective judgment to determine what is in Colin's "best interests."

There are two basic inquiries when a dispute involves chemotherapy treatment over parents' religious objections. The court must first consider the effectiveness of the treatment and determine the child's chances of survival with and without medical care. The court must then consider the nature of the treatments and their effect on the child.

The "best interests" analysis is hardly unique or novel. Federal and State courts have unhesitatingly authorized medical treatment over a parent's religious objection when the treatment is relatively innocuous in comparison to the dangers of withholding medical care. See Application of President & Directors of Georgetown College, Inc., 331 F.2d 1000, 1007 (D.C.Cir.), reh'g denied, 331 F.2d 1010, cert. denied, 377 U.S. 978 (1964) (better than 50% chance of saving life with blood transfusion); Jehovah's Witnesses In State of Washington v. King Co. Hospital Unit No. 1, 278 F.Supp. 488, 503 (W.D.Wash.1967), aff'd, 390 U.S. 598, reh'g denied, 391 U.S. 961 (1968) (blood transfusion authorized where "safe" and necessary); In re Cabrera, 381 Pa. Super 100, 101–02, 552 A.2d 1114, 1115 (1989) (blood transfusion 90% effective to treat illness); In re D.L.E., 645 P.2d 271, 275 (Colo.1982) (authorization of medication to prevent epileptic seizures); Muhlenberg Hospital v. Patterson, 128 N.J.Super. 498, 503, 320 A.2d 518, 521 (Law Div.1974) (authorizing blood transfusion); New Jersey v. Perricone, 37 N.J. 463, 477, 181 A.2d 751, 759, cert. denied, 371 U.S. 890

9. Other jurisdictions have respected and upheld a minor's decision regarding his own medical care only when the child presented clear and convincing evidence that he was mature enough to exercise an adult's judgment and understood the consequences of his decision. See, e.g., In re E.G., 133 Ill.2d 98, 103, 139 Ill.Dec. 810, 815–16, 549 N.E.2d 322, 327–28 (1989); cf. In re Application of L.I. Jewish Med. Ctr., 147 Misc.2d at 730, 557 N.Y.S.2d at 243. Although we decline to comment on the applicability of the "mature minor doctrine" under Delaware law, it is doubtful that even the most precocious three year old could meet the standard. Yet, while not dispositive, there was evidence that Colin overheard some hospital discussion about treating him with chemotherapy. His reaction was one of fright that the proposed treatment would "kill" him. Thus, even at his young age, Colin was able to perceive the very real dangers of the treatment. Given the admittedly poor odds of its success, Colin's fear of chemotherapy was not unjustified.

(1962) (same); People v. Labrenz, 411 Ill. 618, 626, 104 N.E.2d 769, 774 (1952) (same). Accordingly, courts are reluctant to authorize medical care over parental objection when the child is not suffering a life threatening or potential life threatening illness. See In re Green, 448 Pa. 338, 348–49, 292 A.2d 387, 392 (1972) (court refused to authorize corrective spine surgery on minor); In re Seiferth, 309 N.Y. 80, 85–86, 127 N.E.2d 820, 823 (1955) (no authorization to correct cleft palate and harelip on fourteen year old minor); but cf. In re Sampson, 65 Misc.2d 658, 675–76, 317 N.Y.S.2d 641, 657–58 (N.Y.Fam.Ct.1970), aff'd, 29 N.Y.2d 900, 328 N.Y.S.2d 686, 278 N.E.2d 918 (1972) (authorizing corrective surgery on minor where parents' only objection was blood transfusion).

The linchpin in all cases discussing the "best interests of a child", when a parent refuses to authorize medical care, is an evaluation of the risk of the procedure compared to its potential success. This analysis is consistent with the principle that State intervention in the parent-child relationship is only justifiable under compelling conditions. The State's interest in forcing a minor to undergo medical care diminishes as the risks of treatment increase and its benefits decrease.

The New Jersey Supreme Court implicitly recognized this principle in the seminal Quinlan case decided over a decade ago. See In re Quinlan, 70 N.J. 10, 355 A.2d 647, cert. denied, 429 U.S. 922 (1976). In deciding that a legal custodian could authorize the termination of artificial life support in certain circumstances, Quinlan noted that: [T]he State's interest contra weakens and the individual's right to privacy grows as the degree of bodily invasion increases and the prognosis dims. Ultimately there comes a point at which the individual's rights overcome the State interest. It is for that reason that we believe Karen's choice, if she were competent to make it, would be vindicated by the law. Her prognosis is extremely poor,—she will never resume cognitive life. And the bodily invasion is very great,—she requires 24 hour intensive nursing care, antibiotics, the assistance of a respirator, a catheter and feeding tube. Similarly, most courts which have authorized medical treatment on a minor over parental objection have also noted that a different situation exists when the treatment is inherently dangerous and invasive. See, e.g., In re Cabrera, 381 Pa.Super. at 111, 552 A.2d at 1119; Muhlenberg Hospital, 128 N.J.Super. at 503, 320 A.2d at 521 ("if the disputed procedure involved a significant danger to the infant, the parents' wishes would be respected."); Perricone, 37 N.J. at 479–80, 181 A.2d at 760 (strong argument for parents if "there were substantial evidence that the treatment itself posed a significant danger to the infant's life"); Labrenz, 411 Ill. at 624–25, 104 N.E.2d at 773 (same); In re Hudson, 126 P.2d at 777 (court not permitted to authorize treatment "which would probably result in merciful release by death from [minor's] physical ... handicap.").

Applying the foregoing considerations to the "best interests standard" here, the State's petition must be denied. The egregious facts of this case indicate that Colin's proposed medical treatment was highly invasive, painful, involved terrible temporary and potentially permanent side effects, posed an unacceptably low chance of success, and a high risk that the treatment itself would cause his death. The State's authority to intervene in this case, therefore, cannot outweigh the Newmarks' parental preroga-tive and Colin's inherent right to enjoy at least a modicum of human dignity in the short time that was left to him.

IV.

Dr. Meek originally diagnosed Colin's condition as Burkitt's Lympho-ma. She testified that the cancer was "a very bad tumor" in an advanced disseminated state and not localized to only one section of the body. She accordingly recommended that the hospital begin an "extremely intensive" chemotherapy program scheduled to extend for at least six months. The first step necessary to prepare Colin for chemotherapy involved an intrave-nous hydration treatment. This process, alone, posed a significant risk that Colin's kidneys would fail. Indeed, these intravenous treatments had al-ready begun and were threatening Colin's life while the parties were arguing the case to us on September 14, 1990. Thus, if Colin's kidneys failed he also would have to undergo dialysis treatments. There also was a possibility that renal failure could occur during the chemotherapy treat-ments themselves. In addition, Dr. Meek recommended further pretreat-ment diagnostic tests including a spinal tap and a CAT scan.

Dr. Meek prescribed "maximum" doses of at least six different types of cancer-fighting drugs during Colin's chemotherapy. This proposed "maxi-mum" treatment represented the most aggressive form of cancer therapy short of a bone marrow transplant. The side effects would include hair loss, reduced immunological function creating a high risk of infection in the patient, and certain neurological problems. The drugs also are toxic to bone marrow.

The record demonstrates that this form of chemotherapy also would adversely affect other parts of Colin's body. Dr. Meek stated that the doctors would have to administer the treatments through injections in the veins and spinal fluid. The chemotherapy would reduce Colin's white blood count, and it would be extremely likely that he would suffer numerous infections. Colin would require multiple blood transfusions with a resultant additional risk of infection.

The treating physicians also would have to install a catheter in Colin's chest to facilitate a constant barrage of tests and treatments. Colin also would receive food through the catheter because the chemotherapy would depress his appetite. The operation to set the catheter in place would take approximately one hour. The doctors proposed to perform biopsies on both Colin's bone marrow and the lump in his groin during the procedure.

The physicians planned to administer the chemotherapy in cycles, each of which would bring Colin near death. Then they would wait until Colin's body recovered sufficiently before introducing more drugs. Dr. Meek opined that there was no guarantee that drugs alone would "cure" Colin's illness. The doctor noted that it would then be necessary to radiate Colin's testicles if drugs alone were unsuccessful. Presumably, this would have rendered him sterile.

Dr. Meek also wanted the State to place Colin in a foster home after the initial phases of hospital treatment. Children require intensive home monitoring during chemotherapy. For example, Dr. Meek testified that a usually low grade fever for a healthy child could indicate the presence of a potentially deadly infection in a child cancer patient. She believed that the Newmarks, although well educated and financially responsible, were incapable of providing this intensive care because of their firm religious objections to medical treatment.[10]

Dr. Meek ultimately admitted that there was a real possibility that the chemotherapy could kill Colin. In fact, assuming the treatment did not itself prove fatal, she offered Colin at "best" a 40% chance[11] that he would "survive."[12] Dr. Meek additionally could not accurately predict whether, if Colin completed the therapy, he would subsequently suffer additional tumors.

A.

No American court, even in the most egregious case, has ever authorized the State to remove a child from the loving, nurturing care of his parents and subject him, over parental objection, to an invasive regimen of treatment which offered, as Dr. Meek defined the term, only a forty percent chance of "survival." For example, the California Court of Appeals ruled in Eric B., that the State could conduct various procedures as part of an "observation phase" of chemotherapy over the objection of his parents. 189 Cal.App.3d at 1008–1009, 235 Cal.Rptr. at 29. The treatment included bone scans, CT scans, spinal taps and biopsies. The court specifically found that "[t]he risks entailed by the monitoring are minimal." The court also noted that the child would enjoy a 60% chance of survival with the treatments.

The Tennessee Court of Appeals awarded custody of a minor suffering from Ewing's Sarcoma to the State after her parents refused to treat the cancer with medical care. See In re Hamilton, 657 S.W.2d at 429. The child in that case enjoyed an at least 80% chance of temporary remission and a 25%–50% opportunity for long-term "cure". The court specifically noted that various hospitals had successfully treated Ewing's Sarcoma in "a significant number of patients." There was no testimony in Hamilton, however, concerning the magnitude of the proposed chemotherapy.

The Supreme Judicial Court of Massachusetts took custody away from parents who refused to administer "mild" cancer fighting drugs after the child had already undergone more "vigorous" treatment. See Custody of a Minor, 375 Mass. at 755–56, 379 N.E.2d at 1058, 1067. The trial judge, in that case, specifically found that aside from some minor side effects,

---

10. A doctor in a recent related case in Connecticut involving state intervention over a mother's decision to treat her minor child with traditional Chinese remedies rather than "conventional surgery" remarked that " '[i]f you do something where you need the cooperation of the entire family for the child to get better, when it's against the family's wishes your probability of success is vastly reduced.' " N.Y. Times, Dec. 13, 1990, at B5, col. 1.

11. Dr. Meek based her estimate on "historical" data compiled from children who have suffered from Burkitt's Lymphoma.

12. Dr. Meek testified that there was no available medical data to conclude that Colin could survive to adulthood. Rather, she stated that the term "survival", as applied to victims of leukemia or lymphoma, refers only to the probability that the patient will live two years after chemotherapy without a recurrence of cancer.

including stomach cramps and constipation, the chemotherapy "bore no chance of leaving the child physically incapacitated in any way." The trial court also ruled that the chemotherapy gave the child not only a chance to enjoy a long life "but also a 'substantial' chance for cure."

The Ohio Court of Appeals awarded custody of a minor suffering from Osteogenic Sarcoma to the state when his parents consented to chemotherapy, but later refused to authorize an operation to partially remove his shoulder and entire left arm. In re Willmann, 24 Ohio App.3d at 193, 199, 493 N.E.2d at 1383, 1390. Although amputation is ultimately the most invasive type of surgery, there was at least a 60% chance in Willmann that the child would survive with the operation. The court also significantly noted that the child remained at home while receiving the lower court's mandated chemotherapy treatments.

Finally, the New York Supreme Court most recently ruled that the State could intervene and order chemotherapy treatments over a parent's religious objections when the medical care presented a 75% chance of short-term remission but only a 25–30% chance for "cure." See In re Application of L.I. Jewish Med. Ctr., 147 Misc.2d at 725, 557 N.Y.S.2d at 241. The seventeen year old minor in that case suffered from an advanced case of Rhabdomyosarcoma, a type of pediatric cancer affecting potential muscle tissue. This case, however, is not dispositive given the fact that the parents were not wholly opposed to chemotherapy.

The minor and his parents in L.I. Jewish Med. Ctr., were both members of the Jehovah's Witnesses religion and only objected to blood transfusions which were an incidental part of the prescribed medical treatment. There was no evidence that either party objected to the chemotherapy, which included radiation treatments. The treatments were also probably "radical" in nature given the fact that the disease had spread throughout the child's body. This New York decision is therefore in perfect accord with other well-established precedent. Courts have consistently authorized state intervention when parents object to only minimally intrusive treatment which poses little or no risk to a child's health. See supra Part III.C.

B.

The aggressive form of chemotherapy that Dr. Meek prescribed for Colin was more likely to fail than succeed. The proposed treatment was also highly invasive and could have independently caused Colin's death. Dr. Meek also wanted to take Colin away from his parents and family during the treatment phase and place the boy in a foster home. This certainly would have caused Colin severe emotional difficulties given his medical condition, tender age, and the unquestioned close bond between Colin and his family.

In sum, Colin's best interests were served by permitting the Newmarks to retain custody of their child. Parents must have the right at some point to reject medical treatment for their child. Under all of the circumstances here, this clearly is such a case. The State's important and legitimate role in safeguarding the interests of minor children diminishes in the face of this egregious record.

Parents undertake an awesome responsibility in raising and caring for their children. No doubt a parent's decision to withhold medical care is both deeply personal and soul wrenching. It need not be made worse by the invasions which both the State and medical profession sought on this record. Colin's ultimate fate therefore rested with his parents and their faith.[13]

The judgment of the Family Court is, REVERSED.

In re E.G.

Supreme Court of Illinois, 1989.
133 Ill.2d 98, 139 Ill.Dec. 810, 549 N.E.2d 322.

[The text of this opinion is reproduced at p. 170, supra.]

NOTE

During 2007 Virginia's Child Abuse Law, Va. Code Ann. § 63.2–100, was amended to provide that "a decision by parents who have legal authority for the child or, in the absence of parents with legal authority for the child, any person with legal authority for the child, who refuses a particular medical treatment for a child with a life-threatening condition shall not be deemed a refusal to provide necessary care if (i) such decision is made directly by the parents or other person with legal authority and the child; (ii) the child has reached 14 years of age and is sufficiently mature to have an informed opinion on the subject of his medical treatment; (iii) the parents or other person with legal authority and the child have considered alternative treatment options; and (iv) the parents or other person with legal authority and the child believe in good faith that such decision is in the child's best interest. Nothing in this subdivision shall be construed to limit the provisions of § 16.1–278.4." [That section deals with children in need of services.]

In *Commonwealth v. Nixon*, 563 Pa. 425, 761 A.2d 1151 (2000), defendant parents had been convicted of involuntary manslaughter based on their religiously motivated refusal to provide medical care for their sixteen-year-old child, who died from diabetes acidosis (a treatable but not curable condition). On appeal, the Supreme Court of Pennsylvania held that the minor's privacy rights were not violated by the convictions and that Pennsylvania had no "mature minor" rule. The basis for the latter was that a state statute explicitly stated the age (eighteen) at which minors could make medical decisions for themselves. Under those circumstances the court determined that a "mature minor doctrine" could not be asserted as a defense in a criminal action against the parents.

---

13. Tragically, Colin died shortly after we announced our oral decision.

CHAPTER VI

FOSTER CARE AND ITS CHANGING ROLE

A. INTRODUCTION

Orphanages for children without parents largely disappeared long ago in the United States. Today there are far fewer institutions in which to place children without surviving parents or children who have been removed from their homes because of neglect, abuse or dependency, or voluntarily relinquished temporarily by their parents.[1] Instead there is great reliance on foster parents who care for such children with state approval and compensation. At one time foster care ostensibly was an interim placement in which a child would remain until returning home, or to other relatives, or possibly to a new family through adoption if parental rights were terminated. As the material in this chapter indicates, however, "interim" or temporary placement was a fiction in a large number of instances; some foster children even became lost indefinitely in a Kafkaesque system. Recognizing this, some urged that removal of a child from the home and placement in foster care should be a last resort. See, e.g., Robert Mnookin, Foster Care—In Whose Best Interests?, 43 Harv.Ed.Rev. 599 (1973).

NEW YORK SOCIAL SERVICES LAW (MCKINNEY)

§ 383. Care and custody of children

1. The parent of a child remanded or committed to an authorized agency shall not be entitled to the custody thereof, except upon consent of the court, public board, commission, or official responsible for the commitment of such child, or in pursuance of an order of a court or judicial officer of competent jurisdiction, determining that the interest of such child will be promoted thereby and that such parent is fit, competent and able to duly maintain, support and educate such child. The name of such child shall not be changed while in the custody of an authorized agency.

2. The custody of a child placed out or boarded out and not legally adopted or for whom legal guardianship has not been granted shall be vested during his minority, or until discharged by such authorized agency

---

1. In formulating any policy that would attempt to impose limitations on the removal of children from their homes for placement in foster care, it is important to understand that many placements labeled "voluntary" on the part of parents actually result from the threat of proceeding under a neglect or dependency petition. The Juvenile Justice Standards on Abuse and Neglect (Tentative Draft 1977) recognized the potential impact of a voluntary placement and urged all states to adopt a statutory structure regulating voluntary placements.

from its care and supervision, in the authorized agency placing out or boarding out such child and any such authorized agency may in its discretion remove such child from the home where placed or boarded.

. . .

B. Relationships Within the Foster Family

J.M.A. v. State

Supreme Court of Alaska, 1975.
542 P.2d 170.

■ Boochever, Justice.

[A foster parent, licensed by the State of Alaska and receiving a monthly allowance of $233 per child from the State, became concerned that visits to her home by children who were strangers might be related to trafficking in drugs. The foster parent, Mrs. Blankenship, searched the room of her foster child, J.M.A., and listened on an extension telephone to one of his calls without the child's permission. She found a bag of marijuana in one of his pockets and consulted the social worker assigned to J.M.A. for advice on how to deal with the problem. The social worker called the police. A police officer went to the Blankenship home, confronted J.M.A. and questioned him about the marijuana without giving any *Miranda* warnings. At trial, J.M.A.'s counsel moved to suppress the evidence obtained by the foster parent. The motion was denied and J.M.A. was adjudicated a delinquent child and committed to the Department of Social Services to be placed in a correctional or detention facility for an indeterminate period not to extend past his 19th birthday. J.M.A. appeals from the delinquency adjudication and the ruling on the motion to suppress.]

. . . [W]e must determine whether the state and federal constitutional prohibitions[4] against unreasonable searches and seizures apply to a foster parent, licensed and paid by the state, and if so, whether the exclusionary rule, whereby evidence obtained in violation of the constitution is held inadmissible, should apply. Our analysis must initially focus on the question of whether the foster parent stands in such a relationship to the state as to be subject to the constitutional prohibitions against unreasonable searches and seizures. J.M.A. contends that the evidence gathered by Mrs. Blankenship should be suppressed since these warrantless searches were executed while Mrs. Blankenship was acting as an agent of the state, and thus did not comport with constitutional requirements concerning such actions. The state, to the contrary, argues that Mrs. Blankenship, as a foster parent, is not an agent of the state for purposes of the fourth amendment.

---

4. The fourth amendment of the United States Constitution provides in part:

The right of the people to be secure in their persons, houses, papers and effects, against unreasonable searches and seizures, shall not be violated. . . .

. . .

Although the constitutional prohibitions against unreasonable searches and seizures have not been specifically limited to state action, there is little doubt but that was the original intent . . . .

There is a further limitation on the scope of the fourth amendment in that it does not apply to searches engaged in by governmental officials when such officials act for a private purpose or outside the scope of duties related to law enforcement. Such a limitation involves a question of the capacity in which the state agent acts during the course of the search . . . .

. . .

. . . [I]t is apparent that, in some respects, Mrs. Blankenship is an agent of the state. Her home is licensed and regulated by the state, and she is paid by the state for caring for foster children. But she also acts in a private capacity in managing the home for her family and herself. In all likelihood, her search of J.M.A.'s room and her listening to his telephone conversation involved both her state duties and her private functions. In both capacities, she had a need to supervise the young people placed under her control, and, solely as a private person, she had a legitimate concern about the illegal activities taking place in her home.

The mere fact that Mrs. Blankenship may have been acting in part as an agent of the state, however, does not necessarily mean that fourth amendment prohibitions apply . . . .

. . .

A foster parent is required both to assume temporarily the role of a natural parent to the child committed to his custody and to aid in the discharge of the government's obligation to care for and supervise those juveniles who have become the responsibility of the state. In substituting for a natural parent, the foster parent is no more an agent of the police than would be any natural parent. The actions of Mrs. Blankenship were in no manner instigated by the police. She testified that she did not want her children to get into trouble with the police and that she sought to work out such problems without police involvement. In fact, even after discovering the marijuana, she contacted J.M.A.'s social worker rather than the police. There is no reason for regarding Mrs. Blankenship's actions undertaken while fulfilling this parental role, which did not involve collaboration with the police, as being any different from the actions of a private parent, and, therefore, not subject to fourth amendment constitutional restraints.

The second function undertaken by foster parents, that of caring for and supervising foster children on behalf of the state, quite obviously involves the foster parent in a relationship with the state which may be characterized as an agency relationship. At least insofar as the supervision of J.M.A. is concerned, even as an agent of the state, we suggest without deciding that Mrs. Blankenship had the right to search J.M.A.'s room. He had previously been declared a delinquent and was placed in the Blankenship home as an alternative to placement in a correctional institution. Had he been placed in a correctional institution, his room would have been legally subject to searches. "In prison, official surveillance has traditionally been the order of the day."

Thus, if Mrs. Blankenship's relationship with J.M.A. is analogized to that of parent and child, the search did not violate the fourth amendment, and if the relationship were to be construed as similar to that involved had J.M.A. been placed in a correctional institution, again there would be no violation. In this instance, the operator of a foster home is in the extremely difficult position of endeavoring to fulfill the role of parent, and, at the same time, perform the task of supervising the activities of a minor found to be a delinquent. Under the circumstances of such a relationship, a search of the room can hardly be regarded as the type of unreasonable activity constitutionally prohibited. Nevertheless, we believe that the privacy of both natural and foster children should be respected to the fullest extent consistent with parental responsibilities.

Quite obviously, the duties of foster parents do not encompass responsibilities of a law enforcement officer.... Foster parents are not charged with the enforcement of penal statutes or regulations, nor are they entrusted with ensuring the physical security of the public.... They merely supervise on behalf of the state those children committed to their care.... [A]ccordingly, we hold that foster parents are not agents of the state for purposes of the fourth amendment.

Our conclusion that the trial court did not err in denying the motion to suppress is bolstered by application of the policies underlying the exclusionary rule to the facts of this case....

... [T]he purpose of the rule is not to give shelter to those who have violated criminal laws but to insure that the constitutional rights of all citizens will be maintained. Police, knowing that illegally-obtained evidence cannot be used, are encouraged to comply with constitutional provisions. In the instant case, a principal motivating factor of Mrs. Blankenship's actions must have been a desire to aid her foster child as well as to have her home free of illegal drugs and criminal activity. Excluding the evidence seized herein would do nothing to deter similar future conduct by the Blankenships and other foster parents as that interest is entirely separate from a desire to have a person convicted of a crime or adjudged a delinquent. Put another way, the incentive to make a search under the circumstances here involved would not be lessened because of the likelihood that the evidence would be suppressed. In short, the primary purpose to be served by the exclusionary rule would not be served by its application in this case or ones similar to it.

. . .

NOTE

In *Carroll v. Washington Township Zoning Commission*, 63 Ohio St.2d 249, 408 N.E.2d 191 (1980), a married couple who served as foster parents to five or six children under contract with the Ohio Youth Commission sought a declaratory judgment that they were in compliance with township zoning regulations limiting their house to use as a one family residential dwelling unit. The Supreme Court of Ohio upheld a finding that the foster home violated the ordinance, which was a reasonable enactment of the township governing body. The court found that "the children are in effect transients, staying varying periods from six months to a year . . . ."

Brown, J., dissenting, pointed out that "The factors relied upon by the majority to indicate that the Carroll family was not integrated could be used to conclude that any foster family, even a family with only one foster child", would not be permitted to live in a single family residential district. He added that "the policy considerations associated with foster homes . . . weigh in favor of permitting such homes whenever possible in residential neighborhoods."

For a view contrary to that of the Ohio Supreme Court, see *Group House of Port Washington v. Board of Zoning*, 45 N.Y.2d 266, 408 N.Y.S.2d 377, 380 N.E.2d 207 (1978), in which the New York Court of Appeals stated:

> Any foster care program . . . is in a very real way "temporary," since foster care by its very nature is simply a method of caring for children until they can either be returned to their natural parents or until an adoptive home can be found for them. Thus, the argument that petitioner's "group home" is not a family simply because petitioner hopes to eventually return the children to their natural families is unconvincing. . . .

> Petitioner's very purpose is to create a stable, family type environment for children whose natural families unfortunately cannot provide such a home. As such, petitioner's "group home" would in no way detract from the family and youth values which one-family zoning is intended to protect. In fact, petitioner's "group home" might actually support and further those values even more effectively than certain natural families. If petitioner's "group home" is to be a success, it would most appropriately be placed in just such a quiet, residential neighborhood, for that is the very type of atmosphere which it seeks to emulate.

> The surrogate family which petitioner hopes to create is in fact a permanent family structure, and not a temporary residence for transients. Although some of the resident children will be replaced by others as time passes, the family unit itself will continue.

Group homes also have been opposed on the basis of private subdivision covenants restricting use to single family residences. The subject is carefully analyzed in Robert D. Brussack, Group Homes, Families, and Meaning in the Law of Subdivision Covenants, 16 Ga.L.Rev. 33 (1981). See also Gerald Korngold, Single Family Use Covenants: For Achieving a Balance Between Traditional Family Life and Individual Autonomy, 22 U.C. Davis L.Rev. 951 (1989).

Smith v. Organization of Foster Families for Equality and Reform

Supreme Court of the United States, 1977.
431 U.S. 816, 97 S.Ct. 2094, 53 L.Ed.2d 14.

■ MR. JUSTICE BRENNAN delivered the opinion of the Court.

Appellees, individual foster parents[1] and an organization of foster parents, brought this civil rights class action pursuant to 42 U.S.C. § 1983 in the United States District Court for the Southern District of New York,

---

1. Appellee Madeleine Smith is the foster parent with whom Eric and Danielle Gandy have been placed since 1970. The Gandy children, who are now 12 and 9 years old respectively, were voluntarily placed in foster care by their natural mother in 1968, and have had no contact with her at least since being placed with Mrs. Smith. The foster-care agency has sought to remove the children from Mrs. Smith's care because her arthritis, in the agency's judgment makes it difficult

on their own behalf and on behalf of children for whom they have provided homes for a year or more. They sought declaratory and injunctive relief against New York State and New York City officials, alleging that the procedures governing the removal of foster children from foster homes provided in N.Y.Soc.Serv. Law §§ 383(2) and 400 (McKinney 1976), and in 18 N.Y.C.R.R. § 450.14 (1974) violated the Due Process and Equal Protection Clauses of the Fourteenth Amendment.[3] The District Court appointed independent counsel for the foster children to forestall any possibility of

for her to continue to provide adequate care....

Appellees Ralph and Christiane Goldberg were the foster parents of Rafael Serrano, now 14. His parents placed him in foster care voluntarily in 1969 after an abuse complaint was filed against them. It is alleged that the agency supervising the placement had informally indicated to Mr. and Mrs. Goldberg that it intended to transfer Rafael to the home of his aunt in contemplation of permanent placement. This effort has apparently failed. A petition for foster-care review under Soc.Serv. Law § 392 filed by the agency alleges that the Goldbergs are now separated, Mrs. Goldberg having moved out of the house, taking her own child but leaving Rafael. The child is now in a residential treatment center, where Mr. Goldberg continues to visit him.

Appellees Walter and Dorothy Lhotan were foster parents of the four Wallace sisters, who were voluntarily placed in foster care by their mother in 1970. The two older girls were placed with the Lhotans in that year, their two younger sisters in 1972. In June 1974, the Lhotans were informed that the agency had decided to return the two younger girls to their mother and transfer the two older girls to another foster home. The agency apparently felt that the Lhotans were too emotionally involved with the girls and were damaging the agency's efforts to prepare them to return to their mother. The state courts have ordered that all the Wallace children be returned to their mother. We are told that the children have been returned and are adjusting successfully.

3. New York Soc.Serv. Law § 383(2) (McKinney 1976) provides:

"The custody of a child placed out or boarded out and not legally adopted or for whom legal guardianship has not been granted shall be vested during his minority, or until discharged by such authorized agency from its care and supervision, in the authorized agency placing out or boarding out such child and any

such authorized agency may in its discretion remove such child from the home where placed or boarded."

New York Soc.Serv. Law § 400 (McKinney 1976) provides:

"Removal of children

"1. When any child shall have been placed in an institution or in a family home by a commissioner of public welfare or a city public welfare officer, the commissioner or city public welfare officer may remove such child from such institution or family home and make such disposition of such child as is provided by law.

"2. Any person aggrieved by such decision of the commissioner of public welfare or city welfare officer may appeal to the department, which upon receipt of the appeal shall review the case, shall give the person making the appeal an opportunity for a fair hearing thereon and within thirty days render its decision. The department may also, on its own motions, review any such decision made by the public welfare official. The department may make such additional investigation as it may deem necessary. All decisions of the department shall be binding upon the public welfare district involved and shall be complied with by the public welfare officials thereof."

Title 18 N.Y.C.R.R. § 450.14, which was renumbered § 450.10 as of September 18, 1974, provides:

"Removal from foster family care. (a) Whenever a social services official of another authorized agency acting on his behalf proposes to remove a child in foster family care from the foster family home, he or such other authorized agency, as may be appropriate, shall notify the foster family parents, in writing of the intention to remove such child at least 10 days prior to the proposed effective date of such removal, except where

conflict between their interests and the interests asserted by the foster parents. A group of natural mothers of children in foster care[5] were granted leave to intervene on behalf of themselves and others similarly situated.

A divided three-judge District Court concluded that "the pre-removal procedures presently employed by the State are constitutionally defective," holding that "before a foster child can be peremptorily transferred from the foster home in which he has been living, be it to another foster home or to the natural parents who initially placed him in foster care, he is entitled to a hearing at which all concerned parties may present any relevant information to the administrative decisionmaker charged with determining the future placement of the child," Organization of Foster Families v. Dumpson, 418 F.Supp. 277, 282 (1976).... We reverse.

. . .

the health or safety of the child requires that he be removed immediately from the foster family home. Such notification shall further advise the foster family parents that they may request a conference with the social services official or a designated employee of his social services department at which time they may appear, with or without a representative to have the proposed action reviewed, be advised of the reasons therefore and be afforded an opportunity to submit reasons why the child should not be removed. Each social services official shall instruct and require any authorized agency acting on his behalf to furnish notice in accordance with the provisions of this section. Foster parents who do not object to the removal of the child from their home may waive in writing their right to the 10 day notice, provided, however, that such waiver shall not be executed prior to the social services official's determination to remove the child from the foster home and notifying the foster parents thereof.

"(b) Upon the receipt of a request for such conference, the social services official shall set a time and place for such conference to be held within 10 days of receipt of such request and shall send written notice of such conference to the foster family parents and their representative, if any, and to the authorized agency, if any, at least five days prior to the date of such conference.

"(c) The social services official shall render and issue his decision as expeditiously as possible but not later than five days after the conference and shall send a written notice of his decision to the foster family parents and their representative, if any, and to the authorized agency, if any. Such decision shall advise the foster family parents of their right to appeal to the department and request a fair hearing in accordance with section 400 of the Social Services Law.

"(d) In the event there is a request for a conference, the child shall not be removed from the foster family home until at least three days after the notice of decision is sent, or prior to the proposed effective date of removal, whichever occurs later.

"(e) In any agreement for foster care between a social services official or another authorized agency acting on his behalf and foster parents, there shall be contained therein a statement of a foster parent's rights provided under this section."

5. Intervenor Naomi Rodriguez, who is blind, placed her newborn son Edwin in foster care in 1973 because of marital difficulties. When Mrs. Rodriguez separated from her husband three months later, she sought return of her child. Her efforts over the next nine months to obtain return of the child were resisted by the agency, apparently because it felt her handicap prevented her from providing adequate care. Eventually, she sought return of her child in the state courts, and finally prevailed, three years after she first sought return of the child. Rodriguez v. Dumpson, 52 A.D.2d 299, 383 N.Y.S.2d 883 (1976). The other named intervenors describe similar instances of voluntary placements during family emergencies followed by lengthy and frustrating attempts to get their children back.

The expressed central policy of the New York system is that "it is generally desirable for the child to remain with or be returned to the natural parent because the child's need for a normal family life will usually best be met in the natural home, and . . . parents are entitled to bring up their own children unless the best interests of the child would be thereby endangered," Soc.Serv. Law § 384–b(1)(a)(ii) (McKinney Supp. 1976–1977). But the State has opted for foster care as one response to those situations where the natural parents are unable to provide the "positive, nurturing family relationships" and "normal family life in a permanent home" that offer "the best opportunity for children to develop and thrive." §§ 384–b(1)(b), (1)(a)(I).

Foster care has been defined as "[a] child welfare service which provides substitute family care for a planned period for a child when his own family cannot care for him for a temporary or extended period, and when adoption is neither desirable nor possible." Child Welfare League of America, Standards for Foster Family Care Service, 5 (1959).[8] Thus, the distinctive features of foster care are, first, "that it is care in a *family*, it is noninstitutional substitute care," and, second, "that it is for a *planned* period—either temporary or extended. This is unlike adoptive placement, which implies a *permanent* substitution of one home for another." Kadushin 355.

Under the New York scheme children may be placed in foster care either by voluntary placement or by court order. Most foster care placements are voluntary.[9] They occur when physical or mental illness, economic problems, or other family crises make it impossible for natural parents, particularly single parents, to provide a stable home life for their children for some limited period. Resort to such placements is almost compelled when it is not possible in such circumstance to place the child with a relative or friend, or to pay for the services of a homemaker or boarding school.

Voluntary placement requires the signing of a written agreement by the natural parent or guardian, transferring the care and custody of the child to an authorized child welfare agency.[11] Although by statute the terms

8. The term "foster care" is often used more generally to apply to any type of care that substitutes others for the natural parent in the parental role, including group homes, adoptive homes, and institutions, as well as foster family homes. A. Kadushin, Child Welfare Services 355 (1967) (hereafter Kadushin). Cf. Mnookin, Foster Care—In Whose Best Interests?, 43 Harv.Educ.Rev. 599, 600 (1973) (hereafter Mnookin I). Since this case is only concerned with children in foster family homes, the term will generally be used here in the more restricted sense defined in the text.

9. The record indicates that as many as 80% of the children in foster care in New York City are voluntarily placed. Deposition of Prof. David Fanshel, App. 178a. But cf. Child Welfare Information Services, Characteristics of Children in Foster Care, New York City Reports, Table No. 11 (Dec. 31, 1976). Other studies from New York and elsewhere variously estimate the percentage of voluntary placements between 50% and 90%.

11. "Authorized agency" is defined in N.Y.Soc.Serv. Law § 371(10) (McKinney 1976) and "includes any local public welfare children's bureau, such as the defendants New York City Bureau of Child Welfare and Nassau County Children's Bureau, and any voluntary child-care agency under the supervision of the New York State Board of Social Welfare, such as the defendant Catholic

of such agreements are open to negotiation, it is contended that agencies require execution of standardized forms. The agreement may provide for return of the child to the natural parent at a specified date or upon occurrence of a particular event, and if it does not, the child must be returned by the agency, in the absence of a court order, within 20 days of notice from the parent.

The agency may maintain the child in an institutional setting, but more commonly acts under its authority to "place out and board out" children in foster homes. Foster parents, who are licensed by the State or an authorized foster-care agency, provide care under a contractual arrangement with the agency, and are compensated for their services. The typical contract expressly reserves the right of the agency to remove the child on request. Conversely, the foster parent may cancel the agreement at will.[15]

The New York system divides parental functions among agency, foster parents, and natural parents, and the definitions of the respective roles are often complex and often unclear.[16] The law transfers "care and custody" to the agency, but day-to-day supervision of the child and his activities, and most of the functions ordinarily associated with legal custody, are the responsibility of the foster parent. Nevertheless, agency supervision of the performance of the foster parents takes forms indicating that the foster parent does not have the full authority of a legal custodian.[18] Moreover, the natural parent's placement of the child with the agency does not surrender legal guardianship;[19] the parent retains authority to act with respect to the

---

Guardian Society of New York." 418 F.Supp., at 278 n. 5.

An *amicus curiae* brief states that in New York City, 85% of the children in foster care are placed with voluntary child-care agencies licensed by the State, while most children in foster care outside New York City are placed directly with the local Department of Social Services. Brief for Legal Aid Society of City of New York, Juvenile Rights Division, as *Amicus Curiae* 14 n. 22.

15. . . . Evidence in the record indicates that as many as one-third of all transfers within the foster-care system are at the request of the foster parents.

16. The resulting confusion not only produces anomalous legal relationships but also affects the child's emotional status. The foster child's loyalties, emotional involvements, and responsibilities are often divided among three adult authority figures—the natural parent, the foster parent, and the social worker representing the foster-care agency. See, e.g., Kadushin 387–389; see also Mnookin I 624; Wald, State Intervention on Behalf of "Neglected" Children: Standards for Removal of Children from Their Homes, Monitoring the Status of Children in Foster Care, and Termination of Parental Rights, 28 Stan.L.Rev. 623, 645 (1976) (hereafter Wald);

E. Weinstein, The Self–Image of the Foster Child 15 (1960).

18. "The agency sets limits and advances directives as to how the foster parents are to behave toward the child—a situation not normally encountered by natural parents. The shared control and responsibility for the child is clearly set forth in the instruction pamphlets issued to foster parents." Id., at 394. Agencies frequently prohibit corporal punishment; require that children over a certain age be given an allowance; forbid changes in the child's sleeping arrangements or vacations out of State without agency approval; require the foster parent to discuss the child's behavioral problems with the agency. Id., at 394–395. Furthermore, since the cost of supporting the child is borne by the agency, the responsibility, as well as the authority, of the foster parent is shared with the agency. Ibid.

19. Voluntary placement in foster care is entirely distinct from the "surrender" of both "the guardianship of the person and the custody" of a child under Soc.Serv. Law § 384, which frees the child for adoption. § 384(2). "Adoption is the legal proceeding whereby a person takes another person into the legal relation of child and thereby ac-

child in certain circumstances.[20] The natural parent has not only the right but the obligation to visit the foster child and plan for his future; failure of a parent with capacity to fulfill the obligation for more than a year can result in a court order terminating the parent's rights on the ground of neglect.

Children may also enter foster care by court order. The Family Court may order that a child be placed in the custody of an authorized child-care agency after a full adversary judicial hearing under Art. 10 of the New York Family Court Act, if it is found that the child has been abused or neglected by his natural parents. In addition, a minor adjudicated a juvenile delinquent, or "person in need of supervision" may be placed by the court with an agency. The consequences of foster-care placement by court order do not differ substantially from those for children voluntarily placed, except that the parent is not entitled to return of the child on demand pursuant to Soc.Serv. Law § 384–a(2)(a); termination of foster care must then be consented to by the court.[22]

The provisions of the scheme specifically at issue in this litigation come into play when the agency having legal custody determines to remove the foster child from the foster home, either because it has determined that it would be in the child's best interests to transfer him to some other foster home, or to return the child to his natural parents in accordance with the statute or placement agreement. Most children are removed in order to be transferred to another foster home.[23] The procedures by which foster parents may challenge a removal made for that purpose differ somewhat from those where the removal is made to return the child to his natural parent.

Section 383(2), n. 3, supra, provides that the "authorized agency placing out or boarding [a foster] child ... may in its discretion remove such child from the home where placed or boarded." Administrative regulations implement this provision. The agency is required, except in emergencies, to notify the foster parents in writing 10 days in advance of any removal. 18 N.Y.C.R.R. § 450.10(a) (1976). The notice advises the foster parents that if they object to the child's removal they may request a "conference" with the Social Services Department. Ibid. The department schedules requested conferences within 10 days of the receipt of the

---

quires the rights and incurs the responsibilities of parent in respect of such other person." N.Y.Dom.Rel. Law § 110 (McKinney 1964). A child may also be free for adoption by abandonment or consent. § 111 (McKinney Supp. 1976–1977); Soc.Serv. Law § 384–b.

20. "[A]lthough the agency usually obtains legal custody in foster family care, the child still legally 'belongs' to the parent and the parent retains guardianship. This means that, for some crucial aspects to the child's life, the agency has no authority to act. Only the parent can consent to surgery for the child, or consent to his marriage, or permit

his enlistment in the armed forces, or represent him at law." Kadushin 355. But see Soc.Serv. Law § 383–b.

22. The Family Court is also empowered permanently to sever the ties of parent and child if the parent fails to maintain contact with the child while in foster care.

23. The record shows that in 1973–1974 approximately 80% of the children removed from foster homes in New York State after living in the foster home for one year or more were transferred to another foster placement. Thirteen percent were returned to the biological parents, and 7% were adopted.

request. § 450.10(b). The foster parent may appear with counsel at the conference, where he will "be advised of the reasons [for the removal of the child], and be afforded an opportunity to submit reasons why the child should not be removed." § 450.10(a). The official must render a decision in writing within five days after the close of the conference, and send notice of his decision to the foster parents and the agency. § 450.10(c). The proposed removal is stayed pending the outcome of the conference. § 450.10(d).

If the child is removed after the conference, the foster parent may appeal to the Department of Social Services for a "fair hearing," that is, a full adversary administrative hearing, under Soc.Serv.Law § 400, the determination of which is subject to judicial review under N.Y.Civ.Prac.Law § 7801 et seq. (McKinney 1963); Art. 78; however, the removal is not automatically stayed pending the hearing and judicial review.

This statutory and regulatory scheme applies statewide. In addition, regulations promulgated by the New York City Human Resources Administration, Department of Social Services—Special Services for Children (SSC) provide even greater procedural safeguards there. Under SSC Procedure No. 5 (Aug. 5, 1974), in place of or in addition to the conference provided by the state regulations, the foster parents may request a full trial-type hearing *before* the child is removed from their home. This procedure applies, however, only if the child is being transferred to another foster home, and not if the child is being returned to his natural parents.

One further preremoval procedural safeguard is available. Under Soc. Serv. Law § 392, the Family Court has jurisdiction to review, on petition of the foster parent or the agency, the status of any child who has been in foster care for 18 months or longer.[30] The foster parents, the natural parents, and all interested agencies are made parties to the proceeding ...

. . .

Foster care of children is a sensitive and emotion-laden subject, and foster-care programs consequently stir strong controversy. The New York regulatory scheme is no exception. New York would have us view the scheme as described in its brief:

> "Today New York premises its foster care system on the accepted principle that the placement of a child into foster care is solely a temporary, transitional action intended to lead to the future reunion of the child with his natural parent or parents, or if such a reunion is not possible, to legal adoption and the establishment of a new permanent home for the child."

Some of the parties and *amici* argue that this is a misleadingly idealized picture.

. . .

---

30. The agency is required to initiate such a review when a child has remained in foster care for 18 months, § 392(2)(a), and if the child remains in foster care, the court "shall rehear the matter whenever it deems necessary or desirable, or upon petition by any party entitled to notice in proceedings under this section, but at least every twenty-four months." § 392(10).

From the standpoint of natural parents, such as the appellant intervenors here, foster care has been condemned as a class-based intrusion into the family life of the poor. See, e.g., Jenkins, Child Welfare as a Class System, in Children and Decent People 3 (A. Schorr ed. 1974). It is certainly true that the poor resort to foster care more often than other citizens. For example, over 50% of all children in foster care in New York City are from female-headed families receiving Aid to Families with Dependent Children. Minority families are also more likely to turn to foster care; 52.3% of the children in foster care in New York City are black and 25.5% are Puerto Rican. This disproportionate resort to foster care by the poor and victims of discrimination doubtless reflects in part the greater likelihood of disruption of poverty-stricken families. Commentators have also noted, however, that middle-and upper-income families who need temporary care services for their children have the resources to purchase private care. . . .

The extent to which supposedly "voluntary" placements are in fact voluntary has been questioned on other grounds as well. For example, it has been said that many "voluntary" placements are in fact coerced by threat of neglect proceedings . . . Studies also suggest that social workers of middle-class backgrounds, perhaps unconsciously, incline to favor continued placement in foster care with a generally higher-status family rather than return the child to his natural family, thus reflecting a bias that treats the natural parents' poverty and lifestyle as prejudicial to the best interests of the child. This accounts,[35] it has been said, for the hostility of agencies to the efforts of natural parents to obtain the return of their children.

Appellee foster parents as well as natural parents question the accuracy of the idealized picture portrayed by New York. They note that children often stay in "temporary" foster care for much longer than contemplated by the theory of the system. The District Court found as a fact that the median time spent in foster care in New York was over four years. Indeed, many children apparently remain in this "limbo" indefinitely. The District Court also found that the longer a child remains in foster care, the more likely it is that he will never leave: "[T]he probability of a foster child being returned to his biological parents declined markedly after the first year in foster care." 418 F.Supp., at 279 n. 6. It is not surprising then that many children, particularly those that enter foster care at a very early age and have little or no contact with their natural parents during extended stays in foster care, often develop deep emotional ties with their foster parents.[40]

---

35. Other factors alleged to bias agencies in favor of retention in foster care are the lack of sufficient staff to provide social work services needed by the natural parent to resolve their problems and prepare for return of the child; policies of many agencies to discourage involvement of the natural parent in the care of the child while in foster care; and systems of foster-care funding that encourage agencies to keep the child in foster care.

40. The development of such ties points up an intrinsic ambiguity of foster care that is central to this case. The warmer and more homelike environment of foster care is intended to be its main advantage over institutional child care, yet because in theory foster care is intended to be only temporary, foster parents are urged not to become too attached to the children in their care. Mnookin I 613. Indeed, the New York courts have upheld removal from a foster home for the very reason that the foster parents had become

Yet such ties do not seem to be regarded as obstacles to transfer of the child from one foster placement to another. The record in this case indicates that nearly 60% of the children in foster care in New York City have experienced more than one placement, and about 28% have experienced three or more.... [E]ven when it is clear that a foster child will not be returned to his natural parents, it is rare that he achieves a stable home life through final termination of parental ties and adoption into a new permanent family. Fanshel, Status Changes of Children in Foster Care: Final Results of the Columbia University Longitudinal Study, 55 Child Welfare 143, 145, 157 (1976); ...

... [W]e present this summary in the view that some understanding of those criticisms is necessary for a full appreciation of the complex and controversial system with which this lawsuit is concerned.[41] But the issue presented by the case is a narrow one.... The relief sought in this case is entirely procedural. Our task is only to determine whether the District Court correctly held that the present procedures preceding the removal from a foster home of children resident there a year or more are constitutionally inadequate....

Our first inquiry is whether appellees have asserted interests within the Fourteenth Amendment's protection of "liberty" and "property." Board of Regents v. Roth, 408 U.S. 564, 571 (1972).

The appellees have not renewed in this Court their contention, rejected by the District Court, that the realities of the foster-care system in New York gave them a justified expectation amounting to a "property" interest that their status as foster parents would be continued. Our inquiry is therefore narrowed to the question whether their asserted interests are within the "liberty" protected by the Fourteenth Amendment.

The appellees' basic contention is that when a child has lived in a foster home for a year or more, a psychological tie is created between the child and the foster parents which constitutes the foster family the true "psychological family" of the child. See J. Goldstein, A. Freud, & A. Solnit,

---

too emotionally involved with the child. In re Jewish Child Care Assn. (Sanders), 5 N.Y.2d 222, 183 N.Y.S.2d 65, 156 N.E.2d 700 (1959). See also the case of the Lhotans, named appellees in this case, n. 1, supra.

On the other hand, too warm a relation between foster parent and foster child is not the only possible problem in foster care. Qualified foster parents are hard to find, and very little training is provided to equip them to handle the often complicated demands of their role; it is thus sometimes possible that foster homes may provide inadequate care....

41. It must be noted, however, that both appellee foster parents and intervening natural parents present incomplete pictures of the foster-care system. Although seeking relief applicable to all removal situations, the foster parents focus on intra-foster-care transfers, portraying a foster-care system in which children neglected by their parents and condemned to a permanent limbo of foster care are arbitrarily shunted about by social workers whenever they become attached to a foster home. The natural parents, who focus on foster children being returned to their parent, portray a system under which poor and minority parents, deprived of their children under hard necessity and bureaucratic pressures, are obstructed in their efforts to maintain relationships with their children and ultimately to regain custody, by hostile agencies and meddling foster parents. As the experiences of the named parties to this suit, and the critical studies of foster care cited demonstrate, there are elements of truth in both pictures. But neither represents the whole truth about the system.

Beyond the Best Interests of the Child (1973). That family, they argue, has a "liberty interest" in its survival as a family protected by the Fourteenth Amendment. Upon this premise they conclude that the foster child cannot be removed without a prior hearing satisfying due process. Appointed counsel for the children, appellants in No. 76–5200, however, disagrees, and has consistently argued that the foster parents have no such liberty interest independent of the interests of the foster children, and that the best interests of the children would not be served by procedural protections beyond those already provided by New York law. The intervening natural parents of children in foster care, appellants in No. 76–5193, also oppose the foster parents, arguing that recognition of the procedural right claimed would undercut both the substantive family law of New York, which favors the return of children to their natural parents as expeditiously as possible, and their constitutionally protected right of family privacy, by forcing them to submit to a hearing and defend their rights to their children before the children could be returned to them.

. . .

We ... turn to appellees' assertion that they have a constitutionally protected liberty interest—in the words of the District Court, a "right to familial privacy," 418 F.Supp., at 279—in the integrity of their family unit....

It is, of course, true that "freedom of personal choice in matters of ... family life is one of the liberties protected by the Due Process Clause of the Fourteenth Amendment." Cleveland Board of Education v. LaFleur, 414 U.S. 632, 639–640 (1974). There does exist a "private realm of family life which the state cannot enter," Prince v. Massachusetts, 321 U.S. 158 (1944), that has been afforded both substantive and procedural protection. But is the relation of foster parent to foster child sufficiently akin to the concept of "family" recognized in our precedents to merit similar protection?[48] Although considerable difficulty has attended the task of defining "family" for purposes of the Due Process Clause, we are not without guides to some of the elements that define the concept of "family" and contribute to its place in our society.

First the usual understanding of "family" implies biological relationships, and most decisions treating the relation between parent and child have stressed this element. Stanley v. Illinois, 405 U.S. 645, 651 (1972), for example, spoke of "[t]he rights to conceive and to raise one's children" as essential rights, citing Meyer v. Nebraska, 262 U.S. 390 (1923), and Skinner v. Oklahoma, ex rel. Williamson, 316 U.S. 535 (1942). And Prince v. Massachusetts, stated:

"It is cardinal with us that the custody, care and nurture of the child reside first in the parents, whose primary function and freedom include

48. Of course, recognition of a liberty interest in foster families for purposes of the procedural protections of the Due Process Clause would not necessarily require that foster families be treated as fully equivalent to biological families for purposes of substantive due process review. Cf. Moore v. City of East Cleveland, supra, 431 U.S., at 546–547 (White, J., dissenting).

preparation for obligations the state can neither supply nor hinder."
321 U.S., at 166.[49]

A biological relationship is not present in the case of the usual foster
family. But biological relationships are not exclusive determination of the
existence of a family. The basic foundation of the family in our society, the
marriage relationship, is of course not a matter of blood relation. Yet its
importance has been strongly emphasized in our cases:

> "We deal with a right of privacy older than the Bill of Rights—
> older than our political parties, older than our school system. Marriage
> is a coming together for better or for worse, hopefully enduring, and
> intimate to the degree of being sacred. It is an association that
> promotes a way of life, not causes; a harmony in living, not political
> faiths; a bilateral loyalty, not commercial or social projects. Yet it is an
> association for as noble a purpose as any involved in our prior deci-
> sions." Griswold v. Connecticut, 381 U.S. 479 (1965).

See also Loving v. Virginia, 388 U.S. 1, 12 (1967).

Thus the importance of the familial relationship, to the individuals
involved and to the society, stems from the emotional attachments that
derive from the intimacy of daily association, and from the role it plays in
"promot[ing] a way of life" through the instruction of children, Wisconsin
v. Yoder, 406 U.S. 205, 231–233 (1972), as well as from the fact of blood
relationship. No one would seriously dispute that a deeply loving and
interdependent relationship between an adult and a child in his or her care
may exist even in the absence of blood relationship.[51] At least where a child
has been placed in foster care as an infant, has never known his natural
parents, and has remained continuously for several years in the care of the
same foster parents, it is natural that the foster family should hold the
same place in the emotional life of the foster child, and fulfill the same
socializing functions, as a natural family.[52] For this reason, we cannot
dismiss the foster family as a mere collection of unrelated individuals.

But there are also important distinctions between the foster family and
the natural family. First, unlike the earlier cases recognizing a right to
family privacy, the State here seeks to interfere, not with a relationship
having its origins entirely apart from the power of the State, but rather
with a foster family which has its source in state law and contractual
arrangements. The individual's freedom to marry and reproduce is "older
than the Bill of Rights," Griswold v. Connecticut, 381 U.S., at 486.
Accordingly, unlike the property interests that are also protected by the

49. The scope of these rights extends
beyond natural parents. The "parent" in
Prince itself, for example, was the child's
aunt and legal custodian.

51. Adoption, for example, is recognized as the legal equivalent of biological
parenthood. See, e.g., N.Y.Dom.Rel.Law
§ 110, supra, n. 19.

52. The briefs dispute at some length
the validity of the "psychological parent"
theory propounded in J. Goldstein, A. Freud,
& A. Solnit, Beyond the Best Interests of the
Child (1973). That book, on which appellee
foster parents relied to some extent in the
District Court, is indeed controversial. But
this case turns, not on the disputed validity
of any particular psychological theory, but on
the legal consequences of the undisputed fact
that the emotional ties between foster parent
and foster child are in many cases quite close,
and undoubtedly in some as close as those
existing in biological families.

Fourteenth Amendment cf. Board of Regents v. Roth, 408 U.S., at 577, the liberty interest in family privacy has its source, and its contours are ordinarily to be sought, not in state law,[53] but in intrinsic human rights, . . . Here, however, whatever emotional ties may develop between foster parent and foster child have their origins in an arrangement in which the State has been a partner from the outset. . . . In this case, the limited recognition accorded to the foster family by the New York statutes and the contracts executed by the foster parents argue against any but the most limited constitutional "liberty" in the foster family.

A second consideration related to this is that ordinarily procedural protection may be afforded to a liberty interest of one person without derogating from the substantive liberty of another. Here, however, such a tension is virtually unavoidable. Under New York law, the natural parent of a foster child in voluntary placement has an absolute right to the return of his child in the absence of a court order obtainable only upon compliance with rigorous substantive and procedural standards, which reflect the constitutional protection accorded the natural family. Moreover, the natural parent initially gave up his child to the State only on the express understanding that the child would be returned in those circumstances. These rights are difficult to reconcile with the liberty interest in the foster family relationship claimed by appellees. It is one thing to say that individuals may acquire a liberty interest against arbitrary governmental interference in the family-like associations into which they have freely entered, even in the absence of biological connection or state-law recognition of the relationship. It is quite another to say that one may acquire such an interest in the face of another's constitutionally recognized liberty interest that derives from blood relationship, state-law sanction, and basic human right—an interest the foster parent has recognized by contract from the outset.[54] Whatever liberty interest might otherwise exist in the foster family as an institution, that interest must be substantially attenuated where the proposed removal from the foster family is to return the child to his natural parents.

As this discussion suggests, appellees' claim to a constitutionally protected liberty interest raises complex and novel questions. It is unnecessary for us to resolve those questions definitively in this case, however, for like the District Court, we conclude that "narrower grounds exist to support" our reversal. We are persuaded that, even on the assumption that appellees have a protected "liberty interest," the District Court erred in holding that the preremoval procedures presently employed by the State are constitutionally defective.

Where procedural due process must be afforded because a "liberty" or "property" interest is within the Fourteenth Amendment's protection,

---

53. The legal status of families has never been regarded as controlling: "Nor has the [Constitution] refused to recognize those family relationships unlegitimized by a marriage ceremony." Stanley v. Illinois, 405 U.S., at 651.

54. The New York Court of Appeals has as a matter of state law "[p]articularly reject-

ed . . . the notion . . . that third-party custodians may acquire some sort of squatter's rights in another's child." Bennett v. Jeffreys, 40 N.Y.2d 543, 552 n. 2, 387 N.Y.S.2d 821, 829 n. 2, 356 N.E.2d 277, 285 n. 2 (1976).

there must be determined "what process is due" in the particular context. . . .

It is true that "[b]efore a person is deprived of a protected interest, he must be afforded opportunity for some kind of a hearing, 'except for extraordinary situations where some valid governmental interest is at stake that justifies postponing the hearing until after the event.'" Board of Regents v. Roth, 408 U.S., at 570 n. 7. . . . But the hearing required is only one "appropriate to the nature of the case." Mullane v. Central Hanover Bank & Trust Co., 339 U.S. 306, 313, . . . Only last Term, the Court held that "identification of the specific dictates of due process generally requires consideration of three distinct factors: First, the private interest that will be affected by the official action; second, the risk of an erroneous deprivation of such interest through the procedures used, and the probable value, if any, of additional or substitute procedural safeguards; and finally, the Government's interest, including the function involved and the fiscal and administrative burdens that the additional or substitute procedural requirement would entail." Mathews v. Eldridge, 424 U.S. 319, 335 (1976). Consideration of the procedures employed by the State and New York City in light of these three factors requires the conclusion that those procedures satisfy constitutional standards.

Turning first to the procedure applicable in New York City, SSC Procedure No. 5 provides that before a child is removed from a foster home for transfer to another foster home, the foster parents may request an "independent review." . . . Such a procedure would appear to give a more elaborate trial-type hearing to foster families than this Court has found required in other contexts of administrative determinations. Cf. Goldberg v. Kelly, supra, 397 U.S., at 266–271. [The District Court had held below that the review procedure was insufficient because it was available only at the request of foster parents. The Court reasoned that because the child is not able to request review the child's interest would not be protected. The Supreme Court responded: ". . . [i]t is difficult to see what right . . . of the foster child is protected by holding a hearing to determine whether removal would impair his emotional attachments to a foster parent who does not care enough about the child to contest the removal."]

. . . [T]he District Court faulted the city procedure on the ground that participation is limited to the foster parents and the agency and the natural parent and the child are not made parties to the hearing. This is not fatal in light of the nature of the alleged constitutional interests at stake. When the child's transfer from one foster home to another is pending, the interest arguably requiring protection is that of the foster family, not that of the natural parents. Moreover, the natural parent can generally add little to the accuracy of factfinding concerning the wisdom of such a transfer, since the foster parents and the agency, through its caseworkers, will usually be most knowledgeable about conditions in the foster home. Of course, in those cases where the natural parent does have a special interest in the proposed transfer or particular information that would assist the factfinder, nothing in the city's procedure prevents any party from securing his testimony.

... [Another] defect in the city procedure found by the District Court must also be rejected. [It] is that the procedure does not extend to the removal of a child from foster care to be returned to his natural parent. But as we have already held, whatever liberty interest may be argued to exist in the foster family is significantly weaker in the case of removals preceding return to the natural parent, and the balance of due process interests must accordingly be different. If the city procedure is adequate where it is applicable, it is no criticism of the procedure that it does not apply in other situations where different interests are at stake. . . .

Outside New York City, where only the statewide procedures apply, foster parents are provided not only with the procedures of a preremoval conference and postremoval hearing provided by 18 N.Y.C.R.R. § 450.10 (1976) and Soc.Serv. Law § 400, but also with the preremoval *judicial* hearing available on request to foster parents who have in their care children who have been in foster care for 18 months or more, Soc.Serv. Law § 392. . . . [A] foster parent in such case may obtain an order that the child remain in his care.

The District Court found three defects in this full judicial process. First, a § 392 proceeding is available only to those foster children who have been in foster care for 18 months or more. The class certified by the court was broader, including children who had been in the care of the same foster parents for more than one year. Thus, not all class members had access to the § 392 remedy. We do not think that the 18–month limitation on § 392 actions renders the New York scheme constitutionally inadequate. The assumed liberty interest to be protected in this case is one rooted in the emotional attachments that develop over time between a child and the adults who care for him. But there is no reason to assume that those attachments ripen at less than 18 months or indeed at any precise point. Indeed, testimony in the record, see App. 177a, 204a, as well as material in published psychological tests, see e.g., J. Goldstein, A. Freud, & A. Solnit, Beyond the Best Interests of the Child 40–42, 49 (1973), suggests that the amount of time necessary for the development of the sort of tie appellees seek to protect varies considerably depending on the age and previous attachments of the child. In a matter of such imprecision and delicacy, we see no justification for the District Court's substitution of its view of the appropriate cutoff date for that chosen by the New York Legislature, given that any line is likely to be somewhat arbitrary and fail to protect some families where relationships have developed quickly while protecting others where no such bonds have formed. If New York sees 18 months rather than 12 as the time at which temporary foster care begins to turn into a more permanent and family-like setting requiring procedural protection and/or judicial inquiry into the propriety of continuing foster care, it would take far more than this record provides to justify a finding of constitutional infirmity in New York's choice.

. . .

... [T]he § 392 hearing is available to foster parents, both in and outside New York City, even where the removal sought is for the purpose of returning the child to his natural parents. Since this remedy provides a sufficient constitutional preremoval hearing to protect whatever liberty interest might exist in the continued existence of the foster family when the State seeks to transfer the child to another foster home, *a fortiori* the procedure is adequate to protect the lesser interest of the foster family in remaining together at the expense of the disruption of the natural family.

. . . Since we hold that the procedures provided by New York State in § 392 and by New York City's SSC Procedure No. 5 are adequate to protect whatever liberty interest appellees may have, the judgment of the District Court is

Reversed.

■ MR. JUSTICE STEWART, with whom THE CHIEF JUSTICE and MR. JUSTICE REHNQUIST join, concurring in the judgment.

. . . New York confers no right on foster families to remain intact, defeasible only upon proof of specific acts or circumstances. . . .

. . . New York law provides no basis for a justifiable expectation on the part of foster families that their relationship will continue indefinitely. The District Court in this litigation recognized as much, noting that the typical foster-care contract gives the agency the right to recall the child "upon request," and commenting that the discretionary authority vested in the agency "is on its face incompatible with plaintiffs' claim of legal entitlement." 418 F.Supp., at 281. To be sure, the New York system has not operated perfectly. As the state legislature found, foster care has in many cases been unnecessarily protracted, no doubt sometimes resulting in the expectation on the part of some foster families that their relationship will continue indefinitely. But, . . . the New York Court of Appeals has unequivocally rejected the notion that under New York law prolonged third-party custody of children creates some sort of "squatter's rights." . . .

. . . [T]he protection that foster children have is simply the requirement of state law that decisions about their placement be determined in the light of their best interests. See, e.g., Bennett v. Jeffreys, 40 N.Y.2d 543, 387 N.Y.S.2d 821, 356 N.E.2d 277; . . . This requirement is not "liberty or property" protected by the Due Process Clause, and it confers no right or expectancy of any kind in the continuity of the relationship between foster parents and children. See e.g., Bennett, supra, 40 N.Y.2d, at 552 n. 2, 387 N.Y.S.2d, at 829 n. 2, 356 N.E.2d, at 285 n. 2: "Third-party custodians acquire 'rights' . . . only derivatively by virtue of the child's best interests being considered. . . ."

What remains of the appellees' argument is the theory that the relation of the foster parent to the foster child may generate emotional attachments similar to those found in natural families. The Court surmises that foster families who share these attachments might enjoy the same constitutional interest in "family privacy" as natural families.

. . .

But under New York's foster-care laws, any case where the foster parents had assumed the emotional role of the child's natural parents would represent not a triumph of the system, to be constitutionally safeguarded from state intrusion, but a failure. The goal of foster care, at least in New York, is not to provide a permanent substitute for the natural or adoptive home, but to prepare the child for his return to his real parents or placement in a permanent adoptive home by giving him temporary shelter in a family setting. Thus, the New York Court of Appeals has recognized that the development of close emotional ties between foster parents and a child may hinder the child's ultimate adjustment in a permanent home, and provide a basis for the *termination* of the foster family relationship. Perhaps it is to be expected that children who spend unduly long stays in what should have been temporary foster care will develop strong emotional ties with their foster parents. But this does not mean, and I cannot believe, that such breakdowns of the New York system must be protected or forever frozen in their existence by the Due Process Clause of the Fourteenth Amendment.

One of the liberties protected by the Due Process Clause, the Court has held, is the freedom to "establish a home and bring up children." Meyer v. Nebraska, supra, 262 U.S., at 399. If a State were to attempt to force the breakup of a natural family, over the objections of the parents and their children, without some showing of unfitness and for the sole reason that to do so was thought to be in the children's best interest, I should have little doubt that the State would have intruded impermissibly on "the private realm of family life which the state cannot enter." Prince v. Massachusetts, 321 U.S. 158, 166. But this constitutional concept is simply not in point when we deal with foster families as New York law has defined them. The family life upon which the State "intrudes" is simply a temporary status which the State itself has created. It is a "family life" defined and controlled by the law of New York, for which New York pays, and the goals of which New York is entitled to and does set for itself.

NOTES

(1) Although the Supreme Court did not resolve the question whether children in foster care and their foster parents have a protectible "liberty interest" in their relationship, such an argument has been specifically rejected by some U.S. circuit courts. See, e.g., *Kyees v. County Department of Public Welfare*, 600 F.2d 693 (7th Cir.1979); *Drummond v. Fulton County Department of Family & Children's Services*, 563 F.2d 1200 (5th Cir.1977). For a discussion of these decisions, see John J. Musewicz, The Failure of Foster Care: Federal Statutory Reform and the Child's Right to Permanence, 54 So.Cal.L.Rev. 633, 666 et seq. (1981). For another U.S. Circuit Court's comparison of the legal ramifications of "foster care" as distinguished from legal guardianship or adoption, see *Lofton v. Secretary of Department of Children and Family Services*, 358 F.3d 804 (11th Cir.2004).

(2) Persons who serve as foster parents, like almost everyone else who practices a profession or engages in business these days, are typically subject to state licensing requirements. The authority administering the licensure provisions will maintain or be provided with standards with which an applicant or an existing licensee must comply. Often a provisional license may be issued for someone who is temporarily not in compliance with such standards but who submits a plan for overcoming any deficiencies within the time limit of the provisional licensing period.

In *Sherrard v. Owens*, 484 F.Supp. 728 (W.D.Mich.1980), foster parents whose two foster children had been removed from their home when their provisional license expired and was not renewed by the agency sought injunctive and declaratory relief to prevent further action with respect to the children and to secure their return. The court denied any such relief, finding that the plaintiffs had no reasonable expectation of continued licensure as a foster home after expiration of their provisional license and that no liberty right had developed. The Michigan provisions for revocation of foster home licenses also were held to be constitutionally adequate.

(3) Some courts have considered the preference of the children in deciding whether they should be returned from foster homes to their natural parents. In *In re Ross*, 29 Ill.App.3d 157, 329 N.E.2d 333 (1975), two girls, 12 and 14 years old, appealed from a custody decision determining that they should be returned to their natural parents after having lived with foster parents more than 6½ years. In reversing the decision and remanding the cause for taking further evidence and redetermining what would be in the best interests of the children at the present time, the appellate court stated:

> Irrespective of the basis for such feelings, the adamant expression of the girls over the years not to return to their natural parents should be given considerable weight in the court's determination since these children are now 14 and 12 years old and are of average to above-average intelligence.

In re Michael B.

Court of Appeals of New York, 1992.
590 N.Y.S.2d 60, 80 N.Y.2d 299, 604 N.E.2d 122.

■ KAYE, JUDGE.

This appeal from a custody determination, pitting a child's foster parents against his biological father, centers on the meaning of the statutory term "best interest of the child," and particularly on the weight to be given a child's bonding with his long-time foster family in deciding what placement is in his best interest. The biological father (appellant) on one side, and respondent foster parents (joined by respondent Law Guardian) on the other, each contend that a custody determination in their favor is in the best interest of the child, as that term is used in Social Services Law § 392(6), the statute governing dispositions with respect to children in foster care.

The subject of this protracted battle is Michael B., born July 29, 1985 with a positive toxicology for cocaine. Michael was voluntarily placed in foster care from the hospital by his mother, who was unmarried at the time of the birth and listed no father on the birth certificate. Michael's four siblings were then also in foster care, residing in different homes. At three months, before the identity of his father was known, Michael—needing extraordinary care—was placed in the home of intervenor Maggie W.L., a foster parent certified by respondent Catholic Child Care Society (the agency), and the child remained with the L.'s for more than five years, until December 1990. It is undisputed that the agency initially assured Mrs. L. this was a "preadoptive" placement.

Legal proceedings began in May 1987, after appellant had been identified as Michael's father. The agency sought to terminate the rights of both biological parents and free the child for adoption, alleging that for more than a year following Michael's placement the parents had failed to substantially, continuously or repeatedly maintain contact with Michael and plan for his future, although physically and financially able to do so

(Social Services Law § 384–b[7]). Michael's mother (since deceased) never appeared in the proceeding, and a finding of permanent neglect as to her was made in November 1987. Appellant did appear and in September 1987 consented to a finding of permanent neglect, and to committing custody and guardianship to the agency on condition that the children be placed with their two godmothers. That order was later vacated, on appellant's application to withdraw his pleas and obtain custody, because the agency had not in fact placed the children with their godmothers. In late 1987, appellant—a long-time alcohol and substance abuser—entered an 18–month residential drug rehabilitation program and first began to visit Michael.

In August 1988, appellant, the agency and the Law Guardian agreed to reinstatement of the permanent neglect finding, with judgment suspended for 12 months, on condition that appellant: (1) enroll in a program teaching household management and parenting skills; (2) cooperate by attending and complying with the program; (3) remain drug-free, and periodically submit to drug testing, with test results to be delivered to the agency; (4) secure and maintain employment; (5) obtain suitable housing; and (6) submit a plan for the children's care during his working day (see, Family Ct. Act § 631 [b]; § 633). The order recited that it was without prejudice to the agency recalendaring the case for a de novo hearing on all allegations of the petition should appellant fail to satisfy the conditions, and otherwise said nothing more of the consequences that would follow on appellant's compliance or noncompliance.

As the 12–month period neared expiration, the agency sought a hearing to help "determine the status and placement of the children." Although appellant was unemployed (he was on public assistance) and had not submitted to drug testing during the year, Family Court at the hearing held October 24, 1989 was satisfied that "there seem[ed] to be substantial compliance" with the conditions of the suspended judgment. Because the August 1988 order was unclear as to who had responsibility for initiating the drug tests, the court directed that the agency arrange three successive blood and urine tests, and if the tests proved negative, "all subject children may be released to father except Jemel [a 'special needs' child]." The matter was adjourned to December 21, when it was joined with respondents' application for a dispositional order with respect to Michael, whose long residence with the L.'s, they said, raised special concerns.

On December 21, 1989, the Law Guardian presented a report indicating that Michael might suffer severe psychological damage if removed from his foster home, and argued for a "best interests" hearing pursuant to Matter of Bennett v. Jeffreys, 40 N.Y.2d 543, 387 N.Y.S.2d 821, 356 N.E.2d 277, based on Michael's bonding with the L.'s and, by contrast, his lack of bonding with appellant, who had visited him infrequently. Family Court questioned whether it even had authority for such a hearing, but stayed the order directing Michael's discharge to appellant pending its determination. Michael's siblings, then approximately twelve, eight, seven and six years old, were released to appellant in January and July 1990. Litigation continued as to Michael.

In November 1990, Family Court directed Michael's discharge to appellant, concluding that it was without "authority or jurisdiction" to rehear the issue of custody based on the child's best interest, and indeed that Michael had been wrongfully held in foster care. The court noted, additionally, that the Law Guardian's arguments as to Michael's best interest went to issues of bonding with his temporary custodians rather than appellant's insufficiency as a parent—bonding that had been reinforced by the agency's failure to ensure sufficient contacts with appellant during the proceedings. Appellant "should not be denied custody simply because of the actions of the [agency] and the lengthy litigation following final disposition has resulted in the foster parents enjoying a stronger emotional tie to the child than the [appellant]." The court directed that Michael commence immediate weekend visitation with appellant, with a view to transfer within 60 days. Michael was discharged to appellant in December 1990.

The Appellate Division reversed and remitted for a new hearing and new consideration of Michael's custody, concluding that dismissal of a permanent neglect petition cannot divest Family Court of its continuing jurisdiction over a child until there has been a "best interests" custody disposition. As for the relevance of bonding, the Appellate Division held that, given the "extraordinary circumstances" (Matter of Bennett v. Jeffreys, 40 N.Y.2d, at 544, 387 N.Y.S.2d 821, 356 N.E.2d 277, supra)—referring particularly to Michael's long residence with his foster parents—Family Court should have conducted a hearing to consider issues such as the impact on the child of a change in custody. There having been no question of appellant's fitness, however, the Appellate Division permitted Michael to remain with his father pending the new determination.

On remittal, Family Court . . . adhered to its determination that Michael should be released to his father. . . .

Again the Appellate Division reversed Family Court's order, this time itself awarding custody to the foster parents under Social Services Law § 392(6)(b), and remitting the matter to a different Family Court Judge solely to determine appellant's visitation rights. Exercising its own authority—as broad as that of the hearing court—to assess the credibility of witnesses and character and temperament of the parents, the court reviewed the evidence and, while pointing up appellant's many deficiencies, significantly stopped short of finding him an unfit parent, as it had the power to do. Rather, the court looked to Michael's lengthy stay and psychological bonding with the foster family, which it felt gave rise to extraordinary circumstances meriting an award of custody to the foster parents. According to the Appellate Division, the evidence "overwhelmingly demonstrate[d] that Michael's foster parents are better able than his natural father to provide for his physical, emotional, and intellectual needs." (180 A.D.2d, at 794, 580 N.Y.S.2d 430.) Since early 1992, Michael has once again resided with the L.'s.

While prolonged, inconclusive proceedings and seesawing custody of a young child—all in the name of Michael's best interest—could not conceivably serve his interest at all, we granted appellant father's motion for leave to appeal, and now reverse the Appellate Division's central holdings. The opinions of Family Court specifying deficiencies of the agency and foster parents, and the opinions of the Appellate Division specifying inadequacies of the biological parent, leave little question that the only blameless person is the child. But rather than assess fault, our review will address the legal standards that have twice divided Family Court and the Appellate Division, hopefully minimizing recurrences, for this child and others, of the tragic scenario now before us.

Analysis

. . .

What remains the bone of contention in this Court is the scope of the requisite "best interest" inquiry under Social Services Law § 392(6). Appellant urges that in cases of foster care, so long as the biological parent is not found unfit—and he underscores that neither Family Court nor the Appellate Division found him unfit—"best interest of the child" is only a limited inquiry addressed to whether the child will suffer grievous injury if transferred out of foster care to the biological parent. Respondents, by contrast, maintain that extraordinary circumstances—such as significant bonding with foster parents, after inattention and even admitted neglect by the biological parent—trigger a full inquiry into the more suitable placement as between the biological and foster parents. Subsidiarily, appellant challenges the Appellate Division's outright award of custody to the foster parents, claiming that disposition was beyond the Court's authority under Social Services Law § 392(6).

We conclude, first, that neither party advances the correct "best interest" test in the context of temporary foster care placements, but that appellant's view is more consistent with the statutory scheme than the broad-gauge inquiry advocated by respondents and applied by the Appellate Division. Second, we hold that the award of custody to the foster parents was impermissible as we interpret Social Services Law § 392(6).

The Foster Care Scheme

. . .

New York's foster care scheme is built around several fundamental social policy choices that have been explicitly declared by the Legislature and are binding on this Court (Social Services Law § 384–b[1]). Under the statute, operating as written, appellant should have received the active support of both the agency in overcoming his parental deficiencies and the foster parents in solidifying his relationship with Michael, and as soon as return to the biological parent proved unrealistic, the child should have been freed for adoption.

A biological parent has a right to the care and custody of a child, superior to that of others, unless the parent has abandoned that right or is proven unfit to assume the duties and privileges of parenthood, even though the State perhaps could find "better" parents. Looking to the child's rights as well as the parents' rights to bring up their own children, the Legislature has found and declared that a child's need to grow up with a "normal family life in a permanent home" is ordinarily best met in the child's "natural home" (Social Services Law § 384–b[1][a][i], [ii]).

Parents in temporary crisis are encouraged to voluntarily place their children in foster care without fear that they will thereby forfeit their parental rights. The State's first obligation is to help the family with services to prevent its break-up, or to reunite the family if the child is out of the home (Social Services Law § 384–b[1][a][iii]; Santosky v. Kramer, 455 U.S. 745, 748). While a child is in foster care, the State must use diligent efforts to strengthen the relationship between parent and child, and work with the parent to regain custody (Social Services Law § 384–a[2][c][iv]; Matter of Sheila G., 61 N.Y.2d, at 385, 474 N.Y.S.2d 421, 462 N.E.2d 1139, supra).

Because of the statutory emphasis on the biological family as best serving a child's long-range needs, the legal rights of foster parents are necessarily limited (see, Smith v. Organization of Foster Families, 431 U.S. 816, 846). Legal custody of a child in foster care remains with the agency that places the child, not with the foster parents. Foster parents enter into this arrangement with the express understanding that the placement is temporary, and that the agency retains the right to remove the child upon notice at any time.... Foster parents, moreover, have an affirmative obligation—similar to the obligation of the State—to attempt to solidify the relationship between biological parent and child. While foster parents may be heard on custody issues, they have no standing to seek permanent custody absent termination of parental rights.

Fundamental also to the statutory scheme is the preference for providing children with stable, permanent homes as early as possible.... Extended foster care is not in the child's best interest, because it deprives a child of a permanent, nurturing family relationship (see, Matter of Gregory B., 74 N.Y.2d 77, 90, 544 N.Y.S.2d 535, 542 N.E.2d 1052, rearg. denied sub nom. Matter of Willie John B., 74 N.Y.2d 880, 547 N.Y.S.2d 841, 547 N.E.2d 96; Matter of Joyce T., 65 N.Y.2d 39, 47–48, 489 N.Y.S.2d 705, 478 N.E.2d 1306). Where it appears that the child may never be reunited with the biological parents, the responsible agency should institute a proceeding to terminate parental rights and free the child for adoption (Social Services Law § 384–b[1][b]; [3][b]; § 392[6][c]).

Parental rights may be terminated only upon clear and convincing proof of abandonment, inability to care for the child due to mental illness or retardation, permanent neglect, or severe or repeated child abuse (Social Services Law § 384–b[3][g]; [4]).[1] Of the permissible dispositions in a termination proceeding based on permanent neglect, the Legislature—

---

1. Several model statutes would authorize termination of parental rights based on a child's absence from the biological home for a substantial period, with the period depending on the child's age. Such provisions were based on the notion, in circulation prior to and during the formulation of our current parental termination statute, that once a child under the age of three has been in the continuous care of the same adult for a year, it is unreasonable to presume that the child's ties with biological parents are more significant than ties with long-term caretakers (see, Taub, Assessing the Impact of Goldstein, Freud and Solnit's Proposals: An Introductory Overview, 12 NYU Rev.L. & Soc.Change 485, 490). Our Legislature did not recognize prolonged separation as an additional ground for termination of parental rights.

consistent with its emphasis on the importance of biological ties, yet mindful of the child's need for early stability and permanence—has provided for a suspended judgment, which is a brief grace period designed to prepare the parent to be reunited with the child. Parents found to have permanently neglected a child may be given a second chance, (where the court determines it is in the child's best interests), but that opportunity is strictly limited in time. Parents may have up to one year (and a second year only where there are "exceptional circumstances") during which they must comply with terms and conditions meant to ameliorate the difficulty (see, 22 NYCRR 205.50 [spelling out terms and conditions]). Noncompliance may lead to revocation of the judgment and termination of parental rights. Compliance may lead to dismissal of the termination petition with the child remaining subject to the jurisdiction of the Family Court until a determination is made as to the child's disposition pursuant to Social Services Law § 392(6)....

Where parental rights have not been terminated, Social Services Law § 392 promotes the objectives of stability and permanency by requiring periodic review of foster care placements. The agency having custody must first petition for review after a child has been in continuous foster care for 18 months, and if no change is made, every 24 months thereafter. While foster parents who have been caring for such child for the prior 12 months are entitled to notice, and may also petition for review on their own initiative, a petition under section 392 (captioned "Foster care status; periodic family court review") is not an avenue to permanent custody for foster parents where the child has not been freed for adoption.

Upon such review, the court must consider the appropriateness of the agency's plan for the child, what services have been offered to strengthen and reunite the family, efforts to plan for other modes of care, (and other further efforts to promote the child's welfare), and in accordance with the best interest of the child, make one of the following dispositions: (1) continue the child in foster care (which may include continuation with the current foster parents); (2) direct that the child "be returned to the parent, guardian or relative, or [direct] that the child be placed in the custody of a relative or other suitable person or persons"; or (3) require the agency (or foster parents upon the agency's default) to institute a parental rights termination proceeding).

The key element in the court's disposition is the best interest of the child (Social Services Law § 392[6])—the statutory term that is at the core of this appeal, and to which we now turn.

"Best Interest" in the Foster Care Scheme

"Best interest(s) of the child" is a term that pervades the law relating to children—appearing innumerable times in the pertinent statutes, judicial decisions and literature—yet eludes ready definition. Two interpretations are advanced, each vigorously advocated.

Appellant would read the best interest standard of Social Services Law § 392(6) narrowly, urging that Family Court should inquire only into whether the biological parent is fit, and whether the child will suffer grievous harm by being returned to the parent. Appellant urges affirmance of the Family Court orders, which (1) defined the contest as one between foster care agency and biological parent, rather than foster parent and biological parent; (2) focused first on "the ability of the father to care for the subject child," and then on whether "the child's emotional health will be so seriously impaired as to require continuance in foster care;" and (3) concluded that appellant was fit, and that Michael would not suffer irreparable emotional harm if returned to him. Wider inquiry, appellant insists, creates an "unwinnable beauty contest" the biological parent will inevitably lose where foster placement has continued for any substantial time.

Respondents take a broader view, urging that because of extraordinary circumstances largely attributable to appellant, the Appellate Division correctly compared him with the foster parents in determining Michael's custody and concluded that the child's best interest was served by the placement that better provided for his physical, emotional and intellectual needs. Respondents rely on Matter of Bennett v. Jeffreys, 40 N.Y.2d 543, 387 N.Y.S.2d 821, 356 N.E.2d 277, supra, this Court's landmark decision recognizing that a child's prolonged separation from a biological parent may be considered, among other factors, to be extraordinary circumstances permitting the court to inquire into which family situation would be in the child's best interests.

In that Matter of Bennett v. Jeffreys concerned an unsupervised private placement, where there was no directly applicable legislation, that case is immediately distinguishable from the matter before us, which is controlled by a detailed statutory scheme. Our analysis must begin at a different point—not whether there are extraordinary circumstances, but what the Legislature intended by the words "best interest of the child" in Social Services Law § 392(6).

Necessarily, we look first to the statute itself. The question is in part answered by Social Services Law §§ 383 and 384–b, which encourage voluntary placements, with the provision that they will not result in the termination of parental rights so long as the parent is fit. To use the period during which a child lives with a foster family, and emotional ties that naturally eventuate, as a ground for comparing the biological parent with the foster parent undermines the very objective of voluntary foster care as a resource for parents in temporary crisis, who are then at risk of losing their children once a bond arises with the foster families.

Other portions of the statute support this conclusion....

Absent an explicit legislative directive—such as that found in Family Court Act § 631—we are not free to overlook the legislative policies that underlie temporary foster care, including the preeminence of the biological family. Indeed, the legislative history of Social Services Law § 392(5–a), which specifies factors that must be considered in determining the child's best interests, states "this bill clearly advises the Family Court of certain considerations before making an order of disposition. These factors establish a clear policy of exploring all available means of reuniting the child with his family before the Court decides to continue his foster care or to direct a permanent adoptive placement." (Mem. Accompanying Comments on Bill, N.Y. State Bd. of Social Welfare, A 12801–B, July 9, 1976, Governor's Bill Jacket, L.1976, ch. 667.)

We therefore cannot endorse a pure "best interests" hearing, where biological parent and foster parents stand on equal footing and the child's interest is the sole consideration. In cases controlled by Social Services Law § 392(6), analysis of the child's "best interest" must begin not by measuring biological parent against foster parent but by weighing past and continued foster care against discharge to the biological parent, or other relative or suitable person within Social Services Law § 392(6)(b) (see, Matter of Sheila G., 61 N.Y.2d, at 389–390, 474 N.Y.S.2d 421, 462 N.E.2d 1139, supra; . . .)

While the facts of Matter of Bennett v. Jeffreys fell outside the statute, and the Court was unrestrained by legislative prescription in defining the scope of the "best interests" inquiry, principles underlying that decision are also relevant here. It is plainly the case, for example, that a "child may be so long in the custody of the nonparent that, even though there has been no abandonment or persisting neglect by the parent, the psychological trauma of removal is grave enough to threaten destruction of the child" (id., 40 N.Y.2d at 550, 387 N.Y.S.2d 821, 356 N.E.2d 277), and we cannot discount evidence that a child may have bonded with someone other than the biological parent. In such a case, continued foster care may be appropriate although the parent has not been found unfit.

Under Social Services Law § 392, where a child has not been freed for adoption, the court must determine whether it is nonetheless appropriate to continue foster care temporarily, or whether the child should be permanently discharged to the biological parent (or a relative or "other suitable person"). In determining the best interest of a child in that situation, the fitness of the biological parent must be a primary factor. The court is also statutorily mandated to consider the agency's plan for the child, what services have been offered to strengthen and reunite the family, what reasonable efforts have been made to make it possible for the child to return to the natural home, and if return home is not likely, what efforts have been or should be made to evaluate other options (Social Services Law § 392[5–a]). Finally, the court should consider the more intangible elements relating to the emotional well-being of the child, among them the impact on the child of immediate discharge versus an additional period of foster care.

While it is doubtful whether it could be found to be in the child's best interest to deny the parent's persistent demands for custody simply because it took so long to obtain it legally (Matter of Sanjivini K., 47 N.Y.2d, at 382, 418 N.Y.S.2d 339, 391 N.E.2d 1316, supra), neither is a lapse of time necessarily without significance in determining custody. The child's emotional well-being must be part of the equation, parental rights notwithstanding. However, while emotional well-being may encompass bonding to someone other than the biological parent, it includes as well a recognition that, absent termination of parental rights, the nonparent cannot adopt the child, and a child in continued custody with a nonparent remains in legal—

and often emotional—limbo (see, Matter of Bennett v. Jeffreys, 40 N.Y.2d, at 551, 387 N.Y.S.2d 821, 356 N.E.2d 277, supra).[4]

The Appellate Division, applying an erroneous "best interest" test, seemingly avoided that result when it awarded legal custody to the foster parents. We next turn to why that disposition was improper.

Award of Legal Custody to Foster Parents

The Appellate Division awarded legal custody of Michael to the foster parents pursuant to Social Services Law § 392(6)(b), noting that the statute "permits a court to enter an order of disposition directing, inter alia, that a child, whose custody and care have temporarily been transferred to an authorized agency, be placed in the custody of a suitable person or persons." (180 A.D.2d, at 796, 580 N.Y.S.2d 430.) The Court correctly looked to section 392 as the predicate for determining custody, but erroneously relied on paragraph (b) of subdivision (6) in awarding custody to the foster parents.

As set forth above, there are three possible dispositions after foster care review with respect to a child not freed for adoption: continued foster care; release to a parent, guardian, relative or other suitable person; and institution of parental termination proceedings (Social Services Law § 392[6] [a]–[c]).

As the first dispositional option, paragraph (a) contemplates the continuation of foster care, with the child remaining in the custody of the authorized agency, and the arrangement remaining subject to periodic review. As a result of 1989 amendments, disposition under paragraph (a) can include an order that the child be placed with (or remain with) a particular foster family until the next review. Under the statutory scheme, however, foster care is temporary, contractual and supervised.

Paragraph (b), by contrast, contemplates removal of the child from the foster care system by return to "the parent, guardian or relative, or direct[ion] that the child be placed in the custody of a relative or other

---

4. Although the concurrence underscores the extraordinary nature of this case, widely publicized failures of the foster care system indicate that this situation is, regrettably, all too common. To the extent the courts have a role, heartbreak can perhaps be avoided and the statutory goals of early permanence and stability advanced by clear standards and by promptness in addressing child custody matters; no custody determination should be permitted to languish for years. The clear (by no means "constricting") standard set forth by the Court, incorporating all of the relevant considerations, helps to assure that these unfortunate cases will not be caught in an endless loop between trial and appellate courts such as we have here. The concurrence agrees that this case must be reversed on the section 392(6)(b) ground because "a contrary interpretation of that key provision, as used by the Appellate Division, would have internally contradictory implications in the field of temporary foster child placement." (Concurring on. at 318, at 72 of 590 N.Y.S.2d, at 134 of 604 N.E.2d). The same is true of the "best interest" test in that same section, which must be read in the context of our statutory scheme requiring parents and the State to work together toward the preferred goal (so long as it remains realistic) of keeping biological families together. Given that foster parents cannot obtain permanent custody under Social Services Law § 392(6) absent termination of parental rights, the concurrence's call for even greater "flexibility," comparing foster parent to biological parent (see, Matter of Bennett v. Jeffreys, supra), obviously could not further the objectives of finality and certainty in custody determinations.

suitable person or persons." The 1989 statutory revision added as a permissible disposition the placement of children with relatives or other suitable persons. The purpose of this amendment was to promote family stability by allowing placement with relatives, extended family members or persons like them, as an alternative to foster care.

Plainly, the scheme does not envision also including the foster parents—who were the subject of the amendment to paragraph (a)—as "other suitable persons." Indeed, reading paragraph (b) as the Appellate Division did, to permit removal of the child from foster care and an award of legal custody to the foster parents, exacerbates the legal limbo status. The child is left without a placement looking to the establishment of a permanent parental relationship through adoption, or the prospect of subsequent review of foster care status with the possibility of adoption placement at that time, yet has no realistic chance of return to the biological parent.

The terms of paragraph (c), providing for an order that the agency institute a parental termination proceeding, further buttress the conclusion that foster parents are not included in paragraph (b). Pursuant to paragraph (c), if the court finds reasonable cause to believe there are grounds for termination of parental rights, it may order the responsible agency to institute such proceedings. If the agency fails to do so within 90 days, the foster parents themselves may bring the proceeding, unless the court believes their subsequent petition to adopt would not be approved. Thus, in the statutory scheme the Legislature has provided a means for foster parents to secure a temporary arrangement under paragraph (a) and a permanent arrangement under paragraph (c)—both of which specifically mention foster parents. They are not also implicitly included in paragraph (b), which addresses different interests.

We therefore conclude that the Appellate Division erred in interpreting Social Services Law § 392(6) to permit the award of legal custody to respondent foster parents.

Need for Further Inquiry

We have no occasion to apply the proper legal test to the facts at hand, as the parties urge. New circumstances require remittal to Family Court for an expedited hearing and determination of whether appellant is a fit parent and entitled to custody of Michael.

The Court has been informed that, during the pendency of the appeal, appellant was charged with—and admitted—neglect of the children in his custody (not Michael), and that those children have been removed from his home and are again in the custody of the Commissioner of the Social Services. The neglect petitions allege that appellant abused alcohol and controlled substances including cocaine, and physically abused the children. Orders of fact finding have been entered by Family Court, Queens County, recognizing appellant's admission in open court to "substance abuse, alcohol and cocaine abuse." Moreover, an Order of Protection was entered prohibiting appellant from visiting the children while under the influence of drugs or alcohol.

Appellant's request that we ignore these new developments and simply grant him custody, because matters outside the record cannot be considered by an appellate court, would exalt the procedural rule—important though it is—to a point of absurdity. . . . Indeed changed circumstances may have particular significance in child custody matters. This Court would therefore take notice of the new facts and allegations to the extent they indicate that the record before us is no longer sufficient for determining appellant's fitness and right to custody of Michael, and remit the matter to Family Court for a new hearing and determination of those issues. The Appellate Division concluded that the hearing should take place before a different Judge of that court, and we see no basis to disturb that determination. Pending the hearing, Michael should physically remain with his current foster parents, but legal custody should be returned to the foster care agency. . . .

■ BELLACOSA, JUDGE (concurring).

. . . I would not relegate Matter of Bennett v. Jeffreys, 40 N.Y.2d 543, 387 N.Y.S.2d 821, 356 N.E.2d 277 essentially to general relevance only, would not limit the beginning of the analysis to the statutory setting, and would allow for appropriate flexibility as to the range and manner of exercising discretion in the application of the best interests test by the Family Courts and Appellate Divisions.

I believe courts, in the fulfillment of the *parens patriae* responsibility of the State, should, as a general operating principle, have an appropriately broad range of power to act in the best interests of children. We agree that the teachings of Matter of Bennett v. Jeffreys, 40 N.Y.2d 543, 387 N.Y.S.2d 821, 356 N.E.2d 277, supra are still excellent and have served the process and the affected subjects and combatants in custody disputes very well. While the common-law origination in Bennett is a distinguishing feature from the instant case, I do not view that aspect as subordinated to or secondary in the use of its wisdom, even in a predominantly statutory setting, where this case originates. I am not persuaded that there is any support or positive authority for the view that the Legislature meant anything different when it adopted the phrase "best interest of the child" in Social Services Law s 392(6) from the meaning of that phrase articulated in Matter of Bennett v. Jeffreys, supra. Courts must exercise common-law authority in all these circumstances, and the Legislature has not, as far as I can tell, displaced that uniquely judicial function and plenary role. Since the best of Matter of Bennett v. Jeffreys' best interest analysis enjoys continued vitality therefore, it should serve as a cogent, coequal common-law building block. In my view, it provides helpful understanding for and intertwined supplementation to the Social Services Law provisions as applied in these extraordinary circumstances, defined in one aspect of Matter of Bennett v. Jeffreys as "prolonged separation" of parent and child "for most of the child's life" (40 N.Y.2d, at 544, 387 N.Y.S.2d 821, 356 N.E.2d 277, supra). The child in that case was eight years of age and none of the other serious and disquieting features of this case were apparent there.

The nuances, complexity and variations of human situations make the development and application of the general axiom—best interests of the child—exceedingly difficult. As a matter of degree and perspective, however, the Court's test is concededly more limiting than Matter of Bennett v. Jeffreys, supra, and therefore I believe it is more narrow than it should be in this case since I discern no compelling authority for the narrower approach. This 6½–year-old child, born of a long since deceased crack-cocaine mother, has yet to be permanently placed and has suffered a continuing, lengthy, bad trip through the maze of New York's legal system. His father has an extended history of significant substance addiction and other problems, and the child has spent much of his 7½ years with the same foster parents. These graphic circumstances surely present an exceptionally extraordinary and compelling case requiring significant flexibility by the courts in resolving his best interests (see, Matter of Bennett v. Jeffreys, supra)....

After the proper, broad, "pure" Matter of Bennett v. Jeffreys-type best interests hearing was held in Family Court, the Appellate Division on February 24, 1992 added in the order now before us:

> "In light of the lengthy period of time during which Michael resided with and psychologically bonded to his foster parents and given the potential for emotional as well as physical harm to Michael should permanent custody be awarded to his natural father, we find that the requisite extraordinary circumstances are present (see, Matter of Bennett v. Jeffreys, 40 N.Y.2d 543, 545 [387 N.Y.S.2d 821, 356 N.E.2d 277]), and conclude that the best interests of this child will be served by allowing him to return to his foster parents.

> "In view of the testimony presented during the best interests hearing, this court concludes that Michael's natural father is incapable of giving him the emotional support so vital to his well-being (see, Matter of Bennett v. Marrow, 59 A.D.2d 492 [399 N.Y.S.2d 697]). The testimony presented by Dr. Sullivan and Mr. Falco indicated that an emotional void still existed between Michael and his father despite the eight to nine months during which they resided together prior to the best interests hearing and that this void showed no signs of being bridged." (180 A.D.2d 792, 795–796, 580 N.Y.S.2d 430.)

In sum, I cannot agree that the important and pervasive legal axiom "best interests of the child" is or was meant to be as constricted as it is in the Court's application to this case. The governing phrase and test even in this statutory scheme ought to be as all-encompassing as in Matter of Bennett v. Jeffreys, 40 N.Y.2d 543, 387 N.Y.S.2d 821, 356 N.E.2d 277, supra, despite the difference in the procedural origin and setting of the two cases. The approach I urge ... better serves the objectives of finality and certainty in these matters, more realistically takes into account the widely varying human conditions, and allows the Family Courts to achieve more uniformity and evenness of application of the rules. That is a better way to promote the best interests of this youngster with reasonable finality and the best interests of all others affected by the operation of these rules.

C. The Expanded (and Further Shifting) Legal Process

Introductory Note

The foster care system, which by now has been transformed into a large bureaucracy, is now facing new calls for reform. After going through periods of expanding removal from home to protect children (generally from the parents), followed by prolonged attempts at family reunification (often continuing long after this seemed highly unlikely), or keeping children at home, the shift changed toward emphasis on child protection.The Adoption and Safe Families Act (ASFA), enacted in 1997,[1] facilitated earlier termination of parental rights (and thus adoption). The Virginia statute which follows gives an idea of much of the regulation seen in state laws today. Although regulation is basically found in state law, federal provisions such as the ASFA have had considerable impact because the federal government is a major source of funding for foster care.

The new round of reform includes suggestions ranging from the fairly specific, such as more careful judicial assurance of child protection before removing a child from home into a foster placement,[2] to much broader examinations and proposals for children in foster care such as those in a 2004 report of The Pew Commission on Children and Foster Care, Fostering the Future Safety, Permanence and Well–Being for Children in Foster Care (known as the Pew Report).[3]

VIRGINIA CODE ANNOTATED

§ 63.2–900.   Accepting children for placement in homes, facilities, etc., by local boards

A.   . . . [A] local board shall have the right to accept for placement in suitable family homes, children's residential facilities or independent living arrangements . . . such persons under eighteen years of age as may be entrusted to it by the parent, parents or guardian, committed by any court of competent jurisdiction, or placed through an agreement between it and the parent, parents or guardians where legal custody remains with the parent, parents, or guardians.

The Board shall adopt regulations for the provision of foster care services by local boards, which shall be directed toward the prevention of unnecessary foster care placements and towards the immediate care of and permanent planning for children in the custody of or placed by local boards and which shall achieve, as quickly as practicable, permanent placements for such children. . . . The local board shall first seek out kinship care options to keep children out of foster care and as a placement option for those children in foster care, if it is in the child's best interest. . . .

The local board shall, in accordance with the regulations adopted by the Board and in accordance with the entrustment agreement or other order by which such person is entrusted or committed to its care, have

---

1. Adoption and Safe Families Act of 1997, Pub. L. No. 105–89, 111 Stat. 2115 (codified as amended in scattered sections of 2, 42 U.S.C.). For discussion of the Act in the context of foster care, see James G. Dwyer, The Relationship Rights of Children 56 et seq., (Cambridge University Press 2006); Kimberley Carpenter Emery, Family Ties Dismissed: The Unintended Consequences of ASFA, 12 Va.J. Social Pol'y & L. 400 (2005).

2. See Theo Liebmann, What's Missing from Foster Care Reform? The Need for Comprehensive, Realistic, and Compassionate Removal Standards, 28 Hamline J. Public L. & Pol'y 141 (2006).

3. The Report can be found at http:// www.pewfostercare.org.

custody and control of the person so entrusted or committed to it until he is lawfully discharged, has been adopted or has attained his majority.

Whenever a local board places a child where legal custody remains with the parent, parents or guardians, the board shall enter into an agreement with the parent, parents or guardians. The agreement shall specify the responsibilities of each for the care and control of the child.

The local board shall have authority to place for adoption, and to consent to the adoption of, any child properly committed or entrusted to its care when the order of commitment or entrustment agreement between the parent or parents and the agency provides for the termination of all parental rights and responsibilities with respect to the child for the purpose of placing and consenting to the adoption of the child.

. . . The placement of a child in a foster home, whether within or without the Commonwealth, shall not be for the purpose of adoption unless the placement agreement between the foster parents and the local board specifically so stipulates.

B. Prior to the approval of any family for placement of a child, a home study shall be completed as prescribed in regulations adopted by the Board.

. . .

63.2–900.1. Kinship foster care

A. The local board shall, in accordance with regulations adopted by the Board, determine whether the child has a relative who is eligible to become a kinship foster parent.

B. Kinship foster care placements . . . shall be subject to all requirements of, and shall be eligible for all services related to, foster care placement . . .

C. The kinship foster parent shall be eligible to receive payment at the full foster care rate for the care of the child.

63.2–900.2. Placement of sibling groups; visitation

All reasonable steps shall be taken to place siblings . . . together in the same foster home.

Where siblings are placed in separate foster homes, the local department . . . shall develop a plan to encourage frequent and regular visitation or communication between the siblings. . . .

[§ 63.2–901.1 requires obtaining a statewide criminal history record and results of a search of the child abuse and neglect central registry of any person being considered for a placement.]

§ 63.2–902. Agreements with persons taking children

Every local board and licensed child-placing agency shall, with respect to each child placed by it in a foster home or children's residential facility, enter into a written agreement contained in an approved foster care policy with the head of such home or facility, which agreement shall provide that the authorized representatives of the local board or agency shall have access at all times to such child and to the home or facility, and that the head of the home or facility will release custody of the child so placed to the authorized representatives of the local board or agency whenever, in the opinion of the local board or agency, or in the opinion of the Commissioner, it is in the best interests of the child.

[§ 63.2–903 provides for terminations of parental rights and adoption under an entrustment agreement. § 63.2–904 provides for investigation, visitation and supervision of foster homes.]

§ 63.2–905. Foster care services

Foster care services are the provision of a full range of casework, treatment and community services, including but not limited to independent living services, for a planned period of time to a child who is abused or neglected as defined in § 63.2–100 or in need of services as defined in § 16.1–228 and his family when the child (i) has been identified as needing services to prevent or eliminate the need for foster care placement, (ii) has been placed through an agreement between the local board or the public agency designated by the community policy and management team and the parents or guardians where legal custody remains with the parents or guardians, or (iii) has been committed or entrusted to a local board or licensed child placing agency.

§ 63.2–905.1. Independent living services

Local departments and licensed child-placing agencies may provide independent living services to persons between 18 and 21 years of age who are in the process of transitioning from foster care to self-sufficiency....

§ 63.2–912. Visitation of child placed in foster care

The circuit courts and juvenile and domestic relations district courts shall have the authority to grant visitation rights to the natural parents, siblings, and grandparents of any child entrusted or committed to foster care if the court finds (i) that the parent, sibling, or grandparent had an ongoing relationship with the child prior to his being placed in foster care and (ii) it is in the best interests of the child that the relationship continue. The order of the court committing the child to foster care shall state the nature and extent of any visitation rights granted as provided in this section.

§ 16.1–281. Foster care plan

A. In any case in which (i) a local board of social services places a child through an agreement with the parents or guardians where legal custody remains with the parents or guardian, or (ii) legal custody of a child is given to a local board of social services or a child welfare agency, the local department of social services shall prepare a foster care plan for such child, as described hereinafter....

The representatives of such department or agency shall involve the child's parent(s) in the development of the plan, except when parental rights have been terminated ..., [the] parent(s) cannot be located, and any other person or persons standing in loco parentis at the time the board or child welfare agency obtained custody or the board placed the child. The representatives of such department or agency shall involve the child in the development of the plan, if such involvement is consistent with the best interests of the child. . . .

The department or child welfare agency shall file the plan with the juvenile and domestic relations district court within 60 days following the transfer of custody or the board's placement of the child unless the court, for good cause shown, allows an extension of time, which shall not exceed an additional 60 days. . . .

B. The foster care plan shall describe in writing (i) the programs, care, services and other support which will be offered to the child and his parents and other prior custodians; (ii) the participation and conduct which will be sought from the child's parents and other prior custodians, and between the child and his siblings; (iii) the visitation and other contacts which will be permitted between the child and his parents and other prior custodians, and between the child and his siblings; (iv) the nature of the placement or placements which will be provided for the child; (v) for children 14 years of age or older, the child's needs and goals in the areas of counseling, education, housing, employment, and money management skills development, along with specific independent living services that will provided to the child to help him reach these goals; and (vi) where appropriate for children 16 or over, the programs and services which will help the child prepare for the transition from foster care to independent living. If consistent with the child's health and safety, the plan shall be designed to support reasonable efforts which lead to the return of the child to his parents or other prior custodians within the shortest practicable time which shall be specified in the plan. . . .

If the department or child welfare agency concludes that it is not reasonably likely that the child can be returned to his prior family within a practicable time, consistent with the best interests of the child, in a separate section of the plan the department, child welfare agency or team shall (a) include a full description of the reasons for this conclusion; (b) provide information on the opportunities for placing the child with a relative or in an adoptive home; (c) design the plan to lead to the child's successful placement with a relative if a subsequent transfer of custody to the relative is planned, or in an adoptive home within the shortest practicable time, and if neither of such placements is feasible; (d) explain why permanent foster care, independent living for a child 16 years of age or older or continued foster care is the plan for the child. . . .

The local board or other child welfare agency having custody of the child shall not be required by the court to make reasonable efforts to reunite the child with a parent if the court finds that (1) the residual parental rights of the parent regarding a sibling of the child have previously been involuntarily terminated; (2) the parent has been convicted of an offense under the laws of this Commonwealth or a substantially similar law of any other state, the United States or any foreign jurisdiction that constitutes murder or voluntary manslaughter, or a felony attempt, conspiracy or solicitation to commit any such offense, if the victim of the offense was a child of the parent, a child with whom the parent resided at the time such offense occurred or the other parent of the child; (3) the parent has been convicted of an offense under the laws of this Commonwealth or a substantially similar law of any other state, the United States or any foreign jurisdiction that constitutes felony assault resulting in serious bodily injury or felony bodily wounding resulting in serious bodily injury or felony sexual assault, if the victim of the offense was a child of the parent or a child with whom the parent resided at the time of such offense; or (4) based on clear and convincing evidence, the parent has subjected any child to aggravated circumstances, or abandoned a child under circumstances which would justify the termination of residual parental rights pursuant to subsection D of § 16.1–283.

[The statute defines "aggravated circumstances," "chronic abuse," "serious bodily injury" and "severe abuse."]

Within 30 days of making a determination that reasonable efforts to reunite the child with the parents are not required, the court shall hold a permanency planning hearing pursuant to § 16.1–282.1.

C.   [Subsection C first describes all parties receiving notice of the foster care plan.] A hearing shall be held for the purpose of reviewing and approving the foster care plan. The hearing shall be held within 75 days of (i) the child's initial foster care placement, if the child was placed through an agreement between the parents or guardians and the local department of social services or a child welfare agency; (ii) the original preliminary removal order hearing, if the child was placed in foster care pursuant to § 16.1–252; (iii) the hearing on the petition for relief of custody, if the child was placed in foster care pursuant to § 16.1–277.02; or (iv) the dispositional hearing at which the child was placed in foster care ...

C1.   Any order transferring custody of the child to a relative other than the child's prior family shall be entered only upon a finding, based upon a preponderance of the evidence, that the relative is one who, after an investigation as directed by the court, (i) is found by the court to be willing and qualified to receive and care for the child; (ii) is willing to have a positive, continuous relationship with the child; (iii) is committed to providing a permanent, suitable home for the child; and (iv) is willing and has the ability to protect the child from abuse and neglect; and the order shall so state. The court's order transferring custody to a relative should further provide for, as appropriate, any terms or conditions which would promote the child's interest and welfare; ongoing provision of social services to the child and the child's custodian; and court review of the child's placement.

C2.   Any order entered at the conclusion of the hearing that has the effect of achieving a permanent goal for the child by terminating residual parental rights pursuant to §§ 16.1–277.01, 16.1–277.02, 16.1–278.3, or § 16.1–283; by placing the child in permanent foster care pursuant to subdivision A iv of § 16.1–282.1; or by directing the board or agency to provide the child with services to achieve independent living status, if the child has attained the age of 16 years, pursuant to subdivision A v of § 16.1–282.1 shall state whether reasonable efforts have been made to place the child in a timely manner in accordance with the foster care plan and to complete the steps necessary to finalize the permanent placement of the child.

D. The court in which the foster care plan is filed shall be notified immediately if the child is returned to his parents or other persons standing in loco parentis at the time the board or agency obtained custody or the board placed the child.

E. At the conclusion of the hearing at which the initial foster care plan is reviewed, the court shall schedule a foster care review hearing to be held within six months in accordance with § 16.1–282. However, if an order is entered pursuant to subsection C2, the court shall schedule a foster care review hearing to be held within 12 months of the entry of such order in accordance with the provisions of § 16.1–282.2. Parties who are present at the hearing at which the initial foster care plan is reviewed shall be given notice of the date set for the foster care review hearing and parties who are not present shall be summoned as provided in § 16.1–263.

F. ... The court shall appoint an attorney to act as guardian ad litem to represent the child any time a hearing is held to review the foster care plan filed for the child or to review the child's status in foster care.

§ 16.1–282. Foster care review

A. In the case of a child who was the subject of a foster care plan filed with the court pursuant to § 16.1–281, a foster care review hearing shall be held within six months of the dispositional hearing at which the foster care plan pursuant to § 16.1–281 was reviewed if the child: (a) was placed through an agreement between the parents or guardians and the local board of social services where legal custody remains with the parents or guardians and such agreement has not been dissolved by court order; or (b) is under the legal custody of a local board of social services or a child welfare agency and has not had a petition to terminate parental rights granted, filed or ordered to be filed on the child's behalf; has not been placed in permanent foster care; or is age 16 or over and the plan for the child is not independent living.

Any interested party ... may file with the court the petition for a foster care review hearing hereinafter described at any time after the initial foster care placement of the child. However, the board or child welfare agency shall file the petition within five months of the dispositional hearing at which the foster care plan was reviewed pursuant to § 16.1–281.

B. The petition shall:

. . .

3. Describe the placement or placements provided for the child while in foster care and the services or programs offered to the child and his parents and, if applicable, the persons previously standing in loco parentis;

4. Describe the nature and frequency of the contacts between the child and his parents and, if applicable, the persons previously standing in loco parentis;

5. Set forth in detail the manner in which the foster care plan previously filed with the court was or was not complied with and the extent to which the goals thereof have been met; and

6. Set forth the disposition sought and the grounds therefor . . . .

C. Upon receipt of the petition ... the court shall schedule a hearing to be held within 30 days if a hearing was not previously scheduled. [The statute describes all parties entitled to notice of the hearing, which include the child if he is 12 years of age or older; the guardian ad litem; the child's parents; the foster parents and the petitioning board or child welfare agency.]

D. At the conclusion of the hearing, the court shall ... enter any appropriate order of disposition consistent with the dispositional alternatives available to the court at the time of the original hearing. The court order shall state whether reasonable efforts, if applicable, have been made to reunite the child with his parents, guardian or other person standing in loco parentis to the child. Any order entered at the conclusion of this hearing that has the effect of achieving a permanent goal for the child by terminating residual parental rights ...; by placing the child in permanent foster care ....; or, if the child has attained the age of 16 years, and the plan is for independent living, directing the board or agency to provide the necessary services to transition from foster care ... shall state whether reasonable efforts have been made to place the child in a timely manner in accordance with the foster care plan and to complete the steps necessary to finalize the permanent placement of the child.

D1. [This subsection establishes requirements for transferring custody to a relative.]

E. [This subsection establishes the court's continuing jurisdiction as long as the child is in foster care or the parents are subject to conditions. The court is directed to schedule a permanency planning hearing on the case to be held five months thereafter.]

§ 16.1–282.1. Permanency planning hearing for children in foster care

A. In the case of a child who was the subject of a foster care plan filed with the court pursuant to § 16.1–281, a permanency planning hearing shall be held within 11 months of the dispositional hearing at which the foster care plan pursuant to § 16.1–281 was reviewed if the child (a) was placed through an agreement between the parents or guardians and the local board of social services or a public agency designated by the community policy and management team where legal custody remains with the parents or guardians and such agreement has not been dissolved by court order; or (b) is under the legal custody of a local board of social services or a child welfare agency and has not had a petition to terminate parental rights filed on the child's behalf, has not been placed in permanent foster care, or is age 16 or over and the plan for the child is not independent living. The board, public agency or child welfare agency shall file a petition for a permanency planning hearing within 10 months of the dispositional hearing at which the foster care plan was reviewed pursuant to § 16.1–281. The purpose of this hearing is to establish a permanent goal for the child and either to achieve the permanent goal or to defer such action through the approval of an interim plan for the child.

To achieve the permanent goal, the petition for a permanency planning hearing shall seek to (i) transfer the custody of the child to his prior family, or dissolve the board's or public agency's placement agreement and return the child to his prior family; (ii) transfer custody of the child to a relative other than the child's prior family, subject to the provisions of subsection A1; (iii) terminate residual parental rights pursuant to § 16.1–277.01 or s 16.1–283; (iv) place the child in permanent foster care pursuant to § 63.2–908; (v) if the child has attained the age of 16 years or over and the plan is independent living, direct the board or agency to provide the child with services to transition from foster care; or (vi) place the child in another planned permanent living arrangement in accordance with the provisions of subsection A2.

[The statute provides for approval of an interim plan.]

Upon receipt of the petition, if a permanency planning hearing has not already been scheduled, the court shall schedule such a hearing to be held within 30 days. The permanency planning hearing shall be held within 11 months of the dispositional hearing at which the foster care plan was reviewed pursuant to § 16.1–281 . . .

A1. [This subsection establishes requirements for transferring custody to a relative.]

A2. [This subsection establishes requirements for permanent placement in a long term residential treatment facility, an option only if the child has a severe and chronic emotional, physical or neurological disabling condition.]

B. [This subsection establishes requirements for approval of an interim plan for the child in accordance with subsection A.]

. . .

2. Before approving an interim plan for the child, the court shall find:

a. When returning home remains the plan for the child, that the parent has made marked progress toward reunification with the child, the parent has maintained a close and positive relationship with the child, and the child is likely to return home within the near future, although it is premature to set an exact date for return at the time of this hearing; or

b. When returning home is not the plan for the child, that marked progress is being made to achieve the permanent goal identified by the board or child welfare agency and that it is premature to set an exact date for accomplishing the goal at the time of this hearing.

3. Upon approval of an interim plan, the court shall schedule a hearing to be held within six months to determine that the permanent goal is accomplished and to enter an order consistent with alternative (i), (ii), (iii), (iv), or (v) of subsection A. All parties present at the initial permanency planning hearing shall be given notice of the date scheduled for the second permanency planning hearing. Parties not present shall be summoned to appear as provided in § 16.1–263. Otherwise, subsection A shall govern the scheduling and notice for such hearings.

C. At the conclusion of the permanency planning hearing held pursuant to this section, whether action is taken or deferred to achieve the permanent goal for the child, the court shall enter an order that states whether reasonable efforts have been made to reunite the child with the child's prior family, if returning home is the permanent goal for the child; or whether reasonable efforts have been made to achieve the permanent goal identified by the board or agency, if the goal is other than returning the child home. In making this determination, the court shall give consideration to whether the board or agency has placed the child in a timely manner in accordance with the foster care plan and completed the steps necessary to finalize the permanent placement of the child.

D.   FOSTER PARENTS AS ADOPTERS

Unlike foster care, adoption generally serves to sever previous ties with a child's natural parents and fully substitute adoptive parents in their place. Unless the natural parents relinquish a child for extreme circumstances. For this reason, many children who might otherwise be adoptable remain in foster care until they become of age. Ironically, most states permit adoption of an adult without consent of the natural parents, so some children are adopted by their foster parents after reaching majority.

Generally children are placed in foster care with the understanding that they will be relinquished to the placing agency on demand. This may mean when the child becomes legally available for adoption as a result of termination of parental rights or relinquishment. Although the foster parents may have executed a contract specifically agreeing to relinquish the child on demand, some still have sought to assert a preference to be considered for adoption. From the agency's standpoint the question may be viewed as one of determining whether the foster parents would be the best available—or even the appropriate—adopters. Factors such as advanced age might make them seem satisfactory for temporary placement but less so for adoption, which creates a permanent, long-term parent-child relationship.

Some state legislatures have adopted statutes giving foster parents a preference, or at least standing to be considered, in adoptions that take place after a significant period of foster care. For example, N.Y. Social Services Law § 383(3) provides:

> Any adult husband and his adult wife and any adult unmarried person, who, as foster parent or parents, have cared for a child continuously for a period of twelve months or more, may apply to such authorized agency for the placement of said child with them for the purpose of adoption, and if said child is eligible for adoption, the agency shall give preference and first consideration to their application over all other applications for adoption placements. However, final determination of the propriety of said adoption of such foster child shall be within the sole discretion of the court . . .

E.   PERMANENT OR LONG TERM FOSTER PLACEMENT

Courts sometimes face a dilemma in which there are insufficient grounds for statutory termination of parental rights but it is undesirable, inappropriate or dangerous to return a child to the natural parent or parents, particularly after a long period of attachment between foster parent and child to the psychological benefit of the latter. In some such instances a child may simply remain in foster care by default, though this is less likely than once was the case. Formalization of a mechanism for permanent or long term foster care is provided in some states to permit recognition of strong bonds within the foster family, to assure continued stability in the placement, and to give foster parents increased rights of decisionmaking with regard to the child. Continuing contact between the child and the natural parents also is possible under such a scheme. Conceptually this is far different from the ostensibly "interim" or short term foster placement. Virginia uses the term "permanent" foster care, but some other states have rejected such a label or even eliminated specific statutes dealing with the subject.

VIRGINIA CODE ANNOTATED

§ 63.2–908 Permanent foster care placement

A. Permanent foster care placement means the place in which a child has been placed pursuant to the provisions of §§ 63.2–900, 63.2–903 and this section with the expectation and agreement between the placing agency and the place of permanent foster care that the child shall remain in the placement until he reaches the age of majority unless modified by court order or unless removed pursuant to § 16.1–251 or § 63.2–1517. A permanent foster care placement may be a place of residence of any natural person or persons deemed appropriate to meet a child's needs on a long-term basis.

B. A local department or a licensed child-placing agency shall have authority pursuant to a court order to place a child over whom it has legal custody in a permanent foster care placement where the child shall remain until attaining majority or thereafter, until the age of twenty-one years, if such placement is a requisite to providing funds for the care of such child, so long as the child is a participant in an educational, treatment or training program approved pursuant to regulations of the Board. No such child shall be removed from the physical custody of the foster parents in the permanent care placement except upon order of the court or pursuant to § 16.1–251 or § 63.2–1517. The department or agency so placing a child shall retain legal custody of the child. A court shall not order that a child be placed in permanent foster care unless it finds that (i) diligent efforts have been made by the local department to place the child with his natural parents and such efforts have been unsuccessful, and (ii) diligent efforts have been made by the local department to place the child for adoption and such efforts have been unsuccessful or adoption is not a reasonable alternative for a long-term placement for the child under the circumstances.

C. Unless modified by the court order, the foster parent in the permanent foster care placement shall have the authority to consent to surgery, entrance into the armed services, marriage, application for a motor vehicle and driver's license, application for admission into college and any other such activities that require parental consent and shall have the responsibility for informing the placing department or agency of any such actions.

D.   Any child placed in a permanent foster care placement by a local department shall, with the cooperation of the foster parents with whom the permanent foster care placement has been made, receive the same services and benefits as any other child in foster care pursuant to §§ 63.2–319, 63.2–900 and 63.2–903 and any other applicable provisions of law.

E.   The Board shall establish minimum standards for the utilization, supervision and evaluation of permanent foster care placements.

F.   The rate of payment for permanent foster care placements by a local department shall be in accordance with standards and rates established by the Board. The rate of payment for such placements by other licensed child-placing agencies shall be in accordance with standards and rates established by the individual agency.

G.   If the child has a continuing involvement with his natural parents, the natural parents should be involved in the planning for a permanent placement. The court order placing the child in a permanent placement shall include a specification of the nature and frequency of visiting arrangements with the natural parents.

H.   Any change in the placement of a child in permanent foster care or the responsibilities of the foster parents for that child shall be made only by order of the court which ordered the placement pursuant to a petition filed by the foster parents, local department, licensed child-placing agency or other appropriate party.

Martin v. Pittsylvania County Department of Social Services

Court of Appeals of Virginia, 1986.
3 Va.App. 15, 348 S.E.2d 13.

■ KOONTZ, CHIEF JUDGE.

This case involves a controversy between the Pittsylvania County Department of Social Services (hereinafter referred to as "appellee" or "DSS") and Margie Sparks Martin concerning the custody of her son, John, born on June 20, 1976. By order dated June 23, 1985, the circuit court denied Mrs. Martin's petition for custody and directed that the child be placed in permanent foster care pursuant to Code § 63.1–206.1, subject to the visitation rights of Mrs. Martin. Mrs. Martin appeals from that order.

Procedural Background

The procedural background of this case is somewhat involved and we cite it to illustrate the events which led to the entry of the order on appeal. As a result of physical abuse of the child by the father, the Pittsylvania County Juvenile and Domestic Relations District Court, by order dated May 20, 1981, placed John in the appellee's custody. Subsequently, on December 30, 1982, that court granted the petition of the appellee to terminate the parental rights of Mrs. Martin. On appeal, the circuit court denied the petition to terminate Mrs. Martin's parental rights by order dated May 26, 1983. Thereafter, the appellee filed a foster care plan in the juvenile court with the goal being to return John to the custody of Mrs. Martin. The juvenile court approved the plan in November, 1983, but upon review of it in June, 1984, rejected it on the ground that Mrs. Martin would not be a proper custodial parent and ordered the appellee to file a plan with adoption as the goal. At that time Mrs. Martin unsuccessfully sought custody for herself. She appealed both of these determinations to the circuit court. Pending the hearing on appeal, the appellee filed a petition in the circuit court to terminate Mrs. Martin's parental rights. Mrs. Martin's appeal and the appellee's petition were consolidated and heard ore tenus in February and June, 1985. A guardian ad litem was appointed to represent John's interest in these proceedings. On June 23, 1985, the circuit court denied the petition to terminate Mrs. Martin's parental rights, denied her petition for custody, and directed that John be placed in permanent foster care.

During this four year period John remained in foster care and had visitations with his mother. The father voluntarily surrendered his parental rights under an entrustment agreement dated November 5, 1982, and consequently his rights were not involved in the proceedings below and are not involved in this appeal. There is no appeal from the denial of the petition to terminate the parental rights of Mrs. Martin.

Factual Background

At the hearing in the circuit court various caseworkers and mental health professionals, in addition to Mrs. Martin, were called as witnesses. The record reveals that Mrs. Martin had three children by her marriage to Mr. Martin. A fifteen year old son is in the custody of his father and an older daughter is in the custody of Mrs. Martin's brother. Mrs. Martin has little, if any, contact with these children. At the time of the abuse of John by his father in May 1981, Mrs. Martin had gone to Baltimore, Maryland for medical treatment. The precise reason for this trip is unclear from the record. Mrs. Martin testified that she had bronchitis and allergies and that she was treated in the emergency room of a hospital in Baltimore for this condition. She had been taking medication for "nerves" but had discontinued taking the medication. The children had been left in the care of the father's sister, who subsequently relinquished custody of John to his father. Upon learning of the abuse of John, Mrs. Martin returned but has not regained custody of him. Throughout these proceedings Mrs. Martin has remained separated from her husband though not divorced from him.

It is clear from the record that Mrs. Martin has never physically abused John. There is an emotional tie between the two. Pursuant to the first foster care plan, Mrs. Martin, according to her caseworker, for several years, until April 1984, made reasonable progress in establishing a stable home, attending parenting classes and providing care for John during home visitations. At that time John was concerned about alleged arguments between his mother and her boyfriend, that he had to do household chores, and that his mother had placed him inside garbage dumpsters to locate junk. This evidence was admitted by the trial court to establish the reasons the appellee changed the foster care plan goal to adoption rather than return of custody to Mrs. Martin. Mrs. Martin explained that John was in no danger during arguments with her boyfriend, that she considered household chores to be beneficial training, and that she often sold junk for extra income. Her regular income consisted of a monthly social security disability check and food stamps. We do not find that any of these matters were the basis of the trial court's denial of her petition for custody. Furthermore, the issue of their admissibility into evidence is not before us.

The crucial evidence came from the mental health professionals. It is undisputed that Mrs. Martin is mildly to moderately mentally retarded. Her therapist, Gloria Culley, testified that Mrs. Martin could function as a parent but would need supervision and assistance under stressful circumstances. Dr. Ashby, a psychiatrist, testified that Mrs. Martin "does not have the necessary capability to assume responsibility for the custody and care of her son at the present time and likely as not in the foreseeable future." At the direction of the trial judge, Mrs. Martin and John were seen for evaluation by Dr. Frazier, a child psychiatrist. Dr. Frazier testified that John "should not be considered retarded but should be considered a child who is on the low side of average but who needs help with verbal skills." He further testified that "a socially and intellectually stimulating program or environment" would help to improve verbal and arithmetic skills. Dr. Frazier further testified that Mrs. Martin needs "support in parent managing, assertive discipline and to be instructed in the various needs of the different levels of development as he grows," and for that "I think she needs help in managing him and that should continue throughout his life as a child until he becomes an adult." Dr. Frazier testified, however, that severing the maternal relationship would be detrimental to John, but that he should remain in foster care.

Mrs. Martin, in her brief, asserts that there are three issues presented to us in her appeal:

1. In a child custody proceeding involving the natural mother and the local welfare department (DSS), may the court permanently deprive the mother of custody without clear and convincing evidence of her unfitness as a parent?

2. In a child custody proceeding involving the natural mother and DSS, may the court permanently deprive the mother of custody based solely upon the fact that she is mildly mentally retarded without any evidence that she has abused or neglected the child or has been incapable of caring for the child due to such retardation?

3. Is the court's finding in this case that the natural mother was incapable of assuming physical and legal custody of her son supported by substantial evidence on the record?

Discussion

We first consider Mrs. Martin's contention that the trial court's finding that she was incapable of assuming physical and legal custody of John is not supported by substantial evidence. We review the record to determine whether there is clear and convincing evidence to support the determination of the trial court. Under familiar principles we view that evidence and all reasonable inferences in the light most favorable to the prevailing party below. Where, as here, the court hears the evidence ore tenus, its finding is entitled to great weight and will not be disturbed on appeal unless plainly wrong or without evidence to support it. Simmons v. Simmons, 1 Va.App. 358, 361, 339 S.E.2d 198, 199 (1986).

It is well settled that in custody cases involving a controversy between parent and non-parent, there is a presumption that the best interests of the child will be served when the child is placed in the custody of a fit parent with a suitable home. Judd v. Van Horn, 195 Va. 988, 995–96, 81 S.E.2d 432, 436 (1954).

It is necessary to draw a clear distinction between the Judd rule and those cases cited by Mrs. Martin which involve the termination of parental rights.

> The termination of parental rights is a grave, drastic, and irreversible action. When a court orders termination of parental rights, the ties between the parent and child are severed forever and the parent becomes "a legal stranger to the child."

Lowe v. Richmond Dept. of Public Welfare, 231 Va. 277, 343 S.E.2d 70, 72 (1986), (quoting Shank v. Dept. of Social Services, 217 Va. 506, 509, 230 S.E.2d 454, 457 (1976)). With the enactment of Code § 16.1–283 the termination of parental rights must promote the best interests of the child, and where a determination is made that the factors enumerated in the statute are present, such a determination in a given case is tantamount to a finding of parental unfitness. No further finding of parental unfitness is required by the court. Knox v. Lynchburg Division of Social Services, 223 Va. 213, 220, 288 S.E.2d 399, 403 (1982).

In the context of the sufficiency of the evidence to support the trial court's denial of Mrs. Martin's custody petition, her reliance on these termination cases is misplaced. The child had been placed previously in foster care and would remain in foster care if she were unsuccessful in her custody petition. In that context termination of parental rights is not at issue.

In addition, where a prior order formally has divested a parent of custody, the Judd presumption is not applicable and the burden rests on the parent to show that circumstances have so changed that it is in the best interests of the child to return custody to the parent. Dyer v. Howell, 212 Va. 453, 456, 184 S.E.2d 789, 792 (1971). That burden must be met by clear and convincing evidence which was recently defined as follows:

> [T]hat measure or degree of proof which will produce in the mind of the trier of facts a firm belief or conviction as to the allegations sought to be established. It is intermediate, being more than a mere preponderance, but not to the extent of such certainty as is required beyond a reasonable doubt as in criminal cases. It does not mean clear and unequivocal.

Gifford v. Dennis, 230 Va. 193, 198 n. 1, 335 S.E.2d 371, 373 n. 1 (1985).

We now review the record to determine whether Mrs. Martin carried her burden to establish that John's best interests would be served by a return of custody to her.

As previously noted, the evidence established that John has remained in foster care for many years and that Mrs. Martin has been unable to establish a suitable home for him. While there is an emotional tie between them, the psychological evidence established beyond question that she is mildly to moderately retarded, would need supervision and assistance under stressful circumstances, and that throughout his life as a child she would need help in managing and disciplining John. Mrs. Martin's separation from her other children, her apparent inability to profit from parenting classes, the length of time which the child has remained in foster care, and the repeated denial of her custody petitions in the lower courts all evince her inability to provide a suitable home for the child. The psychological evidence established that John's best interests would be furthered by his remaining in a stable placement with the retention of the parental relationship with his mother through visitations and the possibility of a future return of custody to her. Accordingly, we find no error in the trial court's denial of Mrs. Martin's custody petition.

It is unnecessary to resolve the merits of the remaining two issues raised by Mrs. Martin in this appeal because we find that the trial court lacked jurisdiction to order a placement in permanent foster care pursuant to Code § 63.1–206.1. While not raised specifically by Mrs. Martin, lack of jurisdiction may be considered by an appellate court of its own motion. 1B Michie's Jurisprudence, Appeal and Error, § 107 (1980). Under the facts of this case, we are compelled to do so.

In the proceedings below, the trial court had no petition before it seeking a *permanent* foster care placement. The appellee had sought termination of Mrs. Martin's parental rights, Mrs. Martin had appealed a plan with adoption as its goal, and had appealed the denial of her custody petition by the juvenile court. None of these issues presented the trial court with the dispositional alternative of *permanent* foster care. Those dispositional alternatives are initially found in Code § 16.1–279, and a final order of foster care placement had been entered. Thereafter, it was incumbent upon the appellee, pursuant to Code § 16.1–281(B), to file an appropriate plan for permanent foster care upon which Mrs. Martin had the right to petition the court to review the plan. It is implicit in the statutory scheme of Code §§ 16.1–281 and 16.1–282 (providing for foster care review by the court) that the natural parent, at subsequent hearings concerning that child, is entitled to prior and specific notice of the disposition sought by the agency in whose custody a child has been placed. Due process demands it.

A petition for termination of parental rights pursuant to Code § 16.1–283 does not encompass a petition for *permanent* foster care. The latter is not a less drastic form of the former, but rather is a different and distinct alternative. As such, a natural parent in preparing for a hearing on one would not necessarily adequately prepare for the other.

Code § 63.1–206.1 provides the statutory scheme for *permanent* foster care placement. That scheme is intended to provide a more permanent placement for a child in a particular foster home than is generally obtained in regular foster care, and yet does not, as in the case of adoption proceedings, serve as a vehicle for terminating parental rights. Where the child has a continuing involvement with his or her natural parents, the statute provides for a continuation of that involvement through court-ordered visiting arrangements with the natural parents. Legal custody remains with the local department of welfare or social services or a licensed child-placing agency, and physical custody is granted to the foster parent. In this capacity, the foster parent is granted the authority to give parental consent in such matters as surgery, entrance into the armed services, marriage and others. The intended result is stability for the child and the foster parents know the nature and scope of their authority and responsibility. No change can occur in this placement without an order of the court which instituted the placement. A proper petition, filed by the foster parents, local department, licensed child-placing agency or "other appropriate party," is required for such a change. We construe the term "other appropriate party" to include the natural parent. Consequently, the issue of *permanently* depriving Mrs. Martin of the custody of John is not involved in this appeal. However, she has lost substantial parental rights vis-a-vis regular foster care. Where, as here, the natural parent is not given specific notice by a petition seeking a specific placement, and where, as here, substantial parental rights are at stake, we hold that a trial court has no jurisdiction to enter *sua sponte* an order terminating or reducing those parental rights. Our review of the record reveals that the trial judge was very conscientious in finding a placement for the child which would be in his best interests, and we make no determination in this opinion that the placement ordered was inappropriate. Rather, our holding addresses the omission of the necessary procedure to arrive at that placement.

Accordingly, the order of June 23, 1985, insofar as it places the child in *permanent* foster care, is vacated, and this case is remanded for further proceedings consistent with this opinion. The effect of our decision is to affirm the denial of Mrs. Martin's custody petition, and to leave the prior orders placing the child in regular foster care in full force and effect.

. . .

CHAPTER VII

TERMINATION OF PARENTAL RIGHTS

A. INTRODUCTORY NOTE

It is important at the outset to distinguish between custody determinations of all sorts and actions to terminate parental rights. Because of the severe, peremptory and virtually unalterable nature of the results in the latter, contests based on constitutional rights have been at the forefront in many legal actions. Many persons feel that courts have been more concerned with the rights of parents than with the rights of children, with inadequate balancing between them. (Language in the dissenting opinion of Justice Rehnquist in *Santosky* is sometimes regarded as supporting this view.) Some critics feel also that judicial responses often are much too mechanical, and that even after a number of cases overcoming objections about vagueness of termination statutes (many of which have been substantially amended to deal with such objections), there is still inadequate delineation of just what must be proven by "clear and convincing evidence". These are matters to keep in mind while going over the material which follows.

B. REQUIREMENTS OF PROOF AND REPRESENTATION

Santosky v. Kramer

Supreme Court of the United States, 1982.
455 U.S. 745, 102 S.Ct. 1388, 71 L.Ed.2d 599.

■ JUSTICE BLACKMUN delivered the opinion of the Court.

Under New York law, the State may terminate, over parental objection, the rights of parents in their natural child upon a finding that the child is "permanently neglected." N.Y. Soc. Serv. Law §§ 384–b.4.(d), 384–b.7.(a). The New York Family Court Act § 622 requires that only a "fair preponderance of the evidence" support that finding. Thus, in New York, the factual certainty required to extinguish the parent-child relationship is no greater than that necessary to award money damages in an ordinary civil action.

Today we hold that the Due Process Clause of the Fourteenth Amendment demands more than this. Before a State may sever completely and irrevocably the rights of parents in their natural child, due process requires that the State support its allegations by at least clear and convincing evidence.

New York authorizes its officials to remove a child temporarily from his or her home if the child appears "neglected," within the meaning of Art. 10 of the Family Court Act. Once removed, a child under the age of 18 customarily is placed "in the care of an authorized agency," usually a state institution or a foster home. At that point, "the state's first obligation is to help the family with services to ... reunite it...." But if convinced that "positive, nurturing parent-child relationships no longer exist," the State may initiate "permanent neglect" proceedings to free the child for adoption.

The State bifurcates its permanent neglect proceeding into "factfinding" and "dispositional" hearings. Fam.Ct.Act §§ 622, 623. At the factfinding stage, the State must prove that the child has been "permanently neglected," as defined by Fam.Ct.Act §§ 614.1.(a)–(d) and Soc.Serv.Law § 384–b.7.(a). The Family Court judge then determines at a subsequent dispositional hearing what placement would serve the child's best interests.

At the factfinding hearing, the State must establish, among other things, that for more than a year after the child entered state custody, the agency "made diligent efforts to encourage and strengthen the parental relationship." Fam.Ct.Act §§ 614.1.(c), 611. The State must further prove that during that same period, the child's natural parents failed "substantially and continuously or repeatedly to maintain contact with or plan for the future of the child although physically and financially able to do so." § 614.1.(d). Should the State support its allegations by "a fair preponderance of the evidence," § 622, the child may be declared permanently neglected. § 611. That declaration empowers the Family Court judge to terminate permanently the natural parents' rights in the child. §§ 631(c), 634. Termination denies the natural parents physical custody, as well as the rights ever to visit, communicate with, or regain custody of the child.

New York's permanent neglect statute provides natural parents with certain procedural protections.[2] But New York permits its officials to establish "permanent neglect" with less proof than most States require. Thirty-three States, the District of Columbia, and the Virgin Islands currently specify a higher standard of proof, in parental rights termination proceedings, than a "fair preponderance of the evidence." ... The question here is whether New York's "fair preponderance of the evidence" standard is constitutionally sufficient.

Petitioners John Santosky II and Annie Santosky are the natural parents of Tina and John III. In November 1973, after incidents reflecting parental neglect, respondent Kramer, Commissioner of the Ulster County Department of Social Services, initiated a neglect proceeding under Fam.Ct. Act § 1022 and removed Tina from her natural home. About 10 months later, he removed John III and placed him with foster parents. On the day John was taken, Annie Santosky gave birth to a third child, Jed. When Jed was only three days old, respondent transferred him to a foster home on

---

2. Most notably, natural parents have a statutory right to the assistance of counsel and of court-appointed counsel if they are indigent. Fam.Ct.Act § 262(a)(iii).

the ground that immediate removal was necessary to avoid imminent danger to his life or health.

In October 1978, respondent petitioned the Ulster County Family Court to terminate petitioners' parental rights in the three children. Petitioners challenged the constitutionality of the "fair preponderance of the evidence" standard specified in Fam.Ct.Act § 622. The Family Court judge rejected this constitutional challenge, and weighed the evidence under the statutory standard. While acknowledging that the Santoskys had maintained contact with their children, the judge found those visits "at best superficial and devoid of any real emotional content." After deciding that the agency had made " 'diligent efforts' to encourage and strengthen the parental relationship," he concluded that the Santoskys were incapable, even with public assistance, of planning for the future of their children. The judge later held a dispositional hearing and ruled that the best interests of the three children required permanent termination of the Santoskys' custody.[5]

Petitioners appealed, again contesting the constitutionality of § 622's standard of proof. The New York Supreme Court, Appellate Division, affirmed, holding application of the preponderance of the evidence standard "proper and constitutional." In re John AA, 75 App.Div.2d 910, 427 N.Y.S.2d 319, 320 (1980). That standard, the court reasoned, "recognizes and seeks to balance rights possessed by the child ... with those of the natural parents...." Ibid.

The New York Court of Appeals then dismissed petitioners' appeal to that court "upon the ground that no substantial constitutional question is directly involved." ...

Last Term, in Lassiter v. Department of Social Services, 452 U.S. 18 (1981), this Court, by a 5–4 vote, held that the Fourteenth Amendment's Due Process Clause does not require the appointment of counsel for indigent parents in every parental status termination proceeding. The case casts light, however, on the two central questions here—whether process is constitutionally due a natural parent at a State's parental rights termination proceeding, and, if so, what process is due.

In *Lassiter,* it was "not disputed that state intervention to terminate the relationship between [a parent] and [the] child must be accomplished by procedures meeting the requisites of the Due Process Clause." The absence of dispute reflected this Court's historical recognition that freedom of personal choice in matters of family life is a fundamental liberty interest protected by the Fourteenth Amendment.

The fundamental liberty interest of natural parents in the care, custody, and management of their child does not evaporate simply because they have not been model parents or have lost temporary custody of their child to the State. Even when blood relationships are strained, parents retain a

---

5. Since respondent took custody of Tina, John III, and Jed, the Santoskys have had two other children, James and Jeremy. The State has taken no action to remove these younger children. At oral argument, counsel for respondent replied affirmatively when asked whether he was asserting that petitioners were "unfit to handle the three older ones but not unfit to handle the two younger ones."

vital interest in preventing the irretrievable destruction of their family life. If anything, persons faced with forced dissolution of their parental rights have a more critical need for procedural protections than do those resisting state intervention into ongoing family affairs. When the State moves to destroy weakened familial bonds, it must provide the parents with fundamentally fair procedures.

In *Lassiter,* the Court and three dissenters agreed that the nature of the process due in parental rights termination proceedings turns on a balancing of the "three distinct factors" specified in Mathews v. Eldridge, 424 U.S. 319, 335 (1976): the private interests affected by the proceeding; the risk of error created by the State's chosen procedure; and the countervailing governmental interest supporting use of the challenged procedure.

. . .

In *Lassiter,* to be sure, the Court held that fundamental fairness may be maintained in parental rights termination proceedings even when some procedures are mandated only on a case-by-case basis, rather than through rules of general application. 452 U.S., at 31–32 (natural parent's right to court-appointed counsel should be determined by the trial court, subject to appellate review). But this Court never has approved case-by-case determination of the proper *standard of proof* for a given proceeding. Standards of proof, like other "procedural due process rules[,] are shaped by the risk of error inherent in the truth-finding process as applied to the *generality of cases,* not the rare exceptions." Mathews v. Eldridge, 424 U.S., at 344 (emphasis added). Since the litigants and the factfinder must know at the outset of a given proceeding how the risk of error will be allocated, the standard of proof necessarily must be calibrated in advance. Retrospective case-by-case review cannot preserve fundamental fairness when a class of proceedings is governed by a constitutionally defective evidentiary standard.

In parental rights termination proceedings, the private interest affected is commanding; the risk of error from using a preponderance standard is substantial; and the countervailing governmental interest favoring that standard is comparatively slight. Evaluation of the three *Eldridge* factors compels the conclusion that use of a "fair preponderance of the evidence" standard in such proceedings is inconsistent with due process.

"The extent to which procedural due process must be afforded the recipient is influenced by the extent to which he may be 'condemned to suffer grievous loss.' " Whether the loss threatened by a particular type of proceeding is sufficiently grave to warrant more than average certainty on the part of the factfinder turns on both the nature of the private interest threatened and the permanency of the threatened loss.

Lassiter declared it "plain beyond the need for multiple citation" that a natural parent's "desire for and right to 'the companionship, care, custody, and management of his or her children' " is an interest far more precious than any property right. 452 U.S., at 27, quoting Stanley v. Illinois, 405 U.S., at 651. When the State initiates a parental rights termination proceeding, it seeks not merely to infringe that fundamental liberty interest, but to end it. "If the State prevails, it will have worked a unique kind of deprivation.... A parent's interest in the accuracy and justice of the decision to terminate his or her parental status is, therefore, a commanding one." 452 U.S., at 27.

In government-initiated proceedings to determine juvenile delinquency, this Court has identified losses of individual liberty sufficiently serious to warrant imposition of an elevated burden of proof. Yet juvenile delinquency adjudications, civil commitment, deportation, and denaturalization, at least to a degree, are all *reversible* official actions. Once affirmed on appeal, a New York decision terminating parental rights is *final* and irrevocable. Few forms of state action are both so severe and so irreversible.

Thus, the first *Eldridge* factor—the private interest affected—weighs heavily against use of the preponderance standard at a State-initiated permanent neglect proceeding. We do not deny that the child and his foster parents are also deeply interested in the outcome of that contest. But at the factfinding stage of the New York proceeding, the focus emphatically is not on them.

The factfinding does not purport—and is not intended—to balance the child's interest in a normal family home against the parents' interest in raising the child. Nor does it purport to determine whether the natural parents or the foster parents would provide the better home. Rather, the factfinding hearing pits the State directly against the parents. The State alleges that the natural parents are at fault. The questions disputed and decided are what the State did—"made diligent efforts," § 614.1.(c)—and what the natural parents did not do—"maintain contact with or plan for the future of the child." § 614.1.(d). The State marshals an array of public resources to prove its case and disprove the parents' case. Victory by the State not only makes termination of parental rights possible; it entails a judicial determination that the parents are unfit to raise their own children.[10]

At the factfinding, the State cannot presume that a child and his parents are adversaries. After the State has established parental unfitness at that initial proceeding, the court may assume at the *dispositional* stage that the interests of the child and the natural parents do diverge. But until the State proves parental unfitness, the child and his parents share a vital interest in preventing erroneous termination of their natural relationship.[11]

10. The Family Court judge in the present case expressly refused to terminate petitioners' parental rights on a "non-statutory, no-fault basis." Nor is it clear that the State constitutionally could terminate a parent's rights *without* showing parental unfitness. See Quilloin v. Walcott, 434 U.S. 246, 255 (1978) ("We have little doubt that the Due Process Clause would be offended '[i]f a State were to attempt to force the breakup of a natural family, over the objections of the parents and their children, without some showing of unfitness and for the sole reason that to do so was thought to be in the children's best interest,'" quoting Smith v. Or- ganization of Foster Families, 431 U.S. 816, 862–863 (1977) (Stewart, J., concurring in the judgment)).

11. For a child, the consequences of termination of his natural parents' rights may well be far-reaching. In Colorado, for example, it has been noted: "The child loses the right of support and maintenance, for which he may thereafter be dependent upon society; the right to inherit; and all other rights inherent in the legal parent-child relationship not just for [a limited] period ..., but forever." In re K.S., 33 Colo.App. 72, 76, 515 P.2d 130, 133 (1973).

Thus, at the factfinding, the interests of the child and his natural parents coincide to favor use of error-reducing procedures.

However substantial the foster parents' interests may be, they are not implicated directly in the factfinding stage of a State-initiated permanent neglect proceeding against the natural parents. If authorized, the foster parents may pit their interests directly against those of the natural parents by initiating their own permanent neglect proceeding. Fam.Ct.Act §§ 615, 1055(d); Soc.Serv.Law § 392.7.(c). Alternatively, the foster parents can make their case for custody at the dispositional stage of a State-initiated proceeding, where the judge already has decided the issue of permanent neglect and is focusing on the placement that would serve the child's best interests. Fam.Ct.Act §§ 623, 631. For the foster parents, the State's failure to prove permanent neglect may prolong the delay and uncertainty until their foster child is freed for adoption. But for the natural parents, a finding of permanent neglect can cut off forever their rights in their child. Given this disparity of consequence, we have no difficulty finding that the balance of private interests strongly favors heightened procedural protections.

Under Mathews v. Eldridge, we next must consider both the risk of erroneous deprivation of private interests resulting from use of a "fair preponderance" standard and the likelihood that a higher evidentiary standard would reduce that risk. . . .

In New York, the factfinding stage of a State-initiated permanent neglect proceeding bears many of the indicia of a criminal trial. The Commissioner of Social Services charges the parents with permanent neglect. They are served by summons. The factfinding hearing is conducted pursuant to formal rules of evidence. The State, the parents, and the child are all represented by counsel. The State seeks to establish a series of historical facts about the intensity of its agency's efforts to reunite the family, the infrequency and insubstantiality of the parents' contacts with their child, and the parents' inability or unwillingness to formulate a plan for the child's future. The attorneys submit documentary evidence, and call witnesses who are subject to cross-examination. Based on all the evidence, the judge then determines whether the State has proved the statutory elements of permanent neglect by a fair preponderance of the evidence.

At such a proceeding, numerous factors combine to magnify the risk of erroneous factfinding. Permanent neglect proceedings employ imprecise substantive standards that leave determinations unusually open to the subjective values of the judge. In appraising the nature and quality of a complex series of encounters among the agency, the parents, and the child, the court possesses unusual discretion to underweigh probative facts that might favor the parent.[12] Because parents subject to termination proceed-

---

Some losses cannot be measured. In this case, for example, Jed Santosky was removed from his natural parents' custody when he was only three days old; the judge's finding of permanent neglect effectively foreclosed the possibility that Jed would ever know his natural parents.

12. For example, a New York court appraising an agency's "diligent efforts" to provide the parents with social services can excuse efforts *not* made on the grounds that they would have been "detrimental to the moral and temporal welfare of the child."

ings are often poor, uneducated, or members of minority groups, such proceedings are often vulnerable to judgments based on cultural or class bias.

The State's ability to assemble its case almost inevitably dwarfs the parents' ability to mount a defense. No predetermined limits restrict the sums an agency may spend in prosecuting a given termination proceeding. The State's attorney usually will be expert on the issues contested and the procedures employed at the factfinding hearing, and enjoys full access to all public records concerning the family. The State may call on experts in family relations, psychology, and medicine to bolster its case. Furthermore, the primary witnesses at the hearing will be the agency's own professional caseworkers whom the State has empowered both to investigate the family situation and to testify against the parents. Indeed, because the child is already in agency custody, the State even has the power to shape the historical events that form the basis for termination.[13]

The disparity between the adversaries' litigation resources is matched by a striking asymmetry in their litigation options. Unlike criminal defendants, natural parents have no "double jeopardy" defense against repeated state termination efforts. If the State initially fails to win termination, as New York did here, it always can try once again to cut off the parents' rights after gathering more or better evidence. Yet even when the parents have attained the level of fitness required by the State, they have no similar means by which they can forestall future termination efforts.

Coupled with a "preponderance of the evidence" standard, these factors create a significant prospect of erroneous termination. A standard of proof that by its very terms demands consideration of the quantity, rather than the quality, of the evidence may misdirect the factfinder in the marginal case. Given the weight of the private interests at stake, the social cost of even occasional error is sizable.

. . .

The Appellate Division approved New York's preponderance standard on the ground that it properly "balanced rights possessed by the child ... with those of the natural parents...." 75 App.Div.2d, at 910, 427 N.Y.S.2d,

Fam.Ct.Act § 614.1.(c). In determining whether the parent "substantially and continuously or repeatedly" failed to "maintain contact with ... the child." § 614.1.(d), the judge can discount actual visits or communications on the grounds that they were insubstantial or "overtly demonstrat[ed] a lack of affection and concerned parenthood." Soc. Serv.Law § 384–b.7.(b). When determining whether the parent planned for the child's future, the judge can reject as unrealistic plans based on overly optimistic estimates of physical or financial ability. § 384.b.7.(c)....

13. In this case, for example, the parents claim that the State sought court orders denying them the right to visit their children, which would have prevented them from maintaining the contact required by Fam.Ct. Act § 614.1.(d). The parents further claim that the State cited their rejection of social services they found offensive or superfluous as proof of the agency's "diligent efforts" and their own "failure to plan" for the children's future.

We need not accept these statements as true to recognize that the State's unusual ability to structure the evidence increases the risk of an erroneous factfinding. Of course, the disparity between the litigants' resources will be vastly greater in States where there is no statutory right to court-appointed counsel....

at 320. By so saying, the court suggested that a preponderance standard properly allocates the risk of error *between* the parents and the child. That view is fundamentally mistaken.

The court's theory assumes that termination of the natural parents' rights invariably will benefit the child.[15] Yet we have noted above that the parents and the child share an interest in avoiding erroneous termination. Even accepting the court's assumption, we cannot agree with its conclusion that a preponderance standard fairly distributes the risk of error between parent and child. Use of that standard reflects the judgment that society is nearly neutral between erroneous termination of parental rights and erroneous failure to terminate those rights. Cf. In re Winship, 397 U.S., at 371 (Harlan, J., concurring). For the child, the likely consequence of an erroneous failure to terminate is preservation of an uneasy status quo.[16] For the natural parents, however, the consequence of an erroneous termination is the unnecessary destruction of their natural family. A standard that allocates the risk of error nearly equally between those two outcomes does not reflect properly their relative severity.

Two state interests are at stake in parental rights termination proceedings—a *parens patriae* interest in preserving and promoting the welfare of the child and a fiscal and administrative interest in reducing the cost and burden of such proceedings. A standard of proof more strict than preponderance of the evidence is consistent with both interests.

"Since the State has an urgent interest in the welfare of the child, it shares the parent's interest in an accurate and just decision" at the *factfinding* proceeding. As *parens patriae,* the State's goal is to provide the child with a permanent home. Yet while there is still reason to believe that

---

15. This is a hazardous assumption at best. Even when a child's natural home is imperfect, permanent removal from that home will not necessarily improve his welfare. See, e.g., Wald, State Intervention on Behalf of "Neglected" Children: A Search for Realistic Standards, 27 Stan.L.Rev. 985, 993 (1975) ("In fact, under current practice, coercive intervention frequently results in placing a child in a more detrimental situation than he would be in without intervention.").

Nor does termination of parental rights necessarily ensure adoption. See Brief for Community Action for Legal Services, Inc., et al., as *Amicus Curiae* 22–23 (in 1979; only 12% of the adoptable children in foster care in New York City were actually adopted, although some had been waiting for years, citing Redirecting Foster Care, A Report to the Mayor of the City of New York 69, 43 (1980)). Even when a child eventually finds an adoptive family, he may spend years moving between state institutions and "temporary" foster placements after his ties to his natural parents have been severed. See Smith v. Organization of Foster Families, 431 U.S., at

833–838 (describing the "limbo" of the New York foster care system).

16. When the termination proceeding occurs, the child is not living at his natural home. A child cannot be adjudicated "permanently neglected" until, "for a period of more than a year," he has been in "the care of an authorized agency." Soc.Serv.Law § 384–b.7.(a); Fam.Ct.Act § 614.1.(d). See also dissenting opinion, at 20–21.

Under New York law, a judge has ample discretion to ensure that, once removed from his natural parents on grounds of neglect, a child will not return to a hostile environment. In this case, when the State's initial termination effort failed for lack of proof, see n. 4, supra, the court simply issued orders under Fam.Ct.Act § 1055(b) extending the period of the child's foster home placement. See App. 19–20. See also Fam.Ct.Act § 632(b) (when State's permanent neglect petition is dismissed for insufficient evidence, judge retains jurisdiction to reconsider underlying orders of placement); § 633 (judge may suspend judgment at dispositional hearing for an additional year).

positive, nurturing parent-child relationships exist, the *parens patriae* interest favors preservation, not severance, of natural familial bonds.[17] § 384–b.1.(a)(ii). "[T]he State registers no gain towards its declared goals when it separates children from the custody of fit parents." Stanley v. Illinois, 405 U.S., at 652.

The State's interest in finding the child an alternative permanent home arises only "when it is *clear* that the natural parent cannot or will not provide a normal family home for the child." Soc.Serv.Law § 384–b.1.(a)(iv) (emphasis added). At the factfinding, that goal is served by procedures that promote an accurate determination of whether the natural parents can and will provide a normal home.

Unlike a constitutional requirement of hearings, or court-appointed counsel, a stricter standard of proof would reduce factual error without imposing substantial fiscal burdens upon the State. . . .

Nor would an elevated standard of proof create any real administrative burdens for the State's factfinders. New York Family Court judges already are familiar with a higher evidentiary standard in other parental rights termination proceedings not involving permanent neglect. . . . New York also demands at least clear and convincing evidence in proceedings of far less moment than parental rights termination proceedings.

. . .

We . . . express no view on the merits of petitioners' claims. At a hearing conducted under a constitutionally proper standard, they may or may not prevail. Without deciding the outcome under any of the standards we have approved, we vacate the judgment of the Appellate Division and remand the case for further proceedings not inconsistent with this opinion.

■ Justice Rehnquist, with whom the Chief Justice, Justice White, and Justice O'Connor join, dissenting.

. . . New York has created an exhaustive program to assist parents in regaining the custody of their children and to protect parents from the unfair deprivation of their parental rights. And yet the majority's myopic scrutiny of the standard of proof blinds it to the very considerations and procedures which make the New York scheme "fundamentally fair."

[The opinion reviews the procedures of the New York statute both with regard to temporary removal of children from the home and termination of parental rights.]

The three children to which this case relates were removed from petitioners' custody in 1973 and 1974, before petitioners' other two children were born. The removals were made pursuant to the procedures detailed above and in response to what can only be described as shockingly abusive treatment.[10] At the temporary removal hearing held before the

---

17. Any *parens patriae* interest in terminating the natural parents' rights arises only at the dispositional phase, *after* the parents have been found unfit.

10. Tina Apel, the oldest of petitioners' five children, was removed from their custody by court order in November 1973 when she was two years old. Removal proceedings were commenced in response to complaints by

Family Court on September 30, 1974, petitioners were represented by counsel, and allowed the Ulster County Department of Social Services ("Department") to take custody of the three children.

Temporary removal of the children was continued at an evidentiary hearing held before the Family Court in December 1975, after which the court issued a written opinion concluding that petitioners were unable to resume their parental responsibilities due to personality disorders. Unsatisfied with the progress petitioners were making, the court also directed the Department to reduce to writing the plan which it had designed to solve the problems at petitioners' home and reunite the family.

A plan for providing petitioners with extensive counseling and training services was submitted to the court and approved in February 1976. Under the plan, petitioners received training by a mother's aide, a nutritional aide, and a public health nurse, and counseling at a family planning clinic. In addition, the plan provided psychiatric treatment and vocational training for the father, and counseling at a family service center for the mother. Between early 1976 and the final termination decision in April 1979, the State spent more than $15,000 in these efforts to rehabilitate petitioners as parents.

Petitioners' response to the State's effort was marginal at best. They wholly disregarded some of the available services and participated only sporadically in the others. As a result, and out of growing concern over the length of the childrens' stay in foster care, the Department petitioned in September 1976 for permanent termination of petitioners' parental rights so that the children could be adopted by other families. Although the Family Court recognized that petitioners' reaction to the State's efforts was generally "non-responsive, even resentful," the fact that they were "at least superficially cooperative" led it to conclude that there was yet hope of further improvement and an eventual reuniting of the family. Accordingly, the petition for permanent termination was dismissed.

Whatever progress petitioners were making prior to the 1976 termination hearing, they made little or no progress thereafter. In October 1978, the Department again filed a termination petition alleging that petitioners had completely failed to plan for the childrens' future despite the considerable efforts rendered in their behalf. This time, the Family Court agreed. The court found that petitioners had "failed in any meaningful way to take advantage of the many social and rehabilitative services that have not only been made available to them but have been diligently urged upon them." In addition, the court found that the "infrequent" visits "between the parents and their children were at best superficial and devoid of any real emotional

neighbors and reports from a local hospital that Tina had suffered injuries in petitioners' home including a fractured left femur, treated with a homemade splint; bruises on the upper arms, forehead, flank, and spine; and abrasions of the upper leg. The following summer John Santosky III, petitioners' second oldest child, was also removed from petitioners' custody. John, who was less than one year old at the time, was admitted to the hospital suffering malnutrition, bruises on the eye and forehead, cuts on the foot, blisters on the hand, and multiple pin pricks on the back. Jed Santosky, the third oldest of petitioners' children, was removed from his parents' custody when only three days old as a result of the abusive treatment of the two older children.

content." The court thus found "nothing in the situation which holds out any hope that [petitioners] may ever become financially self sufficient or emotionally mature enough to be independent of the services of social agencies. More than a reasonable amount of time has passed and still, in the words of the case workers, there has been no discernible forward movement. At some point in time, it must be said 'enough is enough.' "

In accordance with the statutory requirements set forth above, the court found that petitioners' failure to plan for the future of their children, who were then seven, five, and four years old and had been out of petitioners' custody for at least four years, rose to the level of permanent neglect. At a subsequent dispositional hearing, the court terminated petitioners' parental rights, thereby freeing the three children for adoption.

As this account demonstrates, the State's extraordinary four-year effort to reunite petitioners' family was not just unsuccessful, it was altogether rebuffed by parents unwilling to improve their circumstances sufficiently to permit a return of their children. At every step of this protracted process petitioners were accorded those procedures and protections which traditionally have been required by due process of law. Moreover, from the beginning to the end of this sad story all judicial determinations were made by one family court judge. After four and one-half years of involvement with petitioners, more than seven complete hearings, and additional periodic supervision of the State's rehabilitative efforts, the judge no doubt was intimately familiar with this case and the prospects for petitioners' rehabilitation.

It is inconceivable to me that these procedures were "fundamentally unfair" to petitioners. Only by its obsessive focus on the standard of proof and its almost complete disregard of the facts of this case does the majority find otherwise.[11] ... [S]uch a focus does not comport with the flexible

11. The majority finds, without any reference to the facts of this case, that "numerous factors [in New York termination proceedings] combine to magnify the risk of erroneous factfinding." Among the factors identified by the majority are the "unusual discretion" of the family court judge "to underweigh probative facts that might favor the parent"; the often uneducated, minority status of the parents and their consequent "vulnerab[ility] to judgments based on cultural or class bias"; the "State's ability to assemble its case," which "dwarfs the parents' ability to mount a defense" by including an unlimited budget, expert attorneys, and "full access to all public records concerning the family"; and the fact that "natural parents have no 'double jeopardy' defense against repeated state 'efforts,' with more or better evidence," to terminate parental rights "even when the parents have attained the level of fitness required by the State." In short, the majority characterizes the State as a wealthy and powerful bully bent on taking children away

from defenseless parents. Such characterization finds no support in the record.

The intent of New York has been stated with eminent clarity: "the [S]tate's *first obligation* is to *help* the family with services to *prevent* its break-up or to *reunite* it if the child has already left home." SSL § 384-b(1)(a)(iii) (emphasis added). There is simply no basis in fact for believing, as the majority does, that the State does not mean what it says; indeed, the facts of this case demonstrate that New York has gone the extra mile in seeking to effectuate its declared purpose. More importantly, there should be no room in the jurisprudence of this Court for decisions based on unsupported inaccurate assumptions.

A brief examination of the "factors" relied upon by the majority demonstrates its error. The "unusual" discretion of the family court judge to consider the "affectio[n] and concer[n]" displayed by parents during visits with their children, is nothing more than

standard of fundamental fairness embodied in the Due Process Clause of the Fourteenth Amendment.

In addition to the basic fairness of the process afforded petitioners, the standard of proof chosen by New York clearly reflects a constitutionally permissible balance of the interests at stake in this case. The standard of proof "represents an attempt to instruct the factfinder concerning the degree of confidence our society thinks he should have in the correctness of factual conclusions for a particular type of adjudication." In re Winship, 397 U.S. 358, 370 (1970) (Harlan, J. concurring); Addington v. Texas, 441 U.S. 418, 423 (1979). In this respect, the standard of proof is a crucial component of legal process, the primary function of which is "to minimize the risk of erroneous decisions."[12]

In determining the propriety of a particular standard of proof in a given case, however, it is not enough simply to say that we are trying to minimize the risk of error. Because errors in factfinding affect more than one interest, we try to minimize error as to those interests which we consider to be most important. As Justice Harlan explained in his well-known concurrence to In re Winship:

"In a lawsuit between two parties, a factual error can make a difference in one of two ways. First, it can result in a judgment in favor of

discretion to consider reality; there is not one shred of evidence in this case suggesting that the determination of the family court was "based on cultural or class bias"; if parents lack the "ability to mount a defense," the State provides them with the full services of an attorney, FCA § 262, and they, like the State, have "full access to all *public* records concerning the family" (emphasis added); and the absence of "double jeopardy" protection simply recognizes the fact that family problems are often ongoing and may in the future warrant action that currently is unnecessary. In this case the family court dismissed the first termination petition because it desired to give petitioners "the benefit of the doubt," and a second opportunity to raise themselves to "an acceptable minimal level of competency as parents." It was their complete failure to do so that prompted the second, successful termination petition.

12. It is worth noting that the significance of the standard of proof in New York parental termination proceedings differs from the significance of the standard in other forms of litigation. In the usual adjudicatory setting, the factfinder has had little or no prior exposure to the facts of the case. His only knowledge of those facts comes from the evidence adduced at trial, and he renders his findings solely upon the basis of that evidence. Thus, normally, the standard of proof is a crucial factor in the final outcome of the case, for it is the scale upon which the factfinder weighs his knowledge and makes his decision.

Although the standard serves the same function in New York parental termination proceedings, additional assurances of accuracy are present in its application. As was adduced at oral argument, the practice in New York is to assign one judge to supervise a case from the initial temporary removal of the child to the final termination of parental rights. Therefore, as discussed above, the factfinder is intimately familiar with the case before the termination proceedings ever begin. Indeed, as in this case, he often will have been closely involved in protracted efforts to rehabilitate the parents. Even if a change in judges occurs, the Family Court retains jurisdiction of the case and the newly assigned judge may take judicial notice of all prior proceedings. Given this familiarity with the case, and the necessarily lengthy efforts which must precede a termination action in New York, decisions in termination cases are made by judges steeped in the background of the case and peculiarly able to judge the accuracy of evidence placed before them. This does not mean that the standard of proof in these cases can escape due process scrutiny, only that additional assurances of accuracy attend the application of the standard in New York termination proceedings.

the plaintiff when the true facts warrant a judgment for the defendant. The analogue in a criminal case would be the conviction of an innocent man. On the other hand, an erroneous factual determination can result in a judgment for the defendant when the true facts justify a judgment in plaintiff's favor. The criminal analogue would be the acquittal of a guilty man.

The standard of proof influences the relative frequency of these two types of erroneous outcomes. If, for example, the standard of proof for a criminal trial were a preponderance of the evidence rather than proof beyond a reasonable doubt, there would be a smaller risk of factual errors that result in freeing guilty persons, but a far greater risk of factual errors that result in convicting the innocent. Because the standard of proof affects the comparative frequency of these two types of erroneous outcomes, the choice of the standard to be applied in a particular kind of litigation should, in a rational world, reflect an assessment of the comparative social disutility of each." 397 U.S., at 370–372.

When the standard of proof is understood as reflecting such an assessment, an examination of the interests at stake in a particular case becomes essential to determining the propriety of the specified standard of proof. Because proof by a preponderance of the evidence requires that "[t]he litigants ... share the risk of error in a roughly equal fashion," Addington v. Texas, supra, 441 U.S., at 423, it rationally should be applied only when the interests at stake are of roughly equal societal importance. The interests at stake in this case demonstrate that New York has selected a constitutionally permissible standard of proof.

On one side is the interest of parents in a continuation of the family unit and the raising of their own children. The importance of this interest cannot easily be overstated. Few consequences of judicial action are so grave as the severance of natural family ties. Even the convict committed to prison and thereby deprived of his physical liberty often retains the love and support of family members. "This Court's decisions have by now made plain beyond the need for multiple citation that a parent's desire for and right to 'the companionship, care, custody and management of his or her children' is an important interest that 'undeniably warrants deference and, absent a powerful countervailing interest, protection.' Stanley v. Illinois, 405 U.S. 645, 651." Lassiter v. Department of Social Services, 452 U.S. 18, 27 (1981). In creating the scheme at issue in this case, the New York legislature was expressly aware of this right of parents "to bring up their own children." SSL § 384–b(1)(a)(ii).

On the other side of the termination proceeding are the often counter-vailing interests of the child.[13] A stable, loving homelife is essential to a

13. The majority dismisses the child's interest in the accuracy of determinations made at the factfinding hearing because "[t]he factfinding does not purport ... to balance the child's interest in a normal family life against the parents' interest in raising the child," but instead "pits the State direct-ly against the parents." Only "[a]fter the State has established parental unfitness," the majority reasons, may the court "assume ... that the interests of the child and the natural parents do diverge."

child's physical, emotional, and spiritual well-being. It requires no citation of authority to assert that children who are abused in their youth generally face extraordinary problems developing into responsible, productive citizens. The same can be said of children who, though not physically or emotionally abused, are passed from one foster home to another with no constancy of love, trust, or discipline. If the Family Court makes an incorrect factual determination resulting in a failure to terminate a parent-child relationship which rightfully should be ended, the child involved must return either to an abusive home or to the often unstable world of foster care. The reality of these risks is magnified by the fact that the only families faced with termination actions are those which have voluntarily surrendered custody of their child to the State, or, as in this case, those from which the child has been removed by judicial action because of threatened irreparable injury through abuse or neglect. Permanent neglect findings also occur only in families where the child has been in foster care for at least one year.

In addition to the child's interest in a normal homelife, "the State has an urgent interest in the welfare of the child." Lassiter v. Department of Social Services, supra, at 27.[16] Few could doubt that the most valuable resource of a self-governing society is its population of children who will one day become adults and themselves assume the responsibility of self-governance. "A democratic society rests, for its continuance, upon the healthy, well-rounded growth of young people into full maturity as citizens, with all that implies." Prince v. Massachusetts, 321 U.S. 158, 168 (1944).

This reasoning misses the mark. The child has an interest in the outcome of the factfinding hearing independent of that of the parent. To be sure, "the child and his parents share a vital interest in preventing *erroneous* termination of their natural relationship." (emphasis added). But the child's interest in a continuation of the family unit exists only to the extent that such a continuation would not be harmful to him. An error *in the factfinding hearing* that results in a failure to terminate a parent-child relationship which rightfully should be terminated may well detrimentally affect the child.

The preponderance of the evidence standard, which allocates the risk of error more or less evenly, is employed when the social disutility of error *in either direction* is roughly equal—that is, when an incorrect finding of fault would produce consequences as undesirable as the consequences that would be produced by an incorrect finding of *no* fault. Only when the disutility of error in one direction discernibly outweighs the disutility of error in the other direction do we choose, by means of the standard of proof, to reduce the likelihood of the more onerous outcome. See In re Winship, 397 U.S. 358, 370–372 (1970) (Harlan, J., concurring).

New York's adoption of the preponderance of the evidence standard reflects its conclusion that the undesirable consequence of an erroneous finding of parental unfitness—the unwarranted termination of the family relationship—is roughly equal to the undesirable consequence of an erroneous finding of parental fitness—the risk of permanent injury to the child either by return of the child to an abusive home or by the child's continued lack of a permanent home. Such a conclusion is well within the province of state legislatures. It cannot be said that the New York procedures are unconstitutional simply because a majority of the members of this Court disagree with the New York legislature's weighing of the interests of the parents and the child in an error-free factfinding hearing.

16. The majority's conclusion that a state interest in the child's well-being arises only after a determination of parental unfitness suffers from the same error as its assertion that the child has no interest, separate from that of its parents, in the accuracy of the factfinding hearing.

Thus, "the whole community" has an interest "that children be both safeguarded from abuses and given opportunities for growth into free and independent well-developed ... citizens." Id., at 165.

When, in the context of a permanent neglect termination proceeding, the interests of the child and the State in a stable, nurturing homelife are balanced against the interests of the parents in the rearing of their child, it cannot be said that either set of interests is so clearly paramount as to require that the risk of error be allocated to one side or the other. Accordingly, a State constitutionally may conclude that the risk of error should be borne in roughly equal fashion by use of the preponderance of the evidence standard of proof....

For the reasons heretofore stated, I believe that the Court today errs in concluding that the New York standard of proof in parental-rights termination proceedings violates due process of law. The decision disregards New York's earnest efforts to *aid* parents in regaining the custody of their children and a host of procedural protections placed around parental rights and interests. The Court finds a constitutional violation only by a tunnel-vision application of due process principles that altogether loses sight of the unmistakable fairness of the New York procedure.

Even more worrisome, today's decision cavalierly rejects the considered judgment of the New York legislature in an area traditionally entrusted to state care. The Court thereby begins, I fear, a trend of federal intervention in state family law matters which surely will stifle creative responses to vexing problems. Accordingly, I dissent.

NOTES

(1) Does it seem unusual that the facts of the case were revealed only in a footnote to the dissent? Some persons feel that judicial decisions regarding termination of parental rights have been more concerned with procedural due process than child protection. Is the "level playing field" suggested in the dissent consistent with such an argument? For further discussion of standards for termination, see Douglas E. Cressler, Requiring Proof Beyond a Reasonable Doubt in Termination Cases, 32 U. Louisville J.Fam.L. 785 (1994).

(2) **Standard of Proof in Action by a Parent.** *Santosky* involved a state's action to terminate parental rights. In *In re T.R.*, 502 Pa. 165, 465 A.2d 642 (1983), the Pennsylvania Supreme Court held that although proceedings undertaken by an individual (in the particular case, a parent) may not involve as great a disparity in litigating resources, "the same 'particularly important' parental interests are at stake." Also "the private interest affected is commanding; the risk of error from using a preponderance standard is substantial; and the countervailing governmental interest favoring that standard is comparatively slight." Thus the "clear and convincing" standard was held to apply in all proceedings to terminate parental rights involuntarily. See also *In re Adoption of Atencio*, 539 Pa. 161, 650 A.2d 1064 (1994).

(3) **Constitutional Attacks Asserting Vagueness.** Parental rights termination laws have been challenged under the "void for vagueness" doctrine in a number of states. See, e.g., *Alsager v. District Ct. of Polk Cty.*, 406 F.Supp. 10 (S.D.Iowa 1975). Typically these have focused on statutes with few or no specific criteria for termination. Such challenges were rejected in *In re Doe*, 100 N.M. 92,

666 P.2d 771 (1983), and *In re Brooks*, 228 Kan. 541, 618 P.2d 814 (1980). Newer statutes, such as the Virginia provision that follows at p. 765 infra, typically are more detailed and specific about what conduct can be used to establish unfitness.

(4) **In *M.L.B. v. S.L.J.*,** 519 U.S. 102, 117 S.Ct. 555, 136 L.Ed.2d 483 (1996), the Supreme Court of the United States held that a Mississippi statute conditioning appeal from a trial court's termination of a mother's parental rights on advance payment of record preparation fees (estimated at $2,352.36 in the particular case) violated both equal protection and due process guarantees of the Fourteenth Amendment. The appellant mother's application to appeal in forma pauperis had been denied by the Mississippi Supreme Court because the state allows in forma pauperis proceedings only at the trial level in civil cases.

In a 6–3 decision, the U.S. Supreme Court noted that although the trial judge had stated in his order that the decision to terminate parental rights was based on clear and convincing evidence, the order contained no description of the evidence. In its decision the Supreme Court drew from two lines of cases. The first was based on two family law cases, *Boddie v. Connecticut*, 401 U.S. 371, 91 S.Ct. 780, 28 L.Ed.2d 113 (1971) (holding that a state could not deny access to judicial proceedings for divorce because of inability to pay court costs) and *Lassiter v. Department of Social Services*, 452 U.S. 18, 101 S.Ct. 2153, 68 L.Ed.2d 640 (1981) (discussed in detail in the *Santosky* opinion). The second line stems from *Griffin v. Illinois,* 351 U.S. 12, 76 S.Ct. 585, 100 L.Ed. 891 (1956) and *Mayer v. Chicago,* 404 U.S. 189, 92 S.Ct. 410, 30 L.Ed.2d 372 (1971). The Court noted its past recognition that termination of parental rights cases are "apart from mine run civil actions, even from other domestic relations matters such as divorce, paternity, and child custody." Citing *Lassiter,* it added that "termination decrees 'wor[k] a unique kind of deprivation' ".

In re Guardianship of S.A.W.

Supreme Court of Oklahoma, 1993.
856 P.2d 286.

■ ALMA WILSON, JUSTICE:

The question before this Court is whether the trial court erred in terminating the parental rights of the appellants. We have previously granted certiorari to determine whether independent counsel should have been appointed for the minor child. We conclude that the minor child was entitled to be represented by independent counsel. Because the appellants did not preserve other issues presented in its brief in chief, we address only the issue tendered in the petition for certiorari. . . .

A review of the evidence reveals the facts that follow. S.A.W., born December 22, 1985, is the daughter of the appellants, Eric Winbigler and Deborah McCallum, a/k/a Deborah Winbigler.[2] The appellants have a younger son, who lives with them. Since March 4, 1988, S.A.W. has continuously resided with the appellee, Joan Torres, sister of Winbigler, and her husband, Juan Torres, Jr. Letters of guardianship of S.A.W. were issued to

---

2. Apparently, the appellants are not married. The transcript of the court hearing of January 10, 1990, reveals that the parties had claimed a common-law marriage at an earlier hearing, but they are residents of California, which does not recognize such a marriage. Elden v. Sheldon, 46 Cal.3d 267, 758 P.2d 582, 587, 250 Cal.Rptr. 254, 259 (1988); Norman v. Norman, 121 Cal. 620, 54 P. 143, 146 (1898). The trial judge concluded that they were not married.

appellee on March 21, 1988. Within three months of the issuance of those letters of guardianship, the appellants moved to terminate the guardianship.[3] The motion was denied on July 18, 1988. The denial was affirmed by the Court of Appeals, and mandate issued October 2, 1989.

Within two months of the mandate, the appellee filed a petition to terminate the parental rights of the appellants, and declare S.A.W. eligible for adoption without the consent of the natural parents. The petition was filed November 29, 1989. The sole reason for termination was failure of the appellants to provide support for a period of twelve months preceding the filing of the petition. The guardianship court has not entered any orders for the payment of child support and appellee does not allege otherwise. Because there was no order specifying an amount to be paid by the appellants to the appellee, the petition to terminate alleges failure of the appellants to support consistent with their means and earning capacity.

Hearing was scheduled for January 8, 1990. The appellants appeared without counsel and informed the court that they were indigent. Consequently, the trial court appointed the public defender to represent the appellants and reset the hearing to January 10, 1990. The testimony concerning the financial condition of the appellants was unclear. The testimony revealed that for a portion of 1988, they worked for their landlord in exchange for rent and food. There was no evidence of steady income during the period from March, 1988, to November, 1989. Both appellants testified that during 1990 they were employed in the towing business, although their incomes were subject to expenses for their tow trucks.

The appellants testified they sent Christmas and birthday gifts in 1988, and brought gifts to Oklahoma for Christmas and birthday in 1989. Ms. McCallum made phone calls to the appellee and spoke with her daughter. She sent about eight letters, but the appellee testified that she neither read the letters to S.A.W., nor told her about them. The appellee testified that S.A.W. calls the appellee, her mother and Mr. Torres, her father. She further testified that she had not requested child support.[7]

After hearing the evidence, the trial judge pronounced her judgment. She referred to the evidence in the previous guardianship case, and made the following statement: I think the law is very clear that whether there has been an order for the payment of Child Support, if it can be shown that the parents could, in any way, pay any amount of support and if they failed to make any payments towards support as these parents have failed to do, other than the purchase of "birthday and Christmas gifts" that were sent in nineteen eighty-eight (1988), that the Court must, if it can be shown in any way that they could have sent any amount, terminate their parental rights if it's in the best interest of the child. This child has now been out of their home for almost two (2) years. I don't have to rely on Mrs. Torres' testimony that the child does not know her parents, does not know who they are, or even who she's talking to when they call, or when she calls

---

3. The motion was filed June 6, 1988.

7. Mr. Winbigler testified that Deborah had asked if the Torres wanted anything. He stated that they refused. Both Mrs. Torres and Ms. McCallum testified that support money was never discussed.

them, and I can't believe that it would be in the best interest of the child at this time to return the custody of the child to the parents and I do believe it would be in the best interest of the child for their parental rights to be terminated, and for an adoption proceeding to be had without their consent. And that is the Order of the Court. Transcript of Hearing, January 10, 1990, pp. 108–109.[8]

In their petition for certiorari the appellants argue that independent counsel should have been appointed to protect the interest of S.A.W. in the proceedings to terminate parental rights. They correctly observe that a termination of parental rights has profound implications upon the rights of the child as well as the parents. Siblings may even lose contact with each other. S.A.W., as noted above, has a younger brother. The appellee answers that the child's interests are protected by the appellee because an action to terminate parental rights for wilful failure to support is actually brought for the benefit of the child; that the legal contest is not between the guardian and the parents, but between the child and the non-supporting parents.

In Matter of Chad S., 580 P.2d 983 (Okla.1978), a mother's parental rights to her daughter had been terminated at a hearing in which she was neither represented by counsel, nor advised of any right to court-appointed counsel. In reversing and remanding the matter, this Court held that the mother had a constitutional right to assistance of counsel, and that counsel must be appointed for indigent parents unless knowingly and intelligently waived. This Court found an obligation to advise parents of that right. "Where the assistance of counsel is a constitutional requisite, the right to be furnished counsel does not depend upon request." Chad S., 580 P.2d at 986. The relationship of parents to their children is a fundamental, constitutionally-protected right. Chad S., 580 P.2d at 986. In that case, the Court also noted that Oklahoma has statutory authority for counsel to be appointed for indigent parties to a termination proceeding.[9] If a parent has a right

---

8. Our reversal of the trial court order terminating parental rights is not a determination of custody. Custody of S.A.W. is not an issue herein.

9. Chad S., 580 P.2d at 985. The case cites 10 O.S.1971 §§ 24(a) and 1109(b). Section 24 was amended (1989 Okla.Sess.Laws, ch. 363, § 1) without change to the first paragraph except subsection "(a)" was changed to "A." Subsection A provides: "When it appears to the court that the minor or his parent or guardian desires counsel but is indigent and cannot for that reason employ counsel, the court shall appoint counsel. In any case in which it appears to the court that there is such a conflict of interest between a parent or guardian and child that one attorney could not properly represent both, the court may appoint counsel, in addition to counsel already employed by a parent or guardian or appointed by the court to represent the minor or parent or guardian, provid-

ed that in all counties having public defenders, said public defenders shall assume the duties of representation in proceedings such as above." [Now codified as 10 O.S.1991, § 24(A)]. Section 1109 has been amended eight times since 1971. Subsection B of § 1109 has not changed since 1986 and provides: "If the parents, guardian, or other legal custodian of the child requests an attorney and is found to be without sufficient financial means, counsel shall be appointed by the court if a petition has been filed alleging that the child is a deprived child, a child in need of supervision, or a child in need of treatment, or if termination of parental rights is a possible remedy, provided that the court may appoint counsel without such request, if it deems representation by counsel necessary to protect the interest of the parents, guardian or other legal custodian. If the child is not otherwise represented by counsel, whenever a petition is filed pursuant to the

to be represented in a case involving termination of parental rights, the child, whose own rights are in jeopardy of being terminated, has equal interests at stake and must also be represented. The issue is whether that child must have separate counsel to preserve the child's constitutional rights.

Two years after Chad S., this Court handed down Matter of T.M.H., 613 P.2d 468 (Okla.1980). In that case, the state petitioned to terminate the parental rights of the mother and father of Teresa M. The parents filed a motion to appoint independent counsel to represent their five-year-old daughter, but the motion was denied by the trial court. On appeal, this Court, as in Chad S., cited 10 O.S.1971, §§ 24(a) and 1109(b), and held that these statutes made appointment of counsel mandatory if an indigent so requested counsel. This Court then went on to consider what must be done if no request for counsel was made on behalf of the child.

The Court reasoned that in a termination proceeding, if a child is not represented by independent counsel, the child is caught in the middle while each attorney argues from his client's viewpoint. Although each side phrases arguments in terms of the child's best interests, each attorney desires to prevail for his client, who is not the child. But when the trial court appoints an attorney for the child, testimony is presented and cross-examination is done by an advocate whose only interest is the welfare of the child. After stating that trial judges too often assume the interests of the child are adequately protected by the Department of Human Services, this Court held that under 10 O.S.1971, §§ 24 and 1109, independent counsel must be appointed to represent the children if termination of parental rights is sought. T.M.H., 613 P.2d at 471. The new rule was given prospective application.

Matter of Christopher W., 626 P.2d 1320 (Okla.1980), cited T.M.H., and noted its holding in footnote 1. The issue in Christopher W. was which party would pay the attorney fees of the child. This Court held that parents or other litigants are not responsible for the child's attorney fees and reasoned that 10 O.S.1971, § 24 requires the child's attorney to be paid out of the court fund, or be represented by the Public Defender in counties that have Public Defenders.

Davis v. Davis, 708 P.2d 1102, 1113 (Okla.1985), held that 10 O.S.1981, § 1130 was available only for state initiated cases, and not invocable in a private suit by the custodial parent who seeks termination of parental rights of the noncustodial parent. But in 1986, the legislature added subsection D to § 1130, allowing such a private suit.

We can see no rational reason to hold that in state initiated termination cases, the child is entitled to an attorney, while in privately initiated termination cases based on the same statute, § 1130, the child is not entitled to an attorney. The state would seem to be more likely to remain neutral in a dispute than a private party who has a private interest in

provisions of Section 1103 of this title, the court shall appoint a separate attorney, who shall not be a district attorney, for the child regardless of any attempted waiver by the parent or other legal custodian of the child of the right of the child to be represented by counsel.'' [Now codified at 10 O.S.Supp. 1992, § 1109(B)].

termination of parental rights. A respondent parent has an equally partisan interest in maintaining parental rights.

In applying this rule to the facts of the case it is clear how requiring that S.A.W. be represented by independent counsel could work for her benefit. When the trial court pronounced judgment, the court's concerns were the failure of the parents to make any payment, other than gifts, in the year prior to the filing of the petition to terminate parental rights. Although the trial judge states that she believed that termination of parental rights were in the best interest of the child, there was no independent counsel arguing the child's best interests. The presentation of evidence concentrated on the financial status of the parents, and that evidence was confusing. Independent counsel may have chosen to try to clarify that testimony. Such counsel, although having no objection to the continuation of the guardianship, may have presented evidence that the child's best interests were to maintain parental ties.[11] Whatever such counsel may have chosen to argue is speculative, because S.A.W. had no such advocate. We therefore expand the holding of T.M.H. to include privately initiated petitions for termination of parental rights.

Because S.A.W. was entitled to independent counsel but was not appointed one, we VACATE the decision of the Court of Appeals, and REVERSE and REMAND the judgment of the trial court for disposition of the matter in a manner consistent with the views expressed herein.

NOTES

(1) Some states specifically provide for appointment of counsel for children in parental rights termination cases. It would seem that several obvious duties of such counsel would be to investigate the facts fully and to examine the possible alternatives available under the circumstances. What other functions do you believe that counsel should serve? How much should counsel be an advocate for the child's own choice rather than a neutral evaluator for the court? The March 1996 issue of the Fordham Law Review is devoted in its entirety to Ethical Issues in the Legal Representation of Children. With regard to whether children should have standing to intervene in family law cases in which their interests may be affected, see *Miller v. Miller*, 677 A.2d 64 (Me.1996), supra at page 440.

(2) As the Supreme Court noted in *Santosky,* the question of parental right to counsel in a termination proceeding was addressed earlier in *Lassiter v. Department of Social Services*, 452 U.S. 18, 101 S.Ct. 2153, 68 L.Ed.2d 640 (1981). The petitioner in *Lassiter* was a mother whose infant son had been adjudicated a neglected child and placed in custody of a state agency in 1975. A year later the mother was convicted of second-degree murder and she began serving a 25–40 year prison term. In 1978 a termination proceeding was instituted. Petitioner was brought from prison to the hearing. Finding that she had been given ample time to obtain counsel and that her failure to do so was without just cause, the court did not postpone the proceeding. Because petitioner did not aver that she was indigent,

---

11. Because of the fundamental rights of the child involved, a trial court has inherent discretion in cases involving the termination of parental rights. In re Adoption of A.G.K., 728 P.2d 1, 4–5 (Okla.Ct.App.1986). Title 10 O.S. 1991, § 1130 specifically provides in subsection A that "a court may terminate the rights of a parent to a child" in certain situations. (Emphasis added.) Discretion is granted to avoid a termination that the court finds to be contrary to the best interests of the child.

counsel was not appointed for her. During the hearing petitioner and her mother responded to questions by the court, and petitioner cross-examined a social worker. The court terminated petitioner's parental rights, finding that she had "willfully failed to maintain concern or responsibility for the welfare of the minor." The issue on appeal was whether petitioner had been denied due process because of the court's failure to appoint counsel for her.

Explaining how to determine whether counsel need be appointed in a particular case, the opinion of the Court stated:

> The case of Mathews v. Eldridge, 424 U.S. 319, 335, propounds three elements to be evaluated in deciding what due process requires, viz., the private interests at stake, the government's interest, and the risk that the procedures used will lead to erroneous decisions. We must balance these elements against each other, and then set their net weight in the scales against the presumption that there is a right to appointed counsel only where the indigent, if he is unsuccessful, may lose his personal freedom.

> This Court's decisions have by now made plain beyond the need for multiple citation that a parent's desire for and right to "the companionship, care, custody and management of his or her children" is an important interest that "undeniably warrants deference and, absent a powerful countervailing interest, protection." Stanley v. Illinois, 405 U.S. 645, 651. Here the State has sought not simply to infringe upon that interest but to end it. If the State prevails, it will have worked a unique kind of deprivation. Cf. May v. Anderson, 345 U.S. 528, 533; Armstrong v. Manzo, 380 U.S. 545. A parent's interest in the accuracy and justice of the decision to terminate his or her parental status is, therefore a commanding one.[3]

> Since the State has an urgent interest in the welfare of the child, it shares the parent's interest in an accurate and just decision. For this reason, the State may share the indigent parent's interest in the availability of appointed counsel. If, as our adversary system presupposes, accurate and just results are most likely to be obtained through the equal contest of opposed interests, the State's interest in the child's welfare may perhaps best be served by a hearing in which both the parent and the State acting for the child are represented by counsel, without whom the contest of interests may become unwholesomely unequal. North Carolina itself acknowledges as much by providing that where a parent files a written answer to a termination petition, the State must supply a lawyer to represent the child. N.C.G.S. § 7A–289.29.

> The State's interests, however, clearly diverge from the parent's insofar as the State wishes the termination decision to be made as economically as possible and thus wants to avoid both the expense of appointed counsel and the cost of the lengthened proceedings his presence may cause. But though the State's pecuniary interest is legitimate, it is hardly significant enough to overcome private interests as important as those here, particularly in light of the concession in the respondent's brief that the "potential costs of appointed counsel in termination proceedings . . . is [sic] admittedly *de minimis* compared to the costs in all criminal actions."

> Finally, consideration must be given to the risk that a parent will be erroneously deprived of his or her child because the parent is not represented by counsel.

---

3. Some parents will have an additional interest to protect. Petitions to terminate parental rights are not uncommonly based on alleged criminal activity. Parents so accused may need legal counsel to guide them in understanding the problems such petitions may create.

[The Court details the safeguards prescribed by contemporary N.C. termination procedure.]

. . .

The respondent argues that the subject of a termination hearing—the parent's relationship with her child—far from being abstruse, technical, or unfamiliar, is one as to which the parent must be uniquely well informed and to which the parent must have given prolonged thought. The respondent also contends that a termination hearing is not likely to produce difficult points of evidentiary law, or even of substantive law, since the evidentiary problems peculiar to criminal trials are not present and since the standards for termination are not complicated. In fact, the respondent reports, the North Carolina Departments of Social Services are themselves sometimes represented at termination hearings by social workers instead of by lawyers.

Yet the ultimate issues with which a termination hearing deals are not always simple, however commonplace they may be. Expert medical and psychiatric testimony, which few parents are equipped to understand and fewer still to confute, is sometimes presented. The parents are likely to be people with little education, who have had uncommon difficulty in dealing with life, and who are, at the hearing, thrust into a distressing and disorienting situation. That these factors may combine to overwhelm an uncounselled parent is evident from the findings some courts have made. Thus, courts have generally held that the State must appoint counsel for indigent parents at termination proceedings. The respondent is able to point to no presently authoritative case, except for the North Carolina judgment now before us, holding that an indigent parent has no due process right to appointed counsel in termination proceedings.

The dispositive question . . . is whether the three *Eldridge* factors, when weighed against the presumption that there is no right to appointed counsel in the absence of at least a potential deprivation of physical liberty, suffice to rebut that presumption and thus to lead to the conclusion that the Due Process Clause requires the appointment of counsel when a State seeks to terminate an indigent's parental status. To summarize the above discussion of the *Eldridge* factors: the parent's interest is an extremely important one (and may be supplemented by the dangers of criminal liability inherent in some termination proceedings); the State shares with the parent an interest in a correct decision, has a relatively weak pecuniary interest, and, in some but not all cases, has a possibly stronger interest in informal procedures; and the complexity of the proceeding and the incapacity of the uncounselled parent could be, but would not always be, great enough to make the risk of an erroneous deprivation of the parent's rights insupportably high.

If, in a given case, the parent's interests were at their strongest, the State's interests were at their weakest, and the risks of error were at their peak, it could not be said that the *Eldridge* factors did not overcome the presumption against the right to appointed counsel, and that due process did not therefore require the appointment of counsel. But since the *Eldridge* factors will not always be so distributed, and since "due process is not so rigid as to require that the significant interests in informality, flexibility and economy must always be sacrificed," Gagnon v. Scarpelli, supra, 411 U.S., at 788, neither can we say that the Constitution requires the appointment of counsel in every parental termination proceeding. We therefore adopt the standard found appropriate in Gagnon v. Scarpelli, and leave the decision whether due process calls for the appointment of counsel for indigent parents in termination proceedings to be answered in the first instance by the trial court, subject, of course, to appellate review.

　　·　·　·

　　In its Fourteenth Amendment, our Constitution imposes on the States the standards necessary to ensure that judicial proceedings are fundamentally fair. A wise public policy, however, may require that higher standards be adopted than those minimally tolerable under the Constitution. Informed opinion has clearly come to hold that an indigent parent is entitled to the assistance of appointed counsel not only in parental termination proceedings, but in dependency and neglect proceedings as well. Most significantly, 33 States and the District of Columbia provide statutorily for the appointment of counsel in termination cases. The Court's opinion today in no way implies that the standards increasingly urged by informed public opinion and now widely followed by the States are other than enlightened and wise.

　　For further comment on the meaning of *Lassiter* and some subsequent review standards, see William Wesley Patton, The Right to Appointed Counsel in Child Protection and Parental Severance Cases, 27 Loy.U.Chi.L.J. 195 (1996); Douglas Besharov, Terminating Parental Rights: The Indigent Parent's Right to Counsel after Lassiter v. North Carolina, 15 Fam.L.Q. 205, 216 (1981).

　　(3) In *Peregood v. Cosmides*, 663 So.2d 665 (Fla.App.1995), the Florida Court of Appeals permitted a minor child's declaratory judgment to challenge his adoption by his biological mother. The natural father and mother were never married, but a judgment of paternity was entered establishing the father's parentage and requiring him to pay monthly child support.

　　After animosity developed between the father and mother over visitation, the parents "settled" the dispute by agreeing that the father would forego visitation in exchange for the mother's forfeiture of the monthly child support. Such an arrangement is not enforceable under Florida law, however, and the father would have been exposed to possible arrearages in child support as a result of the order for support.

　　To implement their agreement, each parent executed a consent to the child's adoption. He continued to live with his mother and she petitioned to readopt her own child. A final judgment of adoption was entered, establishing the mother as the sole adoptive parent and terminating the father's parental rights and obligations including any obligation of support.

　　During the adoption proceedings the mother assured the court she would not need to seek public assistance in order to support Michael. However, she later sought and obtained public assistance for her son, who filed a complaint for a declaratory judgment and petition to vacate and rescind the final judgment of adoption, through his best friend, his maternal grandmother.

　　On appeal, the father argued that his minor son lacked standing to bring the declaratory action and that it was improper to challenge the judgment of adoption.

　　The court determined that

　　... where fraud has entered into an adoption proceeding, the adoption decree can be set aside. *Jefferis v. May*, 603 So.2d 84 (Fla. 5th DCA 1992); *Andy v. Lessem*, 595 So.2d 197 (Fla. 3d DCA 1992). The fraudulent procurement of a natural parent's consent to the adoption of a child is sufficient to warrant setting aside the adoption. *Lambert v. Taylor*, 150 Fla. 680, 8 So.2d 393 (1942). It logically follows that consent to an adoption for the purpose of abrogating a parent's obligation of child support is a sham and a sufficient ground to set aside an adoption decree for fraud.

. . .

The procedure utilized by Michael's parents in this case violates the intent and purposes of the Florida adoption law. The Legislative intent under Chapter 63 adoption proceedings is to "protect and promote the well-being of persons being adopted." Section 63.022(1). The courts are instructed to enter orders necessary and suitable to "promote and protect the best interests of the person to be adopted." Section 63.022(2)(1). The actions taken in this case clearly do not protect or promote Michael's well-being. Rather, they have placed him in economic jeopardy, depriving him of a substantial source of financial support, substituting instead, public assistance. The parents' agreement produced a sham adoption, the sole purpose of which was to circumvent the law, or to do that which the law precludes: relieve a parent of support obligations, thereby forcing the child to become dependent upon the state for public assistance.

663 So.2d at 669–70.

The court also rejected the father's arguments that the son could not bring the case as a declaratory action, stating that "The principal purpose of the Declaratory Judgment Act is to obtain a judgment on rights which have never before been determined."

(4) Issues related to the right to and role of counsel are explored more generally in Chapter IX infra.

C. CRITERIA FOR INTERVENTION

VIRGINIA CODE ANNOTATED

§ 16.1–283   Termination of residual parental rights

A.   The residual parental rights of a parent or parents may be terminated by the court as hereinafter provided in a separate proceeding if the petition specifically requests such relief. No petition seeking termination of residual parental rights shall be accepted by the court prior to the filing of a foster care plan, pursuant to § 16.1–281, which documents termination of residual parental rights as being in the best interests of the child. The court may hear and adjudicate a petition for termination of parental rights in the same proceeding in which the court has approved a foster care plan which documents that termination is in the best interests of the child. The court may terminate the residual parental rights of one parent without affecting the rights of the other parent. The local board of social services or a licensed child-placing agency need not have identified an available and eligible family to adopt a child for whom termination of parental rights is being sought prior to the entry of an order terminating parental rights.

Any order terminating residual parental rights shall be accompanied by an order continuing or granting custody to a local board of social services, to a licensed child-placing agency or the granting of custody or guardianship to a relative or other interested individual, subject to the provisions of subsection A1 of this section. However, in such cases the court shall give a consideration to granting custody to relatives of the child, including grandparents. An order continuing or granting custody to a local board of social services or to a licensed child-placing agency shall indicate whether that board or agency shall have the authority to place the child for adoption and consent thereto.

The summons shall be served upon the parent or parents and the other parties specified in § 16.1–263. Written notice of the hearing shall also be provided to the foster parents of the child, a relative providing care for the child, and any preadoptive parents for the child informing them that they may appear as witnesses at the hearing to give testimony and otherwise participate in the proceeding. The persons entitled to notice and an opportunity to be heard need not be made parties to the proceedings. The summons or notice of hearing shall clearly state the consequences of a termination of residual parental rights. Service shall be made pursuant to § 16.1–264.

A1.   Any order transferring custody of the child to a relative or other interested individual pursuant to subsection A of this section shall be entered only upon a finding, based upon a preponderance of the evidence, that the relative or other interested individual is one who, after an investigation as directed by the court, (i) is found by the court to be willing and qualified to receive and care for the child; (ii) is willing to have a positive, continuous relationship with the child; (iii) is committed to providing a permanent, suitable home for the child; and (iv) is willing and has the ability to protect the child from abuse and neglect; and the order shall so state. The court's order transferring custody to a relative or other interested individual should further provide, as appropriate, for any terms and conditions which would promote the child's interest and welfare.

B.   The residual parental rights of a parent or parents of a child found by the court to be neglected or abused and placed in foster care as a result of (i) court commitment, (ii) an entrustment agreement entered into by the parent or parents or (iii) other voluntary relinquishment by the parent or parents may be terminated if the court finds, based upon clear and convincing evidence, that it is in the best interests of the child and that:

1.   The neglect or abuse suffered by such child presented a serious and substantial threat to his life, health or development; and

2.   It is not reasonably likely that the conditions which resulted in such neglect or abuse can be substantially corrected or eliminated so as to allow the child's safe return to his parent or parents within a reasonable period of time. In making this determination, the court shall take into consideration the efforts made to rehabilitate the parent or parents by any public or private social, medical, mental health or other rehabilitative agencies prior to the child's initial placement in foster care.

Proof of any of the following shall constitute prima facie evidence of the conditions set forth in subdivision B 2 hereof:

a.   The parent or parents are suffering from a mental or emotional illness or mental deficiency of such severity that there is no reasonable expectation that such parent will be able to undertake responsibility for the care needed by the child in accordance with his age and stage of development;

b.   The parent or parents have habitually abused or are addicted to intoxicating liquors, narcotics or other dangerous drugs to the extent that proper parental ability has been seriously impaired and the parent, without good cause, has not responded to or followed through with recommended and available treatment which could have improved the capacity for adequate parental functioning; or

c.   The parent or parents, without good cause, have not responded to or followed through with appropriate, available and reasonable rehabilitative efforts on the part of social, medical, mental health or other rehabilitative agencies designed to reduce, eliminate or prevent the neglect or abuse of the child.

C.   The residual parental rights of a parent or parents of a child placed in foster care as a result of court commitment, an entrustment agreement entered into by the parent or parents or other voluntary relinquishment by the parent or parents may be terminated if the court finds, based upon clear and convincing evidence, that it is in the best interests of the child and that:

1.   The parent or parents have, without good cause, failed to maintain continuing contact with and to provide or substantially plan for the future of the child for a period of six months after the child's placement in foster care notwithstanding the reasonable and appropriate efforts of social, medical, mental health or other rehabilitative agencies to communicate with the parent or parents and to strengthen the parent-child relationship. Proof that the parent or parents have failed without good cause to communicate on a continuing and planned basis with the child for a period of six months shall constitute prima facie evidence of this condition; or

2.   The parent or parents, without good cause, have been unwilling or unable within a reasonable period not to exceed twelve months from the date the child was placed in foster care to remedy substantially the conditions which led to the child's foster care placement, notwithstanding the reasonable and appropriate efforts of social, medical, mental health or other rehabilitative agencies to such end. Proof that the parent or parents, without good cause, have failed or been unable to make substantial progress towards elimination of the conditions which led to or required continuation of the child's foster care placement in accordance with their obligations under and within the time limits or goals set forth in a foster care plan filed with the court or any other plan jointly designed and agreed to by the parent or parents and a public or private social, medical, mental health or other rehabilitative agency shall constitute prima facie evidence of this condition. The court shall take into consideration the prior efforts of such agencies to rehabilitate the parent or parents prior to the placement of the child in foster care.

D.   The residual parental rights of a parent or parents of a child found by the court to be neglected or abused upon the ground of abandonment may be terminated if the court finds, based upon clear and convincing evidence, that it is in the best interests of the child and that:

1. The child was abandoned under such circumstances that either the identity or the whereabouts of the parent or parents cannot be determined; and

2. The child's parent or parents, guardian or relatives have not come forward to identify such child and claim a relationship to the child within three months following the issuance of an order by the court placing the child in foster care; and

3. Diligent efforts have been made to locate the child's parent or parents without avail.

E. The residual parental rights of a parent or parents of a child who is in the custody of a local board or licensed child-placing agency may be terminated by the court if the court finds, based upon clear and convincing evidence, that it is in the best interests of the child and that (i) the residual parental rights of the parent regarding a sibling of the child have previously been involuntarily terminated; (ii) the parent has been convicted of an offense under the laws of this Commonwealth or a substantially similar law of any other state, the United States or any foreign jurisdiction that constitutes murder or voluntary manslaughter, or a felony attempt, conspiracy or solicitation to commit any such offense, if the victim of the offense was a child of the parent, a child with whom the parent resided at the time such offense occurred or the other parent of the child; (iii) the parent has been convicted of an offense under the laws of this Commonwealth or a substantially similar law of any other state, the United States or any foreign jurisdiction that constitutes felony assault resulting in serious bodily injury or felony bodily wounding resulting in serious bodily injury or felony sexual assault, if the victim of the offense was a child of the parent or a child with whom the parent resided at the time of such offense; or (iv) the parent has subjected any child to aggravated circumstances.

As used in this section:

"Aggravated circumstances" means torture, chronic or severe abuse, or chronic or severe sexual abuse, if the victim of such conduct was a child of the parent or a child with whom the parent resided at the time such conduct occurred, including the failure to protect such a child from such conduct, which conduct or failure to protect: (i) evinces a wanton or depraved indifference to human life, or (ii) has resulted in the death of such a child or in serious bodily injury to such a child.

"Chronic abuse" or "chronic sexual abuse" means recurring acts of physical abuse which place the child's health, safety and well-being at risk.

"Serious bodily injury" means bodily injury that involves substantial risk of death, extreme physical pain, protracted and obvious disfigurement, or protracted loss or impairment of the function of a bodily member, organ or mental faculty.

"Severe abuse" or "severe sexual abuse" may include an act or omission that occurred only once, but otherwise meets the definition of "aggravated circumstances."

The local board or other child welfare agency having custody of the child shall not be required by the court to make reasonable efforts to reunite the child with a parent who has been convicted of one of the felonies specified in this subsection or who has been found by the court to have subjected any child to aggravated circumstances.

F.   The local board or licensed child-placing agency to which authority is given to place the child for adoption and consent thereto after an order terminating parental rights is entered shall file a written Adoption Progress Report with the juvenile court on the progress being made to place the child in an adoptive home. The report shall be filed with the court every six months from the date of the final order terminating parental rights until a final order of adoption is entered on behalf of the child in the circuit court. At the conclusion of the hearing at which termination of parental rights is ordered and authority is given to the local board or licensed child-placing agency to place the child for adoption, the juvenile court shall schedule a date by which the board or agency shall file the first written Adoption Progress Report required by this section. A copy of the Adoption Progress Report shall be sent by the court to the guardian ad litem for the child. The court may schedule a hearing on the report with or without the request of a party.

G.   Notwithstanding any other provisions of this section, residual parental rights shall not be terminated if it is established that the child, if he is fourteen years of age or older or otherwise of an age of discretion as determined by the court, objects to such termination. However, residual parental rights of a child fourteen years of age or older may be terminated over the objection of the child, if the court finds that any disability of the child reduces the child's developmental age and that the child is not otherwise of an age of discretion.

In re M.N.L.

Court of Appeals of Georgia, 1996.
221 Ga.App. 123, 470 S.E.2d 753.

■ POPE, PRESIDING JUDGE.

The mother of M.N.L. appeals from an order of the juvenile court terminating her parental rights.[1] The two-part question presented is whether (1) there is clear and convincing evidence of parental misconduct or inability, and (2) termination of parental rights is in the best interest of the child. See In the Interest of G.L.H., 209 Ga.App. 146, 149(2), 433 S.E.2d 357 (1993). Concluding that the evidence supports the juvenile court's affirmative answer to both parts of the question, we affirm its decision to terminate the mother's parental rights.

Viewed in a light to support the juvenile court's determination, see G.L.H., 209 Ga.App. at 149(1), 433 S.E.2d 357, the evidence shows that M.N.L. was born prematurely in July 1993. M.N.L.'s mother, who was 27 years old when he was born, used alcohol and drugs throughout her pregnancy and tested positive for cocaine when she was admitted to the hospital to give birth. Concerned about the results of the drug test and other behavioral indicators of drug and alcohol abuse, the hospital recom-

---

1. The father's parental rights were also terminated, but he does not appeal.

mended that the mother spend a couple of days with M.N.L. in the "parenting room" at the hospital, where she could learn to take care of her baby, first with the help of nurses and then on her own. The second night the mother was to spend the entire night with the baby on her own, but instead she left the baby and went off with her boyfriend.

At that point the Department of Family & Children Services ("DFCS") obtained an adjudication that M.N.L. was deprived and took temporary custody of him, with the hope of eventually reuniting the child with his mother. DFCS and the mother agreed to a multi-goal reunification plan, the first step of which was to complete an in-patient treatment program at the Alcohol & Drug Abuse Treatment Center ("ADAC"). When the mother was arrested and posted bail with the "Aid to Families With Dependent Children" funds that she originally intended to use for the ADAC program, DFCS paid for the ADAC program for her. Nonetheless, the mother left before the program was over, and ADAC refused DFCS's request to take her back, saying she was uncooperative and uncommitted. DFCS's efforts to get the mother into out-patient treatment were also unsuccessful, as the mother failed to even show up for an initial interview. To the mother's credit, she was visiting M.N.L. as regularly as possible through the end of 1993, and sent him cards and presents. In January 1994, however, the mother was again arrested, and she has been incarcerated since that time.

The mother's criminal history goes back to her arrest and conviction for burglary when she was 18. Prior to M.N.L.'s birth, she was also convicted of criminal trespass, theft by taking of a truck, and theft by taking of a purse. Then, within a month after M.N.L.'s birth, the mother was arrested for stabbing a male friend. Out on bail, she stabbed another man in January 1994. She was convicted of both aggravated assaults and sentenced to ten years in prison. At first the mother testified that she had no parole date, but she later testified that she might come up for parole after 52 months. Thus, the mother will be incarcerated at least until the latter part of 1998, and possibly a lot longer.

At the time of the hearing on the motion to terminate her parental rights, the mother had been in prison on the latest charges for approximately ten months. She testified that she had been alcohol and drug free during that time, and that for the last six months she had participated in various therapy groups for substance abuse. The mother has no family who can care for the child, but she testified she knew of an agency that takes care of children of inmates and allows them to maintain contact with their incarcerated mothers.

1.   The juvenile court's finding of parental misconduct or inability is supported by clear and convincing evidence that the child is deprived and the deprivation is likely to continue. See OCGA § 15–11–81(b)(4)(A). Although it appears the mother cares for her child, she is unable to take care of him due to her substance abuse as well as her long-term incarceration for her criminal activities. See OCGA § 15–11–81(b)(4)(B)(ii & iii). The mother's efforts to improve herself during her imprisonment are good. However, "[t]he trial court must determine whether a parent's conduct warrants hope of rehabilitation, not an appellate court. [Cit.]" In the Interest of J. R., 201 Ga.App. 199(1), 200, 410 S.E.2d 458 (1991). In light of

the mother's lengthy history of alcohol and drug abuse and her repetitive incarcerations, her testimony regarding her recent progress does not negate the clear and convincing evidence supporting the juvenile court's finding that the child's deprivation is likely to continue. Id.; see also In the Interest of M. R., 213 Ga.App. 460, 467(4), 444 S.E.2d 866 (1994); In the Interest of J.M.C., 201 Ga.App. 173, 410 S.E.2d 368 (1991).

2. Nor did the court err in concluding that termination would serve the best interests of M.N.L. The child has been in foster care since soon after his birth, so no bond between the mother and child has formed. The mother will be in prison for at least two and a half more years (possibly as long as eight more years), and the child would have to be in the care of a foster family or agency until that time if he cannot be adopted. DFCS representatives testified at the hearing that M.N.L.'s prospects for adoption were good at that time—but the older the child gets, the poorer his prospects for adoption become. See In Re M. R., 213 Ga.App. at 464–465(1)(b), 444 S.E.2d 866.

3. The mother also enumerates as error the juvenile court's refusal to reconsider its decision in light of "new evidence" that an agency called Tender Mercy Ministries could care for M.N.L. and allow him to visit her. First of all, this is not really new evidence since the mother described such an agency (though without mentioning the name) in her testimony at the termination hearing. Secondly, the existence of such a possibility simply does not outweigh the factors discussed in Division 2 which clearly establish that termination is in the best interest of the child. DFCS is obligated to pursue alternatives to termination, which it did in this case, but it is not obligated to gamble the child's prospects for a good life on the possibility that the mother will emerge from prison in two and a half to eight years reformed to the point that she can take care of M.N.L. and provide him with a stable home.

Judgment affirmed.

In re E.M.

Supreme Court of Pennsylvania, 1993.
533 Pa. 115, 620 A.2d 481.

■ Flaherty, Justice.

This is an appeal, by allowance, from an order of the Superior Court which affirmed a decree of the Court of Common Pleas of Allegheny County ordering an involuntary termination of parental rights.... The appellant, Elizabeth M., is the natural mother of two boys, Louis C. and Erick C., ages seven and nine respectively at the time of the hearing in this case, to wit, in 1989. Appellant's parental rights were terminated involuntarily because appellant was unable to provide adequate care for her children. The parental rights of the father of the children, Mr. C., were terminated with his consent.

Appellant suffers from mental retardation. Her education consists of a high school diploma from a school for exceptional children. Appellant's children are similarly afflicted. Erick suffers from both physical and mental retardation. He has an impairment in his ability to walk, speak, etc. Louis is learning-disabled and has an attention deficit. The children first came to the attention of the Allegheny County Children and Youth Services (CYS) in 1982. At that time appellant was a victim of Mr. C's domestic violence and was having difficulty with rent payments and food purchases. Mr. C had expensive drug and alcohol habits. By March of 1983 the situation had worsened to such an extent that the family was evicted from its residence and was forced to seek shelter at a Salvation Army facility.

CYS observed major deficiencies in appellant's capacity as a parent. Appellant failed to feed her children properly and failed to maintain clean and sanitary conditions in the living space that was provided for her. She fed her children from dirty bottles of spoiled and diluted milk, left dirty diapers in their living space for days at a time, and was lax about providing medical care. In December of 1983, the children were adjudicated dependent and placed with a foster family. The foster family has cared for the children since that time and now seeks to adopt them.

Prior to 1982 and continuing for approximately six years, appellant received assistance from numerous remedial programs designed to enhance her homemaking and parenting skills. Although she earnestly participated in the programs, she failed to make any substantial progress in improving her skills and competence to meet the needs of her children. Appellant, impaired by her own mental retardation, was simply not able to care for her children, who, likewise, had special needs as a result of their own disabilities. CYS determined that nothing short of 24–hour supervision by an assistant skilled in the care of special needs children would be sufficient to permit appellant to resume caring for her children. The children were unruly, oppositional, and very difficult to manage. Whenever appellant engaged in supervised visits with them, she was unable to control them. Despite this, appellant maintained an interest in the children and continued to visit them on a frequent and regular basis. She continued to hope that someday the children would be returned to her. Inasmuch as the programs designed to improve appellant's parenting skills had proved fruitless, however, CYS determined sometime in 1985 or 1986 that reunification of the family was impossible and that the best interests of the children would be served by a plan of adoption.

In 1987, appellant, who was no longer residing with Mr. C, moved into a clean apartment with her paramour. The paramour expressed a willingness to assist in caring for appellant's children, but admitted that the children have special needs that make it difficult to care for them, and stated that he and appellant would need help if they were to attempt to provide care.

In 1989, to facilitate an adoption by the children's foster parents, CYS filed a petition seeking termination of appellant's parental rights on the ground that appellant was unable to provide for the needs and welfare of her children. The court of common pleas, after a hearing, denied the petition. Exceptions were filed, and, upon reconsideration, the court reversed its decision, thereby granting the petition. An appeal was taken to the Superior Court, and the termination decree was affirmed.

At issue is whether the decree terminating appellant's parental rights was adequately supported by the evidence and was based upon a proper consideration of the needs and welfare of the children. We discern that an important element relating to the needs and welfare of the children, to wit, the emotional bond between appellant and her children, has been inadequately considered in the proceedings below. Accordingly, we reverse and remand for further proceedings to determine whether termination is warranted.

The termination decree was issued by the court of common pleas pursuant to 23 Pa.C.S. § 2511(a)(2), which provides for termination of parental rights in cases where parental incapacity cannot be remedied. In pertinent part, 23 Pa.C.S. § 2511 provides: (a) General rule.—The rights of a parent in regard to a child may be terminated after a petition filed on any of the following grounds: . . . . (2) The repeated and continued incapacity, abuse, neglect or refusal of the parent has caused the child to be without essential parental care, control or subsistence necessary for his physical or mental well-being and the conditions and causes of the incapacity, abuse, neglect or refusal cannot or will not be remedied by the parent. . . . (b) Other considerations.—The court in terminating the rights of a parent shall give primary consideration to the needs and welfare of the child.

It is well established that this provision supplies a basis to terminate parental rights where a child's well-being suffers as a result of the physical or mental impairment of his parent. In re Adoption of J.J., 511 Pa. 590, 607, 515 A.2d 883, 892 (1986). Grounds for termination can consist of lack of capacity and not just affirmative misconduct. . . .

. . . As stated in Matter of Adoption of G.T.M., 506 Pa. 44, 46, 483 A.2d 1355, 1356 (1984), in cases where there has been an involuntary termination of parental rights by the Orphans' Court, the scope of appellate review is limited to the determination of whether the decree of termination is supported by competent evidence. In re Adoption of B.D.S., 494 Pa. 171, 177, 431 A.2d 203, 206 (1981). . . . It is established that, in a proceeding to involuntarily terminate parental rights, the burden of proof is upon the party seeking termination to establish by "clear and convincing" evidence the existence of grounds for doing so. . . .

The record, as heretofore recounted, clearly contains evidence that appellant has been unable to provide proper care for her children. Further, in view of the long time that this incapacity has continued and the failure by appellant to make progress in remedial programs, there is basis to conclude that the incapacity will not be remedied. The fact that there is parental incapacity does not in itself, however, require that parental rights be terminated. Rather, termination must be decreed only where it serves the needs and welfare of the children. 23 Pa.C.S. § 2511(b), supra.

The parties have raised a significant issue in this case that has been inadequately addressed in the record. Specifically, appellant alleges that a strong emotional bond exists between herself and the children and that it would be detrimental to the needs and welfare of the children to have that bond severed through a decree of termination. . . . Where there has not been adequate consideration of the emotional needs of the children, a termination of parental rights cannot be sustained.

The CYS expert witness in this case, a psychologist, testified that the children interacted well with their foster mother and that they had formed a strong bond with her. However, no observation was made by the psychologist of the children's interaction with the foster father. Similarly, the psychologist made no observation of the children's interaction with appellant and was not able to make any recommendation as to whether the children should be placed with appellant. The psychologist testified that a better assessment of the relevant emotional factors could have been made if the foster father had been observed interacting with the children. She also stated that the children's interaction with appellant should have been evaluated from the same standpoint. She further stated, "I think it is important, if there is an issue about terminating parental rights, that that part of the evaluation is conducted." In addition, she testified that the children continue to maintain an emotional bond with appellant. The children have expressed a desire to live with both their foster parents and their natural parents. They also maintain that they have "two mommies and daddies."

Inasmuch as the psychological evaluations so clearly recommended by CYS's own expert witness have not been performed, and given that the burden of proof is upon CYS as the party seeking termination of appellant's rights to show by clear and convincing evidence that termination meets the needs and welfare of the children, it cannot be said that CYS has met its burden. While the fact that there exists some bond between appellant and the children would not per se block a termination of rights, it is at least a factor that, according to CYS's own expert witness, should have been more fully explored.

The Superior Court, in affirming the termination decree, expressly recognized that the question of the bond between appellant and the children had not been fully considered. Nevertheless, the Superior Court held, [O]nce a parent is adjudged incompetent under section 2511(a) whereby family unity cannot be preserved, but where adoption is imminent, then there is no need to ascertain whether a beneficial bonding exists as between the natural parent and the children, nor whether additional factors counsel that continuing the relationship might otherwise serve the needs and welfare of the child. (Emphasis in original). We do not agree. It is clearly conceivable that a beneficial bonding could exist between a parent and child, such that, if the bond were broken, the child could suffer extreme emotional consequences. This is true regardless of whether adoption is imminent. To render a decision that termination serves the needs and welfare of the child without consideration of emotional bonds, in a case such as this where a bond, to some extent at least, obviously exists and where the expert witness for the party seeking termination indicates that the factor has not been adequately studied, is not proper.

Whether the bond exists to such a considerable extent that severing the natural parent-child relationship would be contrary to the needs and welfare of the children is an issue that must be more fully explored by the evidence. Such an intense bond may exist with respect to one, both, or neither of the children. The existing record is simply inadequate in its treatment of this issue.

The order of the Superior Court affirming the decree of the court of common pleas must, therefore, be reversed. The case will be remanded to the court of common pleas for a reevaluation of the needs and welfare of the children, taking into account whatever bonds may currently exist between the children and appellant, as well as other factors having bearing upon whether termination is proper.

In re S.R.

Supreme Court of Vermont, 1991.
157 Vt. 417, 599 A.2d 364.

■ ALLEN, CHIEF JUSTICE.

The parents of S.R., a juvenile, appeal the termination of their residual parental rights. We affirm.

S.R.'s mother argues that the juvenile court's findings concerning her mental illness and conditions in the home did not warrant the termination. She also claims that the court's findings of risk to S.R. were not supported by clear and convincing evidence. Finally, she claims that stagnation in parental capacity was caused primarily by the Vermont Department of Social and Rehabilitation Services (SRS) rather than by fault on her part.

S.R.'s father joins the arguments advanced by the mother. He also raises separate challenges to the sufficiency of the evidence and the court's findings in support of termination of his rights. In addition, he argues that the findings regarding the quality of the preadoptive foster home are irrelevant and violate his constitutional rights.

We hold that the juvenile court's findings are sufficiently supported by the evidence and that those findings in turn support the conclusion that termination of parental rights is in the best interests of S.R. We also find that the court's inquiry into the quality of the preadoptive foster home was relevant and did not violate the father's constitutional rights. For these reasons, we affirm the juvenile court's order terminating the rights of both parents.

I.

S.R., a child with special needs, is the daughter of parents who never married but have lived together for over ten years. Her father has an alcohol problem which causes stress and discord in her relationship with him. Her mother suffers from seizures.

In 1986, when S.R. was nine months old, the juvenile court found her to be a child in need of care and supervision and transferred custody to SRS. This disposition was based on a diagnosis by a psychologist at Boston Children's Hospital that her mother suffered from a rare psychological disorder known as Munchausen syndrome by proxy. It causes a parent, usually the mother, to report or cause a serious illness or injury in her child in order to gain the attention and sympathy of the medical community. This illness, recognized in the psychiatric community and by the courts (see, e.g., People v. Phillips, 122 Cal.App.3d 69, 77–79, 175 Cal.Rptr. 703, 707–09 (1981), and In re Colin R., 63 Md.App. 684, 690, 493 A.2d 1083,

1086 (1985)), can be fatal to the child. In this case, the mother caused breathing difficulties in S.R. requiring extensive medical evaluation of S.R. prior to the Munchausen syndrome by proxy diagnosis.

During the three and one-half years prior to the termination of residual parental rights, SRS provided appropriate and extensive services for S.R. and her parents designed to reunify the family. These services included counseling for the mother, family counseling, parent education, special education for S.R., supervised home visits, and one period of home placement during which S.R. sustained several injuries. These services were largely ineffective because the parents did not acknowledge the diagnosis of Munchausen syndrome by proxy or fully avail themselves of the services offered by SRS to improve their parenting skills. After S.R. left her parents' home in 1988, SRS continued its efforts to reunify the family by continuing to provide counseling and parent education for the mother. Attempts to involve the father in the counseling or to address his alcohol problem were unsuccessful. Seeing no improvement in the capacity of either parent to resume parental duties, SRS sought to terminate both parents' residual rights through the modification of S.R.'s disposition order.

II.

When termination of parental rights is sought at a modification proceeding, 33 V.S.A. § 5532 requires the court to conduct a two-step analysis. In re J.R., 153 Vt. 85, 99, 570 A.2d 154, 161 (1989). First, the court must find a substantial change in material circumstances. Id. Second, the court must find that the best interests of the juvenile require termination of parental rights. Id. at 100, 570 A.2d at 161. Title 33 V.S.A. § 5540 sets forth four factors for the court to consider when evaluating the best interests of the child: (1) The interaction and interrelationship of the child with his natural parents, his foster parents if any, his siblings, and any other person who may significantly affect the child's best interests; (2) The child's adjustment to his home, school, and community; (3) The likelihood that the natural parent will be able to resume his parental duties within a reasonable period of time; and (4) Whether the natural parent has played and continues to play a constructive role, including personal contact and demonstrated love and affection, in the child's welfare. The court's findings must be supported by clear and convincing evidence, and such findings will withstand Supreme Court review unless clearly erroneous. In re H.A., 153 Vt. 504, 515, 572 A.2d 884, 890 (1990). The lower court's conclusions of law, if supported by the findings, will be affirmed. Id.

Both parents argue that termination of parental rights is not supported by sufficient findings of risk to S.R. The detailed and extensive findings of the trial court, as well as the record upon which they are based, sufficiently support the termination order. The court found that S.R. was at risk due to her mother's Munchausen syndrome by proxy and the failure of both parents to acknowledge that disorder. The court also found that S.R. faced risks of injury and developmental harm due to the inadequacy of her parents' supervision, their inability to assist in the delivery of necessary special services, her mother's seizure disorder, and problems between the mother and father which were exacerbated by the father's drinking problem. These findings all find support in the record from ample credible evidence. For example, the psychologist who diagnosed the Munchausen syndrome by proxy testified that S.R. faced a ten-to-twenty percent chance of death based on her parents' denial of that disorder. He also testified that the risk to S.R. due to that denial increased with the level of stress in the home.

The mother and father also argue that the court based its modification of S.R.'s case plan on changed circumstances that were the fault of SRS rather than the parents. When the State seeks modification of a juvenile case plan, the court may find a substantial change in material circumstances based on "stagnation." In re J.R., 153 Vt. at 99, 570 A.2d at 161. Stagnation is the passage of time with no improvement in parental capacity to care properly for the child. Id. While stagnation caused by factors beyond the parents' control could not support termination of parental rights, the claim that SRS caused stagnation in this case is without merit. Prior to termination, SRS worked with S.R.'s parents for well over three years providing services in an effort to effect reunification. In spite of those efforts, the trial court concluded that there had been no improvement in the ability of either parent to provide a safe environment or to care properly for S.R. The court specifically found that the parents refused to participate in regular counseling or provide transportation for S.R. to attend special early education classes. More significantly, they both failed to acknowledge the role of the mother's Munchausen syndrome by proxy. The findings in support of stagnation are well supported by the evidence, and we will not disturb the court's conclusion based on those findings.

In addition to joining the arguments made by S.R.'s mother, the father advances two arguments of his own. First, he argues that the conclusion that he is incapable of properly caring for S.R. was not sufficiently supported by the findings or the evidence. Specifically, he claims that his alcohol problem was not shown to affect S.R. adversely and is therefore irrelevant, that his failure to acknowledge the mother's Munchausen syndrome by proxy is not relevant, that the lack of a safe home environment is not attributable to him, and that his use of corporal punishment was not unreasonable. Second, he argues that findings regarding the quality of the preadoptive foster home are irrelevant and violate his constitutional rights.

Concerning the father's first argument, the court found that the father's alcohol problem caused stress in the home, including frequent arguments and occasional separations, and that this stress had a negative impact on S.R. Similarly, the court found that both parents' failure to acknowledge the Munchausen syndrome by proxy posed a direct threat to the health and safety of S.R., which increased with the level of stress in the home. Both findings are well supported by credible evidence. Furthermore, these findings are but two of several factors upon which the court based its decision to terminate the father's parental rights. The record also supports the finding of lack of safety in the home, which is equally attributable to the father and the mother. Finally, the court below placed no reliance upon the father's use of corporal punishment. It relied on a broader finding of lack of parental ability to care properly for S.R. We find extensive evidence in the record to support the court's findings regarding the father's inability to parent. These findings, in turn, support the conclusion that the father is incapable of properly caring for his daughter.

The father's second argument is that the court's consideration of the quality of S.R.'s preadoptive foster home is irrelevant and violates his constitutional rights. At modification proceedings, the statute requires the court to consider the interaction of the juvenile with foster parents, 33 V.S.A. § 5540(1). Given this statutory requirement, the father's argument that such inquiry is irrelevant and prejudicial is not well founded.

Furthermore, consideration of the preadoptive home does not, as the father argues, violate his fundamental right to care for S.R. in the context of the family. As mentioned above, 33 V.S.A. § 5532 requires the court to conduct a two-step analysis prior to modifying a disposition order. Here, the court first found a change in material circumstances based on stagnation of the parents' ability to properly care for S.R. The father's inability to provide a safe home and care for his daughter finds ample support in the record. Only after satisfying this prerequisite did the court consider whether modification was in the best interest of S.R. As part of this analysis, the court was required by 33 V.S.A. § 5540(1) to consider the relationship between S.R. and her foster parents. The father's reliance on In re N.H., 135 Vt. 230, 373 A.2d 851 (1977), is misplaced. In that case, we held that our statutes do not "allow for intervention simply because a child might be better off somewhere else." Id. at 236, 373 A.2d at 856. We based our decision, however, on the "absence of any convincing proof that the appellant [was] an unfit parent, demonstrably incapable of providing an appropriate home for his child." Id. at 237, 373 A.2d at 857. Here, the court properly followed the required two-step analysis and found the incapacity of both parents before considering the preadoptive home as part of its analysis of the best interests of S.R.

This Court has long recognized the awesome power involved in terminating parental rights. In re H.A., 153 Vt. at 513, 572 A.2d at 889. This power is constrained by procedures set forth in 33 V.S.A. chapter 55 and the holdings of this Court. In this case, the trial court properly followed both. It made appropriate findings based on clear and convincing evidence. These findings are not clearly erroneous and support the court's conclusion that the best interests of S.R. require the termination of her parents' residual rights.

Affirmed.

NOTE

For further discussion of Munchausen Syndrome by Proxy, see the material at p. 535, supra.

In re M.L.G.

Court of Appeals of Georgia, 1984.
170 Ga.App. 642, 317 S.E.2d 881.

(The opinion in this case is reproduced at p. 676 supra.)

NOTE

Much of the judicial activity challenging termination statutes has focused on possible vagueness or on process issues such as those in *Santosky*. There has been less concern about delineating the conduct or incapacity that might form the basis for termination of parental rights even if all procedural due process issues were satisfied. Do the preceding cases help in articulating a minimum level of parental capacity or involvement below which parental rights could be terminated to enable early placement of a child in a home where he or she is wanted? Would such a standard have to be tied to overt, dangerous conduct or flagrant inaction by a parent? What serious constitutional objections might be raised? Is the movement toward according more rights to nonbiological parents likely to cause us to address these issues over the near term?

In re A.C.

District of Columbia Court of Appeals, 1991.
597 A.2d 920.

■ Wagner, Associate Judge:

Appellant, R.R., the father of A.C., challenges an order of the trial court terminating his parental rights under the provisions of D.C.Code § 16–2353 (1989). The child's mother, P.C., whose parental rights were terminated in the same proceeding, did not appeal. R.R. argues that his due process rights were violated by the failure of the District of Columbia Department of Human Services (DHS), the social service agency which had court ordered custody of the child, to make reasonable efforts to reunite him with his child and that the trial court erred by failing to apply a presumption in favor of a fit, natural parent. Appellee, the minor child, contends that the trial court's order is supported by clear and convincing evidence and that appellant was not entitled to a parental preference, having failed to grasp his "opportunity interest." Appellee also argues that reunification efforts by DHS are not a required element of proof under applicable law; nevertheless, DHS made reasonable efforts at reunification, but appellant failed to display any significant interest in the child. We hold that the efforts of a public custodial agency to reunify the family are a relevant factor in the decision-making process in a proceeding to terminate parental rights, but that the agency's defaults in that regard do not preclude termination, if in the child's best interest. Finding no error in the decision to terminate R.R.'s parental rights, we affirm.

I.

A.C. was born on August 10, 1985. When he was only two months old, A.C.'s natural father, R.R., voluntarily placed him in emergency care with DHS after the child's mother could not be located. The parents were never married to each other. Initially, DHS placed A.C. at St. Ann's Infant Home, and later, in an interim foster care placement. In July 1986, A.C. was placed in foster care with the family with whom he remained continuously until the termination hearing in November 1990. The child has bonded with his foster mother. With the exception of one visit during A.C.'s brief hospitalization in October 1985, R.R. has not visited nor otherwise contacted the child. An order providing R.R. reasonable visitation rights was entered on June 23, 1988. Thereafter, DHS workers attempted to locate R.R. without success. Finally, R.R. requested and arranged for a visit with A.C. in February 1989, but he failed to keep the appointment.

In February 1989, the child's mother, P.C., entered a stipulation in the neglect proceeding acknowledging that she had neglected A.C. by leaving him alone or with unwilling caretakers. She also admitted her inability to care for the child because of her incarceration and emotional problems, among other reasons. R.R., then a party to the proceeding, did not sign the stipulation; therefore, the trial date for R.R.'s case was reset, along with the dispositional hearing in P.C.'s case for May 9, 1989.[1] DHS workers could not locate R.R. again until he appeared for the hearing. At that time, R.R. informed a social worker that he was unable to care for A.C. because he was unemployed. The trial court entered an order committing A.C. to the custody of DHS. The neglect case was later dismissed as to R.R. at his attorney's request.[2]

On February 23, 1990, the attorney and guardian *ad litem* for the child filed a motion to terminate parental rights. While incarcerated at Lorton, Virginia, R.R. was personally served with a summons and order to appear for the hearing on the motion. R.R. was brought to court from Lorton for the hearing on August 20, 1990, but the case was postponed until November 5, 1990 to secure proper service on A.C.'s mother. In spite of having been personally served and notified of the continued date at the August proceeding, R.R., who had been released from jail by this time, did not appear for the hearing on the motion to terminate parental rights in November. R.R.'s counsel was present at the hearing which resulted in an order terminating R.R.'s parental rights on November 15, 1990. R.R.'s attorney filed a timely notice of appeal on his behalf.

At the hearing on the motion, the family social worker testified that she did not attempt to enter into a case plan[3] with R.R. because he had said that he was unemployed and unable to care for A.C. Further, R.R. had been difficult for DHS to locate. The family social worker contacted shelters, hospitals, jails and the morgue in an effort to find him. When R.R. appeared at the neglect hearing, he was given information through which he could contact the agency and maintain contact with the child. R.R. provided DHS with only his mother's address. After R.R. failed to make the scheduled visit he had requested with the child in February 1989, neither the social worker nor R.R. initiated any further contact.

---

1. After an adjudication of neglect under D.C.Code § 16–2316 (1989), a predisposition study is made as required by D.C.Code § 16–2319 (1989) followed by a dispositional hearing consistent with D.C.Code § 16–2320 (1989).

2. The motion for an order dismissing R.R. as a party was not filed until June 21, 1990, and the order was entered granting the request on July 13, 1990, nunc pro tunc to May 9, 1989. According to R.R.'s motion, an oral motion had been made for dismissal and granted at the May 9, 1989 hearing, but the action had not been recorded.

3. The family social worker explained that a case plan is an agreement between the parent and the agency worker in which services are identified in order for the family to be reunited. The plan specifies the steps the parents must take to reach the goal of reunification.

An expert witness on adoptions testified, and the trial judge found as fact, that if parental rights were terminated, A.C. would be readily adoptable because of his tender age and lack of physical, emotional or behavioral problems. As of the date of the termination order, an adoptive family had been approved for A.C., and a backup adoptive family had been identified.

II.

Appellant argues that his due process rights were violated by DHS's failure to make reasonable efforts to reunite him with his son. The argument is unpersuasive. The protections afforded by the Due Process Clause of the Fourteenth Amendment to natural parents to direct the upbringing of their children are well established. In re A.B.E., 564 A.2d 751, 754–55 (D.C.1989) (citations omitted). Such rights are not absolute, and they must yield to the child's best interest in a proceeding to terminate parental rights. Id. at 754. In such proceedings, the "parents' constitutional rights are relevant only to the question of what process is due." Id.

As desirable as it might be, appellant's due process rights do not include as a condition precedent to termination of parental rights that the state agency having custody of a minor child make affirmative efforts to reunite the family. The statute in this jurisdiction which governs proceedings to terminate the parental rights of neglected children, D.C.Code § 16–2351 et seq. (1989), contains no express requirement that the agency having custody of a neglected child demonstrate that it has made reasonable efforts to reunite parent and child before the government or a guardian, acting on behalf of the child, can institute termination proceedings nor before the court can decide such cases.

In support of his argument that his due process rights were violated by the failure of DHS to make reasonable efforts to reunite him with his child, appellant relies on cases from states which have statutes requiring proof that the agency having care of the child has made reasonable efforts to strengthen and encourage the family relationship before the petition to terminate can be filed or granted. See In re Lori D., 510 A.2d 421, 424 (R.I.1986) (order dismissing petition reversed where record replete with efforts of state agency to reunite family as required by law);[4] see also Weaver v. Roanoke Dep't of Human Resources, 220 Va. 921, 927–29, 265 S.E.2d 692, 696–97 (1980) (termination order reversed because of lack of evidence indicating reasonable efforts taken by social agencies to remedy conditions leading to foster care).[5] In the absence of similar statutes

4. The statute involved requires proof of parental unfitness and includes in pertinent part the following provision, which was interpreted to require reasonable efforts at reunification of the family: The court shall ... terminate any and all legal rights of the parent to the child ... if the court finds as fact that:

* * *

(c) The parent has or has had a child in the care of a licensed or governmental child

placement agency, either voluntarily or involuntarily, for a period of at least six (6) consecutive months and the court further finds that the integration of the child into the home of the parent is improbable in the foreseeable future due to conduct or conditions not likely to change. R.I.Gen.Laws § 15–7–7 1956 (1981 Reenactment).

5. The section of the Virginia Code under consideration in Weaver, supra, requires proof by clear and convincing evidence that termination of parental rights is in the best

expressly requiring that rehabilitative efforts be offered by state agencies, courts have refused to impose such requirements as a condition precedent to filing a termination proceeding. See In re I.R.A., 487 Pa. 563, 410 A.2d 755, 757 (1980). In Maine, in spite of a statutory provision placing upon the state agency an obligation to facilitate reunification of children in its custody with their parents, the court held that the failure of the agency to fulfill that responsibility would not preclude termination of parental rights absent an express requirement of such proof. In re Daniel C., 480 A.2d 766, 770 (Me.1984).

The controlling statute in this jurisdiction contains no requirement that DHS make affirmative efforts to reunite the family. See D.C.Code § 16–2351 et seq. That is not to suggest that the custodial governmental agency has no obligation in that regard. The statute under which A.C. was adjudicated neglected contains numerous provisions focusing on the roles of the court and public agencies in the reunification process. Following an adjudication of neglect, a predisposition study and report must be prepared which addresses the harms which led to intervention, plans for alleviating them, recommended services and service providers, actions required by the parents to remedy problems, estimated time necessary to reach goals of intervention, and the criteria for determining that continued intervention is no longer necessary. D.C.Code § 16–2319(c)(1). If the child is removed from the care of a parent, guardian or custodian, the report must contain plans for maintaining contact between parent and child and for fostering that relationship, consistent with the child's well-being. D.C.Code § 16–2319(c)(2)(D). The court must consider the plan contained in the report in making its dispositional order. D.C.Code § 16–2320(f); See In re M.C.S., 555 A.2d 463 (D.C.1989); see also In re C.W.M., 407 A.2d 617, 623–24 (D.C.1979). In the disposition order, the court may provide for services by any public agency to the parties deemed necessary, which are within the agency's legal authority. D.C.Code § 16–2320(a)(5). An agency responsible for providing such services must report to the court and the parties if it is unable to do so. D.C.Code § 16–2320(f).

The goal of prompt reunification of parent with child with assistance from various agencies is also reflected in the limited duration of commitment orders and the subjects addressed at periodic reviews. The term of commitment cannot exceed two years, D.C.Code § 16–2322(a)(1), and it can be extended only for additional periods of one year at a time, if necessary to safeguard the child's welfare. D.C.Code § 16–2322(b). The periodic reviews require reports to the court on the services offered or provided the parent, child and guardian, an evaluation of the cooperation of the parents and guardians with the various agencies, and the frequency of visitation. D.C.Code §§ 16–2323(b)(1)–(4). These provisions reflect the temporary character of such commitments and the expectation that the services of

interest of the child and that: 2. The parent or parents, without good cause, have been unwilling or unable within a reasonable period to remedy substantially the conditions which led to the child's foster care placement, notwithstanding the reasonable and appropriate efforts of social, medical, mental health and other rehabilitative agencies to such end. Va.Code Ann. § 16.1–283(C)(2) (Supp.1979).

public agencies will be secured to address the needs of the child and family in an effort to assure their reunification.[6]

In spite of the obligations of the public custodial agency contained in the neglect statute or imposed by court order pursuant to it, there is no statutory requirement that such agencies fulfill these responsibilities as a condition precedent to the filing or disposition of a motion to terminate parental rights under D.C.Code § 16–2353 et seq. There are clear indications in the termination statute to the contrary. Foremost, the condition is not set forth in the statute which specifies the conditions precedent to filing motions to terminate parental rights. The statute includes only that the adjudication of neglect have occurred at least six months before the filing of the motion and that the child be in the custody of an agency or person other than the parent. It is also significant that before any efforts can be made to provide services to the family to address the problems which may hinder reunification, the court has as a dispositional alternative following an adjudication of neglect, termination of the parent-child relationship pursuant to the termination statute, if in the child's best interest. D.C.Code § 16–2320(a)(6).[7] Moreover, the overriding consideration is the best interest of the child, which may compel the filing of a motion to terminate parental rights regardless of the defaults of public agencies in seeking reunification of the family.[8]

Defaults by a custodial agency in failing to provide services or make reasonable efforts to assist in resolving problems that prevent the reunification of parents with their children are a serious matter. If the family could remain together without outside intervention, consistent with the child's welfare, there would have been no need for removing the child from the home in the first place. Thus, the agency's failure to make reasonable efforts to foster reunification of parent and child may impede reunifications which might have been possible otherwise with needed assistance and services. Nevertheless, we cannot read into the statute a condition precedent to termination which is not provided for. Moreover, we cannot impose an interpretation which does not adequately consider the child's interest, which is always paramount under the statute. This court has previously rejected the argument that the primary focus in such cases should be directed towards reunification of the parent and child instead of the child's best interest. In re D.G., 583 A.2d 160, 165 (D.C.1990). The extent of reunification efforts is, however, one factor in the decision-making process where the primary focus is the best interest of the child. Id.

"The legal touchstone in any proceeding to terminate parental rights is the best interest of the child, and that interest is controlling." In re A.B.E., supra, 564 A.2d at 754 (citing D.C.Code § 16–2353(a) (1981)); In re C.O.W., 519 A.2d 711, 713–14 (D.C.1987); In re Adoption of J.S.R., 374 A.2d 860,

---

6. An agency social worker testified in the proceeding below that the first goal of DHS is to achieve family reunification.

7. A motion for termination may be filed immediately for a child who has been adjudicated abandoned or when the parent could not be located for the factfinding hearing for three months preceding the hearing despite reasonable efforts. D.C.Code § 16–2354(b)(1) and (2).

8. A motion to terminate may be filed not only by the government, but by a child through his or her legal guardian. D.C.Code § 16–2354.

864 (D.C.1977). It is also required that due consideration be given to the interest of the parents, D.C.Code § 16–2353(a), and among the statute's general purposes is "that the constitutional rights of all parties are recognized and enforced" in the proceedings "while ensuring that the fundamental needs of children are not subjugated to the interests of others ..." D.C.Code § 16–2351(a)(2). In determining the child's best interest, consideration must be given to the well established principle that such interest is presumptively best served when the child can be placed in the care of a parent who is not unfit, In re S.G., 581 A.2d 771, 784 (D.C.1990), including "a fit unwed father who has grasped his opportunity interest" in developing a relationship with the child. Appeal of H.R., 581 A.2d 1141, 1143 (D.C.1990). The action or inaction of the agency having custody of the child is pertinent to the determination of whether a parent has seized that opportunity interest. Among factors considered in determining whether an unwed, non-custodial father is entitled to due process protection is "the impact, if any, of state action on the father's opportunity to establish a relationship with his child." Id. at 1162. Where state action interferes with the natural father's assertion of his opportunity interest, such circumstances may preclude a finding that the father abandoned his opportunity interest. See id.

The agency's action is relevant to other factors as well. The court must consider the child's need for continuity of care and for timely integration into a permanent home in determining whether parental rights may be terminated, a factor upon which the actions of the public agencies may have impact. See In re D.G., supra, 583 A.2d at 165.[9] The child's chance for realizing a permanent home may be improved significantly, not by terminating parental rights in hopes of an adoptive placement, but by meaningful intervention of the social service agency in the lives of the existing family. Evidence that the agency failed to make prior efforts in that regard may explain the parent's prior inability to meet the child's needs, and leave open the prospect that the child's integration into a permanent home might be better achieved by increased services, rather than by termination of parental rights. See In re A.B.E., supra, 564 A.2d at 755; see also In re D.R.M., 570 A.2d 796, 808 (D.C.1990) (noting agency's efforts to achieve reunification). Therefore, we hold that the effort of the public custodial agency to reintegrate the family is a relevant factor in the decision-making process in a proceeding to terminate parental rights. We also hold that termination of parental rights is not precluded solely because the custodial agency has failed in its responsibility to make efforts to reunify the family. Recognizing these principles, we turn to a review of the trial court's decision under the applicable standard of review.

---

9. The statutory factors relevant in this case to determining whether the child's best interest requires termination of parental rights are: (1) the child's need for continuity of care and caretakers and for timely integration into a stable and permanent home, taking into account the differences in the development and the concept of time of children of different ages; (2) the physical, mental and emotional health of all individuals involved to the degree that such affects the welfare of the child, the decisive consideration being the physical, mental and emotional needs of the child; (3) the quality of the interaction and interrelationship of the child with his or her parent, siblings, relative and/or caretakers, including the foster parent; and (4) to the extent feasible, the child's opinion of his or her own interest in the matter. D.C.Code § 16–2353(b).

III.

Our scope of review of the trial court's order terminating parental rights of a non-custodial parent is limited to whether the decision is supported by clear and convincing evidence in the record. Appeal of U.S.W., 541 A.2d 625, 627 (D.C.1988). To affirm the trial court's decision, this court must be satisfied that there is sufficient evidence "such that the possibility of an erroneous judgment does not lie in equipoise between the two sides." In re K.A., 484 A.2d 992, 996 (D.C.1984). The evidence need not be so compelling as to exclude the likelihood of an erroneous decision, id., but it must be such "that the likelihood of an erroneous decision would be greater if the trial court elected not to terminate parental rights." In re A.B.E., supra, 564 A.2d at 755 (citing In re K.A., supra, 484 A.2d at 996). The trial court's determination of where the best interest of the child lies may be reversed only for an abuse of discretion. Appeal of S.M., 589 A.2d 1252, 1257 (D.C.1991). We review appellant's case against these standards.

IV.

The trial court's careful findings of fact and conclusions of law which resulted in the order terminating R.R.'s parental rights are unassailable. The court applied to its detailed findings of fact the criteria established in D.C.Code §§ 16–2353(b)(1)–(4) (1989), which must be considered in proceedings to terminate parental rights.[10] The court's findings and conclusions in this regard are well summarized in the following excerpt from its opinion:

> A.C. was removed from the care and custody of the natural parents, by voluntary placement in emergency care by the putative birth father, R.R., when he was approximately two (2) months old. A.C. who is now five (5) years old, has had no contact through visitation or contributions to his support and maintenance, with his mother or father since that time. A.C. has resided in the same foster care family since 1986, has bonded with that family and is a healthy and normal child. A.C., having been removed from his biological parents at such a tender age, clearly has no emotional ties or links to his natural parents. Indeed the only mother that A.C. knows is his foster care mother, and A.C. will remain in that home until he is successfully integrated into an adoptive home. An adoptive family has been identified for A.C. It is clearly in his best interest that he be placed in a permanent home. Removal of the only impediment which makes his adoption an "at risk" adoption to an adoption involving a legally-free child will undoubtedly facilitate his adoption and integration into a permanent home.

The trial court also concluded that for virtually all of his tender years, A.C.'s emotional needs had been met successfully by foster parents as a result of which he is healthy and well-adjusted. On the other hand, R.R., who did not even attend the hearings, had no interaction with the child for

---

10. See footnote 9, supra.

CHAPTER 7   TERMINATION OF PARENTAL RIGHTS

at least four years. On this record, the trial court's conclusions that A.C.'s best interest requires termination of parental rights to assure his timely integration into a permanent home and his continued physical, mental and emotional well-being is supported by clear and convincing evidence.[11]

Having outlined and considered the factors identified in Appeal of H.R., supra, 581 A.2d at 1162, for consideration in determining whether an unwed non-custodial father's opportunity interest will be entitled to substantial due process protections,[12] the trial court concluded that R.R. had never seized "the full panoply of interactions, characteristics and attendant responsibilities which define the parent and child relationship." Clear and convincing evidence supports this conclusion. There is no evidence that DHS or any other governmental agency impeded that opportunity. The record reflects and the trial court found, that DHS made exceptional efforts to attempt to locate R.R., who was well aware of how to contact the agency. Not only did he fail to do so, but he missed the only visit he ever scheduled and even failed to participate personally in the termination proceedings. The presumption that a child's best interest is served by being with a parent, extends only to " 'a fit unwed father who has grasped his opportunity interest.' " Appeal of A.H., 590 A.2d 123, 132 (D.C.1991)(citing Appeal of H.R., supra, 581 A.2d at 1143). Without that presumption the record is more than adequate to support the trial court's order terminating R.R.'s parental rights by clear and convincing evidence. Even if the presumption applied, the decision would be the same on this record.

. . . Affirmed.

NOTE

The federal Adoption Assistance and Child Welfare Act, enacted in 1980, requires qualifying state plans for foster care and assistance to needy families to provide "that, in each case, reasonable efforts will be made (A) prior to the placement of a child in foster care, to prevent or eliminate the need for removal of the child from his home, and (B) to make it possible for the child to return to his home." 42 U.S.C.A. § 671(15). For discussion of this provision and what constitutes "reasonable efforts", see David J. Herring, Inclusion of the Reasonable Efforts Requirement in Termination of Parental Rights Statutes: Punishing the Child for the Failures of the State Child Welfare System, 54 U.Pitt.L.Rev. 139 (1992); Alice C. Shotton, Making Reasonable Efforts in Child Abuse and Neglect Cases: Ten Years Later, 26 Cal. Western L.Rev. 223 (1990).

---

11. The trial court did not ascertain A.C.'s opinion as to his best interest because the child does not know his parents. The statute requires consideration of this factor only to the extent feasible. D.C.Code § 16–2353(b)(4).

12. The factors set forth in Appeal of H.R., supra, are: (1) the presence or absence of an established relationship between the child and an existing family; (2) whether the father has established a custodial, personal, or financial relationship with his child, or assumed responsibilities during the mother's pregnancy; (3) the impact, if any, of state action on the father's opportunity to establish a relationship with his child; (4) the age of the child when the action to terminate parental rights is initiated; and (5) the natural father's invocation or disregard of statutory safeguards designed to protect his opportunity interest. Id. at 1162.

D. Safe Haven Laws

A substantial majority of the states in recent years have enacted what are known as "safe haven" statutes. There is much variation between them but their basic approach is to provide that a parent who anonymously leaves a newborn child or young infant at a certain designated location (hospitals, emergency medical service facilities, or a fire station are among locations that have been designated) may avoid giving personal information and prosecution for abandonment except when child abuse is evident. This "legally condoned abandonment" is designed to deal with the significant number of cases in which newborns have been abandoned anonymously, and sometimes found only after their death. A presumption of abandonment arises but the statutes differ regarding the legal procedures that must be taken to assure that parental rights can be terminated under constitutional standards with only minimal steps . Once the rights of the parent have been terminated, an adoption or other placement can take place.

Some statutes are worded in such a fashion as to appear that they apply to a surrender by either a father or a mother, but it has been suggested that they serve largely to permit anonymous surrender by unmarried, genetic mothers who under many statutes need not identify the genetic fathers (or perhaps even themselves). This has raised serious constitutional questions about whether they contravene the spirit, if not the letter, of modern decisions and statutes ostensibly protecting the parental rights of unwed fathers. For further commentary on the statutes, see Annette R. Appell, Safe Havens to Abandon Babies: Part I: The Law, 5 (4) Adoption Quarterly 59 (2002); Appell, supra, Part II: The Fit, 6 (1) Adoption Quarterly 61 (2002); Appell, supra, Part III: The Effects, 6 (2) Adoption Quarterly 67 (2002); Jeffrey A. Parness, Deserting Mothers, Abandoned Babies, Lost Fathers: Dangers in Safe Havens, 24 Quinnipiac L.Rev. 335–349 (2006); Carol Sanger, Infant Safe Haven Laws: Legislating in the Culture of Life, 106 Colum.L.Rev. 753–829 (2006); Christina A. Zawisza, Taking Hold of the Elephant in Child Dependency and Neglect Cases, 17 St. Thomas L.Rev. 531–559 (2005). See also, *Stanley v. Illinois*, at p. 63 supra.

FLORIDA STATUTES ANNOTATED

§ 383.50. Treatment of abandoned newborn infant.

(1) As used in this section, the term "newborn infant" means a child that a licensed physician reasonably believes to be approximately 3 days old or younger at the time the child is left at a hospital, emergency medical services station, or fire station.

(2) There is a presumption that the parent who leaves the newborn infant in accordance with this section intended to leave the newborn infant and consented to termination of parental rights.

(3) Each emergency medical services station or fire station staffed with full-time firefighters, emergency medical technicians, or paramedics shall accept any newborn infant left with a firefighter, emergency medical

technician, or paramedic. The firefighter, emergency medical technician, or paramedic shall consider these actions as implied consent to and shall:

(a) Provide emergency medical services to the newborn infant to the extent he or she is trained to provide those services, and

(b) Arrange for the immediate transportation of the newborn infant to the nearest hospital having emergency services.

A licensee as defined in § 401.23, a fire department, or an employee or agent of a licensee or fire department may treat and transport a newborn infant pursuant to this section. If a newborn infant is placed in the physical custody of an employee or agent of a licensee or fire department, such placement shall be considered implied consent for treatment and transport. A licensee, a fire department, or an employee or agent of a licensee or fire department is immune from criminal or civil liability for acting in good faith pursuant to this section. Nothing in this subsection limits liability for negligence.

(4) Each hospital of this state subject to § 395.1041 shall, and any other hospital may, admit and provide all necessary emergency services and care, as defined in § 395.002(10), to any newborn infant left with the hospital in accordance with this section. The hospital or any of its licensed health care professionals shall consider these actions as implied consent for treatment, and a hospital accepting physical custody of a newborn infant has implied consent to perform all necessary emergency services and care. The hospital or any of its licensed health care professionals is immune from criminal or civil liability for acting in good faith in accordance with this section. Nothing in this subsection limits liability for negligence.

(5) Except where there is actual or suspected child abuse or neglect, any parent who leaves a newborn infant with a firefighter, emergency medical technician, or paramedic at a fire station or emergency medical services station, or brings a newborn infant to an emergency room of a hospital and expresses an intent to leave the newborn infant and not return, has the absolute right to remain anonymous and to leave at any time and may not be pursued or followed unless the parent seeks to reclaim the newborn infant.

(6) A parent of a newborn infant left at a hospital, emergency medical services station, or fire station under this section may claim his or her newborn infant up until the court enters a judgment terminating his or her parental rights. A claim to the newborn infant must be made to the entity having physical or legal custody of the newborn infant or to the circuit court before whom proceedings involving the newborn infant are pending.

(7) Upon admitting a newborn infant under this section, the hospital shall immediately contact a local licensed child-placing agency or alternatively contact the statewide central abuse hotline for the name of a licensed child-placing agency for purposes of transferring physical custody of the newborn infant. The hospital shall notify the licensed child-placing agency that a newborn infant has been left with the hospital and approximately when the licensed child-placing agency can take physical custody of the child. In cases where there is actual or suspected child abuse or neglect, the hospital or any of its licensed health care professionals shall report the

actual or suspected child abuse or neglect in accordance with §§ 39.201 and 395.1023 in lieu of contacting a licensed child-placing agency.

(8) Any newborn infant admitted to a hospital in accordance with this section is presumed eligible for coverage under Medicaid, subject to federal rules.

(9) A newborn infant left at a hospital, emergency medical services station, or fire station in accordance with this section shall not be deemed abandoned and subject to reporting and investigation requirements under § 39.201 unless there is actual or suspected child abuse or until the department takes physical custody of the child.

(10) A criminal investigation shall not be initiated solely because a newborn infant is left at a hospital under this section unless there is actual or suspected child abuse or neglect.

§ 383.51.   Confidentiality; identification of parent leaving newborn infant at hospital, emergency medical services station, or fire station.

The identity of a parent who leaves a newborn infant at a hospital, emergency medical services station, or fire station in accordance with § 383.50 is confidential and exempt from the provisions of § 119.07(1) and § 24(a), Art. I of the State Constitution. The identity of a parent leaving a child shall be disclosed to a person claiming to be a parent of the newborn infant.

NOTE

In a separate, complementary statute, the Florida legislature has set out guidelines and rules for the courts and for licensed agencies who take custody of any infants abandoned to the designated entities. The statute attempts to balance issues of notice to parents for adoption (usually constructive), maintaining confidentiality, not penalizing abandonment, presumptive consent, and confidentiality in a facilitated adoption process. See Fla.Stat.Ann. § 63.0423.

CHAPTER VIII

ADOPTION OF MINORS

A. CONTINUING CHANGE FOR A VENERABLE INSTITUTION

Adoption is best known as a legal procedure for establishing a legal parent-child relationship between persons who are not so related previously.[1] No blood ties are needed. Many centuries ago adoption was used to perpetuate family religious rites or to provide continuity for other purposes, or to serve a function similar to that of the modern will. Although it reached a fairly high degree of formal development in Roman law, it passed into some modern civil law countries as well.

In France, adoption had almost disappeared by the time of the Revolution. Its revival and incorporation into the 1804 Civil Code included the limitation that the adopter must be at least fifty years of age and without legitimate child or other descendant at the time of the adoption, and that the adoptee must have reached majority.[2] Not until well into the 20th century, with the introduction of a process known as adoptive legitimation, did French law provide a method for adopting an infant and fully integrating the child into a normal family situation at an early age.

The common law did not recognize adoption. It was first introduced by statute in England in 1926.[3] Thus adoption law in the United States developed independently of English influence and our courts were often hampered by the tenet of strict construction of statutes in derogation of the common law. Although adoption in the civil law sense was the first to exist in this country because of Spanish influence in Louisiana and Texas,[4] this is unimportant to present considerations because those provisions differed greatly in purpose and effect from the later American version and disappeared early.

Although the American version of adoption draws to some extent on the civil law model, the institution has developed much differently in this country. Our adoption system has as its principal object the promotion of child welfare. As one commentator has put it, adoption in the United States is "a process of selecting fit parents for children, not finding children for

---

1. In some jurisdictions a natural parent of a child born out of wedlock can formally adopt his or her child. See e.g., *Bridges v. Nicely*, 304 Md. 1, 497 A.2d 142 (1985); *Petition of Curran*, 314 Mass. 91, 49 N.E.2d 432 (1943).

2. Civil Code arts. 343, 346 (Fr.1804). See, also, Walter Wadlington, Minimum Age Difference as a Requisite for Adoption, 1966 Duke L.J. 392, 396–7.

3. Adoption of Children Act, 1926, 16 & 17 Geo. 5, c. 29. For discussion of the background of adoption in England, see Stephen B. Presser, The Historical Background of the American Law of Adoption, 11 J.Fam.Law 443 (1971).

4. See, e.g., *Vidal v. Commagère*, 13 La.Ann. 516 (1858); *Fuselier v. Masse*, 4 La. 423 (1832); *Teal v. Sevier*, 26 Tex. 516 (1863).

parents."[5] The oldest of our modern adoption statutes is the 1851 Massachusetts law[6] which served as a model for a number of other states. The 1865 Civil Code of New York, known as the Field Code, included an extensive section on adoption. Though not adopted by the New York legislature, the Field Code greatly influenced adoption law in some of our western states, sometimes enacted by them without substantial change.

More recent influences on state adoption legislation have included the Uniform Adoption Act of 1953 and the suggested language for "An Act for the Adoption of Children", published by the Children's Bureau of the Department of Health, Education and Welfare. A Revised Uniform Adoption Act was approved by the National Conference of Commissioners on Uniform State Laws in 1969. A new and much more detailed Uniform Adoption Act was promulgated by the National Conference of Commissioners on Uniform Laws in 1994.[7] Despite this proliferation of models, however, the legislative development of adoption statutes has been a slow, patchwork process in many states. Early in the past century the most prominent variations between state laws concerned such matters as the need for judicial intervention and approval (as opposed to adoption by deed or contract), the need for investigation of the adoptive home for fitness, and civil effects of an adoption decree. Today judicial intervention and investigation of the adoptive home are standard practices, and most states try to equate the adopter-adoptee relationship with that of parent and legitimate child by blood kinship in all legal respects.

For many years the key focus of adoption practice was to place children with adoptive families as soon after birth as circumstance permitted. Changing attitudes concerning legitimacy, widespread dissemination of information about birth control, the availability of legal abortion and a declining birth rate already have had considerable impact on adoption and on the network of state and private agencies through which the bulk of non-relative placements traditionally have been made. The extent of this change (in a numbers sense) has been cushioned by the fact that many children, typically those with physical handicaps and other children with special needs, had long remained largely outside the adoption process but have now been included within it to a far greater degree.

Ironically we must note that orphanages, once popular beneficiaries of philanthropists interested in helping children, reached a point some years ago when some had significant assets but few orphans in their care. Diversion of their assets was sought in some instances through application of the *cy pres* doctrine.[8] This reflected in part a change in attitudes toward how unwanted or parentless children could best be cared for, as well as changing views toward accepting outsiders into family groups.

5. Sanford Katz, Community Decision—Makers and the Promotion of Values in the Adoption of Children, 4 J.Fam.Law 7, 8 (1964).

6. Mass.Gen.Laws 1836–1853, ch. 324, at 752 (1854).

7. 9 U.L.A. 1 (Supp.1999). The Act also is reproduced in Walter Wadlington and Raymond C. O'Brien, Family Law Statutes, International Conventions and Uniform Laws 1, 3d ed. (Foundation Press 2007).

8. See *In re Milne's Succession*, 230 La. 729, 89 So.2d 281 (1956).

Today there is growing debate over whether there should be increased openness in the adoption process and, if so, how far it should be extended. Key legal proposals for and against this, along with statutory and judicial changes regarding it, will be addressed in the chapter, along with the traditional rules of the game stemming from the latter part of the previous century. It is important to understand that adoption remains largely a creature of state law in our country, which translates into many different judicial and statutory rules and procedures. A favorable outlook toward it today nationally can be illustrated by the availability of federal tax credits.

For a valuable resource on current adoption facts and issues, see Adoption Factbook IV (2007), published by the National Council for Adoption.

B.   WHO CAN ADOPT?: THE IMPORTANCE OF STATE LAWS AND THEIR CONSTRUCTION

Adoption of Tammy

Supreme Judicial Court of Massachusetts, Middlesex, 1993.
416 Mass. 205, 619 N.E.2d 315.

■ GREANEY, JUSTICE.

In this case, two unmarried women, Susan and Helen, filed a joint petition in the Probate and Family Court Department under G.L. c. 210, § 1 (1992 ed.) to adopt as their child Tammy, a minor, who is Susan's biological daughter. Following an evidentiary hearing, a judge of the Probate and Family Court entered a memorandum of decision containing findings of fact and conclusions of law. Based on her finding that Helen and Susan "are each functioning, separately and together, as the custodial and psychological parents of [Tammy]," and that "it is the best interest of said [Tammy] that she be adopted by both," the judge entered a decree allowing the adoption. Simultaneously, the judge reserved and reported to the Appeals Court the evidence and all questions of law, in an effort to "secure [the] decree from any attack in the future on jurisdictional grounds." ... We conclude that the adoption was properly allowed under G.L. c. 210.[1]

We summarize the relevant facts as found by the judge. Helen and Susan have lived together in a committed relationship, which they consider to be permanent, for more than ten years. In June, 1983, they jointly purchased a house in Cambridge. Both women are physicians specializing in surgery. At the time the petition was filed, Helen maintained a private practice in general surgery at Mount Auburn Hospital and Susan, a

---

1. The judge also decreed, as an alternative to the adoption ordered under G.L. c. 210, "[I]t would be in the best interest of the child to permit [Helen] to adopt [Tammy] and [Susan] to retain postadoptive parental rights of custody and visitation pursuant to its equitable powers, under G.L. c. 215." Be- cause we conclude that the adoption was properly allowed under G.L. c. 210, we need not consider the alternative equitable ground relied on by the judge in permitting Helen to adopt Tammy and Susan to maintain postadoptive rights.

nationally recognized expert in the field of breast cancer, was director of the Faulkner Breast Center and a surgical oncologist at the Dana Farber Cancer Institute. Both women also held positions on the faculty of Harvard Medical School.

For several years prior to the birth of Tammy, Helen and Susan planned to have a child, biologically related to both of them, whom they would jointly parent. Helen first attempted to conceive a child through artificial insemination by Susan's brother. When those efforts failed, Susan successfully conceived a child through artificial insemination by Helen's biological cousin, Francis. The women attended childbirth classes together and Helen was present when Susan gave birth to Tammy on April 30, 1988. Although Tammy's birth certificate reflects Francis as her biological father, she was given a hyphenated surname using Susan and Helen's last names.

Since her birth, Tammy has lived with, and been raised and supported by, Helen and Susan. Tammy views both women as her parents, calling Helen "mama" and Susan "mommy." Tammy has strong emotional and psychological bonds with both Helen and Susan. Together, Helen and Susan have provided Tammy with a comfortable home, and have created a warm and stable environment which is supportive of Tammy's growth and over-all well being. Both women jointly and equally participate in parenting Tammy, and both have a strong financial commitment to her. During the work week, Helen usually has lunch at home with Tammy, and on weekends both women spend time together with Tammy at special events or running errands. When Helen and Susan are working, Tammy is cared for by a nanny. The three vacation together at least ten days every three to four months, frequently spending time with Helen's and Susan's respective extended families in California and Mexico. Francis does not participate in parenting Tammy and does not support her. His intention was to assist Helen and Susan in having a child, and he does not intend to be involved with Tammy, except as a distant relative. Francis signed an adoption surrender and supports the joint adoption by both women.

Helen and Susan, recognizing that the laws of the Commonwealth do not permit them to enter into a legally cognizable marriage, believe that the best interests of Tammy require legal recognition of her identical emotional relationship to both women. Susan expressed her understanding that it may not be in her own long-term interest to permit Helen to adopt Tammy because, in the event that Helen and Susan separate, Helen would have equal rights to primary custody. Susan indicated, however, that she has no reservation about allowing Helen to adopt. Apart from the emotional security and current practical ramifications which legal recognition of the reality of her parental relationships will provide Tammy, Susan indicated that the adoption is important for Tammy in terms of potential inheritance from Helen. Helen and her living issue are the beneficiaries of three irrevocable family trusts. Unless Tammy is adopted, Helen's share of the trusts may pass to others. Although Susan and Helen have established a substantial trust fund for Tammy, it is comparatively small in relation to Tammy's potential inheritance under Helen's family trusts.

Over a dozen witnesses, including mental health professionals, teachers, colleagues, neighbors, blood relatives and a priest and nun, testified to the fact that Helen and Susan participate equally in raising Tammy, that Tammy relates to both women as her parents, and that the three form a healthy, happy, and stable family unit. Educators familiar with Tammy testified that she is an extremely well-adjusted, bright, creative, cheerful child who interacts well with other children and adults. A priest and nun from the parties' church testified that Helen and Susan are active parishioners, that they routinely take Tammy to church and church-related activities, and that they attend to the spiritual and moral development of Tammy in an exemplary fashion. Teachers from Tammy's school testified that Helen and Susan both actively participate as volunteers in the school community and communicate frequently with school officials. Neighbors testified that they would have no hesitation in leaving their own children in the care of Helen or Susan. Susan's father, brother, and maternal aunt, and Helen's cousin testified in favor of the joint adoption. Members of both women's extended families attested to the fact that they consider Helen and Susan to be equal parents of Tammy. Both families unreservedly endorsed the adoption petition.

The Department of Social Services (department) conducted a home study in connection with the adoption petition which recommended the adoption, concluding that "the petitioners and their home are suitable for the proper rearing of this child." Tammy's pediatrician reported to the department that Tammy receives regular pediatric care and that she "could not have more excellent parents than Helen and Susan." A court-appointed guardian ad litem, Dr. Steven Nickman, assistant clinical professor of psychiatry at Harvard Medical School, conducted a clinical assessment of Tammy and her family with a view toward determining whether or not it would be in Tammy's best interests to be adopted by Helen and Susan. Dr. Nickman considered the ramifications of the fact that Tammy will be brought up in a "non-standard" family. As part of his report, he reviewed and referenced literature on child psychiatry and child psychology which supports the conclusion that children raised by lesbian parents develop normally. In sum, he stated that "the fact that this parent-child constellation came into being as a result of thoughtful planning and a strong desire on the part of these women to be parents to a child and to give that child the love, the wisdom and the knowledge that they possess ... [needs to be taken into account].... The maturity of these women, their status in the community, and their seriousness of purpose stands in contrast to the caretaking environments of a vast number of children who are born to heterosexual parents but who are variously abused, neglected and otherwise deprived of security and happiness." Dr. Nickman concluded that "there is every reason for [Helen] to become a legal parent to Tammy just as [Susan] is," and he recommended that the court so order. An attorney appointed to represent Tammy's interests also strongly recommended that the joint petition be granted.

Despite the overwhelming support for the joint adoption and the judge's conclusion that joint adoption is clearly in Tammy's best interests, the question remains whether there is anything in the law of the Commonwealth that would prevent this adoption. The law of adoption is purely statutory, is to be strictly followed in all its essential particulars. To the extent that any ambiguity or vagueness exists in the statute, judicial construction should enhance, rather than defeat, its purpose. The primary purpose of the adoption statute, particularly with regard to children under the age of fourteen, is undoubtedly the advancement of the best interests of the subject child.... With these considerations in mind, we examine the statute to determine whether adoption in the circumstances of this case is permitted.

1. The initial question is whether the Probate Court judge had jurisdiction under G.L. c. 210 to enter a judgment on a joint petition for adoption brought by two unmarried cohabitants in the petitioners' circumstances. We answer this question in the affirmative.

There is nothing on the face of the statute which precludes the joint adoption of a child by two unmarried cohabitants such as the petitioners. Chapter 210, § 1, provides that "[a] person of full age may petition the probate court in the county where he resides for leave to adopt as his child another person younger than himself, unless such other person is his or her wife or husband, or brother, sister, uncle or aunt, of the whole or half blood."[2] Other than requiring that a spouse join in the petition, if the petitioner is married and the spouse is competent to join therein, the statute does not expressly prohibit or require joinder by any person.[3] Although the singular "a person" is used, it is a legislatively mandated rule of statutory construction that "[w]ords importing the singular number may extend and be applied to several persons" unless the resulting construction is "inconsistent with the manifest intent of the law-making body or repugnant to the context of the same statute." G.L. c. 4, § 6 (1992 ed.). In the context of adoption, where the legislative intent to promote the best interests of the child is evidenced throughout the governing statute, and the adoption of a child by two unmarried individuals accomplishes that goal, construing the term "person" as "persons" clearly enhances, rather

---

2. There is no question that Helen and Susan each individually satisfy the identity requirements of G.L. c. 210, § 1. Although the adoption statute, as it first appeared (St. 1851, c. 324) precluded a person from adopting his or her own child by birth, the statute was amended to permit adoption by the child's natural parents. Curran, Petition of, 314 Mass. 91, 49 N.E.2d 432 (1943) (natural mother of child born out of wedlock proper party to adoption petition). None of the prohibitions to adoption set forth in § 1 is applicable. Furthermore, there is nothing in the statute that prohibits adoption based on gender or sexual orientation. Contrast Fla.Stat. § 63.042(3) (1991) (prohibiting homosexuals from adopting); N.H.Rev.Stat.Ann. § 170–B:4 (1990) (same). 381 Mass. 563, 579, 410 N.E.2d 1207 (1980).

3. The provision concerning joinder of spouses is a requirement that has been present in the statute since its enactment in 1851.... Adoption by a married person has the effect of changing the legal duties of both spouses because the "infant who is adopted becomes the child not of one but of both." Lee v. Wood, 279 Mass. 293, 295, 181 N.E. 229 (1932). Both spouses must freely consent to join in the adoption petition. If a person falsely claims to be the legal spouse of another, the Probate Court may vacate the adoption decree. The required joinder of spouses, which is jurisdictional in nature, does not by its terms apply to joint petitions by unmarried persons who seek to adopt. See Adoption of B.L.V.B., 628 A.2d 1271 (Vt.1993) (requirement of joinder of spouses in Vermont adoption statute does not bar adoption by same-sex partner of children's natural mother); Matter of A.J.J., 108 Misc.2d 657, 659–660, 438 N.Y.S.2d 444 (N.Y.Sur.Ct.1981) (natural parents decided not to marry; natural father permitted, with mother's consent, to adopt as if he were married to mother); Matter of the Adoption of a Child by A.R., 152 N.J.Super. 541, 545, 378 A.2d 87 (1977) (natural father permitted to adopt his illegitimate child without marrying mother or terminating mother's legal relationship to child).

than defeats, the purpose of the statute. Furthermore, it is apparent from the first sentence of G.L. c. 210, § 1, that the Legislature considered and defined those combinations of persons which would lead to adoptions in violation of public policy. Clearly absent is any prohibition of adoption by two unmarried individuals like the petitioners.

While the Legislature may not have envisioned adoption by same-sex partners, there is no indication that it attempted to define all possible categories of persons leading to adoptions in the best interests of children.[4] Rather than limit the potential categories of persons entitled to adopt (other than those described in the first sentence of § 1), the Legislature used general language to define who may adopt and who may be adopted. The Probate Court has thus been granted jurisdiction to consider a variety of adoption petitions. See Adoption of Thomas, 408 Mass. 446, 449–451, 559 N.E.2d 1230 (1990). The limitations on adoption that do exist derive from the written consent requirements contained in § 2,[5] from specific conditions set forth in § 2A, which must be satisfied prior to the adoption of a child under the age of fourteen,[6] and from several statutory and judicial directives[7] which essentially restrict adoptions to those which have been

---

4. Children in earlier times who lacked two married and living parents, just as many children today, were often adopted into "nonstandard" families. See e.g., Curran, petitioner, supra (child born out of wedlock adopted by unmarried natural mother); Delano v. Bruerton, 148 Mass. 619, 20 N.E. 308 (1889) (grandfather adopted grandson, child of his deceased son). By permitting adoption by unmarried persons, the Legislature clearly sanctioned adoption into "non-standard" families. Moreover, the Legislature could easily have contemplated circumstances leading to adoption by more than one unmarried party, albeit in circumstances different from this case. For example, orphaned children are frequently taken in and raised by relatives, who may be unmarried siblings, aunts or uncles, or cousins of their parents. See, e.g., Merrill v. Berlin, 316 Mass. 87, 89, 54 N.E.2d 674 (1944) (court found that it was in the best interests of two orphaned boys to be raised by their deceased mother's aunt and two female cousins, despite the "wholly feminine" nature of the household).

5. General Laws c. 210, § 2 (1992 ed.), provides in relevant part: "A decree of adoption shall not be made, except as provided in this chapter, without the written consent of the child to be adopted, if above the age of twelve; of the child's spouse, if any; of the lawful parents, who may be previous adoptive parents, or surviving parent; or of the mother only if the child was born out of wedlock and not previously adopted. A person whose consent is hereby required shall not be prevented from being the adoptive parent." Susan's

request to adopt her own child and her consent to Helen's adoption of Tammy satisfies the statute. Although not required by the statute, Francis, the biological father, has provided his written consent to the joint adoption. The written consent of the child's natural parents is not required if the court has terminated the natural parents' legal rights to the child because there has been a showing by clear and convincing evidence that the natural parents are unfit. G.L. c. 210, § 3 (1992 ed.).

6. A decree of adoption may not be entered unless one of five preconditions set forth in G.L. c. 210, § 2A, is satisfied. These preconditions include a showing that "the petitioner is a blood relative of the child sought to be adopted" or that "[t]he petition for adoption has been approved in writing by the department of social services or by an agency authorized by said department." Because both Susan and Helen are blood relatives of Tammy, and the department has approved the adoption, two of the preconditions have been satisfied in this case.

7. The judge is directed to consider "all factors relevant to the physical, mental and moral health of the child" and a decree of adoption may be entered only after the judge has determined that the adopting parties are "of sufficient ability to bring up the child and provide suitable support and education for it, and that the child should be adopted." G.L. c. 210, §§ 5B, 6. Additionally, we have stated, with regard to establishing the status of legal parent, that the judge "must look at the

found by a judge to be in the best interests of the subject child. See Merrill v. Berlin, supra, 316 Mass. at 89, 54 N.E.2d 674 (in dismissing elderly grandparents' petition to adopt following death of children's parents, and retaining custody with three female testamentary guardians, the court stated "[t]he only question [to be considered] is whether the best interests of the children would be served by their adoption").

In this case all requirements in §§ 2 and 2A are met, and there is no question that the judge's findings demonstrate that the directives set forth in §§ 5B and 6, and in case law, have been satisfied. Adoption will not result in any tangible change in Tammy's daily life; it will, however, serve to provide her with a significant legal relationship which may be important in her future. At the most practical level, adoption will entitle Tammy to inherit from Helen's family trusts and from Helen and her family under the law of intestate succession, to receive support from Helen, who will be legally obligated to provide such support, to be eligible for coverage under Helen's health insurance policies, and to be eligible for social security benefits in the event of Helen's disability or death.

Of equal, if not greater significance, adoption will enable Tammy to preserve her unique filial ties to Helen in the event that Helen and Susan separate, or Susan predeceases Helen.[8] As the case law and commentary on the subject illustrate, when the functional parents of children born in circumstances similar to Tammy separate or one dies, the children often remain in legal limbo for years while their future is disputed in the courts. Polikoff, This Child Does Have Two Mothers: Redefining Parenthood to Meet the Needs of Children in Lesbian–Mother and Other Nontraditional Families, 78 Geo.L.J. 459, 508–522 (1990); Comment, Second Parent Adoption for Lesbian–Parented Families: Legal Recognition of the Other Mother, 19 U.C.Davis L.Rev. 729, 741–745 (1986). In some cases, children have been denied the affection of a functional parent who has been with them since birth, even when it is apparent that this outcome is contrary to the children's best interests.[9] Adoption serves to establish legal rights and

relationship [between the parent and the child] as a whole, and consider emotional bonds, economic support, custody of the child, the extent of personal association, the commitment of the [parent] to attending to the child's needs, the consistency of the [parent's] expressed interest ... and any other factors which bear on the nature of the alleged parent-child relationship." C.C. v. A.B., 406 Mass. 679, 690, 550 N.E.2d 365 (1990).

8. Although Susan has designated Helen guardian of Tammy in her will, Helen's custody of Tammy could conceivably be contested in the event of Susan's death, particularly by Francis, members of his family or members of Susan's family. Absent adoption, Helen would not have a dispositive legal right to retain custody of Tammy, because she would be a "legal stranger" to the child.

9. Cases from other jurisdictions demonstrate the difficulties resulting from the

lack of an established legal relationship between a child and its second functional parent. See, e.g., In re the Interest of Z.J.H., 162 Wis.2d 1002, 1033, 471 N.W.2d 202 (1991) (Bablitch, J., dissenting) (former lesbian partner of child's adoptive mother, who had planned on adoption, cultivated "parent-like" relationship with child since his birth, and had been child's primary caretaker, denied both visitation and custody after partners' separation due to lack of legal relationship with child; court refused to consider issue of child's best interests); Nancy S. v. Michele G., 228 Cal.App.3d 831, 840 & n. 8, 279 Cal.Rptr. 212 (1991) (two children conceived by artificial insemination during lesbian couple's relationship deemed legal children of natural mother only, who was granted sole physical and legal custody following the couple's separation; appellate court recognized that adoption would avoid this "unfortunate

responsibilities so that, in the event that problems arise in the future, issues of custody and visitation may be promptly resolved by reference to the best interests of the child within the recognized framework of the law. See G.L. c. 209C, § 10. See also Adoption of B.L.V.B., 628 A.2d 1271 (Vt.1993). There is no jurisdictional bar in the statute to the judge's consideration of this joint petition. The conclusion that the adoption is in the best interests of Tammy is also well warranted.

2. The judge also posed the question whether, pursuant to G.L. c. 210, § 6 (1992 ed.), Susan's legal relationship to Tammy must be terminated if Tammy is adopted. Section 6 provides that, on entry of an adoption decree, "all rights, duties and other legal consequences of the natural relation of child and parent shall . . . except as regards marriage, incest or cohabitation, terminate between the child so adopted and his natural parents and kindred." Although G.L. c. 210, § 2, clearly permits a child's natural parent to be an adoptive parent, § 6 does not contain any express exceptions to its termination provision. The Legislature obviously did not intend that a natural parent's legal relationship to its child be terminated when the natural parent is a party to the adoption petition.

Section 6 clearly is directed to the more usual circumstances of adoption, where the child is adopted by persons who are not the child's natural parents (either because the natural parents have elected to relinquish the child for adoption or their parental rights have been involuntarily terminated). The purpose of the termination provision is to protect the security of the child's newly-created family unit by eliminating involvement with the child's natural parents. Although it is not uncommon for a natural parent to join in the adoption petition of a spouse who is not the child's natural parent, the statute has never been construed to require the termination of the natural parent's legal relationship to the child in these circumstances. Nor has § 6 been construed to apply when the natural mother petitions alone to adopt her child born out of wedlock. See Curran, petitioner, 314 Mass. 91, 49 N.E.2d 432 (1943). Reading the adoption statute as a whole, we conclude that the termination provision contained in § 6 was intended to apply only when the natural parents (or parent) are not parties to the adoption petition.[10]

3. We conclude that the Probate Court has jurisdiction to enter a decree on a joint adoption petition brought by the two petitioners when the judge has found that joint adoption is in the subject child's best interests.

---

situation" noting that "we see nothing in [our statutory] provisions [similar to those in Massachusetts] that would preclude a child from being jointly adopted by someone of the same sex as the natural parent"); In re Pearlman, 15 Fam.L.Rep. (BNA) 1355 (Fla.Cir.Ct. 1989) (unreported) (custody of child conceived by artificial insemination during lesbian couple's relationship awarded to "de facto" parent after four years of litigation with child's maternal grandparents following death of natural mother; child, who had been separated from her functional parent and suffered anxiety as a result, told the court "for

Christmas I don't really want a present. All I want is to live with Neenie ['de facto' parent]").

10. In interpreting a provision similar to G.L. c. 210, § 6, the Vermont Supreme Court, citing support from trial courts in other jurisdictions, likewise concluded that the natural or prior adoptive parent's legal relationship to the child does not terminate when the child is adopted by the same-sex partner of the child's legal parent. See Adoption of B.L.V.B., 628 A.2d 1271 (Vt.1993). . . .

We further conclude that, when a natural parent is a party to a joint adoption petition, that parent's legal relationship to the child does not terminate on entry of the adoption decree.

4.   So much of the decree as allows the adoption of Tammy by both petitioners is affirmed. So much of the decree as provides in the alternative for the adoption of Tammy by Helen and the retention of rights of custody and visitation by Susan is vacated.

■ Nolan, Justice (dissenting).

I write separately in dissent only because I do not agree with the sentiments expressed by my brother Lynch in the first few sentences of his dissent. His dissent is otherwise a faultless analysis of our existing jurisprudence to which I subscribe.

■ Lynch, Justice (dissenting, with whom O'Connor, Justice, joins).

At the outset I wish to make clear that my views are not motivated by any disapproval of the two petitioners here or their life-style. The judge has found that the petitioners have provided the child with a healthy, happy, stable family unit. The evidence supports the judge's findings. Nor is my disagreement with the court related to the sexual orientation of the petitioners. I am firmly of the view that a litigant's expression of human sexuality ought not determine the outcome of litigation as long as it involves consenting adults and is not harmful to others. However, the court's decision, which is inconsistent with the statutory language, cannot be justified by a desire to achieve what is in the child's best interests. Indeed, those interests can be accommodated without doing violence to the statute by accepting the alternative to joint adoption suggested by the Probate Court judge; that is, permitting Helen to adopt Tammy while allowing Susan to retain all her parental rights and obligations. This is essentially what the court accomplishes in part 2 of its opinion. By this simple expedient, all of the court's concerns about protecting filial ties and avoiding legal limits are put to rest without invading the prerogatives of the Legislature and giving legal status to a relationship by judicial fiat that our elected representatives and the general public have, as yet, failed to endorse.

The court concludes that the Probate and Family Court has jurisdiction to grant a joint petition for adoption by two unmarried cohabitants because they meet the statutory requirements of G.L. c. 210, § 1, and it is in the child's best interests to be adopted by both. General Laws c. 210, § 1, enumerates who may petition for adoption. In accordance with the statute, a petitioner of full age may petition to adopt. If a person is married and has a competent spouse, the spouse is required to join in the petition to adopt. If a husband and wife fail jointly to petition for adoption, a decree or judgment granting the adoption is void. A minor may petition for adoption of his or her natural child or may join in the petition of his or her spouse when the child is the natural child of one of the parties. G.L. c. 210, § 1. The court has also interpreted the statute as permitting a biological parent of full age to petition for the adoption of his or her own child. Curran, petitioner, 314 Mass. 91, 95, 49 N.E.2d 432 (1943). There is, however, nothing in the statute indicating a legislative intent to allow two or more unmarried persons jointly to petition for adoption.[2]

Massachusetts became the first common law jurisdiction to authorize judicially approved adoption with parental consent by statute. General jurisdiction over adoptions is granted to the Probate and Family Court, G.L. c. 215, § 3, and can be exercised only as provided by the Legislature with the paramount concern, purpose, and focus of adoption proceedings being the welfare of the child. Since adoption is a creature of the Legislature, and in derogation of the common law, the statute must be strictly construed. The plain meaning of a statute cannot be expanded or altered where the Legislature establishes specific criteria or classifications to be satisfied. Unless one of the enumerated potential petitioners brings an adoption petition, the court lacks the jurisdiction to entertain the petition. In the present case, the petitioners are two unmarried persons seeking to adopt a child. The statute only permits joint petitions for adoption by married persons. See Adoption of Meaux, 417 So.2d 522, 523 (La.Ct.App. 1982) (unmarried natural parents may not jointly adopt own illegitimate child); Matter of Adams, 189 Mich.App. 540, 544, 473 N.W.2d 712 (1991) (inconsistent with purpose and scope of adoption statute to allow joint adoption of two unmarried petitioners); In re Jason C., 129 N.H. 762, 765, 533 A.2d 32 (1987) (two unmarried persons may not jointly adopt child). Contra Adoption of B.L.V.B., 628 A.2d 1271 (Vt.1993) (92–321) (permitting joint petition to adopt by two unmarried persons).

The court opines that the use of the singular form "a person" in the first sentence of the statute should not be construed as prohibiting joint petitions by unmarried persons because such an interpretation would not be in the best interests of the child. I have already demonstrated that, whether the petition be singular or joint, has nothing to do with the best interests of the child. The court's reasoning in part 2 of its opinion amounts to a tacit agreement with this position. Furthermore, on examining § 1 as a whole, I find no inconsistent use of the singular form from the first sentence that "[a] person ... may ... adopt ... another person younger than himself," to the final sentence pertaining to nonresidents who wish to adopt. Throughout the section, the singular is preserved. The only time a second petitioner is contemplated is where the initial petitioner has a living, competent spouse. There is nothing in the statute to suggest that joint petitions other than by spouses are permitted.

A biological mother may petition alone for the adoption of her child. Curran, petitioner, supra. Helen also meets the statutory requirements and may petition alone for the adoption of Tammy with Susan's consent. G.L. c. 210, § 2. Despite the admirable parenting and thriving environment being provided by these two unmarried cohabitants for this child, the statute does not permit their joint petition for adoption of Tammy.

2. There is nothing based on sexual orientation in the statute which would prohibit a homosexual from singly adopting a child. Additionally, a parent may not be deprived of custody of his or her children simply because he or she is a homosexual. Bezio v. Patenaude, 381 Mass. 563, 579, 410 N.E.2d 1207 (1980). Contra Fla.Stat.Ann. § 63.042 (1985) (prohibiting homosexuals from adopting); ...

NOTES

(1) In *In the Interest of Angel Lace M.*, 184 Wis.2d 492, 516 N.W.2d 678 (1994), the Supreme Court of Wisconsin held that their state's statute would not allow a mother's female cohabitant to adopt the child of the mother even though the trial court had held that such an adoption would be in the child's best interests. The court concluded that the adoption statute containing the limitation did not violate either the minor's due process or equal protection rights or the cohabitant's equal protection rights. In *In re Adoption of Luke*, 263 Neb. 365, 640 N.W.2d 374 (2002), the Supreme Court of Nebraska upheld the denial of a petition for adoption jointly filed by a mother and her companion, in which the companion sought to adopt the mother's child. The court, noting that adoption is a statutory creature, held that the child was not eligible for adoption by the companion under the adoption statute as the mother had not relinquished the child.

(2) Florida law prohibits adoption in that state by practicing homosexuals. Fla.Stat.Ann. § 63.042 (3). The United States Court of Appeals for the Eleventh Circuit upheld the constitutionality of the statute in *Lofton v. Secretary of Department of Children and Family Services*, 358 F.3d 804 (11th Cir.2004), *cert. denied* 543 U.S. 1081, 125 S.Ct. 869, 160 L.Ed.2d 825 (2005). Finding no fundamental right to adopt, the court held that the state could rationally choose to place children in adoptive homes with a mother and a father, and the family model may provide a rational basis for the legislative exclusion of adoption by homosexual persons.

(3) The Court of Appeals of New York, in *Matter of Jacob*, 86 N.Y.2d 651, 636 N.Y.S.2d 716, 660 N.E.2d 397 (1995), held that an unmarried heterosexual couple could be permitted to adopt under New York law. The New York court also held that the unmarried partner of a child's biological mother, whether heterosexual or homosexual, who is raising the child together with the biological parent, can become the child's second parent by means of adoption. They further noted that a single homosexual could adopt a child.

With more states permitting same sex marriage and adoption by same sex couples, the likelihood of challenges regarding interstate adoption recognition are likely to increase. In *Finstuen v. Crutcher*, 496 F.3d 1139 (10th Cir.2007), the United States Court of Appeals for the Tenth Circuit upheld a constitutional challenge to an amendment to Okla.Stat. tit. 10, § 7502–1.4(A) providing that "this state, any of its agencies or any court of this state shall not recognize an adoption by more than one individual of the same sex from any other state or foreign jurisdiction." Although the court found that several plaintiffs lacked standing under their facts, they held that the nonbiological parent member of a same sex couple and their adopted child did satisfy the requirements for standing and that the statute violated the Full Faith and Credit Clause.

C. REQUIREMENTS OF NOTICE AND CONSENT

For a child to be eligible for adoption, ordinarily there must be parental consent or parental rights must have been terminated. If there has been no formal consent or termination, the nonconsenting parent must be given notice. Although this was in question at one point, it was made clear by the Supreme Court of the United States in *Armstrong v. Manzo*, 380 U.S. 545, 85 S.Ct. 1187, 14 L.Ed.2d 62 (1965).

Some states have statutes permitting waiver of parental consent in specific instances. See, e.g. Alaska St. 25.23.180(c)(2) (provides for waiver when "parent who does not have custody is unreasonably withholding consent to adoption contrary to the best interests of the child"). Such provisions seemingly have been used only in special situations and a clear and convincing evidentiary standard ordinarily is applied. The provision on standards in Va. Code Ann. § 63.2–1205 is fairly detailed:

> In determining whether the valid consent of any person whose consent is required is withheld contrary to the best interests of the child, or is unobtainable, the circuit court or juvenile and domestic relations district court, as the case may be, shall consider whether the failure to grant the petition pending before it would be detrimental to the child. In determining whether the failure to grant the petition would be detrimental to the child, the circuit court or juvenile and domestic relations district court, as the case may be, shall consider all relevant factors, including the birth parent(s)' efforts to obtain or maintain legal and physical custody of the child; whether the birth parent(s)' efforts to assert parental rights were thwarted by other people; the birth parent(s)' ability to care for the child; the age of the child; the quality of any previous relationship between the birth parent(s) and the child and between the birth parent(s) and any other minor children; the duration and suitability of the child's present custodial environment; and the effect of a change of physical custody on the child.

The states generally wish to avoid revocation of consent by the placing parent except in special circumstances. For example, Va. Code Ann. § 63.2–1204 provides:

> Parental consent to an adoption shall be revocable prior to the final order of adoption (i) upon proof of fraud or duress or (ii) after placement of the child in an adoptive home, upon written, mutual consent of the birth parents and prospective adoptive parents.

1. THE SUPREME COURT AND FATHERS' RIGHTS

(See Chapter 1, p. 63 for this section.)

2. ADOPTION PLACEMENT AND FATHERS' RIGHTS

(See Chapter 1, p. 94 for this section.)

D. PLACEMENT FOR ADOPTION

It is common to divide the adoptive placement process from both legal and record-keeping standpoints according to the method through which a child is placed with prospective adoptive parents or by the prior existence of close ties through consanguinity or affinity. "Independent" or "private" placements are those made by parents either directly to prospective adopters or through a non-licensed intermediary such as a physician, lawyer, relative, or friend. Most "relative" placements are in this category. Special statutes generally have been enacted to facilitate adoptions by stepparents.

Agency placements are those made by a licensed private adoptive agency or an official state agency designated to serve such a function. In the agency placement the child usually is formally "surrendered" or "relinquished" by the parents to the agency, which then acts in place of the parents in seeking to effect a desirable adoptive placement. Agencies also may receive children through judicial disposition in cases in which parental rights have been terminated.

Generally adoption is a two step process, though this varies among states. Usually an initial placement is made and after a probationary period in which the home is monitored an interlocutory decree is rendered, later followed by a final decree. Some states lessen these requirements for stepparent placements.

Some jurisdictions limit the role which can be played by lawyers or others in making private placements. And some even have statutes designed to deal with "trafficking in babies". Special provisions on stepparent adoption typically dispense with the need for a home investigation and one of the two decrees. While placement with relatives has often been encouraged, some states now have specific statutes expressing a preference for this in many instances. California Family Code § 8710 provides:

(a) If a child is being considered for adoption, the department or licensed adoption agency shall first consider adoptive placement in the home of a relative. . . . However, if a relative is not available, if placement with an available relative is not in the child's best interest, or if placement would permanently separate the child from other siblings who are being considered for adoption or who are in foster care and an alternative placement would not require the permanent separation, the foster parent or parents of the child shall be considered with respect to the child along with all other prospective adoptive parents where all of the following conditions are present:

(1) The child has been in foster care with the foster parent or parents for a period of more than four months.

(2) The child has substantial emotional ties to the foster parent or parents.

(3) The child's removal from the foster home would be seriously detrimental to the child's well-being.

(4) The foster parent or parents have made a written request to be considered to adopt the child.

. . .

(c) This section does not apply to a child who has been adjudged a dependent of the juvenile court pursuant to Section 300 of the Welfare and Institutions Code.

THE SPECIAL ROLE AND DUTIES OF A PLACEMENT AGENCY
VIRGINIA CODE ANNOTATED

§ 63.2–1200. Who may place children for adoption

A child may be placed for adoption by:

1. A licensed child-placing agency;

2. A local board;

3. The child's parent or legal guardian if the placement is a parental placement; and

4. Any agency outside the Commonwealth that is licensed or otherwise duly authorized to place children for adoption by virtue of the laws under which it operates.

CALIFORNIA FAMILY CODE (West)

§ 8700. Relinquishment of child to department or a licensed adoption agency; minor parents; rescission; termination of parental rights

(a) Either birth parent may relinquish a child to the department or a licensed adoption agency for adoption by a written statement signed before two subscribing witnesses and acknowledged before an authorized official of the department or agency. The relinquishment, when reciting that the person making it is entitled to the sole custody of the child and acknowledged before the officer, is prima facie evidence of the right of the person making it to the sole custody of the child and the person's sole right to relinquish.

(b) A relinquishing parent who is a minor has the right to relinquish his or her child for adoption to the department or a licensed adoption agency, and the relinquishment is not subject to revocation by reason of the minority.

(c) If a relinquishing parent resides outside this state and the child is being cared for and is or will be placed for adoption by the department or a licensed adoption agency, the relinquishing parent may relinquish the child to the department or agency by a written statement signed by the relinquishing parent before a notary on a form prescribed by the department, and previously signed by an authorized official of the department or agency, that signifies the willingness of the department or agency to accept the relinquishment.

(d) If a relinquishing parent and child reside outside this state and the child will be cared for and will be placed for adoption by the department or a licensed adoption agency, the relinquishing parent may relinquish the child to the department or agency by a written statement signed by the relinquishing parent, after that parent has satisfied the following requirements:

(1) Prior to signing the relinquishment, the relinquishing parent shall have received, from a representative of an agency licensed or otherwise approved to provide adoption services under the laws of the relinquishing parent's state of residence, the same counseling and advisement services as if the relinquishing parent resided in this state.

(2) The relinquishment shall be signed before a representative of an agency licensed or otherwise approved to provide adoption services under the laws of the relinquishing parent's state of residence whenever possible or before a licensed social worker on a form prescribed by the department,

and previously signed by an authorized official of the department or agency, that signifies the willingness of the department or agency to accept the relinquishment.

(e)(1) The relinquishment authorized by this section has no effect until a certified copy is sent to, and filed with, the department. The licensed adoption agency shall send that copy by certified mail, return receipt requested, or by overnight courier or messenger, with proof of delivery, to the department no earlier than the end of the business day following the signing thereof. The relinquishment shall be final 10 business days after receipt of the filing by the department, unless any of the following apply:

(A) The department sends written acknowledgment of receipt of the relinquishment prior to the expiration of that 10–day period, at which time the relinquishment shall be final.

(B) A longer period of time is necessary due to a pending court action or some other cause beyond control of the department.

(2) After the relinquishment is final, it may be rescinded only by the mutual consent of the department or licensed adoption agency to which the child was relinquished and the birth parent or parents relinquishing the child.

(f) The relinquishing parent may name in the relinquishment the person or persons with whom he or she intends that placement of the child for adoption be made by the department or licensed adoption agency.

(g) Notwithstanding subdivision (e), if the relinquishment names the person or persons with whom placement by the department or licensed adoption agency is intended and the child is not placed in the home of the named person or persons or the child is removed from the home prior to the granting of the adoption, the department or agency shall mail a notice by certified mail, return receipt requested, to the birth parent signing the relinquishment within 72 hours of the decision not to place the child for adoption or the decision to remove the child from the home.

(h) The relinquishing parent has 30 days from the date on which the notice described in subdivision (g) was mailed to rescind the relinquishment.

(1) If the relinquishing parent requests rescission during the 30–day period, the department or licensed adoption agency shall rescind the relinquishment.

(2) If the relinquishing parent does not request rescission during the 30–day period, the department or licensed adoption agency shall select adoptive parents for the child.

(3) If the relinquishing parent and the department or licensed adoption agency wish to identify a different person or persons during the 30–day period with whom the child is intended to be placed, the initial relinquishment shall be rescinded and a new relinquishment identifying the person or persons completed.

(i) If the parent has relinquished a child, who has been found to come within Section 300 of the Welfare and Institutions Code or is the subject of a petition for jurisdiction of the juvenile court under Section 300 of the

Welfare and Institutions Code, to the department or a licensed adoption agency for the purpose of adoption, the department or agency accepting the relinquishment shall provide written notice of the relinquishment within five court days to all of the following:

(1) The juvenile court having jurisdiction of the child.

(2) The child's attorney, if any.

(3) The relinquishing parent's attorney, if any.

(j) The filing of the relinquishment with the department terminates all parental rights and responsibilities with regard to the child, except as provided in subdivisions (g) and (h).

(k) The department shall adopt regulations to administer the provisions of this section.

§ 8702. Statement presented to birth parents at time of relinquishment; content; form

(a) The department shall adopt a statement to be presented to the birth parents at the time a relinquishment is signed and to prospective adoptive parents at the time of the home study. The statement shall, in a clear and concise manner and in words calculated to ensure the confidence of the birth parents in the integrity of the adoption process, communicate to the birth parents of a child who is the subject of an adoption petition all of the following facts:

(1) It is in the child's best interest that the birth parent keep the department or licensed adoption agency to whom the child was relinquished for adoption informed of any health problems that the parent develops that could affect the child.

(2) It is extremely important that the birth parent keep an address current with the department or licensed adoption agency to whom the child was relinquished for adoption in order to permit a response to inquiries concerning medical or social history.

(3) Section 9203 of the Family Code authorizes a person who has been adopted and who attains the age of 21 years to request the department or the licensed adoption agency to disclose the name and address of the adoptee's birth parents. Consequently, it is of the utmost importance that the birth parent indicate whether to allow this disclosure by checking the appropriate box provided on the form.

(4) The birth parent may change the decision whether to permit disclosure of the birth parent's name and address, at any time, by sending a notarized letter to that effect, by certified mail, return receipt requested, to the department or to the licensed adoption agency that joined in the adoption petition.

(5) The relinquishment will be filed in the office of the clerk of the court in which the adoption takes place. The file is not open to inspection by any persons other than the parties to the adoption proceeding, their attorneys, and the department, except upon order of a judge of the superior court.

(b) The department shall adopt a form to be signed by the birth parents at the time the relinquishment is signed, which shall provide as follows:

"Section 9203 of the Family Code authorizes a person who has been adopted and who attains the age of 21 years to make a request to the State Department of Social Services, or the licensed adoption agency that joined in the adoption petition, for the name and address of the adoptee's birth parents. Indicate by checking one of the boxes below whether or not you wish your name and address to be disclosed:

[ ] YES

[ ] NO

[ ] UNCERTAIN AT THIS TIME; WILL NOTIFY AGENCY AT LATER DATE."

§ 8706. Medical report; background of child and biological parents; contents; blood sample

(a) An agency may not place a child for adoption unless a written report on the child's medical background and, if available, the medical background of the child's biological parents so far as ascertainable, has been submitted to the prospective adoptive parents and they have acknowledged in writing the receipt of the report.

(b) The report on the child's background shall contain all known diagnostic information, including current medical reports on the child, psychological evaluations, and scholastic information, as well as all known information regarding the child's developmental history and family life.

(c)(1) The biological parents may provide a blood sample at a clinic or hospital approved by the State Department of Health Services. The biological parents' failure to provide a blood sample shall not affect the adoption of the child.

(2) The blood sample shall be stored at a laboratory under contract with the State Department of Health Services for a period of 30 years following the adoption of the child.

(3) The purpose of the stored sample of blood is to provide a blood sample from which DNA testing can be done at a later date after entry of the order of adoption at the request of the adoptive parents or the adopted child. The cost of drawing and storing the blood samples shall be paid for by a separate fee in addition to the fee required under Section 8716. The amount of this additional fee shall be based on the cost of drawing and storing the blood samples but at no time shall the additional fee be more than one hundred dollars ($100).

(d)(1) The blood sample shall be stored and released in such a manner as to not identify any party to the adoption.

(2) Any results of the DNA testing shall be stored and released in such a manner as to not identify any party to the adoption.

§ 8709. Consideration of religious background; best interest of child

(a) The department or licensed adoption agency to which a child has been freed for adoption by either relinquishment or termination of parental rights may consider the child's religious background in determining an appropriate placement.

Mohr v. Commonwealth

Supreme Judicial Court of Massachusetts, Bristol, 1955.
421 Mass. 147, 653 N.E.2d 1104.

■ Before LIACOS, C.J., and WILKINS, ABRAMS and GREANEY, JJ.

■ LIACOS, CHIEF JUSTICE.

The Commonwealth appeals from a judgment awarding the plaintiffs $200,000 based on jury findings that the Commonwealth negligently misrepresented the medical and family history of a child (Elizabeth) adopted by the plaintiffs, and that the Commonwealth was liable for the plaintiffs' uninformed consent to adopt Elizabeth. The plaintiffs cross appeal from a judgment entered in favor of the codefendant, Pamela Tompkins (a social worker in the adoption placement unit of the Department of Public Welfare), on the plaintiffs' claim that Tompkins intentionally failed to disclose to them the mental illness of the child's biological mother.

The plaintiffs commenced this action in January, 1987. They alleged that the defendants negligently failed to provide accurate and complete information about Elizabeth's background, particularly her medical and family history, as well as her probable needs for future treatment and care, and that this negligence caused them harm. The plaintiffs also alleged that Tompkins made misrepresentations and fraudulently concealed from them certain background information about Elizabeth.

The case was tried to a jury in October, 1991. At the close of the evidence, the defendants filed motions for directed verdicts. The judge denied the motions as to the claims against the Commonwealth and the intentional tort claims against Tompkins. In response to special questions, the jury found that the Commonwealth's negligence proximately caused the plaintiffs' injuries, and that the Commonwealth was liable for the plaintiffs' uninformed consent[4]. The jury also found that Tompkins was not liable for an intentional tort. The judge denied the Commonwealth's motion for judgment notwithstanding the verdict or for a new trial, and denied the plaintiffs' motion for a new trial against Tompkins. Both sides timely appealed, and this court granted a joint application for direct appellate review.

On appeal, the Commonwealth asserts that (1) its failure to disclose the biological mother's mental health history was not inherently unknowable at the time of Elizabeth's adoption in 1976, and that the plaintiffs

---

4. The jury found that $3.8 million would fairly and adequately compensate the plaintiffs for their damages. The judge granted the Commonwealth's motion to amend or alter the judgment to $200,000 with no interest, the amount permitted by G.L. c. 258, § 2.

failed to commence the action within the time allowed by the statute of limitations; (2) this court should decline to recognize a cause of action for wrongful adoption based on negligence; (3) the judge erroneously failed to instruct the jury on comparative negligence; (4) the Commonwealth's decision not to disclose information about Elizabeth's biological mother's history of mental illness was a discretionary function entitling the Commonwealth to immunity pursuant to G.L. c. 258, § 10(b) (1994 ed.); (5) the judge erred in instructing the jury to determine whether regulations promulgated in 1972, 1974, or 1976 governed the Commonwealth's duty to disclose certain information to the plaintiffs; and (6) the doctrine of informed consent does not apply to a wrongful adoption action.

In their cross appeal, the plaintiffs contend that the judge erred in instructing the jury that Tompkins would not be liable for an intentional tort if she acted pursuant to orders of her superiors in not disclosing information to the plaintiffs.

Facts. We recite some of the facts that the jury could have found from the evidence admitted.

Elizabeth was born on January 15, 1968. At that time, her mother was a committed patient at Worcester State Hospital and was under the care of the Department of Mental Health. The mother agreed to give up Elizabeth for adoption. Elizabeth was placed in foster care by the Department of Public Welfare (department) for five years. Within a few months after her birth, it became apparent that Elizabeth was missing early developmental milestones. A department social worker took Elizabeth to a neurologist, who concluded that she "show[ed] definite evidence [of] retarded growth and development of unknown etiology." In January, 1969, Elizabeth was admitted to Springfield Hospital for a complete neurological evaluation. Her admission and discharge diagnoses were "mental retardation." Tests conducted while Elizabeth was an inpatient indicated that she had "moderate cerebral atrophy."

In September, 1973, Elizabeth was removed from her foster home and admitted to Springfield Hospital for "failure to thrive." During this hospitalization, a physician recommended that Elizabeth undergo a more complete psychological evaluation. The department did not follow this recommendation. Instead, Elizabeth was discharged with a diagnosis of "[f]ailure to thrive, probably due to environmental deprivation. Prognosis: Good." On discharge, responsibility for Elizabeth's care was transferred from the Springfield regional office of the department to its adoption placement unit in Boston, which placed her in the Nazareth Child Care Center for adoption preparation.

Sometime in the early 1970s, the Mohrs approached the department seeking to adopt a child. They attended several educational meetings sponsored by the department. They knew that the children available for adoption were older children, some of whom had suffered emotional trauma as a result of disruption in their biological families, inadequate foster care, and other factors. The plaintiffs also knew that certain "special needs" children, which included children with psychological or physical handicaps, were available for adoption and that an adoption subsidy would be offered to facilitate placement of such children.[5] Hazel Mohr acknowledged attending meetings at which the available children's emotional and behavioral problems were discussed. She also understood that there was a potential risk of mental illness or retardation, but did not remember any specific discussion of such issues. In their adoption application, the plaintiffs indicated that they would accept a child with a "[c]orrectable medical problem. Emotion[al] problem—we would consider."

In March, 1974, Pamela Tompkins, the social worker responsible for Elizabeth's adoption placement, notified the plaintiffs that six year old Elizabeth was available for adoption. Tompkins told the plaintiffs about Elizabeth's ethnic background, her placement in foster care from birth, and that the department had no background information about the father. Tompkins also told the plaintiffs that Elizabeth's mother had "blonde hair, blue eyes, fair coloring, [was] 5 foot, 1 inch tall, 130 pounds [and that she] liked to cook, liked dogs . . . was young and she wanted to go into nursing." Tompkins also told the plaintiffs that Elizabeth had been removed from foster care because of alleged abuse and had been hospitalized for malnutrition, and that she was small for her age and had been examined for dwarfism. Hazel Mohr testified that Tompkins provided no other information about Elizabeth's medical history or familial background at any time, and that she told the plaintiffs that no medical records concerning Elizabeth were available. Although Tompkins knew of a record stating that Elizabeth's birth mother was schizophrenic, she did not disclose that information to the plaintiffs.

After they learned that Elizabeth was available for adoption, the plaintiffs visited her weekly for several months. In July, 1974, Elizabeth went to live with the plaintiffs. The next month, Tompkins sent Elizabeth's medical records to Dr. Raymond Guillette, whom the plaintiffs had selected to be Elizabeth's pediatrician. The records revealed Elizabeth's medical history, including physicians' concerns about retardation. The records also detailed the birth mother's diagnosis of "Schi[z]ophrenic Reaction Chronic Undifferentiated Type manifested by emotional immaturity and instability."

In November, 1975, the plaintiffs took Elizabeth to Joseph P. Kennedy Jr. Memorial Hospital for neurological testing. Dr. Edward J. Hart, the evaluating physician, described Elizabeth as having a "considerable behavioral disruption" and as "a child of probably low average intelligence" who was two years behind her developmental level. Dr. Hart recommended therapy with the whole family and an inpatient evaluation to determine whether Elizabeth's problems were organic or related to early emotional deprivations. The plaintiffs did not choose to follow this recommendation.

In August, 1976, the plaintiffs adopted Elizabeth after she had lived with them for two years. Nine years later, in January, 1984, they decided to have Dr. Hart conduct the inpatient evaluation that he had suggested in 1975. The admission procedures required that the plaintiffs obtain Eliza-

5. The plaintiffs responded that they did not feel they could consider "special needs" children.

beth's immunization records. In the course of obtaining those records, Hazel Mohr first learned that Dr. Guillette had received medical records from the department. She also then discovered that Elizabeth's birth mother had been diagnosed as schizophrenic[6] and that Elizabeth's early infant development had been stunted. In addition, Hazel Mohr then learned that Elizabeth had been diagnosed with "cerebral atrophy." The plaintiffs testified at trial that they would not have adopted Elizabeth if this information had been disclosed to them.

According to the plaintiffs, the department's employees told them prior to the adoption that the only background information that would not be disclosed to them was the identity of the biological parents. They assert that Tompkins knew, but did not disclose to them, that:

(a) the birth mother was a committed patient at Worcester State Hospital when Elizabeth was born, with a diagnosis of chronic schizophrenia.

(b) the birth mother had an IQ score of eighty-three (dull normal level).

(c) the foster mother with whom Elizabeth was first placed one month after birth was concerned that the infant was not developing as quickly as she should.

(d) a developmental examination at eighteen weeks concluded that Elizabeth's "development is not satisfactory."

(e) a follow-up examination at thirty-nine weeks found that many of Elizabeth's abilities were at the twenty-week level and that "[h]er general maturity level ... is around 24 weeks and this being the second examination to show retardation, it takes on a more serious import."

(f) at an October 31, 1968, examination, a neurologist found that Elizabeth "shows definite evidence [of] retarded growth and development of unknown etiology."

(g) in January, 1969, a complete neurological examination conducted by Springfield Hospital diagnosed "mental retardation." A pneumoencephalogram revealed bilaterally enlarged ventricles, which were interpreted as "diagnostic of moderate cerebral atrophy." Her prognosis was "guarded."

(h) by October, 1973, Elizabeth's height and weight had declined from the fiftieth to the third percentile.

---

6. One of the plaintiffs' experts testified that the familial nature of schizophrenia has been recognized for over one hundred years. He also testified that a child born to a schizophrenic mother would be fifteen times as likely to develop schizophrenia as a child in the general population. He further testified that Elizabeth suffers from borderline or latent schizophrenia, and that the facts concerning her biological mother's schizophrenia would have been very important for a correct assessment of Elizabeth's prognosis when she was presented to the plaintiffs in 1974. Another expert testified that it would have been possible to determine in 1974 that there was not "any way that this young woman would have attained normal cognitive development; have been able to function the way the vast majority of children do ... [and] that there was [not] any way, given this history, that she would have attained normal emotional status."

(i) when Springfield Hospital evaluated Elizabeth in 1973, a physician recommended that she be admitted to the hospital's Child Guidance Center for a complete psychological evaluation. That was not done. Instead, Elizabeth was discharged with a diagnosis of failure to thrive.

(j) the supervisor of social service at the Springfield office of the Division of Family and Children's Services (now the Department of Social Services) objected to transferring "this five year old retarded, emotionally disturbed child whose physical ailments have not yet been diagnosed" to the adoption placement unit in Boston. This objection was not heeded.

Tompkins did not disclose the above information in the petition that she prepared for submission to the Probate Court in connection with Elizabeth's adoption. In the petition, she stated only that Elizabeth "was developing below average due to environmental deprivation, but had potential for further development." Tompkins described the biological mother as "generally in good health," and stated that "[b]ecause of the severe marital problems of [her] parents, [the mother] had a problem with interpersonal relationships and was unable to meet the needs of a baby." The plaintiffs' expert on adoption testified that, by 1974, there was consensus in the field of social work that schizophrenia and mental retardation in the biological family should be disclosed to adoptive parents prior to placement.

At the time of trial, Elizabeth lived at home and was incapable of caring for herself. Medical records admitted in evidence indicated that Elizabeth is mentally retarded, with a verbal scale IQ of seventy-seven and a performance scale IQ of fifty-five. The plaintiffs testified that they would not have adopted or even agreed to meet Elizabeth if facts concerning her retardation during infancy or her mother's schizophrenia had been disclosed. They commenced this action in order to recover sufficient damages to enable them to provide for the structured, residential placement that Elizabeth will need throughout her lifetime.

I. *Statute of limitations . . . .* On appeal, the Commonwealth contends that the judge should have determined as a matter of law that the statute of limitations barred the plaintiffs' action because the biological mother's history of mental illness was not "inherently unknowable" at the time that Elizabeth's adoption was finalized in 1976.

We have recognized the "unfairness of a rule that holds that the statute of limitations has run even before a plaintiff knew or reasonably should have known that she may have been harmed by the conduct of another." *Bowen v. Eli Lilly & Co.,* 408 Mass. 204, 205, 557 N.E.2d 739 (1990). Thus, we have developed a "discovery rule" for determining, in the absence of a governing statute, when a cause of action accrues and triggers the beginning of the statutory period. See *id.* The discovery rule "prescribes as crucial the date when a plaintiff discovers, or any earlier date when she should reasonably have discovered, that she has been harmed or may have been harmed by the defendant's conduct." *Bowen v. Eli Lilly & Co., supra* at 205–206, 557 N.E.2d 739.

In response to special questions, the jury found that "2/84" was "the date when the plaintiffs either or both, knew or in the exercise of reasonable diligence should have known of the material facts which are the basis of this action." Thus, under the discovery rule, the plaintiffs' cause of action accrued in February, 1984. We conclude that the plaintiffs satisfied their burden of proving that they commenced this action within the three year statutory period.

II. *"Wrongful adoption" tort.* We decide today whether we should recognize a cause of action in tort which would allow adoptive parents the right to seek compensatory damages against an adoption agency for the agency's negligent material misrepresentations of fact prior to adoption concerning the adopted child's history.

In 1986, in *Burr v. County Comm'rs of Stark County,* 23 Ohio St.3d 69, 75, 491 N.E.2d 1101 (1986), the Supreme Court of Ohio became the first State supreme court to recognize the tort of "wrongful adoption."[8] In that case, the court affirmed a jury verdict finding an adoption agency liable in tort for making material misrepresentations to adoptive parents about a child's background and physical condition. *Id.* at 78, 491 N.E.2d 1101. During the ensuing years, the child suffered from a number of physical and mental problems and was classified as mentally retarded. Eventually, he was diagnosed as suffering from Huntington's disease, a genetically inherited condition.

When the plaintiffs obtained a court order to open the sealed records concerning the child's background prior to adoption, the records revealed that the biological mother was a thirty-one year old mental patient and that the child was born at a State mental institution. *Id.* The mother shared the child's low intellectual level, had a speech impediment, and was diagnosed as having a "mild mental deficiency, idiopathic, with psychotic reactions." *Id.* The biological father was unknown, but was presumed to be a mental patient. *Id.* In addition, other information provided by the adoption agency about the child apart from his age and sex was untrue. The plaintiffs claimed that they would not have adopted the child had it not been for the defendants' fraudulent conduct.

The Supreme Court of Ohio held that the adoptive parents could recover where they were fraudulently misled to their detriment by an adoption agency's material misrepresentations of fact about the infant's background and condition, so long as they proved each element of the tort of fraud. *Id.* at 73, 491 N.E.2d 1101. Because "the record amply support[ed] the lower courts' decisions that fraud was demonstrated," the court affirmed the jury verdict against the defendants. *Id.* In so holding, the court stated that "[a]s a public agency charged with the legal duty and authority to arrange adoptions ... governing principles of justice ... require that [the defendants] be held accountable for injuries resulting from deceitful and material misrepresentations which we find were foreseeably and justifiably relied on by [the plaintiffs]." *Id.* at 75, 491 N.E.2d 1101.

---

8. The term "wrongful adoption" is commonly used, but it adds no more to a proper analysis than the counterpart term of "wrongful birth." See *Viccaro v. Milunsky,* 406 Mass. 777, 779 n. 3, 551 N.E.2d 8 (1990). As well stated by Justice Murray in *Mallette v. Children's Friend & Serv.,* 661 A.2d 67, 69 (R.I.1995) "[T]he question of whether to recognize causes of action for 'wrongful adoption' simply requires the straightforward application and extension of well-recognized common-law actions, such as negligence and fraud, to the adoption context and not the creation of new torts."

Other jurisdictions subsequently have followed the Ohio Supreme Court in recognizing a cause of action for "wrongful adoption" based upon an adoption agency's misrepresentations to parents prior to adoption. See, e.g., *Roe v. Catholic Charities of the Diocese of Springfield,* 225 Ill.App.3d 519, 524, 538, 167 Ill.Dec. 713, 588 N.E.2d 354 (1992) (agency told three sets of adoptive parents that the particular children they planned to adopt were normal in physical and mental condition as well as level of development, despite its knowledge that children had exhibited violent and uncontrollable behavior while in foster care, and that two children suffered from social and emotional retardation); *M.H. v. Caritas Family Servs.,* 488 N.W.2d 282, 284–285, 288 (Minn.1992) (agency told adoptive parents there was "possibility of incest in the family," despite its knowledge that child's biological parents were a seventeen year old boy and his thirteen year old sister); *Gibbs v. Ernst,* 538 Pa. 193, 217–218, 647 A.2d 882 (1994) (despite specific inquiry by adoptive parents, agency failed to disclose that child had long history of physical and sexual abuse by biological parents, that he had been neglected by biological mother, that he had extensive history of aggressiveness and hostility toward other children, that biological mother at one time attempted to cut off his penis, and that he had been in and out of foster care during his first six years); *Meracle v. Children's Serv. Soc'y of Wis.,* 149 Wis.2d 19, 32–33, 437 N.W.2d 532 (1989) (agency told adoptive parents that child's biological father had tested negative for Huntington's disease and therefore child had no more chance of developing it than any other child, even though paternal grandmother had died of Huntington's disease and no reliable test existed to determine whether biological father had it; child subsequently diagnosed as having Huntington's disease). See *Roe v. Catholic Charities of the Diocese of Springfield, supra* at 524, 167 Ill.Dec. 713, 588 N.E.2d 354 ("Recognition of this cause of action is not a dramatic, radical departure from the well-established common law. . . . It is rather an extension of the doctrine of common law fraud. This is how the common law traditionally grows; it responds to the needs of the society it serves"). See also *Juman v. Louise Wise Servs.,* 159 Misc.2d 314, 320, 608 N.Y.S.2d 612 (1994), aff'd, 211 A.D.2d 446, 620 N.Y.S.2d 371 (1995). We agree that the straightforward application of well-established common law principles supports recognition of a cause of action in tort for an adoption agency's material misrepresentations of fact to adoptive parents about a child's history prior to adoption. See *Mallette v. Children's Friend & Serv.,* 661 A.2d 67, 69 (1995).

Next we must consider whether, as the Commonwealth contends, public policy concerns dictate that we should limit liability for "wrongful adoption" to claims based on intentional conduct. The Commonwealth relies on several cases in which courts have declined to extend liability to cases involving negligent, rather than intentional, misrepresentation by an adoption agency. For example, in *Burr v. County Comm'rs of Stark County, supra* at 78, 491 N.E.2d 1101, the court stated that "[i]t is not the mere failure to disclose the risks inherent in [the] child's background which we hold to be actionable [but] the deliberate act of misinforming [the plaintiffs] which deprived them of their right to make a sound parenting decision and which led to the compensable injuries." Similarly, in *Michael J. v. Los Angeles County Dep't of Adoptions,* 201 Cal.App.3d 859, 874–875,

247 Cal.Rptr. 504 (1988), the California Court of Appeal stated that "an adoption agency cannot be made the guarantor of an infant's future good health and should not be liable for mere negligence in providing information regarding the health of a prospective adoptee." See *Richard P. v. Vista Del Mar Child Care Serv.,* 106 Cal.App.3d 860, 866–867, 165 Cal.Rptr. 370 (1980) (court stated that "no cause of action for negligence should be recognized based on considerations of public policy"); *Foster v. Bass,* 575 So.2d 967, 981 (Miss.1990) (court refused to recognize tort of negligence in adoption context because result not foreseeable). See also *Juman v. Louise Wise Servs.,* 620 N.Y.S.2d 371, 372 (App.Div.1995) (recognizing "wrongful adoption" cause of action grounded in fraud and fraudulent misrepresentation).

Other courts, however, have held that, apart from claims based on allegations of fraud or intentional misrepresentation of material fact, public policy also supports recognizing the tort of negligent misrepresentation in the adoption context. See, e.g., *Roe v. Catholic Charities of the Diocese of Springfield, supra* at 536–537, 167 Ill.Dec. 713, 588 N.E.2d 354; *Gibbs v. Ernst, supra* at 211; *Meracle v. Children's Serv. Soc'y of Wis., supra* at 32–33, 437 N.W.2d 532. See also *M.H. v. Caritas Family Servs., supra* at 288 (allowing negligent misrepresentation action against adoption agency which, having undertaken to disclose information about child's biological parents and medical background to adoptive parents, "negligently withholds information in such a way that the adoptive parents were misled as to the truth"). These courts have emphasized "the compelling need of adoptive parents for full disclosure of medical background information that may be known to the agency on both the child they may adopt and the child's genetic parents, not only to secure timely and appropriate medical care for the child, but also to make vital personal, health and family decisions." *Id.* at 287. See *Roe v. Catholic Charities of the Diocese of Springfield, supra* at 537, 167 Ill.Dec. 713, 588 N.E.2d 354. This need, according to these courts, outweighs any increased burden that is placed on adoption agencies when liability is imposed for negligent as well as intentional misrepresentation. See *id.* In addition, these courts have maintained that allowing negligent misrepresentation claims against adoption agencies does not subject agencies to potentially limitless liability or make them guarantors of adopted children's health. *Meracle v. Children's Serv. Soc'y of Wis., supra* at 32, 437 N.W.2d 532.[9]

In Massachusetts, we have recognized that biological parents have a cause of action in tort for negligent failure properly to perform a sterilization surgical procedure to avoid the birth of even a healthy child. *Burke v. Rivo,* 406 Mass. 764, 772, 551 N.E.2d 1 (1990). Further, as to a child born with a congenital or genetic disorder, we have recognized, and agreed with the principle that, "[i]f a child is born with a congenital or genetic disorder, almost all courts have allowed the parents to recover against a negligent

---

9. We note that, like the plaintiffs in this case, none of the plaintiffs in the above-cited cases sought to nullify the adoption decree because of the adoption agency's alleged misrepresentations. Cf. *County Dep't of* *Pub. Welfare of St. Joseph County v. Morningstar,* 128 Ind.App. 688, 689, 151 N.E.2d 150 (1958); *Allen v. Allen,* 214 Or. 664, 665, 330 P.2d 151 (1958); *In re Lisa Diane G.,* 537 A.2d 131, 132 (R.I.1988).

physician the extraordinary medical, educational, and other expenses that are associated with and are consequences of the disorder." *Viccaro v. Milunsky*, 406 Mass. 777, 780, 551 N.E.2d 8 (1990). Most recently, in regard to adoption, in a case almost on all fours with the case at bar, the Supreme Court of Rhode Island has stated in *Mallette v. Children's Friend & Serv., supra* at 71, "[w]hen [the defendant] began allegedly volunteering information concerning [the child's] and his biological mother's medical and genetic background, the agency assumed a duty to refrain from making negligent misrepresentations." We agree.

Although we acknowledge the "necessity to approach slowly any attempt to make an adoption agency liable for the health of the children that they place," *Foster v. Bass, supra* at 981, we believe that the preferable approach is to allow liability for "wrongful adoption" for claims based on both intentional and negligent misrepresentation to adoptive parents about a child's history prior to adoption. We add that an adoption agency does have an affirmative duty to disclose to adoptive parents information about a child that will enable them to make a knowledgeable decision about whether to accept the child for adoption. See 110 Code Mass.Regs. § 7.213(3) (1994) ("[t]he Department [of Social Services] shall provide the adoptive parent with all relevant information about a child to enable the adoptive parent to knowledgeably determine whether to accept the child for adoption").

Several considerations support our conclusion. First, as noted above, there is a compelling need for full disclosure of a child's medical and familial background not only to enable adoptive parents to obtain timely and appropriate medical care for the child, but also to enable them to make an intelligent and informed decision to adopt. We acknowledge that there always are certain risks associated with having a child, whether biologically or through adoption. "However, just as couples must weigh the risks of becoming natural parents, taking into consideration a host of factors, so too should adoptive parents be allowed to make their decision in an intelligent manner." *Burr v. County Comm'rs of Stark County, supra* at 78, 491 N.E.2d 1101. In order to enable adoptive parents to "assume the awesome responsibility of raising a child with their eyes wide open," *Roe v. Catholic Charities of the Diocese of Springfield, supra* at 537, 167 Ill.Dec. 713, 588 N.E.2d 354, an adoption agency must disclose fully a child's medical and familial background.[11] Full disclosure is particularly necessary in the adoption context, where often the adoption agency is the only party with access to information about a child's medical and genetic background. . . .

Second, our conclusion applies accepted tort principles to the interactions between adoption agencies and potential adoptive parents during the adoption process. We do not believe that adoption agencies should be exempt from tort liability for false statements negligently made during the adoption process. In reaching this conclusion, we note that the Legislature has not acted affirmatively to provide adoption agencies immunity from

---

11. This is not a case where an adoption agency placed a child without discovering and informing the potential adoptive parents about the child's medical and familial background. Thus, we need not and do not address whether and to what extent an agency has a duty to investigate a child's background.

common law sanctions for negligence. See *Gibbs v. Ernst, supra* at 207, 647 A.2d 882 ("The causes of action ... are so well established that we find affirmative action by the legislature, rather than silence, would be necessary to prevent their application in the adoption context").

Third, allowing liability for negligent as well as intentional "wrongful adoption" does not impose any "extraordinary or onerous" burden on adoption agencies. See *M.H. v. Caritas Family Servs., supra* at 287. To avoid liability for "wrongful adoption" based on negligence, an agency need only use due care to ensure that it fully and adequately discloses information about a child's background so as not to mislead potential adoptive parents. Thus, we do not agree with the Commonwealth that allowing liability for negligent misrepresentation would "burden [State] adoption agencies with greater costs for verification of family histories and discovery of hidden genetic-related conditions." Indeed, in light of the emotional, physical and financial problems that can result from an agency's affirmative misrepresentations about a child's medical and familial background, any increased burden upon adoption agencies is slight. Furthermore, "the common law notion of foreseeability as found in the concepts of duty and proximate cause" prevents the tort of negligent "wrongful adoption" from making adoption agencies guarantors of children's future health. See *Gibbs v. Ernst, supra* at 211, 647 A.2d 882.

Fourth, we do not believe that a negligent "wrongful adoption" cause of action conflicts with the biological parents' interest in keeping their identities confidential. Adoption agencies could provide information about a child's medical and familial background without disclosing the biological parents' identities. This disclosure would be similar to that approved in G.L. c. 210, § 5D (1994 ed.), which authorizes the release of "nonidentifying information" concerning a biological parent's "medical, ethnic, socioeconomic, and educational circumstances."

Fifth, we note that G.L. c. 258, § 10(*c*) (1994 ed.) (Massachusetts Tort Claims Act), provides that the statute does not apply to "any claim arising out of an intentional tort, including ... misrepresentation." Thus, under the act, the Commonwealth as a public employer is immune from suits arising from intentional torts. See *Spring v. Geriatric Auth. of Holyoke,* 394 Mass. 274, 284–285, 475 N.E.2d 727 (1985). Absent a "wrongful adoption" cause of action based upon negligence, adoptive parents would have no recourse against the Commonwealth for misrepresentations by a State adoption agency about a child's medical and familial background. We cannot sanction such a result

Last, the Commonwealth asserts that it is immune from liability because of the discretionary function exception to governmental tort liability. See G.L. c. 258, § 10(*b*).[14] Specifically, the Commonwealth contends that a State adoption agency's decision whether to disclose a child's background information to prospective adoptive parents is a decision based on public

14. Section 10(*b*) provides as follows: "The provisions of sections one to eight, inclusive, shall not apply to ... any claim based upon the exercise or performance or the failure to exercise or perform a discretionary function or duty on the part of a public employer or public employee, acting within the scope of his office or employment, whether or not the discretion involved is abused...."

planning and policy, and thus is a discretionary act within the meaning of
G.L. c. 258, § 10(*b*). We disagree. . . .

In this case, Tompkins did not make a policy or planning judgment in
deciding whether to withhold information from the plaintiffs about Elizabeth's background. Rather, according to Tompkins, she acted in accordance
with an agency policy not to disclose a biological parent's mental illness to
prospective adoptive parents. Thus, Tompkins's actions did not constitute a
discretionary function entitled to immunity pursuant to G.L. c. 258,
§ 10(*b*). . . .

III.   *The plaintiffs' cross appeal.* In their cross appeal, the plaintiffs
assert that the judge erroneously instructed the jury that "Tompkins is not
liable for intentional tort if the nondisclosure was pursuant to the orders of
her superiors." A review of the charge, however, demonstrates that the
judge did not give any such instruction. We conclude therefore that the
plaintiffs' cross appeal is without merit, and affirm the judgment in favor of
the defendant Tompkins. We also affirm the judgment for the plaintiffs as
against the Commonwealth.

So ordered.

NOTE

For further discussion of these actions, which have been accorded different
titles in some states, see Madelyn Freundlich & Lisa Peterson, Wrongful Adoption:
Law, Policy and Practice (CWLA Press 1998). Can you think of a better name than
"wrongful adoption"?

INTERETHNIC ADOPTION ACT

42 U.S.C.A. § 1996b

(1) Prohibited conduct

A person or government that is involved in adoption or foster care
placements may not—

(A) deny to any individual the opportunity to become an adoptive or a
foster parent, on the basis of the race, color, or national origin of the
individual, or of the child, involved; or

(B) delay or deny the placement of a child for adoption or into foster
care, on the basis of the race, color, or national origin of the adoptive or
foster parent, or the child, involved.

(2) Enforcement

Noncompliance with paragraph (1) is deemed a violation of title VI of
the Civil Rights Act of 1964 [42 U.S.C.A. § 2000d et seq.].

(3) No effect on the Indian Child Welfare Act of 1978

This subsection shall not be construed to affect the application of the
Indian Child Welfare Act of 1978 [25 U.S.C.A. § 1901 et seq.].

NOTE

There remains significant disagreement between some persons, including social workers and sociologists, about whether transracial adoption should be permitted or discouraged. For a discussion of this debate that includes extensive citations to articles and books by the debaters, see Sarah Ramsey, Fixing Foster Care or Reducing Child Poverty: The Pew Commission Recommendations and the Transracial Adoption Debate, 66 Montana L.Rev. 39 (2004); and Solangel Maldonado, Discouraging Racial Preferences in Adoptions, 39 U.C. Davis L.Rev. 1415 (2006).

Mississippi Band of Choctaw Indians v. Holyfield

Supreme Court of the United States, 1989.
490 U.S. 30, 109 S.Ct. 1597, 104 L.Ed.2d 29.

■ Justice Brennan delivered the opinion of the Court.

This appeal requires us to construe the provisions of the Indian Child Welfare Act that establish exclusive tribal jurisdiction over child custody proceedings involving Indian children domiciled on the tribe's reservation.

The Indian Child Welfare Act of 1978 (ICWA), 92 Stat. 3069, 25 U.S.C. §§ 1901–1963, was the product of rising concern in the mid–1970's over the consequences to Indian children, Indian families, and Indian tribes of abusive child welfare practices that resulted in the separation of large numbers of Indian children from their families and tribes through adoption or foster care placement, usually in non-Indian homes. Senate oversight hearings in 1974 yielded numerous examples, statistical data, and expert testimony documenting what one witness called "the wholesale removal of Indian children from their homes, . . . the most tragic aspect of Indian life today." Indian Child Welfare Program, Hearings before the Subcommittee on Indian Affairs of the Senate Committee on Interior and Insular Affairs, 93d Cong., 2d Sess., 3 (hereinafter 1974 Hearings) (statement of William Byler). Studies undertaken by the Association on American Indian Affairs in 1969 and 1974, and presented in the Senate hearings, showed that 25 to 35 percent of all Indian children had been separated from their families and placed in adoptive families, foster care, or institutions. Adoptive placements counted significantly in this total: in the State of Minnesota, for example, one in eight Indian children under the age of 18 was in an adoptive home, and during the year 1971–1972 nearly one in every four infants under one year of age was placed for adoption. The adoption rate of Indian children was eight times that of non-Indian children. Approximately 90% of the Indian placements were in non-Indian homes. A number of witnesses also testified to the serious adjustment problems encountered by such children during adolescence,[1] as well as the impact of the adoptions on Indian parents and the tribes themselves.

---

1. For example, Dr. Joseph Westermeyer, a University of Minnesota social psychiatrist, testified about his research with Indian adolescents who experienced difficulty coping in white society, despite the fact that they had been raised in a purely white environment:

"[T]hey were raised with a white cultural and social identity. They are raised in a white home. They attended, predominantly white schools, and in almost all cases, attended a church that was predominantly white, and really came to understand very little about Indian cul-

Further hearings, covering much the same ground, were held during 1977 and 1978 on the bill that became the ICWA. While much of the testimony again focused on the harm to Indian parents and their children who were involuntarily separated by decisions of local welfare authorities, there was also considerable emphasis on the impact on the tribes themselves of the massive removal of their children. For example, Mr. Calvin Isaac, Tribal Chief of the Mississippi Band of Choctaw Indians and representative of the National Tribal Chairmen's Association, testified as follows:

"Culturally, the chances of Indian survival are significantly reduced if our children, the only real means for the transmission of the tribal heritage, are to be raised in non-Indian homes and denied exposure to the ways of their People. Furthermore, these practices seriously undercut the tribes' ability to continue as self-governing communities. Probably in no area is it more important that tribal sovereignty be respected than in an area as socially and culturally determinative as family relationships."

Chief Isaac also summarized succinctly what numerous witnesses saw as the principal reason for the high rates of removal of Indian children:

"One of the most serious failings of the present system is that Indian children are removed from the custody of their natural parents by nontribal government authorities who have no basis for intelligently evaluating the cultural and social premises underlying Indian home life and childrearing. Many of the individuals who decide the fate of our children are at best ignorant of our cultural values, and at worst contemptful of the Indian way and convinced that removal, usually to a non-Indian household or institution, can only benefit an Indian child."[4]

ture, Indian behavior, and had virtually no viable Indian identity. They can recall such things as seeing cowboys and Indians on TV and feeling that Indians were a historical figure but were not a viable contemporary social group.

"Then during adolescence, they found that society was not to grant them the white identity that they had. They began to find this out in a number of ways. For example, a universal experience was that when they began to date white children, the parents of the white youngsters were against this, and there were pressures among white children from the parents not to date these Indian children....

"The other experience was derogatory name calling in relation to their racial identity....

. . .

"[T]hey were finding that society was putting on them an identity which they didn't possess and taking from them an identity that they did possess." 1974 Hearings, at 46.

4. One of the particular points of concern was the failure of non-Indian child welfare workers to understand the role of the extended family in Indian society. The House Report on the ICWA noted: "An Indian child may have scores of, perhaps more than a hundred, relatives who are counted as close, responsible members of the family. Many social workers, untutored in the ways of Indian family life or assuming them to be socially irresponsible, consider leaving the child with persons outside the nuclear family as neglect and thus as grounds for terminating parental rights." At the conclusion of the 1974 Senate hearings, Senator Abourezk noted the role that such extended families played in the care of children: "We've had testimony here that in Indian communities throughout the Nation there is no such thing as an abandoned child because when a child does have a need for parents for one reason or another, a relative or a friend will take that child in. It's the extended family concept." 1974 Hearings 473. See also Wisconsin Potowatomies of Hannahville Indian Community v. Houston,

The congressional findings that were incorporated into the ICWA reflect these sentiments. The Congress found:

"(3) that there is no resource that is more vital to the continued existence and integrity of Indian tribes than their children . . .;

"(4) that an alarmingly high percentage of Indian families are broken up by the removal, often unwarranted, of their children from them by nontribal public and private agencies and that an alarmingly high percentage of such children are placed in non-Indian foster and adoptive homes and institutions; and

"(5) that the States, exercising their recognized jurisdiction over Indian child custody proceedings through administrative and judicial bodies, have often failed to recognize the essential tribal relations of Indian people and the cultural and social standards prevailing in Indian communities and families." 25 U.S.C. § 1901.

At the heart of the ICWA are its provisions concerning jurisdiction over Indian child custody proceedings. Section 1911 lays out a dual jurisdictional scheme. Section 1911(a) establishes exclusive jurisdiction in the tribal courts for proceedings concerning an Indian child "who resides or is domiciled within the reservation of such tribe," as well as for wards of tribal courts regardless of domicile. Section 1911(b), on the other hand, creates concurrent but presumptively tribal jurisdiction in the case of children not domiciled on the reservation: on petition of either parent or the tribe, state-court proceedings for foster care placement or termination of parental rights are to be transferred to the tribal court, except in cases of "good cause," objection by either parent, or declination of jurisdiction by the tribal court.

Various other provisions of ICWA Title I set procedural and substantive standards for those child custody proceedings that do take place in state court. The procedural safeguards include requirements concerning notice and appointment of counsel; parental and tribal rights of intervention and petition for invalidation of illegal proceedings; procedures governing voluntary consent to termination of parental rights; and a full faith and credit obligation in respect to tribal court decisions. See §§ 1901–1914. The most important substantive requirement imposed on state courts is that of § 1915(a), which, absent "good cause" to the contrary, mandates that adoptive placements be made preferentially with (1) members of the child's extended family, (2) other members of the same tribe, or (3) other Indian families.

The ICWA thus, in the words of the House Report accompanying it, "seeks to protect the rights of the Indian child as an Indian and the rights of the Indian community and tribe in retaining its children in its society." It does so by establishing "a Federal policy that, where possible, an Indian child should remain in the Indian community," ibid., and by making sure that Indian child welfare determinations are not based on "a white, middle-class standard which, in many cases, forecloses placement with [an] Indian family."

393 F.Supp. 719 (WD Mich.1973) (discussing custom of extended family and tribe assuming responsibility for care of orphaned children).

This case involves the status of twin babies, known for our purposes as B.B. and G.B., who were born out of wedlock on December 29, 1985. Their mother, J.B., and father, W.J., were both enrolled members of appellant Mississippi Band of Choctaw Indians (Tribe), and were residents and domiciliaries of the Choctaw Reservation in Neshoba County, Mississippi. J.B. gave birth to the twins in Gulfport, Harrison County, Mississippi, some 200 miles from the reservation. On January 10, 1986, J.B. executed a consent-to-adoption form before the Chancery Court of Harrison County.[7] W.J. signed a similar form.[8] On January 16, appellees Orrey and Vivian Holyfield filed a petition for adoption in the same court, and the chancellor issued a Final Decree of Adoption on January 28. Id., at 13–14.[10] Despite the court's apparent awareness of the ICWA, the adoption decree contained no reference to it, nor to the infants' Indian background.

Two months later the Tribe moved in the Chancery Court to vacate the adoption decree on the ground that under the ICWA exclusive jurisdiction was vested in the tribal court.[12] On July 14, 1986, the court overruled the motion, holding that the Tribe "never obtained exclusive jurisdiction over the children involved herein. . . ." The court's one-page opinion relied on two facts in reaching that conclusion. The court noted first that the twins' mother "went to some efforts to see that they were born outside the confines of the Choctaw Indian Reservation" and that the parents had promptly arranged for the adoption by the Holyfields. Second, the court stated: "At no time from the birth of these children to the present date have either of them resided on or physically been on the Choctaw Indian Reservation."

The Supreme Court of Mississippi affirmed. 511 So.2d 918 (1987). It rejected the Tribe's arguments that the state court lacked jurisdiction and that it, in any event, had not applied the standards laid out in the ICWA.

---

7. Section 1913(a) of the ICWA requires that any voluntary consent to termination of parental rights be executed in writing and recorded before a judge of a "court of competent jurisdiction," who must certify that the terms and consequences of the consent were fully explained and understood. Section 1913(a) also provides that any consent given prior to birth or within 10 days thereafter is invalid. In this case the mother's consent was given 12 days after the birth.

8. W.J.'s consent to adoption was signed before a notary public in Neshoba County on January 11, 1986. Record 11–12. Only on June 3, 1986, however—well after the decree of adoption had been entered and after the Tribe had filed suit to vacate that decree—did the chancellor of the Chancery Court certify that W.J. had appeared before him in Harrison County to execute the consent to adoption. Id., at 12–A.

10. Mississippi adoption law provides for a 6–month waiting period between interlocutory and final decrees of adoption, but grants the chancellor discretionary authority to waive that requirement and immediately enter a final decree of adoption. See Miss. Code Ann. § 93–17–13 (1972). The chancellor did so here, Record 14, with the result that the final decree of adoption was entered less than one month after the babies' birth.

12. The ICWA specifically confers standing on the Indian child's tribe to participate in child custody adjudications. Section 1914 authorizes the tribe (as well as the child and its parents) to petition a court to invalidate any foster care placement or termination of parental rights under state law "upon a showing that such action violated any provision of sections 1911, 1912, and 1913" of the ICWA. See also § 1911(c) (Indian child's tribe may intervene at any point in state-court proceedings for foster care placement or termination of parental rights). "Termination of parental rights" is defined in § 1903(1)(ii) as "any action resulting in the termination of the parent-child relationship."

The court recognized that the jurisdictional question turned on whether the twins were domiciled on the Choctaw Reservation. It answered that question as follows:

> "At no point in time can it be said the twins resided on or were domiciled within the territory set aside for the reservation. Appellant's argument that living within the womb of their mother qualifies the children's residency on the reservation may be lauded for its creativity; however, apparently it is unsupported by any law within this state, and will not be addressed at this time due to the far-reaching legal ramifications that would occur were we to follow such a complicated tangential course."

The court distinguished Mississippi cases that appeared to establish the principle that "the domicile of minor children follows that of the parents". It noted that "the Indian twins ... were voluntarily surrendered and legally abandoned by the natural parents to the adoptive parents, and it is undisputed that the parents went to some efforts to prevent the children from being placed on the reservation as the mother arranged for their birth and adoption in Gulfport Memorial Hospital, Harrison County, Mississippi." Therefore, the court said, the twins' domicile was in Harrison County and the state court properly exercised jurisdiction over the adoption proceedings. Indeed, the court appears to have concluded that, for this reason, none of the provisions of the ICWA was applicable.... In any case, it rejected the Tribe's contention that the requirements of the ICWA applicable in state courts had not been followed....

... We now reverse.

Tribal jurisdiction over Indian child custody proceedings is not a novelty of the ICWA. Indeed, some of the ICWA's jurisdictional provisions have a strong basis in pre–ICWA case law in the federal and state courts.... In enacting the ICWA Congress confirmed that, in child custody proceedings involving Indian children domiciled on the reservation, tribal jurisdiction was exclusive as to the States.

The state-court proceeding at issue here was a "child custody proceeding." That term is defined to include any " 'adoptive placement' which shall mean the permanent placement of an Indian child for adoption, including any action resulting in a final decree of adoption." 25 U.S.C. § 1903(1)(iv). Moreover, the twins were "Indian children." See 25 U.S.C. § 1903(4). The sole issue in this case is, as the Supreme Court of Mississippi recognized, whether the twins were "domiciled" on the reservation.[16]

---

16. "Reservation" is defined quite broadly for purposes of the ICWA. See 25 U.S.C. § 1903(10). There is no dispute that the Choctaw Reservation falls within that definition.

Section 1911(a) does not apply "where such jurisdiction is otherwise vested in the State by existing Federal law." This proviso would appear to refer to Pub.L. 280, 67 Stat. 588, as amended, which allows States under certain conditions to assume civil and criminal jurisdiction on the reservations. ICWA § 1918 permits a tribe in that situation to reassume jurisdiction over child custody proceedings upon petition to the Secretary of the Interior. The State of Mississippi has never asserted jurisdiction over the Choctaw Reservation under Public Law 280. See F. Cohen, Handbook of Federal Indian Law 362–363, and nn. 122–125 (1982);....

The meaning of "domicile" in the ICWA is, of course, a matter of Congress' intent. The ICWA itself does not define it. The initial question we must confront is whether there is any reason to believe that Congress intended the ICWA definition of "domicile" to be a matter of state law....

First, and most fundamentally, the purpose of the ICWA gives no reason to believe that Congress intended to rely on state law for the definition of a critical term; quite the contrary. It is clear from the very text of the ICWA, not to mention its legislative history and the hearings that led to its enactment, that Congress was concerned with the rights of Indian families and Indian communities vis-à-vis state authorities. More specifically, its purpose was, in part, to make clear that in certain situations the state courts did *not* have jurisdiction over child custody proceedings. Indeed, the congressional findings that are a part of the statute demonstrate that Congress perceived the States and their courts as partly responsible for the problem it intended to correct.... Under these circumstances it is most improbable that Congress would have intended to leave the scope of the statute's key jurisdictional provision subject to definition by state courts as a matter of state law.

Second, Congress could hardly have intended the lack of nationwide uniformity that would result from state-law definitions of domicile. An example will illustrate. In a case quite similar to this one, the New Mexico state courts found exclusive jurisdiction in the tribal court pursuant to § 1911(a), because the illegitimate child took the reservation domicile of its mother at birth—notwithstanding that the child was placed in the custody of adoptive parents two days after its off-reservation birth and the mother executed a consent to adoption ten days later. In re Adoption of Baby Child, 102 N.M. 735, 737–738, 700 P.2d 198, 200–201 (App.1985). Had that mother traveled to Mississippi to give birth, rather than to Albuquerque, a different result would have obtained if state-law definitions of domicile applied. The same, presumably, would be true if the child had been transported to Mississippi for adoption after her off-reservation birth in New Mexico. While the child's custody proceeding would have been subject to exclusive tribal jurisdiction in her home State, her mother, prospective adoptive parents, or an adoption intermediary could have obtained an adoption decree in state court merely by transporting her across state lines. Even if we could conceive of a federal statute under which the rules of domicile (and thus of jurisdiction) applied differently to different Indian children, a statute under which different rules apply from time to time to the same child, simply as a result of her transport from one State to another, cannot be what Congress had in mind.[21]

We therefore think it beyond dispute that Congress intended a uniform federal law of domicile for the ICWA.

It remains to give content to the term "domicile" in the circumstances of the present case. The holding of the Supreme Court of Mississippi that the twin babies were not domiciled on the Choctaw Reservation appears to

---

21. For this reason, the general rule that domicile is determined according to the law of the forum, see Restatement (Second) of Conflict of Laws § 13 (1971) (hereinafter Restatement), can have no application here.

have rested on two findings of fact by the trial court: (1) that they had never been physically present there, and (2) that they were "voluntarily surrendered" by their parents. The question before us, therefore, is whether under the ICWA definition of "domicile" such facts suffice to render the twins nondomiciliaries of the reservation.

. . .

That we are dealing with a uniform federal rather than a state definition does not, of course, prevent us from drawing on general state-law principles to determine "the ordinary meaning of the words used." Well-settled state law can inform our understanding of what Congress had in mind when it employed a term it did not define. Accordingly, we find it helpful to borrow established common-law principles of domicile to the extent that they are not inconsistent with the objectives of the congressional scheme.

"Domicile" is, of course, a concept widely used in both federal and state courts for jurisdiction and conflict-of-laws purposes, and its meaning is generally uncontroverted. "Domicile" is not necessarily synonymous with "residence," and one can reside in one place but be domiciled in another. For adults, domicile is established by physical presence in a place in connection with a certain state of mind concerning one's intent to remain there. Texas v. Florida, 306 U.S. 398, 424 (1939). One acquires a "domicile or origin" at birth, and that domicile continues until a new one (a "domicile of choice") is acquired. Since most minors are legally incapable of forming the requisite intent to establish a domicile, their domicile is determined by that of their parents. In the case of an illegitimate child, that has traditionally meant the domicile of its mother. Under these principles, it is entirely logical that "[o]n occasion, a child's domicil of origin will be in a place where the child has never been." Restatement § 14, Comment *b*.

It is undisputed in this case that the domicile of the mother (as well as the father) has been, at all relevant times, on the Choctaw Reservation. Thus, it is clear that at their birth the twin babies were also domiciled on the reservation, even though they themselves had never been there. The statement of the Supreme Court of Mississippi that "[a]t no point in time can it be said the twins . . . were domiciled within the territory set aside for the reservation," 511 So.2d, at 921, may be a correct statement of that State's law of domicile, but it is inconsistent with generally accepted doctrine in this country and cannot be what Congress had in mind when it used the term in the ICWA.

Nor can the result be any different simply because the twins were "voluntarily surrendered" by their mother. Tribal jurisdiction under § 1911(a) was not meant to be defeated by the actions of individual members of the tribe, for Congress was concerned not solely about the interests of Indian children and families, but also about the impact on the tribes themselves of the large numbers of Indian children adopted by non-Indians. . . .

In addition, it is clear that Congress' concern over the placement of Indian children in non-Indian homes was based in part on evidence of the detrimental impact on the children themselves of such placements outside their culture. Congress determined to subject such placements to the ICWA's jurisdictional and other provisions, even in cases where the parents consented to an adoption, because of concerns going beyond the wishes of individual parents. As the 1977 Final Report of the congressionally established American Indian Policy Review Commission stated, in summarizing these two concerns, "[r]emoval of Indian children from their cultural setting seriously impacts a long-term tribal survival and has damaging social and psychological impact on many individual Indian children."[25]

These congressional objectives make clear that a rule of domicile that would permit individual Indian parents to defeat the ICWA's jurisdictional scheme is inconsistent with what Congress intended. See In re Adoption of Child of Indian Heritage, 111 N.J. 155, 168–171, 543 A.2d 925, 931–933 (1988). The appellees in this case argue strenuously that the twins' mother went to great lengths to give birth off the reservation so that her children could be adopted by the Holyfields. But that was precisely part of Congress' concern. Permitting individual members of the tribe to avoid tribal exclusive jurisdiction by the simple expedient of giving birth off the reservation would, to a large extent, nullify the purpose the ICWA was intended to accomplish.[27] The Supreme Court of Utah expressed this well in its scholarly and sensitive opinion in what has become a leading case on the ICWA:

"To the extent that [state] abandonment law operates to permit [the child's] mother to change [the child's] domicile as part of a scheme to facilitate his adoption by non-Indians while she remains a domiciliary of the reservation, it conflicts with and undermines the operative scheme established by subsections [1911(a)] and [1913(a)] to deal with children of domiciliaries of the reservation and weakens considerably the tribe's ability to assert its interest in its children. The protection of this tribal interest is at the core of the ICWA, which recognizes that the tribe has an interest in the child which is distinct from but on a parity with the interest of the parents. This relationship between Indian tribes and Indian children domiciled on the reservation finds no parallel in other ethnic cultures found in the United States. It is a relationship that many non-Indians find difficult to understand and

25. While the statute itself makes clear that Congress intended the ICWA to reach voluntary as well as involuntary removal of Indian children, the same conclusion can also be drawn from the ICWA's legislative history. For example, the House Report contains the following expression of Congress' concern with both aspects of the problem:

"One of the effects of our national paternalism has been to so alienate some Indian [parents] from their society that they abandon their children at hospitals or to welfare departments rather than entrust them to the care of relatives in the extended family. Another expression of it is the involuntary, arbitrary, and unwarranted separation of families."

27. It appears, in fact, that all Choctaw women give birth off the reservation because of the lack of appropriate obstetric facilities there. In most cases, of course, the mother and child return to the reservation after the birth, and this would presumably be sufficient to make the child a reservation domiciliary even under the Mississippi court's theory. Application of the Mississippi domicile rule would, however, permit state authorities to avoid the tribal court's exclusive § 1911(a) jurisdiction by removing a newborn from an allegedly unfit mother while in the hospital, and seeking to terminate her parental rights in state court.

that non-Indian courts are slow to recognize. It is precisely in recognition of this relationship, however, that the ICWA designates the tribal court as the exclusive forum for the determination of custody and adoption matters for reservation-domiciled Indian children, and the preferred forum for nondomiciliary Indian children. [State] abandonment law cannot be used to frustrate the federal legislative judgment expressed in the ICWA that the interests of the tribe in custodial decisions made with respect to Indian children are as entitled to respect as the interests of the parents." In re Adoption of Halloway, 732 P.2d 962, 969–970 (1986).

We agree with the Supreme Court of Utah that the law of domicile Congress used in the ICWA cannot be one that permits individual reservation-domiciled tribal members to defeat the tribe's exclusive jurisdiction by the simple expedient of giving birth and placing the child for adoption off the reservation. Since, for purposes of the ICWA, the twin babies in this case were domiciled on the reservation when adoption proceedings were begun, the Choctaw tribal court possessed exclusive jurisdiction pursuant to 25 U.S.C. § 1911(a). The Chancery Court of Harrison County was, accordingly, without jurisdiction to enter a decree of adoption; under ICWA § 1914 its decree of January 28, 1986, must be vacated.

We are not unaware that over three years have passed since the twin babies were born and placed in the Holyfield home, and that a court deciding their fate today is not writing on a blank slate in the same way it would have in January 1986. Three years' development of family ties cannot be undone, and a separation at this point would doubtless cause considerable pain.

Whatever feelings we might have as to where the twins should live, however, it is not for us to decide that question. We have been asked to decide the legal question of *who* should make the custody determination concerning these children—not what the outcome of that determination should be. The law places that decision in the hands of the Choctaw tribal court. Had the mandate of the ICWA been followed in 1986, of course, much potential anguish might have been avoided, and in any case the law cannot be applied so as automatically to "reward those who obtain custody, whether lawfully or otherwise, and maintain it during any ensuing (and protracted) litigation." It is not ours to say whether the trauma that might result from removing these children from their adoptive family should outweigh the interest of the Tribe—and perhaps the children themselves—in having them raised as part of the Choctaw community.[28] Rather, "we must defer to the experience, wisdom, and compassion of the [Choctaw] tribal courts to fashion an appropriate remedy."

The judgment of the Supreme Court of Mississippi is reversed and the case remanded for further proceedings not inconsistent with this opinion.

28. We were assured at oral argument that the Choctaw court has the authority under the tribal code to permit adoption by the present adoptive family, should it see fit to do so.

■ JUSTICE STEVENS, with whom THE CHIEF JUSTICE and JUSTICE KENNEDY join, dissenting.

The parents of these twin babies unquestionably expressed their intention to have the state court exercise jurisdiction over them. J.B. gave birth to the twins at a hospital 200 miles from the Reservation, even though a closer hospital was available. Both parents gave their written advance consent to the adoption and, when the adoption was later challenged by the Tribe, they reaffirmed their desire that the Holyfields adopt the two children. As the Mississippi Supreme Court found, "the parents went to some efforts to prevent the children from being placed on the reservation as the mother arranged for their birth and adoption in Gulfport Memorial Hospital, Harrison County, Mississippi." 511 So.2d 918, 927 (1987). Indeed, both parents appear before us today, urging that Vivian Holyfield be allowed to retain custody of B.B. and G.B.

Because J.B.'s domicile is on the reservation and the children are eligible for membership in the Tribe, the Court today closes the state courthouse door to her. I agree with the Court that Congress intended a uniform federal law of domicile for the Indian Child Welfare Act of 1978 (ICWA), and that domicile should be defined with reference to the objectives of the congressional scheme.... I cannot agree, however, with the cramped definition the Court gives that term. To preclude parents domiciled on a reservation from deliberately invoking the adoption procedures of state court, the Court gives "domicile" a meaning that Congress could not have intended and distorts the delicate balance between individual rights and group rights recognized by the ICWA.

The ICWA was passed in 1978 in response to congressional findings that "an alarmingly high percentage of Indian families are broken up by the *removal,* often unwarranted, of their children from them by nontribal public and private agencies" and that "the States, exercising their recognized jurisdiction over Indian child custody proceedings through administrative and judicial bodies, have often failed to recognize the essential tribal relations of Indian people and the cultural and social standards prevailing in Indian communities and families." 25 U.S.C. § 1901(4), (5). (Emphasis added.) The Act is thus primarily addressed to the unjustified removal of Indian children from their families through the application of standards that inadequately recognized the distinct Indian culture.

The most important provisions of the ICWA are those setting forth minimum standards for the placement of Indian children by state courts and providing procedural safeguards to insure that parental rights are protected. The Act provides that any party seeking to effect a foster care placement of, or involuntary termination of parental rights to, an Indian child must establish by stringent standards of proof that efforts have been made to prevent the breakup of the Indian family and that the continued custody of the child by the parent is likely to result in serious emotional or physical damage to the child. §§ 1912(d), (e), (f). Each party to the proceeding has a right to examine all reports and documents filed with the court and an indigent parent or custodian has the right to appointment of counsel. §§ 1912(b), (c). In the case of a voluntary termination, the ICWA provides that consent is valid only if given after the terms and consequences of the consent have been fully explained, may be withdrawn at any time up to the final entry of a decree of termination or adoption, and even then may be collaterally attacked on the grounds that it was obtained through fraud or duress. § 1913. Finally, because the Act protects not only the rights of the parents, but also the interests of the tribe and the Indian children, the Act sets forth criteria for adoptive, foster care, and preadoptive placements that favor the Indian child's extended family or tribe, and that can be altered by resolution of the tribe. § 1915.

The Act gives Indian tribes certain rights, not to restrict the rights of parents of Indian children, but to complement and help effect them. The Indian tribe may petition to transfer an action in state court to the tribal court, but the Indian parent may veto the transfer. § 1911(b). The Act provides for a tribal right of notice and intervention in involuntary proceedings but not in a voluntary ones. §§ 1911(c), 1912(a). Finally, the tribe may petition the court to set aside a parental termination action upon a showing that the provisions of the ICWA that are designed to protect parents and Indian children have been violated. § 1914.[5]

While the Act's substantive and procedural provisions effect a major change in state child custody proceedings, its jurisdictional provision is designed primarily to preserve tribal sovereignty over the domestic relations of tribe members and to confirm a developing line of cases which held that the tribe's exclusive jurisdiction could not be defeated by the temporary presence of an Indian child off the reservation.

. . .

Although parents of Indian children are shielded from the exercise of state jurisdiction when they are temporarily off the reservation, the Act also reflects a recognition that allowing the tribe to defeat the parents' deliberate choice of jurisdiction would be conducive neither to the best interests of the child nor to the stability and security of Indian tribes and families. Section 1911(b), providing for the exercise of concurrent jurisdiction by state and tribal courts when the Indian child is not domiciled on the reservation, gives the Indian parents a veto to prevent the transfer of a state court action to tribal court.[8] "By allowing the Indian parents to

5. Significantly, the tribe can not set aside a termination of parental rights on the grounds that the adoptive placement provisions of § 1915, favoring placement with the tribe, have not been followed.

8. The explanation of this subsection in the House Committee Report reads as follows:

"Subsection (b) directs a State court, having jurisdiction over an Indian child custody proceeding to transfer such proceeding, absent good cause to the contrary, to the appropriate tribal court upon the petition of the parents or the Indian tribe. Either parent is given the right to veto such transfer. The subsection is intended to permit a State court to apply a modified doctrine of forum non conveniens, in appropriate cases, to

insure that the rights of the child as an Indian, the Indian parents or custodian, and the tribe are fully protected." Id., at 21.

In commenting on the provision, the Department of Justice suggested that the section should be clarified to make it perfectly clear that a state court need not surrender jurisdiction of a child custody proceeding if the Indian parent objected. The Department of Justice letter stated:

"Section 101(b) should be amended to prohibit clearly the transfer of a child placement proceeding to a tribal court when any parent or child over the age of 12 objects to the transfer." Id., at 32.

Although the specific suggestion made by the Department of Justice was not in fact implemented, it is noteworthy that there is noth-

'choose' the forum that will decide whether to sever the parent-child relationship, Congress promotes the security of Indian families by allowing the Indian parents to defend in the court system that most reflects the parents' familial standards." Jones, 21 Ariz.L.Rev., at 1141. As Mr. Calvin Isaac, Tribal Chief of the Mississippi Band of Choctaw Indians stated in testimony to the House Subcommittee on Indian Affairs and Public Lands with respect to a different provision:

> "The ultimate responsibility for child welfare rests with the parents and we would not support legislation which interfered with that basic relationship."

If J.B. and W.J. had established a domicile off the Reservation, the state courts would have been required to give effect to their choice of jurisdiction; there should not be a different result when the parents have not changed their own domicile, but have expressed an unequivocal intent to establish a domicile for their children off the Reservation. The law of abandonment, as enunciated by the Mississippi Supreme Court in this case, does not defeat, but serves the purposes of the Act. An abandonment occurs when a parent deserts a child and places the child with another with an intent to relinquish all parental rights and obligations. Restatement (Second) of Conflict of Laws § 22, Comment e (1971) (hereinafter Restatement); In re Adoption of Halloway, 732 P.2d 962, 966 (Utah 1986). If a child is abandoned by his mother, he takes on the domicile of his father; if the child is abandoned by his father, he takes on the domicile of his mother. If the child is abandoned by both parents, he takes on the domicile of a person other than the parents who stands in loco parentis to him. To be effective, the intent to abandon or the actual physical abandonment must be shown by clear and convincing evidence.

When an Indian child is temporarily off the reservation, but has not been abandoned to a person off the reservation, the tribe has an interest in exclusive jurisdiction. The ICWA expresses the intent that exclusive tribal jurisdiction is not so frail that it should be defeated as soon as the Indian child steps off the reservation. Similarly, when the child is abandoned by one parent to a person off the reservation, the tribe and the other parent domiciled on the reservation may still have an interest in the exercise of exclusive jurisdiction. That interest is protected by the rule that a child abandoned by one parent takes on the domicile of the other. But when an Indian child is deliberately abandoned by both parents to a person off the reservation, no purpose of the ICWA is served by closing the state courthouse door to them. The interests of the parents, the Indian child, and the tribe in preventing the unwarranted removal of Indian children from their families and from the reservation are protected by the Act's substantive and procedural provisions. In addition, if both parents have intentionally invoked the jurisdiction of the state court in an action involving a non-Indian, no interest in tribal self-governance is implicated.

The interpretation of domicile adopted by the Court requires the custodian of an Indian child who is off the reservation to haul the child to a

---

ing in the legislative history to suggest that the recommended change was in any way inconsistent with any of the purposes of the statute.

potentially distant tribal court unfamiliar with the child's present living conditions and best interests. Moreover, it renders any custody decision made by a state court forever suspect, susceptible to challenge at any time as void for having been entered in the absence of jurisdiction.[12] Finally, it forces parents of Indian children who desire to invoke state court jurisdiction to establish a domicile off the reservation. Only if the custodial parent has the wealth and ability to establish a domicile off the reservation will the parent be able use the processes of state court. I fail to see how such a requirement serves the paramount congressional purpose of "promot[ing] the stability and security of Indian tribes and families." 25 U.S.C. § 1902.

The Court concludes its opinion with the observation that whatever anguish is suffered by the Indian children, their natural parents, and their adoptive parents because of its decision today is a result of their failure to initially follow the provisions of the ICWA. By holding that parents who are domiciled on the reservation cannot voluntarily avail themselves of the adoption procedures of state court and that all such proceedings will be void for lack of jurisdiction, however, the Court establishes a rule of law that is virtually certain to ensure that similar anguish will be suffered by other families in the future. Because that result is not mandated by the language of the ICWA and is contrary to its purposes, I respectfully dissent.

NOTE

Litigation over applications and possible exceptions to ICWA has continued. Not all of the cases have been released for publication. Some have centered on determining whether one or both parties meet the requirements of tribal membership or whether paternity has been established (ICWA contains no standard for establishing paternity). See e.g. *Matter of Adoption of a Child of Indian Heritage*, 111 N.J. 155, 543 A.2d 925 (1988). The United States Code, 25 U.S.C. § 1915(c), states that "[w]here appropriate, the preference of the Indian child or parent shall be considered." Interpretation of this produced litigation, though the provision would seem to apply only in cases where jurisdiction is not the issue. See, e.g., *Adoption of F.H.*, 851 P.2d 1361 (Alaska 1993). For further, discussion of ICWA in the context of adoption, see Solangel Maldonado, Race, Culture, and Adoption: Lessons from *Mississippi Band of Choctaw Indians v. Holyfield*, 17 Colum. J. Gender & L. 1 (2008); David H. Getches, Conquering the Cultural Frontier: The New Subjectivism of the Supreme Court in Indian Law, 84 Calif.L.Rev. 1573 (1996);

---

12.   The facts of In re Adoption of Halloway, 732 P.2d 962 (Utah 1986), which the Court cites approvingly, vividly illustrate the problem. In that case, the mother, a member of an Indian Tribe in New Mexico, voluntarily abandoned an Indian child to the custody of the child's maternal aunt off the Reservation with the knowledge that the child would be placed for adoption in Utah. The mother learned of the adoption two weeks after the child left the Reservation and did not object and, two months later, she executed a consent to adoption. Nevertheless, some two years after the petition for adoption was filed, the Indian Tribe intervened in the proceeding and set aside the adoption. The Tribe argued successfully that regardless of whether the Indian parent consented to it, the adoption was void because she resided on the Reservation and thus the tribal court had exclusive jurisdiction. Although the decision in *Halloway*, and the Court's approving reference to it, may be colored somewhat by the fact that the mother in that case withdrew her consent (a fact which would entitle her to relief even if there were only concurrent jurisdiction, see 25 U.S.C. § 1913(c)), the rule set forth by the majority contains no such limitation. As the Tribe acknowledged at oral argument, any adoption of an Indian child effected through a state court will be susceptible of challenge by the Indian tribe no matter how old the child and how long it has lived with its adoptive parents.

Philip P. Frickey, Congressional Intent, Practical Reasoning, and the Dynamic Nature of Federal Indian Law, 78 Calif.L.Rev. 1137 (1990); and Ann Atwood, Fighting Over Indian Children: The Uses and Misuses of Judicial Ambiguity, 36 U.C.L.A. L.Rev. 1050 (1989).

E.   ADOPTION OF CHILDREN WITH SPECIAL NEEDS

A subsidized adoption provision was adopted in some states as early as 1968, but there was initial early reluctance to the approach, prompting one commentator to remark that "In a society in which two of the most cherished values are children and money, it is surprising that a proposal holding promise of saving both has met with much resistance." See Kenneth W. Watson, Subsidized Adoption: A Crucial Investment, 51 Child Welfare 220, 224 (1972).

In 1976 A MODEL STATE SUBSIDIZED ADOPTION ACT was published by the Office of Child Development of what is now the Department of Health and Human Services. A model set of regulations accompanied the statutory proposal, along with a comparison of the Model Act with then existing laws. The regulations explained that:

> Subsidized adoption is an ongoing program ... intended to make adoption possible for children who otherwise may not be adopted. It is designed as a supplement to the [State] adoption statutes and as an effective addition to regular recruitment efforts. It is meant to provide the benefits of family security, love and nurture for children in special circumstances, presently under the care of public or licensed voluntary agencies.

Subsidized adoption was given a strong boost by a provision in Public Law 96–272 (1980) requiring state plans for adoption assistance under 42 U.S.C.A. § 602(a)(20). In 1981 the Department also published a MODEL ACT FOR ADOPTION OF CHILDREN WITH SPECIAL NEEDS. See 46 FED.REG. 50,022 (1981). The elaborate and comprehensive proposal, which includes special sections on terminating parental rights of children with special needs, complemented the Model Subsidized Adoption Act.

For some views of the adoption assistance program and a perceptive analysis of problems that have arisen under it, including coordination of medical care payments for children of interstate placements, see Alice Bussiere, Federal Adoption Assistance for Children with Special Needs, 1985 Clearinghouse Rev. 587 and Ellen C. Segal (ed.), Adoption of Children with Special Needs: Issues in Law and Policy (ABA 1985).

VIRGINIA CODE ANNOTATED

CHAPTER 13.   ADOPTION ASSISTANCE FOR CHILDREN WITH SPECIAL NEEDS

§ 63.2–1300.   Purpose and intent of adoption assistance

The purpose of adoption assistance is to facilitate adoptive placements and ensure permanency for children with special needs. Adoption assistance includes subsidy payments made pursuant to requirements set forth in this chapter. A child with special needs is any child (i) in the custody of a local board that has the authority to place the child for adoption and consent thereto in accordance with the provisions of §§ 63.2–900, 63.2–903 and 63.2–1105 or (ii) in the custody of a licensed child-placing agency, for whom it has been determined that it is unlikely that the child will be adopted within a reasonable period of time due to one or more factors including, but not limited to:

1. Physical, mental or emotional condition existing prior to adoption;

2. Hereditary tendency, congenital problem or birth injury leading to substantial risk of future disability; or

3. Individual circumstances of the child related to age, racial or ethnic background or close relationship with one or more siblings.

Child with special needs shall also include a child for whom the factors set out in subdivision 1 or 2 are present at the time of adoption but are not diagnosed until after the final order of adoption is entered and no more than one year has elapsed.

§ 63.2–1301. Subsidy payments; when adoptive parents, etc., eligible

Subsidy payments shall be made to the adoptive parents and other persons on behalf of a child in the custody of the local board or in the custody of a licensed child-placing agency and placed for adoption, pursuant to this chapter, if it is determined that:

(1) The child is a child with special needs; and

(2) The adoptive parents are capable of providing the permanent family relationships needed by the child in all respects except financial.

Such subsidy payments shall be made, however, only after a reasonable but unsuccessful effort has been made to place the child with appropriate adoptive parents without the provision of adoption assistance pursuant to this chapter except in cases where the child has developed significant emotional ties with the prospective adoptive parents while in the care of such parents as a foster child.

§ 63.2–1302. Subsidy payments; maintenance; special needs; payment agreements; continuation of payments when adoptive parents move to another jurisdiction; funds

A. Subsidy payments shall include:

1. A maintenance subsidy which shall be payable monthly to provide for the support and care of the child; however, the maintenance subsidy shall not exceed the maximum regular foster care payment that would otherwise be made for the child; and

2. A special need subsidy to provide special services to the child which the adoptive parents cannot afford and which are not covered by insurance or otherwise, including, but not limited to:

a. Medical, surgical and dental care;

b. Hospitalization;

c. Legal services in effecting adoption;

d. Individual remedial educational services;

e. Psychological and psychiatric treatment;

f.   Speech and physical therapy;

g.   Special services, equipment, treatment and training for physical and mental handicaps; and

h.   Cost of adoptive home study and placement by a child-placing agency other than the local board.

Special need subsidies may be paid to the vendor of the goods or services directly or through the adoptive parents.

Subsidy payments shall cease when the child with special needs reaches the age of eighteen years. If it is determined that the child has a mental or physical handicap, or an educational delay resulting from such handicap, warranting the continuation of assistance, subsidy payments may be made until the child reaches the age of twenty-one years.

B.   Maintenance subsidy payments and special need subsidy payments shall be made on the basis of a subsidy payment agreement entered into by the local board and the adoptive parents or, in cases in which the child is in the custody of a licensed child-placing agency, an agreement between the local board, the licensed child-placing agency and the adoptive parents.

Adoptive parents shall submit annually to the local board within thirty days of the anniversary date of the approved agreement an affidavit which certifies that (i) the child on whose behalf they are receiving subsidy payments remains in their care and (ii) the child's condition requiring subsidy continues to exist. Failure to provide this information may be grounds for suspension of the subsidy payment until such time as the information is provided.

Maintenance subsidy payments made pursuant to this section shall not be reduced unless the circumstances of the child or adoptive parents have changed significantly in relation to the terms of the subsidy agreement.

C.   Responsibility for subsidy payments for a child placed for adoption shall be continued in the event that the adoptive parents live in or move to another jurisdiction, provided that the adoptive parents meet the conditions of the agreement and provided that an agreement can be made with the appropriate agency of the locality within or without the Commonwealth where the adoptive family lives or is moving to provide the necessary assistance in administering the subsidy agreement.

.   .   .

F.   ACCESS TO ADOPTION RECORDS AND CONTACTS WITH BIRTH PARENTS

1.   THE STRICT PRIVACY VIEW

In re Roger B.

Supreme Court of Illinois, 1981.
84 Ill.2d 323, 49 Ill.Dec. 731, 418 N.E.2d 751, appeal dismissed 454 U.S. 806, 102 S.Ct. 80, 70 L.Ed.2d 76.

■ THOMAS J. MORAN, JUSTICE.

The circuit court of Cook County dismissed the amended petition of plaintiff, Roger B., which sought a judgment declaring section 18 of the

Adoption Act unconstitutional. That statute places adoption records and original birth records under seal. The appellate court, in a two-to-one decision, affirmed.

Plaintiff argues before this court that the Section is invalid in that it (1) infringes upon a fundamental right, (2) creates a suspect classification, in violation of the equal protection clause of the United States Constitution, and (3) violates plaintiff's right to receive information.

The facts are uncontradicted. Plaintiff, who was born in 1949, filed an amended petition in the circuit court, asserting that his status as an adult adoptee who had feelings of inadequacy and uncertainty as to his background permitted access to his adoption records. Alternatively, plaintiff alleged that the Section is unconstitutional. At the hearing, plaintiff testified that he had been searching for his biological family for three years. Plaintiff regarded himself as "emotionally, physically, and financially comfortable." He testified that his search was not based on any psychiatric or medical need. Rather, the search emanated from plaintiff's desire to know "information which pertains to [him] as a person." The trial court upheld the validity of the statute. It also found that the statute requires a showing of good cause, which plaintiff failed to establish. The appellate court affirmed, upholding the constitutionality of the Section. The court also held that adulthood, in and of itself, does not constitute good cause to allow access to sealed adoption records.

The Section provides in pertinent part:

> "Upon motion of any party to an adoption proceeding the court shall, or upon the court's own motion the court may, order that the file relating to such proceeding shall be impounded by the clerk of the court and shall be opened for examination only upon specific order of the court, which order shall name the person or persons who are to be permitted to examine such file." (Ill.Rev.Stat.1977, ch. 40, par. 1522.)

A companion statute ... provides that, after an adoption, the original birth certificate shall be sealed from inspection except upon court order.

Neither party disputes the trial court's finding that the statutory scheme allows the records to be unsealed upon a showing of good cause. The statute, unlike those of several other States, does not explicitly provide a good-cause standard. However, the legislature has given the court authority to issue an order providing access to the records....

Plaintiff contends that the right to know his own identity is a fundamental right. He argues that the Section infringes upon this right without serving a compelling State interest, thereby violating the equal protection clause of the Federal Constitution. Plaintiff maintains that the right to determine one's natural identity finds its basis under one's right to privacy. He relies on several Supreme Court cases involving familial relationships, rights of family privacy, and freedom to marry and reproduce....

These cases concern the most intimate areas of personal and marital privacy. The Supreme Court has been very hesitant in expanding the list of fundamental rights.... We have found no case holding that the right of an adoptee to determine his genealogical origin is explicitly or implicitly guaranteed by the Constitution. Several courts, however, have found that the right asserted here is not a fundamental right. Alma Society, Inc. v. Mellon (2d Cir.1979), 601 F.2d 1225, 1231–33; Application of Maples (Mo.1978), 563 S.W.2d 760, 762–64; . . .

In Alma Society, Inc. v. Mellon, the plaintiff adoptees similarly claimed that a statute allowing the sealing of adoption records, unless good cause is shown, violated their fundamental right to "personhood." The court upheld the statute, concluding that the right to unseal birth records does not come within any recognized category of privacy. . . . The court held that the right of an adoptee to discover his identity should not be considered exclusive of the interests of other family members.

Virtually every State statute affects important rights. Although information regarding one's background, heritage, and heredity is important to one's identity, it does not fall within any heretofore delineated zone of privacy implicitly protected within the Bill of Rights. We believe the adoptee does not have a fundamental right to examine his adoption records.

Inasmuch as a fundamental right is not involved, the statute will be upheld if it is not arbitrary and bears a rational relationship to a legitimate State objective.

Section 18 and its related statutes represent a considered legislative judgment that confidentiality promotes the integrity of the adoption process. Confidentiality is needed to protect the right to privacy of the natural parent. The natural parents, having determined it is in the best interest of themselves and the child, have placed the child for adoption. This process is done not merely with the expectation of anonymity, but also with the statutory assurance that his or her identity as the child's parent will be shielded from public disclosure. Quite conceivably, the natural parents have established a new family unit with the expectation of confidentiality concerning the adoption that occurred several years earlier. In Application of Maples, [563 S.W.2d 760 (Mo.1978)], the Missouri Supreme Court stated:

"[T]he state at the behest of those concerned undertook through the adoption process to sever the parental relationship, award custody and establish a new relationship of parent and child. Much of the information coming into the court's records during that process is for good reason treated as a confidence, offering a fresh start to the parties so that natural parents making this agonizing decision are assured the parent-child relationship will be completely severed, both legally and socially and may put behind the mistakes and misfortunes precipitating this fateful act. They are assisted in this traumatic experience by the knowledge that the records may be compromised only on order of court and that neither the child nor the adoptive parents may question why they consented to the adoption or the circumstances of the abandonment or neglect. If it were otherwise, the adopted child might reenter their lives with disastrous results. There must be finality for the natural parents and a new beginning; if there is a right of privacy not to be lightly infringed, it would seem to be theirs." 563 S.W.2d 760, 763.

These interests of the natural parents do not cease when the adoptee reaches adulthood.

Confidentiality also must be promoted to protect the right of the adopting parents. The adopting parents have taken into their home a child whom they will regard as their own and whom they will love, support, and raise as an integral part of the family unit. They should be given the opportunity to create a stable family relationship free from unnecessary intrusion. The Section creates a situation in which the emotional attachments are directed toward the relationship with the new parents. The adoptive parents need and deserve the child's loyalty as they grow older, and particularly in their later years. As stated in *Alma Society:*

> "The adoptee's attainment of majority is a definite event in the adoptee's life; but it occurs independent of either the legally terminated natural family relationship or the legally assumed adoptive one and does not affect termination or continuation of those relationships." 601 F.2d 1225, 1231.

The State's concern of promoting confidentiality to protect the integrity of the adoption process is well expressed by the following excerpt from Klibanoff, Genealogical Information in Adoption: The Adoptees' Quest and the Law, 11 Fam.L.Q. 185, 196–97 (1977):

> "The primary interest of the public is to preserve the integrity of the adoptive process. That is, the continued existence of adoption as a humane solution to the serious social problem of children who are or may become unwanted, abused or neglected. In order to maintain it, the public has an interest in assuring that changes in law, policy or practice will not be made which negatively affect the supply of capable adoptive parents or the willingness of biological parents to make decisions which are best for them and their children. We should not increase the risk of neglect to any child, nor should we force parents to resort to the black market in order to surrender children they can't care for.
>
>   . . .
>
> No one has yet shown that decades of policy protecting the anonymity of the biological parents and the security from intrusion of the parent-child relationship after adoption have been misguided. Quite the contrary. The overwhelming success of adoption as an institution which has provided millions of children with families, and vice versa, cannot be easily attacked.
>
> The public has a strong interest, too, in preserving the confidential non-public nature of the process. Public attitudes toward illegitimacy and parents who neglect or abuse children have not changed sufficiently to warrant careless disclosure of the circumstances leading to adoption.
>
> But the public also has an interest in the mental health of children who have been adopted—in order that they not become burdens to society. Some provision for the relatively small group of adoptees whose psychological needs are compelling would appear necessary."

We note that only three States, Alabama, Florida and Kansas, grant the adoptee access to original birth records. Confidentiality is perceived to promote the efficacy of the adoption process in 42 States, where the statutes provide for sealed birth records.

The State certainly must protect the interest of the adoptee, as well as the rights of the natural and adopting parents. When the adoptee is a minor, there is no dispute that the sealed-record provisions serve this end. The child, in his new family environment, is insulated from intrusion from the natural parents. The child is protected from any stigma resulting from illegitimacy, neglect, or abuse. The preclusion of outside interference allows the adopted child to develop a relationship of love and cohesiveness with the new family unit. Prior to adulthood, the adoptee's interest is consistent with that of the adopting and natural parents.

Upon reaching majority, the adoptee often develops a countervailing interest that is in direct conflict with the other parties, particularly the natural parents. The adoptee wishes to determine his natural identity, while the privacy interest of the natural parents remains, perhaps stronger than ever. The Section recognizes that the right of privacy is not absolute. It allows the court to evaluate the needs of the adoptee as well as the nature of the relationships and choices made by all parties concerned. The statute, by providing for release of adoption records only upon issuance of a court order, does no more than allow the court to balance the interests of all the parties and make a determination based on the facts and circumstances of each individual case.

We find the statute to be rationally related to the legitimate legislative purpose of protecting the adoption process. Consequently, the Section does not unconstitutionally infringe upon an adoptee's right to discover his own identity.

Plaintiff argues that the Section creates a suspect classification for which there is no compelling State justification, thereby violating the equal protection clause of the Constitution. He compares his classification as an adoptee to legislative classifications that have been held suspect, such as race, alienage, national origin, and classifications that have been analyzed as "quasi-suspect," such as illegitimacy and sex. Only race, alienage, and national origin have been definitively recognized as suspect classifications. Just as is true with respect to fundamental rights, the Supreme Court has been very hesitant in expanding the list of suspect classifications.

Again, the Supreme Court has not enunciated specific criteria by which a suspect class is determined, but has suggested that suspect classes are those that suffer from "an immutable characteristic determined solely by the accident of birth" and have had a history of the relegation of the class to an inferior status. Frontiero v. Richardson (1973), 411 U.S. 677, 684–86, 93 S.Ct. 1764, 1769–70, 36 L.Ed.2d 583, 590–91.

The status of adoptee does not result at birth, it is derived from a legal proceeding, the purpose of which is to protect the best interest of the child. Such status, conferred by the Adoption Act, actually improves the position of the child by providing a home, support, a family unit, and loving care that might otherwise not be present. Further, the child inherits from the adopting parents. We find that section 18 of the Adoption Act does not create a suspect classification.

Inasmuch as a suspect classification is not involved, the State need only have a rational basis for the statutory classification.

. . .

As discussed earlier, the legislature perceived a need for confidentiality. This confidentiality performs the socially and legally vital role of balancing the interest of the child, the interest of the natural parents, and the interest of the adopting parents. The prohibition against seeing the records is not restricted to the adoptees. It applies equally to the adoptees, adopting parents, natural parents, and any curious third party who seeks to look at the record. Further, as stated earlier, the preclusion on viewing the records is not absolute. The court may, for good cause, order the records to be seen. Inasmuch as a rational relationship exists between the creation of the status of adoptee and the State's interest in promoting the adoption process, we find no unconstitutional infringement.

Plaintiff also argues that his constitutional right to receive information is violated by the Section. We disagree....

Just as we held that plaintiff's right to know his identity is not absolute, plaintiffs right to receive information cannot be considered at the exclusion of the right of the other concerned parties. As stated earlier, the Section does not totally deny plaintiff access to his birth records. It simply requires a court to determine that sufficient justification exists before releasing the information. This limitation, founded upon protecting the adoption process, is not an unconstitutional exercise of State power.

. . .

In this case, plaintiff's attempt to have his adoption records released did not result from any physical or psychological medical need. It arose from plaintiff's desire to discover his natural identity. Further, the record does not show that the natural parents have ever waived their privacy right by consenting to divulgence of the information. We find that the trial court did not abuse its discretion in concluding that plaintiff's desire to obtain release of the records should not prevail over the potential infringement of the rights of other parties. Accordingly, the judgment of the appellate court is affirmed.

2. INCREASING MOVEMENT TOWARD OPENNESS

Until recently access to adoption records by the adoptee or a relinquishing parent typically would be permitted only by court order based on good cause (not always defined in the statutes). Some states now permit adoptees to gain access to their records on reaching majority or some other specific age without such stringent restrictions. Such a change can be particularly controversial if it does not provide a means for protecting the privacy expectations of the relinquishing parent based on the law at the time of the relinquishment. Note the provision in this regard in California Family Code § 8702, at page 806 supra. Some courts have allowed openness for an adoptee to obtain parental medical records that might be relevant to a child's medical condition, though sometimes this can be accomplished without revealing the name of the natural parent(s).

Kentucky Revised Statutes § 199.575 sets forth a procedure that could facilitate an adopted person seeking to locate a preadoptive sibling:

> In situations where a preadoptive brother or sister relationship existed, and one (1) or more of these siblings was then adopted, the following procedures shall be followed on an inquiry by one (1) or more of the siblings to the Cabinet for Health and Family Services seeking information about his brother or sister:
>
> (1) In all cases, an adopted person eighteen (18) years of age or older or a preadoptive sibling eighteen (18) years of age or older of an adopted person may file information concerning himself, his present location, and his known antecedents with the Cabinet for Health and Family Services, stating his interest in being reunited with his preadoptive siblings and authorizing the cabinet to release such information to his preadoptive siblings who may make similar inquiry.
>
> (2) In any case in which a person eighteen (18) years of age or older requests information about or expresses a desire in being reunited with a preadoptive sibling, the cabinet shall first determine whether such sibling has made similar inquiry pursuant to subsection (1) of this section. If the sibling has previously authorized release of information about himself, the cabinet shall release the information to the sibling making inquiry.

The December 17, 2007, issue of People Magazine, at p. 124, carried an article describing how two women, both in their mid-twenties and best friends, became convinced that they might be related. Along with the mother of one of them (both of them as it turned out), they petitioned the state to open adoption records of one of the "friends." After waiting for a year, impatience mounting, they submitted DNA samples. When the results came back they learned that they were sisters. They also learned that they shared the same biological father. See http://www.people.com/people/archive/article/0,,20170930,00.html.

OPEN ADOPTION

Although "open adoption" has many strong advocates, only recently has it received much favorable attention by legislatures. In fact, the name currently refers to adoptions in states in which courts will approve contracts for visitation after adoption or in which the natural and adoptive parents simply agree and no contest ensues later. Open adoption is a recent development in the law of adoption. It refers to the practice of allowing the birth family and the adoptive family to share information, communications, and contact with the child prior to, during and after the adoption. Without this possibility, the biological family would lose all contact with the child upon the child's adoption. Open adoption was not anticipated in most adoption laws, but some states are now enacting specific provisions providing for it. For commentary, see Rosemary Cabellero, Open Records Adoption: Finding the Missing Piece, 30 S.Ill.U. L.J. 291–313 (2006).

For views on the effectiveness of "open" as compared to "closed" adoptions, see Arnette Barran and Reuben Pannor, Perspectives on Open Adoption, 3 The Future of Children, No. 1 (Spring 1993) at 120; Marianne Berry, Risks and Benefits of Open Adoption, 3 The Future of Children, No. 1 (Spring 1993) at 125; and William L. Pierce, Open Adoption: A Review of the Research, Adoption Factbook III 233 (1999). For a more recent, extensive study concluding that no "one size fits all" approach seems best, see Harold D. Grotevant, Yvette V. Perry, and Ruth G. McRoy, Openness in Adoption: Outcomes for Adolescents within Their Adoptive Kinship Networks, in Psychological Issues in Adoption, David M. Brodzinsky and Jesús Palacios, eds., 167–169, reprinted with permission in Adoption Factbook IV, 439–452 (2007); cf. Thomas C. Atwood, The Jury Is in Regarding Adoption Openness, Adoption Factbook IV 453–454 (2007).

NEW MEXICO STATUTES

§ 32A–5–35.   Open adoptions

A.   The parents of the adoptee and the petitioner may agree to contact between the parents and the petitioner or contact between the adoptee and one or more of the parents or contact between the adoptee and relatives of the parents. An agreement shall, absent a finding to the contrary, be presumed to be in the best interests of the child and shall be included in the decree of adoption. The contact may include exchange of identifying or nonidentifying information or visitation between the parents or the parents' relatives and the petitioner or visitation between the parents or the parents' relatives and the adoptee. An agreement entered into pursuant to this section shall be considered an open adoption.

B.   The court may appoint a guardian ad litem for the adoptee. The court shall adopt a presumption in favor of appointing a guardian ad litem for the adoptee when visitation between the biological family and the adoptee is included in an agreement; however, this requirement may be waived by the court for good cause shown. When an adoptive placement is made voluntarily through an agency or pursuant to Section 32A–5–13 NMSA 1978, the court may, in its discretion, appoint a guardian ad litem. If the child is fourteen years of age or older, the court may appoint an attorney for the child. In all adoptions other than those in which the child is placed by the department, the court may assess the parties for the cost of services rendered by the guardian ad litem or the child's attorney. The duties of the guardian ad litem or child's attorney end upon the filing of the decree, unless otherwise ordered by the court.

C.   In determining whether the agreement is in the adoptee's best interests, the court shall consider the adoptee's wishes, but the wishes of the adoptee shall not control the court's findings as to the best interests of the adoptee.

D.   Every agreement entered into pursuant to provisions of this section shall contain a clause stating that the parties agree to the continuing jurisdiction of the court and to the agreement and understand and intend that any disagreement or litigation regarding the terms of the agreement shall not affect the validity of the relinquishment of parental rights, the adoption or the custody of the adoptee.

E.   The court shall retain jurisdiction after the decree of adoption is entered, if the decree contains an agreement for contact, for the purpose of hearing motions brought to enforce or modify an agreement entered into pursuant to the provisions of this section. The court shall not grant a request to modify the agreement unless the moving party establishes that there has been a change of circumstances and the agreement is no longer in the adoptee's best interests.

STANDBY GUARDIANSHIP

Under standby guardianship, recognized by statute in some states, a standby guardian can be designated by a parent to assume authority for a minor child upon the parent's incapacity or death. It is not actually open adoption but some consider it a variation of it. For an example of a standby guardian statute, see Maryland Estates & Trusts Code Ann. §§ 13–901 et seq.

G.   CIVIL EFFECTS OF ADOPTION

NEW YORK DOMESTIC RELATIONS LAW

§ 117.   Effect of adoption

1.   (a) After the making of an order of adoption the birth parents of the adoptive child shall be relieved of all parental duties toward and of all responsibilities for and shall have no rights over such adoptive child or to his property by descent or succession, except as hereinafter stated.

(b) The rights of an adoptive child to inheritance and succession from and through his birth parents shall terminate upon the making of the order of adoption except as hereinafter provided.

(c) The adoptive parents or parent and the adoptive child shall sustain toward each other the legal relation of parent and child and shall have all the rights and be subject to all the duties of that relation including the rights of inheritance from and through each other and the birth and adopted kindred of the adoptive parents or parent.

(d) When a birth or adoptive parent, having lawful custody of a child, marries or remarries and consents that the stepparent may adopt such child, such consent shall not relieve the parent so consenting of any parental duty toward such child nor shall such consent or the order of adoption affect the rights of such consenting spouse and such adoptive child to inherit from and through each other and the birth and adopted kindred of such consenting spouse.

(e) Notwithstanding the provisions of paragraphs (a), (b) and (d) of this subdivision, as to estates of persons dying after the thirty-first day of August, nineteen hundred eighty-seven, if:

(1) the decedent is the adoptive child's birth grandparent or is a descendant of such grandparent, and

(2) an adoptive parent (i) is married to the child's birth parent, (ii) is the child's birth grandparent, or (iii) is descended from such grandparent,

the rights of an adoptive child to inheritance and succession from and through either birth parent shall not terminate upon the making of the order of adoption.

However, an adoptive child who is related to the decedent both by birth relationship and by adoption shall be entitled to inherit only under the birth relationship unless the decedent is also the adoptive parent, in which case the adoptive child shall then be entitled to inherit pursuant to the adoptive relationship only.

(f) The right of inheritance of an adoptive child extends to the distributees of such child and such distributees shall be the same as if he were the birth child of the adoptive parent.

(g) Adoptive children and birth children shall have all the rights of fraternal relationship including the right of inheritance from each other. Such right of inheritance extends to the distributees of such adoptive children and birth children and such distributees shall be the same as if each such child were the birth child of the adoptive parents.

(h) The consent of the parent of a child to the adoption of such child by his or her spouse shall operate to vest in the adopting spouse only the rights as distributee of a birth parent and shall leave otherwise unaffected the rights as distributee of the consenting spouse.

(i) This subdivision shall apply only to the intestate descent and distribution of real and personal property.

2. (a) Except as hereinafter stated, after the making of an order of adoption, adopted children and their issue thereafter are strangers to any birth relatives for the purpose of the interpretation or construction of a disposition in any instrument, whether executed before or after the order of adoption, which does not express a contrary intention or does not expressly include the individual by name or by some classification not based on a parent-child or family relationship.

(b) As to the wills of persons executed after the thirty-first day of August, nineteen hundred eighty-six, or to lifetime instruments executed after such date whether executed before or after the order of adoption, a designation of a class of persons described in section 2–1.3 of the estates, powers and trusts law shall, unless the will or instrument expresses a contrary intention, be deemed to include an adoptive child who was a member of such class in his or her birth relationship prior to adoption, and the issue of such child, only if:

(1) an adoptive parent (i) is married to the child's birth parent, (ii) is the child's birth grandparent, or (iii) is a descendant of such grandparent, and

(2) the testator or creator is the child's birth grandparent or a descendant of such grandparent.

(c) A person who, by reason of this subdivision, would be a member of the designated class, or a member of two or more designated classes pursuant to a single instrument, both by birth relationship and by adoption shall be entitled to benefit only under the birth relationship, unless the testator or creator is the adoptive parent, in which case the person shall then be entitled to benefit only under the adoptive relationship.

(d) The provisions of this subdivision shall not impair or defeat any rights which have vested on or before the thirty-first day of August, nineteen hundred eighty-six, or which have vested prior to the adoption regardless of when the adoption occurred.

3.   The provisions of law affected by the provisions of this section in force prior to March first, nineteen hundred sixty-four shall apply to the estates or wills of persons dying prior thereto and to lifetime instruments theretofore executed which on said date were not subject to grantor's power to revoke or amend.

NOTE

(1) **Abrogation or annulment.** At one time some state adoption statutes contained what might be described as quasi-warranty provisions that allowed parents to return a child who developed certain major mental or physical conditions not determinable at the time of the adoption. In the spirit of fully integrating a child into the adoptive family, annulment of adoptions generally is not looked on favorably today by courts or legislatures. However, in *In re Adoption of M*, 317 N.J.Super. 531, 722 A.2d 615 (Ch.Div.1998), an adopted daughter was pregnant by her adoptive father and the court permitted revocation of the adoption so that the two could be married. The divorced mother did not object to the relocation and the court seemed to be concerned with legitimating the child born to the daughter.

(2) Relationship by adoption does not fall within either consanguinity or affinity, which are the two bases used historically for prohibiting marriage between persons related too closely by kinship. However some jurisdictions have enacted statutes specifically barring marriage between siblings by adoption. Such a law in Colorado was declared unconstitutional in *Israel v. Allen*, 195 Colo. 263, 577 P.2d 762 (1978). Should there be a difference in any such ban based on the ages of the parties at the time when they became related by adoption? Considering that genetics is not a concern, what is the basis for such a restriction?

H.   EQUITABLE ADOPTION

John Jeffries, Equitable Adoption: They Took Him Into Their Home and Called Him Fred*

58 Va.L.Rev. 727, 727–31 (1972).†

Though not legally adopted, a foster child may in some cases participate in the estate of an intestate foster parent. Courts reach this result under a number of different labels: equitable or virtual adoption, or adoption by estoppel. Generally, "equitable adoption" describes the provision of some judicial remedy for an unperformed contract for legal adoption. Although this doctrine arises in a variety of factual contexts, it most

---

* Kuchenig v. California Co., 410 F.2d 222, 224 (5th Cir.1969).

† Copyright 1972, Virginia Law Review. Reprinted with permission.

commonly involves a child's effort to share in the intestate estate of someone who has agreed to adopt him but has not done so. Typically the foster parents contract for legal adoption with the child, his natural parents, or someone in loco parentis. The child lives with his foster parents, takes their name, loves and obeys them as would a natural child. Upon the death of the foster parents, the child asks a court to treat him as if he were a legally adopted child for purposes of intestate succession.

Whatever remedy is provided, the result is startling: A child's share of the estate goes to one who, in the eyes of the law, stands as a stranger to the deceased. Eight states refuse to allow any such recovery on an unperformed adoption contract. These courts note that adoption is everywhere a creature of statute and insist on strict construction of statutes in derogation of common law. In these jurisdictions the statutory scheme provides the exclusive method of adoption, and no private agreement will suffice to bring the child within the statutes of descent and distribution.

One may ask why any court would consider a claim of equitable adoption in the face of an unambiguous statutory scheme. The answer lies in the extraordinarily persuasive factual situations which may arise. For example, in Wooley v. Shell Petroleum Corporation[8] Mr. and Mrs. Fowler agreed with a widower to adopt his twin infant daughters. Three years later the father and the foster parents apprenticed the girls to the Fowlers, apparently thinking that this proceeding constituted a legal adoption. The Fowlers took the children into their home and raised them as their own. In return, the girls helped and cared for the Fowlers during the apparent poverty of their declining years:

> Evidence could not show more loyal or faithful performance of duty than these girls rendered to the Fowlers. Hardships and privations which they endured in their faithfulness to Mr. and Mrs. Fowler evoke sympathy and consideration, as well as admiration, from all acquainted with the facts.[9]

Courts of some twenty-five other jurisdictions have similarly demonstrated their willingness to go beyond the statutory scheme to meet the demands of conscience.

. . .

Theory of Recovery

At the outset one must distinguish a contract to adopt from a contract to make a will. The latter agreement necessarily involves the disposition of property and may come within the Statute of Frauds, but if written or removed from the Statute by part performance, such a contract will be enforced quite apart from any purported adoption. An agreement to adopt stands on a different footing. Although frequently discussed in relation to an adoption agreement, the Statute of Frauds does not invalidate such a contract. It can be performed within one year and within the lifetime of the promisor, and it need not involve the disposition of property since the promisor remains free to disinherit a child by will. Of course, a single case

8.   39 N.M. 256, 45 P.2d 927 (1935).   9.   Id. at 261, 45 P.2d at 930.

may involve both a contract to make a will and a contract to adopt, and courts sometimes fail to distinguish between them; but the essence of equitable adoption is the provision of a judicial remedy for an unperformed adoption agreement.

Courts that endorse the doctrine of equitable adoption recognize no right in law; they merely agree to provide an equitable and discretionary remedy in a proper case: "Equity, abhorring injustice, and having its origin in the inadequacy of legal remedies, and possessing powers all its own, has developed the remedy ... the granting or denial of which rests in sound discretion."[15] Some courts rest their decisions solely and squarely on the principles of equity. More commonly, courts employ one of several more sophisticated techniques to reach the desired result.

Specific Performance

The most popular theory of recovery is specific performance of the contract to adopt. Courts grant this remedy only against the estate of a deceased promisor; a child cannot enforce an adoption agreement during the lifetime of his adoptive parent:

> The [adoption] statute involves action by the court, looking always to the best interest of the child. Such action could not have been compelled in a suit for specific performance.... [A]doption is not a contract alone between the parties. It requires judicial determination of the advisability of permitting such action, and if a court decrees otherwise, it is not within the power of one person to adopt another. The relationship of parent and child is of the most intimate, personal nature. Equity will not ordinarily enforce a contract to create such relationship.[17]

As against the defaulting promisor's estate, courts characteristically require an adoption agreement and valid consideration for the promise of adoption. This conceptual framework leads to discussions of the authority of the contracting parties and the sufficiency of consideration. Generally, custody of the child, filial companionship and obedience, or change in the child's domestic status will support the promise of the adoptive parent. Transfer of custody to the prospective spouse of the child's natural parent may suffice, but some courts hold that neither the marriage nor the benefits of association consequently enjoyed by the stepparent constitute consideration. Misconduct of the child, including abandonment of the adoptive family, may amount to a failure of consideration, but only where the conduct is flagrant.

Despite its currency, the theory of specific performance of the adoption agreement fits the facts of these cases only passing well. For one thing, courts will grant relief only against the estate of a deceased promisor. Furthermore, a proven contract to adopt will fail to determine custody in a contest between the natural and foster parents. Most importantly, courts that follow this theory do not order specific performance. A deceased promisor cannot adopt the child, and no court has held that the equitably

15. Wooley v. Shell Petroleum Corp., 39 N.M., 256, 264, 45 P.2d 927, 932 (1935).

17. Besche v. Murphy, 190 Md. 539, 544, 59 A.2d 499, 501–02 (1948).

adopted child attains the status of legal adoption. In allowing participation in the estate of a foster parent, the courts do not specifically enforce the contract but merely provide an equitable remedy, limited in application and result.

NOTE

Some states have gradually adopted the doctrine of equitable adoption in the context of intestate succession, allowing for the child equitably adopted to take "from" but not "through" the equitably adopting parent under the state's intestate laws. See e.g., *Lankford v. Wright*, 347 N.C. 115, 489 S.E.2d 604 (1997) (acknowledging that twenty-seven other states have recognized and adopted equitable adoption). In *In re Estate of Ford*, 32 Cal.4th 160, 8 Cal.Rptr.3d 541, 82 P.3d 747 (2004), the Supreme Court of California ruled that the doctrine may only apply if the parties' conduct and statements clearly and convincingly demonstrate an intent to adopt. A close relationship between an adopter and an adoptee is not sufficient to invoke the doctrine of equitable adoption. There must be statements and acts indicating an intent to adopt, or the "parent" consistently holding the child out as the child of the parent.

I. INTERNATIONAL ADOPTIONS

The United States signed the CONVENTION ON PROTECTION OF CHILDREN AND CO-OPERATION IN RESPECT OF INTERCOUNTRY ADOPTION on March 31, 1994. This move signaled that the U.S. would proceed with efforts to ratify it. In 2000 the Senate consented to ratification and Congress enacted implementing legislation, the Intercountry Adoption Act (IAA). In December 2007 a ratification ceremony took place at the Hague, and its provisions started governing intercountry adoptions between the United States and other Hague Convention countries on April 15, 2008. The Department of State has been designated as the "Central Authority."

Intercountry adoptions involving United States adopters totaled roughly between 7,000 and 8,000 children in 1990. This number increased to almost 23,000 in 2006 but declined by some 3,000 in 2007. (The State Department keeps track of the number of foreign adoptions by counting the numbers of visas issued to orphans.)

The rise in foreign adoptions has not been without problems and adverse publicity. Concerns have included national pride of the countries involved whether there has been something akin to baby selling in some jurisdictions, unusual delays in others, and even questions of whether it is certain that the consenting parent is the actual parent. However many adopters who have participated in the process have been pleased with the outcome.

With present concerns about increasing adoptions of foster children in our own country, questions have been raised about whether some adopters seek to enter foreign adoptions rather than participate in transracial adoptions. See, e.g., discussions at pages 819 and 831–32, supra.

CONVENTION ON PROTECTION OF CHILDREN AND CO–OPERATION IN RESPECT OF INTERCOUNTRY ADOPTION

CHAPTER I—SCOPE OF THE CONVENTION

Article 1

The objects of the present Convention are—

a) to establish safeguards to ensure that intercountry adoptions take place in the best interests of the child and with respect for his or her fundamental rights as recognized in international law;

b) to establish a system of co-operation amongst Contracting States to ensure that those safeguards are respected and thereby prevent the abduction, the sale of, or traffic in children;

c) to secure the recognition in Contracting States of adoptions made in accordance with the Convention.

Article 2

(1) The Convention shall apply where a child habitually resident in one Contracting State ("the State of origin") has been, is being, or is to be moved to another Contracting State ("the receiving State") either after his or her adoption in the State of origin by spouses or a person habitually resident in the receiving State, or for the purposes of such an adoption in the receiving State or in the State of origin.

(2) The Convention covers only adoptions which create a permanent parent-child relationship.

Article 3

The Convention ceases to apply if the agreements mentioned in Article 17, sub-paragraph c, have not been given before the child attains the age of eighteen years.

CHAPTER II—REQUIREMENTS FOR INTERCOUNTRY ADOPTIONS

Article 4

An adoption within the scope of the Convention shall take place only if the competent authorities of the State of origin—

a) have established that the child is adoptable;

b) have determined, after possibilities for placement of the child within the State of origin have been given due consideration, that an intercountry adoption is in the child's best interests;

c) have ensured that

(1) the persons, institutions and authorities whose consent is necessary for adoption, have been counselled as may be necessary and duly informed of the effects of their consent, in particular whether or not an adoption will result in the termination of the legal relationship between the child and his or her family of origin,

(2) such persons, institutions and authorities have given their consent freely, in the required legal form, and expressed or evidenced in writing,

(3) the consents have not been induced by payment or compensation of any kind and have not been withdrawn, and

(4) the consent of the mother, where required, has been given only after the birth of the child; and

d) have ensured, having regard to the age and degree of maturity of the child, that

(1) he or she has been counselled and duly informed of the effects of the adoption and of his or her consent to the adoption, where such consent is required,

(2) consideration has been given to the child's wishes and opinions,

(3) the child's consent to the adoption, where such consent is required, has been given freely, in the required legal form, and expressed or evidenced in writing, and

(4) such consent has not been induced by payment or compensation of any kind.

Article 5

An adoption within the scope of the Convention shall take place only if the competent authorities of the receiving State—

a) have determined that the prospective adoptive parents are eligible and suited to adopt;

b) have ensured that the prospective adoptive parents have been counselled as may be necessary; and

c) have determined that the child is or will be authorized to enter and reside permanently in that State.

CHAPTER III—CENTRAL AUTHORITIES AND ACCREDITED BODIES

Article 6

(1) A Contracting State shall designate a Central Authority to discharge the duties which are imposed by the Convention upon such authorities.

(2) Federal States, States with more than one system of law or States having autonomous territorial units shall be free to appoint more than one Central Authority and to specify the territorial or personal extent of their functions. Where a State has appointed more than one Central Authority, it shall designate the Central Authority to which any communication may be addressed for transmission to the appropriate Central Authority within that State.

Article 7

(1) Central Authorities shall co-operate with each other and promote co-operation amongst the competent authorities in their States to protect children and to achieve the other objects of the Convention.

(2) They shall take directly all appropriate measures to—

a) provide information as to the laws of their States concerning adoption and other general information, such as statistics and standard forms;

b) keep one another informed about the operation of the Convention and, as far as possible, eliminate any obstacles to its application.

Article 8

Central Authorities shall take, directly or through public authorities, all appropriate measures to prevent improper financial or other gain in connection with an adoption and to deter all practices contrary to the objects of the Convention.

Article 9

Central Authorities shall take, directly or through public authorities or other bodies duly accredited in their State, all appropriate measures, in particular to—

a) collect, preserve and exchange information about the situation of the child and the prospective adoptive parents, so far as is necessary to complete the adoption;

b) facilitate, follow and expedite proceedings with a view to obtaining the adoption;

c) promote the development of adoption counselling and post-adoption services in their States;

d) provide each other with general evaluation reports about experience with intercountry adoption;

e) reply, in so far as is permitted by the law of their State, to justified requests from other Central Authorities or public authorities for information about a particular adoption situation.

Article 10

Accreditation shall only be granted to and maintained by bodies demonstrating their competence to carry out properly the tasks with which they may be entrusted.

Article 11

An accredited body shall—

a) pursue only non-profit objectives according to such conditions and within such limits as may be established by the competent authorities of the State of accreditation;

b) be directed and staffed by persons qualified by their ethical standards and by training or experience to work in the field of intercountry adoption; and

c) be subject to supervision by competent authorities of that State as to its composition, operation and financial situation.

Article 12

A body accredited in one Contracting State may act in another Contracting State only if the competent authorities of both States have authorized it to do so.

Article 13

The designation of the Central Authorities and, where appropriate, the extent of their functions, as well as the names and addresses of the accredited bodies shall be communicated by each Contracting State to the Permanent Bureau of the Hague Conference on Private International Law.

CHAPTER IV—PROCEDURAL REQUIREMENTS IN INTERCOUNTRY ADOPTION

Article 14

Persons habitually resident in a Contracting State, who wish to adopt a child habitually resident in another Contracting State, shall apply to the Central Authority in the State of their habitual residence.

Article 15

(1) If the Central Authority of the receiving State is satisfied that the applicants are eligible and suited to adopt, it shall prepare a report including information about their identity, eligibility and suitability to adopt, background, family and medical history, social environment, reasons for adoption, ability to undertake an intercountry adoption, as well as the characteristics of the children for whom they would be qualified to care.

(2) It shall transmit the report to the Central Authority of the State of origin.

Article 16

(1) If the Central Authority of the State of origin is satisfied that the child is adoptable, it shall—

a) prepare a report including information about his or her identity, adoptability, background, social environment, family history, medical history including that of the child's family, and any special needs of the child;

b) give due consideration to the child's upbringing and to his or her ethnic, religious and cultural background;

c) ensure that consents have been obtained in accordance with Article 4; and

d) determine, on the basis in particular of the reports relating to the child and the prospective adoptive parents, whether the envisaged placement is in the best interests of the child.

(2) It shall transmit to the Central Authority of the receiving State its report on the child, proof that the necessary consents have been obtained and the reasons for its determination on the placement, taking care not to reveal the identity of the mother and the father if, in the State of origin, these identities may not be disclosed.

Article 17

Any decision in the State of origin that a child should be entrusted to prospective adoptive parents may only remade if—

a) the Central Authority of that State has ensured that the prospective adoptive parents agree;

b) the Central Authority of the receiving State has approved such decision, where such approval is required by the law of that State or by the Central Authority of the State of origin;

c) the Central Authorities of both States have agreed that the adoption may proceed; and

d) it has been determined, in accordance with Article 5, that the prospective adoptive parents are eligible and suited to adopt and that the child is or will be authorized to enter and reside permanently in the receiving State.

Article 18

The Central Authorities of both States shall take all necessary steps to obtain permission for the child to leave the State of origin and to enter and reside permanently in the receiving State.

Article 19

(1) The transfer of the child to the receiving State may only be carried out if the requirements of Article 17 have been satisfied.

(2) The Central Authorities of both States shall ensure that this transfer takes place in secure and appropriate circumstances and, if possible, in the company of the adoptive or prospective adoptive parents.

(3) If the transfer of the child does not take place, the reports referred to in Articles 15 and 16 are to be sent back to the authorities who forwarded them.

Article 20

The Central Authorities shall keep each other informed about the adoption process and the measures taken to complete it, as well as about the progress of the placement if a probationary period is required.

Article 21

(1) Where the adoption is to take place after the transfer of the child to the receiving State and it appears to the Central Authority of that State that the continued placement of the child with the prospective adoptive parents is not in the child's best interests, such Central Authority shall take the measures necessary to protect the child, in particular—

a) to cause the child to be withdrawn from the prospective adoptive parents and to arrange temporary care;

b) in consultation with the Central Authority of the State of origin, to arrange without delay a new placement of the child with a view to adoption or, if this is not appropriate, to arrange alternative long-term care; an adoption shall not take place until the Central Authority of the State of origin has been duly informed concerning the new prospective adoptive parents;

c) as a last resort, to arrange the return of the child, if his or her interests so require.

(2) Having regard in particular to the age and degree of maturity of the child, he or she shall be consulted and, where appropriate, his or her consent obtained in relation to measures to be taken under this Article.

Article 22

(1) The functions of a Central Authority under this Chapter may be performed by public authorities or by bodies accredited under Chapter III, to the extent permitted by the law of its State.

(2) Any Contracting State may declare to the depositary of the Convention that the functions of the Central Authority under Articles 15 to 21 may be performed in that State, to the extent permitted by the law and subject to the supervision of the competent authorities of that State, also by bodies or persons who—

a) meet the requirements of integrity, professional competence, experience and accountability of that State; and

b) are qualified by their ethical standards and by training or experience to work in the field of intercountry adoption.

(3) A Contracting State which makes the declaration provided for in paragraph 2 shall keep the Permanent Bureau of the Hague Conference on Private International Law informed of the names and addresses of these bodies and persons.

(4) Any Contracting State may declare to the depositary of the Convention that adoptions of children habitually resident in its territory may only take place if the functions of the Central Authorities are performed in accordance with paragraph 1.

(5) Notwithstanding any declaration made under paragraph 2, the reports provided for in Articles 15 and 16 shall, in every case, be prepared under the responsibility of the Central Authority or other authorities or bodies in accordance with paragraph 1.

CHAPTER V—RECOGNITION AND EFFECTS OF THE ADOPTION

Article 23

(1) An adoption certified by the competent authority of the State of the adoption as having been made in accordance with the Convention shall be recognized by operation of law in the other Contracting States. The certificate shall specify when and by whom the agreements under Article 17, sub-paragraph c), were given.

(2) Each Contracting State shall, at the time of signature, ratification, acceptance, approval or accession, notify the depositary of the Convention of the identity and the functions of the authority or the authorities which, in that State, are competent to make the certification. It shall also notify the depositary of any modification in the designation of these authorities.

Article 24

The recognition of an adoption may be refused in a Contracting State only if the adoption is manifestly contrary to its public policy, taking into account the best interests of the child.

Article 25

Any Contracting State may declare to the depositary of the Convention that it will not be bound under this Convention to recognize adoptions made in accordance with an agreement concluded by application of Article 39, paragraph 2.

Article 26

(1) The recognition of an adoption includes recognition of

a) the legal parent-child relationship between the child and his or her adoptive parents;

b) parental responsibility of the adoptive parents for the child;

c) the termination of a pre-existing legal relationship between the child and his or her mother and father, if the adoption has this effect in the Contracting State where it was made.

(2) In the case of an adoption having the effect of terminating a pre-existing legal parent-child relationship, the child shall enjoy in the receiving State, and in any other Contracting State where the adoption is recognized, rights equivalent to those resulting from adoptions having this effect in each such State.

(3) The preceding paragraphs shall not prejudice the application of any provision more favourable for the child, in force in the Contracting State which recognizes the adoption.

Article 27

(1) Where an adoption granted in the State of origin does not have the effect of terminating a pre-existing legal parent-child relationship, it may, in the receiving State which recognizes the adoption under the Convention, be converted into an adoption having such an effect—

a) if the law of the receiving State so permits; and

b) if the consents referred to in Article 4, sub-paragraphs c and d, have been or are given for the purpose of such an adoption.

(2) Article 23 applies to the decision converting the adoption.

CHAPTER VI—GENERAL PROVISIONS

Article 28

The Convention does not affect any law of a State of origin which requires that the adoption of a child habitually resident within that State take place in that State or which prohibits the child's placement in, or transfer to, the receiving State prior to adoption.

Article 29

There shall be no contact between the prospective adoptive parents and the child's parents or any other person who has care of the child until the requirements of Article 4, sub-paragraphs a) to c), and Article 5, sub-paragraph a), have been met, unless the adoption takes place within a family or unless the contact is in compliance with the conditions established by the competent authority of the State of origin.

Article 30

(1) The competent authorities of a Contracting State shall ensure that information held by them concerning the child's origin, in particular information concerning the identity of his or her parents, as well as the medical history, is preserved.

(2) They shall ensure that the child or his or her representative has access to such information, under appropriate guidance, in so far as is permitted by the law of that State.

Article 31

Without prejudice to Article 30, personal data gathered or transmitted under the Convention, especially data referred to in Articles 15 and 16, shall be used only for the purposes for which they were gathered or transmitted.

Article 32

(1) No one shall derive improper financial or other gain from an activity related to an intercountry adoption.

(2) Only costs and expenses, including reasonable professional fees of persons involved in the adoption, may be charged or paid.

(3) The directors, administrators and employees of bodies involved in an adoption shall not receive remuneration which is unreasonably high in relation to services rendered.

Article 33

A competent authority which finds that any provision of the Convention has not been respected or that there is a serious risk that it may not be respected, shall immediately inform the Central Authority of its State. This Central Authority shall be responsible for ensuring that appropriate measures are taken.

Article 34

If the competent authority of the State of destination of a document so requests, a translation certified as being in conformity with the original must be furnished. Unless otherwise provided, the costs of such translation are to be borne by the prospective adoptive parents.

Article 35

The competent authorities of the Contracting States shall act expeditiously in the process of adoption.

Article 36

In relation to a State which has two or more systems of law with regard to adoption applicable in different territorial units—

a) any reference to habitual residence in that State shall be construed as referring to habitual residence in a territorial unit of that State;

b) any reference to the law of that State shall be construed as referring to the law in force in the relevant territorial unit;

c) any reference to the competent authorities or to the public authorities of that State shall be construed as referring to those authorized to act in the relevant territorial unit;

d) any reference to the accredited bodies of that State shall be construed as referring to bodies accredited in the relevant territorial unit.

Article 37

In relation to a State which with regard to adoption has two or more systems of law applicable to different categories of persons, any reference to the law of that State shall be construed as referring to the legal system specified by the law of that State.

Article 38

A State within which different territorial units have their own rules of law in respect of adoption shall not be bound to apply the Convention where a State with a unified system of law would not be bound to do so.

Article 39

(1) The Convention does not affect any international instrument to which Contracting States are Parties and which contains provisions on matters governed by the Convention, unless a contrary declaration is made by the States Parties to such instrument.

(2) Any Contracting State may enter into agreements with one or more other Contracting States, with a view to improving the application of the Convention in their mutual relations. These agreements may derogate only from the provisions of Articles 14 to 16 and 18 to 21. The States which have concluded such an agreement shall transmit a copy to the depositary of the Convention.

Article 40

No reservation to the Convention shall be permitted.

Article 41

The Convention shall apply in every case where an application pursuant to Article 14 has been received after the Convention has entered into force in the receiving State and the State of origin.

Article 42

The Secretary General of the Hague Conference on Private International Law shall at regular intervals convene a Special Commission in order to review the practical operation of the Convention.

[ED. NOTE: Articles 43–48 have been omitted.]

CHAPTER IX

THE JUVENILE JUSTICE SYSTEM: CHANGING PERSPECTIVES

A. A LOOK BACK

The subject matter jurisdiction of juvenile and family courts traditionally has included delinquency (conduct by a child that would be a crime if committed by an adult); noncriminal misbehavior (the so-called status offenses unique to children such as truancy, running away from home or engaging in other conduct injurious to the child's health, welfare or morals); and abuse and neglect (failure of parents to provide the minimum tolerable level of care for their children). More recently, some states have structured their juvenile justice systems around full-service family courts that have been given significantly increased jurisdiction, including adoption, child custody, intrafamily assaults, juvenile traffic offenses, or even divorce.

While most observers of the juvenile justice system would point to child custody and neglect adjudications with the possible remedy of permanent termination of parental rights as the most agonizing decisions a juvenile or family court judge must make, it is ironic that until very recently the greatest scrutiny of the system by the United States Supreme Court has focused on delinquency cases. This chapter discusses those decisions as a prelude to and catalyst for modern proposals for juvenile court reform and also provides an introduction to delinquency jurisdiction.

Until the turn of the twentieth century children were treated as adults in court, i.e., there were no special courts for handling children. As early as the beginning of the nineteenth century, concern began to be expressed for the plight of children, particularly with a view toward protection of wayward children (including orphans, paupers and children convicted of crimes in criminal court). In response houses of refuge were established in several cities by well-intentioned reformers anxious to keep youthful offenders separate from adult criminals.[1]

Beginning in the middle of the nineteenth century, progressives called for the creation of special courts to deal with delinquent minors. Although the "delinquent" label covered both vagrant and neglected children, the principal focus of the Illinois Juvenile Court Act of 1899 was criminal conduct by children. The Illinois Act, America's first juvenile code, was a

---

1. Herbert H. Lou, Juvenile Courts in the United States 13–19 (1927). For an historical account of the houses of refuge and other early reform efforts see Robert M. Men- nel, Origins of the Juvenile Court: Changing Perspectives on the Legal Rights of Juvenile Delinquents, 18 Crime & Delinq. 68 (1972).

direct product of the reformers' sense of outrage at the handling of children in the criminal courts. It enshrined the major ideas of what came to be called the Juvenile Court Philosophy:

(1) A special court was created for neglected, dependent or delinquent children under age 16.

(2) The purpose of that court was to rehabilitate children rather than punish them.

(3) Ostensibly, no stigma would attach to a child from a court appearance; all records and proceedings were to be confidential.

(4) The Act required that juveniles be separated from adults when incarcerated or placed in the same institution in order to avoid the corrupting influence of adult criminals on juveniles. All detention of children under 12 in police stations or jails was barred.

(5) Juvenile court proceedings were to be informal. Indeed, these new tribunals were not to operate on a legal model at all; the analogy from the start was medical, reflecting proposals by early reformers utilizing techniques of the then newly-developed social and behavioral sciences to diagnose, treat and cure socially sick children.

In philosophy and focus the juvenile court was a radical departure from its criminal counterpart, as noted by a contemporary of the Juvenile Court Movement:

> ... Why is it not just and proper to treat these juvenile offenders, as we deal with the neglected children, as a wise and merciful father handles his own child whose errors are not discovered by the authorities? Why is it not the duty of the state, instead of asking merely whether a boy or a girl has committed a specific offense, to find out what he is, physically, mentally, morally, and then if it learns that he is treading the path that leads to criminality to take him in charge, not so much to punish as to reform, not to degrade but to uplift, not to crush but to develop, not to make him a criminal but a worthy citizen.
>
>   . . .
>
> The child who must be brought into court should, of course, be made to know that he is face to face with the power of the state, but he should at the same time, and more emphatically, be made to feel that he is the object of its care and solicitude. The ordinary trappings of the court-room are out of place in such hearings. The judge on a bench, looking down upon the boy standing at the bar, can never evoke a proper sympathetic spirit. Seated at a desk, with the child at his side, where he can on occasion put his arm around his shoulder and draw the lad to him, the judge, while losing none of his judicial dignity, will gain immensely in the effectiveness of his work.[2]

The character and structure of the juvenile court also were different, as a result of the dictates of the sociological jurisprudence movement. Another contemporary wrote:

2. Julian Mack, The Juvenile Court, 23   © 1909 by the Harvard Law Review Associa-
Harv.L.Rev. 104, 107, 120 (1909). Copyright   tion. Reprinted with permission.

. . . With the advent of the sociological school of jurisprudence of the present century, which advocates the unification of all social sciences, of which law is but one, law is no longer regarded as a self-centered, self-sufficing science, isolated from the other social sciences. We are realizing more and more that law should be conceived as a means toward social ends. This new conception of law compels us to take account of social causes and social effects in relation to social conditions and social progress. This is sometimes called social justice.

The juvenile court is conspicuously a response to the modern spirit of social justice. . . .

These principles upon which the juvenile court acts are radically different from those of the criminal courts. In place of judicial tribunals, restrained by antiquated procedure, saturated in an atmosphere of hostility, trying cases for determining guilt and inflicting punishment according to inflexible rules of law, we have now juvenile courts, in which the relations of the child to his parents or other adults and to the state or society are defined, and are adjusted summarily according to the scientific findings about the child and his environment. In place of magistrates, limited by the outgrown custom and compelled to walk in the paths fixed by the law of the realm, we have now socially-minded judges, who hear and adjust cases according not to rigid rules of law but to what the interests of society and the interests of the child or good conscience demand. In place of juries, prosecutors, and lawyers, trained in the old conception of law and staging dramatically, but often amusingly, legal battles, as the necessary paraphernalia of a criminal court, we have now probation officers, physicians, psychologists, and psychiatrists, who search for the social, physiological, psychological, and mental backgrounds of the child in order to arrive at reasonable and just solutions of individual cases. In other words, in this new court we tear down primitive prejudice, hatred, and hostility toward the lawbreaker in that most hide-bound of all human institutions, the court of law, and we attempt, as far as possible, to administer justice in the name of truth, love, and understanding.[3]

Modern scholars disagree about the origins of the reform impulses that led to the creation of juvenile courts. Some have advocated the traditional view espoused by the contemporaries of the juvenile court movement, i.e., that its proponents were motivated by genuine concern about the plight of children.[4] Others have argued that proponents of the movement were more concerned with preserving traditional values against the rising threat of increased urbanism and industrialism at the turn of the century than they were by humanitarian concerns.[5]

3. Herbert H. Lou, Juvenile Courts in the United States 1–2 (1927). Copyright © 1927 by the University of North Carolina Press. Used by permission of the publisher.

4. J. Lawrence Schulz, The Cycle of Juvenile Court History, 19 Crime & Delinq. 457 (1973).

5. Anthony M. Platt, The Child Savers: The Invention of Delinquency (2d ed. 1972); Sanford Fox, Juvenile Justice Reform: An Historical Perspective, 22 Stan.L.Rev. 1187 (1970). A more recent, well-written account that lends credence to the Platt and Fox theory, is Ellen Ryerson, The Best–Laid

Between 1899 and 1917, all but three states created special courts for children. Fueled by the Progressive movement in the decade around World War I, the Juvenile Court Philosophy swept the country. Whatever the motivations that led to the creation of juvenile courts, by 1925 the Juvenile Court Philosophy had triumphed almost everywhere.

From their earliest beginnings until Justice Fortas's opinion in *Kent*[6] in 1966, juvenile courts operated without legal oversight or monitoring. Many would say that juvenile courts in this period were not really courts at all. As noted above, there was little or no place for law, lawyers, reporters and the usual paraphernalia of courts; this is not at all surprising because the proponents of the Juvenile Court movement had specifically rejected legal institutions as appropriate to the rehabilitation of children.

When some of the new juvenile court acts were subjected to constitutional challenge they were upheld on the ground that proceedings in juvenile court were civil, not criminal, and rehabilitative rather than punitive in nature.[7] Indeed, this same rationale withstood constitutional scrutiny from the turn of the century through the Arizona Supreme Court's decision in the *Gault* case in 1965.[8]

Beginning with *Kent* and continuing immediately in *Gault*[9] the Supreme Court examined the operation of the juvenile justice system and found, in Justice Fortas's words in *Kent*, that:

> While there can be no doubt of the original laudable purpose of juvenile courts, studies and critiques in recent years raise serious questions as to whether actual performance measures well enough against theoretical purpose to make tolerable the immunity of the process from the reach of constitutional guaranties applicable to adults. There is much evidence that some juvenile courts ... lack the personnel, facilities and techniques to perform adequately as representatives of the State in a *parens patriae* capacity, at least with respect to children charged with law violation. There is evidence, in fact, that there may be grounds for concern that the child receives the worst of both worlds: that he gets neither the protections accorded to adults nor the solicitous care and regenerative treatment postulated for children.[10]

In *Kent* the Court was confronted with a challenge to the process by which a juvenile court makes the decision whether to waive its jurisdiction and transfer a particular case for criminal prosecution as in the case of an adult. Specifically the Court held that (1) juveniles are entitled to a hearing on the question of waiver, (2) counsel is entitled to access to the social records that the court considers in making the waiver determination, and (3) any waiver order must be accompanied by a statement of reasons

Plans: America's Juvenile Court Experiment (1978).

6. *Kent v. United States*, 383 U.S. 541, 86 S.Ct. 1045, 16 L.Ed.2d 84 (1966).

7. See, e.g., *Ex parte Sharp*, 15 Idaho 120, 96 P. 563 (1908); *Commonwealth v. Fisher*, 213 Pa. 48, 62 A. 198 (1905).

8. *In re Gault*, 99 Ariz. 181, 407 P.2d 760 (1965), rev'd, 387 U.S. 1, 87 S.Ct. 1428, 18 L.Ed.2d 527 (1967).

9. *In re Gault*, 387 U.S. 1, 87 S.Ct. 1428, 18 L.Ed.2d 527 (1967).

10. 383 U.S. at 555.

explaining the court's decision to waive its jurisdiction. What was not clear, however, was the basis of the Court's decision in *Kent*. The Court specifically stated that its decision was based on a reading of the District of Columbia statutes rather than the Constitution. Other language in the opinion, however, suggested that the opinion had constitutional dimensions. Certainly most lower courts subsequently read *Kent* as expressing constitutional requirements.

The skepticism and doubt about the currency of the rehabilitative model expressed in *Kent* sharpened further in *Gault* as the Court scrutinized the old model, clearly using constitutional standards this time. Without a doubt *Gault* was the great watershed of the modern juvenile court movement. It constitutionalized the juvenile justice process. Its impact was profound. Lower courts and legislatures fully embraced the spirit of *Gault* and extended it far beyond the scope of the Court's holding. The juvenile court would never be the same.

The Supreme Court decisions that followed *Gault* examined the applicability of other due process rights to the juvenile process and, more importantly, revealed an emerging, evolving analytical framework employed by the Court to fashion a new due process model. This group of cases presents the most significant judicial response to the perceived malfunction of juvenile courts. By the 1970s, however, the main vehicle for reform shifted from judicial decisions to legislation. In the period from 1970 to the present, nearly every state has radically revised its juvenile code—usually to provide more exacting and precise guidelines for the exercise of discretion by juvenile judges, especially in delinquency cases.

More recently, another impetus for change has been the influence of various model legislative proposals, such as the Uniform Juvenile Court Act and the Juvenile Justice Standards. The result has been the emergence of diverging trends that run counter to traditional juvenile court philosophy. Some of the most thought-provoking proposals of recent years are found in the 23 volumes of Juvenile Justice Standards prepared under the auspices of the Institute of Judicial Administration and the American Bar Association. Twenty of the 23 volumes of standards were approved by the A.B.A. House of Delegates. The Standards are intended less as model legislation than as a broad compendium of current thought about juvenile courts and children's rights. As such, their conceptual bases undoubtedly provide building blocks for legislative reform even today.

While only some of the Standards relate to delinquency, certain basic principles that underlie the entire set of standards were capsulized in the summary volume to the 1980 edition of the Drafts: (1) Dispositions should be made in accordance with the principles of proportionality and determinacy and in favor of the least restrictive alternative where possible; (2) jurisdiction over noncriminal misconduct should be abandoned in favor of voluntary community services; (3) proceedings should be more visible in contrast to the closed proceedings dictated by the traditional model; (4) all affected parties should have the right to counsel at all critical stages of the proceedings; (5) juveniles should be empowered to make decisions affecting their lives, except when they are incapable of rationally doing so; (6) the role of parents should be reexamined for possible conflicts of interest between parent and child; (7) limitations should be placed on detention or other handling of juveniles prior to adjudication or disposition; and (8) strict criteria should be established for governing transfer of juveniles to adult court for prosecution as adults. Juvenile Justice Standards Project, Standards for Juvenile Justice: A Summary and Analysis (Second Edition 1982).

The Standards have proved to be one of two emerging trends that run counter to the traditional juvenile court model. The other—and probably more influential—is the post-*Gault* development of a body of statutory and case law that has fashioned juvenile procedure into something more akin to its criminal procedure counterpart, to the point that not much remains to distinguish treatment of juveniles accused of crime from adults. Juveniles, with relatively few exceptions, are treated the same as adults, although as will be seen later in this book they often do not enjoy the same level of constitutional protection as adults. The *Gault* decision, of course, was the catalyst that started it all, and our examination logically begins with a look at the case that had such a profound impact on the juvenile justice process. As one reads the different opinions of the justices one can easily detect the philosophical differences about where the juvenile court has been and the direction it should be taking. In a sense the opinions represent a microcosm of all that has been said about the juvenile court as an institution, and collectively they offer a prelude to all modern reform proposals.

B.   THE JUVENILE COURT AND THE CONSTITUTION: THE *GAULT* CASE

In re Gault

Supreme Court of the United States, 1967.
387 U.S. 1, 87 S.Ct. 1428, 18 L.Ed.2d 527.

■ MR. JUSTICE FORTAS delivered the opinion of the Court.

This is an appeal under 28 U.S.C. § 1257(2) from a judgment of the Supreme Court of Arizona affirming the dismissal of a petition for a writ of habeas corpus. 99 Ariz. 181, 407 P.2d 760 (1965). The petition sought the release of Gerald Francis Gault, appellants' 15–year-old son, who had been committed as a juvenile delinquent to the State Industrial School by the Juvenile Court of Gila County, Arizona. The Supreme Court of Arizona affirmed dismissal of the writ against various arguments which included an attack upon the constitutionality of the Arizona Juvenile Code because of its alleged denial of procedural due process rights to juveniles charged with being "delinquents." The court agreed that the constitutional guarantee of due process of law is applicable in such proceedings. It held that Arizona's Juvenile Code is to be read as "impliedly" implementing the "due process concept." It then proceeded to identify and describe "the particular elements which constitute due process in a juvenile hearing." It concluded that the proceedings ending in commitment of Gerald Gault did not offend those requirements. We do not agree, and we reverse. We begin with a statement of the facts.

I.

On Monday, June 8, 1964, at about 10 a.m., Gerald Francis Gault and a friend, Ronald Lewis, were taken into custody by the Sheriff of Gila County. Gerald was then still subject to a six months' probation order which had been entered on February 25, 1964, as a result of his having been in the company of another boy who had stolen a wallet from a lady's purse. The police action on June 8 was taken as the result of a verbal complaint by a neighbor of the boys, Mrs. Cook, about a telephone call made to her in which the caller or callers made lewd or indecent remarks. It will suffice for purposes of this opinion to say that the remarks or questions put to her were of the irritatingly offensive, adolescent, sex variety.

At the time Gerald was picked up, his mother and father were both at work. No notice that Gerald was being taken into custody was left at the home. No other steps were taken to advise them that their son had, in effect, been arrested. Gerald was taken to the Children's Detention Home. When his mother arrived home at about 6 o'clock, Gerald was not there. Gerald's older brother was sent to look for him at the trailer home of the Lewis family. He apparently learned then that Gerald was in custody. He so informed his mother. The two of them went to the Detention Home. The deputy probation officer, Flagg, who was also superintendent of the Detention Home, told Mrs. Gault "why Jerry was there" and said that a hearing would be held in Juvenile Court at 3 o'clock the following day, June 9.

Officer Flagg filed a petition with the court on the hearing day, June 9, 1964. It was not served on the Gaults. Indeed, none of them saw this petition until the habeas corpus hearing on August 17, 1964. The petition was entirely formal. It made no reference to any factual basis for the judicial action which it initiated. It recited only that "said minor is under the age of eighteen years, and is in need of the protection of this Honorable Court; [and that] said minor is a delinquent minor." It prayed for a hearing and an order regarding "the care and custody of said minor." Officer Flagg executed a formal affidavit in support of the petition.

On June 9, Gerald, his mother, his older brother, and Probation Officers Flagg and Henderson appeared before the Juvenile Judge in chambers. Gerald's father was not there. He was at work out of the city. Mrs. Cook, the complainant, was not there. No one was sworn at this hearing. No transcript or recording was made. No memorandum or record of the substance of the proceedings was prepared. Our information about the proceedings and the subsequent hearing on June 15, derives entirely from the testimony of the Juvenile Court Judge, Mr. and Mrs. Gault and Officer Flagg at the habeas corpus proceeding conducted two months later. From this, it appears that at the June 9 hearing Gerald was questioned by the judge about the telephone call. There was conflict as to what he said. His mother recalled that Gerald said he only dialed Mrs. Cook's number and handed the telephone to his friend, Ronald. Officer Flagg recalled that Gerald had admitted making the lewd remarks. Judge McGhee testified that Gerald "admitted making one of these [lewd] statements." At the conclusion of the hearing, the judge said he would "think about it." Gerald was taken back to the Detention Home. He was not sent to his own home with his parents. On June 11 or 12, after having been detained since June 8, Gerald was released and driven home.[2] There is no explanation in the record as to why he was kept in the Detention Home or why he was released. At 5 p.m. on the day of Gerald's release, Mrs. Gault received a note signed by Officer Flagg. It was on plain paper, not letterhead. Its entire text was as follows:

"Mrs. Gault:

"Judge McGhee has set Monday June 15, 1964 at 11:00 A.M. as the date and time for further Hearings on Gerald's delinquency

"/s/Flagg"

At the appointed time on Monday, June 15, Gerald, his father and mother, Ronald Lewis and his father, and Officers Flagg and Henderson were present before Judge McGhee. Witnesses at the habeas corpus proceeding differed in their recollections of Gerald's testimony at the June 15 hearing. Mr. and Mrs. Gault recalled that Gerald again testified that he had only dialed the number and that the other boy had made the remarks. Officer Flagg agreed that at this hearing Gerald did not admit making the lewd remarks. But Judge McGhee recalled that "there was some admission again of some of the lewd statements. He—he didn't admit any of the more serious lewd statements." Again, the complainant, Mrs. Cook, was not present. Mrs. Gault asked that Mrs. Cook be present "so she could see which boy that done the talking, the dirty talking over the phone." The Juvenile Judge said "she didn't have to be present at that hearing." The judge did not speak to Mrs. Cook or communicate with her at any time. Probation Officer Flagg had talked to her once—over the telephone on June 9.

At this June 15 hearing a "referral report" made by the probation officers was filed with the court, although not disclosed to Gerald or his parents. This listed the charge as "Lewd Phone Calls." At the conclusion of the hearing, the judge committed Gerald as a juvenile delinquent to the State Industrial School "for the period of his minority [that is, until 21], unless sooner discharged by due process of law." An order to that effect was entered. It recites that "after a full hearing and due deliberation the Court finds that said minor is a delinquent child, and that said minor is of the age of 15 years."

No appeal is permitted by Arizona law in juvenile cases. On August 3, 1964, a petition for a writ of habeas corpus was filed with the Supreme Court of Arizona and referred by it to the Superior Court for hearing.

At the habeas corpus hearing on August 17, Judge McGhee was vigorously cross-examined as to the basis for his actions. He testified that

---

2. There is a conflict between the recollection of Mrs. Gault and that of Officer Flagg. Mrs. Gault testified that Gerald was released on Friday, June 12, Officer Flagg that it had been on Thursday, June 11. This was from memory; he had no record, and the note hereafter referred to was undated.

he had taken into account the fact that Gerald was on probation. He was asked "under what section of . . . the code you found the boy delinquent?"

His answer is set forth in the margin.[5] In substance, he concluded that Gerald came within ARS § 8–201–6(a), which specifies that a "delinquent child" includes one "who has violated a law of the state or an ordinance or regulation of a political subdivision thereof." The law which Gerald was found to have violated is ARS § 13–377. This section of the Arizona Criminal Code provides that a person who "in the presence or hearing of any woman or child . . . uses vulgar, abusive or obscene language, is guilty of a misdemeanor. . . ." The penalty specified in the Criminal Code, which would apply to an adult, is $5 to $50, or imprisonment for not more than two months. . . .

. . .

The Superior Court dismissed the writ, and appellants sought review in the Arizona Supreme Court. That court stated that it considered appellants' assignments of error as urging (1) that the Juvenile Code, ARS § 8–201 to § 8–239, is unconstitutional because it does not require that parents and children be apprised of the specific charges, does not require proper notice of a hearing, and does not provide for an appeal; and (2) that the proceedings and order relating to Gerald constituted a denial of due process of law because of the absence of adequate notice of the charge and the hearing; failure to notify appellants of certain constitutional rights including the rights to counsel and to confrontation, and the privilege against self-incrimination; the use of unsworn hearsay testimony; and the failure to make a record of the proceedings. Appellants further asserted that it was error for the Juvenile Court to remove Gerald from the custody of his parents without a showing and finding of their unsuitability, and alleged a miscellany of other errors under state law.

The Supreme Court handed down an elaborate and wide-ranging opinion affirming dismissal of the writ and stating the court's conclusions as to the issues raised by appellants and other aspects of the juvenile process. In their jurisdictional statement and brief in this Court, appellants do not urge upon us all of the points passed upon by the Supreme Court of Arizona. They urge that we hold the Juvenile Code of Arizona invalid on its face or as applied in this case because, contrary to the Due Process Clause of the Fourteenth Amendment, the juvenile is taken from the custody of his parents and committed to a state institution pursuant to proceedings in which the Juvenile Court has virtually unlimited discretion, and in which the following basic rights are denied:

5. "Q. All right. Now, Judge, would you tell me under what section of the law or tell me under what section of—of the code you found the boy delinquent?

"A. Well, there is a—I think it amounts to disturbing the peace. I can't give you the section, but I can tell you the law, that when one person uses lewd language in the pres-ence of another person, that it can amount to—and I consider that when a person makes it over the phone, that it is considered in the presence, I might be wrong, that is one section. The other section upon which I consider the boy delinquent is Section 8–201, Subsection (d), habitually involved in immoral matters."

1. Notice of the charges;

2. Right to counsel;

3. Right to confrontation and cross-examination;

4. Privilege against self-incrimination;

5. Right to a transcript of the proceedings; and

6. Right to appellate review.

. . .

II.

The Supreme Court of Arizona held that due process of law is requisite to the constitutional validity of proceedings in which a court reaches the conclusion that a juvenile has been at fault, has engaged in conduct prohibited by law, or has otherwise misbehaved with the consequence that he is committed to an institution in which his freedom is curtailed. This conclusion is in accord with the decisions of a number of courts under both federal and state constitutions.

This Court has not heretofore decided the precise question. In Kent v. United States, 383 U.S. 541 (1966), we considered the requirements for a valid waiver of the "exclusive" jurisdiction of the Juvenile Court of the District of Columbia so that a juvenile could be tried in the adult criminal court of the District. Although our decision turned upon the language of the statute, we emphasized the necessity that "the basic requirements of due process and fairness" be satisfied in such proceedings.... [N]either the Fourteenth Amendment nor the Bill of Rights is for adults alone.

We do not in this opinion consider the impact of these constitutional provisions upon the totality of the relationship of the juvenile and the state. We do not even consider the entire process relating to juvenile "delinquents." For example, we are not here concerned with the procedures or constitutional rights applicable to the pre-judicial stages of the juvenile process, nor do we direct our attention to the post-adjudicative or dispositional process. We consider only the problems presented to us by this case. These relate to the proceedings by which a determination is made as to whether a juvenile is a "delinquent" as a result of alleged misconduct on his part, with the consequence that he may be committed to a state institution. As to these proceedings, there appears to be little current dissent from the proposition that the Due Process Clause has a role to play.[11] The problem is to ascertain the precise impact of the due process requirement upon such proceedings.

---

11. See Report by the President's Commission on Law Enforcement and Administration of Justice, "The Challenge of Crime in a Free Society" (1967) (hereinafter cited as Nat'l Crime Comm'n Report), pp. 81, 85–86; Standards, p. 71; Gardner, The Kent Case and the Juvenile Court: A Challenge to Lawyers, 52 A.B.A.J. 923 (1966); Paulsen, Fairness to the Juvenile Offender, 41 Minn. L.Rev. 547 (1957); Ketcham, The Legal Renaissance in the Juvenile Court, 60 Nw. U.L.Rev. 585 (1965); Allen, The Borderland of Criminal Justice (1964), pp. 19–23; Harvard Law Review Note, p. 791; Note, Rights and Rehabilitation in the Juvenile Courts, 67 Colum.L.Rev. 281 (1967); Comment, Criminal Offenders in the Juvenile Court: More Brickbats and Another Proposal, 114 U.Pa.L.Rev. 1171 (1966).

From the inception of the juvenile court system, wide differences have been tolerated—indeed insisted upon—between the procedural rights accorded to adults and those of juveniles. In practically all jurisdictions, there are rights granted to adults which are withheld from juveniles. In addition to the specific problems involved in the present case, for example, it has been held that the juvenile is not entitled to bail, to indictment by grand jury, to a public trial or to trial by jury. It is frequent practice that rules governing the arrest and interrogation of adults by the police are not observed in the case of juveniles.

The history and theory underlying this development are well-known, but a recapitulation is necessary for purposes of this opinion. The juvenile court movement began in this country at the end of the last century. From the Juvenile Court statute adopted in Illinois in 1899, the system has spread to every State in the Union, the District of Columbia, and Puerto Rico.[14] The constitutionality of Juvenile Court laws has been sustained in over 40 jurisdictions against a variety of attacks.

The early reformers were appalled by adult procedures and penalties, and by the fact that children could be given long prison sentences and mixed in jails with hardened criminals. They were profoundly convinced that society's duty to the child could not be confined by the concept of justice alone. They believed that society's role was not to ascertain whether the child was "guilty" or "innocent," but "What is he, how has he become what he is, and what had best be done in his interest and in the interest of the state to save him from a downward career."[16] The child—essentially good, as they saw it—was to be made "to feel that he is the object of [the state's] care and solicitude,"[17] not that he was under arrest or on trial. The rules of criminal procedure were therefore altogether inapplicable. The apparent rigidities, technicalities, and harshness which they observed in both substantive and procedural criminal law were therefore to be discarded. The idea of crime and punishment was to be abandoned. The child was to be "treated" and "rehabilitated" and the procedures, from apprehension through institutionalization, were to be "clinical" rather than punitive.

14. See National Counsel of Juvenile Court Judges, Directory and Manual (1964), p. 1. The number of Juvenile Judges as of 1964 is listed as 2,987, of whom 213 are full-time Juvenile Court Judges. Id., at 305. The Nat'l Crime Comm'n Report indicates that half of these judges have no undergraduate degree, a fifth have no college education at all, a fifth are not members of the bar, and three-quarters devote less than one-quarter of their time to juvenile matters. See also McCune, Profile of the Nation's Juvenile Court Judges (monograph, George Washington University, Center for the Behavioral Sciences, 1965), which is a detailed statistical study of Juvenile Court Judges, and indicates additionally that about a quarter of these judges have no law school training at all. About one-third of all judges have no probation and social work staff available to them; between eighty and ninety percent have no available psychologist or psychiatrist. Ibid. It has been observed that while "good will, compassion, and similar virtues are ... admirably prevalent throughout the system ... expertise, the keystone of the whole venture, is lacking." Harvard Law Review Note, p. 809. In 1965, over 697,000 delinquency cases (excluding traffic) were disposed of in these courts, involving some 601,000 children, or 2% of all children between 10 and 17. Juvenile Court Statistics—1965, Children's Bureau Statistical Series No. 85 (1966), p. 2.

16. Julian Mack, The Juvenile Court, 23 Harv.L.Rev. 104, 119–120 (1909).

17. Id., at 120.

These results were to be achieved, without coming to conceptual and constitutional grief, by insisting that the proceedings were not adversary, but that the state was proceeding as parens patriae.[18] The Latin phrase proved to be a great help to those who sought to rationalize the exclusion of juveniles from the constitutional scheme; but its meaning is murky and its historic credentials are of dubious relevance. The phrase was taken from chancery practice, where, however, it was used to describe the power of the state to act in loco parentis for the purpose of protecting the property interests and the person of the child. But there is no trace of the doctrine in the history of criminal jurisprudence. At common law, children under seven were considered incapable of possessing criminal intent. Beyond that age, they were subjected to arrest, trial, and in theory to punishment like adult offenders. In these old days, the state was not deemed to have authority to accord them fewer procedural rights than adults.

The right of the state, as parens patriae, to deny to the child procedural rights available to his elders was elaborated by the assertion that a child, unlike an adult, has a right "not to liberty but to custody." He can be made to attorn to his parents, to go to school, etc. If his parents default in effectively performing their custodial functions—that is, if the child is "delinquent"—the state may intervene. In doing so, it does not deprive the child of any rights, because he has none. It merely provides the "custody" to which the child is entitled. On this basis, proceedings involving juveniles were described as "civil" not "criminal" and therefore not subject to the requirements which restrict the state when it seeks to deprive a person of his liberty.

Accordingly, the highest motives and most enlightened impulses led to a peculiar system for juveniles, unknown to our law in any comparable context. The constitutional and theoretical basis for this peculiar system is—to say the least—debatable. And in practice, as we remarked in the Kent case, supra, the results have not been entirely satisfactory.[23] Juvenile

18. Id., at 109; Paulsen, [Kent v. United States: The Constitutional Context of Juvenile Cases, 1967 Sup.Ct.Review 167], at 173–174. There seems to have been little early constitutional objection to the special procedures of juvenile courts. But see Waite, How Far Can Court Procedure Be Socialized Without Impairing Individual Rights, 12 J.Crim.L. & Criminology 339, 340 (1922): "The Court which must direct its procedure even apparently to do something *to* a child because of what he *has done*, is parted from the court which is avowedly concerned only with doing something *for* a child because of what he *is* and *needs*, by a gulf too wide to be bridged by any humanity which the judge may introduce into his hearings, or by the habitual use of corrective rather than punitive methods after conviction."

23. "There is evidence ... that there may be grounds for concern that the child receives the worst of both worlds: that he gets neither the protections accorded to adults nor the solicitous care and regenerative treatment postulated for children." 383 U.S. at 556, citing Handler, The Juvenile Court and the Adversary System: Problems of Function and Form, 1965 Wis.L.Rev. 7; Harvard Law Review Note; and various congressional materials set forth in 383 U.S. at 546, note 5.

On the other hand, while this opinion and much recent writing concentrate upon the failures of the Juvenile Court system to live up to the expectations of its founders, the observation of the Nat'l Crime Comm'n Report should be kept in mind:

"Although its shortcomings are many and its results too often disappointing, the juvenile justice system in many cities is operated by people who are better educated and more highly skilled, can call on more and better facilities and services, and has more ancillary

Court history has again demonstrated that unbridled discretion, however benevolently motivated, is frequently a poor substitute for principle and procedure. In 1937, Dean Pound wrote: "The powers of the Star Chamber were a trifle in comparison with those of our juvenile courts...."[24] The absence of substantive standards has not necessarily meant that children receive careful, compassionate, individualized treatment. The absence of procedural rules based upon constitutional principle has not always produced fair, efficient, and effective procedures. Departures from established principles of due process have frequently resulted not in enlightened procedure, but in arbitrariness. The Chairman of the Pennsylvania Council of Juvenile Court Judges has recently observed: "Unfortunately, loose procedures, high-handed methods and crowded court calendars, either singly or in combination, all too often, have resulted in depriving some juveniles of fundamental rights that have resulted in a denial of due process."

Failure to observe the fundamental requirements of due process has resulted in instances, which might have been avoided, of unfairness to individuals and inadequate or inaccurate findings of fact and unfortunate prescriptions of remedy. Due process of law is the primary and indispensable foundation of individual freedom. It is the basic and essential term in the social compact which defines the rights of the individual and delimits the powers which the state may exercise. As Mr. Justice Frankfurter has said: "The history of American freedom is, in no small measure, the history of procedure." But in addition, the procedural rules which have been fashioned from the generality of due process are our best instruments for the distillation and evaluation of essential facts from the conflicting welter of data that life and our adversary methods present. It is these instruments of due process which enhance the possibility that truth will emerge from the confrontation of opposing versions and conflicting data. "Procedure is to law what 'scientific method' is to science."

It is claimed that juveniles obtain benefits from the special procedures applicable to them which more than offset the disadvantages of denial of the substance of normal due process. As we shall discuss, the observance of due process standards, intelligently and not ruthlessly administered, will not compel the States to abandon or displace any of the substantive benefits of the juvenile process. But it is important, we think, that the claimed benefits of the juvenile process should be candidly appraised. Neither sentiment nor folklore should cause us to shut our eyes, for example, to such startling findings as that reported in an exceptionally reliable study of repeaters or recidivism conducted by the Stanford Research Institute for the President's Commission on Crime in the District of Columbia. This Commission's Report states:

agencies to which to refer its clientele than its adult counterpart." Id., at 78.

24. Foreword to Young, Social Treatment in Probation and Delinquency (1937), p. xxvii. The 1965 Report of the United States Commission on Civil Rights, "Law Enforcement—A Report on Equal Protection in the South," pp. 80–83, documents numerous instances in which "local authorities used the broad discretion afforded them by the absence of safeguards [in the juvenile process]" to punish, intimidate, and obstruct youthful participants in civil rights demonstrations. See also Paulsen, Juvenile Courts, Family Courts, and the Poor Man, 54 Calif.L.Rev. 694, 707–709 (1966).

"In fiscal 1966 approximately 66 percent of the 16– and 17–year-old juveniles referred to the court by the Youth Aid Division had been before the court previously. In 1965, 56 percent of those in the Receiving Home were repeaters. The SRI study revealed that 61 percent of the sample Juvenile Court referrals in 1965 had been previously referred at least once and that 42 percent had been referred at least twice before." Id., at 773.

Certainly, these figures and the high crime rates among juveniles ... could not lead us to conclude that the absence of constitutional protections reduces crime, or that the juvenile system, functioning free of constitutional inhibitions as it has largely done, is effective to reduce crime or rehabilitate offenders. We do not mean by this to denigrate the juvenile court process or to suggest that there are not aspects of the juvenile system relating to offenders which are valuable. But the features of the juvenile system which its proponents have asserted are of unique benefit will not be impaired by constitutional domestication. For example, the commendable principles relating to the processing and treatment of juveniles separately from adults are in no way involved or affected by the procedural issues under discussion.[30] Further, we are told that one of the important benefits of the special juvenile court procedures is that they avoid classifying the juvenile as a "criminal." The juvenile offender is now classed as a "delinquent." There is, of course, no reason why this should not continue. It is disconcerting, however, that this term has come to involve only slightly less stigma than the term "criminal" applied to adults.[31] It is also emphasized that in practically all jurisdictions, statutes provide that an adjudication of the child as a delinquent shall not operate as a civil disability or disqualify him for civil service appointment. There is no reason why the application of due process requirements should interfere with such provisions.

Beyond this, it is frequently said that juveniles are protected by the process from disclosure of their deviational behavior. As the Supreme Court of Arizona phrased it in the present case, the summary procedures of Juvenile Courts are sometimes defended by a statement that it is the law's policy "to hide youthful errors from the full gaze of the public and bury them in the graveyard of the forgotten past." This claim of secrecy, however, is more rhetoric than reality. Disclosure of court records is discretionary with the judge in most jurisdictions. Statutory restrictions

30. Here again, however, there is substantial question as to whether fact and pretension, with respect to the separate handling and treatment of children, coincide.

While we are concerned only with procedure before the juvenile court in this case, it should be noted that to the extent that the special procedures for juveniles are thought to be justified by the special consideration and treatment afforded them, there is reason to doubt that juveniles always receive the benefits of such a *quid pro quo*....

In fact, some courts have recently indicated that appropriate treatment is essential to the validity of juvenile custody, and therefore that a juvenile may challenge the validity of his custody on the ground that he is not in fact receiving any special treatment.

31. "[T]he word 'delinquent' has today developed such invidious connotations that the terminology is in the process of being altered; the new descriptive phrase is 'persons in need of supervision,' usually shortened to 'pins.'" Harvard Law Review Note, p. 799, n. 140. The N.Y. Family Court Act § 712 distinguishes between "delinquents" and "persons in need of supervision."

almost invariably apply only to the court records, and even as to those the evidence is that many courts routinely furnish information to the FBI and the military, and on request to government agencies and even to private employers. Of more importance are police records. In most States the police keep a complete file of juvenile "police contacts" and have complete discretion as to disclosure of juvenile records. Police departments receive requests for information from the FBI and other law-enforcement agencies, the Armed Forces, and social service agencies, and most of them generally comply. Private employers word their application forms to produce information concerning juvenile arrests and court proceedings, and in some jurisdictions information concerning juvenile police contacts is furnished private employers as well as government agencies.

In any event, there is no reason why, consistently with due process, a State cannot continue, if it deem appropriate, to provide and to improve provision for the confidentiality of records of police contacts and court action relating to juveniles. . . .

Further, it is urged that the juvenile benefits from informal proceedings in the court. The early conception of the Juvenile Court proceeding was one in which a fatherly judge touched the heart and conscience of the erring youth by talking over his problems, by paternal advice and admonition, and in which, in extreme situations, benevolent and wise institutions of the State provided guidance and help "to save him from a downward career." Then, as now, goodwill and compassion were admirably prevalent. But recent studies have, with surprising unanimity, entered sharp dissent as to the validity of this gentle conception. They suggest that the appearance as well as the actuality of fairness, impartiality and orderliness—in short, the essentials of due process—may be a more impressive and more therapeutic attitude so far as the juvenile is concerned. . . . While due process requirements will, in some instances, introduce a degree of order and regularity to Juvenile Court proceedings to determine delinquency, and in contested cases will introduce some elements of the adversary system, nothing will require that the conception of the kindly juvenile judge be replaced by its opposite, nor do we here rule upon the question whether ordinary due process requirements must be observed with respect to hearings to determine the disposition of the delinquent child.

Ultimately, however, we confront the reality of that portion of the Juvenile Court process with which we deal in this case. A boy is charged with misconduct. The boy is committed to an institution where he may be restrained of liberty for years. It is of no constitutional consequence—and of limited practical meaning—that the institution to which he is committed is called an Industrial School. The fact of the matter is that, however euphemistic the title, a "receiving home" or an "industrial school" for juveniles is an institution of confinement in which the child is incarcerated for a greater or lesser time. His world becomes "a building with white-washed walls, regimented routine and institutional hours. . . ." Instead of mother and father and sisters and brothers and friends and classmates, his world is peopled by guards, custodians, state employees, and "delinquents" confined with him for anything from waywardness to rape and homicide.

In view of this, it would be extraordinary if our Constitution did not require the procedural regularity and the exercise of care implied in the phrase "due process." Under our Constitution, the condition of being a boy does not justify a kangaroo court. The traditional ideas of Juvenile Court procedure, indeed, contemplated that time would be available and care would be used to establish precisely what the juvenile did and why he did it—was it a prank of adolescence or a brutal act threatening serious consequences to himself or society unless corrected? Under traditional notions, one would assume that in a case like that of Gerald Gault, where the juvenile appears to have a home, a working mother and father, and an older brother, the Juvenile Judge would have made a careful inquiry and judgment as to the possibility that the boy could be disciplined and dealt with at home, despite his previous transgressions. Indeed, so far as appears in the record before us, except for some conversation with Gerald about his school work and his "wanting to go to ... Grand Canyon with his father," the points to which the judge directed his attention were little different from those that would be involved in determining any charge of violation of a penal statute. The essential difference between Gerald's case and a normal criminal case is that safeguards available to adults were discarded in Gerald's case. The summary procedure as well as the long commitment was possible because Gerald was 15 years of age instead of over 18.

If Gerald had been over 18, he would not have been subject to Juvenile Court proceedings. For the particular offense immediately involved, the maximum punishment would have been a fine of $5 to $50, or imprisonment in jail for not more than two months. Instead, he was committed to custody for a maximum of six years. If he had been over 18 and had committed an offense to which such a sentence might apply, he would have been entitled to substantial rights under the Constitution of the United States as well as under Arizona's laws and constitution. The United States Constitution would guarantee him rights and protections with respect to arrest, search and seizure, and pretrial interrogation. It would assure him of specific notice of the charges and adequate time to decide his course of action and to prepare his defense. He would be entitled to clear advice that he could be represented by counsel, and, at least if a felony were involved, the State would be required to provide counsel if his parents were unable to afford it. If the court acted on the basis of his confession, careful procedures would be required to assure its voluntariness. If the case went to trial, confrontation and opportunity for cross-examination would be guaranteed. So wide a gulf between the State's treatment of the adult and of the child requires a bridge sturdier than mere verbiage, and reasons more persuasive than cliché can provide....

In Kent v. United States, supra, we stated that the Juvenile Court Judge's exercise of the power of the state as parens patriae was not unlimited.... With respect to the waiver by the Juvenile Court to the adult court of jurisdiction over an offense committed by a youth, we said that "there is no place in our system of law for reaching a result of such tremendous consequences without ceremony—without hearing, without effective assistance of counsel, without a statement of reasons." We announced with respect to such waiver proceedings that while "We do not mean ... to indicate that the hearing to be held must conform with all of the requirements of a criminal trial or even of the usual administrative hearing; but we do hold that the hearing must measure up to the essentials of due process and fair treatment." We reiterate this view, here in connection with a juvenile court adjudication of "delinquency," as a requirement which is part of the Due Process Clause of the Fourteenth Amendment of our Constitution.

We now turn to the specific issues which are presented to us in the present case.

III.

NOTICE OF CHARGES

.   .   .

We cannot agree with the court's conclusion that adequate notice was given in this case. Notice, to comply with due process requirements, must be given sufficiently in advance of scheduled court proceedings so that reasonable opportunity to prepare will be afforded, and it must "set forth the alleged misconduct with particularity." It is obvious, as we have discussed above, that no purpose of shielding the child from the public stigma of knowledge of his having been taken into custody and scheduled for hearing is served by the procedure approved by the court below. The "initial hearing" in the present case was a hearing on the merits. Notice at that time is not timely; and even if there were a conceivable purpose served by the deferral proposed by the court below, it would have to yield to the requirements that the child and his parents or guardian be notified, in writing, of the specific charge or factual allegations to be considered at the hearing, and that such written notice be given at the earliest practicable time, and in any event sufficiently in advance of the hearing to permit preparation. Due process of law requires notice of the sort we have described—that is, notice which would be deemed constitutionally adequate in a civil or criminal proceeding.

.   .   .

IV.

RIGHT TO COUNSEL

Appellants charge that the Juvenile Court proceedings were fatally defective because the court did not advise Gerald or his parents of their right to counsel, and proceeded with the hearing, the adjudication of delinquency and the order of commitment in the absence of counsel for the child and his parents or an express waiver of the right thereto. The Supreme Court of Arizona pointed out that "[t]here is disagreement [among the various jurisdictions] as to whether the court must advise the infant that he has a right to counsel." It noted its own decision . . . to the effect "that *the parents* of an infant in a juvenile proceeding cannot be denied representation by counsel of their choosing." (Emphasis added.) It referred to a provision of the Juvenile Code which it characterized as requiring "that the probation officer shall look after the interests of neglected, delinquent and dependent children," including representing their interests in court. The court argued that "The parent and the

probation officer may be relied upon to protect the infant's interests." Accordingly it rejected the proposition that "due process requires that an infant have a right to counsel." It said that juvenile courts have the discretion, but not the duty, to allow such representation; it referred specifically to the situation in which the Juvenile Court discerns conflict between the child and his parents as an instance in which this discretion might be exercised. We do not agree. Probation officers, in the Arizona scheme, are also arresting officers. They initiate proceedings and file petitions which they verify, as here, alleging the delinquency of the child; and they testify, as here, against the child. And here the probation officer was also superintendent of the Detention Home. The probation officer cannot act as counsel for the child. His role in the adjudicatory hearing, by statute and in fact, is as arresting officer and witness against the child. Nor can the judge represent the child. There is no material difference in this respect between adult and juvenile proceedings of the sort here involved. In adult proceedings, this contention has been foreclosed by decisions of this Court. A proceeding where the issue is whether the child will be found to be "delinquent" and subjected to the loss of his liberty for years is comparable in seriousness to a felony prosecution. The juvenile needs the assistance of counsel to cope with problems of law, to make skilled inquiry into the facts, to insist upon regularity of the proceedings, and to ascertain whether he has a defense and to prepare and submit it. The child "requires the guiding hand of counsel at every step in the proceedings against him."
. . .

During the last decade, court decisions, experts, and legislatures have demonstrated increasing recognition of this view. In at least one-third of the States, statutes now provide for the right of representation by retained counsel in juvenile delinquency proceedings, notice of the right, or assignment of counsel, or a combination of these. In other States, court rules have similar provisions.

The President's Crime Commission has recently recommended that in order to assure "procedural justice for the child," it is necessary that "Counsel . . . be appointed as a matter of course wherever coercive action is a possibility, without requiring any affirmative choice by child or parent."
. . .

We conclude that the Due Process Clause of the Fourteenth Amendment requires that in respect of proceedings to determine delinquency which may result in commitment to an institution in which the juvenile's freedom is curtailed, the child and his parents must be notified of the child's right to be represented by counsel retained by them, or if they are unable to afford counsel, that counsel will be appointed to represent the child.

. . .

V.

CONFRONTATION, SELF–INCRIMINATION, CROSS–EXAMINATION

Appellants urge that the writ of habeas corpus should have been granted because of the denial of the rights of confrontation and cross-examination in the Juvenile Court hearings, and because the privilege against self-incrimination was not observed. The Juvenile Court Judge testified at the habeas corpus hearing that he had proceeded on the basis of Gerald's admissions at the two hearings. Appellants attack this on the ground that the admissions were obtained in disregard of the privilege against self-incrimination.

. . .

We shall assume that Gerald made admissions of the sort described by the Juvenile Court Judge, as quoted above. Neither Gerald nor his parents were advised that he did not have to testify or make a statement, or that an incriminating statement might result in his commitment as a "delinquent."

The Arizona Supreme Court rejected appellants' contention that Gerald had a right to be advised that he need not incriminate himself. It said: "We think the necessary flexibility for individualized treatment will be enhanced by a rule which does not require the judge to advise the infant of a privilege against self-incrimination."

In reviewing this conclusion of Arizona's Supreme Court, we emphasize again that we are here concerned only with a proceeding to determine whether a minor is a "delinquent" and which may result in commitment to a state institution. Specifically, the question is whether, in such a proceeding, an admission by the juvenile may be used against him in the absence of clear and unequivocal evidence that the admission was made with knowledge that he was not obliged to speak and would not be penalized for remaining silent. In light of Miranda v. Arizona, 384 U.S. 436 (1966), we must also consider whether, if the privilege against self-incrimination is available, it can effectively be waived unless counsel is present or the right to counsel has been waived.

. . .

The privilege against self-incrimination is, of course, related to the question of the safeguards necessary to assure that admissions or confessions are reasonably trustworthy, that they are not the mere fruits of fear or coercion, but are reliable expressions of the truth. The roots of the privilege are, however, far deeper. They tap the basic stream of religious and political principle because the privilege reflects the limits of the individual's attornment to the state and—in a philosophical sense—insists upon the equality of the individual and the state. In other words, the privilege has a broader and deeper thrust than the rule which prevents the use of confessions which are the product of coercion because coercion is thought to carry with it the danger of unreliability. One of its purposes is to prevent the state, whether by force or by psychological domination, from overcoming the mind and will of the person under investigation and depriving him of the freedom to decide whether to assist the state in securing his conviction.

It would indeed be surprising if the privilege against self-incrimination were available to hardened criminals but not to children. The language of the Fifth Amendment, applicable to the States by operation of the Fourteenth Amendment, is unequivocal and without exception. . . .

. . .

Against the application to juveniles of the right to silence, it is argued that juvenile proceedings are "civil" and not "criminal," and therefore the privilege should not apply. It is true that the statement of the privilege in the Fifth Amendment, which is applicable to the States by reason of the Fourteenth Amendment, is that no person "shall be compelled in any *criminal case* to be a witness against himself." However, it is also clear that the availability of the privilege does not turn upon the type of proceeding in which its protection is invoked, but upon the nature of the statement or admission and the exposure which it invites. The privilege may, for example, be claimed in a civil or administrative proceeding, if the statement is or may be inculpatory.

It would be entirely unrealistic to carve out of the Fifth Amendment all statements by juveniles on the ground that these cannot lead to "criminal" involvement. In the first place, juvenile proceedings to determine "delinquency," which may lead to commitment to a state institution, must be regarded as "criminal" for purposes of the privilege against self-incrimination. To hold otherwise would be to disregard substance because of the feeble enticement of the "civil" label-of-convenience which has been attached to juvenile proceedings. Indeed, in over half of the States, there is not even assurance that the juvenile will be kept in separate institutions, apart from adult "criminals." In those States juveniles may be placed in or transferred to adult penal institutions after having been found "delinquent" by a juvenile court. For this purpose, at least, commitment is a deprivation of liberty. It is incarceration against one's will, whether it is called "criminal" or "civil." And our Constitution guarantees that no person shall be "compelled" to be a witness against himself when he is threatened with deprivation of his liberty—a command which this Court has broadly applied and generously implemented in accordance with the teaching of the history of the privilege and its great office in mankind's battle for freedom.

In addition, apart from the equivalence for this purpose of exposure to commitment as a juvenile delinquent and exposure to imprisonment as an adult offender, the fact of the matter is that there is little or no assurance in Arizona, as in most if not all of the States, that a juvenile apprehended and interrogated by the police or even by the Juvenile Court itself will remain outside of the reach of adult courts as a consequence of the offense for which he has been taken into custody. In Arizona, as in other States, provision is made for Juvenile Courts to relinquish or waive jurisdiction to the ordinary criminal courts. In the present case, when Gerald Gault was interrogated concerning violation of a section of the Arizona Criminal Code, it could not be certain that the Juvenile Court Judge would decide to "suspend" criminal prosecution in court for adults by proceeding to an adjudication in Juvenile Court.

It is also urged, as the Supreme Court of Arizona here asserted, that the juvenile and presumably his parents should not be advised of the juvenile's right to silence because confession is good for the child as the commencement of the assumed therapy of the juvenile court process, and he should be encouraged to assume an attitude of trust and confidence toward the officials of the juvenile process. This proposition has been subjected to widespread challenge on the basis of current reappraisals of the rhetoric and realities of the handling of juvenile offenders.

In fact, evidence is accumulating that confessions by juveniles do not aid in "individualized treatment," as the court below put it, and that compelling the child to answer questions, without warning or advice as to his right to remain silent, does not serve this or any other good purpose. In light of the observations of Wheeler and Cottrell, and others, it seems probable that where children are induced to confess by "paternal" urgings on the part of officials and the confession is then followed by disciplinary action, the child's reaction is likely to be hostile and adverse—the child may well feel that he has been led or tricked into confession and that despite his confession, he is being punished.

Further, authoritative opinion has cast formidable doubt upon the reliability and trustworthiness of "confessions" by children....

The "confession" of Gerald Gault was first obtained by Officer Flagg, out of the presence of Gerald's parents, without counsel and without advising him of his right to silence, as far as appears. The judgment of the Juvenile Court was stated by the judge to be based on Gerald's admissions in court. Neither "admission" was reduced to writing, and, to say the least, the process by which the "admissions" were obtained and received must be characterized as lacking the certainty and order which are required of proceedings of such formidable consequences. Apart from the "admissions," there was nothing upon which a judgment or finding might be based. There was no sworn testimony. Mrs. Cook, the complainant, was not present. The Arizona Supreme Court held that "sworn testimony must be required of all witnesses including police officers, probation officers and others who are part of or officially related to the juvenile court structure." We hold that this is not enough. No reason is suggested or appears for a different rule in respect of sworn testimony in juvenile courts than in adult tribunals. Absent a valid confession adequate to support the determination of the Juvenile Court, confrontation and sworn testimony by witnesses available for cross-examination were essential for a finding of "delinquency" and an order committing Gerald to a state institution for a maximum of six years.

. . .

As we said in Kent v. United States, 383 U.S. 541, 554 (1966), with respect to waiver proceedings, "there is no place in our system of law for reaching a result of such tremendous consequences without ceremony...." We now hold that, absent a valid confession, a determination of delinquency and an order of commitment to a state institution cannot be sustained in the absence of sworn testimony subjected to the opportunity for cross-examination in accordance with our law and constitutional requirements.

VI.

APPELLATE REVIEW AND TRANSCRIPT OF PROCEEDINGS

Appellants urge that the Arizona statute is unconstitutional under the Due Process Clause because, as construed by its Supreme Court, "there is no right of appeal from a juvenile court order...." The court held that there is no right to a transcript because there is no right to appeal and because the proceedings are confidential and any record must be destroyed after a prescribed period of time. Whether a transcript or other recording is made, it held, is a matter for the discretion of the juvenile court.

This Court has not held that a State is required by the Federal Constitution "to provide appellate courts or a right to appellate review at all." In view of the fact that we must reverse the Supreme Court of Arizona's affirmance of the dismissal of the writ of habeas corpus for other reasons, we need not rule on this question in the present case or upon the failure to provide a transcript or recording of the hearings—or, indeed, the failure of the Juvenile Judge to state the grounds for his conclusion. Cf. Kent v. United States, supra, 383 U.S., at 561, where we said, in the context of a decision of the juvenile court waiving jurisdiction to the adult court, which by local law, was permissible: "... it is incumbent upon the Juvenile Court to accompany its waiver order with a statement of the reasons or considerations therefor." As the present case illustrates, the consequences of failure to provide an appeal, to record the proceedings, or to make findings or state the grounds for the juvenile court's conclusion may be to throw a burden upon the machinery for habeas corpus, to saddle the reviewing process with the burden of attempting to reconstruct a record, and to impose upon the Juvenile Judge the unseemly duty of testifying under cross-examination as to the events that transpired in the hearings before him.

For the reasons stated, the judgment of the Supreme Court of Arizona is reversed and the cause remanded for further proceedings not inconsistent with this opinion.

■ MR. JUSTICE BLACK, concurring.

The juvenile court laws of Arizona and other States, as the Court points out, are the result of plans promoted by humane and forward-looking people to provide a system of courts, procedures, and sanctions deemed to be less harmful and more lenient to children than to adults. For this reason such state laws generally provide less formal and less public methods for the trial of children. In line with this policy, both courts and legislators have shrunk back from labeling these laws as "criminal" and have preferred to call them "civil." This, in part, was to prevent the full application to juvenile court cases of the Bill of Rights safeguards, including notice as provided in the Sixth Amendment, the right to counsel guaranteed by the Sixth, the right against self-incrimination guaranteed by the Fifth, and the right to confrontation guaranteed by the Sixth. The Court here holds, however, that these four Bill of Rights safeguards apply to protect a juvenile accused in a juvenile court on a charge under which he can be imprisoned for a term of years. This holding strikes a well-nigh fatal blow to much that is unique about the juvenile courts in the Nation. For this reason, there is much to be said for the position of my Brother Stewart that we should not pass on all these issues until they are more squarely presented. But since the majority of the Court chooses to decide all of these questions, I must either do the same or leave my views unexpressed on the important issues determined. In these circumstances, I feel impelled to express my views.

The juvenile court planners envisaged a system that would practically immunize juveniles from "punishment" for "crimes" in an effort to save them from youthful indiscretions and stigmas due to criminal charges or convictions. I agree with the Court, however, that this exalted ideal has failed of achievement since the beginning of the system. Indeed, the state laws from the first one on contained provisions, written in emphatic terms, for arresting and charging juveniles with violations of state criminal laws, as well as for taking juveniles by force of law away from their parents and turning them over to different individuals or groups or for confinement within some state school or institution for a number of years. The latter occurred in this case. Young Gault was arrested and detained on a charge of violating an Arizona penal law by using vile and offensive language to a lady on the telephone. If an adult, he could only have been fined or imprisoned for two months for his conduct. As a juvenile, however, he was put through a more or less secret, informal hearing by the court, after which he was ordered, or more realistically, "sentenced," to confinement in Arizona's Industrial School until he reaches 21 years of age. Thus, in a juvenile system designed to lighten or avoid punishment for criminality, he was ordered by the State to six years' confinement in what is in all but name a penitentiary or jail.

Where a person, infant or adult, can be seized by the State, charged, and convicted for violating a state criminal law, and then ordered by the State to be confined for six years, I think the Constitution requires that he be tried in accordance with the guarantees of all the provisions of the Bill of Rights made applicable to the States by the Fourteenth Amendment. Undoubtedly this would be true of an adult defendant, and it would be a plain denial of equal protection of the laws—an invidious discrimination— to hold that others subject to heavier punishments could, because they are children, be denied these same constitutional safeguards. I consequently agree with the Court that the Arizona law as applied here denied to the parents and their son the right of notice, right to counsel, right against self-incrimination, and right to confront the witnesses against young Gault. Appellants are entitled to these rights, not because "fairness, impartiality and orderliness—in short, the essentials of due process"—require them and not because they are "the procedural rules which have been fashioned from the generality of due process," but because they are specifically and unequivocally granted by provisions of the Fifth and Sixth Amendments which the Fourteenth Amendment makes applicable to the States.

A few words should be added because of the opinion of my Brother Harlan who rests his concurrence and dissent on the Due Process Clause alone. He reads that clause alone as allowing this Court "to determine what forms of procedural protection are necessary to guarantee the fundamental fairness of juvenile proceedings" "in a fashion consistent with the 'traditions and conscience of our people.' " Cf. Rochin v. People of California, 342 U.S. 165. He believes that the Due Process Clause gives this Court the power, upon weighing a "compelling public interest," to impose on the States only those specific constitutional rights which the Court deems "imperative" and "necessary" to comport with the Court's notions of "fundamental fairness."

I cannot subscribe to any such interpretation of the Due Process Clause. Nothing in its words or its history permits it, and "fair distillations of relevant judicial history" are no substitute for the words and history of the clause itself. The phrase "due process of law" has through the years evolved as the successor in purpose and meaning to the words "law of the land" in Magna Charta which more plainly intended to call for a trial according to the existing law of the land in effect at the time an alleged offense had been committed. That provision in Magna Charta was designed to prevent defendants from being tried according to criminal laws or proclamations specifically promulgated to fit particular cases or to attach new consequences to old conduct. Nothing done since Magna Charta can be pointed to as intimating that the Due Process Clause gives courts power to fashion laws in order to meet new conditions, to fit the "decencies" of changed conditions, or to keep their consciences from being shocked by legislation, state or federal.

And, of course, the existence of such awesome judicial power cannot be buttressed or created by relying on the word "procedural." Whether labeled as "procedural" or "substantive," the Bill of Rights safeguards, far from being mere "tools with which" other unspecified "rights could be fully vindicated," are the very vitals of a sound constitutional legal system designed to protect and safeguard the most cherished liberties of a free people. These safeguards were written into our Constitution not by judges but by Constitution makers. Freedom in this Nation will be far less secure the very moment that it is decided that judges can determine which of these safeguards "should" or "should not be imposed" according to their notions of what constitutional provisions are consistent with the "traditions and conscience of our people." Judges with such power, even though they profess to "proceed with restraint," will be above the Constitution, with power to write it, not merely to interpret it, which I believe to be the only power constitutionally committed to judges.

There is one ominous sentence, if not more, in my Brother HARLAN's opinion which bodes ill, in my judgment, both for legislative programs and constitutional commands. Speaking of procedural safeguards in the Bill of Rights, he says:

> "These factors in combination suggest that legislatures may properly expect only a cautious deference for their procedural judgments, but that, conversely, courts must exercise their special responsibility for procedural guarantees with care to permit ample scope for achieving the purposes of legislative programs. . . . [T]he court should necessarily proceed with restraint."

It is to be noted here that this case concerns Bill of Rights Amendments; that the "procedure" power my Brother HARLAN claims for the Court here relates solely to Bill of Rights safeguards; and that he is here claiming for the Court a supreme power to fashion new Bill of Rights safeguards according to the Court's notions of what fits tradition and conscience. I do not believe that the Constitution vests any such power in judges, either in the Due Process Clause or anywhere else. Consequently, I do not vote to invalidate this Arizona law on the ground that it is "unfair" but solely on the ground that it violates the Fifth and Sixth Amendments made obligatory on the States by the Fourteenth Amendment. Cf. Pointer v. State of Texas, 380 U.S. 400, 412 (Goldberg, J., concurring). It is enough for me that the Arizona law as here applied collides head-on with the Fifth and Sixth Amendments in the four respects mentioned. The only relevance to me of the Due Process Clause is that it would, of course, violate due process or the "law of the land" to enforce a law that collides with the Bill of Rights.

[The separate concurring opinion of Mr. Justice White has been omitted because of space limitations.]

■ MR. JUSTICE HARLAN, concurring in part and dissenting in part.

. . .

No more evidence of the importance of the public interests at stake here is required than that furnished by the opinion of the Court; it indicates that "some 601,000 children under 18, or 2% of all children between 10 and 17, came before juvenile courts" in 1965, and that "about one-fifth of all arrests for serious crimes" in 1965 were of juveniles. The Court adds that the rate of juvenile crime is steadily rising. All this, as the Court suggests, indicates the importance of these due process issues, but it mirrors no less vividly that state authorities are confronted by formidable and immediate problems involving the most fundamental social values. The state legislatures have determined that the most hopeful solution for these problems is to be found in specialized courts, organized under their own rules and imposing distinctive consequences. The terms and limitations of these systems are not identical, nor are the procedural arrangements which they include, but the States are uniform in their insistence that the ordinary processes of criminal justice are inappropriate, and that relatively informal proceedings, dedicated to premises and purposes only imperfectly reflected in the criminal law, are instead necessary.

It is well settled that the Court must give the widest deference to legislative judgments that concern the character and urgency of the problems with which the State is confronted. Legislatures are, as this Court has often acknowledged, the "main guardian" of the public interest, and, within their constitutional competence, their understanding of that interest must be accepted as "well-nigh" conclusive. Berman v. Parker, 348 U.S. 26, 32. This principle does not, however, reach all the questions essential to the resolution of this case. The legislative judgments at issue here embrace assessments of the necessity and wisdom of procedural guarantees; these are questions which the Constitution has entrusted at least in part to courts, and upon which courts have been understood to possess particular competence. The fundamental issue here is, therefore, in what measure and fashion the Court must defer to legislative determinations which encompass constitutional issues of procedural protection.

It suffices for present purposes to summarize the factors which I believe to be pertinent. It must first be emphasized that the deference given to legislators upon substantive issues must realistically extend in part to ancillary procedural questions. Procedure at once reflects and creates substantive rights, and every effort of courts since the beginnings of the common law to separate the two has proved essentially futile. The distinction between them is particularly inadequate here, where the legislature's substantive preferences directly and unavoidably require judgments about procedural issues. The procedural framework is here a principal element of the substantive legislative system; meaningful deference to the latter must include a portion of deference to the former. The substantive-procedural dichotomy is, nonetheless, an indispensable tool of analysis, for it stems from fundamental limitations upon judicial authority under the Constitution. Its premise is ultimately that courts may not substitute for the judgments of legislators their own understanding of the public welfare, but must instead concern themselves with the validity under the Constitution of the methods which the legislature has selected. The Constitution has in this manner created for courts and legislators areas of primary responsibility which are essentially congruent to their areas of special competence. Courts are thus obliged both by constitutional command and by their distinctive functions to bear particular responsibility for the measurement of procedural due process. These factors in combination suggest that legislatures may properly expect only a cautious deference for their procedural judgments, but that, conversely, courts must exercise their special responsibility for procedural guarantees with care to permit ample scope for achieving the purposes of legislative programs. Plainly, courts can exercise such care only if they have in each case first studied thoroughly the objectives and implementation of the program at stake; if, upon completion of those studies, the effect of extensive procedural restrictions upon valid legislative purposes cannot be assessed with reasonable certainty, the court should necessarily proceed with restraint.

The foregoing considerations, which I believe to be fair distillations of relevant judicial history, suggest three criteria by which the procedural requirements of due process should be measured here: first, no more restrictions should be imposed than are imperative to assure the proceedings' fundamental fairness; second, the restrictions which are imposed should be those which preserve, so far as possible, the essential elements of the State's purpose; and finally, restrictions should be chosen which will later permit the orderly selection of any additional protections which may ultimately prove necessary. In this way, the Court may guarantee the fundamental fairness of the proceeding, and yet permit the State to continue development of an effective response to the problems of juvenile crime. . . .

Measured by these criteria, only three procedural requirements should, in my opinion, now be deemed required of state juvenile courts by the Due Process Clause of the Fourteenth Amendment: first, timely notice must be provided to parents and children of the nature and terms of any juvenile court proceeding in which a determination affecting their rights or interests may be made; second, unequivocal and timely notice must be given that counsel may appear in any such proceeding in behalf of the child and its parents, and that in cases in which the child may be confined in an institution, counsel may, in circumstances of indigency, be appointed for them; and third, the court must maintain a written record, or its equivalent, adequate to permit effective review on appeal or in collateral proceedings. These requirements would guarantee to juveniles the tools with which their rights could be fully vindicated, and yet permit the States to pursue without unnecessary hindrance the purposes which they believe imperative in this field. Further, their imposition now would later permit more intelligent assessment of the necessity under the Fourteenth Amendment of additional requirements, by creating suitable records from which the character and deficiencies of juvenile proceedings could be accurately judged. . . .

■ MR. JUSTICE STEWART, dissenting.

The Court today uses an obscure Arizona case as a vehicle to impose upon thousands of juvenile courts throughout the Nation restrictions that the Constitution made applicable to adversary criminal trials. I believe the Court's decision is wholly unsound as a matter of constitutional law, and sadly unwise as a matter of judicial policy.

Juvenile proceedings are not criminal trials. They are not civil trials. They are simply not adversary proceedings. Whether treating with a delinquent child, a neglected child, a defective child, or a dependent child, a juvenile proceeding's whole purpose and mission is the very opposite of the mission and purpose of a prosecution in a criminal court. The object of the one is correction of a condition. The object of the other is conviction and punishment for a criminal act.

In the last 70 years many dedicated men and women have devoted their professional lives to the enlightened task of bringing us out of the dark world of Charles Dickens in meeting our responsibilities to the child in our society. The result has been the creation in this century of a system of juvenile and family courts in each of the 50 States. There can be no denying that in many areas the performance of these agencies has fallen disappointingly short of the hopes and dreams of the courageous pioneers who first conceived them. For a variety of reasons, the reality has sometimes not even approached the ideal, and much remains to be accomplished in the administration of public juvenile and family agencies—in personnel, in planning, in financing, perhaps in the formulation of wholly new approaches.

I possess neither the specialized experience nor the expert knowledge to predict with any certainty where may lie the brightest hope for progress in dealing with the serious problems of juvenile delinquency. But I am certain that the answer does not lie in the Court's opinion in this case, which serves to convert a juvenile proceeding into a criminal prosecution.

The inflexible restrictions that the Constitution so wisely made applicable to adversary criminal trials have no inevitable place in the proceedings of those public social agencies known as juvenile or family courts. And to impose the Court's long catalog of requirements upon juvenile proceedings in every area of the country is to invite a long step backwards into the nineteenth century. In that era there were no juvenile proceedings, and a child was tried in a conventional criminal court with all the trappings of a conventional criminal trial. So it was that a 12–year-old boy named James Guild was tried in New Jersey for killing Catharine Beakes. A jury found him guilty of murder, and he was sentenced to death by hanging. The sentence was executed. It was all very constitutional.[2]

A State in all its dealings must, of course, accord every person due process of law. And due process may require that some of the same restrictions which the Constitution has placed upon criminal trials must be imposed upon juvenile proceedings. For example, I suppose that all would agree that a brutally coerced confession could not constitutionally be considered in a juvenile court hearing. But it surely does not follow that the testimonial privilege against self-incrimination is applicable in all juvenile proceedings. Similarly, due process clearly requires timely notice of the purpose and scope of any proceedings affecting the relationship of parent and child. Armstrong v. Manzo, 380 U.S. 545. But it certainly does not follow that notice of a juvenile hearing must be framed with all the technical niceties of a criminal indictment. See Russell v. United States, 369 U.S. 749.

In any event, there is no reason to deal with issues such as these in the present case. The Supreme Court of Arizona found that the parents of Gerald Gault "knew of their right to counsel, to subpoena and cross examine witnesses, of the right to confront the witnesses against Gerald and the possible consequences of a finding of delinquency." 99 Ariz. 181, 185, 407 P.2d 760, 763. It further found that "Mrs. Gault knew the exact nature of the charge against Gerald from the day he was taken to the detention home." 99 Ariz., at 193, 407 P.2d, at 768. And, as MR. JUSTICE WHITE correctly points out, no issue of compulsory self-incrimination is presented by this case.

I would dismiss the appeal.

NOTES

(1) The *Gault* decision is concerned primarily with the adjudicatory hearing at which the crucial question is: are the facts alleged in the petition true? Justice Fortas suggests that there is nothing about the status of being a child that justifies sloppiness or lack of due process in fact-finding on the ultimate issue of guilt. What impact should the *Gault* reasoning have on the kinds of evidence that should properly be admissible at such adjudicatory hearings? What is the logical impact of Gault on disposition decisionmaking? These questions will be considered in greater detail in Chapter X.

(2) As indicated in the introductory note, most state courts had rejected the application of due process rights to juvenile courts on the ground that delinquency

---

2. State v. Guild, 5 Halst. 163, 18 Am. Dec. 404 (N.J.Sup.Ct.).

"Thus, also, in very modern times, a boy of ten years old was convicted on his own confession of murdering his bedfellow, there appearing in his whole behavior plain tokens of a mischievous discretion; and as the sparing of this boy merely on account of his tender years might be of dangerous consequences to the public, by propagating a notion that children might commit such atrocious crimes with impunity, it was unanimously agreed by all the judges that he was a proper subject of capital punishment." 4 Blackstone, Commentaries 23 (Wendell ed. 1847).

adjudications were not criminal but rather civil proceedings at which such rights as counsel, notice, the Fifth Amendment right and the right to confront and cross-examine were inappropriate. See e.g., *Ex parte Sharp*, 15 Idaho 120, 96 P. 563 (1908); *Moquin v. State*, 216 Md. 524, 140 A.2d 914 (1958); *Commonwealth v. Fisher*, 213 Pa. 48, 62 A. 198 (1905); or the Arizona Supreme Court's decision in Gault, 99 Ariz. 181, 407 P.2d 760 (1965). See also, Robert M. Emerson, Judging Delinquents: Context and Process in Juvenile Court (1969). What is the jurisprudential problem with determining the rights accorded litigants based on the civil or criminal label? Should it make any difference that the state's motivation for Gerald Gault's commitment to the State Industrial School was therapeutic—to rehabilitate rather than punish him? Justice Fortas asserts that involuntary loss of liberty is the appropriate dividing line to determine the applicability of due process requirements. Do you find this functional division constitutionally persuasive?

(3) In 1965 more than one-quarter of all juvenile judges were not legally trained, and most were not full-time judges. The decision to provide attorneys for juveniles meant that for the first time juvenile courts would become law courts. It is not surprising that juvenile judges of the time, some of whom were hostile to the *Gault* decision, were especially unhappy with the prospect of attorneys in delinquency proceedings. Such hostility was fueled by, at best, uncertainty over the role attorneys would play in juvenile court and, at worst, the assumption that they would play an advocacy role.

In order to accommodate the rule of law, the juvenile or family court required a full-time legally trained judge. Between 1968 and 1972 about 40 percent of all juvenile and family court judgeships changed hands usually from laymen to lawyers. In order to attract attorneys as full-time juvenile court judges, many jurisdictions had to upgrade both the staff and prestige of the courts. See Kenneth C. Smith, A Profile of Juvenile Court Judges, (National Council of Juvenile Judges 1972). In rural areas where no one county could support a full-time juvenile judge and an adequate probation staff, regionalization was used to create one full-time court to serve several counties on a circuit riding model. See, e.g., Model Rules for Virginia Regional Juvenile and Domestic Relations Courts, 1968–75.

Ted Rubin, a former juvenile court judge, has reported that since the survey of judges believed to have juvenile responsibilities conducted by the National Council of Juvenile Court judges in the early 1970s, no more recent survey had been conducted some fifteen years later. H. Ted Rubin, Juvenile Justice: Policy, Practice, and Law 373 (2d ed. 1985). At that time, based on responses returned (38.2 percent), most judges were male (96.2 percent), married (93 percent) and licensed to practice law (86.2 percent). Only 12.4 percent devoted their time exclusively to juvenile matters; 86.4 percent spent half or less than half their time on juvenile matters; 66.7 percent, in fact, spent only one-fourth of their time, or even less, on juvenile matters. Id. Rubin subjectively muses that "[m]ore recent observation suggests that today there are fewer nonlawyer judges and more female judges, and that jurists have a greater interest in the legal dimensions of their responsibilities." Id. at 374.

The traditional weaknesses of judges, Rubin further observes, has been their knowledge and application of law, although this area has seen much improvement in the last decade as more well-qualified lawyers have succeeded to the bench. Their strengths lie in their awareness of community resources and their advocacy of improved resources. Id. at 374–75. He predicts that "in the future fewer judges will serve lengthy terms on the juvenile court" and "judges ... will be stronger on law and procedure but will have lessened opportunity to fulfill their unique advocacy role." With the shifting of some of their administrative duties to others, "they will have more time for judging but will become less aware of probation capabilities.'' He concludes:

> With shorter tenure, they will develop less knowledge of community agency services. Their motivation and zeal will take other forms: toward improving the court's legal processes and administration, and community and governmental agency accountability for the effectuation of judicial orders.

Id. at 376.*

(4) For a contemporary analysis of *Gault*, see Monrad G. Paulsen, The Constitutional Domestication of the Juvenile Court, 1967 Sup.Ct.Rev. 233.

C. TESTING THE PREMISES OF *GAULT*: *WINSHIP* AND *McKEIVER*

The first case involving rights of juveniles to reach the Supreme Court after *Gault* was *In re Winship*.[1] *Winship* raised the question of the applicable standard of proof in a case in which a child is charged with an act that would be a crime if committed by an adult. More specifically, the case raised the question of whether due process of law requires that the allegations be proved beyond a reasonable doubt. The New York statute challenged there, as did most statutes at the time, required only that the allegations be proved by a preponderance of the evidence.

At the time of the *Winship* decision, the Supreme Court had never held that proof beyond a reasonable doubt is constitutionally required in criminal proceedings. An often overlooked aspect of the *Winship* case is that before reaching the specific issue presented, the Court first held that proof beyond a reasonable doubt is constitutionally required in criminal prosecutions in state court as a matter of due process of law.

Turning to the more narrow issue before it the Court reiterated its view in *Gault* that "[a] proceeding where the issue is whether the child will be found to be 'delinquent and subjected to the loss of his liberty for years is comparable in seriousness to a felony prosecution.' "[2] The Court then specifically held that " 'where a twelve-year-old child is charged with an act of stealing which renders him liable to confinement for as long as six years, then, as a matter of due process ... the case against him must be proved beyond a reasonable doubt.' "[3]

The fundamental disagreement between Justices Black and Harlan begun in *Gault* continued in *Winship*. In his dissent in *Winship* Justice Black pointed out that the requirement of proof beyond a reasonable doubt is not found in the Bill of Rights and, hence, is not within the scope and meaning of due process of law contained in the Fourteenth Amendment. For that reason, he concluded, it is not a right made applicable to the states by the due process clause. Justice Black's dissent in *Winship* thus repre-

---

* From Juvenile Justice: Policy, Practice, and Law, 2d edition, by H. Ted Rubin (ed.). Copyright © 1985, The McGraw–Hill Companies. Reprinted with permission.

1. 397 U.S. 358, 90 S.Ct. 1068, 25 L.Ed.2d 368 (1970).

2. Id. at 366.

3. Id. at 368.

sents a logical, if problematical consequence of the views he expressed in *Gault*.

The *Winship* decision was compatible with Justice Harlan's more expansive view of the due process clause. Justice Harlan concurred in the judgment in *Winship* largely on the basis of his "traditions and conscience" analysis first expressed in *Gault*. He found the beyond a reasonable doubt standard acceptable because it would not, inter alia, "burden the juvenile courts with a procedural requirement that will make juvenile adjudications significantly more time consuming, or rigid."[4] This last observation would prove instructive when it came time to predict how Justice Harlan would vote on the right to jury trial for juveniles (see *McKeiver v. Pennsylvania*, p. 888 infra).

Chief Justice Burger, newly appointed to the Court, dissented in *Winship* in an opinion in which he was joined by Justice Stewart. Chief Justice Burger's dissent echoed sentiments expressed in Justice Stewart's dissent in *Gault*, but at the end he sounded an ominous note:

> My hope is that today's decision will not spell the end of a generously conceived program of compassionate treatment intended to mitigate the rigors and trauma of exposing youthful offenders to a traditional criminal court; each step we take turns the clock back to the pre-juvenile-court era. I cannot regard it as a manifestation of progress to transform juvenile courts into criminal courts, which is what we are well on the way to accomplishing. We can only hope the legislative response will not reflect our own by having these courts abolished.[5]

Chief Justice Burger had replaced Chief Justice Warren at the time *Winship* was decided, and by his dissent in *Winship* he signaled his opposition to the expanding role of the Constitution in the juvenile process. Justice Stewart had done so even earlier in *Gault*. By the time of the next juvenile rights decision (see *McKeiver*, p. 888 infra) Justice Blackmun had replaced Justice Fortas, the author of the *Kent* and *Gault* opinions. Justices sympathetic to the constitutionalization of the juvenile court were diminishing in number and those opposed were growing in number. The stage was set for a momentous decision by the Court, with Justice Harlan perhaps being the swing vote.

NOTES

(1) The *Winship* holding has had greatest impact in criminal procedure. When may a state require a criminal defendant to raise and prove a particular defense? Are presumptions—whether mandatory or permissive—unconstitutional as shifting the burden of proof to the defendant? See *Mullaney v. Wilbur*, 421 U.S. 684, 95 S.Ct. 1881, 44 L.Ed.2d 508 (1975); *Patterson v. New York*, 432 U.S. 197, 97 S.Ct. 2319, 53 L.Ed.2d 281 (1977); Barbara D. Underwood, The Thumb on the Scales of Justice: Burdens of Persuasion in Criminal Cases, 86 Yale L.J. 1299 (1977); John J. Jeffries & Paul B. Stephan, III, Defenses, Presumptions, and Burden of Proof in the

4. Id. at 375.   **5.** Id. at 376.

Criminal Law, 88 Yale L.J. 1325 (1979); and Ronald J. Allen, More on Constitutional Process-of-Proof Problems in Criminal Cases, 94 Harv.L.Rev. 1795 (1981).

(2) Picking up on the sentiments expressed in Chief Justice Burger's dissenting opinion, some commentators have suggested the abolition of juvenile court jurisdiction over conduct by children that would be criminal if they were adults. For example, as early as 1977 Barry McCarthy advocated abolition of the juvenile court's delinquency jurisdiction in a manner resonant of the central theme in the next chapter of this book. McCarthy was lamenting the fact that the Juvenile Justice Standards favored the continued separate existence of the juvenile court:

> ... [T]he standards' near complete replication of adult criminal procedure argues much more persuasively for abolition of the delinquency jurisdiction of the juvenile courts. Indeed, there are essentially only three areas in which the juvenile standards deviate from the standards proposed by the ABA Criminal Justice Project. These differences fall into the broad categories of intake, sentencing, and disabilities. The question, then, is whether these differences indicate the need for a separate juvenile court system to handle children who commit crimes.

F. Barry McCarthy, Delinquency Dispositions Under the Juvenile Justice Standards: The Consequences of a Change of Rationale, 52 N.Y.U.L.Rev. 1093, 1116 (1977). Other commentators have agreed. See, e.g., Stephen Wizner & Mary F. Keller, The Penal Model of Juvenile Justice: Is Juvenile Court Delinquency Jurisdiction Obsolete?, 52 N.Y.U.L.Rev. 1120 (1977); Barry C. Feld, Juvenile Court Legislative Reform and the Serious Young Offender: Dismantling the "Rehabilitative Ideal," 65 Minn.L.Rev. 167 (1980); Katherine Hunt Federle, The Abolition of the Juvenile Court: A Proposal for the Preservation of Children's Legal Rights, 16 J.Contemp.L. 23 (1990); Janet E. Ainsworth, Re–Imagining Childhood and Reconstructing the Legal Order: The Case for Abolishing the Juvenile Court, 69 N.C.L.Rev. 1083 (1991). For a defense of the traditional view—and still probably the prevailing view—favoring retention of juvenile court jurisdiction, see Irene Merker Rosenberg, Leaving Bad Enough Alone: A Response to the Juvenile Court Abolitionists, 1993 Wis.L.Rev. 163; Ira M. Schwartz, Neil Alan Weiner & Guy Enosh, Nine Lives and Then Some: Why the Juvenile Court Does Not Roll Over and Die, 33 Wake Forest L. Rev. 533 (1998); Sacha M. Coupet, Comment, What to Do with the Sheep in Wolf's Clothing: The Role of Rhetoric and Reality About Youth Offenders in the Constructive Dismantling of the Juvenile Justice System, 148 U.Penn.L.Rev. 1303 (2000); Daniel M. Filler & Austin E. Smith, The New Rehabilitation, 91 Iowa L.Rev. 951 (2006).

McKeiver v. Pennsylvania

Supreme Court of the United States, 1971.
403 U.S. 528, 91 S.Ct. 1976, 29 L.Ed.2d 647.

■ MR. JUSTICE BLACKMUN announced the judgments of the Court and an opinion in which THE CHIEF JUSTICE, MR. JUSTICE STEWART, and MR. JUSTICE WHITE join.

These cases present the narrow but precise issue whether the Due Process Clause of the Fourteenth Amendment assures the right to trial by jury in the adjudicative phase of a state juvenile court delinquency proceeding.

. . .

The details of the McKeiver and Terry offenses are set forth in Justice Roberts's opinion for the Pennsylvania court, 438 Pa., at 341–342, nn. 1 and 2, 265 A.2d, at 351 nn. 1 and 2, and need not be repeated at any length here. It suffices to say that McKeiver's offense was his participating with 20 or 30 youths who pursued three young teenagers and took 25 cents from them; that McKeiver never before had been arrested and had a record of gainful employment; that the testimony of two of the victims was described by the court as somewhat inconsistent and as "weak"; and that Terry's offense consisted of hitting a police officer with his fists and with a stick when the officer broke up a boys' fight Terry and others were watching.

No. 128. Barbara Burrus and approximately 45 other black children, ranging in age from 11 to 15 years,[3] were the subjects of juvenile court summonses issued in Hyde County, North Carolina, in January 1969.

The charges arose out of a series of demonstrations in the county in late 1968 by black adults and children protesting school assignments and a school consolidation plan. Petitions were filed by North Carolina state highway patrolmen. Except for one relating to James Lambert Howard, the petitions charged the respective juveniles with wilfully impeding traffic. The charge against Howard was that he wilfully made riotous noise and was disorderly in the O. A. Peay School in Swan Quarter; interrupted and disturbed the school during its regular sessions; and defaced school furniture. The acts so charged are misdemeanors under North Carolina law.

The several cases were consolidated into groups for hearing before District Judge Hallett S. Ward, sitting as a juvenile court. The same lawyer appeared for all the juveniles. Over counsel's objection, made in all except two of the cases, the general public was excluded. A request for a jury trial in each case was denied.

The evidence as to the juveniles other than Howard consisted solely of testimony of highway patrolmen. No juvenile took the stand or offered any witness. The testimony was to the effect that on various occasions the juveniles and adults were observed walking along Highway 64 singing, shouting, clapping, and playing basketball. As a result, there was interference with traffic. The marchers were asked to leave the paved portion of the highway and they were warned that they were committing a statutory offense. They either refused or left the roadway and immediately returned. The juveniles and participating adults were taken into custody. Juvenile petitions were then filed with respect to those under the age of 16.

The evidence as to Howard was that on the morning of December 5, he was in the office of the principal of the O. A. Peay School with 15 other persons while school was in session and was moving furniture around; that the office was in disarray; that as a result the school closed before noon; and that neither he nor any of the others was a student at the school or authorized to enter the principal's office.

In each case the court found that the juvenile had committed "an act for which an adult may be punished by law." A custody order was entered

---

3. In North Carolina juvenile court procedures are provided only for persons under the age of 16.

declaring the juvenile a delinquent "in need of more suitable guardianship" and committing him to the custody of the County Department of Public Welfare for placement in a suitable institution "until such time as the Board of Juvenile Correction or the Superintendent of said institution may determine, not inconsistent with the laws of this State." The court, however, suspended these commitments and placed each juvenile on probation for either one or two years conditioned upon his violating none of the State's laws, upon his reporting monthly to the County Department of Welfare, upon his being home by 11 p.m. each evening, and upon his attending a school approved by the Welfare Director. None of the juveniles has been confined on these charges.

On appeal, the cases were consolidated into two groups. The North Carolina Court of Appeals affirmed. In re Burrus, 4 N.C.App. 523, 167 S.E.2d 454 (1969); In re Shelton, 5 N.C.App. 487, 168 S.E.2d 695 (1969). In its turn the Supreme Court of North Carolina deleted that portion of the order in each case relating to commitment, but otherwise affirmed. In re Burrus, 275 N.C. 517, 169 S.E.2d 879 (1969). We granted certiorari.

III

It is instructive to review, as an illustration, the substance of Justice Roberts' opinion for the Pennsylvania court. He observes that "[f]or over sixty-five years the Supreme Court gave no consideration at all to the constitutional problems involved in the juvenile court area"; that *Gault* "is somewhat of a paradox, being both broad and narrow at the same time"; that it "is broad in that it evidences a fundamental and far-reaching disillusionment with the anticipated benefits of the juvenile court system"; that it is narrow because the court enumerated four due process rights which it held applicable in juvenile proceedings, but declined to rule on two other claimed rights; that as a consequence the Pennsylvania court was "confronted with a sweeping rationale and a carefully tailored holding,"; that the procedural safeguards "*Gault* specifically made applicable to juvenile courts have already caused a significant 'constitutional domestication' of juvenile court proceedings," that those safeguards and other rights, including the reasonable-doubt standard established by *Winship*, "insure that the juvenile court will operate in an atmosphere which is orderly enough to impress the juvenile with the gravity of the situation and the impartiality of the tribunal and at the same time informal enough to permit the benefits of the juvenile system to operate"; that the "proper inquiry, then, is whether the right to a trial by jury is 'fundamental' within the meaning of *Duncan*, in the context of a juvenile court which operates with *all* of the above constitutional safeguards," and that his court's inquiry turned "upon whether there are elements in the juvenile process which render the right to a trial by jury less essential to the protection of an accused's rights in the juvenile system than in the normal criminal process."

Justice Roberts then concluded that such factors do inhere in the Pennsylvania juvenile system: (1) Although realizing that "faith in the quality of the juvenile bench is not an entirely satisfactory substitute for due process," the judges in the juvenile courts "to take a different view of their role than that taken by their counterparts in the criminal courts." (2) While one regrets its inadequacies, "the juvenile system has available and utilizes much more fully various diagnostic and rehabilitative services" that are "far superior to those available in the regular criminal process." (3) Although conceding that the post-adjudication process "has in many respects fallen far short of its goals, and its reality is far harsher than its theory," the end result of a declaration of delinquency "*is* significantly different from and less onerous than a finding of criminal guilt" and "we are not yet convinced that the current practices do not contain the seeds from which a truly appropriate system can be brought forth." (4) Finally, "of all the possible due process rights which could be applied in the juvenile courts, the right to trial by jury is the one which would most likely be disruptive of the unique nature of the juvenile process." It is the jury trial that "would probably require substantial alteration of the traditional practices." The other procedural rights held applicable to the juvenile process "will give the juveniles sufficient protection" and the addition of the trial by jury "might well destroy the traditional character of juvenile proceedings."

The court concluded that it was confident "that a properly structured and fairly administered juvenile court system can serve our present societal needs without infringing on individual freedoms."

IV

The right to an impartial jury "[i]n all criminal prosecutions" under federal law is guaranteed by the Sixth Amendment. Through the Fourteenth Amendment that requirement has now been imposed upon the States "in all criminal cases which—were they to be tried in a federal court—would come within the Sixth Amendment's guarantee." This is because the Court has said it believes "that trial by jury in criminal cases is fundamental to the American scheme of justice."

This, of course, does not automatically provide the answer to the present jury trial issue, if for no other reason than that the juvenile court proceeding has not yet been held to be a "criminal prosecution," within the meaning and reach of the Sixth Amendment, and also has not yet been regarded as devoid of criminal aspects merely because it usually has been given the civil label. *Kent*, 383 U.S., at 554; *Gault*, 387 U.S., at 17, 49–50; *Winship*, 397 U.S., at 365–366.

Little, indeed, is to be gained by any attempt simplistically to call the juvenile court proceeding either "civil" or "criminal." The Court carefully has avoided this wooden approach. Before *Gault* was decided in 1967, the Fifth Amendment's guarantee against self-incrimination had been imposed upon the state criminal trial. So, too, had the Sixth Amendment's rights of confrontation and cross-examination. Yet the Court did not automatically and peremptorily apply those rights to the juvenile proceeding. A reading of *Gault* reveals the opposite. And the same separate approach to the standard-of-proof issue is evident from the carefully separated application of the standard, first to the criminal trial, and then to the juvenile proceeding, displayed in *Winship*. 397 U.S., at 361 and 365.

Thus, accepting "the proposition that the Due Process Clause has a role to play," *Gault*, 387 U.S., at 13, our task here with respect to trial by jury, as it was in *Gault* with respect to other claimed rights, "is to ascertain the precise impact of the due process requirement." Id. at 13–14.

V

The Pennsylvania juveniles' basic argument is that they were tried in proceedings "substantially similar to a criminal trial." They say that a delinquency proceeding in their State is initiated by a petition charging a penal code violation in the conclusory language of an indictment; that a juvenile detained prior to trial is held in a building substantially similar to an adult prison; that in Philadelphia juveniles over 16 are, in fact, held in the cells of a prison; that counsel and the prosecution engage in plea bargaining; that motions to suppress are routinely heard and decided; that the usual rules of evidence are applied; that the customary common-law defenses are available; that the press is generally admitted in the Philadelphia juvenile courtrooms; that members of the public enter the room; that arrest and prior record may be reported by the press (from police sources, however, rather than from the juvenile court records); that, once adjudged delinquent, a juvenile may be confined until his majority in what amounts to a prison (see In re Bethea, 215 Pa.Super. 75, 76, 257 A.2d 368, 369 (1969), describing the state correctional institution at Camp Hill as a "maximum security prison for adjudged delinquents and youthful criminal offenders"); and that the stigma attached upon delinquency adjudication approximates that resulting from conviction in an adult criminal proceeding.

. . .

VI

All the litigants here agree that the applicable due process standard in juvenile proceedings, as developed by *Gault* and *Winship*, is fundamental fairness. As that standard was applied in those two cases, we have an emphasis on factfinding procedures. The requirements of notice, counsel, confrontation, cross-examination, and standard of proof naturally flowed from this emphasis. But one cannot say that in our legal system the jury is a necessary component of accurate factfinding. There is much to be said for it, to be sure, but we have been content to pursue other ways for determining facts. Juries are not required, and have not been, for example, in equity cases, in workmen's compensation, in probate, or in deportation cases. Neither have they been generally used in military trials. . . .

We must recognize, as the Court has recognized before, that the fond and idealistic hopes of the juvenile court proponents and early reformers of three generations ago have not been realized. The devastating commentary upon the system's failures as a whole, contained in the President's Commission on Law Enforcement and Administration of Justice, Task Force Report: Juvenile Delinquency and Youth Crime 7–9 (1967), reveals the depth of disappointment in what has been accomplished. Too often the juvenile court judge falls far short of that stalwart, protective, and communicating figure the system envisaged.[4] The community's unwillingness to provide people and facilities and to be concerned, the insufficiency of time devoted, the scarcity of professional help, the inadequacy of dispositional alternatives, and our general lack of knowledge all contribute to dissatisfaction with the experiment.[5]

Despite all these disappointments, all these failures, and all these shortcomings, we conclude that trial by jury in the juvenile court's adjudicative stage is not a constitutional requirement. We so conclude for a number of reasons:

1. The Court has refrained, in the cases heretofore decided, from taking the easy way with a flat holding that all rights constitutionally assured for the adult accused are to be imposed upon the state juvenile proceeding....

2. There is a possibility, at least, that the jury trial, if required as a matter of constitutional precept, will remake the juvenile proceeding into a fully adversary process and will put an effective end to what has been the idealistic prospect of an intimate, informal protective proceeding.

. . .

5. The imposition of the jury trial on the juvenile court system would not strengthen greatly, if at all, the factfinding function, and would, contrarily, provide an attrition of the juvenile court's assumed ability to function in a unique manner. It would not remedy the defects of the system. Meager as has been the hoped-for advance in the juvenile field, the alternative would be regressive, would lose what has been gained, and would tend once again to place the juvenile squarely in the routine of the criminal process.

6. The juvenile concept held high promise. We are reluctant to say that, despite disappointments of grave dimensions, it still does not hold promise, and we are particularly reluctant to say, as do the Pennsylvania

---

4. "A recent study of juvenile court judges ... revealed that half had not received undergraduate degrees; a fifth had received no college education at all; a fifth were not members of the bar." Task Force Report 7.

5. "What emerges, then, is this: In theory the juvenile court was to be helpful and rehabilitative rather than punitive. In fact the distinction often disappears, not only because of the absence of facilities and personnel but also because of the limits of knowledge and technique. In theory the court's action was to affix no stigmatizing label. In fact a delinquent is generally viewed by employers, schools, the armed services—by society generally—as a criminal. In theory the court was to treat children guilty of criminal acts in noncriminal ways. In fact it labels truants and runaways as junior criminals." "In theory the court's operations could justifiably be informal, its findings and decisions made without observing ordinary procedural safeguards, because it would act only in the best interest of the child. In fact it frequently does nothing more nor less than deprive a child of liberty without due process of law—knowing not what else to do and needing, whether admittedly or not, to act in the community's interest even more imperatively than the child's. In theory it was to exercise its protective powers to bring an errant child back into the fold. In fact there is increasing reason to believe that its intervention reinforces the juvenile's unlawful impulses. In theory it was to concentrate on each case the best of current social science learning. In fact it has often become a vested interest in its turn, loathe to cooperate with innovative programs or avail itself of forward-looking methods." Task Force Report 9.

appellants here, that the system cannot accomplish its rehabilitative goals. So much depends on the availability of resources, on the interest and commitment of the public, on willingness to learn, and on understanding as to cause and effect and cure. In this field, as in so many others, one perhaps learns best by doing. We are reluctant to disallow the States to experiment further and to seek in new and different ways the elusive answers to the problems of the young, and we feel that we would be impeding that experimentation by imposing the jury trial. The States, indeed, must go forward. If, in its wisdom, any State feels the jury trial is desirable in all cases, or in certain kinds, there appears to be no impediment to its installing a system embracing that feature. That, however, is the State's privilege and not its obligation.

7. Of course there have been abuses.... We refrain from saying at this point that those abuses are of constitutional dimension. They relate to the lack of resources and of dedication rather than to inherent unfairness.

8. There is, of course, nothing to prevent a juvenile court judge, in a particular case where he feels the need, or when the need is demonstrated, from using an advisory jury.

9. "The fact that a practice is followed by a large number of states is not conclusive in a decision as to whether that practice accords with due process, but it is plainly worth considering...." It therefore is of more than passing interest that at least 28 States and the District of Columbia by statute deny the juvenile a right to a jury trial in cases such as these. The same result is achieved in other States by judicial decision. In 10 States statutes provide for a jury trial under certain circumstances.

10. Since *Gault* ... the great majority of States, in addition to Pennsylvania and North Carolina, that have faced the issue have concluded that the considerations that led to the result in those two cases do not compel trial by jury in the juvenile court.

. . .

12. If the jury trial were to be injected into the juvenile court system as a matter of right, it would bring with it into that system the traditional delay, the formality, and the clamor of the adversary system and, possibly, the public trial. It is of interest that these very factors were stressed by the District Committee of the Senate when, through Senator Tydings, it recommended, and Congress then approved, as a provision in the District of Columbia Crime Bill, the abolition of the jury trial in the juvenile court. S.Rep.No.91–620, pp. 13–14 (1969).

13. Finally, the arguments advanced by the juveniles here are, of course, the identical arguments that underlie the demand for the jury trial for criminal proceedings. The arguments necessarily equate the juvenile proceeding—or at least the adjudicative phase of it—with the criminal trial. Whether they should be so equated is our issue. Concern about the inapplicability of exclusionary and other rules of evidence, about the juvenile court judge's possible awareness of the juvenile's prior record and of the contents of the social file; about repeated appearances of the same familiar witnesses in the persons of juvenile and probation officers and social workers—all to the effect that this will create the likelihood of pre-

judgment—chooses to ignore it seems to us, every aspect of fairness, of concern, of sympathy, and of paternal attention that the juvenile court system contemplates.

If the formalities of the criminal adjudicative process are to be super-imposed upon the juvenile court system, there is little need for its separate existence. Perhaps that ultimate disillusionment will come one day, but for the moment we are disinclined to give impetus to it.

Affirmed.

■ Mr. Justice Harlan, concurring in the judgments.

If I felt myself constrained to follow Duncan v. Louisiana, 391 U.S. 145 (1968), which extended the Sixth Amendment right of jury trial to the States, I would have great difficulty, upon the premise seemingly accepted by my Brother Blackmun's opinion, in holding that the jury trial right does not extend to state juvenile proceedings. That premise is that juvenile delinquency proceedings have in practice actually become in many, if not all, respects criminal trials. But see my concurring and dissenting opinion in In re Gault, 387 U.S. 1, 65 (1967). If that premise be correct, then I do not see why, given *Duncan*, juveniles as well as adults would not be constitutionally entitled to jury trials, so long as juvenile delinquency systems are not restructured to fit their original purpose. When that time comes I would have no difficulty in agreeing with my Brother Blackmun, and indeed with my Brother White, the author of *Duncan*, that juvenile delinquency proceedings are beyond the pale of *Duncan*.

I concur in the judgments in these cases, however, on the ground that criminal jury trials are not constitutionally required of the States, either as a matter of Sixth Amendment law or due process. See my dissenting opinion in *Duncan* and my concurring opinion in Williams v. Florida, 399 U.S. 78, 118–119 (1970).

[The concurring opinion of Mr. Justice White, the opinion of Mr. Justice Brennan concurring in the judgment in No. 322 and dissenting in No. 128, and the dissenting opinion of Mr. Justice Douglas, with whom Mr. Justice Black and Mr. Justice Marshall concur, have been omitted.]

NOTES

(1) As the Court points out, some states accord children a right to jury trial either by statute or judicial decision. Today about a dozen states permit jury trials in juvenile cases. See, e.g., Tex.Fam.Code Ann. § 54.03(c). However, a clear majority of jurisdictions have declined to require jury trials in delinquency proceedings.

As Justice Blackmun suggests, judges may elect to use advisory juries. The California Supreme Court has permitted judges to empanel advisory juries to assist in fact-finding. *People v. Superior Court*, 15 Cal.3d 271, 124 Cal.Rptr. 47, 539 P.2d 807 (1975). For a contrary view, see *People ex rel. Carey v. White*, 65 Ill.2d 193, 2 Ill.Dec. 345, 357 N.E.2d 512 (1976).

(2) Where jury trials are available, either by statute or under state constitutional law, are teenagers constitutionally required on juries under the concept of trial by a jury of one's peers? Judge De Ciantis of the Family Court of Providence, Rhode Island, addressed this issue in *In re McCloud*, a 1971 opinion appended to Mr. Justice Douglas's dissent in *McKeiver*, at 570–571:

One of the most interesting questions raised is that concerning the right of a juvenile to a trial by his peers. Counsel has suggested that a jury of a juvenile's peers would be composed of other juveniles, that is, a "teenage jury." Webster's Dictionary, Second Edition, 1966, defines a peer as an equal, one of the same rank, quality, value. The word "peers" means nothing more than citizens. In re Grilli, 110 Misc. 45, 179 N.Y.S. 795, 797. The phrase "judgment of his peers" means at common law, a trial by a jury of twelve men, State v. Simons, 61 Kan. 752, 60 P. 1052. "Judgment of his peers" is a term expressly borrowed from the Magna Charta, and it means a trial by jury, Ex parte Wagner, 58 Okl.Cr. 161, 50 P.2d 1135. The Declaration of Independence also speaks of the equality of *all* men. Are we now to say that a juvenile is a second-class citizen, not equal to an adult? The Constitution has never been construed to say women must be tried by their peers, to wit, by all-female juries, or Negroes by all-Negro juries.

The only restriction on the makeup of the jury is that there can be no systematic exclusion of those who meet local and federal requirements, in particular, voting qualifications.

The Court notes that presently in some states 18–year-olds can vote. Presumably, if they can vote, they may also serve on juries. Our own legislature has given first passage to an amendment to the Constitution to permit 18–year-olds to vote. Thus, it is quite possible that we will have teenage jurors sitting in judgment of their so-called "peers."

For a more current affirmation of the notion that juveniles are not entitled to juries composed of other juveniles, see *In re Welfare of J.K.B.*, 552 N.W.2d 732 (Minn.App.1996).

(3) One pillar of Justice Blackmun's opinion in *McKeiver* is that extension of the right to jury trial would materially disrupt the nature and purpose of the juvenile court. A study of states using juries suggests that the request for jury trial is rare. This was explained in the *McKeiver* decision in a footnote at p. 561. The Public Defender Service for the District of Columbia filed a brief *amicus curiae* in which they presented:

... the results of a survey of jury trials in delinquency cases in the 10 States requiring jury trials plus the District of Columbia are set forth. The cities selected were mostly large metropolitan areas. Thirty juvenile courts processing about 75,000 juvenile cases a year were canvassed:

"[W]e discovered that during the past five and a half years, in 22 out of 26 courts surveyed, cumulative requests for jury trials totaled 15 or less. In the remaining five courts in our sample, statistics were unavailable. During the same period, in 26 out of 29 courts the cumulative number of jury trials actually held numbered 15 or less, with statistics unavailable for two courts in our sample. For example, in Tulsa, Oklahoma, counsel is present in 100% of delinquency cases, but only one jury trial has been requested and held during the past five and one-half years. In the Juvenile Court of Fort Worth, Texas, counsel is also present in 100% of the cases, and only two jury trials have been requested since 1967. The Juvenile Court in Detroit, Michigan, reports that counsel is appointed in 70–80% of its delinquency cases, but thus far in 1970, it has had only four requests for a jury. Between 1965 and 1969 requests for juries were reported as 'very few.'

"In only four juvenile courts in our sample has there clearly been a total during the past five and one-half years of more than 15 jury trial requests and/or more than 15 such trials held."

The four courts showing more than 15 requests for jury trials were Denver, Houston, Milwaukee, and Washington, D.C.

(4) As the introductory note to this chapter states, one of the significant trends in recent years has been the move away from the rehabilitative model toward a punitive model that emphasizes accountability, proportionality of sentences, determinate sentencing, and punishment. In light of this shift in purpose, some have argued that the day Justice Blackmun was loath to say had arrived has now come, and as a consequence juveniles are entitled to the right to jury trial. See Carol R. Berry, Comment, A California Juvenile's Right to Trial By Jury: An Issue Now Overripe for Consideration, 24 San Diego L.Rev. 1223 (1987).

Courts, however, are reluctant to agree. In Washington, following sweeping changes to the juvenile code resulting in a more punitive model and tougher sentencing guidelines, a juvenile argued that the shift away from a rehabilitative purpose and toward a punitive purpose meant that juvenile proceedings were now criminal in nature and that he was entitled to a jury trial. The court, however, disagreed, holding that while the code had been substantially revised, the basic rehabilitative purpose survived sufficiently to warrant the continued distinction between juvenile and criminal proceedings. *State v. Lawley*, 91 Wn.2d 654, 591 P.2d 772 (1979). Following more recent reexamination, the *Lawley* decision was reaffirmed in *State v. Schaaf*, 109 Wn.2d 1, 743 P.2d 240 (1987). See *In re L.C.*, 273 Ga. 886, 548 S.E.2d 335 (2001).

(5) *Gault*—and its progeny—have not been without criticism. The criticism of *Gault* in recent years has focused principally on the notion that the rationale of *Gault*—the "fundamental fairness" or due process model—has led to such adverse decisions (viewed from the perspective of juveniles' rights) as *McKeiver* and more recently, decisions in the areas of First and Fourth Amendment rights. See, e.g., Barry C. Feld, A Century of Juvenile Justice: A Work in Progress or a Revolution that Failed?, 34 N.Ky.L.Rev. 189 (2007); Emily Buss, The Missed Opportunity in Gault, 70 U.Chi.L.Rev. 39 (2003); Sacha M. Coupet, Comment, What to Do with the Sheep in Wolf's Clothing: The Role of Rhetoric and Reality About Youth Offenders in the Constructive Dismantling of the Juvenile Justice System, 148 U.Penn.L.Rev. 1303 (2000).

McKEIVER: A "JUVENILE" CASE OR A "JURY TRIAL" CASE?

The majority's concern in *McKeiver* about the impact of a jury trial requirement on the informal process of the juvenile court perhaps reflects the influence—some might say triumph—of Justice Harlan's concept of due process outlined in his opinions in *Gault* and *Winship*. Justice Harlan's opinion in *McKeiver* is included here not because he continues to expound on that theme but because he takes a new tack, namely that the right to jury trial is not required by due process in state court juvenile proceedings because it is not required by due process, in his view, in state court criminal proceedings. As he points out, he dissented in *Duncan v. Louisiana*, 391 U.S. 145, 88 S.Ct. 1444, 20 L.Ed.2d 491 (1968), the decision that extended the right to jury trial to the states, at least in criminal proceedings, as a matter of due process of law.

Justice Harlan's view that due process does not include the right to jury trial raises an interesting question. Would the Court that decided *McKeiver* have decided *Duncan* differently? Some of the Court's other decisions affecting the right to jury trial have diminished the right. In *Williams v. Florida*, 399 U.S. 78, 90 S.Ct. 1893, 26 L.Ed.2d 446 (1970), for example, the Court held that the traditional jury structure calling for juries of twelve persons was an "historical accident" and was not binding; juries of six, therefore, were appropriate. In *Johnson v. Louisiana*, 406 U.S. 356, 92 S.Ct. 1620, 32 L.Ed.2d 152 (1972), and *Apodaca v. Oregon*, 406 U.S. 404, 92 S.Ct. 1628, 32 L.Ed.2d 184 (1972), the Court held that less than unanimous verdicts, such as 10–2 or 9–3, were constitutional. The Court has drawn a line beyond which it is unwilling to go, however, holding juries of five unconstitutional, *Ballew v. Georgia*, 435 U.S. 223, 98 S.Ct. 1029, 55 L.Ed.2d 234 (1978), and holding less than unanimous verdicts on juries of six unconstitutional, *Burch v. Louisiana*, 441 U.S. 130, 99 S.Ct. 1623, 60 L.Ed.2d 96 (1979).

Viewing *McKeiver* against the constitutional backdrop of other jury trial cases gives one a different perspective. One tends to view *McKeiver* as a "juvenile rights" case. Certainly the tendency at the time was to view *McKeiver* as a setback to the expanding due process model envisioned in *Gault* and *Winship*, and in particular to the analytical framework that emerged from those cases. Perhaps *McKeiver* is better understood, however, not as a "juvenile" case but as a "jury trial" case and more properly as one in a series of jury trial cases in which the Court diluted the constitutional importance of the right to jury trial. When viewed in this light *McKeiver* is seen as less of a turning point or abandonment of the due process analysis begun in *Gault* and more of a continuation of that analytical approach. Such a view of *McKeiver* makes the Court's subsequent decisions more understandable.

D. BEYOND *MCKEIVER*

Many commentators and Court analysts suggested that *McKeiver* signaled the end of the extension of adult constitutional protections to children's cases. The unanimous decision in the very next case, *Breed v. Jones*, 421 U.S. 519, 95 S.Ct. 1779, 44 L.Ed.2d 346 (1975), indicated that earlier predictions were a bit premature. In *Breed v. Jones* the Court held the Fifth Amendment's double jeopardy prohibition applicable to juveniles in state court proceedings via the due process clause of the Fourteenth Amendment. A better set of conclusions would seem to be that (1) use of the civil label to bar extension of due process rights in juvenile cases is finally over (see the quoted language from *Breed v. Jones* below), and (2) the Court is especially likely to extend adult protections where there will be little disruption to state practice in doing so.

In *Breed v. Jones* the juvenile court had entered a delinquency adjudication but had not yet entered a disposition. Having given further thought to the question of the appropriateness of the case for juvenile treatment, the court waived its jurisdiction and transferred the case for criminal prosecution. Following transfer, the juvenile was convicted of robbery in criminal court. Speaking for a unanimous Court, Chief Justice Burger noted:

> We believe it is simply too late in the day to conclude, as did the District Court in this case, that a juvenile is not put in jeopardy at a

proceeding whose object is to determine whether he has committed acts that violate a criminal law and whose potential consequences include both the stigma inherent in such a determination and the deprivation of liberty for many years.

421 U.S. at 529.[1]

In *Fare v. Michael C.*, 442 U.S. 707, 99 S.Ct. 2560, 61 L.Ed.2d 197 (1979), the Court held that a juvenile's right to speak to his probation officer did not operate to invoke his Fifth Amendment privilege against self-incrimination, and the fact that he waived his rights and made a statement in the absence of a parent did not, per se, render his statement inadmissible. In so holding, however, the Court did not deny to juveniles a right enjoyed by adults in the criminal process. It did not, for example, hold that *Miranda v. Arizona*, 384 U.S. 436, 86 S.Ct. 1602, 16 L.Ed.2d 694 (1966), is inapplicable to juvenile custodial interrogations. In fact, it applied to juveniles the same totality-of-the-circumstances test used in evaluating waivers of *Miranda* rights by adults. *Fare v. Michael C.* is discussed more thoroughly in the next chapter.

In *Schall v. Martin*, 467 U.S. 253, 104 S.Ct. 2403, 81 L.Ed.2d 207 (1984), the Supreme Court upheld New York's preventive detention statute against a due process challenge. The statute allows the juvenile court to order the continued detention of a juvenile, pending an adjudicatory hearing, where "there is a serious risk that he may before the return date commit an act which if committed by an adult would constitute a crime." N.Y.Fam.Ct.Act § 320.5. The Supreme Court upheld the statute on the ground that it effectuates the state's legitimate interest in protecting both society and the juvenile from the harmful consequences of pretrial crime, and under the statutory scheme sufficient procedural safeguards exist to safeguard against unnecessary detention. Language in the Court's opinion suggested that preventive detention statutes for adults might be constitutionally valid as well, so *Schall v. Martin* does not represent a case in which juveniles were denied a right that adults enjoy. Indeed, subsequent to its decision in *Schall v. Martin*, the Court held that preventive detention for adults, with appropriate safeguards, is constitutional. *United States v. Salerno*, 481 U.S. 739, 107 S.Ct. 2095, 95 L.Ed.2d 697 (1987). *Schall v. Martin* also is discussed more fully in the next chapter.

---

1. The Court revisited the double jeopardy issue in *Swisher v. Brady*, 438 U.S. 204, 98 S.Ct. 2699, 57 L.Ed.2d 705 (1978). Maryland, like many states, allows initial hearings before referees, who make factual and legal findings and make recommendations to the juvenile court. The Maryland rule at issue in this case permitted the juvenile court to review the findings and proposals of a referee by reviewing the record itself but did not permit a de novo hearing. The Supreme Court held that, since the prohibition against double jeopardy is designed to prevent exposure to two successive trials (or hearings), no violation occurred under the Maryland procedure because the juveniles were subjected to only one hearing.

The Court concluded that the juvenile court's review of the record constituted a continuation of the original hearing before the referee rather than commencement of a new hearing. This conclusion in turn was based on the nature of the Maryland procedure itself, specifically that the referee's findings are advisory only, subject to acceptance, modification, or rejection by the juvenile court, and that the juvenile court cannot conduct a de novo hearing.

In *New Jersey v. T.L.O.*, 469 U.S. 325, 105 S.Ct. 733, 83 L.Ed.2d 720 (1985), the Court adopted a "reasonable suspicion" standard that allows school personnel to search a student whom they reasonably suspect has violated or is violating the law or a school rule. In adopting a reduced Fourth Amendment standard the Court emphasized the uniqueness of the public school environment, which calls for relaxation of the warrant and probable cause requirements. In so doing the Court approved differential treatment not so much for juveniles as opposed to adults but for students as opposed to nonstudents. Viewed in this manner, *T.L.O.* does not represent a case in which juveniles are denied a right that is available to adults in the criminal process. *New Jersey v. T.L.O.* was discussed in Chapter III and also will receive expanded treatment in the next chapter.

In a subsequent Fourth Amendment case, *Vernonia School District 47J v. Acton*, 515 U.S. 646, 115 S.Ct. 2386, 132 L.Ed.2d 564 (1995), the Court upheld a school district's policy authorizing the random suspicionless urinalysis drug testing of high school athletes. Although the Court concluded that such random testing constituted a "search" under the Fourth Amendment, it held that the searches were reasonable when balancing the minimal intrusion on the individual interests involved against the legitimate governmental interests of deterring drug use by schoolchildren and minimizing risk of physical harm to athletes in particular. On the one hand, the Court in so holding gave credence to the paternalism it has permitted the states to exercise in its handling of children dating back to *Prince v. Massachusetts*, 321 U.S. 158, 64 S.Ct. 438, 88 L.Ed. 645 (1944), and continuing up through *Hazelwood School District v. Kuhlmeier*, 484 U.S. 260, 108 S.Ct. 562, 98 L.Ed.2d 592 (1988). On the other hand, the Court's decision is also consistent with its treatment of identical or similar issues involving adults. For example, it has upheld random suspicionless drug testing of railroad employees, *Skinner v. Railway Labor Executives' Association*, 489 U.S. 602, 109 S.Ct. 1402, 103 L.Ed.2d 639 (1989), and federal customs agents, *National Treasury Employees v. Von Raab*, 489 U.S. 656, 109 S.Ct. 1384, 103 L.Ed.2d 685 (1989), as well as the use of automobile checkpoints to look for illegal immigrants and contraband, *United States v. Martinez–Fuerte*, 428 U.S. 543, 96 S.Ct. 3074, 49 L.Ed.2d 1116 (1976), and drunk drivers, *Michigan Department of State Police v. Sitz*, 496 U.S. 444, 110 S.Ct. 2481, 110 L.Ed.2d 412 (1990). *Acton* was noted in Chapter III and is covered in greater depth in the next chapter.

Most recently, in *Board of Education of Independent School District No. 92 of Pottawatomie County v. Earls*, 536 U.S. 822, 122 S.Ct. 2559, 153 L.Ed.2d 735 (2002), the Supreme Court extended its rationale in *Acton* to uphold a school district's policy requiring drug testing of students who wished to participate in *any* extracurricular activity, including, in addition to athletics, choir, band, academic team, cheerleading, pom-pom, and Future Farmers of America and Future Homemakers of America activities. The Court held that the policy was "a reasonable means of furthering the School District's important interest in preventing and deterring drug use among its schoolchildren." 536 U.S. at 838, 122 S.Ct. at 2569, 153 L.Ed.2d at 750. *Earls* also is treated more extensively in the next chapter.

Despite the expansiveness of the *Gault* decision, *McKeiver* was a reminder of the self-imposed limitations of *Gault*. The Court in *Gault* warned: "We do not mean . . . to indicate that the hearing to be held must conform with all of the requirements of a criminal trial or even of the usual administrative hearing; but we do hold that the hearing must measure up to the essentials of due process and fair treatment." 387 U.S. at 30. This statement was not simply an abstention from deciding questions that were not presented; the Court meant to establish an analytical framework whereby each right subsequently claimed would be scrutinized under due process analysis and an independent determination would be made whether due process requires application of the right to the juvenile process. In *McKeiver*, for example, the Court simply felt that due process of law could be accorded juveniles without requiring a trial by jury.

With regard to the adjudicatory hearing itself, the Court does not favor applicability of any procedure that will be disruptive of the informal juvenile process, that will cause unnecessary delay, that will tend to transform it into a fully adversary process, or that will largely frustrate the ameliorative purposes of the juvenile court. The more difficult question, of course, is the Court's uncertain direction in the area of pre-and post-hearing rights, as illustrated by its decisions in *Fare v. Michael C., Schall v. Martin, New Jersey v. T.L.O.*, and *Vernonia School District 47J v. Acton*.

The Court's decisions in the latter areas, e.g., interrogation and search and seizure, have to be viewed in larger contexts. Thus, the Court's view of a juvenile's rights during interrogation must be viewed in the larger context of the Court's views of Fifth Amendment rights generally. Its decision in *Fare v. Michael C.* is explainable in part by its adherence to a long-standing refusal to expand the scope of the *Miranda* decision itself. Similarly, *T.L.O.* and *Acton* are more easily understood as part of a move toward a more restrictive view of the Fourth Amendment generally. Moreover, *T.L.O.* and *Acton* should be viewed in the context of an overall retrenchment of rights of students in the public school setting. See, e.g., *Bethel School District No. 403 v. Fraser*, 478 U.S. 675, 106 S.Ct. 3159, 92 L.Ed.2d 549 (1986), *Hazelwood School District v. Kuhlmeier*, 484 U.S. 260, 108 S.Ct. 562, 98 L.Ed.2d 592 (1988), and *Morse v. Frederick*, 551 U.S. ___, 127 S.Ct. 2618, 168 L.Ed.2d 290 (2007), discussed in Chapter III supra.

While *McKeiver* did not mark the end of the expansion of due process rights for juveniles, it did mark the beginning of a new analytical framework for determining which rights were required by due process of law. Juvenile cases can no longer be viewed in narrow isolation as juvenile cases only, without considering them as part of a larger landscape. This theme will be explored in greater detail in Chapter X infra.

E. Participation of Counsel in the Juvenile Process

1. Scope of the Right to Counsel

The key language in *Gault* relating to the right to representation by counsel is:

... A proceeding where the issue is whether the child will be found to be "delinquent" and subjected to the loss of his liberty for years is comparable in seriousness to a felony prosecution. The juvenile needs the assistance of counsel to cope with problems of law, to make skilled inquiry into the facts, to insist upon regularity of the proceedings, and to ascertain whether he has a defense and to prepare and submit it. The child "requires the guiding hand of counsel at every step in the proceedings against him." ...

387 U.S. at 36.

Basing its decision on this realization the Court held:

We conclude that the Due Process Clause of the Fourteenth Amendment requires that in respect of proceedings to determine delinquency which may result in commitment to an institution in which the juvenile's freedom is curtailed, the child and his parents must be notified of the child's right to be represented by counsel retained by them, or if they are unable to afford counsel, that counsel will be appointed to represent the child.

387 U.S. at 41.

Early in its opinion, however, the Court limited the scope of its holding:

We do not in this opinion consider the impact of these constitutional provisions upon the totality of the relationship of the juvenile and the state. We do not even consider the entire process relating to juvenile "delinquents." For example, we are not here concerned with the procedures or constitutional rights applicable to the pre-judicial stages of the juvenile process, nor do we direct our attention to the post-adjudicative or dispositional process. We consider only the problems presented to us by this case. These relate to the proceedings by which a determination is made as to whether a juvenile is a "delinquent" as a result of alleged misconduct on his part, with the consequence that he may be committed to a state institution....

387 U.S. at 13.

One can clearly see, then, that the specific mandate of *Gault* was that a juvenile is entitled to representation by counsel at the (1) adjudicatory stage of a (2) delinquency proceeding (3) in which the juvenile may be committed to a juvenile institution. The Court did not address whether the right to counsel attaches at other stages of the proceedings, whether it applies in cases alleging noncriminal misbehavior wherein the same risk of commitment is present, or whether parents under some circumstances might have a right to counsel. Despite the limited nature of the Court's decision, the states have expanded the right to counsel beyond the literal mandate of *Gault*. This expansion is covered to some degree in the next chapter in the material dealing with police investigation. See pp. 1120–43 infra.

One finds an incredible variety among the right to counsel statutes. Many simply state that "a party" or "the child" or "the child and his parent, custodian, or guardian" is entitled to representation by counsel "at all stages of the proceedings." If parents are not specifically mentioned, "party" presumably would include persons other than the juvenile, e.g., parents in a termination of parental rights proceeding. Since no limitation appears, the right to counsel would seem to extend to cases other than those nominally labeled "delinquency" cases, e.g., cases of noncriminal misbehavior and even those alleging neglect and abuse. See, e.g., 42 Pa.Cons.Stat.Ann. § 6337.

Another group of states simply provide that the juvenile (and sometimes the parent) has the right to representation by counsel without specifying whether this right extends to all stages of the proceedings or applies to cases other than delinquency cases. See, e.g., Ill.Comp.Stat.Ann. ch. 705, § 405/1–5(1).

A few states provide for a more limited right to counsel. They require the court to appoint counsel only when the juvenile requests counsel and is financially unable to retain counsel of his own choice. See, e.g., S.D.Comp. Laws Ann. §§ 26–7A–30, 26–7A–31.

Finally, a number of states clearly provide that the right to counsel is applicable not only in delinquency cases, i.e., cases alleging a violation of law, but noncriminal misbehavior cases and even neglect and dependency cases. See, e.g., Va.Code Ann. §§ 16.1–266, 16.1–268; *State ex rel. Von Rossum*, 515 So.2d 582 (La.Ct.App.1987). A few states specifically extend the child's right to counsel to noncriminal misbehavior cases but do not extend it to neglect and dependency cases. See, e.g., N.M.Stat.Ann. § 32A–2–14(H). Legislative extension of the right to counsel to neglect and dependency cases is particularly significant in that it clearly goes beyond the mandate of *Gault* since delinquency, in the sense of a violation of law, is not involved and since, unless the petition also alleges delinquent conduct, no risk of commitment is generally present.

Courts on occasion have been called on to resolve the issue of applicability of the right to counsel in nondelinquency cases, with somewhat interesting results. In *State ex rel. Juvenile Department of Multnomah County v. Wade*, 19 Or.App. 314, 527 P.2d 753 (1974), for example, the court held that a child is entitled to counsel in juvenile court proceedings to terminate parental rights. Two years later, in a case involving the right to counsel of a child in an adoption proceeding also involving termination of parental rights, the court agreed that there was no distinction between the two kinds of cases, but rather than extend the child's right to counsel to adoption proceedings it rescinded its earlier rule and held that a child has no right to counsel in either proceeding. *In re D.*, 24 Or.App. 601, 547 P.2d 175 (1976). In somewhat similar fashion the Pennsylvania Supreme Court held that although a child has a statutory right to counsel in a dependency proceeding in juvenile court (see the Pennsylvania statute cited at page 902 supra), a child does not have a statutory or constitutional right to counsel in an adoption proceeding. *In re Kapcsos*, 468 Pa. 50, 360 A.2d 174 (1976).

The child dependency cases involving possible termination of parental rights raise the issue of a parent's right to counsel in such proceedings. Some statutes specifically provide that parents in neglect or dependency proceedings have a right to counsel, including the right to court-appointed counsel if they are indigent. See, e.g., Va.Code Ann. § 16.1–266(C).

The United States Supreme Court has held that due process does not require a court to appoint counsel for an indigent parent in all termination proceedings. In *Lassiter v. Department of Social Services*, 452 U.S. 18, 101 S.Ct. 2153, 68 L.Ed.2d 640 (1981), the Court held that the issue of appointment of counsel in these proceedings is to be decided on a case-by-case basis in the first instance by the trial court, subject to appellate review. The Court stated that a presumption exists that an indigent person only has a right to appointed counsel when he faces a risk of loss of liberty, although other factors must be weighed against this presumption, namely the private interest at stake, the government's interest, and the risk that the procedures employed may lead to erroneous decisions. The Court did acknowledge:

> In its Fourteenth Amendment, our Constitution imposes on the States the standards necessary to ensure that judicial proceedings are fundamentally fair. A wise public policy, however, may require that higher standards be adopted than those minimally tolerable under the Constitution. Informed opinion has clearly come to hold that an indigent parent is entitled to the assistance of appointed counsel not only in parental termination proceedings, but in dependency and neglect proceedings as well. Most significantly, 33 States and the District of Columbia provide statutorily for the appointment of counsel in termination cases. The Court's opinion today in no way implies that the standards increasingly urged by informed public opinion and now widely followed by the States are other than enlightened and wise.

452 U.S. at 33–34.

In those states already providing a statutory right to counsel for indigent parents in termination proceedings the *Lassiter* decision will have no impact. Moreover, it will have no impact in those states that have found such a right based in whole or in part on state constitutional law, e.g., *Department of Public Welfare v. J.K.B.*, 379 Mass. 1, 393 N.E.2d 406 (1979). Where it will have an impact is in those states whose courts have held, on the basis of federal constitutional law, that indigent parents have a right to appointed counsel, e.g., *In re B.*, 30 N.Y.2d 352, 334 N.Y.S.2d 133, 285 N.E.2d 288 (1972), unless, of course, the legislatures in those states choose to provide a statutory right, as New York's subsequently did, N.Y.Fam.Ct. Act § 262(a)(i), or the courts in future cases base their decisions on state law, see, e.g., *State ex rel. S.N.*, 573 So.2d 1178 (La.Ct.App.1991).

State ex rel. J. M. v. Taylor

Supreme Court of Appeals of West Virginia, 1981.
166 W.Va. 511, 276 S.E.2d 199.

■ HARSHBARGER, CHIEF JUSTICE:

We have consolidated these three juvenile cases because they present common issues.

G.E. was a few days shy of eighteen when he had a probation revocation hearing for participating in an interstate automobile theft ring. The judge asked him if he wanted counsel and told him that if he were indigent, the court would appoint an attorney; but he and his father waived this right. After the hearing, his probation was revoked and he was committed to the Department of Corrections for examination at Pruntytown (our "industrial school" for boys), then to forestry camp for an indeterminate term until he was twenty-one. He got a lawyer who presented a habeas corpus petition to us, and we ordered the circuit court to determine whether G. E. voluntarily waived counsel; and the learned trial judge decided that he did.

J.M., then sixteen, was accused of breaking and entering a market with intent to steal. He did not have counsel at preliminary, adjudicatory or dispositional hearings, pled guilty, and was committed to the Department of Corrections until he became twenty-one years old.

The third juvenile, A. H., was sixteen when his father and mother filed multiple petitions against him for assault, forging checks, and possession of marijuana with intent to deliver. A. H., with his father present, waived counsel. We have no record of the preliminary hearing, but relevant colloquy from his adjudicatory hearing transcript is:

COURT: At that [preliminary] hearing the Court, I think, in some detail explained to the infant and his parents that he had the right to be represented by counsel. I don't see counsel here today.

. . .

[A. H.], are you ready to proceed with this hearing without being represented by an attorney?

JUVENILE: Yes, sir.

After he pled guilty and was adjudicated delinquent:

COURT: . . . Again, at that dispositional hearing you have the right to be represented by an attorney.

Do you want to be represented by an attorney?

JUVENILE: Should I?

COURT: Well, that's not for me to say. I just want to inform you that you definitely have that right if you want to be represented by an attorney.

JUVENILE: No, sir.

. . .

COURT: All right. I realize, of course, that being an infant that you are without funds, and if that's the only drawback, then if the parents would not furnish counsel for you, this court would appoint an attorney to serve you in this case, and his expenses would be paid by the State of West Virginia. Do you understand that?

JUVENILE: Yes, sir.

I.

A juvenile's constitutional right to counsel was recognized by the Supreme Court in 1967 in In re Gault, 387 U.S. 1. That right is in

W.Va.Const. art. 3, § 14, codified at W.Va.Code, 49–5–1(c) and is recognized in many state cases, . . .

Any defendant may relinquish constitutional rights by knowing and intelligent waiver. Johnson v. Zerbst, 304 U.S. 458 (1938); State v. Rissler, W.Va., 270 S.E.2d 778 (1980). In Von Moltke v. Gillies, 332 U.S. 708, 723–24 (1948), the Supreme Court discussed adult waiver of counsel:

> To discharge this duty [of determining whether there is an intelligent and competent waiver] properly in light of the strong presumption against waiver of the constitutional right to counsel, a judge must investigate as long and as thoroughly as the circumstances of the case before him demand. The fact that an accused may tell him that he is informed of his right to counsel and desires to waive this right does not automatically end the judge's responsibility. To be valid such waiver must be made with an apprehension of the nature of the charges, the statutory offenses include within them, the range of allowable punishments thereunder, possible defenses to the charges and circumstances in mitigation thereof, and all other facts essential to a broad understanding of the whole matter. A judge can make certain that an accused's professed waiver of counsel is understandingly and wisely made only from a penetrating and comprehensive examination of all the circumstances under which such a plea is tendered. (Footnotes omitted.)

We have written about waivers of constitutional rights generally:

> But waiver of a constitutional right is not to be lightly regarded, and if such a waiver is to be implied at all, it can only be in situations in which it is clear that the accused has not only a full knowledge of all facts and of his rights, but a full appreciation of the effects of his voluntary relinquishment. Holland v. Boles, 225 F.Supp. 863 (N.D.W.Va.1963). This Court has held that courts indulge every reasonable presumption against waiver of a constitutional right and will not presume acquiescence in the loss of such fundamental right. State ex rel. Calloway v. Boles, 149 W.Va. 297, 140 S.E.2d 624 (1965); syl. pt. 2, State ex rel. May v. Boles, 149 W.Va. 155, 139 S.E.2d 177 (1964). An accused may, by declaration and conduct, waive a fundamental right protected by the Constitution, but it must be demonstrated that the waiver was made knowingly and intelligently. State ex rel. Grob v. Blair [214 S.E.2d 330], supra. State v. Eden, W.Va., 256 S.E.2d 868, 873 (1979).

Courts, scholars, and legislatures have developed two juvenile waiver tests. One weighs the "totality of circumstances"; the other keys on whether there was an interested adult present when the waiver occurred.*

The "totality of circumstances" analysis was made in Haley v. Ohio, 332 U.S. 596 (1948), and Gallegos v. Colorado, 370 U.S. 49 (1962), wherein juvenile waivers of counsel and privileges against self-incrimination were not accepted because circumstances indicated that they were not knowingly and intelligently made.

---

* Waiver of constitutional rights, including the right to counsel, in connection with police interrogation is discussed at pp. 1120–43 infra.

Most cases about juvenile waiver involve custodial interrogations and confessions, and factors such as age, mental age, previous police or court experience, advice of parent or counsel, physical condition, whether held incommunicado, methods of interrogation, education, knowledge of the substance of a charge, and the nature of rights waived, must also be evaluated.

A more objective and workable standard simply invalidates juvenile waivers not secured with counsel, guardian, parent or interested adult present. An interested, friendly adult is supposed to protect an infant from governmental coercion or pressure and to allow someone capable of understanding the nature and consequences of the waiver to help in the decision and to protect the child from inaccurate accounts of his statements at proceedings in which waiver is made. . . .

Some states have legislatively mandated that an adult be present when a juvenile waives. Our code prevents interrogation of juveniles without the presence of a parent or counsel, W.Va.Code, 49–5–8(d), reflecting a legislative judgment that a juvenile is not capable of knowingly waiving his Fifth Amendment privilege against self-incrimination.

But a parent or other adult, even one intensely involved in and interested in a child's welfare, may not be sufficiently knowledgeable, educated or informed about constitutional law to competently waive protections. Commonwealth v. Webster, 466 Pa. 314, 353 A.2d 372 (1975). Sometimes parents' interests may even be opposite a child's, as A.H.'s record here illustrates.

Courts have had difficulty defining an "interested adult". Is a probation officer an interested adult? Is a grandparent? Is a parent who initiated the complaint? or is drunk? or is apathetic? See generally Fare v. Michael C., 442 U.S. 707 (1979), reh. denied, 444 U.S. 887.

In its *Standards Relating to Adjudication*, the Juvenile Justice Standards Project has drafted Rule 1.2:

1.2   Attorneys for respondent and the government.

The juvenile court should not begin adjudication proceedings unless the respondent is represented by an attorney who is present in court and the government is represented by an attorney who is present in court.

A commentary teaches that the juvenile right to counsel should be non-waivable, citing a 1967 recommendation by the President's Commission on Law Enforcement and Administration of Justice, IJA/ABA Juvenile Justice Standards Project, Standards Relating to Adjudication, § 1.2 (1977).

We admire this rule, but are confronted with a suggestion that our Legislature intended that there could be knowing waiver of counsel. Our statute about the preliminary hearing stage of juvenile proceedings provides that a court or juvenile referee shall:

(2) Appoint counsel by order entered of record, if counsel has not already been retained, appointed *or knowingly waived.* (Emphasis added.) Code, 49–5–9(a)(2).

Juvenile waiver of constitutional rights obviously must be more carefully proscribed than adult waiver because of the unrebuttable presumption, long memorialized by courts and legislatures, that juveniles lack the capacity to make legally binding decisions. No juvenile legal status is treated the same as that of an adult, to our knowledge. Examples of legislative recognition of juvenile incapacity are statutes requiring guardians ad litem for infants: in civil actions when a minor is a defendant, Code, 56–4–10; if a minor is plaintiff in a lawsuit (next friend or guardian) § 56–4–9; in eminent domain proceedings involving land in which a minor has an interest, § 54–2–4; for will probate in solemn form, § 41–5–5; for the sale, lease or mortgage of real property owned by a minor, §§ 37–1–3, 37–1–4 and 37–1–12; for sale or lease of real or personal property subject to a future interest, § 36–2–5; for depositions to preserve testimony in which an infant is affected, § 57–4–7; and for actions proving the contents of lost records or papers, § 39–3–7. A child is also given the right to his own counsel in civil neglect proceedings, Code, 49–6–2. There is no statutory authority that counsel can be waived in any of these instances that require a lawyer or a counselor for infants.

We therefore recognize that juvenile waiver has been contemplated by our Legislature; but must also observe that it seems to be a contradiction that an infant might waive his constitutional right to counsel in proceedings wherein his very liberty is threatened, but not do so if someone is about to force sale of a piece of land in which he owns even a $1.00 interest.

We will, therefore, accommodate the statutory implication that he can waive his right to counsel, by requiring that he can do so, but only upon advice of counsel. Only then can there be knowing waiver.

.   .   .

Writs granted.

NOTES

(1) **Texas Family Code Annotated (Vernon)**

§ 51.09. **Waiver of Rights**

Unless a contrary intent clearly appears elsewhere in this title, any right granted to a child by this title or by the constitution or laws of this state or the United States may be waived in proceedings under this title if:

(1) the waiver is made by the child and the attorney for the child;

(2) the child and the attorney waiving the right are informed of and understand the right and the possible consequences of waiving it;

(3) the waiver is voluntary; and

(4) the waiver is made in writing or in court proceedings that are recorded.

§ 51.10. **Right to Assistance of Attorney; Compensation**

(a) A child may be represented by an attorney at every stage of proceedings under this title, including:

(1) the detention hearing required by Section 54.01 of this code;

(2) the hearing to consider transfer to criminal court required by Section 54.02 of this code;

(3) the adjudication hearing required by Section 54.03 of this code;

(4) the disposition hearing required by Section 54.04 of this code;

(5) the hearing to modify disposition required by Section 54.05 of this code;

(6) hearings required by Chapter 55 of this code;*

(7) habeas corpus proceedings challenging the legality of detention resulting from action under this title; and

(8) proceedings in a court of civil appeals or the Texas Supreme Court reviewing proceedings under this title.

(b) The child's right to representation by an attorney shall not be waived in:

(1) a hearing to consider transfer to criminal court as required by Section 54.02 of this code;

(2) an adjudication hearing as required by Section 54.03 of this code;

(3) a disposition hearing as required by Section 54.04 of this code;

(4) a hearing prior to commitment to the Texas Youth Commission as a modified disposition in accordance with Section 54.05(f) of this code; or

(5) hearings required by Chapter 55 of this code.

. . . .

(f) The court shall appoint an attorney to represent the interest of a child entitled to representation by an attorney, if:

(1) the child is not represented by an attorney;

(2) the court determines that the child's parent or other person responsible for support of the child is financially unable to employ an attorney to represent the child; and

(3) the child's right to representation by an attorney:

(A) has not been waived under Section 51.09 of this code; or

(B) may not be waived under Subsection (b) of this section.

(g) The juvenile court may appoint an attorney in any case in which it deems representation necessary to protect the interests of the child.

. . . .

Some commentators have urged that other state legislatures follow Texas's lead in providing for an unwaivable right to counsel. See, e.g., Barry C. Feld, A Century of Juvenile Justice: A Work in Progress or a Revolution That Failed?, 34 N.Ky. L.Rev. 189, 217–30 (2007). Feld points out that the most common reason that many juveniles are unrepresented is waiver of counsel. 34 N.Ky.L.Rev. at 221. Others agree that juveniles should have an unwaivable right to counsel. See Mary Berkheiser, The Fiction of Juvenile Right to Counsel: Waiver in the Juvenile Courts, 54 Fla.L.Rev. 577 (2002); Robert E. Shepherd, Jr., In re Gault at 40: Still Seeking the Promise, 22 Juv. Justice 53 (Fall 2007).

* Chapter 55 concerns children with mental illness, retardation, disease or defect.—Ed.

(2) The Juvenile Justice Standards Relating to Pretrial Court Proceedings, Standards 5.1–5.3 (1980) provide for mandatory representation by counsel at all stages of the proceedings. The right attaches at the time the juvenile is taken into custody, when a petition is filed, or at the first appearance in court, whichever occurs first. In the case of a conflict of interest between parent and child where the parent has retained counsel for the juvenile, the Standards require that parent and counsel be cautioned about the attorney's duty of loyalty to the juvenile's interests.

Should the juvenile court appoint an attorney for the child over parental objection? This long has been the practice since *Gault*, as the *Taylor* case indicates (see quotes from the record). Should children have an independent right to counsel? Some have argued that courts invade family autonomy unduly when they appoint counsel for children against the wishes of their parents. For example:

> The appointment of counsel for a child without regard to the wishes of parents is a drastic alteration of the parent-child relationship. Indeed, it is in effect a disposition by the state. It intrudes upon the integrity of the family and strains the psychological bonds that hold it together. Therefore it cannot take place until the presumption of parental autonomy has been overcome—until the protective insulation that parents give children from the law has been broken by the establishment at adjudication of a ground for intervention.

Joseph Goldstein, Anna Freud, and Albert J. Solnit, Before the Best Interests of the Child 112 (1979).*

(3) Over two decades after *Gault*, some commentators argued that the right to counsel for juveniles existed more in form than substance and that in many jurisdictions less than half or barely more than half of the juveniles appearing in juvenile court were represented by counsel. See, e.g., Barry C. Feld, The Right to Counsel in Juvenile Court: An Empirical Study of When Lawyers Appear and the Difference They Make, 79 J.Crim.L. & Criminology 1185, 1188–89 (1989); Barry C. Feld, In re Gault Revisited: A Cross–State Comparison of the Right to Counsel in Juvenile Court, 34 Crime & Delinq. 393, 402 (1988); Stevens H. Clarke & Gary G. Koch, Juvenile Court: Therapy or Crime Control, and Do Lawyers Make a Difference?, 14 Law & Soc'y Rev. 263 (1980). Feld suggested several reasons that might explain this phenomenon:

> parental reluctance to retain an attorney; inadequate public-defender legal services in nonurban areas; a judicial encouragement of and readiness to find waivers of the right to counsel in order to ease administrative burdens on the courts; a continuing judicial hostility to an advocacy role in a traditional, treatment-oriented court; or a judicial predetermination of dispositions with nonappointment of counsel where probation is the anticipated outcome.

Barry C. Feld, In re Gault Revisited: A Cross–State Comparison of the Right to Counsel in Juvenile Court, 34 Crime & Delinq. 393, 395 (1988).

Perhaps more alarming is the finding by the same commentators that in cases in which juveniles were represented by counsel, the dispositions were more severe. One might suspect the reason for this phenomenon is that juveniles are more likely to be represented by counsel in cases involving the most serious allegations, and, therefore, one naturally would find the most severe dispositions in such cases. Empirical studies do not support this conclusion, however, and show instead that the presence of an attorney exerts an independent effect on the severity of the disposition. Feld also suggested several possible explanations for this effect:

* From BEFORE THE BEST INTERESTS OF THE CHILD by Joseph Goldstein, Anna Freud, and Albert Solnit. Copyright © 1979, by The Free Press, a division of Simon & Schuster. Reprinted with permission of the publisher. All rights reserved.

Organizational pressures to cooperate, judicial hostility toward adversarial litigants, role ambiguity created by the dual goals of rehabilitation and punishment, reluctance to help juveniles ''beat a case,'' or an internalization of a court's treatment philosophy may compromise the role of counsel in juvenile court.

Feld, supra, at 395.*

Feld—and others—also suggested that attorneys in juvenile court might simply be incompetent and prejudice their clients' cases. He also observed that public defender offices often assigned their least experienced or least capable attorneys to juvenile cases to get trial experience and that these attorneys might receive less supervision than their prosecutorial counterparts. Finally, he suggests that court-appointed counsel may feel beholden to the judges who appointed them and may be more concerned with maintaining the relationship with the judge than with protecting the interests of their clients. 34 Crime & Delinq. at 419.

More recent studies have borne out the weaknesses both in the right to counsel and the effectiveness of counsel observed by Professor Feld. Many of them are recounted in N. Lee Cooper, Patricia Puritz & Wendy Shang, Fulfilling the Promise of In re Gault: Advancing the Role of Lawyers for Children, 33 Wake Forest L Rev. 651, 654–63 (1998). In Ellen Marrus, Best Interests Equals Zealous Advocacy: A Not So Radical View of Holistic Representation for Children Accused of Crime, 62 Md.L.Rev. 288, 296–326 (2003), the author joins Professor Feld in decrying the disparity between the promise of *Gault* and the reality in practice.

Feld himself argues that even 40 years after the *Gault* decision, little has changed—many juveniles still are not represented by counsel, and those who are often fare worse when it comes to disposition than do those who are unrepresented. Barry C. Feld, A Century of Juvenile Justice: A Work in Progress or a Revolution That Failed?, 34 N.Ky.L.Rev. 189, 217–30 (2007). He assigns waiver of counsel as the most prevalent reason that many juveniles are unrepresented. 34 N.Ky.L.Rev. at 221. Others agree with Feld that even today *Gault* has failed to live up its promise. See, e.g., Mary Berkheiser, The Fiction of Juvenile Right to Counsel: Waiver in the Juvenile Courts, 54 Fla.L.Rev. 577 (2002); Robert E. Shepherd, Jr., In re Gault at 40: Still Seeking the Promise, 22 Juv. Justice 53 (Fall 2007).

In re A.R.

Court of Appeals of Illinois, First District, 1998.
295 Ill.App.3d 527, 230 Ill.Dec. 391, 693 N.E.2d 869.

■ PRESIDING JUSTICE CERDA delivered the opinion of the court:

Respondent, 15–year–old A.R., was found delinquent on the basis of two counts of aggravated battery and aggravated discharge of a firearm. He was sentenced to five years' probation. On appeal, respondent asserts that (1) he was not proven guilty beyond a reasonable doubt; and (2) he received ineffective assistance of counsel. For the following reasons, we vacate the conviction and remand this cause for further proceedings.

Javier Perez testified that he went to a gangway at 72nd and Washtenaw Streets, Chicago, to see Cory Ellis, on April 2, 1996. When he arrived, four men, including respondent and Cory Ellis, were present. Five to ten minutes later, while Perez was talking with Ellis, one of the men said something like "what is up," pulled a gun from his pocket, and shot Perez in his side. Respondent was standing next to the shooter. After being shot, Perez fell to the ground, then dragged himself to the front yard, where a passerby helped him. As a result of the gunshot wound, Perez suffered a spinal cord injury, which left him paralyzed.

Cory Ellis testified that respondent's brother, Kenneth Robinson, called him several times on April 2, 1996, to buy marijuana from him. When Ellis went to a house at 72nd and Washtenaw Streets at about 6 p.m. for a pre-arranged meeting with Robinson, Robinson and respondent accompanied Ellis to the backyard. Robinson was looking at the marijuana when Ellis's friend, Perez, walked toward them. Ellis told Robinson to hurry up, but Robinson seemed to be stalling. As Perez walked down the gangway, he told Ellis he would wait for him in the front. At that point, Robinson took a gun from his pocket and shot Perez once. At the time of the shooting, respondent was behind Robinson, watching.

Chicago police detective Roland Paulintsky testified that he investigated the shooting. After going to the hospital where Perez was being treated, Paulintsky went to the scene of the shooting. In the gangway, he saw blood splatters and a shell casing. He then went into the house and spoke with respondent. Respondent's younger brother and stepfather were also in the house. After speaking with respondent's stepfather, Paulintsky advised respondent of his Miranda rights and took him to the police station. After respondent gave an oral confession at the police station, Paulintsky contacted a youth officer.

When respondent's biological father arrived, respondent repeated his confession in front of his father, Chicago police youth officer Cheryl Guratowski, Detective Paulintsky, and assistant State's Attorney Montel Gayles. In his statement, respondent said that he overheard his brother and cousin talking about buying marijuana from Ellis on April 2, 1996. His brother Kenneth said that they would stick-up Ellis and take the marijuana, which Kenneth would sell. His brother planned to keep the money. Respondent heard Kenneth call Ellis three or four times and inquire about buying a pound and a half of marijuana.

Before Ellis arrived around 6 p.m., respondent warned Kenneth that it was not a good idea to rob Ellis because something might happen to their house or their family. Kenneth agreed, but then told respondent that when Ellis arrived, he should act like he did not know Kenneth and should do everything that Kenneth told the others to do.

When Ellis came to the house, Kenneth told respondent to come outside with him and Ellis. Respondent followed the two men into the backyard. Ten seconds later, Perez arrived. After Ellis took three plastic baggies filled with marijuana out of a backpack, Kenneth complained that Ellis had shorted him the last time. After Perez denied that he had shorted Kenneth earlier, Kenneth turned his back and looked at the marijuana. He then turned back toward the men and pulled a gun from his pocket. Perez tried to run, but Kenneth told him to stay. Kenneth hit Ellis in the mouth with the gun, then told everyone to get on ground. When no one got on the ground, Kenneth shot Perez in the chest. Ellis and Kenneth ran, but respondent stayed to help Perez. He returned home until the police arrived later that evening.

After closing arguments, the trial court found respondent guilty of two counts of aggravated battery and aggravated discharge of a firearm based on his written statement. The court found that both Ellis and Perez were not credible witnesses. After being found delinquent, respondent was sentenced to five years' probation.

The first issue is whether defendant received ineffective assistance of counsel because his attorney failed to file a motion to quash his arrest and suppress evidence or to refile a motion to suppress his statements.

In order to establish ineffective assistance of counsel, a defendant generally must prove that his counsel was deficient and that he was prejudiced by that deficiency. Strickland v. Washington, 466 U.S. 668, 687, 104 S.Ct. 2052, 2064, 80 L.Ed.2d 674, 693 (1984); People v. Albanese, 104 Ill.2d 504, 525, 85 Ill.Dec. 441, 473 N.E.2d 1246 (1984). To show prejudice, the defendant must demonstrate that there was a reasonable probability that, but for counsel's unprofessional errors, the result of the proceeding would have been different. Strickland, 466 U.S. at 694, 104 S.Ct. at 2068, 80 L.Ed.2d at 698. A reasonable probability is a probability sufficient to undermine confidence in the outcome. Strickland, 466 U.S. at 694, 104 S.Ct. at 2068, 80 L.Ed.2d at 698. In making a determination of prejudice, the court must examine the totality of the circumstances. Strickland, 466 U.S. at 695, 104 S.Ct. at 2069, 80 L.Ed.2d at 698.

To prevail on a claim that his trial counsel was ineffective for failing to file a motion to quash arrest or suppress statements, the defendant must show that there was a reasonable probability that the motion would have been granted and that the outcome of the trial would have been different if the arrest had been quashed or the statements suppressed. People v. Morris, 229 Ill.App.3d 144, 157, 171 Ill.Dec. 112, 593 N.E.2d 932 (1992); People v. Bennett, 222 Ill.App.3d 188, 201, 164 Ill.Dec. 426, 582 N.E.2d 1370 (1992); People v. Mendez, 221 Ill.App.3d 868, 873, 164 Ill.Dec. 321, 582 N.E.2d 1265 (1991).

Defendant argues that he was arrested without probable cause and that his statements were involuntary. In determining whether an arrest has occurred, the court must make an objective determination whether a reasonable person, innocent of any crime, would have considered himself or herself arrested or free to leave. Michigan v. Chesternut, 486 U.S. 567, 573, 108 S.Ct. 1975, 1979, 100 L.Ed.2d 565, 572 (1988); People v. Holveck, 141 Ill.2d 84, 95, 152 Ill.Dec. 237, 565 N.E.2d 919 (1990). The factors to consider include the time, place, length, mood, and mode of the interrogation; the number of police officers present; any indicia of formal arrest or evidence of restraint; the intention of the officers; the extent of the officers' knowledge; the focus of the officers' investigation (People v. Brown, 136 Ill.2d 116, 124–25, 143 Ill.Dec. 281, 554 N.E.2d 216 (1990)); the subjective belief of the detainee concerning his arrest status (People v. Booker, 209 Ill.App.3d 384, 393, 154 Ill.Dec. 211, 568 N.E.2d 211 (1991)); any statement or non-verbal conduct by the police indicating that the detainee was not free to leave (People v. Langlo, 153 Ill.App.3d 636, 641–42, 106 Ill.Dec. 547, 505 N.E.2d 1338 (1987)); and whether the detainee was told that he was free to leave or that he was under arrest. Holveck, 141 Ill.2d at 95, 152 Ill.Dec. 237, 565 N.E.2d 919; People v. Reynolds, 257 Ill.App.3d 792, 799, 196 Ill.Dec. 14, 629 N.E.2d 559 (1994). The police officer's subjective belief that the detainee was free to leave is not determinative if it was not communicated to the defendant. People v. Stofer, 180 Ill.App.3d 158, 168, 128 Ill.Dec. 682, 534 N.E.2d 1287 (1989). No one factor is dispositive. A determination will vary with all of the circumstances surrounding the detention in each case. Chesternut, 486 U.S. at 572, 108 S.Ct. at 1978, 100 L.Ed.2d at 571.

Whether or not probable cause for an arrest exists depends on the totality of the facts and circumstances known to the officers when the arrest was made. People v. James, 118 Ill.2d 214, 223, 113 Ill.Dec. 86, 514 N.E.2d 998 (1987). Probable cause "requires more than mere suspicion, but it does not require the arresting officers to have in their hands evidence sufficient to convict the defendant." In re D.G., 144 Ill.2d at 409, 163 Ill.Dec. 494, 581 N.E.2d 648.

For a confession to be admissible at trial, it must be free, voluntary, and not obtained by any direct or implied promises, however slight, nor by the exertion of any improper influence. Malloy v. Hogan, 378 U.S. 1, 84 S.Ct. 1489, 12 L.Ed.2d 653 (1964); People v. Thomas, 137 Ill.2d 500, 516, 148 Ill.Dec. 751, 561 N.E.2d 57 (1990). The test for the voluntariness of a confession is whether, under the totality of the circumstances, the statement was made freely, without compulsion or inducement, with consideration given to the characteristics of the accused and the details of the interrogation. Thomas, 137 Ill.2d at 516, 148 Ill.Dec. 751, 561 N.E.2d 57.

Under the Juvenile Court Act, a law enforcement officer who takes a minor into custody shall immediately make a reasonable attempt to notify the parent and shall without unnecessary delay take the minor to the nearest juvenile officer. The purpose of the "notice" requirement is to permit, where possible, a parent to confer and counsel with the juvenile before interrogation and confession. People v. Montanez, 273 Ill.App.3d 844, 210 Ill.Dec. 295, 652 N.E.2d 1271 (1995).

Factors to be considered in determining whether the confession was voluntary include the defendant's age, education, intelligence, experience and physical condition; the length and intensity of the interrogation; the existence of any threats, promises, or physical coercion; whether the confession was induced by police deception; and whether defendant was informed of his constitutional rights. People v. Martin, 102 Ill.2d 412, 427, 80 Ill.Dec. 776, 466 N.E.2d 228 (1984); People v. MacFarland, 228 Ill. App.3d 107, 117, 170 Ill.Dec. 35, 592 N.E.2d 471 (1992). When a juvenile's confession is at issue, additional factors come into play, including the time of day and the presence of a parent or other adult interested in the juvenile's welfare. People v. Brown, 235 Ill.App.3d 479, 490, 176 Ill.Dec. 492, 601 N.E.2d 1190 (1992).

Although the presence of a youth officer does not per se make a juvenile's confession voluntary, it is a significant factor. In re Lashun H., 284 Ill.App.3d 545, 557, 219 Ill.Dec. 823, 672 N.E.2d 331 (1996). The failure to have a juvenile officer present is material to determining the voluntariness of defendant's statement. People v. Knox, 186 Ill.App.3d 808, 815, 134

Ill.Dec. 564, 542 N.E.2d 910 (1989). The presence or absence of a parent is also a factor in evaluating the voluntary nature of a confession. Montanez, 273 Ill.App.3d at 854, 210 Ill.Dec. 295, 652 N.E.2d 1271; In re J.O., 231 Ill.App.3d 853, 855, 173 Ill.Dec. 406, 596 N.E.2d 1285 (1992). The relevant inquiry is whether the absence of an adult interested in the defendant's welfare contributed to the coercive circumstances surrounding the interview, not whether contact with a parent was denied. Knox, 186 Ill.App.3d at 814, 134 Ill.Dec. 564, 542 N.E.2d 910.

The following cases are helpful in deciding whether the confession in this case was voluntary. In Montanez, 273 Ill.App.3d 844, 210 Ill.Dec. 295, 652 N.E.2d 1271, the confession was involuntary. The court stated:

> " 'Notice' here must be understood to have some purpose, namely to allow, where possible, the concerned adult to confer and counsel with the juvenile before interrogation and confession. Yes, an attempt was made to contact a youth officer before the statement was taken; but the interrogation went forward anyway within minutes. And yes, the parent here was 'notified' but in the same breath she was told she could not see her child until called. These circumstances demonstrate the intended fulfillment of notice here was simply a charade." Montanez, 273 Ill.App.3d at 850, 210 Ill.Dec. 295, 652 N.E.2d 1271.

Montanez further held that the failure to have the opportunity to confer was material in determining the voluntariness of a minor defendant's statement. 273 Ill.App.3d at 852, 210 Ill.Dec. 295, 652 N.E.2d 1271.

In In re J.O., 231 Ill.App.3d 853, 173 Ill.Dec. 406, 596 N.E.2d 1285, the parents of a minor respondent went to the police station, but did not ask to talk to the respondent. As a result, they were not taken to see him. Instead, they waited in the police station lobby while the respondent was being questioned. The court stated:

> "A juvenile's age and the fact that the interrogation occurred in the middle of the night may properly be considered in evaluating the voluntary nature of a confession. [Citation] Additionally, if parents have indicated an interest by their presence, then they should be allowed to confer with their children before any questioning occurs. [Citation] The presence or absence of a parent is a factor in evaluating the voluntary nature of a confession under the totality of the circumstances test. [Citation] Accordingly, because the trial court's ruling was based on the totality of the circumstances and the court considered proper factors in making its determination, we affirm its granting of the motion to suppress." In re J.O., 231 Ill.App.3d at 855, 173 Ill.Dec. 406, 596 N.E.2d 1285.

In People v. R.B., 232 Ill.App.3d 583, 173 Ill.Dec. 905, 597 N.E.2d 879 (1992), the 15–year-old defendant maintained that his statement was involuntary. The court explained in deciding the case:

> "This court has stated that the failure to telephone a juvenile's parents, or the absence of a parent during questioning, is a factor in determining voluntariness, but is not determinative of whether defendant's confession should be suppressed. [Citation]

However, where the State failed to take appropriate steps to ensure that a juvenile defendant had an opportunity to confer with an interested adult, either a parent or a youth officer, this court has held that the police conduct rendered his confession inadmissible. [Citation] R.B., 232 Ill.App.3d at 593, 173 Ill.Dec. 905, 597 N.E.2d 879.

The court then held that the confession was involuntary.

In this case, the totality of the circumstances suggests that respondent was arrested before he gave an oral confession, which was likely involuntary since no adult interested in his welfare was present. The defendant was given his Miranda rights and taken into custody to the police station by Officer Paulintsky. At the police station, he gave an oral confession. There was no parent present and the police did not contact a youth officer until after respondent gave his confession. This case is similar to the recent case of People v. Fuller, 292 Ill.App.3d 651, 226 Ill.Dec. 657, 686 N.E.2d 6 (1997), in which this court ruled that the minor defendant's first confession was involuntary because it was given without a parent present and before the police contacted a youth officer.

It is disturbing that respondent was questioned without an interested adult being present and before the police even contacted the youth officer. Receiving an incriminating statement by a juvenile in the absence of counsel is a sensitive concern requiring great care to assure that the juvenile's confession was neither coerced, suggested, nor the product of fright or despair. People v. Prude, 66 Ill.2d 470, 476, 6 Ill.Dec. 689, 363 N.E.2d 371 (1977). As a result, courts scrutinize custodial statements by juvenile suspects with particular care, given that the potential for coercion is enhanced. *Brown*, 235 Ill.App.3d at 490, 176 Ill.Dec. 492, 601 N.E.2d 1190.

We do not know if the police asked respondent's step-father to come to the police station or contacted his biological parents before questioning him. We do know, however, that his biological father arrived after he gave his oral confession and that the youth officer was not contacted until after he had given that confession. While the absence of a parent or youth officer does not per se make a juvenile's confession involuntary, the police must make every reasonable effort to have a parent, youth officer, or other interested adult present before they question a juvenile.

Nevertheless, we do not have to decide whether the arrest was illegal or the confession involuntary. The issue in this case is whether respondent received ineffective assistance of counsel because his attorney failed to challenge the legality of the arrest or voluntariness of his confession. Based on the foregoing, we find that there was enough evidence to suggest that there was a reasonable probability that, but for counsel's unprofessional errors, the result of the proceeding would have been different. Strickland, 466 U.S. at 694, 104 S.Ct. at 2068, 80 L.Ed.2d at 698.

Because we conclude that respondent received ineffective assistance of counsel, we are vacating his conviction and remanding this cause to the circuit court for a hearing on his motion to quash arrest and suppress statements. If the circuit court grants the motion, a new trial is ordered. If, however, the circuit court denies the motion, the conviction is affirmed.

.   .   .

Vacated and remanded with instructions.

■ McNAMARA AND BURKE, JJ., concur.

NOTES

(1) More recently, the Supreme Court reaffirmed the two-part test first announced in *Strickland v. Washington* for resolving claims of ineffective assistance of counsel, in *Williams v. Taylor*, 529 U.S. 362, 120 S.Ct. 1495, 146 L.Ed.2d 389 (2000).

(2) Courts have sustained ineffective assistance of counsel claims in other circumstances as well. See, e.g., *Miller v. Straub*, 299 F.3d 570 (6th Cir.2002), cert. denied, 537 U.S. 1179, 123 S.Ct. 995, 154 L.Ed.2d 927 (2003) (failure of counsel to advise juvenile of possibility that he could receive mandatory life sentence without possibility of parole when he pleaded guilty to first-degree murder); *S.T. v. State*, 764 N.E.2d 632 (Ind.2002) (failure of counsel to object to exclusion of testimony of juvenile's mother and his friend, as sanction for juvenile's failure to comply with court rule requiring disclosure of witness list ten days before hearing); *In re R.D.B.*, 20 S.W.3d 255 (Tex.Ct.App.2000) (failure of counsel to seek assistance of mental health professional to determine whether brain injury could have caused juvenile's antisocial and disruptive behavior). But see *Brown v. Crosby*, 249 F.Supp.2d 1285 (S.D.Fla.2003) (counsel's strategy on motion to suppress was not objectively unreasonable and did not constitute ineffective assistance of counsel; court will not second-guess deliberate strategy where chosen course is not objectively unreasonable).

(3) The significance of the second part of the *Strickland* test—the showing of actual prejudice—cannot be overlooked. If a juvenile is not prejudiced as a result of counsel's failure, the ineffective assistance claim fails. See, e.g., *Coley v. Morrow*, 183 Or.App. 426, 52 P.3d 1090, review denied, 335 Or. 104, 59 P.3d 1279 (2002). In the adult context, see *Lockhart v. Fretwell*, 506 U.S. 364, 113 S.Ct. 838, 122 L.Ed.2d 180 (1993).

2.   THE ROLE OF COUNSEL

Following *Gault*, many attorneys had no idea how adversary their role should be and how it should differ if at all from representation in an adult criminal case. See, e.g., the language of *Samuel W. v. Family Court*, 24 N.Y.2d 196, 199, 202, 299 N.Y.S.2d 414, 417, 419, 247 N.E.2d 253, 255, 257, reversed on other grounds sub nom. *In re Winship*, 397 U.S. 358, 90 S.Ct. 1068, 25 L.Ed.2d 368 (1970):

> A lawyer's traditional professional duty in an adversary proceeding is to do what he can and fight as hard as he can, to see his client wins. In the criminal case this is to see his client acquitted, the charge reduced, or the punishment minimized. But a child's best interest is not necessarily, or even probably, promoted if he wins in the particular inquiry which may bring him to the juvenile court.

.   .   .

It seems probable we cannot have the best of two worlds. If the emphasis is on constitutional rights something of the essential freedom of method and choice which the sound juvenile court Judge ought to have is lost; if range be given to that freedom, rights which the law gives to criminal offenders will not be respected. But the danger is that we may lose the child and his potential for good while giving him his constitutional rights.

Even before *Gault* many urged that attorneys should serve as vigorous advocates in juvenile delinquency adjudicatory hearings. A defense of the vigorous advocate in juvenile court comes from the President's Commission on Law Enforcement and the Administration of Justice:

> The case against counsel in juvenile proceedings rests in part on the fear that lawyers will inject into juvenile court proceedings the worst features of criminal trials: Emphasis on technical and legalistic points without regard to the larger interests at stake; use of dilatory devices such as needless requests for adjournments; preoccupation with "getting the client off" rather than concern for furthering the interests of child and state.

> First, even to the extent those fears are well-grounded, the pervasive and fundamental commitment to fairness and the unfortunate experience with departure from procedural regularity in the juvenile courts require provision of counsel. But some of the consequences of introducing lawyers are not at all undesirable. Effective representation of the rights and interests of the offender inevitably appears to those accustomed to complete freedom of decision making as needless obstreperousness and dilatoriness. Of course law is an irksome restraint upon the free exercise of discretion. But its virtue resides precisely in the restraints it imposes on the freedom of the probation officer and the judge to follow their own course without having to demonstrate its legitimacy or even the legitimacy of their intervention.

Task Force Report: Juvenile Delinquency and Youth Crime 33 (1967). Further, a study by sociologists Wheeler and Cottrell urged: "Unless appropriate due process of law is followed, even the juvenile who has violated the law may not feel that he is being fairly treated and may therefore resist the rehabilitative efforts of court personnel." Stanton Wheeler & Leonard S. Cottrell, Juvenile Delinquency:—Its Prevention and Control (1966). See also W. Vaughn Stapleton & Lee E. Teitelbaum, In Defense of Youth: A Study of the Role of Counsel in American Juvenile Courts (1972).

By the early 1970s despite lamentation from Chief Justice Burger and others (see dissenting opinion of Burger, C.J., in *In re Winship*, 397 U.S. 358, 376, 90 S.Ct. 1068, 25 L.Ed.2d 368 (1970)), advocacy was the rule rather than the exception in post-*Gault* courts. Debate continues, however, over whether counsel's role in a juvenile proceeding should be that of an advocate or that of, for example, a guardian. In the excerpt from its opinion in *Samuel W. v. Family Court* supra, the New York Court of Appeals spoke of a lawyer's "professional duty." What is a lawyer's "professional duty" in representing a juvenile? What guidance if any is afforded by rules governing the professional conduct of lawyers? The pertinent rules are set forth below, followed by commentary on some of the dilemmas they pose as well as commentary on the approach taken in the Juvenile Justice Standards, Standards Relating to Counsel for Private Parties.

AMERICAN BAR ASSOCIATION, MODEL RULES OF PROFESSIONAL CONDUCT, 2008 EDITION*

Rule 1.14(a)

When a client's ability to make adequately considered decisions in connection with the representation is impaired, whether because of minority, mental disability or for some other reason, the lawyer shall, as far as reasonably possible, maintain a normal client-lawyer relationship with the client.

Comment

The normal client-lawyer relationship is based on the assumption that the client, when properly advised and assisted, is capable of making decisions about important matters. When the client is a minor or suffers from a mental disorder or disability, however, maintaining the ordinary client-lawyer relationship may not be possible in all respects. In particular, an incapacitated person may have no power to make legally binding decisions. Nevertheless, a client lacking legal competence often has the ability to understand, deliberate upon, and reach conclusions about matters affecting the client's own well-being. Furthermore, to an increasing extent the law recognizes intermediate degrees of competence. For example, children as young as five or six years of age, and certainly those of ten or twelve, are regarded as having opinions that are entitled to weight in legal proceedings concerning their custody. . . .

Ellen Marrus, Best Interests Equals Zealous Advocacy: A Not So Radical View of Holistic Representation for Children Accused of Crime

62 Maryland Law Review 288 (2003).**

INTRODUCTION

A lawyer in adult criminal court represents an eighteen-year-old client charged with burglary who does not want to plead guilty, even though he is guilty. The lawyer explains that quantitatively and qualitatively there is more than sufficient evidence to convict. Furthermore, counsel advises the accused of the unpleasant facts that over ninety percent of defendants in state criminal courts plead guilty, and that sentences after trial tend to be higher than those obtained by plea. Under these circumstances, the attorney advises her client to plead guilty. If, however, the client persists, defense counsel will put on her advocate hat and use all her professional skills to gain an acquittal. If that fails, she will try to prevent incarceration or limit the prison term by presenting mitigating evidence at sentencing, such as: the client's mother is a junkie, there is no food at home, and the client grew up in a chaotic household. The probation department recommends a two-year prison sentence. Although the defendant's record demonstrates that he will undoubtedly need the lawyer's services again in the very near future, the attorney succeeds in getting probation for her client. Nobody blinks an eye.

Transport that lawyer to a delinquency proceeding in juvenile court. This time she represents a sixteen-year-old client accused of burglary who does not want to plead guilty, even though he is, and even though there is more than sufficient evidence to establish his guilt. Almost all children in juvenile court plead guilty.[7] But they do so, at least in large part, because the "best interests of the child" is the accepted mantra, and any "bargaining" that might hinder the child's rehabilitation would theoretically conflict with that notion. The attorney pressures her client to admit his complicity. After the plea and considering the youth's past record, the lawyer simply accepts the "expert" recommendation of probation and that the boy needs a "structured environment." The child is sentenced to two years in a state prison for juveniles, euphemistically called a training school. The fact that his mother is a junkie, there is no food at home, and he lives in a chaotic environment are what primarily motivates the probation department to recommend commitment. Nobody blinks an eye.

What happened to the advocate hat that the lawyer wore in criminal court? She left it there, because, after all, the juvenile court system is benign, the records are sealed, the proceedings are confidential, there is no punishment, just treatment, and last, but not least, her client needs "help."

Although they are becoming increasingly punitive,[17] the juvenile courts still try to obfuscate the similarities between criminal court and juvenile court by using a different vocabulary. The child is a respondent, not a defendant; a child is not indicted for the commission of a crime, a petition for delinquency is filed; there is no bail hearing, rather a detention hearing; there is no trial, only an adjudicatory hearing; there is no guilty plea, the child either admits or stipulates to the allegations of the petition; there is no criminal conviction, merely a finding of fact or an adjudication that the child engaged in delinquent conduct; there is no sentence, just a disposi-

---

7. See *State ex rel. C. A. H. v. Strickler*, 162 W.Va. 535, 251 S.E.2d 222, 226 (1979) (noting that "most juvenile cases are resolved by guilty pleas"); Wallace J. Mlyniec, A Judge's Ethical Dilemma: Assessing a Child's Capacity to Choose, 64 Fordham L.Rev. 1873, 1898 (1996) (stating that "courts accept pleas of guilty in the vast majority of juvenile delinquency cases").

17. See Barry C. Feld, The Transformation of the Juvenile Court—Part II: Race and the "Crack Down" on Youth Crime, 84 Minn. L.Rev. 327, 328 (1999) (arguing that we are

seeing more juvenile offenders being tried as adults as well as "jurisprudential changes that de-emphasize rehabilitation and escalate punitive sanctions for ordinary delinquents"); Julianne P. Sheffer, Note, Serious and Habitual Juvenile Offender Statutes: Reconciling Punishment and Rehabilitation Within the Juvenile Justice System, 48 Vand. L.Rev. 479, 483–84 (1995) (stating that evidence indicates that "the juvenile court is becoming more punitive").

tional hearing; and the child is not sentenced to prison, but rather committed to a treatment facility or training school.

The nomenclature in juvenile court may be different from that in criminal court, but the essentials are much the same . . . Providing effective assistance of counsel to children accused of delinquency requires lawyers to evaluate realistically what is going on in these courts and to protect their clients just as they would in a typical adult criminal court. The attorney needs to understand her role. She is not a guardian ad litem, appointed by the court to seek the "best interests of the child." She is an advocate. Instead of pandering to the supposed benevolence of the kiddie court—telling the child-client what to do, betraying confidential information, spending insufficient time on the case and with the client—she should protect her client by embracing a model, which I call "holistic lawyering."[33]

Holistic lawyering, in part, is based on my experience as a public defender representing children accused of crime in Solano County, California. I also base this model on my many years as a public school teacher and administrator. Holistic lawyering embodies the quality of legal representation that is necessary to assure that alleged delinquents receive the true right to counsel that the Court in *Gault* intended to grant.

. . . .

II. The False Dichotomy of Zealous Advocacy Versus the Child's Best Interests

The deficiencies noted above are often compounded by lawyers' confusion about their proper role when they represent a juvenile. Many attorneys practicing in juvenile court view their role in representing minors in delinquency cases more as guardian ad litems who seek the child's best interests,[204] than as zealous advocates for the child-client.[205] The attorneys who see themselves as guardian ad litems are often passive and somewhat

---

33. Prior to *Gault*, juvenile court judges did not welcome lawyers in their courtrooms. See Barry C. Feld, The Right to Counsel in Juvenile Court: An Empirical Study of When Lawyers Appear and the Difference They Make, 79 J.Crim.L. & Criminology 1185, 1192 (1989) (noting that juvenile court judges were hostile to lawyers in juvenile proceedings because they "regarded lawyers as both irrelevant and an impediment to their 'child-saving' mission").

204. Many courts agree with this viewpoint. See, e.g., *In re K.M.B.*, 123 Ill.App.3d 645, 78 Ill.Dec. 917, 462 N.E.2d 1271, 1273 (1984) (finding that it was entirely appropriate for the child's attorney to express her opinion that the minor's out of home placement would be in her best interests, despite the fact that K.M.B. wanted to remain at home). The court concluded that the "recommendation [of counsel] was based on her professional evaluation . . . and indicate[d] . . . not only that K.M.B. received counsel but

that she received [a] very conscientious counsel . . . [who] is to be highly commended." Id.

Recently, students taking my Children's Rights course at the University of Houston Law Center informed me that several attorneys had told them that they saw themselves more as guardian ad litems than as an attorney representing a client charged with a criminal offense.

205. The IJA/ABA Juvenile Justice Standards state that an attorney in delinquency proceedings "should ordinarily be bound by the client's definition of his or her interests with respect to admission or denial of the facts or conditions alleged," Juvenile Justice Standards Annotated § 3.1(b)(ii)[a] (1996), and that "[t]he active participation of counsel at disposition is often essential to protection of clients' rights and . . . the lawyer's most valuable service to clients will be rendered at this stage of the proceeding," id. § 9.1.

uncomfortable dealing with "criminal matters" in the juvenile court atmosphere.[206] Conflict is seen not only as unnecessary, but harmful.[207] To such attorneys, serving the best interests of the child-client usually means following the disposition recommended by the probation department, even if it is incarceration, and even though one might argue that the best interests of the child-client would be better served by keeping the child out of prison-like detention facilities. The term "kiddie court" is a revealing aphorism denoting informality, the absence of traditional lawyering, social work attitudes, and either the dispensing of slaps on the wrist punishment or therapeutic treatment.[209]

Even some criminal law attorneys are guilty of acquiring a paternalistic attitude when they practice in juvenile court. They are accustomed to adult court and adult sentences; therefore, they often mistake juvenile court dispositions as being of minor consequence. To them, the juvenile court system is benign and incomparable to the criminal justice system in terms of restraints on personal liberty.[211] Indeed, the juvenile court is considered more of a child welfare agency than a true court.[212] What many people fail to appreciate is that the juvenile court has become increasingly punitive. Many juvenile codes now openly speak of the need to punish children for wrongdoing and prescribe mandatory and often lengthy sentences for delinquents.[213]

206. To some degree it is understandable that attorneys react in this manner. For years, the juvenile court was seen as an institution that was there to help the child and do what was in the child's best interests. This mindset can influence all the actors in juvenile court. See Janet E. Ainsworth, Re-Imagining Childhood and Reconstructing the Legal Order: The Case for Abolishing the Juvenile Court, 69 N.C.L.Rev.1083, 1129–30 (1991) (discussing that the "reason for less than zealous defense advocacy is the ambiguity felt by many juvenile court lawyers concerning their proper role"); David A. Harris, The Criminal Defense Lawyer in the Juvenile Justice System, 26 U.Tol.L.Rev. 751, 762–63 (1995) (discussing how an attorney either cooperates with the court and gets to contribute to the decision, or advocates to the hilt, falls in disfavor with the court, and becomes cut out of the loop).

207. See Ainsworth, supra note 206, at 1129 (stating that attorneys who exhibit "excessive zeal" in representing their clients are often reminded by the court that such attitudes are "inappropriate and counter-productive").

209. See Ainsworth, supra note 206, at 1130 (describing the general belief that the sentences in juvenile courts are "palliative" and "radically less severe" than those given in adult courts); see also Harris, supra note

206, at 762–63 (explaining the role of attorneys and judges in juvenile courtrooms).

211. Cf. *Schall v. Martin*, 467 U.S. 253, 255–57 (1984) (upholding a statute authorizing pretrial detention of a child alleged to be a delinquent if there was "a serious risk" he would commit a crime). Indeed, the Supreme Court itself has fostered such a belief. See id. at 265 (arguing that although children have an "interest in freedom from institutional restraints, . . . that interest must be qualified by the recognition that juveniles, unlike adults, are always in some form of custody").

212. Professor Harris describes the situation in the following way:

See Harris, supra note 206, at 763–64 (footnote omitted).

213. Several states have changed their juvenile codes to place a stronger emphasis on punishment and to hold juveniles accountable. See, e.g., Colo.Rev.Stat.Ann. § 19–2–102(1) (West Supp. 2002) (stating that in order to protect the public, the juvenile system "will appropriately sanction juveniles who violate the law"). For a further discussion on the changes of the juvenile justice system from rehabilitation to punishment, see Giardino, supra note 8, at 228–49 (discussing the increasingly punitive goals of state juvenile justice systems, switching their emphasis from the best interest of the child to public safety).

The judge may [be seen as] little more than a super social worker in a robe ... doing what was "necessary" to help the child ... [and, therefore,] commit[ting] all [individuals]—even defense counsel—to a nonlegal, helping approach.... Simply put, no one in the system wants counsel assigned to represent juvenile offenders to act as a "real" lawyer would.

Furthermore, a two-or three-year sentence for a child who is in the midst of rapid development may be more harmful than a ten-year sentence for an adult. To children, even adolescents, time is measured differently from adults and the same two-year sentence may have much more severe consequences. Removing a child from his or her home, school, and community can have devastating effects, including recidivism both as a child and as an adult. Moreover, in some jurisdictions, a sentence rendered in juvenile court can be as long as the sentence imposed for a comparable crime committed by an adult offender.[217] Sentences imposed by juvenile courts may even extend beyond the period when the child offender is legally under the jurisdiction of the juvenile authorities.[218] In California, for example, when the child reaches eighteen, he or she may be transferred to an adult facility, and at twenty-five the prisoner must be transferred.[219]

This blurring of the distinction between juvenile and criminal court is also exemplified by the Texas determinate sentencing law. The statute, as amended in 1995, was designed as a compromise between those who wanted to expand the category of children subject to waiver to criminal court by lowering the age threshold and expanding the class of offenses subject to waiver and those opposed to such expansion of the waiver provisions.[220] The compromise was a determinate sentencing law which permits children between ten and sixteen years of age who are charged with one of a dozen plus crimes to be tried in juvenile court,[221] but subjected to imprisonment for longer periods than ordinary delinquents, and to be transferred to adult correctional facilities upon reaching maturity.[222] Given these recent changes in both the practice and ideology of the

---

217. See, e.g., Cal.Welf. & Inst. Code § 726 (West 1998) (stating that a minor can be confined up to the maximum term of imprisonment that an adult would receive for the same penal offense).

218. See, e.g., id. § 607(b) (declaring that the juvenile court can maintain jurisdiction of a juvenile until the age of twenty-five if the minor has been committed to the California Youth Authority).

219. Id.

220. Prior to 1995, the waiver provision applied only to fifteen- and sixteen-year-olds who were charged with having committed a felony. In 1995, the age was lowered to fourteen, if the child was alleged to have committed one of three very serious felonies, "a capital felony, an aggravated controlled substance felony, or a felony of the first degree." Tex.Fam.Code Ann. § 54.02(a)(2)(A) (Vernon 2002).

221. See id. § 53.045(a)(1)–(16). Originally the determinate sentencing law applied only to six very serious offenses. The amendments include such offenses as, murder, capital murder, manslaughter, aggravated kidnapping, sexual assault or aggravated sexual assault, aggravated assault, aggravated robbery, injury to a child or an elderly or disabled person, felony deadly conduct involving discharging a firearm, aggravated controlled substance felony, criminal solicitation, indecency with a child, criminal solicitation of a minor, attempted murder or capital murder, arson, and intoxication manslaughter. Id.

222. Tex.Hum.Res. Code Ann. § 61.079 (Vernon 2002) (stating that when the juvenile is between the ages of sixteen and twenty-one, the Texas Youth Commission may seek to transfer the child to the Texas Department of Criminal Justice if "(1) the child has not completed the sentence; and (2) the

juvenile justice system, it is difficult to justify any attorney assuming a guardian role, rather than an advocate role, when practicing in juvenile court.

Many attorneys go along with the probation department's recommendation that the child remain at home under supervision. This disposition seems innocuous because the child remains with his family and the probation officer may be able to help the child. However, the probation officer often has a caseload of one hundred or more cases; he or she triages and spends little time with those that do not seem to be most at risk. In these circumstances, it is likely that the child will violate probation. This time around, the disposition invariably will be more harsh because the child has demonstrated that he cannot live at home and that probation supervision, which may have been minimal, is insufficient to help the child.

. . .

Boot camps are being touted as an efficacious and less expensive alternative. These facilities are typically isolated geographically and have a military style curriculum. They purportedly provide juveniles with a rigorous, disciplined routine that encourages the youth to accept responsibility, build self-esteem, and develop trust of others. Juveniles are often given group punishments for violations of rules rather than encouragement for behaving correctly. Some are not licensed and thus there is little oversight and their employees are often not sufficiently trained. There have been a number of deaths of children in such facilities, and recently the director of such a boot camp was indicted for murder because a fourteen-year-old died after being required to remain in one-hundred-degree heat without water.[235] Another available, yet objectionable facility, is the state training school. These facilities are lock-ups and resemble prisons.[237] By and large there is little medical care or schooling.[238] There is, however, a lot of brutality in many of these places.[239] The cases reveal cruelty that may be even more extreme than in adult prisons.

During the 1970s a number of class action lawsuits were brought in federal courts to correct the deplorable conditions that existed in juvenile locked facilities.[240] In Rhode Island children were kept in small, dark cement rooms where the only opening was a small barred window.[241] Often

child's conduct . . . indicates that the welfare of the community requires the transfer'').

235. Associated Press, Boot Camp Chief Held In Boy's Death, L.A. Times, Feb. 16, 2002, at A20.

237. See Inmates of the Boys' Training Sch. v. Affleck, 346 F.Supp. 1354, 1359–61 (D.R.I.1972) (describing the conditions of the training school); Lollis v. N.Y. State Dep't of Soc. Servs., 322 F.Supp. 473, 475–76 (S.D.N.Y.1970) (describing the child's room conditions).

238. See Affleck, 346 F.Supp. at 1359, 1361; Jennifer Warren, Suit Assails Conditions at Youth Prisons, L.A. Times, Jan. 25,

2002, at B8 (giving examples of deficient medical care and limited educational programming).

239. See Nelson v. Heyne, 491 F.2d 352, 354 (7th Cir.1974) (citing routine beatings administered by staff members); Morales v. Turman, 364 F.Supp. 166, 169–73 (E.D.Tex. 1973) (finding that staff members routinely administered physical beatings, including blows to the face, and used tear gas).

240. See Nelson, 491 F.2d at 353; Morales, 364 F.Supp. at 169; Affleck, 346 F.Supp. at 1357.

241. See Affleck, 346 F.Supp. at 1359.

the window was boarded up and with no artificial lighting, the room would be totally dark. In one of the buildings, the children were allowed out of their cells only for a daily shower and to receive their meals which had to be eaten in their cell. The children were unable to exercise. Many children would receive nothing to eat for sixteen hours, as the last meal of the day was given at three o'clock in the afternoon, and no other food was provided until seven o'clock the next morning. Lack of education was another major problem. The state provided only one and a half to two hours of education a day, which consisted mostly of math problems. Visitors were also limited, and many children went months without being able to see their parents or other relatives.

Facilities in Indiana,[249] Texas,[250] and New York[251] were not any better. . . .

Have these conditions changed? Recently a suit was filed against the California Youth Authority (CYA) alleging some of these same conditions.[259] Young offenders are forcibly given mind-altering drugs while being denied proper psychiatric care. They are sometimes placed in small "metal cages," where, the CYA contends, the youths are given educational opportunities and exercise. Children are allegedly raped by other inmates and are not protected by the guards. In 2001, Maryland began to phase out two juvenile detention facilities due to similar conditions.[263] In Louisiana, the state took over the operations of a privately run juvenile facility because of the appalling conditions,[264] which still existed months after the state took control.[265] Juveniles are disciplined with extreme force and sufficient education is still not provided.

Can anyone say that such facilities are in a child's best interests? It is true that there are dangerous children who must be incarcerated to protect society, but nothing requires that they be abused. Protecting society is the same rationale given for sentencing adult defendants to prison. Prison sentences may protect society, but no one claims that incarceration is in the adult offender's best interests.

The role of an attorney in juvenile court was perhaps best expressed by Justice Fortas in *Kent v. United States*, which held that a child being considered for waiver to adult criminal court is entitled to a hearing, an attorney with access to probation files, and a statement detailing the

---

249. See *Nelson v. Heyne*, 491 F.2d 352, 353–54, 356–58 (7th Cir.1974).

250. See *Morales v. Turman*, 535 F.2d 864, 867–69 (5th Cir.1976), rev'd on other grounds, 430 U.S. 988 (1977).

251. See *Lollis v. N.Y. State Dep't of Soc. Servs.*, 328 F.Supp. 1115, 1117 (S.D.N.Y. 1971).

259. Warren, supra note 238.

263. Maureen O'Hagan, Maryland to Phase Out Troubled Youth Center; Most Juveniles to Move to Community Programs, Wash. Post, Dec. 28, 2001, at B04.

264. See Fox Butterfield, Settling Suit, Louisiana Abandons Private Youth Prisons, N.Y. Times, Sept. 8, 2000, at A14 (explaining that children were beaten by the guards regularly, denied food and clothing, and were not provided proper medical treatment).

265. See Joe Gyan, Jr., Judge Frees Youth, Blasts Prison, Advocate, Dec. 20, 2001, at 6–B (citing the continued violence in the youth prison, even after the state was running the facility).

reasons for the transfer.[268] The circuit court of appeals in the case had justified the denial of access to probation reports on the ground that it was not counsel's role to "denigrate" probation recommendations.[269] In reversing, the Supreme Court stated, "it is precisely the role of counsel to 'denigrate' such matter."[270] Justice Fortas eloquently noted that "[t]he right to representation by counsel is not a formality. It is not a grudging gesture to a ritualistic requirement. It is of the essence of justice."[271] This moving description of counsel's role is not merely flowery rhetoric. Rather, the provision of adequate counsel is of profound importance to the well-being of children in juvenile court.

III. HOLISTIC LAWYERING

The model of holistic lawyering that I propose permits, and indeed requires the lawyer to act as a lawyer. While zealous advocacy informs the entire model, the attorney also is associated with other professionals in a team. The combined skills of each team member contribute to the kind of advocacy that truly ensures the best interests of the child. This model requires money, access to professionals in other disciplines, a keen appreciation of the dangers of the juvenile court system, attitudinal changes regarding the attorney child-client relationship, the necessity for adversarial representation, and expertise in child development and criminal, juvenile, and civil court law and practice. Even attorneys with limited means can employ aspects of this model. The differences between the ideal and real worlds are more in degree than in kind, and, as with most things, ultimately rest on the extent of available resources.

A. Ideal Holistic Lawyering

1. The Value of a Team Approach.—Simply stated, my proposal of ideal holistic lawyering for minors charged with juvenile delinquency encompasses a team approach. The team should include attorneys who specialize in juvenile law, social workers, educators, therapists, psychologists, psychiatrists, investigators, and criminal and civil law attorneys who work together to provide high quality representation for the child-client.

. . .

How would this approach play out for attorneys representing children in delinquency matters? As noted above, representation of children charged with crimes is no easy job. Juvenile court procedures are usually termed civil matters; that requires the attorney to know civil law—how to preserve the record, motions, discovery, rules of appellate practice, etc. The reality, however, is that the child is charged with committing a penal offense, and therefore the attorney must know both substantive criminal law and criminal procedure. But that is not enough. The attorney must also know juvenile law and practice, which may differ from both civil and

268. 383 U.S. 541, 561–63 (1966) (stating the child's "rights are meaningless—an illusion, a mockery—unless counsel is given an opportunity to function").

269. *Kent v. United States*, 343 F.2d 247, 258 (D.C.Cir.1964), rev'd, 383 U.S. 541.

270. *Kent*, 383 U.S. at 563. The Court granted counsel access to probation reports "within reasonable limits having regard to the theory of the Juvenile Court Act." Id.

271. Id. at 561.

criminal law. If the child is found guilty, dispositional alternatives become critical. The attorney cannot rely on an overworked probation officer to explore all possibilities. The attorney needs a social worker who is experienced in such matters and knows of private treatment facilities that are specially geared for the child's particular problem and that are less prison-like. Psychiatrists and psychologists will provide necessary information on the particular child's intelligence and emotional state, the differences in child development, and how to communicate effectively with minor children. Educational specialists can determine why the child hates school and is doing poorly there. While some such services are provided by the juvenile courts, there is often a long waiting period to receive them, and these professionals, paid by the state, are not always sympathetic to the child's perspective. Furthermore, they are not available on a day to day basis to assist the attorney and child in communicating.

In one case, I represented a young girl whose mother had remarried and the girl, Joan, did not get along with her step-father. In addition, she was required to spend a lot of time babysitting a new sibling. Joan ran away from home and in the process was arrested for joyriding. She was found guilty, and the question at the dispositional hearing was Joan's placement. Many of the typical teenage-parent problems were present; however, despite the parents' ambivalence, Joan did want to return home.

I arranged for a local psychologist to interview Joan, and with Joan's consent, to talk with the mother and step-father. The psychologist discussed a program he had developed in another community that he believed would meet the needs of Joan and her family. He explained to Joan what would be involved and received her input regarding the workability of the program. Joan agreed it was something she wanted to try. At this stage, the parents agreed it was best for Joan to remain with them. The probation department, on the other hand, was recommending placement in a group home. The psychologist testified to the appropriateness of the suggested plan and Joan's willingness to cooperate. Joan was able to take the stand and intelligently discuss what was involved in the treatment program for her, her mother, and step-father. She also clearly indicated her involvement with the development of the plan and her acceptance of it. The judge, who routinely followed the probation department's recommendation, was impressed with the psychologist's and Joan's participation. She permitted Joan to remain at home, and ordered her and the family to engage in the program with this particular psychologist.

.   .   .

Unlike many portraits from the eighteenth century, children are not merely miniature adults. People who, in other contexts recognize and relate to children differently than to adults, when faced with criminal activities by juveniles, suddenly no longer see the child as a child, but rather as a super-predator adult criminal deserving of adult punishment. If the juvenile court system is a recognition that children are different from adults, and that the best interests of the child must govern, lawyers for child-clients must utilize the skills of all professionals who can help to bridge the gap between adult and child.

2. *The Dynamics of Ideal Holistic Lawyering.*—To get the full benefits of such a team approach, it must be structured in such a way as to assure that the professional participants freely interact with each other and provide optimal input. Studies show that when professional teams are hierarchically structured with the doctor or lawyer at the top, the other professional team members are more reluctant to speak out, and the patient or client has less control over his treatment or representation. Group members may avoid this problem by voting on the leader, or making decisions based on a majority vote. Ethical problems, however, may result from such practices. The attorney must ultimately rely on his or her own professional judgment in representing a client,[294] regardless of what other team members conclude when, in his or her view, such conclusions may be detrimental to the child's legal defenses.[295] Indeed, the United States Supreme Court has held in *Jones v. Barnes*,[296] that an attorney need not obey even the client's directive to pursue or raise even non-frivolous claims, notwithstanding [the ruling in *Faretta v. California*] permitting defendants to represent themselves in criminal cases.[298]

The permissibility of such a hierarchical arrangement between attorney and client allowed by *Jones* is perplexing, particularly after the *Faretta* decision. If the accused may dispense with counsel altogether, surely after being advised of the options, he or she must make the ultimate decisions affecting their representation, as long as it does not involve committing a crime, providing ineffective assistance of counsel, or impinging on the lawyer's ability to make instantaneous trial decisions.

Does the fact that the client is a child change my view? In general, no. Children, when properly informed of all matters by the team, can make good decisions regarding their representation. Unless there are compelling circumstances, the child, if he or she wishes, should be present for team meetings and have access to reports. The issues must be explained in a way that is child-friendly, and the client should be urged to provide feedback and direction to team members. Children in juvenile court often do not understand what is happening to them, what the possible consequences are, or how selecting different choices can affect their lives. At the very least, children in juvenile court have to be kept informed. Many children will ultimately ask the lawyer to make the decision, particularly when the juvenile is very young. That is fine, because the child is deciding to let the lawyer decide. What is important is that the child knows he or she has a say in the outcome. Of course, the older the child, the greater the likelihood that the child, after being informed, will elect to make the ultimate decision. Realistically, however, based on my experience, almost all children, even older adolescents, will elect to follow their attorney's recommendation. That too is fine, because the child is still the decisionmaker.

---

294. Model Rules of Prof'l Conduct R. 5.4(c) (2002); Model Code of Prof'l Responsibility DR 5–107(B) (1999).

295. See Lisa A. Stanger, Note, Conflicts Between Attorneys and Social Workers Representing Children in Delinquency Proceedings, 65 Fordham L.Rev. 1123, 1135–40

(1996) (explaining that independent zealous representation must outweigh all other assessments).

296. 463 U.S. 745 (1983).

298. 422 U.S. 806, 819–20 (1975).

However, if the attorney agrees with this view of lawyering in the juvenile court, he or she must be careful not to *unduly* influence the client. Children naturally look to authority figures to make decisions for them. If the attorney under the guise of providing information overwhelms the child, he or she implicitly becomes a guardian rather than a lawyer. For example, consider an attorney that is representing a child charged with a hate crime. The child sees nothing wrong with his actions since his parents, who are anti-Semitic, supported his decision to paint a swastika on a Jewish classmate's garage. The lawyer is appalled by the child-client's actions and thinks it would be good for the child to be removed from his home environment lest he grows up to be a violent "skinhead." Although the lawyer may want to influence his client and encourage him to take responsibility for his actions, if he believes there is a lack of evidence and that he could get a dismissal, the lawyer needs to present this information to the child in an unbiased fashion and live with the outcome of the trial.

This viewpoint is not shared by all. Indeed, the high profile aggressive criminal defense attorney Leslie Abramson claims:

> With adults, it's ethically appropriate to do whatever your client wants, so long as it's legal.... But when it's a kid who's being wrongheaded, you have to recognize that the child doesn't necessarily have the maturity to make wise choices. You overrule him when necessary. And you try to do something that will make his life better, even if he doesn't see the logic.[307]

In my idealistic model, all members of the team should understand and appreciate the importance of the child-client directing his or her own representation within the proper parameters. The team approach also has to overcome the normative differences within various professional disciplines. For example, the lawyer's role is to provide zealous advocacy.[308] A mental health worker seeks the client's best interests. Sometimes the two coincide, but sometimes, they do not, or at least do not appear to. Suppose a child charged with committing a criminal act tells his representational team that he is guilty, but wants to "get off" and remain at home, notwithstanding severe abuse by his parents, information that he wishes to keep secret. Because of his or her advocacy view of representation, the lawyer's duty may be to keep the information confidential[311] and to try to get an acquittal, or failing that, probation while the child lives at home. The social worker's professional responsibility is to report the abuse so that the child is moved to a protective environment. It is not that all social workers believe that removal of the child is necessary in all cases of abuse, and indeed, they know that some alternative placements can be extremely destructive for a child as well. However, their code of ethics requires that the information be relayed to the court. Under some circumstances, some social workers may instinctively urge that the child plead guilty to the

307. Leslie Abramson, The Defense Is Ready: Life in the Trenches of Criminal Law 105 (1997).

308. See Model Rules of Prof'l Conduct R. 1.3 cmt. 1 (2002); Model Code of Prof'l Responsibility EC 7–1 (2000).

311. See Model Rules of Prof'l Conduct R. 1.6(a) (forbidding disclosure of information without client's consent); see also Model Code of Prof'l Responsibility EC 4–1, DR 4–101(A)–(B) (explaining the ethical obligation of keeping the client's secrets).

alleged offense so that the child will remain within the court's jurisdiction, thus actively opposing a trial that may result in an acquittal or a disposition that results in the child remaining at home.

In my view, the attorney's mandate to protect confidential communications must trump the social worker's code of ethics. Thus, professionals who want to be part of the representational team must also include themselves in the attorney-client confidential relationship. Without that adherence, the child-client may be unwilling to speak freely with all members of the team. In addition, confidentiality by all members of the team would be important for the attorney too and would accomplish the purposes of a team approach. If confidentiality is not preserved, the attorney will not feel comfortable releasing information to the team members. At Legal Services for Children in San Francisco, each child-client is assigned a social worker and an attorney. The confidential relationship exists between the child-client, the attorney and the social worker, and between the social worker and attorney.

. . .

Is there a downside to my model of holistic lawyering, particularly if it results in a factually guilty child's acquittal? While it may be distasteful for some to facilitate such a result, I view it as no worse than doing the same for an adult defendant. Indeed, an argument could be made that "getting children off" in juvenile court is even more important than in adult criminal court. Many children commit criminal acts, even serious ones, and then outgrow their impulsive behavior even without juvenile court intervention. In fact, it is more likely that the child will develop normally without the labeling and incarceration that the juvenile court imposes. Studies show that children adjudicated delinquents are more likely to become recidivists as adults.[321]

But are we teaching the child that crime is okay as long as you have good lawyers? Furthermore, are trials not simply a waste of time and resources since most children are, in fact, guilty, and there is usually enough evidence to support an adjudication of delinquency? Starting backwards with the "efficiency" and "everyone charged is guilty" arguments, the difficulty is that most adults charged with a crime are also guilty. Yet few argue that they should not have a right to test the government's proof, even though the lawyer in defense of a "guilty" person may have to cross-examine witnesses who are telling the truth so as to make it appear that they are lying or mistaken. Moreover, there is an even stronger argument that children, even if guilty, should have a trial. A trial brings home to children the realization that they committed criminal acts and are deserving of punishment. A guilty plea may obviate that lesson and children may feel that they are being punished for their confession of guilt rather than their criminal acts. Furthermore, a plea of not guilty necessarily slows

321. [Ira M. Schwartz, (In)Justice for Juveniles: Rethinking the Best Interests of the Child (1989)] at 51 (finding that out of 303 youths released from two juvenile facilities in Florida, sixty percent re-offended within one year). Of course, children who are adjudicated delinquent may be more prone to violence, and thus the recidivism may not be due to the juvenile court intervention, but rather to the child himself.

down the treadmill dispensing of justice that is prevalent both in adult and juvenile court. The judge is forced to listen and see the child not just as another burglar, but as an individual with unique characteristics. I am not suggesting that there should be a trial in every case. For various strategic and tactical reasons it may be better for the child to plead guilty, such as in cases where the facts are so horrendous it would be better that the judge not hear the gruesome and overwhelming evidence.

With respect to the argument that getting guilty children off can result in future crime because it engenders an attitude of being able to get away with anything as long as you have a good lawyer, it is well to remember that such a belief is grounded in reality. By insisting on proof beyond a reasonable doubt, the child is learning another, perhaps more important lesson; he or she is valued by the system, and that the system, although imperfect, assures that individuals count and that it is better to free a guilty person than to convict an innocent one. It has also been shown that when people understand how the system works and the rules to be followed, they are more likely to become law-abiding citizens. Alternatively, children may see the acquittal as getting a second chance, particularly when they are told why they "got off." Children are likely to recognize that the circumstances leading to the acquittal may not occur again in the future and will take this opportunity as a way of staying out of trouble.

B.   *Holistic Lawyering in the Real World*

Why do I offer an approach to legal representation for minors that I acknowledge in its most fulsome form is probably unattainable, at least here and now? The response is that even when we cannot provide the very best approach, it is important to look at its components, to see if there are parts of the very best that we can adapt and use towards the betterment of our current state.

Some of these components can be seen at work in a number of specialized juvenile public defender offices throughout the country. Attorneys who go to work in these offices are there because they want to be. They are permanently assigned to the juvenile division and are not rotated to the other criminal law units. Moreover, within the juvenile division, attorneys specialize in particular kinds of proceedings such as waiver, juvenile delinquency, or appeals. Some of these offices come close to the idealistic team approach, but they too suffer from a lack of funds. Their virtues are expertise in juvenile law, training programs for new juvenile law attorneys, access to sister criminal defender units for advice, political clout, and some money for hiring outside experts when necessary. There are also stand-alone public defender offices for children. They are not part of a larger public defender system with other units, and thus, do not have access to sister criminal law divisions.

Most of these public defender offices for children, whether part of a larger unit or stand alone, are funded by the state and may have associated investigators, social workers, psychiatrists, and psychologists. Many of these offices are very child advocate oriented and actively seek to assure that children charged with crimes receive quality legal representation. Attorneys in these offices have a special interest in juvenile law, and they share similar beliefs in protecting children from the often brutal vagaries of the juvenile court system. This advocacy orientation is not universally admired, particularly by judges.

. . .

Many jurisdictions, however, do not have public defender offices with juvenile law divisions; indeed, in many areas, there is no public defender office. Instead, private attorneys are appointed by the court to represent indigent juvenile respondents. They often receive less money than private attorneys appointed to represent indigent adult defendants, thus making it more likely that experienced, competent attorneys will not practice in juvenile court. When these attorneys request outside experts, the applications are subjected to very intense scrutiny and almost routinely rejected except in extraordinary circumstances. Lawyers who are too aggressive in requesting outside expert assistance or who practice zealous advocacy, refusing to plead their clients guilty and challenging probation recommendations, are very often not reappointed.

Because of these constraints, many appointed attorneys plead their clients guilty choosing not to seek alternative placement options to probation recommendations. I am not suggesting that all appointed counsel in juvenile court are not doing their job despite the hurdles. Many are. However, many are not. What then can solo practitioners or individual public defenders, who want to provide quality legal representation for children, do to achieve that goal?

[The author next discusses four means by which solo practitioners or individual public defenders might achieve the goal of providing quality legal representation for children. The first three are (1) training programs, where they are available, (2) certification in juvenile law, currently offered in only one state, and (3) informal networking with other attorneys who practice in the area of juvenile law. The fourth follows.]

4.   Lawyer's Commitment and Attitude.—The biggest and least expensive change the solo attorney can make is rethinking the role of counsel in juvenile delinquency proceedings. The best way to represent children in juvenile court is to provide zealous advocacy. This requires that the attorney spend numerous hours with the client, treating the client with respect and allowing the child to participate in the process. The lawyer must be committed to providing quality representation to the child, just as he or she would give to an adult, refusing to treat the court and its personnel with velvet gloves unless it inures to the benefit of the child. I am not advocating rudeness or snarling, but the attorney must be willing to buck the paternalism and the "we know what is best" attitude of the juvenile court. Perhaps most importantly, the lawyer must be a creative thinker who will delve beyond the surface issues of guilt and innocence.

Take for example, the case of a young man who had been placed at the California Youth Authority (CYA), a state youth prison. He took advantage of schooling, counseling and work opportunities in his placement. He was released on parole, enrolled in high school to get his diploma, obtained a part-time job, developed a relationship with a very nice young woman, and lived at home, helping his mother and providing emotional support for his younger brother. He had also secured a guarantee of employment upon his graduation from high school. Shortly before graduation he was arrested because of an incident that had occurred prior to his CYA placement. He admitted that he was in the fight and had knifed the other boy. His main concerns, however, were missing his graduation, losing his part-time job, possibly losing his future employment, and destroying his image as a role model for his younger brother. Because the attorney took the time to talk to him and elicit his concerns, she was able to persuade his teachers, principal, employer, and parole officer to all testify on his behalf. In addition, she was able to get his employer to hold his job and his future employment placement, all in time for him to attend his high school graduation. He was the first member of his family to graduate from high school. The judge recognized what this meant to the family and particularly to his younger sibling. What is important to note is that money is not what made the difference. There was no need to call in outside experts. All that was necessary was that the lawyer listened to her client and used all her professional skills to assure that her client did not go back to CYA.

Another example involves a youth charged with burglary. He also failed to attend school regularly, which ordinarily leads to a harsher disposition for a child. To provide proper representation, the lawyer must not only try to get the child acquitted, but if that fails, to get the best possible disposition. That in turn requires the lawyer to find out why the child is a truant. Merely asking the child if it is true that she does not go to school regularly will not ferret out the whole problem. Does the mother use the child as a translator to deal with welfare officials? Does the child have health problems, physical or mental, that result in irregular attendance? Is the child a victim of school phobia or is she being bullied beyond endurance? Does the child suffer from any form of learning disabilities? Is one of the teachers picking on her and exposing her to ridicule? Is the teacher making sexual advances? Does the child not have enough clean clothes to wear to school? Does the minor have a part-time job that keeps her up late, causing her to oversleep, waking too late to go to school?

Or suppose the juvenile runs away from home. Why? Many court personnel see this behavior on the part of girls as accompanying sexual acting out. Studies show, however, that a large percentage of girls who leave home are being sexually abused.[387] This information is the most difficult to elicit. The parents will hide it and so will the girl who often feels shame or is afraid she will not be believed.

The need to dig below the surface is necessary even in cases that seem straightforward. Suppose a teenager is charged with committing arson of the family home and readily admits it. The lawyer who accepts that and pleads her guilty, condemns the girl to a locked state facility, because private treatment centers, for insurance and liability reasons, usually do

---

387. A.B.A. & Nat'l Bar Ass'n, Justice by Gender: The Lack of Appropriate Prevention, Diversion and Treatment Alternatives for Girls in the Justice System 10 (2001). Fifty-nine percent of all arrests for runaways in 1999 were girls. Id. at 17–18. Delinquent girls usually have several things in common: a history of sexual abuse, fragmented families from death and divorce, serious physical and mental problems, drug-abuse problems, and home lives affected by lack of consistency and conflict. Id. at 6–8.

not take arsonists. What the lawyer may not know is that the girl was systematically sexually abused by the father for years with the complicity of the mother. The girl simply saw no other way out.

One final example is the last case I tried as a public defender. My client was a sixteen-year-old charged with assault who had previously been adjudicated a delinquent. The victim was lying on the ground, bleeding, and surrounded by several people, including my client. When the police officer arrived at the scene, he observed blood on my client's pants. He told me that he had been in the park and his dog had fought another dog, and that is how the blood got on his pants. I requested that the prosecutor do a DNA test. For unknown reasons, he refused. I had promised my client, who was being detained, that I would try his case before I left. I subpoenaed twenty witnesses who had observed the dog fight. On the trial date, the prosecutor took one look at the twenty witnesses, and requested a continuance to do the DNA test. I opposed that request because my client was locked up, the district attorney had had time to do the test, and it was my last week of work. The judge dismissed the case with prejudice.

The type of representation I am describing is necessarily time-consuming. The problem for the lawyer is caseload and money, which are intimately related. The lawyers in solo practice face difficult choices—their ethical responsibility for representing their clients in a competent manner, and the need to pay their rent and provide for their families. This is very hard. If the lawyer takes fewer cases, allowing him or her to spend more time with each client, but not providing enough financial gain to pay the bills, he or she will not be able to stay in the practice. As a result, the child-client may not have any source for legal representation. Political clout to increase the fees paid to appointed attorneys in juvenile court becomes a necessity.

. . .

I have no easy answer to the problem of low fees and large caseloads. To avoid the money issue I worked for the public defenders office. But, it did not, and typically does not, solve the caseload problem. The organization itself, and the lawyers, must put a cap on the number of cases each attorney can take. They must make clear that they are not going to provide ineffective assistance of counsel, and money must be made available to hire additional attorneys. The private attorney must do the same.

One might argue that the funds for increased quality representation should instead be used to improve the actual programs and facilities for children in juvenile court. I might agree with that view if I believed the states would put sufficient resources into these programs and facilities. But even if the states should do that, money for high-quality representation is still necessary to assure that children, whether guilty or innocent, receive due process of law, and that only those children who need treatment receive it.

CONCLUSION

I wrote this Article in the hope of inspiring dialogues and discussions about how to increase the quality of legal representation in juvenile court delinquency proceedings. Some will view my beliefs as naive, idealistic, and unnecessary. My own experience, and that of many colleagues across the country, tells me otherwise. I do agree, however, that my views on the attorney-client relationship are somewhat radical. I have great trust in children and their abilities to solve problems if they are given the necessary tools and information to do so. Treating children as objects to whom things are done, infantilizes them and makes effective treatment less likely to succeed. Dealing with children as persons who have a large stake in the proceedings and whose input is respected is the most likely means of keeping children out of trouble. Thus, when I represent children as respected individuals, I am not just providing effective assistance of counsel, I am also, in some way, helping those children develop the necessary skills and sense of self that will enable them to survive and indeed, to prevail.

NOTES

(1) The role of counsel may vary depending on the setting or type of proceeding in which counsel is undertaking to represent a child. For further discussion of the role of counsel in settings other than delinquency or status offense cases, see Martin Guggenheim, The Right To Be Represented But Not Heard: Reflections on Legal Representation for Children, 59 N.Y.U.L.Rev. 76 (1984) (general); Charles L. Hobson, Appointed Counsel to Protect the Child Victim's Rights, 21 Pacific L.J. 691 (1990) (child abuse proceedings); Stephen Wizner & Miriam Berkman, Being a Lawyer for a Child Too Young to be a Client: A Clinical Study, 68 Neb.L.Rev. 330 (1989) (divorce proceedings); Kim J. Landsman & Martha L. Minow, Note, Lawyering for the Child: Principles of Representation in Custody and Visitation Disputes Arising from Divorce, 87 Yale L.J. 1126 (1978).

Guggenheim, in particular, is concerned about the role of the attorney in representing a very young child, too young to direct his or her attorney. In the article cited above he explores different roles—the "champion" and the "investigator"—in different types of proceedings and concludes that judges, legislators, and practitioners might wish to reconsider the need for appointed counsel in every case in which the client is too young to express his or her wishes in the litigation. He concludes that in divorce-custody cases, for example, there is no need for independent counsel for the child—either as champion or investigator. Guggenheim, supra, at 125–26.

More recently, confessing an oversight in his earlier piece, Guggenheim proposed a "paradigm" for determining the role of counsel in representing very young children, a paradigm that has less to do with the process of lawyering than it does with the substantive rights of the child in the particular kind of litigation:

> A common error commentators make in divining the purpose of counsel is unduly concentrating on the rule that lawyers for adults must allow their clients to set the objectives of representation. Although this rule is certainly important, what is even more important is its underlying policy.... [T]he reason an adult's lawyer must let the adult set the objectives has little to do with an inherent aspect of lawyering. Instead, it has everything to do with the legal rights and powers adults possess.

> A lawyer's first role is to enforce and advance her clients' legal rights. Everything else is secondary to this. When clients such as unimpaired adults or pregnant minors have autonomy rights to control their own destiny, lawyers are obligated to let them set the objectives of the case. Moreover, in such circumstances, lawyers are not only permitted, but required, to forcefully

advocate for the results chosen by their clients. In dramatic contrast, however, when clients do not have autonomy rights (such as young children in most, but not all situations), lawyers should not allow their clients to set the objectives.

For these reasons, when determining the role of counsel for children it is essential to engage in a careful study of the legal rights and powers children enjoy in the particular subject matter implicated by the proceeding. The role of counsel for young children necessarily will vary across a variety of legal matters. This is because the role of counsel is not developed in a vacuum. What a lawyer for a young child must or may do will depend directly on the rights of the young child in the particular matter involved. Because lawyers, above all else, are the enforcers of their client's rights, the principal task when determining counsel's role for young children is to examine the relevant legislation and case law in the particular subject area. Once those rights have been identified, the only remaining inquiry is to determine the most effective way to enforce them.

Martin Guggenheim, A Paradigm for Determining the Role of Counsel for Children, 64 Fordham L.Rev. 1399, 1420–21 (1996).*

(2) The moral and ethical dilemmas encountered when an attorney represents a child have been explored by many commentators. The March 1996 issue of Fordham Law Review is devoted specially to the topic Ethical Issues in the Legal Representation of Children. Other commentary includes: Guggenheim, supra; Samuel M. Davis, The Role of the Attorney in Child Advocacy, 32 J.Fam.L. 817 (1994); Bruce C. Hafen, Children's Rights and Legal Representation: The Proper Roles of Children, Parents, and Attorneys, 7 Notre Dame J.L.Ethics & Pub. Pol'y 423 (1993); Howard A. Davidson, The Child's Right to Be Heard and Represented in Judicial Proceedings, 18 Pepp.L.Rev. 255 (1991); Jan C. Costello, Ethical Issues in Representing Juvenile Clients: A Review of the IJA–ABA Standards on Representing Private Parties, 10 N.M.L.Rev. 255 (1980).

In representing children, particularly those charged with criminal misconduct, attorneys need to develop expertise in the area of child development, e.g., the ability to detect an incompetence issue and the ability to identify and access sources of help within the community such as school records, health records and the like. Some of the ethical dilemmas that arise in representing adults in criminal court are even more complex when representing children. An attorney also may need to educate and inform the court about child development and its application in the case at hand. For an excellent analysis and discussion of these and other issues, see Lynda E. Frost & Adrienne E. Volenik, The Ethical Perils of Representing the Juvenile Defendant Who May Be Incompetent, 14 Wash.U.J.L. & Pol'y 327 (2004). For analysis of ethical and professional issues in a particular jurisdiction, which has broader application, see Donna Sheen, Professional Responsibilities Toward Children in Trouble with the Law, 5 Wyo.L.Rev. 483 (2005).

(3) Costello, supra Note (2), discusses the lawyer's role during the disposition hearing and makes the point that a lawyer's role during the dispositional stage is as critical or perhaps more critical to effective representation than the role played during the adjudicatory stage. Consider *State ex rel. D.D.H. v. Dostert*, which follows.

(4) The subject of adolescent competence generally was examined toward the end of Chapter III. Recalling the cases and materials from Chapter III and considering the treatment of this issue above, how might immature understanding and judgment affect the youthful defendant's ability to assist counsel? Consider also

the excerpt from an article by Thomas Grisso et al., Juveniles' Competence to Stand Trial: A Comparison of Adolescents' and Adults' Capacities as Trial Defendants, 27 Law & Hum.Behav. 333 (2003), in Chapter X at p. 1175 infra.

The subject of competency can arise in other contexts as well, e.g., in determining the validity of a waiver of *Miranda* rights or whether a confession was knowingly given. This issue is covered in Chapter X at pp. 1133–36. Competency also is an issue in determining whether a juvenile is incompetent to stand trial, whether a juvenile should be able to claim insanity as a defense and in some cases whether a juvenile should be able to claim an infancy defense. These issues also are covered in Chapter X at pp. 1167–80.

State ex rel. D. D. H. v. Dostert

Supreme Court of Appeals of West Virginia, 1980.
165 W.Va. 448, 269 S.E.2d 401.

■ NEELY, CHIEF JUSTICE:

In this case we shall endeavor, with some apprehension, to clarify the proper procedures at the dispositional stage of a juvenile proceeding. . . .

. . .

I

At the outset it is important to recognize that the juvenile law in West Virginia has been in substantial turmoil since this court's decision in State ex rel. Harris v. Calendine, W.Va., 233 S.E.2d 318 (1977) which, among other things, prompted an entire revision of the statutory juvenile law. Historically, protecting society from juvenile delinquency and helping juvenile offenders modify their behavior have been seen as complementary goals of the juvenile law; however, it is now generally recognized that caring for the juvenile and controlling the juvenile are often quite contradictory processes. Much of our juvenile law at the moment is predicated upon a healthy skepticism about the capacity of the State and its agents to help children when they are incarcerated in one of the juvenile detention facilities. Thus, the control of juveniles and the treatment of juveniles (if the expression can be used without conjuring Kafkaesque images) are frequently irreconcilable goals. Furthermore, children can be dangerous, destructive, abusive, and otherwise thoroughly anti-social, which prompts an entirely understandable expectation in society of protection, even if we have matured beyond expecting retribution.

The dispositional stage of a juvenile proceeding is designed to do something which is almost impossible, namely, to reconcile: (1) society's interest in being protected from dangerous and disruptive children; (2) society's interest in nurturing its children in such a way that they will be productive and successful adults; (3) society's interest in providing a deterrent to other children who, but for the specter of the juvenile law, would themselves become disruptive and unamenable to adult control; (4) the citizen's demand that children be responsible for invasion of personal rights; and, (5) the setting of an example of care, love, and forgiveness by the engines of the state in the hope that such qualities will be emulated by the subject children.[8] While retribution is considered an unhealthy instinct and, conceivably, an immoral instinct in an enlightened society, nonetheless, State imposed retribution has historically been the *quid pro quo* of the State's monopoly of force and its proscription of individual retribution. Retribution is merely another way of saying that children are to be treated as responsible moral agents.

II

It is possible to make the dispositional stage of a juvenile proceeding so burdensome in requiring exhaustive examination of all "less restrictive alternatives," no matter how speculative, that we, in effect, direct lower courts to abandon all hope of confining a child.[9] That is not the clear purport, however, of W.Va. Code, 49–5–13(b) [1978] which says:

> In disposition the court shall not be limited to the relief sought in the petition and shall give precedence to the least restrictive of the

---

8. Many states have been wrestling with some statutory reconciliation of these competing goals. In this regard it is interesting to compare the 1977 amendment to W.Va. Code, 49–1–1(a), the purpose clause for the child welfare chapter, with the 1978 amendment to the same section. The difference is subtle, but it demonstrates a recognition that child welfare cannot be completely "child centered." W.Va. Code, 49–1–1(a) [1977] says:

> The purpose of this chapter is to provide a comprehensive system of child welfare throughout the State which will assure to each child such care and guidance, preferably in his own home, as will serve the spiritual, emotional, mental and physical welfare of the child; preserve and strengthen the child's family ties whenever possible with recognition to the fundamental rights of parenthood and with recognition of the state's responsibility to assist the family in providing the necessary education and training and protect the welfare of the general public. In pursuit of these goals it is the intention of the legislature to provide for removing the child from the custody of parents only when the child's welfare or the safety and protection of the public cannot be adequately safeguarded without removal; and, when the child has to be removed from his own family, to secure for him custody, care and discipline as nearly as possible equivalent to that which should have been given by his parents, consistent with the child's best interests.

W.Va. Code, 49–1–1(a) [1978] says:

The purpose of this chapter is to provide a comprehensive system of child welfare throughout the State which will assure to each child such care and guidance, preferably in his own home, as will serve the spiritual, emotional, mental and physical welfare of the child; preserve and strengthen the child's family ties whenever possible with recognition to the fundamental rights of parenthood and with recognition of the state's responsibility to assist the family in providing the necessary education and training *and to reduce the rate of juvenile delinquency and to provide a system for the rehabilitation or detention of juvenile delinquents and protect the welfare of the general public.* In pursuit of these goals it is the intention of the legislature to provide for removing the child from the custody of parents only when the child's welfare or the safety and protection of the public cannot be adequately safeguarded without removal; and, when the child has to be removed from his own family, to secure for him custody, care and discipline *consistent with the child's best interests and other goals herein set out.* [Emphasis supplied by the Court]

9. Our Court has recently examined the procedures that must be followed before a juvenile may be properly committed to a juvenile correctional facility in State ex rel. S.J.C. v. Fox, W.Va., 268 S.E.2d 56 (1980). We followed the same procedure established in State ex rel. E.D. v. Aldredge, W.Va., 245 S.E.2d 849 (1978) which required that the court set forth a finding on the record that no less restrictive alternative was available before a transfer to criminal jurisdiction could be effected. . . .

following alternatives *consistent with the best interests and welfare of the public and the child* . . . .

[Emphasis supplied by the Court.]

W.Va. Code 49–5–13(b)(5) [1978] says:

> Upon a finding that no less restrictive alternative would accomplish the requisite rehabilitation of the child, and upon an adjudication of delinquency pursuant to subdivision (1), section four [§ 49–1–4], article one of this chapter, commit the child to an industrial home or correctional institution for children. Commitments shall not exceed the maximum term for which an adult could have been sentenced for the same offense, with discretion as to discharge to rest with the director of the institution, who may release the child and return him to the court for further disposition; . . . .

As David Dudley Field, author of the *Field Code*, once pointed out, substantive law can be "gradually secreted in the interstices of procedure." Consequently, it is important to explain exactly what the elaborate procedure at the dispositional stage is designed to do. Unless there are clear, understandable standards, procedure becomes confounding at best and disguised legislation at worst.

Chapter 49 of the W.Va. Code covering child welfare is clearly committed to the rehabilitative model. As we noted in State ex rel. Harris v. Calendine, W.Va., 233 S.E.2d 318, 325 (1977),

> The Legislature could choose to punish children guilty of criminal conduct in the same manner as it punishes adults, but as a matter of public policy the Legislature provided instead for a comprehensive system of child welfare. The aim of this system is to protect and rehabilitate children, not to punish them.

The rehabilitative model requires a great deal of information about the child at the dispositional hearing. Much of that information must necessarily focus on the critical issue of whether it is *possible* for the State or other social service agencies to help the child. Although helping the child is the first concern of the juvenile law, it is not the only concern, since at the *operational* rather than *theoretical* level, the rehabilitative approach has dramatic limitations, preeminent among which is that it interferes both with the deterrence of other children and the protection of society. While *Code,* 49–5–13(b) explicitly recognizes this problem, we have not yet refined an approach which intelligently uses procedure to arrive at sufficient information to permit a balancing of the child's liberty interest with society's need for protection and deterrence.

. . .

IV

At the dispositional stage of the juvenile proceeding there are a number of actors whose roles have been established by statute. The first major actor is obviously the judge who, according to W.Va. Code, 49–5–13(a) [1978], is entitled to request the juvenile probation officer or State department worker to make an investigation of the environment of the child and the alternative dispositions possible. The second actor is the probation officer or State department worker who must fulfill this obligation, and the third actor is the counsel for the petitioner who is entitled to review any report made by the probation officer or welfare worker seventy-two hours before the dispositional hearing. In addition there is the child and his parents, guardian, or adult relatives, and the representatives of any social service agencies, including the schools, which have been involved in the case. Since the threshold question at any dispositional hearing is whether the child is delinquent because of his own free will or for environmental reasons which society can attack directly, all of the actors in the dispositional drama should concentrate their attention initially on that one subject. Obviously this is a question which the trial judge has always answered in his own mind. However, the thrust of the formal procedural model which has been evolving is that this question be developed on the record and reasons for determining a particular disposition be articulated for appellate review. We shall now focus on the role of each major actor.

THE ROLE OF COURT APPOINTED COUNSEL:

The dispositional stage of any juvenile proceeding may be the most important stage in the entire process; therefore, it is the obligation of any court appointed or retained counsel to continue active and vigorous representation of the child through that stage. We have already held that counsel has a duty to investigate all resources available to find the least restrictive alternative, State ex rel. C.A.H. v. Strickler, W.Va., 251 S.E.2d 222 (1979), and here we confirm that holding. Court appointed counsel must make an independent investigation of the child's background. Counsel should present to the court any facts which could lead the court to conclude that the child's environment is a major contributing factor to his misbehavior. In this regard counsel should investigate the child's performance in school, his family background, the level of concern and leadership on the part of his parents, the physical conditions under which the child is living, and any health problems. Counsel must also inform himself in detail about the facilities both inside and outside the State of West Virginia which are able to help children.[13]

Armed with adequate information, counsel can then present the court with all reasonable alternative dispositions to incarceration and should have taken the initial steps to secure the tentative acceptance of the child into those facilities. It is not sufficient to suggest upon the record as an abstract proposition that there are alternatives; it is the affirmative obligation of counsel to advise the court of the exact terms, conditions, and

---

13. The Department of Welfare must prepare a descriptive catalogue of its juvenile programs and services at least once a year and those catalogues are to be readily available under W.Va. Code, 49–5B–7 [1979]. Furthermore, the West Virginia Child Care Association (WVC CA) publishes a Residential Child Care Directory which describes available services. In addition, the WVCCA maintains a Resource Center with a statewide telephone information service designed to assist social workers, agencies, lawyers and others in placing young people in the most appropriate group home or group child care agency. Their office is open Monday–Friday, 8:30 a.m.–5:00 p.m. and their telephone number is (304) 335–6211.

costs of such alternatives, whether the Department of Welfare or any other source can pay for such alternative, and under what conditions any alternative facilities would be willing to accept the child.

The faithful discharge of these duties requires substantial industry; however, appointed counsel is entitled to be compensated for his time up to the statutory limit set for the criminal charges fund. Furthermore, energetic advocacy implies that the court must accommodate an adversarial proceeding at the disposition stage. In the case at bar, the court reacted to the legitimate efforts of the appointed attorney to arrange an alternative disposition by finding him in contempt and removing him from his appointment. Such practices are obviously condemned since it is envisaged that the child shall have an advocate who will make a record.[14]

The court undermined the efforts of counsel from the outset of the trial: counsel was given approximately thirty minutes to prepare before the first detention hearing, after which petitioner was placed in the Jefferson County Jail; after counsel obtained release of petitioner she was again placed in the Jefferson County Jail for failing to attend school and counsel received no notice of the second detention hearing; after counsel obtained release of petitioner she was arrested and taken before the court who placed her in the Morgan County Jail again without notice or presence of the child's counsel and with no record save the summary order; after petitioner was adjudicated delinquent, counsel represented the willingness of the Odyssey House in Morgantown to take petitioner for a trial period but the court refused all less restrictive alternatives; and, after placement in the Industrial Home for Girls counsel continued actively to pursue probation for petitioner to which the court reacted by withdrawing the appointment of counsel and requiring his appearance at a contempt hearing. This conduct is so unjustifiable that the State chose not even to address the validity of the contempt citation in its brief. . . .

THE ROLE OF THE PROBATION OFFICER OR WELFARE WORKER:

The probation officer or welfare worker when requested by the judge is also responsible for discovering whether there are forces which are at work upon the child which either the Department of Welfare or other social service agencies can correct. In the case before us it is obvious that the petitioner had no adult supervision whatsoever and that she was left to fend for herself in the back streets. Obviously, before incarcerating a first offender like the petitioner it would have been incumbent upon the Department of Welfare to find a suitable environment for her. The record amply demonstrates from the history of the petitioner *after* this Court released her from the industrial school, that the petitioner is a somewhat unmanageable and ungovernable child who, at the time, would not remain in a juvenile refuge.[15] Nonetheless, absent at least one predisposition

14. For a cogent analysis of the defense counsel's role in dispositions, *see* IJA/ABA Juvenile Justice Standards Project, Standards Relating to Juvenile Counsel for Private Parties, pp. 168–87 (1977).

15. Petitioner was placed in the Odyssey House, a group home, after her petition for a writ of habeas corpus was granted by this Court and she ran away from that placement. Evidence that is before our Court, but which was not before the circuit court, indi-

incidence of flight from a reasonable alternative, it was quite improper for the court to place her in the first instance in the industrial school. Upon remand the court must focus on her level of cooperation at the time she is again considered for disposition at the remand.

The record before us also demonstrates that the Department of Welfare did not intervene with this child upon her initial arrest, although any inquiry into her background would have disclosed at the detention hearing that she was in need of help. The appropriate time for the Department of Welfare or the juvenile probation officer to intervene is at the first sign of trouble.

THE ROLE OF THE COURT:

It is the obligation of the court to hear all witnesses who might shed light upon the proper disposition of a child and before incarcerating a child, to find facts *upon the record* which would lead a reasonable appellate court to conclude in the words of the statute, either that "no less restrictive alternative would accomplish the requisite rehabilitation of the child ..." or "the welfare of the public" requires incarceration. Where the court directs incarceration, he should affirmatively find upon the record either that the child's behavioral problem is not the result of social conditions beyond the child's control, but rather of an intentional failure on the part of the child to conform his actions to the law, or that the child will be dangerous if any other disposition is used, or that the child will not cooperate with any rehabilitative program absent physical restraint. Where the court concludes that simple punishment will be a more effective rehabilitative device than anything else, the conclusion is certainly legitimate and within the discretion of the trial court; nonetheless, the trial court must elaborate on the record his reasons for that conclusion.

If the proceeding is merely the last in a long series involving the same child, the court should set forth any "less restrictive alternatives" which have already been tried and the actions of the child after those alternatives were implemented. Even when the child's behavior results from environmental factors, the court may find the child to pose an imminent danger to society because he will flee from all but secure facilities and, therefore, conclude that incarceration is the only *reasonable* alternative.

The court has a duty to insure that the child's social history is reviewed intelligently so that an individualized treatment plan may be designed when appropriate. This information also insures that the disposition decision is not made simply by reference to the very misbehavior which is the ground for the juvenile proceeding. The effectiveness of treatment is disputed to say the least, and this is particularly true whenever commitment to an institution is involved. Therefore, the judge making the dispositional determination should not place a child who is not dangerous and who can be accommodated elsewhere in an institution under the guise of "treating" the child.

cates that petitioner was apprehended in a stolen car on at least two other occasions after her initial disposition.

While in the hearing before this Court it appeared that progress has been made in providing basic education and counseling in the State's industrial schools, the fact that these schools have improved does not make them the proper place for "rehabilitation" unless it appears that the child is either dangerous or must be restrained in a secure facility in order to prevent his flight.

.   .   .

When . . . , there is a consistent pattern of noncooperation which makes alternative rehabilitative programs impossible, the court should set forth the facts upon the record so that this Court will understand why the trial court concludes that there are no alternatives to placement in an institution.[19]

.   .   .

NOTE

As the principal case points out, the attorney is but one of the players in a juvenile court proceeding. For a look at roles played by various others, see Kristin Henning, It Takes a Lawyer to Raise a Child?: Allocating Responsibilities Among Parents, Children, and Lawyers in Delinquency Cases, 6 Nev.L.Rev. 836 (2006). For further comment on the role played by the child's attorney, see Kristen Henning, Loyalty, Paternalism, and Rights: Client Counseling Theory and the Role of Child's Counsel in Delinquency Cases, 81 Notre Dame L.Rev. 285 (2005). Consider the role of counsel in representing a juvenile as you read the problem that follows. Also consider why it is so important for an attorney representing juveniles to be knowledgeable about child development as well as community resources in order to represent a child effectively. See Lynda E. Frost & Adrienne E. Volenik, The Ethical Perils of Representing the Juvenile Defendant Who May Be Incompetent, 14 Wash.U.J.L. & Pol'y 327 (2004).

19. Some states have been more specific in rewriting their purpose clauses to reflect the legislative determination that rehabilitation alone does not exhaust the purposes of the juvenile justice system. For example, California added the [italicized] sections to its purpose clauses:

(a) The purpose of this chapter is to secure for each minor under the jurisdiction of the juvenile court such care and guidance, preferably in his own home, as will serve the spiritual, emotional, mental, and physical welfare of the minor and the best interests of the state; *to protect the public from criminal conduct by minors; to impose on the minor a sense of responsibility for his own acts*; to preserve and strengthen the minor's family ties whenever possible, removing him from the custody of his parents only when necessary for his welfare or for the safety and protection of the public . . . and, when the minor is removed from his own family, to secure for him custody, care, and discipline as nearly as possible equivalent to that which should have been given by his parents. This chapter shall be liberally construed to carry out these purposes.

(b) *The purpose of this chapter also includes the protection of the public from the consequences of criminal activity, and to such purpose probation officers, peace officers, and juvenile courts shall take into account such protection of the public in their determinations under this chapter. Cal.* [Welf. & Inst.] *Code,* § 202 [1977]. (Emphasis added.)

In Virginia the old purpose clause focused solely on the welfare of the child, Va. Code § 16.1–140 [1956], while the revised statute includes the purpose of "protect[ing] the community against those acts of its citizens which are harmful to others and . . . reduc[ing] the incidence of delinquent behavior." Va.Code § 16.1–227 [1977].

PROBLEM

Susie Quinlan, a 16–year-old minor, admitted the allegations of a petition filed under the Juvenile Court Code, section 15–11–5, charging her with violation of Criminal Code section 16–8–5 (obtaining telephone services by fraud).

The acts forming the basis of the present petition occurred during a four-month period while Susie was residing part-time at the Florence Crittenton home. The Crittenton home is a half-way house for troubled youth, and Susie's attendance there was pursuant to an agreement entered into by Susie and the juvenile court as a means of informally resolving an earlier petition against Susie alleging that she was an unruly child. While at the Crittenton home Susie placed unauthorized long distance telephone calls to her boyfriend (44 times), her mother (11 times), her aunt (4 times), her probation officer (1 time), and friends (51 times), totaling $338.53 in charges. She admitted that she made the calls "on whims" almost every day despite frequent warnings not to and even after her telephone privileges had been suspended. At the insistence of her social worker, Susie paid $50 of the money she earned while at Crittenton to the telephone company.

At the end of four months, Susie went home and refused to return to Crittenton. She remained home, living with her mother and five younger siblings, and so far as appears on the record she has not been involved in any delinquent behavior.

Susie's mother and father are divorced. Her mother is ill and receives public assistance. The family receives no support from Susie's father, whose whereabouts are unknown. Susie does not have a part-time job after school. Her mother feels that Susie is needed at home to help care for the younger siblings and to help run the household. The home is a three-bedroom rented house in a lower socio-economic area of town.

Susie does not get along with her mother. She defies her mother by staying out late at night, sometimes all night. The strain in the mother-daughter relationship has been exacerbated by Susie's new-found relationship with her 18–year-old boyfriend. Most of her time is spent with the boyfriend, whom the mother does not like.

To make matters worse, Susie has been missing a lot of school. During her stay at Crittenton she showed marked improvement in her school performance, but since returning home and particularly since her difficulties with her mother and the newly created relationship with her boyfriend, she has missed school frequently, fallen behind in her school work, and suffered a rather serious drop in her grades.

Susie resents having to run the household and act as mother to her younger siblings. She would like to have a part-time job and be able to earn her own spending money. Without a job, of course, she has no income from which to repay the telephone company for the unauthorized calls.

The available dispositions under the Code are:

1. Commitment to the Youth Authority, which involves an indeterminate commitment to a juvenile institution for up to two years;

2. Payment of a fine, up to $1,000;

3. Payment of restitution, in an amount the juvenile can afford;

4. Performance of public service, such as cleaning up parks, removing graffiti from public buildings, and the like; and

5. Probation, on such terms and under such conditions as the court reasonably may impose.

The problem is based in part on the facts in *In re Carrie W.*, 89 Cal.App.3d 642, 152 Cal.Rptr. 690 (1979). As Susie's attorney, what role would you play in fashioning an appropriate disposition in her case, and what do you think that disposition should be?

CHAPTER X

DELINQUENCY: DIFFERENTIAL TREATMENT OF JUVENILE AND ADULT OFFENDERS

RESHAPING JUVENILE JUSTICE IN THE POST-*GAULT* WORLD

The effect of the Supreme Court's decision in *In re Gault*, supra page * * *, was almost as profound as the advent of the juvenile court itself. Courts and legislatures alike were occupied for years following *Gault* in an attempt to address the many constitutional issues raised by the decision. In general, the analytical framework was usually the same: To what extent did due process of law mandate that the same safeguards available to adults in the criminal process apply equally to children in the juvenile process? This framework was explored, in different contexts (e.g., standard of proof, right to jury trial, and protection against double jeopardy), in the previous chapter.

In grasping for a rationale for denying juveniles the right to jury trial in *McKeiver v. Pennsylvania*, Justice Blackmun observed, perhaps prophetically: "If the formalities of the criminal adjudicative process are to be superimposed upon the juvenile justice system, there is little need for its separate existence. Perhaps that ultimate disillusionment will come one day, but for the moment we are disinclined to give impetus to it." 403 U.S. at 551. Today the juvenile court in many regards is quite similar to an ordinary criminal court. The time has come to shift the focus from analysis of all aspects of the juvenile justice process, most of which are identical to their criminal counterparts with few exceptions, to analysis of areas in which the two processes are different.

Gault, after all, was decided over 40 years ago. We are no longer in the immediate post-*Gault* period in which each element of the juvenile process has to be examined in light of its implications. We are well into the post-*Gault* era, a period defined by the constitutionalization of the juvenile process and assimilation of most, but not all, of the criminal safeguards into the juvenile process.

This chapter, therefore, dwells on the differences between the criminal and juvenile justice systems. To be sure, the differences are significant in kind and in number, from allocation of jurisdiction between courts (how cases end up in one court or the other) to disposition (what is done with juveniles following adjudication).

A. ALLOCATION OF JURISDICTION BETWEEN COURTS

In the early stages decisions are made that affect the process by which a case will be handled as well as the outcome of the case. These decisions determine whether a person within the age range of the juvenile court's jurisdiction will be tried as a juvenile in juvenile court and subjected to juvenile court dispositions, or will be tried as an adult in criminal court, with adult sanctions.

There are several statutory models by which jurisdiction is allocated between juvenile and criminal courts. One is to exclude certain offenses from the jurisdiction of the juvenile court, or legislative allocation. (See, e.g., the Illinois statute below.) Another is to leave the decision to the discretion of the prosecutor, as in the Arkansas statute at p. 956 infra. Still another method is to provide for concurrent jurisdiction between the juvenile and criminal courts over certain offenses or classes of offenses. (See, e.g., the Georgia statute at p. 961 infra.) The most common method is to leave the decision to the discretion of the juvenile court judge, as illustrated by the California statute, p. 964 infra. Finally, some or all transfer decisions may be made by the criminal court judge in what is known as reverse certification, exemplified by the Pennsylvania statute, p. 990 infra. Some states use a combination of these methods. The following statutes, cases, and other materials illustrate how the various alternatives function.

1. LEGISLATIVE ALLOCATION OF JURISDICTION

ILLINOIS COMPILED STATUTES ANNOTATED, CHAPTER 705 (Smith–Hurd)

§ 405/5–130. Criminal Prosecutions Limited

(1)(a) The definition of delinquent minor under Section 5–120 of this Article shall not apply to any minor who at the time of an offense was at least 15 years of age and who is charged with (i) first degree murder, (ii) aggravated criminal sexual assault, (iii) aggravated battery with a firearm where the minor personally discharged a firearm as defined in Section 2–15.5 of the Criminal Code of 1961, (iv) armed robbery when the armed robbery was committed with a firearm, or (v) aggravated vehicular hijacking when the hijacking was committed with a firearm.

These charges and all other charges arising out of the same incident shall be prosecuted under the criminal laws of this State.

(b)(i) If before trial or plea an information or indictment is filed that does not charge an offense specified in paragraph (a) of this subsection (1), the State's Attorney may proceed on any lesser charge or charges, but only in Juvenile Court under the provisions of this Article. The State's Attorney may proceed under the Criminal Code of 1961 on a lesser charge if before trial the minor defendant knowingly and with advice of counsel waives, in writing, his or her right to have the matter proceed in Juvenile Court.

(ii) If before trial or plea an information or indictment is filed that includes one or more charges specified in paragraph (a) of this subsection (1) and additional charges that are not specified in that paragraph, all of the charges arising out of the same incident shall be prosecuted under the Criminal Code of 1961.

(c)(i) If after trial or plea the minor is convicted of any offense covered by paragraph (a) of this subsection (1), then, in sentencing the minor, the court shall have available any or all dispositions prescribed for that offense under Chapter V of the Unified Code of Corrections.

(ii) If after trial or plea the court finds that the minor committed an offense not covered by paragraph (a) of this subsection (1), that finding shall not invalidate the verdict or the prosecution of the minor under the criminal laws of the State; however, unless the State requests a hearing for the purpose of sentencing the minor under Chapter V of the Unified Code of Corrections, the court must proceed under Sections 5–705 and 5–710 of this Article.* To request a hearing, the State must file a written motion within 10 days following the entry of a finding or the return of a verdict. Reasonable notice of the motion shall be given to the minor or his or her counsel. If the motion is made by the State, the court shall conduct a hearing to determine if the minor should be sentenced under Chapter V of the Unified Code of Corrections. In making its determination, the court shall consider among other matters: (a) whether there is evidence that the offense was committed in an aggressive and premeditated manner; (b) the age of the minor; (c) the previous history of the minor; (d) whether there are facilities particularly available to the Juvenile Court or the Department of Juvenile Justice for the treatment and rehabilitation of the minor; (e) whether the security of the public requires sentencing under Chapter V of the Unified Code of Corrections; and (f) whether the minor possessed a deadly weapon when committing the offense. The rules of evidence shall be the same as if at trial. If after the hearing the court finds that the minor should be sentenced under Chapter V of the Unified Code of Corrections, then the court shall sentence the minor accordingly having available to it any or all dispositions so prescribed.

. . .

(3)(a) The definition of delinquent minor under Section 5–120 of this Article shall not apply to any minor who at the time of the offense was at least 15 years of age and who is charged with a violation of the provisions of paragraph (1), (3), (4), or (10) of subsection (a) of Section 24–1 of the Criminal Code of 1961** while in school, regardless of the time of day or the time of year, or on the real property comprising any school, regardless of the time of day or the time of year. School is defined, for purposes of this Section as any public or private elementary or secondary school, community college, college, or university. These charges and all other charges arising

---

* Sections 5–705 and 5–710 provide for available dispositions in delinquency cases. The effect of this limitation is that, if a juvenile pleads guilty to or is convicted of a lesser offense in criminal court, the criminal court retains jurisdiction to determine whether the juvenile should be sentenced as a juvenile or as an adult.

** These sections describe various weapons offenses.

out of the same incident shall be prosecuted under the criminal laws of this State.

[The remainder of this subsection (3) is virtually identical to the provisions set forth in subsection (1)(b)–(c).]

(4)(a) The definition of delinquent minor under Section 5–120 of this Article shall not apply to any minor who at the time of an offense was at least 13 years of age and who is charged with first degree murder committed during the course of either aggravated criminal sexual assault, criminal sexual assault, or aggravated kidnaping. However, this subsection (4) does not include a minor charged with first degree murder based exclusively upon the accountability provisions of the Criminal Code of 1961.

[The remainder of this subsection (4) is virtually identical to the provisions set forth in subsection (1)(b)–(c).]

(5)(a) The definition of delinquent minor under Section 5–120 of this Article shall not apply to any minor who is charged with a violation of subsection (a) of Section 31–6* or Section 32–10** of the Criminal Code of 1961 when the minor is subject to prosecution under the criminal laws of this State as a result of the application of the provisions of Section 5–125, or subsection (1) or (2) of this Section. These charges and all other charges arising out of the same incident shall be prosecuted under the criminal laws of this State.

[The remainder of this subsection (5) is virtually identical to the provisions set forth in subsection (1)(b)–(c).]

(6) The definition of delinquent minor under Section 5–120 of this Article shall not apply to any minor who, pursuant to subsection (1), (2), or (3) or Section 5–805,*** or 5–810,**** has previously been placed under the jurisdiction of the criminal court and has been convicted of a crime under an adult criminal or penal statute. Such a minor shall be subject to prosecution under the criminal laws of this State.

.   .   .

People v. M.A.

Supreme Court of Illinois, 1988.
124 Ill.2d 135, 124 Ill.Dec. 511, 529 N.E.2d 492.

■ Justice Ryan delivered the opinion of the court:

The defendant, M.A., a minor, was arrested and charged with the offense of unlawful use of weapons on school grounds. (Ill.Rev.Stat.1985, ch. 38, par. 24–1(a)(12).) Pursuant to the automatic-transfer provision of the Juvenile Court Act (Ill.Rev.Stat.1985, ch. 37, par. 702–7(6)(a) (now Ill.Rev.Stat.1987, ch. 37, par. 805–4(6)(a))), the defendant's case was trans-

---

* This section deals with the offense of escape.

** This section deals with violation of a bail bond.

*** This section deals with transfer of juveniles from juvenile court to criminal court.

**** This section deals with juveniles who are designated as extended jurisdiction juveniles

ferred to criminal court so that he could be prosecuted as an adult. Following a hearing, the trial court held that the automatic-transfer provision of the Juvenile Court Act (Ill.Rev.Stat.1985, ch. 37, par. 702–7(6)(a)) is unconstitutional as applied to the charge of unlawful use of weapons on school grounds (Ill.Rev.Stat.1985, ch. 38, par. 24–1(a)(12)). Because the statute was declared unconstitutional as applied, this case is here on direct appeal by the State.

The defendant asserts that section 2–7(6)(a) of the Juvenile Court Act is invalid because it deprives him of due process and equal protection of the laws. Section 2–7(6)(a) of the Juvenile Court Act provides:

"(a) The definition of delinquent minor under Section 2–2 of this Act shall not apply to any minor who at the time of an offense was at least 15 years of age and who is charged with murder, aggravated criminal sexual assault, armed robbery when the armed robbery was committed with a firearm, *or violation of the provisions of subsection 24–1(a)(12) of the Criminal Code of 1961, as amended.* These charges and all other charges arising out of the same incident shall be prosecuted pursuant to the Criminal Code of 1961, as amended." (Emphasis added.)

The italicized language was added by an amendment in 1985, adding the offense of unlawful use of weapons on school grounds (Ill.Rev.Stat. 1985, ch. 38, par. 24–1(a)(12)) to those offenses required to be transferred automatically to the jurisdiction of the criminal court. (Pub. Act 84–1075, eff. Dec. 2, 1985.) The statute, Unlawful Use of Weapons (Ill.Rev.Stat.1985, ch. 38, par. 24–1(a)(12)), provides in relevant part:

"(a) A person commits the offense of unlawful use of weapons when he knowingly:

(12) Carries or possesses on or about his person any bludgeon, black-jack, sling-shot, sand-club, sandbag, metal knuckles, switchblade knife, tear gas gun projector bomb or any object containing noxious liquid gas, pistol or revolver or other firearm, bomb, grenade, bottle or other container containing an explosive substance of over one-quarter ounce, or cartridge while in the building or on the grounds of any elementary or secondary school, community college, college or university. . . ."

The State raises one issue on appeal: whether the trial court erred in holding that it is unconstitutional for the legislature to provide that 15 and 16 year olds charged with unlawful use of weapons on school grounds shall be automatically transferred to the criminal court for disposition.

The trial court found there was no rational basis for automatically transferring 15 or 16 year olds charged with unlawful use of weapons on school grounds when other 15 or 16 year olds charged with attempted murder or other Class X felonies are entitled to a hearing before the case is transferred. (Ill.Rev.Stat.1985, ch. 37, par. 702–7(3).) The trial court concluded that to automatically transfer juveniles charged with unlawful use of weapons on school grounds without a hearing violates due process and equal protection.

The defendant claims that the trial court correctly found that the inclusion of unlawful use of weapons on school grounds in the class of crimes excluded from the Juvenile Court Act violates equal protection because other similarly situated defendants fall within the scope of the Juvenile Court Act. Additionally, the defendant urges this court to apply the strict scrutiny standard to juveniles because as a class they are uniquely powerless. In support of this assertion, defendant relies on the fact that minors have no right to vote. (See also Stern, *The Burger Court and the Diminishing Constitutional Rights of Minors: A Brief Overview,*1985 Ariz.St.L.J. 865, 894.) The defendant asserts that juveniles fall within the definition of a "suspect class" set forth in *San Antonio Independent School District v. Rodriguez* (1973), 411 U.S. 1, 28, 93 S.Ct. 1278, 1294, 36 L.Ed.2d 16, 40: a class "regulated to such a position of political powerlessness as to command extraordinary protection from the majoritorian political process."

Courts, however, have routinely held that age is not a suspect class for purposes of equal protection analysis, and thus the rational basis standard applies (See, *e.g., Massachusetts Board of Retirement v. Murgia* (1976), 427 U.S. 307, 96 S.Ct. 2562, 49 L.Ed.2d 520; *Trafelet v. Thompson* (7th Cir.1979), 594 F.2d 623; *Shorez v. City of Dacono, Colorado* (D.C.Colo. 1983), 574 F.Supp. 130.) The Supreme Court has held that strict scrutiny is appropriate for classifications based upon "immutable characteristics determined solely by accident of birth" such as sex, race, and national origin because these classes have been historically discriminated against politically. (See *Frontiero v. Richardson* (1973), 411 U.S. 677, 685, 93 S.Ct. 1764, 1769, 36 L.Ed.2d 583, 591.) While it is true that juveniles are not entitled to vote, they have not been historically discriminated against and age is clearly not an immutable characteristic. Thus, this court's prior holdings that the rational basis standard is applicable to juveniles comports with decisions of the United States Supreme Court. See *In re Sekeres* (1971), 48 Ill.2d 431, 270 N.E.2d 7.

In *People v. J.S.* (1984), 103 Ill.2d 395, 83 Ill.Dec. 156, 469 N.E.2d 1090, this court upheld the validity of section 2–6 as it read before the 1985 amendment, and it is only the provision added by that amendment that is under consideration in this case. In *People v. J.S.,* this court applied the rational basis test, which we have indicated above is applicable here. Also in *People v. J.S.,* the defendants argued, as does the defendant in this case, that the classification of the crimes was arbitrary. In *People v. J.S.,* this court held that the inclusion of murder, rape, deviate sexual assault, and armed robbery with a firearm-to the exclusion of other Class X felonies-in the class of cases in which minor defendants over 15 years of age would be prosecuted under the Criminal Code of 1961, and not the Juvenile Court Act, was a rational classification.

The defendant here also asserts that even under the rational basis test the classification is unconstitutional because the legislature has arbitrarily denied the defendant a benefit (treatment under the Juvenile Court Act) which is granted to others who are similarly situated. Specifically, the defendant argues that a juvenile who is charged with unlawful use of weapons on school grounds commits intrinsically the same quality of offense whether he is on school grounds or at a park district playground. Although the defendant acknowledges that the legislature has the authority to define the limits of juvenile court jurisdiction, he asserts that the distinction which is drawn in section 2–7(6)(a) of the Juvenile Court Act, which includes unlawful use of weapons on school grounds, but not other similar offenses in the class of cases in which a minor defendant shall be prosecuted under the Criminal Code, is arbitrary. We do not agree.

The juvenile court system was created by the legislature. "Nowhere in the Federal or in this State's constitution is there found the right to be treated as a juvenile for jurisdictional purposes." (*People v. J.S.* (1984), 103 Ill.2d 395, 402, 83 Ill.Dec. 156, 469 N.E.2d 1090.) In determining whether the classification violates the equal protection clause, it must be noted that the classification is presumed valid and that the party challenging the classification has the burden of showing invalidity. (*People v. McCabe* (1971), 49 Ill.2d 338, 340, 275 N.E.2d 407.) The classification will not be set aside as a denial of equal protection if facts reasonably may be conceived to justify it. (*Begich v. Industrial Comm'n* (1969), 42 Ill.2d 32, 36, 245 N.E.2d 457.) "Whether the enactment is wise or unwise; . . . whether it is the best means to achieve the desired results, and whether the legislative discretion within its prescribed limits should be exercised in a particular manner are matters for the judgment of the legislature, and the honest conflict of serious opinion does not suffice to bring them within the range of judicial cognizance." (*Thillens, Inc. v. Morey* (1957), 11 Ill.2d 579, 593, 144 N.E.2d 735.) Thus we must be concerned with the purpose of the classification and whether a rational basis exists to justify the classification. *McCabe,* 49 Ill.2d at 341, 275 N.E.2d 407.

The State asserts that the legislature has drawn a rational distinction because the presence of weapons on school grounds could lead to a series of other crimes. Comments by the sponsor of the Act indicate that the provision concerning unlawful use of weapons on school grounds was designed to remedy perceived problems that occur in and around school buildings and property:

"[This Act] creates the safe school zones in and around school property and deals severely with the bringing of firearms, the selling of . . . hard drugs in and around schools. It deals with adults trying to recruit juveniles into . . . gangs. This is a . . . result of hearings over six months in schools throughout the State of Illinois, we've seen statistics about the dropout rate and surveys . . . [indicate] that the major reason for the dropout rate has been gangs. This is our message to those gangs that we're not going to tolerate drugs, firearms, gang recruitment in and around the schools. . . ." (84th Ill.Gen.Assem., Senate Proceedings, July 1, 1985, at 40 (statements of Senator Maro-vitz).)

It is true, as defendant maintains, that juveniles charged with unlawful use of weapons on school grounds commit intrinsically the same offense whether they are on school grounds or not. However, the legislature could have rationally concluded that deterring juveniles from carrying weapons on school grounds is more important because attendance at school is compulsory and therefore the State has a duty to create a safe environment.

Moreover, this court has upheld classifications against equal protection challenges when the situs of the crime warranted a stricter penalty. (*People v. Bales* (1985), 108 Ill.2d 182, 91 Ill.Dec. 171, 483 N.E.2d 517.) In *Bales* this court held that there was a rational basis for classifying residential burglary as a Class 1 felony and burglary as a Class 2 felony. (108 Ill.2d at 192, 91 Ill.Dec. 171, 483 N.E.2d 517.) This court stated that there was a rational basis for the classification because "residential burglary contains more possibility for danger and serious harm than that of places not used as dwellings." (*Bales,* 108 Ill.2d at 193, 91 Ill.Dec. 171, 483 N.E.2d 517, quoting *People v. Gomez* (1983), 120 Ill.App.3d 545, 549, 76 Ill.Dec. 165, 458 N.E.2d 565.) Similarly, in this case the legislature could have rationally concluded that the unlawful use of weapons on school grounds poses a greater chance of injury and danger to persons in the school environment than elsewhere.

Additionally, the defendant contends that automatically transferring juveniles charged with unlawful use of weapons on school grounds is arbitrary because more serious crimes with a closer nexus to gang activity are not included in the automatic-transfer statute when committed on school grounds. (See, *e.g.,* Ill.Rev.Stat.1985, ch. 38, par. 12–6 (intimidation); Ill.Rev.Stat.1985, ch. 38, par. 12–6.1 (compelling membership in a gang).) "[A] classification which has some reasonable basis is not unconstitutional because it is not made with mathematical nicety or because in practice it results in some inequality." (*City of Chicago v. Vokes* (1963), 28 Ill.2d 475, 480, 193 N.E.2d 40.) Moreover, Public Act 84–1075 created and amended numerous pieces of legislation in addition to adding the offense of unlawful use of weapons on school grounds to those offenses required to be automatically transferred to criminal court. For example, the Act enhanced the penalty for "compelling organization membership of persons" into gangs from a Class 3 to a Class 2 felony. (Ill.Rev.Stat.1985, ch. 38, par. 12–6.1.) The Illinois Controlled Substances Act was also amended to increase the penalty for violations if the offense took place on or around school grounds. (Ill.Rev.Stat.1985, ch. 56 1/2 , par. 1407.) Thus, even if the classification results in some inequality, it is not unconstitutional because it was rational for the legislature to conclude that juveniles that are charged with unlawful use of weapons on school grounds posed the greatest threat to the school environment. See *People v. J.S.* (1984), 103 Ill.2d 395, 403, 83 Ill.Dec. 156, 469 N.E.2d 1090.

The defendant next contends that automatically transferring juveniles charged with unlawful use of weapons on school grounds violates due process. Because a transfer from juvenile to criminal court creates the possibility that the child will be deprived of liberty for a longer period of time and under more punitive conditions, it must comport with due process. (*In re Gault* (1967), 387 U.S. 1, 87 S.Ct. 1428, 18 L.Ed.2d 527.) Our analysis of whether the statute violates the due process clause must begin, as did our equal protection analysis, with the presumption that the statute is valid. Similarly, the burden of showing the statute is invalid is on the defendant. *People v. Bales* (1985), 108 Ill.2d 182, 91 Ill.Dec. 171, 483 N.E.2d 517.

Generally, the legislature has wide discretion to prescribe penalties for defined offenses. (*People v. Bradley* (1980), 79 Ill.2d 410, 417, 38 Ill.Dec. 575, 403 N.E.2d 1029.) However, the legislature's power to fix penalties is subject to the constitutional limitation which prohibits the deprivation of liberty without due process of law. (*Bradley,* 79 Ill.2d 410, 38 Ill.Dec. 575, 403 N.E.2d 1029; *Heimgaertner v. Benjamin Electric Manufacturing Co.* (1955), 6 Ill.2d 152, 128 N.E.2d 691.)

> "We have consistently stated that the standard of a proper exercise of the police power is whether the statute is reasonably designed to remedy the evils which the legislature has determined to be a threat to the public health, safety and general welfare." (*Heimgaertner,* 6 Ill.2d at 159, 128 N.E.2d 691.)

Thus, the test focuses on the purpose of the statute and the problem the legislature was attempting to alleviate thereby.

The defendant maintains that the legislature has acted arbitrarily and irrationally in mandating the adult prosecution of juveniles charged with unlawful use of weapons on school grounds, a Class 4 felony, while providing that minors charged with more serious crimes retain the benefits of the Juvenile Court Act. Additionally, the defendant asserts that the purpose of automatically transferring juveniles charged with unlawful use of weapons on school grounds was to root out the evil of gangs in Illinois schools. Accordingly, the defendant contends that the statute is irrational because minors charged with crimes more serious and directly related to gang activity retain the protections of the Juvenile Court Act. See, *e.g.,*Ill.Rev.Stat.1985, ch. 38, par. 12–6 (intimidation); Ill.Rev.Stat.1985, ch. 38, par 12–6.1 (compelling organization membership).

In support of his substantive due process contention, defendant relies on *People v. Bradley* (1980), 79 Ill.2d 410, 38 Ill.Dec. 575, 403 N.E.2d 1029. *Bradley* involved the validity of the penalty for possession of a controlled substance, which was higher than that for delivery of the same substance. This court noted that the purpose of the Illinois Controlled Substances Act was to penalize more severely those engaged in the traffic of the substances than the occasional user. This court in *Bradley* concluded that the statute violated due process because it imposed a greater sentence for possession than for delivery, which was in contravention of the express intent of the legislature. 79 Ill.2d at 418, 38 Ill.Dec. 575, 403 N.E.2d 1029.

We do not agree with defendant's assertion that the legislature has acted arbitrarily and irrationally. As was previously noted, the purpose of the Act was to reduce crime in schools and lessen gang activity. The fact that the offense of compelling organization membership of persons is not subject to automatic transfer is not dispositive of defendant's due process claim. The legislature chose to attack the gang-crime situation in a variety of ways, and automatically transferring juveniles charged with unlawful use of weapons on school grounds was but one of the methods chosen. This court has stated that: "The reasonableness of a police regulation is not necessarily what is best but what is fairly appropriate under all circumstances...." *City of Chicago v. Vokes* (1963), 28 Ill.2d 475, 479–80, 193 N.E.2d 40.

Finally, it should be noted that, unlike *Bradley,* providing that juveniles charged with the unlawful use of weapons on school grounds be criminally prosecuted is not in contravention to the express legislative intent. Thus, the legislature could have rationally concluded that unlawful use of weapons on school grounds is unique in being a catalyst for other, more serious offenses and therefore there is a greater need to deter such activity.

The differences in treatment created by the statute in question is not in the penalty provided for different offenses, as was the case in *People v. Bradley*. A minor confined under the Juvenile Court Act by order of the court may be confined just as long, and possibly longer, than a person sentenced under the Criminal Code. It is the method of treatment that differs under the two procedures. Because of this difference, a finding of delinquency and disposition under the Juvenile Court Act does not have the same effect insofar as creating a criminal record is concerned. There is a different effect from a juvenile disposition insofar as subsequent criminal convictions are concerned than there is if the defendant is prosecuted criminally and convicted. It has been argued in this court, and not seriously contested, that because of the differences in the resulting criminal record created by treatment under the two statutes, juveniles are often recruited as "gunmen" by adult gang members and recruiters. Therefore, in the particular area covered by this statute the legislature may have felt it advisable to remove the cloak of protection afforded by treatment under the Juvenile Court Act. The legislature was addressing a series of problems involving the school environment. Whether these problems could have been more effectively dealt with in a different manner is not for this court to say.

We hold that section 2–7(6)(a) of the Juvenile Court Act, requiring minors charged with unlawful use of weapons on school grounds to be prosecuted as adults, does not deprive minors of due process or equal protection of the law.

We reverse the judgment of the circuit court of Cook County and remand this case to that court for further proceeding.

REVERSED and REMANDED.

■ JUSTICE STAMOS took no part in the consideration or decision of this case.

NOTES

(1) An earlier version of the Illinois statute set forth above, page 949, was upheld against constitutional claims in *People v. J.S.*, 103 Ill.2d 395, 83 Ill.Dec. 156, 469 N.E.2d 1090 (1984), which is cited and discussed in *People v. M.A.* The current statute, like its predecessor, specifically excludes certain offenses when committed by a juvenile 15 or older, or in some cases 13 or older, which means that the case originates in criminal court. Other states similarly exclude certain offenses from the juvenile court's jurisdiction. See, e.g., Cal.Welf. & Inst.Code § 602(b); Ind.Code Ann. § 31-30-1-4; La. Children's Code Ann. art. 305(A). The Louisiana statute similarly was upheld against challenges that it violated equal protection of the laws, *State v. Leach*, 425 So.2d 1232 (La.1983), and due process of law, *State v. Perique*, 439 So.2d 1060 (La.1983). Some jurisdictions achieve the same result by mandating that certain cases originating in juvenile court be transferred to criminal court. Indeed, the Illinois statutes elsewhere require that certain cases are automatically transferred to criminal court. Ill.Comp.Stat.Ann. ch. 705, § 405/5-805(1). This statute was upheld, of course, in *People v. M.A.*, 124 Ill.2d 135, 124 Ill.Dec. 511, 529 N.E.2d 492 (1988). Other states make similar provision. See, e.g., Minn.Stat.Ann. § 260B.125(5); N.C.Gen.Stat. § 7B-2200; 42 Pa.Cons.Stat.Ann. § 6355(e). Still oth-

er states achieve the same result with "once waived, always waived" statutes, which provide that once jurisdiction over a juvenile is waived, it is deemed waived with respect to any offense with which he or she might be charged subsequently. See, e.g., Cal.Welf. & Inst.Code § 707.01(a)(5)–(6); Fla.Stat.Ann. § 985.556(1), (5); Wn. Rev.Code Ann. § 13.40.020(14). These statutes, too, generally have been upheld because they constitute an exercise of legislative prerogative rather than judicial discretion. See, e.g., *State v. Sharon*, 100 Wn.2d 230, 668 P.2d 584 (1983).

(2) Is legislative allocation of jurisdiction (through exclusion of certain offenses) a stalking horse for prosecutorial discretion (covered in the next section)? The prosecutor, after all, decides what to charge or what degree of an offense to charge, and the exclusion statutes turn on charge alone.

(3) What if a child charged with one of the excluded offenses pleads guilty to or is convicted of a lesser included offense in criminal court? Is the criminal court's exercise of jurisdiction proper, even though the offense of which he is convicted is one that would have been triable in juvenile court and one over which the criminal court would not have had original jurisdiction at all?

Suppose, for example, that a 15–year-old juvenile is charged in Louisiana with first-degree murder, which means that his case will originate in criminal court, but when he gets to criminal court he pleads guilty to or is convicted of voluntary manslaughter, an offense that would not have resulted in original jurisdiction in the criminal court. The juvenile code provides that in these circumstances the criminal court retains jurisdiction. La.Children's Code Ann. art. 863(A). The same result is reached elsewhere. See, e.g., Del.Code Ann. tit. 10, § 921(2)(b), 1010(d); Ind.Stat. Ann. § 31–30–1–4; *People v. Self*, 63 Cal.App.4th 58, 73 Cal.Rptr.2d 501 (1998); *State v. Morales*, 240 Conn. 727, 694 A.2d 758 (1997); *Commonwealth v. Williams*, 427 Mass. 59, 691 N.E.2d 553 (1998); *People v. Veling*, 443 Mich. 23, 504 N.W.2d 456 (1993); *State v. Behl*, 564 N.W.2d 560 (Minn.1997). The Illinois statute, p. 947 supra, in subsec. (1)(c)(ii) anticipates this dilemma and provides for retention of jurisdiction by the criminal court but imposition of a juvenile sentence, unless the state requests a hearing on the matter, in which case the court as a result of the hearing may impose either a juvenile sentence or an adult sentence. Other states provide that if the juvenile pleads guilty to or is convicted of a lesser offense, he or she must be remanded to the juvenile court for sentencing. See, e.g., Kan.Stat.Ann. § 38–2347(i); Or.Rev.Stat. § 419C.361(1).

This question usually comes up in connection with waiver of jurisdiction, in cases in which the child has been transferred to criminal court and is convicted of or pleads guilty to a lesser included offense that would not have been waivable in the first instance. See note (6) at p. 971 infra.

2.   PROSECUTORIAL DISCRETION

ARKANSAS CODE ANNOTATED (Lexis–Nexis)

§ 9–27–318. Filing and transfer to the criminal division of circuit court.

. . .

(c) A prosecuting attorney may charge a juvenile in either the juvenile or criminal division of circuit court when a case involves a juvenile:

(1) At least sixteen (16) years old when he or she engages in conduct that, if committed by an adult, would be any felony; or

(2) Fourteen (14) or fifteen (15) years old when he or she engages in conduct that, if committed by an adult, would be:

    (A) Capital murder, § 5–10–101;

    (B) Murder in the first degree, § 5–10–102;

    (C) Kidnapping, § 5–11–102;

    (D) Aggravated robbery, § 5–12–103;

    (E) Rape, § 5–14–103;

    (F) Battery in the first degree, § 5–13–201; or

    (G) Terroristic act, § 5–13–310.

(d) If a prosecuting attorney can file charges in the criminal division of circuit court for an act allegedly committed by a juvenile, the state may file any other criminal charges that arise out of the same act or course of conduct in the same division of the circuit court case if, after a hearing before the juvenile division of circuit court, a transfer is so ordered.

(e) Upon the motion of the court or of any party, the judge of the division of circuit court in which a delinquency petition or criminal charges have been filed shall conduct a transfer hearing to determine whether to transfer the case to another division of circuit court.

(f) The court shall conduct a transfer hearing within thirty (30) days if the juvenile is detained and no longer than ninety (90) days from the date of the motion to transfer the case.

(g) In the transfer hearing, the court shall consider all of the following factors:

(1) The seriousness of the alleged offense and whether the protection of society requires prosecution in the criminal division of circuit court;

(2) Whether the alleged offense was committed in an aggressive, violent, premeditated, or willful manner;

(3) Whether the offense was against a person or property, with greater weight being given to offenses against persons, especially if personal injury resulted;

(4) The culpability of the juvenile, including the level of planning and participation in the alleged offense;

(5) The previous history of the juvenile, including whether the juvenile had been adjudicated a juvenile offender and, if so, whether the offenses were against persons or property, and any other previous history of antisocial behavior or patterns of physical violence;

(6) The sophistication or maturity of the juvenile as determined by consideration of the juvenile's home, environment, emotional attitude, pattern of living, or desire to be treated as an adult;

(7) Whether there are facilities or programs available to the judge of the juvenile division of circuit court that are likely to rehabilitate the juvenile before the expiration of the juvenile's twenty-first birthday;

(8) Whether the juvenile acted alone or was part of a group in the commission of the alleged offense;

(9) Written reports and other materials relating to the juvenile's mental, physical, educational, and social history; and

(10) Any other factors deemed relevant by the judge.

(h)(1) The court shall make written findings on all of the factors set forth in subsection (g) of this section.

(2) Upon a finding by clear and convincing evidence that a case should be transferred to another division of circuit court, the judge shall enter an order to that effect.

(i) Upon a finding by the criminal division of circuit court that a juvenile fourteen (14) through seventeen (17) years of age and charged with the crimes in subdivision (c)(2) of this section should be transferred to the juvenile division of circuit court, the criminal division of circuit court may enter an order to transfer as an extended juvenile jurisdiction case.

(j) If a juvenile age fourteen (14) or fifteen (15) is found guilty in the criminal division of circuit court for an offense other than an offense listed in subsection (b) or subdivision (c)(2) of this section, the judge shall enter a juvenile delinquency disposition under § 9–27–330.

(k) If the case is transferred to another division, any bail or appearance bond given for the appearance of the juvenile shall continue in effect in the division to which the case is transferred.

(*l*) Any party may appeal from a transfer order.

(m) The circuit court may conduct a transfer hearing and an extended juvenile jurisdiction hearing under § 9–27–503 at the same time.

NOTES

(1) Wyoming authorizes the prosecutor to decide the court—criminal or juvenile—in which to proceed in the case of any juvenile charged with a misdemeanor, a juvenile 17 or older charged with a felony, or a juvenile 14 or older charged with a violent felony or charged with a felony who has been adjudicated delinquent twice previously for felonies. Wyo.Stat.Ann. §§ 14–6–203(c)–(f), 14–6–211; see Colo.Rev. Stat. § 19–2–517; La.Children's Code Ann. art. 305(B); Neb.Rev.Stat. § 43–276.

Prior to legislative changes in 1984 that produced the statute in its current form, the Wyoming statute authorized the prosecutor to decide the court in which to proceed in *all* cases alleging delinquency. The old statute was the subject of critical analysis in Jeffrey C. Brinkerhoff, Comment, Prosecution as a Juvenile or Adult? Is the Discretion Vested in the District Attorney by Section 14–6–203(c) of the Wyoming Statutes Unconstitutional and Violative of the Proper Role of a Prosecutor?, 19 Land & Water L.Rev. 187 (1984). That comment was written in reaction to the case of 16–year-old Richard Jahnke, who was convicted of voluntary manslaughter in the shooting death of his father despite his defense that the shooting was in response to many years of parental abuse. His conviction was affirmed on appeal. *Jahnke v. State*, 682 P.2d 991 (Wyo.1984).

The *Jahnke* case is representative of a fact pattern that sadly—and all too frequently—is repeated: the trial of a child who is charged with the killing of a parent, claiming the killing was in response to a long period of persistent abuse, invoking a fear of imminent danger or even death. For another example, in which the court held that expert testimony on battered child syndrome is admissible in appropriate cases to aid in proof of self-defense, see *State v. Janes*, 121 Wn.2d 220, 850 P.2d 495 (1993).

(2) Some states, while employing other allocation models, have created the functional equivalent of the prosecutorial model, thus allowing the prosecutor to make some allocation decisions. This point was made in the preceding section, for example, with respect to the legislative allocation model (see note (2), supra p. 956). In addition, Georgia provides for traditional juvenile waiver but also provides for concurrent jurisdiction between the juvenile and criminal courts over certain offenses (see the Georgia statute on page 961 infra). The prosecutor, by charging one of these offenses, causes the case to be handled in criminal court. Other examples are Fla.Stat.Ann. §§ 985.56(1), 985.557(1); S.D.Comp.Laws Ann. § 26–11–3. In New York (the statutory scheme is described in note (2) at page 999 infra), certain enumerated offenses are initially excluded from the juvenile court's jurisdiction, but the criminal court has discretion to transfer appropriate cases to the juvenile court. Even if the evidence will support only a lesser offense the prosecutor, by charging a juvenile with a more serious offense, can assure that the case will at least originate in criminal court.

The District of Columbia statutory scheme differs only slightly. There certain statutorily designated offenses are excluded altogether from the jurisdiction of the juvenile court. By deciding what offense to charge, the prosecutor, in effect, determines the court in which the juvenile will be tried. D.C. Code § 16–2301(3)(A); *United States v. Bland*, 472 F.2d 1329 (D.C.Cir.1972); *Pendergrast v. United States*, 332 A.2d 919 (D.C.1975). See Charles H. Whitebread & Robert Batey, Transfer Between Courts: Proposals of the Juvenile Justice Standards Project, 63 Va.L.Rev. 221, 233–35 (1977).

Some have argued for additional safeguards in all of the above settings as protection against potential prosecutorial abuse. For example:

[A]t the very least the criminal court should be required to hold a hearing at which the prosecutor must establish probable cause to believe the child has committed the offense charged in criminal court. Under New York procedure, for example, if a child charged with an offense over which the criminal court has original jurisdiction is arraigned prior to grand jury action, he is entitled to a probable cause hearing. If probable cause supporting the serious offense is shown, the case is bound over for grand jury action. If probable cause to support a lesser offense over which the juvenile court would have exercised original jurisdiction is shown, the case is transferred to the juvenile court. If no probable cause is found, the case is dismissed. As a minimal safeguard, this kind of procedure should be followed in all cases in which a child is brought before a criminal court as a result of prosecutorial discretion or as a result of the criminal court having exclusive, original, or concurrent jurisdiction over the offense charged.

Furthermore, in states granting original jurisdiction to the criminal court over certain kinds of offenses, with authority to transfer exceptional cases to the juvenile court, more should be required. These "reverse waiver" procedures should be attended by the same procedural safeguards required in a judicial waiver determination in juvenile court. Specifically, a waiver hearing should be required, and the child should have the same rights in this hearing that *Kent* guarantees in juvenile waiver proceedings.

The importance of the decision to the child is the same. In a juvenile waiver proceeding the juvenile court cannot arbitrarily determine which cases are exceptional and ought to be handled in criminal court. Likewise, the criminal court should not be allowed arbitrarily to determine which cases are exceptional and ought to be handled in juvenile court. In each case the presumption as to how children should be treated is reversed, but the result of the decision-making process is the same—some children are treated as juveniles and some are subjected to criminal prosecution. Such a decision, regardless of the court in which it is made, should be subject to the procedural safeguards required by *Kent*. Indeed, a reverse waiver procedure in the absence of sufficient safeguards may create a constitutionally impermissible presumption of competency to commit crime.

Samuel M. Davis, The Efficacy of a Probable Cause Requirement in Juvenile Proceedings, 59 N.C.L.Rev. 723, 743–44 (1981).*

(3) The issue immediately raised by such statutes is whether the exercise of the discretion vested by statute in a prosecutor to charge a person with certain enumerated offenses and thus initiating that person's prosecution as an adult violates due process. However, these statutes have been upheld time and again against attacks on due process or equal protection grounds, and against the argument in *United States v. Bland* (note (2) supra) that the statute negates the presumption of innocence. See *Woodard v. Wainwright*, 556 F.2d 781 (5th Cir.1977); *Russell v. Parratt*, 543 F.2d 1214 (8th Cir.1976); *Cox v. United States*, 473 F.2d 334 (4th Cir.1973); *Myers v. District Court*, 184 Colo. 81, 518 P.2d 836 (1974); *State v. Cain*, 381 So.2d 1361 (Fla.1980); *People v. Sprinkle*, 56 Ill.2d 257, 307 N.E.2d 161 (1974); *State v. Grayer*, 191 Neb. 523, 215 N.W.2d 859 (1974); *Sherfield v. State*, 511 P.2d 598 (Okl.Cr.App.1973). But in *State v. Butler*, 294 Mont. 17, 977 P.2d 1000 (1999), the court held that, where under the statutory scheme the prosecutor had discretion to seek the district court's permission to file an information directly in district court but the decision was actually made by the court, not the prosecutor, a hearing on the issue of transfer was constitutionally required. The statute subsequently was amended to require a hearing on transfer. Following the amendment, *Butler* was overruled to the extent it required a transfer hearing *before* the filing of the information. *State v. McKee*, 330 Mont. 249, 127 P.3d 445 (2006).

(4) Vesting the prosecutor with even limited discretion raises the specter of prosecutorial abuse. While the traditional waiver process is replete with due process safeguards as a result of *Kent*, what safeguards assure fair decisionmaking by the prosecutor? What is to prevent the prosecutor from charging an offense over which the criminal court has concurrent jurisdiction when the evidence will support at best commission of a lesser offense over which the juvenile court has original jurisdiction? Or charging an offense that is excluded from the juvenile court's jurisdiction, even though the evidence will only support commission of a lesser offense? Or, in a jurisdiction in which certain offenses must originate in the criminal court, from charging such an offense even though the evidence will not support an offense of that grade? In all of these examples overcharging could be used, in effect, as a means of prosecutorial allocation of jurisdiction between courts while avoiding the necessity of a waiver hearing in juvenile court.

In Vermont, the statutes provide for waiver and transfer to criminal court of a juvenile who was over 10 but under 14 at the time of the alleged commission of any one of certain enumerated offenses. Vt.Stat.Ann. tit. 33, § 5506(a). The statutes further provide, however, that if the juvenile is not convicted of one of the enumerated offenses but is only convicted of a lesser offense, the case shall be remanded to juvenile court for disposition, the conviction shall be treated as a delinquency adjudication and the case shall be treated as though it had remained in juvenile court at all times. Id. § 5506(h). Should a similar safeguard exist for juveniles whose cases originate in criminal court as a result of prosecutorial discretion rather than judicial discretion? See Davis, supra note (2).

3. CONCURRENT JURISDICTION

GEORGIA CODE ANNOTATED (Lexis–Nexis)

§ 15–11–28. Jurisdiction over juveniles

. . .

(b) *Criminal jurisdiction.* (1) Except as provided in paragraph (2) of this subsection, the court shall have concurrent jurisdiction with the superior court over a child who is alleged to have committed a delinquent act which would be considered a crime if tried in a superior court and for which the child may be punished by loss of life, imprisonment for life without possibility of parole, or confinement for life in a penal institution.

(2)(A) The superior court shall have exclusive jurisdiction over any matter concerning any child 13 to 17 years of age who is alleged to have committed any of the following offenses:

    (i) Murder;

    (ii) Voluntary manslaughter;

    (iii) Rape;

    (iv) Aggravated sodomy;

    (v) Aggravated child molestation;

    (vi) Aggravated sexual battery; or

    (vii) Armed robbery if committed with a firearm.

. . .

(B) After indictment, the superior court may after investigation and for extraordinary cause transfer any case involving a child 13 to 17 years of age alleged to have committed any offense enumerated in subparagraph (A) of this paragraph which is not punishable by loss of life, imprisonment for life without possibility of parole, or confinement for life in a penal institution. . . . Upon such a transfer by the superior court, jurisdiction shall vest in the juvenile court and jurisdiction of the superior court shall terminate. . . .

(C) Before indictment, the district attorney may, after investigation and for extraordinary cause, decline prosecution in the superior court of a child 13 to 17 years of age alleged to have committed an offense specified in subparagraph (A) of this paragraph. Upon declining such prosecution in the superior court, the district attorney shall immediately cause a petition to be filed in the appropriate juvenile court for adjudication. . . .

(D) The superior court may transfer any case involving a child 13 to 17 years of age alleged to have committed any offense enumerated in subparagraph (A) of this paragraph and convicted of a lesser included offense not included in subparagraph (A) of this paragraph to the juvenile court of the county of the child's residence for disposition. Upon such a transfer by the superior court, jurisdiction shall vest in the juvenile court and jurisdiction of the superior court shall terminate.

. . .

NOTES

(1) Concurrent jurisdiction comes in various forms. In some instances it applies only to older juveniles, regardless of the seriousness of the offense charged; in others it applies to juveniles charged with categorical offenses (e.g., felonies or capital felonies) or certain enumerated offenses, regardless of age; and in still others, it applies based on a combination of age and offense factors. See, e.g., Colo.Rev.Stat.Ann. § 19–2–805(1); Fla.Stat.Ann. §§ 985.56(1), 985.557(1); Mich. Comp.Laws Ann. § 712A.2(d); Wyo.Stat.Ann. §§ 14–6–203(c)–(f), 14–6–211. For a critical analysis of Utah's statutory scheme as a response to public concern over a perceived rise in juvenile crime, see Michael Norman & L. Kay Gillespie, Changing Horses: Utah's Shift in Adjudicating Serious Juvenile Offenders, 12 J.Contemp.L. 85 (1986).

(2) Concurrent jurisdiction sometimes can result from judicial construction of statutory and constitutional provisions. The typical case involves a conflict between the juvenile code, which grants the juvenile court exclusive original jurisdiction over all juveniles, and a constitutional grant of jurisdiction to a court of general jurisdiction to try "all criminal cases" or "all offenses punishable by death or life imprisonment." In the face of such a jurisdictional conflict, some courts have held that the statutory grant of jurisdiction to the juvenile court must yield to the constitutional grant of jurisdiction to another court, resulting in the two courts having concurrent jurisdiction. *Jackson v. Balkcom*, 210 Ga. 412, 80 S.E.2d 319 (1954); *State v. Lindsey*, 78 Idaho 241, 300 P.2d 491 (1956); *State v. McCoy*, 145 Neb. 750, 18 N.W.2d 101 (1945).

Most courts in these circumstances, however, have concluded that the statutory grant of jurisdiction to the juvenile court is valid, that there is no conflict with the constitutional grant of jurisdiction to another court. See, e.g., *People ex rel. Terrell v. District Court*, 164 Colo. 437, 435 P.2d 763 (1967); *Mallory v. Paradise*, 173 N.W.2d 264 (Iowa 1969); *State ex rel. Knutson v. Jackson*, 249 Minn. 246, 82 N.W.2d 234 (1957); *State ex rel. Slatton v. Boles*, 147 W.Va. 674, 130 S.E.2d 192 (1963); *Gibson v. State*, 47 Wis.2d 810, 177 N.W.2d 912 (1970). One reason given is that such statutes do not deprive another court of jurisdiction but rather provide procedures (i.e., waiver of jurisdiction) that must be followed before the criminal jurisdiction of the other court attaches. *State ex rel. Knutson v. Jackson*, 249 Minn. at 250–51, 82 N.W.2d at 237–38. Another rationale is that there is no conflict because grants of jurisdiction to other courts usually refer to *criminal* cases, whereas a delinquency case is a civil, not a criminal proceeding. *People ex rel. Rodello v. District Court*, 164 Colo. 530, 535, 436 P.2d 672, 675 (1968); *State ex rel. Slatton v. Boles*, 147 W.Va. at 683–85, 130 S.E.2d at 198–99.

(3) Notice that the Georgia statute is not a "pure" concurrent jurisdiction model. It contains elements of other allocation models as well. For example, subsection (b)(2)(A) resembles the "legislative allocation" model in that it excludes certain enumerated offenses from those over which the juvenile and criminal courts have concurrent jurisdiction; subsection (b)(2)(B) resembles the "reverse certification" model in that it grants the criminal court discretion to transfer some cases that otherwise are excluded to the juvenile court for handling; subsection (b)(2)(C) resembles the "prosecutorial discretion" model since it gives the prosecutor discretion, in cases that otherwise are excluded, to file a petition in juvenile court rather than to seek an indictment.

4. Judicial Transfer by the Juvenile Court

a. THE CONSTITUTIONAL IMPLICATIONS

KENT v. UNITED STATES: A CONSTITUTIONAL DECISION?

In *Kent v. United States,* 383 U.S. 541, 86 S.Ct. 1045, 16 L.Ed.2d 84 (1966), Morris Kent, age 16, was accused of committing a number of robberies and housebreakings in the District of Columbia. One robbery victim was raped. The principal evidence against Kent was a latent fingerprint left at the scene of the robbery and rape. Kent was on probation from the juvenile court at the time of his apprehension. He was interrogated over a seven-hour period and confessed to several housebreakings. Kent and his mother met with the social service director of the juvenile court who informed them Kent might be transferred for trial in adult court. Kent's attorney sought a court order to provide for psychiatric evaluation and for access to any social reports on Kent in the court's possession. Without a hearing, the juvenile judge transferred Kent's case to the criminal court; after a denial of his motion to dismiss Kent was tried there. He presented an insanity defense in the criminal proceeding. The jury found Kent guilty of robbery and housebreaking but not guilty by reason of insanity on the rape charge. Sentenced to serve 90 years in prison on the charges as to which he was found guilty, Kent first was sent to a mental hospital for the treatment mandated in the District of Columbia when a defendant is found not guilty by reason of insanity. Time in the mental hospital was to be credited against his prison sentence. Kent appealed his conviction and the court of appeals affirmed.

Kent was a precursor to *In re Gault,* decided the following year. As indicated in the previous chapter, supra pp. 860–61, the Supreme Court in *Kent* held that in cases in which the juvenile court is considering transfer to criminal court, (1) juveniles are entitled to a hearing, (2) counsel is entitled to access to the social records that the court considers in making its decision, and (3) any transfer order must include a statement of reasons explaining the court's decision. One of the chief issues following the Court's decision was whether it was a decision affecting only the juvenile court in the District of Columbia, since the case involved construction of a local statute, or instead was a decision of constitutional dimensions.

On the one hand, the Court said:

> This concern [that juveniles receive neither the rehabilitative treatment afforded by the juvenile court nor the procedural protections afforded adults in criminal court] . . . does not induce us in this case to accept the invitation to rule that constitutional guaranties which would be applicable to adults charged with the serious offenses for which Kent was tried must be applied in juvenile court proceedings concerned with allegations of law violation. The Juvenile Court Act and the decisions of the United States Court of Appeals for the District of Columbia Circuit provide an adequate basis for decision of this case, and we go no further.

383 U.S. at 556.

On the other hand, the Court, after setting forth its requirements, stated: "We believe that this result is required by the statute read in the context of constitutional principles relating to due process and the assistance of counsel." 383 U.S. at 557. Later in the opinion the Court added: "We do not mean by this to indicate that the hearing to be held must conform with all of the requirements of a criminal trial or even of the usual administrative hearing; but we do hold that the hearing must measure up to the essentials of due process and fair treatment." 383 U.S. at 562.

The latter statement in particular, because it was reiterated in *Gault*, led some observers to conclude that *Kent* was a decision with constitutional implications. Certainly it was treated by lower courts (and legislatures) as a decision of constitutional magnitude. See, e.g., *Powell v. Hocker*, 453 F.2d 652 (9th Cir.1971), overruled, *Harris v. Procunier*, 498 F.2d 576 (9th Cir.1974) (on the issue of the retroactivity of *Kent*); *In re Harris*, 67 Cal.2d 876, 64 Cal.Rptr. 319, 434 P.2d 615 (1967).

Kent's attorney also challenged certain post-arrest police practices. The Court did not rule on these claims because it grounded its decision in the impropriety of the waiver of juvenile court jurisdiction. In what might be considered a prelude to *Gault*, Justice Fortas remarked in passing:

> These contentions raise problems of substantial concern as to the construction of and compliance with the Juvenile Court Act. They also suggest basic issues as to the justifiability of affording a juvenile less protection than is accorded to adults suspected of criminal offenses, particularly where, as here, there is an absence of any indication that the denial of rights available to adults was offset, mitigated or explained by action of the Government, as *parens patriae*, evidencing the special solicitude for juveniles commanded by the Juvenile Court Act. However, because we remand the case on account of the procedural error with respect to waiver of jurisdiction, we do not pass upon these questions.

387 U.S. at 551–52.

b.   THE STATUTORY CRITERIA

CALIFORNIA WELFARE AND INSTITUTIONS CODE (West)

§ 606.   Subjecting minor to criminal prosecution

When a petition has been filed in a juvenile court, the minor who is the subject of the petition shall not thereafter be subject to criminal prosecution based on the facts giving rise to the petition unless the juvenile court finds that the minor is not a fit and proper subject to be dealt with under this chapter and orders that criminal proceedings be resumed or instituted against him, or the petition is transferred to a court of criminal jurisdiction pursuant to subdivision (b) of Section 707.01.*

§ 707.   Fitness hearing

(a)(1) In any case in which a minor is alleged to be a person described in Section 602(a) by reason of the violation, when he or she was 16 years of

---

* Section 707.01(b) requires mandatory transfer of certain cases to criminal court.

age or older, of any criminal statute or ordinance except those listed in subdivision (b), upon motion of the petitioner made prior to the attachment of jeopardy the court shall cause the probation officer to investigate and submit a report on the behavioral patterns and social history of the minor being considered for a determination of unfitness. Following submission and consideration of the report, and of any other relevant evidence that the petitioner or the minor may wish to submit, the juvenile court may find that the minor is not a fit and proper subject to be dealt with under the juvenile court law if it concludes that the minor would not be amenable to the care, treatment, and training program available through the facilities of the juvenile court, based upon an evaluation of the following criteria:

(i) The degree of criminal sophistication exhibited by the minor.

(ii) Whether the minor can be rehabilitated prior to the expiration of the juvenile court's jurisdiction.

(iii) The minor's previous delinquent history.

(iv) Success of previous attempts by the juvenile court to rehabilitate the minor.

(v) The circumstances and gravity of the offense alleged in the petition to have been committed by the minor.

A determination that the minor is not a fit and proper subject to be dealt with under the juvenile court law may be based on any one or a combination of the factors set forth above, which shall be recited in the order of unfitness. In any case in which a hearing has been noticed pursuant to this section, the court shall postpone the taking of a plea to the petition until the conclusion of the fitness hearing, and no plea that may already have been entered shall constitute evidence at the hearing.

(2)(A) This paragraph shall apply to a minor alleged to be a person described in Section 602 by reason of the violation, when he or she has attained 16 years of age, of any felony offense when the minor has been declared to be a ward of the court pursuant to Section 602 on one or more prior occasions if both of the following apply:

(i) The minor has previously been found to have committed two or more felony offenses.

(ii) The offenses upon which the prior petition or petitions were based were committed when the minor had attained 14 years of age.

(B) Upon motion of the petitioner made prior to the attachment of jeopardy the court shall cause the probation officer to investigate and submit a report on the behavioral patterns and social history of the minor being considered for a determination of unfitness. Following submission and consideration of the report, and of any other relevant evidence that the petitioner or the minor may wish to submit, the minor shall be presumed to be not a fit and proper subject to be dealt with under the juvenile court law unless the juvenile court concludes, based upon evidence, which evidence may be of extenuating or mitigating circumstances, that the minor would be amenable to the care, treatment, and training program available through the facilities of the juvenile court, based upon an evaluation of the following criteria:

(i) The degree of criminal sophistication exhibited by the minor.

(ii) Whether the minor can be rehabilitated prior to the expiration of the juvenile court's jurisdiction.

(iii) The minor's previous delinquent history.

(iv) Success of previous attempts by the juvenile court to rehabilitate the minor.

(v) The circumstances and gravity of the offense alleged in the petition to have been committed by the minor.

A determination that the minor is a fit and proper subject to be dealt with under the juvenile court law shall be based on a finding of amenability after consideration of the criteria set forth above, and findings therefor recited in the order as to each of the above criteria that the minor is fit and proper under each and every one of the above criteria. In making a finding of fitness, the court may consider extenuating and mitigating circumstances in evaluating each of the above criteria. In any case in which the hearing has been noticed pursuant to this section, the court shall postpone the taking of a plea to the petition until the conclusion of the fitness hearing and no plea which may already have been entered shall constitute evidence at the hearing. If the minor is found to be a fit and proper subject to be dealt with under the juvenile court law pursuant to this subdivision, the minor shall be committed to placement in a juvenile hall, ranch camp, forestry camp, boot camp, or secure juvenile home pursuant to Section 730, or in any institution operated by the Department of Corrections and Rehabilitation, Division of Juvenile Facilities.

(3) If, pursuant to this subdivision, the minor is found to be not a fit and proper subject for juvenile court treatment and is tried in a court of criminal jurisdiction and found guilty by the trier of fact, the judge may commit the minor to the Department of Corrections and Rehabilitation, Division of Juvenile Facilities, in lieu of sentencing the minor to the state prison, unless the limitations specified in Section 1732.6 apply.

(b) Subdivision (c) shall be applicable in any case in which a minor is alleged to be a person described in Section 602 by reason of the violation of one of the following offenses:

(1) Murder.

(2) Arson [of an inhabited building].

(3) Robbery.

(4) Rape with force or violence or threat of great bodily harm.

(5) Sodomy by force, violence, duress, menace, or threat of great bodily harm.

(6) Lewd or lascivious act as provided in subdivision (b) of Section 288 of the Penal Code.

(7) Oral copulation by force, violence, duress, menace, or threat of great bodily harm.

(8) Any offense specified in subdivision (a) of Section 289 of the Penal Code [sexual penetration by force, violence, duress, menace, threat of immediate and unlawful bodily injury, or threat to retaliate in the future].

(9) Kidnapping for ransom.

(10) Kidnapping for purpose of robbery.

(11) Kidnapping with bodily harm.

(12) Attempted murder.

(13) Assault with a firearm or destructive device.

(14) Assault by any means of force likely to produce great bodily injury.

(15) Discharge of a firearm into an inhabited or occupied building.

(16) Any offense described in Section 1203.09 of the Penal Code [crimes against elderly or disabled persons].

(17) Any offense described in Section 12022.5 [use of firearm, assault weapon or machine gun in commission of or attempt to commit a felony] or 12022.53 [use or discharge of firearm in commission of enumerated felonies] of the Penal Code.

(18) Any felony offense in which the minor personally used a weapon listed in subdivision (a) of Section 12020 of the Penal Code.

(19) Any felony offense described in Section 136.1 [intimidation of witness or victim] or 137 [influencing testimony or information given to law enforcement official] of the Penal Code.

(20) Manufacturing, compounding, or selling one-half ounce or more of any salt or solution of a controlled substance specified in subdivision (e) of Section 11055 of the Health and Safety Code.

(21) Any violent felony, as defined in subdivision (c) of Section 667.5 of the Penal Code, which would also constitute a felony violation of subdivision (b) of Section 186.22 of the Penal Code.

(22) Escape, by the use of force or violence, from any county juvenile hall, home, ranch, camp, or forestry camp in violation of subdivision (b) of Section 871 where great bodily injury is intentionally inflicted upon an employee of the juvenile facility during the commission of the escape.

(23) Torture as described in Sections 206 and 206.1 of the Penal Code.

(24) Aggravated mayhem as described in Section 205 of the Penal Code.

(25) Carjacking, as described in Section 215 of the Penal Code, while armed with a dangerous or deadly weapon.

(26) Kidnapping for purposes of sexual assault, as punishable in subdivision (b) of Section 209 of the Penal Code.

(27) Kidnapping, as punishable in Section 209.5 of the Penal Code.

(28) The offense described in subdivision (c) of Section 12034 of the Penal Code [driver or owner of vehicle permitting firearms in vehicle or discharge of firearms from vehicle].

(29) The offense described in Section 12308 of the Penal Code [explosion or attempt to explode or ignite destructive device or explosive with intent to murder].

(30) Voluntary manslaughter, as described in subdivision (a) of Section 192 of the Penal Code.

(c) With regard to a minor alleged to be a person described in Section 602 by reason of the violation, when he or she was 14 years of age or older, of any of the offenses listed in subdivision (b), upon motion of the petitioner made prior to the attachment of jeopardy the court shall cause the probation officer to investigate and submit a report on the behavioral patterns and social history of the minor being considered for a determination of unfitness. Following submission and consideration of the report, and of any other relevant evidence that the petitioner or the minor may wish to submit, the minor shall be presumed to be not a fit and proper subject to be dealt with under the juvenile court law unless the juvenile court concludes, based upon evidence, which evidence may be of extenuating or mitigating circumstances, that the minor would be amenable to the care, treatment, and training program available through the facilities of the juvenile court based upon an evaluation of each of the following criteria:

(1) The degree of criminal sophistication exhibited by the minor.

(2) Whether the minor can be rehabilitated prior to the expiration of the juvenile court's jurisdiction.

(3) The minor's previous delinquent history.

(4) Success of previous attempts by the juvenile court to rehabilitate the minor.

(5) The circumstances and gravity of the offenses alleged in the petition to have been committed by the minor.

A determination that the minor is a fit and proper subject to be dealt with under the juvenile court law shall be based on a finding of amenability after consideration of the criteria set forth above, and findings therefor recited in the order as to each of the above criteria that the minor is fit and proper under each and every one of the above criteria. In making a finding of fitness, the court may consider extenuating or mitigating circumstances in evaluating each of the above criteria. In any case in which a hearing has been noticed pursuant to this section, the court shall postpone the taking of a plea to the petition until the conclusion of the fitness hearing and no plea which may already have been entered shall constitute evidence at the hearing. If, pursuant to this subdivision, the minor is found to be not a fit and proper subject for juvenile court treatment and is tried in a court of criminal jurisdiction and found guilty by the trier of fact, the judge may commit the minor to the Department of Corrections and Rehabilitation, Division of Juvenile Facilities, in lieu of sentencing the minor to the state prison, unless the limitations specified in Section 1732.6 apply.

(d)(1) Except as provided in subdivision (b) of Section 602,* the district attorney or other appropriate prosecuting officer may file an accusatory

---

* Section 602(b) provides that any person who, when he or she was 14 years of age or older, is alleged to have committed murder (where aggravating circumstances are shown

pleading in a court of criminal jurisdiction against any minor 16 years of age or older who is accused of committing an offense enumerated in subdivision (b).

(2) Except as provided in subdivision (b) of Section 602, the district attorney or other appropriate prosecuting officer may file an accusatory pleading against a minor 14 years of age or older in a court of criminal jurisdiction in any case in which any one or more of the following circumstances apply:

(A) The minor is alleged to have committed an offense that if committed by an adult would be punishable by death or imprisonment in the state prison for life.

(B) The minor is alleged to have personally used a firearm during the commission or attempted commission of a felony, as described in Section 12022.5 or 12022.53 of the Penal Code.

(C) The minor is alleged to have committed an offense listed in subdivision (b) in which any one or more of the following circumstances apply:

(i) The minor has previously been found to be a person described in Section 602 by reason of the commission of an offense listed in subdivision (b).

(ii) The offense was committed for the benefit of, at the direction of, or in association with any criminal street gang, as defined in subdivision (f) of Section 186.22 of the Penal Code, with the specific intent to promote, further, or assist in any criminal conduct by gang members.

(iii) The offense was committed for the purpose of intimidating or interfering with any other person's free exercise or enjoyment of any right secured to him or her by the Constitution or laws of this state or by the Constitution or laws of the United States and because of the other person's race, color, religion, ancestry, national origin, disability, gender, or sexual orientation, or because the minor perceives that the other person has one or more of those characteristics, as described in Title 11.6 (commencing with Section 422.6) of Part 1 of the Penal Code.

(iv) The victim of the offense was 65 years of age or older, or blind, deaf, quadriplegic, paraplegic, developmentally disabled, or confined to a wheelchair, and that disability was known or reasonably should have been known to the minor at the time of the commission of the offense.

(3) Except as provided in subdivision (b) of Section 602, the district attorney or other appropriate prosecuting officer may file an accusatory pleading in a court of criminal jurisdiction against any minor 16 years of age or older who is accused of committing one of the following offenses, if the minor has previously been found to be a person described in Section 602 by reason of the violation of any felony offense, when he or she was 14 years of age or older:

and the juvenile is alleged to have been the principal) or one of several enumerated sex offenses, shall be prosecuted as an adult.

(A) Any felony offense in which it is alleged that the victim of the offense was 65 years of age or older, or blind, deaf, quadriplegic, paraplegic, developmentally disabled, or confined to a wheelchair, and that disability was known or reasonably should have been known to the minor at the time of the commission of the offense;

(B) Any felony offense committed for the purposes of intimidating or interfering with any other person's free exercise or enjoyment of any right secured to him or her by the Constitution or laws of this state or by the Constitution or laws of the United States and because of the other person's race, color, religion, ancestry, national origin, disability, gender, or sexual orientation, or because the minor perceived that the other person had one or more of those characteristics, as described in Title 11.6 (commencing with Section 422.6) of Part 1 of the Penal Code; or

(C) The offense was committed for the benefit of, at the direction of, or in association with any criminal street gang as prohibited by Section 186.22 of the Penal Code.

(4) In any case in which the district attorney or other appropriate prosecuting officer has filed an accusatory pleading against a minor in a court of criminal jurisdiction pursuant to this subdivision, the case shall then proceed according to the laws applicable to a criminal case. In conjunction with the preliminary hearing as provided for in Section 738 of the Penal Code, the magistrate shall make a finding that reasonable cause exists to believe that the minor comes within this subdivision. If reasonable cause is not established, the criminal court shall transfer the case to the juvenile court having jurisdiction over the matter.

(5) For any offense for which the prosecutor may file the accusatory pleading in a court of criminal jurisdiction pursuant to this subdivision, but elects instead to file a petition in the juvenile court, if the minor is subsequently found to be a person described in subdivision (a) of Section 602, the minor shall be committed to placement in a juvenile hall, ranch camp, forestry camp, boot camp, or secure juvenile home pursuant to Section 730, or in any institution operated by the Department of Corrections and Rehabilitation, Division of Juvenile Facilities.

(6) If, pursuant to this subdivision, the minor is found to be not a fit and proper subject for juvenile court treatment and is tried in a court of criminal jurisdiction and found guilty by the trier of fact, the judge may commit the minor to the Department of Corrections and Rehabilitation, Division of Juvenile Facilities in lieu of sentencing the minor to the state prison, unless the limitations specified in Section 1732.6 apply.

. . .

NOTES

(1) The most common way the waiver decision is made is to leave that determination to the discretion of the juvenile court. As will be seen below, standards of varying specificity are sometimes provided to guide or limit that discretion. It is here that the procedural rights provided by *Kent* and its progeny become significant. See *Donald L. v. Superior Court*, 7 Cal.3d 592, 102 Cal.Rptr. 850, 498 P.2d 1098 (1972).

(2) The Juvenile Justice Standards adopt traditional judicial waiver by the juvenile court as the exclusive means of allocating jurisdiction between courts. Standard 1.1 of the Standards Relating to Transfer Between Courts posits original jurisdiction over all juveniles (persons under 17 years of age) in the juvenile court and provides that the criminal court can exercise jurisdiction in appropriate cases only upon transfer from the juvenile court following a waiver hearing. Standards 2.1 through 2.4 deal with waiver procedures, including the requirement of a hearing.

(3) In some states in connection with waiver proceedings the child may request to be tried as an adult. See, e.g., Fla.Stat.Ann. § 985.556(1); Ill.Comp.Stat.Ann. ch. 705, § 405/5–130(9); *State ex rel. Sumner v. Williams*, 304 So.2d 472 (Fla.App.1974) (court rule in Florida that child may be waived on demand is mandatory, not discretionary, with juvenile court judge); accord, *People v. Thomas*, 34 Ill.App.3d 1002, 341 N.E.2d 178 (1976); see also *United States v. Hill*, 538 F.2d 1072 (4th Cir.1976) (18 U.S.C.A. § 5032 permits the child on advice of counsel to be waived on demand to be tried as an adult). The juvenile's decision to be tried as an adult must be knowing and voluntary. See, e.g., *State v. N.G.*, 305 N.J.Super. 132, 701 A.2d 976 (1997). Unless the statutory scheme provides for the right of a juvenile to demand waiver, a juvenile does not have a right to be tried as an adult, and waiver can only be ordered on the prosecution's motion or the court's own motion. See, e.g., *In re D.B.*, 187 Ga.App. 3, 369 S.E.2d 498 (1988); *In re K.A.A.*, 410 N.W.2d 836 (Minn.1987); see also *State ex rel. Romley v. Superior Court*, 170 Ariz. 339, 823 P.2d 1347 (App.1991); *J.D.C. v. District Court*, 910 P.2d 684 (Colo.1996).

(4) In some cases waiver is mandatory, generally in the case of a juvenile charged with one of certain enumerated offenses or a juvenile with a prior record. See, e.g., Ga.Code Ann. §§ 15–11–30.2(b)(3)–(4), 15–11–30.3; Ill.Comp.Stat.Ann. ch. 705, § 405/5–805(1); Ind.Code Ann. § 31–30–1–4; Minn.Stat.Ann. § 260B.125(5); N.C.Gen.Stat. § 7B–2200; Pa.Stat.Ann. tit. 42, § 6355(e). This kind of statutory mandate is tantamount to exclusion of certain offenses from the juvenile court's jurisdiction. See subdivision 1, Legislative Allocation of Jurisdiction, page 947 supra. Such statutes generally have been upheld against constitutional challenge. See, e.g., *People v. P.H.*, 145 Ill.2d 209, 164 Ill.Dec. 137, 582 N.E.2d 700 (1991). Delaware's statute, however, was held invalid on both equal protection and due process grounds because, in providing for automatic waiver of children charged with a felony who turn 18 while awaiting an adjudicatory hearing, the statute gave unbridled discretion to the prosecutor. *Hughes v. State*, 653 A.2d 241 (Del.1994).

(5) Some states have "once waived, always waived" statutes. These statutes provide that once jurisdiction over a child is waived it is deemed waived for any offense with which the child might be charged in the future. See, e.g., Ala.Code §§ 12–15–1(8), 12–15–34(j); Cal.Welf. & Inst.Code Ann. § 707.01(a)(5)–(6); Miss. Code Ann. § 43–21–157(8); Ohio Rev.Code Ann. §§ 2152.02(C)(5), 2152.12(A)(2)(a); Wash.Rev.Code Ann. § 13.40.020(14). These statutes also have been upheld, on the ground that they constitute a permissible exercise of legislative prerogative rather than judicial discretion as in *Kent*. See, e.g., *State v. Sharon*, 100 Wn.2d 230, 668 P.2d 584 (1983), aff'g 33 Wn.App. 491, 655 P.2d 1193 (1982).

(6) Suppose a juvenile's case is transferred to criminal court, where he or she pleads guilty to or is convicted, following trial, of a lesser offense that would not have been transferable in the first instance. Does the criminal court still have jurisdiction over the juvenile? In *Castro v. State*, 703 S.W.2d 804 (Tex.App.1986), the court held that where the juvenile was transferred on a charge of murder, her plea of guilty to and conviction of burglary were valid where both charges arose out of the same incident. See also *People v. Dean*, 198 Mich.App. 267, 497 N.W.2d 223 (1993) (having acquired original jurisdiction over juvenile charged with assault with intent to murder, as a result of automatic waiver provision, circuit court did not lose

jurisdiction when juvenile pleaded guilty to lesser offense that would not have been automatically transferable).

To the contrary, several states take the view that under the above circumstances the case must be remanded to the juvenile court unless the juvenile is charged by accusatory instrument with a transferable offense in criminal court. See, e.g., Ky.Rev.Stat. Ann. § 640.010(3); Or.Rev.Stat. § 419C.361(1); see also *State v. Torres*, 206 Conn. 346, 538 A.2d 185 (1988) (where criminal court found lack of probable cause to sustain murder charge on basis of which juvenile had been transferred, and state substituted an information charging manslaughter, manslaughter charge should have been remanded to juvenile court); *Jenkins v. State*, 700 S.W.2d 759 (Tex.App.1985) (where following transfer, grand jury returned a no bill, subsequent indictment was invalid and jurisdiction reverted to juvenile court). But see *Fuller v. State*, 700 S.W.2d 5 (Tex.App.1985) (where following transfer, indictment was handed up prior to probable cause hearing and was subsequently quashed, second indictment following probable cause hearing was valid).

The Texas cases and the problem generally are discussed in Robert O. Dawson, Prosecution of Juveniles in Texas Criminal Courts: Eliminating the Jurisdictional Requirement of an Examining Trial, 23 Hous.L.Rev. 1067 (1986). A broader analysis of the problem is found in Samuel M. Davis, The Efficacy of a Probable Cause Requirement in Juvenile Proceedings, 59 N.C.L.Rev. 723 (1981).

Some states also provide that if the juvenile is convicted of a lesser included offense, the juvenile is to be returned to the juvenile court for disposition. See, e.g., Or.Rev.Stat. § 419C.361; Vt.Stat.Ann. tit. 33, § 5506(h).

If a transferable offense is transferred to criminal court, the criminal court usually has jurisdiction over all related offenses committed as part of the same occurrence. See, e.g., *State v. Karow*, 154 Wis.2d 375, 453 N.W.2d 181 (App.1990). In fact, in most jurisdictions the juvenile court, if it is contemplating waiving jurisdiction at all, is compelled to waive jurisdiction over all offenses or else waive jurisdiction over none. See, e.g., *Romley v. Superior Court*, 174 Ariz. 126, 847 P.2d 627 (App.1993); *Richardson v. State*, 770 S.W.2d 797 (Tex.Crim.App.1989).

c.   THE NATURE OF A TRANSFER HEARING

GENERAL STATUTES OF NORTH CAROLINA (West)

§ 7B–2200. Transfer of jurisdiction of juvenile to superior court

After notice, hearing, and a finding of probable cause the court may, upon motion of the prosecutor or the juvenile's attorney or upon its own motion, transfer jurisdiction over a juvenile to superior court if the juvenile was 13 years of age or older at the time the juvenile allegedly committed an offense that would be a felony if committed by an adult. If the alleged felony constitutes a Class A felony and the court finds probable cause, the court shall transfer the case to the superior court for trial as in the case of adults.

§ 7B–2202. Probable cause hearing

(a) The court shall conduct a hearing to determine probable cause in all felony cases in which a juvenile was 13 years of age or older when the offense was allegedly committed. The hearing shall be conducted within 15 days of the date of the juvenile's first appearance.

(b) At the probable-cause hearing:

(1) A prosecutor shall represent the State;

(2) The juvenile shall be represented by counsel;

(3) The juvenile may testify, call, and examine witnesses, and present evidence; and

(4) Each witness shall testify under oath or affirmation and be subject to cross-examination.

(c) The State shall by nonhearsay evidence, or by evidence that satisfies an exception to the hearsay rule, show that there is probable cause to believe that the offense charged has been committed and that there is probable cause to believe that the juvenile committed it, except:

(1) A report or copy of a report made by a physicist, chemist, firearms identification expert, fingerprint technician, or an expert or technician in some other scientific, professional, or medical field, concerning the results of an examination, comparison, or test performed in connection with the case in issue, when stated in a report by that person, is admissible in evidence;

(2) If there is no serious contest, reliable hearsay is admissible to prove value, ownership of property, possession of property in a person other than the juvenile, lack of consent of the owner, possessor, or custodian of property to the breaking or entering of premises, chain of custody, and authenticity of signatures.

(d) Counsel for the juvenile may waive in writing the right to the hearing and stipulate to a finding of probable cause.

(e) If probable cause is found and transfer to superior court is not required by G.S. 7B–2200, upon motion of the prosecutor or the juvenile's attorney or upon its own motion, the court shall either proceed to a transfer hearing or set a date for that hearing. If the juvenile has not received notice of the intention to seek transfer at least five days prior to the probable cause hearing, the court, at the request of the juvenile, shall continue the transfer hearing.

(f) If the court does not find probable cause for a felony offense, the court shall:

(1) Dismiss the proceeding, or

(2) If the court finds probable cause to believe that the juvenile committed a lesser included offense that would constitute a misdemeanor if committed by an adult, either proceed to an adjudicatory hearing or set a date for that hearing.

§ 7B–2203.   Transfer hearing

(a) At the transfer hearing, the prosecutor and the juvenile may be heard and may offer evidence, and the juvenile's attorney may examine any court or probation records, or other records the court may consider in determining whether to transfer the case.

(b) In the transfer hearing, the court shall determine whether the protection of the public and the needs of the juvenile will be served by transfer of the case to superior court and shall consider the following factors:

(1) The age of the juvenile;

(2) The maturity of the juvenile;

(3) The intellectual functioning of the juvenile;

(4) The prior record of the juvenile;

(5) Prior attempts to rehabilitate the juvenile;

(6) Facilities or programs available to the court prior to the expiration of the court's jurisdiction under this Subchapter and the likelihood that the juvenile would benefit from treatment or rehabilitative efforts;

(7) Whether the alleged offense was committed in an aggressive, violent, premeditated, or willful manner; and

(8) The seriousness of the offense and whether the protection of the public requires that the juvenile be prosecuted as an adult.

(c) Any order of transfer shall specify the reasons for transfer. When the case is transferred to superior court, the superior court has jurisdiction over that felony, any offense based on the same act or transaction or on a series of acts or transactions connected together or constituting parts of a single scheme or plan of that felony, and any greater or lesser included offense of that felony.

(d) If the court does not transfer the case to superior court, the court shall either proceed to an adjudicatory hearing or set a date for that hearing.

SOME RECURRING ISSUES

RIGHT TO COUNSEL

Kent did not finally decide the issue of right to counsel at the waiver hearing, since the Court was not faced with that issue. Morris Kent had retained counsel. Yet the Court did state that "there is no place in our system of law for reaching a result of such tremendous consequences without ceremony—without hearing, without effective assistance of counsel." 383 U.S. at 554. In subsequent cases courts, using a "critical stage" analysis, made clear that under *Kent* and *Gault* a juvenile is constitutionally entitled to counsel at a waiver hearing. See, e.g., *Kemplen v. Maryland*, 428 F.2d 169 (4th Cir.1970); *Inge v. Slayton*, 395 F.Supp. 560 (E.D.Va. 1975).

Counsel has a critical role to play at juvenile waiver hearings. The child's counsel can gather information favorable to the client, scrutinize the reports of the social staff, and suggest alternatives for handling the child within the juvenile process. "The child's advocate should search for a plan, or perhaps a range of plans, which may persuade the court that the welfare of the child and the safety of the community can be served without waiver." *Haziel v. United States*, 404 F.2d 1275 (D.C.Cir.1968). For an excellent discussion of the role of counsel at the waiver hearing see Thomas F. Geraghty & Will Rhee, Learning from Tragedy: Representing Children in Discretionary Waiver Hearings, 33 Wake Forest L.Rev. 595 (1998).

Providing the child with a right to counsel implies a right to effective or competent counsel. The combined effect of a failure to appoint counsel until a waiver hearing was about to begin and "counsel's notable lack of zeal" in attempting to present the court alternatives to waiver of the child, led the Seventh Circuit to conclude the juvenile had been denied the effective assistance of counsel, rendering his transfer to adult court invalid. *Geboy v. Gray*, 471 F.2d 575 (7th Cir.1973). Mere lateness of appointment of counsel does not establish ineffective assistance. In *People v. Banks*, 29 Ill.App.3d 923, 331 N.E.2d 561 (1975), the court held that an attorney appointed to represent the child was not denied adequate time to prepare when the transfer hearing was held on the day of counsel's appointment, especially in light of counsel's prior representation of the child in other recent delinquency proceedings. Should lateness of appointment create a presumption of ineffective assistance? What if counsel in *Banks* had objected to going forward with the transfer hearing? The issue of competency of counsel in a waiver hearing is thoroughly discussed in *State v. Jack*, 144 N.J. 240, 676 A.2d 545 (1996), in which the court remanded the case to the trial court for a determination of whether counsel's strategy in refraining from presenting case of potential for rehabilitation was acceptable and whether prejudice to juvenile resulted.

A difficult issue is that of waiver of the right to counsel at a transfer hearing. The Juvenile Justice Standards Relating to Transfer Between Courts do not permit waiver of the right to counsel at a transfer hearing. The Commentary to Standard 2.3(A) stresses the critical importance of the presence of counsel at the transfer hearing, concluding that the absolute prohibition of waiver of counsel at that stage is the better rule.

The issue usually arises when the juvenile pleads guilty or goes to trial in the criminal court without having objected to the failure to appoint counsel at the waiver hearing. The general rule is that a guilty plea operates to waive any nonjurisdictional defects. Courts disagree, however, over whether procedural irregularities constitute jurisdictional defects. *Acuna v. Baker*, 418 F.2d 639 (10th Cir.1969) held that a guilty plea by a juvenile in the criminal court waives denial of the right to counsel at the waiver hearing. *Powell v. Hocker*, 453 F.2d 652 (9th Cir.1971), overruled on other grounds, *Harris v. Procunier*, 498 F.2d 576 (9th Cir.1974), reached the opposite conclusion, holding that a guilty plea in the subsequent adult case does not waive a defect in the transfer proceedings. *Crumley v. State*, 3 Tenn.Cr.App. 385, 462 S.W.2d 252 (1970) and *Neller v. State*, 79 N.M. 528, 445 P.2d 949 (1968), are cases in accord with the Tenth Circuit's decision in *Acuna*. On the other hand, in *State v. Grenz*, 243 N.W.2d 375 (N.D. 1976), the court held that denial of the right to counsel at the waiver hearing is a jurisdictional defect not waived by the guilty plea in criminal court, and *James v. Cox*, 323 F.Supp. 15 (E.D.Va.1971), held that a juvenile's failure to request counsel at the transfer proceeding did not amount to a waiver. Of course, if the juvenile is represented by competent counsel and fails to raise any claim of irregularities during the transfer proceedings, the guilty plea operates as a waiver of the irregularities. *State v. LePage*, 536 S.W.2d 834 (Mo.App.1976).

In Texas the juvenile court must conduct a diagnostic study of the child as a mandatory precondition to transfer to adult court. Where the child's attorney refused to permit him to answer any questions concerning the homicide he was alleged to have committed it was error for the juvenile court judge to hold such refusal a waiver of the right to the diagnostic study. Further the appellate court held the attorney alone could not make an effective waiver of any substantial right of the child without the presence and concurrence of the subject child. *R.E.M. v. State*, 532 S.W.2d 645 (Tex.Civ.App.1975).

NOTICE

Notice of the waiver hearing to the child, his parents and counsel is a constitutional requirement. Reasonable notice of the waiver hearing and the charge to be considered and a reasonable opportunity to prepare a defense must be given. See *State v. McArdle*, 156 W.Va. 409, 194 S.E.2d 174 (1973), where the waiver was held invalid for lack of prior notice and opportunity to prepare a defense even though the child's parents and counsel were present at the waiver hearing. See also *State v. Grenz*, 243 N.W.2d 375 (N.D.1976), in which the court held adequate notice constitutionally required.

Reed v. State, 125 Ga.App. 568, 188 S.E.2d 392 (1972), held that the failure to meet statutory notice requirements was not waived by the appearance of the parents at the hearing since they may not have known the purpose of the hearing. *Ferguson v. Slayton*, 340 F.Supp. 276 (W.D.Va. 1972), is another case where the failure to notify parents of a transfer hearing rendered a subsequent conviction void. In *L.C.L. v. State*, 319 So.2d 133 (Fla.App.1975) the court held it reversible error to proceed with a waiver hearing where defendant's mother had not been sent a summons even though the child's sister with whom he was living was present and he was represented by counsel. Similarly, in *In re D.W.M.*, 562 S.W.2d 851 (Tex.1978), the court held that failure to give notice to the *juvenile* as required by statute invalidated the waiver and transfer; accord, *Alaniz v. State*, 2 S.W.3d 451 (Tex.App.1999).

There are, however, cases to the contrary on the issue of waiver of the right to notice. A Colorado notice requirement that parents be served with a summons prior to the beginning of a transfer proceeding was found to be waived in *People ex rel. G.A.T.*, 183 Colo. 111, 515 P.2d 104 (1973), when the mother voluntarily appeared at the hearing. In *Turner v. Commonwealth*, 216 Va. 666, 222 S.E.2d 517 (1976), the court held that failure to give notice is a procedural rather than jurisdictional defect, and the defect was cured in this case because all necessary parties actually appeared at the waiver hearing. Subsequently, Virginia amended its statutes to provide that an indictment in criminal court cures any defect in juvenile court waiver proceedings except with respect to the juvenile's age. Va.Code Ann. § 16.1–269.1(E). The Virginia Supreme Court has held that indictment cures any defects in juvenile proceedings where the offense occurred after the effective date of the statute. *Moore v. Commonwealth*, 259 Va. 405, 527 S.E.2d 415 (2000). Even with respect to an offense occurring prior to its effective date, the court has held that lack of notice to a parent is waived if it was not raised in a timely fashion. *Nelson v. Warden*, 262 Va. 276, 552 S.E.2d 73 (2001). Failure to notify the natural father and adoptive mother of the transfer hearing was not error where the child's natural mother acted as guardian ad litem and he was represented by counsel. *In re Honsaker*, 539 S.W.2d 198 (Tex.Civ.App.1976). In that case the court stated: "The natural father and adoptive mother are not parties to the lawsuit, and no contention is advanced that they have parental rights which might be affected by the [transfer] hearing." See also *In re Juvenile*, 364 Mass. 531, 306 N.E.2d 822 (1974).

PRESENTATION OF EVIDENCE

A juvenile has a right to the production of witnesses and records that are needed to resist a petition for waiver to an adult court. *In re Brown*, 183 N.W.2d 731 (Iowa 1971).

The Juvenile Justice Standards Relating to Transfer Between Courts, Standard 2.3(C), provides for the services of expert witnesses to resist the motion for transfer at court expense for indigents.

Some state statutes guarantee the child and his attorney access to social reports prepared by the court or its probation staff. See, e.g., Tex.Fam.Code Ann. § 54.02(e).

RULES OF EVIDENCE

The rules of evidence are not always strictly followed at a waiver hearing, largely because courts tend to view the waiver hearing as dispositional in nature. Representative cases to that effect are *People v. Taylor*, 76 Ill.2d 289, 29 Ill.Dec. 103, 391 N.E.2d 366 (1979); *People v. Hana*, 443 Mich. 202, 504 N.W.2d 166 (1993); *In re Eduardo L.*, 136 N.H. 678, 621 A.2d 923 (1993); and *In re S.J.M.*, 922 S.W.2d 241 (Tex.App.1996). Thus, social reports, though hearsay in character, are admissible. See, e.g., *People v. Taylor*, supra; *In re Murphy*, 15 Md.App. 434, 291 A.2d 867 (1972). Of course, this is tempered by the *Kent* mandate that the juvenile's counsel must have access to social reports to be used at a waiver proceeding and an opportunity to challenge or impeach the findings. *Hazell v. State*, 12 Md.App. 144, 277 A.2d 639 (1971). Probation officers' reports, law enforcement officers' reports and arrest records are other items that may be admitted though in the nature of hearsay. *In re T.D.S.*, 289 N.W.2d 137 (Minn.1980); *Sheppard v. Rhay*, 73 Wn.2d 734, 440 P.2d 422 (1968). Even illegally seized evidence, where it was found to be reliable, has been held admissible in a waiver hearing. *Marvin v. State*, 95 Nev. 836, 603 P.2d 1056 (1979). In *In re S.J.M.*, supra, the court held that the Sixth Amendment right of confrontation and cross-examination did not apply to a waiver hearing; thus, statements by co-actors were properly admitted. For an argument that the privilege against self-incrimination should be extended to waiver hearings, see Sarah Freitas, Comment, Extending the Privilege Against Self–Incrimination to the Juvenile Waiver Hearing, 62 U.Chi. L.Rev. 301 (1995).

Is a waiver hearing dispositional if in addition to a finding of non-amenability a state requires a finding of probable cause to believe the juvenile committed the alleged delinquent act? Some states take the view that hearsay or other incompetent evidence is not admissible to support a probable cause finding. See, e.g., N.C.Gen.Stat. § 7B–2202(c); *R.J.D. v. State*, 799 P.2d 1122 (Okl.Cr.App.1990). The Juvenile Justice Standards recognize the distinction between the two required findings. Standard 2.2(B) of the Standards Relating to Transfer Between Courts provides that only evidence that would be admissible in an adjudicatory hearing is admissible to support a finding of probable cause in a waiver hearing, whereas Standard 2.2(C) provides that on the issue of nonamenability evidence is admissible that would be admissible in a dispositional hearing. The rationale for this view is set forth in the Commentary to Standard 2.2(B) at pp. 37–39: to encourage reliable fact finding and judicial economy. Use of evidence that would not be admissible in a subsequent adjudicatory hearing or criminal trial would be a waste of time and effort. See *People v. Hana*, supra (incriminating statements admissible at nonamenability phase of the waiver hearing but not at probable cause phase); *In re P.W.N.*, 301 N.W.2d 636 (N.D.1981) (hearsay admissible on nonamenability but not on probable cause).

Would it be helpful if the probable cause and the amenability determinations were conducted in separate phases? Some states so provide and further provide that more formal rules attach to the probable cause phase. See, e.g., Ariz.R.Juv.Proc. 34(F); Me.Rev.Stat.Ann. tit. 15, § 3101(4)(B).

Even if hearsay or other incompetent evidence is admissible in support of a transfer decision there may be some point at which the sole ground of the state's case for transfer is hearsay. When this occurs, it may be argued the juvenile's constitutional rights to confront and cross-examine the witnesses against him has been denied. See *In re Harris*, 218 Kan. 625, 544 P.2d 1403 (1976) (all state's evidence of nonamenability to juvenile treatment based on written reports admitted over hearsay objection of juvenile's attorney—held transfer order error); *People ex rel. Guggenheim v. Mucci*, 77 Misc.2d 41, 352 N.Y.S.2d 561 (Sup.Ct., Kings County 1974), aff'd 46 A.D.2d 683, 360 N.Y.S.2d 71 (1974) (due process requires that probable cause determination not be based solely on hearsay); *Comer v. Tom A.M.*, 184 W.Va. 634, 403 S.E.2d 182 (1991). In *O.M. v. State*, 595 So.2d 514 (Ala.Crim.App.1991), the court held that not only may hearsay not constitute the sole basis for a finding of probably cause to support transfer, it is not admissible at all if it violates the juvenile's right to confrontation.

One might think that occasionally a juvenile might benefit from relaxed application of the rules of evidence. In *People v. Reese*, 90 Ill.App.3d 284, 45 Ill.Dec. 597, 412 N.E.2d 1179 (1980), however, the court, while holding hearsay admissible to sustain a nonamenability finding, emphasizing the differences between a waiver hearing and an adjudicatory hearing or criminal trial, held that the trial court did not abuse its discretion in refusing to admit the juvenile's offer of polygraph evidence to refute the hearsay offered by the state.

STANDARD OF PROOF

The standard of proof applied at the waiver hearing varies from jurisdiction to jurisdiction, from substantial evidence, *People v. Dunbar*, 423 Mich. 380, 377 N.W.2d 262 (1985), to clear and convincing evidence, Minn.Stat.Ann. § 260B.125(2)(6)(ii), to perhaps the most common standard, preponderance of the evidence, Md.Cts. & Jud.Proc.Code Ann. § 3–8A–06(d); *State ex rel. Juvenile Dep't v. George*, 124 Or.App. 257, 862 P.2d

531 (1993). Suppose the statute does not provide a standard of proof? In *Stout v. Commonwealth*, 44 S.W.3d 781 (Ky.Ct.App.2000), the court upheld such a statute against a constitutional due process claim, noting that "[o]bviously, the decision must be supported by substantial evidence to pass judicial review; however, no greater standard need be applied." 44 S.W.3d at 788. *In re Winship*, 397 U.S. 358, 90 S.Ct. 1068, 25 L.Ed.2d 368 (1970), which held that the applicable standard of proof in delinquency cases is proof beyond a reasonable doubt, was expressly limited to the adjudicatory hearing.

The Juvenile Justice Standards Relating to Transfer Between Courts reject the preponderance standard for the requirement of a finding by clear and convincing evidence in 2.2(C). "A finding that a juvenile is not a proper person to be handled by the juvenile court must include determinations, *by clear and convincing evidence, . . .*" (emphasis added). Will the choice of standard of proof really make a functional difference at transfer hearings?

Can the burden of proof ever constitutionally be placed on the juvenile to show amenability to juvenile treatment? Section 707(c) of California's Welfare and Institutions Code provides:

> With regard to a minor alleged to be [delinquent] by reason of the violation, when he or she was 14 years of age or older, of any of the offenses listed in subdivision (b) [murder, arson, robbery, forcible rape and other sex offenses, kidnapping, attempted murder, aggravated assault, various firearms offenses, various controlled substance offenses, carjacking, and numerous other serious crimes], upon motion of the petitioner made prior to the attachment of jeopardy the court shall cause the probation officer to investigate and submit a report on the behavioral patterns and social history of the minor being considered for a determination of unfitness. Following submission and consideration of the report, and of any other relevant evidence that the petitioner or the minor may wish to submit, the minor shall be presumed to be not a fit and proper subject to be dealt with under the juvenile court law unless the juvenile court concludes, based upon evidence, which evidence may be of extenuating or mitigating circumstances, that the minor would be amenable to the care, treatment, and training program available through the facilities of the juvenile court. . . .

In *Sheila O. v. Superior Court*, 125 Cal.App.3d 812, 178 Cal.Rptr. 418 (1981) the court upheld as constitutional the § 707 presumption of unfitness for juvenile court treatment, saying:

> Petitioner . . . contends that the presumed fact of unfitness cannot reasonably be said . . . to flow from the proved fact of age and the charge of a serious crime. But the tangible effect of the new language in Section 707 was to lower the age of adult criminal responsibility for specified crimes unless the minor could show reasons why he should be treated as a juvenile. That change in juvenile court law was well within the power of the Legislature.

178 Cal.Rptr. at 421.

For application of the California statute, see *Hicks v. Superior Court*, 36 Cal.App.4th 1649, 43 Cal.Rptr.2d 269 (1995). The Kansas statute, Kan.Stat.

Ann. § 38–2347(a)(2), which creates a rebuttable presumption that older youths charged with certain serious offenses be treated as adults, also was upheld against constitutional challenge in *State v. Coleman*, 271 Kan. 733, 26 P.3d 613 (2001). See also *Commonwealth v. Wallace*, 495 Pa. 295, 433 A.2d 856 (1981), upholding a similar Pennsylvania statute requiring a juvenile seeking transfer to juvenile court to bear the burden of showing his or her need of and amenability to juvenile court treatment.

At a time when § 707(c) provided for presumptive transfer of juveniles over 16 charged with certain serious offenses, compared with the present statute's age limit of 14, statistics from Los Angeles County strongly indicated that the shift in the burden of proof to 16 and 17 year olds pursuant to § 707(c) had resulted in far more transfers from juvenile to adult court. In 1979, when the statute did not provide for presumptive transfer at all, 602 transfer hearings were held resulting in 250 (42%) transfers. In 1980, under the new § 707(c), 814 hearings were held producing 507 (62%) transfers. Juvenile Court Coordinators Yearly Judicial Workload Report (Delinquency) Los Angeles County, California 1979 and 1980. With lowering of the age of eligibility from 16 to 14 and the increase in the number of qualifying offense, even more transfers might be expected.

SELF INCRIMINATION

Commonwealth v. Ransom, 446 Pa. 457, 288 A.2d 762 (1972), held that evidence given at a waiver hearing shall not be admissible as evidence against the child in any case or proceeding in any other court. See also *State v. Ross*, 516 S.W.2d 311 (Mo.App.1974) and Mo.Ann.Stat. § 211.271(3).

Standard 2.3(I) of the Juvenile Justice Standards reads: "The juvenile may remain silent at the waiver hearing. No admission by the juvenile during the waiver hearing should be admissible to establish guilt or to impeach testimony in any subsequent proceeding, except a perjury proceeding." Should the juvenile's refusal to confess be used as an index of nonamenability and uncooperative attitude to justify a transfer? See *R.E.M. v. State*, 532 S.W.2d 645 (Tex.Civ.App.1975). Should the protection of § 2.3(I) of the Transfer Standards be extended to bar the admissibility of the child's statements made at the transfer hearing at a subsequent adjudicatory hearing if juvenile court jurisdiction is retained?

In *Sheila O. v. Superior Court*, 125 Cal.App.3d 812, 178 Cal.Rptr. 418 (1981) the court held that statements made by a juvenile at his or her transfer hearing are inadmissible at the subsequent adjudicatory hearing except for the purpose of impeaching the juvenile's testimony.

APPEAL

States differ over whether a waiver order is directly appealable. Sometimes statutory law provides for the kinds of orders that are directly appealable. See, e.g., Haw.Rev.Stat. § 571–22.5; Idaho Code § 20–528; Md.Cts. & Jud.Proc.Ann. § 3–8A–06(g). If the courts are called on to decide the question, many require a final judgment on the merits in adult court before appellate review of the transfer decision is allowed. See, e.g., *People v. Browning*, 45 Cal.App.3d 125, 119 Cal.Rptr. 420 (1975), overruled on other grounds, *People v. Williams*, 16 Cal.3d 663, 128 Cal.Rptr. 888, 547 P.2d 1000 (1976); *D.H. v. People*, 192 Colo. 542, 561 P.2d 5 (1977); *Robinson v. State*, 704 A.2d 269 (Del.1998); *In re Clay*, 246 N.W.2d 263 (Iowa 1976); *W.C.H. v. Matthews*, 536 S.W.2d 679 (Tex.Civ.App.1976).

On the other hand, some states allow immediate appeal of a waiver order on the ground that it is a final order in the sense that it terminates the jurisdiction of the juvenile court. See, e.g., *In re Doe I*, 50 Hawaii 537, 444 P.2d 459 (1968); *In re I.Q.S.*, 309 Minn. 78, 244 N.W.2d 30 (1976); *State v. T.D.R.*, 347 N.C. 489, 495 S.E.2d 700 (1998); *State ex rel. Atcheson*, 575 P.2d 181 (Utah 1978).

In still other states appealability of a waiver order depends on which party seeks to appeal. Illinois does not permit the juvenile to appeal because the waiver order is reviewable on appeal of the conviction in criminal court, *People v. Jiles*, 43 Ill.2d 145, 251 N.E.2d 529 (1969), but does permit the state to appeal a denial of motion to transfer because such an order is not reviewable at the conclusion of the proceedings in juvenile court, *People v. Martin*, 67 Ill.2d 462, 10 Ill.Dec. 563, 367 N.E.2d 1329 (1977). But in Oregon the juvenile is allowed to appeal because the effect of an order transferring jurisdiction to the criminal court is to terminate the jurisdiction of the juvenile court, *State v. Little*, 241 Or. 557, 407 P.2d 627 (1965), whereas the state cannot appeal because the effect of an order denying the state's motion to transfer is that the status quo is maintained and jurisdiction continues in the juvenile court, *In re Brown*, 33 Or.App. 423, 576 P.2d 830 (1978).

Sometimes it is not clear whether the appropriate procedure is appeal of the waiver order or motion to dismiss the indictment on the adult prosecution. See, e.g., *Murphy v. State*, 403 So.2d 314 (Ala.Crim.App.1981); *State v. Abbott*, 654 S.W.2d 260 (Mo.App.1983).

For the problems caused when the subject juvenile outgrows the maximum age for juvenile court jurisdiction while awaiting appeal of the waiver order, see *Brown v. Cox*, 319 F.Supp. 999 (E.D.Va.1970), reversed and remanded, 467 F.2d 1255 (4th Cir.1972). In light of this problem, Standard 2.4 provides that transfer decisions are appealable and stays criminal court jurisdiction until the appeal is decided or the time to file an appeal has elapsed.

See H. Allen Glover, Jr., Note, Review of Improper Transfer Hearings, 60 Va.L.Rev. 818 (1974), in which the author recommends the direct appeal of waiver orders because of the difficulties of reviewing improper transfer hearings at a later date.

STATEMENT OF REASONS

The requirement set forth in *Kent* of a statement of reasons by the juvenile court judge justifying the decision to transfer the child to adult court lessens the chance that the judge will consider the waiver decision lightly, and make a hasty and unreasoned decision. See Charles H. Whitebread & Robert Batey, Transfer Between Courts: Proposals of the Juvenile Justice Standards Project, 63 Va.L.Rev. 221, 240–41 (1977). The written statement of reasons also enhances meaningful review by the appellate court. As the court stated in *Gregory v. State*, 270 Ind. 435, 386 N.E.2d 675 (1979), even when a waiver hearing is required and statutory criteria are provided, that "does not vitiate the requirement of the case law that the findings be sufficiently clear to permit review." 270 Ind. at 442.

If a juvenile court's order is not accompanied by a sufficient statement of reasons, the waiver order is invalid. See *C.L.A. v. State*, 137 Ga.App. 511, 224 S.E.2d 491 (1976); *People v. Dunbar*, 423 Mich. 380, 377 N.W.2d 262 (1985); *Hopkins v. State*, 209 So.2d 841 (Miss.1968); *State v. Kemper*, 535 S.W.2d 241 (Mo.App.1975); and *J.T.P. v. State*, 544 P.2d 1270 (Okl.Cr.App. 1975). Contra, *State v. Jiminez*, 109 Ariz. 305, 509 P.2d 198 (1973) (failure of the juvenile court to provide a written statement of reasons for the transfer was harmless error). How formal should the required statement be? See *In re Honsaker*, 539 S.W.2d 198 (Tex.Civ.App.1976); *O.A.H. v. State*, 332 So.2d 641 (Fla.App.1976); and especially *In re I.B.*, 619 S.W.2d 584 (Tex.Civ.App.1981), where the transferring juvenile court judge merely parroted the statutory language in his statement of reasons for transfer. The Texas Court of Civil Appeals found that, so long as those reasons have evidentiary support in the record, no more detailed statement is required.

d.   WHO SHOULD BE WAIVED? ASSESSING STATUTORY CRITERIA

In re K.A.P.

Court of Appeals of Minnesota, 1996.
550 N.W.2d 9.

OPINION

■ HAROLD W. SCHULTZ, JUDGE.

This appeal is from an order certifying appellant K.A.P. to stand trial as an adult on charges of second-degree murder. See Minn.Stat. § 609.19(1) (1994) (intentional murder), Minn.Stat. § 609.19(2) (1994) (felony murder); Minn.Stat. § 260.125, subd. 2a (1994) (presumption of certification for 16 or 17–year-old who commits an offense with a guidelines presumptive executed sentence).

FACTS

The state filed a delinquency petition alleging that on May 25, 1995, K.A.P., then age 17, caused the death of Ronderick Dewayne Skipper, by stabbing him. Witnesses told police that Skipper was arguing with K.A.P., who entered the apartment building where he lived, followed a short time later by Skipper. K.A.P. told police that he had gone into his apartment, where he retrieved a kitchen knife for his own protection. He heard Skipper in the hallway outside, opened the door, and stabbed him in the chest, although Skipper had not made a move towards him.

The state immediately filed a motion to certify K.A.P. to stand trial as an adult. After the trial court found probable cause to believe K.A.P. committed the offense, it ordered a psychological evaluation.

The psychological evaluation found no mental illness, nor any "underlying emotional disturbance." Patrick Carroll, the psychologist who prepared the evaluation, testified that K.A.P. has a lot of "positives" and strengths, but exhibits behavioral problems associated with a lack of impulse control and control over anger. He testified that K.A.P. had no psychological, or chemical dependency, problems. He recommended retaining K.A.P. in the juvenile system at a residential treatment program. He testified that if the proceeding was designated as an extended jurisdiction juvenile (EJJ) proceeding, with juvenile court jurisdiction continuing until age 21, the length of time was sufficient to serve public safety. He testified that it was highly unlikely that K.A.P. would commit a similar offense and that three years of treatment and probation would reveal whether K.A.P. had solved his behavioral problems.

The probation officer who completed the certification study, Don Bellmont, reached a different conclusion. He testified that although K.A.P. had the ability to turn his life around, he needed to be under some type of supervision longer than three and one-half years. He testified that K.A.P. had no prior juvenile adjudications. K.A.P., however, had two fifth-degree assault petitions pending at the time of the alleged homicide. Each of these was for striking a woman, including one victim who was allegedly pregnant. K.A.P. also was a possible suspect in three other incidents from December 1994 to April 1995, involving fights or verbal confrontations.

K.A.P. presented testimony establishing that he had been accepted into two residential treatment programs that handled serious juvenile offenders and that he was considered an appropriate candidate for a third.

The trial court granted the certification motion, concluding that the juvenile system provided inadequate punishment for K.A.P. The court compared the three and one-half years remaining in the juvenile system with the 306–month presumptive adult sentence. The court found that the two residential treatment programs to which K.A.P. had been admitted were appropriate but did not allow for an adequate period of supervision.

ISSUE

Did the trial court abuse its discretion in ordering certification to adult court?

ANALYSIS

K.A.P. challenges the trial court's determination that he did not rebut by clear and convincing evidence the presumption of certification. A juvenile certification order "will not be reversed unless its findings are clearly erroneous so as to constitute an abuse of discretion." In re Welfare of T.L.J., 495 N.W.2d 237, 240 (Minn.App.1993).

K.A.P. concedes that the statutory presumption of certification applies because he is charged with committing second-degree murder and was 17 years old at the time of the offense. See Minn.Stat. § 260.125, subd. 2a (1994). The statute provides that in such a case:

> If the court determines that probable cause exists to believe the child committed the alleged offense, the burden is on the child to rebut this presumption by demonstrating by clear and convincing evidence that retaining the proceeding in the juvenile court serves public safety.

Id.

As K.A.P. points out, the choice in a presumptive certification case is between adult certification and designation as an EJJ proceeding. See Minn.Stat. § 260.125, subd. 5 (if certification is not ordered in a presumptive certification case, the court "shall designate" the proceeding an EJJ prosecution). Thus, the alternative to adult certification is not simply juvenile court jurisdiction to age 19, but rather EJJ jurisdiction to age 21, with an adult criminal sentence to be executed if K.A.P. should violate the provisions of the juvenile disposition order or commit a new offense. See Minn.Stat. § 260.126, subd. 4(2) (1994).

The certification statute lists six factors to consider in determining whether the public safety is served by certifying the juvenile as an adult:

> (1) the seriousness of the alleged offense in terms of community protection, including the existence of any aggravating factors recognized by the sentencing guidelines, the use of a firearm, and the impact on any victim;

> (2) the culpability of the child in committing the alleged offense, including the level of the child's participation in planning and carrying out the offense and the existence of any mitigating factors recognized by the sentencing guidelines;

> (3) the child's prior record of delinquency;

> (4) the child's programming history, including the child's past willingness to participate meaningfully in available programming;

> (5) the adequacy of the punishment or programming available in the juvenile justice system; and

> (6) the dispositional options available for the child.

Minn.Stat. § 260.125, subd. 2b (1994). The statute also instructs the court how to weigh these factors:

> In considering these factors, the court shall give greater weight to the seriousness of the alleged offense and the child's prior record of delinquency than to the other factors listed in this subdivision.

Id.

K.A.P. acknowledges that the first factor, the seriousness of the offense, favors certification. He argues, however, that by presenting favorable evidence on the other, non-offense related, factors in Minn.Stat. § 260.125, subd. 2b, he has rebutted the presumption of certification. On the facts of this case, it was not an abuse of discretion to find otherwise.

Under earlier versions of the certification statute, it has been held that the state must present evidence of dangerousness other than the offense charged in the petition itself. E.g., In re Welfare of K.P.H., 289 N.W.2d 722, 725 (Minn.1980). This court has held that the requirement of "non-offense related evidence of dangerousness" applies to EJJ designations. In re Welfare of S.W.N., 541 N.W.2d 14, 17 (Minn.App.1995), review denied (Minn. Feb. 9, 1996). But in EJJ designations, the state still bears the burden of proof. Minn.Stat. § 260.126, subd. 2. In a presumptive certification case, the state can rest its argument on proof of the juvenile's age at the time of the offense and on the seriousness of the offense.

The current statute requires the court in a presumptive certification case to consider factors other than the seriousness of the offense. Minn. Stat. § 260.125, subd. 2b. Therefore, it is still true, as before, that the charged offense alone does not determine the risk to public safety. But now the other evidence must be considered in light of the shifting of the burden of proof to the juvenile.

The seriousness of the charged offense is not the only statutory factor favoring adult certification in this case. The statute provides that the court should consider "the adequacy of the punishment or programming available in the juvenile justice system." Minn.Stat. § 260.125, subd. 2b(5). The trial court compared the presumptive adult criminal sentence (306 months) to the time remaining in the juvenile system under EJJ (three and one-half years). The trial court determined that this time remaining under EJJ did not provide an adequate period of supervision.

K.A.P.'s rebuttal of the state's case relied heavily on the psychological evaluation. The psychologist, however, admitted that he had some concern about the short time available in the juvenile system. He concluded that if K.A.P. had an uncontrollable behavioral problem, it would show up in the time remaining under EJJ jurisdiction and provide grounds for imposing the adult sentence. He also noted that K.A.P. did not have a long track record of aggression. His evaluation, however, did not take into consideration several incidents shown in K.A.P.'s school records.

The trial court acknowledged that in ordering adult certification it was relying in part on unadjudicated conduct, but emphasized it was doing so because that conduct showed a pattern. The unadjudicated assault petitions involved alleged conduct occurring within seven months of the charged offense. We conclude that to require the trial court to ignore the two pending assault charges would unduly limit the court's ability to accurately assess the risk to public safety. At the least, the pending charges are relevant to the conclusions in the psychological evaluation.

The trial court's order reflects a careful balancing of the seriousness of the second-degree murder charges and the existence of mitigating factors. The court acknowledged that there was evidence that the victim was the aggressor, and that there was little, if any, indication of planning by K.A.P. The trial court, however, noted the concern with the lack of time for punishment, or even adequate supervision, in the juvenile court system. K.A.P. presented a psychological evaluation concluding that he was motivated towards, and capable of, changing his behavior. But the trial court had to determine what weight to place on that evaluation. We conclude that the trial court did not abuse its discretion in concluding that K.A.P. failed to present clear and convincing evidence to rebut the presumption of certification.

DECISION

The trial court did not abuse its discretion in ordering appellant certified to stand trial as an adult.

Affirmed.

OKLAHOMA STATUTES ANNOTATED, TITLE 10, CHILDREN (West)

§ 7303–4.3.   Certification proceedings

. . .

B.   Except as otherwise provided by law, if a child is charged with delinquency as a result of an offense which would be a felony if committed by an adult, the court on its own motion or at the request of the district attorney shall conduct a preliminary hearing to determine whether or not there is prosecutive merit to the complaint. If the court finds that prosecutive merit exists, it shall continue the hearing for a sufficient period of time to conduct an investigation and further hearing to determine if the child should be held accountable for acts of the child as if the child were an adult if the child should be found to have committed the alleged act or omission.

Consideration shall be given to:

1.   The seriousness of the alleged offense to the community, and whether the alleged offense was committed in an aggressive, violent, premeditated or willful manner;

2.   Whether the offense was against persons or property, greater weight being given to transferring the accused person to the adult criminal justice system for offenses against persons and, if personal injury resulted, the degree of personal injury;

3.   The sophistication and maturity of the juvenile and capability of the juvenile of distinguishing right from wrong as determined by consideration of psychological evaluation of the juvenile, home, environmental situation, emotional attitude and pattern of living;

4.   The record and previous history of the accused person, including previous contacts with community agencies, law enforcement agencies, schools, juvenile or criminal courts and other jurisdictions, prior periods of probation or prior commitments to juvenile institutions;

5.   The prospects for adequate protection of the public;

6.   The likelihood of reasonable rehabilitation of the juvenile if the juvenile is found to have committed the alleged offense, by the use of procedures and facilities currently available to the juvenile court; and

7.   Whether the offense occurred while the juvenile was escaping or in an escape status from an institution for delinquent children.

After the investigation and hearing, the court may in its discretion proceed with the juvenile proceeding, or it shall state its reasons in writing and shall certify, based on clear and convincing evidence, that the child shall be held accountable for acts of the child as if the child were an adult and shall be held for proper criminal proceedings for the specific offense charged, by any other division of the court which would have trial jurisdiction of the offense if committed by an adult. The juvenile proceeding shall not be dismissed until the criminal proceeding has commenced and if no criminal proceeding commences within thirty (30) days of the date of the certification, unless stayed pending appeal, the court shall proceed with the juvenile proceeding and the certification shall lapse.

If not included in the original summons, notice of a hearing to consider whether a child should be certified for trial as an adult shall be given to all persons who are required to be served with a summons at the commencement of a juvenile proceeding, but publication in a newspaper when the address of a person is unknown is not required. The purpose of the hearing shall be clearly stated in the notice.

. . .

D. Any child who has been certified to stand trial as an adult pursuant to any certification procedure provided by law, or who has been tried as an adult pursuant to any reverse certification procedure provided by law, and is subsequently convicted of the alleged offense, or against whom the imposition of judgment and sentencing has been deferred, shall be tried as an adult in all subsequent criminal prosecutions, and shall not be subject to the jurisdiction of the juvenile court or be eligible to be tried as a youthful offender in any further proceedings.

E. Any child seventeen (17) years of age or older who has been certified to stand trial as an adult pursuant to any certification procedure of any other state and subsequently convicted of the alleged offense, or who has been tried and convicted as an adult in any other state, or against whom the imposition of judgment and sentencing has been deferred, shall be tried as an adult in all subsequent criminal prosecutions, and shall not be subject to the jurisdiction of the juvenile court or be eligible to be tried as a youthful offender in any further proceedings.

F. An order either certifying a person as a child pursuant to subsection B of this section or denying such certification shall be a final order, appealable when entered.

NOTES

(1) Few states have waiver statutes that formulate precise criteria to guide the judge when making the transfer decision. More often the statutes contain only general phrases, such as "the best interest of the child or public," which leave a great deal to the discretion of the juvenile court judge. The Juvenile Justice Standards Project reports that 36 of the states have statutes that elaborate conditions sufficient to justify waiver: Of these, 27 states cite the public interest in treating the juvenile as a factor, while 24 states list the nonamenability of the juvenile to rehabilitation through juvenile facilities.

With increased enactment of new juvenile court codes or amendment of existing ones, the trend is toward setting forth specific waiver criteria in the statutes. In addition to the Oklahoma statute, supra, representative statutes are: Ala.Code § 12–15–34(d); Ill.Comp.Stat.Ann. ch. 705, § 405/5–805(3)(b); Md.Cts. & Jud.Proc. Code Ann. § 3–8A–06(e); Mich.Comp.Laws Ann. § 712A.4(4); Tex.Fam.Code Ann. § 54.02(f).

Is a waiver statute unconstitutional for lack of sufficient standards? The Louisiana Supreme Court so held in *State ex rel. Hunter*, 387 So.2d 1086 (La.1980). The statute, which lacked even a general nonamenability standard, allowed waiver of juveniles who were 15 or older at the time of the alleged offense and charged with one of certain enumerated serious offenses. The waiver hearing was, in effect, a probable cause hearing. The court held the statute unconstitutional on due process grounds as well as on state constitutional grounds. The waiver statute was subsequently amended to include a general nonamenability standard and to furnish specific criteria as well. La.Children's Code Ann. art. 862(A)(2).

The Supreme Court of California, on the other hand, rejected such an attack on § 707 of the California Welfare and Institutions Code. In *Donald L. v. Superior Court*, 7 Cal.3d 592, 102 Cal.Rptr. 850, 498 P.2d 1098 (1972), disapproved on other grounds, *In re Winnetka V.*, 28 Cal.3d 587, 169 Cal.Rptr. 713, 620 P.2d 163 (1980), the court concluded that the statutory phrases "not amenable" and "not a fit and proper subject" were not unconstitutionally vague. The great majority of courts that have considered constitutional challenges to statutes employing a general nonamenability standard have held them valid. In addition to the California decision see *Davis v. State*, 297 So.2d 289 (Fla.1974); *State v. Gibbs*, 94 Idaho 908, 500 P.2d 209 (1972); *Summers v. State*, 248 Ind. 551, 230 N.E.2d 320 (1967); *State v. Smagula*, 117 N.H. 663, 377 A.2d 608 (1977); *In re Bullard*, 22 N.C.App. 245, 206 S.E.2d 305 (1974), appeal dismissed 285 N.C. 758, 209 S.E.2d 279. In most of these cases the courts held the general standard sufficient, leaving the courts free to fashion specific criteria to be applied by judges in making waiver decisions. Such judicial criteria are, in effect, incorporated into the waiver statute. See, e.g., *Speck v. Auger*, 558 F.2d 394 (8th Cir.1977) (Iowa waiver statute not unconstitutionally vague as interpreted by Iowa Supreme Court, which, in *State v. Halverson*, 192 N.W.2d 765 (Iowa 1971), set forth criteria to be considered).

(2) How do the provisions of the Oklahoma statute differ from those of the Minnesota statute in *K.A.P.*?

Ordinarily, unless by statute seriousness of the offense requires no nonamenability finding, that factor alone does not give rise to a presumption that the child should be transferred to adult court. It is a permissible factor to be considered in the overall calculus of the transfer decision. See, e.g., *State v. Kemper*, 535 S.W.2d 241 (Mo.App.1975). Indeed, cases abound in which courts have held that waiver cannot be based on a single factor alone, at least where the judge simply cites the factor without elaboration of *why* the juvenile for that reason is not amenable to juvenile treatment. See, e.g., *Commonwealth v. Greiner*, 479 Pa. 364, 388 A.2d 698 (1978) (nature of the crime); *J.G.B. v. State*, 136 Ga.App. 75, 220 S.E.2d 79 (1975) (number and severity of the alleged offenses); *Duvall v. State*, 170 Ind.App. 473, 353 N.E.2d 478 (1976) (seriousness of the offense and consent of the juvenile); *In re Dahl*, 278 N.W.2d 316 (Minn.1979) (age of the juvenile and seriousness of the offense); *S.H. v. State*, 555 P.2d 1050 (Okl.Cr.App.1976), overruled on other grounds, *State ex rel. Coats v. Rakestraw*, 610 P.2d 256 (Okla.Crim.App. 1980) (a finding that the juvenile knows the difference between right and wrong). As the principal case illustrates, however, the applicable statute may provide that age and seriousness of the offense are sufficient to show nonamenability to juvenile treatment.

Similarly, suppose the nonamenability determination is based solely on the court's conclusion that no facilities are available to the court for treatment of the juvenile. For a decision upholding such a waiver determination, see *In re Pima County, Juvenile Action No. J–218–1*, 22 Ariz.App. 327, 527 P.2d 104 (1974). Contra, *In re J.E.C.*, 302 Minn. 387, 225 N.W.2d 245 (1975). In *People v. Joe T.*, 48 Cal.App.3d 114, 121 Cal.Rptr. 329 (1975), disapproved on other grounds, *People v. Chi Ko Wong*, 18 Cal.3d 698, 135 Cal.Rptr. 392, 557 P.2d 976 (1976), where "the finding of unfitness was based solely on the referee's belief that the sentencing alternatives in the adult court would be better suited for appellant than the local treatment programs available through the juvenile court," the waiver order was held invalid. In the latter case the court pointed out that where the standard for waiver is nonamenability to juvenile treatment (or unfitness), absence of the required finding of unfitness is a jurisdictional defect and the waiver order is a nullity.

In assessing nonamenability to juvenile court treatment, should the state's mistakes on the child's prior court contacts give rise to a concept of contributory negligence by the state barring transfer? In *People v. Browning*, 45 Cal.App.3d 125, 119 Cal.Rptr. 420 (1975), overruled on other grounds, *People v. Williams*, 16 Cal.3d 663, 128 Cal.Rptr. 888, 547 P.2d 1000 (1976), the child's attorney argued that the California Youth Authority had been grossly negligent in letting his client run away from a foster home placement and live in another less constructive environment. This negligence by the state although characterized by the juvenile judge as "grossly stupid" and "incomprehensible" was no bar to a nonamenability finding.

Of what value is so-called expert opinion on the determination of nonamenability? One source of considerable disillusionment about the conduct of juvenile courts has been disappointment with the inability of the social and behavioral sciences to live up to their early promise. See Stephen J. Morse & Charles H. Whitebread, The Implications of the Juvenile Justice Standards for Mental Health Professionals in Gary Melton (ed.) Child and Youth Services and the Law 6 (Haworth 1982). What should we expect experts to say and who will those experts be? The use of psychiatrists and psychologists in criminal cases has been the subject of extensive scholarly debate. See Stephen J. Morse, Crazy Behavior, Morals, and Science: An Analysis of Mental Health Law, 51 So.Cal.L.Rev. 527 (1978); Richard Bonnie & Christopher Slobogin, The Role of the Mental Health Professional in the Criminal Process: The Case for Informed Speculation, 66 Va.L.Rev. 427 (1980); and Stephen J. Morse, Failed Expectations and Criminal Responsibility: Experts and the Unconscious, 68 Va.L.Rev. 971 (1982).

(3) The required finding of probable cause (or prosecutive merit) contained in the Oklahoma statute as a prerequisite to transfer is typical. See, e.g., Va.Code § 16.1–269.1(A)(2). Some states permit the juvenile judge to assume the existence of probable cause at the waiver hearing. Md.Cts. & Jud.Proc.Code Ann. § 3–8A–06(d)(2). How does this square with the time-honored presumption of innocence? Should the juvenile court's finding of probable cause at the waiver hearing be a sufficient substitute for the usual preliminary hearing in adult proceedings if the child is transferred? See Samuel M. Davis, The Efficacy of a Probable Cause Requirement in Juvenile Proceedings, 59 N.C.L.Rev. 723, 735–37 (1981) for a discussion of the problem.

(4) Suppose a juvenile is suffering from a mental, emotional or behavioral disorder. Should the court be authorized to waive jurisdiction and transfer the juvenile for criminal prosecution? The Uniform Juvenile Court Act (and those states that follow its model) provides in § 34(a)(4) for certain prerequisites for waiver of jurisdiction, among them that "the child is not committable to an institution for the mentally retarded or mentally ill." Of course, the juvenile may be suffering from a mental, emotional or behavioral disorder that falls short of qualifying for institutional commitment but that nevertheless touches on the juvenile's competency. In such case, some have argued that the juvenile should not be transferred for criminal prosecution. See Vanessa L. Kolbe, Note, A Proposed Bar to Transferring Juveniles with Mental Disorders to Criminal Court: Let the Punishment Fit the Culpability, 14 Va.J.Soc. Pol'y & L. 418 (2007).

Suppose the juvenile is not suffering from a mental, emotional or behavioral disorder but simply is laboring under the disability of immaturity, a normative behavior for juveniles, particularly the very young. Even in that case some have argued against prosecution of juveniles as adults, whether by transfer or by some other means. See David O. Brink, Immaturity, Normative Competence, and Juvenile Transfer: How (Not) to Punish Minors for Major Crimes, 82 Tex.L.Rev. 1557 (2004).

5.   REVERSE CERTIFICATION

PURDON'S PENNSYLVANIA CONSOLIDATED STATUTES ANNOTATED (West)

TITLE 42.   JUDICIARY AND JUDICIAL PROCEDURE

§ 6302.   Definitions

The following words and phrases when used in this chapter shall have, unless the context clearly indicates otherwise, the meanings given to them in this section:

. . .

"Delinquent act."

(1) The term means an act designated a crime under the law of this Commonwealth, or of another state if the act occurred in that state, or under Federal law, or under local ordinances. . . .

(2) The term shall not include:

(i) The crime of murder.

(ii) Any of the following prohibited conduct where the child was 15 years of age or older at the time of the alleged conduct and a deadly weapon as defined in 18 Pa.C.S. § 2301 (relating to definitions) was used during the commission of the offense, which, if committed by an adult, would be classified as:

(A) Rape. . . .

(B) Involuntary deviate sexual intercourse. . . .

(C) Aggravated assault. . . .

(D) Robbery. . . .

(E) Robbery of motor vehicle. . . .

(F) Aggravated indecent assault. . . .

(G) Kidnapping. . . .

(H) Voluntary manslaughter.

(i) An attempt, conspiracy or solicitation to commit murder or any of these crimes. . . .

(iii) Any of the following prohibited conduct where the child was 15 years of age or older at the time of the alleged conduct and has been previously adjudicated delinquent of any of the following prohibited conduct which, if committed by an adult, would be classified as:

(A) Rape. . . .

(B) Involuntary deviate sexual intercourse. . . .

(C) Robbery. . . .

(D) Robbery of motor vehicle. . . .

(E) Aggravated indecent assault. . . .

(F) Kidnapping. . . .

(G) Voluntary manslaughter.

(H) An attempt, conspiracy or solicitation to commit murder or any of these crimes. . . .

(iv) Summary offenses, unless the child fails to comply with a lawful sentence imposed thereunder, in which event notice of such fact shall be certified to the court.

(v) A crime committed by a child who has been found guilty in a criminal proceeding for other than a summary offense.

. . .

§ 6322. Transfer from criminal proceedings

(a) General rule.—Except as provided in 75 Pa.C.S. § 6303 (relating to rights and liabilities of minors) or in the event the child is charged with murder or any of the offenses excluded by paragraph (2)(ii) or (iii) of the definition of "delinquent act" in section 6302 (relating to definitions) or has been found guilty in a criminal proceeding, if it appears to the court in a criminal proceeding that the defendant is a child, this chapter shall immediately become applicable, and the court shall forthwith halt further criminal proceedings, and, where appropriate, transfer the case to the division or a judge of the court assigned to conduct juvenile hearings, together with a copy of the accusatory pleading and other papers, documents, and transcripts of testimony relating to the case. If it appears to the court in a criminal proceeding charging murder or any of the offenses excluded by paragraph (2)(ii) or (iii) of the definition of "delinquent act" in section 6302, that the defendant is a child, the case may similarly be transferred and the provisions of this chapter applied. In determining whether to transfer a case charging murder or any of the offenses excluded from the definition of "delinquent act" in section 6302, the child shall be required to establish by a preponderance of the evidence that the transfer will serve the public interest. In determining whether the child has so established that the transfer will serve the public interest, the court shall consider the factors contained in section 6355(a)(4)(iii) (relating to transfer to criminal proceedings).

(b) Order.—If the court finds that the child has met the burden under subsection (a), the court shall make findings of fact, including specific references to the evidence, and conclusions of law in support of the transfer order. If the court does not make its finding within 20 days of the hearing on the petition to transfer the case, the defendant's petition to transfer the case shall be denied by operation of law.

. . .

(e) Transfer of convicted criminal cases.—If in a criminal proceeding, the child is found guilty of a crime classified as a misdemeanor, and the child and the attorney for the Commonwealth agree to the transfer, the case may be transferred for disposition to the division or a judge of the court assigned to conduct juvenile hearings.

Commonwealth v. Cotto

Supreme Court of Pennsylvania, 2000.
562 Pa. 32, 753 A.2d 217.

■ CASTILLE, JUSTICE.

This Court granted allocatur in this matter to determine whether certain 1995 amendments to the Juvenile Act, 42 Pa.C.S. § 6301 et seq., violate the Fourteenth Amendment of the United States Constitution and Article I, Section 9, of the Pennsylvania Constitution. For the reasons that follow, we hold that the amendments are constitutional and, therefore, we affirm.

On April 23, 1996, appellant and two accomplices, armed with a handgun, robbed the owner, an employee and two customers of the Mane Magic Beauty Salon in Lancaster, Pennsylvania. Subsequently, on May 8, 1996, appellant and three accomplices, again armed with a handgun, robbed the Parkhill Jewelry Store, its employees and one customer. On July 29, 1996, appellant was charged with four counts of robbery and one count of criminal conspiracy arising out of the April 23 incident and with two counts of robbery and one count of criminal conspiracy arising out of the May 8 incident.

Appellant, who was fifteen years old at the time of both robberies, was charged in criminal court as an adult pursuant to § 6302 of the Juvenile Act, which excludes robbery from the definition of a delinquent act when, as in the case sub judice, (1) it was committed by a child who was fifteen years old or older and (2) a deadly weapon was used during the commission of the offense.[1] On February 28, 1997, appellant filed a motion to transfer the proceedings to juvenile court and a petition for a writ of habeas corpus alleging that the 1995 amendments to the Juvenile Act governing transfer were unconstitutional on two grounds: because they were void for vagueness and because they unconstitutionally placed the burden of proof on the juvenile seeking transfer to juvenile court.

The trial court promptly scheduled a hearing, which was held on March 20, 1997. After receiving briefs from the parties, the trial court issued an opinion on May 12, 1997, denying both motions. In the opinion, the trial court engaged in an exhaustive analysis of the statutory factors governing the decision to transfer a case to juvenile court. See 42 Pa.C.S. § 6355(a)(4)(iii).

One week later, on May 19, 1997, appellant entered a negotiated guilty plea to all charges and was sentenced to eight concurrent terms of five to ten years' imprisonment. Pursuant to the plea agreement, appellant specifically reserved the right to appeal his twin challenges to the constitutionality of the amendments to the Juvenile Act. On appeal, appellant did not challenge the trial court's discretionary denial of his transfer motion, but raised only his two challenges to the constitutionality of the amendments. The Superior Court held that the amendments were constitutional. Commonwealth v. Cotto, 708 A.2d 806 (Pa.Super.1998).

---

1. Those offenses that the amended Juvenile Act requires to be initiated in criminal court when committed by juveniles are known as "direct file" cases.

In his appeal to this Court, as in the Superior Court, appellant contends that the 1995 amendments to the Juvenile Act are unconstitutional in two respects. Initially, we note that a statute is presumed to be constitutional and will not be declared unconstitutional unless it clearly, palpably and plainly violates the Constitution. Commonwealth v. Hendrickson, 555 Pa. 277, 280–81, 724 A.2d 315, 317 (1999); Commonwealth v. Barud, 545 Pa. 297, 304, 681 A.2d 162, 165 (1996). Therefore, the party challenging the constitutionality of a statute has a heavy burden of persuasion. *Barud*, supra.

As amended in 1995, the Juvenile Act vests original jurisdiction in the criminal courts for specified violent felonies, e.g., rape, aggravated assault and robbery committed by minors aged fifteen or older who either used a deadly weapon in the commission of the offense or were previously adjudicated delinquent for such crimes. Prior to the amendments, those serious felonies initially came within the jurisdiction of the juvenile courts, subject to certification and transfer to adult court. The 1995 amendments reflect a legislative judgment that the most serious violent felonies should be treated in the same manner as murder charges, i.e., as adult crimes in adult court, at least in the first instance.

The amendments, however, also provide a mechanism for a minor to prove to the court that he does not belong in criminal court. Thus, § 6322 of the Juvenile Act allows a defendant to petition to have his case transferred to juvenile court. The standard governing such transfers is as follows:

> ... In determining whether to transfer a case charging murder or any of the offenses excluded from the definition of "delinquent act" in section 6302, the child shall be required to establish by a preponderance of the evidence that the transfer will serve the public interest. In determining whether the child has so established that the transfer will serve the public interest, the court shall consider the factors contained in section 6355(a)(4)(iii) (relating to transfer to criminal proceedings).

42 Pa.C.S. § 6322(a).

First, appellant contends that this section is unconstitutionally vague because the "serve the public interest" standard is not defined. A statute is constitutionally void only if it is so vague that "persons of 'common intelligence must necessarily guess at its meaning and differ as to its application.'" Fabio v. Civil Service Commission of the City of Philadelphia, 489 Pa. 309, 314, 414 A.2d 82, 84 (1980), quoting Connally v. General Construction Co., 269 U.S. 385, 391, 46 S.Ct. 126, 70 L.Ed. 322 (1926). "A vague law impermissibly delegates basic policy matters to policemen, judges, and juries for resolution on an ad hoc and subjective basis, with the attendant dangers of arbitrary and discriminatory application." Grayned v. City of Rockford, 408 U.S. 104, 108–09, 92 S.Ct. 2294, 33 L.Ed.2d 222 (1972). However, a statute will not be deemed unconstitutionally vague if the terms, when read in context, are sufficiently specific that they are not subject to arbitrary and discriminatory application. *Hendrickson*, supra; *Barud*, supra.

In support of his vagueness argument, appellant cites several cases in which this and other courts have held that statutes that provide for determinations to be made based upon the "public interest" standard have been found to be void for vagueness. See Bell Telephone Co. of Pa. v. Driscoll, 343 Pa. 109, 21 A.2d 912 (1941); Bykofsky v. Borough of Middletown, 401 F.Supp. 1242 (M.D.Pa.1975), aff'd per curiam, 535 F.2d 1245 (3d Cir.1976), cert. denied, 429 U.S. 964, 97 S.Ct. 394, 50 L.Ed.2d 333 (1976); People v. Saad, 105 Cal.App.2d Supp. 851, 234 P.2d 785 (Cal.App. Dep't Super.Ct.1951); Whitaker v. Dept. of Ins. and Treasurer, 680 So.2d 528 (Fla.Dist.Ct.App.1996). What appellant fails to recognize, however, is that in each of those cases the determination that the statute was unconstitutionally vague was based on the fact that the term "public interest" was not further defined in the statute. E.g., Bell Telephone, supra at 116, 21 A.2d at 915 (implied standard of public interest not proper unless further defined or limited in its meaning).

The amended Juvenile Act decidedly does not suffer from this infirmity. The amendments further define "public interest" by mandating that the court consider the factors set forth in § 6355, which provides, in pertinent part:

In determining whether the public interest can be served, the court shall consider the following factors:

(A) the impact of the offense on the victim or victims;

(B) the impact of the offense on the community;

(C) the threat to the safety of the public or any individual posed by the child;

(D) the nature and circumstances of the offense allegedly committed by the child;

(E) the degree of the child's culpability;

(F) the adequacy and duration of dispositional alternatives available under this chapter and in the adult criminal justice system; and

(G) whether the child is amenable to treatment, supervision or rehabilitation as a juvenile by considering the following factors:

(I) age;

(II) mental capacity;

(III) maturity;

(IV) the degree of criminal sophistication exhibited by the child;

(V) previous records, if any;

(VI) the nature and extent of any prior delinquent history, including the success or failure of any previous attempts by the juvenile court to rehabilitate the child;

(VII) whether the child can be rehabilitated prior to the expiration of the juvenile court jurisdiction;

(VIII) probation or institutional reports, if any;

(IX) any other relevant factors . . .

42 Pa.C.S. § 6355(a)(4)(iii). This extensive list of factors—specifically focusing on the background of the juvenile, the impact of his crime, the safety of the community and the juvenile's treatment and rehabilitation prospects-clearly provides definite standards for a court to apply in determining whether the public interest would be served by transfer of the matter to juvenile court.

Moreover, the purpose of the amended Act itself provides guidance as to the meaning of "public interest." The Statement of Purpose provides, in pertinent part:

> Consistent with the protection of the public interest, to provide for children committing delinquent acts programs of supervision, care and rehabilitation which provide balanced attention to the protection of the community, the imposition of accountability for offenses committed and the development of competencies to enable children to become responsible and productive members of the community.

42 Pa.C.S. § 6301(b)(2). When read in the context of the clearly elaborated legislative purpose, and given the extensive list of factors to be considered in determining whether to transfer a case to juvenile court, the term "public interest" is not vague at all. To the contrary, courts are provided with a carefully crafted framework for evaluating these often-difficult issues. Therefore, we find that the statute as amended is not unconstitutionally vague.

Appellant also claims that the Juvenile Act as amended is unconstitutional because the factors set forth may be mutually exclusive—i.e., the rehabilitative needs of the defendant and the safety of the community may weigh in favor of different conclusions—and the Juvenile Act does not provide any guidance as to the weight to be given individual factors. Appellant argues that such a construct invites arbitrary and discriminatory application. However, both this Court and the United States Supreme Court have held that a legislative decision not to assign specific weight to a series of various relevant factors does not render a statutory scheme unconstitutional. This Court addressed a similar challenge in Commonwealth v. Zettlemoyer, 500 Pa. 16, 454 A.2d 937 (1982), cert. denied, 461 U.S. 970, 103 S.Ct. 2444, 77 L.Ed.2d 1327 (1983), reh'g denied, 463 U.S. 1236, 104 S.Ct. 31, 77 L.Ed.2d 1452 (1983). In *Zettlemoyer*, the appellant argued that Pennsylvania's death penalty statute was unconstitutionally vague because the jury was not given guidance as to the specific weight to be given to the competing aggravating and mitigating factors that a jury is required to consider in the penalty phase. In rejecting that claim, the Court, quoting federal precedent, stated:

> While these questions and decisions may be hard, they require no more line drawing than is commonly required of a factfinder in a lawsuit. For example, juries have traditionally evaluated the validity of defenses such as insanity or reduced capacity, both of which involve the same considerations as some of the above-mentioned mitigating circumstances. While the various factors to be considered by the sentencing authorities do not have numerical weights assigned to them, the requirements of Furman [v. Georgia, 408 U.S. 238, 92 S.Ct. 2726, 33 L.Ed.2d 346 (1972),] are satisfied when the sentencing author-

ity's discretion is guided and channeled by requiring examination of specific factors that argue in favor of or against imposition of the death penalty, thus eliminating total arbitrariness and capriciousness in its imposition.

> The directions given to judge and jury by the Florida statute are sufficiently clear and precise to enable the various aggravating circumstances to be weighed against the mitigating ones. As a result, the trial court's sentencing discretion is guided and channeled by a system that focuses on the circumstances of each individual homicide and individual defendant in deciding whether the death penalty is to be imposed.

Id. at 66–67, 454 A.2d at 963–64, quoting Proffitt v. Florida, 428 U.S. 242, 257–58, 96 S.Ct. 2960, 49 L.Ed.2d 913 (1976).

Under the Juvenile Act, the decision-maker has discretion in determining whether to transfer a direct file case to juvenile court. However, that discretion, like the discretion provided to juries under the death penalty statute, is guided by the specific factors that must be considered in making that determination. That the relevant factors may weigh in favor of different results is neither surprising nor problematic; rather, it reflects reality. Although each juvenile is an individual, he is also a member of a community. The needs of an individual are often at odds with the needs of society. The exercise of discretion routinely requires a balancing of competing concerns. Furthermore, nothing in the Juvenile Act countenances or encourages arbitrariness in the balancing process. In contrast, the interpretation that appellant suggests is constitutionally required would essentially eliminate discretion entirely. But the constitution does not disfavor discretion. Therefore, the transfer provisions of the Juvenile Act are not unconstitutional merely because they provide for flexibility and discretion rather than for the rigid assignment of a specific weight to each of the factors to be considered in determining whether transfer is in the public interest.[3]

Second, appellant contends that the amended Act is unconstitutional because it impermissibly places the burden of proof for transfer on the accused. At the outset, we should emphasize that, as this Court noted in Commonwealth v. Williams, 514 Pa. 62, 522 A.2d 1058 (1987), the special treatment provided to criminal offenders by the Juvenile Act is not a constitutional requirement. It is a statutory creation. That does not mean,

---

3. We note that other jurisdictions faced with similar challenges have also held that juvenile transfer provisions based on the public interest are not unconstitutionally vague, even where the statute does not set forth factors to be considered at transfer hearings. See, e.g., People v. Moseley, 193 Colo. 256, 259–60, 566 P.2d 331 (1977) (six statutory factors with no weight assigned to the factors); State v. Stanley, 60 Haw. 527, 592 P.2d 422, 426–27 (1979), cert. denied, 444 U.S. 871, 100 S.Ct. 149, 62 L.Ed.2d 97 (1979) (no factors); People v. Taylor, 76 Ill.2d 289, 29 Ill.Dec. 103, 391 N.E.2d 366, 373–74 (1979) (six statutory factors with no weight assigned to the factors); State v. Speck, 242 N.W.2d 287, 289–94 (Iowa 1976) (no factors); State ex rel. Londerholm v. Owens, 197 Kan. 212, 416 P.2d 259, 271 (1966) (no factors); In re a Juvenile, 364 Mass. 531, 306 N.E.2d 822, 826–27 (1974) (no factors); Lewis v. State, 86 Nev. 889, 478 P.2d 168, 171 (1970) (no factors); State v. Doyal, 59 N.M. 454, 286 P.2d 306, 310–11 (1955) (no factors); In the Interest of L.V.A., 248 N.W.2d 864, 866 (S.D.1976) (no factors); State in Interest of Salas, 520 P.2d 874, 875 (Utah 1974) (no factors); and State v. F.R.W., 61 Wis.2d 193, 212 N.W.2d 130 (1973) (no factors).

of course, that the due process clause plays no role in questions of transfer. As we recognized in a matter construing a former version of the Juvenile Act, in a proceeding to determine whether to transfer a juvenile, "the youth is entitled to notice of the charges against him, to a counseled hearing where he may present evidence and cross-examine witnesses, access to social records and probation or similar reports, and a statement of the reasons for the Court's determination." Commonwealth v. Pyle, 462 Pa. 613, 621 n. 10, 342 A.2d 101, 105 n. 10 (1975), citing Kent v. United States, 383 U.S. 541, 557, 86 S.Ct. 1045, 16 L.Ed.2d 84 (1966).

With respect to the specific question of the constitutional propriety of placing the burden on a juvenile defendant to prove that he is amenable to treatment in juvenile court, we do not write upon a blank slate. To the contrary, the burden of showing amenability to treatment justifying transfer to juvenile court was first placed on Pennsylvania juveniles not by the legislature, but by this Court in *Pyle*. In determining that it does not violate the Constitution to place the burden of proof for transfer of a murder case to juvenile court on the juvenile, the *Pyle* Court reasoned that:

> The decision to transfer has no bearing on either the procedural or substantive aspects of the criminal conviction in criminal court (i.e., it is still the Commonwealth's burden to prove every fact necessary to constitute murder beyond a reasonable doubt). Consequently, placing the burden on a petitioner in this manner in no way denied him his due process safeguards.

Id. at 623 n. 12, 342 A.2d at 107 n. 12 (citations omitted). We have reaffirmed this holding in later cases. Commonwealth v. Johnson, 542 Pa. 568, 579, 669 A.2d 315, 321 (1995); *Williams*, supra at 71–74, 522 A.2d at 1063–64; Commonwealth v. Pettus, 492 Pa. 558, 561, 424 A.2d 1332, 1335–36 (1981); Commonwealth v. Sourbeer, 492 Pa. 17, 25, 422 A.2d 116, 119 (1980); Commonwealth v. Greiner, 479 Pa. 364, 369–71, 388 A.2d 698, 701–02 (1978). Furthermore, this Court has held that the rationale of *Pyle* is applicable to charges other than murder where those charges arise out of the same criminal transaction as a murder charge. Commonwealth v. Romeri, 504 Pa. 124, 137–39, 470 A.2d 498, 505 (1983), cert. denied, 466 U.S. 942, 104 S.Ct. 1922, 80 L.Ed.2d 469 (1984); Commonwealth v. Keefer, 470 Pa. 142, 147–48, 367 A.2d 1082, 1084–85 (1976). The rationale of these cases is equally applicable here. The only distinction is that the legislature has determined in its judgment that, in certain instances, violent felonies in addition to murder are sufficiently serious to merit vesting original jurisdiction in the criminal courts, while affording the defendant an opportunity to show that his is the exceptional case warranting juvenile treatment.

Appellant contends, however, that *Pyle* and its progeny must be limited to the murder cases at issue therein. Obviously, those cases spoke only of murder prosecutions because, under the previous version of the Juvenile Act, those were the only cases directly filed in criminal court. But there is nothing unconstitutional in the legislature determining, in light of continued experience with violent juvenile crime, that other serious conduct also warrants criminal court treatment. In *Williams*, supra, this Court, in addressing the propriety of the legislature's determination that a juvenile charged with murder should be prosecuted as an adult, noted that "[m]urder is a heinous and serious crime, and the legislature's assumption that one who commits murder is in need of adult discipline and restraint is a reasonable one." *Williams*, supra at 71, 522 A.2d at 1063. That rationale is equally applicable to the violent offenses that were excluded from the definition of a delinquent act under the most recent amendments to the Juvenile Act. Armed robbery, too, for example, is a heinous and serious crime, and the legislature's informed determination that juveniles fifteen years of age and older who commit such offenses are not initially amenable to rehabilitation under the Juvenile Act, unless they prove otherwise by a preponderance of the evidence, is equally reasonable. There is nothing in the Constitution to prevent the legislature from making such a judgment.

Although it is true, as appellant notes, that murder has always been excluded from the jurisdiction of the juvenile courts, it is also true that, prior to the twentieth century, there were no juvenile courts in this Commonwealth at all.[4] The fact that the legislature chose in the past to presumptively extend the benefits of the juvenile system to older juveniles charged with armed robbery and other serious violent offenses does not act as a constitutional restraint upon it to make a different judgment in response to changing societal conditions. It is no less the legislature's prerogative now to limit those benefits than it was to extend them in the first place. Therefore, appellant's claim that it was unconstitutional to place the burden of proof upon him to prove that it would serve the public interest if he were transferred to juvenile court must fail.[5]

---

4. Juvenile courts were first established in this Commonwealth by the Act of May 21, 1901, P.L. 279.

5. The parties requested, and were granted, leave to file supplemental briefs addressing this Court's recent decision in Commonwealth v. Williams, 557 Pa. 285, 733 A.2d 593 (1999), cert. denied, 528 U.S. 1077, 120 S.Ct. 792, 145 L.Ed.2d 668 (2000). In *Williams*, the Court held, over this author's objection, that 42 Pa.C.S. §§ 9791–9799.6 ("Megan's Law") violated federal due process requirements by imposing a presumption that a person convicted of a sexually violent offense is a sexually violent predator, placing the burden on the offender to rebut that presumption, and providing for significantly enhanced penalties, up to a mandatory life term of imprisonment, if the offender failed to rebut the presumption. The transfer provision of the amended Juvenile Act is distinguishable from Megan's Law's sentencing procedure in several respects.

First, Megan's Law created a statutory presumption that persons convicted of certain crimes were sexually violent predators. 42 Pa.C.S. § 9794(b). The Juvenile Act, on the other hand, does not create any statutory presumption about the juvenile, but merely excludes certain violent offenses from the definition of delinquent acts and provides a

transfer provision that places the burden of proof on the defendant. 42 Pa.C.S. § 6302. More significantly, the *Williams* Court concluded that the "full panoply" of due process protections, including placing the burden of proof on the Commonwealth, see 557 Pa. at 304 n. 12, 733 A.2d at 602 n. 12, was required because the enhanced punishment proceeding was "a separate factual determination, the end result of which is the imposition of criminal punishment...." *Williams*, supra at 304, 733 A.2d at 603 (emphasis added). In such a circumstance, this Court held that the United States Supreme Court's decision in Specht v. Patterson, 386 U.S. 605, 87 S.Ct. 1209, 18 L.Ed.2d 326 (1967), controlled. *Specht* held that separate proceedings, requiring new findings of fact and leading to additional punishment, required that the "full panoply" of due process rights be provided. 386 U.S. at 608–09, 87 S.Ct. 1209. The transfer proceeding in the Juvenile Act is not a separate factual proceeding leading to punishment. Even if the defendant fails to establish that it would serve the public interest to transfer his case to juvenile court, punishment will result only if and when the defendant is convicted. That conviction, in turn, will only occur following a trial at which all due process protections are afforded. As this Court noted in *Pyle*, because the Commonwealth continues

For the foregoing reasons, we hold that the 1995 amendments to the Juvenile Act are constitutional and, accordingly, we affirm the order of the Superior Court.

■ JUSTICE NEWMAN concurs in the result.

NOTES

(1) Is the effect of reverse certification statutes to give more discretion to prosecutors and, therefore, to cause more cases involving juveniles (particularly those involving older juveniles charged with more serious offenses) to be handled in criminal court without the necessity of a transfer hearing as contemplated by *Kent*? Prosecutors, after all, determine the charge, and the reverse certification statutes turn on charge alone. Moreover, if the underlying assumption in cases originating in juvenile court is that most of those cases will be retained in juvenile court and only a few exceptional (egregious) cases will be transferred to criminal court, would not the same be true for cases originating in criminal court, i.e., that most of those cases will be retained in criminal court and only a few exceptional (deserving) cases will be transferred to juvenile court?

(2) Only two states—New York and Nebraska—authorize the criminal court to make all judicial transfer decisions. The New York statutory scheme is very similar to the Pennsylvania scheme in that certain cases originate in criminal court, which has discretion to transfer appropriate cases to the juvenile court. See N.Y.Fam.Ct. Act § 301.2(1)(b); N.Y.Penal Law §§ 10(18), 30; N.Y.Crim.Proc.Law §§ 180.75, 190.71, 210.43, 220.10(5)(g). The Nebraska procedure differs from the New York statutory scheme in that the juvenile and criminal courts have concurrent jurisdiction over juveniles charged with a felony and juveniles 16 or older charged with any offense. Neb.Rev.Stat. § 43–247. No provision is made for waiver of jurisdiction by the juvenile court. The prosecutor decides the court in which any such case shall be handled, id. § 43–276, and the criminal court is given discretionary authority to transfer appropriate cases to the juvenile court, id. § 43–261. Thus, in Nebraska the prosecutor and the criminal court share in the decision to allocate jurisdiction between the juvenile and criminal courts, although only the criminal court may make a *transfer* decision.

At least 10 other states authorize the criminal court to make some transfer decisions. In Maryland, for example, the criminal court has original jurisdiction over children 14 years of age and older who are charged with an offense punishable by death or life imprisonment and children 16 and older who are charged with one of several enumerated serious offenses, but the criminal court has discretion to transfer some cases to juvenile court. Md.Cts. & Jud.Proc.Ann. § 3–8A–03(d); Md.Crim.Proc.Code Ann.4–202. In Vermont, the maximum jurisdictional age for the juvenile court is 16, but the criminal court has discretion to transfer juveniles over 16 but under 18 to juvenile court. Vt.Stat.Ann. tit. 33, §§ 5502(a)(1), 5505(b), 5516(c). In Arkansas the juvenile and criminal courts have concurrent jurisdiction in certain cases, and the prosecutor has discretion to choose the court in which these cases will be handled, but the criminal court has discretion to transfer some cases to juvenile court. Ark.Code Ann. § 9–27–318(c), (e)–(i), supra p. 956. See also Del.Code Ann. tit. 10, §§ 1010(a), (e), 1011; Mich.Comp.Laws Ann. § 712A.2(d); Miss.Code Ann. §§ 43–21–105(j), 43–21–157(8), 43–21–159(4), (7); Okla.Stat.Ann. tit. 10, §§ 7306–1.1, 7306–2.5.

to bear the burden of establishing every element of the crime charged before any punishment will result, there is no due process infirmity. *Pyle*, supra at 623 n. 12, 342 A.2d at 107 n. 12. Accordingly, *Williams* is inapplicable to the Juvenile Act.

(3) In the principal case the court rejected the juvenile's claim that the "serve the public interest" standard was impermissibly vague. The court pointed out that the statute incorporates by reference the criteria contained elsewhere in the waiver statute. In an earlier case, *Commonwealth v. Pyle*, 462 Pa. 613, 342 A.2d 101 (1975), which the court in *Cotto* cites, the court held that the same standards that provide for transfer from juvenile court to criminal court are applicable also to transfers from criminal court to juvenile court. The only difference is that in the latter cases the burden of proof is reversed, i.e., the burden is on the juvenile to show amenability to treatment as a juvenile. The statute subsequently was amended to include the reference to waiver criteria. See Pa.Stat.Ann., tit. 42, § 6322(a), supra p. 990. Other states also place the burden of proof on the juvenile on the issue of amenability to juvenile treatment, in certain cases, even in transfer proceedings in juvenile court. See, e.g., Cal.Welf. & Inst.Code § 707(c), supra p. 964.

(4) Reverse certification statutes generally have withstood constitutional challenge, usually on the rationale that such a statutory scheme bears a rational relationship to the state's legitimate interest in protecting public safety and welfare. In addition to *Cotto*, see *In re Ricky B.*, 43 Md.App. 645, 406 A.2d 690 (1979); *Vega v. Bell*, 47 N.Y.2d 543, 419 N.Y.S.2d 454, 393 N.E.2d 450 (1979); *State ex rel. Coats v. Rakestraw*, 610 P.2d 256 (Okla.Cr.App.1980); *State v. Martin*, 191 Wis.2d 646, 530 N.W.2d 420 (App.1995).

The Oklahoma statutory scheme was criticized in Tom R. Cornish, Where Have All the Children Gone?—Reverse Certification, 35 Okla.L.Rev. 373 (1982). More recently, however, the Oklahoma court reaffirmed its earlier decision in *Rakestraw*. *Douma v. State*, 749 P.2d 1163 (Okla.Cr.App.1988).

The New York reverse certification scheme has been criticized because it does not go far enough. Lucia Beadel Whisenand & Edward J. McLaughlin, Completing the Cycle: Reality and the Juvenile Justice System in New York State, 47 Albany L.Rev. 1 (1982). The statutory scheme also has been criticized on the ground that if its purpose is deterrence, it has been a failure. Simon I. Singer & David McDowall, Criminalizing Delinquency: The Deterrent Effects of the New York Juvenile Offender Law, 22 L. & Society Rev. 521 (1988).

(5) In a case attracting national attention, the Pennsylvania Supreme Court held that the criminal court abused its discretion in denying 9-year-old Eric Kocher's petition to have his case transferred to juvenile court. *Commonwealth v. Kocher*, 529 Pa. 303, 602 A.2d 1308 (1992). Two justices concurred in the court's judgment on the ground that, as a matter of law, a 9-year-old child may not be criminally prosecuted for murder. 529 Pa. at 315, 602 A.2d at 1315 (Flaherty, J., concurring).

(6) Should a juvenile be advised that he or she has the right to petition for transfer to the juvenile court for treatment as a juvenile? In some cases, such advice may be required. See, e.g., Okla.Stat.Ann. tit. 10, § 7306–1.1(D)(1). If so, failure so to advise the juvenile is error. See, e.g., *Gilley v. State*, 848 P.2d 578 (Okla.Crim. App.1992).

(7) Many statutes give adult courts that are properly exercising jurisdiction over a juvenile the power to try the juvenile as a juvenile court would, or to sit as a criminal court but to make a juvenile disposition. See, e.g., Va. Code Ann. § 16.1–272; see also Ill.Comp.Stat.Ann. ch. 705, § 405/5–130(1)(c)(ii), (2)(c)(ii), (3)(c)(ii), (4)(c)(ii), (5)(c)(ii); Or.Rev.Stat. § 419C.361(1). "Blended sentencing," in which the juvenile and criminal courts share sentencing powers, is covered in the section on Dispositions, infra pp. 1215–24.

THE RELATIONSHIP OF TRANSFER TO THE FUTURE OF THE JUVENILE COURT

In the past several years legislatures have reacted to concern for the level of juvenile crime and to skepticism about the ability of the juvenile justice system to rehabilitate youthful offenders by enacting (or modifying) statutes that take a tougher stance toward juveniles charged with serious crimes. The underlying premise that juvenile crime is on the rise and is increasing in severity has been questioned. See, e.g., Frank Zimring, American Youth Violence (1998); Samuel M. Davis, The Criminalization of Juvenile Justice: Legislative Responses to "The Phantom Menace," 70 Miss.L.J. 1 (2000); Elizabeth S. Scott & Laurence Steinberg, Blaming Youth, 81 Tex.L.Rev. 799, 803–11 (2003). Nevertheless, the popular perception is that youth crime is on the rise, and legislative bodies are responding to public clamor that something needs to be done about it. These statutes include those that lower the age required for transfer, those that exclude serious offenses from juvenile court jurisdiction, those that permit more transfers of 16 and 17 year olds to adult criminal court, and those that call for more cases to remain in criminal court. Typical is the shift in the burden of proof in Cal. Welf. & Inst. Code § 707(c), supra at p. 964. Minnesota has created a presumption of nonamenability in the case of older juveniles charged with certain serious offenses. Minn.Stat.Ann. § 260B.125(3). If a juvenile 16 or older is charged with such an offense and the court finds probable cause to believe the juvenile committed it, he or she shall be certified for criminal prosecution unless the presumption is rebutted by clear and convincing evidence that the juvenile court's retaining jurisdiction would serve public safety. See *In re K.A.P.*, 550 N.W.2d 9 (Minn.App.1996), supra p. 982. The net result of this general trend is that increasing numbers of juvenile cases are being handled in criminal court.

As juvenile court proceedings become more like adult criminal prosecutions, does any reason remain for a separate juvenile court system? Some commentators recently have suggested that a possible solution to the transfer problem might be to try all offenders regardless of age in the same courts with the same full set of procedural rights. Dispositions could then vary based on age, prior record, and the availability of appropriate programs and facilities. Barry Feld has argued:

> The recent changes in juvenile court jurisdiction, sentencing, and procedures reflect ambivalence about the role of juvenile courts and the control of children. As juvenile courts converge procedurally and substantively with criminal courts, is there any reason to maintain a separate court whose only distinctions are procedures under which no adult would agree to be tried?

> The juvenile court is at a philosophical crossroads that cannot be resolved by simplistic formulations, such as treatment versus punishment. In reality, there are no practical or operational differences between the two. Acknowledging that juvenile courts punish, imposes an obligation to provide all criminal procedural safeguards because, in the words of *Gault*, "the condition of being a boy does not justify a kangaroo court." While procedural parity with adults may sound the death-knell of the juvenile court, to fail to do so perpetuates injustice.

To treat similarly situated juveniles differently, to punish them in the name of treatment, and to deny them basic safeguards fosters a sense of injustice that thwarts any efforts to rehabilitate.

Abolishing juvenile courts is desirable both for youths and society. After more than two decades of constitutional and legislative reform, juvenile courts continue to deflect, co-opt, ignore, or absorb ameliorative tinkering with minimal institutional change. Despite its transformation from a welfare agency to a criminal court, the juvenile court remains essentially unreformed. The quality of justice youths receive would be intolerable if it were adults facing incarceration. Public and political concerns about drugs and youth crime foster a "get tough" mentality to repress rather than rehabilitate young offenders. With fiscal constraints, budget deficits, and competition from other interest groups, there is little likelihood that treatment services for delinquents will expand. Coupling the emergence of punitive policies with our societal unwillingness to provide for the welfare of children in general, much less to those who commit crimes, there is simply no reason to believe that the juvenile court can be rehabilitated.

Without a juvenile court, an adult criminal court that administers justice for young offenders could provide children with all the procedural guarantees already available to adult defendants and additional enhanced protections because of the children's vulnerability and immaturity. The only virtue of the contemporary juvenile court is that juveniles convicted of serious crimes receive shorter sentences than do adults. Youthfulness, however, long has been recognized as a mitigating, even if not an excusing, condition at sentencing. The common law's infancy defense presumed that children below age fourteen lacked criminal capacity, emphasized their lack of fault, and made youthful irresponsibility explicit. Youths older than fourteen are mature enough to be responsible for their behavior, but immature enough as to not deserve punishment commensurate with adults. If shorter sentences for diminished responsibility is the rationale for punitive juvenile courts, then providing an explicit "youth discount" to reduce adult sentences can ensure an intermediate level of just punishment. Reduced adult sentences do not require young people to be incarcerated with adults; existing juvenile prisons allow the segregation of offenders by age.

Barry C. Feld, The Transformation of the Juvenile Court, 75 Minn.L.Rev. 691, 722–24 (1991).*

Some commentators have long called for the abolition of the juvenile court, or at least its exercise of delinquency jurisdiction. See, e.g, F. Barry McCarthy, Delinquency Dispositions Under the Juvenile Justice Standards: The Consequences of a Change in Rationale, 52 N.Y.U.L.Rev. 1093 (1977); Stephen Wizner & Mary F. Keller, The Penal Model of Juvenile Justice: Is Juvenile Court Delinquency Jurisdiction Obsolete?, 52 N.Y.U.L.Rev. 1120 (1977). In recent years more and more voices have been added to Feld's in arguing for abolition of the juvenile court. See, e.g., Katherine Hunt

* Copyright © 1991, Minnesota Law Review. Reprinted with permission.

Federle, The Abolition of the Juvenile Court: A Proposal for the Preservation of Children's Legal Rights, 16 J.Contemp.L. 23 (1990); Janet E. Ainsworth, Re–Imagining Childhood and Reconstructing the Legal Order: The Case for Abolishing the Juvenile Court, 69 N.C.L.Rev. 1083 (1991). Irene Rosenberg, however, has argued forcefully against abolition:

> I oppose the abolitionists despite hard-earned experience that tugs me in their direction. . . . [A]s much as I agree with Barry Feld that the juvenile courts impose punishment in the name of treatment and give reduced constitutional and procedural protection to children, I do not share his belief in the abolitionist solution, even though it is prompted by a despair that I do share. The proposed alternative of trial in the adult criminal courts, where I also have practiced, is even worse than what we now have.

> Before deciding whether to abandon the juvenile courts, two basic questions must be addressed: (1) is the disparity in procedural and constitutional protection between the adult and juvenile courts significant enough to justify opting out of the juvenile justice system; and (2) if children are tried in the criminal courts, will their immaturity and vulnerability be taken into account adequately in assessing culpability and determining sentences? In my view, the answers to these questions are no and no.

> . . .

> Abandoning the juvenile court is an admission that its humane purposes were misguided or unattainable. I do not believe that. We should stay and fight—fight for a reordering of societal resources, one that will protect and nourish children. . . . We can and should seek both procedural and dispositional reform in the juvenile courts.

> Despite all their failings, of which there are many, the juvenile courts do afford benefits that are unlikely to be replicated in the criminal courts, such as the institutionalized intake diversionary system, anonymity, diminished stigma, shorter sentences, and recognition of rehabilitation as a viable goal. We should build on these strengths rather than abandon ship.

> It is important to take into account both the chimerical quality of enhanced constitutional safeguards in the criminal courts and the significant benefits afforded to minors even by the existing juvenile justice system, before relegating children to criminal courts and prisons with no guarantee that their immaturity will be adequately considered or their vulnerability meaningfully protected.

Irene Merker Rosenberg, Leaving Bad Enough Alone: A Response to the Juvenile Court Abolitionists, 1993 Wis.L.Rev. 163, 165–66, 184–85;* see also Ira M. Schwartz, Neil Alan Weiner & Guy Enosh, Nine Lives and Then Some: Why the Juvenile Court Does Not Roll Over and Die, 33 Wake Forest L.Rev. 533 (1998); Sacha M. Coupet, Comment, What to Do with the Sheep in Wolf's Clothing: The Role of Rhetoric and Reality About Youth Offenders in the Constructive Dismantling of the Juvenile Justice System, 148 U.Penn.L.Rev. 1303 (2000); Daniel M. Filler & Austin E. Smith, The New Rehabilitation, 91 Iowa L.Rev. 951 (2006).

In many instances the juvenile court has taken on some of the attributes of criminal courts. For example, some states allow "blended sentencing," which authorizes the juvenile court, in cases of older youths adjudicated delinquent for certain serious offenses, to impose both a juvenile disposition and a criminal sentence. The criminal sentence is stayed while the juvenile fulfills the terms and conditions of the juvenile disposition, failure to do which results in revocation of the stay and imposition of the adult sentence. See, e.g., Ill.Comp.Stat.Ann., ch. 705, § 405/5–810; Minn.Stat.Ann. § 260B.130(4). Blended sentencing has its advocates, as a means of fulfilling the dual purposes of punishment and deterrence in the interest of public safety. See, e.g., Christian Sullivan, Juvenile Delinquency in the Twenty–First Century: Is Blended Sentencing the Middle–Road Solution for Violent Kids?, 21 N.Ill.U.L.Rev. 483 (2001); Kristen L. Caballero, Note, Blended Sentencing: A Good Idea for Juvenile Sex Offenders?, 19 St. John's J.Leg.Comment. 379 (2005); Christine Chamberlin, Note, Not Kids Anymore: A Need for Punishment and Deterrence in the Juvenile Justice System, 42 B.C.L.Rev. 391 (2001). It also has been criticized as a "net-widening" measure that has caused criminal sanctions to be imposed on an increasing number of juveniles without achieving the purpose for which it was intended. See, e.g., Marcy R. Podkopacz & Barry C. Feld, The Back–Door to Prison: Waiver Reform, "Blended Sentencing," and the Law of Unintended Consequences, 91 J.Crim.L. & Criminol. 997 (2001).

Blended sentencing and other "get tough" measures have been enacted in recent years as a means of dealing with what is perceived as an alarming rise in juvenile crime. In fact, many have argued that the claim of rising rates in juvenile crime is a misperception, advanced by the media, often in response to a particularly sensational crime committed by a juvenile or juveniles. See, e.g., Frank Zimring, American Youth Violence (1998); Elizabeth S. Scott & Laurence Steinberg, Blaming Youth, 81 Tex.L.Rev. 799 (2003); Samuel M. Davis, The Criminalization of the Juvenile Court: Legislative Responses to "The Phantom Menace," 70 Miss.L.J. 1 (2000).

As you study delinquency adjudication and disposition in the following sections, consider this possible convergence of the adult and juvenile systems. Does recent scholarship and legislative reform inexorably press in the direction of a unified court system or abolition of separate juvenile court jurisdiction over conduct by children that would be criminal if they were adults?

B.   INTAKE AND DIVERSION

1.   INTRODUCTION

After a juvenile is apprehended but before formal court proceedings, some member of the probation staff must decide whether to file a petition that will lead to adjudication by the court or to divert the juvenile from the court system entirely by informal adjustment or referral to a non-court social service agency. At this stage—usually called intake—the probation officer will usually meet with the child, his parents, perhaps the police officer or complaining witness, and sometimes an attorney for the child. In this meeting, the intake officer may decide the matter can be settled without a court appearance, in which case several options are available including dismissal of the case, informal probation or referral to some other social service agency or youth service bureau.

Intake and diversion present an early opportunity to exercise discretion in the juvenile justice system. The decision whether to proceed to adjudication or divert has a profound effect on the juvenile and his family. In fact, the study of juvenile law is to some extent misleading in focusing so heavily on adjudication and disposition because some research indicates petitions are filed in less than half the cases. See Juvenile Justice Standards Relating to the Juvenile Probation Function: Intake and Predisposition Investigative Services (hereinafter "Standards Relating to the Juvenile Probation Function"), Commentary to Standard 2.2 at page 32. Thus, the decisions made at intake may be the most significant ones in the whole process for an allegedly delinquent youth.

NORTH DAKOTA CENTURY CODE (Lexis–Nexis)

§ 27–20–10. Informal adjustment.

1. Before a petition is filed, the juvenile supervisor or other officer of the court designated by it, subject to its direction, may give counsel and advice to the parties and impose conditions for the conduct and control of the child with a view to an informal adjustment if it appears:

> a. The admitted facts bring the case within the jurisdiction of the court;
>
> b. Counsel, advice and conditions, if any, for the conduct and control of the child without an adjudication would be in the best interest of the public and the child; and
>
> c. The child and his parents, guardian, or other custodian consent thereto with knowledge that consent is not obligatory.

2. The giving of counsel and advice and any conditions imposed for the conduct and control of the child cannot extend beyond nine months from the day commenced unless extended by the court for an additional period not to exceed six months and does not authorize the detention of the child if not otherwise permitted by this chapter. If the child admits to driving or being in actual physical control of a vehicle in violation of section 39–08–01 or an equivalent ordinance, the child may be required to pay a fine as a condition imposed under this section.

3. An incriminating statement made by a participant to the person giving counsel or advice and in the discussions or conferences incident thereto may not be used against the declarant over objection in any hearing except in a hearing on disposition in a juvenile court proceeding or in a criminal

proceeding against the declarant after conviction for the purpose of a presentence investigation.

———

At intake, (1) the juvenile's case can be referred for formal judicial proceedings by filing a petition; (2) the complaint can be dismissed; or, (3) as the North Dakota statutory example illustrates, the complaint can be handled through "nonjudicial disposition."

The Juvenile Justice Standards Relating to the Juvenile Probation Function delineate the existing types of nonjudicial dispositions: (1) "nonjudicial probation," which involves supervision of the juvenile by juvenile court personnel for a limited period of time during which some restrictions may be imposed (similar to regular probation except that it is not judicially imposed); (2) "provision of intake services," which involves direct provision of services to the juvenile by juvenile court personnel; and (3) "conditional dismissal of a complaint," which is the dismissal of the complaint subject to certain conditions not involving acceptance of nonjudicial supervision or intake services; it would include a "community agency referral," which is a referral to a community agency for services. Standard 2.4(B).

The Standards go on to provide that nonjudicial supervision, provision of intake services, and conditional dismissal (other than community agency referral) are not intake dispositional options under the Standards. Standard 2.4(D). The only option permitted by the Standards is the community agency referral, i.e., referral to youth service bureaus or other community agencies. Standard 2.4(C).

Why do you think the Standards disapprove nonjudicial probation, the provision of intake services and conditional dismissal of a complaint? What do you think of the use of these options? Do you see the potential for substantial intervention in a juvenile's life for a significant period without truly voluntary and knowing consent by the juvenile or his or her parents, or for abuse where intake officers have virtually unlimited discretion in intake decisionmaking, or for unequal treatment of juveniles based on external factors? See Standards Relating to the Juvenile Probation Function (1980), Introduction at 2–3.

NOTE

In one sense, labeling a single phase of the juvenile system Intake and Diversion is misleading. Diversion can actually occur when the police first have contact with the juvenile. Police may decide at the scene not to intervene if they are convinced that the juvenile is not in serious danger of engaging in further antisocial behavior. In making this decision, police usually consider the juvenile's demeanor and his past contacts with police in addition, of course, to the juvenile's observed behavior.

The police may merely warn a juvenile and release him to his parents or take him to the police station and then release him without further formal action. In addition, the police may resolve a minor dispute involving a juvenile by requiring immediate restitution from the juvenile to the complainant. These examples of "police diversion" are really examples of police discretion. Police discretion involves such legal issues as whether it is appropriate to vest such power in the police, where the discretion should be exercised (on the street or at the station) and how to avoid the discriminatory impact of discretion on minorities and the poor. A thorough discussion of police discretion, however, is outside the scope of this book. For complete development of these issues, see A.B.A. Project on Standards for Criminal Justice, Standards Relating to the Urban Police Function (1973); Kenneth Culp Davis, Police Discretion (1975); Herman Goldstein, Policing a Free Society (1977); Albert J. Reiss, Jr., The Police and the Public (1971); Charles E. Silberman, Criminal Violence, Criminal Justice (2d ed. 1980) (esp. ch. 7); Jerome Skolnick, Justice Without Trial (3d ed. 1994); Symposium, Police Practices, 36 Law & Contemp. Prob. 445–588 (1971).

2. Rights at Intake

IN RE ANTHONY S, 73 Misc.2d 187, 341 N.Y.S.2d 11 (Fam.Ct., Richmond County 1973). Stanley Gartenstein, Judge:

. . .

Respondent ... moves for an order of dismissal based upon the undisputed contention that he was not represented by counsel in the informal pre-court intake conference at which time he had the opportunity to have this matter adjusted before a petition was drawn. He argues that this deprived him of his constitutional right to counsel.

. . .

RIGHT TO COUNSEL AT INTAKE CONFERENCE

The informal conference prior to judicial proceedings is unique to the system of juvenile justice in the United States. It is a clearing house in which solutions are worked out under the protective eye of court sanctioned social workers which insures the fact that lessons will be learned and the prospective respondent put back into the community with all possible assurance that, having had his brush with the law, he will not return either to this or the Criminal Court. This "preventive medicine" stage, unique to the juvenile courts, insures that no one will come to the "fail safe" point in contact with the Court and not be able to turn back. Sometimes a simple apology will soothe ruffled feelings; often restitution can be worked out to everyone's satisfaction buttressed by voluntary probation and supervision. Even novel solutions such as cleaning subway graffiti are utilized. In point of fact, with everyone satisfied and the youthful perpetrator having permanently learned his lesson, in this county alone, for a period between January and November, 1972, statistics show that of 515 delinquency matters handled at Intake, 360 were adjusted while 155 were referred to Court, a ratio in excess of two-thirds disposed of informally.

Should an aggrieved party insist on his right to be heard in court after informal Intake has been exhausted, that party may not be prevented from filing a petition and bringing the matter on for adjudication (Family Court Rules, rule 7.3; 22 NYCRR 2502.4). Moreover, whether or not a case is adjusted at Intake, Section 735 of the Family Court Act provides:

"No statement made during a preliminary conference may be admitted into evidence at a factfinding hearing. . . ."

Does the constitutional right to counsel attach to the Intake conference?

PRIOR HOLDINGS OF THE SUPREME COURT

The convulsions now being felt throughout the juvenile justice system are the result of a chain of holdings by the United States Supreme Court and the problem of ascertaining what areas were or were not affected.

. . .

From these decisions, the Court in *McKeiver* stressed that although the *hearing* (added emphasis) must measure up to essentials of due process, not all rights in connection therewith guaranteed to adults were guaranteed to juveniles, lest this destroy the very fabric of the unique nature of the juvenile court, and in the words of the Court, "deprive it of its 'informality, flexibility or speed.'"

It is significant that the *McKeiver* Court quotes with approval the opinion of Justice Roberts of the Pennsylvania Supreme Court in that matter that "'of all the possible due process rights which could be applied in the juvenile courts, the right to trial by jury is the one which would most likely be disruptive of the unique nature of the juvenile process.'" Thus, the criteria of "disruptive of the unique nature of the juvenile process" must, by mandate of the Supreme Court, temper and further define the impact of the *Kent–Gault–Winship* emphasis on "fundamental fairness" with particular reference to fact-finding procedures.

At all times, the courts must heed the warning of the *McKeiver* Court that we are not to "remake the juvenile proceeding into a fully adversary process and . . . put an effective end to what has been the idealistic prospect of an intimate, informal protective proceeding."

. . .

This Court recognizes that the presence of counsel at informal Intake would in effect convert that conference to a formal rigid adversary proceeding, halting the free exchange of ideas which is buttressed by statutory absolute privilege, and relegating this conference to the redundancy of a minor trial prior to trial, thereby emasculating the innovative techniques of Probation services.

The Court holds that the informal Intake conference is not part of the adjudication process, therefore not subject in the first instance to *Kent–Gault–Winship*. However, should future holding deem it to be part of the hearing procedure, thereby subject to the admonitions of *Kent–Gault–Winship*, the court holds that *McKeiver's* criteria of "disruptive of the juvenile process" would form sufficient basis for excluding the right to counsel at the Intake conference, especially in view of the absolute statutory privilege of Section 735.

It is always in order to recall the admonition of the *McKeiver* Court, 403 U.S. on page 551:

> "If the formalities of the criminal adjudicative process are to be super-imposed upon the juvenile court system, there is little need for its separate existence."

The motion is accordingly denied.

. . .

NOTES

(1) *In re Anthony S* represents the majority view that juveniles are not constitutionally entitled to counsel at intake. However, in most jurisdictions, if the juvenile has retained an attorney, the attorney is permitted to participate in the intake process. More importantly, in many juvenile codes today juveniles are provided a statutory right to counsel "at all stages of the proceedings." See, e.g., 42 Pa.Cons.Stat.Ann. § 6337; Tex.Fam.Code Ann. § 51.10(a)–(b).

Considering the impact an attorney can have at intake, should all juveniles be entitled to representation at this stage? For arguments supporting the right to counsel at intake, see Andrew W. Maron, Constitutional Problems of Diversion of Juvenile Delinquents, 51 Notre Dame L.Rev. 22, 38–41 (1975).

(2) Do you agree that the provision of attorneys at the intake conference will convert it into "a formal rigid adversary proceeding"? What is the appropriate role of counsel at intake? Aren't there grave dangers in the attorney's becoming overbearing and counterproductive? If an attorney persistently raises legal points with intake staff, they may very well let the attorney obtain a more receptive audience: the juvenile court judge. Isn't it possible that intake staff might prefer attorneys present at these conferences?

Consider the following roles of the attorney in representing his or her client at intake:

> 1. To assess and make recommendations as to available non-court programs for which the juvenile qualifies.

> 2. To arrange restitution.

> 3. To interpret the proceeding to the child and his family and to present the family's preferred course of action to the intake officer.

> 4. To collect and present relevant school, medical and social records.

For a general discussion of the role of attorneys at intake, see Monrad G. Paulsen & Charles H. Whitebread, Juvenile Law and Procedure 23–31 (1974).

3. WHO GETS DIVERTED?

Juvenile intake officers generally consider a variety of factors in deciding whether a juvenile should be diverted including:

1. The child's attitude toward the offense: has the child admitted the misbehavior or does he deny involvement?

2. Parental control over the youth.

3. The child's school and/or employment status.

4. The psychiatric history of the child.

5. The willingness of the child and his parents to participate in a diversion program.

6. The age of the juvenile.

7. The nature of the offense.

Under the traditional rehabilitative model of juvenile justice, the seventh factor theoretically was not a major consideration. In reality, however, the nature of the misbehavior was always part of the diversion calculus. A child who has raped or killed is less likely to be diverted to a youth service bureau than a child who violated a curfew. The public clamor over juvenile crime has put even more pressure on probation officers to ensure that juveniles who engage in violent behavior go to court.

In recent years, intake staff have published specific guidelines for the exercise of discretion. California probation officers, in accord with this modern trend, have developed the following guidelines for the processing of both alleged delinquents and status offenders. Recent changes in California Rules of Court references are noted in brackets. Changes in the substance of the Rules, though minimal, also are indicated by brackets.

CALIFORNIA JUVENILE COURT PRACTICE (Robert N. Waxman Feb. 1998 Update), CHAPTER TWO: MINOR'S ARREST AND INTAKE*

Intake Guidelines

[§ 2.14]   Juvenile Court Rules

California Rules of Court [5.514] and [5.516] have been substantially rewritten to reflect both statutory and philosophical changes in the juvenile court law. Rule [5.514] now encourages the prepetition settlement of juvenile cases through either nonaction, community treatment referrals, or informal supervision, suggesting that formal proceedings be undertaken only when necessary for the welfare of the child or the protection of the community. Cal Rules of Ct [5.514(b)]. Of course, there is an exception to this for cases that must be referred for prosecution. Cal Rules of Ct [5.514(d)]; see § 2.13.

Although Cal Rules of Ct [5.514—5.516] ... establish guidelines for the probation officer to use at intake, these guidelines are not mandatory. Because the probation officer is required by Welf & I C § 652 and Welf & I C § 653.5 to make whatever investigation he or she "deems necessary," investigation that falls far short of that suggested by Rule [5.514] appears to be acceptable. Raymond B. v. Superior Court (1980) 102 CA3d 372, 162 CR 506. Under this standard, the probation officer apparently need not make any investigation at all. Alsavon M. v. Superior Court (1981) 124 CA3d 586, 593, 177 CR 434, 438. [Note: Rule 5.514(c) now states that the probation officer "must" conduct an investigation.]

Alsavon M. concerned the Los Angeles County Juvenile Justice Center, a pilot program set up in the Watts area of Los Angeles. Under the juvenile justice center concept, the initial intake review is made before a panel consisting of representatives from the sheriff's department, the police department, the probation department, and the schools. The minor is not allowed to attend, nor is he or she allowed to be represented by counsel. The panel, on review of the case, makes a recommendation about the action to be taken. According to a declaration file in *Alsavon M.* by the director of the Juvenile Justice Center, the director, who is a probation officer, makes the final decision; however, documents submitted to the court of appeal indicated that the probation officer followed the "recommendation" of the panel 100 percent of the time. Besides holding that the probation officer need make no personal investigation, the court also held that the minor had neither the right to notice of the hearing nor the right to attend. 124 CA3d at 595, 177 CR at 440. [Again, Rule 5.514(c), as amended in 2007, now states that the probation officer "must" conduct an investigation.]

Because it appears that courts are not going to force probation departments to screen cases thoroughly, attorneys should make every effort to contact the probation officer and set up a proper screening. As a practical matter, probation officers, with their heavy caseloads, often do very little investigation prior to filing, particularly in busy urban areas. Therefore, counsel should present in an easily assimilable form all the information he or she wishes the probation officer to consider. Generally, if counsel can do an effective selling job at intake, the probation officer will look on the case more favorably. The judicial retreat from the requirements of the Rules of Court makes counsel's early intervention very important.

Inadequate funding will not excuse a probation department from providing informal supervision to a juvenile who otherwise deserves it. John O. v. Superior Court (1985) 169 CA3d 823, 215 CR 592. The probation officer in *John O.* informed the court that the probation department had suffered budget cuts, making it impossible to operate an adequate program of informal supervision under Welf & I C § 654. The only available program was an unsupervised referral to a community agency. Because the minor needed more supervision than the existing program provided, the trial court refused to place the minor on informal supervision. The court of appeal held that the lack of proper funding was not a proper ground to deny informal supervision and ordered the trial court to reconsider the minor's application, ruling that the informal supervision decision must comply with the criteria set forth in Cal Rules of Ct [5.516(b)....]

While the actual decision in *John O.* will have limited application (if one assumes that probation officers are hesitant in saying that minors are rejected for budgetary reasons), the rule that informal supervision decisions must be made under the criteria stated in Cal Rules of Ct [5.516(b)] is significant. This will eliminate many of the "personal" reasons that probation officers and judges give for denying informal supervision and will provide them with a more rational framework....

The probation department may not institute a policy of rejecting minors for informal supervision because they deny guilt of the charged offense. The juvenile court has the authority to order the probation department to consider a minor's eligibility for informal supervision. Paul D. v. Superior Court (1984) 158 CA3d 838, 205 CR 77.

The factors considered in deciding whether to dismiss the charges are now found in Cal Rules of Ct [5.516(a)]:

(1) Whether there is sufficient evidence of a condition or conduct to bring the child within the jurisdiction of the ... court;

(2) If the [alleged] condition or conduct is not considered serious, whether the child has previously presented ... significant problems in the home, school, or community;

(3) Whether the matter appears to have arisen from a temporary problem within the family [that] has been or can be resolved;

(4) Whether any agency or other resource in the community is [available to offer services to] the child [and the child's family to prevent or eliminate the need to remove the child from the child's home];

(5) The attitudes of the child , ... the parent or guardian [and any affected persons];

(6) The age, maturity, and capabilities of the [child];

(7) [The dependency or delinquent history, if any, of the child];

(8) The recommendation, if any, of the referring party or agency; [and]

(9) Any other circumstances that indicate that settling the matter at intake would be consistent with the welfare of the child and the ... protection of the public.

. . .

NOTES

(1) Will the California guidelines really remove discretion from the intake and diversion process? In addition to the skepticism (and the need for attorney input) expressed in the above excerpt, consider the following:

> Even in probation departments with official diversion policies, diversion is likely to occur only if the intake officers want it to occur. Although these men surely are influenced by the policies, programs, and philosophies favored by their superiors—especially their immediate supervisors—they still have great latitude to decide who shall be diverted and who shall not. The degree and direction in which juvenile offenders are diverted is influenced by the individual intake officer's conception of justice and his philosophy and theory of correction, as well as by his knowledge of community resources, by his relationships with other professional welfare workers both within and without his department, by his personal assumptions, attitudes, biases, and prejudices, by the size of his case load and the work load of his department, and by many other subtle conditions. He cannot easily be ordered to make his decisions in a specified way. Ultimately, then, decisions to divert or not divert are his to make. Pressuring him to make his decisions in a certain way, overruling his decisions, and even hesitant questioning of his decisions are usually viewed as unwarranted interference by both intake officers and their superiors.

Donald R. Cressey & Robert A. McDermott, Diversion from the Juvenile Justice System 12–13 (1973).*

(2) California permits informal probation, or supervision. Recall that the Standards indicate that informal probation is "impermissible." What are the benefits of informal probation? What are the dangers inherent in informal probation? Should there be any time limits on an informal probation period? See Colo.Rev.Stat.Ann. § 19–3–501(1)(c)(II).

(3) Intake officers have begun to focus not just on the social history and psychological make-up of the juvenile, but also on the "legal facts" involved. In determining whether to file a petition it is now considered important to view the seriousness of the offense, prior offense records, prior dispositions, and the possibility of obtaining a favorable adjudication from the prosecutor's standpoint. See Juveniles in Justice: A Book of Readings 226–27 (H. Ted Rubin ed. 1980). In fact, in some states there is criticism that prosecutors have begun to dominate the decision-making process. Id. at 227. Nevertheless, the trend is to eliminate the prosecutor's ability to file a complaint over the objection of the intake staff. Under California Rule of Court 5.514(c) the probation officer makes the decision whether to request that a petition be filed. However, under Rule 5.514(d) the probation officer *must* refer certain cases to the prosecutor, i.e., juveniles charged with certain serious offenses regardless of age and those 16 or older with a prior history. Most states do not permit the complainant to force a juvenile to court if the intake staff decides to divert. But see Ill.Comp.Stat.Ann. ch. 705, § 405/2–12; N.Y.Fam.Ct.Act § 735(b), (f)–(g). The juvenile, however, can almost always go to court if he desires. Can you think of any cases in which a juvenile would want to go to court when the intake staff has proposed diversion?

(4) The Standards require that the intake officer should "make an initial determination of whether the complaint is legally sufficient for the filing of a petition." Juvenile Justice Standards Relating to the Juvenile Probation Function, Standard 2.7. If the intake officer is unsure about such legal sufficiency, the officer should ask the appropriate prosecuting official. Is it sensible to require non–lawyers to determine the legal sufficiency of a complaint, including whether the court has jurisdiction and whether there is enough evidence to support the charges against the juvenile?

(5) Must the juvenile admit his behavior in order to be diverted? Some jurisdictions require an admission before diversion on the rationale that admission is essential to rehabilitation. Some states, however, permit diversion so long as the juvenile agrees that he or she does not want to contest the allegations. In *Kody P. v. Superior Court*, 137 Cal.App.4th 1030, 40 Cal.Rptr.3d 763 (2006), the court held that the probation department's policy of categorically excluding juveniles who refuse to admit an offense from consideration for informal supervision violates statutory law as well as court rules that provide specific criteria. The issue of admission is rarely raised, however, because juveniles often confess and admit their conduct and want to avoid an adjudication of delinquency. In other words, they cooperate to qualify for diversion. This common occurrence raises the issue of whether the state is conditioning a benefit upon a "compelled" confession, thereby violating the juvenile's Fifth Amendment privilege against self-incrimination.

A related issue is whether a juvenile's statements during intake are admissible against him at a later court proceeding. Some states permit statements during intake to be used against the juvenile, but the Juvenile Justice Standards disagree. Standard 2.12 of the Standards Relating to the Juvenile Probation Function provides that juveniles are entitled to the privilege against self-incrimination when being questioned by intake personnel during the intake process. It further provides that any statement made to intake personnel or information derived directly or indirectly from such a statement is inadmissible in any proceeding prior to an adjudication of delinquency unless the statement was made following consultation with and in the presence of counsel. See Ill.Comp.Laws Ann. ch. 705, § 405/2–12 (4); N.Y.Fam.Ct.Act § 735(h).

(6) Is it possible, or advisable, to move diversion to an even earlier point, i.e., can court service workers predict who is most at risk for juvenile crime and intervene at an early stage before any offense has been committed? For an argument that a correlation exists between truancy and commission of juvenile offenses and describing an early intervention program in Los Angeles County, California, see Charles Edward Pell, Note, Pre–Offense Monitoring of Potential Juvenile Offenders: An Examination of the Los Angeles County Probation Department's Novel Solution to the Interrelated Problems of Truancy and (Juvenile) Crime, 73 S.Cal.L.Rev. 879 (2000).

4.   WHY ARE WE DIVERTING?

Commentators and juvenile authorities have long extolled the benefits of diverting youths from the juvenile court to increase the likelihood of rehabilitation. Several aspects of diversion make rehabilitation more likely. First, diversion is nonstigmatizing or at least less stigmatizing than formal adjudication. Second, diversion programs often begin soon after the juvenile has engaged in the delinquent behavior. Utilizing social services for the juvenile at this crisis point increases the possibility that the juvenile may modify his antisocial behavior. Finally, diversion programs usually involve intervention by agencies that are not associated with law enforcement. Rehabilitation becomes more likely because troubled youths generally react more favorably toward probation officers and mental health professionals than toward police officers. See Edwin Schur, Radical Non–Intervention: Rethinking the Delinquency Problem (1973); Edwin M. Lemert, Instead of Court: Diversion in Juvenile Justice (1971).

Whatever its impact on the likelihood of rehabilitation, diversion serves the additional function of reducing court backlog and congestion. Is that result sufficiently beneficial to be regarded as a major factor in favor of diversion? One of the best-known commentators on diversion, Paul Nejelski, has argued that reduced case loads have drawn attention away from the need for more fundamental reform of juvenile justice, and that diversion programs often reduce the visibility of "coercive state intervention" in the lives of juveniles, which permits administrators to act discriminatorily. Nejelski explains:

> In the adult system, society is coming to realize the impracticability of processing drunks or alcoholics as criminals. In contrast, where there is case by case diversion of minor cases, especially in the so-called status offenses, there is little pressure for radical change; sentiment for the repeal of the statutes which form the basis for state intervention does not develop. Instead, an administrator is deciding privately that some "juvenile offenders" are better treated in noncourt systems. Such a scheme currently calls for ad hoc decisions in individual cases by someone in the large system which deals with children in trouble. This discretion has low visibility and may be exercised in a discriminatory or arbitrary fashion.

> Discretionary screening of cases, which has the most serious impact on the poor and minorities, may have the unfortunate result of postponing more basic reform.... Outright abolition, and not passing the buck to anonymous administrators, may be a more appropriate solution in dealing with status offenses.

Paul Nejelski, Diversion: Unleashing the Hounds of Heaven?, in Pursuing Justice for the Child 94, 115 (Margaret Rosenheim ed. 1976).*

Furthermore, Nejelski contends diversion presents a more basic problem in that it may increase "coercive intervention in the lives of children and families without proper concern for their rights." Despite his criticism of diversion programs, Nejelski concludes that when properly monitored, such programs have "considerable promise." See also Paul Nejelski, Diversion: The Promise and the Danger, 22 Crime & Delinq. 393 (1976).

Some commentators have been more critical of diversion programs. For example, Margo Andriessen studied American diversion programs because she planned to establish similar programs in Holland. She concluded that the majority of programs were not diversion at all, but rather extensions of the criminal justice system. Current programs, according to Andriessen, are designed not for diversion but to appease critics of the juvenile system. Margo Andriessen, A Foreigner's View of American Diversion, 26 Crime & Delinq. 70 (1980). Others have argued that diversion programs have not furnished an alternative to the juvenile justice system but rather have "widened the net" of the system to include juveniles who otherwise would not have been included in the system at all. Kenneth Polk, Juvenile Diversion: A Look at the Record, 30 Crime & Delinq. 648 (1984). Critics also have argued that diversion has produced a form of sex discrimination (because of the proportionately large number of females who are in diversion programs) and has resulted in loss of procedural rights and even arbitrary treatment (because of the informality of the process). Polk, supra; Dean G. Rojek, Juvenile Diversion and the Potential of Inappropriate Treatment for Offenders, 12 New Eng.J. on Crim. & Civ. Confinement 329 (1986). Other scholars have defended diversion against these and similar criticisms. Arnold Binder & Gilbert Geis, Ad Populum Argumentation in Criminology: Juvenile Diversion as Rhetoric, 30 Crime & Delinq. 309 (1984).

NOTES

(1) For a discussion of the history of diversion, see Andrew W. Maron, Constitutional Problems of Diversion of Juvenile Delinquents, 51 Notre Dame L.Rev. 22, 26–28 (1975). Maron notes that diversion was "well established" by 1926 and chronicles the growth of diversion programs during the late 1960s and 1970s as a result of a recommendation from a Presidential Task Force extolling the benefits of diversion.

(2) For one proposal for establishing a beneficial diversion program based on the idea that some deviant behavior is essentially "normal" and need not be viewed as portending future pathology, see Margaret Rosenheim, Notes on Helping Juve-

nile Nuisances, in Pursuing Justice for the Child 43, 60 (Margaret Rosenheim ed. 1976).

5.   DIVERSION TO WHAT?

One of the most striking features of juveniles in trouble may be their sense that no one cares about them or their problems. Psychologists and child development experts have long indicated that misbehavior often reflects the juvenile's need for some type of love and care. What implications does this have for diversion programs? Consider the following example of a diversion program in Kenton County, Kentucky, that used volunteers in theater production to work intensively with diverted youths. The Kentucky program was patterned after a Washington program, Theatre Inside, that matched actors and other theater professionals with incarcerated juveniles:

> The actors conduct a fast-paced workshop in which the students take part in exercises facilitated by the teachers, all of whom have had experience or training in dramatic performance. Teachers and students begin work in small groups, then prepare to stage a production. The actors make no attempt to offer psychological therapy or rehabilitative instruction, nor do they teach acting techniques per se. Unlike the kind of drama taught in a high school drama class, which stresses techniques of internalization and characterization for example, Theatre Inside emphasizes a flexible, criticism-free interaction between students and teachers. The program uses the study of drama to provide a forum in which to instill cooperation, create relationships, build self-esteem, and cultivate imagination.
>
>   . . .
>
> . . . In working with the facilitators, the juvenile participants found someone who took an interest in them. As the relationship with these teachers grew, the youth began to recognize the value of building links with people outside their immediate peer groups. The values displayed by the facilitator provided an alternative to the subcultural values they had come with, and as the juveniles began to reflect these values, the promise of resiliency revealed itself.
>
> Rehearsing and giving the performance reinforced a sense of togetherness. For the production to take place as scheduled, each individual had to make a commitment to the group. When one came late to practice lines, others indicated their disapproval which underscored the importance of being on time and fulfilling agreements. Together, the troupe solved problems of equipment shortages, scheduling, and other day-to-day obstacles. Getting to the performance meant that the group had learned more than acting; they had learned about working cooperatively as a group.
>
> The dramatic production linked youth with their community. From the mayor to parents, the production brought together community members. At-risk youth were exposed to the importance of community participation. Community leaders witnessed youth working together to improve the quality of social life. In a kind of role reversal,

alienated youth participated in community outreach. Rather than undermining social cohesion by acting out, they had become community organizers by acting and had improved the quality of life in an urban neighborhood.

Sue Larison, Deborah Williamson & Paul Knepper, Dress Rehearsal for Citizenship: Using Theatre to Teach Law–Related Education to Diverted Youth, 45 Juv. & Fam.Ct.J. 55, 59, 61 (Spring 1994).* An earlier program used student volunteers to work intensively, one-on-one, with diverted juveniles. The program is described more fully in Michelle Bauer, Gilda Bordeaux, John Cole, William S. Davidson, Arnoldo Martinez, Christina Mitchell & Dolly Singleton, A Diversion Program for Juvenile Offenders: The Experience of Ingham County, Michigan, 31 Juv. & Fam.Ct.J. 53 (August 1980).

Another innovative approach, the Juvenile Conference Committee operated statewide in New Jersey, is described in David Twain & Laura Maiello, Juvenile Conference Committees: An Evaluation of the Administration of Justice at the Neighborhood Level, 16 J.Crim.Just. 451 (1988). The primary focus is on juveniles charged with minor delinquent behavior, although in some cases the court may refer a status offender to a Committee. Each Committee is made up of six to nine members from the business and residential communities. In addition, a Committee includes a police liaison, a probation liaison, and a school attendance counselor. The role of the latter members is to provide helpful information in their areas of expertise. Because of its informal nature, a Committee may not order the confinement of a juvenile, place a juvenile on probation, remove a juvenile from his or her family, or impose a fine. It may not order any formal sanction but may only recommend a course of action. It may decide to counsel the juvenile or it may choose from a wide range of creative dispositional alternatives, such as restitution or community service. In 1988 there were about 300 of these neighborhood Committees in New Jersey, and it was estimated that they handled between 15 and 25 percent of the cases coming to the juvenile court.

Yet another innovation that is enjoying increased use and visibility is the "teen court" program. The program is available principally for juveniles charged with minor offenses (stealing, vandalism and the like). Few adults are involved in the process. Juveniles themselves (student volunteers as well as youth who have gone through the program successfully) determine the "punishment," which might include, e.g., community service, restitution, payment of a fine, or something as simple as an apology to the victim. Recidivism rates for those who go through the program typically are lower than for juveniles who are adjudicated. For a description of the teen court process see Jeffrey A. Butts, Janeen Buck & Mark B. Coggeshall, The Impact of Teen Court on Young Offenders (The Urban Institute April 2002). A 2002 study shows that one state has established procedures for teen court, seven others specifically mention it as a diversion alternative, and 28 others, while not specifically mentioning it, would allow it as an

* Copyright © 1994, by the National   Reprinted with permission.
Council of Juvenile and Family Court Judges.

option in an existing diversion scheme. Madelynn M. Herman, Teen Courts—A Juvenile Justice Diversion Program, in 2002 Report on Trends in the State Courts (National Center for State Courts 2002).

NOTES

(1) Diversion programs are as diverse as the juveniles who enter them. In many jurisdictions there is simply a youth service bureau designed to handle all diversions. In larger cities, however, diversion programs become quite specialized and often include drug and alcohol rehabilitation, vocational training and remedial education. In addition, some jurisdictions have Outward Bound programs or some type of wilderness appreciation program. Finally, in some instances the only necessary intervention may be referral to a physician for medical treatment. Sometimes frustrating physical disorders contribute to a youth's inability to perform in school and to resultant antisocial behavior.

(2) Many churches sponsor programs for their young people. Should intake officers utilize these programs when diverting juveniles? Are there constitutional questions raised by such referrals?

(3) The Standards and a few jurisdictions permit intake personnel, the juvenile and the juvenile's family to enter into a consent decree that has the force of a court order but is not a formal adjudication. The use of decrees may hold a great deal of rehabilitative promise because they allow a juvenile to help fashion his own diversion program. See Juvenile Justice Standards Relating to the Juvenile Probation Function, Standard 2.5 at 53–57.

C.   Pretrial Detention

1.   Introduction

Detention of juveniles before any adjudication or disposition has occurred is one of the most serious problems in the administration of juvenile justice today. The range of problems includes the large number of juveniles detained during the pre-adjudicatory stage each year, the sometimes harsh conditions in which they are confined, the high costs associated with such detention, and the harmful after-effects that such detention can produce. In addition, these difficulties often are exacerbated by disturbing inadequacies in the system of juvenile justice itself, namely, inadequacies in the decision-making process that can lead to detention, delays between taking into custody and final disposition, and the pervasive lack of visibility and accountability in the process.

In contrast, the post-adjudicative dispositional process is characterized by greater care and sensitivity in terms of the quality and character of facilities and the availability of alternatives to incarceration. For juveniles the result, ironically, is less frequent detention under better conditions once the presumption of innocence has been set aside.

Reform in the area of pretrial detention of juveniles should focus on the importance and integrity of pretrial decisionmaking and the development of an expedited, informed process. Standards should be formulated and rules imposed to narrow the function of the process to that of the historic function of bail in the criminal process, i.e., ensuring the presence of the accused at subsequent court proceedings. These standards also should acknowledge one of the de facto functions that bail in the adult criminal process plays, namely, that in some cases the evidence of guilt and the danger to others are sometimes too great to warrant a reasonable judicial officer in releasing an accused suspect. Juvenile Justice Standards Relating to Interim Status: The Release, Control, and Detention of Accused Juvenile Offenders Between Arrest and Disposition, Introduction at 1–3 (1980).

2. STATUTORY LIMITATIONS

Schall v. Martin

Supreme Court of the United States, 1984.
467 U.S. 253, 104 S.Ct. 2403, 81 L.Ed.2d 207.

■ JUSTICE REHNQUIST delivered the opinion of the Court.

Section 320.5(3)(b) of the New York Family Court Act authorizes pretrial detention of an accused juvenile delinquent based on a finding that there is a "serious risk" that the child "may before the return date commit an act which if committed by an adult would constitute a crime." Appellees brought suit on behalf of a class of all juveniles detained pursuant to that provision. The District Court struck down § 320.5(3)(b) as permitting detention without due process of law and ordered the immediate release of all class members. United States ex rel. Martin v. Strasburg, 513 F.Supp. 691 (S.D.N.Y.1981). The Court of Appeals for the Second Circuit affirmed, holding the provision "unconstitutional as to all juveniles" because the statute is administered in such a way that "the detention period serves as punishment imposed without proof of guilt established according to the requisite constitutional standard." Martin v. Strasburg, 689 F.2d 365, 373–374 (1982). We noted probable jurisdiction, 460 U.S. 1079 (1983), and now reverse. We conclude that preventive detention under the FCA serves a legitimate state objective, and that the procedural protections afforded pretrial detainees by the New York statute satisfy the requirements of the Due Process Clause of the Fourteenth Amendment to the United States Constitution.

I

Appellee Gregory Martin was arrested on December 13, 1977, and charged with first-degree robbery, second-degree assault, and criminal possession of a weapon based on an incident in which he, with two others, allegedly hit a youth on the head with a loaded gun and stole his jacket and sneakers. Martin had possession of the gun when he was arrested. He was 14 years old at the time and, therefore, came within the jurisdiction of New York's Family Court. The incident occurred at 11:30 at night, and Martin lied to the police about where and with whom he lived. He was consequently detained overnight.[5]

---

5. When a juvenile is arrested, the arresting officer must immediately notify the parent or other person legally responsible for the child's care. FCA § 305.2(3). Ordinarily,

A petition of delinquency was filed, and Martin made his "initial appearance" in Family Court on December 14th, accompanied by his grandmother. The Family Court Judge, citing the possession of the loaded weapon, the false address given to the police, and the lateness of the hour, as evidencing a lack of supervision, ordered Martin detained under § 320.5(3)(b) (at that time § 739(a)(ii)). A probable cause hearing was held five days later, on December 19th, and probable cause was found to exist for all the crimes charged. At the factfinding hearing held December 27–29, Martin was found guilty on the robbery and criminal possession charges. He was adjudicated a delinquent and placed on two years' probation. He had been detained pursuant to § 320.5(3)(b), between the initial appearance and the completion of the factfinding hearing, for a total of 15 days.

. . .

II

There is no doubt that the Due Process Clause is applicable in juvenile proceedings. "The problem," we have stressed, "is to ascertain the precise impact of the due process requirement upon such proceedings." In re Gault, 387 U.S. 1, 13–14 (1967). We have held that certain basic constitutional protections enjoyed by adults accused of crimes also apply to juveniles. See Id., at 31–57 (notice of charges, right to counsel, privilege against self-incrimination, right to confrontation and cross-examination); In re Winship, 397 U.S. 358 (1970) (proof beyond a reasonable doubt); Breed v. Jones, 421 U.S. 519 (1975) (double jeopardy). But the Constitution does not mandate elimination of all differences in the treatment of juveniles. See, e.g., McKeiver v. Pennsylvania, 403 U.S. 528 (1971) (no right to jury trial). The State has "a parens patriae interest in preserving and promoting the welfare of the child," Santosky v. Kramer, 455 U.S. 745, 766 (1982), which makes a juvenile proceeding fundamentally different from an adult criminal trial. We have tried, therefore, to strike a balance—to respect the "informality" and "flexibility" that characterize juvenile proceedings, In re Winship, supra, 397 U.S., at 366, and yet to ensure that such proceedings comport with the "fundamental fairness" demanded by the Due Process Clause. Breed v. Jones, supra, 421 U.S., at 531; *McKeiver*, supra, 403 U.S., at 543 (plurality opinion).

the child will be released into the custody of his parent or guardian after being issued an "appearance ticket" requiring him to meet with the probation service on a specified day. § 307.1(1). See n. 9, infra. If, however, he is charged with a serious crime, one of several designated felonies, see § 301.2(8), or if his parent or guardian cannot be reached, the juvenile may be taken directly before the Family Court. § 305.2. The Family Court judge will make a preliminary determination as to the jurisdiction of the court, appoint a law guardian for the child, and advise the child of his or her rights, including the right to counsel and the right to remain silent.

Only if, as in Martin's case, the Family Court is not in session and special circumstances exist, such as an inability to notify the parents, will the child be taken directly by the arresting officer to a juvenile detention facility. § 305.2(4)(c). If the juvenile is so detained, he must be brought before the Family Court within 72 hours or the next day the court is in session, whichever is sooner. § 307.3(4). The propriety of such detention, prior to a juvenile's initial appearance in Family Court, is not at issue in this case. Appellees challenged only judicially ordered detention pursuant to § 320.5(3)(b).

The statutory provision at issue in these cases, § 320.5(3)(b), permits a brief pretrial detention based on a finding of a "serious risk" that an arrested juvenile may commit a crime before his return date. The question before us is whether preventive detention of juveniles pursuant to § 320.5(3)(b) is compatible with the "fundamental fairness" required by due process. Two separate inquiries are necessary to answer this question. First, does preventive detention under the New York statute serve a legitimate state objective? See Bell v. Wolfish, 441 U.S. 520, 534, n. 15 (1979); Kennedy v. Mendoza–Martinez, 372 U.S. 144, 168–169 (1963). And, second, are the procedural safeguards contained in the FCA adequate to authorize the pretrial detention of at least some juveniles charged with crimes? See Mathews v. Eldridge, 424 U.S. 319, 335 (1976); Gerstein v. Pugh, 420 U.S. 103, 114 (1975).

A

Preventive detention under the FCA is purportedly designed to protect the child and society from the potential consequences of his criminal acts. When making any detention decision, the Family Court judge is specifically directed to consider the needs and best interests of the juvenile as well as the need for the protection of the community.... As an initial matter, therefore, we must decide whether, in the context of the juvenile system, the combined interest in protecting both the community and the juvenile himself from the consequences of future criminal conduct is sufficient to justify such detention.

The "legitimate and compelling state interest" in protecting the community from crime cannot be doubted....

The juvenile's countervailing interest in freedom from institutional restraints, even for the brief time involved here, is undoubtedly substantial as well. But that interest must be qualified by the recognition that juveniles, unlike adults, are always in some form of custody. Lehman v. Lycoming County Children's Services, 458 U.S. 502, 510–511 (1982); In re Gault, supra, 387 U.S., at 17. Children, by definition, are not assumed to have the capacity of take care of themselves. They are assumed to be subject to the control of their parents, and if parental control falters, the State must play its part as parens patriae. See State v. Gleason, 404 A.2d 573, 580 (Me.1979); People ex rel. Wayburn v. Schupf, supra, at 690, 385 N.Y.S.2d, at 522, 350 N.E.2d, at 910; Baker v. Smith, 477 S.W.2d 149, 150–151 (Ky.1971). In this respect, the juvenile's liberty interest may, in appropriate circumstances, be subordinated to the State's "*parens patriae* interest in preserving and promoting the welfare of the child."

The New York Court of Appeals, in upholding the statute at issue here, stressed at some length "the desirability of protecting the juvenile from his own folly." People ex rel. Wayburn v. Schupf, supra, at 688–689, 385 N.Y.S.2d, at 520–521, 350 N.E.2d, at 909.[15] Society has a legitimate interest

15. "Our society recognizes that juveniles in general are in the earlier stages of their emotional growth, that their intellectual development is incomplete, that they have had only limited practical experience, and that their value systems have not yet been clearly identified or firmly adopted...."

in protecting a juvenile from the consequences of his criminal activity—both from potential physical injury which may be suffered when a victim fights back or a policeman attempts to make an arrest and from the downward spiral of criminal activity into which peer pressure may lead the child. . . .

. . .

Of course, the mere invocation of a legitimate purpose will not justify particular restrictions and conditions of confinement amounting to punishment. It is axiomatic that "[d]ue process requires that a pretrial detainee not be punished." Bell v. Wolfish, 441 U.S., at 535, n. 16. Even given, therefore, that pretrial detention may serve legitimate regulatory purposes, it is still necessary to determine whether the terms and conditions of confinement under § 320.5(3)(b) are in fact compatible with those purposes. Kennedy v. Mendoza–Martinez, 372 U.S., at 168–169. "A court must decide whether the disability is imposed for the purpose of punishment or whether it is but an incident of some other legitimate governmental purpose." Bell v. Wolfish, supra, 441 U.S., at 538. Absent a showing of an express intent to punish on the part of the State, that determination generally will turn on "whether an alternative purpose to which [the restriction] may rationally be connected is assignable for it, and whether it appears excessive in relation to the alternative purpose assigned [to it]." Kennedy v. Mendoza–Martinez, supra, 372 U.S., at 168–189. See Bell v. Wolfish, supra, 441 U.S., at 538; Flemming v. Nestor, 363 U.S. 603, 613–614 (1960).

There is no indication in the statute itself that preventive detention is used or intended as a punishment. First of all, the detention is strictly limited in time. If a juvenile is detained at his initial appearance and has denied the charges against him, he is entitled to a probable-cause hearing to be held not more than three days after the conclusion of the initial appearance or four days after the filing of the petition, whichever is sooner. FCA § 325.1(2). If the Family Court judge finds probable cause, he must also determine whether continued detention is necessary pursuant to § 320.5(3)(b).

Detained juveniles are also entitled to an expedited factfinding hearing. If the juvenile is charged with one of a limited number of designated

"For the same reasons that our society does not hold juveniles to an adult standard of responsibility for their conduct, our society may also conclude that there is a greater likelihood that a juvenile charged with delinquency, if released, will commit another criminal act than that an adult charged with crime will do so. To the extent that self-restraint may be expected to constrain adults, it may not be expected to operate with equal force as to juveniles. Because of the possibility of juvenile delinquency treatment and the absence of second-offender sentencing, there will not be the deterrent for the juvenile which confronts the adult. Perhaps more significant is the fact that in consequence of lack of experience and comprehension the juvenile does not view the commission of what are criminal acts in the same perspective as an adult. . . . There is the element of gamesmanship and the excitement of 'getting away' with something and the powerful inducement of peer pressures. All of these commonly acknowledged factors make the commission of criminal conduct on the part of juveniles in general more likely than in the case of adults." People ex rel. Wayburn v. Schupf, 39 N.Y.2d, at 687–688, 385 N.Y.S.2d, at 520–521, 350 N.E.2d, at 908–909.

felonies, the factfinding hearing must be scheduled to commence not more than 14 days after the conclusion of the initial appearance. § 340.1. If the juvenile is charged with a lesser offense, then the factfinding hearing must be held not more than three days after the initial appearance. In the latter case, since the times for the probable-cause hearing and the factfinding hearing coincide, the two hearings are merged.

Thus, the maximum possible detention under § 320.5(3)(b) of a youth accused of a serious crime, assuming a 3–day extension of the factfinding hearing for good cause shown, is 17 days. The maximum detention for less serious crimes, again assuming a 3–day extension for good cause shown, is six days. These time frames seem suited to the limited purpose of providing the youth with a controlled environment and separating him from improper influences pending the speedy disposition of his case.

. . .

Pretrial detention need not be considered punitive merely because a juvenile is subsequently discharged subject to conditions or put on probation. In fact, such actions reinforce the original finding that close supervision of the juvenile is required. Lenient but supervised disposition is in keeping with the Act's purpose to promote the welfare and development of the child. As the New York Court of Appeals noted:

> "It should surprise no one that caution and concern for both the juvenile and society may indicate the more conservative decision to detain at the very outset, whereas the later development of very much more relevant information may prove that while a finding of delinquency was warranted, placement may not be indicated." People ex rel. Wayburn v. Schupf, 39 N.Y.2d, at 690, 385 N.Y.S.2d, at 522, 350 N.E.2d, at 910.

Even when a case is terminated prior to fact finding, it does not follow that the decision to detain the juvenile pursuant to § 320.5(3)(b) amounted to a due process violation. A delinquency petition may be dismissed for any number of reasons collateral to its merits, such as the failure of a witness to testify. The Family Court judge cannot be expected to anticipate such developments at the initial hearing. He makes his decision based on the information available to him at that time, and the propriety of the decision must be judged in that light. Consequently, the final disposition of a case is "largely irrelevant" to the legality of a pretrial detention. Baker v. McCollan, 443 U.S. 137, 145 (1979).

It may be, of course, that in some circumstances detention of a juvenile would not pass constitutional muster. But the validity of those detentions must be determined on a case-by-case basis. Section 320.5(3)(b) is not invalid "on its face" by reason of the ambiguous statistics and case histories relied upon by the court below.[23] We find no justification for the

---

23. Several *amici* argue that similar statistics obtain throughout the country. See, e.g., Brief for American Bar Association as Amicus Curiae 23; Brief for Association for Children of New Jersey as Amicus Curiae 8, 11; Brief for Youth Law Center et al. as Amicus Curiae 13–14. But even if New York's experience were duplicated on a national scale, that fact would not lead us, as *amici* urge, to conclude that every State and the

conclusion that, contrary to the express language of the statute and the judgment of the highest state court, § 320.5(3)(b) is a punitive rather than a regulatory measure. Preventive detention under the FCA serves the legitimate state objective, held in common with every State in the country, of protecting both the juvenile and society from the hazards of pretrial crime.

B

Given the legitimacy of the State's interest in preventive detention, and the nonpunitive nature of that detention, the remaining question is whether the procedures afforded juveniles detained prior to factfinding provide sufficient protection against erroneous and unnecessary deprivations of liberty.

. . .

In sum, notice, a hearing, and a statement of facts and reasons are given prior to any detention under § 320.5(3)(b). A formal probable-cause hearing is then held within a short while thereafter, if the fact-finding hearing is not itself scheduled within three days. These flexible procedures have been found constitutionally adequate under the Fourth Amendment, see Gerstein v. Pugh, and under the Due Process Clause, see Kent v. United States, supra, 557. Appellees have failed to note any additional procedures that would significantly improve the accuracy of the determination without unduly impinging on the achievement of legitimate state purposes.

Appellees argue, however, that the risk of erroneous and unnecessary detentions is too high despite these procedures because the standard for detention is fatally vague. Detention under § 320.5(3)(b) is based on a finding that there is a "serious risk" that the juvenile, if released, would commit a crime prior to his next court appearance. We have already seen that detention of juveniles on that ground serves legitimate regulatory purposes. But appellees claim, and the District Court agreed, that it is virtually impossible to predict future criminal conduct with any degree of accuracy. Moreover, they say, the statutory standard fails to channel the discretion of the Family Court judge by specifying the factors on which he should rely in making that prediction. The procedural protections noted above are thus, in their view, unavailing because the ultimate decision is intrinsically arbitrary and uncontrolled.

Our cases indicate, however, that from a legal point of view there is nothing inherently unattainable about a prediction of future criminal conduct. Such a judgment forms an important element in many decisions,

United States are illicitly punishing juveniles prior to their trial. On the contrary, if such statistics obtain nationwide, our conclusion is strengthened that the existence of the statistics in these cases is not a sufficient ground for striking down New York's statute. As already noted: "The fact that a practice is followed by a large number of states is not conclusive in a decision as to whether that practice accords with due process, but it is plainly worth considering in determining whether the practice 'offends some principle of justice so rooted in the traditions and conscience of our people as to be ranked as fundamental.' Snyder v. Massachusetts, 291 U.S. 97, 105 (1934)." Leland v. Oregon, 343 U.S. 790, 798 (1952).

and we have specifically rejected the contention, based on the same sort of sociological data relied upon by appellees and the District Court, "that it is impossible to predict future behavior and that the question is so vague as to be meaningless." Jurek v. Texas, 428 U.S. 262, 274 (1976) (opinion of Stewart, Powell and Stevens, JJ.); id., at 279, (White, J., concurring in judgment).

We have also recognized that a prediction of future criminal conduct is "an experienced prediction based on a host of variables" which cannot be readily codified. Judge Quinones of the Family Court testified at trial that he and his colleagues make a determination under § 320.5(3)(b) based on numerous factors including the nature and seriousness of the charges; whether the charges are likely to be proved at trial; the juvenile's prior record; the adequacy and effectiveness of his home supervision; his school situation, if known; the time of day of the alleged crime as evidence of its seriousness and a possible lack of parental control; and any special circumstances that might be brought to his attention by the probation officer, the child's attorney, or any parents, relatives, or other responsible persons accompanying the child. Testimony of Judge Quinones, App. 254–267. The decision is based on as much information as can reasonably be obtained at the initial appearance. Ibid.

Given the right to a hearing, to counsel, and to a statement of reasons, there is no reason that the specific factors upon which the Family Court judge might rely must be specified in the statute. As the New York Court of Appeals concluded, People ex rel. Wayburn v. Schupf, 39 N.Y.2d, at 690, 385 N.Y.S.2d, at 522, 350 N.E.2d, at 910, "to a very real extent Family Court must exercise a substitute parental control for which there can be no particularized criteria." There is also no reason, we should add, for a federal court to assume that a state court judge will not strive to apply state law as conscientiously as possible.

. . .

III

The dissent would apparently have us strike down New York's preventive detention statute on two grounds: first, because the preventive detention of juveniles constitutes poor public policy, with the balance of harms outweighing any positive benefits either to society or to the juveniles themselves, and, second, because the statute could have been better drafted to improve the quality of the decisionmaking process. But it is worth recalling that we are neither a legislature charged with formulating public policy nor an American Bar Association committee charged with drafting a model statute. The question before us today is solely whether the preventive detention system chosen by the State of New York and applied by the New York Family Court comports with constitutional standards. Given the regulatory purpose for the detention and the procedural protections that precede its imposition, we conclude that § 320.5(3)(b) of the New York FCA is not invalid under the Due Process Clause of the Fourteenth Amendment.

The judgment of the Court of Appeals is

Reversed.

■ JUSTICE MARSHALL, with whom JUSTICE BRENNAN and JUSTICE STEVENS join, dissenting.

. . .

The Court today holds that preventive detention of a juvenile pursuant to § 320.5(3)(b) does not violate the Due Process Clause. Two rulings are essential to the Court's decision: that the provision promotes legitimate government objectives important enough to justify the abridgment of the detained juveniles' liberty interests; and that the provision incorporates procedural safeguards sufficient to prevent unnecessary or arbitrary impairment of constitutionally protected rights. Because I disagree with both of those rulings, I dissent.

I

The District Court made detailed findings, which the Court of Appeals left undisturbed, regarding the manner in which § 320.5(3)(b) is applied in practice. Unless clearly erroneous, those findings are binding upon us, see Fed.Rule Civ.Proc. 52(a), and must guide our analysis of the constitutional questions presented by these cases.

. . .

The actual decision whether to detain a juvenile under § 320.5(3)(b) is made by a Family Court judge at what is called an "initial appearance"—a brief hearing resembling an arraignment. The information on which the judge makes his determination is very limited. He has before him a "petition for delinquency" prepared by a state agency, charging the juvenile with an offense, accompanied with one or more affidavits attesting to the juvenile's involvement. Ordinarily the judge has in addition the written report and recommendation of the probation officer. However, the probation officer who prepared the report rarely attends the hearing. Nor is the complainant likely to appear. Consequently, "[o]ften there is no one present with personal knowledge of what happened."

In the typical case, the judge appoints counsel for the juvenile at the time his case is called. Thus, the lawyer has no opportunity to make an independent inquiry into the juvenile's background or character, and has only a few minutes to prepare arguments on the child's behalf. The judge ordinarily does not interview the juvenile, makes no inquiry into the truth of allegations in the petition, and does not determine whether there is probable cause to believe the juvenile committed the offense. The typical hearing lasts between 5 and 15 minutes, and the judge renders his decision immediately afterward.

Neither the statute nor any other body of rules guides the efforts of the judge to determine whether a given juvenile is likely to commit a crime before his trial. In making detention decisions, "each judge must rely on his own subjective judgment, based on the limited information available to him at court intake and whatever personal standards he himself has developed in exercising his discretionary authority under the statute." Ibid. Family Court judges are not provided information regarding the behavior of juveniles over whose cases they have presided, so a judge has no way of refining the standards he employs in making detention decisions.

After examining a study of a sample of 34 cases in which juveniles were detained under § 320.5(3)(b) along with various statistical studies of pretrial detention of juveniles in New York, the District Court made findings regarding the circumstances in which the provision habitually is invoked. Three of those findings are especially germane to appellees' challenge to the statute. First, a substantial number of "first offenders" are detained pursuant to § 320.5(3)(b). For example, at least 5 of the 34 juveniles in the sample had no prior contact with the Family Court before being detained and at least 16 had no prior adjudications of delinquency. Second, many juveniles are released—for periods ranging from five days to several weeks—after their arrests and are then detained under § 320.5(3)(b), despite the absence of any evidence of misconduct during the time between their arrests and "initial appearances." Sixteen of the thirty-four cases in the sample fit this pattern. Third, "the overwhelming majority" of the juveniles detained under § 320.5(3)(b) are released either before or immediately after their trials, either unconditionally or on parole. At least 23 of the juveniles in the sample fell into this category. Martin v. Strasburg, 689 F.2d 365, 369, n. 19 (C.A.2 1982); see 513 F.Supp., at 695–700.

Finally, the District Court made a few significant findings concerning the conditions associated with "secure detention" pursuant to § 320.5(3)(b). In a "secure facility," "[t]he juveniles are subjected to strip-searches, wear institutional clothing and follow institutional regimen. At Spofford [Juvenile Detention Center], which is a secure facility, some juveniles who have had dispositional determinations and were awaiting placement (long term care) commingle with those in pretrial detention (short term care)."

It is against the backdrop of these findings that the contentions of the parties must be examined.

II

A

. . .

To comport with "fundamental fairness," § 320.5(3)(b) must satisfy two requirements. First, it must advance goals commensurate with the burdens it imposes on constitutionally protected interests. Second, it must not punish the juveniles to whom it applies.

The majority only grudgingly and incompletely acknowledges the applicability of the first of these tests, but its grip on the cases before us is undeniable. It is manifest that § 320.5(3)(b) impinges upon fundamental rights. If the "liberty" protected by the Due Process Clause means anything, it means freedom from physical restraint. Only a very important government interest can justify deprivation of liberty in this basic sense.

The majority seeks to evade the force of this principle by discounting the impact on a child of incarceration pursuant to § 320.5(3)(b). The curtailment of liberty consequent upon detention of a juvenile, the majority contends, is mitigated by the fact that "juveniles, unlike adults, are always in some form of custody." In any event, the majority argues, the conditions of confinement associated with "secure detention" under § 320.5(3)(b) are not unduly burdensome. These contentions enable the majority to suggest that § 320.5(3)(b) need only advance a "legitimate state objective" to satisfy the strictures of the Due Process Clause.

The majority's arguments do not survive scrutiny. Its characterization of preventive detention as merely a transfer of custody from a parent or guardian to the State is difficult to take seriously. Surely there is a qualitative difference between imprisonment and the condition of being subject to the supervision and control of an adult who has one's best interests at heart. And the majority's depiction of the nature of confinement under § 320.5(3)(b) is insupportable on this record.... [T]he District Court found that secure detention entails incarceration in a facility closely resembling a jail and that pretrial detainees are sometimes mixed with juveniles who have been found to be delinquent....

In short, fairly viewed, pretrial detention of a juvenile pursuant to § 320.5(3)(b) gives rise to injuries comparable to those associated with imprisonment of an adult. In both situations, the detainee suffers stigmatization and severe limitation of his freedom of movement. Indeed, the impressionability of juveniles may make the experience of incarceration more injurious to them than to adults; all too quickly juveniles subjected to preventive detention come to see society at large as hostile and oppressive and to regard themselves as irremediably "delinquent." Such serious injuries to presumptively innocent persons—encompassing the curtailment of their constitutional rights to liberty—can be justified only by a weighty public interest that is substantially advanced by the statute.

The applicability of the second of the two tests is admitted even by the majority. In Bell v. Wolfish, 441 U.S. 520, 535 (1979), the Court held that an adult may not be punished prior to determination that he is guilty of a crime. The majority concedes, as it must, that this principle applies to juveniles. Thus, if the only purpose substantially advanced by § 320.5(3)(b) is punishment, the provision must be struck down.

For related reasons, § 320.5(3)(b) cannot satisfy either of the requirements discussed above that together define "fundamental fairness" in the context of pretrial detention.

B

Appellants and the majority contend that § 320.5(3)(b) advances a pair of intertwined government objectives: "protecting the community from crime," and "protecting a juvenile from the consequences of his criminal activity." More specifically, the majority argues that detaining a juvenile for a period of up to 17 days prior to his trial has two desirable effects: it protects society at large from the crimes he might have committed during that period if released; and it protects the juvenile himself "both from potential physical injury which may be suffered when a victim fights back or a policeman attempts to make an arrest and from the downward spiral of criminal activity into which peer pressure may lead the child."

Appellees and some amici argue that public purposes of this sort can never justify incarceration of a person who has not been adjudicated guilty of a crime, at least in the absence of a determination that there exists probable cause to believe he committed a criminal offense. We need not reach that categorical argument in these cases because, even if the purposes identified by the majority are conceded to be compelling, they are not sufficiently promoted by detention pursuant to § 320.5(3)(b) to justify the concomitant impairment of the juveniles' liberty interests. To state the case more precisely, two circumstances in combination render § 320.5(3)(b) invalid *in toto:* in the large majority of cases in which the provision is invoked, its asserted objectives are either not advanced at all or are only minimally promoted; and, as the provision is written and administered by the state courts, the cases in which its asserted ends are significantly advanced cannot practicably be distinguished from the cases in which they are not.

1

Both of the courts below concluded that only occasionally and accidentally does pretrial detention of a juvenile under § 320.5(3)(b) prevent the commission of a crime. Three subsidiary findings undergird that conclusion. First, Family Court judges are incapable of determining which of the juveniles who appear before them would commit offenses before their trials if left at large and which would not. In part, this incapacity derives from the limitations of current knowledge concerning the dynamics of human behavior. On the basis of evidence adduced at trial, supplemented by a thorough review of the secondary literature, the District Court found that "no diagnostic tools have as yet been devised which enable even the most highly trained criminologists to predict reliably which juveniles will engage in violent crime." The evidence supportive of this finding is overwhelming. An independent impediment to identification of the defendants who would misbehave if released is the paucity of data available at an initial appearance. The judge must make his decision whether to detain a juvenile on the basis of a set of allegations regarding the child's alleged offense, a cursory review of his background and criminal record, and the recommendation of a probation officer who, in the typical case, has seen the child only once. In view of this scarcity of relevant information, the District Court credited the testimony of appellees' expert witness, who "stated that he would be surprised if recommendations based on intake interviews were better than chance and assessed the judge's subjective prognosis about the probability of future crime as only 4% better than chance—virtually wholly unpredictable."

Second, § 320.5(3)(b) is not limited to classes of juveniles whose past conduct suggests that they are substantially more likely than average juveniles to misbehave in the immediate future. The provision authorizes the detention of persons arrested for trivial offenses and persons without any prior contacts with juvenile court. Even a finding that there is probable cause to believe a juvenile committed the offense with which he was charged is not a prerequisite to his detention.

Third, the courts below concluded that circumstances surrounding most of the cases in which § 320.5(3)(b) has been invoked strongly suggest that the detainee would not have committed a crime during the period before his trial if he had been released. In a significant proportion of the cases, the juvenile had been released after his arrest and had not committed any reported crimes while at large; it is not apparent why a juvenile would be more likely to misbehave between his initial appearance and his trial than between his arrest and initial appearance. Even more telling is the fact that "the vast majority" of persons detained under § 320.5(3)(b) are released either before or immediately after their trials. The inference is powerful that most detainees, when examined more carefully than at their initial appearances, are deemed insufficiently dangerous to warrant further incarceration.

The rarity with which invocation of § 320.5(3)(b) results in detention of a juvenile who otherwise would have committed a crime fatally undercuts the two public purposes assigned to the statute by the State and the majority. The argument that § 320.5(3)(b) serves "the State's 'parens patriae interest in preserving and promoting the welfare of the child,'" now appears particularly hollow. Most juveniles detained pursuant to the provision are not benefited thereby, because they would not have committed crimes if left to their own devices (and thus would not have been exposed to the risk of physical injury or the perils of the cycle of recidivism). On the contrary, these juveniles suffer several serious harms: deprivation of liberty and stigmatization as "delinquent" or "dangerous," as well as impairment of their ability to prepare their legal defenses. . . .

The argument that § 320.5(3)(b) protects the welfare of the community fares little better. Certainly the public reaps no benefit from incarceration of the majority of the detainees who would not have committed any crimes had they been released. Prevention of the minor offenses that would have been committed by a small proportion of the persons detained confers only a slight benefit on the community. Only in occasional cases does incarceration of a juvenile pending his trial serve to prevent a crime of violence and thereby significantly promote the public interest. Such an infrequent and haphazard gain is insufficient to justify curtailment of the liberty interests of all the presumptively innocent juveniles who would have obeyed the law pending their trials had they been given the chance.

. . .

C

The findings reviewed in the preceding section lend credence to the conclusion reached by the courts below: § 320.5(3)(b) "is utilized principally, not for preventive purposes, but to impose punishment for unadjudicated criminal acts."

The majority contends that, of the many factors we have considered in trying to determine whether a particular sanction constitutes "punishment," the most useful are "whether an alternative purpose to which [the sanction] may rationally be connected is assignable for it, and whether it appears excessive in relation to the alternative purpose assigned". Assuming, arguendo, that this test is appropriate, it requires affirmance in these cases. The alternative purpose assigned by the State to § 320.5(3)(b) is the prevention of crime by the detained juveniles. But, as has been shown, that objective is advanced at best sporadically by the provision. Moreover, § 320.5(3)(b) frequently is invoked under circumstances in which it is extremely unlikely that the juvenile in question would commit a crime while awaiting trial. The most striking of these cases involve juveniles who have been at large without mishap for a substantial period of time prior to their initial appearances and detainees who are adjudged delinquent and are nevertheless released into the community. In short, § 320.5(3)(b) as administered by the New York courts surely "appears excessive in relation to" the putatively legitimate objectives assigned to it.

. . .

III

If the record did not establish the impossibility, on the basis of the evidence available to a Family Court judge at a § 320.5(3)(b) hearing, of reliably predicting whether a given juvenile would commit a crime before his trial, and if the purposes relied upon by the State were promoted sufficiently to justify the deprivations of liberty effected by the provision, I would nevertheless still strike down § 320.5(3)(b) because of the absence of procedural safeguards in the provision. As Judge Newman, concurring in the Court of Appeals observed, "New York's statute is unconstitutional because it permits liberty to be denied, prior to adjudication of guilt, in the exercise of unfettered discretion as to an issue of considerable uncertainty—likelihood of future criminal behavior."

Appellees point out that § 320.5(3)(b) lacks two crucial procedural constraints. First, a New York Family Court judge is given no guidance regarding what kinds of evidence he should consider or what weight he should accord different sorts of material in deciding whether to detain a juvenile. For example, there is no requirement in the statute that the judge take into account the juvenile's background or current living situation. Nor is a judge obliged to attach significance to the nature of a juvenile's criminal record or the severity of the crime for which he was arrested. Second, § 320.5(3)(b) does not specify how likely it must be that a juvenile will commit a crime before his trial to warrant his detention. The provision indicates only that there must be a "serious risk" that he will commit an offense and does not prescribe the standard of proof that should govern the judge's determination of that issue.

Not surprisingly, in view of the lack of directions provided by the statute, different judges have adopted different ways of estimating the chances whether a juvenile will misbehave in the near future. . . . This discretion exercised by Family Court judges in making detention decisions gives rise to two related constitutional problems. First, it creates an excessive risk that juveniles will be detained "erroneously"—i.e., under circumstances in which no public interest would be served by their incarceration. Second, it fosters arbitrariness and inequality in a decisionmaking process that impinges upon fundamental rights.

. . .

IV

The majority acknowledges—indeed, founds much of its argument upon—the principle that a State has both the power and the responsibility to protect the interests of the children within its jurisdiction. See Santosky v. Kramer, supra, at 766. Yet the majority today upholds a statute whose net impact on the juveniles who come within its purview is overwhelmingly detrimental. Most persons detained under the provision reap no benefit and suffer serious injuries thereby. The welfare of only a minority of the detainees is even arguably enhanced. The inequity of this regime, combined with the arbitrariness with which it is administered, is bound to disillusion its victims regarding the virtues of our system of criminal justice. I can see—and the majority has pointed to—no public purpose advanced by the statute sufficient to justify the harm it works.

I respectfully dissent.

NOTES

(1) *Schall v. Martin* has been the subject of a great deal of scholarly commentary. For example, in an article written immediately following the *Schall* decision, Irene Rosenberg criticized the Court's decision as a return to pre-*Gault* jurisprudence:

A contrary decision in *Schall* might not have made much of a practical difference with respect to pre-trial detention of children. The judges who previously conscientiously applied the appropriate criteria and safeguards would have presumably continued to do so after being so mandated by the legislature—and, unfortunately, *vice versa*. The primary value of invalidation of such a vague preventive detention statute would have been reaffirmation of the application of the rule of law to children. What *Schall* instead does it to reinforce unbridled state authority at the expense of both children and their parents.

The ruling in *Schall* cuts against the grain of the Court's prior cases dealing with juveniles and may also adversely affect the rights of adults. One can only hope that Justice Cardozo was right when he said, "The work of a judge is in one sense enduring and in another sense ephemeral. What is good in it endures. What is erroneous is pretty sure to perish."

Irene Merker Rosenberg, Schall v. Martin: A Child is a Child is a Child, 12 Am.J.Crim.L. 253, 278 (1984).*

(2) Would your views be different with regard to detention of adults as potentially dangerous?

In 1987, the Supreme Court of the United States upheld a provision in the 1984 Bail Reform Act that authorized pretrial detention of adults charged with serious felonies and determined to present a threat to the safety of others. The Court held that the provision did not violate Fifth Amendment due process rights or the Eighth Amendment prohibition of excessive bail. Citing *Schall*, the Court found that the detention of arrestees based on prediction of future dangerousness served a legitimate regulatory goal and was not punishment. In so holding, the Court rejected a "general rule" against pretrial detention for adults unless the person was likely to leave the jurisdiction or was incompetent to stand trial. *United States v. Salerno*, 481 U.S. 739, 107 S.Ct. 2095, 95 L.Ed.2d 697 (1987).

What effect is the decision in *Salerno* likely to have on the significance of *Schall*? *Salerno* relied heavily on the rationale of *Schall* in concluding that pretrial detention serves a regulatory rather than a punitive purpose, and the Court did not discuss the fundamental differences between juveniles and adults that might call for differential treatment in terms of detention policy. *Salerno*, then, would seem to be a broader statement of the validity of preventive detention. One can argue, however, that *Schall* is the broader of the two decisions because the statute approved in *Schall* authorized preventive detention of any juvenile for any offense, whereas the one in *Salerno* was more focused and seemingly limited in reach to persons accused of serious crimes. See, e.g., Marc Miller & Martin Guggenheim, Pretrial Detention and Punishment, 75 Minn.L.Rev. 335, 354 (1990). The authors argue that *Schall* by itself does not answer the question whether preventive detention of adults is constitutional, and they further argue that *Salerno* was wrongly decided. Miller & Guggenheim, 75 Minn.L.Rev. at 349–54.

Often persons who have been released on bail or other forms of pre-trial release, including juveniles, will have conditions attached to their release. One such condition, in cases involving drug-related offenses, is a "stay-away" order, which means that the accused must stay away from the scene of the crime or stay away from a known drug area. Suppose a juvenile who is subject to a "stay-away" order is seen in the prohibited area. Is that fact alone sufficient grounds for arrest and detention in light of *Schall v. Martin* and *United States v. Salerno*, given that the purpose of taking the person into custody is a crime prevention measure? This issue among others is discussed in Robert J. Prince, Note, A Line in the Sand: Implementing Scene of the Crime Stay–Away Orders As a Condition of Pretrial Release in Community Prosecutions, 92 Va.L.Rev. 1899, 1933, 1945–46 (2006), primarily from the point of view of adult offenders, with implications for juveniles. The author concludes that, with certain safeguards, such an approach is constitutional as a preventive detention measure.

The argument has been made that *Salerno* and *Schall v. Martin* have furthered a diminution of the right to bail and the presumption of innocence, leading to an increased reliance on preventive detention. See Joseph L. Lester, Presumed Innocent, Feared Dangerous: The Eighth Amendment's Right to Bail, 32 N.Ky.L.Rev. 1 (2005).

(3) As in New York, most states have enacted statutory criteria for determining whether a juvenile shall be released or detained pending trial. For example, California's Welfare and Institutions Code, § 635, provides that:

[U]nless it appears that such minor has violated an order of the juvenile court or has escaped from the commitment of the juvenile court or that it is a matter of immediate and urgent necessity for the protection of the minor or reasonably necessary for the protection of the person or property of another that he or she be detained or that the minor is likely to flee to avoid the jurisdiction of the court, the court shall make its order releasing such minor from custody.

The circumstances and gravity of the alleged offense may be considered, in conjunction with other factors, to determine whether it is a matter of immediate and urgent necessity for the protection of the minor or reasonably necessary for the protection of the person or property of another that the minor be detained.

Similarly, Texas Family Code § 53.02 requires that:

(b) A child taken into custody may be detained prior to hearing on the petition only if:

(1) the child is likely to abscond or be removed from the jurisdiction of the court;

(2) suitable supervision, care, or protection for the child is not being provided by a parent, guardian, custodian, or other person;

(3) the child has no parent, guardian, custodian, or other person able to return the child to the court when required;

(4) the child is accused of committing a felony offense and may be dangerous to himself or herself or the child may threaten the safety of the public if released;

(5) the child has previously been found to be a delinquent child or has previously been convicted of a penal offense punishable by a term in jail or prison and is likely to commit an offense if released; or

(6) the child's detention is required under Subsection (f).

. . .

(f) A child who is alleged to have engaged in delinquent conduct and to have used, possessed, or exhibited a firearm ... in the commission of the offense shall be detained until the child is released at the direction of the judge of the juvenile court, a substitute judge ..., or a referee ..., including an oral direction by telephone, or until a detention hearing is held....

(4) Should any limitations be imposed on the fairly wide discretion accorded judges in ordering pretrial detention, to assure consistency and fairness? In *In re William M.*, 3 Cal.3d 16, 89 Cal.Rptr. 33, 473 P.2d 737 (1970), a juvenile court judge had followed a policy of detaining all children charged with illegal sale of drugs. The Supreme Court of California declared that practice a violation of the statutorily formulated policy of the state (see Cal.Welf. & Inst.Code § 635, note (3) supra), because the judge was not actually considering the particularized relevant facts with respect to each individual case. In *In re G.M.B.*, 483 P.2d 1006 (Alaska 1971), the Supreme Court of Alaska held that a family court master's temporary detention order stating that "[the] child should be detained for his own protection in view of present offense and past violations" was insufficiently specific to show that incarceration was necessary for the protection of the juvenile and therefore was void.

In *Commonwealth ex rel. Sprowal v. Hendrick*, 438 Pa. 435, 265 A.2d 348 (1970), a juvenile was detained, apparently to ensure his appearance at subsequent judicial proceedings. Although the court stated that this could be a valid reason for detention, it cautioned that "[s]uch measures should be utilized ... only when the hearing court determines that there is *no other less coercive method whereby future attendance can be reasonably assured and places the reasons for this finding on the record.*" 265 A.2d at 349 [Emphasis added].

(5) The divergence of factors that a detention officer must be prepared to take into consideration is illustrated by *Kinney v. Lenon*, 425 F.2d 209 (9th Cir.1970), even though it is a case that is factually restrictive as to application. Appellant, a black youth of 17, was being detained on charges arising out of a schoolyard fight. He claimed that there were many witnesses to the fight who he did not know by name but could recognize on sight, and that because his potential witnesses were all black his white attorneys would have great difficulty in preparing his defense unless he were free to aid them. The court of appeals, in ordering his release, stated:

This is not a case where release from detention is sought simply for the convenience of the appellant. There is here a strong showing that the appellant is the only person who can effectively prepare his own defense. We may take notice, as judges and lawyers, of the difficulties often encountered, even by able and conscientious counsel, in overcoming the apathy and reluctance of potential witnesses to testify. It would require blindness to social reality not to understand that these difficulties may be exacerbated by the barriers of age and race.

Yet the alternative to some sort of release for appellant is to cast the entire burden of assembling witnesses onto his attorneys, with almost certain prejudice to appellant's case.

Id. at 210.

(6) The Juvenile Justice Standards take a position favoring release or the least intrusive alternative, and do not provide for preventive detention. See Juvenile Justice Standards Relating to Interim Status: The Release, Control, and Detention of Accused Juvenile Offenders Between Arrest and Disposition 3.1–3.5, 4.2, 5.1, 5.6, 9.2 (1980). For a dissenting view from the approach taken in the Standards on Interim Status, see the Statement of Commissioner Wilfred W. Nuernberger at p. 107 of the Standards. In a critique of the preventive detention of allegedly dangerous juveniles in which he approves of the position taken in the Standards, Martin Guggenheim points out the enhanced negative impact of preventive detention where juveniles are concerned:

> Not only do the conventional considerations, like interference with the construction of a criminal defense, obtain, but the disposition of the case itself may also be influenced because it usually rests on the juvenile's amenability to treatment or supervision in the community. Confinement before trial prevents the juvenile from demonstrating a capacity to remain in his home setting, and misbehavior during confinement may be taken as evidence that the youngster should not be allowed to return to his community. Incarceration, moreover, can be a devastating personal experience, involving a traumatic removal from one's family and placement, perhaps for the first time, in a prison. Wrongful detention can have a particularly negative effect.

Martin Guggenheim, Paternalism, Prevention, and Punishment: Pretrial Detention of Juveniles, 52 N.Y.U.L.Rev. 1064, 1064–65 (1977).*

(7) Should a juvenile who is later adjudicated delinquent and sent to a juvenile institution be entitled to credit against his "sentence" for the time spent detained prior to disposition? See *In re Ricky H.*, 30 Cal.3d 176, 178 Cal.Rptr. 324 at 329–333, 636 P.2d 13 at 18–22 (1981).

3. CONSTITUTIONAL ISSUES

a. PROBABLE CAUSE TO DETAIN

Bell v. Superior Court

Court of Appeals of Arizona, Division 2, 1977.
117 Ariz. 551, 574 P.2d 39.

■ RICHMOND, JUDGE.

Is a juvenile detained while awaiting adjudication of a delinquency charge entitled to bail and a probable cause hearing? Although we deny relief because the question has become moot as to petitioner, ... we assume jurisdiction to answer it as one of statewide concern that is likely to recur.

Petitioner was arrested by Tucson police officers on September 30, 1977, and immediately transported to the Pima County Juvenile Court Center.... On October 3, 1977, while he was still in detention, the state filed a formal petition alleging that petitioner was a delinquent child in that he had violated the law as follows:

"(RECEIVING STOLEN PROPERTY)

"On or about the 30 day of September 1977, DENNIS BELL bought, sold, possessed, concealed, or received stolen personal property, valued at $100, or more, to wit: four Mag wheels and tires; one car seat, all in violation of A.R.S. § 13–621, as amended, 13–1645, and 13–1647, as amended."

The following day petitioner, his mother, and his attorney appeared before a juvenile court referee at a detention hearing. No evidence was presented as to the alleged delinquent act. Petitioner requested a probable cause hearing and that bail be fixed in a reasonable amount. The requests were denied and the referee recommended that petitioner be detained because he lacked custodial supervision, would be a danger to himself or others if released, and might not be present for trial. The recommendation was appealed to the juvenile court judge and the matter was heard the same day. Petitioner, by counsel, requested the court to order the state to produce forthwith evidence of the alleged crime, receiving stolen property, so as to establish probable cause for detaining him, and that bond be set in a reasonable amount. The court ruled adversely to petitioner and found that it was not required to hold a probable cause hearing or set bond in a reasonable amount.

The Rules of Procedure for Juvenile Court, A.R.S. 17A, contain no provision for release on bail. Rule 3(b), however, sets forth the only conditions for detention:

"A child shall be detained only if there are reasonable grounds to believe:

"(1) That otherwise he will not be present at any hearing; or

"(2) That he is likely to commit an offense injurious to himself or others; or

"(3) That he must be held for another jurisdiction; or

"(4) That the interests of the child or the public require custodial protection."

Unless the situation falls within one of these specified categories, release from custody is mandated. It is unnecessary to reach the question of whether there is a constitutional right to bail in juvenile proceedings. When Rule 3(b) is applied consistent with the requirements of due process, an adequate substitute for bail is provided. . . .

We agree with petitioner, however, that pre-trial detention of juveniles without determination of probable cause violates the Fourth Amendment. Several courts have held that a probable cause determination is required if the juvenile is at the risk of being incarcerated before trial. . . .

In Gerstein v. Pugh, 420 U.S. 103 (1975), the United States Supreme Court held that arrest and detention under a prosecutor's information violated the Fourth Amendment because of failure to afford a probable cause determination by a magistrate. The court noted:

". . . [A] policeman's on-the-scene assessment of probable cause provides legal justification for arresting a person suspected of crime, and for a brief period of detention to take the administrative steps incident to arrest. Once the suspect is in custody, however, the reasons that justify dispensing with the magistrate's neutral judgment evaporate. There no longer is any danger that the suspect will escape or commit further crimes while the police submit their evidence to a magistrate. And, while the State's reasons for taking summary action subside, the suspect's need for a neutral determination of probable cause increases significantly.... Accordingly, we hold that the Fourth Amendment requires a judicial determination of probable cause as a prerequisite to extended restraint of liberty following arrest."

The state relies on the requirement in Rule V, Local Rules of Procedure for the Pima County Juvenile Court, that an adjudicatory hearing be held no later than 15 days from the filing of the petition when a juvenile is detained. We do not believe this 15–day requirement obviates the need for a probable cause determination as a prerequisite to detention in addition to the other grounds enumerated in Rule 3(b), Rules of Procedure for Juvenile Court, supra.

We are of the opinion, and so hold, that a finding of probable cause— i.e., of "facts and circumstances, 'sufficient to warrant a prudent man in believing that the [suspect] had committed or was committing an offense,' " *Gerstein*, supra, 95 S.Ct. at 862—is required to justify pre-trial detention of a juvenile. As stated in Moss v. Weaver, [525 F.2d 1258, 1260 (5th Cir.1976)]:

> "A finding of probable cause ... is central to the [Fourth] Amendment's protections against official abuse of power. Pre-trial detention is an onerous experience, especially for juveniles, and the Constitution is affronted when this burden is imposed without adequate assurance that the accused has in fact committed the alleged crime."

The state argues that the philosophy of the juvenile court system to expedite juvenile matters and to afford juveniles special treatment would be subverted by requiring a probable cause hearing. We agree with the state that the Fourth Amendment itself does not require adversary safeguards. We cannot agree, however, that detained juveniles have less Fourth Amendment protection than detained adults in adult felony criminal proceedings. In Gerstein v. Pugh, supra, the court indicated that the standard to be applied in determining whether there is probable cause for detention is the same as that for arrest. The court also observed in *Gerstein* that the question of probable cause has for many years been resolved "in a nonadversary proceeding on hearsay and written testimony," 95 S.Ct. at 866, usually in the context of a magistrate's decision whether or not to issue an arrest warrant.

In holding that judicial determination of probable cause to believe that an alleged juvenile delinquent has committed an offense is constitutionally required before a juvenile may be detained pending the adjudicatory hearing, we do not believe that a hearing is required in every instance. The record, whether in the form of affidavit or a description of the circumstances of the offense in the delinquency petition, may suffice to satisfy a detached judicial officer that probable cause does exist. However, the mere filing of a petition in juvenile court charging an act which if committed by an adult would constitute a crime is not a sufficient showing of probable cause for issuance of an arrest warrant, and is not sufficient to support an independent judicial determination.

Because no factual materials sufficient to warrant a prudent man in believing that petitioner had committed an offense were presented by sworn statement or otherwise, the state failed to establish a prima facie case of probable cause to detain and petitioner's request for a probable cause hearing should have been granted.

Relief denied solely on the grounds of mootness.

NOTE

How long must a juvenile be in detention before he or she is entitled to a probable cause hearing? In the principal case the court cites the U.S. Supreme Court's decision in *Gerstein v. Pugh*, in which the Court held that in the criminal process the accused is entitled to a timely *judicial* determination of probable cause. Subsequent to its decision in *Gerstein v. Pugh*, the Court held in *County of Riverside v. McLaughlin*, 500 U.S. 44, 111 S.Ct. 1661, 114 L.Ed.2d 49 (1991), that a statute or judicial decision requiring a judicial determination of probable cause within 48 hours of arrest normally will comply with *Gerstein*'s "promptness" requirement. Should the requirement be any different for juveniles? In *Alfredo A. v. Superior Court*, 6 Cal.4th 1212, 26 Cal.Rptr.2d 623, 865 P.2d 56, cert. denied, 513 U.S. 822, 115 S.Ct. 86, 130 L.Ed.2d 38 (1994), the California Supreme Court, while holding the promptness requirement applicable to juveniles, upheld California's statutory scheme requiring a detention hearing within 72 hours of arrest, citing the differences between juveniles and adults that allow for a degree of differential treatment.

b.   DURATION AND TIMING

The Juvenile Justice Standards Relating to Interim Status provide that a juvenile taken into custody who has not already been released is entitled to a judicial hearing within 24 hours of the filing of a petition for a release hearing. The juvenile, his parents, and their counsel are entitled to immediate notice of the detention review hearing if an intake officer decides not to release the juvenile pending the hearing. At the initial detention hearing, the state has the burden to establish probable cause that the juvenile committed the offense charged. Juvenile Justice Standards Relating to Interim Status: The Release, Control, and Detention of Accused Juvenile Offenders Between Arrest and Disposition 7.6 (A)–(B), (F) (1980).

In *Cox v. Turley*, 506 F.2d 1347 (6th Cir.1974), a 16–year-old youth was arrested and detained for a curfew violation. After his confinement from Saturday evening until the following Wednesday, he was told by the judge to have his hair cut and then was released to his father. On appeal from dismissal of his suit for injunctive and declaratory relief, it was held that the youth's due process rights had been violated "by reason of his confinement ... without being taken before any judicial officer 'at the earliest possible time'...." The court found that "both the Fourth Amendment and the Fifth Amendment were violated because there was no prompt determination of probable cause—a constitutional mandate that protects juveniles as well as adults." Id. at 1352, 1353. See *Palmer v. State*, 626 A.2d 1358 (Del.1993); *People v. C.R.H.*, 163 Ill.2d 263, 206 Ill.Dec. 100, 644 N.E.2d 1153 (1994).

On the other hand, confinement for a shorter period of time, e.g., 10 hours, has been held not to violate the juvenile's due process rights. *Bergren v. City of Milwaukee*, 811 F.2d 1139 (7th Cir.1987).

c. PRESENCE OF COUNSEL

In recent years the importance of counsel at detention hearings has received greater emphasis. A good explanation was given by the National Advisory Commission on Criminal Justice Standards:

> Because a child's liberty is at stake, a child and his parents should have the right to counsel at each phase of the formal juvenile justice process, detention, adjudication, and disposition hearing. The right to counsel should be a non-waiverable right. In the interest of an equitable and more uniform process, a juvenile taken into custody should be referred immediately to court intake services. Professionally trained personnel must again inform him of his rights in a version of *Miranda* that, it is hoped, he can understand. His parents, if not already present, should be notified immediately and informed of their child's rights. At this point, the intake worker would gather the information necessary to decide whether or not an informal disposition is desirable.*

Standard 7.6C. of the Juvenile Justice Standards Relating to Interim Status, dealing with release hearings, recognizes that an attorney for the accused juvenile should be present and adds that "no waiver should be valid unless made in writing by the juvenile and his or her counsel."

In *Doe v. State*, 487 P.2d 47 (Alaska 1971), the Supreme Court of Alaska stated that

> [D]ue process standards must be observed at a detention inquiry since it may result in the deprivation of the child's liberty. Due process requires at the very least that detention orders be based on competent, sworn testimony, that the child have the right to be represented by counsel at the detention inquiry, and that the detention order state with particularity the facts supporting it.

In *T.K. v. State*, 126 Ga.App. 269, 190 S.E.2d 588 (1972), the court described a juvenile detention hearing as serving a function analogous to a preliminary hearing in the criminal process and thus a proceeding in which it is intended that procedural due process requirements be observed. The court further explained that the statutory and constitutional right to be represented by counsel at a juvenile detention hearing includes the right to a reasonable opportunity to secure counsel.

d. BAIL

State v. M.L.C.

Supreme Court of Utah, 1997.
933 P.2d 380.

■ RUSSON, JUSTICE:

M.L.C., a minor, appeals from an order of the third district juvenile court denying him bail from the time he was charged with aggravated

---

* National Advisory Commission on Criminal Justice Standards and Goals: Task Force on Corrections, Ch. 8, Juvenile Intake and Detention 257 (1973).

robbery by criminal information in juvenile court until he was bound over to district court to be tried as an adult pursuant to the Serious Youth Offender Act. We affirm.

BACKGROUND

In October 1995, when he was sixteen years of age, M.L.C. was charged by criminal information in the third district juvenile court with aggravated robbery, a first degree felony in violation of section 76–6–302 of the Utah Code, and a firearm sentencing enhancement pursuant to section 76–3–203 of the Utah Code. This information was filed in accordance with the Serious Youth Offender Act, Utah Code Ann. § 78–3a–25.1 (Supp.1995),[1] which required a determination by the juvenile court as to whether M.L.C. should be bound over to district court to be tried as an adult pursuant to the criminal information or whether he should remain in juvenile court and the criminal information be treated as though it were a juvenile petition.

Prior to the determination hearing, M.L.C. moved the juvenile court to set bail. The juvenile court denied the motion on the basis of sections 78–3a–30(10) and 78–3a–25.1 of the Utah Code. Section 78–3a–30(10) provides that provisions of the law relating to bail are generally not applicable to children under eighteen years of age.[2] Section 78–3a–25.1 provides that juveniles charged in juvenile court with certain aggravated offenses may be bound over to the district court to be tried and sentenced as adults and that, once bound over, such juveniles have the same right to bail as do adult defendants.

Subsequently, the juvenile court conducted the determination hearing. This hearing was required to determine whether there was probable cause to believe that M.L.C. had committed the alleged aggravated robbery and, if so, whether certain conditions existed that would nevertheless require the matter to remain in juvenile court as provided by section 78–3a–25.1(3) of the Utah Code. The juvenile court determined that M.L.C., indeed, should be bound over to district court to be tried as an adult and set bail at $20,000.[3] Thereafter, M.L.C. appealed the juvenile court's initial order denying bail pending the bindover determination.[4]

M.L.C. argues on appeal that he was entitled to bail immediately upon the filing of a criminal information in juvenile court under the serious youth offender statute, even though the juvenile court had not yet deter-

---

1. In 1996, the Utah Legislature recodified this section as 78–3a–602. However, we use the section numbers in place at the time of appeal throughout this opinion. Unless otherwise indicated, all references to the Utah Code are to the 1995 Supplement.

2. "Child" is defined by section 78–3a–2(5) as "a person less than 18 years of age." Utah Code Ann. § 78–3a–2(5) (Supp.1995).

3. The case before us deals only with the bail issue. However, we note that M.L.C.

also appealed the juvenile court's order of bindover to the Utah Court of Appeals. See M.C. v. State, 916 P.2d 914, 918 (Utah Ct. App.1996) (holding that juvenile court's bindover determination is a final appealable order).

4. Section 77–20–1(3) of the Utah Code provides, "An appeal may be taken from an order of any court denying bail to the Supreme Court. . . ."

mined, pursuant to the statute, whether he would be bound over to district court to be tried as an adult or remain in juvenile court and have the information treated as a juvenile petition. He argues that at the time of the filing of the criminal information in juvenile court, he was a "person charged with a crime" and, thus, entitled to the right to bail guaranteed by article I, section 8 of the Utah Constitution, which provides, with certain enumerated exceptions, "All persons charged with a crime shall be bailable. . . ." M.L.C. also argues that the denial of bail prior to a determination of his status violates the unnecessary rigor clause of article I, section 9 of the Utah Constitution, as well as the Excessive Bail Clause of the Eighth Amendment of the United States Constitution. In addition, M.L.C. argues that the denial of bail violates the Equal Protection Clause of the Fourteenth Amendment of the United States Constitution and the uniform operation of laws clause of article I, section 24 of the Utah Constitution inasmuch as juveniles and adults charged with the same crimes are treated disparately.

The State responds that serious youth offenders are not entitled to bail unless and until the juvenile court determines that bindover to adult district court is appropriate. Until bindover, the State argues, the juvenile does not have the status of a criminal defendant and, thus, does not have a federal or state constitutional right to bail. Additionally, the State argues that denying bail to charged serious youth offenders prior to bindover does not implicate the uniform operation of laws clause of the Utah Constitution or the Fourteenth Amendment to the United States Constitution inasmuch as there is no basis for treating adult and juvenile offenders as similarly situated groups and, moreover, all juveniles, including serious youth offenders, are denied preadjudication bail eligibility.

STANDARD OF REVIEW

Whether sections 78–3a–25.1(5) and 78–3a–30(10) violate the bail provisions of the Eighth Amendment of the United States Constitution and article I, sections 8 and 9 of the Utah Constitution are questions of law, which this court reviews for correctness. State v. Mohi, 901 P.2d 991, 995 (Utah 1995). Likewise, whether such statutory provisions violate the Equal Protection Clause of the Fourteenth Amendment of the United States Constitution and the uniform operation of laws clause of article I, section 24 of the Utah Constitution are questions of law, which we review for correctness. Id. Doubts regarding the constitutionality of a statute should be resolved in favor of its constitutionality. Id.

ANALYSIS

M.L.C.'s appeal became technically moot once he was bound over to the district court and immediately became eligible for bail. While we typically refrain from adjudicating moot questions, we recognize an exception to this rule where the "alleged wrong is 'capable of repetition yet evading review.'" In re Giles, 657 P.2d 285, 286 (1982) (quoting Southern Pac. Terminal Co. v. Interstate Commerce Comm'n, 219 U.S. 498, 515, 31 S.Ct. 279, 283, 55 L.Ed. 310 (1911)). Section 78–3a–25.1 provides that persons charged under the statute will either be bound over to district court where the statute explicitly states that they will be eligible for bail, Utah Code

Ann. § 78–3a–25.1(5), or be retained in juvenile court as if charged by petition. Utah Code Ann. § 78–3a–25.1(3)(d), (4). A challenge to the denial of bail prior to bindover, as in the instant case, is likely to be mooted by either of these statutory procedures. Thus, the issues presented by this appeal are likely to evade review in the future. Accordingly, we proceed to address the issues presented.

Article I, section 8 of the Utah Constitution provides that "[a]ll persons charged with a crime shall be bailable," with certain enumerated exceptions not at issue here. However, juveniles appearing in juvenile court proceedings have been treated differently from adults appearing in adult court with respect to bail issues. In particular, section 78–3a–30(10) of the Utah Code provides, "Provisions of law regarding bail are not applicable to children detained or taken into custody...." And section 78–3a–44 provides, "Proceedings in children's cases shall be regarded as civil proceedings, with the court exercising equitable powers."

In R. v. Whitmer, 30 Utah 2d 206, 208, 515 P.2d 617, 619–20 (1973), this court held that the excessive bail provision of article I, section 9 did not apply to juvenile court proceedings because "[t]he section of our Constitution proscribing excessive bail has application to criminal cases, where a presumption of innocence prevails, and does not apply to the proceedings in Juvenile Courts."

Moreover, most courts considering whether the excessive bail provision of the Eighth Amendment of the United States Constitution confers a right to bail upon juveniles have held that juveniles do not have a constitutional right to bail. See, e.g., D.B. v. Tewksbury, 545 F.Supp. 896, 906 (D.Or.1982) ("[C]hildren are not entitled to a jury trial, to indictment by Grand Jury, or to bail."); L.O.W. v. District Court, 623 P.2d 1253, 1258–59 (Colo.1981) (en banc) (holding that juveniles do not have right to bail under United States or Colorado constitution); Aubry v. Gadbois, 50 Cal.App.3d 470, 123 Cal. Rptr. 365, 367 (1975) ("The Eighth Amendment ... confers a right to bail on no one, whether adult or juvenile."); see also Joseph T. Bockrath, Annotation, Right of Bail in Proceedings in Juvenile Courts, 53 A.L.R.3d 848, 851 (1973).

In 1995, the Utah Legislature passed the Serious Youth Offender Act, whereby a criminal information could be filed against a juvenile between the ages of sixteen and eighteen in juvenile court as to certain enumerated felonies but requiring the juvenile court to determine whether the juvenile should be bound over to district court or remain in juvenile court. Utah Code Ann. § 78–3a–25.1. M.L.C. argues that a juvenile charged under the serious youth offender statute is, in fact, a person "charged with a crime" within the meaning of article I, section 8 of the Utah Constitution and, thus, is entitled to bail. We disagree.

While a "criminal information" may be filed in juvenile court, it has no legal effect as such until the juvenile court so determines. A hearing must be held in juvenile court to determine whether the minor will remain in juvenile court and have the criminal information treated as though it were a juvenile petition or whether the juvenile should be bound over to district court to be tried as an adult on the criminal information. At such hearing, the State has the burden to establish probable cause that the minor committed one of the nine felonies enumerated in the statute before the juvenile court judge can bind him over to trial in district court. Utah Code Ann. § 78–3a–25.1(3). However, even if the State establishes probable cause, the juvenile is given the opportunity, pursuant to the statute, to prove the existence of certain factors which would require that the juvenile remain in juvenile court. Id. If such factors were established, the juvenile court judge would be compelled to treat the information as a juvenile petition and the juvenile would be held for trial as a juvenile. Utah Code Ann. § 78–3a–25.1(3)(d). In such a case, the matter would continue as a civil matter, pursuant to section 78–3a–44 of the Utah Code, and the juvenile would not be entitled to bail. See Whitmer, 30 Utah 2d at 208, 515 P.2d at 619–20. On the other hand, if probable cause were established and the juvenile did not prove the existence of the retention factors, the juvenile court would be compelled to order the juvenile bound over to district court to be tried as an adult on the criminal information. At that time, the juvenile would immediately be entitled to the same rights to bail applicable to all persons charged in district court. See Utah Code Ann. § 78–3a–25.1(5).[11] Accordingly, while the juvenile is before the juvenile court for such determination and until the juvenile is bound over to district court on the criminal information, he or she is not a person actually "charged with a crime" within the meaning of article I, section 8 of the Utah Constitution, and thus, denial of bail prior to bindover does not violate this provision.[12]

At the time of a bind over to district court a criminal warrant of arrest shall issue. The defendant shall have the same right to bail as any other criminal defendant and shall be advised of that right by the juvenile court judge. The juvenile court shall set initial bail in accordance with Title 77, Chapter 20, Bail.

. . .

M.L.C. also argues that denying bail to juveniles charged under the serious youth offender statute violates the Eighth Amendment to the United States Constitution. The Eighth Amendment provides, "Excessive bail shall not be required, nor excessive fines imposed, nor cruel and unusual punishments inflicted." U.S. Const. amend. VIII. M.L.C. concedes that the Eighth Amendment "says nothing about whether bail shall be available at all." United States v. Salerno, 481 U.S. 739, 752, 107 S.Ct. 2095, 2104, 95 L.Ed.2d 697 (1987). In fact, the United States Supreme Court has observed that the Eighth Amendment "fails to say all arrests must be bailable." Carlson v. Landon, 342 U.S. 524, 546, 72 S.Ct. 525, 537, 96 L.Ed. 547 (1952). Furthermore, the United States Supreme Court has

---

11. Section 78–3a–25.1(5) of the Utah Code provides:

At the time of a bind over to district court a criminal warrant of arrest shall issue. The defendant shall have the same right to bail as any other criminal defendant and shall be advised of that right by the juvenile court judge. The juvenile court shall set initial bail in accordance with Title 77, Chapter 20, Bail.

12. Because we hold that serious youth offenders are not "persons charged with a crime" for purposes of article I, section 8 of the Utah Constitution, it is not necessary to consider whether serious youth offenders otherwise fall within article I, section 8's exceptions to bailability.

not addressed whether juveniles have a constitutional right to bail under the Eighth Amendment. See In re Whittington, 391 U.S. 341, 88 S.Ct. 1507, 20 L.Ed.2d 625 (1968).

For essentially the same reasons that led us to determine in *Whitmer* that the excessive bail provisions of the Utah Constitution do not apply to juveniles, we hold that the denial of bail to a juvenile prior to bindover under section 78–3a–25.1 does not violate the excessive bail provisions of the Eighth Amendment. Until bindover, the juvenile is still subject to the jurisdiction of the juvenile court and the juvenile court may retain jurisdiction. Moreover,

> juveniles seeking release pending adjudication are not situated like adults applying for bail pending trial. A child does not have the unqualified right of individual liberty that an adult has because a child is subject to parental control. Therefore, the full basis for bail does not exist with regard to children, for a child released on bail would not gain individual freedom from custody but would simply be restored to parental control.

Morris v. D'Amario, 416 A.2d 137, 140 (R.I.1980); see also Pauley v. Gross, 1 Kan.App.2d 736, 574 P.2d 234, 240 (1977) (denying bail to child is different from denying bail to adult because children are already subject to parental or other control). Accordingly, denying bail to charged serious youth offenders prior to bindover does not violate the Excessive Bail Clause of the Eighth Amendment to the United States Constitution.

M.L.C. also contends that denying bail to juveniles charged under the serious youth offender statute violates the uniform operation of laws clause of article I, section 24 of the Utah Constitution and the Fourteenth Amendment to the United States Constitution inasmuch as the statute's provisions deny bail to juveniles charged with certain enumerated crimes until bindover, while adults charged with the same offenses are eligible for bail.

Article I, section 24 of the Utah Constitution provides, "All laws of a general nature shall have uniform operation." M.L.C. argues that because both adults and juveniles may be charged with the aggravated offenses enumerated in section 78–3a–25.1(1), juveniles and adults are appropriately grouped together for purposes of an article I, section 24 analysis. M.L.C. also argues that section 78–3a–25.1 divides this class of persons into two groups, adults who are taken before a magistrate and routinely allowed bail and juveniles who are denied bail until bindover. Because the crimes charged are identical and the potential punishments are identical, M.L.C. argues that the different treatment afforded juveniles and adults violates article I, section 24.

In analyzing claims under article I, section 24,

> we must first determine what classifications, if any, are created by the statute. Second, we must determine whether different classes or subclasses are treated disparately. Finally, if any disparate treatment exists between classes or subclasses, we must determine whether the legislature had any reasonable objective that warrants the disparity.

Mohi, 901 P.2d at 997; see also Malan v. Lewis, 693 P.2d 661, 670 (Utah 1984).

This court has already held that the different treatment afforded juveniles and adults with respect to bail is not unconstitutional. *Whitmer*, 30 Utah 2d at 208, 515 P.2d at 619. Furthermore, as we have already determined, a juvenile charged under the serious youth offender statute is to be considered a juvenile in juvenile court unless and until the juvenile court makes a determination that such juvenile should be bound over to district court to stand trial on the criminal information.

Treating a juvenile—including a juvenile charged under the serious youth offender statute prior to bindover—differently from an adult with respect to bail is not arbitrary but is reasonably related to the purposes of the Juvenile Courts Act, including section 78–3a–25.1, which M.L.C. does not challenge. In part, the purposes of the Juvenile Courts Act are to

(a) promote public safety and individual accountability by the imposition of appropriate sanctions on persons who have committed acts in violation of law;

(b) order appropriate measures to promote guidance and control, preferably in the child's own home, as an aid in the prevention of future unlawful conduct and the development of responsible citizenship;

(c) where appropriate, order rehabilitation, reeducation, and treatment for persons who have committed acts bringing them within the court's jurisdiction;

. . . ;

(g) consistent with the ends of justice, strive to act in the best interests of the children in all cases and attempt to preserve and strengthen family ties where possible.

Utah Code Ann. § 78–3a–102(5) (1996). The protective and rehabilitative purposes of the Juvenile Courts Act are reasonably related to denying bail to juveniles, including a juvenile charged under the serious youth offender statute prior to a determination that he or she will be bound over to district court. Accordingly, denying a charged serious youth offender bail until bindover to district court does not violate article I, section 24 of the Utah Constitution.

Likewise, because prior to bindover, juveniles and adults are not in the same class, we need not address M.L.C.'s contention that the denial of prebindover bail violates equal protection under the Fourteenth Amendment of the United States Constitution. See State v. Taylor, 541 P.2d 1124, 1125 (Utah 1975) ("All that is required, under the Fourteenth Amendment, is equality among members of each class."); *Malan*, 693 P.2d at 669.

CONCLUSION

On the basis of the foregoing, we hold that the juvenile court did not err in denying bail to M.L.C. prior to the time he was bound over to district court to be tried as an adult. We therefore affirm.

■ ZIMMERMAN, C.J., STEWART, ASSOCIATE C.J., and HOWE and DURHAM, JJ., concur.

NOTES

(1) As the principal case illustrates, the right to bail is one of the rights that adults generally enjoy in the criminal process that juveniles do not enjoy in the juvenile process, at least not as a result of caselaw. Several courts earlier had held that juveniles do not have a right to bail in juvenile proceedings, focusing on the existence of "adequate alternatives" as a reason for not holding bail constitutionally required in the juvenile justice system. See, e.g., *Doe v. State*, 487 P.2d 47 (Alaska 1971); *In re William M.*, 3 Cal.3d 16, 89 Cal.Rptr. 33, 473 P.2d 737 (1970); *Fulwood v. Stone*, 394 F.2d 939 (D.C.Cir.1967); *Baldwin v. Lewis*, 300 F.Supp. 1220 (E.D.Wis. 1969), reversed on other grounds 442 F.2d 29 (7th Cir.1971). See also *Pauley v. Gross*, 1 Kan.App.2d 736, 574 P.2d 234 (1977), *Baker v. Smith*, 477 S.W.2d 149 (Ky.1971) and *Morris v. D'Amario*, 416 A.2d 137 (R.I.1980), both of which are cited in the *M.L.C.* opinion. Contra, *State in Interest of Banks*, 402 So.2d 690 (La.1981).

In *Baldwin v. Lewis*, supra, Judge Reynolds more clearly explained the "adequate alternatives" rationale:

> Petitioner contends that the refusal of the State courts to admit him to bail is a violation of his rights under the Eighth Amendment to the United States Constitution. I find it unnecessary to reach the question of whether there is a "constitutional right to bail" in juvenile proceedings, because I believe that the Wisconsin Children's Code, when applied consistent with the ... requirements of due process, provides an adequate substitute for bail.

> The Wisconsin Children's Code, specifically § 48.29, requires that a juvenile *shall* be released to the custody of his parents unless there is a finding that because of the circumstances, including the gravity of the alleged crime, the nature of the juvenile's home life, and the juvenile's previous contacts with the court, the parents or guardian of the juvenile are incapable under the circumstances to care for him. Only if such a finding is made may the juvenile be detained pending trial of the accusations against him. As I have already held, the hearing at which the question of detention of the juvenile is determined must satisfy the requirements of due process of law. When this is done, the interest of the juvenile is protected, and he is not subjected to the arbitrary confinement which the Eighth Amendment is designed to prohibit.

300 F.Supp. at 1233.

In an earlier case, *Trimble v. Stone*, 187 F.Supp. 483, 488 (D.D.C.1960), the court found otherwise:

> It was the beneficent purpose of the progressive legislation creating juvenile courts to ameliorate some of the rigidity and formality of the criminal law in cases in which the accused is a juvenile. The objective was to introduce more leniency, humanity, and informality in dealing with juvenile offenders....

> The Court recognizes that it may be desirable in the interest of the public, or even in the interest of the individual, in some instances to confine the accused while awaiting final disposition of his case, instead of permitting him to be liberated on bail. These considerations are as applicable to some adult offenders as to juveniles. Yet the Constitution forbids this result. It is far more important to preserve the basic safeguards of the Bill of Rights, which were developed as a result of centuries of experience, than it is to sacrifice any one of them in order to achieve a desirable result in an individual case no matter how beneficial it may seem to be for the moment....

> The Court concludes that the right to bail exists in cases pending in the Juvenile Court and that hence the petitioner should be admitted to bail until the outcome of the proceeding against him in the Juvenile Court.

(2) Judicial inquiry may be precluded when state statutes speak specifically to the issue of whether or not bail is required. Only a few states, however, have clearly delineated this issue through legislation. A very small number actually deny juveniles the right to bail. See, e.g., Haw.Rev.Stat. § 571–32(h); Or.Rev.Stat. § 419C.179. Several states have enacted laws expressly granting juveniles the right to bail. See, e.g., Mass.Gen.Laws Ann. ch. 119, § 67; Okla.Stat.Ann. tit. 10, § 7303–4.3(C). (Some of the latter statutes use the word "bond".)

In the majority of jurisdictions the granting of bail either is made a matter of discretion or is not mentioned at all. It is expressly or impliedly left to the hearing officer's discretion in several states. See, e.g., Minn.Stat.Ann. § 260B.176(1); Tenn. Code Ann. § 37–1–117(e). Fully half the states and the District of Columbia have no statutory provision with regard to a juvenile's right to bail; it is in this group that the "adequate alternative" jurisprudence has flourished. Standard 4.7 of the Juvenile Justice Standards Relating to Interim Status prohibits "use of bail bonds in any form as an alternate interim status . . . ."

(3) The issue of whether bail must be extended to juveniles reached the court through an imaginative argument in *Aubry v. Gadbois*, 50 Cal.App.3d 470, 123 Cal.Rptr. 365 (1975). A taxpayer sought to enjoin an asserted illegal expenditure of funds by a judge with juvenile jurisdiction. Plaintiff theorized that since a juvenile could be detained without bail pursuant to Calif.Welf. & Inst.Code §§ 635 and 636 for 15 judicial days before a hearing on the offense, while an adult charged with a similar offense would be entitled to bail pending trial, this was a denial of the juvenile's due process rights, equal protection rights, or both. Therefore, because such pretrial detention of juveniles is illegal, it was asserted to involve unlawful expenditure of public funds. Relying on the jurisprudence differentiating between treatment of juvenile and adult offenders, however, the court held that bail was not required by either the California or United States Constitution.

e. PLACE OF DETENTION

D.B. v. Tewksbury

United States District Court, District of Oregon, 1982.
545 F.Supp. 896.

FINDINGS OF FACT, CONCLUSIONS OF LAW, and ORDER

■ FRYE, DISTRICT JUDGE:

This is a civil rights action brought pursuant to 42 U.S.C. § 1983. Plaintiffs and members of plaintiffs' class are all children who are presently confined, or who are subject to confinement in the Columbia County Correctional Facility (CCCF), an adult jail, in St. Helens, Oregon. Plaintiffs challenge the constitutionality of defendants' actions in confining plaintiffs and members of their class in CCCF. Plaintiffs seek declaratory and injunctive relief.

. . .

SPECIAL FINDINGS OF FACT

. . .

CCCF houses both adults and children in the same facility. Many adults are convicted prisoners serving time on sentences already imposed. All children held in CCCF are pretrial detainees, i.e., there has been no adjudication with regard to these children's acts, status, or behavior. They range in age from 12 to 18. Many of the children are "status offenders." Status offenders are children who, by virtue of their ages, are confined for being beyond parental control or running away from home. Of 101 children held at CCCF during a nine month period in 1980, 36 were held on status offense charges. The remaining children during this period were held for acts which, if they had been done by an adult, would constitute crimes. Sometimes children are placed in CCCF for shelter care: for example, a child who has been raped can be placed in CCCF.

Children do not stay in CCCF for long periods of time, but status offenders ordinarily are confined longer than those detained for criminal acts. In any event, 70 percent of the children who were confined in CCCF in 1981 were released within 24 hours. Nearly 75 percent of the children held in CCCF are released to their parents. A small number pose an immediate threat to community safety or their own safety or may flee from the court's jurisdiction. In 1980, of 124 children confined in CCCF, during a nine month period, only 25 required secure custody. The others could have been released without posing a serious threat to community safety, personal safety, or court jurisdiction.

.   .   .

Children detained in CCCF are usually placed in quarters consisting of multiple-occupancy cells with a common day space. They may be placed in isolation cells, however. Each multiple-occupancy cell contains steel bed frames, a toilet-sink installation, one overhead light, and a steel-barred wall with a sliding door. Children are locked inside the cells from 10 p.m. to 6 a.m.

The day room area, i.e., the common room, contains a metal picnic table, fluorescent lighting fixtures, and a single shower unit. There is no natural light in the cells occupied by children. Illumination is sufficient for overall visibility. All walls, floors, and ceilings are solid concrete or concrete block materials. The walls are painted blue.

Doors entering into these areas are either steel bars or solid metal. Each door contains a small viewing window and a food service slot. Children are detained in cells geared for as many as three children. Sometimes children ranging in age from 12 to 17 years are placed in the same cell.

Children held in CCCF are not issued sheets, mattress covers, or pillows. They sleep on mattresses covered with urethane and they are given a wool blanket. Occasionally children are not given mattresses. Those children placed in isolation cells sleep on cement floors.

Female children are not advised by matrons that sanitary napkins or tampons are available. If requested, however, they are made available. Matrons are not stationed within the secure detention area of CCCF. They are stationed in the front office area and are in the jail only to make checks on the female children. In order to obtain a sanitary napkin or tampon, female children must strike their cell doors or yell to attract the attention of a male corrections officer, who in turn contacts a matron. There are no full-time matrons available during night shifts, but if a female child is detained during the night, a part-time matron is called and is available.

There is no 24–hour a day intake screening process at CCCF. The intake process at CCCF is essentially an admissions process rather than a screening process. Part of the reason that children are detained at CCCF rather than being placed elsewhere is that there are no written criteria upon which to make decisions regarding who should be detained in CCCF. There is no policy as to who makes a decision when a child is to be lodged in jail. There is a phone list for jail staff to use to try to reach juvenile counselors, but counselors are sometimes unavailable. Children are then lodged based upon the decision of the corrections officer (jailer). If an arresting officer can locate a juvenile counselor, there is nothing in writing that tells the officer or the juvenile counselor when to lodge the child. For example, D.P. was arrested with a friend. D.P.'s friend was released to his parents who came to pick him up. D.P., however, was lodged in CCCF because his custodial grandmother did not have a car and therefore could not pick him up. Even if a juvenile counselor is available, the juvenile counselor does not speak directly with the child before he or she makes an intake decision. There are no written procedures for how to handle physically, mentally, or emotionally handicapped children. Jail personnel testified that none of these children are ever detained.

All clothing of children detained in CCCF is confiscated. Children are issued jail clothes which consist of jeans, a shirt, and socks for boys, and slacks, a blouse, and socks for girls. No child lodged in CCCF may have underwear.[2]

Toilet facilities at CCCF are not screened from view and children using these toilet facilities are visible to other children and to corrections officers. The day room area has a shower which can be used at all times when the children are not locked in their cells. On occasion showers in CCCF are not equipped with shower curtains. Children showering are visible to other children and to corrections officers. Female children using the toilet or shower are visible to male corrections officers. Male children using the toilet or shower are visible to matrons.

Children in CCCF are sometimes placed in either of two isolation cells. These are 8′ X 8′ windowless concrete block rooms, barren of all furniture and furnishings. Sometimes it is very cold in the isolation cells. Near the center of the isolation cell there is a sewer hole which is the only facility for urination and defecation.

Lighting and the mechanism for flushing the sewer hole for each isolation cell are controlled outside the cell by the corrections staff. Lights in the isolation cells are sometimes left on or off for long periods of time. Sometimes the sewer hole is not flushed for long periods. When the mechanism for the sewer hole is flushed by a corrections staff officer, water and sewage gushes onto the cell floor.[4]

---

2. For sanitary reasons personal clothing is confiscated from children and adult prisoners. Adults at CCCF can, however, have underwear brought to them, and children cannot.

4. This court in its tour of CCCF witnessed the water erupt several inches above

The isolation cells are located across a corridor from the adult male dormitory cell which holds up to 18 prisoners. For a child to be placed in isolation, that child must be moved down a corridor immediately outside the adult male dormitory cell. The child can see the adult male prisoners, and the adult male prisoners can see him or her. When the isolation cell door is closed, children in isolation and the adults in the dormitory cell can and do communicate by talking in loud voices. Children may also encounter adult inmates during the intake process.

There are no written standards for placement of children in isolation. There is no one designated to determine if and when a child should be placed in isolation. There is no absolute limit to the period of time that a child can be held in isolation. Isolation cells have been used when children were intoxicated or under the influence of drugs. Children have also been placed in isolation for perceived offenses or disputes between children held in the same cell. There is no psychological screening of children placed in isolation. No log is maintained when a child is placed in isolation.

   . . .

No medical screening procedure is used for children admitted to CCCF other than a visual inspection by an untrained corrections officer. Children who are intoxicated or under the influence of drugs are admitted to CCCF. Corrections officers have no training in identifying or meeting the needs of intoxicated or drug dependent children. These children may be placed in isolation. For example, one of the plaintiffs, D.P., was arrested while intoxicated and was placed in isolation for uncooperative behavior. He received no counseling or assistance from anyone trained to deal with an intoxicated child. After shattering his finger and breaking out several teeth, he was transported to Dammasch Hospital.

K.K. was also detained at CCCF while intoxicated. Because of belligerent behavior, he was placed in a juvenile section in handcuffs. He received no medical screening, monitoring, or assistance, and was later found on his cell floor in a pool of vomit and urine. He was then taken to Columbia District Hospital where he was admitted for observation.

   . . .

Corrections officers determine whether a child needs medical treatment based upon perception, common sense, and experience. If a child believes he or she is ill, the child notifies a corrections officer, who decides whether the child should be taken to a doctor. There are no written criteria for corrections officers to follow in determining whether a child should see a doctor.

   . . .

Children are treated considerably differently from adults. Adults have access to books, television, radio, cards, and other recreational materials; children do not. Adults are allowed to have underwear brought to them at CCCF; children are not. Adults have regular visitation and may visit with

the floor and splash on the cell floor around the sewer hole. A Columbia County Special Grand Jury recommended that the isolation cell not be used in its condition.

friends as well as families; children have no regularly scheduled visitation. Adults are allowed to send and receive mail; children are not allowed to send or receive mail. Adults are provided paper, writing material, envelopes, and stamps. Children are not allowed to have paper, writing material, envelopes, or stamps. Adults are allowed to make one phone call upon admission; children are not allowed to make a phone call upon admission. Adults are allowed to make phone calls during their period of incarceration. Children at CCCF, prior to the court entering its preliminary injunction dated June 10, 1981, were prohibited from making phone calls without Juvenile Department permission. When an attorney comes to CCCF to see an adult inmate, this visitation is allowed. If an attorney comes to CCCF to see a child, the attorney must go through the Juvenile Department to gain access to the child.[7] An inmate manual governs the conduct of adults held in CCCF. Children are not advised what behavior will result in disciplinary action or sanctions. There are no grievance procedures for children.

Parents are not allowed to visit children confined in CCCF without permission of the Juvenile Department. Jailers do not have the authority to allow parent-child visitation. Visitation with children in CCCF is controlled by the Juvenile Department and not the jail. The visitation policy for children is not in writing. There are no standards within the Juvenile Department for granting or denying visits with children in CCCF. No contact visits are allowed. Parents and detained children must talk to one another by means of a telephone and are separated by shatter-proof glass. Jailers sometimes will not tell inquiring parents whether or not their child is, in fact, in jail.

There are no formal written policies and procedures pertaining to the care and treatment of juveniles at CCCF. The policies that do exist are developed informally and handed down verbally. Therefore, many policies are in a constant state of flux and/or confusion. Furthermore, it is impossible to determine which policies are promulgated by the Juvenile Department and which policies are promulgated by the Sheriff's Department. There is no written contract between the Juvenile Department and the Sheriff's Department or jail regarding confinement of children.

There are no written rules governing the conduct of children held in CCCF. Therefore, children are not notified of what behavior is expected of them. What behavior is expected of them is left to the individual whims and caprices of the various corrections officers in charge. For example, it is up to an individual officer's discretion to decide if a child should be locked in isolation. It is up to an individual officer's discretion what restraining physical tactic to employ in dealing with a child.

All full-time corrections officers at CCCF are men. There are three part-time matrons who are employed to handle female children. Matrons are not stationed within the security detention area of CCCF. The part-time matrons are not required to receive training that male corrections officers receive. If a female child wants to get the attention of a matron, she

---

7. An attorney appointed by a Juvenile Court Judge may have access to a child without permission of the Juvenile Department. All of the plaintiffs and presumably many of the class, had no appointed attorney while detained in CCCF.

first must get the attention of a male guard, who in turn contacts the matron. Ordinarily, female children are not informed by jail staff as to how to get the attention of a matron. Frequently only one corrections officer staffs the jail.

Corrections officers at CCCF are basically jail staff. They have no training and little time to work with children. For example, if a child locked in a cell is screaming or yelling, the officer may go to the cell and yell, "Quiet down." The personnel at CCCF are not prepared or trained to treat children in other than a manner consistent with a maximum security lock-up facility.

Although there is no evidence to indicate physical abuse such as beatings, there is evidence that corrections personnel have made verbal threats toward detained children and have refused to tell them the time of day when requested. Since there is no natural light in the children's cells and since there are no clocks, children often become disoriented as to time.

Generally, the corrections staff has been insensitive to the needs of children in stressful situations. For example, when C.H. called for help when he and his brother were being harassed by older juveniles, the staff did not respond for a long time. One jailer told L.B. and other girls that they could bleed to death if they wanted to during an incident when the girls had broken a light bulb and were carving on their bodies. When D.B. called for help when he saw an adult inmate lying on the ground with slashed wrists, the corrections officer told him to "Shut up or go to the isolation cell." When D.P. refused to sign a paper during the booking process, a corrections officer grabbed D.P. by the hair and used an arm lock to pull D.P. to his cell. One corrections officer threatened to put D.P. in a cell with a "buck nigger" and showed D.P. a bloody shirt which the officer claimed indicated what happened to the last person who shared a cell with a "buck nigger."

Children in CCCF are allowed to see and hear adult inmates. All entry ways, passages, and exits to and from the facility are the same for juveniles and adults. Children in both isolation and regular cells can and do communicate with adult inmates. Several of the plaintiffs have been subjected to sexually suggestive comments from adults. Corrections officers do not invite child-adult communication; however, they cannot prevent it.

In January, 1980, the Columbia County Circuit Judge appointed a special investigating Grand Jury to make a complete investigation into the conditions at CCCF. That Grand Jury inspected the jail and took testimony. In May, 1980, the Grand Jury found numerous deficiencies in the facility and specifically recommended that children not be kept in CCCF until these conditions were remedied. The Grand Jury further expressed "hope" that alternatives to confinement of children in CCCF would be developed.

After the Federal Defender for the District of Oregon investigated conditions in CCCF, the United States Marshals Service discontinued placement of federal prisoners in CCCF.

Columbia County has some cost-effective alternative facilities for housing children. Shelter care is available. Defendants agree that removal of children from CCCF could result in a potential financial saving to Columbia County. Facilities in Cowlitz County, Washington, and at the Multnomah County Juvenile Detention Facilities, in Portland, Oregon are available. Columbia County participates in the Juvenile Services Act and in the 1981–82 biennium received approximately $100,000 under that act. Columbia County has been negotiating for and could receive funds in the amount of $36,000 under the Boys and Girls Aid Jail Removal Initiative Proposal. Columbia County has a special fund of approximately $25,000 given as a bequest for the betterment of conditions for children.

Data from a contiguous county, Clackamas County, indicate that children requiring secure custody in Clackamas County are housed in Multnomah County's Juvenile Detention Facility and that this program does not cost Clackamas County any more money than putting children into jails. Columbia County can request free technical assistance through the Federal Office of Juvenile Justice and Delinquency Prevention. At no cost to Columbia County, procedures, practices, programs, and planning can be provided so that Columbia County has access to expertise and planning and monitoring skills of experts in the field of juvenile care. It would take approximately 30 days to effect a 100% removal of children from CCCF and set up alternatives.

Current literature in the field of juvenile justice indicates that behavior modification of socially-deviant children is best achieved when children are diverted from the criminal justice system and its jails and punishments whenever possible. Studies also indicate that whenever restraints of children are necessary for the protection of society or protection of the children themselves, these restraints are best carried out through diversion programs, home detention, shelter care, crisis or emergency centers, or through intensive counseling and monitoring. As a last resort, the literature indicates, children who need to be confined should be held—not in jails or dungeons—but in juvenile detention centers geared to meet the needs of these children.

The jailing of children in maximum security adult jails such as CCCF stigmatizes (or brands) them as criminals. This interferes with their relationships with their families, schools, and communities—and most of all with their ability to confront adolescent crises and emerge from those crises as law-abiding productive adults. It increases the chance that they will forever be "criminals." The fact that the confinement is brief does not reduce the harm.

The plaintiffs were credible witnesses. Details of their stories were corroborated by the testimony of defendants, themselves, the Columbia County Grand Jury report, the Federal Defender's report, the CCCF jail records (and absence of records), and the expert witnesses.

Defendant Tewksbury has publicly described CCCF as "pretty much a bare lock-up, just like the adult jail, but the kids don't get the same privileges ... It's a boring place, a helluva place." He has further stated "Detention is punishment and I try to make it as unappetizing as possible. The last place a child wants to be."

GENERAL FACTUAL FINDINGS

CCCF is designed for the purpose of confinement, without regard for human dignity or need. Nothing over and above the basic minimums necessary for the maintenance of bodily functions is provided to children at CCCF. Nothing at CCCF is responsive to the emotional and physical needs of children in conflict with the law and their families. CCCF is a maximum security lock-up facility.

Placement of children within cells without regard to their ages or levels of maturity and without adequate supervision by trained corrections staff and without regard to the reasons why they are being held, increases antisocial behavior such as violence and physical abuse.

To require a female child to strike a cell door or to yell for assistance in order to receive sanitary napkins causes needless embarrassment and humiliation to such child. To require any child to go without underwear in a culture in which underwear is considered a requirement of dress causes needless embarrassment and humiliation for the child.

The requirement that children wear jail "uniforms," and the lack of privacy for the use of showers and bathrooms contribute to feelings of anxiety and loss of self-esteem which are counterproductive to the goals of the juvenile justice system. The failure to provide counseling or psychiatric care for children in CCCF is also counterproductive to these goals.

The lack of programs and the method of "treatment" reflect policies of the Juvenile Department and the institution, rather than inadequate resources. These policies result in harsher treatment for pretrial detainee children than for adult prisoners, many of whom have been convicted and sentenced. The denial of access to family and friends by way of regularly scheduled visits, use of telephone, and use of mail, needlessly creates or intensifies children's fears, hostilities, and rages, and is, again, counterproductive to the goals of the juvenile justice system.

The failure to have a written policy results in confusion, arbitrary decisions, and different treatment under similar situations. Without written rules children are at the mercy of the corrections staff and therefore subject to unnecessary anxieties about what to do or expect. There is nothing for children to do while confined at CCCF. This creates needless idleness, boredom, acute anxiety, fear, depression, and hostility. Idle, unattended, confined children present special supervisory problems. They frequently become destructive and cause physical harm to each other, themselves, or to their surroundings.

CCCF is inadequately staffed and the staff is inadequately trained to handle children. As a result, there is a lack of proper care of children. Jailers without special training in dealing with children under stress or emotionally distressed children are not qualified to provide the kind of counseling and therapy which is consistent with the goals of the juvenile justice system.

Confinement in CCCF is clearly and fundamentally intended to punish children. Punishment is the treatment of choice of Columbia County's Juvenile Department for its detained children. This "treatment" has little or nothing to do with simple detention, rehabilitation, or even the protection of society.

. . .

CONFINEMENT IN CCCF AS PUNISHMENT

Oregon statutory law allows a child to be detained in local correctional facilities such as CCCF so long as the portion of the facility holding the child is screened from the sight and sound of adult prisoners. ORS 419.575, ORS 169.079 (1979)(amended 1981; renumbered ORS 169.740). Under Oregon law, then, plaintiffs may legitimately be incarcerated in CCCF prior to an adjudication of their status or guilt. It is the scope of their federal constitutional rights during this period of confinement before a hearing that is the focus of this case.

The Due Process Clause of the Fourteenth Amendment to the United States Constitution requires that a pretrial detainee not be punished. Bell v. Wolfish, 441 U.S. 520 (1979). A state does not acquire the power to punish a person—adult or child (assuming a child is convicted of committing a crime)—until after it has secured a formal adjudication of guilt in accordance with due process of law. Not every disability imposed in preadjudication detention amounts to "punishment," however. The very fact of detention implies a measure of restriction of movement, choice, privacy, and comfort.

This court must determine whether the conditions imposed upon plaintiffs are imposed for the purpose of punishment or whether they are incidents of some other legitimate governmental purpose. In this case the determination is simple. Defendant Tewksbury has stated publicly and expressly that he intends to punish children detained in CCCF. It is the express intent of defendants that plaintiffs' confinements in CCCF be punishments. The intent to punish is carried out in the extraordinary conditions of confinement imposed on plaintiffs while confined in CCCF. Confinement of child pretrial detainees in CCCF as it now exists is punishment prior to an adjudication of guilt.

Defendants have violated plaintiffs' due process rights under the Fourteenth Amendment to be free from pretrial punishments by confining plaintiffs in CCCF. Those extraordinary conditions which alone and in combination constitute punishment are:

1. Failure to provide any form of work, exercise, education, recreation, or recreational materials.

2. Failure to provide minimal privacy when showering, using toilets, or maintaining feminine hygiene.

3. Placement of intoxicated or drugged children in isolation cells without supervision or medical attention.

4. Placement of younger children in isolation cells as a means of protecting them from older children.

5. Failure to provide adequate staff supervision to protect children from harming themselves and/or other children.

6. Failure to allow contact between children and their families.

7.   Failure to provide an adequate diet.

8.   Failure to train staff to be able to meet the psychological needs of confined children.

9.   Failure to provide written institutional rules, sanctions for violation of those rules, and a grievance procedure.

10.   Failure to provide adequate medical care.

CONFINEMENT IN JAILS AS PUNISHMENT FOR STATUS OFFENDERS

Plaintiffs also contend and ask the court to rule that even if the conditions of confinement at CCCF are corrected, plaintiffs and plaintiffs' class may not be detained in CCCF because the confinement of plaintiffs and plaintiffs' class in any adult jail constitutes punishment per se and is therefore unconstitutional. The court will address this contention first as it relates to status offenders, i.e., runaway children or children who are out of parental control.

The impact that a runaway child or a child out of the control of his or her parents has on the family and may have on the community causes alarm and often leads to the necessity for societal intervention. The runaway or out-of-control child can jeopardize the lives and property of other people as well as his own life. The question is: Does the status of such a child justify placing that child in a jail?

Society has historically used terror, confinement, and punishment as a means of dealing with "status." For example, insane people used to be beaten and imprisoned. Lepers were sent to remote and undesirable geographical areas. As recently as 1962 the legislature of the State of California enacted a law which made being a narcotic addict a crime for which punishment could be inflicted. That law was ruled unconstitutional by the United States Supreme Court. Robinson v. State of California, 370 U.S. 660 (1962).

A child who has run away from home or is out of parental control is clearly a child in distress, a child in conflict with his family and his society. But nobody contends he is a criminal. A runaway child or a child out of control, as an addict or an insane person, may be confined for treatment or for the protection of society, but to put such a child in a jail—any jail—with its criminal stigma—constitutes punishment and is a violation of that child's due process rights under the Fourteenth Amendment to the United States Constitution. No child who is a status offender may be lodged constitutionally in an adult jail.

CONFINEMENT IN JAILS FOR CHILDREN ACCUSED OF COMMITTING CRIMES

The court must now turn to the issue of whether it is constitutionally permissible to lodge children who have been accused of committing crimes in adult jails pending adjudication of the charges against them. The court has above ruled that confining children in CCCF pending adjudication of crimes or status constitutes punishment, and the court has further ruled that detaining children in any jails on the basis of their status or condition constitutes punishment and is an unconstitutional deprivation of due process. The court must now deal with children charged with committing crimes and must suppose that the jails in which these children are lodged are modern, "enlightened" kinds of jails—ones which provide different methods of discipline, care, and treatment appropriate for individual children according to age, personality, and mental and physical condition. The court must further suppose that these jails are adequately staffed and provide reasonable measures of comfort, privacy, medical care, food, and recreation. Would it be constitutionally permissible to lodge children accused of committing crimes in these jails?

In deciding this issue, the court declines to rule on the "punishment" aspect of the due process clause of the 14th Amendment. Instead the court will rely on the "fundamental fairness" doctrine enunciated in In re Gault, 387 U.S. 1 (1967) and juvenile cases decided after the *Gault* decision.

Due process—or fundamental fairness—does not guarantee to children all the rights in the adjudication process which are constitutionally assured to adults accused of committing crimes. For example, children are not entitled to a jury trial, to indictment by Grand Jury, or to bail. In lieu of these constitutional rights, children are not to be treated or considered as criminals. An adjudication of a child as guilty does not have the effect of a conviction nor is such child deemed a criminal. Even upon a finding of "guilt" as to the criminal charges, the child may not be imprisoned in adult jails as punishment for his acts. ORS 419.507, 419.509.

Juvenile proceedings, in the State of Oregon as elsewhere, are in the nature of a guardianship imposed by the state as parens patriae to provide the care and guidance that under normal circumstances would be furnished by the natural parents. It is, then, fundamentally fair-constitutional—to deny children charged with crimes rights available to adults charged with crimes if that denial is offset by a special solicitude designed for children.

But when the denial of constitutional rights for children is not offset by a "special solicitude" but by lodging them in adult jails, it is fundamentally unfair.[11] When children who are found guilty of committing criminal acts cannot be placed in adult jails, it is fundamentally unfair to lodge children accused of committing criminal acts in adult jails.

In 1966 the United States Supreme Court envisioned the problem confronting this court: "... There is evidence, in fact, that there may be grounds for concern that the child receives the worst of both worlds: that he gets neither the protections accorded to adults nor the solicitous care and regenerative treatment postulated for children." Kent v. United States, 383 U.S. 541, 556 (1966).

The supervisors at jails are guards—not guardians. Jails hold convicted criminals and adults charged with crimes. Jails are prisons, with social stigmas. Children identify with their surroundings. They may readily perceive themselves as criminals, for who goes to jail except for criminals?

---

11. This opinion does not apply to children who are remanded to adult criminal courts and who are afforded all of the constitutional rights accorded to adults charged with crimes. This opinion also does not apply to children temporarily detained in police stations pending the obtaining of identifying information.

A jail is not a place where a truly concerned natural parent would lodge his or her child for care and guidance. A jail is not a place where the state can constitutionally lodge its children under the guise of parens patriae.

To lodge a child in an adult jail pending adjudication of criminal charges against that child is a violation of that child's due process rights under the Fourteenth Amendment to the United States Constitution.

CONCLUSION

Plaintiffs are entitled to a permanent injunction and to reasonable attorneys' fees including reasonable attorneys' fees for the hearing on the motion for preliminary injunction. Plaintiffs' counsel shall submit to the court a proposed judgment order disposing of this case. Plaintiffs' counsel shall at the same time file their claims for attorneys' fees with supporting data and a memorandum. Defendants' counsel shall have 20 days to object to the form of the judgment and to request a hearing on the amount of the attorneys' fees. If the court receives no objection or request for hearing, it will sign the judgment order and will allow such attorneys' fees as it deems reasonable in accordance with law.

NOTE

Perhaps the primary premise underlying our juvenile justice system today is that it should be separate and distinct from the adult criminal justice system. Consonant with this premise, the notion that juveniles should not be detained in jails with adults has long been recognized. Section 10.2 of the Juvenile Justice Standards Relating to Interim Status states a prohibition against "interim detention of accused juveniles in any facility or part thereof also used to detain adults...." The federal Juvenile Justice and Delinquency Prevention Act links state eligibility for federal funds with a requirement that juveniles not be detained in adult jails or lockups, although some latitude is allowed in exceptional cases. 42 U.S.C.A. § 5633(a)(11)–(13). Even so, cases continue to arise in which such detention practices exist, perhaps through lack of proper training and disciplining of intake personnel or, more likely, through lack of proper facilities for juveniles. Kristina H. Chung, Note, Kids Behind Bars: The Legality of Incarcerating Juveniles in Adult Jails, 66 Ind.L.J. 999, 1005–07 (1991). *Swansey v. Elrod,* 386 F.Supp. 1138 (N.D.Ill.1975), is not atypical in this regard.

In *Swansey,* juveniles between ages 13 and 17 were detained in Cook County Jail, an adult facility, pending criminal prosecution. Several of them commenced a civil rights action alleging that confinement in such a location constituted cruel and unusual punishment and violated the equal protection clause. Granting the motion of the juveniles for a preliminary injunction against transferring any more youths to the Cook County jail and denying the defendants' motion to dismiss, the court ruled that there was "sufficient likelihood of success" on both of plaintiffs' claims. As to the Eighth Amendment argument, it held that though the juveniles had been transferred to adult authority and would thereby receive the "full panoply of criminal constitutional rights" to which an adult would be entitled, this did not mean that juveniles were entitled to no higher degree of care than any other detainee in the criminal justice system. Rather, juveniles still warrant fundamentally different treatment from adults, and a showing by the plaintiffs of possible devastating psychological harm and reprehensible physical results from detention with adults was sufficient to establish a likelihood of success as to their claim.

As to the assertion of a violation of equal protection, the court stated that since juveniles convicted as adults are incarcerated in separate facilities from adults where they can receive adequate rehabilitative services, "incarcerated juveniles under adult jurisdiction who are unconvicted can receive no less." Id. at 1143. Such differential treatment was not justified upon any rational reason by the defendants, and thus the court ruled that plaintiffs had demonstrated a likelihood of success on this claim also.

For other cases containing admonitions against detaining juveniles in adult jails, see *Schaffer v. Green*, 496 P.2d 375 (Okl.Cr.App.1972); *Cox v. Turley*, 506 F.2d 1347 (6th Cir.1974); *Osorio v. Rios*, 429 F.Supp. 570 (D.P.R.1976); and *Miller v. Carson*, 392 F.Supp. 515 (M.D.Fla.1975), modified and remanded, 563 F.2d 741 (5th Cir.1977).

Virtually all states require at a minimum that juveniles be separated from adults in detention facilities. Chung, supra at 1016 (1991). This result is driven largely by the provision in the Juvenile Justice and Delinquency Prevention Act requiring separation as a condition of eligibility for federal funds. 42 U.S.C.A. § 5633(a)(13). An example is found in Ga.Code Ann. § 15–11–48, which generally prohibits juveniles from being detained in adult facilities but allows exceptions, and in the latter cases, separation is required. A 1980 study found that only Arizona, Maryland, Mississippi, Pennsylvania and Rhode Island absolutely prohibit the detention of juveniles in adult jails. Many more states would prohibit jail detention of children under a certain age. J. King, A Comparative Analysis of Juvenile Codes 39–40 (Washington: Office of Juvenile Justice and Delinquency Prevention, 1980). Of course, in some instances more recent legislation may impose tougher restrictions on the detention of juveniles. See David Steinhart, California Legislature Ends the Jailing of Children: The Story of a Policy Reversal, 34 Crime & Delinq. 169 (1988) for one such legislative development.

A special problem is posed with juveniles who are detained as "enemy combatants." For a discussion of the complexities arising from housing juveniles with adults in the prison at Guantanamo Bay, Cuba, including application of international law, as well as some suggested protections, see Melissa A. Jamison, Detention of Juvenile Enemy Combatants at Guantanamo Bay: The Special Concerns of the Children, 9 U.Cal. Davis J.Juv.L. & Pol'y 127 (2005).

f.   LENGTH OF DETENTION AND RIGHT TO SPEEDY TRIAL

In re Thomas J.

Court of Appeals of Maryland, 2002.
372 Md. 50, 811 A.2d 310.

■ Bell, C.J.

The issue this case presents is whether the constitutional right to a speedy trial applies to juvenile proceedings, where, in this case, there was a delay of three years and four months between the detention of the juvenile and the subsequent adjudicatory hearing. The Circuit Court for Prince George's County, sitting as a juvenile court, found that there was no denial of the right to a speedy trial and, therefore, denied the motion to dismiss filed by Thomas J., the respondent. The Court of Special Appeals, following an independent constitutional appraisal of the undisputed facts, reversed, determining that Thomas J. had been denied his right to a speedy trial. We shall affirm.

I.

Evidence gathered during a police investigation of an attempted robbery led to the arrest of Thomas J. on January 18, 1996. Later that day, Thomas J. was released into the custody of his mother ("Mrs. J.") pending further proceedings. Subsequently, a delinquency petition was filed on May 2, 1996, but because Mrs. J. and Thomas J. had moved, they did not receive the summonses issued on May 8, 1996. The summonses were reissued on two occasions, May 28, 1996 and May 30, 1996. As a result of the failed attempts at service by the State, the petitioner, a writ of attachment was issued on June 24, 1996. This writ was reviewed annually for three years, and finally returned on April 22, 1999–three years and four months after the arrest. At the adjudicatory hearing on May 20, 1999, Thomas J. filed a preliminary Motion to Dismiss, "based upon denial of a speedy trial."

The State argues that neither the Fourteenth, nor the Sixth Amendment is applicable to juvenile delinquency proceedings, in light of the Maryland Juvenile Causes Act ("MJCA"), infra, which already has in place rigid time limitations for the commencement of juvenile proceedings. Moreover, the State argues, Mrs. J. signed a form release requiring her to "immediately notify the Clerk of the Juvenile Court at the Court House, Upper Marlboro, Maryland of any new address for [her] or the child." She failed to do so and, thus, the State submits, the delay should be attributed to Thomas J.:

> "And the fact that there had been an outstanding writ, that is not attributable to us. We have absolutely no obligation to go out and find him. That is what a writ is for. That is what a bench warrant is for. In the adult system, we use the bench warrant. Bench warrants can be outstanding for years. And if they are served, they are served. Same thing with a writ. The writ works as a bench warrant in juvenile court."

Thomas J., of course, sees it much differently. Noting that the form release was not admitted into evidence, he disputes that Mrs. J. was notified of an affirmative duty to notify the clerk of the juvenile court of any change of address. Rather, Mrs. J. did what she reasonably could have by giving the detective in the case her phone number at work, notifying that same detective of her change of address, and also in notifying the post office of her change of address. Moreover, even after the move, Thomas J. remained a student in the Prince George's County Public School System. Arguing that both the Fourteenth and Sixth Amendment of the United States Constitution should be applicable to juvenile proceedings, and that the delay should be attributed to the State, defense counsel stated:

> "I am not aware of what efforts the State made to serve the respondent. But I would venture to guess that there were essentially none. Had the State's Attorney's Office contacted the detective, the detective could have contacted the mother. Had the State's Attorney's Office or their investigators gone to the school, they could have found this man, this respondent. So they are going to have to justify the reasons for why they did not serve the respondent."

Subsequently, Thomas J.'s Motion to Dismiss was denied. Consequently, Thomas J. noted an appeal to the Court of Special Appeals. The intermediate appellate court reversed the judgment of the trial court. In re Thomas J., 132 Md.App. 396, 752 A.2d 699 (2000). Balancing the four factors set forth in Barker v. Wingo, 407 U.S. 514, 530, 92 S.Ct. 2182, 2191, 33 L.Ed.2d 101, 116 (1972) (assessing length of the delay, reasons for the delay, appellant's assertion of his right to a speedy trial, and prejudice to the appellant), that court, *In re Thomas J.*, at 404–12, 752 A.2d at 703–07, opined:

> "This length of delay [of more than three years and four months] is especially egregious considering that the opportunity to rehabilitate and treat, the purpose of our juvenile justice system, was lost during some of the more formative years of Thomas's life."

> * * *

> "[T]he record shows that the State made three attempts to summons Thomas and his mother, contrary to Thomas's contention that the State made only one attempt. Although we recognize that the State probably could have located Thomas and could have issued the writ of body attachment earlier, rather than allow it to remain outstanding for years, we do not find this case to be deliberate and knowing inaction, but rather, 'less-than-diligent action.' ... Because the State was less than diligent in finding Thomas, we will weigh the Reasons for Delay factor against the State, although not heavily."

> * * *

> "It is undisputed that Thomas never asserted his right to a speedy trial, but, rather made a motion to dismiss at the adjudicatory hearing on May 20, 1999. '[A] defendant's failure to demand a speedy trial during the period when he was unaware of the charge, cannot be weighed against him.' Brady v. State, 288 Md. 61, 69, 415 A.2d 1126, [1130] (1980)."

> * * *

> "[I]n this case, Thomas was suddenly detained for an incident that occurred more than three years before. We place particular emphasis on the fact that Thomas was fourteen years of age when the incident occurred and he was served with the writ at the age of seventeen. As we noted above, these three years are some of the most formative years in a person's life. For a teenager, three years and four months may seem a lifetime.... We therefore find that Thomas suffered at least some prejudice beyond mere anxiety.... [And moreover,] we find that the delay of over three years reached that critical point of being a 'substantial' delay where a presumption of prejudice arose."

We then granted the Petitioner's Petition for Writ of Certiorari, In re Thomas J., 360 Md. 485, 759 A.2d 230 (2000), to address this case of first impression.

II.

A.

We have previously noted that while "juvenile proceedings are civil and not criminal in nature, this does not mean that a juvenile gives up all rights that a person would be entitled to in a criminal proceeding." In re Anthony R., 362 Md. 51, 69, 763 A.2d 136, 146 (2000). The respondent adopts this premise and asserts (I) a speedy trial claim based on the Due Process Clause of the Fourteenth Amendment to the United States Constitution and Article 24 of the Maryland Declaration of Rights; and (ii) a speedy trial claim based on the Sixth Amendment to the United States Constitution and Article 21 of the Maryland Declaration of Rights.

The Sixth Amendment to the United States Constitution contains protections specifically granted to a criminal defendant in a criminal prosecution. Therefore, those rights are properly asserted by an accused in a criminal prosecution. The Supreme Court has been reluctant to transfer wholesale all the rights specifically granted to the criminal defendant to the juvenile offender. See McKeiver v. Pennsylvania, 403 U.S. 528, 545, 91 S.Ct. 1976, 1986, 29 L.Ed.2d 647, 661 (1971) ("[t]he Court has refrained ... from taking the easy way with a flat holding that all rights constitutionally assured for the adult accused are to be imposed upon the state juvenile proceeding."). See also In re Gault, 387 U.S. 1, 30, 87 S.Ct. 1428, 1445, 18 L.Ed.2d 527, 548 (1967); Kent v. United States, 383 U.S. 541, 562, 86 S.Ct. 1045, 1057, 16 L.Ed.2d 84, 97 (1966) ("we do not mean ... that the hearing to be held must conform with all of the requirements of a criminal trial"). Consequently, any federal constitutional relief Thomas J. is afforded must stem from a violation of his due process rights protected by the Fourteenth Amendment.

. . .

The State, however, argues that any rights afforded Thomas J. are sufficiently contained in the MJCA, Md.Code (1974, 1998 Repl.Vol., 2000 Supp.), Courts and Judicial Proceedings Article, § 3–801 et seq. and Md. Rule 11–114.[2] In theory, the statutory scheme provided by the MJCA and

---

2. Section 3–810(p), in pertinent part, provides:

"(p) Time for filing complaint.—(1) Except as provided in paragraph (2) of this subsection, within 15 days after a law enforcement officer takes a child into custody the law enforcement officer shall file a complaint with an intake officer."

After the complaint is filed, § 3–810(d) provides:

"(d) Authorization decision.—(1) The intake officer or the local department may authorize the filing of a petition if, based upon the complaint and the inquiry, the intake officer or the local department concludes that the court has jurisdiction over the matter and that judicial action

is in the best interests of the public or the child."

Once authorized, a petition should be filed in the following manner, in accord with § 3–812(b) and (d):

"(b) Petitions alleging delinquency or violation of § 3–831.—Petitions alleging delinquency or violation of § 3–831 of this subtitle shall be prepared and filed by the State's Attorney. A petition alleging delinquency shall be filed within 30 days after the receipt of a referral from the intake officer, unless that time is extended by the court for good cause shown. Petitions alleging that a child is in need of supervision shall be filed by the intake officer. Petitions alleging that

Rule 11–114 ought to provide Thomas J. with sufficient protection against any delay of considerable length, but it does not do so. Section 3–812(d) of the MJCA provides that the juvenile "procedures to be followed by the court, shall be specified in the Maryland Rules." In turn, the applicable Rule, Md. Rule 11–114 provides for the release of any juvenile in detention unless an "adjudicatory hearing shall be held within thirty days from the date on which the court ordered continued detention or shelter care." In addition, that Rule also provides for the release of any juvenile not in detention or shelter care unless an "adjudicatory hearing shall be held within sixty days after the juvenile petition is served on the respondent...." Thus, Rule 11–114 provides protection against delayed juvenile adjudicatory proceeding in two specific circumstances: (1) to detained juveniles who are not given an adjudicatory hearing within thirty days of the court ordered detention or shelter care; and (2) to non-detained juveniles who are not given an adjudicatory hearing within sixty days after the petition is served upon them.

In the case sub judice, Thomas J. was not detained and the petition was not served on him until three years and four months after his arrest. The statutory and regulatory scheme fails to provide protection when an alleged juvenile is not detained and has no notice of a petition being filed. Simply because a court conducted an annual writ review and directed it to remain outstanding does not work to extend the time within which the adjudicatory hearing may be held, pursuant to Rule 11–114(b)(1). Indeed, as the respondent's Brief notes, "there was a delay of considerable length, sufficient to invoke a due process concern, but not one which was protected by the statute and rule." This belies the State's argument that the provisions of the MJCA ensure prompt adjudicatory hearings to juveniles.

a child is in need of assistance shall be filed by the local department. If the local department does not file the petition, the person or agency that made the complaint to the local department may submit the denial to the Department of Juvenile Justice Area Director for filing.

. . .

"(d) Applicability of Maryland Rules.— The form of petitions, peace order requests, and all other pleadings, and except as otherwise provided in this subtitle, the procedures to be followed by the court, shall be as specified in the Maryland Rules."

The applicable Maryland Rule, 11–114, in turn, provides in pertinent part:

"b. Scheduling of hearing. 1. *Adjudicatory hearing*. An adjudicatory hearing shall be held within sixty days after the juvenile petition is served on the respondent unless a waiver petition is filed, in which case an adjudicatory hearing shall be held within thirty days after the court's

decision to retain jurisdiction at the conclusion of the waiver hearing. However, upon motion made on the record within these time limits by the petitioner or the respondent, the administrative judge of the county or a judge designated by him, for extraordinary cause shown, may extend the time within which the adjudicatory hearing may be held. The judge shall state on the record the cause which requires an extension and specify the number of days of the extension.

2. *Pre-hearing detention or shelter care*. If the respondent is in detention or shelter care, the adjudicatory hearing shall be held within thirty days from the date on which the court ordered continued detention or shelter care. If an adjudicatory hearing is not held within thirty days, the respondent shall be released on the conditions imposed by the court pending an adjudicatory hearing, which hearing shall be held within the time limits set forth in subsection 1 of this section."

Consequently, we look to the Due Process Clause of the Fourteenth Amendment and Article 21 of the Maryland Declaration of Rights, for guidance.

B.

The United States Supreme Court, albeit in the adult context, determined that a defendant may assert due process violations to challenge delay both before and after official accusation, because:

> " 'Inordinate delay between arrest, indictment, and trial may impair a defendant's ability to present an effective defense. But the major evils protected against by the speedy trial guarantee exist quite apart from actual or possible prejudice to an accused's defense. To legally arrest and detain, the Government must assert probable cause to believe the arrestee has committed a crime. Arrest is a public act that may seriously interfere with the defendant's liberty, whether he is free on bail or not, and that may disrupt his employment, drain his financial resources, curtail his associations, subject him to public obloquy, and create anxiety in him, his family and his friends.' "

United States v. MacDonald, 456 U.S. 1, 7, 102 S.Ct. 1497, 1502, 71 L.Ed.2d 696, 703 (1982) (quoting United States v. Marion, 404 U.S. 307, 320, 92 S.Ct. 455, 463, 30 L.Ed.2d 468, 478 (1971)). By point of reference, the Due Process Clause of the Fourteenth Amendment provides, "nor shall any State deprive any person of life, liberty, or property, without due process of the law." U.S. Const. amend. XIV. . . .

Thomas J. asserts a violation of due process and speedy trial rights where his right to a prompt adjudication was delayed beyond three years. Moreover, he contends that "the statutory and regulatory control of juvenile proceedings is no more the exclusive guarantor of a juvenile's constitutional right to due process than is Md.Code (1957, 1996 Repl.Vol.), Art. 27, § 591 and Md. Rule 4–271 the exclusive guarantor of an adult's constitutional right to speedy trial." The State, however, points to *In re Gault*, supra, arguing that while the requirement of due process applies in juvenile proceedings, "only a showing of denial of due process warrants dismissal of juvenile proceedings, and given that Thomas J. was not detained . . . and was responsible for the delay," his rights were not violated.

Prior to *Gault*, proceedings involving juveniles were determined to be unique proceedings that were not subject to the provisions of either the state or federal constitutions applicable to criminal cases, and, thus, juveniles did not enjoy the attendant constitutional protections afforded in criminal prosecution of adults. See *Kent v. United States*, supra, 383 U.S. at 555, 86 S.Ct. at 1054, 16 L.Ed.2d at 94 (noting that in the juvenile proceedings, delinquents had not been entitled to bail, to indictment by grand jury, to a speedy and public trial, to trial by jury, to immunity against self-incrimination, to confrontation of their accusers, and in some jurisdictions, they are not entitled to counsel); Ex parte Cromwell, 232 Md. 305, 310, 192 A.2d 775, 778 (1963) (holding that failure to provide bail in juvenile proceedings was not a violation of the Federal Constitution). . . .

. . .

The *Gault* Court ... held that "delinquency" determinations within a state juvenile court proceeding "must measure up to the essentials of due process and fair treatment." Id. at 30, 407 P.2d 760, 87 S.Ct. at 1445, 18 L.Ed.2d at 548. Moreover, the Due Process Clause of the Fourteenth Amendment requires states to observe certain fundamental rights in connection with juvenile court proceedings. In so holding, the *Gault* Court specifically acknowledged that the right to written notice of the specific charge(s) in advance of the hearing; notification of the right to counsel, and to appointed counsel in case of indigence; the privilege against self-incrimination; and the right to a hearing based on sworn testimony, with the corresponding right of cross-examination were constitutionally protected rights within state juvenile proceedings.

In In re Winship, 397 U.S. 358, 364, 90 S.Ct. 1068, 1073, 25 L.Ed.2d 368, 375 (1970), the Court extended the *Gault* holding when it held that the Due Process Clause of the Fourteenth Amendment requires that the proof beyond a reasonable doubt standard, applicable in adult criminal cases, must be applied in the adjudication stage of juvenile proceedings. For an inapposite application, however, see *McKeiver*, supra, 403 U.S. at 545, 91 S.Ct. at 1986, 29 L.Ed.2d at 661, where the Court held that a defendant does not have a constitutional right to a jury in juvenile proceedings. Of particular importance to the Court was the determination that because of the impact a constitutionally required jury would have on juvenile proceedings, "fundamental fairness" did not require a jury trial. Id. at 543–51, 91 S.Ct. at 1985–89, 29 L.Ed.2d at 659–64.

. . .

We commence our analysis of whether a prompt hearing and adjudication in a juvenile proceeding is among the "essentials of due process and fair treatment" by reviewing the case law of our sister jurisdictions. Our review reveals that many of our sister jurisdictions have extended the constitutional right to a speedy trial to youthful offenders in juvenile proceedings. In Commonwealth v. Dallenbach, 1999 Pa. Super 101, 729 A.2d 1218 (1999), for example, a juvenile had his hearing postponed, resulting in an eighteen month delay following the filing of the juvenile petition.... The court formally held that the right to a speedy trial applied to juvenile proceedings. *Dallenbach*, supra, 729 A.2d at 1222.

See also In re P.V., 199 Colo. 357, 359–60, 609 P.2d 110, 111 (1980) (citing to prior decisions that held that certain judiciary created rules and legislative enactments which are premised on fundamental constitutional rights must, as a matter of fundamental fairness, be applied to juveniles and holding that a statute requiring a speedy trial for adult offenders be applied to juveniles); Piland v. Clark County Juvenile Court Services, 85 Nev. 489, 492, 457 P.2d 523, 524–525 (1969) (holding that although *Gault* does not expressly enumerate the right to a speedy trial as one of the safeguards of due process, the right is axiomatic to the mandates announced in *Gault* and to rule otherwise would emasculate the safeguards that were expressly enumerated: adequate notice of hearing, right to counsel, right to cross-examination of witnesses and privilege against self-incrimination—and that to hold otherwise the youthful offender might never be provided a forum in which to enjoy the basic rights of due process specifically granted in *Gault*). See generally, In re R.D.F., 266 Ga. 294, 301, 466 S.E.2d 572 (1996) (Carley J., concurring) (noting that *Gault* "required in appropriate situations the same constitutional standards apply to juveniles as to adults.").

. . .

We have stated, supra, that the *Gault* fundamental fairness standard requires that we emphasize its application in the fact finding process. We note that one of the significant justifications for a speedy trial in the criminal proceeding is the safeguarding of the fact-finding process, see *Barker*, supra, 407 U.S. at 521, 92 S.Ct. at 2187 ("[a]s the time between the commission of the crime and trial lengthens, witnesses may become unavailable or their memories may fade"). As the Supreme Court of Nevada made clear, without a speedy trial, "a youthful offender might never be provided a forum in which he could enjoy the basic rights of due process specifically granted in *Gault*." *Piland v. Clark County*, supra, 85 Nev. at 492, 457 P.2d at 525. Inasmuch as the rights (adequate notice of hearing, right to counsel, right to cross-examination of witnesses, privilege against self-incrimination and burdens of proof) specifically acknowledged by *Gault* and its progeny were determined to stem from fundamental fairness, this Court finds the right to a speedy trial in a juvenile proceeding to be consistent with the protections enumerated in *Gault*. We therefore hold, as a matter of fundamental fairness, that the Due Process Clause of the Fourteenth Amendment and Article 21 of the Maryland Declaration of Rights require that juveniles be afforded a speedy trial. We decline to engage in rule making by stating a specified period that would result in a violation of the right. Consequently, we rely on our case law to determine whether Thomas' constitutional due process right to a speedy trial has been violated in this case.

III.

The test identified by the Supreme Court in Barker v. Wingo, 407 U.S. 514, 92 S.Ct. 2182, 33 L.Ed.2d 101 (1972), as adopted by this Court for the determination of whether violations of a criminally accused's right to a speedy trial in this state, see Divver v. State, 356 Md. 379, 388, 739 A.2d 71, 76 (1999), has been violated, provides the standard as to the application of speedy trial principles to a prompt adjudicatory hearing. When presented with the similar issue, courts in our sister states have arrived at consistent results—the *Barker* Sixth Amendment test is applicable to juvenile proceedings. For example, in *Dallenbach* the court extended the "fundamental fairness" doctrine and held, "[a]fter careful consideration ... the due process clause of the 14th Amendment makes applicable to juveniles a 6th Amendment speedy trial right in delinquency proceedings." *Dallenbach*, supra, 729 A.2d at 1222. The court then applied the four *Barker* factors and determined that, although the delay in the case was unreasonable, on remand the trial court must find "actual prejudice." Id. at 1226.

. . .

We too adopt the *Barker* test in order to determine whether the respondent's constitutional right to a speedy trial has been violated in the case sub judice.

In *Barker*, the United States Supreme Court adopted a four-part balancing test to determine whether an accused has been denied the right to a speedy trial under the Sixth Amendment. The factors identified to be considered are: (1) the length of delay; (2) the reason for the delay; (3) the assertion of the right to a speedy trial by the accused; and (4) the prejudice to the accused resulting from the delay. See *Barker*, 407 U.S. at 530–532, 92 S.Ct. at 2192–2193, 33 L.Ed.2d at 117–118; *Divver*, supra, 356 Md. at 388, 739 A.2d at 76. "Until there is some delay which is presumptively prejudicial, there is no necessity for inquiry into the other factors that go into the balance." State v. Henson, 335 Md. 326, 333, 643 A.2d 432, 435 (1994) (quoting *Barker*, 407 U.S. at 530, 92 S.Ct. at 2192, 33 L.Ed.2d at 117). Once the existence of a presumptively prejudicial delay has been determined, "none of the four factors [is] either a necessary or sufficient condition . . . [r]ather they are related factors and must be considered together with such other circumstances as may be relevant." *Divver* at 394, 739 A.2d at 79 (quoting Epps v. State, 276 Md. 96, 107, 345 A.2d 62, 70 (1975) (quoting *Barker*, 407 U.S. at 533, 92 S.Ct. at 2193, 33 L.Ed.2d at 118)).

1. Length of Delay

As previously stated, the length of delay factor is a triggering mechanism and is not necessarily, in and of itself, sufficient to compel dismissal. What may seem, on its face, an outrageous delay may, indeed, be deemed reasonable. See e.g., *Barker*, 407 U.S. at 533–36, 92 S.Ct. at 2193–95, 33 L.Ed.2d at 118–120 (holding delay of five years not violative of constitutional right to speedy trial); State v. Bailey, 319 Md. 392, 415, 572 A.2d 544, 555 (1990) (deciding "the various periods of delay [amounting to two years and nine days] in this case do not mount up to a denial of any constitutional right."); Wilson v. State, 281 Md. 640, 651, 382 A.2d 1053, 1062 (1978) ("Applying the balancing test by assessing the four factors relevant in determining whether Wilson was deprived of his right to a speedy trial in the circumstances of the delay here, [four years and two months] the conclusion that he was not denied the right is crystal clear."); cf. *Epps*, 276 Md. at 111, 345 A.2d at 72 (delay of one year and fourteen days was "sufficiently inordinate to constitute a 'triggering mechanism' to engage in the 'sensitive balancing process' ").

"For speedy trial purposes the length of delay is measured from the date of arrest or filing of indictment, information, or other formal charges to the date of trial." *Divver* at 388–89, 739 A.2d at 76 (citing State v. Gee, 298 Md. 565, 569, 471 A.2d 712, 714 (1984)). In the case sub judice, the date of arrest was January 18, 1996 and the date on which the writ was returned was April 22, 1999. Thus, the delay of three years and four months raises a presumption of prejudice and is of sufficient duration to trigger a consideration of the remaining three elements of the *Barker* analysis.

2. Reason For Delay

"Closely related to length of delay is the reason the government assigns to justify the delay . . . [and] different weights should be assigned to different reasons." *Barker*, 407 U.S. at 531, 92 S.Ct. at 2192, 33 L.Ed.2d at 117. By way of guidance, the *Barker* Court provided:

> "A deliberate attempt to delay the trial in order to hamper the defense should be weighed heavily against the government. A more neutral reason such as negligence or over-crowded courts should be weighed less heavily but nevertheless should be considered since the ultimate responsibility for such circumstances must rest with the government rather than with the defendant. Finally, a valid reason, such as a missing witness, should serve to justify appropriate delay."

Id. at 531, 92 S.Ct. at 2192, 33 L.Ed.2d at 117 (footnote omitted); accord *Divver*, 356 Md. at 391, 739 A.2d at 78; *Bailey*, 319 Md. at 412, 572 A.2d at 553.

. . .

In the instant case, the State asserts that the reason for the delay is "solely attributable to Thomas J. and his mother, who moved shortly after Thomas J.'s delinquent acts without providing notice of their new address." It contends that Thomas J. and his mother had an affirmative duty to notify the court of the change of address; Mrs. J. signed a form when Thomas J. was released into her custody, requiring notification of any change of address. Thomas J., however, asserts no such affirmative duty was present and that his mother properly notified the person with whom she was in contact, in a reasonable manner when she,

> "provided a change of address to the Post Office and the police, and gave the detective in the case information about where she worked, which remained unchanged after the move. With only minimal effort, Thomas argues, the State could have located him either by: (1) contacting his mother at work, or (2) searching the database of pupils within the Prince George's County school system in which Thomas remained after the move."

In re Thomas J., 132 Md.App. at 405, 752 A.2d at 703. (Footnote omitted).

There is no evidence in the record of this case that the State intended to hamper the defense of the respondent. Nor is there any evidence that the respondent or his mother intended to hide from or elude the juvenile proceedings. But, there is an obligation of the State to at least attempt, in a reasonable manner, to locate alleged delinquents. The State's assertion that the writ serves as a warrant, especially in light of the goal of the juvenile statutory and regulatory scheme is not satisfactory. . . .

Therefore, because the respondent reasonably kept in contact with the proper authorities and the State simply relied upon a writ, in lieu of contacting respondents' mother or school, we hold that "a prolongation due to the negligence of the State," *Bailey*, 319 Md. at 412, 572 A.2d at 553, would be weighed, albeit less heavily, against the State.

3. Assertion of the Right

"It is undisputed that Thomas [J.] never asserted his right to a speedy trial, but, rather, made a motion to dismiss at the adjudicatory hearing on May 20, 1999." *In re Thomas J.*, 132 Md.App. at 407, 752 A.2d at 704.

Therefore, ordinarily, this "failure to assert the right will make it difficult for a defendant to prove that he was denied a speedy trial." *Barker*, 407 U.S. at 532, 92 S.Ct. at 2193, 33 L.Ed.2d at 118. But, "a defendant's failure to demand a speedy trial during the period when he was unaware of the charge, cannot be weighed against him." *Brady*, 288 Md. 61, 69, 415 A.2d 1126, 1130 (1980), rev'd on other grounds, Brady v. State, 291 Md. 261, 434 A.2d 574 (1981) ("*Brady II*"). Because there is no evidence that the respondent was aware that a delinquency petition had been filed, we shall not weigh this factor against him.

4.   Prejudice to the Accused

Prejudice, in respect to the right of a speedy trial, has been defined to include not merely an "impairment of defense" but [also] "any threat to what has been termed an accused's significant stakes, psychological, physical and financial, in the prompt termination of a proceeding which may ultimately deprive him of life, liberty or property." U.S. v. Dreyer, 533 F.2d 112, 115 (3d Cir.1976). It is to be assessed in light of the interests that the speedy trial constitutional right was designed to protect. The *Barker* Court has expressly "identified three such interests: (I) to prevent oppressive pretrial incarceration; (ii) to minimize anxiety and concern of the accused; and (iii) to limit the possibility that the defense will be impaired." *Barker*, 407 U.S. at 532, 92 S.Ct. at 2193, 33 L.Ed.2d at 118. We have also, see *Bailey*, supra, 319 Md. at 415, 572 A.2d at 555, citing *Brady v. State*, 288 Md. at 66, 415 A.2d at 1129, "made clear that *Barker* expressly rejected the notion that an affirmative demonstration of prejudice was necessary to prove a denial of the constitutional right to a speedy trial." As to the first interest, prevention of oppressive pretrial incarceration, the respondent was arrested and released into the custody of his mother, all on the same day of January 18, 1996. Thereafter, once the writ of attachment was served on April 2, 1999, Thomas J. was detained until his arraignment on April 22, 1999. He was then released into the custody of his mother once again. Therefore, like the intermediate appellate court, we do not believe that Thomas J. was oppressively incarcerated pending the outcome of the juvenile proceedings.

Regarding the second interest, minimizing the anxiety and concern of the accused, the lack of awareness of any outstanding charges may indicate that the accused was neither anxious nor concerned. We have, however, recognized that a "sudden awareness ... [of existing] charges which had been dismissed the year before, must have generated a response more than mere anxiety.... [Defendant] had to be frustrated." *Brady II*, 291 Md. at 268, 434 A.2d at 578. Here, as we have previously indicated, Thomas J. was unaware that a delinquency petition had been filed against him until he was served with the writ and suddenly detained for an incident that was over three years old. At the time that Thomas J. was arrested he was fourteen years of age and when the writ was served he was seventeen. Indeed, these three years are some of the most formative years in a person's life. As indicated in In re Benjamin L., 92 N.Y.2d 660, 667, 685 N.Y.S.2d 400, 708 N.E.2d 156, 160 (1999), "[m]inimizing the time between arrest and disposition in juvenile delinquency cases may be especially desirable because of the nature of adolescence."

In the instant matter, minimizing the time between arrest and disposition, so as to prevent anxiety and psychological harm, was a goal chargeable to the State—one which it failed to discharge. Thomas J., however, has never expressly asserted the existence of anxiety or psychological harm. The lack of this assertion is telling, where we have stated a preference for particularity when claiming anxiety and concern. See *Bailey*, 319 Md. at 417, 572 A.2d at 556 (holding that bald assertion of anxiety and concern have little significance). To be sure, however, the lack of success of showing a violation of this interest is not dispositive, because of the three interests, "the most serious is the last...." *Barker*, 407 U.S. at 532, 92 S.Ct. at 2193, 33 L.Ed.2d at 118.

Assessing the third interest, limiting the possibility that the defense will be impaired, we note that it speaks more to presumed prejudice, rather than the actual prejudice to a defendant's ability to present an effective defense. This is because actual prejudice can be difficult to prove....

This is one of the reasons why we have long recognized that a substantial delay gives rise to a presumption of prejudice. In *Bailey*, 319 Md. at 415, 572 A.2d at 555, we said that a delay of two years and nine days was presumptively prejudicial and "the presumption of prejudice always remains a factor to be weighed in the balance, because no one circumstance, such as the lack of actual prejudice, is controlling in deciding whether the defendant has been denied a speedy trial."

. . .

The United States Supreme Court has also recently affirmed that a presumption of prejudice increases with the length of delay. See Doggett v. United States, 505 U.S. 647, 655–56, 112 S.Ct. 2686, 2693, 120 L.Ed.2d 520, 531 (1992). In *Doggett*, the Government claimed that the petitioner failed to make any affirmative showing that the eight and one-half year delay weakened his ability to raise specific defenses, elicit specific testimony, or produce specific items of evidence. Holding that a petitioner could prevail on a speedy trial claim predicated upon presumed prejudice, the Supreme Court opined that:

> "*Barker* explicitly recognized that impairment of one's defense is the most difficult form of speedy trial prejudice to prove because time's erosion of exculpatory evidence and testimony 'can rarely be shown.' And though time can tilt the case against either side one cannot generally be sure which of them it has prejudiced more severely. Thus, we generally have to recognize that excessive delay presumptively compromises the reliability of a trial in ways that neither party can prove or, for that matter, identify. While such presumptive prejudice cannot alone carry a Sixth Amendment claim without regard to the other Barker criteria it is part of the mix of relevant facts, and its importance increases with the length of delay."

Doggett, 505 U.S. at 655–56, 112 S.Ct. at 2692–93, 120 L.Ed.2d at 531 (citations omitted)

The delay in the case sub judice of more than three years was presumptively prejudicial. Not only was the time period in excess of those found above, i.e., from ten months to two years, but it was also identical to the time period of forty months found presumptively prejudicial by the Delaware Supreme Court.

Based on the foregoing, we conclude that the Respondent's due process and speedy trial rights, as guaranteed by the Fourteenth Amendment of the United States Constitution and Article 21 of the Maryland Declaration of Rights, were violated when his juvenile proceeding was not adjudicated until three years and four months after his arrest.

JUDGMENT AFFIRMED, WITH COSTS.

■ HARRELL, J.

I respectfully dissent. I do not quarrel with the Majority with respect to: (1) its reasoning and conclusion extending to juvenile proceedings in Maryland constitutional due process speedy trial protection; (2) its reasoning and conclusion that the *Barker v. Wingo* factors supply the appropriate analytical paradigm for consideration of a speedy trial issue in the juvenile proceeding context; or, indeed, (3) much of the Majority's weighing of the *Barker v. Wingo* factors on the record of the present case (for example, the "length of delay" and "assertion of the right.") I part company with the Majority, however, in its weighing and analysis of the remaining *Barker v. Wingo* factors and its resultant conclusion based on the record of this case.

The Majority's conclusion as to the weight to be accorded the facts under the "reason for delay" factor, although better sifted than in the Court of Special Appeals's opinion (which concluded that they should be weighted "heavily in Thomas's favor," 132 Md.App. at 404, 752 A.2d 699), should have resulted in a neutral conclusion, rather than one weighed against the State, "albeit less heavily." In my view, both the State and Thomas J. shared equally the blame for the delay, to such an extent that I would not weigh this factor against either party.

At the 20 May 1999 hearing on Thomas J.'s motion to dismiss, no witnesses testified. The "facts" were proffered by Thomas J.'s attorney and the prosecutor and, without objection, accepted by the Court for purposes of the motion. No documentary exhibits were introduced or formally received in evidence, although the transcript reflects that the judge and counsel at times reviewed documents either in the court file or a party's

The proffer by Thomas J.'s counsel was to the effect that Thomas and his mother moved from their residence on 23rd Parkway in Forest Heights to "another location within Prince George's County" three weeks after the offense was alleged to have been committed on 18 January 1996. As a consequence of the move, Thomas changed schools from Benjamin Stoddert Middle School to Andrew Jackson Middle School in Prince George's County. His mother, the judge was informed, would have claimed to have supplied her work telephone number to the police detective "in the case."[3] She also would have testified that she provided a change of address to the Post Office.[4],[5]

___

3. The proffer did not include when she did this.

4. Again, the proffer was silent as to when the Post Office was so notified.

5. It is worth taking judicial notice that, at the pertinent times in this case, the U.S. Postal regulations provided that, unless requested otherwise, the Post Office forwards

Notwithstanding that Thomas J.'s mother wholly failed to notify the court directly of the change of residence address, as it appears she had agreed on 18 January 1996 to do, Respondent argues that it was entirely the State's fault that he was not located until 2 April 1999. He ventures that the State's Attorney failed to contact the police detective "in the case" to learn of the mother's work telephone number and failed to assign an investigator to check the County school system to find him. Indeed, the State may be faulted for merely sticking to routine gestures and "paper-pushing" in its efforts to bring Thomas J. to a prompt adjudication.

By the same token, Thomas J. and his mother were not models of civic responsibility. The Majority blesses the mother's efforts in "reasonably" keeping in contact with the proper authorities. The record does not support this characterization. The proffer to the juvenile court judge did not include when she notified the unnamed detective "in the case" or when she notified the Post Office of her change of address. Absent this chronological information, I fail to see how the label of reasonableness is so quickly bestowed. Of greater moment, however, is the question of whether the mother notified the Post Office of the address change at all. The return of the 28 May 1996 summons could be viewed as contradicting that assertion. If one assumed Thomas J.'s mother informed the Post Office on or about of the date of the move (some three weeks after 18 January 1996, or approximately 8 February 1996) and gave no instruction for a longer forwarding period, it could be inferred reasonably that the Post Office would forward her or Thomas J.'s mail through at least August 1996. See n. 5, supra. Yet, the Post Office returned the 28 May 1996 summons marked "unable to forward." Finally, common sense compels me to question whether a reasonable person, knowing that her child was subject to juvenile proceedings, would move and fail to notify the court of her new address (and her son's).

I do not purport to engage in fact finding regarding potentially disputed facts or inferences. My point is only that the weighing of the "reason for delay" factor should result in no prejudice to either party. There is more than enough blame on this score to share proportionately.

I also quarrel with the Majority's analysis of the "prejudice to the accused" factor, to the extent it posits some unexplained degree of weight against the State based on presumed prejudice to Thomas J. I agree that the record reflects no pre-adjudication incarceration, no anxiety or concern claimed by Thomas J., and no evidence that his defense was impaired by the delay. Nonetheless, the Majority apparently weighs this factor against the State solely on the ephemeral concept of presumed prejudice, which, on the record of this case, is a form without substance. The Majority leaps from legal abstracts identifying the cases and courts that recognize the existence of this presumption to a conclusion that it exists in this case, premised solely on the duration of the delay. Even assuming this presumption applies here, largely because Thomas J. lost the potential benefits of a disposition under our juvenile system of justice when he was 14 years old

mail for 6 months to a change of address after notification. See 39 C.F.R. § 111.5 (Domestic Mail Manual, F020, § 1.1, Issue 55, 10 January 2000). If requested, the Post Office will forward mail up to 18 months after notice.

(at the time of the misconduct) rather than at 17 when he was located and his case tried, I fail to see how the Majority, in a most conclusory fashion, races from there to the result of a constitutional violation.

According to my *Barker v. Wingo* "score card," Thomas J. has the better of the threshold "length of delay" and marginally the "prejudice" factors; however, the important "reason for delay" factor is a "push." The "assertion of the right" factor is concededly of no significance. On so thin a weighing, I would not find that his right to a speedy trial was abridged. Accordingly, I would reverse the judgment of the Court of Special Appeals.

NOTES

(1) Appellant, a 13–year–old charged with bank robbery, asserted that his right to speedy trial under 18 U.S.C.A. § 5036 had been violated. *United States v. Cuomo,* 525 F.2d 1285 (5th Cir.1976). The court responded:

> Section 5036 of Title 18 provides:

> If an alleged delinquent who is in detention pending trial is not brought to trial within thirty days from the date upon which such detention was begun, the information shall be dismissed on motion of the alleged delinquent or at the direction of the court, unless the Attorney General shows that additional delay was caused by the juvenile or his counsel, or consented to by the juvenile and his counsel, or would be in the interest of justice in the particular case. Delays attributable solely to court calendar congestion may not be considered in the interest of justice. Except in extraordinary circumstances, an information dismissed under this section may not be reinstituted.

> The appellant vigorously contends that he was "detained", within the ambit of § 5036, from the time he was arrested and throughout the time he was released from custody on restrictive bail conditions. Since there were seventy days between the time of his arrest and the time of his trial, he asserts that the information against him must be dismissed. The government, on the other hand, argues that Cuomo was "in detention" only while he was in the El Paso County Jail.

After a discussion as to the meaning of the word "detention", drawing on such sources as the legislative history of the statute, language in other statutes, the "understanding of juvenile court specialists", and judicial opinions, the court stated:

> Our conclusion is that the phrase "in detention" in § 5036 means "in physically restrictive detention amounting to institutionalization". Section 5036 was not transgressed by Cuomo's prosecution.

(2) In the *Thomas J.* case the length of delay (three years and four months) was extraordinarily long. What if the delay had been significantly shorter, e.g., a matter of months or even weeks? See *P.V. v. District Court,* 199 Colo. 357, 609 P.2d 110 (1980) (nine months), cited in the *Thomas J.* opinion; *In re J.G.B.,* 443 N.W.2d 867 (Minn.App.1989) (31 days); *In re Anthony* P., 104 Misc.2d 1024, 430 N.Y.S.2d 479 (Fam.Ct., N.Y. Co. 1980) (18 months).

In *United States v. Calloway,* 505 F.2d 311 (D.C.Cir.1974), appellant, a 17–year–old youth, had been charged with rape and tried and convicted as an adult. On appeal he claimed that he had been denied a speedy trial by the 15–month delay between arrest and trial, during which time he was incarcerated in the D.C. jail. The court reversed appellant's convictions and ordered dismissal of the indictment "for lack of a speedy trial", noting:

The personal prejudice resulting from pre-trial incarceration was exacerbated in the present case by two factors. First, the defendant was a youth being confined in an adult jail. As Judge Wright warned in his dissent in *United States v. Bland*, 153 U.S.App.D.C. 254, 472 F.2d 1329, 1349–1350 (1972)—in which this court upheld the D.C. statute permitting youths aged 16 and 17 to be tried as adults solely on the basis of the charge filed by the prosecutor—"*I am confident that a child is unlikely to succeed in the long, difficult process of rehabilitation when his teachers during his confinement are adult criminals.*" Subsequent events have shown that this confidence was well placed. Speaking of the D.C. Jail—the institution in which Calloway was confined for almost two years—Judge Wright later wrote:

> The recent prisoners' riot ... tragically demonstrates the inhumanity as well as the danger of treating children as adults for the purposes of correction and rehabilitation. Apparently one of the causes of the prison riot was the homosexual assaults by the adult prisoners on the 16– and 17–year old children being held in the jail as "adult" prisoners.

The record in this case, too, lends heavy support to the view that confining young offenders with hardened criminals is equivalent to simply abandoning them. In Calloway's jail records there are several entries in which he claims he was homosexually assaulted by other inmates. Moreover, Calloway (and apparently others) were able to secure enough drugs to induce a seizure. As a result he became so hostile and uncommunicative that his lawyers requested permission to withdraw from the case. Finally, when, after serving two years in the D.C. Jail, Calloway was sentenced under the Youth Corrections Act, he immediately "tr[ied] to be a leader of his peers ... [by] impress[ing] the other inmates with his belligerent attitude." From the date of his arrival at the Youth Center the authorities noted that he "will probably be a problem in the future."

(3) Juveniles may be entitled to a right to speedy trial under state constitutional law as well, and factors in addition to those enumerated in *Barker v. Wingo* may be considered. See, e.g., *In re Benjamin L.*, 92 N.Y.2d 660, 708 N.E.2d 156, 685 N.Y.S.2d 400 (1999). The *Benjamin L.* case is analyzed in Stephanie Beige, Casenote, Right to a Speedy Trial: In the Matter of Benjamin L., 16 Touro L.Rev. 719 (2000).

NEW MEXICO CHILDREN'S COURT RULES (West)

Rule 10–226. Adjudicatory hearing; time limits.

A. Child in Detention. If the child is in detention, the adjudicatory hearing shall be commenced within thirty (30) days from whichever of the following events occurs latest:

(1) the date the petition is served on the child;

(2) the date the child is placed in detention;

(3) if an issue is raised concerning the child's competency to participate at the adjudicatory hearing, the date an order is entered finding the child is competent to participate at the adjudicatory hearing. The court may order periodic judicial reviews pending completion of the competency evaluation. At each judicial review the child's attorney shall advise the court of the status of the evaluation;

(4) if the proceedings have been stayed pursuant to Rule 10–221 NMRA on a finding of incompetency to stand trial, the date an order is filed finding the child competent to participate in an adjudicatory hearing;

(5) if a mistrial is declared or a new adjudicatory hearing is ordered by the children's court, the date such order is filed;

(6) in the event of an appeal, the date the mandate or order is filed in the children's court disposing of the appeal;

(7) if the child fails to appear at any time set by the court, the date the child is taken into custody after the failure to appear or the date an order is entered quashing the warrant for failure to appear;

(8) the date the court allows the withdrawal of a plea or rejects a plea; or

(9) if a notice of intent has been filed alleging the child is a "youthful offender", as that term is defined in the Children's Code, the return of an indictment or the filing of a bind over order that does not include a "youthful offender" offense.

B. Child not in Detention. If the child is not in detention, or has been released from detention prior to the expiration of the time limits set forth in this rule for a child in detention, the adjudicatory hearing shall be commenced within one-hundred twenty (120) days from whichever of the following events occurs latest:

(1) the date the petition is served on the child;

(2) if an issue is raised concerning the child's competency to participate at the adjudicatory hearing, the date an order is entered finding the child is competent to participate at the adjudicatory hearing;

(3) if the proceedings have been stayed on a finding of incompetency to participate in the adjudicatory hearing, the date an order is filed finding the child competent to participate in an adjudicatory hearing;

(4) if a mistrial is declared or a new adjudicatory hearing is ordered by the children's court, the date such order is filed;

(5) in the event of an appeal, the date the mandate or order is filed in the children's court disposing of the appeal;

(6) if the child fails to appear at any time set by the court, the date the child is taken into custody after the failure to appear or the date an order is entered quashing the warrant for failure to appear;

(7) the date the court allows the withdrawal of a plea or rejects a plea; or

(8) if a notice of intent has been filed alleging the child is a "youthful offender", as that term is defined in the Children's Code, the return of an indictment or the filing of a bind over order that does not include a "youthful offender" offense.

C. Multiple Petitions. If more than one petition is pending, the time limits applicable to each petition shall be determined independently.

D. Extension of Time by Children's Court. For good cause shown, the time for commencement of an adjudicatory hearing may be extended by the children's court judge provided that the aggregate of all extensions granted by the children's court judge may not exceed sixty (60) days.

E. Extension of Time by Supreme Court. For good cause shown, the time for commencement of an adjudicatory hearing may be extended by the Supreme Court, a justice thereof, or a judge designated by the Supreme Court. The party seeking an extension of time shall file with the clerk of the Supreme Court a verified petition for extension concisely stating the facts petitioner deems to constitute good cause for an extension of time to commence the adjudicatory hearing. The petition shall be filed within the applicable time limits prescribed by this rule, except that it may be filed within ten (10) days after the expiration of the applicable time limits if it is based on exceptional circumstances beyond the control of the state or children's court which justify the failure to file the petition within the applicable time limit. A party seeking an extension of time shall forthwith serve a copy thereof on opposing counsel. Within five (5) days after service of the motion, opposing counsel may file an objection to the extension setting forth the reasons for such objection. No hearing shall be held except upon order of the Supreme Court. If the Supreme Court finds that there is good cause for the granting of an extension beyond the applicable time limit, it shall fix the time limit within which the adjudicatory hearing must be commenced.

F. Effect of Noncompliance with Time Limits. If the adjudicatory hearing on any petition is not begun within the times specified in Paragraph A or B of this rule or within the period of any extension granted as provided in this rule, the petition shall be dismissed with prejudice.

NOTE

Most states have statutory provisions similar to the New Mexico rule dealing with when a petition must be filed and when an adjudicatory hearing must be held. See, e.g., Ga.Code Ann. § 15–11–39(a). Such statutes or court rules often are strictly enforced. See, e.g., *Doe v. State,* 88 N.M. 644, 545 P.2d 1022 (App.1976), in which the court held that failure to comply with the time requirements, in the absence of excusable delay, necessitated a dismissal with prejudice. Even if the statute or court rule does not call for dismissal with prejudice, courts sometimes approve of dismissal with prejudice. See, e.g., *In re L.R.T.,* 209 Mont. 421, 680 P.2d 579 (1984). In addition to statutory requirements, such delays may violate the constitutional right to a speedy trial. See, e.g., *In re J.G.B.,* 443 N.W.2d 867 (Minn.App.1989). On the other hand, in some states such delays, if they violate only the statutory time requirements but not the court's sense of what constitutes a speedy trial, the dismissal is without prejudice. See, e.g., *In re R.D.F.,* 266 Ga. 294, 466 S.E.2d 572 (1996), overruling *J.B.H. v. State,* 139 Ga.App. 199, 228 S.E.2d 189 (1976), which had required dismissal with prejudice for a speedy trial violation where the statutory time requirements were not met.

D. ARREST AND SEARCH AND SEIZURE

1. TAKING INTO CUSTODY

THE LAW OF ARREST AND JUVENILES

The first encounter a juvenile has with the juvenile justice system is often with the police at the point of arrest, or as it euphemistically called, "taking into custody." Historically, of course, both statutes[1] and caselaw[2] emphasized the protective rather than the punitive purpose of the juvenile process. For that reason, prior to *Gault*[3] police had every reason to believe they had a free hand in taking juveniles into custody, in particular that the usual limitations applicable to the arrest of adults did not apply to juveniles.[4] After *Gault* the prevalent attitude among police toward the applicability of the law of arrest was one of uncertainty. This uncertainty might have been fueled by some of the earlier statutory formulations, patterned after § 16 of the Standard Juvenile Court Act (1959), to the effect that taking a juvenile into custody does not amount to an arrest.[5]

On the other hand, § 13(b) of the Uniform Juvenile Court Act (1968), formulated after *Gault*, provides that taking a juvenile into custody does not amount to an arrest "except for the purpose of determining its validity under the Constitution of this State or of the United States." Several states that have adopted the Uniform Act in whole or in part have identical or similar provisions,[6] the obvious implication of which is that the law of arrest applies to juveniles in the same manner in which it applies to adults. Caselaw on this issue, while still rare, supports the view that constitutional, as well as statutory, limitations associated with the law of arrest apply to adults and juveniles alike.[7] The rarity of such decisions is probably due to the assumption by most courts that the law of arrest is so clearly applicable to juveniles that the issue of its applicability does not warrant discussion.[8]

The Juvenile Justice Standards provide that the arrest process should be the same for juveniles as for adults, except that in some circumstances greater constitutional protection may be necessary for juveniles because of their peculiar vulnerability.[9] It is precisely because of the latter concern that special procedures have been developed for the handling of juveniles that do not arise in the case of adults. Indeed, the focus of this chapter is on those areas in which juveniles are treated differentially from adults.

---

1. See, e.g., Ga.Code Ann. § 15–11–1; N.J.Stat.Ann. § 2A:4A–21.

2. See, e.g., *Ex parte Sharpe*, 15 Idaho 120, 126–28, 96 P. 563, 564–65 (1908); *State v. Monahan*, 15 N.J. 34, 38, 104 A.2d 21, 23 (1954); *In re Gault*, 99 Ariz. 181, 192, 407 P.2d 760 (1965), rev'd, 387 U.S. 1, 87 S.Ct. 1428, 18 L.Ed.2d 527 (1967).

3. *In re Gault*, 387 U.S. 1, 87 S.Ct. 1428, 18 L.Ed.2d 527 (1967).

4. Although the caselaw is sparse, in one pre-*Gault* decision the court held that the law of arrest did not apply to juveniles. *In re James L.*, 25 Ohio Op.2d 369, 194 N.E.2d 797 (Juv. Ct., Cuyahoga County 1963).

5. Some of these statutes still contain this rather general language. See, e.g., Minn. Stat.Ann. § 260B.175(2).

6. See, e.g., Ga.Code Ann. § 15–11–45(b); Ohio Rev.Code Ann. § 2151.31(B)(1);

Tenn.Code Ann. § 37–1–113(b); see also Iowa Code Ann. § 232.2(54).

7. See, e.g., *In re J.B.*, 131 N.J.Super. 6, 328 A.2d 46 (Juv. & Dom.Rel.Ct., Union Co. 1974), overruled on other grounds, *State ex rel. J.M.*, 339 N.J.Super. 244, 771 A.2d 651 (2001); see also *Lanes v. State*, 767 S.W.2d 789 (Tex.Crim.App.1989).

8. See, e.g., *In re D.G.*, 144 Ill.2d 404, 163 Ill.Dec. 494, 581 N.E.2d 648 (1991). The same sort of assumption is seen in other areas as well, e.g., the applicability to juveniles of the law of search and seizure and the applicability of limitations on police interrogation of suspects, covered elsewhere in this chapter.

9. Juvenile Justice Standards Project, Standards Relating to Police Handling of Juvenile Problems 3.2 (1980).

Some of these issues, in the context of the process that begins with taking into custody, are explored in the notes that follow.

NOTES

(1) One typically thinks of the applicability of the law of arrest to juveniles who are being taken into custody for a violation of criminal law. Juvenile courts, of course, have broad jurisdiction over juveniles who engage in noncriminal conduct as well, e.g., truancy, running away from home, and disobedience to parents. See e.g., Ohio Rev.Code Ann. § 2151.31(A)(3); Wis.Stat.Ann. § 48.19(1)(d). These statutes indicate that the decision to take a youth into custody is regarded primarily as a police decision. A serious question that arises is whether a police officer should be allowed unchecked discretion in deciding whether to take into custody a youth not charged with a criminal violation. New York's juvenile jurisdiction statute, N.Y.Fam.Ct.Act § 305.2(2), provides that a person under the age of 16 may be taken into custody without a warrant only when he is committing an act that if performed by an adult would justify an arrest. The statute does not authorize taking a juvenile into custody for noncriminal conduct without a summons.

Cases may arise, of course, in which the child's immediate safety is in peril, and in such cases the officer may need to act immediately to prevent harm to the child. In *State v. Hunt*, 2 Ariz.App. 6, 406 P.2d 208 (1965), an officer responded to the call of a babysitter who had discovered a 5-year-old child lying on the floor of a furnace room, her hands tied behind her back, her head under the hot water heater, and blood on her face from what appeared to be strap marks. The court held the police officer had not only a right but a duty to enter the home immediately to protect the child and that he would have been remiss to have sought a warrant or delayed in any way in the face of such exigent circumstances. The police officer acted properly to remove the child quickly from immediate risk of substantial harm. In *White ex rel. White v. Pierce County*, 797 F.2d 812 (9th Cir.1986), the court similarly upheld the action of deputies in entering a house to investigate a report of suspected child abuse. The same emergency removal authority may be exercised by social services workers as well. See, e.g., *Doe v. Kearney*, 329 F.3d 1286 (11th Cir.2003).

Under the New York statutory scheme, warrantless emergency removal of a child in situations such as those described above is authorized. N.Y.Fam.Ct.Act § 1024(a).

(2) Following the decision to take the child into custody, the police officer must then decide whether to invoke the formal juvenile justice process. While most police officers are well aware of the inevitable stigmatizing effect of this second decision, they often lack the resources and opportunities to conduct extensive inquiries into individual cases. As a result, stereotypes may exert inordinate influence. Young people whose backgrounds indicate that they have bright futures may be treated differently from those whose situation indicates that their prospects are not so auspicious. To minimize this undesirable result, the Juvenile Justice Standards propose that police not make formal referrals to the juvenile justice process unless the juvenile manifests serious or repeated criminal behavior or, in the event of less serious criminal behavior, less restrictive alternatives are not appropriate. Juvenile Justice Standards Project, Juvenile Justice Standards Relating to Police Handling of Juvenile Problems 2.3 (1980).

(3) State statutes typically require police officers to handle arrested juveniles in special ways. The following are examples of some of the special duties imposed on the police. Consider how and why these duties differ from those imposed when the arrestee is an adult. Do you feel in each instance that the difference in treatment is justified as a matter of legislative policy?

(a) *Notification of Parents, the Court, and Others*

California Welf. & Inst.Code § 308 (West):

(a) When a peace officer or social worker takes a minor into custody pursuant to this article, he or she shall take immediate steps to notify the minor's parent, guardian, or a responsible relative that the minor is in custody and that the child has been placed in a facility authorized by law to care for the child, and shall provide a telephone number at which the minor may be contacted. . . .

(b) Immediately after being taken to a place of confinement pursuant to this article and, except where physically impossible, no later than one hour after he or she has been taken into custody, a minor 10 years of age or older shall be advised that he or she has the right to make at least two telephone calls from the place where he or she is being held, one call completed to his or her parent, guardian, or a responsible relative, and another call completed to an attorney. The calls shall be at public expense, if the calls are completed to telephone numbers within the local calling area, and in the presence of a public officer or employee. Any public officer or employee who willfully deprives a minor taken into custody of his or her right to make these telephone calls is guilty of a misdemeanor.

(b) *Duties of Peace Officer after Taking into Custody or on Delivery by Private Person*

New York Fam.Ct.Act § 724 (McKinney):

(a) If a peace officer or a police officer takes into custody or if a person is delivered to him under section seven hundred twenty-three, the officer shall immediately notify the parent or other person legally responsible for his care, or the person with whom he is domiciled, that he has been taken into custody.

(b) After making every reasonable effort to give notice under paragraph (a), the officer shall:

(i) release the youth to the custody of his or her parent or other person legally responsible for his or her care upon the written promise, without security, of the person to whose custody the child is released that he or she will produce the child before the lead agency designated pursuant to section seven hundred thirty five of this article in that county at a time and place specified in writing; or

(ii) forthwith and with all reasonable speed take the youth directly, and without first being taken to the police station house, to the designated lead agency located in the county in which the act occasioning the taking into custody allegedly was done, unless the officer determines that it is necessary to question the youth, in which case he or she may take the child to a facility designated by the chief administrator of the courts as a suitable place for the questioning of youth or, upon the consent of a parent or other person legally responsible for the care of the youth, to the youth's residence and there question him or her for a reasonable period of time; or

(iii) take a youth in need of crisis intervention or respite services to an approved runaway program or other approved respite or crisis program; or

(iv) take the youth directly to the family court located in the county in which the act occasioning the taking into custody was allegedly done, provided that the officer affirms on the record that he or she attempted to exercise the options identified in paragraphs (i), (ii) and (iii) of this subdivision, was unable to exercise these options, and the reasons therefor.

(c) In the absence of special circumstances, the peace officer shall release the child in accord with paragraph (b)(i).

(d) In determining what is a "reasonable period of time" for questioning a child, the child's age and the presence or absence of his parents or other person legally responsible for his care shall be included among the relevant considerations.

(c) *Separate Detention and Incarceration*

Alaska Stat. § 47.12.240 (Lexis–Nexis):

(a) When the court commits a minor to the custody of the department, the department shall arrange to place the minor in a detention home, work camp, or another suitable place that the department designates for that purpose. Except when detention in a correctional facility is authorized by (c) of this section, the minor may not be incarcerated in a correctional facility that houses adult prisoners.

. . .

(c) Notwithstanding (a) of this section, a minor may be incarcerated in a correctional facility

(1) if the minor is the subject of a petition filed with the court under this chapter seeking adjudication of the minor as a delinquent minor or if the minor is in official detention pending the filing of that petition; however, detention in a correctional facility under this paragraph may not exceed the lesser of

(A) six hours, except under the criteria listed in (e) of this section; or

(B) the time necessary to arrange the minor's transportation to a juvenile detention home or comparable facility for the detention of minors;

(2) if, in response to a petition of delinquency filed under this chapter, the court has entered an order closing the case under AS 47.12.100(a), allowing the minor to be prosecuted as an adult;

(3) if the incarceration constitutes a protective custody detention of the minor that is authorized by AS 47.37.170(b); or

(4) if the minor is at least 16 years of age and the court has entered an order under AS 47.12.160(e) imposing an adult sentence and transferring custody of the minor to the Department of Corrections.

(d) When a minor is detained under (c)(1) or (3) of this section and incarcerated in a correctional facility, the minor shall be

(1) assigned to quarters in the correctional facility that are separate from quarters used to house adult prisoners so that the minor cannot communicate with or view adults who are in official detention;

(2) provided admission, health care, hygiene, and food services and recreation and visitation opportunities separate from services and opportunities provided to adults who are in official detention.

(e) Notwithstanding the limitation on detention set out in (c)(1) of this section, a minor whose detention is authorized by (c)(1) of this section may be detained in a correctional facility for up to 24 hours when the authority having jurisdiction over the minor under this chapter is outside a metropolitan statistical area under the current designation of the United States Bureau of the Census and the authority has no existing acceptable alternative placement available for the minor. The minor may be held in secure custody beyond the

24–hour period if the criteria set out in this subsection are met and if the correctional facility is located where conditions of

(1) distance to be traveled or the lack of highway, road, or other ground transportation do not allow for court appearances within 24 hours, in which case the minor may be held for up to an additional 48 hours at the correctional facility; or

(2) lack of safety exist, such as severely adverse, life-threatening weather conditions that do not allow for reasonably safe travel, in which case the time for an appearance may be delayed until 24 hours after the time that the conditions become safe.

(f) A detention authorized by (e) of this section may not exceed the time necessary to satisfy the requirement of (c)(1)(B) of this section.

. . .

(d) *Limitations on the Taking and the Distribution of Fingerprints and Photographs as a Means of Identification*

Kan.Stat.Ann. § 38–2313:

(a) Fingerprints or photographs shall not be taken of any juvenile who is taken into custody for any purpose, except that:

(1) Fingerprints or photographs of a juvenile may be taken if authorized by a judge of the district court having jurisdiction;

(2) a juvenile's fingerprints shall be taken, and photographs of a juvenile may be taken, immediately upon taking the juvenile into custody or upon first appearance or in any event before final sentencing, before the court for an offense which, if committed by an adult, would constitute . . . a felony, a class A or B misdemeanor or assault . . .;

(3) fingerprints or photographs of a juvenile may be taken . . . if the juvenile has been: (A) Prosecuted as an adult . . .; or (B) taken into custody for [a traffic offense where the juvenile is 14 or older or a game and fish violation where the juvenile is 16 or older];

(4) fingerprints or photographs shall be taken of any juvenile admitted to a juvenile correctional facility; and

(5) photographs may be taken of any juvenile placed in a juvenile detention facility. Photographs taken under this paragraph shall be used solely by the . . . facility for the purposes of identification, security and protection and shall not be disseminated to any other person or agency except after an escape and necessary to assist in apprehension.

(b) Fingerprints and photographs taken under subsection (a)(1) or (a)(2) shall be kept readily distinguishable from those of persons of the age of majority. Fingerprints and photographs taken under subsections (a)(3) and (a)(4) may be kept in the same manner as those of persons of the age of majority.

(c) Fingerprints and photographs of a juvenile shall not be sent to a state or federal repository, except that:

(1) Fingerprints and photographs may be sent to the state and federal repository if authorized by a judge of the district court having jurisdiction;

(2) a juvenile's fingerprints shall, and photographs of a juvenile may, be sent to the state and federal repository if taken under subsection (a)(2) or (a)(4); and

(3) fingerprints or photographs taken under subsection (a)(3) shall be processed and disseminated in the same manner as those of persons of the age of majority.

(d) Fingerprints or photographs of a juvenile may be furnished to another juvenile justice agency . . . if the other agency has a legitimate need for the fingerprints or photographs.

. . .

(e) *In the Interest of Confidentiality, Limitations May be Placed on Distribution to Other Law Enforcement Agencies*

Ill.Comp.Stat.Ann. ch. 705, § 405/1–7(B):

(1) Except as provided in paragraph (2) no law enforcement officer or other person or agency may knowingly transmit to the Department of Corrections, Adult Division or the Department of State Police or to the Federal Bureau of Investigation any fingerprint or photograph relating to a minor who has been arrested or taken into custody before his or her 17th birthday, unless the court in proceedings under this Act authorizes the transmission or enters an order under Section 5–805 permitting or requiring the institution of criminal proceedings.

(2) Law enforcement officers or other persons or agencies shall transmit to the Department of State Police copies of fingerprints and descriptions of all minors who have been arrested or taken into custody before their 17th birthday for the offense of unlawful use of weapons under Article 24 of the Criminal Code of 1961, a Class X or Class 1 felony, a forcible felony as defined in Section 2–8 of the Criminal Code of 1961, or a Class 2 or greater felony under the Cannabis Control Act, the Illinois Controlled Substances Act, or Chapter 4 of the Illinois Vehicle Code, pursuant to Section 5 of the Criminal Identification Act. Information reported to the Department pursuant to this Section may be maintained with records that the Department files pursuant to Section 2.1 of the Criminal Identification Act. Nothing in this Act prohibits a law enforcement agency from fingerprinting a minor taken into custody or arrested before his or her 17th birthday for an offense other than those listed in this paragraph (2).

(f) *Separate and Confidential Police Records (Sometimes Including the Possibility of Expungement)*

Kan.Stat.Ann. § 38–2310:

(a) All records of law enforcement officers and agencies and municipal courts concerning an offense committed or alleged to have been committed by a juvenile under 14 years of age shall be kept readily distinguishable from criminal and other records and shall not be disclosed to anyone except:

(1) The judge of the district court and members of the staff of the court designated by the judge;

(2) parties to the proceedings and their attorneys;

(3) the department of social and rehabilitation services;

(4) the juvenile's court appointed special advocate, any officer of a public or private agency or institution or any individual having custody of a juvenile under court order or providing educational, medical or mental health services to a juvenile;

(5) any educational institution, to the extent necessary to enable the educational institution to provide the safest possible environment for its pupils and employees;

(6) any educator, to the extent necessary to enable the educator to protect the personal safety of the educator and the educator's pupils;

(7) law enforcement officers or county or district attorneys, or their staff, when necessary for the discharge of their official duties;

(8) the central repository . . ., for use only as a part of the juvenile offender information system . . .;

(9) juvenile intake and assessment workers;

(10) the juvenile justice authority;

(11) juvenile community corrections officers;

(12) any other person when authorized by a court order, subject to any conditions imposed by the order; and

(13) as provided in subsection (c).

(b) The provisions of this section shall not apply to records concerning:

(1) A violation, by a person 14 or more years of age, of any provision of chapter 8 of the Kansas Statutes Annotated . . . or of any city ordinance or county resolution which relates to the regulation of traffic on the roads, highways or streets or the operation of self-propelled or nonself-propelled vehicles of any kind;

(2) a violation, by a person 16 or more years of age, of any provision of chapter 32 of the Kansas Statutes Annotated . . .; or

(3) an offense for which the juvenile is prosecuted as an adult.

(c) All records of law enforcement officers and agencies and municipal courts concerning an offense committed or alleged to have been committed by a juvenile 14 or more years of age shall be subject to the same disclosure restrictions as the records of adults. Information identifying victims and alleged victims of sex offenses . . ., shall not be disclosed or open to public inspection under any circumstances. Nothing in this section shall prohibit the victim or any alleged victim of any sex offense from voluntarily disclosing such victim's identity.

(d) Relevant information, reports and records shall be made available to the department of corrections upon request and a showing that the former juvenile has been convicted of a crime and placed in the custody of the secretary of the department of corrections.

. . .

In re D.M.

Supreme Court of Pennsylvania, 2001.
566 Pa. 445, 781 A.2d 1161.

■ CAPPY, JUSTICE.

We originally issued an opinion in this matter on December 27, 1999, wherein we held that a police officer did not possess the requisite cause to stop appellant pursuant to the Fourth Amendment of the United States Constitution and Article 1, Section 8 of the Pennsylvania Constitution. In the Interest of D.M., 560 Pa. 166, 743 A.2d 422 (1999) (hereinafter "D.M."). The United States Supreme Court issued a per curiam order vacating our prior decision and remanding the case for further consideration in light of its opinion in Illinois v. Wardlow, 528 U.S. 119, 120 S.Ct. 673, 145 L.Ed.2d 570 (2000). We now reverse our original decision.

The facts and procedural history, as reported in the previous opinion, established the following:

On June 24, 1996, at approximately 6:00 p.m., Officer Chris Frazier received a radio call regarding a man with a gun at 28th and Cecil B. Moore Avenues in Philadelphia. The officer was only one block from the location at the time of the call. The radio call included a description of the "man with a gun" as a black male, wearing a white t-shirt, blue jeans and white sneakers.

Upon arriving at the scene, the officer saw appellant, D.M., who matched the description given by the radio call. Officer Frazier exited his vehicle and told appellant to come over. Appellant ran away from the officer. Police back up approached the scene and appellant was stopped between the two cars. Officer Frazier asked appellant to put his hands on the hood of the car in front of him and proceeded to pat appellant down for the officer's own protection. Officer Frazier felt a hard object resembling a handgun in appellant's crotch area. A .32 caliber handgun fell out of appellant's right pants leg. At that point, Officer Frazier secured the gun and arrested appellant.

Appellant filed a motion to suppress alleging violations of both the United States and Pennsylvania Constitutions. Following a hearing, the trial court denied appellant's motion to suppress. That same day, the court adjudicated appellant delinquent and placed him on Intensive Probation. The Superior Court affirmed in a memorandum opinion. This court granted the petition for allowance of appeal in order to address the issue of whether the officer possessed reasonable suspicion to stop appellant based on an anonymous tip, where appellant fled at the time he was approached by the officer. D.M., 743 A.2d at 424.

On appeal, we held that the officer did not possess a reasonable suspicion to stop appellant and reversed the lower courts. The United States Supreme Court remanded this matter for our reconsideration in light of *Wardlow*. Once again, the sole issue before our court is whether the police demonstrated the requisite cause to stop appellant, based on an anonymous tip, where appellant fled when the officer approached him.

Appellant has filed a Petition for Clarification and/or Affirmance of this Court's Judgment as Resting Upon State Constitutional Grounds. Appellant argues that under Article 1, Section 8 of the Pennsylvania Constitution, the police could not properly stop him since the detention must be justified at its inception. According to appellant, the critical inquiry is whether the police had the requisite cause to stop him at the time they initially approached him rather than at the time they actually effectuated the stop. Appellant asserts that case law, decided under the Pennsylvania Constitution, supports his position. However, for the reasons stated herein, we cannot agree with appellant's argument.

It is well settled that the purpose of both the Fourth Amendment of the United States Constitution and Article 1, Section 8 of the Pennsylvania Constitution is to protect citizens from unreasonable searches and seizures. Commonwealth v. Jackson, 548 Pa. 484, 698 A.2d 571, 573 (1997). In the seminal case of Terry v. Ohio, 392 U.S. 1, 88 S.Ct. 1868, 20 L.Ed.2d 889 (1968), the United States Supreme Court indicated that police may stop and frisk a person where they had a reasonable suspicion that criminal activity is afoot. In order to determine whether the police had a reasonable suspicion, the totality of the circumstances—the whole picture—must be considered. United States v. Cortez, 449 U.S. 411, 417, 101 S.Ct. 690, 66 L.Ed.2d 621 (1981). "Based upon that whole picture the detaining officers must have a particularized and objective basis for suspecting the particular person stopped of criminal activity." Id. at 417–18, 101 S.Ct. 690. Pennsylvania courts have consistently followed *Terry* in stop and frisk cases, including those in which the appellants allege protections pursuant to Article 1, Section 8 of the Pennsylvania Constitution. Jackson; see also Commonwealth v. Cook, 558 Pa. 50, 735 A.2d 673, 677 (1999).

Appellant now asks this court to depart from this longstanding practice of following *Terry*. However, we see no reason at this juncture to embrace a standard other than that adhered to by the United States Supreme Court. Appellant is correct that our case law has questioned the relevancy of flight in reviewing the totality of the circumstances. Indeed, in our original opinion in D.M., we concluded that flight was not a factor that would weigh in favor of finding reasonable suspicion or probable cause under the totality of the circumstances test. D.M., 743 A.2d at 426. Nevertheless, this conclusion has been directly contradicted by the United States Supreme Court's recent decision in *Wardlow*.

In *Wardlow*, the Chicago police sent a four-car caravan into a high crime area to investigate drug activity. *Wardlow*, 528 U.S. at 121, 120 S.Ct. 673. One of the officers in the last vehicle observed the respondent on a corner with an opaque bag in his hand. Id. at 121–22, 120 S.Ct. 673. The respondent looked at the officers and fled. The officers cornered the respondent and upon exiting their car, immediately conducted a brief pat-down search for weapons. Id. at 122, 120 S.Ct. 673. During the pat-down search of the respondent, the officer discovered a gun. The issue before the court was whether sudden flight in a high crime area created a reasonable suspicion justifying a *Terry* stop. Id. at 123, 120 S.Ct. 673.

In explaining that such a seizure was justified, the Court reiterated the *Terry* standard and concluded that an officer "may, consistent with the Fourth Amendment, conduct a brief, investigatory stop when the officer has a reasonable, articulable suspicion that criminal activity is afoot." Id. at 124, 120 S.Ct. 673. The Court acknowledged that mere presence in a high crime area was insufficient to support a finding of reasonable suspicion. However, a court could consider "the fact that the stop occurred in a 'high crime area'" in assessing the totality of the circumstances. Id. Similarly, the Court held that unprovoked flight could be considered among the relevant contextual considerations, since "nervous, evasive behavior is a pertinent factor in determining reasonable suspicion" and "[h]eadlong flight—wherever it occurs—is the consummate act of evasion...." Id.

Based upon respondent's unprovoked flight in a high crime area, the Court concluded that the officer was justified in suspecting that criminal activity was afoot.

Following this decision, it is evident that unprovoked flight in a high crime area is sufficient to create a reasonable suspicion to justify a *Terry* stop under the Fourth Amendment. In light of this recent case law, it is clear that our original analysis in this case was contrary to the United States Supreme Court's subsequent analysis in *Wardlow*.

In the instant case, the police received an anonymous telephone call reporting that appellant was on a specific corner with a gun. The caller also described what appellant was wearing. This information standing alone was insufficient to support a finding of reasonable suspicion. *Jackson*, 698 A.2d at 574–75. However, as the police officer approached appellant, he turned and fled the scene. As the Court indicated in *Wardlow*, flight is the consummate act of evasion. Thus, appellant's flight coupled with the anonymous caller's information was sufficient to arouse the officer's suspicion that criminal activity was afoot at the time he stopped appellant.

Appellant argues that he was "seized" at the time the police initially approached him and that the initial detention must be justified by reasonable suspicion. According to appellant, flight precipitated by unjustified police conduct cannot be used in the determination of reasonable suspicion because the flight occurs only after the police have initiated an unjustified seizure. Commonwealth v. Matos, 543 Pa. 449, 672 A.2d 769 (1996).

Appellant's interpretation of *Matos* is incorrect. In *Matos*, we explained that the *pursuit* of an appellant by police officers amounted to a seizure. *Matos*, 672 A.2d at 771 (emphasis added). Thus, the officer must demonstrate either probable cause to make the seizure or reasonable suspicion to stop and frisk. However, *Matos* did not address whether the police needed some level of requisite cause at the time they initially approached the appellant.

Rather, that question is governed by the type of encounter that the police initiated when they approached the appellant.

> Traditionally, this Court has recognized three categories of encounters between citizens and the police. These categories include (1) a mere encounter, (2) an investigative detention, and (3) custodial detentions.

Commonwealth v. Polo, 563 Pa. 218, 759 A.2d 372, 375 (2000). Further, the police may approach anyone in a public place to talk to him, without any level of suspicion, but the citizen "has a right to ignore the police and go about his business." *Wardlow*, 528 U.S. at 125, 120 S.Ct. 673 (citing Florida v. Royer, 460 U.S. 491, 103 S.Ct. 1319, 75 L.Ed.2d 229 (1983)); see also *Polo* ("a 'mere encounter' (or request for information), which need not be supported by any level of suspicion, but carries no official compulsion to stop and respond"); Commonwealth v. Mendenhall, 552 Pa. 484, 715 A.2d 1117, 1119 (1998).

In the instant case, at the time the police initially approached the appellant it was unclear whether the police intended to do anything other than talk to him. Thus, the initial approach did not need to be justified by any level of suspicion. Rather, the appropriate time to consider whether the police had reasonable suspicion is at the time the police actually effectuated the seizure of the appellant and the totality of the circumstances test, by its very definition, requires that the whole picture be considered when determining whether the police possessed the requisite cause to stop appellant. Cortez. Here, the police effectuated the stop following appellant's flight from the scene, thus, flight was clearly relevant in determining whether the police demonstrated reasonable suspicion to justify a *Terry* stop under the totality of the circumstances.

Accordingly, for the reasons stated herein, we reverse our earlier decision and reinstate the Order of the Superior Court affirming the judgment of sentence.[2]

■ JUSTICE ZAPPALA files a dissenting opinion in which CHIEF JUSTICE FLAHERTY and JUSTICE NIGRO join.

■ ZAPPALA, JUSTICE, dissenting.

Because the United States Supreme Court's decision in Illinois v. Wardlow, 528 U.S. 119, 120 S.Ct. 673, 145 L.Ed.2d 570 (2000), does not affect our prior decision in this case pursuant to Article 1, Section 8 of the Pennsylvania Constitution, holding that the officer involved did not possess reasonable suspicion to stop Appellant based on an anonymous tip, where Appellant fled at the time he was approached by the officer, I dissent.

I find the majority writer's present change of position regarding our disposition of this matter pursuant to Article 1, Section 8 perplexing. In our original opinion addressing this matter, we relied upon both the Fourth Amendment to the United States Constitution and Article 1, Section 8 of the Pennsylvania Constitution in holding that the police officer here did not possess the requisite cause to stop appellant based upon flight alone. In re D.M., 560 Pa. 166, 743 A.2d 422 (1999). While the United States Supreme Court's decision in *Wardlow* impacts upon our analysis as it relates to the Fourth Amendment, the Court's decision is not dispositive of our state constitutional analysis. Moreover, regardless of the majority writer's current disagreement with his prior disposition of the case pursuant to Article 1, Section 8, principles of stare decisis mandate that such disposition, a majority opinion of this Court, remains the law of this case and of the Commonwealth. As Justice Cappy cogently noted in Commonwealth v. Tilghman, 543 Pa. 578, 673 A.2d 898 (1996), a majority opinion of this Court is binding not only on the parties before us, under the doctrine of law of the case, but is precedent as to different parties in cases involving substantially similar facts, pursuant to the rule of stare decisis.

In Commonwealth v. Matos, 543 Pa. 449, 672 A.2d 769 (1996), this Court considered whether police officers were required to establish reasonable suspicion pursuant to Article 1, Section 8 in order to recover contra-

2. As noted supra ..., subsequent to the remand from the United States Supreme Court, appellant filed a Petition for Clarification and/or Affirmance of this Court's Judgment as Resting Upon State Constitutional Grounds. We grant the Petition to the extent that we have considered appellant's argu- ments raised in the petition herein. Following reflection, however, as discussed more fully above, we have concluded that appellant's arguments raised in that Petition do not entitle him to relief on independent state grounds.

band by a person fleeing the police. *Matos* responded to the Supreme Court's decision in California v. Hodari D., 499 U.S. 621, 111 S.Ct. 1547, 113 L.Ed.2d 690 (1991), wherein the Court concluded that police officers could recover contraband from a fleeing suspect, since no seizure occurred for purposes of the Fourth Amendment. *Matos* involved three cases, which were consolidated for appeal.

In the lead opinion, Commonwealth v. Matos,, 23 E.D. Appeal Docket 1994, the facts established that two Philadelphia police officers responded to a radio broadcast that unknown persons were selling narcotics in the vicinity of Reese Street. As the police approached a group of three men in a nearby playground, the men fled. The police pursued the men and one of the pursuing officers observed Matos discarding a plastic bag of cocaine. The police recovered the bag. The issue before our Court was whether the police pursuit amounted to a seizure under Article 1, Section 8 of the Pennsylvania Constitution.

We rejected the decision in *Hodari D.* under our heightened privacy considerations pursuant to Article 1, Section 8 of the Pennsylvania Constitution. Rather, we determined that police pursuit amounted to a seizure, which must be justified by either a reasonable suspicion or probable cause. Ultimately, we concluded that the facts and circumstances surrounding *Matos* did not create a reasonable suspicion that criminal activity was afoot.

Once again, in Commonwealth v. Cook, 558 Pa. 50, 735 A.2d 673 (1999), we considered the relevancy of flight in determining the existence of a reasonable suspicion. In *Cook*, the police officer observed what he believed to be a drug transaction between appellant and another individual. When the officer approached appellant, the appellant began backing away and began to run "in almost a dead sprint." Id. at 674. As the appellant was running away, the officer observed appellant discard two pagers and a sandwich bag. The officers apprehended appellant and retrieved the sandwich bag. Id. The bag contained eighteen large rocks of crack cocaine. The sole issue before us was whether the officer demonstrated a reasonable suspicion to stop appellant. Id.

In reviewing the issue, we reiterated that "a police officer's pursuit of a person fleeing the officer was a seizure for purposes of Article 1, Section 8 of the Pennsylvania Constitution." *Cook*, 735 A.2d at 675 (citing *Matos*). Thus, in order to recover contraband from a fleeing suspect the police officer needed to demonstrate either a reasonable suspicion or probable cause. Id. In examining whether a reasonable suspicion existed, all the facts and circumstances surrounding the stop can be considered. Id. at 677. However, certain facts considered alone, like flight, cannot establish a reasonable suspicion. Id. Rather, a combination of these facts is necessary to establish the requisite cause for the stop. Id. In the end, we concluded that the officer demonstrated a reasonable suspicion based upon his first hand observations of appellant.

In the original *D.M.* opinion authored by the majority writer herein, we found the analysis employed in *Cook* to be instructive in reviewing the issue therein.

[I]n *Cook*, this court made clear that flight alone does not establish reasonable suspicion. 735 A.2d at 677. However, flight along with other facts, may demonstrate a reasonable suspicion that criminal activity is afoot. Id. In making the determination that reasonable suspicion existed, we relied upon the fact that the officer made firsthand observations of suspicious conduct, which based upon his experience, indicated that criminal activity was afoot, before he even approached appellant. Id. Moreover, we explained that flight could be considered in establishing reasonable suspicion, since the officer's suspicions were already aroused at the time appellant fled. Id. at 677–78. Accordingly, *Cook* makes clear that the appellant's subsequent flight becomes a relevant factor, in determining reasonable suspicion, only when the officer's suspicions are already aroused.

In re D.M., 743 A.2d at 426.

The analysis in *Cook*, which is cited extensively in *D.M.*, was clearly rooted in Pennsylvania's heightened privacy considerations pursuant to Article 1, Section 8 as interpreted by this Court in *Matos*. Moreover, our conclusion in the original *D.M.* opinion was consistent with both *Matos* and *Cook*. The facts in *Matos* were almost identical to the facts of the instant case, except in this case, the man was allegedly carrying a gun instead of drugs and did not abandon anything as he was fleeing the police. We have previously indicated that a radio call regarding a man with a gun does not create a reasonable suspicion that criminal activity is afoot. Commonwealth v. Jackson, 548 Pa. 484, 698 A.2d 571 (1997); Commonwealth v. Hawkins, 547 Pa. 652, 692 A.2d 1068 (1997). Thus, there are no facts in the instant case justifying a departure from *Matos*. In addition, the instant case is distinct from the situation in *Cook*, since in that case we emphasized that it was the police officer's firsthand observations of suspicious activity rather than the ensuing flight that created a reasonable suspicion. In this case, there were no comparable firsthand observations on the part of the police officer creating a reasonable suspicion that criminal activity was afoot.

Accordingly, since there are no facts in the instant case justifying a departure from prior case law under Article 1, Section 8 of the Pennsylvania Constitution, this Court is compelled to affirm our prior decision reversing the Superior Court and granting appellant's motion to suppress the contraband. As the Court's position has inexplicably changed, I dissent.

■CHIEF JUSTICE FLAHERTY and JUSTICE NIGRO join this dissenting opinion.

NOTES

(1) The *D.M.* case illustrates the practical reality that for purposes of the law of arrest, juveniles and adults are treated alike. Notice that neither the majority opinion nor the dissent contains a discussion of whether the law of arrest should be any different when applied to juveniles. The case illustrates another point as well, a point of disagreement between the majority opinion and the dissent, whether juveniles—or for that matter, adults—might be entitled to greater protection under state constitutional law than under the U.S. Constitution.

(2) The dissent mentions the case of *California v. Hodari D.*, 499 U.S. 621, 111 S.Ct. 1547, 113 L.Ed.2d 690 (1991), in which the Supreme Court held that a

"seizure" does not occur until the police actually bring a fleeing suspect under their control. In this case, even though the officer's initiation of a pursuit was a show of force, when the juvenile ignored the order to halt and fled, the seizure did not occur until the officer actually tackled the juvenile. The practical effect of the case was that a rock of crack cocaine that the juvenile discarded during the chase but before he was captured was not a product of a search and seizure and, therefore, was admissible.

(3) The majority opinion discusses at some length the Supreme Court's decision in *Terry v. Ohio*, 392 U.S. 1, 88 S.Ct. 1868, 20 L.Ed.2d 889 (1968), the Court's seminal "stop and frisk" case giving law enforcement officers limited authority to conduct a pat-down search, for weapons, of a suspect they have stopped based on a reasonable suspicion that he or she might be involved in illegal activity, for the officers' own protection. What kind of information must an officer possess in order to form a "reasonable suspicion"? In *Florida v. J.L.*, 529 U.S. 266, 120 S.Ct. 1375, 146 L.Ed.2d 254 (2000), the Court held that officers lacked reasonable suspicion for the stop of a 15–year-old juvenile where the only information they possessed was furnished by an anonymous informant to the effect that a young black male standing at a particular bus stop and wearing a plaid shirt was carrying a gun. The Court pointed out that an anonymous tip is not as reliable as a tip from a known informant who has proved to be reliable in the past. While an anonymous tip is not per se unreliable, it must have certain indicia of reliability if it is to furnish the basis of a stop and frisk for weapons. 529 U.S. at 270–72.

The Court's decision in *Florida v. J.L.* has been characterized as a narrow one that should not create heightened expectations for juvenile rights advocates. Irene Merker Rosenberg, Florida v. J.L. and the Fourth Amendment Rights of Juvenile Delinquents: Peekaboo!, 69 U.Cin.L.Rev. 289 (2000). Indeed, at about the same time it decided *Florida v. J.L.*, the Supreme Court in *Illinois v. Wardlow*, 528 U.S. 119, 120 S.Ct. 673, 145 L.Ed.2d 570 (2000)—the decision that prompted the Court to remand *In re D.M.* to the Pennsylvania Supreme Court for reconsideration—held that police officers had reasonable suspicion to stop a suspect where the encounter occurred in an area known for high-volume drug trafficking and where the suspect fled when approached by the officers.

2.   SEARCH AND SEIZURE

The Fourth Amendment's application to juveniles was explored in Chapter III as part of the overall theme of that chapter, children's rights and school authority. Specifically, we looked at the issue in the context of searches and seizures that take place in the public school setting. The same issue is reexamined here for an important reason. By and large, judicial analysis of search and seizure issues is the same for children as it is for adults, i.e., whether a case involves a search incident to arrest, a "hot pursuit" search, an automobile search, or a border search, courts tend to analyze the issues in the same way regardless of whether the subject of the search is an adult or a minor. The glaring exception to this generality, however, is the different treatment accorded students in the public school environment. Because of that differential treatment, the school search cases reviewed earlier dominate the focus of Fourth Amendment analysis generally where juveniles are concerned, particularly where some degree of police involvement is present.

New Jersey v. T.L.O.

Supreme Court of the United States, 1985.
469 U.S. 325, 105 S.Ct. 733, 83 L.Ed.2d 720.

(The opinion of the Court is reproduced at p. 351, supra.)

NOTES

(1) The Supreme Court in *T.L.O.* left open the question of the exclusionary rule's applicability to school search cases in which the evidence is illegally seized. See *T.L.O.*, 469 U.S. at 333 n.3. The case originally was scheduled for oral argument during the 1983 term solely on this issue but was carried over to the 1984 term for argument on the broader issue of the applicable standard for such searches. How should the exclusionary rule issue be resolved?

In *State v. Young*, 234 Ga. 488, 216 S.E.2d 586, cert. denied, 423 U.S. 1039, 96 S.Ct. 576, 46 L.Ed.2d 413 (1975), the Georgia Supreme Court held the exclusionary rule inapplicable to school search cases, even those in which the evidence has been illegally seized. Cf. *In re Lance W.*, 37 Cal.3d 873, 210 Cal.Rptr. 631, 694 P.2d 744 (1985) (1982 amendment to state constitution abolished exclusionary rule for violations of search and seizure provisions of state constitution).

(2) In *T.L.O.* the Court also left open the question of whether the applicable standard would be more stringent if the search is conducted "in conjunction with or at the behest of law enforcement agencies." See *T.L.O.*, 469 U.S. at 341 n.7. Consider the following facts.

A student reports to the vice-principal that items have been stolen from her gym locker and describes the items. Present at the time is a police officer who is assigned to the school as a liaison officer, although she is a plainclothes officer and drives an unmarked car. The vice-principal decides to investigate and the officer accompanies her.

The vice-principal questions some students who give her the names of four students, including S.C., who were seen in the vicinity of the gym lockers at the time preceding the theft and at a time when they were not in gym class. The vice-principal verifies that the four students were not scheduled to be in gym class at that hour.

The vice-principal, accompanied by the officer, questions the four students individually. The officer, while present, does not participate in the questioning. While questioning S.C., the vice-principal asks to search her purse. Upon dumping the contents of the purse on a shelf she discovers a coin purse matching the description of one of the stolen items. The officer then conducts a pat-down search of S.C. as she stands spread-eagle with her hands against the wall. S.C. then admits the theft and implicates one of the other students.

S.C. files suit in federal court alleging that her civil rights have been violated as a result of an unlawful search, specifically alleging that police involvement in the search raised the applicable standard to probable cause and invoked the warrant requirement. What result?

On these facts, the Eighth Circuit held that the search was reasonable. *Cason v. Cook*, 810 F.2d 188 (8th Cir.), cert. denied, 482 U.S. 930, 107 S.Ct. 3217, 96 L.Ed.2d 704 (1987). The court observed that the search in this instance was not conducted at the *behest* of the police; therefore, more stringent standards would have to rest on the basis that it was conducted *in conjunction with* the police. Viewed in this light the police involvement with the search was "limited" and not of sufficient magnitude to change the character of the search. A similar result was reached in

People in Interest of P.E.A., 754 P.2d 382 (Colo.1988); *In re Murray*, 136 N.C.App. 648, 525 S.E.2d 496 (2000). What sort of involvement or participation by the police *would* change the character of the search? Consider, e.g., the drug-sniffing dog cases, infra.

THE JUVENILE JUSTICE STANDARDS

As mentioned in note (2) above, *T.L.O.* does not address the issue of whether police participation in a school search might change the character of the search and, therefore, the applicable standard under the Fourth Amendment. The Juvenile Justice Standards take the position that Fourth Amendment limitations apply fully to searches conducted by law enforcement officers in the school setting. Juvenile Justice Standards Project, Standards Relating to Schools and Education 8.1 (1977). A search of a student or a protected area is viewed as unreasonable unless it is made pursuant to a valid search warrant, a lawful arrest, or a lawful stop, or is made with the student's consent or under exigent circumstances on the basis of a recognized exception to the search warrant requirement. The Standards further require that, to be reasonable, the search must entail no greater intrusion than is necessary under the conditions that justify the search. Standard 8.2.

"Protected student area" includes (1) an assigned desk if the student sits at that desk on a regular basis, is authorized to store in that desk items belonging to the student, and has authority to lock the desk (regardless of whether others, including school personnel, have a key or the combination to the lock; school personnel have issued regulations regarding what may or may not be stored in desks; the student has consented to or agreed to any such restrictions; or the student has paid a fee for use of the desk); (2) a locker if the student has exclusive use of the locker or shares it with one or two other students and has authority to lock the locker (regardless of whether: others, including school personnel, have a key or the combination to the lock; school personnel have issued regulations regarding what may or may not be stored in lockers; the student has consented to or agreed to any such restrictions; or the student has paid a fee for use of the locker); and (3) a motor vehicle that is located on or near school premises if it is either owned by the student or operated by the student with the owner's permission. Standard 8.3.

A personal search under the Standards includes a search of the student's body, clothing worn or carried by the student, or any container used by the student for carrying personal items, such as a pocketbook, briefcase, duffel bag, bookbag, or backpack, if in the student's possession or immediate proximity. Standard 8.4.

Under the Standards, a search by law enforcement officers is not validated by the fact that it is conducted with the consent of school personnel or by the student's parent except to the extent the parent's consent might be necessary to validate the student's consent. Standard 8.5.

The Standards provide that if a school official searches a student or a protected area at the behest of or in cooperation with law enforcement officers, or for a noneducation-related reason, i.e., to obtain evidence that might be turned over to law enforcement authorities for use in a criminal proceeding, the school official's actions are governed by the same requirements applicable to law enforcement officers. Standard 8.6(A). In addition, a search conducted by a school official for the purpose of gathering evidence of student conduct that might result in disciplinary sanctions is reasonable only if it is conducted pursuant to a valid search warrant or the student's consent, or is based on the school official's reasonable decision that it was not possible to detain the student or secure the protected area until law enforcement officers could arrive and that failure to conduct the search would pose a danger or result in loss of evidence or the flight of the student. In a case in which the possible sanction would include expulsion, long-term suspension, or transfer to an alternative school, the requirements for school officials are the same as those for law enforcement personnel. Standard 8.7.

The Standards employ the exclusionary rule as the sanction for any evidence seized in violation of the standards set forth above. Standards 8.8 & 8.9.

DISCUSSION PROBLEMS

BOMB THREAT

An anonymous phone call informs the high school principal that a bomb has been placed in one of the student lockers. The police are called in and along with school officials conduct a search of every locker. They do not find a bomb, but during the investigation seize a pound of marijuana from one of the lockers.

Do the Standards say anything about whether the marijuana is admissible in a subsequent delinquency proceeding? A subsequent disciplinary proceeding? Note that the same conduct by a student may result in both a delinquency disposition and a disciplinary action. As attorney for the student, can you think of any basis to argue for suppression? See *Horton v. Goose Creek Independent School District*, 690 F.2d 470 (5th Cir.1982), and other cases, supra p. 373.

GIRARD SCHOOL

Refer to the facts of this problem in Chapter III, supra at p. 368. Assume that the search of the desks did not turn up the money. The police, operating on the knowledge that Kerry is the school "troublemaker," come to the school and search Kerry's person without a warrant and over her objection. Would this be a valid search? Could school officials have performed such a search under *T.L.O.*? Under the Standards? What if the police had obtained prior consent from Kerry's mother, who did not believe her little angel would do anything wrong? Do you believe that parental consent should bind a minor? Should the minor be informed of her right to refuse a search? Consider the material on third-party consent infra at p. 1117.

Vernonia School District 47J v. Acton

Supreme Court of the United States, 1995.
515 U.S. 646, 115 S.Ct. 2386, 132 L.Ed.2d 564.

■ JUSTICE SCALIA delivered the opinion of the Court.

The Student Athlete Drug Policy adopted by School District 47J in the town of Vernonia, Oregon, authorizes random urinalysis drug testing of students who participate in the District's school athletics programs. We granted certiorari to decide whether this violates the Fourth and Fourteenth Amendments to the United States Constitution.

I

[After observing a sharp increase in drug use in the mid-to-late 80s, and discovering that student athletes were the drug culture leaders, the Vernonia School District (District) brought in speakers and offered classes in order to deter drug use. When the drug problems persisted, the District proposed a drug testing program for student athletes. The drug testing program received unanimous approval from parents who attended a parent "input night" on the proposal, and was subsequently approved by the school board in the fall of 1989. The drug testing program required all interscholastic athletes to sign a form consenting to drug testing which would occur at the beginning of the season for their sport and at random during the season. Acton signed up for football when he was in seventh grade but was not allowed to play because he and his parents would not consent to the drug testing. The Actons filed suit in federal district court seeking declaratory and injunctive relief, claiming that the drug testing program violated the Fourth and Fourteenth Amendments. The district court denied the claims after a bench trial, but the United States Court of Appeals for the Ninth Circuit reversed, holding that the drug testing program violated the Fourth and Fourteenth Amendments.

The Supreme Court, after granting review to determine whether the drug testing program constituted an unreasonable search and seizure under the Fourth Amendment, held six to three, that the drug testing program, designed to curb district-wide drug use, was not an unreasonable search and seizure under the Fourth Amendment.]

II

The Fourth Amendment to the United States Constitution provides that the Federal Government shall not violate "[t]he right of the people to be secure in their persons, houses, papers, and effects, against unreasonable searches and seizures, ..." We have held that the Fourteenth Amendment extends this constitutional guarantee to searches and seizures by state officers, Elkins v. United States, 364 U.S. 206, 213 (1960), including public school officials, New Jersey v. T.L.O., 469 U.S. 325, 336–337 (1985). In Skinner v. Railway Labor Executives' Assn., 489 U.S. 602, 617 (1989), we held that state-compelled collection and testing of urine, such as that required by the Student Athlete Drug Policy, constitutes a "search" subject to the demands of the Fourth Amendment. See also Treasury Employees v. Von Raab, 489 U.S. 656, 665 (1989).

As the text of the Fourth Amendment indicates, the ultimate measure of the constitutionality of a governmental search is "reasonableness." At least in a case such as this, where there was no clear practice, either approving or disapproving the type of search at issue, at the time the constitutional provision was enacted, whether a particular search meets the reasonableness standard " 'is judged by balancing its intrusion on the individual's Fourth Amendment interests against its promotion of legitimate governmental interests.' " *Skinner*, supra, at 619 (quoting Delaware v. Prouse, 440 U.S. 648, 654 (1979)). Where a search is undertaken by law enforcement officials to discover evidence of criminal wrongdoing, this Court has said that reasonableness generally requires the obtaining of a judicial warrant, *Skinner*, supra, at 619. Warrants cannot be issued, of course, without the showing of probable cause required by the Warrant Clause. But a warrant is not required to establish the reasonableness of all government searches; and when a warrant is not required (and the Warrant Clause therefore not applicable), probable cause is not invariably required either. A search unsupported by probable cause can be constitutional, we have said, "when special needs, beyond the normal need for law enforcement, make the warrant and probable-cause requirement impracticable." Griffin v. Wisconsin, 483 U.S. 868, 873 (1987) (internal quotation marks omitted).

We have found such "special needs" to exist in the public-school context. There, the warrant requirement "would unduly interfere with the maintenance of the swift and informal disciplinary procedures [that are] needed," and "strict adherence to the requirement that searches be based upon probable cause" would undercut "the substantial need of teachers and administrators for freedom to maintain order in the schools." *T.L.O.*, supra, 469 U.S., at 340, 341. The school search we approved in *T.L.O.*, while not based on probable cause, was based on individualized suspicion of wrongdoing. As we explicitly acknowledged, however, " 'the Fourth Amendment imposes no irreducible requirement of such suspicion,' " id., at 342, n. 8 (quoting United States v. Martinez–Fuerte, 428 U.S. 543, 560–561 (1976)). We have upheld suspicionless searches and seizures to conduct drug testing of railroad personnel involved in train accidents, see *Skinner*, supra; to conduct random drug testing of federal customs officers who carry arms or are involved in drug interdiction, see *Von Raab*, supra; and to maintain automobile checkpoints looking for illegal immigrants and contraband, *Martinez-Fuerte*, supra, and drunk drivers, Michigan Dept. of State Police v. Sitz, 496 U.S. 444 (1990).

III

The first factor to be considered is the nature of the privacy interest upon which the search here at issue intrudes. The Fourth Amendment does not protect all subjective expectations of privacy, but only those that society recognizes as "legitimate." *T.L.O.*, 469 U.S., at 338. What expectations are legitimate varies, of course, with context, id., at 337, depending, for example, upon whether the individual asserting the privacy interest is at home, at work, in a car, or in a public park. In addition, the legitimacy of certain privacy expectations vis-a-vis the State may depend upon the individual's legal relationship with the State. For example, in *Griffin*, supra, we held that, although a "probationer's home, like anyone else's, is protected by the Fourth Amendmen[t]," the supervisory relationship between probationer and State justifies "a degree of impingement upon [a probationer's] privacy that would not be constitutional if applied to the public at large." 483 U.S., at 873, 875. Central, in our view, to the present case is the fact that the subjects of the Policy are (1) children, who (2) have been committed to the temporary custody of the State as schoolmaster.

Traditionally at common law, and still today, unemancipated minors lack some of the most fundamental rights of self-determination—including even the right of liberty in its narrow sense, i.e., the right to come and go at will. They are subject, even as to their physical freedom, to the control of their parents or guardians. When parents place minor children in private schools for their education, the teachers and administrators of those schools stand in loco parentis over the children entrusted to them. In fact, the tutor or schoolmaster is the very prototype of that status. As Blackstone describes it, a parent "may ... delegate part of his parental authority, during his life, to the tutor or schoolmaster of his child; who is then in loco parentis, and has such a portion of the power of the parent committed to his charge, viz. that of restraint and correction, as may be necessary to answer the purposes for which he is employed." 1 W. Blackstone, Commentaries on the Laws of England 441 (1769).

In *T.L.O.* we rejected the notion that public schools, like private schools, exercise only parental power over their students, which of course is not subject to constitutional constraints. *T.L.O.*, 469 U.S., at 336. Such a view of things, we said, "is not entirely 'consonant with compulsory education laws,'" ibid. (quoting Ingraham v. Wright, 430 U.S. 651, 662 (1977)), and is inconsistent with our prior decisions treating school officials as state actors for purposes of the Due Process and Free Speech Clauses, *T.L.O.*, supra, at 336. But while denying that the State's power over schoolchildren is formally no more than the delegated power of their parents, *T.L.O.* did not deny, but indeed emphasized, that the nature of that power is custodial and tutelary, permitting a degree of supervision and control that could not be exercised over free adults. "[A] proper educational environment requires close supervision of schoolchildren, as well as the enforcement of rules against conduct that would be perfectly permissible if undertaken by an adult." 469 U.S., at 339. While we do not, of course, suggest that public schools as a general matter have such a degree of control over children as to give rise to a constitutional "duty to protect," see DeShaney v. Winnebago County Dept. of Social Servs., 489 U.S. 189, 200 (1989), we have acknowledged that for many purposes "school authorities ac[t] in loco parentis," Bethel School Dist. No. 403 v. Fraser, 478 U.S. 675, 684 (1986), with the power and indeed the duty to "inculcate the habits and manners of civility," id., at 681 (internal quotation marks omitted). Thus, while children assuredly do not "shed their constitutional rights ... at the schoolhouse gate," Tinker v. Des Moines Independent Community School Dist., 393 U.S. 503, 506 (1969), the nature of those rights is what is appropriate for children in school. See, e.g., Goss v. Lopez, 419 U.S. 565, 581–582 (1975) (due process for a student challenging disciplinary suspension requires only that the teacher "informally discuss the alleged misconduct with the student minutes after it has occurred"); *Fraser*, supra, 478 U.S., at 683 ("[I]t is a highly appropriate function of public school education to prohibit the use of vulgar and offensive terms in public discourse"); Hazelwood School Dist. v. Kuhlmeier, 484 U.S. 260, 273 (1988) (public school authorities may censor school-sponsored publications, so long as the censorship is "reasonably related to legitimate pedagogical concerns"); *Ingraham*, supra, 430 U.S., at 682 ("[I]mposing additional administrative safeguards [upon corporal punishment] ... would ... entail a significant intrusion into an area of primary educational responsibility").

Fourth Amendment rights, no less than First and Fourteenth Amendment rights, are different in public schools than elsewhere; the "reasonableness" inquiry cannot disregard the schools' custodial and tutelary responsibility for children. For their own good and that of their classmates, public school children are routinely required to submit to various physical examinations, and to be vaccinated against various diseases.... Particularly with regard to medical examinations and procedures, therefore, "students within the school environment have a lesser expectation of privacy than members of the population generally." *T.L.O.*, 469 U.S., at 348 (POWELL, J., concurring).

Legitimate privacy expectations are even less with regard to student athletes. School sports are not for the bashful. They require "suiting up" before each practice or event, and showering and changing afterwards. Public school locker rooms, the usual sites for these activities, are not notable for the privacy they afford. The locker rooms in Vernonia are typical: no individual dressing rooms are provided; shower heads are lined up along a wall, unseparated by any sort of partition or curtain; not even all the toilet stalls have doors. As the United States Court of Appeals for the Seventh Circuit has noted, there is "an element of 'communal undress' inherent in athletic participation," Schaill by Kross v. Tippecanoe County School Corp., 864 F.2d 1309, 1318 (1988).

There is an additional respect in which school athletes have a reduced expectation of privacy. By choosing to "go out for the team," they voluntarily subject themselves to a degree of regulation even higher than that imposed on students generally. In Vernonia's public schools, they must submit to a preseason physical exam (James testified that his included the giving of a urine sample), they must acquire adequate insurance coverage or sign an insurance waiver, maintain a minimum grade point average, and comply with any "rules of conduct, dress, training hours and related matters as may be established for each sport by the head coach and athletic director with the principal's approval." Somewhat like adults who choose to participate in a "closely regulated industry," students who voluntarily participate in school athletics have reason to expect intrusions upon normal rights and privileges, including privacy. See *Skinner*, 489 U.S., at 627; United States v. Biswell, 406 U.S. 311, 316 (1972).

IV

Having considered the scope of the legitimate expectation of privacy at issue here, we turn next to the character of the intrusion that is complained of. We recognized in *Skinner* that collecting the samples for urinalysis intrudes upon "an excretory function traditionally shielded by great privacy." *Skinner*, 489 U.S., at 626. We noted, however, that the degree of intrusion depends upon the manner in which production of the urine sample is monitored. Ibid. Under the District's Policy, male students produce samples at a urinal along a wall. They remain fully clothed and are only observed from behind, if at all. Female students produce samples in an enclosed stall, with a female monitor standing outside listening only for sounds of tampering. These conditions are nearly identical to those typically encountered in public restrooms, which men, women, and especially school children use daily. Under such conditions, the privacy interests compromised by the process of obtaining the urine sample are in our view negligible.

The other privacy-invasive aspect of urinalysis is, of course, the information it discloses concerning the state of the subject's body, and the materials he has ingested. In this regard it is significant that the tests at issue here look only for drugs, and not for whether the student is, for example, epileptic, pregnant, or diabetic. See *Skinner*, supra, at 617. Moreover, the drugs for which the samples are screened are standard, and do not vary according to the identity of the student. And finally, the results of the tests are disclosed only to a limited class of school personnel who have a need to know; and they are not turned over to law enforcement authorities or used for any internal disciplinary function.

Respondents argue, however, that the District's Policy is in fact more intrusive than this suggests, because it requires the students, if they are to avoid sanctions for a falsely positive test, to identify in advance prescription medications they are taking. We agree that this raises some cause for concern. In Von Raab, we flagged as one of the salutary features of the Customs Service drug-testing program the fact that employees were not required to disclose medical information unless they tested positive, and, even then, the information was supplied to a licensed physician rather than to the Government employer. See *Von Raab*, 489 U.S., at 672–673, n. 2. On the other hand, we have never indicated that requiring advance disclosure of medications is per se unreasonable. Indeed, in *Skinner* we held that it was not "a significant invasion of privacy." *Skinner*, 489 U.S., at 626, n. 7. It can be argued that, in *Skinner*, the disclosure went only to the medical personnel taking the sample, and the Government personnel analyzing it, see id., at 609, but see id., at 610 (railroad personnel responsible for forwarding the sample, and presumably accompanying information, to the Government's testing lab); and that disclosure to teachers and coaches—to persons who personally know the student—is a greater invasion of privacy. Assuming for the sake of argument that both those propositions are true, we do not believe they establish a difference that respondents are entitled to rely on here.

The General Authorization Form that respondents refused to sign, which refusal was the basis for James's exclusion from the sports program, said only (in relevant part): "I ... authorize the Vernonia School District to conduct a test on a urine specimen which I provide to test for drugs and/or alcohol use. I also authorize the release of information concerning the results of such a test to the Vernonia School District and to the parents and/or guardians of the student." While the practice of the District seems to have been to have a school official take medication information from the student at the time of the test, that practice is not set forth in, or required by, the Policy, which says simply: "Student athletes who ... are or have been taking prescription medication must provide verification (either by a copy of the prescription or by doctor's authorization) prior to being tested."

It may well be that, if and when James was selected for random testing at a time that he was taking medication, the School District would have permitted him to provide the requested information in a confidential manner—for example, in a sealed envelope delivered to the testing lab. Nothing in the Policy contradicts that, and when respondents choose, in effect, to challenge the Policy on its face, we will not assume the worst. Accordingly, we reach the same conclusion as in *Skinner*: that the invasion of privacy was not significant.

V

Finally, we turn to consider the nature and immediacy of the governmental concern at issue here, and the efficacy of this means for meeting it. In both *Skinner* and *Von Raab*, we characterized the government interest motivating the search as "compelling." *Skinner*, supra, 489 U.S., at 628 (interest in preventing railway accidents); *Von Raab*, supra, 489 U.S., at 670 (interest in insuring fitness of customs officials to interdict drugs and handle firearms). Relying on these cases, the District Court held that because the District's program also called for drug testing in the absence of individualized suspicion, the District "must demonstrate a 'compelling need' for the program." The Court of Appeals appears to have agreed with this view. It is a mistake, however, to think that the phrase "compelling state interest," in the Fourth Amendment context, describes a fixed, minimum quantum of governmental concern, so that one can dispose of a case by answering in isolation the question: Is there a compelling state interest here? Rather, the phrase describes an interest which appears important enough to justify the particular search at hand, in light of other factors which show the search to be relatively intrusive upon a genuine expectation of privacy. Whether that relatively high degree of government concern is necessary in this case or not, we think it is met.

That the nature of the concern is important—indeed, perhaps compelling—can hardly be doubted. Deterring drug use by our Nation's schoolchildren is at least as important as enhancing efficient enforcement of the Nation's laws against the importation of drugs, which was the governmental concern in *Von Raab*, supra, 489 U.S., at 668, or deterring drug use by engineers and trainmen, which was the governmental concern in *Skinner*, supra, at 628. School years are the time when the physical, psychological, and addictive effects of drugs are most severe. "Maturing nervous systems are more critically impaired by intoxicants than mature ones are; childhood losses in learning are lifelong and profound"; "children grow chemically dependent more quickly than adults, and their record of recovery is depressingly poor." Hawley, The Bumpy Road to Drug–Free Schools, 72 Phi Delta Kappan 310, 314 (1990). And of course the effects of a drug-infested school are visited not just upon the users, but upon the entire student body and faculty, as the educational process is disrupted. In the present case, moreover, the necessity for the State to act is magnified by the fact that this evil is being visited not just upon individuals at large, but upon children for whom it has undertaken a special responsibility of care and direction. Finally, it must not be lost sight of that this program is directed more narrowly to drug use by school athletes, where the risk of immediate physical harm to the drug user or those with whom he is playing his sport is particularly high. Apart from psychological effects, which include impairment of judgment, slow reaction time, and a lessening of the perception of pain, the particular drugs screened by the District's Policy have been demonstrated to pose substantial physical risks to athletes. . . .

As for the immediacy of the District's concerns: We are not inclined to question—indeed, we could not possibly find clearly erroneous—the District Court's conclusion that "a large segment of the student body, particularly those involved in interscholastic athletics, was in a state of rebellion," that "[d]isciplinary actions had reached 'epidemic proportions,'" and that "the rebellion was being fueled by alcohol and drug abuse as well as by the student's misperceptions about the drug culture." That is an immediate crisis of greater proportions than existed in *Skinner*, where we upheld the Government's drug testing program based on findings of drug use by railroad employees nationwide, without proof that a problem existed on the particular railroads whose employees were subject to the test. See *Skinner*, 489 U.S., at 607. And of much greater proportions than existed in *Von Raab*, where there was no documented history of drug use by any customs officials. See *Von Raab*, 489 U.S., at 673; id., at 683 (SCALIA, J., dissenting).

As to the efficacy of this means for addressing the problem: It seems to us self-evident that a drug problem largely fueled by the "role model" effect of athletes' drug use, and of particular danger to athletes, is effectively addressed by making sure that athletes do not use drugs. Respondents argue that a "less intrusive means to the same end" was available, namely, "drug testing on suspicion of drug use." We have repeatedly refused to declare that only the "least intrusive" search practicable can be reasonable under the Fourth Amendment. *Skinner*, supra, at 629, n. 9 (collecting cases). Respondents' alternative entails substantial difficulties—if it is indeed practicable at all. It may be impracticable, for one thing, simply because the parents who are willing to accept random drug testing for athletes are not willing to accept accusatory drug testing for all students, which transforms the process into a badge of shame. Respondents' proposal brings the risk that teachers will impose testing arbitrarily upon troublesome but not drug-likely students. It generates the expense of defending lawsuits that charge such arbitrary imposition, or that simply demand greater process before accusatory drug testing is imposed. And not least of all, it adds to the ever-expanding diversionary duties of schoolteachers the new function of spotting and bringing to account drug abuse, a task for which they are ill prepared, and which is not readily compatible with their vocation. Cf. *Skinner*, supra, at 628 (quoting 50 Fed.Reg. 31526 (1985)) (a drug impaired individual "will seldom display any outward 'signs detectable by the lay person or, in many cases, even the physician.'"); *Goss*, 419 U.S., at 594 (POWELL, J., dissenting) ("There is an ongoing relationship, one in which the teacher must occupy many roles—educator, adviser, friend, and, at times, parent-substitute. It is rarely adversary in nature . . .") (footnote omitted). In many respects, we think, testing based on "suspicion" of drug use would not be better, but worse.

VI

Taking into account all the factors we have considered above—the decreased expectation of privacy, the relative unobtrusiveness of the search, and the severity of the need met by the search—we conclude Vernonia's Policy is reasonable and hence constitutional.

We caution against the assumption that suspicionless drug testing will readily pass constitutional muster in other contexts. The most significant element in this case is the first we discussed: that the Policy was undertaken in furtherance of the government's responsibilities, under a public school system, as guardian and tutor of children entrusted to its care. Just as when the government conducts a search in its capacity as employer (a warrantless search of an absent employee's desk to obtain an urgently needed file, for example), the relevant question is whether that intrusion upon privacy is one that a reasonable employer might engage in, see O'Connor v. Ortega, 480 U.S. 709 (1987); so also when the government acts as guardian and tutor the relevant question is whether the search is one that a reasonable guardian and tutor might undertake. Given the findings of need made by the District Court, we conclude that in the present case it is.

We may note that the primary guardians of Vernonia's schoolchildren appear to agree. The record shows no objection to this districtwide program by any parents other than the couple before us here—even though, as we have described, a public meeting was held to obtain parents' views. We find insufficient basis to contradict the judgment of Vernonia's parents, its school board, and the District Court, as to what was reasonably in the interest of these children under the circumstances.

* * *

The Ninth Circuit held that Vernonia's Policy not only violated the Fourth Amendment, but also, by reason of that violation, contravened Article I, § 9 of the Oregon Constitution. Our conclusion that the former holding was in error means that the latter holding rested on a flawed premise. We therefore vacate the judgment, and remand the case to the Court of Appeals for further proceedings consistent with this opinion.

It is so ordered.

[In a brief concurring opinion Justice Ginsburg expresses reservations whether a policy such as the one in this case, limited as it is to student athletes, could be applied more broadly to students generally. Justice O'Connor, joined by Justice Stevens and Justice Souter, dissented, arguing that drug testing of student athletes can only be reasonable when justified by some level of suspicion. Suspicionless searches, according to Justice O'Connor, have historically been held to be unreasonable, but recently have been permitted only where "a suspicion-based regime would be ineffectual."]

NOTES

(1) Much of the commentary following *Acton* was critical of the Court's decision, ranging from those who thought it was just wrong, see, e.g., Amanda E. Bishop, Note, Students, Urinalysis & Extracurricular Activities: How Vernonia's Aftermath is Trampling Fourth Amendment Rights, 10 Health Matrix 217 (2000), to those who thought it lacked sufficient clarity to guide courts in applying it in

subsequent cases, see, e.g., Benjamin Gerald Dusing, Constitutional Standards for Suspicionless Student Drug Testing: A Moving Target, 88 Ky.L.J. 687 (2000).

(2) *Acton* seems to be having the greatest influence in two kinds of cases: Those that are similar on the facts and those that, at least before *Acton*, might have presented close questions on the issue of reasonableness of the search. As to the first kind, one might expect there would be few cases factually similar to *Acton*. As an example of one such case, see *People v. Pruitt*, 278 Ill.App.3d 194, 214 Ill.Dec. 974, 662 N.E.2d 540 (1996). In that case the Illinois Court of Appeals upheld the general suspicionless search of students through use of a magnetometer (metal detector), resulting in the discovery and seizure of a handgun. In so holding, the court relied on *T.L.O.* but also on *Acton*:

> In *Vernonia*, the Supreme Court approved a school district drug policy that authorized random urinalysis drug testing of student athletes. The decision was based on the students' decreased expectation of privacy—they were public school students, the relative unobtrusiveness of the search—producing urine samples, and the severity of the need met by the search—deterring drug use by children. The policy satisfied the Fourth Amendment's reasonableness requirement, said the Court. No individualized suspicion was required.
>
> .　.　.
>
> The searches of Pruitt and all the other Fenger students were directed and controlled by school officials, although actually carried out by Chicago police officers. The metal detectors belonged to the school board. The purpose of the screening was to protect and maintain a proper educational environment for all students, not to investigate and secure evidence of a crime. Because all students were required to walk through the detectors no official discretion or opportunity to harass was involved. The intrusion was minimal, not involving any physical touching until the metal detector reacted. (Certainly it was less intrusive than the acts required of the student athletes in the Vernonia school district.) Once the metal detector reacted, the facts were sufficient to justify a frisk.

278 Ill.App.3d at 204–05, 662 N.E.2d at 547. Other courts have agreed. See, e.g., *In re Latasha W.*, 60 Cal.App.4th 1524, 70 Cal.Rptr.2d 886 (1998); *In re S.S.*, 452 Pa.Super. 15, 680 A.2d 1172 (1996).

An example of the other kind of case in which *Acton* has been influential is *People v. Dilworth*, 169 Ill.2d 195, 214 Ill.Dec. 456, 661 N.E.2d 310 (1996). In *Dilworth* the Illinois Supreme Court upheld a warrantless school search conducted by a police liaison officer. The officer was an employee of the Joliet Police Department (rather than the school district) but was assigned to the school full time as a member of its staff. His primary purpose at the school was to prevent criminal activity, although he also handled some school disciplinary problems. The court held that the officer had reasonable suspicion to conduct the search, although the real issue was whether the search was one "conducted by school officials in conjunction with or at the behest of law enforcement agencies," to borrow the language from *T.L.O.* The court borrowed from the "special needs" analysis of *Acton*:

> ... There, the United States Supreme Court utilized a three-prong test for determining whether special needs beyond normal law enforcement require a departure from the usual Fourth Amendment standard of probable cause and a warrant. The competing interests of the individual and the State were balanced by an examination of the following: (1) the nature of the privacy interest upon which the search intrudes, (2) the character of the search, and (3) the nature

and immediacy of the governmental concern at issue, and the efficacy of the means for meeting it.

An analysis of each of these three factors supports our holding that reasonable suspicion, not probable cause, is the proper Fourth Amendment standard to be applied in this case. As to the first factor, the nature of the privacy interest upon which the search intrudes, it must be remembered that we are dealing with schoolchildren here. In this respect, the *Vernonia* majority stated:

> "Fourth Amendment rights ... are different in public schools than elsewhere; the 'reasonableness' inquiry cannot disregard the schools' custodial and tutelary responsibility for children. For their own good and that of their classmates, public school children are routinely required [to do a variety of things].... '[S]tudents within the school environment have a lesser expectation of privacy than members of the population generally.' *T.L.O.*, 469 U.S., at 348 (Powell, J., concurring)." *Vernonia*, 515 U.S. at ___, 115 S.Ct. at 2392.

The second factor is the character of the search. The intrusion complained of in this case is the seizure and search of defendant's flashlight by a school liaison officer. Of utmost significance, the liaison officer had an *individualized* suspicion that defendant's flashlight contained drugs. He confirmed his suspicion by searching only that flashlight. Thus, we find this search as conducted to be minimally intrusive.

The final factor—the nature and immediacy of the governmental concern at issue, and the efficacy of the means for meeting it—also weighs in favor of the reasonable suspicion standard here. There is no doubt that the State has a compelling interest in providing a proper educational environment for students, which includes maintaining its schools free from the ravages of drugs. As to the efficacy of the means for meeting this interest, it is relevant that the search at issue took place at the alternate school for students with behavioral disorders. In order to maintain a proper educational environment at this particular school, school officials found it necessary to have a full-time police liaison as a member of its staff. The liaison officer assisted teachers and school officials with the difficult job of preserving order in this school.

169 Ill.2d at 208–10, 661 N.E.2d at 318. The Supreme Court denied certiorari in the *Dilworth* case. *Dilworth v. Illinois*, 517 U.S. 1197, 116 S.Ct. 1692, 134 L.Ed.2d 793 (1996). Other courts similarly have upheld searches at school in which the determination of reasonableness was aided by the *Acton* special needs analysis. See, e.g., *Commonwealth v. Cass*, 551 Pa. 25, 709 A.2d 350 (1998); *In re Patrick Y.*, 358 Md. 50, 746 A.2d 405 (2000).

In perhaps the most sweeping extension of the *Acton* special needs analysis, the California Supreme Court held that school officials, because of their broad authority over student behavior, school safety, and the learning environment, have the power to stop a student in order to ask questions or to conduct an investigation, even in the absence of reasonable suspicion, as long as such authority is not exercised in an arbitrary, capricious, or harassing manner. In *In re Randy G.*, 26 Cal.4th 556, 110 Cal.Rptr.2d 516, 28 P.3d 239 (2001), the court upheld a search, conducted by a school security officer, that produced a knife with a locking blade. The court saw no reason to draw a distinction between school security officers and other school personnel who delegate to them responsibility for school safety.

School safety, particularly in light of the Columbine tragedy, is an issue of paramount concern. Schools have a duty to ensure the safety of all students in their care; Justice Scalia in *Acton* referred to it as the school's role as both "custodian" and "tutor." At the same time, students are entitled, to some degree at least, to protection of their privacy under the Fourth Amendment. Balancing the two interests is fraught with constitutional peril. Schools, particularly if they cannot afford metal detectors, might opt to frisk all students as they enter school buildings. For an analysis of the constitutional dilemma posed, see Michael A. Sprow, The High Price of Safety: May Public Schools Institute a Policy of Frisking Students As They Enter the Building?, 54 Baylor L.Rev. 133 (2002). The author concludes that under the three-pronged test announced by the Court in *Acton*, such a policy would be unconstitutional because, despite the state's interest in student safety, the invasion of privacy is too great in the absence of individualized suspicion. Id. at 158–66. This analysis, however, was written before the Court's decision in *Board of Education v. Earls*, which follows. After reading *Earls*, re-think the question of the legitimacy of frisking students.

(3) Following *Acton*, Anne Proffitt Dupre reviewed the Court's long line of decisions touching on the nature and scope of school authority in the context of both the First and Fourth Amendments. Professor Dupre describes two models of public education:

> In the social reconstruction model, the school is an institution where power is necessary only to facilitate the child in his attempts to reconstruct a new social order. In fact, the primary mission of the school under this model is to effect "cultural change" in an attempt to move toward a new "planet-wide democratic order." The school as a force in reconstructing a new social order was a reverse of the traditional function of public education in American society, in which the power of the school was necessary to inculcate—to reproduce—society's traditions and habits.

> In contrast to the social reproduction model, which would allow the school the power it needed to mold children in society's image, the social reconstruction model would allow the student the power the student needs to avoid perpetuating society's flaws. To achieve its goal, the reconstruction model endeavors to support those students who rebut the values that the school is trying to inculcate.

Anne Proffitt Dupre,* Should Students Have Constitutional Rights? Keeping Order in the Public Schools, 65 Geo.Wash.L.Rev. 49, 65 (1996).

Dupre views *Acton* as a renunciation of *Tinker* and the social reconstruction model and an endorsement of the social reproduction model. She argues that, while *Acton* has logical (and historical) flaws, it nevertheless represents a major step toward restoring some modicum of order in the public schools and reviving public confidence in the public school as an institution. The latter point is important, she maintains: "The amount of power we are willing to confer upon our institutions is a function of the confidence we have in those institutions to wield that power effectively." Id. at 64.

(4) If suspicionless searches in the form of random urinalysis can be conducted in the case of athletes, would such random drug-testing be permissible in the case of students in other groups, e.g., band, drama club, chorus, and cheerleading? Does the school district have to demonstrate a prevalent drug problem and that the drug problem seems to center around students in that particular group, as in *Acton*? Consider the case that follows.

Board of Education of Independent School District No. 92 of Pottawatomie County v. Earls

Supreme Court of the United States, 2002.
536 U.S. 822, 122 S.Ct. 2559, 153 L.Ed.2d 735.

■ JUSTICE THOMAS delivered the opinion of the Court.

The Student Activities Drug Testing Policy implemented by the Board of Education of Independent School District No. 92 of Pottawatomie County (School District) requires all students who participate in competitive extracurricular activities to submit to drug testing. Because this Policy reasonably serves the School District's important interest in detecting and preventing drug use among its students, we hold that it is constitutional.

I

... In practice, the Policy has been applied only to competitive extracurricular activities sanctioned by the Oklahoma Secondary Schools Activities Association, such as the Academic Team, Future Farmers of America, Future Homemakers of America, band, choir, pom-pom, cheerleading, and athletics. Under the Policy, students are required to take a drug test before participating in an extracurricular activity, must submit to random drug testing while participating in that activity, and must agree to be tested at any time upon reasonable suspicion....

At the time of their suit, both respondents attended Tecumseh High School. Respondent Lindsay Earls was a member of the show choir, the marching band, the Academic Team, and the National Honor Society. Respondent Daniel James sought to participate in the Academic Team. Together with their parents, Earls and James brought a § 1983 action against the School District, challenging the Policy both on its face and as applied to their participation in extracurricular activities. They alleged that the Policy violates the Fourth Amendment as incorporated by the Fourteenth Amendment and requested injunctive and declarative relief. They also argued that the School District failed to identify a special need for testing students who participate in extracurricular activities, and that the "Drug Testing Policy neither addresses a proven problem nor promises to bring any benefit to students or the school."

Applying the principles articulated in Vernonia School Dist. 47J v. Acton, 515 U.S. 646, 115 S.Ct. 2386, 132 L.Ed.2d 564 (1995), in which we upheld the suspicionless drug testing of school athletes, the United States District Court for the Western District of Oklahoma rejected respondents' claim that the Policy was unconstitutional and granted summary judgment to the School District. The court noted that "special needs" exist in the public school context and that, although the School District did "not show a drug problem of epidemic proportions," there was a history of drug abuse starting in 1970 that presented "legitimate cause for concern." The District Court also held that the Policy was effective because "[i]t can scarcely be disputed that the drug problem among the student body is effectively addressed by making sure that the large number of students participating in competitive, extracurricular activities do not use drugs."

The United States Court of Appeals for the Tenth Circuit reversed, holding that the Policy violated the Fourth Amendment. The Court of Appeals agreed with the District Court that the Policy must be evaluated in the "unique environment of the school setting," but reached a different conclusion as to the Policy's constitutionality. Before imposing a suspicion-less drug testing program, the Court of Appeals concluded that a school "must demonstrate that there is some identifiable drug abuse problem among a sufficient number of those subject to the testing, such that testing that group of students will actually redress its drug problem." The Court of Appeals then held that because the School District failed to demonstrate such a problem existed among Tecumseh students participating in competitive extracurricular activities, the Policy was unconstitutional. We granted certiorari, and now reverse.

II

The Fourth Amendment to the United States Constitution protects "[t]he right of the people to be secure in their persons, houses, papers, and effects, against unreasonable searches and seizures." Searches by public school officials, such as the collection of urine samples, implicate Fourth Amendment interests. See *Vernonia, supra,* at 652, 115 S.Ct. 2386; cf. New Jersey v. T.L.O., 469 U.S. 325, 334, 105 S.Ct. 733, 83 L.Ed.2d 720 (1985). We must therefore review the School District's Policy for "reasonableness," which is the touchstone of the constitutionality of a governmental search.

In the criminal context, reasonableness usually requires a showing of probable cause. See, e.g., Skinner v. Railway Labor Executives' Assn., 489 U.S. 602, 619, 109 S.Ct. 1402, 103 L.Ed.2d 639 (1989). The probable-cause standard, however, "is peculiarly related to criminal investigations" and may be unsuited to determining the reasonableness of administrative searches where the "Government seeks to *prevent* the development of hazardous conditions." Treasury Employees v. Von Raab, 489 U.S. 656, 667–668, 109 S.Ct. 1384, 103 L.Ed.2d 685 (1989). The Court has also held that a warrant and finding of probable cause are unnecessary in the public school context because such requirements " 'would unduly interfere with the maintenance of the swift and informal disciplinary procedures [that are] needed.' " *Vernonia, supra,* at 653, 115 S.Ct. 2386 (quoting *T.L.O., supra,* at 340–341, 105 S.Ct. 733).

Given that the School District's Policy is not in any way related to the conduct of criminal investigations, see Part II–B, *infra,* respondents do not contend that the School District requires probable cause before testing students for drug use. Respondents instead argue that drug testing must be based at least on some level of individualized suspicion. It is true that we generally determine the reasonableness of a search by balancing the nature of the intrusion on the individual's privacy against the promotion of legitimate governmental interests. See Delaware v. Prouse, 440 U.S. 648, 654, 99 S.Ct. 1391, 59 L.Ed.2d 660 (1979). But we have long held that "the Fourth Amendment imposes no irreducible requirement of [individualized] suspicion." United States v. Martinez–Fuerte, 428 U.S. 543, 561, 96 S.Ct. 3074, 49 L.Ed.2d 1116 (1976). "[I]n certain limited circumstances, the Government's need to discover such latent or hidden conditions, or to prevent their development, is sufficiently compelling to justify the intrusion on privacy entailed by conducting such searches without any measure of individualized suspicion." *Von Raab, supra,* at 668, 109 S.Ct. 1384; see also *Skinner, supra,* at 624, 109 S.Ct. 1402. Therefore, in the context of safety and administrative regulations, a search unsupported by probable cause may be reasonable "when 'special needs, beyond the normal need for law enforcement, make the warrant and probable-cause requirement impracticable.' " Griffin v. Wisconsin, 483 U.S. 868, 873, 107 S.Ct. 3164, 97 L.Ed.2d 709 (1987) (quoting *T.L.O., supra,* at 351, 105 S.Ct. 733 (Blackmun, J., concurring in judgment)); see also *Vernonia, supra,* at 653, 115 S.Ct. 2386; *Skinner, supra,* at 619, 109 S.Ct. 1402.

Significantly, this Court has previously held that "special needs" inhere in the public school context. See *Vernonia, supra,* at 653, 115 S.Ct. 2386; *T.L.O., supra,* at 339–340, 105 S.Ct. 733. While schoolchildren do not shed their constitutional rights when they enter the schoolhouse, see Tinker v. Des Moines Independent Community School Dist., 393 U.S. 503, 506, 89 S.Ct. 733, 21 L.Ed.2d 731 (1969), "Fourth Amendment rights . . . are different in public schools than elsewhere; the 'reasonableness' inquiry cannot disregard the schools' custodial and tutelary responsibility for children." *Vernonia,* 515 U.S., at 656, 115 S.Ct. 2386. In particular, a finding of individualized suspicion may not be necessary when a school conducts drug testing.

In *Vernonia,* this Court held that the suspicionless drug testing of athletes was constitutional. The Court, however, did not simply authorize all school drug testing, but rather conducted a fact-specific balancing of the intrusion on the children's Fourth Amendment rights against the promotion of legitimate governmental interests. See *id.,* at 652–653, 115 S.Ct. 2386. Applying the principles of *Vernonia* to the somewhat different facts of this case, we conclude that Tecumseh's Policy is also constitutional.

A

We first consider the nature of the privacy interest allegedly compromised by the drug testing. See *id.,* at 654, 115 S.Ct. 2386. As in *Vernonia,* the context of the public school environment serves as the backdrop for the analysis of the privacy interest at stake and the reasonableness of the drug testing policy in general. See *ibid.* ("Central . . . is the fact that the subjects of the Policy are (1) children, who (2) have been committed to the temporary custody of the State as schoolmaster"); see also *id.,* at 665, 115 S.Ct. 2386 ("The most significant element in this case is the first we discussed: that the Policy was undertaken in furtherance of the government's responsibilities, under a public school system, as guardian and tutor of children entrusted to its care"); *ibid.* ("[W]hen the government acts as guardian and tutor the relevant question is whether the search is one that a reasonable guardian and tutor might undertake").

A student's privacy interest is limited in a public school environment where the State is responsible for maintaining discipline, health, and safety. Schoolchildren are routinely required to submit to physical examinations and vaccinations against disease. See *id.,* at 656, 115 S.Ct. 2386. Securing order in the school environment sometimes requires that students be subjected to greater controls than those appropriate for adults. See *T.L.O.,* 469 U.S., at 350, 105 S.Ct. 733 (Powell, J., concurring) ("Without first establishing discipline and maintaining order, teachers cannot begin to educate their students. And apart from education, the school has the obligation to protect pupils from mistreatment by other children, and also to protect teachers themselves from violence by the few students whose conduct in recent years has prompted national concern").

Respondents argue that because children participating in nonathletic extracurricular activities are not subject to regular physicals and communal undress, they have a stronger expectation of privacy than the athletes tested in *Vernonia.* This distinction, however, was not essential to our decision in *Vernonia,* which depended primarily upon the school's custodial responsibility and authority.

In any event, students who participate in competitive extracurricular activities voluntarily subject themselves to many of the same intrusions on their privacy as do athletes. Some of these clubs and activities require occasional off-campus travel and communal undress. All of them have their own rules and requirements for participating students that do not apply to the student body as a whole. . . .

B

Next, we consider the character of the intrusion imposed by the Policy. See *Vernonia, supra,* at 658, 115 S.Ct. 2386. Urination is "an excretory function traditionally shielded by great privacy." *Skinner,* 489 U.S., at 626, 109 S.Ct. 1402. But the "degree of intrusion" on one's privacy caused by collecting a urine sample "depends upon the manner in which production of the urine sample is monitored." *Vernonia, supra,* at 658, 115 S.Ct. 2386.

Under the Policy, a faculty monitor waits outside the closed restroom stall for the student to produce a sample and must "listen for the normal sounds of urination in order to guard against tampered specimens and to insure an accurate chain of custody." App. 199. The monitor then pours the sample into two bottles that are sealed and placed into a mailing pouch along with a consent form signed by the student. This procedure is virtually identical to that reviewed in *Vernonia,* except that it additionally protects privacy by allowing male students to produce their samples behind a closed stall. Given that we considered the method of collection in *Vernonia* a "negligible" intrusion, 515 U.S., at 658, 115 S.Ct. 2386, the method here is even less problematic.

In addition, the Policy clearly requires that the test results be kept in confidential files separate from a student's other educational records and released to school personnel only on a "need to know" basis. . . .

Moreover, the test results are not turned over to any law enforcement authority. Nor do the test results here lead to the imposition of discipline or have any academic consequences. Cf. *Vernonia, supra,* at 658, and n. 2, 115 S.Ct. 2386. Rather, the only consequence of a failed drug test is to limit the student's privilege of participating in extracurricular activities. . . .

Given the minimally intrusive nature of the sample collection and the limited uses to which the test results are put, we conclude that the invasion of students' privacy is not significant.

C

Finally, this Court must consider the nature and immediacy of the government's concerns and the efficacy of the Policy in meeting them. See *Vernonia,* 515 U.S., at 660, 115 S.Ct. 2386. This Court has already articulated in detail the importance of the governmental concern in preventing drug use by schoolchildren. See *id.,* at 661–662, 115 S.Ct. 2386. The drug abuse problem among our Nation's youth has hardly abated since *Vernonia* was decided in 1995. In fact, evidence suggests that it has only grown worse. As in *Vernonia,* "the necessity for the State to act is magnified by the fact that this evil is being visited not just upon individuals at large, but upon children for whom it has undertaken a special responsibility of care and direction." *Id.,* at 662, 115 S.Ct. 2386. The health and safety risks identified in *Vernonia* apply with equal force to Tecumseh's children. Indeed, the nationwide drug epidemic makes the war against drugs a pressing concern in every school.

Additionally, the School District in this case has presented specific evidence of drug use at Tecumseh schools. Teachers testified that they had seen students who appeared to be under the influence of drugs and that they had heard students speaking openly about using drugs. A drug dog found marijuana cigarettes near the school parking lot. Police officers once found drugs or drug paraphernalia in a car driven by a Future Farmers of America member. And the school board president reported that people in the community were calling the board to discuss the "drug situation." We decline to second-guess the finding of the District Court that "[v]iewing the evidence as a whole, it cannot be reasonably disputed that the [School District] was faced with a 'drug problem' when it adopted the Policy."

Respondents consider the proffered evidence insufficient and argue that there is no "real and immediate interest" to justify a policy of drug testing nonathletes. We have recognized, however, that "[a] demonstrated problem of drug abuse ... [is] not in all cases necessary to the validity of a testing regime," but that some showing does "shore up an assertion of special need for a suspicionless general search program." Chandler v. Miller, 520 U.S. 305, 319, 117 S.Ct. 1295, 137 L.Ed.2d 513 (1997). The School District has provided sufficient evidence to shore up the need for its drug testing program.

Furthermore, this Court has not required a particularized or pervasive drug problem before allowing the government to conduct suspicionless drug testing. For instance, in *Von Raab* the Court upheld the drug testing of customs officials on a purely preventive basis, without any documented history of drug use by such officials. See 489 U.S., at 673, 109 S.Ct. 1384....

Given the nationwide epidemic of drug use, and the evidence of increased drug use in Tecumseh schools, it was entirely reasonable for the School District to enact this particular drug testing policy. We reject the Court of Appeals' novel test that "any district seeking to impose a random suspicionless drug testing policy as a condition to participation in a school activity must demonstrate that there is some identifiable drug abuse problem among a sufficient number of those subject to the testing, such that testing that group of students will actually redress its drug problem." Among other problems, it would be difficult to administer such a test. As we cannot articulate a threshold level of drug use that would suffice to justify a drug testing program for schoolchildren, we refuse to fashion what would in effect be a constitutional quantum of drug use necessary to show a "drug problem."

. . .

We also reject respondents' argument that drug testing must presumptively be based upon an individualized reasonable suspicion of wrongdoing because such a testing regime would be less intrusive. In this context, the Fourth Amendment does not require a finding of individualized suspicion, and we decline to impose such a requirement on schools attempting to prevent and detect drug use by students. Moreover, we question whether testing based on individualized suspicion in fact would be less intrusive. Such a regime would place an additional burden on public school teachers who are already tasked with the difficult job of maintaining order and discipline. . . .

Finally, we find that testing students who participate in extracurricular activities is a reasonably effective means of addressing the School District's legitimate concerns in preventing, deterring, and detecting drug use. While in *Vernonia* there might have been a closer fit between the testing of athletes and the trial court's finding that the drug problem was "fueled by the 'role model' effect of athletes' drug use," such a finding was not essential to the holding. 515 U.S., at 663, 115 S.Ct. 2386; cf. *id.*, at 684–685, 115 S.Ct. 2386 (O'CONNOR, J., dissenting) (questioning the extent of the drug problem, especially as applied to athletes). *Vernonia* did not require the school to test the group of students most likely to use drugs, but rather considered the constitutionality of the program in the context of the public school's custodial responsibilities. Evaluating the Policy in this context, we conclude that the drug testing of Tecumseh students who participate in extracurricular activities effectively serves the School District's interest in protecting the safety and health of its students.

III

Within the limits of the Fourth Amendment, local school boards must assess the desirability of drug testing schoolchildren. In upholding the constitutionality of the Policy, we express no opinion as to its wisdom. Rather, we hold only that Tecumseh's Policy is a reasonable means of furthering the School District's important interest in preventing and deterring drug use among its schoolchildren. Accordingly, we reverse the judgment of the Court of Appeals.

It is so ordered.

■ [The concurring opinion of Justice Breyer has been omitted.]

■ [The separate dissenting opinion of Justice O'Connor, joined by Justice Souter, has been omitted.]

■ Justice Ginsburg, with whom Justice Stevens, Justice O'Connor, and Justice Souter join, dissenting.

Seven years ago, in Vernonia School Dist. 47J v. Acton, 515 U.S. 646, 115 S.Ct. 2386, 132 L.Ed.2d 564 (1995), this Court determined that a school district's policy of randomly testing the urine of its student athletes for illicit drugs did not violate the Fourth Amendment. In so ruling, the Court emphasized that drug use "increase[d] the risk of sports-related injury" and that Vernonia's athletes were the "leaders" of an aggressive local "drug culture" that had reached " 'epidemic proportions.' " *Id.,* at 649, 115 S.Ct. 2386. Today, the Court relies upon *Vernonia* to permit a school district with a drug problem its superintendent repeatedly described as "not ... major," to test the urine of an academic team member solely by reason of her participation in a nonathletic, competitive extracurricular activity-participation associated with neither special dangers from, nor particular predilections for, drug use.

"[T]he legality of a search of a student," this Court has instructed, "should depend simply on the reasonableness, under all the circumstances, of the search." New Jersey v. T.L.O., 469 U.S. 325, 341, 105 S.Ct. 733, 83 L.Ed.2d 720 (1985). Although " 'special needs' inhere in the public school context," (quoting *Vernonia,* 515 U.S., at 653, 115 S.Ct. 2386), those needs are not so expansive or malleable as to render reasonable any program of student drug testing a school district elects to install. The particular testing program upheld today is not reasonable; it is capricious, even perverse: Petitioners' policy targets for testing a student population least likely to be at risk from illicit drugs and their damaging effects. I therefore dissent.

I

A

A search unsupported by probable cause nevertheless may be consistent with the Fourth Amendment "when special needs, beyond the normal need for law enforcement, make the warrant and probable-cause requirement impracticable." Griffin v. Wisconsin, 483 U.S. 868, 873, 107 S.Ct. 3164, 97 L.Ed.2d 709 (1987) (internal quotation marks omitted). In *Vernonia,* this Court made clear that "such 'special needs' ... exist in the public school context." 515 U.S., at 653, 115 S.Ct. 2386 (quoting *Griffin,* 483 U.S., at 873, 107 S.Ct. 3164)....

The *Vernonia* Court concluded that a public school district facing a disruptive and explosive drug abuse problem sparked by members of its athletic teams had "special needs" that justified suspicionless testing of district athletes as a condition of their athletic participation.

This case presents circumstances dispositively different from those of *Vernonia.* True, as the Court stresses, Tecumseh students participating in competitive extracurricular activities other than athletics share two relevant characteristics with the athletes of *Vernonia.* First, both groups attend public schools. "[O]ur decision in *Vernonia,*" the Court states, "depended primarily upon the school's custodial responsibility and authority." Concern for student health and safety is basic to the school's caretaking, and it is undeniable that "drug use carries a variety of health risks for children, including death from overdose."

Those risks, however, are present for *all* schoolchildren. *Vernonia* cannot be read to endorse invasive and suspicionless drug testing of all students upon any evidence of drug use, solely because drugs jeopardize the life and health of those who use them. Many children, like many adults, engage in dangerous activities on their own time; that the children are enrolled in school scarcely allows government to monitor all such activities. If a student has a reasonable subjective expectation of privacy in the personal items she brings to school, see *T.L.O.,* 469 U.S., at 338–339, 105 S.Ct. 733, surely she has a similar expectation regarding the chemical composition of her urine. Had the *Vernonia* Court agreed that public school attendance, in and of itself, permitted the State to test each student's blood or urine for drugs, the opinion in *Vernonia* could have saved many words. See, e.g., 515 U.S., at 662, 115 S.Ct. 2386 ("[I]t must not be lost sight of that [the Vernonia School District] program is directed . . . to drug use by school athletes, where the risk of immediate physical harm to the drug user or those with whom he is playing his sport is particularly high.").

The second commonality to which the Court points is the voluntary character of both interscholastic athletics and other competitive extracurricular activities. "By choosing to 'go out for the team,' [school athletes] voluntarily subject themselves to a degree of regulation even higher than that imposed on students generally." *Id.,* at 657, 115 S.Ct. 2386. Comparably, the Court today observes, "students who participate in competitive extracurricular activities voluntarily subject themselves to" additional rules not applicable to other students.

The comparison is enlightening. While extracurricular activities are "voluntary" in the sense that they are not required for graduation, they are part of the school's educational program; for that reason, the petitioner (hereinafter School District) is justified in expending public resources to make them available. Participation in such activities is a key component of school life, essential in reality for students applying to college, and, for all participants, a significant contributor to the breadth and quality of the educational experience. See Brief for Respondents 6; Brief for American Academy of Pediatrics et al. as *Amici Curiae* 8–9. Students "volunteer" for extracurricular pursuits in the same way they might volunteer for honors classes: They subject themselves to additional requirements, but they do so in order to take full advantage of the education offered them. . . .

Voluntary participation in athletics has a distinctly different dimension: Schools regulate student athletes discretely because competitive school sports by their nature require communal undress and, more important, expose students to physical risks that schools have a duty to mitigate. For the very reason that schools cannot offer a program of competitive athletics without intimately affecting the privacy of students, *Vernonia* reasonably analogized school athletes to "adults who choose to participate in a closely regulated industry." 515 U.S., at 657, 115 S.Ct. 2386. Industries fall within the closely regulated category when the nature of their activities requires substantial government oversight. See, e.g., United States v. Biswell, 406 U.S. 311, 315–316, 92 S.Ct. 1593, 32 L.Ed.2d 87 (1972).

Interscholastic athletics similarly require close safety and health regulation; a school's choir, band, and academic team do not.

In short, *Vernonia* applied, it did not repudiate, the principle that "the legality of a search of a student should depend simply on the reasonableness, *under all the circumstances,* of the search." *T.L.O.,* 469 U.S., at 341, 105 S.Ct. 733 (emphasis added). Enrollment in a public school, and election to participate in school activities beyond the bare minimum that the curriculum requires, are indeed factors relevant to reasonableness, but they do not on their own justify intrusive, suspicionless searches. *Vernonia,* accordingly, did not rest upon these factors; instead, the Court performed what today's majority aptly describes as a "fact-specific balancing." Balancing of that order, applied to the facts now before the Court, should yield a result other than the one the Court announces today.

B

Vernonia initially considered "the nature of the privacy interest upon which the search [there] at issue intrude[d]." 515 U.S., at 654, 115 S.Ct. 2386. The Court emphasized that student athletes' expectations of privacy are necessarily attenuated:

> "Legitimate privacy expectations are even less with regard to student athletes. School sports are not for the bashful. They require 'suiting up' before each practice or event, and showering and changing afterwards. Public school locker rooms, the usual sites for these activities, are not notable for the privacy they afford. The locker rooms in Vernonia are typical: No individual dressing rooms are provided; shower heads are lined up along a wall, unseparated by any sort of partition or curtain; not even all the toilet stalls have doors.... [T]here is an element of communal undress inherent in athletic participation." *Id.,* at 657, 115 S.Ct. 2386.

Competitive extracurricular activities other than athletics, however, serve students of all manner: the modest and shy along with the bold and uninhibited. Activities of the kind plaintiff-respondent Lindsay Earls pursued-choir, show choir, marching band, and academic team-afford opportunities to gain self-assurance, to "come to know faculty members in a less formal setting than the typical classroom," and to acquire "positive social supports and networks [that] play a critical role in periods of heightened stress."

On "occasional out-of-town trips," students like Lindsay Earls "must sleep together in communal settings and use communal bathrooms." But those situations are hardly equivalent to the routine communal undress associated with athletics; the School District itself admits that when such trips occur, "public-like restroom facilities," which presumably include enclosed stalls, are ordinarily available for changing, and that "more modest students" find other ways to maintain their privacy.

After describing school athletes' reduced expectation of privacy, the *Vernonia* Court turned to "the character of the intrusion ... complained of." 515 U.S., at 658, 115 S.Ct. 2386. Observing that students produce urine samples in a bathroom stall with a coach or teacher outside, *Vernonia* typed the privacy interests compromised by the process of obtaining samples "negligible." *Ibid.* . . . [T]he Court concluded that Vernonia's athletes faced no significant invasion of privacy.

In this case, however, Lindsay Earls and her parents allege that the School District handled personal information collected under the policy carelessly, with little regard for its confidentiality. . . .

In granting summary judgment to the School District, the District Court observed that the District's "[p]olicy expressly provides for confidentiality of test results, and the Court must assume that the confidentiality provisions will be honored." The assumption is unwarranted. Unlike *Vernonia,* where the District Court held a bench trial before ruling in the School District's favor, this case was decided by the District Court on summary judgment. At that stage, doubtful matters should not have been resolved in favor of the judgment seeker. . . .

Finally, the "nature and immediacy of the governmental concern," *Vernonia,* 515 U.S., at 660, 115 S.Ct. 2386, faced by the Vernonia School District dwarfed that confronting Tecumseh administrators. Vernonia initiated its drug testing policy in response to an alarming situation: "[A] large segment of the student body, particularly those involved in interscholastic athletics, was in a state of rebellion . . . fueled by alcohol and drug abuse as well as the student[s'] misperceptions about the drug culture." *Id.,* at 649, 115 S.Ct. 2386 Tecumseh, by contrast, repeatedly reported to the Federal Government during the period leading up to the adoption of the policy that "types of drugs [other than alcohol and tobacco] including controlled dangerous substances, are present [in the schools] but have not identified themselves as major problems at this time." 1998–1999 Tecumseh School's Application for Funds under the Safe and Drug–Free Schools and Communities Program. As the Tenth Circuit observed, "without a demonstrated drug abuse problem among the group being tested, the efficacy of the District's solution to its perceived problem is . . . greatly diminished."

. . .

Not only did the Vernonia and Tecumseh districts confront drug problems of distinctly different magnitudes, they also chose different solutions: Vernonia limited its policy to athletes; Tecumseh indiscriminately subjected to testing all participants in competitive extracurricular activities. Urging that "the safety interest furthered by drug testing is undoubtedly substantial for all children, athletes and nonathletes alike," *ante,* at 2568, the Court cuts out an element essential to the *Vernonia* judgment. Citing medical literature on the effects of combining illicit drug use with physical exertion, the *Vernonia* Court emphasized that "the particular drugs screened by [Vernonia's] Policy have been demonstrated to pose substantial physical risks to athletes." 515 U.S., at 662, 115 S.Ct. 2386; see also *id.,* at 666, 115 S.Ct. 2386 (GINSBURG, J., concurring) (*Vernonia* limited to "those seeking to engage with others in team sports"). We have since confirmed that these special risks were necessary to our decision in *Vernonia.* See *Chandler,* 520 U.S., at 317, 117 S.Ct. 1295 (*Vernonia* "emphasized the importance of deterring drug use by schoolchildren and the risk of injury a drug-using student athlete cast on himself and those engaged with him on the playing field''); . . .

. . .

Nationwide, students who participate in extracurricular activities are significantly less likely to develop substance abuse problems than are their less-involved peers. See, *e.g.,* N. Zill, C. Nord, & L. Loomis, Adolescent Time Use, Risky Behavior, and Outcomes 52 (1995) (tenth graders "who reported spending no time in school-sponsored activities were . . . 49 percent more likely to have used drugs" than those who spent 1–4 hours per week in such activities). Even if students might be deterred from drug use in order to preserve their extracurricular eligibility, it is at least as likely that other students might forgo their extracurricular involvement in order to avoid detection of their drug use. Tecumseh's policy thus falls short doubly if deterrence is its aim: It invades the privacy of students who need deterrence least, and risks steering students at greatest risk for substance abuse away from extracurricular involvement that potentially may palliate drug problems.

To summarize, this case resembles *Vernonia* only in that the School Districts in both cases conditioned engagement in activities outside the obligatory curriculum on random subjection to urinalysis. The defining characteristics of the two programs, however, are entirely dissimilar. The Vernonia district sought to test a subpopulation of students distinguished by their reduced expectation of privacy, their special susceptibility to drug-related injury, and their heavy involvement with drug use. The Tecumseh district seeks to test a much larger population associated with none of these factors. It does so, moreover, without carefully safeguarding student confidentiality and without regard to the program's untoward effects. A program so sweeping is not sheltered by *Vernonia;* its unreasonable reach renders it impermissible under the Fourth Amendment.

II

In *Chandler,* this Court inspected "Georgia's requirement that candidates for state office pass a drug test"; we held that the requirement "d[id] not fit within the closely guarded category of constitutionally permissible suspicionless searches." 520 U.S., at 309, 117 S.Ct. 1295. Georgia's testing prescription, the record showed, responded to no "concrete danger," *id.,* at 319, 117 S.Ct. 1295, was supported by no evidence of a particular problem, and targeted a group not involved in "high-risk, safety-sensitive tasks," *id.,* at 321–322, 117 S.Ct. 1295. . . .

Close review of Tecumseh's policy compels a similar conclusion. That policy was not shown to advance the " 'special needs' [existing] in the public school context [to maintain] . . . swift and informal disciplinary procedures . . . [and] order in the schools," *Vernonia,* 515 U.S., at 653, 115 S.Ct. 2386. What is left is the School District's undoubted purpose to heighten awareness of its abhorrence of, and strong stand against, drug abuse. But the desire to augment communication of this message does not trump the right of persons—even of children within the schoolhouse gate—

to be "secure in their persons ... against unreasonable searches and seizures." U.S. Const., Amdt. 4.

In *Chandler,* the Court referred to a pathmarking dissenting opinion in which "Justice Brandeis recognized the importance of teaching by example: 'Our Government is the potent, the omnipresent teacher. For good or for ill, it teaches the whole people by its example.'" 520 U.S., at 322, 117 S.Ct. 1295. That wisdom should guide decisionmakers in the instant case: The government is nowhere more a teacher than when it runs a public school.

It is a sad irony that the petitioning School District seeks to justify its edict here by trumpeting "the schools' custodial and tutelary responsibility for children." *Vernonia,* 515 U.S., at 656, 115 S.Ct. 2386. In regulating an athletic program or endeavoring to combat an exploding drug epidemic, a school's custodial obligations may permit searches that would otherwise unacceptably abridge students' rights. When custodial duties are not ascendant, however, schools' tutelary obligations to their students require them to "teach by example" by avoiding symbolic measures that diminish constitutional protections. "That [schools] are educating the young for citizenship is reason for scrupulous protection of Constitutional freedoms of the individual, if we are not to strangle the free mind at its source and teach youth to discount important principles of our government as mere platitudes." West Virginia Bd. of Ed. v. Barnette, 319 U.S. 624, 637, 63 S.Ct. 1178, 87 L.Ed. 1628 (1943).

* * *

For the reasons stated, I would affirm the judgment of the Tenth Circuit declaring the testing policy at issue unconstitutional.

NOTES

(1) Would drug-testing of any student who applies for an on-campus parking permit be permissible under *Earls*? See Jared M. Hartman, Note, Pee-to-Park: Should Public High School Students Applying for On–Campus Parking Privileges Be Required to Pass a Drug Test, 18 J.L. & Health 229 (2004). Would the logic of *Earls* go so far as to permit random drug-testing of all students? If one agrees with Justice Thomas's assertion that the central compelling feature of *Acton* is the custodial and tutelary duty that the state owes to schoolchildren—and apparently a majority of the Court does—what is to prevent such a broad interpretation?

(2) Following *Earls,* the commentary on both *Acton* and *Earls* continued to be very critical. See, e.g., Irene Merker Rosenberg, The Public Schools Have a "Special Need" for Their Students' Urine, 31 Hofstra L.Rev. 303 (2002); Floralynn Einesman & Howard Taras, Drug Testing of Students: A Legal and Public Health Perspective, 23 J.Contemp. Health L. & Pol'y 231 (2007); M. Casey Kucharson, Note, Please Report to the Principal's Office, Urine Trouble: The Effect of Board of Education v. Earls on America's Schoolchildren, 37 Akron L.Rev. 131 (2004); Thomas Proctor, Comment, Constitutionality of Testing High School Male Athletes for Steroids under Vernonia School District v. Acton and Board of Education v. Earls, 2005 B.Y.U.L.Rev. 1335; Kari L. Higbee, Comment, Student Privacy Rights: Drug Testing and Fourth Amendment Protections, 41 Idaho L.Rev. 361 (2005); John F. Donaldson, Note, Life, Liberty, and the Pursuit of Urinalysis: The Constitutionality of Random Suspicionless Drug Testing in Public Schools, 41 Val.U.L.Rev. 815 (2006); Jacob L. Brooks, Case Note, Constitutional Law—Suspicionless Drug

Testing of Students Participating in Non–Athletic Competitive School Activities: Are All Students Next? Board of Education v. Earls, 536 U.S. 822 (2002), 4 Wyo.L.Rev. 365 (2004).

3. THIRD PARTY CONSENT TO SEARCH OF JUVENILE'S PERSON OR BELONGINGS

AMERICAN LAW INSTITUTE, MODEL CODE OF PRE–ARRAIGN-MENT PROCEDURE (1975)*

§ 240.2   Requirements of Effective Consent

(1) *Persons from Whom Effective Consent May Be Obtained*. The consent justifying a search and seizure ... must be given, in the case of

(a) Search of an individual's person, by the individual in question or, if the person be under the age of 16, by such individual's parent or guardian;

. . .

(2) *Required Warning to Persons Not in Custody or Under Arrest.* Before undertaking a search, ... an officer present shall inform the individual whose consent is sought that he is under no obligation to give such consent and that anything found may be taken and used in evidence.

(3) *Required Warning to Persons in Custody or Under Arrest.* If the individual whose consent is sought ... is in custody or under arrest at the time such consent is offered or invited, such consent shall not justify a search and seizure ... unless in addition to the warning required by Subsection (2), such individual has been informed that he has the right to consult an attorney, either retained or appointed, and to communicate with relatives or friends, before deciding whether to grant or withhold consent.

NOTES

(1) Can school searches be upheld on the ground that school officials have the power to consent for the child? See *People v. Overton*, 20 N.Y.2d 360, 283 N.Y.S.2d 22, 229 N.E.2d 596 (1967), remanded per curiam 393 U.S. 85, 89 S.Ct. 252, 21 L.Ed.2d 218 (1968), for reconsideration of the consent issue.

(2) May school officials extending the *in loco parentis* concept claim that because parents could consent to a search of the child they should enjoy that power by analogy as well? While some earlier decisions drew on the *in loco parentis* doctrine for support, the doctrine seemingly was abandoned by the Supreme Court in *T.L.O.* Does it appear that the Court has revived the doctrine in *Acton*?

For a case holding parents may not lawfully consent to warrantless search of a 17–year–old's toolbox where he was present and objected to the police conduct, see *In re Scott K.*, 24 Cal.3d 395, 155 Cal.Rptr. 671, 595 P.2d 105 (1979) where the California Supreme Court said in part:

A 17–year–old defendant appeals from an order declaring him a juvenile court ward and placing him on probation. The order was based on the court's finding that defendant unlawfully possessed marijuana for purpose of sale in violation of section 11359 of the Health and Safety Code. The question is whether a warrantless, parent-approved, police search of defendant's personal property was permissible.

Defendant's mother found marijuana in his desk drawer. She gave it to an off-duty police officer who lived in the neighborhood and told him that conversations with other parents led her to believe that her son might be selling marijuana. A week later that officer's report was given to Narcotics Officer Schian for follow-up. He telephoned the father to advise that he was about to arrest defendant. The conversation was as follows: "In substance, I advised the father that I was in charge of the follow-up investigation of the marijuana that his wife had turned over to the police officer; that an arrest would result from this situation, arrest of the son; that I intended to come out and arrest his son if his son was home, and then I received the information that he was working on his motorcycle in the garage.

"And I asked him, 'Is it all right with you then that I go to the garage and arrest your boy there and do you wish to join us out there then, or what shall we do to make easy on maybe the rest of the family?'

"And he indicated, 'Why don't you just come on inside after you have arrested him?' "

Without warrant, Schian and other officers went to the garage. Schian arrested defendant and took him to the house, where the father gave permission to search defendant's bedroom. The search disclosed a locked toolbox. The father told Schian that he had no key and that it was defendant's box. When asked about the key, defendant replied he had lost it. Schian said, "Your father already told me I could break the toolbox open if I couldn't find a key, but it's not in my interest to destroy the lock. Let me see the keys you have in your pocket." Defendant gave Schian his keys, one of which opened the box. Inside were nine baggies of marijuana.

.   .   .

The People argue that, because a parent is responsible for minor children and may himself inspect their property, police search of that property when pursuant to parental consent is reasonable and accordingly constitutional. Implicit is the notion that the father here could effectively waive his son's right to be secure in the son's effects. We reject that view.

.   .   .

The trial court here held that the father's authority was based on the combined circumstance of his ownership of the home and his duty to control his son. Yet neither fact shows the requisite link between the father's interest and the property inspected. Common authority over personal property may not be implied from the father's proprietary interest in the premises. (United States v. Matlock, supra, 415 U.S. 164, 171, fn. 7, 94 S.Ct. 988.) Neither may it be premised on the nature of the parent-child relation.[10]

10. Courts have not previously embraced the notion that the government can use the relationship between parties to impute "common authority" to the consenting party when one in fact existed. (Cf. *People v. Daniels*, 16 Cal.App.3d 36, 93 Cal.Rptr. 628 (1971); *People v. Murillo*, 241 Cal.App.2d 173, 50 Cal.Rptr. 290 (1966); also see dictum in *People v. Terry*, 2 Cal.3d 362, 392, 85 Cal. Rptr. 409, 428, 466 P.2d 961, 980 (1970), where this court held the wife could give valid consent to police search of her husband's property because "[t]here is no evidence that the murder weapon was in a sealed box or other container belonging to Terry [the husband], which Mrs. Terry might not have had authority to permit to be searched.")

Juveniles are entitled "to acquire and hold property, real and personal" (Estate of Yano (1922) 188 Cal. 645, 649, 206 P. 995, 997); and a "minor child's property is his own ... not that of his parents." (Emery v. Emery (1955) 45 Cal.2d 421, 432, 289 P.2d 218, 225; see also Civ.Code § 202) Parents may have a protectible interest in property belonging to children, but that fact may not be assumed. When a warrantless search is challenged the People must show that it was reasonable. Here the People did not establish that the consenting parent had a sufficient interest under search and seizure law. The father claimed no interest in the box or its contents. He acknowledged that the son was owner, and the son did not consent to the search. Because those facts were known to the police there was not justification for their relying on the father's consent to conduct the search. . . .

In its decision in *Scott K.* the court refers to the Supreme Court's 1974 decision in *United States v. Matlock* . *Matlock* stands for the proposition that an occupant's consent to search premises commonly shared with an absent co-occupant is valid. In *Georgia v. Randolph*, 547 U.S. 103, 126 S.Ct. 1515, 164 L.Ed.2d 208 (2006), the Court distinguished *Matlock* somewhat in a case in which a wife had consented to a search of the marital residence, even though her husband was present and objected to the search. He moved to suppress evidence of cocaine discovered during the search. His motion to suppress was denied, but the Georgia Court of Appeals reversed, finding the search to be invalid. The Georgia Supreme Court affirmed. The U.S. Supreme Court affirmed, holding the search unreasonable. The Court's decision stands for the proposition that if an occupant consents to a search of premises commonly shared with a co-occupant, but the co-occupant is present and objects to the search, the consent and the search are invalid as to the co-occupant.

What implications does the *Randolph* decision have for consent by a parent to search of the family residence where the child is present and objects? Is the parent-child relationship different from the husband-wife relationship, or the relationship between co-occupants of a dwelling? The *Randolph* case is thoroughly analyzed in Shane E. Eden, Picking the Matlock: Georgia v. Randolph and the U.S. Supreme Court's Re–Examination of Third–Party Consent Authority in Light of Social Expectations, 52 S.D. L.Rev. 171 (2007).

Is the character of the area to be searched important? Compare *People v. Bunker*, 22 Mich.App. 396, 177 N.W.2d 644 (1970) (upholding parental consent to search an area commonly accessible to all members of the household), with *People v. Flowers*, 23 Mich.App. 523, 179 N.W.2d 56 (1970) (disallowing parental consent to search of child's room).

For a commentary advocating a warrant requirement for searches of a child's room or property (in the absence of any recognized exception) see Rachel Crevans & Lori Ortenstone, Comment, "Who's Been Searching in My Room?" Parental Waiver of Children's Fourth Amendment Rights, 17 U.C.Davis L.Rev. 359 (1983).

(3) May children consent to warrantless police searches of their parents' homes? See generally, Charles H. Whitebread & Christopher Slobogin, Criminal Procedure: An Analysis of Cases and Concepts 309–13 (5th ed. 2008). Age may be the most important factor in determining the authority of a child to give a third party consent to search the parent's home. In addition to age, other factors include whether the minor is living at home, his right of access, and his right of invitation. See *United States v. Clutter*, 914 F.2d 775 (6th Cir.1990); *Atkins v. State*, 254 Ga. 641, 331 S.E.2d 597 (1985). Compare *People v. Jacobs*, 43 Cal.3d 472, 233 Cal.Rptr. 323, 729 P.2d 757 (1987) (11–year-old incapable of giving valid consent to search of home to locate and arrest her father; children "do not have coequal dominion over

the family home" even though parents "may choose to grant their minor children joint access and mutual use of the home") with *Pesterfield v. Commissioner of Public Safety*, 399 N.W.2d 605 (Minn.App.1987) (17-year-old could give valid consent to police entry of family home to question her mother about nearby auto accident they suspected was caused by the mother). All of this assumes the parents are not at home. If the parents are home and object to the search, surely the consent by the child, and any search, would be invalid as to the parents. See discussion of *Georgia v. Randolph* in note (2) supra.

E.   INTERROGATION

THE LEGACY OF *MIRANDA*

Prior to *Miranda v. Arizona*, 384 U.S. 436, 86 S.Ct. 1602, 16 L.Ed.2d 694 (1966), the test of admissibility of statements made in response to questioning by the police was voluntariness, i.e., whether the statements were made voluntarily or were the result of police coercion, viewing the totality of circumstances. In *Miranda*, the Supreme Court shifted away from its voluntariness approach and focused on the Fifth Amendment privilege against self-incrimination and the Sixth Amendment right to counsel. The Court set forth certain requirements that must be met before any statement made by a defendant while in police custody can be used at a criminal trial:

> To summarize, we hold that when an individual is taken into custody or otherwise deprived of his freedom by the authorities in any significant way and is subjected to questioning, the privilege against self-incrimination is jeopardized. Procedural safeguards must be employed to protect the privilege, and unless other fully effective means are adopted to notify the person of his right of silence and to assure that the exercise of the right will be scrupulously honored, the following measures are required. He must be warned prior to any questioning that he has the right to remain silent, that anything he says can be used against him in a court of law, that he has the right to the presence of an attorney, and that if he cannot afford an attorney one will be appointed for him prior to any questioning if he so desires. Opportunity to exercise these rights must be afforded to him throughout the interrogation. After such warnings have been given, and such opportunity afforded him, the individual may knowingly and intelligently waive these rights and agree to answer questions or make a statement. But unless and until such warnings and waiver are demonstrated by the prosecution at trial, no evidence obtained as a result of interrogation can be used against him.

384 U.S. at 478–79. The "*Miranda* warnings" are now part of the popular culture.

Prior to *In re Gault*, 387 U.S. 1, 87 S.Ct. 1428, 18 L.Ed.2d 527 (1967), the test of admissibility of statements by juveniles likewise was voluntariness. In *Haley v. Ohio*, 332 U.S. 596, 68 S.Ct. 302, 92 L.Ed. 224 (1948), and *Gallegos v. Colorado*, 370 U.S. 49, 82 S.Ct. 1209, 8 L.Ed.2d 325 (1962), both of which involved juveniles convicted of crimes in criminal court, the

Supreme Court held statements inadmissible that were obtained in viola-tion of Fourteenth Amendment due process standards.

In *Haley*, which concerned a 15–year-old defendant, Justice Douglas acknowledged that the circumstances "would make us pause for careful inquiry if a mature man were involved," and went on to add: "And when, as here, a mere child—an easy victim of the law—is before us, special care in scrutinizing the record must be used." 332 U.S. at 599. Justice Douglas also wrote the opinion for the Court in *Gallegos*, which involved a 14–year-old defendant. Describing the test to be employed in such cases, he observed: "There is no guide to the decision of cases such as this, except the totality of circumstances that bear on the ... factors we have men-tioned. The youth of the petitioner, the long detention, the failure to send for his parents, the failure immediately to bring him before the judge of the Juvenile Court, the failure to see to it that he had the advice of a lawyer or a friend—all these combine to make us conclude that the formal confession on which this conviction may have rested was obtained in violation of due process." 370 U.S. at 55.

Subsequently, in *Gault* the Court held the Fifth Amendment privilege against self-incrimination applicable to juveniles during a fact-finding hear-ing to determine delinquency, where the juvenile is exposed to the possibili-ty of commitment to an institution. The Court specifically refrained, however, from passing on the question of applicability of its holding to the pre-judicial, investigatory phase of proceedings. 387 U.S. at 13. Perhaps significantly, however, the Court, in holding the Fifth Amendment privilege against self-incrimination applicable to juveniles, quoted from its earlier decision in *Haley*: "No friend stood at the side of this 15–year old boy as the police, working in relays, questioned him hour after hour, from mid-night until dawn. No lawyer stood guard to make sure that the police went so far and no further, to see to it that they stopped short of the point where he became the victim of coercion. No counsel or friend was called during the critical hours of questioning." 387 U.S. at 45–46.

In any event, following *Gault*, courts uniformly held the *Miranda* requirements to be applicable to juvenile proceedings. See, e.g., *In re M.*, 70 Cal.2d 444, 75 Cal.Rptr. 1, 450 P.2d 296 (1969); *In re William L.*, 29 A.D.2d 182, 287 N.Y.S.2d 218 (1968); *Leach v. State*, 428 S.W.2d 817 (Tex.Civ.App. 1968). In some instances the *Miranda* requirements were held applicable to juveniles even prior to the *Gault* decision. *In re Knox*, 53 Misc.2d 889, 280 N.Y.S.2d 65 (Fam.Ct., Monroe County 1967); *In re Rust*, 53 Misc.2d 51, 278 N.Y.S.2d 333 (Fam.Ct., Kings County 1967).

The principal issues in the aftermath of *Miranda* and *Gault*—unique to juveniles—have focused on the circumstances under which a juvenile may waive *Miranda* rights, i.e., whether the juvenile may waive rights by himself or herself without a parent or other friendly adult present; the circumstances under which a juvenile may invoke the right to remain silent, i.e., whether a request to speak to a parent, grandparent or other friendly adult operates the same as a request to speak to an attorney; and whether, even though *Miranda* warnings are given and understood, a confession nevertheless might be involuntary. The cases that follow address those issues.

Fare v. Michael C.

Supreme Court of the United States, 1979.
442 U.S. 707, 99 S.Ct. 2560, 61 L.Ed.2d 197.

■ MR. JUSTICE BLACKMUN delivered the opinion of the Court.

In Miranda v. Arizona, 384 U.S. 436 (1966), this Court established certain procedural safeguards designed to protect the rights of an accused, under the Fifth and Fourteenth Amendments, to be free from compelled self-incrimination during custodial interrogation. The Court specified, among other things, that if the accused indicates in any manner that he wishes to remain silent or to consult an attorney, interrogation must cease, and any statement obtained from him during interrogation thereafter may not be admitted against him at his trial. Id., at 444–445, 473–474.

In this case, the State of California, in the person of its acting chief probation officer, attacks the conclusion of the Supreme Court of California that a juvenile's request, made while undergoing custodial interrogation, to see his *probation officer* is *per se* an invocation of the juvenile's Fifth Amendment rights as pronounced in *Miranda*.

I

Respondent Michael C. was implicated in the murder of Robert Yeager. The murder occurred during a robbery of the victim's home on January 19, 1976. A small truck registered in the name of respondent's mother was identified as having been near the Yeager home at the time of the killing, and a young man answering respondent's description was seen by witnesses near the truck and near the home shortly before Yeager was murdered.

On the basis of this information, Van Nuys, Cal., police took respondent into custody at approximately 6:30 p.m. on February 4. Respondent then was 16½ years old and on probation to the Juvenile Court. He had been on probation since the age of 12. Approximately one year earlier he had served a term in a youth corrections camp under the supervision of the Juvenile Court. He had a record of several previous offenses, including burglary of guns and purse snatching, stretching back over several years.

Upon respondent's arrival at the Van Nuys station house two police officers began to interrogate him. The officers and respondent were the only persons in the room during the interrogation. The conversation was tape recorded. One of the officers initiated the interview by informing respondent that he had been brought in for questioning in relation to a murder. The officer fully advised respondent of his *Miranda* rights. The following exchange then occurred, as set out in the opinion of the California Supreme Court, In re Michael C., 21 Cal.3d 471, 473–474, 146 Cal.Rptr. 358, 359–360, 579 P.2d 7, 8 (1978) (emphasis added by that court):

"Q.   ... Do you understand all of these rights as I have explained them to you?

"A.   Yeah.

"Q.   Okay, do you wish to give up your right to remain silent and talk to us about this murder?

"A.   What murder? I don't know about no murder.

"Q. I'll explain to you which one it is if you want to talk to us about it.

"A. Yeah, I might talk to you.

"Q. Do you want to give up your right to have an attorney present here while we talk about it?

"A. *Can I have my probation officer here?*

"Q. Well I can't get a hold of your probation officer right now. You have the right to an attorney.

"A. How I know you guys won't pull no police officer in and tell me he's an attorney?

"Q. Huh?

"A. [How I know you guys won't pull no police officer in and tell me he's an attorney?]

"Q. Your probation officer is Mr. Christiansen.

"A. Yeah.

"Q. Well I'm not going to call Mr. Christiansen tonight. There's a good chance we can talk to him later, but I'm not going to call him right now. If you want to talk to us without an attorney present, you can. If you don't want to, you don't have to. But if you want to say something you can, and if you don't want to say something you don't have to. That's your right. You understand that right?

"A. Yeah.

"Q. Okay, will you talk to us without an attorney present?

"A. Yeah I want to talk to you."

Respondent thereupon proceeded to answer questions put to him by the officers. He made statements and drew sketches that incriminated him in the Yeager murder.

Largely on the basis of respondent's incriminating statements, probation authorities filed a petition in Juvenile Court alleging that respondent had murdered Robert Yeager, in violation of Cal. Penal Code Ann. § 187 (West Supp. 1979), and that respondent therefore should be adjudged a ward of the Juvenile Court, pursuant to Cal. Welf. & Inst. Code Ann. § 602 (West Supp. 1979).[1] App. 4–5. Respondent thereupon moved to suppress the statements and sketches he gave the police during the interrogation. He alleged that the statements had been obtained in violation of *Miranda* in that his request to see his probation officer at the outset of the questioning constituted an invocation of his Fifth Amendment right to remain silent, just as if he had requested the assistance of an attorney. Accordingly, respondent argued that since the interrogation did not cease until he had a

---

1. The petition also alleged that respondent had participated in an attempted armed robbery earlier on the same evening Yeager was murdered. The Juvenile Court, however, held that the evidence was insufficient to support this charge and it was dismissed. No issue relating to this second charge is before the Court.

chance to confer with his probation officer, the statements and sketches could not be admitted against him in the Juvenile Court proceedings....

. . .

On appeal, the Supreme Court of California took the case by transfer from the California Court of Appeal and, by a divided vote, reversed. In re Michael C., 21 Cal.3d 471, 146 Cal.Rptr. 358, 579 P.2d 7 (1978). The court held that respondent's "request to see his probation officer at the commencement of interrogation negated any possible willingness on his part to discuss his case with the police [and] thereby invoked his Fifth Amendment privilege." Id., at 474, 579 P.2d, at 8. The court based this conclusion on its view that, because of the juvenile court system's emphasis on the relationship between a probation officer and the probationer, the officer was "a trusted guardian figure who exercises the authority of the state as *parens patriae* and whose duty it is to implement the protective and rehabilitative powers of the juvenile court." Id., at 476, 579 P.2d, at 10. As a consequence, the court found that a minor's request for his probation officer was the same as a request to see his parents during interrogation, and thus under the rule of *Burton* constituted an invocation of the minor's Fifth Amendment rights.

. . .

The court accordingly held that the probation officer would act to protect the minor's Fifth Amendment rights in precisely the way an attorney would act if called for by the accused....

We ... believe it clear that the probation officer is not in a position to offer the type of legal assistance necessary to protect the Fifth Amendment rights of an accused undergoing custodial interrogation that a lawyer can offer. The Court in *Miranda* recognized that "the attorney plays a vital role in the administration of criminal justice under our Constitution." 384 U.S., at 481. It is this pivotal role of legal counsel that justifies the *per se* rule established in *Miranda*, and that distinguishes the request for counsel from the request for a probation officer, a clergyman, or a close friend. A probation officer simply is not necessary, in the way an attorney is, for the protection of the legal rights of the accused, juvenile or adult. He is significantly handicapped by the position he occupies in the juvenile system from serving as an effective protector of the rights of a juvenile suspected of a crime.

The California Supreme Court, however, found that the close relationship between juveniles and their probation officers compelled the conclusion that a probation officer, for purposes of *Miranda,* was sufficiently like a lawyer to justify extension of the *per se* rule. 21 Cal.3d, at 476, 146 Cal.Rptr. at 361, 579 P.2d, at 10. The fact that a relationship of trust and cooperation between a probation officer and a juvenile might exist, however, does not indicate that the probation officer is capable of rendering effective legal advice sufficient to protect the juvenile's rights during interrogation by the police, or of providing the other services rendered by a lawyer. To find otherwise would be "an extension of the *Miranda* requirements [that] would cut this Court's holding in that case completely loose from its own explicitly stated rationale." Beckwith v. United States, 425

U.S. 341, 345 (1976). Such an extension would impose the burdens associated with the rule of *Miranda* on the juvenile justice system and the police without serving the interests that rule was designed simultaneously to protect. If it were otherwise, a juvenile's request for almost anyone he considered trustworthy enough to give him reliable advice would trigger the rigid rule of *Miranda*.

Similarly, the fact that the State has created a statutory duty on the part of the probation officer to protect the interests of the juvenile does not render the probation officer any more capable of rendering legal assistance to the juvenile or of protecting his legal rights, especially in light of the fact that the State has also legislated a duty on the part of the officer to report wrongdoing by the juvenile and serve the ends of the juvenile court system. The State cannot transmute the relationship between probation officer and juvenile offender into the type of relationship between attorney and client that was essential to the holding of *Miranda* simply by legislating an amorphous "duty to advise and care for the juvenile defendant." 21 Cal.3d, at 477, 146 Cal.Rptr. at 361, 579 P.2d, at 10. Though such a statutory duty might serve to distinguish to some degree the probation officer from the coach and the clergyman, it does not justify the extension of *Miranda* to requests to see probation officers. If it did, the State could expand the class of persons covered by the *Miranda per se* rule simply by creating a duty to care for the juvenile on the part of other persons, regardless of whether the logic of *Miranda* would justify that extension.

Nor do we believe that a request by a juvenile to speak with his probation officer constitutes a *per se* request to remain silent. As indicated, since a probation officer does not fulfill the important role in protecting the rights of the accused juvenile that an attorney plays, we decline to find that the request for the probation officer is tantamount to the request for an attorney. And there is nothing inherent in the request for a probation officer that requires us to find that a juvenile's request to see one necessarily constitutes an expression of the juvenile's right to remain silent. As discussed below, courts may take into account such a request in evaluating whether a juvenile in fact had waived his Fifth Amendment rights before confessing. But in other circumstances such a request might well be consistent with a desire to speak with the police. In the absence of further evidence that the minor intended in the circumstances to invoke his Fifth Amendment rights by such a request, we decline to attach such overwhelming significance to this request.

We hold, therefore, that it was error to find that the request by respondent to speak with his probation officer *per se* constituted an invocation of respondent's Fifth Amendment right to be free from compelled self-incrimination. It therefore was also error to hold that because the police did not then cease interrogating respondent the statements he made during interrogation should have been suppressed.

. . .

■ MR. JUSTICE MARSHALL, with whom MR. JUSTICE BRENNAN and MR. JUSTICE STEVENS join, dissenting.

. . .

It is therefore critical in the present context that we construe *Miranda*'s prophylactic requirements broadly to accomplish their intended purpose—"dispel[ling] the compulsion inherent in custodial surroundings." 384 U.S., at 458. To effectuate this purpose, the Court must ensure that the "protective device" of legal counsel, id., at 465–466, 469, be readily available, and that any intimation of a desire to preclude questioning be scrupulously honored. Thus, I believe *Miranda* requires that interrogation cease whenever a juvenile requests an adult who is obligated to represent his interests. Such a request, in my judgment, constitutes both an attempt to obtain advice and a general invocation of the right to silence. For, as the California Supreme Court recognized, " '[i]t is fatuous to assume that a minor in custody will be in a position to call an attorney for assistance,' " 21 Cal.3d 471, 475–476, 146 Cal.Rptr. 358, 360, 579 P.2d 7, 9 (1978), quoting People v. Burton, 6 Cal.3d 375, 382, 491 P.2d 793, 797 (1971), or that he will trust the police to obtain a lawyer for him.[1] A juvenile in these circumstances will likely turn to his parents, or another adult responsible for his welfare, as the only means of securing legal counsel. Moreover, a request for such adult assistance is surely inconsistent with a present desire to speak freely. Requiring a strict verbal formula to invoke the protections of *Miranda* would "protect the knowledgeable accused from stationhouse coercion while abandoning the young person who knows no more than to ask for the ... person he trusts." Chaney v. Wainwright, 561 F.2d 1129, 1134 (C.A.5 1977) (Goldberg, J., dissenting).

On my reading of *Miranda*, a California juvenile's request for his probation officer should be treated as a *per se* assertion of Fifth Amendment rights. The California Supreme Court determined that probation officers have a statutory duty to represent minors' interests and, indeed, are "trusted guardian figure[s]" to whom a juvenile would likely turn for assistance. 21 Cal.3d, at 476, 146 Cal.Rptr., at 361, 579 P.2d, at 10. In addition, the court found, probation officers are particularly well suited to assist a juvenile "on such matters as to whether or not he should obtain an attorney" and "how to conduct himself with police." Id., at 476, 477, 146 Cal.Rptr., at 361, 579 P.2d, at 10. Hence, a juvenile's request for a probation officer may frequently be an attempt to secure protection from the coercive aspects of custodial questioning.

This Court concludes, however, that because a probation officer has law enforcement duties, juveniles generally would not call upon him to represent their interests, and if they did, would not be well served. But that conclusion ignores the California Supreme Court's express determination that the officer's responsibility to initiate juvenile proceedings did not negate his function as personal adviser to his wards. I decline to second-guess that court's assessment of state law. Further, although the majority here speculates that probation officers have a duty to advise cooperation with the police—a proposition suggested only in the concurring opinion of two justices below, 21 Cal.3d, at 479, 146 Cal.Rptr., at 363, 579 P.2d, at 11–

1. The facts of the instant case are illustrative. When the police offered to obtain an attorney for respondent, he replied: "How I know you guys won't pull no police officer in and tell me he's an attorney?" Significantly, the police made no attempt to allay that concern.

12 (Mosk, J., concurring)—respondent's probation officer instructed all his charges "not to go and admit openly to an offense, [but rather] to get some type of advice from ... parents or a lawyer." Absent an explicit statutory provision or judicial holding, the officer's assessment of the obligations imposed by state law is entitled to deference by this Court.

Thus, given the role of probation officers under California law, a juvenile's request to see his officer may reflect a desire for precisely the kind of assistance *Miranda* guarantees an accused before he waives his Fifth Amendment rights. At the very least, such a request signals a desire to remain silent until contact with the officer is made. Because the Court's contrary determination withdraws the safeguards of *Miranda* from those most in need of protection, I respectfully dissent.

■ [The separate dissenting opinion of Justice Powell has been omitted.]

NOTES

(1) For the immediate reaction of the state courts in California to the *Fare* decision, consider the following opinion by Kingsley, Acting Presiding Justice, in *In re Patrick W.*, 104 Cal.App.3d 615, 163 Cal.Rptr. 848 (1980):

> The minor was found by the juvenile court to be a person coming under section 602 of the Welfare & Institutions Code in that he had committed murder in violation of section 187 of the Penal Code. He was committed to the Youth Authority; he has appealed; we reverse.

> The case for the People is that, angry at his father, a police officer, the minor had intentionally shot and killed him. Alerted by school authorities and other persons, deputy sheriffs arrested the minor and took him to the station for interrogation. Admittedly they gave him the formal *Miranda* rights and also asked if he desired to talk to the "parents." Quite understandably the minor declined to face his mother, whom he had just widowed. It is the contention of the minor here that, since his grandparents were available and had sought to speak to the minor, the deputies were under an obligation to ask him if he desired to talk to them and that the deputies had not done so.

> This is the second time that this case has been before this court. On September 1, 1978, we held that the order of commitment must be reversed because of that failure. (In re Patrick W. (1978) 84 Cal.App.3d 520, 148 Cal.Rptr. 735.) On October 23, 1978, our Supreme Court denied hearing. The People then sought certiorari and, on June 25, 1979, the United States Supreme Court remanded the case to us "for further consideration in the light of Fare v. Michael C. (1979) 442 U.S. 707."

> In In re Michael C. (1978) 21 Cal.3d 471, 146 Cal.Rptr. 358, 579 P.2d 7, our Supreme Court had held that a confession obtained from a minor after his request to see his probation officer had been denied, was obtained in violation of the minor's *Miranda* rights. It was that holding which the United States Supreme Court reversed, primarily on the ground that a probation officer, by virtue of his dual allegiance, was not the kind of person on whom a minor was entitled, within the purpose of *Miranda*, to rely.

> It is clear that the United States Supreme Court's decision in *Michael C.* rests on facts distinguishable from those before us on this appeal. The grandparents here did not have the official ambivalence that the Supreme Court saw in the *Michael C.* case. They fall more in the group of which our Supreme Court said, in People v. Burton (1971) 6 Cal.3d 375, at page 382, 99 Cal.Rptr. 1, at

page 5, 491 P.2d 793, at page 797, "person to whom he [a minor] normally looks" for help. Admittedly there is *language* in the Supreme Court opinion that might be interpreted as indicating that that court would take a similar view of a right to see grandparents. However, in its action in the case before us, the United States Supreme Court did not reverse our judgment on the authority of *Michael C.* but merely directed us to reconsider our opinion "in the light of" that opinion. We have obeyed that direction.

In a footnote the court stated:

> It is here immaterial to speculate over whether the minor would have exhibited the same reluctance to facing his grandparents as he had to facing his mother. The choice was his; he was never given that choice.

Following this decision by the California Court of Appeals, the Supreme Court denied certiorari. *California v. Patrick Steven W.*, 449 U.S. 1096, 101 S.Ct. 893, 66 L.Ed.2d 824, 66 L.Ed.2d 824 (1981).

More recently, however, different divisions of the California Court of Appeals have held admissible statements given by juveniles whose parents were at the police station asking to see them. *In re Aven S.*, 1 Cal.App.4th 69, 1 Cal.Rptr.2d 655 (1991); *In re John S.*, 199 Cal.App.3d 441, 245 Cal.Rptr. 17, cert. denied, 488 U.S. 928, 109 S.Ct. 316, 102 L.Ed.2d 334 (1988).

(2) In the adult context the Supreme Court has held that an adult need not be advised of the presence of his or her attorney if the adult has not requested an opportunity to speak to his or her attorney. *Moran v. Burbine*, 475 U.S. 412, 106 S.Ct. 1135, 89 L.Ed.2d 410 (1986). Some state courts, however, have declined to follow *Moran v. Burbine* and have held instead, on the basis of state law, that any interrogation must cease and the accused given an opportunity to speak with his or her attorney. See, e.g., *People v. Houston*, 42 Cal.3d 595, 230 Cal.Rptr. 141, 724 P.2d 1166 (1986), abrogated by constitutional amendment as stated in *People v. Ledesma*, 204 Cal.App.3d 682, 251 Cal.Rptr. 417 (1988) (adopting the rule in *Burbine*); *People v. McCauley*, 163 Ill.2d 414, 206 Ill.Dec. 671, 645 N.E.2d 923 (1994).

In the juvenile context, some state courts have held that if an attorney is present and seeking to assist a juvenile, interrogation must cease and the juvenile provided an opportunity to speak to his or her attorney. See, e.g., *Haliburton v. State*, 514 So.2d 1088 (Fla.1987), cert. denied, 501 U.S. 1259, 111 S.Ct. 2910, 115 L.Ed.2d 1073 (1991). More to the point, some courts have held that the adult rule is inapplicable to juveniles and that a juvenile must be advised of a *parent's* presence. See, e.g., *In re Lucas F.*, 68 Md.App. 97, 510 A.2d 270 (1986); see also *People v. Knox*, 186 Ill.App.3d 808, 134 Ill.Dec. 564, 542 N.E.2d 910, cert. denied, 127 Ill.2d 630, 136 Ill.Dec. 598, 545 N.E.2d 122 (1989). But see *State v. Presha*, 163 N.J. 304, 748 A.2d 1108 (2000) (16–year-old juvenile's confession admissible based on totality of circumstances even though he was aware of his mother's presence and his mother's request to speak to him was not honored).

(3) If, as the Supreme Court held in *Fare v. Michael C.*, a juvenile's request to speak to his probation officer is not the equivalent of a request to speak to an attorney, suppose the juvenile asks to speak to a *parent*? Given the tenor of the Court's discussion comparing the role of an attorney and the role of a probation officer, is it likely that a request to speak to *anyone* other than an attorney, even a parent, is going to be treated as an invocation of Fifth and Sixth Amendment rights?

Given its decision that a juvenile's request to speak to a probation officer is not a per se invocation of the right to counsel, the Court in *Fare v. Michael C.* glossed over the question of whether such a request invokes the right to remain silent. Could you argue that a juvenile's request to speak to a parent is the same as a request to stop or terminate the interrogation and that the interrogation should cease in any event?

Some lower courts have held that a juvenile's request to speak to a parent during questioning is equivalent to a request to speak to an attorney, and any statement the juvenile thereafter gives in the absence of a parent is inadmissible under the Fifth and Sixth Amendments or state law. The leading case is *People v. Burton*, 6 Cal.3d 375, 99 Cal.Rptr. 1, 491 P.2d 793 (1971). See also *Dowst v. State*, 336 So.2d 375 (Fla.App.), cert. denied, 339 So.2d 1172 (Fla.1976). Other courts, however, have disagreed, particularly in light of *Fare v. Michael C.* See, e.g., *State v. Whitaker*, 215 Conn. 739, 578 A.2d 1031 (1990); *State v. Jones*, 566 N.W.2d 317 (Minn.1997).

Although decided prior to *Fare v. Michael C.*, the *Burton* decision has since been reaffirmed, based on state law. *People v. Rivera*, 41 Cal.3d 388, 221 Cal.Rptr. 562, 710 P.2d 362 (1985). Should a child's request to speak to a parent be treated the same as a request to speak to an attorney, for the reason that a child's relationship to a parent is different from that between the child and anyone else? The rationale of courts holding a child's request to speak to a parent equivalent to a request to speak to an attorney is that, while an adult normally requests an attorney's assistance, a child is more likely to express his or her desire for help and his or her unwillingness to proceed alone by asking for a parent. See *People v. Burton*, supra. Moreover, in the case of a child, the right to assistance of counsel is hollow unless a parent is present, for a parent is normally the only avenue through which the child may obtain an attorney. See *Commonwealth v. Cain*, 361 Mass. 224, 229 n.3, 279 N.E.2d 706, 710 n.3 (1972).

In *State v. Whitaker*, supra, although the court held a 17–year-old juvenile's confession admissible even though his request to speak to his mother was denied, the court indicated that the result might have been otherwise had the evidence shown that his request was for the purpose of having her obtain an attorney for him. 215 Conn. at 749–50, 578 A.2d at 1037. In a similar Pennsylvania case, the court treated a juvenile's request to be allowed to call his mother to have her obtain an attorney for him as an invocation of the right to counsel and held his subsequent statement inadmissible. *Commonwealth v. Zook*, 520 Pa. 210, 553 A.2d 920, cert. denied, 493 U.S. 873, 110 S.Ct. 203, 107 L.Ed.2d 156 (1989).

Some states grant juveniles a statutory right to the presence of a parent if the juvenile requests a parent's presence. See, e.g., Ala.R.Juv.P. 11(A); Ark.Code Ann. § 9–27–317(h)(2)(C); N.C.Gen.Stat. § 7B–2101(a)(3). In interpreting these provisions, courts have held that if a juvenile requests communication with or presence of a parent, any statement thereafter given in response to police questioning and in the absence of a parent is inadmissible. *Weaver v. State*, 710 So.2d 480 (Ala.Crim. App.1997); *State v. Smith*, 317 N.C. 100, 343 S.E.2d 518 (1986), abrogated (on other grounds) by *State v. Buchanan*, 353 N.C. 332, 543 S.E.2d 823 (2001). If the juvenile's request is ambiguous, police must clarify it before beginning or resuming questioning. *E.C. v. State*, 623 So.2d 364 (Ala.Crim.App.1992). On the latter point, cf. *Davis v. United States*, 512 U.S. 452, 114 S.Ct. 2350, 129 L.Ed.2d 362 (1994), in which the Supreme Court held that a request to speak to counsel must be unambiguous and that police do not have a duty to clarify an ambiguous request.

In Alabama, the juvenile court rules also require that a juvenile be advised that he or she has a right to communicate with his or her parents. See *Smith v. State*, 623 So.2d 369 (Ala.Crim.App.1992), cert. denied, 510 U.S. 1030, 114 S.Ct. 650, 126 L.Ed.2d 607 (1993). Cf. *Carr v. State*, 545 So.2d 820 (Ala.Crim.App.1989) (juvenile's confession admissible where he was advised of right to consult with parent but did not request parent's presence before making statements). If there is no *statutory* requirement to advise a juvenile of the right to confer with a parent, however, there may be no requirement at all. See, e.g., *In re Aven S.*, 1 Cal.App.4th 69, 1 Cal.Rptr.2d 655 (1991) (while request to speak to a parent invokes Fifth Amendment rights, juvenile is not entitled to be advised of right to speak to a parent).

(4) Should a child be incapable of waiving his rights as a matter of law by analogy to other legal disabilities of childhood? The majority view is that age alone is no bar to knowing and intelligent waiver of constitutional rights. See *People v. Lara*, 67 Cal.2d 365, 62 Cal.Rptr. 586, 432 P.2d 202 (1967), cert. denied 392 U.S. 945, 88 S.Ct. 2303, 20 L.Ed.2d 1407 (1968). For a later statement to the same effect see *Quick v. State*, 599 P.2d 712 (Alaska 1979) where the court wrote:

> The mere fact that a person is under the age of majority does not automatically render him incapable of making a knowing and voluntary waiver. The surrounding circumstances must be considered in each case to determine whether a particular juvenile had sufficient knowledge and maturity to make a reasoned decision. Among the factors to be considered are age, intelligence, length of the questioning, education, prior experience with law enforcement officers, mental state at the time of the waiver, and whether there has been any prior opportunity to consult with a parent, guardian, or attorney.[9]

> It is unquestionably a better practice to see to it that a juvenile consults with an adult before he waives his *Miranda* rights, but, at least in those cases where it has not been requested, we decline to adopt a rule requiring such consultation. The state has always had the burden of proof to show that a waiver was knowing and voluntary. Where a juvenile is concerned, the burden on the state is even heavier than it would be with an adult. We believe that the careful scrutiny to be afforded an unsupervised waiver is sufficient to ensure that the rights of a juvenile suspect will be safeguarded.

Other applications of the totality-of-circumstances test in which the age of the defendant is an important but not dispositive factor include *State v. Jackson*, 118 Ariz. 270, 576 P.2d 129, 131 (1978); *Riley v. State*, 237 Ga. 124, 226 S.E.2d 922, 926 (1976); *State v. Young*, 220 Kan. 541, 552 P.2d 905 (1976); *State v. Fernandez*, 712 So.2d 485 (La.1998); *State v. Luoma*, 88 Wn.2d 28, 558 P.2d 756, 761 (1977). See also ALI Model Code of Pre–Arraignment Procedure, Commentary to § 140.6, at 361–63 n. 4 (1975).

In *Fare* the Court stated that the totality-of-circumstances approach mandates inquiry into a juvenile's "age, experience, education, background, and intelligence, and into whether he has the capacity to understand the warnings given him, the nature of his Fifth Amendment rights, and the consequences of waiving those rights." 442 U.S. at 725. In an earlier case, *West v. United States*, 399 F.2d 467 (5th Cir.1968), the court set forth the circumstances to be considered in resolving the waiver issue:

> (1) age of the accused; (2) education of the accused; (3) knowledge of the accused as to both the substance of the charge, if any has been filed, and the nature of his rights to consult with an attorney and remain silent; (4) whether the accused is held incommunicado or allowed to consult with relatives, friends or an attorney; (5) whether the accused was interrogated before or after formal charges had been filed; (6) methods used in interrogation; (7) length of interrogations; (8) whether vel non the accused refused to voluntarily give

---

9. Fare v. Michael C., 442 U.S. 707, 724, 99 S.Ct. 2560, 61 L.Ed.2d 197 (1979). See Peterson v. State, 562 P.2d 1350, 1363 (Alaska 1977); cf. Gregory v. State, 550 P.2d 374, 380 (Alaska 1976) (court can be certain that defendant's waiver of counsel at guilty plea hearing is voluntary only after examining circumstances under which the plea is made, including mental condition, age, education, experience, complexity of the case, and other factors).

statements on prior occasions; and (9) whether the accused had repudiated an extra judicial statement at a later date.

399 F.2d at 469.

Age is clearly the most critical factor considered by courts. Virtually without exception the cases that have held that age alone is not determinative of the effectiveness of the waiver have involved children 14 years of age or older, most often 16 or 17. The younger the child the more important the age factor becomes. See, for example, *In re Peter G.*, 110 Cal.App.3d 576, 168 Cal.Rptr. 3 (1980), where the California Court of Appeals held involuntary a purported waiver after hearing the *Miranda* warnings by a 100–pound, 13–year-old boy who had been drinking before the interrogation. See also *People v. Brown*, 182 Ill.App.3d 1046, 131 Ill.Dec. 534, 538 N.E.2d 909 (1989); *State v. Benoit*, 126 N.H. 6, 490 A.2d 295 (1985); *State v. Ellvanger*, 453 N.W.2d 810 (N.D.1990).

A juvenile's mental age, as opposed to his chronological age, is occasionally taken into account in determining the effectiveness of a waiver. Thus, some courts applying the totality of circumstances test have determined that juveniles who are mentally deficient lack the capacity to understand and waive their rights alone, without advice of counsel or a parent. *State in re Holifield*, 319 So.2d 471 (La.App.1975) (14–year-old boy with I.Q. of 67 who attended school for mentally retarded children, functioned on a third grade level, and exhibited the behavior of an 8–year-old child, held incompetent to make a knowing, understanding waiver); *In re Appeal No. 245 from the Circuit Court of Kent County*, 29 Md.App. 131, 349 A.2d 434 (1975) (confession of 17–year-old boy whose I.Q. had tested 73 on one occasion and 81 on a later occasion, held invalid). But see *In re W.C.*, 167 Ill.2d 307, 212 Ill.Dec. 563, 657 N.E.2d 908 (1995) (confession by 13–year-old juvenile who was moderately retarded held admissible).

In the adult context, in *Miller v. Dugger*, 838 F.2d 1530 (11th Cir.), cert. denied, 486 U.S. 1061, 108 S.Ct. 2832, 100 L.Ed.2d 933 (1988), the court held that under *Miranda* a confession must be intelligently made, and that an accused's mental illness may render his confession inadmissible. In contrast, in *Colorado v. Connelly*, 479 U.S. 157, 107 S.Ct. 515, 93 L.Ed.2d 473 (1986), the Supreme Court held that under both due process and *Miranda*, the confession of a mentally ill person nevertheless can be voluntary (as opposed to intelligent) *in the absence of police coercion or overreaching.*

The Court in *Fare* stated that a juvenile's "capacity to understand the warnings given him" is but one factor to consider. "Capacity" or "incapacity" might raise a question not only of mental illness or disability but also the infirmity of youth itself. Are juveniles *inherently* unable to understand the *Miranda* warnings, for reason of age alone? See the discussion in note (8) infra.

(5) *Lewis v. State*, 259 Ind. 431, 288 N.E.2d 138 (1972):

> We hold ... that a juvenile's statement or confession cannot be used against him at a subsequent trial or hearing unless both he and his parents or guardian were informed of his rights to an attorney, and to remain silent. Furthermore, the child must be given an opportunity to consult with his parents, guardian or an attorney representing the juvenile as to whether or not he wishes to waive those rights. After such consultation the child may waive his rights if he so chooses provided of course that there are no elements of coercion, force or inducement present. This approach has been advocated by several commissions who have studied this area and we believe it represents the best solution to a difficult and reoccurring problem. Model Rules for Juvenile Courts, Rule 25, Evidence (1969), proposed by the Council of Judges of the National Council on Crime and Delinquency; Proposed Indiana Rules of Juve-

nile Procedure, Rule 9. Having a familiar and friendly influence present at the time the juvenile is required to waive or assert his fundamental rights assures at least some equalization of the pressures borne by a juvenile and an adult in the same situation.

> The rule adopted here does not mean that a minor's confession is per se inadmissible but merely holds that, as a result of the age of the accused, the law requires certain specific and concrete safeguards to insure the voluntariness of a confession. The long standing tradition, that juveniles can waive their right to silence or to an attorney is continued, but at the same time another long termed tradition, that such waivers require special precautions to insure it be done knowingly and intelligently, is recognized.

> We believe that this rule goes far in protecting the juvenile from waiving his rights simply because of the unfamiliarity or hostility of his surroundings. At the same time it lays down a concrete and specific procedure for the authorities to follow in order to dispel some of the confusion and doubt which confronts them in the area of juvenile interrogation and waiver of rights.

259 Ind. at 439–440, 288 N.E.2d at 142–143.

Since the *Lewis* court's decision requiring parental presence was based on an interpretation of federal constitutional requirements, does it represent valid law following *Fare v. Michael C.*? The question appears to be moot since the *Lewis* decision has been superseded by statute. Ind.Code Ann. § 31–32–5–1(1)–(2) (requiring counsel or parental presence and participation in any waiver of the child's rights). Compare *Commonwealth v. Henderson*, 496 Pa. 349, 437 A.2d 387 (1981), in which the Pennsylvania Supreme Court held that its "interested adult" requirement survived *Fare v. Michael C.* because the rule is based on state law; therefore, the independent state ground for the rule makes it immune from review by the United States Supreme Court.

Pennsylvania has since abandoned its "interested adult" rule in favor of a pure totality-of-circumstances test. *Commonwealth v. Williams*, 504 Pa. 511, 475 A.2d 1283 (1984). For a subsequent application of the totality-of-circumstances test see *In re C.L.*, 714 A.2d 1074 (Pa.Super.1998). Other states employing an "interested adult" rule include Kansas, *In re B.M.B.*, 264 Kan. 417, 955 P.2d 1302 (1998), Massachusetts, *Commonwealth v. A Juvenile (No. 1)*, 389 Mass. 128, 449 N.E.2d 654 (1983), and Vermont, *In re E.T.C.*, 141 Vt. 375, 449 A.2d 937 (1982).

In contrast to the trend of other state judicial decisions extending the requirement of parental notification prior to taking an admissible statement from a juvenile, the Missouri Supreme Court has refused to follow an earlier decision of the intermediate appellate court requiring access to parents. *In re A.D.R.*, 603 S.W.2d 575 (Mo.1980). Footnote 7 of the opinion states:

> In whatever respect State v. White, 494 S.W.2d 687 (Mo.App.1973) and In re K.W.B., 500 S.W.2d 275 (Mo.App.1973), cited by movant, suggest a test for the admissibility of juvenile confessions other than "the totality of the circumstances standard" reenunciated herein, those cases are not to be followed.

For an argument in favor of requiring presence of an "interested adult" or parent during any interrogation, see Raymond Chao, Mirandizing Kids: Not as Simple as A–B–C, 21 Whittier L.Rev. 521 (2000); David T. Huang, Note, "Less Unequal Footing": State Courts' Per Se Rules for Juvenile Waivers During Interrogations and the Case for Their Implementation, 86 Cornell L.Rev. 437 (2001).

(6) Some states have made a parent's presence mandatory through legislation. Colo.Rev.Stat.Ann. § 19–2–511(1) provides in pertinent part:

No statements or admissions of a juvenile made as a result of the custodial interrogation of such juvenile by a law enforcement official concerning delinquent acts alleged to have been committed by the juvenile shall be admissible in evidence against such juvenile unless a parent, guardian, or legal or physical custodian of the juvenile was present at such interrogation and the juvenile and his parent, guardian, or legal or physical custodian were advised of the juvenile's right to remain silent and that any statements made may be used against him or her in a court of law, of his or her right to the presence of an attorney during such interrogation, and of his or her right to have counsel appointed if he or she so requests at the time of the interrogation; except that, if a public defender or counsel representing the juvenile is present at such interrogation, such statements or admissions may be admissible in evidence even though the juvenile's parent, guardian, or legal or physical custodian was not present.

For application of the Colorado statute, see *People v. L.A.*, 199 Colo. 390, 609 P.2d 116 (1980) holding the statute applies only to custodial police interrogation, not to volunteered statements. See also Conn.Gen.Stat.Ann. § 46b–137(a); Okla.Stat.Ann. tit. 10, § 7303–3.1(A) (requires that warnings be given both to parent and child).

For an argument that parental presence should be a requirement and that juveniles should be informed of the right to have a parent present before any questioning may take place, see Robert E. McGuire, Note, A Proposal to Strengthen Juvenile Miranda Rights: Requiring Parental Presence in Custodial Interrogations, 53 Vand.L.Rev. 1355 (2000).

(7) Will the presence of parents insulate children from police pressure or simply add another impetus to confess? See, e.g., *Harden v. State*, 576 N.E.2d 590 (Ind.1991), in which the court held a 20–minute conversation between a juvenile and his father adequate, even though the boy was distraught and crying and the father's "advice" was that police had said things would go better for the boy if he cooperated.

One study has found that only 10 percent of Israeli children under police investigation told their parents and that nearly half of parents expressed anger as their first reaction on hearing of the child's involvement with the police. Nevertheless, about three-quarters of parents expressed a clear desire to be present during police interrogation of their children. For the complete results of this study, which argues in favor of requiring the presence of parents, see Yael Hassin, Presence of Parents During Interrogation of Their Children, 32 Juv. & Fam.Ct.J. 33 (August 1981).

Some commentators have urged that parental presence raises an inherent conflict of interest and more often than not adds a further impetus to confess. They argue, therefore, that parental presence is insufficient to protect the rights of juveniles and that more, e.g., presence of an attorney, is required. See, e.g., Hillary B. Farber, The Role of the Parent/Guardian in Juvenile Custodial Interrogations: Friend or Foe?, 41 Am.Crim.L.Rev. 1277 (2004); see also Andy Clark, Comment, "Interested Adults" with Conflicts of Interest at Juvenile Interrogations: Applying the Close Relationship Standard of Emotional Distress, 68 U.Chi.L.Rev. 903 (2001).

(8) Empirical research questions juveniles' (especially those under 15) capacity to understand and meaningfully waive *Miranda* rights. In one of the earliest studies, published in 1980, Thomas Grisso reported the following results from his extensive testing of juveniles and adults as to their understanding of *Miranda* warnings:

The results of Study I and Study II support the following conclusions regarding juveniles' abilities to waive the rights to remain silent and to legal counsel conveyed by standard *Miranda* warning statements and hypothetical interrogation situations.

(1) As a class, juveniles younger than fifteen years of age failed to meet both the absolute and relative (adult norm) standards for comprehension measured in Study I and in Study II. The vast majority of these juveniles misunderstood at least one of the four standard *Miranda* statements, and compared with adults, demonstrated significantly poorer comprehension of the nature and significance of the *Miranda* rights.

(2) As a class, fifteen- and sixteen-year-old juveniles with IQ scores below 80 also failed to meet both the absolute and relative standards.

(3) As a class, sixteen-year-olds (and, more equivocally, fifteen-year-olds) understood their rights as well as seventeen- to twenty-two-year-old adults. It should be noted that between one-third to one-half of fifteen- to sixteen-year-olds with IQ scores above 80 exhibited inadequate comprehension using the absolute criterion, however.

(4) Juveniles' sex and socioeconomic status were not significantly related to comprehension of the *Miranda* rights. Race was related only among juveniles with low IQ scores, black juveniles having poorer *Miranda* comprehension.

(5) Prior court experience bore no direct relation to understanding the words and phrases in the *Miranda* warning. However, it was related to increased understanding of the function and significance of the rights to remain silent and to counsel.

Thomas Grisso, Juveniles' Capacities to Waive Miranda Rights: An Empirical Analysis, 68 Calif.L.Rev. 1134, 1160 (1980).*

From these test results, Grisso argued for adoption of a requirement that counsel be present during interrogation. He rejected other palliatives such as the use of simplified *Miranda* warnings, pre–interrogation screening of the child's comprehension level and requiring the presence of a parent or other non-legally trained adult at the interrogation. Following Grisso's study, others concurred with his argument favoring presence of counsel during interrogation of juveniles and his general criticism of the totality-of-circumstances approach. See, e.g., Barry C. Feld, Criminalizing Juvenile Justice: Rules of Procedure for the Juvenile Court, 69 Minn.L.Rev. 141, 169–90 (1984); see also Larry E. Holtz, Miranda in a Juvenile Setting: A Child's Right to Silence, 78 J.Crim.L. & Criminology 534 (1987) (proposing a set of warnings adapted for use with juveniles).

A more recent study by Grisso and others** casts further doubt on the cognitive abilities of adolescents and their maturity level to make various decisions with legal implications. Thomas Grisso et al., Juveniles' Competence to Stand Trial: A Comparison of Adolescents' and Adults' Capacities as Trial Defendants, 27 Law & Hum.Behav. 333 (2003). Although the study primarily focused on the capacity to stand trial, it sheds light on the capacity of juveniles to make other kinds of decisions as well. This study is covered in greater detail in section F 3 infra, dealing with mental capacity. A similar report on a study undertaken by the MacArthur Foundation, also focusing on trial competence, is Elizabeth S. Scott & Thomas Grisso, Developmental Incompetence, Due Process, and Juvenile Justice Policy, 83 N.C.L.Rev. 793 (2005).

In recent years a flood of scholarly commentary has questioned whether juveniles possess the capacity, because of their lack of cognitive development, to understand the *Miranda* warnings and to waive those rights without sufficient guidance. See, e.g., Barry C. Feld, Juveniles' Competence to Exercise Miranda Rights: An Empirical Study of Policy and Practice, 91 Minn.L.Rev. 26 (2006); Barry C. Feld, Police Interrogation of Juveniles: An Empirical Study of Policy and Practice, 97 J.Crim.L. & Criminol. 219 (2006); Hillary B. Farber, Constitutionality, Competence, and Conflicts: What is Wrong with the State of the Law When It Comes to Juveniles and Miranda?, 32 N.Eng.J. on Crim. & Civ. Confinement 29 (2006); David S. Tanenhouse & Steven A. Drizin, "Owing to the Extreme Youth of the Accused": The Changing Legal Response to Juvenile Homicide, 92 J.Crim.L. & Criminol. 641 (2002); Lisa M. Krzewinski, Note, But I Didn't Do It: Protecting the Rights of Juveniles During Interrogation, 22 B.C. Third World L.J. 355 (2002).

Perhaps in response to such empirical studies, commentary and other pressures, some states are experimenting with various models of waiver of rights by juveniles. In Montana, a child 16 years of age or older may waive his or her rights. If the child is under 16 years of age the child and the parent may waive the child's rights, but if they are unable to agree, the child may waive his or her rights only with the advice of an attorney. Mont.Code Ann. § 41–5–331(1). In North Carolina, in the case of a child under 14 years of age, no statement of the child is admissible unless made in the presence of a parent, legal custodian, or attorney, and the parent as well as the child must be advised of the child's rights unless an attorney is present. N.C.Gen.Stat. § 7B–2101(b). In applying the statute, the North Carolina Court of Appeals held that a parent could not waive the rights of a 10–year-old juvenile. *In re Ewing*, 83 N.C.App. 535, 350 S.E.2d 887 (1986). See *In re S.W.T.*, 277 N.W.2d 507, 512–13 (Minn.1979) (parent cannot waive rights of child). The North Carolina statute further provides that in the case of a child 14 years of age or older, the child has a right to have a parent present during questioning. N.C.Gen.Stat. § 7B–2101(a)(3).

Many of the difficulties in determining the competence of juveniles to understand and to comprehend stems from societal and legislative misperceptions of who is a "child" and who is an "adult" for certain purposes. In some cases young people are considered "children," and the law takes a paternalistic and protective view toward them. In other cases they are considered "adults," capable of making certain decisions and being held accountable as in the case of any other adult. For a thorough discussion of the issues see Elizabeth S. Scott, The Legal Construction of Adolescence, 29 Hofstra L.Rev. 547 (2000).

(9) Should a juvenile be entitled to the presence of *counsel* before an effective waiver of rights can be made? In *Ezell v. State*, 489 P.2d 781 (Okl.Crim.App.1971), the court held statements by a juvenile inadmissible even though his parent and legal guardian were present when he was advised of his constitutional rights. The basis of the court's decision was that neither the parent nor legal guardian was knowledgeable about the law nor in a position to counsel the juvenile or make an effective waiver for him; therefore, only the presence of an attorney would have effectuated the juvenile's right to counsel and enabled him to make a knowing, understanding waiver of his right to remain silent if he so chose. 489 P.2d at 783–84. See *Rummel v. J.D.Z.*, 431 N.W.2d 272 (N.D.1988).

In an earlier Texas case the court held a statement given by a juvenile to police officers inadmissible even though he had been advised of his *Miranda* rights and even though his mother was present, because his attorney was not present and did not participate in the waiver of the right to remain silent as then required by statute. *In re R.E.J.*, 511 S.W.2d 347 (Tex.Civ.App.1974). The statute subsequently was amended to provide for the admissibility of statements following an uncounseled waiver where (1) the child has been advised of his rights by a magistrate and the magistrate is satisfied that the waiver is knowing and voluntary; (2) the statement is corroborated; (3) the statement is made as a part of the res gestae of the conduct; (4) the statement is made in open court or other formal proceeding; or (5) the statement was recorded electronically with appropriate safeguards. Tex.Fam. Code Ann. § 51.095(a). See also Iowa Code Ann. § 232.11(1)(a), (2) (child under 16 cannot waive right to counsel for interrogation purposes without written consent of parent or custodian; waiver of counsel by child 16 or older valid only if good faith effort has been made to notify parent or custodian that child is in custody, what act child is alleged to have committed, location of child, and that parent or custodian has right to visit and confer with child).

Most courts have specifically rejected the necessity of counsel where a parent was present. See, e.g., *State v. Hinkle*, 206 Kan. 472, 479 P.2d 841 (1971); *State v. Fernald*, 248 A.2d 754 (Me.1968); *State v. Sinderson*, 455 S.W.2d 486 (Mo.1970). Moreover, most courts would now apply the totality-of-circumstances test in any event, particularly after *Fare v. Michael C.*

Even where counsel is present, the presence of counsel does not always guarantee that a juvenile's rights will be adequately protected. In *In re J.B.*, 159 Vt. 321, 618 A.2d 1329 (1992), even though the parents were present and the parents and the 12–year-old juvenile were advised of his rights, his confession was held inadmissible because of ineffective assistance of counsel, in that counsel did not adequately advise the juvenile of his right not to speak to police and of the consequences of waiving that right.

Much of the scholarly commentary favors representation by counsel (as opposed to a parent or interested adult) as the means most likely to protect the Fifth Amendment rights of juveniles. See, e.g., Ellen Marrus, Can I Talk Now?: Why Miranda Does Not Offer Adolescents Adequate Protections, 79 Temple L.Rev. 515 (2006); Kenneth J. King, Waving Childhood Goodbye: How Juvenile Courts Fail to Protect Children from Unknowing, Unintelligent, and Involuntary Waivers of Miranda Rights, 2006 Wisc.L.Rev. 431; see also Kimberly Larson, Note, Improving the "Kangeroo Courts": A Proposal for Reform in Evaluating Juveniles' Waiver of Miranda, 48 Vill.L.Rev. 629 (2003) (would require counsel for juveniles under 16; for those over 16 any waiver would be presumed invalid, and the burden would be on the prosecution to show by a preponderance of evidence that the waiver was knowing and voluntary).

(10) A caveat is in order. *Miranda* itself has been limited by more recent decisions of the Supreme Court and lower courts. Do those same limitations apply to the juvenile process? For example, *Miranda* applies only to custodial interrogation, a limitation the Court set forth in the *Miranda* opinion itself, 384 U.S. at 444, and in subsequent decisions dealing with the custody issue. See e.g., *Thompson v. Keohane*, 516 U.S. 99, 116 S.Ct. 457, 133 L.Ed.2d 383 (1995); *Beckwith v. United States*, 425 U.S. 341, 96 S.Ct. 1612, 48 L.Ed.2d 1 (1976). The Court has applied this limitation in the case of a criminal defendant who was a juvenile at the time of the confession. *Yarborough v. Alvarado*, 541 U.S. 652, 124 S.Ct. 2140, 158 L.Ed.2d 938 (2004). A noncustodial confession, of course, must be voluntary. *Beckwith*, 425 U.S. at 348. Following this lead, lower courts have held that *Miranda* does not apply to noncustodial questioning of juveniles, although here, too, the statements must have been made voluntarily. See, e.g., *In re Joseph R.*, 65 Cal.App.4th 954, 76 Cal.Rptr.2d 887 (1998); *People v. Matheny*, 46 P.3d 453 (Colo.2002); *State v. Heritage*, 152 Wash.2d 210, 95 P.3d 345 (2004).

In *Harris v. New York*, 401 U.S. 222, 91 S.Ct. 643, 28 L.Ed.2d 1 (1971), the Court held that even though a statement obtained in violation of *Miranda* must be suppressed as direct evidence, it may be used to impeach a criminal defendant who testifies in his own behalf. Accord, *Michigan v. Harvey*, 494 U.S. 344, 110 S.Ct. 1176, 108 L.Ed.2d 293 (1990). The same limitation has been applied to juvenile proceedings. See, e.g., *State v. Kent*, 371 So.2d 1319 (La.1979); *In re Larson's Welfare*, 254 N.W.2d 388 (Minn.1977). In the adult context, the Court has held that a request for counsel must be unambiguous before statements made thereafter will be suppressed. *Davis v. U.S.*, 512 U.S. 452, 114 S.Ct. 2350, 129 L.Ed.2d 362 (1994).

In *Oregon v. Elstad*, 470 U.S. 298, 105 S.Ct. 1285, 84 L.Ed.2d 222 (1985), the Court held that an accused's statement given prior to being informed of *Miranda* rights does not so taint a subsequent statement made following the giving of the warnings as to render the second statement inadmissible, provided the original statement was made voluntarily. This ruling has been applied to hold statements of juveniles admissible under similar circumstances. See, e.g., *Cleveland v. State*, 555 So.2d 302 (Ala.Crim.App.1989).

Following *Miranda*, the Supreme Court held that an accused's silence may not be used against him or her, either in federal proceedings, *United States v. Hale*, 422 U.S. 171, 95 S.Ct. 2133, 45 L.Ed.2d 99 (1975), or in state court proceedings, *Doyle v. Ohio*, 426 U.S. 610, 96 S.Ct. 2240, 49 L.Ed.2d 91 (1976). This rule also has been applied to juveniles in the juvenile process. See, e.g., *S.N. v. State*, 563 So.2d 202 (Fla.Dist.Ct.App.1990).

In *New York v. Quarles*, 467 U.S. 649, 104 S.Ct. 2626, 81 L.Ed.2d 550 (1984), the Court approved the so-called "public safety" exception to *Miranda*, i.e., that in narrow circumstances the need for answers to questions in a situation posing a threat to public safety might outweigh the need for protection of the suspect's privilege against self-incrimination. This limitation likewise has been applied to juvenile cases. See, e.g., *In re J.D.F.*, 553 N.W.2d 585 (Iowa 1996); *Commonwealth v. Alan A.*, 47 Mass.App.Ct. 271, 712 N.E.2d 1157 (1999).

Lower courts have construed *Miranda* to be inapplicable to questioning by private citizens, e.g., private security guards. See, e.g., *People v. Raitano*, 81 Ill.App.3d 373, 36 Ill.Dec. 597, 401 N.E.2d 278 (1980). The same limitation has been applied to juvenile cases, in which the questioning is performed by security guards or, especially recently, by school officials. See, e.g., *In re Deborah C.*, 30 Cal.3d 125, 177 Cal.Rptr. 852, 635 P.2d 446 (1981); *In re Phillips*, 128 N.C.App. 732, 497 S.E.2d 292 (1998). Typically, the school official is a principal or teacher. But what if the school official happens to be a school security officer, often a member of a local law enforcement agency assigned to the school? In *People in re P.E.A.*, 754 P.2d 382 (Colo.1988), the court held that the principal and school security officer were not acting as agents of the police in questioning a juvenile about alleged possession of drugs without giving him the *Miranda* warnings. But in *In re R.H.*, 568 Pa. 1, 791 A.2d 331 (2002), the court held that school police were law enforcement officers for *Miranda* purposes. Of course, even private citizens with no connection to law enforcement may be governed by *Miranda* if the questioning is conducted for prosecutorial purposes. See, e.g., *United States v. D.F.*, 63 F.3d 671 (7th Cir.1995), cert. granted and judgment vacated on other grounds, 517 U.S. 1231, 116 S.Ct. 1872, 135 L.Ed.2d 169 (1996), aff'd on remand, 115 F.3d 413 (7th Cir.1997) (juvenile's confession coerced by staff at mental health facility, which had prosecutorial purpose in mind). Many of these cases and the issue of "schoolhouse" confessions generally are discussed in Meg Penrose, Miranda, Please Report to the Principal's Office, 33 Fordham Urb.L.J. 775 (2006).

Although the Court indicated in *Miranda* that a suspect has a right to stop the questioning at any point or to prevent it altogether, it did not include among the warnings that have to be given a specific warning that the suspect has such a right. In the adult context, lower courts generally have concluded that such a warning does not have to be given. See, e.g., the cases cited in *State v. McGhee*, 280 N.W.2d

436, 441 (Iowa 1979). Likewise, lower courts have concluded that juveniles do not have to warned that they may foreclose or stop the questioning at any time. See, e.g., *State v. McGhee* supra.

Commonwealth v. Leon L.

Appeals Court of Massachusetts, 2001.
52 Mass.App.Ct. 823, 756 N.E.2d 1162.

■ GREENBERG, J.

In Worcester, an historic one hundred year old dining car, which had graced various public places over the years, suffered severe damage on October 20, 1998. Vandals set it ablaze at East Park late at night. Every effort was made to douse the fire, but the diner sustained severe damage. A police investigation ensued that focused on two juveniles, Leon and Carl, whose statements to the police are the subject of this appeal. Complaints filed in the Juvenile Court charged them with burning a building (G.L. c. 266, § 2); malicious destruction of personal property valued at less than $250 (G.L. c. 266, § 127); and breaking and entering in the daytime with intent to commit a felony (G.L. c. 266, § 18). The juveniles moved to suppress statements they made to the police, contending that the statements were elicited in violation of Miranda v. Arizona, 384 U.S. 436, 86 S.Ct. 1602, 16 L.Ed.2d 694 (1966). This is the Commonwealth's appeal of an order of a Juvenile Court judge allowing the juveniles' joint motion to suppress the confessions.

We give a condensed account of the motion judge's findings, with amplification of uncontested facts from the record. On October 20, 1998, Detectives Michael Sabatalo and Michael Mulvey of the Worcester police arson squad drove to fourteen year old Leon's home to question him. Once there, Sabatalo found that Leon's mother spoke no English. A neighbor was called to translate. Leon was not home. His mother left to bring him back from a nearby basketball court.

When Leon and his mother returned to the house, Mulvey observed that Leon spoke and understood only "broken English." The detectives made a decision to take the mother and son to the police station. They agreed, and Sabatalo drove them in an unmarked police van while Mulvey traveled in a separate vehicle. There was no one to interpret en route, but it does not appear that any conversation of consequence occurred. At the station, Leon and his mother waited in an interview room for the interpreter to arrive. While waiting for the interpreter, Sabatalo began speaking to Leon in a raised voice and banging his open hand on the table. Leon's mother did not understand what Sabatalo said, but his anger was so apparent that she broke down and cried.

The tension was broken when Officer Miguel Lopez, who was bilingual and had no part in the investigation of the fire, came to interpret for Leon and his mother. Lopez explained Leon's Miranda rights in English and Spanish. Both Leon's and his mother's signatures appear on the Miranda warnings form, his signature appearing below the English version and hers beneath the Spanish one.

After Lopez completed the Miranda warnings, Sabatalo and two other officers left the room so that Leon and his mother could speak with each other alone. When the officers returned, the questioning began, with Officer Lopez translating. Leon denied any involvement with the fire. Sabatalo told him that someone named Michael Brown had spoken to the police and had implicated Leon and thirteen year old Carl as the persons who set the fire. After speaking with his mother and with Officer Lopez, Leon, in response to Sabatalo's questions, broke down and admitted being a participant. His answers were transcribed, and it was this document that he sought to suppress.

Carl arrived at the police station after Leon. Miranda warnings, in Spanish and English, were read to him and his mother. Lopez again served as an interpreter. Both Carl and his mother signed a waiver card indicating their understanding of the warnings. At first, Carl denied any wrongdoing. Carl was crying, and his mother was nervous. His mother left the room briefly to use the ladies' room. When she returned, Carl was in the process of making a statement confessing his involvement in the fire. Carl's mother was having difficulty understanding the nature of the interrogation. She became distraught and uncertain as to what to do. In her testimony, she described Carl as "nervous" and "crying" throughout the time he made the statement.

The judge concluded that the juveniles' motion to suppress should be allowed because the Commonwealth had not shown that either mother was an "interested adult" under Commonwealth v. Philip S., 414 Mass. 804, 809–810, 611 N.E.2d 226 (1993), and that "[e]ven with the assistance of an interpreter, the mothers did not sufficiently understand their sons' situations." As an alternative basis for allowing suppression, the judge concluded that Sabatalo's conduct and the totality of the circumstances surrounding the questioning of the juveniles intimidated the juveniles to the extent their statements were involuntary. In reaching the conclusion about involuntariness, the judge relied on Sabatalo's overbearing demeanor, the juveniles' lack of experience with police questioning procedure, and the chilling effect Sabatalo's behavior had on the mothers' ability to counsel their sons. In reviewing the judge's action, we accept "the judge's subsidiary findings of fact absent clear error, give substantial deference to the judge's ultimate findings and conclusions of law, but independently review the correctness of the judge's application of constitutional principles to the facts found." Commonwealth v. Mello, 420 Mass. 375, 381 n. 8, 649 N.E.2d 1106 (1995).

1. *The interested adult issue.* Such limits as bear on the ability of the police to interview a juvenile suspected of committing a crime were discussed in Commonwealth v. Berry, 410 Mass. 31, 570 N.E.2d 1004 (1991), and Commonwealth v. Philip S., 414 Mass. at 809–810, 611 N.E.2d 226. In questioning a juvenile who has attained the age of fourteen, the police must provide a genuine opportunity for a meaningful consultation with an interested adult prior to obtaining a Miranda waiver. Commonwealth v. McCra, 427 Mass. 564, 567, 694 N.E.2d 849 (1998). Juveniles like Carl, under age fourteen, must actually consult with the interested adult before a valid waiver of rights can occur. Id. at 567 n. 2, 694 N.E.2d 849. The interested adult must understand the meaning of the juvenile's rights. See

Commonwealth v. Guyton, 405 Mass. 497, 501, 541 N.E.2d 1006 (1989).[4] The adult, viewed from the perspective of the officials conducting the interview, assessed by objective standards, must have the capacity to appreciate the juvenile's situation and render advice. See Commonwealth v. Philip S., 414 Mass. at 809, 611 N.E.2d 226. Concerning the consultation between the interested adult and the juvenile, there is no fixed rule that requires the police to inform them that they may confer in private. See Commonwealth v. Ward, 412 Mass. 395, 397, 590 N.E.2d 173 (1992). It is required, however, for the police to at least provide an opportunity for the parent, attorney, or other interested adult to meet alone before questioning begins. "The ultimate question is whether the juvenile has understood his rights and the potential consequences of waiving them before talking to the police." Commonwealth v. Berry, 410 Mass. at 35, 570 N.E.2d 1004, quoting from Commonwealth v. MacNeill, 399 Mass. 71, 78, 502 N.E.2d 938 (1987).

The judge stated in her findings that both mothers were not interested adults because they did not sufficiently understand the significance or meaning of the Miranda warnings. Lopez, who was called by Sabatalo to act as an interpreter for Leon's mother and who played no role in the investigation of the fire, testified that after conversing with her, she stated to him that she understood the warnings. When Leon's mother was questioned by defense counsel on the point, she responded, "I didn't understand but I could see [Sabatalo's] character coming through because he was talking to [Leon] really loud, and he was hitting the table, and he was pressuring him."

It appears from the record that each juvenile briefly spoke alone with his mother: once before signing the waiver and a second time during the interrogation process. As the two questioning sessions progressed, each mother repeatedly interrupted to ask Lopez about what was happening, and each juvenile conferred with Lopez on his own prior to answering Sabatalo's questions. Given these circumstances and the narrowly tailored test described in the Philip S. case, it appears that the officers conducting the interview had before them "objective facts indicating that [the mothers were] parent[s] who comprehended the events that occurred and were occurring and who could assist [the juveniles] in the choices [they] had to make." Commonwealth v. Philip S., 414 Mass. at 810, 611 N.E.2d 226.

2. *The voluntariness issue.* Although we conclude that the waivers were knowingly executed, the second question raised in this appeal is whether the ensuing answers to the questions put by Sabatalo were voluntary. That determination involves examining "the totality of the circumstances surrounding the making of the statements themselves in an effort to determine whether they were the product of a 'rational intellect'

---

4. Where a juvenile over fourteen years of age does not have an opportunity to consult with a parent, adult, or attorney prior to making a statement, that circumstance by itself does not render the juvenile's inculpatory statement inadmissible. See Commonwealth v. King, 17 Mass.App.Ct. 602, 610– 611, 460 N.E.2d 1299 (1984). Other factors include the maturity of the juvenile for his age, his experience with police procedures, whether he or she was subjected to physical or psychological pressures, and whether he or she was kept in a noncoercive environment. Ibid.

and a 'free will.'" Commonwealth v. Edwards, 420 Mass. 666, 673, 651 N.E.2d 398 (1995), quoting from Commonwealth v. Selby, 420 Mass. 656, 662, 651 N.E.2d 843 (1995). Due process requires a separate inquiry into the voluntariness of the statement, apart from the validity of the Miranda waiver. See ibid. The factors we take into consideration include "promises or other inducements, conduct of the [juvenile], the [juvenile's] age, education, intelligence and emotional stability, experience with and in the criminal justice system, physical and mental condition, the initiator of the discussion of a deal or leniency (whether the [juvenile] or the police), and the details of the interrogation, including the recitation of Miranda warnings." Commonwealth v. LeBlanc, 433 Mass. 549, 554, 744 N.E.2d 33 (2001), quoting from Commonwealth v. Mandile, 397 Mass. 410, 413, 492 N.E.2d 74 (1986). See Commonwealth v. Tavares, 385 Mass. 140, 152, 430 N.E.2d 1198, cert. denied, 457 U.S. 1137, 102 S.Ct. 2967, 73 L.Ed.2d 1356 (1982).

Of Leon's background and experience, we know that he came from the Dominican Republic to Worcester in 1994, four years prior to the events in question. At the station house he was frightened and upset. In and of itself, such manifestations may be insufficient to render a confession involuntary, but taken together with other factors, they warrant the judge's findings. As the interview began, Sabatalo slammed his hand on the table where Leon sat. According to the judge's findings, "Sabatalo was speaking loudly ... and pressuring [Leon] to make a statement." The judge emphasized in her findings that "the circumstances surrounding the juvenile['s] making [his] statement [ ] intimidated [him] to the extent that [the] statement [ ] [was] involuntary." At first, Leon denied any complicity starting the fire; then he spoke with Lopez, who urged him to admit any wrongdoing.

As for Carl's biography, we know less than of the defendant Leon because Carl chose not to argue his case or file a brief. From the transcript, however, we learn that the family moved to the United States from Puerto Rico in 1997, and that at the time of the fire, Carl had failed to complete the sixth grade. He was thirteen years of age at the time of the police interview. He initially denied any involvement in setting the fire. When he finally confessed, he was crying, nervous, and "not allowed to take a break." At some point while answering Sabatalo's questions or shortly thereafter, Carl stated to his mother that the police had told him that if he did not plead guilty, he would be locked up alone.

The judge was within her discretion in finding that Leon and Carl, who had only been in the United States for a short time, were unable to withstand the pressure to confess. There was strong evidence that their admissions were the product of Sabatalo's inquisitorial style. The juveniles' emotional states and those of their mothers, as described in the judge's findings, indicate a loss of mental freedom of action. There is lacking proof beyond a reasonable doubt, see Commonwealth v. Allen, 395 Mass. 448, 456–457, 480 N.E.2d 630 (1985), of the juveniles' voluntary participation at the point Sabatalo pressured each of them to confess.[5] Nor did the motion

---

5. In Commonwealth v. Tavares, the Supreme Judicial Court held that the Com-   monwealth must prove the voluntariness of a defendant's statement beyond a reasonable

judge make any finding that the situation changed during any stage of the interrogation.

It is instructive to compare the instant cases to Commonwealth v. LeBlanc, 433 Mass. 549, 554–556, 744 N.E.2d 33 (2001), in which the defendant, when he did decide to tell his story, narrated his version slowly and carefully and the court held it was "not the product of 'inquisitorial activity.'" We also distinguish Commonwealth v. Williams, 388 Mass. 846, 853–856, 448 N.E.2d 1114 (1983), in which a seventeen year old defendant who had no relatives available, but who appeared to the interrogating officer to be nineteen to twenty years old, did not demonstrate any factor, including his age and the absence of relatives, that "interfer[ed] with the defendant's ability to make a voluntary and knowing waiver...." By contrast, in the instant case, the judge found that each of the juveniles was emotionally upset throughout the interview. Given their youth, the persistent nature of the questioning, the overbearing demeanor of Sabatalo, and the threats, there is enough to support the judge's ultimate conclusion that the juveniles' admissions resulted from police pressure and unfair tactics.[6]

We thus agree with the motion judge's conclusion that the Commonwealth failed to sustain its burden on the issue of the voluntariness of the juveniles' statements. Accordingly, we affirm the order allowing the juveniles' motions to suppress.

So ordered.

NOTES

(1) While the issues of whether the *Miranda* rights were knowingly and voluntarily waived and whether the confession was knowingly and voluntarily made are two separate issues and often are discussed separately by the courts, the principal case illustrates that different conclusions can be reached on the separate issues. In *Brown v. Crosby*, 249 F.Supp.2d 1285 (S.D.Fla.2003), the court in granting federal habeas corpus relief found that, although the juvenile's confession was voluntary in that there was no showing of police coercion, his waiver of *Miranda* rights was not knowingly and intelligently given. In contrast to the principal case, in *State v. Scott*, 584 N.W.2d 412 (Minn.1998), the court concluded

doubt before submission to the trier of fact. 385 Mass. at 152, 430 N.E.2d 1198. See Commonwealth v. Allen, supra at 456–457, 480 N.E.2d 630. The standard was imposed on the basis of Massachusetts "humane practice" and is not constitutionally compelled. See Commonwealth v. Harris, 371 Mass. 462, 469–470, 358 N.E.2d 982 (1976).

6. In Commonwealth v. Coleman, 49 Mass.App.Ct. 150, 155, 727 N.E.2d 103 (2000), where the issue was whether a custodial interrogation took place, we described a situation paralleling the judge's findings in the instant case with respect to the "voluntariness" issue: "Nature of interrogation. The questioning was aggressive and persistent. The defendant's denials were scorned and overridden. Indeed, the interview was largely one-sided; there was little contribution by the defendant. Although voices may not have been raised, and a conversational tone maintained, the substance of what was said was harsh and intended by the questioner to be so. The interrogatory part of 'custodial interrogation' looks to 'any words or actions on the part of the police (other than those normally attendant to arrest and custody) that the police should know are reasonably likely to elicit an incriminating response from the suspect,' and such was the interrogation here" (citation omitted).

that the juvenile voluntarily waived his *Miranda* rights and also voluntarily confessed to the crime with which he was charged.

(2) Cases are legion in which statements of juveniles have been held inadmissible based on the totality of circumstances, including the age of the juvenile, the length of questioning, whether or not the juvenile had any prior experience with the police, whether the juvenile faced his interrogators in isolation, whether he was given food and drink, whether he was denied access to a parent or other friendly adult, whether any intimidation was employed in the questioning, whether he was promised leniency in exchange for his confession, as well as other factors that might be unique to the circumstances of the case. See e.g., *In re Andre M.*, 207 Ariz. 482, 88 P.3d 552 (2004); *In re Shawn D.*, 20 Cal.App.4th 200, 24 Cal.Rptr.2d 395 (1993); *In re V.L.T.*, 292 Ill.App.3d 728, 226 Ill.Dec. 700, 686 N.E.2d 49 (1997); *In re Joshua David C.*, 116 Md.App. 580, 698 A.2d 1155 (1997). On the other hand, many cases can be found in which courts have held statements of juveniles voluntary, also based on consideration of the totality of the circumstances. See e.g., *Attaway v. State*, 244 Ga.App. 5, 534 S.E.2d 580 (2000); *People v. Cunningham*, 332 Ill.App.3d 233, 265 Ill.Dec. 918, 773 N.E.2d 682 (2002); *State v. Presha*, 163 N.J. 304, 748 A.2d 1108 (2000); *In re R.J.H.*, 79 S.W.3d 1 (Tex. 2002). The differences in the facts can be very subtle but yet outcome determinative.

If police are not allowed to use coercive tactics (e.g., prolonged interrogation, isolation of the suspect, deprivation of food and water, not to mention physical coercion), may they employ deception? See Patrick M. McMullen, Comment, Questioning the Questions: The Impermissibility of Police Deception in Interrogations of Juveniles, 99 Nw.U.L.Rev. 971 (2005), which condemns the use of such tactics (e.g., claims to have eyewitnesses, a murder weapon, fingerprints, or DNA evidence) when employed against juveniles because of their unique vulnerability to such pressures.

(3) As the court in the principal case correctly points out, the state bears the burden of proving that statements were made voluntarily and knowingly, although it makes the point that the state must do so by proof beyond a reasonable doubt. The reasonable doubt standard, the court concedes, is not constitutionally required. The Supreme Court has declared that the appropriate standard of proof governing the issue of voluntariness is preponderance of the evidence. *Lego v. Twomey*, 404 U.S. 477, 92 S.Ct. 619, 30 L.Ed.2d 618 (1972).

As a practical matter, the trial court's determination on the question of voluntariness is generally viewed as a factual finding that will not be disturbed on appeal unless it is contrary to the manifest weight of the evidence. As attorney for the juvenile, one therefore must make the strongest arguments at the time of the first motion to suppress the confession.

(4) Suppose the state's evidence consists solely of an extra-judicial (i.e. out of court) confession, and at the delinquency hearing the state presents no other evidence that a crime was actually committed. A motion for a directed verdict of acquittal should succeed under the general doctrine applicable to criminal law that an extra-judicial confession alone is insufficient to convict. There must be independent evidence that a crime was committed. The required evidence of the crime is called the *corpus delicti*, or body of the crime. See *In re Way*, 319 So.2d 651 (Miss.1975). See also Wayne R. LaFave, Criminal Law 20–23 (4th ed. 2003).

F. DIFFERENCES IN TREATMENT—WHAT REMAINS?
INTRODUCTION

At the risk of appearing repetitious, we return to the prophetic words of Justice Blackmun in *McKeiver*, expressing a cynical view of the future of the juvenile justice process while rejecting the right to jury trial for juveniles:

> If the formalities of the criminal adjudicative process are to be superimposed upon the juvenile court system, there is little need for its separate existence. Perhaps that ultimate disillusionment will come one day, but for the moment we are disinclined to give impetus to it.

403 U.S. at 551.

The reality today is that most of the formalities of the criminal adjudicative process have been superimposed on the juvenile court, at least in delinquency cases. Little difference is seen between the two processes in most respects, e.g., notice, discovery, the right to counsel, rules of evidence, standard of proof, privilege against self-incrimination, the guilty-plea process, and confrontation and cross-examination. Some areas remain, however, in which the two processes are different. This section focuses on four of those areas: jury trial, speedy and public trial, mental capacity, and, perhaps most importantly, dispositions.

1. JURY TRIAL

McKeiver v. Pennsylvania

Supreme Court of the United States, 1971.
403 U.S. 528, 91 S.Ct. 1976, 29 L.Ed.2d 647.

(The opinion in this case is reproduced at p. 888, supra.)

NOTES

(1) The Supreme Court in *McKeiver* simply held that due process does not require states to afford jury trials in juvenile proceedings. The Court's decision does not prevent states from choosing to do so. Speaking for a four-member plurality, Justice Blackmun stated: "If in its wisdom, any State feels the jury trial is desirable in all cases, or in certain kinds, there appears to be no impediment to its installing a system embracing that feature. That, however, is the State's privilege and not its obligation." 403 U.S. at 547. For an argument favoring jury trial for juveniles, in part on the basis that Justice Blackmun's opinion announcing the judgment of the Court was a plurality opinion and should not be persuasive to state courts, see Sandra M. Ko, Comment, Why Do They Continue to Get the Worst of Both Worlds?: The Case for Providing Louisiana's Juveniles with the Right to a Jury in Delinquency Adjudications, 12 Am.U.J. Gender Soc. Pol'y & L. 161 (2004).

A number of states provide for jury trial in juvenile proceedings, either by statute or judicial decision. Mass.Gen.Laws Ann. ch. 119, § 55A; Mich.Comp.Laws Ann. § 712A.17(2); Mont.Code Ann. § 41–5–1502(1); N.M.Stat.Ann. § 32A–2–16(A); Okla.Stat.Ann. tit. 10, § 7303–4.1; Tex.Fam.Code Ann. § 54.03(c); W.Va.Code § 49–5–6; Wyo.Stat.Ann. § 14–6–223(c); *RLR v. State*, 487 P.2d 27 (Alaska 1971).[†] The great majority of states, however, have elected not to provide for jury trials in adjudicatory hearings, or have decided that jury trials are not constitutionally

[†] The Alaska Supreme Court's decision in *RLR v. State* actually postdated *McKeiver*, but the court based its decision on state constitutional law.

required. The numerous statutes and cases are cited in Samuel M. Davis, Rights of Juveniles: The Juvenile Justice System § 5:3, n.5 (2d ed. 2008).

(2) The Juvenile Justice Standards provide that a juvenile is entitled to trial by jury on demand in any case in which he has denied the allegations contained in the petition. The Standards would require a minimum of six jurors and would require that all jury verdicts be unanimous. Juvenile Justice Standards Project, Standards Relating to Adjudication 4.1 (1980).

The commentary to Standard 4.1 articulates several reasons for the position favoring jury trials in juvenile proceedings: neutralization of the biased judge; enhanced visibility of the adjudicative process; articulation of the applicable law through jury instructions, which facilitates appellate review of the legal issues; and avoidance of the blurring of evidentiary issues that occurs because of the universal presumption (in the absence of a jury) that the judge has disregarded inadmissible evidence and relied only on competent evidence in arriving at a decision. Juvenile Justice Standards Relating to Adjudication, Commentary at 53–54 (1980).

(3) In recent years several states have revised their juvenile court codes as part of a general "reform" effort to deal more harshly with juveniles, particularly those accused of serious offenses and those with prior records of criminal misbehavior. Claims have been raised that these changes are punitive in nature and have the effect of transforming juvenile proceedings into criminal proceedings, and, therefore, juveniles now have a right to jury trial.

In Washington, for example, the juvenile court code was revised to provide for accountability of juveniles for their acts and for proportional punishment for some juveniles, based on age, prior record, and seriousness of the offense. Wash.Rev.Code Ann. §§ 13.40.010(2)(c)–(d), 13.40.030, 13.40.0357, 13.40.160, 13.40.180. In rejecting a claim that under the revised code juveniles were entitled to jury trial, the Washington Supreme Court held that although "the philosophy and methodology of addressing the personal and societal problems of juvenile offenders" had changed, the fundamentally rehabilitative purpose of the court remained, and viewed in light of *McKeiver* the code's provision for hearings without juries measured up to the essentials of due process. *State v. Lawley*, 91 Wn.2d 654, 591 P.2d 772 (1979). *Lawley* later was reaffirmed in *State v. Schaaf*, 109 Wn.2d 1, 743 P.2d 240 (1987). Moreover, following further amendments to the juvenile court code in 1997, the Washington courts once again rejected the claim that punitive statutory measures give rise to a right to jury trial. *State v. J.H.*, 96 Wash.App. 167, 978 P.2d 1121 (1999), cert. denied, 529 U.S. 1130, 120 S.Ct. 2005, 146 L.Ed.2d 956 (2000). See also *In re L.C.*, 273 Ga. 886, 548 S.E.2d 335 (2001).

This issue is discussed in broader context in Barry C. Feld, Juvenile Court Legislative Reform and the Serious Young Offender: Dismantling the "Rehabilitative Ideal," 65 Minn.L.Rev. 167, 197–203 (1980). For a persuasive argument favoring the right to jury trial in juvenile court because of changes in the nature and focus of the juvenile process, see Carol R. Berry, Comment, A California Juvenile's Right to Trial By Jury: An Issue Now Overripe for Consideration, 24 San Diego L.Rev. 1223 (1987). For a similar argument that California's new "three strikes" provision, which treats juvenile adjudications for felonies the same as felony convictions for sentencing purposes, has changed juvenile proceedings in such a fundamental way that juveniles now should be accorded jury trials, see David C. Owen, Comment, Striking Out Juveniles: A Reexamination of the Right to Jury Trial in Light of California's "Three Strikes" Legislation, 29 U.C.Davis L.Rev. 437 (1996). In *In re Myresheia W.*, 61 Cal.App.4th 734, 72 Cal.Rptr.2d 65 (1998), however, the California Court of Appeals rejected the argument that juveniles are entitled to jury trial because of the "three strikes and you're out" provision.

(4) The argument also has been made that juveniles should have the right to a jury trial when criminal consequences attach to a juvenile adjudication. In *Apprendi v. New Jersey*, 530 U.S. 466, 120 S.Ct. 2348, 147 L.Ed.2d 435 (2000), the Court held that due process requires that any factual determination, *other than a prior conviction*, authorizing an increase in a defendant's sentence beyond the statutory maximum must be made by a jury on the basis of proof beyond a reasonable doubt. The "prior conviction" exception was allowed because defendants in any criminal trial have the right to jury trial and the right to have any case proved beyond a reasonable doubt. Does a juvenile adjudication where the juvenile did not have the right to a jury trial fall within the "prior conviction" exception?

Relying on *Apprendi*, the Louisiana Supreme Court in *State v. Brown*, 879 So.2d 1276 (La. 2004), cert. denied, 543 U.S. 1177, 125 S.Ct. 1310, 161 L.Ed.2d 161 (2005), held that, even though jury trials generally are not required in juvenile proceedings, using a prior juvenile adjudication to enhance an adult sentence where the juvenile did not receive a jury trial is unconstitutional. In Daniel J. Kennedy, Note, Nonjury Adjudications As Prior Convictions under Apprendi, 2004 U.Ill. L.Rev. 267, the author argues that nonjury adjudications fall within the "prior conviction" exception and, therefore, should be allowed to enhance an adult sentence. For an opposite view, that juvenile adjudications should not be used to enhance a criminal sentence, see Ellen Marrus, "That Isn't Fair, Judge": The Costs of Using Prior Juvenile Delinquency Adjudications in Criminal Court Sentencing, 40 Hous.L.Rev. 1323 (2004); Audrey Dupont, The Eighth Amendment Proportionality Analysis and Age and the Constitutionality of Using Juvenile Adjudications to Enhance Adult Sentences, 78 Denver U.L.Rev. 255 (2000). An excellent analysis of *Apprendi* and its impact on the right to jury trial for juveniles is Barry C. Feld, The Constitutional Tension between Apprendi and McKeiver: Sentence Enhancements Based on Delinquency Convictions and the Quality of Justice in Juvenile Courts, 38 Wake Forest L.Rev. 1111 (2003).

The Supreme Court reaffirmed its decision in *Apprendi* four years later in *Blakely v. Washington*, 542 U.S. 296, 124 S.Ct. 2531, 159 L.Ed.2d 403 (2004). In *In re Welfare of J.C.P., Jr.*, 716 N.W.2d 664 (Minn.Ct.App. 2006), the court applied *Blakely* in holding that a juvenile was not entitled to have a jury determine the facts supporting his certification to criminal court for trial as an adult.

Courts have held that the right to jury trial attaches when other criminal consequences may result from a juvenile adjudication. In *In re C.B.*, 708 So.2d 391 (La.1998), the court held that a statute authorizing transfer of adjudicated delinquents to adult correctional facilities at age 17 violates due process of law where the juveniles did not receive a jury trial. As it would later note in *State v. Brown*, supra, the court reached this decision despite the fact that it had held in *State ex rel. D.J.*, 817 So.2d 26 (La. 2002), that juveniles generally are not constitutionally entitled to the right to jury trial. In *In re Hezzie R.*, 219 Wis.2d 848, 580 N.W.2d 660 (1998), cert. denied sub. nom. *Ryan D.L. v. Wisconsin*, 525 U.S. 1150, 119 S.Ct. 1051, 143 L.Ed.2d 56 (1999), the court held that while the statute eliminating jury trials from juvenile proceedings is constitutionally valid, in cases in which juveniles can be subjected to incarceration in adult correctional facilities, juveniles are constitutionally entitled to the right to jury trial. In some states by statute juveniles are granted the right to jury trial in cases with more serious dispositional consequences, even though the right to jury trial is not generally available. See, e.g., Ark. Code Ann. §§ 9–27–325(a), 9–27–505(a); Colo.Rev.Stat. § 19–2–107; Ill.Comp.Stat.Ann. ch. 705, §§ 405/5–605(1), 405/5–810(3), 405/5–815(d), 405/5–820(d).

Following the Louisiana Supreme Court's decision in *State ex rel. D.J.*, supra, rejecting any general constitutional right to trial by jury for juveniles, the argument has been made that juveniles should have a right to jury trial, in large part because

Justice Blackmun's opinion announcing the judgment of the Court in *McKeiver* was a plurality opinion and should not be a basis for reliance by state courts. Sandra M. Ko, Comment, Why Do They Continue to Get the Worst of Both Worlds?: The Case for Providing Louisiana's Juveniles with the Right to a Jury in Delinquency Adjudications, 12 Am.U.J. Gender Soc. Pol'y & L. 161 (2004).

(5) Texas permits jury trials in juvenile hearings. The Texas Court of Civil Appeals, however, held that since juvenile proceedings are civil in nature, the rule in civil cases allowing less than unanimous verdicts (10 out of 12) was applicable in juvenile cases as well. *In re V.R.S.*, 512 S.W.2d 350 (Tex.Civ.App.1974). Unanimous verdicts are constitutionally required in felony cases in Texas, and the delinquent act alleged in this case was a felony. Subsequent to the court's decision the statute allowing jury trials in juvenile hearings was amended to require unanimous jury verdicts. Tex.Fam.Code Ann. § 54.03(c).

(6) *People ex rel. R.A.D.*, 196 Colo. 430, 586 P.2d 46 (1978):

A juvenile, like an adult, is entitled to the essentials of due process before his freedom may be curtailed. Fundamental fairness mandates that the charges against a juvenile be evaluated by a fair and impartial jury. Thus we hold that the rule allowing one charged in an adult criminal prosecution to challenge for cause a prospective juror who is employed by a law enforcement agency, must also be applied in juvenile delinquency proceedings.

Logically the same likelihood of bias affects the law enforcement employee whether an adult or a child is charged with an offense. Logically the same rule should govern both situations. Due process, in the sense of obvious, fundamental fairness, should have prompted the trial judge here to sustain the appellant's challenge for cause.

The appellant was deprived of his statutorily guaranteed number of peremptory challenges, for he was forced to employ one of them to excuse a juror who should have been excused for cause. Had the challenge been sustained, the composition of the jury would have been different. No one can tell what effect this might have had upon the trial's outcome and it is not for us to speculate.

(7) Illinois makes no provision for jury trials in juvenile proceedings. Nevertheless, in *In re Staley*, 67 Ill.2d 33, 7 Ill.Dec. 85, 364 N.E.2d 72 (1977), the Illinois Supreme Court held that requiring a juvenile to appear at the adjudicatory hearing while handcuffed constituted reversible error:

The State points out that there was no trial by jury here. The possibility of prejudicing a jury, however, is not the only reason why courts should not allow the shackling of an accused in the absence of a strong necessity for doing so. The presumption of innocence is central to our administration of criminal justice. In the absence of exceptional circumstances, an accused has the right to stand trial "with the appearance, dignity, and self-respect of a free and innocent man." It jeopardizes the presumption's value and protection and demeans our justice for an accused without clear cause to be required to stand in a courtroom in manacles or other restraints while he is being judged. Also, ... shackling restricts the ability of an accused to cooperate with his attorney and to assist in his defense. The reasons for forbidding shackling are not limited to trials by jury. Section 4.1(C) of the ABA Standards relating to trial by jury, ... while it does concern the conduct of jury trials, does not limit its disapproval of physical restraint of a defendant to such trials. The commentary to section 4.1 provides:

"... [T]he matter of custody and restraint of defendants and witnesses at trial is not of concern solely in those cases in which there is a jury. Obviously, a defendant should be able to consult effectively with counsel in all cases. Prison attire and unnecessary physical restraint are offensive even when there is no jury. . . .

> . . .

(c) . . . Because the rule rests only in part upon the possibility of jury prejudice, it should not be limited to jury trials." ABA Standards, Trial by Jury sec. 4.1, Commentary 92–94 (1968).

2.   Speedy and Public Trial

a.   RIGHT TO SPEEDY TRIAL

(See materials on speedy trial at page 1059 et seq. supra.)

b.   PUBLIC TRIAL AND CONFIDENTIALITY

In re J.S.

Supreme Court of Vermont, 1981.
140 Vt. 458, 438 A.2d 1125.

■ Underwood, Justice.

A juvenile, J.S., appeals from an order of the juvenile court allowing the public to attend proceedings to adjudge him a delinquent child for his alleged participation in the murder of one girl and the sexual assault of another.

In an attempt to comply with the confidentiality provisions of our juvenile shield law, 33 V.S.A. § 651, one trial judge issued an order of closure which barred the public from the proceedings. The Burlington Free Press was granted permission to intervene for the sole purpose of being heard on its petition for access to any and all of the proceedings involving J.S. A second trial judge granted the petition, holding that 33 V.S.A. § 651(c) violated the First Amendment. He ordered that J.S.'s juvenile proceedings be held in open court and that the public and the news media be permitted to attend.

J.S. sought relief from this order by two means. He was granted this interlocutory appeal . . . from the order opening the proceedings, and at the same time he filed a petition for extraordinary relief, . . . seeking to vacate the order and to exclude the public.

> . . .

The principal question before us is whether the limited holding of Richmond Newspapers, Inc. v. Virginia, 448 U.S. 555 (1980), that the First Amendment contains a right of access to criminal trials extends to a juvenile proceeding to determine delinquency and treatment. We must also consider additional arguments put forward by the Free Press in support of public proceedings.

Only a brief recital of the facts is necessary to enable us to grapple with the legal issues raised in this appeal. Two 12–year-old Essex Junction girls were brutally assaulted by two persons in or near an area park. One was killed. The other, left for dead, managed to survive. J.S. and a 16–year-old are the alleged assailants. J.S., who is 15, has been charged as a juvenile delinquent and will have his proceedings heard in juvenile court. The 16–year-old is awaiting trial as an adult in superior court on charges of first-degree murder and sexual assault.*

Our juvenile shield law requires that juvenile court proceedings be confidential. The relevant portions of that law provide:

(c) Except in hearings to declare a person in contempt of court, the general public shall be excluded from hearings under this chapter and only the parties, their counsel, witnesses and other persons accompanying a party for his assistance and such other person as the court finds to have a proper interest in the case or in the work of the court, may be admitted by the court. If the court finds that it is to the best interest and welfare of the child, his presence may be temporarily excluded, except while a charge of his delinquency is being heard at the hearing on the petition.

(d) There shall be no publicity given by any person to any proceedings under the authority of this chapter except with the consent of the child and his parent or guardian.

33 V.S.A. § 651.

On appeal, J.S. contends that 33 V.S.A. § 651(c) mandates that the juvenile proceedings be closed to the public and the news media, and that closed proceedings are perfectly consistent with the United States and Vermont Constitutions. The State, in effect, concurs. Both J.S. and the State ask us to reverse the court below and close the proceedings.

The Free Press makes three arguments in support of public proceedings: (1) The court below was correct in holding that 33 V.S.A. § 651(c) was unconstitutional. (2) Even if the statute is constitutional, the proceedings should be public because the court below erroneously found itself without discretion under § 651(c) to admit reporters, and in the proper exercise of that discretion, they should be admitted. (3) Even if we disagree with the first two arguments, the publicity involving J.S. has been and will be so pervasive that the reasons for confidentiality no longer exist, so a special

---

* The jurisdictional age in Vermont for juveniles alleged to be delinquent is 16, and until recently no provision was made for waiver of jurisdiction. The criminal court was given discretion to transfer to the juvenile court a person who was over 16 but under 18 at the time of the alleged offense; the juvenile court then had jurisdiction over these older youths. Following recent amendments, the criminal court still has original jurisdiction over these older youths with discretion to transfer some of them to the juvenile court and, in addition, has original jurisdiction over juveniles who were 14 or older but under 6 at the time of commission of any one of certain enumerated serious offenses, with discretion to transfer some cases to juvenile court. Vt. Stat.Ann. tit. 33, §§ 5505(b), 5516(c). Moreover, the juvenile court is now authorized to waive jurisdiction and transfer for criminal prosecution a juvenile who was 10 or older but under 14 at the time of commission of one of the serious offenses enumerated in the statute. Id. § 5506(a).

Under either the former provisions or the current law, the case of the 16–year-old accomplice would have originated in criminal court, which, perhaps because of the seriousness of the offenses (murder and sexual assault), would not have been disposed to transfer the case to juvenile court. Had the current law been applicable to J.S., his case would have originated in criminal court because of his age and because the offenses charged are among those set forth in the statute. Id. §§ 5505(b), 5506(a), 5516(c).

exception from the general requirement of confidentiality should be made in this case to allow public access. We disagree with all three arguments and therefore reverse.

I.

The Free Press claims that *Richmond Newspapers*, supra, dictates that the general public and the news media have a First Amendment right to attend juvenile delinquency proceedings and to publicly report what they see and hear in the juvenile court during those proceedings.

The question facing the Supreme Court in the *Richmond Newspapers* case, however, was whether the public and press possess a constitutional right of access to criminal trials. *Richmond Newspapers*, supra, 448 U.S. at 558. The Supreme Court concluded that such a right existed. The plurality held that the combination of the unbroken tradition of open criminal trials at common law and the fact that openness of criminal trials serves important First Amendment goals requires public access, absent overriding interests. That limited holding, however, does not extend to the case at hand.

Far from a tradition of openness, juvenile proceedings are almost invariably closed. All 50 states, in fact, have some sort of juvenile shield law to limit public access. Smith v. Daily Mail Publishing Co., 443 U.S. 97, 105 (1979). Further, juvenile proceedings are not criminal prosecutions, a fact which makes at least some of the First Amendment purposes served by open criminal trials inapplicable. Finally, inherent in the very nature of juvenile proceedings are compelling interests in confidentiality which the Supreme Court itself has endorsed in cases cited below, and which we hold override any remaining First Amendment goals which access might serve.

A.

The holding in *Richmond Newspapers* applies only to criminal trials. Our juvenile law expressly provides that juvenile proceedings are not criminal. The very purpose of the juvenile delinquency law is to provide an alternative to criminal prosecutions of children. Thus, the Legislature has stated:

(a) The purposes of this chapter are:

.   .   .

(2) to remove from children committing delinquent acts the taint of criminality and the consequences of criminal behavior. . . .

.   .   .

(b) The provisions of this chapter shall be construed as superseding the provisions of the criminal law of this state to the extent the same are inconsistent herewith.

33 V.S.A. § 631.

An order of the juvenile court in proceedings under this chapter shall not be deemed a conviction of crime. . . .

33 V.S.A. § 662(a).

We underscored the fundamental characteristic of a juvenile proceeding in In re Rich, 125 Vt. 373, 375, 216 A.2d 266, 267–68 (1966):

> It is a protective proceeding entirely concerned with the welfare of the child, and is not punitive. The procedures supersede the provisions of the criminal law and laws affecting minors in conflict with the authorizations of the juvenile court statutes. The inquiry relates to proper custody for the child, not his guilt or innocence as a criminal offender.

The only issue in a juvenile proceeding is "the care, needs and protection of the minor and his rehabilitation and restoration to useful citizenship." In re Delinquency Proceedings, 129 Vt. 185, 191, 274 A.2d 506, 510 (1970).

B.

The court below compared the similarities and differences of juvenile proceedings and criminal trials, cited the United States Supreme Court decisions in Breed v. Jones, 421 U.S. 519 (1975); In re Winship, 397 U.S. 358 (1970); and In re Gault, 387 U.S. 1 (1967), and concluded that a juvenile proceeding was a juvenile prosecution for the purposes of the First Amendment. The differences and similarities it discussed were irrelevant in light of the fundamental distinction between the punitive purpose of a criminal prosecution and the rehabilitative purpose of a juvenile proceeding.

The cases cited by the court below do not support the proposition for which they were cited. Each merely extended certain procedural protections to the juvenile. Nothing in any one of them suggests that the Legislature may not further protect the juvenile by closing the proceedings. If anything, the great concern for the welfare of the child that they demonstrate suggests that the child's interests should prevail when in conflict with public access. To the extent that they are relevant at all, the precedents cited by the court below indicate that confidentiality is appropriate.

Thus it appears to us that a juvenile proceeding is so unlike a criminal prosecution that the limited right of access described in *Richmond Newspapers* does not govern. Certainly, neither the United States nor Vermont Constitutions expressly mandate a right of access. Nor do our opinions or those of the United States Supreme Court hint that such a right exists. The court below was in error when it held otherwise.

C.

Even if there were some constitutional right of access which presumptively reached juvenile proceedings, public access would not automatically follow. Rather, the First Amendment interests would first have to be weighed against the countervailing interests in confidentiality. See Richmond Newspapers, supra, 448 U.S. at 581 (plurality opinion), 585–86, 598 (Brennan, J., concurring).

The punitive purpose of criminal proceedings raises First Amendment issues which are not present here. There, public access serves as a check against unjust conviction, excessive punishment and the undeserved taint of criminality. See id. at 564–74 (plurality opinion), 589–98 (Brennan, J., concurring). The juvenile proceeding, by contrast, involves no criminal conviction, no punishment, and, when confidential, no taint of criminality. Thus fewer First Amendment interests are at stake here than was the case in *Richmond Newspapers*.

The other side of the balance, however, is more heavily weighted here than in *Richmond Newspapers*. The compelling interests in confidential juvenile proceedings have been recognized and implicitly endorsed by the United States Supreme Court. See, e.g., Smith v. Daily Mail Publishing Co., supra, 443 U.S. at 104–05; In re Gault, supra; In re Winship, supra.

Justice Rehnquist has reiterated the Supreme Court's concern for maintaining the confidentiality of juvenile proceedings:

> It is a hallmark of our juvenile justice system in the United States that virtually from its inception at the end of the last century its proceedings have been conducted outside of the public's full gaze and the youths brought before our juvenile courts have been shielded from publicity. This insistence on confidentiality is born of a tender concern for the welfare of the child, to hide his youthful errors and "bury them in the graveyard of the forgotten past." The prohibition of publication of a juvenile's name is designed to protect the young person from the stigma of his misconduct and is rooted in the principle that a court concerned with juvenile affairs serves as a rehabilitative and protective agency of the State.

Smith v. Daily Mail Publishing Co., supra, 443 U.S. at 107 (Rehnquist, J., concurring) (citations omitted).

Even Davis v. Alaska, cited by the Free Press for the proposition that the State's interest in keeping juvenile matters confidential must yield to an overwhelming First Amendment right, supports the opposite conclusion. The Court there assumed the propriety of confidentiality in juvenile proceedings when it said, "We do not and need not challenge the State's interest as a matter of its own policy in the administration of criminal justice to seek to preserve the anonymity of a juvenile offender." Davis v. Alaska, 415 U.S. 308, 319 (1974). If a right of access existed, there certainly could be no anonymity.

The holding in the *Davis* case only went so far as to protect the defendant's Sixth Amendment right to cross-examination in the context of the factual situation confronting that court. Id. The Court concluded that the State's witness, a juvenile called to identify the defendant, must submit to cross-examination about his juvenile delinquency record, because the defendant's right outweighed the state interest. Id.

Any right of the Free Press to report what takes place in juvenile court is hardly equivalent to the defendant's right to cross-examine the witness who fingered him as the prime suspect in a breaking and entering case, especially where a possible motive of the juvenile for turning State's witness was to take the heat off himself as a suspect in the same crime.

There are, however, many reasons why the State's compelling interests in the confidential juvenile proceedings prescribed by 33 V.S.A. § 651(c) and 33 V.S.A. § 651(d) override the countervailing interests of the public and the news media in access to those proceedings and the news media's interest in publicly disseminating what its reporters learn while attending.

Publication of the youth's name could impair the rehabilitative goals of the juvenile justice system. Confidential proceedings protect the delinquent from the stigma of conduct which may be outgrown and avoids the possibility that the adult is penalized for what he used to be, or worse yet, the possibility that the stigma becomes self-perpetuating, thereby making change and growth impossible. Publication of a delinquent's name may handicap his prospects for adjustment into society, for acceptance by the public, or it may cause him to lose employment opportunities. Public proceedings could so embarrass the youth's family members that they withhold their support in rehabilitative efforts. See Note, Freedom of the Press vs. Juvenile Anonymity: A Conflict Between Constitutional Priorities and Rehabilitation, 65 Iowa L.Rev. 1471, 1484–85 (1980).

The argument of the Free Press that its pervasive newspaper publicity has already compromised these goals and so it ought to be allowed to attend and publicize the proceedings concerning J.S., ignores still another purpose served by confidentiality. Publicity sometimes serves as a reward for the hardcore juvenile delinquent, thereby encouraging him to commit further antisocial acts to attract attention. Id. Further, the legislative goals of expunging the juvenile's delinquency record are vitiated if the same information could at any subsequent time be obtained freely from newspaper morgues.

Neither the Vermont nor the United States Constitution, as interpreted by the United States Supreme Court or our Court, provides a right of public access which overrides the compelling interests served by our juvenile confidentiality shield statutes. The trial court erred in holding otherwise and must be reversed.

II.

The Free Press insists, however, that its reporters are among those persons contemplated by the Legislature as having "a proper interest in the case or in the work of the court," 33 V.S.A. § 651(c), and that the second judge erred when he intimated in his order that the statute gave him no discretion to grant news reporters access to juvenile proceedings.

This argument collides with 33 V.S.A. § 651(d), which specifically prohibits any of those persons admitted under § 651(c) from publicly disseminating information gained from a juvenile hearing "except with the consent of the child and his parent or guardian." No provision is made in either § 651(c) or § 651(d) to give the judge discretion to permit public dissemination of these proceedings.

The Free Press, however, would have us hold that § 651(c) gives the judge discretion to admit their reporters and that § 651(d) forbids them from publishing what they learn once admitted. So construed, they say, § 651(d) is unenforceable as an unconstitutional prior restraint of the press in violation of the First Amendment. Oklahoma Publishing Co. v. District Court, 430 U.S. 308 (1977); Nebraska Press Ass'n v. Stuart, 427 U.S. 539 (1976).

This statutory interpretation runs afoul of common sense and the canons of construction which we observe to keep ourselves within the bounds of judicial authority. Our function is not to pass upon the validity of a legislative concern or the wisdom of the means the Legislature chooses to address that concern, but merely to make sure that no constitutional bounds are exceeded.

When faced with a choice, we assume that the Legislature intended a constitutional result and construe statutes accordingly. Further, we avoid a construction which leads to absurd or irrational results. Reading § 651(c) and § 651(d) together, to give effect to each, leads to the inescapable result that a desire to publicly disseminate the facts of a juvenile proceeding is not "a proper interest in the case or in the work of the court."

These two sections of the juvenile shield law are clear and unambiguous. The Legislature did not intend that either the news media or the general public should attend juvenile hearings or report what transpired there. We do not base this conclusion on a single sentence or word or phrase in a sentence, but we have looked at the provisions of the whole juvenile law, 33 V.S.A. Chapter 12, and to its objects and its policy.

III.

The Free Press and other members of the news media apparently obtained the name of J.S. and his involvement in the murder and sexual assault of the two young girls in Essex Junction after examining the affidavits of probable cause in the two cases pending against the 16–year-old adult in superior court. Information about the juvenile will inevitably be disclosed at the adult's trial. Because this legally obtained information has been flagrantly publicized by the news media, and because more is to come, the Free Press next argues there is no longer any reason for the confidentiality imposed by 33 V.S.A. § 651(c) and § 651(d) and the Court should drop the barriers for this case as a special exception.

This argument also has several flaws. First, as we have already noted, publicity sometimes serves as a reward for incorrigible delinquents, encouraging the very behavior sought to be deterred. Secondly, this approach calls for a case by case analysis to determine if, when, and to what extent access to juvenile proceedings should be limited. Third, such a case by case analysis lets the news media determine which juvenile proceedings will be open to the public simply by turning up the volume of publicity concerning any case that strikes their fancy. Fourth, decisions to open proceedings will then be based, not on the child's needs, but on chance circumstances. Finally, it is not just the name of delinquents which are protected by the juvenile shield law. Other matters which surface in a juvenile proceeding are just as worthy of anonymity as the juvenile's name. They include the very fact of the adjudication of delinquency and the taint of criminality emanating therefrom; the specific program of treatment, training and rehabilitation ordered and the locale in which it takes place; the name of the individual or organization to whom custody of the juvenile may be entrusted; the fact and conditions of probation; disposition reports and recommendations made by the commissioner of social and rehabilitation services or the commissioner of corrections to the juvenile court; the disposition order of the juvenile court; law enforcement reports and files concerning the minor, as well as fingerprints and photographs, and the files and records of the juvenile court itself, including dismissal of the petition. These are all part and parcel of the record of a young person's life which the Legislature shielded from public access.

IV.

To summarize, the Free Press has failed to establish that any right of access to J.S.'s juvenile proceeding is contained in the United States or Vermont Constitutions. The juvenile shield law does not give the court below discretion to make the proceedings public. The fact that J.S.'s name is already a household word in Essex Junction, and that the nature of the offense and his alleged participation with a named adult defendant in certain crimes will be disclosed in the trial of the adult, is no reason to dismantle our juvenile court system. Confidential proceedings continue to serve overriding interests.

Any limitations in the juvenile justice system will not be cured by a public trial of J.S. If the Free Press feels that the underlying purposes of our juvenile laws are outmoded and no longer valid, it should not look to this Court, but to the Legislature to change the law. Only the Legislature has the power to relax the limitations imposed by 33 V.S.A. § 651(c) and § 651(d) upon the general public and the news media if it believes that would be more desirable than the present law. As of the commencement of these juvenile proceedings against J.S., however, the legislative intent is clear. Juveniles, as a class, are shielded from public exposure of any proceedings conducted in juvenile court to determine delinquency.

The order of the District Court of Vermont, Unit No. 2, Chittenden Circuit, granting the public and the press the right to attend any and all proceedings in juvenile court concerning J.S. is reversed.

NOTES

(1) Since the Supreme Court's decision in *Richmond Newspapers, Inc. v. Virginia*, 448 U.S. 555, 100 S.Ct. 2814, 65 L.Ed.2d 973 (1980), which the Vermont court distinguished in the principal case, the Court held in *Globe Newspaper Co. v. Superior Court*, 457 U.S. 596, 102 S.Ct. 2613, 73 L.Ed.2d 248 (1982), that a state statute *requiring* closure of the courtroom during testimony of a minor victim in a sexual offense trial was unconstitutional as violative of the First Amendment right of the press and the public to free access to criminal trials. In a dissenting opinion, Chief Justice Burger criticized the disparity in treatment of juveniles that allows states to close juvenile proceedings from the public and press and yet prohibits them from closing criminal trials during a juvenile victim's testimony. At least one commentator has suggested that the disparity be removed by opening juvenile proceedings. See Note, The Public Right of Access to Juvenile Delinquency Hearings, 81 Mich.L.Rev. 1540 (1983). Cf. Susan Cohn, Note, Protecting Child Rape Victims from the Public and Press after Globe Newspaper and Cox Broadcasting, 51 Geo.Wash.L.Rev. 269 (1983).

Globe Newspaper does not prohibit the closure of criminal trials, but only the *mandatory* closure in all cases in which a minor victim testifies. The Court recognized that closure might be appropriate in certain cases, to be decided on a case-by-case basis. The Vermont court in *J.S.* appears to reject the notion that closure can be decided on a case-by-case basis, adhering instead to a rule that requires closure of juvenile proceedings in all cases. In most cases today, however, courts tend to hold that closure of juvenile hearings is appropriate as long as the public or the press is provided an opportunity to present evidence and argument that in a given case the state's or juvenile's right to privacy is outweighed by concern for public safety or a similar public interest. For such applications see *Florida Publishing Co. v. Morgan*, 253 Ga. 467, 322 S.E.2d 233 (1984) (statute providing for closed juvenile court hearings valid if public or press has opportunity to present evidence and argument that in given case state's or juvenile's right to privacy is overridden by public interest); *State ex rel. St. Louis Post–Dispatch v. Garvey*, 179 S.W.3d 899 (Mo.2005) (trial court erred in granting juvenile's motion to close hearing to public where statute allows an exception in a case, such as this one, in which the juvenile is charged with a Class A or B felony); *State ex rel. Plain Dealer Publishing Co. v. Floyd*, 111 Ohio St.3d 56, 855 N.E.2d 35 (2006) (juvenile court may restrict access of public and media to delinquency proceedings if, after hearing evidence and argument on the matter, it determines that (1) opening proceedings would be harmful to child or would affect the fairness of the hearing; (2) potential for harm outweighs benefit of public access, and (3) there are no reasonable alternatives to closure); *State v. Loukaitis*, 82 Wn.App. 460, 918 P.2d 535 (1996) (trial court erred in granting juvenile's motion to close hearing to public where statute allows an exception in a case, such as this one, in which the juvenile is charged with a Class A or B felony).

The public's right to know, weighed against the individual's (and the state's) need for confidentiality, seems to be gaining ground. Some have argued that a "quiet revolution" has been going on in the last 15 years or so, whereby more and more courts are opening up juvenile hearings to media access. See, e.g., William McHenry Horne, Note, The Movement to Open Juvenile Courts: Realizing the Significance of Public Discourse in First Amendment Analysis, 39 Ind.L.Rev. 659 (2006). The public's need to know is especially great where the threat to public safety is greatest, in cases involving serious crime. It is precisely in those cases that some have argued for greater public and media access. See, e.g., Kristin Henning, Eroding Confidentiality in Delinquency Proceedings: Should Schools and Public Housing Authorities Be Notified?, 79 N.Y.U.L.Rev. 520 (2004); Melissa C. Walker, Comment, Revealing Mississippi Youth Court: The Consequences of Lifting Confidentiality Requirements on Juvenile Justice in Mississippi, 71 Miss.L.J. 999 (2002).

(2) In *Smith v. Daily Mail Publishing Co.*, 443 U.S. 97, 99 S.Ct. 2667, 61 L.Ed.2d 399 (1979), to which reference is made in the principal case, the Supreme Court held unconstitutional a West Virginia statute subjecting newspapers to a criminal penalty for publishing the name of a juvenile offender without written authorization of the juvenile court. There, the name of the juvenile had been obtained by interviewing witnesses at the scene of the crime. The Court held that the state's interest in protecting the anonymity of the juvenile offender, which in turn would aid in his rehabilitation, did not outweigh the significant First Amendment rights involved. The Court, however, limited the scope of its decision:

> Our holding in this case is narrow. There is no issue before us of unlawful press access to confidential judicial proceedings; there is no issue here of privacy or prejudicial pretrial publicity. At issue is simply the power of a state to punish the truthful publication of an alleged juvenile delinquent's name lawfully obtained by a newspaper. The asserted state interest cannot justify the statute's imposition of criminal sanctions on this type of publication.

443 U.S. at 105–06, 99 S.Ct. at 2672–73.

The Court pointed out that all 50 states had statutes that, like West Virginia's, seek to protect the confidentiality of juvenile proceedings, but that only five states, including West Virginia, provided for a criminal penalty for publication of a juvenile offender's name. The Court listed the others as Colorado, Georgia, New Hampshire, and South Carolina. The Colorado provision was repealed in 1979, and the South Carolina statute was held unconstitutional, in reliance on *Smith v. Daily Mail*, in *State ex rel. The Times and Democrat*, 276 S.C. 26, 274 S.E.2d 910 (1981). The statutes remaining are: Ga.Code Ann. § 15–11–83(g)(1); N.H.Rev.Stat.Ann. §§ 169–B:37, 169–B:38. The scope of the Georgia statute is limited to juveniles appearing before the court for the first time. In the case of a juvenile appearing before the court for a second or subsequent time, the judge is *mandated* to release the name of the juvenile. Ga.Code Ann. § 15–11–83(g)(2).

In pointing out that most states have found means other than the criminal sanction for accomplishing the objective of protecting the confidentiality of a juvenile offender, the Supreme Court noted:

> The approach advocated by the National Council of Juvenile Court Judges is based on cooperation between juvenile court personnel and newspaper editors. It is suggested that if the courts make clear their purpose and methods then the press will exercise discretion and generally decline to publish the juvenile's name without some prior consultation with the juvenile court judge. See Conway, Publicizing the Juvenile Court: A Public Responsibility, 16 Juv.Ct. Judges J. 21, 21–22 (1965); Riederer, Secrecy or Privacy? Communications Problems in the Juvenile Court Field, 17 J.Mo.Bar 66, 69–70 (1961).

443 U.S. at 105 n.3.

The issue is explored generally in Jill K. McNulty, First Amendment Versus Sixth Amendment: A Constitutional Battle in the Juvenile Courts, 10 N.M.L.Rev. 311 (1980).

(3) Sometimes cases initially start out in criminal court and may be transferred to juvenile court or vice versa. Should the presumption of openness apply for the time such a case is in criminal court? Compare *F.T.P. v. Courier–Journal*, 774 S.W.2d 444 (Ky.1989), cert. denied, 498 U.S. 890, 111 S.Ct. 232, 112 L.Ed.2d 193 (1990) (proper to bar press from hearing and to deny press access to juvenile records, even though hearing was in circuit court on appeal of juvenile court's transfer order, since case could still be remanded to juvenile court for handling as a juvenile case) with *In re K.F.*, 151 Vt. 211, 559 A.2d 663 (1989) (where case originated in criminal court and court was considering transfer to juvenile court, hearing required to be open to the public and the press until such time, if at all, case is transferred to juvenile court). As a practical matter, once a case has been covered by the media during the initial criminal phase of the proceedings, can the media be barred from further coverage once the proceedings are transferred to juvenile court?

(4) On whom should the burden of proof be placed, the party seeking to close the hearing or the party seeking to open it? Statutes often place the burden on one party or the other, and increasingly, the burden seems to be placed on the party seeking to close the hearing. For differences in treatment compare *In re M.C.*, 527 N.W.2d 290 (S.D.1995) (party seeking to open hearing has burden of showing compelling reason for opening hearing, and newspaper failed to establish reason) with *State in re Presha*, 291 N.J.Super. 454, 677 A.2d 806 (1995) (statutory presumption favoring public access may be overcome only where juvenile shows likelihood of specific harm from opening hearing to public and media, and juvenile failed to meet burden); *In re Application for News Media Coverage in the Matter of M.S.*, 173 Misc.2d 656, 662 N.Y.S.2d 207 (Fam.Ct., Westchester Co. 1997) (media access to delinquency hearing granted in absence of evidence that closure was necessary to preserve higher values and was carefully tailored to serve that interest).

(5) Should the rule be different depending on whether the proceedings are delinquency proceedings alleging a violation of law or neglect or dependency proceedings? See *In re Application for News Media Coverage in the Matter of M.S.*, supra note (4), where the court in ruling that a delinquency hearing should be open to media coverage, stated that the result might be different in child neglect or abuse proceedings where the child is the victim and not the accused. Courts generally seem to be more protective of a child's privacy in proceedings alleging neglect, abuse or dependency or in other proceedings in which delinquent conduct is not alleged. See, e.g., *In re T.R.*, 52 Ohio St.3d 6, 556 N.E.2d 439, cert. denied, 498 U.S. 958, 111 S.Ct. 386, 112 L.Ed.2d 396 (1990); *State ex rel. Garden State Newspapers, Inc. v. Hoke*, 205 W.Va. 611, 520 S.E.2d 186 (1999); see also *Pack v. Kings Cty. Hum. Serv. Agency*, 89 Cal.App.4th 821, 107 Cal.Rptr.2d 594 (2001). For arguments favoring continued protection of the privacy of children in abuse and dependency cases see William Wesley Patton, Revictimizing Child Abuse Victims: An Empirical Rebuttal to the Open Juvenile Dependency Court Reform Movement, 38 Suffolk U.L.Rev. 303 (2005); William Wesley Patton, Pandora's Box: Opening Child Protection Cases to the Press and Public, 27 W.St.U.L.Rev. 181 (2000).

(6) May a court attach conditions to opening a hearing to public and media access? Compare *In re Hughes Cty. Action No. JUV 90–3*, 452 N.W.2d 128 (S.D. 1990) (proper for trial court to bar media from adjudicatory hearing where media refused to abide by condition not to publish names of juveniles and where it was clear that story would be sensationalized) with *Baltimore Sun Co. v. State*, 340 Md. 437, 667 A.2d 166 (1995) (order conditioning newspaper's access to hearing on publication by newspaper of court's order setting forth conditions of access was unconstitutional denial of freedom of press). Attaching conditions to media access to juvenile hearings might promote the value of informing the public while at the same time protecting the privacy of individual juveniles and their families. See Emily Metzgar, Neither Seen Nor Heard: Media in America's Juvenile Courts, 12 Comm.L. & Pol'y 177 (2007).

(7) In *In re J.S.* the court also cited and discussed *Davis v. Alaska*, 415 U.S. 308, 94 S.Ct. 1105, 39 L.Ed.2d 347 (1974), in which the Supreme Court was confronted with the issue of whether a defendant in a criminal prosecution may impeach a prosecution witness by using evidence of a prior delinquency adjudication of the witness. Typical of most states, Alaska statutes and rules provided for the confidentiality of juvenile records and prohibited their use as evidence in subsequent proceedings, except for use in presentencing procedures in a criminal case. The Court held that the state's interest in protecting the confidentiality of juvenile records must yield to a criminal defendant's Sixth Amendment right to confrontation, which includes the right to effective cross examination of an adverse witness.

Should the prosecution be allowed to use a delinquency adjudication to impeach a defense witness? Is the balancing of interests the same as in *Davis v. Alaska*? Results have varied. In *State v. Wilkins*, 215 Kan. 145, 523 P.2d 728 (1974), impeachment of a defense witness was allowed, the court reasoning that the rule operates the same whether the witness is called by the prosecution or by the defendant. On the other hand, in *State v. Thomas*, 536 S.W.2d 529 (Mo.App.1976), the court held that permitting a defense witness to be cross examined about his prior juvenile record was improper because the state in a criminal prosecution has no Sixth Amendment right to confrontation to offset the state's interest in protecting the confidentiality of juvenile proceedings.

May a witness for the defendant be cross examined about the *defendant's* juvenile adjudications? In *Wilburn v. State*, 289 Ark. 224, 711 S.W.2d 760 (1986), the court held that while a juvenile's adjudication cannot be used to impeach the juvenile, it can be used in cross examination of a character witness who testifies for him. In *State v. Rygh*, 206 W.Va. 295, 524 S.E.2d 447 (1999), the court held that a character witness who testifies to the defendant's good character may be cross examined about the defendant's juvenile adjudications. In *Rogers v. United States*, 566 A.2d 69 (D.C. 1989), the court held that a character witness may be questioned about the defendant's juvenile arrest record.

May a juvenile who is the subject of a delinquency proceeding be asked about his prior juvenile record? In *State ex rel. K.P.*, 167 N.J.Super. 290, 400 A.2d 840 (1979), the court held that the prosecutor's cross examination of the juvenile about his prior juvenile record was improper. The court observed that such cross examination would have been improper even had the juvenile been an adult in a criminal trial because the applicable statute allows cross examination only with respect to prior convictions of crime. Accord, *People v. Sanchez*, 170 Cal.App.3d 216, 216 Cal.Rptr. 21 (1985); *Lavinder v. Commonwealth*, 12 Va.App. 1003, 407 S.E.2d 910 (1991); *State v. Christian*, 142 Wis.2d 742, 419 N.W.2d 319 (App.1987). On the other hand, courts in several states have held that adjudications may be used for impeachment purposes if the juvenile testifies in a subsequent proceeding. See, e.g., *State v. Morales*, 120 Ariz. 517, 587 P.2d 236 (1978); *Commonwealth v. Erie*, 361 Pa.Super. 44, 521 A.2d 464 (1987); see also *State v. Wilson*, 755 S.W.2d 707 (Mo.App.1988) (while prior juvenile adjudications may be used to impeach for bias when juvenile authorities still have control over witness and he therefore has motive to lie, they may not be used in a general attack on the witness's credibility).

(8) A number of states allow delinquency adjudications to be used in the sentencing stage of a criminal proceeding. See, e.g., Mass.Gen.Laws Ann. ch. 119, § 60; S.D.Comp.Laws Ann. § 26–7A–106; *State v. LaMunyon*, 259 Kan. 54, 911 P.2d 151 (1996); *People v. Smith*, 437 Mich. 293, 470 N.W.2d 70 (1991); *State v. Taylor*, 128 N.C.App. 394, 496 S.E.2d 811, aff'd, 349 N.C. 219, 504 S.E.2d 785 (1998). The Juvenile Justice Standards Project, Standards Relating to Juvenile Records and Information Systems 18.4(A)(1980) also takes the position that delinquency adjudications may be used in a subsequent disposition or sentencing hearing. The commentary explains that when an adjudication is used for this purpose, relevancy of the prior misconduct outweighs the reasons for preserving confidentiality. But see *In re L.G.S.*, 568 N.W.2d 182 (Minn.Ct.App.1997) (juvenile adjudication not a conviction for adult sentence enhancement); see also *In re D.D.*, 564 So.2d 1224 (Fla.App.1990) (per curiam) (denial of due process to use juvenile arrests, as opposed to adjudications, to establish serious juvenile offender status); *Lane v. State*, 551 N.E.2d 897 (Ind.App.1990) (prior adjudication as CHINS (child in need of supervision) cannot be used to aggravate adult sentence).

Under California's "Three Strikes and You're Out" law, certain prior juvenile adjudications may be counted as prior strikes for sentencing purposes. See *People v. Davis*, 15 Cal.4th 1096, 64 Cal.Rptr.2d 879, 938 P.2d 938 (1997). Conversely, under Pennsylvania's "Three Strikes" law, juvenile adjudications may not be used as prior convictions for purposes of sentence enhancement. See *Commonwealth v. Thomas*, 1999 PA Super 301, 743 A.2d 460 (1999).

In *Apprendi v. New Jersey*, 530 U.S. 466, 120 S.Ct. 2348, 147 L.Ed.2d 435 (2000), the Court held that due process requires that any factual determination, *other than a prior conviction*, authorizing an increase in a defendant's sentence beyond the statutory maximum must be made by a jury on the basis of proof beyond a reasonable doubt. The "prior conviction" exception was allowed because defendants in any criminal trial are entitled to certain fundamental guarantees, e.g., the right to jury trial and the right to have any case proved beyond a reasonable doubt. Does a juvenile adjudication fall within the "prior conviction" exception? There is a split among federal circuits on this issue. Compare *U.S. v. Burge*, 407 F.3d 1183 (11th Cir.), cert. denied, 546 U.S. 981, 126 S.Ct. 551, 163 L.Ed.2d 467 (2005) (juvenile adjudications fall within prior conviction exception and may be used to enhance an adult sentence); *U.S. v. Jones*, 332 F.3d 688 (3d Cir.2003), cert. denied, 540 U.S. 1150, 124 S.Ct. 1145, 157 L.Ed.2d 1044 (2004) (same); *U.S. v. Smalley*, 294 F.3d 1030 (8th Cir.2002) (same) with *U.S. v. Tighe*, 266 F.3d 1187 (9th Cir.2001) (juvenile adjudications do not fall within the prior conviction exception because that exception encompasses only proceedings that provide defendant with basic constitutional guarantees, e.g., jury trial; therefore, adjudications are not prior convictions within meaning of *Apprendi*). In denying certiorari in *Burge* and *Jones*, the Supreme Court passed on an opportunity to resolve the conflict.

In Daniel J. Kennedy, Note, Nonjury Adjudications As Prior Convictions under Apprendi, 2004 U.Ill.L.Rev. 267, the author argues that delinquency adjudications fall within the "prior conviction" exception and, therefore, should be allowed to enhance an adult sentence. For an opposite view, that juvenile adjudications should not be used to enhance a criminal sentence, see Ellen Marrus, "That Isn't Fair, Judge": The Costs of Using Prior Juvenile Delinquency Adjudications in Criminal Sentencing, 40 Hous.L.Rev. 1323 (2004).

A juvenile adjudication also may be used as the predicate offense for a separate offense, e.g., possession of a firearm by a person previously convicted of or adjudicated for a crime of violence. See, e.g., *State v. Cheatham*, 80 Wn.App. 269, 908 P.2d 381 (1996); see also *Griffin v. Commonwealth*, 33 Va.App. 413, 533 S.E.2d 653 (2000).

(9) Use of juvenile records for any of the preceding purposes may be limited by other considerations. For example, most states provide for the eventual sealing or expungement of juvenile records after passage of a certain period of time. See, e.g., Ga.Code Ann. § 15–11–79.2; N.J.Stat.Ann. § 2A:4A–62; Tex.Fam.Code Ann. § 58.003. As a practical matter, if the records have been sealed or expunged, they will be unavailable for use for any purpose. See, e.g., *State ex rel. N.L.*, 345 N.J.Super. 25, 783 A.2d 260 (2001).

In addition, suppose the prior adjudication is constitutionally infirm. May it be used, for example, for impeachment or sentencing purposes? In *Loper v. Beto*, 405 U.S. 473, 92 S.Ct. 1014, 31 L.Ed.2d 374 (1972), the Supreme Court held that a prior conviction in a prosecution in which the accused was not represented by counsel is not useable for impeachment because the right to counsel goes to the integrity of the fact-finding process, and a conviction obtained without representation by counsel therefore lacks reliability. In the juvenile context, in *Rizzo v. United States*, 821 F.2d 1271 (7th Cir.1987), the court held use of a prior juvenile adjudication in which the juvenile was not represented by counsel impermissible for sentencing purposes.

(10) As the Supreme Court observed in *Smith v. Daily Mail*, supra, all states have provisions protecting the confidentiality of juvenile records. Access to records typically is limited to court personnel; the juvenile, his or her parents, and counsel; law enforcement personnel under certain circumstances; and other courts and agencies for purposes of preparing presentence reports, parole recommendations, and the like. In addition, as mentioned in the preceding note, provision is usually made for sealing or expungement of records. Representative statutes are: Ga.Code Ann. §§ 15–11–79, –82; N.J.Stat.Ann. §§ 2A:4A–60, –61; Tex.Fam.Code Ann. §§ 58.002, 58.007. Recent legislation in Georgia and New Jersey, however, makes records available to school officials under certain circumstances. See, e.g., Ga.Code Ann. § 15–11–80; N.J.Stat.Ann. § 2A:4A–60(d)–(e). As an example of the courts' reluctance to allow access to juvenile records see *People v. James H.*, 154 Cal. App.4th 1078, 65 Cal.Rptr.3d 410 (2007) (trial court had no authority to order release of sealed juvenile records to Parole Board, to assist it in determining whether criminal defendant could be declared a sexually violent predator).

The Juvenile Justice Standards Relating to Juvenile Records and Information Systems (1980) provide for extensive regulations to protect the confidentiality of juvenile court records. In addition to furnishing general standards on dissemination of information, Standards 5.1–5.8, the Standards provide for specific standards on access to juvenile court records, Standards 15.1–15.8.

The Standards also restrict access to social histories and provide for their eventual destruction, Standards 9.1 and 10.1; provide for eventual destruction of juvenile court records, Standards 17.1–17.7; and regulate the use of, limit access to, and provide for the destruction of law enforcement records, Standards 19.1–22.1. In a more general fashion the Standards also provide for establishment of a privacy committee with investigatory powers and authority to recommend policies and practices with respect to record-keeping operations, provide for civil, criminal, and administrative penalties for improper record-keeping or dissemination of information contained in records, and furnish procedures for correction and periodic audit of records. Standards 2.1–2.8.

For a discussion of what constitutes "legitimate research" under a statute permitting access to confidential files for such a purpose, see *Seattle Times Co. v. County of Benton*, 99 Wn.2d 251, 661 P.2d 964 (1983).

RLR v. State

Supreme Court of Alaska, 1971.
487 P.2d 27.

■ RABINOWITZ, JUSTICE.

This appeal raises significant issues regarding the constitutional rights of a child to a public jury trial, . . .

A probation officer for the Division of Corrections, Department of Health and Welfare, filed a petition alleging that RLR, a person under 18 years old, had unlawfully sold lysergic acid diethylamide (LSD) to Joseph Want on or about December 11, 1968, and praying that RLR be adjudicated a delinquent. RLR denied the allegations. Initially, a hearing was held to perpetuate the testimony of one William J. Gowans, a chemist employed by the United States Department of Justice. RLR was not present at this proceeding, although his attorney was present. Gowans testified that a substance he had received from the Fairbanks police department was, in his opinion, LSD. At a full adjudicative hearing with RLR present, Joseph W. Want, apparently a part-time secret informer for the Fairbanks police department, testified that he had purchased "a hit" from RLR at a pool hall on December 11 or 12, 1968, and had given the tablet to a police officer. Paul W. Tannenbaum, a Fairbanks police officer, testified that he had given Want money to buy drugs and several hours later Want had given him the tablet Gowans identified as LSD. RLR testified that he had been in school at the time the alleged sale was made, and did not sell LSD to Want. The court found that the allegations of the petition had been proved and adjudicated RLR a delinquent. At the disposition hearing, which was presided over by a judge other than the one who presided at the adjudicative hearing, the court decided to continue custody in the Division of Corrections, Department of Health and Welfare, for an indefinite time up to RLR's 21st birthday, on the understanding that he was to be boarded at a ranch south of Fairbanks on a trial basis. One week later a formal disposition order was entered in which it was ordered that the Department of Health and Welfare have custody of RLR and authority to place him in a foster home, detention home, or other facility without further application to the court. This appeal followed.

. . .

PUBLIC TRIAL

The Federal and Alaska's Constitutions provide that "[i]n all criminal prosecutions, the accused shall enjoy ['have' in Alaska's Constitution] the right to a ... public trial...." The sentence guaranteeing the right also guarantees the rights to speedy trial and an impartial jury. The leading case on public trial, Re Oliver,[51] holds that the Due Process Clause of the Fourteenth Amendment prohibits secret trials in criminal proceedings. *Oliver* says that the traditional Anglo–American distrust for secret trials has been attributed to the despotism of the Spanish Inquisition, the English Court of Star Chamber, and the French lettre de cachet, and quotes Bentham's charge that secret proceedings produce "indolent and arbitrary" judges, unchecked no matter how "corrupt" by recordation and appeal. The court cites as values of a public trial that it safeguards against attempts to employ the courts as instruments of persecution, restrains abuse of judicial power, brings the proceedings to the attention of key witnesses not known to the parties, and teaches the spectators about their government and gives them confidence in their judicial remedies. In a concurring opinion in Estes v. Texas,[54] Justice Harlan says that

> [e]ssentially, the public-trial guarantee embodies a view of human nature, true as a general rule, that judges, lawyers, witnesses, and jurors will perform their respective functions more responsibly in an open court than in secret proceedings.... A fair trial is the objective, and "public trial" is an institutional safeguard for attaining it.
>
> Thus the right of "public trial" is not one belonging to the public, but one belonging to the accused, and inhering in the institutional process by which justice is administered.

Appellant argues that he was denied his constitutional right to a public trial by AS 47.10.070. That statute provides in relevant part that

> [t]he public shall be excluded from the hearing, but the court, in its discretion, may permit individuals to attend a hearing, if their attendance is compatible with the best interest of the minor.

Rules of Children's Procedure 12(d)(2) provides that

> [c]hild hearings shall not be open to the general public. The court may, however, in its discretion after due consideration for the welfare of the child and of the public interest, admit particular individuals to the hearing.

The federal constitutional guarantee has not been construed to mean that all judicial proceedings must be open to any interested member of the public at any time. Some authorities hold that the right to public trial

---

51.   333 U.S. 257 (1948).   **54.**   381 U.S. 532 (1965).

belongs to the public as well as the defendant so public trial is not subject to defendant's waiver, while others hold that the guarantee is for the benefit of the accused, and may be asserted or waived only by him. In both the federal and Alaska's constitutions, the right to public trial is part of a list of rights explicitly stated to be rights of the accused. Some jurisdictions hold that the general public may be excluded consistently with the public trial guarantee so long as the defendant has an opportunity to designate those whom he desires to have present. Others take the view that the general public cannot be excluded in this way. Where the right has been denied, no prejudice need be shown, since such a showing would be almost impossible to make. The right may be waived. We held in Flores v. State[62] that unintentional brief exclusion of a newspaper reporter from part of the reading back to the jury of a section of testimony previously given, when at least one other spectator was present, did not deny the right to public trial.

In re Burrus[63] holds that despite *Gault*, juveniles are not constitutionally entitled to public trial. It is weak authority, however, since it so concludes merely by labeling delinquency proceedings non-criminal, rather than by analyzing the purposes of the public trial requirement to see whether they would be served by applying the right to delinquency proceedings. Many authorities favor a policy in delinquency proceedings of avoiding total secrecy by admitting persons with a special interest in the case or the work of the court, including perhaps the press, but prohibiting disclosure of juveniles' names and excluding the general public.[64] Various reasons are given for this policy. It is said that permitting an audience to attend the hearing would interfere with the "case work relationship" between the judge and the child. Publicity is condemned on the grounds that it is an additional and excessive punishment to that prescribed by the court, or in the alternative that it encourages delinquency by permitting a youngster to "flaunt his unregeneracy."[65] Publication of names of juvenile delinquents is condemned on the ground that it confirms the child in his delinquent identity and impedes his integration into law-abiding society by reducing his ability to obtain legitimate employment, qualify for licenses and bonds, and join the armed services.[66] An important commentator on this subject recommends that the general public be excluded from juvenile hearings, but that the press should be admitted, though prohibited from publishing data which would identify particular juveniles; if he so desires, however, the juvenile should have a public hearing.[67] These social policy consider-

---

62. 475 P.2d 37, 39 (Alaska 1970).

63. 275 N.C. 517, 169 S.E.2d 879 (1969).

64. Children's Bureau, Standards of Juvenile and Family Courts 76–77 (1966); Children's Bureau, Legislative Guide for Drafting Family and Juvenile Court Acts sec. 29(c), at 30 (1969); New Jersey Juv. & Dom.Rel.Ct. Rule 5:9–1(a) (1969).

65. President's Commission on Law Enforcement and Administration of Justice,

Task Force Report: Juvenile Delinquency and Youth Crime 38 (1967).

66. Id. at 38–39.

67. Geis, Publicity and Juvenile Court Proceedings, 30 Rocky Mt.L.Rev. 101, 125–26 (1958); see also Geis, In Re: Juvenile Court Publicity, 16 Juv.Ct.Judges J. 12 (1965), reprinted in O. Ketcham & M. Paulsen, Cases and Materials Relating to Juvenile Courts 407 (1967).

ations are based on empirical propositions which may be false and have not been tested.[68] Some commentary favors open court proceedings for juveniles on the grounds that secrecy and the informality engendered thereby hinders rehabilitation partly by misleading juveniles and their parents into underestimating the seriousness of delinquency.[69] Recent commentary tends to be critical of secrecy because it screens from public view arbitrariness and lawlessness by juvenile courts.[70]

Just as alleged, bad motives of the legislature cannot be considered in determining constitutionality and construction of statutes, so we cannot withhold application of federal and state constitutional provisions on the grounds that those who created various systems of governmental activity such as the juvenile court acted from benevolent motives. Nor will constitutional problems be ignored in deference to untested empirical propositions about what sorts of judicial proceedings succeed in rehabilitating persons charged with misconduct; as between these sorts of prescriptions for what is good for society and constitutional prescriptions, the latter are authoritative. The reasons for the constitutional guarantees of public trial apply as much to juvenile delinquency proceedings as to adult criminal proceedings.[71] Delinquency proceedings as much as adult criminal prosecutions can be used as instruments of persecution, and may be subject to judicial abuse. The appellate process is not a sufficient check on juvenile courts, for problems of mootness and the cost of prosecuting an appeal screen most of what goes on from appellate court scrutiny. We cannot help but notice that the children's cases appealed to this court have often shown much more extensive and fundamental error than is generally found in adult criminal cases, and wonder whether secrecy is not fostering a judicial attitude of casualness toward the law in children's proceedings. In any event, civil labels and good intentions do not themselves obviate the need for criminal due process safeguards in juvenile courts, for "[a] proceeding where the issue is whether the child will be found to be 'delinquent' and subjected to the loss of his liberty for years is comparable in seriousness to a felony prosecution."[73]

68. Geis, Publicity and Juvenile Court Proceedings, 30 Rocky Mt.L.Rev. 101, 124 (1958).

69. Parker, Instant Maturation for the Post–Gault "Hood", 4 Fam.L.Q. 113 (1970). See also Handler, The Juvenile Court and the Adversary System: Problems of Function and Form, 1965 Wisc.L.Rev. 7, 19–21 (1965). Handler argues that the high degree of informality in juvenile court interferes with rehabilitation by producing in the juvenile frustration, distrust, contempt, fear, and cynicism. "The word 'help,' coming from such a person in a position of power, is, in the mind of the adolescent, a familiar signal of danger." Handler at 21.

70. Note, Minnesota Juvenile Court Rules: Brightening One World for Juveniles,

54 Minn.L.Rev. 303, 324–325 (1969); Note, Criminal Offenders in the Juvenile Court: More Brickbats and Another Proposal, 114 U.Pa.L.Rev. 1171, 1185–1186 (1966).

71. Some of these reasons parallel those underlying the constitutional guarantees of jury trial. In one commentator's view, the jury provides the citizenry, in their capacity as jurors, with a vehicle to directly participate in government; that the jury system induces public confidence in the administration of justice; and that the jury system helps to insure the independence and the quality of the judges. Foley, Juveniles and Their Right to a Jury Trial, 15 Villanova L.Rev. 972 (1970).

73. In re Winship, 397 U.S. 358, 365–366 (1970).

Therefore, we hold that children are guaranteed the right to a public trial by the Alaska Constitution.

One additional facet of the child's right to a public trial remains to be considered. AS 47.10.070,[74] and the similar Children's Rule 12(d)(2), provide for the exclusion of the public from children's hearings. Rules of Children's Procedure 12(d)(2), which governs, provides that,

> Child hearings shall not be open to the general public. The court may, however, in its discretion after due consideration for the welfare of the child and of the public interest, admit particular individuals to the hearing.

This flexible rule must be interpreted and applied in a manner consistent with the child's constitutional right to public trial. The evils of secrecy may be avoided by permitting the child to open the adjudicative and dispositive hearings to any individuals. Where the child's choice may be adverse to his own interests, a guardian ad litem may be appointed under the principles discussed in the preceding section dealing with the right to trial by jury. It is an abuse of discretion for the court to refuse admittance to individuals whose presence is favored by the child, except in special circumstances such as the unavailability of a courtroom sufficiently large to hold all the individuals whose presence is sought. If the child or his guardian ad litem wants the press, friends, or others to be free to attend, then the hearing must be open to them. The area of discretion in the rule, where the court may refuse to open the hearing, involves persons whose presence is not desired by the child. Since we have determined that the case must be reversed on other grounds, we find it unnecessary to decide whether the denial of a public trial in the adjudicative stage in the case at bar was plain error.

. . .

The superior court's adjudicative and dispositive orders are vacated and reversed, and the matter remanded for appropriate proceedings.

NOTES

(1) Most states provide by statute that the general public shall be excluded from hearings in juvenile court, although the court usually has discretion to admit

---

74. AS 47.10.070 provides in part that:

The public shall be excluded from the hearing, but the court, in its discretion, may permit individuals to attend a hearing, if their attendance is compatible with the best interests of the minor.

The statute providing for exclusion of the public from juvenile hearings is procedural, so is outside the scope of legislative authority unless two-thirds of each house of the legislature votes to change the rule promulgated by the supreme court in this matter. Alaska Const. art. IV, sec. 15. Children's proceedings are among the "civil and criminal cases in all courts" over which this constitutional provision gives this court rule-making authority which is intended to be plenary and not capable of reduction by re-labeling of proceedings. Cf. Silverton v. Marler, 389 P.2d 3 (Alaska 1964).

The statute making criminal the publication by newspapers, radio stations, and television stations of juvenile delinquents' names, AS 47.10.090(b), and the similar rule, Rules of Children's Procedure 26, are not challenged in this appeal.

persons who are interested in the proceedings. See, e.g., N.Y.Fam.Ct.Act § 341.1; 42 Pa.Cons.Stat.Ann. § 6336(d). Cf. N.M.Stat.Ann. § 32A–2–16(B), (C):

> B.   All hearings to declare a person in contempt of court and all hearings on petitions pursuant to the provisions of the Delinquency Act shall be open to the general public, except where the court in its discretion, after a finding of exceptional circumstances, deems it appropriate to conduct a closed delinquency hearing. Only the parties, their counsel, witnesses and other persons approved by the court may be present at a closed hearing. Those other persons the court finds to have a proper interest in the case or in the work of the court may be admitted by the court to closed hearings on the condition that they refrain from divulging any information concerning the exceptional circumstances that resulted in the need for a closed hearing. Accredited representatives of the news media shall be allowed to be present at closed hearings subject to the condition that they refrain from divulging information concerning the exceptional circumstances that resulted in the need for a closed hearing and subject to such enabling regulations as the court finds necessary for the maintenance of order and decorum and for the furtherance of the purposes of the Delinquency Act.

> C.   Those persons or parties granted admission to a closed hearing who intentionally divulge information in violation of Subsection B of this section are guilty of a petty misdemeanor.

Some states today have modified previous policies favoring closed hearings to allow for open hearings in delinquency cases involving serious crimes. See, e.g., Cal.Welf. & Inst. Code § 676(a); Mass.Gen.Laws Ann. ch. 119, § 65; Minn.Stat.Ann. § 260B.163(1)(c); 42 Pa.Cons.Stat.Ann. § 6336(e). The Missouri statute, e.g., provides for closed hearings "except in cases where the child is accused of . . . a class A or B felony; or . . . a class C felony, if the child has previously been formally adjudicated for the commission of two or more unrelated acts which would have been class A, B or C felonies, if committed by an adult." Mo.Ann.Stat. § 211.171(6). In *State ex rel. St. Louis Post–Dispatch v. Garvey*, 179 S.W.3d 899 (Mo.2005), the court held that the trial court erred in granting a juvenile's motion to close the hearing to the public, where the offense charged was first-degree murder, a Class A felony, clearly within the statutory exception. For discussion and analysis of the trend toward opening up juvenile delinquency hearings to the public see William McHenry Horne, Note, The Movement to Open Juvenile Courts: Realizing the Significance of Public Discourse in First Amendment Analysis, 39 Ind.L.Rev. 659 (2006). Others have argued for greater public and media access to hearings, particularly where serious crime is charged and the threat to public safety is at its greatest. See, e.g., Kristin Henning, Eroding Confidentiality in Delinquency Proceedings: Should Schools and Public Housing Authorities Be Notified?, 79 N.Y.U.L.Rev. 520 (2004); Melissa C. Walker, Comment, Revealing Mississippi Youth Court: The Consequences of Lifting Confidentiality Requirements on Juvenile Justice in Mississippi, 71 Miss.L.J. 999 (2002).

(2) The Juvenile Justice Standards Relating to Adjudication (1980) grant the respondent in a juvenile proceeding the right to a jury trial, Standard 4.1, as well as a right to a public trial, Standard 6.1. A dissenting view to both positions was filed by Commissioner Justine Wise Polier on the basis that such an alteration in the traditional posture of the juvenile court would leave little difference between juvenile and criminal proceedings and would destroy the privacy now afforded to juveniles. Her statement reflects the strongly held belief that the juvenile court as a separate institution ought to be preserved. Juvenile Justice Standards Relating to Adjudication, Dissenting View, at 77–78.

3. Mental Capacity: Competency to Stand Trial and the Insanity Defense

State in re Causey

Supreme Court of Louisiana, 1978.
363 So.2d 472.

■ Tate, Justice.

At the instance of a juvenile made defendant in juvenile proceedings, we granted certiorari to determine whether a juvenile has a right to plead not guilty by reason of insanity and a right to a hearing to determine his mental capacity to assist in his defense.

Facts

Pate Causey, age 16, was petitioned into the Orleans Parish juvenile court, charged with armed robbery. His attorney filed a motion, the substance of which was that defendant be allowed to plead not guilty and not guilty by reason of insanity, and that the judge appoint a panel of psychiatrists to perform comprehensive tests to determine whether defendant was legally insane at the time the act was committed, and also whether defendant was legally competent to aid in his own defense.

Several psychological tests had been performed upon the defendant, and the report of the testing psychologists had recommended psychiatric evaluation. A psychiatrist had interviewed the defendant, without access to the psychological test results. Defense counsel wished to subpoena the psychiatrist, whose report he had been given by the judge at the time of the hearing on the motion. After indicating his inclination to deny the motion, the judge asked the defense attorney if he would "submit it [the question whether defendant was competent to assist in his defense] on that [the psychiatrist's report]." Defense counsel responded, "I submit on the report," and the court denied the motion.

The Right of a Juvenile to Plead Insanity

There is no statutory right to plead not guilty by reason of insanity in a Louisiana juvenile proceeding, since such proceedings are conducted as civil proceedings, with certain enumerated differences. We hold, however, that the due process guaranties of the Fourteenth Amendment to the United States Constitution, and of Article I, Section 2 of the Louisiana Constitution, require that a juvenile be granted this right.

The only courts ever squarely confronted with the issue have held that, at least in adult proceedings, the denial of the right to plead insanity, with no alternative means of exculpation or special treatment for an insane person unable to understand the nature of his act, violates the concept of fundamental fairness implicit in the due process guaranties. Sinclair v. State, 161 Miss. 142, 132 So. 581 (1931); State v. Strasburg, 60 Wash. 106, 110 P. 1020 (1910). Some recent federal cases have also spoken of the insanity plea in terms indicating that the right to assert it has constitutional dimensions of a due process (fundamental fairness) nature.

The insanity defense, and the underlying notion that an accused must understand the nature of his acts in order to be criminally responsible (the *mens rea* concept), are deeply rooted in our legal tradition and philosophy, . . .

However, not every constitutional right guaranteed to adults by the concept of fundamental fairness is automatically guaranteed to juveniles.

The United States Supreme Court has undertaken a case-by-case analysis of juvenile proceedings, making not only the historical inquiry into whether the rights asserted were part of fundamental fairness, but also a functional analysis of whether giving the particular right in question to the juvenile defendant would interfere with any of the beneficial aspects of a juvenile proceeding. Only those rights that are both "fundamental" and "essential," in that they perform a function too important to sacrifice in favor of the benefits theoretically afforded by a civil-style juvenile proceeding, have been held to be required in such proceedings. McKeiver v. Pennsylvania, 403 U.S. 528 (1971); In re Winship, 397 U.S. 358 (1970); In re Gault, 387 U.S. 1 (1967).

The same approach was adopted by a majority of this court in determining which due process rights are guaranteed to juveniles by the Louisiana Constitution, in State in Interest of Dino, 359 So.2d 586 (La.1978). (Since we ultimately find this defendant's right to plead insanity to be guaranteed by the state and federal due process clauses, we need not reach the additional equal protection argument advanced, by which juveniles would be denied the equal protection of the laws if they were not permitted as are adults to be exculpated by insanity from criminal responsibility.)

McKeiver, Winship, and *Gault* imposed on juvenile proceedings a host of traditional criminal trial safeguards—the right to appropriate notice, to counsel, to confrontation and cross-examination, and the privilege against self-incrimination—and declined to impose only one safeguard, the right to a jury trial.

While the due process right to a jury trial has been held to be an element of "fundamental fairness," at least in non-petty adult proceedings, Duncan v. Louisiana, 391 U.S. 145 (1968), the court's emphasis in *McKeiver* was not on the degree of "fundamentality," but on the *function* served by the jury trial. The plurality saw the jury as a component in the factfinding process, and as such, *not* "a necessary component of accurate factfinding." Only after finding that the jury trial—although "fundamental" for adults—was not really "essential" to a fair trial proceeding, i.e., did not perform a function that could not be adequately performed by some other procedure, did the court examine the impact of a jury trial upon the beneficial effects of the juvenile system, and conclude that it would "bring with it into that system the traditional delay, the formality, and the clamor of the adversary system and, possibly, the public trial."

In *Winship,* the court held that a juvenile could not be adjudged to have violated a criminal statute by a mere preponderance of the evidence. The standard of proof "beyond a reasonable doubt" was held to play "a vital role in the American scheme of criminal procedure. It is a prime instrument for reducing the risk of convictions resting on factual error. . . .

'[A] person accused of a crime ... would be at a severe disadvantage ... if he could be adjudged guilty and imprisoned for years on the strength of the same evidence as would suffice in a civil case.' "

Underlying the functional analysis of the two procedures examined in *McKeiver* and *Winship*, was not only the consideration of whether equally effective safeguards existed to the rights sought to be imported into juvenile proceedings, but also a consideration of the realistic role played by these two rights in safeguarding juvenile rights at actual trials: the "beyond a reasonable doubt standard" actually kept the juvenile in *Winship* out of jail, whereas there was no evidence that a jury trial in *McKeiver* would have done so.

The availability of some procedure for differentiating between those who are culpably responsible for their act and those who are merely ill is, as we have seen, a part of "fundamental fairness." Moreover, it is hard to see that any important aim of the juvenile system is thwarted by affording such a distinction to the mentally ill juvenile.

The function of the insanity plea is much more akin to that of the burden of proof imposed on juvenile proceedings in *Winship*, than of the jury trial involved in *McKeiver* and *Dino*. An insanity defense, like a high burden of proof, will generically spell the difference between conviction and acquittal. That there is perhaps a lesser stigma associated with an adjudication of juvenile delinquency than with an adult criminal conviction, and that juvenile incarceration is theoretically calculated to rehabilitate rather than to punish, were deemed constitutionally insignificant in *Winship*.

In the present case, further, the state expressly does not contest the issue whether this juvenile should be allowed to plead not guilty and not guilty by reason of insanity when charged with a serious crime.

. . .

[The court reaches the same conclusion as to competency to stand trial.]

The state does not suggest any special reason that a juvenile should be denied this right due an adult. The only reason that comes to mind is the argument that *many* juveniles, "sane" as well as "insane," "normal" as well as "retarded," are incompetent to assist in their own defenses, at least by normal adult standards. This, indeed, is a large part of the rationale for the special juvenile system. Where a juvenile is "incompetent" primarily because of his tender years, it might be unnecessary and perhaps unwise to substitute the full-dress examinations and hearings designed for adult incompetents, in place of procedures designed especially to deal with youth and inexperience.

But that is not the case here. Pate Causey was reported, by the psychologists who examined him for the court, to vary "from the upper end of the range of moderate mental retardation with regard to non-verbal intelligence ... to the range of mild mental retardation with regard to verbal intelligence.... " He was reported to have "poor fine motor control, spatial disorientation, and problems in angling ... suggestive of neuropsychological dysfunction," with "memory problems and the possibility of episodic 'blanking out' " as "further evidence of possible neuropathy." Psychiatric evaluation was recommended.

A psychiatrist did meet with the boy, without access to test results; the gist of his conclusions was that the boy was dull and a liar rather than retarded and psychotic.

The reports were given by the judge to the defense attorney at the trial, to read for five minutes before arguing the motion relating to incompetence. This data, inconclusive and perhaps contradictory but suggestive of possible problems, is much like that which, in *Bennett*, this court held to require further testing.

Conclusion

The right not to be tried while incompetent to assist in one's own defense is a fundamental due process right. The right to plead insanity, absent some other effective means of distinguishing mental illness from moral culpability, is also fundamental. There is no compelling reason to deny either of these constitutional rights to juveniles charged with conduct that would be serious crimes if committed by adults.

Here, there were facts in the record to put the trial court on notice that the defendant might be mentally retarded or insane. A defendant in a juvenile proceeding has the right to plead not guilty and not guilty by reason of insanity. Under the showing made, this defendant also had the right to a more thorough mental (psychiatric) examination, followed by a contradictory hearing.

. . .

REVERSED AND REMANDED.

■ [The dissenting opinion of Sanders, C.J., is omitted.]

NOTES

(1) In *Dusky v. United States*, 362 U.S. 402, 80 S.Ct. 788, 4 L.Ed.2d 824 (1960) (per curiam), the United States Supreme Court held that the standard for determining competence to stand trial is whether the defendant has "sufficient present ability to consult with his lawyer with a reasonable degree of rational understanding" and has "a rational as well as factual understanding of the proceedings against him." More recently the Court held that this standard also is applicable to determining the defendant's competence to plead guilty or to waive the right to assistance of counsel, rejecting the argument that there should be a higher standard for waiver of constitutional rights than for determining competence to stand trial. *Godinez v. Moran*, 509 U.S. 389, 113 S.Ct. 2680, 125 L.Ed.2d 321 (1993).

What standard should be used to determine whether a juvenile is competent to stand trial? In *In re W.A.F.*, 573 A.2d 1264 (D.C.1990), the District of Columbia Court of Appeals held that the standard used to determine a child's competency to stand trial is the same as that used for adults, namely whether the accused is able to understand the proceedings against him or her and to assist in his or her defense.

(2) As the principal case illustrates, the question of mental capacity can arise at different stages of juvenile and adult proceedings: First is the pretrial stage, which addresses the juvenile's (or the defendant's) competence to stand trial; second is the

trial itself, where the issue of capacity arises in the form of the insanity defense. For an example of the latter see *In re S.W.T.*, 277 N.W.2d 507 (Minn.1979).

Other courts have agreed with the Louisiana court in the principal case that juveniles are entitled to raise a claim of incompetency to stand trial. See, e.g., *State ex rel. Dandoy v. Superior Court*, 127 Ariz. 184, 619 P.2d 12 (1980); *Golden v. State*, 341 Ark. 656, 21 S.W.3d 801, cert. denied, 531 U.S. 1022, 121 S.Ct. 588, 148 L.Ed.2d 504 (2000); *In re E.V.*, 190 Ill.App.3d 1079, 138 Ill.Dec. 354, 547 N.E.2d 521 (1989); *In re S.W.T.*, supra. The *Golden* decision was criticized in William Clayton Taylor, II, Case Note, Golden v. State: Should the Insanity Defense Exist in Juvenile Court?, 54 Ark.L.Rev. 703 (2001).

Few statutes address the issue of incompetence. One exception is Maine Revised Statutes Annotated, Title 15:

§ 3318. Mentally ill or incapacitated juveniles

1. Suspension of proceedings. If it appears that a juvenile may be mentally ill or incapacitated ... the court shall suspend the proceedings on the petition and shall either:

A. Initiate proceedings for voluntary or involuntary commitments ... or

B. Order that the juvenile be examined by a physician or psychologist and refer the juvenile to a suitable facility or program for the purpose of examination, the costs of such examination to be paid by the court. If the report of such an examination is that the juvenile is mentally ill or incapacitated to the extent that short-term or long-term hospitalization or institutional confinement is required, the Juvenile Court shall initiate proceedings for voluntary or involuntary commitment.... The court shall continue the proceedings when a juvenile is voluntarily or involuntarily committed.

2. Resumption of proceedings. The court shall set a time for resuming the proceeding when:

A. The report of the examination made pursuant to subsection 1, paragraph B states that the child is not mentally ill or incapacitated to the extent that short-term or long-term hospitalization or institutional confinement is required; or

B. The child is not found by the appropriate court to be mentally ill or incapacitated as defined in section 101–B and in Title 34, section 2616, subsection 1.

See also D.C.Code § 16–2315(a), (c)–(d).

The matter of a juvenile's competence to stand trial has been the subject of a great deal of scholarly commentary, some of it from a social sciences perspective, including some guideposts for attorneys who represent juveniles in delinquency cases. See, e.g., Randy K. Otto, Considerations in the Assessment of Competence to Proceed in Juvenile Court, 34 N.Ky.L.Rev. 323 (2007); Richard E. Redding & Lynda Frost, Adjudicative Competence in the Modern Juvenile Court, 9 Va.J.Soc. Pol'y & L. 353 (2001); Kellie M. Johnson, Note, Juvenile Competency Statutes: A Model for State Legislation, 81 Ind.L.J. 1067 (2006); Twila A. Wingrove, Note, Is Immaturity a Legitimate Source of Incompetence to Avoid Standing Trial As a Juvenile?, 86 Neb.L.Rev. 488 (2007); Tamera Wong, Comment, Adolescent Minds, Adult Crimes: Assessing a Juvenile's Mental Health and Capacity to Stand Trial, 6 U.C. Davis J. Juv. L. & Pol'y 163 (2002).

(3) New Jersey's experience in addressing the applicability of the insanity defense in juvenile proceedings furnishes an interesting study. When the issue was first considered the courts took the position that insanity could not be raised as a

defense during the adjudicatory hearing but that mental competency of the juvenile was a relevant consideration during dispositional proceedings. *State ex rel. H.C.*, 106 N.J.Super. 583, 256 A.2d 322 (1969). Subsequently the juvenile court code was substantially revised, and one of the additions was a provision entitling juveniles to all defenses available to an adult in a criminal proceeding. N.J.Stat.Ann. § 2A:4A–40. Interpreting this statute as overriding the earlier decision in *H.C.*, the New Jersey appellate courts held that a juvenile is entitled to raise an insanity defense in an adjudicatory hearing and is entitled to a separate hearing on the question of mental competency. *State ex rel. R.G.W.*, 135 N.J.Super. 125, 342 A.2d 869 (1975), affirmed 70 N.J. 185, 358 A.2d 473 (1976).

Other courts have agreed with the Louisiana court in *State ex rel. Causey* that, even in the absence of a statutory right, juveniles are entitled to raise the insanity defense in juvenile proceedings. See, e.g., *Winburn v. State*, 32 Wis.2d 152, 145 N.W.2d 178 (1966); see also *In re Ramon M.*, 22 Cal.3d 419, 149 Cal.Rptr. 387, 584 P.2d 524 (1978) (idiocy defense). However, some have concluded that in the absence of statutory authority juveniles are not entitled to raise an insanity defense either as a matter of due process of law, *K.M. v. State*, 335 Ark. 85, 983 S.W.2d 93 (1998), or equal protection of the laws, *Golden v. State*, supra note (2). For arguments supporting availability of the insanity defense in juvenile delinquency proceedings see Paul E. Antill, Comment, Unequal Protection? Juvenile Justice and the Insanity Defense, 22 J.Juv.L. 50 (2002); Emily S. Pollock, Note, Those Crazy Kids: Providing the Insanity Defense in Juvenile Courts, 85 Minn.L.Rev. 2041 (2001).

(4) The Louisiana Supreme Court in the principal case seems to equate sanity with mens rea. Is it correct in this view? As a result of *Winship* due process requires the state to prove each element of an offense beyond a reasonable doubt in both criminal and juvenile proceedings. However, in *Leland v. Oregon*, 343 U.S. 790, 72 S.Ct. 1002, 96 L.Ed. 1302 (1952), the Supreme Court upheld the constitutionality of a statute requiring a defendant in a criminal case to prove his or her insanity beyond a reasonable doubt. One might argue that *Winship* has superseded *Leland*; however, in *Rivera v. Delaware*, 429 U.S. 877, 97 S.Ct. 226, 50 L.Ed.2d 160 (1976), the Court dismissed an appeal challenging a state statute placing the burden on a defendant to prove his or her insanity by a preponderance of the evidence, on the ground that no substantial federal question was presented.

What conclusions should be drawn from these cases? While they do not necessarily mean that a state may deprive a criminal defendant or an alleged delinquent of the insanity defense altogether, they certainly raise doubts whether the defense is guaranteed by due process of law. Furthermore, the cases indicate that responsibility for one's conduct is not to be equated with mens rea, nor is responsibility, unlike mens rea, an element of the offense that the state must prove beyond a reasonable doubt. Viewed in this light, was the Louisiana court's decision correct, at least on the basis of the reasons given? Consider the arguments presented by the Court of Appeals of the District of Columbia in the case discussed in the note following.

(5) The District of Columbia Code provides as follows:

§ 16–2315. Physical and mental examinations

(a)(1) At any time following the filing of a petition, on motion of the Corporation Counsel or counsel for the child, or on its own motion, the Division may order a child to be examined to aid in determining his physical or mental condition.

. . .

(d) The results of an examination under this section shall be admissible in a transfer hearing pursuant to section 16–2307, in a dispositional hearing under this subchapter, or in a commitment proceeding under chapter 5 or 11 of title 21. The results of examination may be admitted into evidence at a factfinding hearing to aid the Division in determining a material allegation of the petition relating to the child's mental or physical condition, but not for the purpose of establishing a defense of insanity.

. . .

In upholding the constitutionality of this statute against claims that prohibiting an insanity defense during an adjudicatory hearing was a denial of due process and equal protection, the Court of Appeals of the District of Columbia stated:

Appellant urges that because of the statutory prohibition, he was deprived of the opportunity, available to any adult criminal defendant, to obtain acquittal by showing that he did not at the time of the commission of the offense possess the requisite intent. . . .

By this argument, appellant demonstrates a misconception of the nature and purpose of the insanity defense, for there is a fundamental difference between the concept of *mens rea* and the insanity defense.

Moreover, it is well settled in this jurisdiction that proof of insanity at the time of the commission of an offense does not negate intent nor, without more, does it require an outright acquittal, since the trier of fact may not even consider the issue of insanity until after the government has established the essential elements of the offense, including intent.

Consequently, even if the defense of insanity had been permitted and appellant had been successful in obtaining an acquittal by reason of insanity, it would not have established his innocence of the charged offense because "[a]n acquittal by reason of insanity, which . . . includes mental defects, is a determination of guilt beyond a reasonable doubt of the acts charged."

Thus, the function of the insanity defense is not to establish the innocence of the accused, but rather to absolve him of the moral and penal consequences of his criminal act.

Insisting, however, that D.C.Code 1973, § 16–2315(d) violates the Fifth Amendment guarantees of due process and equal protection, appellant urges that because the statute precludes a child from raising the insanity defense at the factfinding hearing, he or she is afforded less protection than that afforded an adult offender who is found to have been insane at the time of the commission of the offense. . . .

. . .

That there are substantial differences between the criminal and juvenile justice systems is of course apparent from an examination of the controlling statutes. However, the relevant differences come into focus only after completion of the first phase of the bifurcated proceedings conducted in this jurisdiction when a criminal defendant interposes the defense of insanity.

In a criminal case, the trier of fact may not even consider the issue of insanity until the government has established the essential elements of the offense, including intent in the first phase of that proceeding. The second phase is held only if the government is successful in proving guilt beyond a reasonable doubt and, only then, may the trier of fact reach the question of insanity. At this point, a criminal defendant may raise an insanity defense, which serves to permit the jury to decide whether the criminal defendant should be absolved of the criminal responsibility and penal consequences of his acts.

The first phase of a bifurcated criminal proceeding is analogous to the factfinding proceeding of the juvenile process during which the Division is permitted to determine only whether the juvenile committed the act charged. Accordingly, contrary to appellant's argument, precluding a juvenile from raising an insanity defense at a factfinding hearing denies him no right that is otherwise accorded an adult.

A juvenile delinquency proceeding concededly does not incorporate the second step. Nevertheless, it is well settled now that unlike a criminal trial a juvenile factfinding hearing does not result in a determination of criminal responsibility. Nor is the succeeding dispositional hearing intended to result in the imposition of any penal sanction on the child. Rather, the purpose is to determine the treatment required to rehabilitate him. Accordingly, the insanity defense would be superfluous in a juvenile delinquency proceeding.

This conclusion, however, does not end our analysis. Appellant contends that the insanity defense in a criminal proceeding serves the secondary, but equally important purpose of providing a criminal defendant with procedural safeguards not otherwise available to a child. He concedes however that an adult offender found not guilty by reason of insanity must be committed to a hospital for the mentally ill until such time as he is able to establish his eligibility for release.... In contrast, appellant maintains that D.C.Code 1973, § 16–2315(d) does not require the Family Division to consider the result of any mental examination or make specific findings respecting a child's mental illness. Because of the broad discretion vested in the Division for dispositional purposes, appellant contends, as a possibility, that a child who was mentally ill at the time of the offense, but not at the time of disposition, could be "incarcerated for a lengthy period as an adjudicated delinquent," and that a child who was still mentally ill at the time of disposition could be institutionalized in a setting where psychiatric care is not available. We have found no support in the statute for these contentions.

We recognize that although the juvenile justice system is not intended to impose penal sanctions, the Family Division frequently orders forms of rehabilitation that a child might regard as punishment. We also recognized that an insanity acquittee, because morally blameless, may not be subject to any form of punishment. Of course, as pointed out above, an adjudication of delinquency does not result in the imposition of any penal sanction. Consequently it cannot be said with rationality that a disposition of a child offender deemed, by the Division, to serve his best interests, is punishment. Nevertheless we deem it to be an indispensable element of fundamental fairness that a mentally ill child offender be accorded the same opportunity for psychiatric treatment and ultimate release as a similarly situated adult. For these reasons, we have examined closely the statutory scheme governing the treatment of mentally ill child offenders in order to determine whether they are being denied any required procedural protections to ensure fundamental fairness. We conclude that the statutes and rules regulating juvenile delinquency proceedings in the District of Columbia presently provide adequate means of ensuring that any mentally ill child offender receives care and treatment similar to that provided for mentally ill criminal defendants.

In re C.W.M., 407 A.2d 617, 619–23 (D.C.1979).

On the related issue of infancy, one commentator has urged that in the "new" juvenile court, with its emphasis on blameworthiness and punishment rather than the traditional goal of rehabilitation, the state should bear the burden of proving that the respondent understood the wrongfulness of his or her act. Andrew Walkover, The Infancy Defense in the New Juvenile Court, 31 U.C.L.A.L.Rev. 503 (1984). Some courts have agreed. See, e.g., *State v. J.P.S.*, 135 Wn.2d 34, 954 P.2d 894 (1998). A more recent argument favoring the infancy defense is found in Andrew M. Carter, Age Matters: The Case for a Constitutionalized Infancy Defense, 54 U.Kan.L.Rev. 687 (2006).

Thomas Grisso, Laurence Steinberg, Jennifer Woolard, Elizabeth Cauffman, Elizabeth Scott, Sandra Graham, Fran Lexcen, N. Dickon Reppucci & Robert Schwartz, Juveniles' Competence to Stand Trial: A Comparison of Adolescents' and Adults' Capacities as Trial Defendants

27 Law & Human Behavior 333, 356–60 (2003).*

Review of Findings

Our results indicate that juveniles aged 15 and younger are significantly more likely than older adolescents and young adults to be impaired in ways that compromise their ability to serve as competent defendants in a criminal proceeding. On the basis of criteria established in studies of mentally ill adult offenders, approximately one third of 11– to 13–year-olds, and approximately one fifth of 14– to 15–year-olds are as impaired in capacities relevant to adjudicative competence as are seriously mentally ill adults who would likely be considered incompetent to stand trial by clinicians who perform evaluations for courts. Our results also indicate that the competence-relevant capacities of 16– and 17–year-olds as a group do not differ significantly from those of young adults. These patterns of age differences are robust across groups defined by gender, ethnicity, and SES [socioeconomic status], and they are evident among individuals in the justice system and in the community. Not surprisingly, juveniles of below-average intelligence are more likely than juveniles of average intelligence to be impaired in abilities relevant for competence to stand trial. Because a greater proportion of youths in the juvenile justice system than in the community are of below-average intelligence, the risk for incompetence to stand trial is therefore even greater among adolescents who are in the justice system than it is among adolescents in the community.

The results are consistent with findings from earlier studies of youths' capacities in legal contexts. For example, in a study of youths' abilities to understand and appreciate *Miranda* warnings, Grisso (1981) found that "understanding . . . was significantly poorer among juveniles who were 14 years of age or younger than among 15–16–year-old juveniles or adult offenders . . ." and that those deficits were even more pronounced among youths with low IQ scores, including youths who were 15 and 16 years of age. Similarly, prior research on youths' understanding and reasoning related to trial participation, although fragmentary, has been fairly consistent in suggesting poorer abilities among youths under 14 years of age.

Moving beyond formal competence to stand trial criteria, the results of our examination of adolescents' and young adults' responses to decision-making vignettes indicate that psychosocial immaturity may affect the performance of youths as defendants in ways that extend beyond the elements of understanding and reasoning that are explicitly relevant to competence to stand trial. Adolescents are more likely than young adults to make choices that reflect a propensity to comply with authority figures, such as confessing to the police rather than remaining silent or accepting a prosecutor's offer of a plea agreement. In addition, when being interrogated by the police, consulting with an attorney, or evaluating a plea agreement, younger adolescents are less likely, or perhaps less able, than others to recognize the risks inherent in the various choices they face or to consider the long-term, and not merely the immediate, consequences of their legal decisions. As is the case with capacities relevant for competence to stand trial, these patterns of age differences in legal decision making generally do not vary with gender, ethnicity, or SES.

. . .

Implications

. . .

The findings of the study should also focus attention on the issue of competence to stand trial in juvenile court delinquency proceedings. Many states extend the competence requirement to juvenile court adjudications, but most focus on mental illness and disability as the sources of incapacity. An important consideration in expanding the doctrinal framework to include incompetence as a result of immaturity is whether the competence standard applied in juvenile court should be less demanding than that applied in adult criminal court. This is important because the standard for competence in juvenile court will determine whether youths adjudicated incompetent as adults can be tried as juveniles. If a less demanding standard operates in juvenile court proceedings, many younger defendants who lack the capacity to be adjudicated as adults can be tried in this venue. Otherwise, the question of how to respond to these immature defendants presents a daunting challenge.

We believe that a more relaxed competence standard in juvenile court is compatible with the demands of constitutional due process. The Supreme Court has made it clear that the requirements of due process in delinquency proceedings are not identical to those that regulate criminal trials (*McKeiver v. Pennsylvania*, 1971). The justification for a separate juvenile court rests in part on the fact that it is not an exact replica of criminal court. If juvenile court jurisdiction ends when the minor reaches adulthood (an important "if"), then the stakes of a delinquency proceeding are not as high as those faced by a youth charged with a felony in adult court. Under these conditions, no constitutional bar would restrict the use of a more relaxed standard of adjudicative competence in juvenile court. As Bonnie and Grisso (2000) have argued, in an ordinary juvenile court delinquency proceeding, the minimal criteria for adjudication are satisfied if the youth "has a basic understanding of the purpose of the proceedings and can communicate rationally with counsel".

This approach not only is constitutionally legitimate, but also offers a practical solution to the challenges that may follow when courts recognize incompetence due to developmental immaturity. Most children and adolescents who are found incompetent to proceed in criminal court because of immaturity could likely be adjudicated in a juvenile delinquency proceeding under a more relaxed competence standard. In most cases, this avoids the dispositional problem of dealing with young defendants who cannot be tried as adults and are not likely to become competent in a reasonable time. Several courts that have considered competence to stand trial in juvenile court assume that the competence demands of a delinquency proceeding are lower than in an adult trial, and that youths who cannot be transferred to criminal court because of incompetence can be tried in juvenile court (e.g., *In the Matter of W.A.F.*, 1990; *Ohio v. Settles*, 1998).

The two-tier standard also minimizes the extent to which delinquency proceedings will be burdened by the incorporation of developmental immaturity as a basis for incompetence. If youths in juvenile court must meet adult standards of competence, prosecutors legitimately might worry that defense attorneys in delinquency proceedings will routinely petition for competence assessments. This will be unlikely if the competency standard in juvenile court is understood to be a modest one. Those who care about the welfare of youths and those who worry about the efficiency of the justice process share a common interest in promoting practices that implement due process without creating an undue burden on the court system.

. . .

NOTES

(1) Since the article excerpted above, summarizing the results of a study sponsored by the MacArthur Foundation, two of the authors collaborated on an additional article. Elizabeth S. Scott & Thomas Grisso, Developmental Incompetence, Due Process, and Juvenile Justice Policy, 83 N.C.L.Rev. 793 (2005). In it the authors explore in depth the issue of developmental immaturity by examining the historical and constitutional basis of the trial competence requirement and its application to juveniles, the scientific bases for knowledge of the psychological development of juveniles and what that knowledge reveals about their trial competence, and finally, the implications of that research for developing legal policy that assures fundamental fairness for juveniles.

(2) In a highly publicized case involving the first-degree murder conviction of 12-year-old Lionel Tate for the death of a six-year-old playmate allegedly while performing a wrestling move, the Florida District Court of Appeal reversed his conviction on the ground that a CST (competency to stand trial) hearing was not ordered in his case, despite the fact that his mental age was 9 or 10 and his IQ was in the 90–91 range. *Tate v. State*, 864 So.2d 44 (Fla.Dist.Ct.App.2003). The court rejected all nine of Tate's other arguments, including the argument that the mandatory life sentence to which he was sentenced was inappropriate. It declared on the competency hearing issue, however, that Tate was entitled to a new trial:

> The denial of defense counsel's post-trial request to have Tate evaluated, based on sworn testimony from a neuropsychologist and two attorneys raising bona fide doubts as to Tate's competency, and the trial court's failure to order, sua sponte, a pre-trial competency evaluation, constitute a violation of Tate's due process rights.

Tate, age twelve at the time of the crime, was indicted by a grand jury and convicted of the first-degree murder of six-year-old Tiffany Eunick in 1999. The general verdict included charges of both felony murder, based on committing aggravated child abuse, and premeditated murder. The trial and sentence, in light of Tate's age, has been the focus of considerable public interest reflected in the multiple amicus briefs filed in this appeal.

The evidence was clear that the victim was brutally slain, suffering as many as thirty-five injuries, including a fractured skull, brain contusions, twenty plus bruises, a rib fracture, injuries to her kidneys and pancreas, and a portion of her liver was detached. It was undisputed that it would take tremendous force to inflict these injuries. None of the experts, not even those for the defense, believed that the injuries were consistent with "play fighting," or that they were accidentally inflicted.

. . .

The question we resolve, here, is whether, due to his extremely young age and lack of previous exposure to the judicial system, a competency evaluation was constitutionally mandated to determine whether Tate had sufficient present ability to consult with his lawyer with a reasonable degree of rational understanding and whether he had a rational, as well as factual, understanding of the proceedings against him. We conclude that it was. See *Pate v. Robinson*, 383 U.S. 375, 86 S.Ct. 836, 15 L.Ed.2d 815 (1966); *Hill v. State*, 473 So.2d 1253 (Fla.1985); see also *Dusky v. United States*, 362 U.S. 402, 80 S.Ct. 788, 4 L.Ed.2d 824 (1960); *Kelly v. State*, 797 So.2d 1278 (Fla. 4th DCA 2001).

. . .

At trial, neuropsychologist, Dr. Mittenberg, testified that Tate had a mental delay of about three to four years, "which means that Lionel has an age equivalent of nine or ten years old." It is undisputed that Tate's IQ is approximately 90. Dr. Joel Klass, a child psychiatrist, testified for the defense at trial that Tate had the social maturity of a six-year-old and delays in inferential thinking. Dr. Sheri Bourg–Carter, called by the state as a rebuttal witness, likewise acknowledged Tate's immaturity.

. . .

We recognize that factually, particularly without the assistance of testimony from trial counsel, the present case differs from *Robinson* and *Hill*. In *Robinson*, witnesses testified that they believed Robinson to be insane, he had a long history of disturbed behavior, had been hospitalized on several occasions for psychiatric disturbances, had shot and killed his son, and tried to commit suicide several years before he murdered his wife. 383 U.S. at 378, 86 S.Ct. 836. There, the Supreme Court concluded that the evidence before the court mandated an inquiry into his competence to stand trial, even in the face of his apparent mental alertness at trial and his counsel's failure to raise the issue. Id. at 385, 86 S.Ct. 836.

The state correctly notes that here, in contrast to *Robinson*, Tate had been seen by Dr. Bourg–Carter, even though no competency hearing was held, and her opinion was that Tate was competent to stand trial. Further, the state emphasized the absence of facts in the pre-trial or trial record showing that Tate was not competent to stand trial. Tate also had psychological experts available to the defense throughout the process, along with his lawyer and mother.

In *Hill*, the defendant was mentally retarded. 473 So.2d at 1255. At a hearing on his motion for post-conviction relief, an investigator testified that Hill was difficult to communicate with and was of no help in preparing his defense. Moreover, at his trial, Hill exhibited unusual behavior. Id. Incident to the post-conviction proceedings, Hill was evaluated and mental health professionals testified he had a low I.Q. and was unable to recall details of events even ninety minutes in the past, and one opined that Hill could not cooperate with his attorney, assist in his defense, or have any rational or factual understanding of the proceedings. Id.

The Florida Supreme Court, in *Hill*, recognized that the trial judge has an independent duty under *Robinson* and Florida Rules of Criminal Procedure to determine the competency of the defendant to stand trial and, finding that the evidence raised sufficient doubt as to Hill's competency to stand trial, should have required a hearing. The supreme court vacated Hill's conviction and sentence and remanded the case, allowing a second prosecution after a new determination that Hill was competent to stand trial. Id.

We also recognize that competency hearings are not, per se, mandated simply because a child is tried as an adult. However, in light of Tate's age, the facts developed pre-trial and post-trial, and his lack of previous exposure to the judicial system, a competency hearing should have been held, particularly given the complexity of the legal proceedings and the fact that he was denied this protection afforded children fourteen and older under section 985.226(2), Florida Statutes, which provides for a waiver hearing to determine whether the child should be tried as an adult. Further, the brief plea colloquy, taken alone, was not adequate to evaluate competency given his age, immaturity, his nine or ten-year-old mental age, and the complexity of the proceedings.

Even if a child of Tate's age is deemed to have the capacity to understand less serious charges, or common place juvenile court proceedings, it cannot be determined, absent a hearing, whether Tate could meet competency standards incident to facing a first-degree murder charge involving profound decisions regarding strategy, whether to make disclosures, intelligently analyze plea offers, and consider waiving important rights.

The record reflects that questions regarding Tate's competency were not lurking subtly in the background, but were readily apparent, as his immaturity and developmental delays were very much at the heart of the defense. It is also alleged that his I.Q. of 90 or 91 means that 75% of children his age scored higher, and that he had significant mental delays.

Applying the principles enunciated in *Robinson* and *Hill*, we conclude that it was error to fail to, sua sponte, order a competency hearing pre-trial and, in any event, to deny the post-trial request for a competency hearing.

In light of the fact-based professional doubts expressed post-trial concerning Tate's competency, Tate was entitled to a complete evaluation and hearing at that time, if for no other reason than to clarify the record, notwithstanding that the trial court may have been correct in concluding that Tate's demeanor and disinterest did not necessarily mean that he did not understand the proceedings and that his incompetency was not previously raised despite defense counsel's continuing access to professional help. Under the principle recognized in *Robinson*, the trial court's reasoning is insufficient justification to override the testimony regarding Tate's reduced mental functioning, his possible inability to understand the charges and decisions to be made, the potential penalty, and the professional opinion that a competency evaluation and hearing was necessary. 383 U.S. at 384–85, 86 S.Ct. 836.

Upon remand, Tate is entitled to a new trial because a hearing at this late date to determine the present competency of a maturing adolescent cannot adequately retroactively protect his rights. See *Jones v. State*, 740 So.2d 520 (Fla.1999); *Tingle v. State*, 536 So.2d 202, 204 (Fla.1988).

Here, if either a pre-trial or post-trial competency hearing had been ordered, the court would have been able to properly assess Tate's appreciation of the charges, the range and nature of possible penalties, determine whether he understood the adversary nature of the legal process, his capacity to disclose to his attorney pertinent facts surrounding the alleged offense, his ability to relate to his attorney, his ability to assist his attorney in planning his defense, his capacity to realistically challenge prosecution witnesses, his ability to manifest appropriate courtroom behavior, his capacity to testify relevantly, and his motivation to help himself in the legal process, as well as his ability to evaluate and make a decision concerning the plea offer.

At a minimum, under the circumstances of this case, the court had an obligation to ensure that the juvenile defendant, who was less than the age of fourteen, with known disabilities raised in his defense and who faced mandatory life imprisonment, was competent to understand the plea offer and the ramifications thereof, and understood the defense being raised and the state's evidence to refute the defense position, so as to ensure that Tate could effectively assist in his defense.

Significantly, the trial court's reasoning in rejecting the post-trial motion overlooks the argument that the proper inquiry was whether the defendant may be incompetent, not whether he is incompetent. *Walker v. State*, 384 So.2d 730, 733 (Fla. 4th DCA 1980).

The Lionel Tate case has been the subject of much controversy and scholarly commentary. See, e.g., Steven Bell, Tate v. State: Highlighting the Need for a Mandatory Competency Hearing, 28 Nova L.Rev. 575 (2004); Michael J. Dale, Making Sense of the Lionel Tate Case, 28 Nova L.Rev. 467 (2004); Joseph Yalon, Constitutional Right to a Competency Hearing, 26 J.Juv.L. 127 (2006).

4. DISPOSITION

THE DEATH PENALTY FOR JUVENILES: *ROPER v. SIMMONS*

This section addresses dispositions imposed in juvenile court following an adjudication of delinquency. It does not address, with one exception, sentences imposed against juveniles, or those who were juveniles at the time of commission of the crime, who are convicted in criminal court. Until recently, one of the sentencing options available to the criminal court in some states included the death penalty. Because of the Supreme Court's decision in *Roper v. Simmons*, 543 U.S. 551, 125 S.Ct. 1183, 161 L.Ed.2d 1 (2005), see below, the authors thought it a good idea to include the *Roper* decision in this section on dispositions, as well as the following background material summarizing the lead-up to *Roper*.

More than two-thirds of the states and the District of Columbia define "juvenile" as one under 18 years of age. Using 18 as the dividing line between juvenile and adult, since the first satisfactorily documented execution in 1642, some 581 people who were juveniles at the time of the offense have been executed in the United States, the majority of them—190—in the 20th century. Few juvenile executions have been carried out since November 1, 1986, but as of that date juvenile executions in any given decade never accounted for more than 4.11 percent of the total number of executions, except for the 1980s when they accounted for 4.76 percent of the total. Victor Streib, Death Penalty for Juveniles 55–56 (1987). Two juveniles were executed in 1986, and the next juvenile execution did not occur until 1990. Including the 1990 execution, 19 juveniles were executed, up until April 3, 2003, when the last one occurred. Victor Streib, The Juvenile Death Penalty Today: Death Sentences and Executions for Juvenile Crimes, January 1, 1973–February 28, 2005, http://www.law.onu.edu/faculty_staff/faculty_profiles/coursematerials/streib/juvdeath.pdf (last updated on Oct. 7, 2005) (as visited on Feb. 16, 2008).

Prior to the 20th century, two 10–year-old juveniles were executed, as well as one 11–year-old and five 12–year-old juveniles. In the 20th century no juveniles so young were executed, but one 13–year-old was executed, as well as five 14–year-olds, 15 15–year-olds and 50 16–year-olds. The rest, 119, were all 17 at the time of the offense. Victor Streib, Death Penalty for Juveniles 55–56 (1987).

The issue of the constitutionality of executing juveniles was presented to the Supreme Court in 1982 in *Eddings v. Oklahoma*, 455 U.S. 104, 102 S.Ct. 869, 71 L.Ed.2d 1 (1982). Eddings was 16 years old at the time he, along with several younger companions, shot and killed a police officer. He was convicted of first-degree murder and sentenced to death. 455 U.S. at 105–09. A divided Supreme Court vacated his death sentence and remanded the case for a new sentencing hearing, but not for reason of the petitioner's age or opposition to the death penalty. Rather, his death sentence was vacated because the sentencing judge had declined to consider mitigating evidence offered by Eddings. 455 U.S. at 109–16.

The issue re-surfaced six years later in *Thompson v. Oklahoma*, 487 U.S. 815, 108 S.Ct. 2687, 101 L.Ed.2d 702 (1988). Thompson was 15 years old at the time he committed a brutal murder. He was convicted of first-degree murder and sentenced to death. A plurality of the Court concluded that the Eighth Amendment prohibits imposition of the death penalty on any person who was under the age of 16 at the time of the offense. 487 U.S. at 838. Justice Stevens announced the judgment of the Court in an opinion in which Justices Brennan, Marshall and Blackmun joined. Justice O'Connor proved to be the swing vote, concurring in the result. The Court specifically declined to address the issue of the constitutionality of execution of a person under age 18, principally because the issue was not before the Court, given that Thompson was 15 at the time of the murder. 487 U.S. at 838.

The next year in two companion cases, *Stanford v. Kentucky* and *Wilkins v. Missouri*, 492 U.S. 361, 109 S.Ct. 2969, 106 L.Ed.2d 306 (1989) (known collectively as *Stanford v. Kentucky*), the Court confronted the issue of the constitutionality of the death penalty for a person 16 or older but under 18 at the time of the offense. In *Stanford* the petitioner was 17 at the time he murdered his victim, and in *Wilkins* the petitioner was 16 at the time of the murder. A five-member majority of the Court held that imposition of the death penalty on 16– and 17–year-old juveniles did not violate the Eighth Amendment's prohibition against cruel and unusual punishment. Three of the five (Chief Justice Rehnquist and Justices Scalia and White) had dissented in *Thompson*, and they were joined in *Stanford* by Justice Kennedy, who took no part in *Thompson*, and Justice O'Connor, who had concurred in *Thompson* (she also wrote a separate concurring opinion in *Stanford* and once again proved to be the swing vote). As part of their reasoning they noted the absence of any national consensus against imposing the death penalty on 16– and 17–year-old juveniles. 492 U.S. at 372–73. The same Justices who had formed the four-member plurality in *Thompson* (Justices Brennan, Marshall, Blackmun and Stevens) dissented in *Stanford*. 492 U.S. at 382.

The decision in *Stanford* was clear evidence that the Court was closely divided on the issue of the constitutionality of the death penalty for 16– and 17–year-old juveniles. In *In re Stanford*, 537 U.S. 968, 123 S.Ct. 472, 154 L.Ed.2d 364 (2002), the Court denied certiorari in a juvenile death penalty case in which four Justices dissented from the denial of certiorari. Justice Stevens wrote the dissenting opinion (joined by Justices Souter, Ginsburg and Breyer, all new to the Court since its decision in the earlier *Stanford* case), in which he argued that in light of the Court's decision in *Atkins v. Virginia*, 536 U.S. 304, 122 S.Ct. 2242, 153 L.Ed.2d 335 (2002), prohibiting execution of persons who are mentally retarded, the Court should reconsider the position it had taken in the first *Stanford* case. He further argued that in the interim since *Stanford*, a national consensus had emerged against imposition of the death penalty on 16 –and 17–year-old juveniles. About two months prior to the denial of certiorari in *In re Stanford*, three of the four Justices who dissented from denial of certiorari in *Stanford* dissented from denial of a stay of execution in *Patterson v. Texas*, 536 U.S. 984, 123 S.Ct. 24, 153 L.Ed.2d 887 (2002), a case in which the petitioner was 17 at the time of the murder. About three months after *Stanford*, the Court denied certiorari in *Hain v. Mullin*, 537 U.S. 1173, 123 S.Ct. 993, 154 L.Ed.2d 916 (2003), another case in which the petitioner was 17 at the time of the double murder. No dissents were filed.

Shortly thereafter, the Missouri Supreme Court thought it sensed a shift among members of the Supreme Court on the issue of the death penalty for juveniles under 18, and in *State ex rel. Simmons v. Roper*, 112 S.W.3d 397 (Mo. 2003), the court, in a four to three decision, held that executing juveniles under age 18 at the time of the offense was unconstitutional in violation of the Eighth and Fourteenth Amendments. The court concluded that since the time of the Supreme Court's decision in *Stanford* negating the argument, a national consensus against imposing the death penalty on 16– and 17–year-old juveniles had emerged. The Missouri court stated, "... this Court finds the Supreme Court would today hold such executions are prohibited by the Eighth and Fourteenth Amendments." 112 S.W.3d at 400.

The U.S. Supreme Court granted certiorari. Their decision follows.

Roper v. Simmons

Supreme Court of the United States, 2005.
543 U.S. 551, 125 S.Ct. 1183, 161 L.Ed.2d 1.

■ JUSTICE KENNEDY delivered the opinion of the Court.

This case requires us to address ... whether it is permissible under the Eighth and Fourteenth Amendments to the Constitution of the United

States to execute a juvenile offender who was older than 15 but younger than 18 when he committed a capital crime. In *Stanford v. Kentucky,* 492 U.S. 361(1989), a divided Court rejected the proposition that the Constitution bars capital punishment for juvenile offenders in this age group. We reconsider the question.

I

At the age of 17, when he was still a junior in high school, Christopher Simmons ... committed murder. About nine months later, after he had turned 18, he was tried and sentenced to death. There is little doubt that Simmons was the instigator of the crime. Before its commission Simmons said he wanted to murder someone. In chilling, callous terms he talked about his plan, discussing it for the most part with two friends, Charles Benjamin and John Tessmer, then aged 15 and 16 respectively. Simmons proposed to commit burglary and murder by breaking and entering, tying up a victim, and throwing the victim off a bridge. Simmons assured his friends they could "get away with it" because they were minors.

The three met at about 2 a.m. on the night of the murder, but Tessmer left before the other two set out.... Simmons and Benjamin entered the home of the victim, Shirley Crook, after reaching through an open window and unlocking the back door ... Mrs. Crook called out, "Who's there?" In response Simmons entered Mrs. Crook's bedroom, where he recognized her from a previous car accident involving them both. Simmons later admitted this confirmed his resolve to murder her.

Using duct tape to cover her eyes and mouth and bind her hands, the two perpetrators put Mrs. Crook in her minivan and drove to a state park. They reinforced the bindings, covered her head with a towel, and walked her to a railroad trestle spanning the Meramec River. There they tied her hands and feet together with electrical wire, wrapped her whole face in duct tape and threw her from the bridge, drowning her in the waters below.

By the afternoon of September 9, Steven Crook had returned home from an overnight trip, found his bedroom in disarray, and reported his wife missing. On the same afternoon fishermen recovered the victim's body from the river. Simmons, meanwhile, was bragging about the killing, telling friends he had killed a woman "because the bitch seen my face."

. . .

II

The prohibition against "cruel and unusual punishments," like other expansive language in the Constitution, must be interpreted according to its text, by considering history, tradition, and precedent, and with due regard for its purpose and function in the constitutional design. To implement this framework we have established the propriety and affirmed the necessity of referring to "the evolving standards of decency that mark the progress of a maturing society" to determine which punishments are so disproportionate as to be cruel and unusual.

. . .

Three Terms ago [in *Atkins v. Virginia*, 536 U.S. 304 (2002)] . . . [w]e held that standards of decency have evolved . . . and now demonstrate that the execution of the mentally retarded is cruel and unusual punishment. The Court noted objective indicia of society's standards, as expressed in legislative enactments and state practice with respect to executions of the mentally retarded. When *Atkins* was decided only a minority of States permitted the practice, and even in those States it was rare. . . .

. . .

III

A

The evidence of national consensus against the death penalty for juveniles is similar, and in some respects parallel, to the evidence *Atkins* held sufficient to demonstrate a national consensus against the death penalty for the mentally retarded. When *Atkins* was decided, 30 States prohibited the death penalty for the mentally retarded. This number comprised 12 that had abandoned the death penalty altogether, and 18 that maintained it but excluded the mentally retarded from its reach. By a similar calculation in this case, 30 States prohibit the juvenile death penalty, comprising 12 that have rejected the death penalty altogether and 18 that maintain it but, by express provision or judicial interpretation, exclude juveniles from its reach. *Atkins* emphasized that even in the 20 States without formal prohibition, the practice of executing the mentally retarded was infrequent. . . . In the present case, too, even in the 20 States without a formal prohibition on executing juveniles, the practice is infrequent. . . .

There is, to be sure, at least one difference between the evidence of consensus in *Atkins* and in this case. Impressive in *Atkins* was the rate of abolition of the death penalty for the mentally retarded. Sixteen States that permitted the execution of the mentally retarded at the time of *Penry* [upholding the execution of mentally retarded offenders] had prohibited the practice by the time we heard *Atkins*. By contrast, the rate of change in reducing the incidence of the juvenile death penalty, or in taking specific steps to abolish it, has been slower. Five States that allowed the juvenile death penalty at the time of *Stanford* have abandoned it in the intervening 15 years—four through legislative enactments and one through judicial decision.

Though less dramatic than the change from *Penry* to Atkins, we still consider the change from *Stanford* to this case to be significant. As noted in *Atkins*, . . . "[i]t is not so much the number of these States that is significant, but the consistency of the direction of change." The number of States that have abandoned capital punishment for juvenile offenders since *Stanford* is smaller than the number of States that abandoned capital punishment for the mentally retarded after *Penry;* yet we think the same consistency of direction of change has been demonstrated. Since *Stanford,* no State that previously prohibited capital punishment for juveniles has reinstated it. This fact, coupled with the trend toward abolition of the juvenile death penalty, carries special force in light of the general popularity of anticrime legislation, and in light of the particular trend in recent years toward cracking down on juvenile crime in other respects, see Scott & Grisso, The Evolution of Adolescence: A Developmental Perspective on Juvenile Justice Reform, 88 J.Crim. L. & C. 137, 148 (1997). . . .

The slower pace of abolition of the juvenile death penalty over the past 15 years, moreover, may have a simple explanation. When we heard *Penry,* only two death penalty States had already prohibited the execution of the mentally retarded. When we heard *Stanford,* by contrast, 12 death penalty States had already prohibited the execution of any juvenile under 18, and 15 had prohibited the execution of any juvenile under 17. If anything, this shows that the impropriety of executing juveniles between 16 and 18 years of age gained wide recognition earlier than the impropriety of executing the mentally retarded. . . .

. . .

As in *Atkins,* the objective indicia of consensus in this case—the rejection of the juvenile death penalty in the majority of States; the infrequency of its use even where it remains on the books; and the consistency in the trend toward abolition of the practice—provide sufficient evidence that today our society views juveniles, in the words *Atkins* used respecting the mentally retarded, as "categorically less culpable than the average criminal."

B

A majority of States have rejected the imposition of the death penalty on juvenile offenders under 18, and we now hold this is required by the Eighth Amendment.

Because the death penalty is the most severe punishment, the Eighth Amendment applies to it with special force. *Thompson,* 487 U.S., at 856 (O'CONNOR, J., concurring in judgment). Capital punishment must be limited to those offenders who commit "a narrow category of the most serious crimes" and whose extreme culpability makes them "the most deserving of execution." *Atkins* [536 U.S. 304 (2002)] at 319. . . .

Three general differences between juveniles under 18 and adults demonstrate that juvenile offenders cannot with reliability be classified among the worst offenders. First, as any parent knows and as the scientific and sociological studies respondent and his *amici* cite tend to confirm, "[a] lack of maturity and an underdeveloped sense of responsibility are found in youth more often than in adults and are more understandable among the young. These qualities often result in impetuous and ill-considered actions and decisions." *Johnson [509 U.S. 350 (1993)],* at 367; see also *Eddings, [455 U.S. 104 (1982)],* at 115–116 ("Even the normal 16–year-old customarily lacks the maturity of an adult"). It has been noted that "adolescents are overrepresented statistically in virtually every category of reckless behavior." Arnett, Reckless Behavior in Adolescence: A Developmental Perspective, 12 Developmental Review 339 (1992). In recognition of the comparative immaturity and irresponsibility of juveniles, almost every State prohibits those under 18 years of age from voting, serving on juries, or marrying without parental consent.

The second area of difference is that juveniles are more vulnerable or susceptible to negative influences and outside pressures, including peer pressure. *Eddings, supra,* at 115 ("Youth is more than a chronological fact. It is a time and condition of life when a person may be most susceptible to influence and to psychological damage"). This is explained in part by the prevailing circumstance that juveniles have less control, or less experience with control, over their own environment. See Steinberg & Scott, Less Guilty by Reason of Adolescence: Developmental Immaturity, Diminished Responsibility, and the Juvenile Death Penalty, 58 Am. Psychologist 1009, 1014 (2003) (hereinafter Steinberg & Scott) ("As legal minors, [juveniles] lack the freedom that adults have to extricate themselves from a crimino-genic setting").

The third broad difference is that the character of a juvenile is not as well formed as that of an adult. The personality traits of juveniles are more transitory, less fixed. See generally E. Erikson, Identity: Youth and Crisis (1968).

These differences render suspect any conclusion that a juvenile falls among the worst offenders. The susceptibility of juveniles to immature and irresponsible behavior means "their irresponsible conduct is not as morally reprehensible as that of an adult." *Thompson, supra,* at 835 (plurality opinion). Their own vulnerability and comparative lack of control over their immediate surroundings mean juveniles have a greater claim than adults to be forgiven for failing to escape negative influences in their whole environment. The reality that juveniles still struggle to define their identity means it is less supportable to conclude that even a heinous crime committed by a juvenile is evidence of irretrievably depraved character. From a moral standpoint it would be misguided to equate the failings of a minor with those of an adult, for a greater possibility exists that a minor's character deficiencies will be reformed. Indeed, "the relevance of youth as a mitigating factor derives from the fact that the signature qualities of youth are transient; as individuals mature, the impetuousness and recklessness that may dominate in younger years can subside." *Johnson, supra,* at 368; see also Steinberg & Scott 1014 ("For most teens, [risky or antisocial] behaviors are fleeting; they cease with maturity as individual identity becomes settled. Only a relatively small proportion of adolescents who experiment in risky or illegal activities develop entrenched patterns of problem behavior that persist into adulthood").

In *Thompson,* a plurality of the Court recognized the import of these characteristics with respect to juveniles under 16, and relied on them to hold that the Eighth Amendment prohibited the imposition of the death penalty on juveniles below that age. 487 U.S., at 833–838. We conclude the same reasoning applies to all juvenile offenders under 18.

Once the diminished culpability of juveniles is recognized, it is evident that the penological justifications for the death penalty apply to them with lesser force than to adults. We have held there are two distinct social purposes served by the death penalty: " 'retribution and deterrence of capital crimes by prospective offenders.' " *Atkins*, 536 U.S., at 319 (quoting *Gregg* v. *Georgia*, 428 U.S. 153, 183 (1976) (joint opinion of Stewart, Powell, and STEVENS, JJ.)). As for retribution, we remarked in *Atkins* that "if the culpability of the average murderer is insufficient to justify the most extreme sanction available to the State, the lesser culpability of the mentally retarded offender surely does not merit that form of retribution." 536 U.S., at 319. The same conclusions follow from the lesser culpability of the juvenile offender. Whether viewed as an attempt to express the community's moral outrage or as an attempt to right the balance for the wrong to the victim, the case for retribution is not as strong with a minor as with an adult. Retribution is not proportional if the law's most severe penalty is imposed on one whose culpability or blameworthiness is diminished, to a substantial degree, by reason of youth and immaturity.

As for deterrence, it is unclear whether the death penalty has a significant or even measurable deterrent effect on juveniles, as counsel for the petitioner acknowledged at oral argument. In general we leave to legislatures the assessment of the efficacy of various criminal penalty schemes. Here, however, the absence of evidence of deterrent effect is of special concern because the same characteristics that render juveniles less culpable than adults suggest as well that juveniles will be less susceptible to deterrence. In particular, as the plurality observed in *Thompson*, "the likelihood that the teenage offender has made the kind of cost-benefit analysis that attaches any weight to the possibility of execution is so remote as to be virtually nonexistent." 487 U.S., at 837. To the extent the juvenile death penalty might have residual deterrent effect, it is worth noting that the punishment of life imprisonment without the possibility of parole is itself a severe sanction, in particular for a young person.

In concluding that neither retribution nor deterrence provides adequate justification for imposing the death penalty on juvenile offenders, we cannot deny or overlook the brutal crimes too many juvenile offenders have committed. Certainly it can be argued, although we by no means concede the point, that a rare case might arise in which a juvenile offender has sufficient psychological maturity, and at the same time demonstrates sufficient depravity, to merit a sentence of death. Indeed, this possibility is the linchpin of one contention pressed by petitioner and his *amici*. They assert that even assuming the truth of the observations we have made about juveniles' diminished culpability in general, jurors nonetheless should be allowed to consider mitigating arguments related to youth on a case-by-case basis, and in some cases to impose the death penalty if justified. . . .

We disagree. The differences between juvenile and adult offenders are too marked and well understood to risk allowing a youthful person to receive the death penalty despite insufficient culpability. . . .

It is difficult even for expert psychologists to differentiate between the juvenile offender whose crime reflects unfortunate yet transient immaturity, and the rare juvenile offender whose crime reflects irreparable corruption. See Steinberg & Scott 1014–1016. As we understand it, this difficulty underlies the rule forbidding psychiatrists from diagnosing any patient under 18 as having antisocial personality disorder, a disorder also referred to as psychopathy or sociopathy, and which is characterized by callousness, cynicism, and contempt for the feelings, rights, and suffering of others. American Psychiatric Association, Diagnostic and Statistical Manual of Mental Disorders 701–706 (4th ed. text rev. 2000); see also Steinberg & Scott 1015. If trained psychiatrists with the advantage of clinical testing and observation refrain, despite diagnostic expertise, from assessing any juvenile under 18 as having antisocial personality disorder, we conclude that States should refrain from asking jurors to issue a far graver condemnation—that a juvenile offender merits the death penalty. When a juvenile offender commits a heinous crime, the State can exact forfeiture of some of the most basic liberties, but the State cannot extinguish his life and his potential to attain a mature understanding of his own humanity.

Drawing the line at 18 years of age is subject, of course, to the objections always raised against categorical rules. The qualities that distinguish juveniles from adults do not disappear when an individual turns 18. By the same token, some under 18 have already attained a level of maturity some adults will never reach. For the reasons we have discussed, however, a line must be drawn. . . . The age of 18 is the point where society draws the line for many purposes between childhood and adulthood. It is, we conclude, the age at which the line for death eligibility ought to rest.

. . .

IV

Our determination that the death penalty is disproportionate punishment for offenders under 18 finds confirmation in the stark reality that the United States is the only country in the world that continues to give official sanction to the juvenile death penalty. This reality does not become controlling, for the task of interpreting the Eighth Amendment remains our responsibility. Yet at least from the time of the Court's decision in *Trop,* the Court has referred to the laws of other countries and to international authorities as instructive for its interpretation of the Eighth Amendment's prohibition of "cruel and unusual punishments.". . .

. . .

Respondent and his *amici* have submitted, and petitioner does not contest, that only seven countries other than the United States have executed juvenile offenders since 1990: Iran, Pakistan, Saudi Arabia, Yemen, Nigeria, the Democratic Republic of Congo, and China. Since then each of these countries has either abolished capital punishment for juveniles or made public disavowal of the practice. In sum, it is fair to say that the United States now stands alone in a world that has turned its face against the juvenile death penalty.

. . .

The Eighth and Fourteenth Amendments forbid imposition of the death penalty on offenders who were under the age of 18 when their crimes were committed. The judgment of the Missouri Supreme Court setting aside the sentence of death imposed upon Christopher Simmons is affirmed.

[The concurring opinion of Justice Stevens, joined by Justice Ginsburg, is omitted.]

■ Justice O'Connor, dissenting.

[In the introduction to her dissent, Justice O'Connor, who concurred in *Stanford* and was the deciding vote, gives as her principal reason for disagreeing with the majority her objection to the Court's categorical prohibition against the death penalty for juveniles, regardless of the individual characteristics of juveniles or the individual circumstances of each crime.

In part I of her dissent, Justice O'Connor outlines her agreement "with much of the Court's description of the general principles that guide our Eighth Amendment jurisprudence."

In part II, she criticizes the Missouri Supreme Court's decision to ignore U.S. Supreme Court precedent (*Stanford*), and is critical of the Court's failure to admonish the Missouri court for doing so:

> ... As a preliminary matter, I take issue with the Court's failure to reprove, or even to acknowledge, the Supreme Court of Missouri's unabashed refusal to follow our controlling decision in *Stanford*....

> Because the Eighth Amendment draw[s] its meaning from ... evolving standards of decency, significant changes in societal mores over time may require us to reevaluate a prior decision. Nevertheless, it remains *this* Court's prerogative *alone* to overrule one of its precedents.

In addition, Justice O'Connor disagrees with the majority's conclusion that a national consensus against execution of juveniles under 18 had emerged since the Court's decision in *Stanford*.

She then continues:]

It is beyond cavil that juveniles as a class are generally less mature, less responsible, and less fully formed than adults, and that these differences bear on juveniles' comparative moral culpability.... But even accepting this premise, the Court's proportionality argument fails to support its categorical rule.

First, the Court adduces no evidence whatsoever in support of its sweeping conclusion.... The fact that juveniles are generally *less* culpable for their misconduct than adults does not necessarily mean that a 17–year-old murderer cannot be *sufficiently* culpable to merit the death penalty. At most, the Court's argument suggests that the average 17–year-old murderer is not as culpable as the average adult murderer. But an especially depraved juvenile offender may nevertheless be just as culpable as many adult offenders considered bad enough to deserve the death penalty.... Surely there is an age below which no offender, no matter what his crime, can be deemed to have the cognitive or emotional maturity necessary to warrant the death penalty. But at least at the margins between adolescence and adulthood—and especially for 17–year-olds such as respondent—the relevant differences between "adults" and "juveniles" appear to be a matter of degree, rather than of kind....

Indeed, this appears to be just such a case. Christopher Simmons' murder of Shirley Crook was premeditated, wanton, and cruel in the extreme. Well before he committed this crime, Simmons declared that he wanted to kill someone. On several occasions, he discussed with two friends (ages 15 and 16) his plan to burglarize a house and to murder the victim by tying the victim up and pushing him from a bridge. Simmons said they could " 'get away with it' " because they were minors. In accord with this plan, Simmons and his 15–year-old accomplice broke into Mrs. Crook's home in the middle of the night, forced her from her bed, bound her, and drove her to a state park. There, they walked her to a railroad trestle spanning a river, "hog-tied" her with electrical cable, bound her face completely with duct tape, and pushed her, still alive, from the trestle. She drowned in the water below. *Id.,* at 4. One can scarcely imagine the terror that this woman must have suffered throughout the ordeal leading to her death. Whatever can be said about the comparative moral culpability of 17–year-olds as a general matter, Simmons' actions unquestionably reflect " 'a consciousness materially more "depraved" than that of' ... the average murderer." And Simmons' prediction that he could murder with impunity because he had not yet turned 18—though inaccurate—suggests that he *did* take into account the perceived risk of punishment in deciding whether to commit the crime. Based on this evidence, the sentencing jury certainly had reasonable grounds for concluding that, despite Simmons' youth, he "ha[d] sufficient psychological maturity" when he committed this horrific murder, and "at the same time demonstrate[d] sufficient depravity, to merit a sentence of death."

The Court's proportionality argument suffers from a second and closely related defect: It fails to establish that the differences in maturity between 17–year-olds and young "adults" are both universal enough and significant enough to justify a bright-line prophylactic rule against capital punishment of the former. The Court's analysis is premised on differences *in the aggregate* between juveniles and adults, which frequently do not hold true when comparing individuals. Although it may be that many 17–year-old murderers lack sufficient maturity to deserve the death penalty, some juvenile murderers may be quite mature. Chronological age is not an unfailing measure of psychological development, and common experience suggests that many 17–year-olds are more mature than the average young "adult."... Indeed, the age-based line drawn by the Court is indefensibly arbitrary....

For purposes of proportionality analysis, 17–year-olds as a class are qualitatively and materially different from the mentally retarded. "Mentally retarded" offenders, as we understood that category in *Atkins,* are *defined* by precisely the characteristics which render death an excessive punishment. A mentally retarded person is, "by definition," one whose cognitive and behavioral capacities have been proven to fall below a certain minimum.... [A] mentally retarded offender is one whose demonstrated impairments make it so highly unlikely that he is culpable enough to deserve the death penalty or that he could have been deterred by the threat of death, that execution is not a defensible punishment....

The proportionality issues raised by the Court clearly implicate Eighth Amendment concerns. But these concerns may properly be addressed not by means of an arbitrary, categorical age-based rule, but rather through individualized sentencing in which juries are required to give appropriate mitigating weight to the defendant's immaturity, his susceptibility to outside pressures, his cognizance of the consequences of his actions, and so forth. . . .

Although the prosecutor's apparent attempt to use respondent's youth as an aggravating circumstance in this case is troubling, that conduct was never challenged with specificity in the lower courts and is not directly at issue here. . . . The Court argues that sentencing juries cannot accurately evaluate a youthful offender's maturity or give appropriate weight to the mitigating characteristics related to youth. But, again, the Court presents no real evidence—and the record appears to contain none—supporting this claim. Perhaps more importantly, the Court fails to explain why this duty should be so different from, or so much more difficult than, that of assessing and giving proper effect to any other qualitative capital sentencing factor. . . .

[Justice O'Connor also downplays the significance of international law: "Because I do not believe that a genuine *national* consensus against the juvenile death penalty has yet developed, and because I do not believe the Court's moral proportionality argument justifies a categorical, age-based constitutional rule, I can assign no such *confirmatory* role to the international consensus described by the Court."

She then concludes her dissent:]

In determining whether the Eighth Amendment permits capital punishment of a particular offense or class of offenders, we must look to whether such punishment is consistent with contemporary standards of decency. We are obligated to weigh both the objective evidence of societal values and our own judgment as to whether death is an excessive sanction in the context at hand. In the instant case, the objective evidence is inconclusive; standing alone, it does not demonstrate that our society has repudiated capital punishment of 17–year-old offenders in all cases. Rather, the actions of the Nation's legislatures suggest that, although a clear and durable national consensus against this practice may in time emerge, that day has yet to arrive. By acting so soon after our decision in Stanford, the Court both pre-empts the democratic debate through which genuine consensus might develop and simultaneously runs a considerable risk of inviting lower court reassessments of our Eighth Amendment precedents.

. . .

Reasonable minds can differ as to the minimum age at which commission of a serious crime should expose the defendant to the death penalty, if at all. Many jurisdictions have abolished capital punishment altogether, while many others have determined that even the most heinous crime, if committed before the age of 18, should not be punishable by death. Indeed, were my office that of a legislator, rather than a judge, then I, too, would be inclined to support legislation setting a minimum age of 18 in this context. But a significant number of States, including Missouri, have decided to make the death penalty potentially available for 17–year-old capital murderers such as respondent. Without a clearer showing that a genuine national consensus forbids the execution of such offenders, this Court should not substitute its own inevitably subjective judgment on how best to resolve this difficult moral question for the judgments of the Nation's democratically elected legislatures. I respectfully dissent.

■ JUSTICE SCALIA, with whom THE CHIEF JUSTICE and JUSTICE THOMAS join, dissenting.

In urging approval of a constitution that gave life-tenured judges the power to nullify laws enacted by the people's representatives, Alexander Hamilton assured the citizens of New York that there was little risk in this, since [t]he judiciary ... ha[s] neither FORCE nor WILL but merely judgment. The Federalist No. 78, p. 465 (C. Rossiter ed.1961). . . . What a mockery today's opinion makes of Hamilton's expectation, announcing the Court's conclusion that the meaning of our Constitution has changed over the past 15 years—not, mind you, that this Court's decision 15 years ago [in *Stanford*] was *wrong,* but that the Constitution *has changed.* The Court reaches this implausible result by purporting to advert, not to the original meaning of the Eighth Amendment, but to the evolving standards of decency, of our national society. It then finds, on the flimsiest of grounds, that a national consensus which could not be perceived in our people's laws barely 15 years ago now solidly exists. Worse still, the Court says in so many words that what our people's laws say about the issue does not, in the last analysis, matter. . . .

[In part I of his dissent, Justice Scalia disagrees with the Court's conclusion that a national consensus opposing the death penalty for juveniles had emerged since its decision in *Stanford* in 1989. This conclusion, he claims, was based on very weak evidence. He criticizes the Court's reliance on the fact that 18 states that allow capital punishment prohibit it for persons who were under 18 at the time of the crime. He points out that those 18 states make up less than 50 percent of the states that allow capital punishment. The views of those states do not constitute a national consensus, he argues.

In part II, he continues:]

Of course, the real force driving today's decision is not the actions of four state legislatures [in abolishing the death penalty for juveniles under 18 since *Stanford* was decided], but the Court's " ' "own judgment" ' " that murderers younger than 18 can never be as morally culpable as older counterparts (quoting *Atkins* (in turn quoting *Coker* [v. Georgia, 433 U.S. 584 (1977)])).

. . .

Today's opinion provides a perfect example of why judges are ill equipped to make the type of legislative judgments the Court insists on making here. To support its opinion that States should be prohibited from imposing the death penalty on anyone who committed murder before age 18, the Court looks to scientific and sociological studies, picking and choosing those that support its position. It never explains why those particular studies are methodologically sound; none was ever entered into evidence or tested in an adversarial proceeding. As The Chief Justice has explained:

"Methodological and other errors can affect the reliability and validity of estimates about the opinions and attitudes of a population derived from various sampling techniques. Everything from variations in the survey methodology, such as the choice of the target population, the sampling design used, the questions asked, and the statistical analyses used to interpret the data can skew the results." *Atkins, supra,* at 326–327 (dissenting opinion) (citing R. Groves, Survey Errors and Survey Costs (1989); 1 C. Turner & E. Martin, Surveying Subjective Phenomena (1984)).

In other words, all the Court has done today, to borrow from another context, is to look over the heads of the crowd and pick out its friends.

We need not look far to find studies contradicting the Court's conclusions. As petitioner points out, the American Psychological Association (APA), which claims in this case that scientific evidence shows persons under 18 lack the ability to take moral responsibility for their decisions, has previously taken precisely the opposite position before this very Court. In its brief in *Hodgson* v. *Minnesota,* 497 U.S. 417 (1990), the APA found a "rich body of research" showing that juveniles are mature enough to decide whether to obtain an abortion without parental involvement. Brief for APA as *Amicus Curiae,* O. T. 1989, No. 88–805 etc., p. 18. The APA brief, citing psychology treatises and studies too numerous to list here, asserted: "By middle adolescence (age 14–15) young people develop abilities similar to adults in reasoning about moral dilemmas, understanding social rules and laws, [and] reasoning about interpersonal relationships and interpersonal problems." *Id.,* at 19–20 (citations omitted). Given the nuances of scientific methodology and conflicting views, courts—which can only consider the limited evidence on the record before them—are ill equipped to determine which view of science is the right one. Legislatures "are better qualified to weigh and 'evaluate the results of statistical studies in terms of their own local conditions and with a flexibility of approach that is not available to the courts.'" *McCleskey* v. *Kemp,* 481 U.S. 279, 319 (1987) (quoting *Gregg, supra,* at 186).

Even putting aside questions of methodology, the studies cited by the Court offer scant support for a categorical prohibition of the death penalty for murderers under 18. At most, these studies conclude that, *on average,* or *in most cases,* persons under 18 are unable to take moral responsibility for their actions. Not one of the cited studies opines that all individuals under 18 are unable to appreciate the nature of their crimes.

Moreover, the cited studies describe only adolescents who engage in risky or antisocial behavior, as many young people do. Murder, however, is more than just risky or antisocial behavior. It is entirely consistent to believe that young people often act impetuously and lack judgment, but, at the same time, to believe that those who commit premeditated murder are—at least sometimes—just as culpable as adults. Christopher Simmons, who was only seven months shy of his 18th birthday when he murdered Shirley Crook, described to his friends *beforehand*—"in chilling, callous terms," as the Court puts it—the murder he planned to commit. He then broke into the home of an innocent woman, bound her with duct tape and electrical wire, and threw her off a bridge alive and conscious. . . .

. . .

Nor does the Court suggest a stopping point for its reasoning. If juries cannot make appropriate determinations in cases involving murderers under 18, in what other kinds of cases will the Court find jurors deficient? We have already held that no jury may consider whether a mentally deficient defendant can receive the death penalty, irrespective of his crime. See *Atkins*, 536 U.S., at 321. Why not take other mitigating factors, such as considerations of childhood abuse or poverty, away from juries as well? Surely jurors "overpowered" by "the brutality or cold-blooded nature" of a crime, could not adequately weigh these mitigating factors either.

[In part III of his dissent, Justice Scalia elaborates on his disagreement with the Court's reliance on international law in interpreting our own Constitution.

In part IV of his dissent, he concludes with a criticizm of the Court's willingness to allow the Missouri Supreme Court to dictate a change in course and to ignore the Court's own precedent:]

To add insult to injury, the Court affirms the Missouri Supreme Court without even admonishing that court for its flagrant disregard of our precedent in *Stanford*. Until today, we have always held that it is this Court's prerogative alone to overrule one of its precedents. That has been true even where changes in judicial doctrine ha[ve] significantly undermined our prior holding, . . . and even where our prior holding appears to rest on reasons rejected in some other line of decisions, Today, however, the Court silently approves a state-court decision that blatantly rejected controlling precedent.

. . .

ADOLESCENT DEVELOPMENTAL IMMATURITY AS A MITIGATING FACTOR

In his proportionality analysis in *Roper*, Justice Kennedy draws on the work of law professor Elizabeth Scott and developmental psychologist Laurence Steinberg, who have analyzed the link between developmental immaturity in adolescence and criminal culpability in a series of articles and a book. Elizabeth S. Scott & Laurence D. Steinberg, Blaming Youth, 81 Tex.L.Rev. 799 (2003); Laurence D. Steinberg & Elizabeth S. Scott, Less Guilty By Reason of Adolescence: Developmental Immaturity, Diminished Responsibility and the Juvenile Death Penalty, 58 American Psychologist 1009 (Dec. 2003); Elizabeth S. Scott & Laurence D. Steinberg, Rethinking Juvenile Justice (2008). In the essay excerpted below, written after *Roper*, Scott explains the mitigation framework that was the basis of the Court's conclusion that juveniles should not receive the death penalty because they are less culpable than adults.

Elizabeth Scott, Adolescence and the Regulation of Youth Crime, 79 Temple L. Rev. 337 (2006).*

Drawing on research in developmental psychology, the Court pointed to several dimensions of adolescence that distinguish young offenders from adults in ways that mitigate culpability. These include deficiencies in decision-making ability, greater vulnerability to external coercion, and the relatively unformed nature of adolescent character. Although the Court did not elaborate, each of these attributes of adolescence corresponds to a conventional source of mitigation in criminal law—and together they offer strong evidence that young offenders are not as culpable as adults. . . .

First, consider diminished capacity. Under standard criminal law doctrine, actors whose decision-making capacities are impaired, by mental illness or retardation for example, are deemed less blameworthy than typical offenders. . . . There is considerable evidence that children and adolescents are less capable decision makers than adults in ways that are relevant to their criminal choices.

. . . [B]y mid-adolescence, most teens are close to adults in their ability to reason and to understand information—what you might call "pure" cognitive capacities—at least in the abstract. The reality, however, is that they are likely less capable than are adults in using these capacities in making real-world choices, partly because of lack of experience and partly because teens are less efficient than adults in processing information. In life, and particularly on the street, the ability to quickly marshal information may be essential to competent decision making.

Also, other aspects of psychological development that affect decision making lag behind cognitive development and undermine adolescent competence. . . . [T]he decisions of teenagers are subject to psychosocial and emotional influences that contribute to immature judgment, which can lead them to make bad choices.

. . .

. . . [First,] teens tend to lack what developmentalists call "future orientation." That is, as compared to adults, adolescents are more likely to focus on the here and now and less likely to think about the long-term consequences of their choices or actions, and when they do, they are inclined to assign less weight to future consequences than to immediate risks and benefits. . . .

Substantial research evidence also supports the conventional wisdom that teens are more oriented toward peers and more responsive to peer influence than are adults. . . . [A]dolescents are more likely than either children or adults to change their decisions and alter their behavior in response to peer pressure.

. . . Teens appear to seek peer approval, especially in group situations. Thus, perhaps it is not surprising that young offenders are far more likely than adults to commit crimes in groups.

. . .

Justice Kennedy in *Roper* noted another psychosocial factor that contributes to immature judgment—adolescents are both less likely to perceive risks and less risk-averse than adults.... In the abstract—on paper and pencil tests—adolescents are capable of perceiving risks almost as well as adults. In the real world, however, risk preference and other dimensions of psychosocial immaturity interact to encourage risky choices.

. . .

Another (compatible) account of why adolescents take more risks than adults is that they may evaluate both the risks and benefits of risky activity differently.... Studies suggest that ... adolescents may discount risks and assign greater weight to the rewards of a choice than do adults.... What distinguishes adolescents from adults in this regard, then, is not the fact that teens are less knowledgeable about risks, but, rather, that they attach different value to the rewards that risk taking provides.

. . .

In addition to age differences in susceptibility to peer influence, future orientation, and risk preference and assessment, adolescents and adults also differ with respect to their ability to control impulsive behavior and choices....

These psychosocial and emotional factors contribute to immature judgment in adolescence and likely play a role in decisions by teens to engage in criminal activity. It is easy to imagine how individuals whose choices are subject to these developmental influences—susceptibility to peer influence, poor (real-world) risk assessment, sensation seeking, a tendency to discount future consequences of choices and focus on immediate consequences, and poor impulse control—might decide to engage in criminal conduct.

. . .

... [R]esearch in the last few years indicates that some of these psychological factors may have biological underpinnings. Recent studies of brain development show that important structural changes take place during adolescence in the frontal lobes, most importantly in the prefrontal cortex. This region of the brain is central to what psychologists call "executive functions"—advanced thinking processes that are employed in planning ahead, regulating emotions, controlling impulses, and weighing the costs and benefits of decisions before acting. Thus, the immature judgment of teens to some extent may be a function of hard wiring.

... [T]wo other sources of mitigation in criminal law also apply to adolescents—and reinforce the conclusion that young offenders are less blameworthy than their adult counterparts.

The second source of mitigation involves situations in which a person offends in response to extreme external pressures. (Think about the defenses of provocation and duress.) The criminal law does not require exceptional forbearance or bravery; a defense (or a reduced sentence) may be available if an ordinary (i.e., "reasonable") person might have responded to the situation in the same way the defendant did. Because of the coercive circumstances, the actor is deemed less blameworthy than other offenders.

In *Roper*, the Court recognized that "ordinary" adolescents are subject to peer pressure to a far greater extent than adults, including pressure to commit crimes.... In some high-crime neighborhoods, peer pressure to commit crimes is so powerful that only exceptional kids escape. As Jeffrey Fagan and others have found, in these settings, resisting this pressure can result in loss of status, ostracism, and vulnerability to physical assault. The circumstances many teens face in these social contexts are similar to those involved in claims of duress, provocation, necessity, or domination by codefendants and are appropriately deemed mitigating of culpability. As the *Roper* Court also noted, the case for mitigation on this ground seems all the more compelling because, unlike adults, adolescents as legal minors are not free to leave their schools, homes, and neighborhoods.... Young adults can avoid the pressure by removing themselves from the social setting in which avoiding involvement in crime is difficult. Thus, it is reasonable that adults can not claim this kind of situational mitigation.

A third source of mitigation in criminal law is evidence that a criminal act was out of character. At sentencing, offenders can often introduce evidence of their general good character to demonstrate that the offense was an aberrant act. Here mitigation applies to the crimes of young offenders as well—not because of their good character per se—but because their characters are unformed.

Beginning with Erik Erikson, psychologists have explained that an important developmental task of adolescence is the formation of personal identity.... During adolescence, identity is fluid—values, plans, attitudes, and beliefs are likely to be tentative as teens struggle to separate from their parents and figure out who they are. This process involves a lot of experimentation, which for many kids means engaging in ... risky activities ..., including involvement in crime. Self-report studies have found that a very high percent of teenage boys admit to committing crimes for which they could be incarcerated, leading one psychologist to describe involvement in criminal activity as "a normal part of teen life."

But, the typical teenage delinquent does not grow up to be an adult criminal. The statistics consistently show that seventeen-year-olds commit more crimes than any other age group. After that age, the crime rate declines steeply. Most adolescents literally grow out of their antisocial tendencies as they attain psychosocial maturity and individual identity becomes settled....

The research supports that much juvenile crime stems from experimentation typical of this developmental stage rather than moral deficiencies reflecting bad character. It is fair to assume that most adults who engage in criminal conduct act on subjectively defined values and preferences and that their choices can be charged to deficient moral character. Thus, an impulsive adult whose "adolescent traits" lead him to get involved in crime is quite different from a risk-taking teen. Adolescent traits are not typical of adulthood. The values and preferences that motivate the adult criminal are not developmental, but characterological, a part of personal identity. This cannot be said of the crimes of typical juvenile offenders, whose choices, while unfortunate, are shaped by developmental factors that are constitutive of adolescence. Like the adult who offers evidence of good character, most adolescent offenders lack a key component of culpability—the connection between the bad act and the offender's bad character. The Court in *Roper* recognized this, rejecting the notion that we can be confident that "even a heinous crime by an adolescent is the product of an irretrievably depraved character."

The reality, of course, is that not all young offenders grow up to be persons of good character—some grow up to be criminals. Psychologist Terrie Moffitt, in a major longitudinal study, has placed adolescent offenders in two rough categories: (1) a large group of what she calls "adolescent-limited" offenders typical delinquents whose involvement in crime begins and ends in adolescence, and (2) a much smaller group that she labels "life-course-persistent offenders." The latter are youths whose antisocial conduct often begins in childhood and continues through adolescence into adulthood; many are in the early stages of criminal careers. In adolescence, the criminal conduct of kids in these two groups looks pretty similar, but the underlying causes and the prognosis are different.

This raises an important issue: Even if adolescents (including seventeen-year-olds) generally are less mature than adults, why should immaturity not be considered on an individualized basis as is typical of most mitigating conditions? . . . This question was critical in the context of the juvenile death penalty, but it is also important in the broader arena of juvenile justice policy. In his *Roper* dissent, Justice Scalia argued that there was no reason to abandon the practice of allowing capital juries to evaluate the immaturity of juveniles on a case-by-case basis.

. . . The problem with individualized assessment is that we currently lack the diagnostic tools to evaluate psychosocial maturity and identity formation on an individualized basis so as to separate savvy young career criminals from ordinary adolescents. Justice Kennedy noted the potential for error in distinguishing incipient psychopaths from youths whose crimes reflect, as he described it, "transient immaturity," and he expressed concern that the brutality of the offense might often overwhelm consideration of youth and immaturity. Indeed, the prosecutor had argued to the jury that Chris Simmons's youth was not mitigating, but *aggravating*. . . .

There is something else to worry about if maturity is litigated on a case-by-case basis. Research evidence suggests that racial and ethnic biases influence attitudes about the punishment of young offenders; thus, decision makers may be inclined to discount the mitigating impact of immaturity in minority youths. The integrity of any individualized decision-making process is vulnerable to contamination from racist attitudes or from unconscious racial stereotyping that operates even among those who may lack overt prejudice. There is evidence that African American youths are viewed as more mature than same-aged white kids, and all offenders will look more like adults at the time of sentencing than at the time of the crime.

NOTES

(1) Following the Supreme Court's decision in *Atkins*, and while the Court's decision in *Roper v. Simmons* was pending, Professor Barry Feld wrote a well-researched article on the developmental incapacity of adolescents. In addition to his

thoughtful analysis, he urged the Court to reconsider its earlier decision in *Stanford*, to affirm the Missouri Supreme Court's decision in *Simmons* and to hold unconstitutional the execution of persons who were under 18 at the time of commission of the crime, as a logical extension of the Court's decision in *Atkins*. He further argued that diminished developmental capacity of adolescents goes beyond the death penalty, that it has implications for proportionality in the sentencing of adolescents generally. Barry C. Feld, Competence, Culpability and Punishment: Implications of *Atkins* for Executing and Sentencing Adolescents, 32 Hofstra L.Rev. 463 (2003).

Professor Mary Berkheiser also wrote in opposition to the juvenile death penalty prior to the Court's decision in *Roper v. Simmons*. She, too, argued for stronger adherence to the notion of proportionality in sentencing for juveniles. Mary Berkheiser, Capitalizing Adolescents: Juvenile Offenders on Death Row, 59 U. Miami L.Rev. 135 (2005). See also Audrey Dupont, The Eighth Amendment Proportionality Analysis and Age and the Constitutionality of Using Juvenile Adjudications to Enhance Adult Sentences, 78 Denver U.L.Rev. 255 (2000). A general analysis of the concept of proportionality under the Eighth Amendment, with implications for sentencing of juveniles, is Richard S. Frase, Excessive Prison Sentences, Punishment Goals, and the Eighth Amendment: "Proportionality" Relative to What?, 89 Minn.L.Rev. 571 (2005).

(2) If the death penalty cannot constitutionally be imposed on juveniles—and consistent with the notion of proportionality as applied to juveniles—what about a sentence of life without possibility of parole? Some courts have held that LWOP for juveniles does not violate the Eighth Amendment. See, e.g., *Harris v. Wright*, 93 F.3d 581 (9th Cir.1996); *People v. Launsbury*, 217 Mich.App. 358, 551 N.W.2d 460 (1996); *Commonwealth v. Carter*, 855 A.2d 885 (Pa.Super.), appeal denied, 581 Pa. 670, 863 A.2d 1142 (2004). Other courts in some earlier decisions held LWOP to be unconstitutional. See, e.g., *Workman v. Commonwealth*, 429 S.W.2d 374 (Ky. 1968); *Naovarath v. State*, 105 Nev. 525, 779 P.2d 944 (1989). Feld, Berkheiser and Dupont, supra, oppose LWOP for juveniles on proportionality principles and point out that the Supreme Court in cases involving less than the death penalty has been "soft" on finding LWOP to be within the meaning of cruel and unusual punishment. For a very thoughtful and timely analysis of the issue see Victor Streib & Bernadette Schrempp, Life Without Parole for Children, 21 Crim.Just. 4 (Winter 2007).

THEORETICAL JUSTIFICATION FOR COERCIVE DISPOSITIONS

The dispositional, or sentencing, phase in delinquency cases presents theoretical problems that pervade not only juvenile courts but the criminal justice system as well. In order to determine what to do with a child who has been adjudicated delinquent, one must first decide the purpose of the court's use of coercive sanctions. No consistent theory of disposition is possible without first deciding the goals of delinquency dispositions.

Historically, rehabilitation was the underlying goal of the juvenile justice system. Rehabilitation required a focus on the particular needs of the offender and the programs of reform available to meet those needs. To achieve the rehabilitative goal, juvenile court judges were given enormous, generally unreviewable, discretion in fashioning a disposition appropriate to the child's needs. The clearest example was the practice of indeterminate commitment whereby a juvenile could be committed to an institution for an indeterminate period until the age of majority.

Beginning with the skepticism expressed by Justice Fortas in *Kent v. United States* that the child "receives the worst of both worlds: that he gets neither the protections accorded to adults nor the solicitous care and regenerative treatment postulated for children," 383 U.S. at 555, the pendulum slowly began to swing toward a more punitive rationale for the juvenile process.

The punitive, or "just desserts" model, found full expression in the Juvenile Justice Standards:

> The purpose of the juvenile correctional system is to reduce juvenile crime by maintaining the integrity of the substantive law proscribing certain behavior and by developing individual responsibility for lawful behavior. This purpose should be pursued through means that are fair and just, that recognize the unique characteristics and needs of juveniles, and that give juveniles access to opportunities for personal and social growth.

Juvenile Justice Standards Project, Standards Relating to Dispositions, Standard 1.1 (1980).

An increasing number of states revised their juvenile codes to reflect the shift from a rehabilitative purpose to a more punitive purpose. See, e.g., Cal.Welf. & Inst.Code. § 202(a)–(b), (e); Wash.Rev.Code Ann. § 13.40.010(2)(c)–(d). In Barry C. Feld, The Juvenile Court Meets the Principle of Offense: Punishment, Treatment, and the Difference It Makes, 68 B.U.L.Rev. 821 (1988), the author analyzes the legislative trend toward punishment as the purpose of juvenile dispositions. Some commentators have argued that the trend toward "get tough" legislation does not spell the demise of the rehabilitative model and that rehabilitative and punitive goals are compatible in an integrated system for dealing with serious and habitual juvenile offenders. See, e.g., Julianne P. Sheffer, Note, Serious and Habitual Juvenile Offender Statutes: Reconciling Punishment and Rehabilitation Within the Juvenile Justice System, 48 Vanderbilt L.Rev. 479 (1995). Likewise, the argument has been made that rehabilitation and punishment are not mutually exclusive, that punishment rather is a means toward the rehabilitative end. Catherine J. Ross, Disposition in a Discretionary Regime: Punishment and Rehabilitation in the Juvenile Justice System, 36 B.C.L.Rev. 1037 (1995).

In addition to adopting punishment as the underlying rationale for imposition of sanctions, the Standards embrace the concept of proportionality, i.e., making the punishment fit the crime. Thus, the Standards reject the traditional indeterminate model in favor of a determinate model based on the proportionality principle for all dispositions, including commitment, fines, and community service. Juvenile Justice Standards Project, Standards Relating to Dispositions, Standards 1.1, 1.2, 3.2 (1980). Some states have adopted the proportionality model as well, not only with respect to fines and community service, see, e.g., Conn.Gen.Stat.Ann. § 46b–140(b), (e); Ky.Rev.Stat.Ann. §§ 635.080, 635.085(1); N.Y.Fam.Ct.Act § 353.6; N.C.Gen.Stat. § 7B–2506(5)–(6), (23); S.C.Code Ann. § 20–7–7805(A)(3), but even with respect to commitment, see, e.g., Wash.Rev.Code Ann. §§ 13.40.030, 13.40.0357, 13.40.160, 13.40.180; see also Ind.Code Ann. § 31–37–19–10; N.C.Gen.Stat. §§ 7B–2506(24), 7B–2513(b); Tenn.Code Ann. § 37–1–137(A)(1)(b), (h).

Courts, too, have shown an occasional retreat from the rehabilitative philosophy. In *Scott L. v. State*, 104 Nev. 419, 760 P.2d 134 (1988), for example, the court upheld a punitive disposition not only on a deterrence theory but on a "just desserts" theory, the theory that he "deserved" it.

At the same time the shift from the rehabilitative model toward a punitive model was taking place, changes occurred as well in the dispositions available to the juvenile court. Traditional dispositions were limited to commitment or probation. Gradually, more and more states added other dispositions, including restitution, fines and community service, as well as more creative conditions of probation. The most dramatic changes, however, have been those with correctional implications, e.g., "blended sentencing," which allows imposition of adult sentences, and transfer to the adult correctional system on reaching the age of majority, to serve out an adult sentence.

These developments signal a distinct trend toward harsher treatment of juveniles, especially those who are older and charged with the most serious offenses. In many ways chronicling this trend toward progressively harsher treatment of juveniles is to explore the philosophical underpinnings of the juvenile court itself as an institution. Perhaps fittingly, this section examining the differential treatment of juveniles and the issues associated with it, concludes with a perspective on dispositions, where historically the differential has been widest. As you read this section, think about what the goals of the juvenile justice system should be and how those goals can best be implemented at the dispositional phase.

a.   TRADITIONAL DISPOSITIONS

NORTH DAKOTA CENTURY CODE (Lexis)

§ 27–20–31.   Disposition of delinquent child.

If the child is found to be a delinquent child, the court may make any of the following orders of disposition best suited to the child's treatment, rehabilitation, and welfare:

1.   Any order authorized ... for the disposition of a deprived child;

2.   Placing the child on probation under the supervision of the juvenile supervisor, probation officer, or other appropriate officer of the court or of the court of another state ... or the director of the county social service board under conditions and limitations the court prescribes;

3.   Ordering the child to pay a fine if the delinquent act committed by the child constitutes manslaughter resulting from the operation of a motor vehicle ...; negligent homicide ...; or driving or being in actual physical control of a vehicle in violation of section 39–08–01, or an equivalent ordinance. The court may suspend the imposition of a fine imposed pursuant to this subsection upon such terms and conditions as the court may determine ...;

4.   Placing the child in an institution, camp, or other facility for delinquent children operated under the direction of the court or other local public authority;

5. Committing the child to the division of juvenile services or to another state department to which commitment of delinquent or unruly children may be made. When necessary, the commitment order may provide that the child initially be placed in a secure facility;

6. Ordering the child to make monetary restitution to the victim of the offense or to complete a specified number of hours of community service as determined by the court, or both;

7. Ordering the periodic testing for the use of illicit drugs or alcohol pursuant to rules or policies adopted by the supreme court; or

8. Under section 27–20–31.1, order the driver's license or permit of the child to be delivered to the juvenile supervisor, probation officer, or other appropriate officer of the court and to inform the director of the department of transportation of the child's suspension of driving privileges and the duration of the suspension of privileges.

In re Gregory S.

California Court of Appeal, 1978.
85 Cal.App.3d 206, 149 Cal.Rptr. 216.

■ PARAS, ASSOCIATE JUSTICE.

The minor, Gregory S., appeals from orders adjudicating him a ward of the court under Welfare and Institutions Code section 602, and committing him to the Youth Authority.

Pending disposition of earlier adjudications in which Gregory was found to have violated Penal Code sections 242 (battery) and 148 (resisting arrest), both misdemeanors, a petition was filed on October 18, 1977 charging him with kidnapping for the purpose of robbery (Pen.Code, § 209), assault with a deadly weapon (Pen.Code, § 245, subd. a), robbery (Pen.Code, § 211), and auto theft (Veh.Code, § 10851). On October 21st another petition was filed charging him with robbery (Pen.Code, § 211), burglary of a residence (Pen.Code, § 459), and burglary of a motor vehicle (Pen.Code, § 459). On October 24th and on November 4th, two more petitions were filed charging him with seven more burglaries (Pen.Code, § 459).

Following the jurisdictional hearing on the offenses charged in the October 18th petition, the court found the first three charges of the petition, kidnapping for the purpose of robbery, assault with a deadly weapon, and robbery to be true and that the latter two offenses merged with the kidnapping offense. Thereafter, having properly been advised of his *Boykin-Tahl* rights with the understanding that all remaining charges and petitions would be dismissed, Gregory admitted two of the three offenses charged in the petition of October 21st (robbery and burglary). The dispositional hearing was held on January 9, 1978.

I

[The court held that the evidence was sufficient to support the adjudication for kidnapping for the purpose of robbery. The facts of the case are contained in this section of the opinion and are set forth below.]

Robert Huiras testified that on October 18, 1977, at approximately 10:50 p. m., while walking down Bianchi Street, three males approached him. One of them, armed with a .38 caliber revolver, ordered Huiras to walk to and enter a white 1962 or 1963 Chevrolet. The larger of the three then put a headlock on him and forced him into the vehicle. He was there asked if he had money and responded that all he had was 50 cents but could get more. They drove around for approximately 15 to 20 minutes, then Huiras was ordered out of the car and told to take off his clothes; after the three took his clothes, his wallet, and the 50 cents, they struck him with the gun on the head, rendering him unconscious and causing him to fall; they then started kicking him. When Huiras regained consciousness, the three were gone. Huiras identified Gregory as one of the three participants.

Later that night Officer William Thompson clocked a vehicle, a 1964 Chevrolet, at 70 miles per hour. He turned on his red light and followed it off the freeway; it came to a stop, and as Thompson got out of his patrol car, it sped off. Thompson pursued again with red light and siren activated; the Chevrolet slowed to about five miles an hour, and at that speed its three occupants, including Gregory, exited and ran. The area was surrounded, and in due course Gregory was apprehended. Huiras' wallet and a loaded revolver were found on the front seat of the Chevrolet.

After indicating that he understood and waived his *Miranda* rights, Gregory told Thompson that Michael McCormick and Derick Hill had been driving around and picked him up; they drove on until they saw Huiras; they made a "U" turn, stopped, and McCormick and Hill forced Huiras into the car. After driving around North Stockton, they stopped and McCormick and Hill forced Huiras out of the car, and beat him. Although Gregory denied to Thompson any participation in the kidnapping, robbery, and beating, when later questioned by police officer, David Duly, he admitted his active involvement.

. . .

II

[The court concluded that the 13–year-old juvenile appreciated the wrongfulness of his acts.]

III

Gregory also contends that the juvenile court abused its discretion in committing him to the Youth Authority. He relies on the principle enunciated in *In re Aline D.* (1975) 14 Cal.3d 557, 564, 121 Cal.Rptr. 816, 536 P.2d 65, that the Juvenile Court Law contemplates a progressively restrictive and punitive series of disposition orders with Youth Authority placement as a last resort. (See also *In re Arthur N.* (1976) 16 Cal.3d 226, 237, 127 Cal.Rptr. 641, 545 P.2d 1345; *In re Michael R.* (1977) 73 Cal.App.3d 327, 334–335, 140 Cal.Rptr. 716.) He points out that at the time of the offense he was but 13 years old, had never been adjudged a ward of the court under section 602, and this was his first serious offense.

A commitment to the Youth Authority is within the sound discretion of the juvenile court and its decision will not be reversed unless there is a showing that the court abused its discretion. (*In re Michael R.*, supra, 73 Cal.App.3d at pp. 332–333, 140 Cal.Rptr. 716; *In re Clarence B.* (1974) 37 Cal.App.3d 676, 682, 112 Cal.Rptr. 474.) The reviewing court must indulge in all reasonable inferences to support the findings of the juvenile court and such findings will not be disturbed on appeal when there is substantial evidence to support them. (Ibid.)

In most instances commitments to the Youth Authority are to be made only in the most serious cases and only after all else has failed. (*In re Aline D.*, supra, 14 Cal.3d at p. 564, 121 Cal.Rptr. 817, 536 P.2d 65; *In re Michael R.*, supra, 73 Cal.App.3d at p. 334, 140 Cal.Rptr. 716.) However, the circumstances in a particular case may well suggest the desirability of a Youth Authority commitment despite the availability of alternative dispositions such as placement in a county camp or ranch. (See *In re John H.* (1978) 21 Cal.3d 18, 27, 145 Cal.Rptr. 357, 577 P.2d 177.) We find this to be such a case.

Both the psychiatrist, Thomas English, and the clinical psychologist, John Hannon, indicated that in light of Gregory's aggressive behavior, which was becoming progressively more anti-social and dangerous, he needed a structured placement, preferably a locked facility, since he had threatened to run away from any placement he did not like or at which he was retained too long. The observation of Dr. English was that the majority of out-of-home placements did not deal well with the aggressive and anti-social child. Hannon observed that Gregory was "street-wise" and opined that if he did not like his placement, he was very likely to run away and probably commit additional crimes.

The court summarized the facts and considerations upon which it based its order. Although only 13 years old, Gregory was very aggressive and violent; pending disposition regarding two violent acts, battery and resisting arrest, he committed other more serious and more violent acts, armed robbery, burglary, and kidnapping for the purpose of robbery with physical assault upon a 15–year-old victim. Even though intelligent, Gregory seldom attended school and made no effort to assist himself. His threats to run away from any type of long-term placement required consideration of the need for a locked facility for his own good. The public was entitled to protection from further criminal acts of Gregory, further necessitating use of a locked facility. Gregory would benefit from the Youth Authority's educational facilities and a commitment to the Youth Authority was in his own best interests.

It is readily apparent from these comments that the court did not act arbitrarily. The facts and circumstances indicate the propriety of the Youth Authority commitment. (See *In re John H.*, supra; *In re Willy L.* (1976) 56 Cal.App.3d 256, 265, 128 Cal.Rptr. 592.) This case is readily distinguishable from such cases as *In re Aline D.*, supra, and *In re Michael R.*, supra. Moreover the Legislature in 1977 (effective January 1, 1978) amended Welfare and Institutions Code section 202 to provide that one of the purposes of the Juvenile Court Law is "to protect the public from criminal conduct by minors." This long overdue objective of juvenile justice was correctly taken into account in deciding upon the commitment.

The orders appealed from are affirmed.

■ Puglia, P. J., concurs.

■ Reynoso, Associate Justice, concurring in the result.

. . .

We deal with a youngster who, at the time of the hearing, was 13 years old and weighed 95 pounds.

The statute declares that such a youngster cannot be committed to the Youth Authority without a finding on the part of the juvenile court that the incarceration is in the boy's best interest. (Welf. & Inst. Code, s 734.)[2] The trial court has thus ruled that the minor will be benefitted by such incarceration. The statute places the juvenile court in a position of deciding that it is in the best interest of a 13–year-old to be incarcerated with older, criminally prone, juveniles in a setting where physical assaults, including sexual attacks, are all too common. How can this be?

The statutory scheme contemplates a Youth Authority very different from today's reality. The Youth Authority was initially established to benefit youngsters of tender years who would benefit from the educational, rehabilitative, and other helpful efforts. In fact, today's Youth Authority is reserved for "the most severely delinquent youths" (*In re Aline D.*, supra, 14 Cal.3d at p. 564, 121 Cal.Rptr. 817, 536 P.2d 65), many of whom reach the Youth Authority through the criminal courts rather than through the juvenile courts. The legislative ideal of rehabilitation has never been a reality, and it is far less so today than yesteryear.

The officials who enforce the law against juveniles have always been far more realistic than the statutes contemplate. Thus, juvenile court judges have traditionally viewed their priorities in dealing with youths as follows: first, rehabilitation; second, deterrence; third, protection of society; and fourth, punishment. When dealing with a crime of violence, even with a boy as young as Gregory, the probation department official tried to balance the interest of the child with the interest of protecting society. That is reality.

Let us examine the sad facts of this case. We deal with a Black youngster who had gotten into the company of some older boys. With them he committed a series of crimes, some of violence. The youngster, according to the probation officer, was used as a mascot by the older boys.

At the dispositional hearing, the juvenile court considered only those matters which were the subject of findings or admissions. . . .

. . . While the youth had a propensity for assaultive behavior the probation department rejected the notion of committing him to the Youth Authority for three related reasons. . . .

---

2. Welfare and Institutions Code section 734 reads as follows:

"No ward of the juvenile court shall be committed to the Youth Authority unless the judge of the court is fully satisfied that the mental and physical condition and qualifications of the ward are such as to render it probable that he will be benefited by the reformatory educational discipline or other treatment provided by the Youth Authority."

The first reason for rejection of Youth Authority by the probation department deals with rehabilitation. Gregory, the probation officer reported, would have a far better opportunity if placed with the Ezell James Group Home in Riverside, California. The probation officer had confidence that that home could control Gregory, that a male role model would be afforded, and that he would learn to deal with community standards. This ties to the testimony of the psychologist who found nothing emotionally wrong with Gregory but found that he was conforming to his concepts (rather than community norms) of what a young man growing into adulthood should do. Gregory had been living with his grandmother. What happened to his mother and father does not appear in the record. It does appear that Gregory appears to have had a mother who gave him a good, solid emotional foundation in the first few years of his life.

The second reason deals with the Youth Authority. Because of Gregory's age and small stature, the probation department felt that he would be subject to assault, including sexual assault, in the Youth Authority facilities. Were he to avoid that result, he would do so only by aligning himself with some bigger, tougher youngsters with even greater criminal dispositions. That is, Gregory would learn to be a "better" criminal.

Third, the interest of society would be protected without resort to the Youth Authority. Gregory needed the close supervision at the group home. Perhaps society would be saved the further trauma of another life dedicated to crime. One of the problems with Gregory, all witnesses agreed, was that he lived in an unstructured environment where involvement in violent criminal behavior seemed to have its own rewards.

The probation office tried to balance the interest of helping the minor and that of protecting society. According to the probation officer, "unless there is such a threat to society that society's welfare takes precedence over the potential treatment versus punishment of the individual," the youngster should not be placed in a "purely punitive setting."

. . .

The prosecutor argued at the dispositional hearing that the type of facility that could be most beneficial to Gregory was simply not available. The prosecution argued: "We just don't have anything available other than Youth Authority in that regard, at least in our county, or as far as I'm aware, statewide." Thus, the prosecution's recommendation was that the youth be sent to the Youth Authority "for protection of society." There was no pretense that the youth would be benefited.

A youngster who violates the law by involving himself in a crime of violence expects to be punished. The record indicates that Gregory expected such punishment. Youngsters, however, have a greater capacity to change than do adults. Further, we as a society have a greater responsibility to attempt to socialize the young than we do with respect to adults. Finally, a youngster is far more subject to peer pressure in becoming involved in criminal behavior (as was Gregory); he can become involved in criminal behavior without yet being a hardened criminal (and Gregory was not a hardened criminal). Thus we cannot give up on the notion of rehabilitation.

The juvenile laws, since they found their way into the California statutes in 1915, support the commonsensical approach of rehabilitation and protection of society. Thus present Welfare and Institutions Code section 202 indicates that the purpose of juvenile law is "to secure for each minor" the care and guidance which will serve the "spiritual, emotional, mental and physical welfare" of that given minor. Deterrence is also mentioned, for another purpose is to protect the "best interest of the state" and to protect the public from "criminal conduct by the minors." Also an aim is "the protection of the public from the consequences of criminal activity" of the minors and "to impose on the minor a sense of responsibility for his own acts." It seems manifest that the best rehabilitative interest of the minor, together with the protection of society, demands punishment when a crime of violence has been committed. Only retributive punishment is proscribed.

Except in the most extreme case, the law, in the case of a 13–year-old, should not contemplate giving up its rehabilitative aim. The juvenile court seems to have done just that.

The reasons given by the juvenile judge for commitment to the Youth Authority (schooling, discipline and control) could also be met by a placement in a boys' ranch, or to a lesser extent, the home placement....

There is a saving grace. The law contemplates that the Youth Authority may form its own judgment as to whether or not it will accept a youngster. (Welf. & Inst. Code, s 736.) In rare cases, perhaps this one, the Youth Authority will refuse to accept the placement.

■ Rehearing denied; Mosk and Newman, JJ., dissenting.

NOTES

(1) Both opinions in *Gregory S.* cite the California Supreme Court's decision in *In re Aline D.*, 14 Cal.3d 557, 121 Cal.Rptr. 816, 536 P.2d 65 (1975). That decision, perhaps more than any other, gave voice to the "least restrictive alternative" philosophy. The court held that under California's statutory procedures a child may not be committed to a juvenile institution, i.e., to the California Youth Authority, solely on the basis that no suitable alternatives exist. Rather, the state must show that the child will benefit from the commitment. While both opinions in *Gregory S.* conclude that the trial court did not abuse its discretion in ordering commitment of the 13–year-old juvenile, one clearly can see the tension that exists between the judges over the propriety of commitment in this case.

Other courts have embraced the "least restrictive alternative" philosophy. See, e.g., *R.P. v. State*, 718 P.2d 168 (Alaska Ct.App.1986); *In re Michael QQ*, 225 A.D.2d 940, 638 N.Y.S.2d 851 (1996); *In re J.F.*, 241 Mont. 434, 787 P.2d 364 (1990); see also *In re J.S.S.*, 610 N.W.2d 364 (Minn.Ct.App.2000). The philosophy also has found increased expression in state statutes. See, e.g., Ark.Stat.Ann. § 9–27–329(d); Iowa Code Ann. § 232.52(1); La.Children's Code Ann. art. 901(B).

(2) For what length of time may a juvenile be committed? Traditionally, a commitment to the California Youth Authority—or the appropriate state agency in any given state—was an indeterminate commitment, often for the remainder of the juvenile's minority. Recall that in the *Gault* case at age 15 Gerald Gault was committed to the State Industrial School "for the period of his minority [i.e., until

21]'' for making an obscene phone call, an offense for which in Arizona an adult could have been fined $5 to $50 or imprisoned for not more than two months.

The indeterminate model still prevails in most jurisdictions. See, e.g., Alaska Stat. § 47.12.120(b)(1); Conn.Gen.Stat.Ann. § 46b–141; Idaho Code § 20–520(1). Thus, a juvenile may be committed to an institution for the remainder of his minority, which may, in fact, mean until age 21. See, e.g., D.C.Code § 16–2322(a)(4); Va.Code Ann. § 16.1–285; see also Miss.Code Ann. § 43–21–605(1)(g)(iii) (until age 20); Tenn.Code Ann. §§ 37–1–103(c), –137(a)(1)(A) (until age 19). The agency to which the juvenile is committed, rather than the juvenile court, typically decides when the juvenile has been "rehabilitated" and is ready for release from confinement. See, e.g., *In re AB, Jr.*, 663 So.2d 580 (Miss.1995); *In re B.L.T.*, 258 Mont. 468, 853 P.2d 1226 (1993). In many states today, even though the indeterminate model is followed, commitment is limited in duration, usually for a two-year maximum. See, e.g., Ga.Code Ann. § 15–11–70; N.D.Cent.Code § 27–20–36(2). Additional two-year periods are authorized if a new hearing is held to determine whether further commitment is required. See, e.g., *People v. Steven S.*, 76 Cal. App.4th 349, 90 Cal.Rptr.2d 290 (1999).

Under the indeterminate disposition model, a juvenile might be committed for a longer period than would be possible in the case of an adult convicted of the same offense, as in the *Gault* case. Is such disparate treatment constitutionally permissible? Historically, the answer was yes, based on the notion that the juvenile court is protective not punitive in nature, that a juvenile is committed to an institution not for purposes of punishment but rather for rehabilitation, and that a longer commitment might be necessary in order to achieve the latter purpose. See, e.g., *In re Eric J.*, 25 Cal.3d 522, 159 Cal.Rptr. 317, 601 P.2d 549 (1979); *People in re M.C.*, 774 P.2d 857 (Colo.1989); *In re T.A.S.*, 244 Mont. 259, 797 P.2d 217 (1990); but see *In re Wilson*, 438 Pa. 425, 264 A.2d 614 (1970). With the trend toward a more punitive philosophy, however, is differential treatment still defensible today? Some states provide by statute that the period of commitment for a juvenile may not exceed what would be authorized in the case of an adult. See, e.g., N.C.Gen.Stat. § 7B–2513(a)–(b); see Ill.Comp.Stat.Ann. ch. 705, § 405/5–710(7); La.Children's Code Ann. art. 898(A); Tenn.Code Ann. § 37–1–137(a)(1)(B).

Increasingly, states are turning toward determinate dispositions based on the principle of proportionality. Some states have adopted the proportionality model with respect to fines and community service, the amount of the fine or the number of hours of community service varying according to the seriousness of the offense. See, e.g., Conn.Gen.Stat.Ann. § 46b–140(b), (e); Ky.Rev.Stat.Ann. §§ 635.080, 635.085(1); N.Y.Fam.Ct.Act § 353.6; N.C.Gen.Stat. § 7B–2506(5)–(6), (23); S.C.Code Ann. § 20–7–7805(A)(3). The clearest example of the movement toward determinate commitment, however, is the State of Washington, which provides the equivalent of sentencing guidelines, allowing commitment within certain ranges set by a state board, as well as commitment beyond the normal range in certain cases. Wash.Rev.Code Ann. §§ 13.40.030, 13.40.0357, 13.40.160, 13.40.180; see also Ind. Code Ann. § 31–37–19–10; N.C.Gen.Stat. §§ 7B–2506(24), 7B–2513(b); Tenn.Code Ann. § 37–1–137(A)(1)(b), (h). The statutes also provide for the setting of release dates in accordance with guidelines similar to those set for adult parole. Wash.Rev. Code Ann. §§ 13.40.205, 13.40.210. As an example of the application of the Washington sentencing guidelines, see *State v. T.C.*, 99 Wn.App. 701, 995 P.2d 98 (2000), in which the court approved a disposition of 104 weeks, outside the standard range of 15 to 36 weeks, under the "manifest injustice" exception.

(3) Some states authorize the juvenile court to impose what is known as a "juvenile life" sentence, i.e., mandatory commitment until age 21 without possibility of parole, probation or other early release—the functional equivalent of life

without possibility of parole but, of course, only until age 21. See, e.g., Ill.Comp. Stat.Ann. ch. 705, §§ 405/5–815(f), 405/5–820(f); La.Children's Code Ann. art. 897.1(A). Does such a commitment raise constitutional concerns? The Illinois statutory scheme has been upheld against both due process and equal protection claims. *In re M.G.*, 301 Ill.App.3d 401, 234 Ill.Dec. 733, 703 N.E.2d 594 (1998). In *State in re A.A.S.*, 711 So.2d 319 (La.Ct.App.1998), the Louisiana Court of Appeals upheld the Louisiana statute and held that a commitment for "juvenile life" was not excessive in the case of a 13–year-old juvenile adjudicated delinquent for rape of an 11–year-old girl. On appeal, however, the Louisiana Supreme Court vacated the decision and remanded the case to the trial court for reconsideration in light of its decision in *State v. Johnson*, 709 So.2d 672 (La.1998). In the latter case the court had set forth an analytical format for determining when a trial court might depart from statutorily mandated sentences.

(4) Some states authorize "restrictive placement" of certain juveniles. In New York, e.g., if a juvenile is adjudicated delinquent for committing at age 13 to 15 an act that would be a Class A felony if committed by an adult (first-or second-degree murder, kidnaping in the first degree, or arson in the first degree), he or she may be committed to the Division for Youth for an initial period of five years—the first 12 to 18 months of which must be spent in a secure facility and the second 12 months of which are to be spent in a residential facility, without possibility of early release from either facility during these periods. Motion for discharge from custody cannot be made until three years of the five-year placement have expired. N.Y.Fam.Ct.Act §§ 301.2(8)–(11), 353.5(1)–(4). Similarly, if the juvenile is adjudicated delinquent for a designated felony other than a Class A felony he or she may be committed for an initial period of three years—the first six to 12 months of which must be spent in a secure facility, followed by a period of six to 12 months in a residential facility, with no possibility of release from either facility during these periods. Early discharge is not allowed. Id. § 353.5(5). Other states have similar restrictive placement schemes. See, e.g., Colo.Rev.Stat. § 19–2–601; Ga.Code Ann. § 15–11–63; Va.Code Ann. § 16.1–285.1. The constitutionality of the Georgia and New York restrictive placement provisions have been upheld. *In re A.M.*, 248 Ga.App. 241, 545 S.E.2d 688 (2001); *In re Quinton A.*, 49 N.Y.2d 328, 425 N.Y.S.2d 788, 402 N.E.2d 126 (1980).

In re Frank V.

Court of Appeal of California, 1991.
233 Cal.App.3d 1232, 285 Cal.Rptr. 16.

■ WALLIN, ASSOCIATE JUSTICE.

Frank V. appeals the judgment declaring him a ward of the court, contending the trial court improperly denied his motion to suppress evidence and restricted his right to association by imposing an overbroad condition of probation. We affirm.

* * *

At about 9:45 p.m., Officers Michael Luke and Gary Kirby were dispatched to investigate a report of reckless motorcycle driving on a street in an active gang area. There was no traffic when the officers arrived, but Officer Luke noticed a motorcycle pulling away from the curb in front of a house known for gang activity. The officers made a u-turn, intending to make a traffic stop. As soon as they turned the motorcycle pulled to the curb, even though the officers did not use their overhead lights or siren or signal in any other fashion.

As the officers approached the motorcycle, the driver held out what appeared to be a driver's license in his left hand. Frank, the passenger, was looking straight ahead with both hands in the front pockets of a bulky leather jacket. On Officer Luke's order, Frank took his hands out of his pockets. When he tried to put them back in, Luke told him to keep them out. Officer Luke did a patdown search of Frank for weapons and discovered a gun in Frank's right front jacket pocket.

Frank was adjudged a ward of the court and granted probation. The terms included orders that he obey all gang terms and conditions of probation and not associate with anyone disapproved of by his probation officer.

I

[The court concluded that the juvenile's motion to suppress evidence was properly denied.]

II

Frank contends the juvenile court improperly restricted his right to association by imposing an overbroad condition of probation. Not so. In explaining the condition to Frank, the court stated: "The terms and conditions that I have indicated, the gang terms and conditions, are terms and conditions of association. [¶] If your father or your mother tells you that they don't want you to hang around with certain people, you can't hang around with those people. And if your father should find out that you have been hanging around with those people against his orders, all he has to do is tell the probation officer, and they will tell me, and I will have you put back in custody. [¶] The probation officer will also tell you about people that you can't hang out with. If you hang out with those people, and I find out about it, you will be placed back in custody. [¶] You understand that?"

Welfare and Institutions Code section 730 authorizes courts in juvenile cases to "impose and require any and all reasonable conditions that it may determine fitting and proper to the end that justice may be done and the reformation and rehabilitation of the ward enhanced." A probation condition "will not be held invalid unless it '(1) has no relationship to the crime of which the offender was convicted, (2) relates to conduct which is not in itself criminal, and (3) requires or forbids conduct which is not reasonably related to future criminality. . . .' " (*People v. Lent* (1975) 15 Cal.3d 481, 486, 124 Cal.Rptr. 905, 541 P.2d 545.) All three requirements must be met before the condition is invalidated. (Id. at p. 486, fn. 1, 124 Cal.Rptr. 905, 541 P.2d 545.)

However, a court's discretion is not boundless. "A probationer has the right to enjoy a significant degree of privacy, or liberty, under the Fourth, Fifth and Fourteenth Amendments to the federal Constitution. . . ." (People v. Hodgkin (1987) 194 Cal.App.3d 795, 802, 239 Cal.Rptr. 831.) " 'Where a condition of probation requires a waiver of precious constitutional rights, the condition must be narrowly drawn; to the extent it is overbroad it is not reasonably related to the compelling state interest in reformation and rehabilitation and is an unconstitutional restriction on the exercise of fundamental constitutional rights....'" (People v. Pointer (1984) 151 Cal.App.3d 1128, 1139, 199 Cal.Rptr. 357.)

Frank cites several cases where probation was considered overbroad, unreasonable, and unconstitutional.[4] However, they all pertained to adult offenders. "A condition of probation which is impermissible for an adult criminal defendant is not necessarily unreasonable for a juvenile receiving guidance and supervision from the juvenile court." (In re Todd L. (1980) 113 Cal.App.3d 14, 19, 169 Cal.Rptr. 625; see also *In re Michael D.* (1989) 214 Cal.App.3d 1610, 1616, 264 Cal.Rptr. 476.)

The United States Supreme Court has been reluctant to define the "totality of the relationship" between minors and the state. (*In re Gault* (1967) 387 U.S. 1, 13, 87 S.Ct. 1428, 1436, 18 L.Ed.2d 527). See also *Carey v. Population Services International* (1977) 431 U.S. 678, 97 S.Ct. 2010, 52 L.Ed.2d 675; *In re Scott K.* (1979) 24 Cal.3d 395, 401, 155 Cal.Rptr. 671, 595 P.2d 105. Although minors possess constitutional rights, "[i]t is equally well established ... that the liberty interest of a minor is not coextensive with that of an adult. '[E]ven where there is an invasion of protected freedoms "the power of the state to control the conduct of children reaches beyond the scope of its authority over adults."' [Citations.] Parents, of course, have powers greater than that of the state to curtail a child's exercise of the constitutional rights he may otherwise enjoy, for a parent's own constitutionally protected 'liberty' includes the right to 'bring up children' [citation,] and to 'direct the upbringing and education of children.' [Citation.]" (*In re Roger S.* (1977) 19 Cal.3d 921, 928, 141 Cal.Rptr. 298, 569 P.2d 1286.)

Frank was declared a ward of the court, which acts in parens patriae. He only challenges as overbroad the condition limiting his right of association to those approved by his probation officer or parents. His purchase of the .38–caliber automatic discovered in his jacket from an unknown "person on the streets" demonstrates the need for such control and the rational relation between the crime and the condition. The juvenile court could not reasonably be expected to define with precision all classes of persons which might influence Frank to commit further bad acts. It may instead rely on the discretion of his parents, and the probation department acting as parent, to promote and nurture his rehabilitation.

The probation condition is consistent with the rehabilitative purpose of probation and constitutional parental authority. Frank's constitutional right of association has not been impermissibly burdened.

The judgment is affirmed.

■ SILLS, P.J., AND MOORE, J., concur.

NOTES

(1) The *Frank V.* decision provides a three-part test for determining whether a particular condition of probation is valid. In contrast to the court's decision in

---

4. *In re White* (1979) 97 Cal.App.3d 141, 158 Cal.Rptr. 562 [blanket prohibition against being in a designated area of Fresno "anytime, day or night,"]; *People v. Beach* (1983) 147 Cal.App.3d 612, 195 Cal.Rptr. 381 [condition that appellant relocate from her home and community of 24 years]; *People v. Bauer* (1989) 211 Cal.App.3d 937, 260 Cal. Rptr. 62 [invalid to require probation officer's approval of residence].

Frank V., in a more recent case a different division of the California Court of Appeals held a condition that the juvenile not associate with persons not approved by his probation officer overbroad, although it upheld a condition banning his association with a person involved in the fight that was the basis of his adjudication of delinquency. *In re Kacy S.*, 68 Cal.App.4th 704, 80 Cal.Rptr.2d 432 (1998). See also *In re J.G.*, 295 Ill.App.3d 840, 230 Ill.Dec. 60, 692 N.E.2d 1226 (1998) (condition of probation banning juvenile from a certain village was invalid as not reasonably related to rehabilitation where the incidents giving rise to his adjudication did not occur in the village and victims had no connection to the village); *In re M.G.*, 103 Wn.App. 111, 11 P.3d 335 (2000) (restricting at-risk juvenile's freedom of movement in areas in which she abused alcohol and engaged in frequent shoplifting was proper, but restricting her freedom of movement in area near university was improper absent showing that visiting area posed a risk to her).

What other kinds of conditions of probation might be permissible? What about a condition that the juvenile obtain passing grades in school? See *In re Angel J.*, 9 Cal.App.4th 1096, 11 Cal.Rptr.2d 776 (1992). That the juvenile attend Sunday school or church or take part in religious training programs? See *L.M. v. State*, 587 So.2d 648 (Fla.Dist.Ct.App.1991) (per curiam). That the juvenile have gang-related tattoos removed? See *In re M.P.*, 297 Ill.App.3d 972, 232 Ill.Dec. 223, 697 N.E.2d 1153 (1998). Banning the juvenile from watching television for one year? See *In re McDonald*, 133 N.C.App. 433, 515 S.E.2d 719 (1999). Requiring the juvenile to submit to DNA testing? See *In re Maricopa Cty. Juvenile Action Numbers JV–512600 and JV–512797*, 187 Ariz. 419, 930 P.2d 496 (Ct.App.1996). Ordering the juvenile to undergo AIDS testing? See *In re Khonsavanh S.*, 67 Cal.App.4th 532, 79 Cal.Rptr.2d 80 (1998). Requiring the juvenile on request of a law enforcement officer or probation officer to submit to urine testing to determine the presence of alcohol or drugs? See *In re Kacy S.*, supra.

(2) Every state has some form of a law requiring sexual predators or offenders to register with the state and providing for notification of communities in which they live. These laws collectively are known as "Megan's Laws" after seven-year-old Megan Kanka, who was raped and murdered in 1994 by a paroled sex offender who had moved into her New Jersey neighborhood. In numerous cases courts have upheld as a condition of probation a requirement that juveniles register as sex offenders. See, e.g., *In re J.W.*, 204 Ill.2d 50, 272 Ill.Dec. 561, 787 N.E.2d 747 (2003); *In re C.D.N.*, 559 N.W.2d 431 (Minn.Ct.App.1997); *In re Ronnie A.*, 355 S.C. 407, 585 S.E.2d 311 (2003); but see *C.C.M. v. State*, 782 So.2d 537 (Fla.Dist.Ct.App. 2001).

NORTH CAROLINA GENERAL STATUTES (West)

§ 7B–2506.   Dispositional alternatives for delinquent juveniles.

The court exercising jurisdiction over a juvenile who has been adjudicated delinquent may use the following alternatives in accordance with the dispositional structure set forth in G.S. 7B–2508:

. . .

(4) Require restitution, full or partial, up to five hundred dollars ($500.00), payable within a 12–month period to any person who has suffered loss or damage as a result of the offense committed by the juvenile. The court may determine the amount, terms, and conditions of the restitution. If the juvenile participated with another person or persons, all participants should be jointly and severally responsible for the payment of restitution; however, the court shall not require the juvenile to make

restitution if the juvenile satisfies the court that the juvenile does not have, and could not reasonably acquire, the means to make restitution.

(5) Impose a fine related to the seriousness of the juvenile's offense. If the juvenile has the ability to pay the fine, it shall not exceed the maximum fine for the offense if committed by an adult.

(6) Order the juvenile to perform up to 100 hours supervised community service consistent with the juvenile's age, skill, and ability, specifying the nature of the work and the number of hours required. The work shall be related to the seriousness of the juvenile's offense and in no event may the obligation to work exceed 12 months.

. . .

(22) Require restitution of more than five hundred dollars ($500.00), full or partial, payable within a 12–month period to any person who has suffered loss or damage as a result of an offense committed by the juvenile. The court may determine the amount, terms, and conditions of restitution. If the juvenile participated with another person or persons, all participants should be jointly and severally responsible for the payment of the restitution; however, the court shall not require the juvenile to make restitution if the juvenile satisfies the court that the juvenile does not have, and could not reasonably acquire, the means to make restitution.

(23) Order the juvenile to perform up to 200 hours supervised community service consistent with the juvenile's age, skill, and ability, specifying the nature of work and the number of hours required. The work shall be related to the seriousness of the juvenile's offense.

. . .

NOTES

(1) Is a court limited in setting the amount of restitution? The North Carolina statute states that, with respect to an amount greater than $500.00 "the court shall not require the juvenile to make restitution if the juvenile satisfies the court that the juvenile does not have, and could not reasonably acquire, the means to make restitution." In *In re McKoy*, 138 N.C.App. 143, 530 S.E.2d 334 (2000), the court held that ordering seven-and eight-year-old juveniles to pay restitution without findings that they had the means to make restitution and that restitution would be in their best interests was improper. The court in *McKoy* also made clear that it is the juvenile's ability to pay, not the parent's that is taken into account. Other courts also have held that restitution is improper where it is in an amount greater than the juvenile's ability to pay. See, e.g., *R.F. v. State*, 549 So.2d 1169 (Fla.Dist. Ct.App.1989) (per curiam); *State v. Kristopher G.*, 201 W.Va. 703, 500 S.E.2d 519 (1997). If the juvenile lacks the present ability to pay, may the court take into account future ability to pay? For decisions in the affirmative see *In re Maricopa Cty. Juvenile Action No. JV–503009*, 171 Ariz. 272, 830 P.2d 484 (Ct.App.1992); *People in re A.R.M.*, 832 P.2d 1093 (Colo.Ct.App.1992).

(2) May parents be required to pay restitution? A number of states by statute authorize the court to order parents to make restitution. See, e.g., Ark.Code Ann. § 9–27–330(a)(7); Md.Cts. & Jud.Proc.Code Ann. § 3–8A–28; Miss.Code Ann. § 43–21–619(2). In the absence of such statutory authority, however, courts generally have held that trial courts lack the authority to order parents to make restitution.

See, e.g., *In re C.R.D.*, 197 Ga.App. 571, 398 S.E.2d 845 (1990); *C.M. v. State*, 676 So.2d 498 (Fla.Dist.Ct.App.1996). Whether the juvenile, the parents or both the juvenile and the parents are ordered to make restitution, ability to pay is still a necessary consideration. See, e.g., *In re Don Mc.*, 344 Md. 194, 686 A.2d 269 (1996) (abuse of discretion to order juvenile and his mother to pay restitution without considering their ability to pay); *In re Delric H.*, 150 Md.App. 234, 819 A.2d 1117 (2003) (ordering juvenile and his mother to pay restitution in the amount of $6,693.89, payable in monthly installments of $50.00, was appropriate in light of court's reasoned inquiry into their ability to pay, even though juvenile was only 12 years old and his mother, a single parent with four children, only made $250.00 per week).

(3) For what kinds of expenses may courts order a juvenile or the juvenile's parents to make restitution? Property damage presents the easiest case. If the jurisdiction has a statute authorizing restitution, much may depend on the language of the statute, i.e., whether it limits restitution to property loss or loss generally. If the statute limits restitution to damage to property, the court has no authority to require it for non-property loss such as medical expenses. See, e.g., *In re Miller*, 110 Idaho 298, 715 P.2d 968 (1986). Following the *Miller* decision, the Idaho statute was amended to cover any "economic loss." Idaho Code § 20–520(3). In addition to property loss, courts have approved payment of restitution for losses such as the victim's medical expenses, see, e.g., *K.M.C. v. State*, 485 So.2d 1296 (Fla.Dist.Ct. App.1986) and, occasionally, lost wages, see, e.g., *In re Erica V.*, 194 Ariz. 399, 983 P.2d 768 (Ct.App.1999), although some courts have held restitution for lost wages improper, see, e.g., *J.S. v. State*, 717 So.2d 175 (Fla.Dist.Ct.App.1998); see also *In re Maricopa Cty. Juvenile Action No. J–96304*, 147 Ariz. 153, 708 P.2d 1344 (Ct.App. 1985) (while restitution for lost wages is permissible, restitution for lost real estate commissions improper because too speculative). What about restitution for teacher and administrative staff salaries for days on which a juvenile made false bomb threats causing evacuation of a school? See *B.D.A. v. State*, 695 So.2d 399 (Fla.Dist. Ct.App.1997).

Restitution sometimes is deemed improper because the loss that occurred is not directly causally related to the offense committed. What factors should a court take into account in determining the amount of restitution? In *State ex rel. Juvenile Dep't of Josephine Cty. v. Dickerson*, 100 Or.App. 95, 784 P.2d 1121 (1990), the court set forth three prerequisites for awarding restitution: (1) criminal activity; (2) pecuniary damages; and (3) a causal relationship between the criminal conduct and the damage that occurs. In *In re Jason W.*, 94 Md.App. 731, 619 A.2d 163 (1993), the court held that a juvenile could not be ordered to pay restitution for damage to the police cruiser involved in his chase and capture, in the absence of evidence that he caused the damage. But in *State v. Donahoe*, 105 Wn.App. 97, 18 P.3d 618 (2001), the court held that sufficient causation was established between the juvenile's offense of possession of a stolen vehicle and damage to a fence and garage resulting from his leaving his nine-year-old brother in the car alone to authorize the court to order him to make restitution to the owners.

(4) What are the consequences of failure to pay restitution? May a juvenile be committed to an institution for failure to pay restitution as ordered? See, e.g., *V.H. v. State*, 498 So.2d 1011 (Fla.Dist.Ct.App.1986) (improper to commit juvenile because of her inability to pay restitution); *State v. M.D.J.*, 169 W.Va. 568, 289 S.E.2d 191 (1982) (improper for court to revoke probation and order juvenile committed where restitution was set in an amount that exceeded his ability to pay); *In re Carroll*, 260 Pa.Super. 23, 393 A.2d 993 (1978) (court without authority to change original order placing juvenile on probation and requiring his mother to pay restitution to an order committing him to institution solely for the reason that his mother could not afford to pay restitution). Restitution as a disposition is discussed

in William Staples, Restitution as a Sanction in Juvenile Court, 32 Crime & Delinq. 177 (1986); Anne Larason Schneider & Jean Shumway Warner, The Role of Restitution in Juvenile Justice Systems, 5 Yale L. & Pol'y Rev. 382 (1987).

(5) The North Carolina statute authorizes imposition of a fine either as an outright disposition or as a condition of probation. Other states also permit imposition of fines as an appropriate disposition. See, e.g., Ky.Rev.Stat.Ann. § 635.085(1); Pa.Stat.Ann. tit. 42, § 6352(a)(5)–(6); S.C.Code Ann. § 20–7–7805(A)(3). What if fines are not authorized by statute? Courts that have considered the question have concluded that in such an instance a juvenile court is without authority to impose a fine. See, e.g., *In re Timothy E.*, 99 Cal.App.3d 349, 160 Cal.Rptr. 256 (1979); *E.P. v. State*, 130 Ga.App. 512, 203 S.E.2d 757 (1973). Apparently the latter view is premised on the notion that fines are punitive, in contrast to the rehabilitative purpose of the juvenile court. In light of the shift toward a more punitive rationale for juvenile dispositions, is this view any longer realistic? Where fines are authorized by statute, e.g., courts readily acknowledge that they may be levied for a purely punitive purpose. See, e.g., *Walker v. State*, 548 A.2d 492 (Del.Super.Ct.1987), aff'd, 547 A.2d 131 (Del.1988); *State in re L.M.*, 229 N.J.Super. 88, 550 A.2d 1252 (1988).

(6) The North Carolina statute also authorizes the juvenile court to order a juvenile to perform public work or community service as an alternative disposition. Other states likewise permit the community service disposition, with the number of hours of service often proportional to the seriousness of the offense. See, e.g., Conn.Gen.Stat.Ann. § 46b–140(b), (e); Ky.Rev.Stat.Ann. § 635.080; N.Y.Fam.Ct.Act § 353.6; S.C.Code Ann. § 20–7–7805(A)(3). Does requiring a juvenile to perform community service violate the Thirteenth Amendment's prohibition against involuntary servitude? At least one court has held that it does not. *In re Erickson*, 24 Wn.App. 808, 604 P.2d 513 (1979). Community service as a form of restitution is discussed in H. Ted Rubin, Community Service Restitution by Juveniles: Also in Need of Guidance, 37 Juv. & Fam.Ct.J. 1 (1986).

b. SEVERE DISPOSITIONS

ILLINOIS COMPILED STATUTES ANNOTATED, CHAPTER 705 (Smith–Hurd)

§ 405/5–810. Extended jurisdiction juvenile prosecutions.

(1)(a) If the State's Attorney files a petition, at any time prior to commencement of the minor's trial, to designate the proceeding as an extended jurisdiction juvenile prosecution and the petition alleges the commission by a minor 13 years of age or older of any offense which would be a felony if committed by an adult, and, if the juvenile judge assigned to hear and determine petitions to designate the proceeding as an extended jurisdiction juvenile prosecution determines that there is probable cause to believe that the allegations in the petition and motion are true, there is a rebuttable presumption that the proceeding shall be designated as an extended jurisdiction juvenile proceeding.

. . .

(4) Sentencing. If an extended jurisdiction juvenile prosecution under subsections (1) results in a guilty plea, a verdict of guilty, or a finding of guilt, the court shall impose the following:

(i) one or more juvenile sentences under Section 5–710; and

(ii) an adult criminal sentence in accordance with the provisions of Chapter V of the Unified Code of Corrections, the execution of which shall be stayed on the condition that the offender not violate the provisions of the juvenile sentence.

. . .

(6) When it appears that a minor convicted in an extended jurisdiction juvenile prosecution under subsection (1) has violated the conditions of his or her sentence, or is alleged to have committed a new offense upon the filing of a petition to revoke the stay, the court may, without notice, issue a warrant for the arrest of the minor. After a hearing, if the court finds by a preponderance of the evidence that the minor committed a new offense, the court shall order execution of the previously imposed adult criminal sentence. After a hearing, if the court finds by a preponderance of the evidence that the minor committed a violation of his or her sentence other than by a new offense, the court may order execution of the previously imposed adult criminal sentence or may continue him or her on the existing juvenile sentence with or without modifying or enlarging the conditions. Upon revocation of the stay of the adult criminal sentence and imposition of that sentence, the minor's extended jurisdiction juvenile status shall be terminated. The on-going jurisdiction over the minor's case shall be assumed by the adult criminal court and juvenile court jurisdiction shall be terminated and a report of the imposition of the adult sentence shall be sent to the Department of State Police.

(7) Upon successful completion of the juvenile sentence the court shall vacate the adult criminal sentence.

. . .

In re S.L.M.

Supreme Court of Montana, 1997.
287 Mont. 23, 951 P.2d 1365.

■ Leaphart, Justice.

The appellants in these five appeals challenge the Extended Jurisdiction Prosecution Act, §§ 41–5–1601 through –1607, MCA, (EJPA) as being unconstitutional under the equal protection, due process and double jeopardy clauses of the United States and Montana constitutions, as well as under Article II, Section 15 of the Montana Constitution.... Since we determine that the EJPA violates Article II, Section 4 (equal protection) of the Montana Constitution and Article II, Section 15 (rights of minors) of the Montana Constitution, we need not address the double jeopardy and due process challenges.

. . .

DISCUSSION

I. *Overview of the Extended Jurisdiction Prosecution Act*

In 1995, the legislature substantially revised the Montana Youth Court Act, including amending the Declaration of Purpose to effectuate the following purpose:

> to prevent and reduce youth delinquency through immediate, consistent, enforceable, and avoidable consequences of youths' actions and to establish a program of supervision, care, rehabilitation, detention, competency development, community protection, and, in appropriate cases, restitution as ordered by the youth court[.]

Section 41–5–102(2), MCA (1995).

. . .

A youth court case may be designated an "extended jurisdiction juvenile prosecution" when the offender is at least 14 years of age, the county attorney requests that the case be designated an extended jurisdiction juvenile prosecution, a hearing is held, and the youth court designates the case as such. Section 41–5–1602, MCA. If, after a hearing, the county attorney has shown by clear and convincing evidence that designating the case an extended jurisdiction prosecution serves the public safety, the youth court may so designate. Section 41–5–1603(3), MCA.

A case may also fall under the EJPA if the youth is alleged to have committed one or more of the offenses listed under § 41–5–206, MCA, and the county attorney designates the case as an extended jurisdiction prosecution. Section 41–5–1602(1)(b), MCA. The case may also fall under the EJPA if the youth was at least 12 years of age, allegedly committed an offense which, if committed by an adult, would be punishable as a felony, and allegedly used a firearm in the commission of the offense. Section 41–5–1602(1)(b), MCA. Additionally, the case may be designated an extended jurisdiction prosecution if, after a hearing on the motion to transfer the case for prosecution in district court under § 41–5–206, MCA, the youth court designates the case an extended jurisdiction prosecution. Section 41–5–1602(1)(c), MCA.

After the case is designated an extended jurisdiction prosecution, the case proceeds to an adjudicatory hearing as provided in § 41–5–1502, MCA. If the youth admits to committing, or is adjudicated to have committed, an offense which would be a felony if committed by an adult, the youth court must impose one or more of the juvenile dispositions under § 41–5–1512, MCA, and any sentence which could be imposed on an adult offender of the same offense. The statute expressly provides that execution of the sentence imposed "must be stayed on the condition that the youth not violate the provisions of the disposition order and not commit a new offense." Section 41–5–1604(1)(b), MCA.

If the court is subsequently informed that any condition of the disposition has been violated, or if it is alleged that the youth has committed a new offense, the court may, without notice, order the youth be taken into custody. Section 41–5–1605(1), MCA. The district court must then notify the youth, in writing, of the reasons alleged for revocation of the stay. Section 41–5–1605(1), MCA.

If the youth challenges the reasons for the revocation, the court must hold a hearing at which the youth is entitled to notice, an opportunity to be heard, right to counsel, and the right to cross-examine witnesses. Section 41–5–1605(2), MCA. If, after the hearing, the court finds by a preponderance of the evidence that the conditions of the stay have been violated or that the youth has committed a new offense, the court shall provide a written statement of the reasons for the revocation and shall: 1) continue the stay and place the youth on probation; 2) impose one or more dispositions under §§ 41–5–1512 or –1513, MCA, if the youth is under age 18; or 3) subject to §§ 41–5–206(6) and (7), MCA, order execution of the sentence imposed under § 41–5–1604(1)(b), MCA. Section 41–5–1605(2)(b), MCA.

Upon revocation and disposition, the youth court shall transfer the case to the district court. Section 41–5–1605(3), MCA. Upon transfer, the offender's extended jurisdiction juvenile status is terminated, and the youth court jurisdiction is terminated. Section 41–5–1605(3), MCA. Ongoing supervision of the offender is with the Department of Corrections rather than with the youth court's juvenile probation services. Section 41–5–1605(3), MCA.

II. *Standing*

[The court concluded that the youths had standing to challenge provisions of the act.]

III. *Does the EJPA violate the equal protection clauses of the United States Constitution and/or the Montana Constitution and the rights of minors under Article II, Section 15 of the Montana Constitution?*

Resolution of this issue involves a question of constitutional law. Accordingly, we review to determine whether the court's interpretation of the law is correct. *State v. Schnittgen* (1996), 277 Mont. 291, 295, 922 P.2d 500, 503.

Equal protection challenges to legislation are reviewed under one of three different levels of scrutiny. When the legislation in question infringes upon a fundamental right or discriminates against a suspect class, we employ the most stringent standard, strict scrutiny. "Strict scrutiny has been limited to those instances when either a fundamental right has been infringed or a suspect classification has been established. Strict scrutiny requires the government to show a compelling state interest for its action." *Davis v. Union Pacific Railroad Co.* (1997), 282 Mont. 233, ___, 937 P.2d 27, 31, 54 St.Rep. 328, 331.

. . .

... The youths argue that imposition of an adult sentence in addition to a juvenile disposition is an infringement upon their physical liberty and that physical liberty is a fundamental right. This question was answered in *Matter of C.H.* (1984), 210 Mont. 184, 683 P.2d 931. C.H. contended that placing a truant status offender in an institution for a 45–day predispositional evaluation was an infringement upon the fundamental right of physical liberty, a right which must be protected absent a compelling state interest. *Matter of C.H.*, 683 P.2d at 938. She also contended that § 41–5–103(12), MCA, is unconstitutional in that it authorizes the youth court to reclassify a youth in need of supervision who has violated a court order as a delinquent youth. *Matter of C.H.*, 683 P.2d at 938. She contended that this classification violated equal protection guarantees by allowing the court to treat youths in the same class, i.e., youthful contemnors, differently.

While physical liberty is not specifically guaranteed under either the United States Constitution or the Montana Constitution, we noted in *Matter of C.H.*, 683 P.2d at 940, that the concept of "liberty" is very much a part of our state constitution. The preamble to the Montana Constitution states in part: "We the people of Montana . . . desiring . . . to secure the blessings of liberty . . . do ordain and establish this constitution." Further, Article II, Section 3 states in part: "All persons are born free and have certain inalienable rights. They include . . . the rights of . . . enjoying and defending their lives and liberties. . . ." Article II, Section 17, the due process clause, states: "No person shall be deprived of life, liberty, or property without due process of law."

In *Matter of C.H.*, 683 P.2d at 940, we concluded: "Reading the preamble and these sections of our constitution together, we hold that under the Montana Constitution physical liberty is a fundamental right, without which other constitutionally guaranteed rights would have little meaning." We then analyzed the interplay between the guarantee of equal protection and Article II, Section 15's guarantee to minors of all the fundamental rights of Article II unless specifically precluded by laws which enhance the protection of such persons. We held that "a juvenile's right to physical liberty must be balanced against her right to be supervised, cared for and rehabilitated." *Matter of C.H.*, 683 P.2d at 941.

. . . .

In the present appeals, the EJPA's imposition of an adult sentence in addition to a juvenile disposition infringes on the juvenile's physical liberty, which is a fundamental right. As in *Matter of C.H.*, 683 P.2d at 941, we must therefore apply a strict scrutiny analysis and determine whether there is a compelling state interest sufficient to justify such an infringement and whether such an infringement is consistent with the mandates of Article II, Section 15 of the Montana Constitution.

Article II, Section 15 provides:

Rights of persons not adults. The rights of persons under 18 years of age shall include, but not be limited to, all the fundamental rights of this Article unless specifically precluded by laws which enhance the protections of such persons.

This section must be read in conjunction with the guarantee of equal protection found in Article II, Section 4. The report of the Bill of Rights Committee of the Constitutional Convention indicates that one of the primary purposes of Article II, Section 15 was to remedy the fact that minors had not been accorded full recognition under the equal protection clause of the United States Constitution. The Bill of Rights Committee's Comments are as follows:

The committee took this action in recognition of the fact that young people have not been held to possess basic civil rights. Although it has been held that they are "persons" under the due process clause of the Fourteenth Amendment, the Supreme Court has not ruled in their favor under the equal protection clause of that same amendment. What this means is that persons under the age of majority have been accorded certain specific rights which are felt to be a part of due process. However, the broad outline of the kinds of rights young people possess does not yet exist. This is the crux of the committee proposal: to recognize that persons under the age of majority have the same protections from governmental and majoritarian abuses as do adults. In such cases where the protection of the special status of minors demands it, exceptions can be made on clear showing that such protection is being enhanced.

Montana Constitutional Convention, Vol. II at 635–36.

Clearly under Article II, Section 15, minors are afforded full recognition under the equal protection clause and enjoy all the fundamental rights of an adult under Article II. Furthermore, if the legislature seeks to carve exceptions to this guarantee, it must not only show a compelling state interest but must also show that the exception is designed to enhance the rights of minors.

In *Matter of C.H.*, 683 P.2d at 941, we held that the state had a compelling interest in removing the element of retribution and instead rehabilitating youths before they became adult offenders. At the time *Matter of C.H.* was decided, the stated purpose of the Youth Court Act was "to remove from youth committing violations of the law the element of retribution and to substitute therefor a program of supervision, care, rehabilitation, and, in appropriate cases, restitution as ordered by the youth court." Section 41–5–102(2), MCA (1983). However, the purposes of the Youth Court Act have since been considerably broadened. As of the 1995 amendments, the Declaration of Purpose now states the following goals:

> [T]o prevent and reduce youth delinquency through an immediate, consistent, enforceable, and avoidable consequences of youths' actions and to establish a program of supervision, care, rehabilitation, detention, competency development, community protection, *36 and, in appropriate cases, restitution as ordered by the youth court[.]

Section 41–5–102(2), MCA (1995) (emphasis added).

As compared to the pre–1995 Declaration of Purpose, the Act now espouses much more preventative, if not punitive, goals; that is, the Act now seeks to prevent delinquency through imposition of enforceable and immediate consequences and to establish programs of detention and community protection. The State asserts that the EJPA was designed by the legislature to address the rising tide of juvenile criminal conduct in Montana and dispel the notion held by some juveniles that their criminal conduct holds no consequences for them. The EJPA, as noted by the State, gives the courts "a bigger stick to help keep kids in line—to let them know their crimes are serious and this is their last chance to cooperate." Obviously, it is no longer accurate to reason, as we did in *Matter of C.H.*, 683 P.2d at 941, that Youth Court Act infringements upon a juvenile's physical liberty are legitimate means of enhancing their protection. Indeed, in requiring the court to impose an adult sentence in addition to the juvenile disposition, the EJPA goes beyond mere rehabilitation and injects the specter of retribution. Our holding in *Matter of C.H.* is thus distinguishable on that basis.

All juveniles subject to the EJA are at risk of serving an adult sentence in addition to their juvenile disposition. Thus, the EJPA, on its face, violates the equal protection clause of Article II, Section 10 by treating EJPA offenders more harshly than their adult counterparts. The EJPA also violates Article II, Section 15 by reducing, rather than enhancing, a juvenile's rights as compared to an adult's. The State, relying solely on its contention that age is not a suspect classification, does not address the fundamental right analysis and has not suggested any compelling state interest to justify the EJPA's infringement on the fundamental right of physical liberty. While the State has a clear interest in deterring serious juvenile crime and while it can, within the limits of equal protection, further this interest by increasing the sanctions imposed upon juveniles, it has no compelling state interest in treating them as adults and restricting their physical liberty beyond the restrictions which are imposed upon an adult for the same offense.

As an example, one of the appeals before us, Matter of J.L.C., Cause No. 96–220, Hill County, involves a 17–year-old youth who pled guilty to one count of negligent homicide, a violation of § 45–5–104, MCA. Pursuant to the EJPA, J.L.C. received a juvenile disposition committing him to formal probation until age 21 plus an adult sentence of 5 years with the Department of Corrections, suspended on the condition that he comply with the probation until age 21. Thus, while the "adult" portion of his sentence is only 5 years, the total sentence with both juvenile and adult aspects combined could equal 9 years, nearly twice as long as the 5–year adult sentence under similar circumstances. Clearly, although the law purports to treat J.L.C. as an "adult," he is treated differently than an adult and in such a manner that his rights are lessened rather than enhanced, as mandated by Article II, Section 15. Thus, the EJPA, both on its face and as applied to J.L.C., violates equal protection under Article II, Section 4 and a minor's rights to enhanced protection under Article II, Section 15 of the Montana Constitution.

In addition to *Matter of C.H.*, 683 P.2d at 931, discussed above, we have twice addressed equal protection challenges to the different treatment of offenders based upon age. As the following analysis indicates, we find both of these decisions distinguishable.

A. Our Decision in *Matter of Wood*:

In *Matter of Wood* (1989), 236 Mont. 118, 768 P.2d 1370, we addressed an equal protection challenge by a 16–year-old youth to the process whereby jurisdiction over his homicide case was mandatorily transferred from youth court to district court. The Youth Court Act, § 41–5–206(1)(a)(I), MCA, provided that a youth aged 12 years or older who had committed deliberate homicide or mitigated deliberate homicide may be transferred, after a hearing, to district court. Wood contended that, as a 16–year-old, he was entitled to the same due process (i.e., a hearing) as a younger person and that § 41–5–206(3), MCA, denied equal protection when it provided that youths 16 years or older who have allegedly committed deliberate homicide must be transferred to district court, without any requirement of a hearing. *Matter of Wood*, 768 P.2d at 1372. We held that procedural due process is not a fundamental right nor is age a suspect class requiring strict scrutiny. *Matter of Wood*, 768 P.2d at 1375. We applied the rational basis test and concluded that treatment as a juvenile is not an inherent right, that the legislature may restrict or qualify that right, and that the legislative classification based upon age and gravity of the offense was rationally related to the legitimate state objective of deterring homicides committed by teenagers and protecting society from these violent offenders. *Matter of Wood*, 768 P.2d at 1376.

Matter of Wood, 768 P.2d at 1370, is distinguishable from the case sub judice. *Matter of Wood* involves the right to procedural due process, which we held is not a fundamental right. In this case, the appellants are challenging the actual loss of physical liberty, in addition to challenging the process by which sentence is imposed. As we stated earlier, physical liberty is a fundamental right requiring strict scrutiny. Also, *Matter of Wood*, 768 P.2d at 1374–76, involved the transfer statute, § 41–5–206, MCA, and an alleged right to be treated as a juvenile. The present appeals involve the EJPA, which while purporting to treat juveniles as adults in fact treats them more harshly than adults under similar circumstances. Our decision in *Matter of Wood* is thus not controlling of the issues presented herein.

B.   Our Decision in *Matter of C.S.*:

We addressed an equal protection challenge to the disparate application of sentencing laws to minors as compared to adults in *Matter of C.S.* (1984), 210 Mont. 144, 687 P.2d 57. At the age of 15, C.S. was adjudged a delinquent youth for having committed the offense of violation of privacy in communication, a misdemeanor as provided in § 45–8–213, MCA. *Matter of C.S.*, 687 P.2d at 58. At the dispositional hearing, C.S. was committed to the Department of Institutions until age 21, unless the Department deemed an earlier release appropriate. Thus, the maximum amount of time C.S. could have spent in the custody of the Department was six years. *Matter of C.S.*, 687 P.2d at 58. This was considerably longer than the six-month maximum to which an adult could be sentenced for committing the same offense. For that reason, C.S. argued that her term of commitment violated the equal protection clause. *Matter of C.S.*, 687 P.2d at 58. We concluded that adults and minors are not similarly situated with respect to Montana's sentencing laws for three reasons. *Matter of C.S.*, 687 P.2d at 59.

The three reasons propounded were: 1) a juvenile commitment is different from a criminal conviction because, given the stated policy of the Youth Court Act in 1984, a juvenile commitment is strictly for rehabilitation, not retribution; 2) in contrast to an adult, the liberty interests of a minor are subject to reasonable regulation by the State under the doctrine of parens patriae; and 3) other jurisdictions have employed the parens patriae doctrine under similar youth court acts. *Matter of C.S.*, 687 P.2d at 59.

Our decision in *Matter of C.S.*, 687 P.2d at 57, predates the adoption of the EJPA. After review of the EJPA and the revised Youth Court Act, we conclude that the three distinctions drawn in *Matter of C.S.* between minors and adults do not apply in the context of these acts. As stated above in our discussion of *Matter of C.H.*, given the new breadth of purpose of the Youth Court Act and the adult sentencing provisions of the EJPA, it is no longer accurate to state, as we did in *Matter of C.S.*, 687 P.2d at 59, that a Youth Court disposition is "strictly for rehabilitation, not retribution." Our holding in *Matter of C.S.* is thus distinguishable on that basis.

Furthermore, where the offender is sanctioned with an "adult" sentence, as under the EJPA, we cannot rely on the doctrine of parens patriae to distinguish between the treatment of juveniles and adults. Parens patriae traditionally refers to the role of the State as sovereign or guardian of persons who are under a legal disability, such as juveniles—"the principle that the state must care for those who cannot take care of themselves, such as minors who lack proper care and custody from their parents." BLACK'S LAW DICTIONARY 1114 (6th ed.1990). Where, as under the EJPA, the offender is no longer sentenced solely as a juvenile, but as an adult as well, the doctrine's paternalistic rationale no longer applies.

Finally, the doctrine of parens patriae must be applied consistently with Article II, Section 15 of the Montana Constitution which provides: "The rights of persons under 18 years of age shall include, but not be limited to, all the fundamental rights of this Article unless specifically precluded by laws which enhance the protection of such persons." (Emphasis added.) In light of this clear constitutional guarantee, a juvenile enjoys all the rights and privileges of an adult unless the law at issue affords more, not less, protection to the juvenile. Our decision in *Matter of C.S.*, 687 P.2d at 57, did not address the provisions of Article II, Section 15 and does not conflict with our conclusion that infringement of an EJPA offender's liberty for a longer period of time than an adult under like circumstances does not enhance the juvenile's rights.

CONCLUSION

Under the framework of the EJPA, a juvenile receives a juvenile disposition plus an adult sentence. If the juvenile violates the terms of the juvenile disposition, it is possible for the youth to serve a longer term of detention or imprisonment than an adult who has committed the same offense. The State has not shown a compelling interest to be advanced by this unequal treatment of similarly situated persons, nor has it shown that the EJPA provides juveniles with increased, rather than decreased, protection under the law. Therefore, we hold that the EJPA violates Article II, Section 4 (equal protection) and Article II, Section 15 (rights of minors).

. . .

■ TURNAGE, C.J., and HUNT, NELSON, GRAY and REGNIER, JJ., concur.

[In a separate opinion concurring specially, TRIEWEILER, J., thought that the Montana statutory scheme violated the prohibition against double jeopardy and for that reason found the scheme unconstitutional.]

NOTES

(1) The "extended jurisdiction juvenile" or "blended sentencing" option has found increasing favor as a dispositional alternative. See, e.g., Kan.Stat.Ann. § 38–2364(a)–(b); Minn.Stat.Ann. § 260B.130(4); Mont.Code Ann. § 41–5–1604(1). As the Illinois statute illustrates, the option authorizes the juvenile court to impose a juvenile disposition *and* an adult sentence to be stayed on condition that the juvenile successfully complete the juvenile disposition and not commit another offense, failure to fulfill the conditions of which will result in revocation of the stay and imposition of the adult sentence. In addition, some jurisdictions allow the juvenile court to impose *either* a juvenile disposition *or* an adult sentence with respect to older juveniles charged with one of enumerated serious offenses. See, e.g., N.M.Stat.Ann. § 32A–2–20.

Following the decision in *In re S.L.M.* holding the Montana statutory scheme unconstitutional under provisions of the state constitution, the statute was amended in an effort to correct the equal protection problem on which the court based its decision. 1999 Mont. Laws ch. 537, § 5. The statute now provides that the combined period of time for the juvenile disposition and the adult sentence may not exceed the maximum period of time allowed for the adult sentence. Mont.Code Ann. § 41–5–1604(1)(b).

In contrast to the Montana Supreme Court's decision in *In re S.L.M.*, the Minnesota Court of Appeals upheld the Minnesota extended jurisdiction juvenile statute against separation of powers and vagueness claims in *In re L.J.S.*, 539 N.W.2d 408 (Minn.Ct.App.1995). The court was not confronted with equal protection or due process challenges to the extended jurisdiction juvenile statute.

(2) "Blended sentencing" statutory schemes were devised for the most part as a response to a perceived rise in the number and severity of crimes committed by juveniles. This perception, some commentators have argued, is false and is the product of media and public hysteria inflamed by sensational cases and over-zealous legislators. See, e.g., Frank Zimring, American Youth Violence (1998); Samuel M. Davis, The Criminalization of the Juvenile Justice: Legislative Responses to "The Phantom Menace," 70 Miss.L.J. 1 (2000); Elizabeth S. Scott & Laurence Steinberg, Blaming Youth, 81 Tex.L.Rev. 799 (2003). For an excellent analysis of application of Minnesota's blended sentencing statutory scheme in Hennepin County, Minnesota, and a general commentary on the concept of blended sentencing see Marcy R. Podkopacz & Barry C. Feld, The Back–Door to Prison: Waiver Reform, "Blended Sentencing," and the Law of Unintended Consequences, 91 J.Crim.L. & Criminol. 997 (2001). The authors conclude that blended sentencing, which was conceived as a middle-ground option for youths who were not such threats to public safety that they should be transferred for criminal prosecution and yet were not appropriate for traditional juvenile dispositions, has produced a "net-widening" effect resulting in criminal sanctions being imposed against an increasing number of youths. Blended sentencing also has its supporters, those who argue that it is necessary in order to protect public safety and that it serves the dual purposes of deterrence and punishment . See, e.g., Christian Sullivan, Juvenile Delinquency in the Twenty–First Century: Is Blended Sentencing the Middle–Road Solution for Violent Kids?, 21 N.Ill.U.L.Rev. 483 (2001); Kristen L. Caballero, Note, Blended Sentencing: A Good Idea for Juvenile Sex Offenders?, 19 St. John's J.Leg.Comment. 379 (2005); Christine Chamberlin, Note, Not Kids Anymore: A Need for Punishment and Deterrence in the Juvenile Justice System, 42 B.C.L.Rev. 391 (2001).

TEXAS FAMILY CODE ANNOTATED (Vernon)

§ 53.045. Violent or Habitual Offenders

(a) Except as provided by Subsection (e), the prosecuting attorney may refer the petition to the grand jury of the county in which the court in which the petition is filed presides if the petition alleges that the child engaged in delinquent conduct that constitutes habitual felony conduct as described by Section 51.031 or that included the violation of any of the following provisions:

(1) Section 19.02, Penal Code (murder);

(2) Section 19.03, Penal Code (capital murder);

(3) Section 19.04, Penal Code (manslaughter);

(4) Section 20.04, Penal Code (aggravated kidnapping);

(5) Section 22.011, Penal Code (sexual assault) or Section 22.021, Penal Code (aggravated sexual assault);

(6) Section 22.02, Penal Code (aggravated assault);

(7) Section 29.03, Penal Code (aggravated robbery);

(8) Section 22.04, Penal Code (injury to a child, elderly individual, or disabled individual), if the offense is punishable as a felony, other than a state jail felony;

(9) Section 22.05(b), Penal Code (felony deadly conduct involving discharging a firearm);

(10) Subchapter D, Chapter 481, Health and Safety Code, if the conduct constitutes a felony of the first degree or an aggravated controlled substance felony (certain offenses involving controlled substances);

(11) Section 15.03, Penal Code (criminal solicitation);

(12) Section 21.11(a)(1), Penal Code (indecency with a child);

(13) Section 15.031, Penal Code (criminal solicitation of a minor);

(14) Section 15.01, Penal Code (criminal attempt), if the offense attempted was an offense under Section 19.02, Penal Code (murder), or Section 19.03, Penal Code (capital murder), or an offense listed by Section 3g(a)(1), Article 42.12, Code of Criminal Procedure;

(15) Section 28.02, Penal Code (arson), if bodily injury or death is suffered by any person by reason of the commission of the conduct; or

(16) Section 49.08, Penal Code (intoxication manslaughter); or

(17) Section 15.02, Penal Code (criminal conspiracy), if the offense made the subject of the criminal conspiracy includes a violation of any of the provisions referenced in Subdivisions (1) through (16).

(b) A grand jury may approve a petition submitted to it under this section by a vote of nine members of the grand jury in the same manner that the grand jury votes on the presentment of an indictment.

. . .

(d) If the grand jury approves of the petition, the fact of approval shall be certified to the juvenile court, and the certification shall be entered in the record of the case. For the purpose of the transfer of a child to the Texas Department of Criminal Justice as provided by Section 61.084(c), Human Resources Code, a juvenile court petition approved by a grand jury under this section is an indictment presented by the grand jury.

(e) The prosecuting attorney may not refer a petition that alleges the child engaged in conduct that violated Section 22.011(a)(2), Penal Code, or Sections 22.021(a)(1)(B) and (2)(B), Penal Code, unless the child is more than three years older than the victim of the conduct.

§ 54.04. Disposition Hearing

(a) The disposition hearing shall be separate, distinct, and subsequent to the adjudication hearing. There is no right to a jury at the disposition hearing unless the child is in jeopardy of a determinate sentence under Subsection (d)(3) or (m), in which case, the child is entitled to a jury of 12 persons to determine the sentence. . . .

. . .

(c) No disposition may be made under this section unless the child is in need of rehabilitation or the protection of the public or the child requires that disposition be made. If the court or jury does not so find, the court shall dismiss the child and enter a final judgment without any disposition . . .

(d) If the court or jury makes the finding specified in Subsection (c) allowing the court to make a disposition in the case:

. . .

(3) if the court or jury found at the conclusion of the adjudication hearing that the child engaged in delinquent conduct that included a violation of a penal law listed in Section 53.045(a) and if the petition was approved by the grand jury under Section 53.045, the court or jury may sentence the child to commitment in the Texas Youth Commission with a possible transfer to the Texas Department of Criminal Justice for a term of:

(A) not more than 40 years if the conduct constitutes:

(i) a capital felony;

(ii) a felony of the first degree; or

(iii) an aggravated controlled substance felony;

(B) not more than 20 years if the conduct constitutes a felony of the second degree; or

(C) not more than 10 years if the conduct constitutes a felony of the third degree;

. . .; or

(5) if applicable, the court or jury may make a disposition under Subsection (m).

. . .

(g) If the court orders a disposition under Subsection (d)(3) or (m) and there is an affirmative finding that the defendant used or exhibited a deadly weapon during the commission of the conduct or during immediate flight from commission of the conduct, the court shall enter the finding in the order. If there is an affirmative finding that the deadly weapon was a firearm, the court shall enter that finding in the order.

. . .

(k) Except as provided by Subsection (m), the period to which a court or jury may sentence a person to commitment to the Texas Youth Commission with a transfer to the Texas Department of Criminal Justice under Subsection (d)(3) applies without regard to whether the person has previously been adjudicated as having engaged in delinquent conduct.

. . .

(m) The court or jury may sentence a child adjudicated for habitual felony conduct as described by Section 51.031 to a term prescribed by Subsection (d)(3) and applicable to the conduct adjudicated in the pending case if:

(1) a petition was filed and approved by a grand jury under Section 53.045 alleging that the child engaged in habitual felony conduct; and

(2) the court or jury finds beyond a reasonable doubt that the allegation described by Subdivision (1) in the grand jury petition is true.

. . .

(q) If a court or jury sentences a child to commitment in the Texas Youth Commission under Subsection (d)(3) for a term of not more than 10 years, the court or jury may place the child on probation under Subsection (d)(1) as an alternative to making the disposition under Subsection (d)(3). The court shall prescribe the period of probation ordered under this subsection for a term of not more than 10 years. The court may, before the sentence of probation expires, extend the probationary period under Section 54.05, except that the sentence of probation and any extension may not exceed 10 years. The court may, before the child's 18th birthday, discharge the child from the sentence of probation. If a sentence of probation ordered under this subsection and any extension of probation ordered under Section 54.05 will continue after the child's 18th birthday, the court shall discharge the child from the sentence of probation on the child's 18th birthday unless the court transfers the child to an appropriate district court under Section 54.051.

. . .

NOTE

The Texas statutory scheme is perhaps the most ambitious of provisions allowing commitment of juveniles to a correctional facility. Yet the statutory scheme has been upheld against claims that it violates equal protection of the laws, on the basis that it furthers the compelling state interest of balancing the need to protect children and the need to protect and guarantee security for the public generally. *In re S.B.C.*, 805 S.W.2d 1 (Tex.App.1991); *In re R.L.H.*, 771 S.W.2d 697 (Tex.App. 1989), abrogated on other grounds, *In re C.O.S.*, 988 S.W.2d 760 (1999). The provision allowing transfer to the adult correctional system at age 16, Tex.Hum.Res. Code Ann. §§ 61.079, 61.084, likewise has been upheld against claims that it violates equal protection, due process and the prohibition against double jeopardy.

In re T.D.H., 971 S.W.2d 606 (Tex.App.1998) (also rejects separation of powers argument); *In re J.G.*, 905 S.W.2d 676 (Tex.App.1995). Transfer decisions have been upheld against non-constitutional claims as well, e.g., that they constitute an abuse of discretion by the juvenile court. See, e.g., *Garrett v. State*, 847 S.W.2d 268 (Tex.App.1992).

The Texas determinate sentencing scheme has been criticized and the argument made that a preferable alternative would be a statutory scheme creating a presumption of adult treatment for the most serious juvenile offenders. Tamara L. Reno, Comment, The Rebuttable Presumption for Serious Juvenile Crimes: An Alternative to Determinate Sentencing in Texas, 26 Tex.Tech L.Rev. 1421 (1995).

INDEX

References are to pages.

†